Europe's Long Century

Society, Politics, and Culture
1900–Present

Combined Volume

SPENCER M. DI SCALA
University of Massachusetts Boston

New York   Oxford
OXFORD UNIVERSITY PRESS

Oxford University Press is a department of the University of Oxford.
It furthers the University's objective of excellence in research, scholarship,
and education by publishing worldwide.

Oxford New York
Auckland Cape Town Dar es Salaam Hong Kong Karachi
Kuala Lumpur Madrid Melbourne Mexico City Nairobi
New Delhi Shanghai Taipei Toronto

With offices in
Argentina Austria Brazil Chile Czech Republic France Greece
Guatemala Hungary Italy Japan Poland Portugal Singapore
South Korea Switzerland Thailand Turkey Ukraine Vietnam

For titles covered by Section 112 of the US Higher Education
Opportunity Act, please visit www.oup.com/us/he for the latest
information about pricing and alternate formats.

Published by Oxford University Press
198 Madison Avenue, New York, New York 10016
http://www.oup.com

Library of Congress Cataloging-in-Publication Data
Di Scala, Spencer.
Europe's long century: politics, society, culture, 1900-present / Spencer Di Scala.
p. cm.
Includes bibliographical references and index.
ISBN 978-0-19-977850-8 (acid-free paper)—ISBN 978-0-19-977851-5—ISBN 978-0-19-977852-2
1. Europe—History—20th century.   2. Europe—Politics and government—20th century.
3. Europe—Biography.   I. Title.
D424.D497 2012
940.5—dc23   2012015473

Printing Number: 9 8 7 6 5 4 3 2 1

Printed in the United States of America
on acid-free paper

CONTENTS

PREFACE

The twentieth century has been interpreted as a short century marked by extremes. According to this view, the century lasted only from 1914 to 1989 or 1991. These dates coincide with the rise and fall of communism, which came to power in Russia in 1917 and ended with the fall of the Berlin wall (1989) or that of the Soviet Union (1991). Thus, the concept of a short century seems to be influenced by a cold war perspective that considers the struggle between communism and capitalism the overriding aspect of the past century.

What I have learned as a result of my research for this book is that, in contradistinction to the idea of the "short" twentieth century, we are talking about a "long" century that lasted approximately from 1900 to 2000, characterized by three overriding movements, with antecedents before the century began, that continued to be elaborated after it ended. In international politics, a struggle for hegemony that pitted the German Empire against its British and French rivals intensified. The Germans challenged the British and French for control of Europe and, indeed, the world. After World War I, the struggle continued with the rise of Nazism, which, albeit with a radically different and odious ideology, reinvigorated the German challenge. The German defeat of 1945 brought the fear that Soviet Russia would rule the entire continent and, more clearly than had been the case of Germany, perhaps the world. Complicating these fights were exasperated nationalism, religious differences, and the desire to right what one side or another considered historical wrongs. International communism submerged these disputes in an all-embracing ideology, but they resurfaced after it collapsed.

In fact, it will be increasingly necessary to view the hundred years of the twentieth century in a post–cold war perspective. In my opinion, the issues that antedate or were independent of the cold war, even if they were enmeshed with it, will forcefully emerge as more important than they were seen during the cold war itself or in the years that immediately followed its end. Despite the importance and duration of the Communist movement, it was, in the context of modern European and world history, a transitory phase that is unlikely to recur. The concept of an age of extremes is also less helpful than appears at first sight because extremes have always characterized European history. The twentieth century witnessed unparalleled atrocities, also because new technology made it possible to commit them. It is important not only to learn from the lessons of a violent age, but to focus on developments during the period that had earlier origins and perhaps more permanent effects.

In this book, I have emphasized another factor that seems to have been neglected in the past: modern science. The past hundred or so years have been characterized by great innovations in science and technology, both of which now affect the common person with unparalleled speed, a trend that may be seen throughout the past century. However, the changes in mentality that twentieth-century science brought about were not confined to scientists, but eventually filtered down to ordinary people and influenced them even if they were unaware of it. This is clear not only in the concrete case of nuclear physics, for example, which developed nuclear weapons under whose shadow the world has lived under since 1945, but in the modern mentality. The "uncertainty" (or "indeterminacy") principle that came out of quantum mechanics affected the culture of most of the twentieth century, and who can argue that the discovery of DNA and the genetic engineering that it made possible during the latter part of the century has not affected people's thinking and society itself?

I have tried to bring these questions to the fore in this book while covering a large amount of information. In my many years of teaching, I have been struck by the intellectual curiosity of students who constantly challenged the opinions of even the most celebrated historians. In my discussions with them, the students always resisted quick explanations. In a twist that might be considered ironic, given the present-mindedness of the current age, when I presented relevant material to them, they were always interested in going back further to understand the origins of a particular dispute, war, social condition, or cultural phenomenon. It slowly dawned on me that full explanations of events must be given in their *historical* contexts, so that, for example, twentieth-century events may have been influenced by facts dating from the nineteenth or previous centuries. If such facts are relevant for a complete understanding of certain developments, I have considered them in this book, so that the reader should not be surprised to find information on the Turkish occupation in the discussion of the states of southeastern Europe, or a reference to the seventeenth century when considering social conditions in modern Spain.

Perhaps fuller explanations will make history, even modern history, less remote. I have always wondered why history seems so boring to many people and have come to at least a tentative conclusion. Professional historians are frequently carried away by generalizations, trying to make everything fit into a scheme. To a certain extent, this is necessary, but historians risk being too abstract, making history "dry" and of seemingly doubtful relevance to the present. I have attempted to strike a balance among political, social, and cultural history. Because history deals primarily with people, I have tried to bring the real lives of people into the picture, not only at strategic points in the book, but in another significant way. I have included "Biographical Sketches" within each chapter. These sketches tell about the lives of prominent—but not necessarily the most important—persons during the period discussed. They emphasize the *life* of a person as a whole, not just the factor that made him or her significant. Real people do not live by their accomplishments alone, but by their hopes and disappointments, achievements and sorrows. The great German scientist Max Planck, for example, will live in history for his formulation of the quantum theory, but that achievement makes Planck remote from most of humanity. His suffering when the Nazis executed his son brings him closer to us on a human level. Another important aspect of this book is the extensive bibliographical essay that I have included for each chapter. This essay, wide-ranging in scope, attempts to give an idea of the arguments confronted by the books that are cited in it. The "Note on the Bibliographical Essay" provides a more detailed explanation of the purposes of the essay.

After World War II Europe underwent a profound transformation. It responded to the two world wars by earnestly seeking economic and political unity. The ideal of European unity as an antidote to war has a long and respectable history, even though it had few practical results before the mid-twentieth century. Because of national cultural differences, creating a European political unity had, by the end of the century, produced an imperfect but viable union with a world role. In domestic politics and society, the contrast between the beginning of the century and its end could hardly be greater. In 1900, elite governments, staffed primarily by aristocrats and very wealthy men, ruled throughout Europe. In most countries, ordinary people and workers had little voice in governing themselves. The ruling classes frowned on governmental intervention in the economy to help the weaker sectors of society. Many men and all women could not vote. Women chafed under the tutelage of their fathers and husbands; lacked social, economic, and sexual equality; and did not have control of their own resources. Socialist parties struggled to alter the political and social system, encountering stiff and sometimes violent resistance.

At the end of the century, wealth and social standing, while still important, were not considered criteria that automatically qualified people for governing—frequently the opposite. Governments claimed the right to rule on grounds of competence and because they had the sanction of the majority in elections in which all persons over a minimum age could vote. Members of the middle and lower classes regularly rose in politics to the highest offices, despite real practical difficulties. Governments paid great attention to the principle of political and social equality of the sexes, even if this ideal remained a work in progress. The European welfare state helped redress the social inequality between the rich and the poor, and governmental officials openly guided the economy. Indeed, the scope and cost of the welfare state provoked a backlash in the latter years of the century.

The increasingly important role of science and technology also characterized European life. The century began with a revolution in physics and ended with one in biology. Work done by European scientists during the early years of the century allowed them to discover nuclear fission, an event that led to both new energy sources and weapons of mass destruction. The last years of the century found Europeans in the forefront with Americans engaged in genetic engineering, on the brink of cloning humans, and confronting new ethical questions raised by the biological revolution.

This book is unusual in considering the smaller countries in detail because the inhabitants of all the countries of Europe, not just the large ones, contributed to the progress of politics, society, and science in the twentieth century. In keeping with the emphasis on science, the book points out that smaller countries were important in the development of atomic physics, as exemplified by Copenhagen as a prime center in the revolution in physics and the prominence of Hungarian scientists as pioneers in the same field. The Scandinavian countries pioneered the social democracy and the emancipation of women that spread all over Europe. Belgium, the Netherlands, and Luxembourg provided a model for the European economic cooperation that knit the continent together. The practical influence of the smaller states in economics and politics increased as the century progressed, and the EU's structure ensured that the trend would intensify.

The high level of violence in Europe and the crucial political events that marked the past century are properly the focus of this book, but so are the end of the struggle for hegemony, the establishment of common economic and political institutions, the affirmation of social democracy, and the stunning advance of science.

A NOTE ON THE BIBLIOGRAPHICAL ESSAY

The aim of the Bibliographical Essay is to give the reader the possibility to expand on the issues discussed in the text. I have attempted to achieve this goal in three ways. First, I have included general works that allow readers to broaden their knowledge of an entire period. Second, specialized books on important themes facilitate the investigation of relevant topics in depth. Third, while these two categories necessarily include points of view, I have also cited books that are notable primarily for their interpretations, even when controversial.

I hope that in this manner readers will not only become familiar with major topics that are relevant to the history of twentieth-century Europe, but will be better able to investigate those of their choice in greater depth and from various points of view. Readers who are interested in further investigation should also remember to take advantage of the Internet sources, of reference bibliographies, and of bibliographies in individual books that could not be mentioned here, in addition to other research tools that are available in libraries. Internet resources should be integrated with books to get a fuller and more accurate discussion of important issues. In order not to weigh down the text, I have not included footnotes. I have cited the sources for the quotations used in the text in the Bibliographical Essay.

Spencer M. Di Scala
Boston, Massachusetts
May 2012

ACKNOWLEDGMENTS

No one writes a book without incurring debts of all kinds with persons who have given their time willingly and generously. I am grateful to the staff of Oxford University Press who were connected with the development and production of this work not only for their skills, but for their kindness; they gave me their much-needed encouragement and suggestions as the book went through its different phases from planning to writing to production. I am particularly grateful to my editor Charles Cavaliere, who shepherded this book though its planning stages and its production, for his encouragement, wise counsel, and excellent suggestions. I also thank Assistant Editor Lauren Aylward, who did the difficult and sometimes maddening technical work of getting this book into production, Marianne Paul, the Production Editor who took it through the production process, and Wendy Ameleh, the Copyeditor.

I want to thank the persons who read the manuscript and gave me their suggestions for improvement, from which I greatly profited: Eugene Boia, Cleveland State University; John Cox, Florida Gulf Coast University; Axel Fair-Schulz, SUNY Potsdam; Martin Menke, Rivier College; David A. Messenger, University of Wyoming; Thomas J. Schaeper, St. Bonaventure University; Robin Underhill, University of Delaware.

I would also like to thank my students at the University of Massachusetts, Boston, for their probing questions, their interest and curiosity, and even their skepticism, all of which spurred me to think about issues that are discussed in this book in ways I would not otherwise have done.

Finally, I would like to acknowledge my two most important personal debts. Although she does not suspect it, my daughter Ashley (not a history buff) gave me valuable insight into the thinking of young people and to what may be most important to them in learning about the past as they mature. To my wife Laura, to whom this book is dedicated, my thanks once again for putting up with too many bouts of introspection alternating with too much boring talk of the past, for reading portions of the manuscript at crucial intervals, for making essential suggestions—and for making the book possible.

ABOUT THE AUTHOR

Spencer M. Di Scala is full professor, Research Professor, and past Graduate Program Director in the history department at the University of Massachusetts Boston. He has been awarded Fulbright scholarships and has published numerous books and articles in modern Italian and European history. His books are: *Dilemmas of Italian Socialism: The Politics of Filippo Turati*; *Renewing Italian Socialism: Nenni to Craxi*; *Italian Socialism Between Politics and History*; *Italy: From Revolution to Republic* (1st ed., 1995; 2nd ed., 1999; 3rd ed., 2004; 4th ed., 2009); *European Political Thought, 1815–1989* (with Salvo Mastellone); *Twentieth Century Europe*; *Makers of the Modern World. Vittorio Orlando: Italy*. *Italy: From Revolution to Republic* was chosen as an alternate selection of the History Book Club and three of his other books have been translated. He has published over 250 articles in scholarly journals, encyclopedias, historical dictionaries, and newspapers in the United States and Europe. Di Scala has also edited a book series on Italian and Italian-American history. In 2011 he held visiting professorships at the University of Rome "Tor Vergata" and at the Free Italian University of the Social Sciences "Guido Carli" (LUISS). Di Scala is President of the Dante Alighieri Society of Massachusetts, the largest Italian-American cultural association in New England. He travels and lectures widely in Europe, consults regularly with European statesmen, and serves on the editorial boards of scholarly journals.

In 1995 Spencer Di Scala was named "Commander" in the Order of Merit of the Italian Republic for the excellence of his research. He received the 2006 award from the New England Chapter of the University Continuing Education Association (UCEA) "in recognition of outstanding teaching, programming, and service." In 2007 UCEA presented him with its national "Excellence in Teaching" award. He teaches face-to-face and online courses.

More information can be found at www.spencerdiscala.com.

Introduction: What Is Europe?

✒

What characterizes Europe, and how do Europeans characterize themselves? Europe does not encompass a large landmass, but its topography and climate are extraordinarily varied. Europe diverges from the lowlands of the Netherlands to the heights of Mont Blanc; from the moderate, wet climate of the British Isles to the extreme cold of Russia; and from Scandinavia to the torrid summers of Greece, Spain, and southern Italy.

EUROPE AS A CULTURAL CONCEPTION

Definitions of people are more difficult to summarize. People compare themselves to others in defining themselves but frequently discover who they are not. The ancient Greeks first fixed the limits of Europe but rejected a geographic for a cultural definition. For the Greek orator Isocrates, Europe meant Greece, that is, Greek culture. With the spread of Greek civilization, the "father of history," Herodotus, extended the idea of Europe to include areas that were influenced by Greek culture. Even persons living within the geographic confines of Europe were not European, Herodotus wrote, if they did not live in cities and were not politically free. In his account of the Persian Wars (6th century BC), in which the Greek city-states defeated the Persian Empire's attempt to conquer them, Herodotus interpreted the conflict as one between liberty (Europe) and despotism (Asia). Both the Greeks and their cultural heirs, the Romans, viewed struggles between themselves and their enemies as civilization versus barbarism.

These ideas remained in the consciousness of Europeans into the twentieth century and still do. In his massive *Decline and Fall of the Roman Empire,* the eighteenth-century British historian Edward Gibbon emphasized how Roman acceptance of despotic Asiatic forms of government signaled the empire's degradation.

THE IDEA OF EUROPE AND CHRISTIANITY

Far from ending the identification of Europe as a cultural unit counterposed against common enemies, the political dismemberment of the Roman Empire marked continuation of the idea, thanks to the empire's conversion to Christianity in the fourth century and to Rome's survival as a unifying ideal. Paradoxically, powerful German tribes that settled in the former Roman Empire converted to Christianity, defended the empire's religion, and championed its political revival. In the ninth century, the Frankish king, Charlemagne, unified large parts of what had been the Roman Empire in the West, and, in a conscious attempt to reclaim Rome's heritage, had himself crowned emperor by the pope. By then, the term *Frank* included both descendants of Teutons and Latins, and western Europeans considered themselves the same people, primarily because of their common religion. A new religious consciousness—East versus West—replaced German against Roman. The bishop of Cremona labeled the East as the land of heresies, while "we westerners" extirpated them. In 960, proclamation of the Holy Roman Empire, based in Germany, demonstrated that Europe remained identified with Rome and Christianity and that these concepts had triumphed in the former homeland of barbarism.

Both popes and secular leaders equated Europe with Christendom when the Muslims invaded Europe in the seventh and eighth centuries. Later, the growing power of the church provoked a reaction by the European monarchs of the twelfth and thirteenth centuries and the decline of papal power in the fourteenth. Even with the weakening of church power, however, the cry went out for Europe to unite against the Turks during the next century when the Muslim threat increased with the rise of the Ottoman Turks, demonstrating the identification of Europe with Christianity.

Within this context of intertwined religious and political conflict, the idea of Europe took hold. The contemporaneous decline of the papacy and the Holy Roman Empire in the fourteenth and fifteenth centuries favored the emergence of individual states with their own interests. This situation made it difficult to unite and oppose the Turkish threat. In 1458, the Italian humanist Aeneas Sylvius Piccolomini, elected Pope Pius II, specifically identified Europe and Christendom. In trying to rally Europe, Pius cataloged the power of the individual "Christian" nations—all European—and warned the Turks that the closer they came to the center of Christendom, the more Europeans would unify. In the course of his discussion, Pius turned the word *Europe* into the adjective—*European*—a linguistic change that enjoyed little support in classical Latin.

THE EUROPEAN IDEA BECOMES SECULARIZED

Pius's yearning for a unified Europe to fight the Muslims remained unfulfilled as the Europeans continued their wars. The idea of Europe as a *cultural* unit, however, survived and became secularized, thanks to the Italian political philosopher Niccolò Machiavelli. Machiavelli defined Europe according to the government and political styles of the individual states, not their religion. States are governed either by one person, with everyone being a servant of the ruler, or by a prince and other groups who have independent power bases, Machiavelli wrote in his famous treatise *The Prince*. In the first case, the ruler may do anything he wishes, while in the second, law, custom, and habit limit monarchs. Machiavelli argued that the second case characterized European states, whether republics or monarchies, but led to conflicts. However, this competition produced diversity and differentiation that favored creative energy and stimulated individual virtue.

This idea led Machiavelli to define Europe by what it is not. Asia, characterized by despotism, permanently repressed the individual. In Europe, political diversity had encouraged the concept of individual liberty. During the seventeenth and eighteenth centuries, European writers strengthened this political interpretation because it fitted well with the existence in Europe of a multiplicity of states.

Unfortunately, constant warfare turned out to be the pernicious other side of the coin of the emergence of powerful states. Many European thinkers considered conflict a necessary evil for the maintenance of freedom. In order to preserve the independence of the individual states and to prevent any one from dominating

Since antiquity, Europe has traditionally been represented as a woman. The painting shown here, by the sixteenth-century Italian artist Titian, depicts a famous Greek myth—"The Rape of Europa." The god Zeus, in the form of a bull, ravishes Europa.

the entire continent, the balance of power concept emerged. First developed in fourteenth-century Italy, this concept spread throughout the continent. Maintaining a political equilibrium required continual diplomatic vigilance and military preparedness that heightened tensions and increased the risk of warfare. Opposing this concept, however, some utopian thinkers elaborated projects for European international organizations that would be capable of keeping the peace and replacing the balance of power while ensuring liberty. As European conflicts became bloodier over the centuries, the desire for some kind of supranational organization strengthened and reached its culmination after World War II.

During the eighteenth-century Enlightenment, the most influential philosophe (a French term signifying Enlightenment intellectuals) of the period, Voltaire, compared Europe to a republic consisting of many states, with diverse forms of government, but fundamentally linked by Christianity and common legal and political principles found nowhere else. Voltaire believed that the principle of freedom for women set the tone for European society, even if women, as most men, did not enjoy political rights. By the eighteenth century, the habit of defining Europe by "who we are not" had become widespread because the discovery of America and subsequent explorations had revealed the existence of peoples living in radically different societies. Paradoxically, the philosophes exploited these exotic societies as a means of criticizing the West by citing their unspoiled character but contrasted European sophistication to the primitivism of other cultures. As more of these different cultures became known, Europeans realized how similar they were despite their own diversity.

The growth of science strengthened this common bond. The scientific revolution of the seventeenth century convinced European thinkers that the scientific method of investigation had ramifications beyond science: Intellectuals considered it an ideal for the secular organization of society and the guiding principle of human development. Ever since then, science, pure, applied, and social, has retained an authority in Europe that has only recently been emulated in other parts of the world. Thus, their scientific culture helped convince Europeans that they were different from, and superior to, other peoples.

In his definition of Europe, Voltaire excluded Russia. If Europe meant a way of life, Russia did not qualify as European. European writers continued to disagree about Russia's character as an Asiatic or a European entity. Even if some observers conceded that, geographically, Russia was in Europe, most agreed that it had the characteristics of an Asian not a European state. Depending on the author, Russia might be included or excluded from the schemes for closer cooperation that emerged from the pens of European writers. In the seventeenth century, Tsar Peter the Great attempted to westernize his country by introducing Western economic methods, but his campaign did not resolve the important issue. If Europe stood for liberty, and Asia for despotism, Russia clearly fit into the latter camp.

During the nineteenth century, however, Russia played a significant role in defeating Napoleon, whose enemies considered him a despot, but it was still generally considered "Asiatic." Only during the late nineteenth and twentieth centuries did Russia become more acceptable as a European country, largely because of an extraordinary series of great writers who reflected important European values, but the debate about whether it was truly European continued not only among West

Europeans. but among Russians themselves. The discussion over Russia's position illustrates how the definition of *Europe* continued to revolve around culture rather than geography.

The increasingly brutal wars, however, encouraged European thinkers and statesmen to focus on unity as a means of ending them and maximizing the continent's potential. The methods for accomplishing this aim can be broadly viewed as either hegemonic or ideological.

HEGEMONY VERSUS CONSENSUS

In substance, the "hegemonic" method meant conquering diverse areas and integrating their inhabitants socially, culturally, and economically into a cohesive, centralized political unit. Proponents of the "ideological" technique, based on consensus instead of force, considered Europe a unit and Europeans as sharing basic beliefs, institutions, and values. In short, despite their differences, Europeans had a common outlook. If they emphasized their common traits, they could form a single economic and political unit on a voluntary basis in order to improve their lot. Concretely, advocates of this ideal believed that a federation would respect the diversity among Europeans while uniting them politically.

The hegemonic ideal can be traced to the Roman Empire. Rome conquered all of known Europe in ancient times and imposed its culture and the Pax Romana, a long-term peace that Europeans considered a golden age. In the Middle Ages, the Roman example inspired imitators, such as Charlemagne, the Holy Roman emperors, and the popes. During the eighteenth century, France seemed destined to conquer all of Europe, first under its powerful monarchs and then under the ideological and political impact of the French Revolution and Napoleon. This last development created a new paradox. Napoleon asserted that he favored a European confederation, with common political and judicial institutions, laws, monetary system, and weights and measures. He would have created a community of European peoples, he professed, ending war among Europeans. Napoleon set up states run by natives that introduced French-style reforms into different areas of Europe; he established a multinational army to invade Russia in 1812 that might be seen as the forerunner of a European army.

Despite Napoleon's claims, he and his French revolutionary predecessors retained real control of the areas they "liberated." At the same time, French revolutionary ideology stimulated the growth of nationalism: the idea that all nationalities should have control of the areas in which they lived and should be free to follow their own interests. Paradoxically, this belief provoked powerful revolts against the French themselves and, later, competition among the various European nationalities. The French Revolution thus created a new tension between the idea of a common European identity and a fight for supremacy among nation-states, each convinced of its superiority. This heightened nationalism culminated in the ruinous wars of the twentieth century, but the theme of a common cultural heritage led Europeans to search for a balance between individuality and commonality when those wars ended.

When the fear of French hegemony faded, the German threat followed. After German unification in 1871, Germany's industrial development eclipsed Britain's and France's. Had Germany won in World War I, its war aims envisioned economic and military domination of the continent through the creation of Middle Europe, a combination of strategic annexations and a customs union, and of Middle Africa to ensure raw materials. Germany also desired the breakup of Russia. German culture, already extremely influential, would have become paramount.

Following Germany's defeat in 1918 and its treatment after the war, the rise of Nazism signaled the approach of a new conflict of the kind that Europeans increasingly considered "a civil war between the forces of oligarchy, aristocracy, authoritarianism, Fascism and those of popular democracy, socialism, revolution." Italian Fascism found support in such traditionally democratic countries as France, England, and Belgium. In France, the triumph of a leftist electoral alliance, including the Communists, and a Jewish Socialist prime minister, forced industrialists to accept the Matignon Agreements that extended benefits for French workers and enraged the industrialists. The far right popularized the slogan, "Better Hitler than Blum." When the Nazis overran Europe in the early days of World War II, they found willing collaborators in the different parts of the continent, and later the Resistance movements took on a clearer civil war aspect. For a continent that considered itself family, wars among its member nations had been civil conflicts for some time, and World War II intensified this feeling.

In their attempt to control the continent, even the Nazis exploited the idea of a common heritage and feeling for European unity and claimed that they defended European interests from "Asian" Bolshevism. In this context, the defeat of Russia was an important step in the process of uniting Europe, which would exclude Russia. According to a German-drafted European Charter, no European country could maintain its freedom and economic viability acting alone.

The grotesque Nazi attempt to exploit Europeanist ideas marked the last gasp of the hegemonic model. The emphasis now shifted to doing so by consensus. Although various ideas to unite the continent had circulated for centuries, only the conditions following World War II's devastation allowed European intellectuals and statesmen to take concrete steps toward some form of unity.

The modern beginnings of an ideological concept of Europe can be found in the eighteenth-century Enlightenment and the French Revolution, during which ideas for all-European institutions combining common principles, the desire for peace, and the basic political restructuring of the continent were discussed. The trend accelerated in the nineteenth century with the growth of democratic and revolutionary movements. French revolutionary thinkers built on philosopher Jean-Jacques Rousseau's concept of the general will. Although subject to different interpretations, the general will opposed rule by divine-right monarchs and was perceived as the people governing by a majority vote. French revolutionaries believed that their reforms, along with "Liberty, Equality, and Fraternity," were the birthright of all nations.

French armies carried these ideals to other European countries despite their ruthlessness. After the Revolution's defeat, the conservative powers banded together to prevent the diffusion of Liberal and Nationalist sentiments that had been unleashed by revolutionary ideology that shook the continent in 1820 and 1821, 1830 and 1831, and especially in the "year of revolutions," 1848. Democratic leftist leaders called for revolutionary Europe to band together against the conservative powers. Italian patriot Giuseppe Mazzini established a secret society to fight for Italian freedom and favored the establishment of similar societies to struggle against the monarchs in favor of Europe's common Liberal heritage. In addition to "Young Italy," Mazzini inspired the foundation of similar organizations in other countries, capped off by Young Europe, which he defined as "a federation of peoples, based on the principles of national independence and the freedom of each in internal affairs." The French utopian Socialist Claude-Henri de Saint Simon called for common European political institutions in which national parliaments would select a European Parliament to elect a king of Europe. This European federation would end war and stimulate industry. Similarly, the nineteenth-century pacifist movement advocated a European federation as a means of eliminating war. It looked to the American model and coined the term "United States of Europe," a popular concept during the nineteenth century. European Socialists preached peace and cooperation on a worldwide scale and coordinated their actions through the Second International.

The outbreak of World War I destroyed the International and seemed to make a mockery of peace based on collaboration among nations, but the idea of European unity survived that conflict. Discussing the shape of a postwar Europe in 1916, former French foreign minister Gabriel Hanotaux advocated a "Constituent Assembly of united European states," a European government with legislative, judicial, and executive powers commanding an armed force capable of enforcing its decisions. Similarly, during the war's early months, the British press emphasized that only a United States of Europe could bring permanent peace to the continent. In Italy in 1917, Fiat owner Giovanni Agnelli and University of Genoa professor Attilio Cabiati argued for the establishment of a European federal structure complete with a parliament and an army as the only means of reconciling European nationality with the political, strategic, and economic goals of different states, and German writers expressed like ideas.

THE IDEAL OF UNITY BETWEEN THE
TWO WORLD WARS

In the 1920s and 1930s, books, the press, conferences, and high governmental officials advocated European unification. The debut of the United States on the world scene stimulated the discussion because World War I had left the European powers exhausted and bankrupt; with the United States eclipsing Europe, many Europeans believed that only a unified continent would be capable of confronting American economic and political power. In the 1920s, the hopes for a practical outcome to projects for European unity seemed bright because the French and Germans resolved some of the important diplomatic problems left over from the war, and a new spirit of cooperation between them emerged. While no concrete results appeared, the discussion on unity between the wars set the tone for practical action after World War II. The editor of the French newspaper *Le Figaro* answered the old question "What is Europe?" He wrote: "Geographically, racially, and linguistically, Europe is characterized by diversity, but in its intellectual and spiritual tradition, it is a unity. The essence of this unity is a fusion of Hebrew religion, Greek intelligence, and Roman law."

The increasing interest that influential statesmen took in the question of unity was demonstrated in talks on the subject among French foreign minister Aristide Briand, German chancellor Gustav Stresemann, and other European statesmen. These talks ultimately failed because the Germans linked unity to a revision of the Versailles settlement, the British believed that their destiny lay with their colonies and dominions, and, predictably, the nationalistic Italian Fascist regime was unsympathetic. But Briand insisted, stating in a July 16, 1929, speech to the Chamber of Deputies that he advocated a European federation as a means of preventing future European wars. On May 17, 1930, the French Foreign Office followed up the speech by releasing a long memorandum on a federal union for Europe. This document linked a European union to the new League of Nations by replicating that body's organization by establishing a European Conference—a general assembly representing all member states—a permanent Political Committee composed only of certain nations, and a Secretariat working closely with the League Secretariat. The union would retain enough flexibility to consider the sovereign needs of nations but would be firm enough to guarantee the benefits of collective security. In the economic sphere, the union would create a common market to achieve the highest standard of living possible for Europeans.

In September 1930, the French attempted to secure the adoption of Briand's proposal by the Europeans, but by then the rise of the Nazis in Germany had already begun. While the political and economic crises of the 1930s scuttled Briand's initiative, it was an important anticipation of the efforts to create the European Union following World War II.

THE EUROPEAN CONCEPT DURING THE LATE TWENTIETH CENTURY

The brutality of World War II, the concentration camps, the persecutions, and the division between resisters and collaborators in Nazi-occupied Europe produced a definitive turn toward the idea of a united Europe as the only way to end the wars that systematically destroyed the European continent. The armed European Resistance itself took on the aspect of a pan-European movement, with fighters of diverse nationalities taking part in different national resistance movements. Even though the Communists were major elements in the resistance, its domination by Moscow prevented it from taking a major role in the new drive for European unity, which came most prominently through the writings of moderate Liberals and Catholics. In Italy, the earliest postwar center of major ideas and leadership for the Europeanist ideal, the Communist-dominated Resistance did not have a major role in the 1943 elaboration of the "Ventotene Manifesto" (from the name of a Mediterranean island used as a prison). Inspired by Mazzini's ideas of a United States of Europe, this declaration linked the postwar European structure to the development of European unity. Altiero Spinelli, one of postwar Europe's most influential advocates for unity, found the cause of wars in the nature of the nation-state itself, regardless of its social or political organization. Patriotism produced degenerate nationalism, Spinelli argued, and federalism was the antidote. In 1944, a conference held in Geneva adopted a "Manifesto of European Resistance" advocating a European Federal Alliance. In addition, the postwar Catholic movement would produce great parties in Germany, Italy, and France that strongly supported European unity.

For Europeans, World War II forcefully posed the question of how to create common European institutions, not whether to do so. Given American predominance and the danger that the continent would rapidly be transformed into an American economic colony, French statesmen Jean Monnet and Robert Schuman prodded the Europeans to cooperate on the economic plane, calculating that economic collaboration would favor political agreements. In fact, Western European economic collaboration culminated in the European Economic Community and, with the demise of its British-led rival, the European Free Trade Association, its enlargement and transformation first into the European Community and then into the EU. East Europe's attempt at cooperation among Communist countries beginning in 1949 (the Council for Mutual Economic Assistance) failed not only because of its domination by the USSR but also because of the inequality among the different member states. Following the fall of communism between 1989 and 1991, the Eastern European countries applied for admission to the EU, which, in the meantime, had eliminated tariff barriers and had established a common currency.

Despite difficulties and crises, the EU proceeded apace in its development of common political institutions and in its efforts to refine its decision-making powers. These institutions included a European Parliament regularly elected by EU citizens and an executive body, the European Commission, consisting of commissioners from the different nations that made policy and uniformly enforced legislation. The Europeans also attempted with less success to work out a common foreign policy and to set up a common armed force. Given Europe's divisive history despite its common heritage, however, these successes did not come easily and were threatened by the crisis following the attack on the United States on September 11, 2001. The process of European unity periodically went through grave political and economic crises, alternating between periods of optimism and pessimism. However, there is no doubt about the substantial success of the experiment, with Europe emerging as a major trading bloc and as a major influence in the world through its influence ("soft power"), rather than through its military strength. Europeans understand that without the EU, they would scarcely count for much in the world. They have evolved their own perspectives on modern economic and social problems that contrast with those of the United States, once more defining themselves as what they "are not."

A POST–COLD WAR PERSPECTIVE

This rapid survey illustrates how the history of Europe transcends short-term events. After World War II, European influence fell to its lowest point in modern times, and the continent became a battleground for the struggle between the United States and the Soviet Union for world domination. Because the cold war lasted almost fifty years, observers assumed that it would be a permanent feature in European history. This turned out to be a false perspective. Long-term

European trends that seemed to have disappeared, especially in the Soviet bloc, rapidly reasserted themselves following the fall of the Soviet Union. Crucial and important as it was, the cold war turned out to be an episode in time that is unlikely to be repeated. In considering the history of Europe, therefore, this book emphasizes long-term trends and tendencies that have determined the continent's course, have marked Europe in the past, and seem likely to do so in the future— along with new developments, such as the great increase in immigration, that are likely to change it. It seems judicious to keep in mind that tendencies that seem minor or that were overwhelmed by more spectacular events, such as the cold war, can later come to the fore, sometimes as the result of those events.

This is the case with the desire for unity, muted but always present in the European background; with nationalism, suppressed by the USSR in the East and overwhelmed by guilt in the West; and with religion, given new life by the challenge of Muslim immigration. The twentieth century opened with the European nations dominating the world but poised for a disastrous civil war. It ended with great progress toward the establishment of what the Soviet Union's last leader, Mikhail Gorbachev, dubbed a "Common Home" because, despite the conflicts, Europeans did have much in common and needed to stop the wars. Thus, their future during the twenty-first century will depend on whether they can truly cooperate to make Europe a working economic and political unit while preserving their individuality. The answer to this question promises to affect Europe and the world.

Bibliographical Essay

There is an ample literature on the topics treated in this section. A good, brief, introduction is Denys Hay, *Europe: The Emergence of an Idea* (New York, 1966). Denis de Rougemont, *The Idea of Europe* (New York, 1966), is a fuller treatment of the themes. Anthony Pogden, *The Idea of Europe: From Antiquity to the European Union* (Washington, D.C., 2002), includes a broad range of essays analyzing the European idea from the distant past up to the most important contemporary issues. Alexander Tchoubarian, *The European Idea in History in the Nineteenth and Twentieth Centuries: A View from Moscow* (Essex, UK, 1994), is full of interesting information that is difficult to get in one source, despite a sometimes naive tone and some printing errors. Carl H. Pegg's *Evolution of the European Idea, 1914–1932* (Chapel Hill, N.C., 1983) is a well-researched work on the period, from which the quote by Lucien Romier was taken (p. 57). The quotation on the period between the First and Second World Wars as the approach of civil strife may be found on p. 13 of Donald Cameron Watt, *Too Serious a Business: European Armed Forces and the Approach to the Second World War* (New York, 1975). The book edited by Peter M. R. Stirk, *European Unity in Context: The Interwar Period* (London, 1989), examines the period from 1918 to 1940. Stirk and David Willis also edited a collection of essays on important themes discussed after World War II, *Shaping Postwar Europe: European Unity and Disunity, 1945–1957* (New York, 1991). Martin Dedman published a good introduction to the subject of the EU: *The Origins and Development of the European Union 1945–2008* (London and New York, 2010). A critical work that brings the question past the cold war's end and takes a skeptical view of European unity, Gerald Delanty's *Inventing Europe: Idea, Identity, Reality* (New York, 1995) argues that the idea of Europe is based more on adversity than on unity and that there is little within the national traditions fostering unity; the work emphasizes a political science rather than a historical approach. As Europe became increasingly more important because of its economy and social policies, the debate about whether the American or European ways of life were better heated up. Jeremy Rifkin, *The European Dream: How Europe's Vision of the Future Is Quietly Eclipsing the American Dream* (New York, 2004), argues for the superiority of the European approach to life and believes that it is eclipsing America's style by emphasizing cooperation and social networks instead of competition and individualism. Mark Leonard's *Why Europe Will Run the 21st Century* (New York, 2005) reasons that Europe will become supreme not through military means ("hard power") but by making use of its enormous and rising cultural and economic influence in the world ("soft power"). Another book favoring the European lifestyle is Steven Hill's *Europe's Promise: Why the European Way Is the Best Hope in an Insecure Age* (Berkeley, Calif., 2010). Alberto Alesina and Francesco Giavazzi take the opposite—and more pessimistic view—arguing in *The Future of Europe: Reform or Decline* (Cambridge, Mass., 2006) that the American economic system is more efficient that that of Europe and assures greater prosperity for its people. Although not specifically concerned with unification, Sam Huntington in *The Clash of Civilizations* (New York, 1996) argues that Europe's borders are those of Western Christianity and have became increasingly relevant after the terroristic attacks on the West after September 11, 2001.

ABBREVIATIONS

ABM	Anti-Ballistic Missile
ACCs	Allied Control Commissions
AN	National Alliance
ARP	Protestant Anti-Revolutionary Party
AVH	Hungarian Communist Secret Police
BANU	Bulgarian Agrarian Party
BBC	British Broadcasting Corporation
BCP	Bulgarian Communist Party
BEF	British Expeditionary Force
BENELUX	Belgium-Netherlands-Luxembourg
BSP	Bulgarian Socialist Party
BVP	Bavarian People's Party
CAP	Common Agricultural Policy
CDA	Christian Democratic Appeal
CDU	Christian Democratic Union
CEDA	Confederation of Autonomous Rightist Groups
CERN	European Council for Nuclear Research
CGIL	Confederation of Italian Workers
CGL	General Confederation of Labor (Italy)
CGT	General Confederation of Labor (France)
CIS	Commonwealth of Independent States
CMEA	Council for Mutual Economic Assistance (same as COMECON)
COMECON	Council for Mutual Economic Assistance (same as CMEA)
COMINFORM	Communist information Bureau
COMINTERN	Communist International
CNT	Anarchist Labor Union
CPA	Centre for Policy Studies
CPC	Communist Party of Czechoslovakia
CPSU	Communist Party of the Soviet Union

CSU	Christian Social Union
DAF	German Labor Front
DAP	German Workers' Party
DC	Christian Democrats
DGB	German Federation of Trade Unions
DNVP	German Nationalist Party
DS	Democrats of the Left
EC	European Commission
EC	European Community
ECB	European Central Bank
ECSC	European Coal and Steel Community
EDC	European Defense Community
EDES	Greek Monarchist Resistance Movement
EEC	European Economic Community
EFTA	European Free Trade Association
ELAS	Greek Communist Resistance Movement
ELF	Eritrean Liberation Front
EMU	European Monetary Union
EP	European Parliament
EPC	European Political Community
EPU	European Payments Union
ETA	Basque Separatist Organization
EU	European Union
EURATOM	European Agency for Atomic Research
FDP	Free Democratic Party
FFI	French Forces of the Interior
FI	Forza Italia
FIDESZ	Federation of Young Democrats-Hungarian Civic Party
GATT	General Agreement on Tariffs and Trade
GDR	German Democratic Republic
GDP	Gross Domestic Product
Gestapo	Nazi Secret Police
GNP	Gross National Product
GUF	Fascist University Youth
GULAG	Chief Administration of Corrective Labor Camps
ICBM	Intercontinental Ballistic Missile
IEA	Institute for Economic Affairs
ILP	Independent Labour Party
IMF	International Monetary Fund
IMRO	Macedonian Revolutionary Organization
INF	Intermediate Nuclear Force Agreement
IRA	Irish Republican Army
IRBM	Intermediate Range Ballistic Missile
IRG	Interregional Group
IRI	Institute for Industrial Reconstruction
KGB	Soviet Secret Police

KLA	Kosovo Liberation Army
KKE	Greek Communist Party
KOR	Committee for Workers' Defense
KPD	German Communist Party
MIRV	Multiple Independently Targetable Reentry Vehicle
MRP	Popular Republican Movement
MSI	Italian Social Movement
ND	New Democracy
NDP	National Democratic Party of Germany
NEM	New Economic Mechanism
NEP	New Economic Policy
NKVD	Soviet Secret Police
NSDAP	National Socialist German Workers' Party (Nazi)
NSF	Nazi Women's Group
NSF	National Salvation Front
OAS	Secret Armed Organization
OECD	Organization for Economic Cooperation and Development
OEEC	Organization for European Economic Cooperation
ONB	Italian Fascist Youth Movement (Balilla)
OND	Italian Fascist Leisure Movement (Dopolavoro)
OPEC	Organization of Petroleum Exporting Countries
OSS	Office of Strategic Services
OVRA	Italian Fascist Secret Police
OZN	Camp of National Unity
PASOK	Socialist Party (Greece)
PCF	French Communist Party
PCI	Italian Communist Party
PDL	"People of Liberty" party
PDS	Democratic Party of the Left
PNF	National Fascist Party
PP	Popular Party (Spanish)
PPF	French Popular Party
PPI	Italian Popular Party
PPS	Polish Socialist Party
PS	Socialist Party (Portugal)
PSD	Portuguese Social Democrats
PSI	Italian Socialist Party
PSOE	Spanish Socialist Workers' Party
RAI	Italian Radio (later Radio and Television) Agency
RSFSR	Russian Soviet Federated Socialist Republic
SALT	Strategic Arms Limitation Talks
SD	Security Service (Nazi)
SDI	Strategic Defense Initiative ("Star Wars")
SEATO	Southeast Asia Treaty Organization
SFIO	French Socialist Party
SPD	German Socialist Party

SS	Security Guards
SSC	Superconducting Supercollider
TUC	Trades Union Congress
UDF	Union of Democratic Forces
UGT	Spanish Trade Workers' Union
UIL	Italian Workers' Union
UN	United Nations
USPD	Independent Social Democratic Party
USSR	Union of Soviet Socialist Republics
VAT	Value Added Tax
WTO	Warsaw Treaty Organization (Warsaw Pact)

PART I

The European Age

✍

December 14, 1900

Chronology aside, some centuries seem to arrive early; others, late. It can be argued that the eighteenth century began in 1715 with the death of France's Sun King, Louis XIV, which removed the political obstacles to the full application of Enlightenment ideas. The nineteenth century may have begun late, in 1815, with the end of the Napoleonic wars, or early, in 1789, with the French Revolution. In considering when historical periods begin or end, historians look at the defining characteristics of an age, then attempt to determine when those attributes became dominant and when they ceased to be so.

THE TWENTIETH CENTURY: SCIENCE AND IDEOLOGY

In this sense, the twentieth century appears unusual, generally being considered an age of conflict, or extremes, beginning in 1914 with the First World War. Certainly the peaceful age preceding World War I lends credence to this interpretation, but it also may mislead observers because wars do not come out of nowhere. A detailed examination of the pre-1914 period is essential to understand the causes of World War I, but this leads also to the conclusion that the attributes of a new age that had already emerged before it.

In volume 5 of his collected papers, philosopher Isaiah Berlin identified the factors characterizing the twentieth century as the dramatic development of the natural sciences and technology and the ideological cyclones that affected everyone's life: totalitarianism of different political hues, nationalism, and racism.

3

If Berlin is correct in his assessment, the twentieth century entered the scene right on time. On December 14, 1900, German physicist Max Planck elaborated the quantum theory. This hypothesis was the foundation of new theories of the atom, motion, and the universe eventually worked out by Albert Einstein and others over the next thirty years. The early years of the century were also the seedtime for new political movements—populist nationalism, fascism, and communism. Both trends shook the comfortable assumptions that had been painfully constructed in Europe over the previous two centuries, even if economic and social changes increased self-confidence. Most Europeans were unaware that they were living an all-too-brief optimistic moment and that their lives were in the process of being pulled apart.

EUROPEAN SOCIETY

In 1900, French philosopher Charles Peguy noted that society had changed more in the past thirty years than it had since the birth of Christ. Indeed, the period from 1890 to 1914 witnessed the second industrial revolution—the spread of heavy industry, electrification, construction of a telephone network, improved transportation, rapid urbanization, increased purchasing power, and a general improvement of living conditions. Europeans were the first to adjust to this rapid modernization of society. However, because large sectors of the population remained desperately poor and resentful, they mobilized politically to oppose existing governments, and socialist parties grew rapidly during the "belle époque."

Private Lives in a Modernizing Society

Interestingly enough, much of the discontent at the twentieth century's dawn appears to have been owing to rising expectations. People expected that life would improve even more rapidly and continuously. Those classes whose lot improved slowly resented being left behind. Yet, despite the high levels of poverty that existed in Europe when compared to the late twentieth century, the continent (and the United States) led the world in the extent and depth of its economic development. After the 1890s, a greater proportion of the European populace enjoyed more goods and services at a lower price than ever before in history. In Britain, a worker's purchasing power increased by 40 percent in only two decades, and real wages also rose dramatically for other Western European workers. An agricultural depression that lasted from the 1870s to the early 1890s lowered the price of food. Coupled with a great increase in industrial production, this drop allowed Europeans to spend a smaller percentage than before of their income on food, clothes, health, entertainment, and education. Moreover, the crisis on the land forced many peasants to move to the cities, which grew enormously. Greater London's population exploded from 1,405,000 in 1891 to 2,045,000 at Queen Victoria's death in 1901, and other European cities had a similar growth pattern. Conditions in the cities were miserable for these new residents, but eventually their children were better off than if they had remained in rural areas.

While heavy industry accounted for much of the increase in Western Europe's prosperity, light industry, stimulated by technological advances, contributed to the greater comfort of its inhabitants. The increased manufacture of such amenities as soap, processed foods, and newspapers raised the standard of living for ordinary people. With the proliferation of trams (initially horse-drawn, then electric), subways, bicycles, and the creation of dense railway networks, a revolution in transportation occurred. Growing numbers of department stores, telephone networks, and other service-sector industries such as teaching, and the typewriter, enabled women to find employment outside the home in greater numbers. Women still suffered discrimination and were obliged to resign from their jobs when they married, but the process of emancipation had begun.

The increased efficiency and lower prices brought about improvements in transportation, and banking increased the pace of economic activity. Improved sanitary conditions reduced the death rate, and Europe's population grew at the extraordinary rate of about 1 percent a year between 1890 and 1914. The increase in production, however, counterbalanced the population expansion and created greater wealth, while the bigger population and improved technology stimulated demand. For example, in the home, heaters capable of warming several rooms efficiently became more common; matches—once very expensive—became cheap; economical and efficient coal- or gas-burning stoves appeared; electric irons replaced their coal-burning predecessors; and iceboxes kept foods fresh. Frozen meats and exotic fruits, such as bananas and coconuts, arrived from faraway places.

Men's lives changed dramatically in the last years of the nineteenth and the first decade of the twentieth century. Paternal authoritarianism in the extended family had afflicted young men in different ways than it had women, but was equally stifling. Fathers kept a tight financial rein on their children's lives and controlled them even if they were away at school, but now real salaries rose and men could live in their own homes with their wives after marriage. National governments sponsored reduced railway fares, encouraging tourism and attendance at sports events in different cities, and the ubiquitous tourist with a Kodak camera slung around his neck appeared. Participation in individual sports, such as swimming, canoeing, and mountain climbing, became common middle-class activities. Politics also aroused their enthusiasm, since by 1900 most men could vote, and more of them participated in discussions in the many cafés. Life for men became less provincial.

The City

Life in the expanding city changed significantly. In places long characterized by pollution, areas of extreme poverty, and unhealthful conditions, better illumination and improved sanitation reduced crime and disease. Electric street lighting gradually replaced gaslights and encouraged people to stay out late at night in greater safety in cafés and theaters or to attend movies—a new art form. Their evening over, electrified streetcars whisked the revelers home. The rapid transportation systems had an important impact on city government by stimulating the incorporation of once outlying regions into major metropolitan areas. In personal transportation, the bicycle, formerly made of wood, acquired rubber tires and gears and revolutionized personal mobility. The first automobiles, expensive and unreliable, did not clog city streets on December 14, 1900, when Max Planck elaborated his quantum theory.

Despite the great improvements in health care and city services, social and economic conditions remained backward by present standards. Only an estimated 20 percent to 30 percent of people belonged to the middle class in England, Europe's most advanced industrial and urban region. Almost 31 percent lived in dire poverty in London in 1900, the world's most advanced city, according to a study in that year. This extreme poverty meant constant hunger and cold, frequent death on the street, and burial in a pauper's grave. Nevertheless, these statistics demonstrate that poverty afflicted a smaller percentage of Europeans than the rest of the world population, and municipalities began keeping records on the changes in daily life—births, marriages, deaths—that are fundamental in implementing governmental support for ordinary people.

The Countryside

In addition to changes in the cities, the agricultural depression's end in the late 1890s produced major alterations in the countryside. The depression forced many rural wage earners and marginal farmers off the land, but the decrease in the labor supply gradually resulted in an improved income for those who remained. Taking advantage of new machinery, such as threshers and reapers, and stimulated by knowledge of improving city life brought to them by newspapers, peasants aspired to higher living standards and organized politically to achieve them. Denmark stands out as a country that transformed its agriculture. It decided to specialize in the production of dairy products for export, resulting in increased agricultural wages at a time when politics dictated high tariff policies for the big European powers. In France and other Western European countries, incomes also increased significantly during the century's first decade, but there political action instead of crop changes played a major role. When phylloxera devastated vineyards in southern France, for example, peasant demonstrations forced the government to intervene in their favor, and similar developments occurred in other countries.

Land tenure varied in different parts of Europe and influenced the economic well-being of rural areas. In France, small independent proprietors and tenant farmers accounted for a large proportion of males who were engaged in agriculture (70 percent), while both categories declined significantly in England. In central and southern Europe, conditions differed considerably. In southern Italy, large latifundia owned by the rich and worked by day laborers contrasted with scattered landholdings that were too small to support a family, a large number of very poor day laborers, and peasant villages located at long distances from farms; these conditions and the lack of industry favored large-scale emigration from the South to other parts of Europe, the United States, and Latin America. In southern Spain and Prussia east of the Elbe river, most peasants did not own land and worked for large landowners, while many German, Czech, Austrian, Hungarian, and Polish peasant families worked their own land. In Russia the peasants were the worst off. The serfs had been emancipated in 1861 and in 1900 could not own land as individuals. Peasants lived in village communities that owned the land and regulated how they paid their taxes and the fees owed to local landowners for land purchased from them. Peasants also required permission from the head of the household and the commune to leave their village for any length of time.

Peasant psychology differed dramatically from that of city folk. Peasants incorporated technological advances into their farming readily enough, but they stubbornly adhered to their traditional cultures and abhorred the changing social attitudes of the cities. Eastern European peasants considered themselves "the people," thought city dwellers strange, and rejected outsiders, especially intellectuals. Russian peasants attacked radical university students who came to the countryside to help them. As a rule, peasants proved impervious to outside movements that hoped to win them over to revolutionary ideals, but they frequently rose spontaneously when circumstances provoked them.

Women

Despite these anomalies, alterations in social conditions affected the lives of social groups everywhere in Europe to a much greater extent than had been true in the past. The breakup of the large extended family and better economic conditions improved women's lives. Living in their own homes instead of with their extended families had become socially acceptable and economically feasible by 1900. Economic progress and better transportation allowed middle-class families to take vacations, and, in general, leisure time increased. In 1900 women still had more children than they did in 1914, but, because peasant girls preferred to come to the city to work as maids, rather than toil in the fields, plentiful domestic help made it easier for middle-class women to go out by themselves, especially in northern Europe, but in some areas women still could not to go out on their own or stay in hotels even if accompanied by their husbands. Where they went out by themselves, shopping was a favorite activity for women, and they changed the whole experience. With more female customers, the shops that had been primarily warehouses acquired a modern aspect with windows that attractively displayed merchandise. In the past women had sewn the family's clothes, but the new century brought more ready-made clothing. Fashion reflected women's new mobility and freedom as skirts shortened and women's suits became more common. More of their offspring survived because of better hygienic practices, so women married later and had fewer children as the century advanced. Fewer children meant more independence for women and allowed more of the middle class's resources to be spent on education and other amenities.

As women became freer, they attended school in greater numbers and in Western Europe studied the same subjects as their male counterparts and made important contributions in diverse fields. In 1894 Maria Montessori became the first woman in Italy to win a medical degree. Specializing in education, she lectured on pedagogy at the University of Rome from 1901 to 1907 and developed educational methods that worked effectively that she applied in a special school she founded in 1906; her educational techniques spread throughout the world. Several women won Nobel Prizes in literature, and in science Madame Marie Curie shared a Nobel Prize and was awarded one for chemistry in 1911.

The real improvements in conditions for women did not bring full equality to women, however,. The doors of Russian institutions of higher learning were still closed to women, and in Maria Montessori's Italy lawyers argued against women's entrance to the bar. Women had only restricted control over their own property and faced discrimination in many professions. As late as the 1920s and 1930s, women were expected to resign from their jobs when they married, and governments placed quotas on the number of women who could be employed in state service. Women could not vote except in some Scandinavian countries, and the major West European countries gave them the vote in general elections only after World War I or II. Women rebelled by establishing feminist organizations, participating in political life, founding newspapers and other publications to advance their cause, and demonstrating. Socialist parties welcomed them into their organizations, but their leaders gave priority to the struggle for men's rights. European Socialism nevertheless numbered among its most innovative thinkers and key political leaders Rosa Luxemburg, Anna Kuliscioff, Angelica Balabanoff, and Clara Zetkin.

Social Classes

Despite the accelerating modernization of European society, the social classes remained separate and distinct in 1900. Part of the aristocracy still boasted

Feminist associations and publications were widespread by the beginning of the twentieth century. This photo dates from the early 1900s and shows suffragists holding a copy of the newspaper *The Vote.*

fabulous wealth and had political power out of proportion to its numbers. In Britain, unlike the continent, the aristocracy had its own house in Parliament, the House of Lords, which wielded real power and comprised a significant bloc in the House of Commons. Nobles dominated the established churches; the higher ranks of the military; the bureaucracies, especially in the East; and society. Suave cosmopolitanism distinguished the European aristocracy, and nobles in different countries had more in common with each other than with the lower or middle classes of their own nations. A common mentality distinguished European nobles: "He [an aristocrat] behaved as if his birth and leisure made him superior but never argued the point."

BIOGRAPHICAL SKETCHES

Anna Kuliscioff
Cofounder of Italian Socialism

Born in Russia on January 9, 1854, the flame-haired Anna Kuliscioff attended the University of Zurich in 1871 to study engineering because Russian institutions of higher learning excluded women. At Zurich, a center of Russian exile activity, she became a revolutionary. Upon returning to her homeland in 1874, she participated in the return-to-the-people movement, an ill-fated attempt to convert Russian peasants to revolutionary activity. Forced to flee the country for Switzerland, she began a liaison with Andrea Costa, a prominent Italian Anarchist, and had a leading role in the European anarchism of the period. In the late 1870s she converted to Marxism and influenced Costa to make a similar change.

When her relationship with Costa ended, Kuliscioff moved to Naples with their daughter Andreina and fell in love with Milanese democrat Filippo Turati. She exercised a decisive influence on Turati, who converted to Marxism. In the meantime, she received a medical degree and practiced medicine among the poor in Milan (this did not stop her from resisting Turati's pleas to stop smoking). The partners founded the country's most important Socialist journal, *Critica Sociale,* and the Milanese Socialist League became a cell for the county's first modern political organization in 1892, the Italian Socialist Party. The articles in *Critica Sociale* and Kuliscioff's salon located in Milan's famous Galleria converted Italy's most famous intellectuals to Marxist socialism. Kuliscioff advised Turati during his many years in Parliament, and the two are still revered as icons of Italian democracy. In 1898, the Italian government cracked down on Socialists, imprisoning the couple. Released after some months, they later guided the Socialist Party in its drive for social and political reforms.

Within the party, the couple fought the revolutionary wing, led after 1912 by Benito Mussolini. The two had political differences, with Kuliscioff pushing for an immediate campaign in favor of women's suffrage and Turati advocating for more gradual action. Kuliscioff headed the feminist movement and in 1911–12 edited its newspaper *La Difesa delle Lavoratrici* [Defense of Women Workers]. Following World War I, the pair led the Socialist revisionists in an unsuccessful fight to block the rise of fascism. Kuliscioff was so closely identified with the antifascist

continued

continued

resistance that when she died on December 29, 1925, her funeral procession to Milan's Monumental Cemetery provided the occasion for the last epic street battle between Socialists and Fascists. Her companion died in exile fighting fascism on March 29, 1932, and joined her in the same cemetery after World War II.

Kuliscioff's daughter married a rich Catholic Milanese businessman, which prompted Kuliscioff to write dejectedly that there must be a balancing force in the world: She rebelled against everyone and everything, while her daughter, raised by two revolutionaries, conformed to bourgeois life. She would have appreciated the irony when her grandson became a monk.

Below the aristocracy, the upper middle class enjoyed life at the beginning of the new century. Composed of administrators, successful entrepreneurs, and professionals, this group made up between 10 percent and 15 percent of the population in the most developed Western European societies, but much less in Eastern and Southern Europe. Seeking to imitate aristocratic values, the group honored intellectual pursuits, such as reading and listening to good music. They valued a good general culture but disdained the specialized knowledge that doctors or skilled craftsmen might possess to earn their living.

The lower middle class, estimated at 20 percent to 30 percent of Western Europe's working population, in turn, emulated the upper bourgeoisie. Consisting of persons, such as craftsmen, elementary schoolteachers, office clerks, bank employees, shop assistants, and white-collar employees, this class dreaded being thrown into the lower class that they resented. Members of the lower-middle class earned about the same as skilled industrial workers, but prided themselves on earning salaries instead of wages and not getting their hands dirty to make a living and flaunted social and cultural mannerisms copied from the upper classes.

All social groups looked down on the working classes, among whom important differences existed. In Northern Europe they were more stable than in the South. Because industrialization had begun earlier, by 1900 they were two or three generations removed from the farm, had organized politically, and were less violent; in southern Europe the industrial revolution had begun later, and workers frequently took to the streets seeking to overthrow the established political system. Even in the North, however, the workers' past unruly behavior fixed their image among the middle classes, who considered them riotous, lawless, and inferior. In the new century, workers still frequently led segregated, miserable lives in isolated city neighborhoods or, as in the case of miners, subdivisions outside the cities. They drank hard and kept to themselves.

At the beginning of the twentieth century, a "second" industrial revolution brought important technical changes, such as electrification, greater mechanization, an increased work pace, larger industrial organizations, and more impersonal relationships with employers that rapidly transformed the workplace by demanding greater skills from workers than in the past. As a consequence, a larger proportion of the workers in the new century had more education, were better paid, and were family oriented. Children, earlier seen solely as sources of income and sent into the factories at a tender age, tended to be withdrawn from the labor force to receive more education, while the average age of male workers increased and more women entered the labor force.

Along with opportunities, however, shifting economic conditions brought new insecurity. Workers adapted to the new conditions with increasing difficulty, men felt threatened by women workers, and the wages that had risen earlier leveled off in the early years of the twentieth century. Work became more routine and monotonous, and workers objected to the legal discrimination against them in such matters as debt and divorce and to the increasingly harsh police methods. Workers became convinced that they and their children had very little chance for advancement and flocked to join Socialist parties and other opposition groups.

Emigration

These factors heavily influenced another characteristic of Europe during the early twentieth century: migration. Emigration and immigration had been common throughout the nineteenth century, but from the 1890s on, movements of populations between and within countries accelerated because several important elements came together. Europe's population jumped from 266 million in 1850 to

The massive emigration of people from Europe to other parts of the world in the late nineteenth and early twentieth centuries had an enormous effect on the continent and on the lands in which the immigrants settled. Here is a picture of immigrants arriving at Ellis Island in New York Harbor in 1904.

429 million in 1900. Old barriers to emigration within countries, such as serfdom, broke down at the same time that the transportation infrastructure was being extended and economies were modernizing. Accelerating industrialization in countries, such as Italy and Russia, brought new employment opportunities abroad or in different areas of the same country. More opportunities to work stimulated travel, widened horizons, intensified communications, broke down traditional communities, increased social mobility, and inspired a desire to move. Even where industrialization did not spread, such as southern Italy, or among populations left behind, such as Russian Jews, industrializing countries needing cheap labor beckoned to people in search of a better life.

The geographic target areas and qualitative nature of the great European migration deserve special emphasis. The emigrant trek across the Atlantic Ocean to the United States, Argentina, Brazil, and Canada is only part of the story. Europeans first migrated within the continent, especially to France. By 1911, the Italian-born population of France was one-third that of the United States, and the country counted large numbers of Poles, Spaniards, and Belgians. Italy, the largest source of immigrants during this period, also sent people to Germany during Germany's intense industrialization after 1890, as did Austria-Hungary. Skilled craftsmen regularly left their native regions to work in other European countries; British technicians transferred advanced technology to the entire European continent as far as Russia; Scottish engineers designed railways the world over; Welsh foundry men developed iron making in France, Russia, and Pennsylvania; Greeks labored in Romania and Bulgaria and traded in Turkey before going to Africa, North America, and South America; Sicilian and Greek peasants tilled the soil in Tunis and the Argentine wheat fields or worked in the American construction industry. Many emigrants started their own businesses, and a sizable number returned home with a nest egg large enough to buy property in their native regions. The money they brought or sent back buoyed the old country's economy, and their foreign experience influenced their country's politics.

The Jewish exodus from Eastern Europe was an important feature of the European migration of the early twentieth century and illustrates the wide-ranging effects of the population movement. Although religious persecution and pogroms played an important role in this vast migration, the decline of the non-Jewish market in proportion to the high percentage of small tradesmen among Jews and workers in consumer-goods industries seems to have had a greater role. An estimated 1.5 million Jews migrated to the United States between 1899 and 1914, many of whom contributed to the growth of the garment trade in New York City.

The great population movements of the late nineteenth and early twentieth centuries brought Europeans into contact with different peoples and customs, preparing them for the late twentieth-century immigration into Europe.

CHANGING CULTURAL AND POLITICAL OUTLOOKS

Unbeknownst to most people at the time, ferment and change also characterized European culture. In 1900 the majority of Europeans led their lives according to comfortable assumptions that had originated during the Enlightenment two hundred years earlier. However, while ordinary Europeans would easily have recognized and subscribed to a common set of ideas and assumptions, new ideas circulating among the cultural elite drastically changed the cultural outlook of ordinary people over the next quarter century.

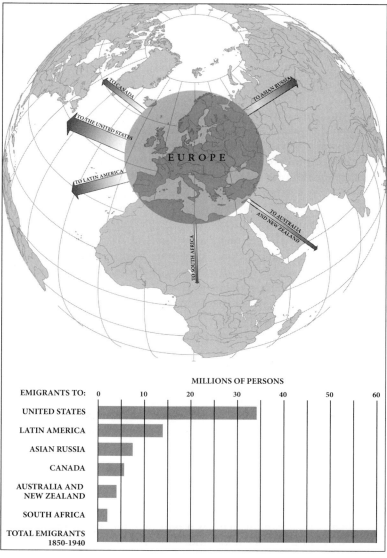

European Exodus. This map and graph give a good idea of where the approximately 60 million emigrants from Europe went between 1850 and 1940. People leaving the different European countries brought a new social and cultural diversity, stimulated the export of manufactured goods and capital from the old continent, and increased European economic influence throughout the world.

The Nation as a Community

Europeans believed in the nation as the ideal form of organization for a community. Before the eighteenth century, generals frequently led armies of a different nationality against their own countries of origin, and foreigners could lead countries. With the French Revolution in 1789, this attitude changed as the French fought savagely to defend their fatherland because of the benefits the Revolution had bestowed on them. During the revolutionary era, French armies fought to extend those advantages to other areas and encouraged the development of nationalism in the hope of utilizing it against the former rulers. However, nationalism worked not only against the old regimes but backfired against the French as different national groups preferred independence under their own leaders who they hoped would implement French-style reforms. Conflicts between the champions of oppressed nationalities and of the status quo marked the early and mid-nineteenth century. In the West, the major enemy of nationalism was Austria, whose existence nationalism threatened because it was composed of many nationalities but ruled by German-speaking Austrians. The struggle produced waves of revolutionary disorder in 1820 to 1821, 1830 to 1831, and 1848 and several wars between 1859 and 1870 and was an important cause of World War I.

Nationalism resulted in a united Italy and Germany, the high point of nineteenth-century nationalism, and, despite the continuing struggle of East European nationalities to free themselves from Austrian, Russian, or German domination, in the West the nation-state seemed to provide the essential framework necessary to confront the demands of the second industrial revolution. Modern industrial economies demanded more educated workers, for example, and modern nation-states created popular school systems with compulsory attendance to provide these workers.

Accelerating industrialization, secular schools and the population shift from the countryside to the cities weakened traditional habits and religious beliefs. Intellectuals confidently predicted the disappearance of traditional churches as the nation-state increasingly inherited the mystique, loyalties, and emotions that religions once possessed and took over the role of the medieval church—regulating public and private business and behavior, controlling education, and replacing charity with social assistance, such as pensions, unemployment insurance, poor relief, and medical help.

The nation-state gave people an identity and appeared as the concrete emanation of a nationality's collective personality and pride. It implemented economic and social principles for the benefit of all, created a legal structure to mediate disputes, set policy to protect the community's interests, and built armed forces to defend them. Because of the benefits it provided, the nation-state legitimately demanded sacrifices and cooperation from different classes and replaced the political struggles of the early and mid-nineteenth century with internal peace. Unfortunately, Europeans considered colonies essential for economic development and big-power status, and the resulting competition intensified tensions among them, stimulated racist ideas, and made war more likely.

Liberalism

Liberalism, the ideology that pervaded the West, originated in eighteenth-century Britain at the dawn of the industrial revolution, when manufacturers demanded that governments cease interfering in economic processes because they believed that the free operation of the market stabilized society. From economics they extended this theory into a political one, according to which the state should intervene only minimally in the lives of free individuals and concern itself only with defense and maintaining internal order.

Throughout the nineteenth century, liberalism was the antithesis of French revolutionary Jacobinism, which called for greater state regulation on behalf of the poor. By the beginning of the twentieth century, the bourgeoisie had become supreme in Western Europe, and liberalism had changed. In the late nineteenth century, Liberal thinkers, such as John Stuart Mill, adapted bourgeois liberalism to changing social, economic, and political conditions by acknowledging an expanded role for the state, although not a dominant one. In 1911 liberal theory reached its culmination with L. T. Hobhouse's famous essay *Liberalism*. Hobhouse argued that the state must interfere in society as little as possible but that it must help create conditions to enable all citizens to obtain everything necessary to their own well-being through their own efforts.

While in theory Liberals continued to believe that the law of supply and demand must be allowed the freest possible reign and that the government must keep out of individuals' lives, in practice the bourgeoisie sought to blunt the social struggles that threatened the economic order and its own political supremacy. Thus, bourgeois-dominated governments favored social legislation to soften the harshest effects that the economic system had on workers and peasants. Moreover, in the early 1900s, many Liberals believed that individuals could achieve their fullest expression within the nation-state's framework. Liberal theory favored free trade, but when confronted with fierce foreign competition that threatened to drive them out of business, Liberals turned to their governments for protection. They argued that jobs would disappear and that the nation would become vulnerable to hostile powers if industrial capacity diminished. In brief, they identified their own interests with the national interest and argued that governmental support of business would stimulate the economy, create jobs, and boost national prestige. For the same reasons, Liberals believed that the nation should help industrialists gain cheap raw materials and world markets and consequently supported the imperialism that had an important role in the foreign policy of the major powers.

Ironically, because the best-paid workers benefitted from these policies, an important segment of the working class supported them, while the bourgeoisie supported labor reforms because they brought economic and social peace. These measures included extension of the right to vote (by 1912 all Western countries had granted universal male suffrage), functioning parliamentary systems, strengthened civil rights, compulsory elementary education, unemployment compensation, old-age pensions, industrial accident insurance, and legislation protecting woman and child labor. In addition, skilled, organized workers in the most advanced industries directly benefited from the protectionist and imperialist policies of the bourgeoisie because they favored good jobs and high salaries. This situation created divisions among sectors of the working class.

Socialism

Despite concessions, the bourgeois refusal to accept the working class as a major partner in government stimulated the growth of Socialist parties, which, however, split on conflicting interpretations of how socialism would come to power.

This is the philosophical crux of Karl Marx's argument predicting the triumph of socialism: Economic relationships (the substructure) determine social relationships (the superstructure). Economic changes demand corresponding alterations in the governmental and the legal structure of society. As the productive system develops, however, the governing class, which was put into power by previous economic conditions (the bourgeoisie), refuses to abdicate. The new means of production and the class it has produced (the workers) come into conflict with the dominant political class; continued development of the new economic system, combined with resistance by the old government, culminates in revolution and the victory of the workers and socialism.

In elaborating his theory, Marx described certain concrete developments that would signal the decline of capitalism—deeper and more frequent economic crises would produce a revolution. When Marx's predictions did not materialize, Socialist theoreticians closely examined his analysis. In *Evolutionary Socialism* (1899), the German Socialist Eduard Bernstein argued that the signs of capitalism's impending collapse not only had failed to appear, but that the opposite seemed to be happening. Economic crises were less frequent and milder, and the middle class was increasing instead of disappearing. Bernstein concluded that Marx was wrong and advocated achieving socialism not by revolution but gradually through parliamentary reforms.

Before World War I, the Bernstein Debate wracked all European Socialist movements as social democratic revisionists or reformists fought with orthodox Marxist revolutionaries for control of the Socialist parties. In general, the revisionists gained control of the organizations against stiff opposition and followed a reformist policy, but stopped short of revising official party theory that called for the violent overthrow of capitalism. In all European countries, Socialist parties split into warring social-democratic and revolutionary factions.

The Belief in Science

The importance of Marx and Liberal economic theories illustrated the European penchant for applying scientific precepts to the analysis of society. This tendency, unique to Europe, originated during the eighteenth-century Enlightenment, when Isaac Newton's scientific method had been applied to the examination of social problems (social Newtonianism). In the nineteenth century, sociologists applied biological precepts to society. Ideas coming both from physics and biology were still important for the ordinary European during the first decade of the twentieth century.

In 1859, Charles Darwin's *The Origin of Species* enunciated the principles of evolution, including natural selection, which Social Darwinists transformed

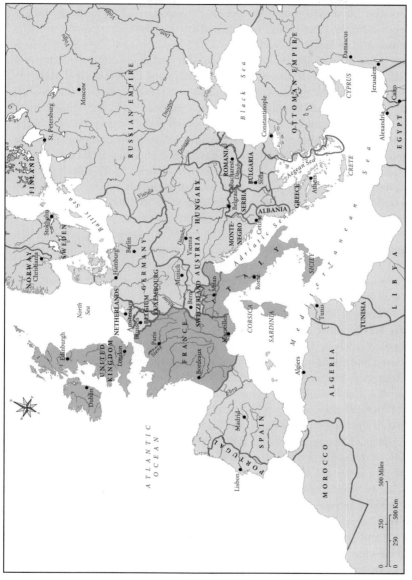

Although the United Kingdom, France, and Italy had unresolved problems, their governments were responsible to parliaments rather than to the monarchs. They were the three large powers of the prewar period that could be considered parliamentary democracies.

17

into the survival of the fittest. They argued that, through a process of struggle, nature selected certain families, classes, nations, or races to rule over others while reserving on inferior status for other groups. This tendency contributed to racist theories that justified imperialism. Philosopher Hannah Arendt wrote that European race-thinking was based primarily on an interpretation of Darwin's survival of the fittest and that it would have disappeared had it not served as an excuse for imperialism. Racism persisted in the European psyche until its culmination as a fundamental Nazi tenet.

The application of scientific principles to different fields of human endeavor abetted materialism, another concept in which many Europeans believed. As science explained more material phenomena, the trend toward a diminished religiosity intensified, and the ability of religion to impose limits on human behavior diminished. Protestant Liberals responded by seeking to demonstrate that the religious and scientific spheres were separate, although most Protestants seemed to believe that science and the Bible should be harmonious because God had revealed both. The Catholic Church, led by Pius X, frowned on new scientific doctrines. As the new century opened, a struggle raged over modernism, an attempt to apply new scientific and social theories to religious dogma that gained some success among Protestants but brought excommunication to its Catholic adherents. Both the more flexible Protestant approach and the rigid Catholic method failed to halt the declining appeal of the churches for the urban masses.

However, the twentieth century overthrew not only traditional religion but the comforting worldview based upon the scientific precepts and cultural assumptions of the Enlightenment.

Scientific Revolution

For Europeans, science had been important for the technological improvements it engendered and for how it defined the world. The diffusion of Newton's physics among eighteenth-century intellectuals had fundamental effects on politics and society. In the fourth century, St. Augustine's view of history as the unfolding of God's will justified the church's prominent role in politics because God directly intervened in the affairs of the world through His church. A universe composed of spheres pushed by angels completed this picture of God's direct intervention in human affairs. Newton, however, argued that the universe operated automatically, according to a series of laws that he described: God had created the universe and left it to run by itself like a clock. Because God did not intervene directly in the running of the universe, He did not directly intervene in the operation of society through the clergy. This rationale bolstered the claim that secular governments should rule and reduced the church's role in politics. Enlightenment intellectuals extended Newton's concept to all society and attempted to discover its fundamental laws of operation. They described the universe, and society, as a smooth-running machine with easily understandable laws, a view to which most people still subscribed in 1900.

During the early years of the twentieth century, however, a new scientific revolution that had its roots in the last years of the previous decade overthrew Newtonianism's comfortable worldview. This new science gradually shattered previous assumptions and fundamentally changed European culture and society.

The old conception of matter went first. The way in which most people understood matter in 1900 had its roots in the Greek philosophy of the fifth century B.C. The ancient Greeks had reasoned that by continually cutting a material, eventually the smallest indivisible piece of matter would be achieved—the atom—but in the last years of the nineteenth century, this commonsense argument broke down, and in the early years of the new one, it was proved false. In 1895, the German physicist Wilhelm Roentgen accidentally discovered X-rays and learned that when he passed them through a gas, they dislodged minute, electrically charged particles. In 1897, the Englishman J. J. Thompson, working at the famous Cavendish laboratory in Cambridge, England, reasoned that bodies made up of *parts* of atoms accounted for electricity, a conclusion independently reached by the Dutch physicist Hendrik Lorentz, who named the particles "electrons." Scientists had demonstrated that atoms consisted of smaller parts and therefore were not irreducible, as had been believed for over two thousand years. Further investigation into the atom made use of quantum and relativity theories elaborated by German physicists Max Planck and Albert Einstein in 1900 and 1905. Additional research by two of Thompson's collaborators at the Cavendish laboratory—the New Zealand-born and educated Ernest Rutherford (1911) and the Dane Niels Bohr (1913)—produced a model of the atom resembling a miniature solar system.

The roster of names involved in crucial discoveries confirms that early twentieth-century science was a common European endeavor. Roentgen sent a reprint of his work to the famous French mathematician Henri Poincaré, who passed it on to physicist Henri Becquerel, discoverer of uranium's radioactive properties in 1896. Inspired by Becquerel, a young Polish-born graduate student at the Sorbonne, Maria Sklodowska, began work in the new field, and, in collaboration with her French husband Pierre Curie, she discovered two new elements that won the couple and Becquerel a Nobel Prize in 1903. The implications of the Curies' research into radioactivity was proof positive that different particles made up the atom and that elements could be changed or transmuted by changing particles within an atom. In April 1902, Rutherford and his colleague Frederick Soddy demonstrated that radioactivity is not only a "manifestation of subatomic chemical change," but produces "new kinds of matter." Their work blazed the way for an understanding of the forces encapsulated within the atom's nucleus over the next forty years. This research influenced society by spurring intellectuals to delve into the characteristics of reality that were not visible.

Indeed, even more revolutionary developments in theoretical physics gave impetus to this search. While examining questions related to the intensity of colors in the radiation emerging from a small hole in an electric oven (cavity radiation), Max Planck, a professor of theoretical physics at the University of Berlin, concluded that energy was emitted not in different amounts but *only* in standard packets he called the "quantum of action." The science historian J. L. Heilbron explained the concept in the following words: "In ordinary or classical physics, energy is a continuous quantity and can be . . . [dispensed] as ordinary people drink beer, in any quantity they wish; in Planck's theory as reinterpreted by

Einstein, the . . . energy [can be dispensed] only in certain amounts, as a guzzler who insists on consuming only by the pint. Why nature guzzles rather than sips became a fundamental problem for physicists."

Max Planck's presentation of his quantum theory at a scientific meeting on December 14, 1900, proved fundamental in touching off the twentieth-century scientific revolution. Applied initially by Planck only to the field of thermodynamics, the quantum concept of the discontinuity of energy contradicted Newton's system, which assumed continuity in all of nature's causal relationships. It soon became clear to scientists that quantum theory was relevant not only to thermodynamics but to many other fields, and the quantum became recognized as a constant of nature fundamental to the study of X-rays, gases, the photochemical effects of light, and atomic structures. During the rest of the century, quantum theory (and its offshoot, quantum mechanics) had increasingly greater revolutionary implications about the nature of matter and its behavior so as to make reality at the subatomic level seem downright bizarre.

Albert Einstein utilized Planck's quantum theory in his famous 1905 paper describing his special theory of relativity (one of three brilliant papers published that year) by demonstrating that light also emits energy in packets or quanta. Relativity proved to be an equally revolutionary formulation that Planck forcefully defended, along with its author, so that, an observer commented: "Einstein may be considered Planck's second great discovery in physics."

BIOGRAPHICAL SKETCHES

Max Planck
An Upright German

A mild man with a conventional demeanor, the scientist who revolutionized twentieth-century physics led an upright public life and a tragic personal one. Born in 1858, descended from a long line of pastors and scholars, Max Planck appeared to his teachers as a steady but not a brilliant student with no special aptitude for physics. His first wife died in 1909 after twenty-three years of marriage. He remarried at age fifty and led a pleasant life with his second wife and four children for an all-too-brief while. An accomplished pianist, Planck composed songs and an operetta as a boy. As a university professor, he kept up with his music at his villa in a Berlin suburb by acting as a choirmaster, by playing the organ at services, and by inviting guests to regular musical evenings. The most famous participants included Albert Einstein, who played along on his violin, and Lise Meitner and Otto Hahn, both renowned for their research into nuclear fission.

After he achieved fame by enunciating the quantum theory, Planck spared no effort to help his fellow scientists and his students. Einstein found in him his first and greatest supporter. Planck's students praised his clear and brilliantly organized lectures and flocked to them. He sat through 650 doctoral examinations. Many of his students became famous, two of them winning Nobel Prizes. Although he believed that nature had determined that women should be mothers and homemakers, he sympathized with their causes and gave them permission to attend his lectures. When he was rector in 1913 to 1914, 770 women attended courses at the University of Berlin. He also appointed as his assistant Austrian physicist Lise Meitner, the first scientist to explain nuclear fission.

On October 4, 1914, Planck signed the "Appeal to the Cultural Peoples of the World," a declaration by ninety-three German intellectuals denying that German troops had committed atrocities and identifying themselves with the army. He later regretted this action and championed the cause of international cooperation among scientists when nationalist sentiments threatened to destroy it. After the war, he helped save German science during the difficult times of hyperinflation by securing grants from the Rockefeller Foundation, the General Electric Corporation, and a Japanese industrialist.

Planck's world changed in January 1933, when Adolf Hitler came to power. In May he attempted to convince Hitler that his anti-Semitic policies would ruin German science, causing the Fuehrer to fly into a rage. Planck attempted to find posts for dismissed Jewish scientists and, if necessary, help them emigrate. He fought Nazi scientists who attacked "Jewish" physics, not openly but indirectly, an attitude that later earned him criticism from some quarters. He continued the battle even after his forced retirement at age eighty, despite the heartache that weighed him down. His oldest son Karl died of his wounds in World War I. His twin daughters both died within two years of each other following childbirth. Bombing during World War II completely destroyed his home and possessions, with all their memories, but that loss paled in comparison to a blow that almost killed him. In February 1945 the Nazis executed his son Erwin, an opponent of the regime, just when the father had high hopes for a pardon.

War and declining health brought more suffering. As he fled from the last bombings of the conflict, his vertebra fused, causing him immense pain. Before his death from a stroke on October 4, 1947, at age 89, he at least had the satisfaction of seeing Germany's premier research institution, the Kaiser Wilhelm Institute, renamed after him and staffed by his friends.

Einstein's relativity theory revolutionized scientific thinking and its implications were still important at the end of the twentieth century. The theory's departure is the constancy of the speed of light for all observers everywhere, conclusively demonstrated in a famous 1887 experiment by two Americans, Albert Michelson and Edward Morley. The only way the speed of light can remain constant is for space and time to change according to one's framework. Einstein's theory produced consequences that ordinary persons would consider weird. Relativity required people to give up their conventional and commonsense ideas of space and time as universal constants that remained the same everywhere for all people. Einstein's theory also postulated that mass and energy were convertible one into the other, as represented by the famous equation $E = MC^2$ (where E is energy, M is mass, and C is the speed of light). Because the speed of light is such a large number, the destruction of even a small amount of mass would produce amounts of energy so great that they were inconceivable at the time. This equation eventually made the atomic bomb possible.

Quantum theory and relativity created conceptions of space, time, motion, and matter that struck observers as fantastic and bounded only by the imagination of individual scientists. By the 1920s, this idea proceeded even further as the "uncertainty (or indeterminacy) principle" elaborated by German physicist Werner Heisenberg disrupted the ordinary person's view of the universe. The uncertainty principle stated that it was possible, at a given moment, to know either the speed or the position of a particle, but not both. Uncertainty evolved into a dominant principle of the cosmos, which had to be interpreted according to statistics. Intellectuals would learn from science not only that reality lay hidden from view and was mysterious, but was, like time and space, flexible.

Taken together, the theories of Planck and Einstein shattered the Newtonian worldview, substituting a cosmos that was difficult to comprehend, apparently unstable, contrary to common sense, irrational, and variable according to a person's frame of reference. The comforting assumption that ordinary people had of the universe as a smooth-operating machine disappeared.

Cultural Rebellion

In 1919 British scientists confirmed relativity by observing the bending of light during a solar eclipse as Einstein's theory predicted, but the new ideas had had an impact on European intellectuals. Max Planck himself acknowledged the close relationship between the natural and intellectual sciences and their mutual influences. Unfortunately, for many nonscientists, "Mistakenly but perhaps inevitably, relativity became confused with relativism [the idea that truth depends on the individuals or groups holding them]." This notion circulated at a popular level primarily after World War I, but long before then, intellectuals demolished the Enlightenment values underpinning European culture and society that were linked to the Newtonian worldview, igniting the cultural and political revolutions that marked the twentieth century.

Like the physicist Einstein, French philosopher Henri Bergson contemplated the nature of time. He declared it a subjective experience, a duration that is lived differently by each individual. In that sense, reality was relative for Bergson. A mystical life force flowed somewhere, Bergson believed, and individuals must be in touch with it through "intuition," rather than rational analysis. Reality was not universal but differed for each individual, and artists or thinkers who understood that were superior to those who did not. In his 1907 book, *Creative Evolution,* Bergson enunciated the concept of the élan vital, the quality that enables people to keep in touch with the mysterious wellspring of life. Bergson's philosophy paralleled physics by stressing the sources of life that were not susceptible to simple rational analysis and varied for different people. Intuition had as great a role in life as it did in science.

In the course of his work, Bergson emphasized psychology, arguing for the importance of dreams, referring to the false realities that people construct as masks. He also considered unconscious influences, a field in which the Austrian physician Sigmund Freud opened up an entirely new dimension for humanity. Successfully working with a patient whose disorder had proved intractable by getting her to remember long-forgotten incidents that had affected her—through free association—Freud became convinced that many mental disorders could be traced back to traumatic, repressed childhood sexual events. He discovered that individuals lived an intense unconscious life. In short, reason alone did not determine people's behavior, but the unconscious—hidden and mysterious. Freud's work cast further doubt on the dominant role of rationality as developed during the Enlightenment in the eighteenth century.

In the cases of Bergson and Freud, as in science, the clear-cut, commonsense approach to life that characterized the beliefs of ordinary people broke down, and the same development occurred in art. In Germany, the Russian-born painter Wassily Kandinsky condemned the materialism that determined the outlook of traditional artists, scientists, leftist politicians, and ordinary people. These materialists, he wrote in 1910, "know nothing of the vital impulse of life." For Kandinsky, the scientific revolution of those years had "cast doubt on that very matter which was yesterday the foundation of everything, so the whole universe is shaken." Kandinsky is an outstanding example of how, stimulated by new scientific developments and philosophical currents uncovering mysterious impelling forces, artists turned to the intuitive study of underlying reality, producing Expressionism— an artistic style affecting all spheres of thought between 1910 and 1924. Thus, Kandinsky, the movement's theoretician, stated that art must appeal to the emotions. In painting, for example, this meant examining the nature and impact of color. Kandinsky explained that colors produce a spiritual vibration in the observer

This painting illustrates some of the central themes of Futurism. "Brawl in the Galleria," by Umberto Boccioni (1882-1916), pictures a riot in Milan's famous Galleria Vittorio Emanuele II. The painting illustrates the sights and sounds of violence among the elegant shops and restaurants of the northern Italian industrial city's famous landmark.

and should, therefore, be chosen *for their psychic effect*. He favored abstract painting for that reason, bolstering his argument by citing the emotional force of music, the least representational of the arts. In line with these ideas, German Expressionist painters of the Blue Rider school founded by Kandinsky produced abstract pictures that attempted to transmit extreme feeling primarily through intense color.

Kandinsky had been greatly influenced by artistic developments in Paris during a 1906–07 stay. In Paris, the Fauves (Wild Beasts) employed violent color and distorted, flat forms in their paintings, even though their best-known representative, Henri Matisse, did not paint in a completely abstract manner. Another artistic school centered in Paris, Cubism, attempted to get at inner reality through the structure of paintings and distorted forms. Cubism counted Pablo Picasso and Georges Braque as its major representatives. Like Kandinsky, Picasso emphasized emotion and considered painting visual music. Although the different schools debated about which one best conveyed emotions on canvas, avant-garde artists of this period broke with earlier naturalistic traditions representing external reality in an attempt to get at the real nature of things, as science had done. Their work included "references to the artist's thoughts, feelings, and unconscious impulses, to the perceptions of his or her nonvisual senses, or to the physical laws governing the universe." The denial of external aspects of life in favor of its intangible and mysterious qualities accelerated the decline of the rationalism that the twentieth century had inherited from the Enlightenment, confirming artists' views of themselves as revolutionaries against the bourgeois world of their elders.

Most avant-garde artists seemed to be interested in social and political issues only tangentially. The great exception was the most iconoclastic of the prewar movements, Italian Futurism. Futurism's political and social outlook formed a whole with its artistic philosophy and had wide-ranging implications. Primarily concerned with reviving Italy from bottom to top, the Futurists issued a manifesto in the Parisian *Le Figaro* on February 20, 1909. Inspired by Egyptian-born, 33-year-old, well-off, well-dressed poet Filippo Tommaso Marinetti, the manifesto took the European art world by storm.

The Futurists felt compelled to speak because "Time and Space died yesterday." They aimed to "break down the doors of the mysterious Impossible" and never look back. This task required an all-out war on the past, against the bourgeoisie, existing society in all its manifestations, and all their supporters (Pastists). Among the instruments and values of the past that were slated for destruction were museums and libraries, schools, and academies, "moralism, feminism, vile and utilitarian opportunism."

The Futurists glorified modern civilization—a culture dominated by speed, the machine, and technology. They aimed to bring this new civilization to Italy in anticipation of a modern Italian art. The great Renaissance tradition weighed heavily on Italian artists and writers, which explains why so many Futurist artists rebelled, why they congregated in Paris, and why they published their founding manifesto in the French capital. They dedicated themselves to the theme of speed and industrialization—symbolized by the airplane, the automobile, and the machine—attempting to reproduce the sounds, noises, and smells of modern life.

Futurist painter Umberto Boccioni portrayed rising cities and speed on his canvases; architects, such as Antonio Sant'Elia, designed ultramodern cities; and poets composed sacred hymns to coal and electricity. Futurists shocked audiences with their weird and violent behavior that was designed to ridicule the placid bourgeoisie during infamous Futurist evenings that ended in riots as the artists jumped from the stage and "dynamically altered" the faces of people in the audience by beating them. Italian Futurism influenced subsequent artistic movements, such as Dadaism.

From Cultural to Political Revolt

The Futurist lifestyle, dominated by danger and rebellion, culminated in a love for war, which the Futurists glorified as the "hygiene of the world." Marinetti saw action in the Libyan War (1911–12) and covered the Balkan Wars (1912–13), and Marinetti and the Futurists pushed for Italian entrance into World War I and volunteered for action in World War I and World War II. He linked up with former revolutionary Socialist and founder of fascism Benito Mussolini. Like Futurism, Italian Fascism adored violence, loved action, and aimed to destroy bourgeois society. (From now on in the book, Fascism with a capital means the Italian movement and the lower case, fascism, refers to the generic movement.) Both movements hated pacifist socialism and its goal of a comfortable materialistic life. In 1919, Futurists and Fascists collaborated in violent physical attacks on their enemies that was the hallmark of early fascism.

The path to fascism, however, was complex. During the century's first decade, political thinkers attempted to connect with the mystical life sources not only of individuals, but of nations. In Italy, intellectuals were obsessed with Italian weakness and the parliamentary rule of pragmatist Prime Minister Giovanni Giolitti, whom they blamed for the country's flaws. The nineteenth-century movement for national unification, the Risorgimento, they believed, had been betrayed, and they dreamed of moral regeneration, grandeur, and a new political system. The primary political exponents of these ideas were the Nationalists, whose theoretician Enrico Corradini founded an influential journal in 1903. Corradini believed that the nation was the highest expression of fellowship and embodied the instincts of association and struggle. Because civilization without war was impossible, imperialism was the natural consequence of nationalism. Corradini stated that since Italy was a poor, "proletarian" nation, it must lead a revolutionary struggle against the rich countries that held it down. Using the Socialist analogy, he argued that this struggle required internal unity that parliaments destroyed and, internationally, a war of the proletarian nations led by Italy against the rich countries. This emphasis on war, antiparliamentarianism, and internal revolution linked the Nationalists and Futurists and, after World War I, the Fascists.

Similar developments occurred in France, exacerbated by the case of Alfred Dreyfus, a Jew accused of treason. This famous case split French society between his accusers and supporters, stimulating French nationalism and anti-Semitism (the strongest in Europe at the time), and bringing together groups that hoped for a national regeneration through authority and force, action and strong leaders, and antiparliamentarianism. Two prominent thinkers provided ideological consistency, clarity, and force to this movement, Maurice Barrès and Charles Maurras. Barrès argued in 1902 that a French essence defined the French people and emphasized the importance of the nation as a tight-knit community working together—organic nationalism. Barrès saw the fatherland as resembling the individual in that it is the sum of a long history of effort, sacrifice, loyalty, and a long struggle against internal and external enemies for survival. Similarly, Charles Maurras developed integral nationalism between 1900 and 1909. Maurras viewed the monarchy as the culminating institution of the French nation, the only one capable of representing it and of imposing a truly national policy. Maurras denounced parliaments as the embodiment of egotistical minorities that a prince who based his dictatorial authority on the French people would eliminate. In the case of both Barrès and Maurras, the French nation embodied the mystical qualities that excluded not only foreigners but French opponents of their ideas.

In Germany as well, to intellectuals, the central theme was the harm that liberalism and parliamentary government had done to the Germans. The intellectuals railed against parliamentary corruption and demanded the ethical revamping of bourgeois society and a culture that would put politics on a new course. The brilliant philosopher and theoretician of the "superman," Friedrich Nietzsche, was repeatedly cited as the enemy of democratic mediocrity. German nationalist exponents demanded a leader who would unite German society, rid it of its impure elements, and lead the country to glory. As in France, the anti-Semitic component of this current of thought was powerful, and the Jew was considered the primary scoundrel. The cultural discontent expressed by these intellectuals had a great influence on German politics and pointed the way toward ideas expressed by Adolf Hitler in the 1930s.

Reinforcing these feelings were the critics of the prevailing European political systems who examined the rules of political behavior. Gaetano Mosca had criticized the corruption and mediocrity of elected parliaments that, he believed, made democracy a sham. Best known for his 1896 work, *The Ruling Class*, Mosca argued that the only real classes in any form of government are the governing (always a minority) and the governed (the majority). Vilfredo Pareto, an Italian political thinker teaching in Switzerland, reaffirmed this view by arguing that in every society, the upper classes constitute an aristocracy or an elite. When the social equilibrium is stable, the power elite appears competent and is accepted; when crises cause political systems to fail, a new elite replaces the old. This cycle always repeats itself, Pareto wrote, no matter what the form of government. The German political theoretician Robert Michels expanded these ideas to party organizations, including democratic ones, in *Political Parties: A Sociological Study of the Oligarchic Tendencies of Modern Democracies* (1911). This work stated his "iron law of oligarchy": in every organization, including democratic parties and parliaments, political groups that cannot be removed have real control.

The ideas seemed to confirm "scientifically" the feelings of avant-garde artists, nationalists, and intellectuals that an underlying reality determined the visible one in politics, a view that permeated Marxism as well. By the end of the nineteenth century, the European Socialist parties, dominated by revisionism, had lost their revolutionary edge. In France and Italy, a new political philosophy, revolutionary syndicalism, incited workers to organize in unions, overthrow the bourgeois political and economic system, and create a new society based on their organizations. The French philosopher Georges Sorel and his Italian disciples put into effect what historian Zeev Sternhell called the revolutionary revision of Marxism. In his *Reflections on Violence* (1906), Sorel lauded violence as the necessary element of change. Because the economic forces that Marx believed would produce a revolution had failed to do so, Sorel emphasized the power of myths, which could mobilize the proletarian to overthrow the bourgeoisie by violence. Sorel thus shifted the main emphasis of Marxist doctrine from economics to psychology by injecting irrationalism into Marxism. Given their limited ability to influence the established French and Italian Socialist parties, revolutionary syndicalist theoreticians turned to the nationalism existing in both France and Italy and, with the objective of "the destruction of the liberal democratic regime and its intellectual norms and moral values," contributed to the birth of Fascist ideology.

A Society in Movement

At the beginning of the twentieth century, European society presented a curious picture of a civilization balanced between stability and transformation. Europeans were better off economically than they had ever been, despite the existence of deep pockets of poverty. However, instead of bringing peace, the new prosperity generated resentment among the categories that were left out or could not keep up with the speed of economic and technical change. These groups linked up with influential intellectuals who aimed to destroy existing society just as quantum and relativity demonstrated that reality could no longer be understood by relying upon appearances and was destroying Newtonianism. Artists and intellectuals went on a search for the hidden and mystical aspects of life, resulting in a cultural and political rebellion that shattered the intellectual basis of the European world even before World War I destroyed its political, economic, and social foundations and brought to power irrational movements that formed in the crucible of early twentieth-century thought.

Bibliographical Essay

A good survey of social conditions at the beginning of the twentieth century is Edward R. Tannenbaum, *1900: The Generation before the Great War* (Garden City, N.Y., 1976). Wider ranging, more complete, and possessing a wealth of historical statistics is Peter N. Stearns, *European Society in Upheaval: Social History Since 1800* (New York, 1967). An older work that gives a good idea of the social life of this period is B. Seebohm Rowntree, *Poverty: A Study of Town Life* (New York, 1971); originally published in 1901, this is the classic study of British social conditions that modern scholars rely on. Peter Laslett, *The World We Have Lost* (New York, 1965), discusses Britain before the industrial revolution but has an excellent chapter on the beginning of the twentieth century; the work includes a wealth of interesting information. Asa Briggs, *Victorian Cities* (New York, 1963), presents a good picture of urban living in approximately the same period as discussed in this chapter. An indispensable starting point in understanding the nature of European population movements during this period is Frank Thistlethwaite's chapter "Migration from Europe Overseas in the Nineteenth and Twentieth Centuries," in Herbert Möller, ed., *Population Movement in Modern European History* (New York, 1964), pp. 73–92.

D. V. Glass and Roger Revelle, eds., *Population and Social Change* (London, 1972), collects a number of papers mostly dealing with Europe. Sandra Halperin, *War and Social Change in Europe: the Great Transformation Revisited* (Cambridge, UK, 2004) describes the continuation of the traditional classes. J. M. Houston's *A Social Geography of Europe*, rev..ed.. (New York, 1963), looks at the development of European cities in historical perspective. Gerold Ambrosius and William H. Hubbard published *A Social and Economic History of Twentieth-Century Europe* (Cambridge, MA, 1989). Books that include material on twentieth-century social conditions in Europe include Robert Clifford Ostergren and John G. Rice, *The Europeans: A Geography of People, Culture and Environment* (New York, 2004), and Richard Vinen, *A History in Fragments: Europe in the Twentieth Century* (Cambridge, Mass., 2001).

On the issue of women, the memoirs of Angelica Balabanoff, *My Life as a Rebel* (New York, 1968), originally published in 1938, not only provides excellent portraits of the important characters she knew well, such as Mussolini and Lenin, but is a mine of information on the period. The British feminist Emmeline Pankhurst wrote her autobiography, first published in 1914, *My Own Story* (London, 1979); see also the biography by her daughter, E. Sylvia Pankhurst, *The Life of Emmeline Pankhurst* (London, 1969). Sandra Stanley Holton, *Feminism and Democracy: Women's Suffrage and Reform Politics in Britain, 1900–1918* (Cambridge, 1986), is a clear, brief overview of the women's movement for reform and the vote in Britain between 1900 and 1918. For France, there is Steven C. Hause and Anne R. Kenney, *Women's Suffrage and Social Politics in the French Third Republic* (Princeton, N.J., 1984), a work seeking to combine the political and social history of the issue, especially between the 1890s and 1920s. Two general histories that consider this period are Deborah Simonton, *The Routledge History of Women in Europe Since 1700* (London, 2006), and Olwen H. Hufton, *The Prospect Before Her: A History of Women in Western Europe* (New York, 1996). Lynn Abrams wrote *The Making of Modern Woman: Europe 1789–1918* (Harlow, 2002), which includes material on the 20th century. Tito Boeri et al. present problems faced by working women in *Women at Work: An Economic Perspective* (Oxford 2005).

Immigration from Europe has been well covered, but it is more difficult to find sources on the material presented in this volume. The following books are helpful: Andrew Geddes, *The Politics of Migration and Immigration in Europe* (London, 2003), an overview of problems linked to immigration; Walter T. K. Nugent, *Crossings: The Great Transatlantic Migrations, 1870–1914* (Bloomington, 1992), an account of migration to the New World that includes some of the countries discussed here; and Eli Lederhendler, *Jewish Immigrants and American Capitalism, 1880–1920: From Caste to Class* (Cambridge, UK, 2009), an account of European Jews and immigration.

Good general surveys of the entire period, which also deal with social and cultural issues in addition to the political and diplomatic, include Carlton J. H. Hayes, *A Generation of Materialism, 1871–1900* (New York, 1941), from which the quotation regarding Darwinism was taken (p. 12), and Oron J. Hale, *The Great Illusion, 1900–1914* (New York, 1971). Hannah Arendt's opinion, cited on the connection between imperialism and racism and its results, is found in her *The Origins of Totalitarianism*, rev..ed...(New York, 1966), pp. 183–84.

Unfortunately, the history of socialism in the twentieth century has been neglected in recent scholarship, and many of the good books are also old. George Lichtheim, *Marxism: An Historical and Critical Study* (New York, 1961), provides a one-volume introduction to the subject. G. D. H. Cole, *A History of Socialist Thought* (New York, 1953), is a thorough examination in five volumes. Peter Gay, *The Dilemma of Democratic Socialism: Edward Bernstein's Challenge to Marx* (New York, 1962), is a classic analysis of Eduard Bernstein's revisionism and its problems and implications. Albert S. Lindemann, *A History of European Socialism* (New Haven, Conn., 1983), examines the European movements. Good studies of socialism, too numerous to cite here, exist for most of the individual European countries during this period. Daryl Glaser et al., *Twentieth Century Marxism: A Global Introduction* (London, 2007) is a recent book. Sheri Berman's *The Primacy of Politics: Social Democracy and the Making of Europe's Twentieth Century* (New York, 2006) emphasizes revisionism and social democracy.

Although the scientific revolution of the early twentieth century has received attention, books that make the issues understandable to nonscientists are unfortunately not plentiful. Thomas H. Kuhn's *The Structure of Scientific Revolutions* (Chicago, 1972), first published in 1962, emphasized the role of paradigms in the history or science; this work achieved a wide following, but his concept of scientific revolutions has been challenged. Alfred North Whitehead's *Science and the Modern World* (Cambridge, U.K., 1929) is a readable classic with a good discussion of relativity and the quantum theory and their impact on modern science. James B. Conant, *On Understanding Science* (New Haven, Conn., 1947), remains useful.

Max Planck attempted to explain the principles of modern physics and their relationship to a philosophy of life in a brief work, *The Philosophy of Physics* (New York, 1936). J. L. Heilbroner, *The Dilemmas of an Upright Man: Max Planck as a Spokesman for German Science* (London, 1986), discusses Planck's discoveries and his role in German physics up to his death; the citation describing the nature of the "quantum" is taken from this work, p. 21, and the quote regarding his relationship to Einstein is from p. 28. Jane Weir has written a more recent biography, *Max Planck: Revolutionary Physicist* (Minneapolis, 2009). Lise Meitner received a well-deserved biography by Patricia Rife, *Lise Meitner and the Dawn of the Nuclear Age* (Boston, 1999). The reader will find biographies of Einstein readily available but no easy description of his relativity theory, even though the effort has been made. The best biography for the nonspecialist is Michael White and John Gribbin, *Einstein: A Life in Science* (New York, 1994); a more detailed work is Ronald W. Clark, *Einstein: The Life and Times* (New York, 1971). Both Denis Brian, *Einstein: A Life* (New York, 1996), and Walter Isaacson's *Einstein: His Life and Universe* (New York, 2007), are excellent. Stanley Goldberg's *Understanding Relativity: Origin and Impact of a Scientific Revolution* (Boston, 1984), is more technical than one would wish, although an indication of its impact is provided. A clearer work about the implications of relativity on the concept of time and some of its strange derivations is Paul Davies, *About Time: Einstein's Unfinished Revolution* (New York, 1995); Davies uses the term *unfinished revolution* to describe the continuing effects of Einstein's theories. An interesting work comparing the influence of science at the beginning of the twentieth century and at its end is Gerald Holton, *Einstein, History, and Other Passions* (Reading, Mass., 1996); this book also provides interesting insights into Einstein's personal life. Susan Quinn's biography, *Marie Curie: A Life* (New York, 1995), is an insightful work dealing with the personal and research aspects of the science of the period. The segments of letters reproduced in Ilse Rosenthal-Schneider, *Reality and Scientific Truth: Discussions with Einstein, von Laue, and Planck* (Detroit, 1980), edited by Thomas Braun, gives a fascinating glimpse of the views that the era's most famous scientists had of their own findings.

A clear analysis of Bergson's thought, especially his concept of time, is Leszek Kolakowski, *Bergson* (Oxford, 1985), to which must be added the more recent *Thinking in Time: An Introduction to Henri Bergson* (Ithaca, N.Y., 2006) by Suzanne Guerlac. Thomas Hama, ed., *The Bergsonian Heritage* (New York, 1962), includes essays on those aspects of Bergson's thought that survive. The collection of essays edited by

P. A. Y. Gunter, *Bergson and the Evolution of Physics* (Knoxville, Tenn., 1969), turns the tables and discusses Bergson's insights on the physical sciences and on the philosophy of science. The reader will find many treatments of the different aspects of Freud's work and thought. The classic biography is the massive three-volume work by a close friend of the early period, but see especially the first volume, Ernest Jones, *The Life and Work of Sigmund Freud. Volume I: The Formative Years and the Great Discoveries, 1856–1900* (New York, 1953). The best one-volume biography is Peter Gay, *Freud: A Life for Our Time* (New York, 1988).

Paul Johnson makes the application of relativity to politics and society the main theme of his *Modern Times: The World from the Twenties to the Eighties* (New York, 1983), in which the reader may find the remark on relativity and relativism (p. 4). Wassily Kandansky's brief, influential work, originally published in 1910, is *Concerning the Spiritual in Art*, translated by M. D. H. Sadler (New York, 1977); the relevant citations are found on pp. 12 and 24. An excellent brief general introduction to Expressionism in its different aspects is R. S. Furness, *Expressionism* (London, 1973); a fuller treatment is Richard Samuel and R. Hinton Thomas, *Expressionism in German Life, Literature and the Theatre (1910–1924)* (Philadelphia, 1971); for a more recent book, see Ashley Bassie's *Expressionism* (New York, 2008). The best work on Picasso during the crucial decade mentioned in the text is John A. Richardson, *A Life of Picasso. Volume 2: 1907–1917*. Matisse is covered in Alfred H. Barr, *Matisse: His Art and His Public* (New York, 1966).

Probably the best work on the active political lives of painters and a smattering of other intellectuals during this period is Theda Shapiro, *Painters and Politics: The European Avant-Garde and Society, 1900–1925* (New York, 1976), on p. 91 of which may be found the citation about artists bringing into their work the invisible elements and the physical laws of the universe. There is an excellent portrait of Marinetti, his action, influence, and link to fascism in James Joll, *Three Intellectuals in Politics* (New York, 1965); the citation regarding Futurism is on p. 144. The quotations in the text regarding Futurist theory are taken from the 1909 Manifesto that founded the movement. Walter L. Adamson examines the crucial role of the Florentine milieu and Futurism in *Avant-Garde Florence: From Modernism to Fascism* (Cambridge, Mass., 1993). The impact of Futurism and its aesthetics on avant-garde European writers and artists is thoroughly discussed by Marjorie Perloff, *The Futurist Moment: Avant-garde, Avant guerre, and the Language of Rupture* (Chicago, 1986). For the technological themes in the movement, see the essays in Gunter Berghaus, *Futurism and the Technological Imagination* (Amsterdam, 2009). Robert C. Williams, *Artists in Revolution: Portraits of the Russian Avantgarde, 1905–1925* (Bloomington, Ind., 1977), discusses the Russian avant-garde at the beginning of the century.

Michael Curtis examines the attacks of three intellectuals discussed in the text against the political and social structure of France during this period: *Three Against the Third Republic: Sorel, Barrès, and Maurras* (Westport, Conn., 1976). The standard work on Germany is Fritz Stern's *The Politics of Cultural Despair: A Study in the Rise of the Germanic Ideology* (Berkeley, Calif., 1963). Armand Patrucco's *The Critics of the Italian Parliamentary System, 1860–1915* (New York, 1992) is an excellent discussion of the ideas of Mosca, Pareto, and Michels in action.

Richard D. Humphrey, *Georges Sorel: Prophet Without Honor* (Cambridge, Mass., 1951), is a general study of Sorel's contribution to the analysis of modern social forces while Larry Portis, *Georges Sorel* (London, 1980) is a biography. John Stanley, *The Sociology of Virtue* (Berkeley, Calif., 1981), concentrates on Sorel's early work and on his revolutionary syndicalism. J. R. Jennings, *Georges Sorel: The Character and Development of His Thought* (New York, 1985), is a good discussion of Sorel's complexity and contradictions.

Mark Antiff's *Avant-garde Fascism: The Mobilization of Myth, Art, and Culture in France, 1909–1939* (Durham, N.C., 2007) discusses some of the themes elaborated on these pages. Jack J. Roth, *The Cult of Violence: Sorel and the Sorelians* (Berkeley, Calif., 1980) remains a good study of the general impact of Sorel and the Sorelians.

The major work on the link between revolutionary syndicalism, Sorel, and Fascist ideology is Zeev Sternhell, *Birth of Fascist Ideology: From Cultural Rebellion to Political Revolution* (Princeton, N.J., 1994); the quotation is on p. 22.

CHAPTER 2

✍

The Democracies and
Their Dilemmas

CHAPTER OUTLINE

Britain: Accommodation and Militancy • France Muddles Through •
Italian Democracy in the Making

BIOGRAPHICAL SKETCHES

Emmeline Pankhurst, "Votes for Women!" • Jean-Joseph-Marie-Auguste
Jaurès, Martyr

At the beginning of the twentieth century, the major European states could be divided into two categories according to their political structure. Three had functioning parliamentary systems that included ministerial responsibility, the principle that no government could be installed or continue to rule without the majority approval of a popularly elected Parliament. Furthermore, members of Parliament could call a vote of confidence that might provoke the fall of a cabinet at any moment. If the government lost such a vote, it had to resign, whether or not the king or president (the executive) agreed. This procedure gave the legislative branch real power in these countries, the outcome of a centuries-long dispute between kings and elected assemblies.

Despite a variety of political, social, and still-unresolved governmental problems, Great Britain, France, and Italy fit the category of parliamentary democracies. In three other major European states—Germany, Austria-Hungary, and Russia—the governments were responsible not to parliaments, but to the monarchs. According to the constitutional structures of these states, the emperors named governmental ministers who served at their pleasure, not the Parliament's. As the new century opened, a number of serious domestic issues faced both the parliamentary democracies and the authoritarian states.

BRITAIN: ACCOMMODATION AND MILITANCY

Following a reign of sixty-three years, Queen Victoria died on January 22, 1901, and because of her longevity at the height of the country's power, her name symbolized the age. Considered rather dull, she at least took her duties seriously.

The opposite is true of her son, who succeeded her as Edward VII at age sixty. Edward loved hobnobbing with the rich and representing his country during a showy age, but, unsuited for governmental affairs, "his reign marks the real transition of the English monarchy from a significant political institution to its present primarily social function." In 1910, his son succeeded him as George V. Solemn and serious, this king resembled his grandmother but ably carried on the reduced role that his father had conferred on the monarchy.

Parliament and Reform

In contrast to the monarchy's decline, the English Parliament still represented the classic parliamentary model, with a long tradition of opposing groups alternating in power, cabinet stability, and parliamentary responsibility but faced a major institutional problem that threatened its ability to meet the growing social demands of modern society: the House of Lords was better able and ready to veto legislation than were the French and Italian senates. As Britain faced the growing lower-class demands, the anomaly of a hereditary branch of Parliament capable of blocking pressing reforms appeared intolerable.

The struggle to reduce the power of the Lords had been ongoing, but the Tories had blocked major changes. In July 1895 they had beaten back a challenge from radicals working with the Liberal Party and won a crushing victory in the general election. Conservative domination of British politics remained secure, despite the poor British performance in the South African Boer War (1899–1902), and continued with the elections of 1900 and 1902, when the new Conservative leader Arthur Balfour controlled the office of prime minister for the next three years.

Nevertheless, Conservative strength slowly eroded. In 1902, the Conservatives passed the Education Act, which alienated Dissenters because they perceived it as strengthening schools run by the Church of England. The temperance movement had brought general recognition that the great number of pubs constituted a grave social problem, but the method of reducing the number of pubs under the Licensing Act of 1904 created dissension, as did the question of whether owners whose licenses to sell alcoholic beverages had not been renewed should be compensated.

In 1903 and 1904, an economic downturn and long-term industrial changes increased labor agitation and spurred inflation. Labor power had ironically grown because of a 1901 House of Lords ruling stating that labor unions did not have immunity from suits and could be sued for the actions of their agents. Anger ignited resistance among the unions, whose political action committee successfully elected two candidates to Parliament, including labor's most notable leader Keir Hardie. Labor's growing clout and the increased industrial unrest came at a bad time for the Conservatives, who were split between the free-trade majority and advocates of protectionism and closer economic links with the British colonies led by Joseph Chamberlain. An attempted compromise and a cabinet reshuffle by

Balfour did not resolve the issue; Chamberlain challenged the prime minister for control of the party, and Balfour resigned in December 1905.

The Conservative decline altered Britain's political complexion. A wealthy, good-looking Scot, Liberal leader Sir Henry Campbell-Bannerman—known as CB—installed a cabinet and prepared for new elections with a successful appeal to Britons who were tired of the high cost of living and sick of the conservative inefficiency. Most important, the Liberals had powerful union support that established the well-organized Labour party. The January 1906 elections resulted in a Liberal majority of eighty-four seats, with twenty-nine seats going to its Labour allies.

CB's new cabinet was committed to reform and included Herbert Henry Asquith, future prime minister, as chancellor of the exchequer (treasury secretary) and Edward Grey, who directed British foreign policy until World War I. The Liberals embraced a serious social reform program based on the ideas of the Fabians, Socialist intellectuals led by Beatrice and Sidney Webb who pressed for reforms that would allow the country to catch up with social legislation that had already been implemented on the continent. The Liberal social-reform program included improvements in education, regulation of the liquor business, and health and accident insurance for working people.

The Liberals addressed the problems of children with legislation in 1906 and 1907 that provided free meals and medical attention for poor children in the schools. Furthermore, in a move aimed at breaking down class barriers in British society, the Liberals obliged every secondary school that received state aid, including private ones, to reserve a quarter of their places for graduates of state elementary schools. In 1908, the Children's Act banned imprisonment of children under age 14 and improved the reformatory system. In a related area, a royal commission recommended modifications in Britain's stringent Poor Laws, but divisions and World War I delayed changes until 1929.

The Liberals also favored the workers who had helped them come to power. In 1908, miners received the eight-hour day. In the same year, the government established old-age pensions and provided for retirement at age seventy, marking acceptance of an important principle by the British. Two other important pieces of labor legislation, backed by Winston Churchill, passed in 1909: creating labor exchanges that matched up workers and employers with available jobs and instituting mixed bodies of workers, employers, and state representatives with the power to set wages (subject to approval of a higher body, the Board of Trade) in industries that were noted for sweatshop conditions. In 1911 legislation patterned on the pioneering German social insurance law of 1889 was passed, the British National Insurance Act. This law established unemployment-limited insurance, national health insurance, maternity assistance, and sick pay, all funded by a modern contributory system.

Struggle with the House of Lords

In the course of implementing this ambitious reform platform, the Liberals ran into stiff opposition from the House of Lords, which it lost.

The Lords hoped to wear down the government by defeating land reform bills in 1907 and an important temperance measure in 1908. Liberal losses in by-elections signaled that the strategy was working, and the Liberals were further weakened by CB's death in 1908 and by the need for his successor Asquith to raise new funds to pay for the expensive social legislation and for new warships to meet the German naval challenge.

Fiery Chancellor of the Exchequer David Lloyd George decided to resolve both the monetary and the political problem in one bold stroke. In 1909 he presented a budget proposal that sharply increased existing estate and luxury taxes and introduced new duties aimed at the rich. His proposal included a supertax on incomes over 5,000 pounds, a 20 percent capital gains tax on land, and a levy on the value of undeveloped land. The high amounts involved, the principle of taxing high income, and the land duties shocked the Lords, who summarily rejected the proposed budget following its passage by the House of Commons. This development raised an important constitutional issue: constitutional experts agreed that the elected House of Commons had complete control of finance measures that should not be subject to reversal by the hereditary House of Lords. Lloyd George took his case to the people in an effective campaign in which he stated ironically: "a fully equipped duke costs as much to keep up as two Dreadnoughts; and dukes are just as great a terror and they last longer."

The Liberals won the January 1910 elections, fought over these issues, keeping their majority in the Commons with 377 seats to 275 with the help of its Labour and Irish Nationalist allies who won forty and eighty-two seats, respectively. This result induced the Lords to accept Lloyd George's budget, but the principle of whether they should have power at all had been raised. The problem the Liberals faced would be that the Lords would veto the legislation when the bill reached their chamber. The only way to get around the obstacle was to have the monarch appoint enough new peers to reverse the majority in the House of Lords, a procedure that had been used in the past. King Edward, therefore, had to agree, but he insisted on a second election, which took place in December 1910 and yielded similar results as the previous election. In the meantime, Edward died, and his successor George V, favored negotiations, but the Lords still rejected the bill and set the stage for its reintroduction under George V's threat to create new peers in case of a new rejection.

In August 1911 the bill became law. It deprived the Lords of their veto power by providing that the budget (or any bill certified as a money bill by the Speaker of the House of Commons) would become law without the consent of the House of Lords after a month. The Lords could hold up legislation other than money bills only for two years if the legislation passed in the Commons three times during that period. Finally, the duration of a parliament was reduced from seven years to five. In this way, the House of Commons gained control of the country's political affairs with the possibility of interference by the Lords reduced to a minimum.

The disputes over constitutional issues and social legislation weakened the British political system's ability to confront other questions threatening the country's stability. Despite British labor's success in attaining social reforms, salaries failed to catch up with the rising cost of living. In 1909, acting in its judicial capacity, the House of Lords dealt a blow to unions by ruling that they could not use members' dues to finance political action (the Osborne case).

Liberal Chancellor of the Exchequer David Lloyd George took on the House of Lords in 1909 with a famous program taxing the rich in a successful attempt to extend social programs and bolster the country's defenses by appealing to the British people. Lloyd George had a long career and led Britain to victory during World War I. Here is a picture of the "People's Champion" at ease with his dog, "Peggy."

The Liberals attempted to nullify the ruling in 1911 and 1913 by instituting salaries for members of Parliament and establishing criteria regulating the utilization of union funds for politics. The Labour Party saw these measures as a compromise, but the workers interpreted them as a sign that the party had been seduced by the parliamentary system. The increased aggressiveness of British workers coincided with agitation in Australia and the rise of revolutionary syndicalism in France and Italy. This ideology criticized parliamentary blandishments and advocated the supremacy of workers in politics and direct action through strikes. The British had won the right to strike in 1906, and labor leaders who had recently returned from Australia urged them to exercise it frequently.

Increasing Militancy

Labor militancy increased dramatically between 1906 and World War I. Union membership doubled, and in 1908 strikes caused the loss of more hours in one year than in the previous ten. Strikes particularly affected the mining, shipping, and railway industries. In 1911 striking seamen and firemen won important concessions. The first national railway strike took place during the same year and paralyzed the nation for two days. In 1912 the dockers' strike brought violence. The government's response ranged from conciliation to force, and the strike met defeat, as did similar actions by the miners. Frustrated by the spotty success of their strike tactics and dissatisfied with governmental concessions, the militant miners', transport, and railway unions signed an agreement to coordinate their action, the triple alliance, in June 1914. Before the agreement could be formally implemented, however, World War I broke out, and the government had little trouble persuading the unions to end their agitation on patriotic grounds—but the labor agitation brought a foretaste of future developments.

Militancy also increased among other groups, especially women. Before 1907, women had attained the vote in local elections, but the "suffragettes" demanded the ballot in national elections. Prime Minister Asquith remained cool to the request. In 1908 and 1909, Emmeline Pankhurst, founder of the Women's Social and Political Union (WSPU), led her organization to adopt militant tactics—demonstrations, violence, and destruction of property. In 1910 the government seemed willing to consider concessions, but the fight with the Lords and parliamentary maneuvering subsequently delayed legislation that was designed to grant them. In the meantime, the WSPU split because of the authoritarian manner in which the Pankhurst family administered the organization. Emmeline then quarreled with her daughters over ideology—were women repressed as a sex or a class? The women, however, like the workers, put the struggle for their rights on hold after the outbreak of war.

BIOGRAPHICAL SKETCHES

Emmeline Pankhurst
"Votes for Women!"

When Emmeline Pankhurst was born on July 14, 1858, her father Robert Goulden exclaimed: "She should have been a lad!" She very quickly learned to play the piano at sight, and her ability to spell earned her the nickname "the dictionary." Growing up in Manchester, then the center of the movement for the right of women to vote, fourteen-year-old Emmeline asked to be taken along when her mother attended a lecture by an advocate for the franchise. The event inspired her life's work.

In 1878, Emmeline and her parents attended a lecture by Dr. Richard Marsden Pankhurst, a strong advocate of equal suffrage for both sexes. The cab pulled up close to the family, and Pankhurst's delicate hand reached out to open the door. Her daughter Sylvia wrote: "Thenceforward all happened as if by magic." They married in the winter of 1879, and within a short time had four children. Emmeline had entered the political world and, spurred by the death of a son who she believed would have survived had the family been better off, became a Socialist and a champion of the poor.

Mrs. Pankhurst campaigned for the rights of married women during debates on a law that would allow women to vote on the local level. Politicians argued that married women should not have the vote because of the protection their husbands afforded them. In fact, once married, a woman did not exist legally. Her property became her husband's, and she could neither sue nor be sued in court.

continued

continued

Mrs. Pankhurst won her battle, and in 1894 all women gained local voting rights without regard to marriage.

During the early years of the new century, she took the lead in the women's movement and instituted militant means to obtain voting rights for women in national elections. Mrs. Pankhurst was intimately involved with the nascent Labour Party, but this organization disappointed her. She founded the WSPU as the instrument of fighting for women's rights. Its slogan was "Votes for Women!" Its members employed disruptive techniques, with many going to jail. During her career, courts sentenced Emmeline to a total of four years in prison, and she served several months. Her jail time compromised her delicate health, as it did that of other militant women who undertook hunger strikes and whom the authorities force-fed. When World War I broke out, Mrs. Pankhurst ended her militant campaign, giving top priority to supporting the war. In 1917, she led a WSPU delegation to Russia to convince that country to remain in the war against Germany. During the trip, she developed an abiding hatred for Bolshevism, an attitude that alienated her from her daughter Sylvia. In 1918 the climax of her campaign came, when women aged thirty and older received the right to vote and ironically the right to be elected to Parliament at age twenty-one.

Mrs. Pankhurst had a difficult relationship with her daughters, but suffered from her daughter Christabel's loss in her attempt to be the first woman elected to Parliament and from the subsequent collapse of her Women's Party. She remained active, however, in helping war orphans and in a number of other worthy causes. In 1928 she surprised the country when she agreed to present herself as a Conservative candidate for Parliament. During the campaign, she fell ill with the jaundice that had plagued her since her prison days. In May her daughters moved her into a nursing home, but she died on June 14, 1928, leaving her worldly possessions of eighty-six pounds to Christabel. In March 1930, a statue of Britain's Gentle Amazon was unveiled in Victoria Square Gardens near the House of Commons. An observer wrote: "There are literal minds which suppose that Mrs. Pankhurst faced obloquy and prison to win votes for women. She did a greater thing than that. She suffered to remove from the mind of every young girl the sense that she is born to a predestined inferiority."

The Irish question proved more recalcitrant. The British hoped to resolve the centuries-old Irish problem with Home Rule—establishment of an Irish parliament. Asquith presented a Home Rule bill in 1912, but the Irish question inflamed passions, and Tory opponents shouted down proponents and the prime minister. This behavior encouraged resistance in Ulster, the Protestant and economically advanced northern part of Ireland. The northerners feared that deputies from the Catholic and agrarian South would swamp their interests in a parliament representing all Ireland.

The northerners organized militarily to fight home rule, and the government dispatched troops to Ulster. This policy caused opposition among the British themselves and even British army officers requested exemptions should military action prove necessary. When the government refused, they resigned in protest—a mutiny that extended to the War Office—and Conservative leader Bonar Law pledged to back Ulster. In response, southern Irish volunteers organized

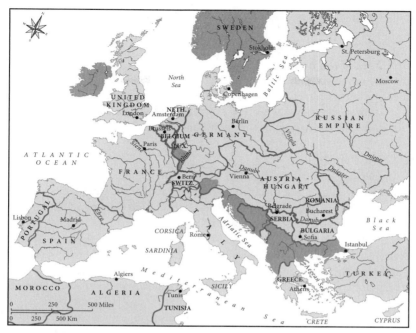

Europe in 1900. In this map of Europe in 1900, the major trouble spots are shaded. The most important problems were a dispute over Alsace-Lorraine, which caused bad blood between France and Germany, and the Balkans. Before 1912–1913, Turkey still occupied most of this peninsula, which was the scene of contests among the small and large powers located in the area's proximity. Italy was unhappy about Austrian mistreatment of the Italians in historically Italian areas still held by Austria-Hungary (Trent, the Trentino, Trieste, and the Dalmatian coast). Ireland, occupied for centuries by Britain, still festered. Sweden and Norway were one country, but the Norwegians chafed at Swedish supremacy. However, in 1905, this was the only issue to be peacefully resolved.

themselves, and a new urban working-class movement under Jim Larkin emerged and pledged to seek Irish freedom. In 1913 a serious tramway strike broke out in Dublin, with militant workers joining Sinn Fein, a nationalist organization demanding independence from Britain. In 1914 the Irish dispute escalated when the British army that had ignored military activities in Ulster fired on southern volunteers in Dublin. In the meantime, the Lords utilized their few remaining powers to delay the home rule bill. The postponement had drastic consequences because, in the meantime, World War I broke out, stymied resolution of the problem, and further radicalized the Irish situation. Ireland seemed on the brink of civil war; the Irish refused to put aside their claims during the conflict.

By 1914 Britain presented a mixed picture. Significant reforms had been adopted, but agitation increased at all levels of British society. It has also been suggested that the increasingly serious disturbances encouraged the coming of war because sectors of British society believed it would increase patriotic sentiment and calm domestic differences. It has been argued that England had "offered the world a remarkable experiment in liberal, capitalist democracy," but, if so, World War I ended it.

France Muddles Through

In the late nineteenth and early twentieth centuries, France resolved the major political problems forcefully posed during the great revolution that had begun in 1789: power sharing between the executive and legislative branches, whether France should be a kingdom or a republic, and the role of the Catholic Church.

The Third Republic

A parliamentary crisis that began on May 16, 1877, ended in an understanding that cabinets would be responsible to a majority vote of the Chamber of Deputies elected by universal male suffrage. An indirectly elected Senate had little effective power, and the president was transformed into a figurehead.

The Third Republic had thus been established, but the fight between secularism and the Catholic Church continued. The church opposed liberalism and republicanism and was strongly allied to the forces in French society opposing both, especially the army, which resisted civilian control and supported the conservative forces in French society. The army favored a war of revenge on Germany and blamed the politicians for their failure to lead the country in a fight to recover the provinces of Alsace and Lorraine that had been lost to Germany in 1871 following the Franco-Prussian War.

In the 1890s the Dreyfus affair brought the struggle between conservatives and liberals to the fore. Captain Alfred Dreyfus, a Jew, was convicted by the army of betraying French military secrets to the Germans and was shipped off to Devil's Island. Supported by their conservative and clerical allies, military leaders eliminated Jews, Protestants, and republicans from influential army positions. These developments convinced Liberals, Radicals, Socialists, and anticlericals to unite in a Leftist bloc, and French society split on the issues of justice, authority, clericalism, anti-Semitism, political prejudice, and democratic rule. The struggle escalated when novelist Émile Zola published a famous letter in defense of Dreyfus. New evidence emerged demolishing the army's case against Dreyfus, but the military refused to reverse its decision. Dreyfus's innocence or guilt became irrelevant as different sectors of the French population staked out positions depending on their views of the future of French society

The battle's fortunes tilted in the Left 's favor with the constitution of a government of republican defense under René Waldeck-Rousseau, with Dreyfus's rehabilitation, and the electoral victory of the Leftist bloc in 1902. Ex-seminary student and anticlerical Émile Combes became prime minister, and the Left passed legislation against church congregations and favoring the army's republicanization, an intense period that culminated in 1905 with the separation of church and state.

The Rise of Nationalism

The Dreyfus affair finally resolved the political question of the church's position in France and reduced the French army's threat but did not end nationalist hatred for the Third Republic. Indeed, the Dreyfus case exacerbated French

The famous Dreyfus case divided France at the end of the nineteenth and beginning of the twentieth century. Captain Alfred Dreyfus, a Jew, was convicted of betraying his country. In reality, this event brought to the fore domestic issues over which France had been fighting for a century: Church vs. State, Monarchy vs. Republic, Military vs. Civilian Control, rich vs. poor. This contemporary image shows Dreyfus receiving a dishonorable discharge from the French army after his conviction. He was later reinstated and fought in World War I.

anti-Semitism, probably the strongest in Europe, and stimulated the rise of a new, mystical, nationalism. Nationalists continued to accuse Jews of being disloyal: "There is not any likelihood that Dreyfus is innocent," they argued, "but it is absolutely certain that France is innocent." The champions of the new nationalism, Maurice Barrès and Charles Maurras, "felt that anti-Semitism filled a certain gap, supplied a need, and that without it nationalism could not survive." Maurras's *Action Française,* founded in 1899, pledged to end the evil Republic dominated by Jews, Freemasons, Protestants, and foreigners and argued that only restoration of the king could save France: "that is, *France* personified by the descendant and heir of forty chiefs who have made, enlarged, maintained, and developed it." *Action Française* presented itself as defending French tradition and accused the republic of destroying French culture by persecuting Catholics, corrupting French youths, and killing workers.

This last point illustrates how the nationalistic right appealed to the proletariat that it considered an integral part of the nation. Its leaders pledged to defend working-class rights by restoring the king, who alone could achieve social progress, maintain order, and "protect, organize and securely install the working class as his ancestors installed the bourgeoisie." Historian Zeev Sterhnell described France during this period as a "laboratory in which the original political syntheses of our time were created" and maintained that this grafting of workers' rights onto traditional nationalist ideology was the beginning of a national socialist or Fascist ideology.

The "Modern Challenge" and France's Failure

This phenomenon gave rise to revolutionary syndicalism, which urged strikes and violent revolution because the workers' own political parties betrayed them. The rise of this movement illustrates the Third Republic's difficulty in responding to the "modern challenge."

Historian David Thompson defined the modern challenge as the task of resolving the issues "of the great present-day problems of unemployment and social insecurity, of industrial despotism and world economy, of aggression and international disorder." A solution necessitated fashioning a new compromise between the industrial elite and the proletariat, which the French proved unable to craft. During the first decade of the twentieth century, no durable agreement between these two forces emerged, despite an increase of per capita industrial production of 57 percent between 1901 and 1913, compared to a European average of 37 percent. The social basis for this failure was the Third Republic's domination by the petite bourgeoisie who were entrenched in the bureaucracy and the major parties—Republicans, Radicals, and Radical-Socialists, which were neither radical nor socialist. The political story of this failure played out amid the backdrop of momentous labor battles and epic oratorical duels in the Chamber of Deputies between France's most notable prewar politician, Georges Clemenceau—the Tiger—and Socialist leader Jean Jaurès over social legislation, strikes, and unionization.

As the new century opened, French Socialists were split into revolutionary and reformist parties. The revolutionaries, led by Jules Guesde, advocated taking power by violence, while the reformists, headed by Jean Jaurès, believed that socialism could be achieved gradually through parliamentary reforms. In 1905 these parties merged into the French Section of the Workers' International (SFIO), with Jaurès as its leader. Following the leftist victory in the Dreyfus affair, the Leftist bloc disintegrated, and the differences reemerged as Clemenceau responded to Jaurès's demand for collectivization: "The real France is founded on property, property, property."

BIOGRAPHICAL SKETCHES

Jean-Joseph-Marie-Auguste Jaurès
Martyr

Jean Jaurès, heroic figure of prewar French socialism, was born in Castres, France, on September 3, 1859. The son of an unsuccessful businessman, Jaurès attended the country's best school on a scholarship—the École Normale Supérieure.
He taught at a lycée from 1881 to 1883 and lectured in philosophy at the University of Toulouse between 1883 and 1885.

In 1885 Jaurès won election to the Chamber of Deputies but was defeated for reelection in 1889. Following his defeat, he pursued graduate studies and earned a doctorate. He ran for Parliament again and won a seat from a working-class district in 1893. By this time Jaurès had converted to socialism, and when the Dreyfus affair touched off the greatest crisis in French politics and society before the 1930s Jaurès sought to reverse Dreyfus's conviction. This position contributed to his defeat in the 1898 elections, but it was his last loss, and Jaurès won reelection to the Chamber of Deputies in 1902, 1906, 1910, and 1914. Besides his political career, Jaurès devoted a great deal of time to scholarship, publishing a massive *Socialist History of the French Revolution, The Franco-German War,* and *The New Army.*

Jaurès belonged to a generation of remarkable Socialist leaders who believed in the gradual achievement of socialism through parliamentary reforms, but like most European Socialists of the age, the French split on this question. In 1904 Jaurès cofounded and edited *L'Humanité,* which helped spread his ideas. Jaurès dueled with Jules Guesde, leader of the revolutionary Socialist party, and Guesde's failure to garner much support set the stage for a merger in 1905 when the revolutionaries joined with Jaurès and, under his leadership, formed the SFIO. In Parliament, Jaurès became the champion of the working class and the great antagonist of Georges Clemenceau.

Besides his struggle for social reforms, Jaurès concentrated on foreign affairs. He feared above all the outbreak of a war in Europe, believing that French foreign policy—particularly its alliances with Russia and Britain—increased the danger of a conflagration and advocated international arbitration to assure continued peace. These views and what they perceived as a pro-German attitude brought violent extremist nationalist denunciations and a call for his assassination. In the summer of 1914, as Europe approached the outbreak of World War I, Jaurès threw his weight behind peace negotiations and argued that if France pressured Russia and the Germans pressed the Austrians, they could save the peace.

On the evening of July 31, 1914, Jaurès, some of his fellow Socialist deputies, and the *Humanité* staff dined at the Café Croissant in the Rue Montmartre—a popular meeting place for French and foreign journalists. Jaurès and his friends ate dinner seated on a bench with their backs to one of the restaurant's open windows. At about 9:30, just as he was finishing, a French nationalist who favored war with Germany pumped two pistol shots from the street through the window into the back of Jaurès's head. The Socialist leader died instantly.

The murder shocked France and Europe just as the conflict was breaking out. Jaurès's friend and Italian Socialist counterpart, Filippo Turati, expressed the feeling of many Europeans in his obituary that Europe could never have gone to war without first killing Jean Jaurès.

On March 14, 1906, Clemenceau became minister of the interior just as the largest French labor union, the Confédération Générale du Travail (CGT) adopted revolutionary syndicalist principles, which favored strikes and violence to overthrow bourgeois society. On May 1, 1906, the CGT planned a great demonstration in favor of the eight-hour day, and fear of the supposed imminent collapse of capitalism sowed panic in the hearts of the middle classes. Instead, Clemenceau arrested CGT officials, earning the undying enmity of Jaurès, who reproached him in Parliament for the next three years. At the same time, new elections produced a majority for a coalition of moderate Leftists and Centrists and a Clemenceau cabinet opposed to radical social or economic changes.

The Clemenceau government's performance turned out to be lackluster. Real wages for workers had lagged since 1902. The bill with the greatest potential for effecting social change would have established an income tax, but the government did not get it through the legislature until 1909, and implementation was delayed until 1914, then postponed again because of World War I. Another serious issue, women's rights, did not find a solution. Married women received control of their earnings in 1907, some acceptance in the bureaucracy, and the right to vote for professional bodies, but these steps left the women's movement unsatisfied because it demanded the right to vote in national elections. Efforts in Parliament to extend the vote to women got nowhere because France's largest party, the Radicals, and Clemenceau himself, resisted on the grounds that women would be influenced by priests to elect clerical candidates and jeopardize the republic.

Similarly, Clemenceau's government opposed union activities, especially in the public sector. When several public service unions joined the CGT in 1906 and 1907, Clemenceau fired their officers and proposed restricting unionization. This time Clemenceau came under fire for different reasons both by the Left and by conservatives who demanded he ban the CGT. Clemenceau refused, but the bitter debate with the Socialists over labor issues produced an irrevocable break. Several clamorous strikes, in which the police fired on the workers, killing six and wounding fifty, prompted an angry Jaurès to declare that there could be no rapprochement between the government and the Socialists. As a result, little in the field of social legislation had been accomplished by July 20, 1909, when the Clemenceau cabinet fell. By then foreign policy issues took precedence, and the opportunity to give France a modern social security system before the conflict had been lost.

France's inability to build an acceptable social security apparatus, to make the working class a partner in the government through meaningful collaboration with the Socialists, and to give workers a greater stake in the country caused the Third Republic to continue losing support among the proletariat. Reformist Socialists advocated participating in Parliament in order to share power, win reforms that would increase working-class living standards, and gradually achieve socialism, but an increasing number of workers agreed with intellectuals who charged that Socialist leaders had sold them out by participating in bourgeois politics that had robbed socialism of its revolutionary impetus. At the same time, the rightists beckoned them toward nationalism. After World War I, both the leftist and rightist movements increasingly had international links to which many French workers had a stronger allegiance than to the Third Republic. The Third Republic's failure to retain the primary loyalty of important segments of the population contributed to its growing weakness and eventual demise.

ITALIAN DEMOCRACY IN THE MAKING

Unlike France and Britain, Italy was a new democracy. Its constitution, the Statuto, proclaimed by the king of Sardinia in 1848, established a parliament but reserved to the monarch the right to name and dismiss governments. With the proclamation of the Kingdom of Italy on March 17, 1861, the Statuto was extended to the new state. The Statuto had the advantage of evolving almost immediately into a liberal-democratic instrument, with a legislature that, in practice, mandated that cabinets win a vote of confidence in order to rule, and the influence of the directly elected Chamber of Deputies overshadowed that of the appointed Senate. Nevertheless, the Italian king retained important privileges that neither the British monarch nor the French president enjoyed, such as the capacity to name the war minister that often had serious indirect results.

Italian Constitutional Weaknesses

Italian conditions following unification limited the importance of the parliamentary system. The level of political participation was very low because gender, tax, and literacy requirements restricted the suffrage to about 2 percent of the population until 1882, when men who could read and write received the vote. Still, the elevated level of illiteracy (about 73 percent in 1870) presented a formidable barrier until 1912, when a new reform act introduced quasi-universal suffrage for men by giving illiterates the right to vote. Women could not vote, and devout Catholics refrained from doing so.

The Catholic question was particularly serious. Italian unification had taken place in opposition to the church's wishes and had destroyed its temporal power, but the church remained a powerful force in Italian society and challenged the new state's existence. In a decree called the *non expedit*, Pope Pius IX ordered Catholics to boycott national elections, a policy that prompted devout Catholics to question the idea of a unified Italy. In addition, the pope called on Catholic powers, such as France and Austria, to restore the papal state, causing the Italian government its most serious diplomatic problems before World War I and stimulating the Italians to respond by adopting anticlerical legislation.

When the church failed to break up the new state, it changed tactics. In 1898 a response to a serious rise in the cost of bread touched off riots; the government struck out violently against all opponents that challenged the state's existence, including Catholics, Anarchists, and Socialists. Stung by its identification with subversives, the church switched its policy to one of unofficial cooperation with the state against its leftist enemies, and relations between the church and state improved. When the country's first general strike in 1904 raised the specter of a Socialist electoral victory, Pius X sanctioned limited Catholic participation in the general elections of that year. The state in return did not enforce anticlerical legislation, and in 1909 the church extended participation.

In 1913 the first general election under male universal suffrage took place. Liberal Prime Minister Giovanni Giolitti understood that the participation of masses of peasants who could not read and write in the elections and the church's heavy influence had altered the political equation. Giolitti reached an unofficial understanding with Catholic leaders in order to ensure victory. The so-called Gentiloni Pact permitted collaboration between Catholic and governmental candidates that allowed the Catholics to enter the Italian political system in force—they subsequently claimed that more than half the deputies had been elected with their help.

In 1919 the pope repealed the *non expedit,* and the Catholics formed a powerful party that greatly increased the church's influence in Italian politics.

The state had less luck in integrating other political opponents into normal life. On the left, anarchism advocated the state's complete destruction by violent means. Italian anarchists threw bombs, attempted revolutions, and in 1900 assassinated the king. Anarchism was the dominant ideology among leftist intellectuals until the early 1890s, but had little popular appeal and lost its intellectual attractiveness.

Socialism replaced anarchism as the strongest movement on the left. In 1892 Filippo Turati, son of a former governmental official, and the Russian revolutionary Anna Kuliscioff established the Italian Socialist party (PSI), born of Marxism and pledged to overthrow the state. Turati and Kuliscioff were reformists who advocated political intransigence—that is, no cooperation with bourgeois political parties—but modified their views when the 1898 disorders shook the country. They argued that the PSI should collaborate with progressive political forces in order to fight conservatives who aimed to restrict civil and political rights and destroy the constitution.

The Rise of Extremism

This was a crucial change. In 1901 a Liberal government came to office with Giovanni Giolitti as its most influential member. Because of the delicate balance of political forces, a negative Socialist vote or abstention would have brought to power Sidney Sonnino, a politician who wanted to modify the constitution in a conservative direction, so the Socialist deputies led by Turati voted in favor of the government. This violation of explicit party orders set off a long-smoldering fight between reformists and revolutionaries in the PSI. Italian reformists (or revisionists) like Turati favored a gradual, parliamentary road to socialism, including case-by-case political alliances with progressive bourgeois forces, while the revolutionaries advocated political intransigence and violence.

The years between 1901 and 1903, the golden age of Italian reformism, brought significant improvements in wages and working conditions for northern industrial and rural workers. In 1903 this progress slowed significantly as the government altered its benevolent attitude because, as in France, strikes spread to the public sector. Giolitti formed a new government and offered Turati a post, but mounting party opposition forced the Socialist leader to refuse. To everyone's surprise, Giolitti formed a more conservative cabinet and went on to dominate the Italian political scene until 1914. Over the years, Giolitti and the Socialists played a cat-and-mouse game, occasionally hostile, sometimes friendly, but never collaborating as closely as they had in 1901, despite his successful support of important measures, such as old-age, sickness, and accident insurance; protection for women and children working in industry and for emigrants; land reclamation; legislation favoring malaria and pellagra-stricken areas of the country; reduction of the workday; longer weekends; and representative institutions that formed the basis of a Labor ministry. As in France, however, the working class as represented by the PSI never reached a position of power in the government. Giolitti and Turati, like

Clemenceau and Jaurès, failed to come to an agreement that might have stabilized the country.

While reformist fortunes declined, revolutionary ideology gained widespread support. In 1904 the first general strike paralyzed the nation and touched off a long wave of disorder. Within the PSI the ideological struggle continued, and in 1912 a young revolutionary, Benito Mussolini, came to the fore.

As a young Socialist, Mussolini wrote for a Milanese revolutionary syndicalist newspaper, denouncing electoral politics and advocating violence. He achieved local fame in his native Romagna region until his arrest for opposing Italy's war against Turkey in 1911–12, and his violent rhetoric, brought him to national prominence. Socialist inability to prevent the conflict produced a backlash against the reformists, and in 1912 delegates to the party congress hailed him and adopted his motion expelling some of the leading reformists. Mussolini's newfound fame allowed him to claim the editorship of the party's daily newspaper *Avanti!*, which gave him a platform to incite revolution. In June 1914, a revolt known as Red Week took place in his own Emilia-Romagna region. Mussolini hailed it as the beginning of the Socialist revolution, but its suppression destroyed Mussolini's faith in Marxism as an instrument for mobilizing the masses for revolution, and he looked around for other means. His open break with the party came after the beginning of World War I, when the PSI supported Italian neutrality and Mussolini advocated intervention as a means of stimulating revolution.

Mussolini's disillusionment with Marxism and his contacts with Italian Nationalist and Futurist groups drew him to the national socialist ideology that was being elaborated by Italian and French intellectuals. In Mussolini, this doctrine would find a leader well versed in the Socialist aspect of the dogma and with the political capacity to implement it.

Divisive Economic and Social Issues

Besides growing extremism, important economic and social questions confronted Italy in the new century. Because the country had practically no coal and iron, it lagged behind the other large European countries in industrialization. In 1878 and 1887, Parliament passed tariffs and other measures to create an iron and steel industry. This legislation spurred industrial and economic growth, which was mainly confined to the northern "industrial triangle" bounded by Milan, Turin, and Genoa and failed to reverse the disparity between the North and South. This failure spurred emigration, and in some years almost a million southerners left for other European countries and for North and South America in what became the largest mass migration in modern times.

Italy's southern problem had important political ramifications. Given the high illiteracy rate in the region, only a small proportion of southerners could vote, and only a relatively few ballots had to be changed for determined groups to secure election to the Parliament. This situation presented the government with too great a temptation not to intervene in favor of its candidates. In 1909, Socialist writer and historian Gaetano Salvemini published an influential tract describing the process, *Il ministro della mala vita* (The Minister of the Underworld).

Salvemini claimed that Giolitti allied with local elites and with the criminal associations endemic in the South to stuff ballot boxes, prevent political rivals from organizing, and stop opponents from voting. As a result of these tactics, Salvemini argued, Giolitti controlled almost the entire southern contingent in the Chamber of Deputies, which, when added to his northern supporters, gave him an unshakable majority. He advocated universal suffrage as a solution because otherwise the Socialists would never be in a position to pass important reforms in the Chamber of Deputies. Salvemini's desire to put the campaign for universal suffrage at the top of the Socialist agenda split the reformists because Turati and other reformist leaders believed that universal suffrage for illiterates would only increase the power of the Catholic church. The reformist split and Salvemini's withdrawal from the party favored the revolutionary takeover of the PSI.

The question of the vote for women was intimately linked to the debate on universal suffrage. The conditions of life for Italian women improved during the 1890s, and by 1900 hundreds of them had earned university degrees in the same fields as men. Women had begun working outside the home, although their jobs, such as teachers and telephone operators, paid poorly. Despite these improvements, however, Italian women suffered from an inferior legal, economic, and social status. Only women could be punished for adultery, and women needed their husbands' permission to open a bank account or administer their own property. Politicians acting in concert with the church regularly defeated divorce bills, claiming that they would destabilize society. In theory the Socialists favored the vote for women, and Salvemini made it a major component of his demand for universal suffrage, but other reformist leaders believed that it should be given a lower priority than winning the ballot for men because they feared that the women would vote for clerical candidates and strengthen the church's influence.

As a result of its weaknesses, Italy had a more fragile parliamentary system than either France or England despite the economic and social progress that occurred during Giolitti's tenure. Giolitti's political acumen allowed him to dominate the Italian political system for fifteen years, longer than any major European politician. In the process, however, Parliament practically became identified with him, transforming the fight his enemies conducted against the man into a denunciation of the parliamentary order. It is no coincidence that the major scholarly critics of the parliamentary system discussed in the previous chapter—Mosca, Pareto, and Michels—were either Italian or worked in Italy for many years. With every crisis came an attempt by his critics to shake Giolitti's hold on power without regard for the damage their methods might inflict on Parliament. Important instances of the confusion between unseating Giolitti and damaging Parliament came with the outbreak of the Libyan War against Turkey and culminated during the debate on whether Italy should intervene in World War I. The impact of the war on Italy completed the job of discrediting Parliament and made a major contribution to the rise of fascism.

Bibliographic Essay

There are many general books on modern Britain, but perhaps R. K. Webb's *Modern England* (New York, 1973), remains the most elegantly written, complete, and thoughtful work. The remark on the significance of Edward VII's reign is on p. 448, and Webb's citation of Lloyd George's remark about the cost of dukes may be found on p. 459. Other general histories that are still very useful include the classic work by R. C. K. Ensor, *England 1870–1914* (Oxford, UK, 1936); J. B. Conacher, *Waterloo to the Common Market* (New York, 1975); and a briefer account, James Butler, *A History of England 1815–1939,* 2nd ed. (London, 1960). For more specific topics, Gary Bryan Magee and Andrew S. Thomson's *Empire and Globalisation: Networks of People, Goods and Capital, 1850–1914* (Cambridge, UK, and New York, 2010), emphasizes economics, migration and investment. *Social Classes and Social Relations in Britain, 1850–1914* (Cambridge, UK, and New York, 1995), by Alastair J. Reid, discusses economics and social conditions. Free trade and its influence is examined by Frank Trentmann, *Free Trade Nation: Commerce, Consumption and Civil Society in Modern Britain* (Oxford, UK, 2009). Ernest P. Hennock, *The Origin of the Welfare State in England and Germany: 1850–1914* (Cambridge, UK, and New York, 2007), compares the social policies of both countries. On socialism in Britain, and changing views, consult Edward J. Bristow, *Individualism versus Socialism in Britain, 1880–1914* (New York, 1987). On Balfour, Kenneth Young's *Arthur James Balfour: The Happy Life of the Politician, Prime Minister, Statesman, and Philosopher* (London, 1963), the complete life, is based upon many unpublished documents. A more up-to-date biography is R. J. Q. Adams, *Balfour: The Last Grandee* (London, 2007).

A clear, concise account of the tenure and action of the Liberal government during the period discussed is Colin Cross, *The Liberals in Power (1905–1914)* (London, 1963). Good works on the major British politicians include John Wilson, *CB: A Life of Sir Henry Campbell-Bannerman* (London, 1973); this detailed biography argues that Campbell-Bannerman was an unusual personality to lead a great political party. A portrait of CB (in addition to those of many other British statesmen) may be found in Keith Laybour, *British Political Leaders: A Biographical Dictionary* (Santa Barbara, Calif., 2001). As might be expected, Asquith has received great attention, and there is an official biography written by J. A. Spender and Cyril Asquith, *Life of Henry Herber: Asquith, Lord Oxford and Asquith,* 2 vols. (London, 1932). Thirty years later, Roy Jenkins wrote *Asquith* (New York, 1964), using material opened to him by the family; this is a reasonable attempt to portray not only the man but the age. At any rate, the reader may also wish to consult a work independent of the family's possible influence: Stephen Koss, *Asquith: Portrait of a Man and an Era* (London, 1976). Interesting insights into how Asquith's cabinet worked are provided by the recollections of a member, Edward David, ed., *Inside Asquith's Cabinet: From the Diaries of Charles Hobhouse* (London, 1977). Given Lloyd George's continuing importance, there are many works on him. Emyr Price, *David Lloyd George* (Cardiff, 2006) is a general biography. An excellent and detailed description of Lloyd Georges's policy during the period covered in this chapter is John Grigg, *Lloyd George: The People's Champion 1902–1911* (Berkeley, Calif., 1978). A biography of Asquith is also in the Haus Publishers series on British prime ministers of the twentieth century, Stephen Bates, *H H Asquith* (London, 2006). The essay by H. C. G. Matthew, "The Liberal Age (1851–1914), in Kenneth O. Morgan's *The Oxford History of Britain* (Oxford, UK, 2009) analyzes some of the themes discussed in this chapter; the quotation that ends this section may be found on p. 581.

On the women's movement in Britain, Sandra Stanley Holton, *Feminism and Democracy* (Cambridge, UK, 1986), mentioned previously, a brief, well-organized work, is particularly interesting; it discusses how, in addition to sex equality, the movement became involved with class issues and the Labour party and argues that these themes became central. Cheryl R. Jorgensen-Earp examines the *Speeches and Trials of the Militant Suffragettes: The Women's Social and Political Union, 1903-1918* (Madison, N.J., 1999); she has also published a book on the WPSU, *The Transfiguring Sword* (Tuscaloosa,

Ala., 1997). Unusual aspects of the women's movement in Britain may be found in Krista Cowman, *Women of the Right Spirit* (Manchester, UK, 2007), which discusses paid functionaries of the WSPU between 1904 and 1918, and Mitzi Auchterlonie, *Conservative Suffragists* (London, 2007), which looks at women and the Tories.

There are many general histories of Ireland that have chapters on this period; consult, for example, Edward Norman, *A History of Modern Ireland* (Coral Gables, Fla., 1971). For particular themes, with good coverage of the Edwardian period, see D. George Boyce, *Nationalism in Ireland*, 3rd ed. (London, 1995); Lawrence J. McCaffrey, *The Irish Question*, 2nd ed. (Lexington, Ky., 1995); R. B. McDowell, *The Irish Administration 1801–1914* (London, 1964); and Eric Strauss, *Irish Nationalism and British Democracy* (New York, 1951). On social conditions, see Timothy Guinnane, *The Vanishing Irish: Households, Migration, and the Rural Economy in Ireland, 1850–1914* (Princeton, N.J., 1997).

On France, David Thompson, *Democracy in France Since 1870*, 5th ed. (London, 1969), a classic account, is stimulating and manageable; the citation regarding France and the modern challenge may be found on p. 171 of this book. Robert Stuart, *Marxism and National Identity: Socialism, Nationalism, and National Socialism During the French Fin de Siècle* (Albany, N.Y., 2006) touches on some of the issues raised in this chapter. D. W. Brogan, *France Under the Republic: The Development of Modern France* (New York, 1940), also a classic work, is a detailed. A brief account is Alexander Sedgwick, *The Third French Republic 1870–1914* (New York, 1968). Theodore Zeldin's *France 1848–1945*, 2 vols (Oxford, UK., 1973) is a social history that includes all aspects of French life during the period indicated and can profitably be utilized as a reference work. General works on economics also include a standard work, J. H. Clapham, *The Economic Development of France and Germany 1814–1914* (Cambridge, UK, 1921). Shepard B. Clough's *France: A History of National Economics 1789–1914* (Cambridge, UK, 1961) contains difficult-to-find information. Patrick O'Brien and Caglar Keyder, *Economic Growth in Britain and France 1780–1914: Two Paths to the Twentieth Century* (London, 1978), is a good comparative study. Peter Campbell, *French Electoral Systems and Elections since 1789* (Hamden, Conn., 1965) has an excellent section on the electoral organization of the Third Republic.

On some of the issues involved and their significance, see Frederic H. Seager, *The Boulanger Affair: Political Crossroad of France, 1886–1889* (Ithaca, N.Y., 1969), an important affair involving a possible military takeover. Many books have been written on the Dreyfus affair, including one by Dreyfus himself. Good introductions are Guy Chapman, *The Dreyfus Trials* (London, 1972), the complete story of the trials in clear prose, and Jean-Denis Bredin, *The Affair: The Case of Alfred Dreyfus* (New York, 1983), a detailed account that also discusses the implications of the case. The state of French Catholicism in relation to the Dreyfus affair was examined by Maurice Larkin, *Church and State after the Dreyfus Affair* (New York, 1974); this book looks at the issue in its wider historical and political context. The whole affair has been reexamined in a comprehensive manner by Ruth Harris, *Dreyfus: Politics, Emotion, and the Scandal of the Century* (New York, 2010). On the threat to French democracy at the end of the century, see Robert Kaplan, *Forgotten Crisis* (Oxford, 1995). Much has been written on anti-Semitism in France, and a good collection of essays on this theme may be found in Frances Malino and Bernard Wasserstein, eds., *The Jews in Modern France* (Hanover, Vt., 1985).

C. Stuart Doty wrote a good account of Barrès and his influence, including an account of his national socialism, *From Cultural Rebellion to Counterrevolution: The Politics of Maurice Barrès* (Athens, Ohio, 1976), on p. 162 of which is the citation on the nationalist view of the Dreyfus case. Charles Maurras's politics is considered by William Curt Buthman, *The Rise of Integral Nationalism in France* (New York, 1970), but this work is useful for all aspects of integral nationalism, from the reasons for its rise to an examination of its other proponents and their ideas. See also Michael Sutton, *Nationalism,*

Postivism, and Catholicism: The Politics of Charles Maurras and French Catholics, 1890–1914 (New York, 1982). On some of the other themes discussed with respect to Barres and Maurras, see *French Literary Fascism: Nationalism, Anti-Semitism, and the Ideology of Culture* (Princeton, N.J., 1994), by David Carroll. The quotations regarding Action Française principles are taken from a declaration of principles (March 23, 1908), translated by Leslie Derfler and published in an appendix to his excellent summary, *The Third French Republic 1870–1940* (Princeton, N.J., 1966). Michael Sutton, *Nationalism, Positivism and Catholicism: The Politics of Charles Maurras and French Catholics, 1890–1914* (Cambridge, UK, 1982), examines Maurras's links to Catholic tradition and to the French Catholics. Oscar L. Arnal argues that the church took a consistently conservative and defensive political and social line in *Ambivalent Alliance: The Catholic Church and the Action Française 1899–1939* (Pittsburgh, 1985).

As might be imagined, Clemenceau has received much attention because of his role in World War I (books on this aspect are cited in the appropriate chapter), but less attention is now given to his domestic politics. The most detailed work is David Robin Watson, *Georges Clemenceau: A Political Biography* (Plymouth, UK, 1974), sympathetic and well argued. Gregor Dallas *At the Heart of a Tiger: Clemenceau and His World, 1841–1929* (New York, 1993). Geoffrey Bruun, *Clemenceau* (Hamden, Conn., 1968), is a shorter treatment by a well-respected scholar. Hampden Jackson, *Clemenceau and the Third Republic* (New York, 1948), is also a brief, clear work. F. F. Ridley wrote about revolutionary syndicalism and the CGT during this period: *Revolutionary Syndicalism in France; The Direct Action of Its Time* (Cambridge, UK, 2008).

There are also several good biographies of Clemenceau's great Socialist antagonist; a detailed, well-constructed study is Harvey Goldberg, *The Life of Jean Jaurès* (Madison, Wisc., 1968), from which the Clemenceau quote on property is taken (p. 363); reprinted in a digital edition in 2005. Zeev Sternhell has discussed the developments in France that led to the elaboration of a Fascist ideology, a controversial topic. The reader will find this theory elaborated—especially with regard to the revolutionary revisionism of Marx and the revolutionary syndicalists—in his *The Birth of Fascist Ideology* (Princeton, N.J., 1994), previously cited, but the Israeli scholar made similar arguments earlier in *Neither Right Nor Left: Fascist Ideology in France* (Princeton, N.J., 1986); it is from this book that the citations on anti-Semitism (p. 46) and prewar France as a laboratory are taken (p. 14). Kenneth H. Tucker looks at revolutionary syndicalism from a different angle: *French Revolutionary Syndicalism and the Public Sphere* (New York, 2005). Edward J. Arnold's *The Development of the Radical Right in France: From Boulanger to Le Pen* (New York, 2000) includes an essay on this period.

General works on Italy during the approximate period covered in this chapter include a good summary by Salvatore Saladino, *Italy from Unification to 1919* (New York, 1970). René Albrecht-Carrié, *Italy from Napoleon to Mussolini* (New York, 1949), wrote under the influence of recent developments, fascism and World War II. Christopher Seton-Watson, *Italy from Liberalism to Fascism 1870–1925* (London, 1967), is a particularly detailed account. Denis Mack Smith, *Italy* (Ann Arbor, Mich., 1959), is a critical view of Italy's history. An interesting topic that is not usually covered but that was an important part of Italy during the prewar period is discussed in Frank Snowden, *The Conquest of Malaria; Italy, 1900–1962* (New Haven, Conn., 2006).

Spencer M. Di Scala, *Italy: From Revolution to Republic, 1700 to the Present*, 4th ed. (Boulder, 2009), is a more recent general account that brings in debates and has an extensive bibliographical essay that outlines the historiographical debate over various issues. Edward R. Tannenbaum and Emiliana P. Noether's *Modern Italy: A Topical History Since 1861* (New York, 1974) contains a series of still-useful essays. Richard Drake, *Byzantium for Rome: The Politics of Nostalgia in Umbertian Italy, 1878–1900*

(Chapel Hill, N.C., 1980), is a good study. The standard work on the Giolittian Era is A. William Salomone, *Italy in the Giolittian Era: Italian Democracy in the Making 1900–1914* (Philadelphia, 1960); he coined the phrase "Italian democracy in the making." The book includes a valuable introductory essay by Gaetano Salvemini; the quotation from that essay is on p. xxi. This edition of the book, originally published in 1945, contains a long section on a debate that the work and the essay generated: "Giolittian Italy Revisited." The best political biography of Giolitti is Alexander De Grand, *The Hunchback's Tailor: Giovanni Giolitti and Liberal Italy from the Challenge of Mass Politics to the Rise of Fascism, 1882–1922* (Westport, Conn., 2001). The all-imprtant topic of Catholicism has been examined by John F. Pollard, *Catholicism in Modern Italy: Religion, Society and Politics Since 1861* (London, 2008). Italian Socialist issues, with particular emphasis on Turati and the role of Giolitti, is the theme of Spencer Di Scala's *Dilemmas of Italian Socialism* (Amherst, Mass., 1980). On the Socialists in the Giolittian era, there is also James Edward Miller, *From Elite to Mass Politics: Italian Socialism in the Giolittian Era, 1900–1914* (Kent, Ohio, 1990). Good essays on different aspects of the Giolittian period may be found in the first part of Spencer M. Di Scala, ed., *Italian Socialism Between Politics and History* (Amherst, Mass., 1996). Alexander De Grand wrote the history of the Nationalist Association, *The Italian Nationalist Association and the Rise of Fascism in Italy* (Lincoln, Nebr., 1978). Futurism is discussed by Christine Poggi, *Inventing Futurism: The Art and Politics of Artificial Optimism* (Princeton, N.J., 2009). Charles Killinger published a life of Salvemini, *Gaetano Salvemini: A Biography* (Westport, Conn., 2002). An important but neglected social and legal thinker and the implications of his thought receives excellent treatment in Mary Gibson's *Born to Crime: Cesare Lombroso and the Origins of Biological Criminology* (Westport, Conn., 2002). Jonathan Dunnage concentrated on social issues in *Twentieth Century Italy: A Social History* (London, 2002).

Economics, with chapters on this period, are considered in Shepard B. Clough's *The Economic History of Italy* (New York, 1964); the more technical Vera Zamagni, *The Economic History of Italy* (Oxford, UK, 1993); and Gianni Toniolo, *An Economic History of Liberal Italy* (London and New York, 1990). The southern problem is put into perspective by Gustav Schachter, *The Italian South* (New York, 1965).

CHAPTER 3

The Authoritarian States

CHAPTER OUTLINE

The German Empire: Greater Prussia • "That ramshackle realm":
Austria-Hungary • Imperial Russia: "Institutions are of no importance"

BIOGRAPHICAL SKETCHES

Friedrich Wilhelm Viktor Albrecht of Hohenzollern,
Failure • Karl Lueger, Mayor of Vienna

In 1900, the parliamentary systems of Germany and Austria-Hungary were not as fully developed as those of the liberal regimes previously discussed because governments were responsible to the monarch and could not be changed without their permission. Although the monarchs would have preferred to have the support of their parliaments, rather than be opposed by them, and did not wish to alienate them, they refused to give up any power despite the challenges of the representative bodies in their countries that wanted to emulate the Western parliamentary regimes. The German and Austrian monarchs' lack of accountability in government and foreign policy threatened European and world stability. Russia did not have a parliament until after the revolution of 1905, after which a parliamentary regime resembling that of the first two was set up.

THE GERMAN EMPIRE: GREATER PRUSSIA

The manner of German unification, completed in 1871, helps explain the weak position of Parliament in the German Empire. In contrast to Italy, unified during the same period, which has been described as a democracy in the making, Germany was a failed democracy despite the strong liberal tradition exhibited in that country during the revolutions of 1848. In 1862 a battle over the issues of popular representation, cabinet responsibility, and civilian control of the military raged in Prussia, the state that unified Germany. The regent who later became German emperor as Wilhelm I appointed the brilliant conservative Otto von

Bismarck as chancellor. Bismarck thwarted Liberal aspirations to introduce popular control over cabinets and the army, but he was much more than an old-
fashioned reactionary. He understood Liberal yearning for a unified Germany
and, more important, believed that Liberals would support unification even at the
cost of their liberalism. Consequently, Bismarck managed to defeat the Liberals
in the Prussian Diet, to strengthen the military, and to use that army to unify Germany. At the end of the process, Parliament itself blessed his action by passing a
bill that sanctioned the expenditures had been made against the Diet's will.

The Constitutional Structure of United Germany

Bismarck pleased the Liberals by agreeing that the new German representative
assembly (Reichstag) would be elected by universal male suffrage (aged twenty-
five or older). Universal suffrage had long been a Liberal aim, but Bismarck conceived of it as window-dressing. The Reichstag had no control over chancellors,
governmental ministers, or cabinets, a privilege reserved for the emperor, and
German constitutional practice over the next half century did not substantially
extend the Reichstag's power. The body could not question ministers (with
the exception of the minister for war, whom the general staff kept uninformed
for precisely that reason) and had a restricted role in economic, military, and
foreign policy. The upper house, the Bundesrat (Federal Council), represented the
different German states and could block legislation passed by the Reichstag. The
Reichstag did possess powers, such as the right to vote on the budget and military
appropriations, that, if further developed over the years, could have transformed
Germany into a true parliamentary system. In the course of several crises up to
World War I, the Reichstag might have been transformed into a Western-style
Parliament, but the emperors always thwarted it.

Other flaws blocked Germany's evolution into a parliamentary democracy. These flaws included Prussia's special position in the empire as the largest
German state containing two-thirds of Germany's population and, therefore, wielding enormous influence. However, Prussia's own constitution was undemocratic,
with 15 percent of the population representing wealthy landowners and bourgeois
ruling it through a Prussian representative assembly (the *Abgeordnetenhaus*), in
which the highest taxpayers had two-thirds' representation (the three-class voting
system). The Prussian king was also German emperor and appointed the imperial
chancellor and the ministers. The imperial chancellor held the post of Prussian
minister president and foreign secretary. The state of Prussia dominated both the
Reichstag and the Bundesrat by electing 236 out of 397 Reichstag members and
through its seventeen votes in the Bundesrat, with only fourteen needed to veto
constitutional changes. Moreover, legislation could not be passed by the Reichstag
alone but required the Bundesrat's assent.

There were other undemocratic features. In 1878, Bismarck instituted secretaries of state for various functions, bureaucratic administrators who oversaw
specific departments. After his dismissal in 1890, his successors could not keep
them under control. These secretaries had direct access to the kaiser, who could
make decisions over which Parliament had little control. An outstanding example
was Admiral Alfred von Tirpitz, father of the German navy, who went directly to

The career of Alfred von Tirpitz, father of the German navy, shows how the weakness of the German constitutional structure before World War I could be exploited for self-serving interests. When Tirpitz needed funds for his navy, he bypassed the Reichstag and went directly to the Emperor. Britain perceived the massive growth of the German navy as a direct challenge to its security.

Wilhelm II in order to gain support for a naval buildup that touched off an arms race with Britain, a principal cause of World War I.

The Tariff and Its Implications

Complex economic and social changes sweeping Europe in the late nineteenth and early twentieth centuries combined with German parliamentary weakness and had grave consequences for all Europe. In 1873 long-term improvements in transportation provoked a long-lived agricultural crisis because cheap American and Russian grain could be sold more inexpensively in Europe than the Europeans could grow it. This change produced demands for protection. In Germany, Bismarck dropped the free trade policies he had formerly supported and called for a protective tariff that passed in 1879. This tariff, which remained in effect after the agrarian crisis ended, protected the large landowners east of the Elbe River, the Junkers, but raised the price of food and consequently the wages that industrialists had to pay their workers. When the industrialists complained, the government compensated them by increasing its orders for military hardware. This deal between large landowners and industrialists resulted from *Sammlungspolitik,* supposedly the collaboration of national groups, but which can be more accurately described as a landowner-capitalist coalition to maintain the tariff and resist democratic reform.

A complex web of interests supported this arrangement. For example, a Navy League materialized to stimulate the popular demand for a bigger battle fleet necessary to win a large German colonial empire, but a larger navy boosted the profits of industrialists and talk of a world empire contributed to the British decision to defend their own possessions through new alliances. The tariffs, passed for seven years at a time, also had the effect of helping pay the Reich's bills and reducing parliamentary leverage over the budget.

German fiscal policy had deleterious effects throughout society. Import duties raised the price of food, while increased taxation for arms expenditures put further pressure on household budgets, causing more ordinary Germans to vote for opposition parties, especially the German Socialist party (*Sozialdemokratische Partei Deutschlands*, SPD). From 1900 to 1914 German industrial development reached unprecedented levels, but, because of the political and social domination of capitalists and landowners, the benefits barely filtered down to the population at large. Between 1890 and 1914, the growth of real wages in Germany has been calculated at 1 percent in comparison to 4 percent in Britain and France. Because of technological developments, the establishment of cartels, and governmental policies favoring industrialists and large landowners, German unemployment rates remained high, and economic growth was seriously unbalanced among different groups of workers, disparate regions, and rural and urban areas. The economic situation stimulated the entrance of wives into the workplace to make ends meet and an exodus from the land and the smaller cities to the large urban areas. This population shift from conservative rural areas to the cities did not result in a reapportionment of the Reichstag, however, and Junker influence remained strong as the least progressive areas of the country continued to be overrepresented in the legislature. In 1914, for example, a deputy from Berlin represented about 100,000 inhabitants compared to a rural Prussian deputy's approximately 24,000.

German Society

Conservative values appeared preeminent in prewar German society. They inculcated fierce loyalty to the Reich, militaristic attributes, and hatred for external and internal enemies. The family's authoritarian structure reinforced these attitudes by giving power to the father and transmitting an absolutistic image strengthened by other institutions, especially the schools. German secondary education did a good job of teaching literacy, but education generally did not improve one's social status; rather, the reverse. A student's social position usually determined his educational success. Moreover, the state mandated the teaching of patriotism and directed the schools to combat Socialist ideas.

While formal education generally ended with elementary school, some went on to an inadequate vocational education, and a small percentage successfully made it through the extremely difficult requirements for entrance to grammar school that opened the door to the university. Most grammar school students came from university-educated middle-class and civil service families, the lower classes rarely receiving a university education. Reflecting the generally limited access of Europeans to the academy during this period, the German university population in 1900 has been estimated at 34,000, out of a population of 56 million

(640 per million). German universities were renowned and universally imitated for their high standards, research, and scholarship, but imposed political conformity on students and faculty.

Because the universities shaped Germany's elite, strong mechanisms assured loyalty to the political and social system. Student fraternities and clubs imposed a neo-aristocratic code on boys of bourgeois origin, "inculcating them with norms and values intended to bind the potential representatives of future middle-class politics to the pre-industrial aristocratic ruling groups." Dueling societies encouraged fights, recalling medieval times, and students collected scars that, combined with an air of superiority, marked them as prestigious members of a learned elite. The successful graduate who avoided subversive ideas and a Jewish wife could count on an effective network that guaranteed him a good economic and social future.

German churches represented another powerful level of control. The dominant Protestant religion, Lutheranism, inspired the identification of church and state that deterred antigovernmental viewpoints and encouraged conservatism. Anti-Catholic prejudices that had their latest manifestation in the Kulturkampf (Bismarck's political struggle against the Catholics) were deeply imbued in German society. Bismarck ended the Kulturkampf in 1879 because he needed Catholic Center Party votes to pass the tariff, and that accommodation set the tone for future relations between Catholics and the state during the late nineteenth and early twentieth centuries. The Center Party, a highly disciplined organization with its base in Catholic southern Germany, provided crucial support for the government, which excluded overt political discrimination against Catholics. The Protestant majority, however, continued to include Catholics in an array of internal enemies not to be trusted, and Catholics never ceased regarding Protestant Prussia as the enemy. The Center Party and Catholic associations opposed liberalism, socialism, and modern trade unionism and hoped to dictate policy regarding education, the family, and social affairs in Catholic areas. Despite their dislike for each other, however, Germany's two most powerful religious denominations did not challenge the Reich's political or social structure.

Racism and Intolerance

The categorization of Catholics as enemies in the minds of many Germans revealed a common phenomenon linked to the authoritarian structure of society. Bismarck and his successors skillfully mobilized nationalist sentiment against foreign enemies, such as France, and against domestic outsiders, such as Catholics, Socialists, and national minorities, that were discriminated against in public employment and in the armed forces and singled out as actual or potential threats to the country. The largest pariah group in German society was the Jews. A great influx of Jews from Eastern Europe followed German unification. These new immigrants, along with longtime Jewish inhabitants, ran into a wall of intolerance encouraged by the idea of medieval Christianity that condemned the Jews for having killed Christ. This belief meshed with old economic and cultural myths—such as the image of the rapacious Jew using interest to exploit ordinary Germans or the Jew as incapable of being assimilated—reinforced by new ones. Anti-Semitism rose sharply with increasing industrialization and the rise of socialism, with Jews being viewed contradictorily both as conspiratorial capitalists who exploited workers and as internationalist Socialist plotters who were out to destroy German culture. As in most of Europe, these notions cut across all German society and transformed the Jew into the scapegoat that many Germans needed to confirm their anti-Western ideas.

By the late nineteenth century, anti-Semitism had been transformed for many German thinkers (as well as for other Europeans) from the cultural to the biological variety. Writers advocated the purification of the German spirit by eliminating all things Jewish. A Völkisch culture emerged according to which race determined everything. The conception that people are the product of their heredity came into vogue. Mixing science with moral and cultural stereotypes of the Jew resulted for many Germans in the feeling that the Jewish character had certain permanent qualities. Racist writers attributed unfavorable characteristics to the Jewish "race" as a whole that conversion to Christianity or assimilation could not alter. By the early twentieth century, therefore, both cultural and biological anti-Semitism was widespread in Germany as in the rest of Europe. Although overtly anti-Semitic political parties did not attract large memberships, they did not probably because of the strength of anti-Semitism in the traditional political organizations. Such views favored ideas regarding biological predetermination and depersonalization of the Jews and, although present in other European countries, later served the Nazis well in their campaign to exterminate Jews and other groups.

Serious problems with other minority groups also troubled prewar Germany, especially the Poles who lived in Prussia. The Prussian Diet made German the official language in the Polish areas, including the schools, and created a mechanism to buy Polish land for German peasants. When the attempt failed, it adopted an expropriation law against the Poles in 1908, and German officials discussed expelling Poles wholesale from the areas they had occupied for centuries. As early as 1885, Bismarck had ordered the deportation of thirty thousand Poles (one-third of whom were Jews) from East Prussia, and in 1914 German war aims included a provision for clearing Poles from the areas they inhabited (the Frontier Strip) and turning the land over to German settlers. The smaller French and Danish minorities also experienced official discrimination.

German Women

Women similarly had difficulties in prewar Germany. The government lifted restrictions on women who wished to work in the universities only in 1909, but whether to educate them remained a question mark. Some German writers argued that it was racial suicide to educate women because women would leave the home for the professions, and the family's downfall would follow. One book that purported to prove the physiological feeblemindedness of women went into twelve editions. The editor of an encyclopedia offered to publish a scientific article by physicist Lise Meitner, who would later be the first to describe nuclear fission, and refused when he discovered that she was a woman.

In 1900 new legislation improved the situation of women slightly by removing the obligation for a wife to have her husband's consent to work, but a woman's property still became her husband's upon marriage, along with any property that came to her during the marriage. Husbands had the legal right to make decisions for the family and had control over the children, divorce was difficult to obtain, and in criminal cases women were considered unreliable witnesses. The state regulated prostitution, but only for the purpose of making it easier for young men to be initiated into the rites of sex.

After 1902 the number of women's associations, membership in them, and activity all increased, but women did not win the right to vote. Prussia and other states forbade women from engaging in political activity, but, as women defied them, they were relaxed after 1908. Disappointed with the lack of support even in leftist parties, German women linked up with similar movements in other countries, particularly Britain. The German women's movement, however, split between radicals and moderates and by 1914 was in turmoil. The political clout of feminism thus remained minimal.

German Socialism

The German Socialists presented the state with a more complicated picture. Bismarck had attacked them between 1878 and 1890, and discrimination followed after that year. Ironically, although SPD rhetoric remained revolutionary, in practice both the party and revisionist thinker Eduard Bernstein influenced the large unions affiliated with the SPD, and they both pursued a de facto policy of winning reforms to raise wages and improve working conditions. This policy did not change substantially after 1905, when, influenced by the atmosphere following the Russian Revolution of that year, growing dissatisfaction with the SPD majority produced a new radicalism that culminated in a formal split in 1917. The SPD had a proved capacity to appeal to voters, but an enlarged Reichstag SPD contingent held out little immediate promise for changing Germany's authoritarian political structure. The question was this: if the Socialists and their allies became a majority, would they be able to transform Germany into a parliamentary democracy?

This concern encouraged German governments to implement policies that historians have called social imperialism, an approach also found in other countries but was the clearest in Germany. "Social imperialism" is the attempt by conservatives to combat growing liberalizing movements by gaining popular support for imperialistic aims by convincing the common people that they have something to gain from those policies. Although traditional conservatives frowned on such notions, elections in 1912 favored candidates who held them. This development has been interpreted as amounting "to a definitive popularization of right-wing politics, and makes it possible to speak for the first time perhaps of a radical right." In this manner, Germany's increasing challenge to the existing world order was supposedly influenced by domestic considerations—the attempt of the German ruling class to defend its power by utilizing foreign adventure and an aggressive new, popular image of Germany's world role.

The Emperor

The continuing failure of the German political system to limit the executive branch's control of the government had a fundamental role in this development. The German constitution made the German emperor the most powerful man in the "world," and its flaws became glaringly obvious when the boastful and erratic Wilhelm II came to power as kaiser in 1888. Bismarck described the new kaiser's personality: "The Emperor is like a balloon," he stated; "if one did not hold him fast on a string, he would go no one knows whither." Two years later, the kaiser broke the string by dropping Bismarck as chancellor.

Although Wilhelm's swaggering and irrational statements have raised questions in the minds of historians as to his willingness to follow through on what he said, there is little doubt that he greatly influenced domestic and foreign affairs. Wilhelm favored the old-line Prussian Conservatives and large agrarian interests, both of whom remained entrenched in the bureaucracy and the army and who refused to make concessions to peasants and industrial workers. As for the liberal middle class whose presence increased because of the enormous growth of industry, its political clout diminished even while Wilhelm supported its economic aims.

The Failure of Reform

The German political scene in the years before World War I is littered with failed opportunities to reform the German Constitution and to adjust to changing social and economic conditions. Between 1894 and 1896, a crisis occurred between the kaiser and his own government. The dispute began over a legal issue but culminated in the question as to whether the emperor could refuse to dismiss a minister the cabinet wished to discharge, a fight the cabinet lost.

During the early years of the new century, the demand for constitutional reform gained momentum as middle-class opinion increasingly seemed to turn against Wilhelm and to favor the steadily advancing Social Democrats. If the Liberals, Social Democrats, and the Center had joined together, the support they enjoyed in the country might have produced a demand for a stronger Parliament, favored by the rise of the Center's left left wing led by Matthias Erzberger.

The year 1906 witnessed a constitutional crisis originating in a dispute between the Center Party and the chancellor, Bernhard von Bülow, because the Colonial Office refused to acknowledge any control by the Reichstag. The quarrel prompted the normally placid Center to vote against part of the financial assessment for German Southwest Africa. Since the Social Democrats supported the Center, the government found itself in the minority. Instead of resigning, Bülow dissolved the Reichstag, put together an electoral coalition consisting of the Conservatives, the middle-class National Liberals, and Progressives, and won the 1907 elections. However, this "Bülow bloc" proved unstable because the Conservatives wished to reestablish an alliance with the Center, a crucial division that made it impossible to revise constitutional procedures even though a new scandal created an opportunity to do so.

BIOGRAPHICAL SKETCHES

Friedrich Wilhelm Viktor Albrecht of Hohenzollern
Failure

Kaiser Wilhelm II hoped to outshine Bismarck and win a place in the sun for Germany, but history recognizes him as a failure.

Wilhelm, grandson of Queen Victoria of England, the son of her eldest daughter Princess Victoria and Crown Prince Frederick, was born in Berlin on January 27, 1859, with a useless, withered left hand. With training, he seemed to overcome this handicap, but observers speculated that it left psychological scars and contributed to his bombastic, vain personality. His parents gave Wilhelm a liberal education, but perhaps under the influence of Bismarck, he grew up a conservative who developed into an anti-Semite and militarist drawn to power politics. In 1881, he married Augusta Victoria, duchess of Schleswig-Holstein, and had seven children.

Wilhelm's father Frederick, a liberal whom Bismarck feared, became emperor in 1888 but died of throat cancer after three months in office. Although only twenty-nine when he inherited the throne, Wilhelm chafed at Bismarck's tutelage and dropped him as chancellor in 1890. Wilhelm believed that he had a right to rule with minimal input from Parliament, and his domestic policy contributed to Germany's failure to develop into a parliamentary democracy. In foreign affairs, he devalued the Russian connection that Bismarck held dear because it prevented a possible two-front war that he believed Germany could not win. When the Russians joined up with the French, the Germans sought a military solution to their encirclement with Wilhelm's approval. In addition, Wilhelm's diplomacy, noted for its clumsiness, alienated the other great powers.

During World War I, Wilhelm faded into the background as the army took effective control of the country and his popularity dropped. After four years of war, the Allies made it clear that Wilhelm himself was an obstacle to peace and, on November 9, 1918, his country in revolt, he abdicated. He fled to Doorn, in the neutral Netherlands, purchasing an estate where he lived until his death. The Dutch refused Allied demands to hand him over as a war criminal.

In exile, Wilhelm worked for his restoration and briefly flirted with Hitler when he thought the Nazis might accept him as emperor. His second wife, whom he married in 1922, was pro-Nazi, as was a son who joined the Nazi SA Storm Troopers. When France fell in 1940, the old kaiser sent Hitler a congratulatory telegram because the Fuehrer's generals had received their training under his rule, but relations remained cool. When Wilhelm's grandson died in combat, Hitler resented the show of sympathy that Berliners demonstrated at his funeral and secretly ordered all Hohenzollern relatives drummed out of the armed forces. When the Germans took over the Netherlands, the British offered him asylum, but Wilhelm refused. After the emperor died on June 5, 1941, Hitler hoped to hold a funeral in Germany for propaganda purposes, but Wilhelm's will stated that he should be buried at Doorn and that there should be no swastikas at the funeral. In retaliation, Hitler ordered that no German military officers attend the services and buried news of his death in the back pages of the newspapers.

Wilhelm II lies buried in a small mausoleum on his estate, now Dutch government property. He is the object of veneration by German monarchists who periodically visit, marching to military music and carrying banners. The old emperor awaits his return to Germany—as he ordered in his will—when the monarchy is restored.

On October 28, 1908, the kaiser released an interview to the British news-paper, the *Daily Telegraph,* that managed to alienate Britain, Japan, King Edward VII, and the Boers. Before its publication, Wilhelm sent a copy of the interview to Bülow who was too busy to read it. When the interview aroused a firestorm of criticism, the Reichstag, with Bülow's support, issued a timid statement criticizing Wilhelm, who promised to be more discrete in the future. Wilhelm was furious with Bülow but did not fire him because of the country's intense reaction to his bungled interview. Under the circumstances, the country seemed likely to have supported Bülow and the bloc if they had tried to take greater control over foreign policy and name a cabinet responsible to the Reichstag, thus bringing Germany closer to the West European parliamentary mainstream. It is doubtful that Bülow supported such a move, but at any rate the Conservatives feared liberalization and in 1909 seized on a minor difference with the government to desert the Bülow bloc and ally once again with the Center Party. Bülow resigned, ending the crisis and permitting Wilhelm to reassert his autocratic ways. Wilhelm appointed as chancellor a bureaucrat who was unlikely to challenge his authority, Theobald von Bethmann-Hollweg.

The *Daily Telegraph* affair's sorry end angered the liberal parties, who, unlike the Center, resolved to support the Social Democrats in reforming the German con-stitution. The Progressives and National Liberals joined a loose coalition with the Social Democrats in the 1912 elections, increasing their representation while the representation of the Conservatives and Center dropped. In 1913 to 1914, another constitutional crisis flared, and the Reichstag censured the government with little effect. Constitutional reform thus proved impossible in prewar Germany.

Major historical schools have interpreted these events differently. The older school, represented by historian Arthur Rosenberg, viewed the emperor's policies as serious errors. Wilhelm's stifling of reform had two results, he argued. The lack of control in foreign policy made it easier to blunder into a major war, and the impossibility of implementing reforms peacefully increased the chances of a rev-olution and the empire's overthrow. For Rosenberg, Wilhelmine Germany was on the road to crisis and revolution even if war had not broken out.

For historian Hans-Ulrich Wehler, the situation was more complex. Wehler argued for the continuity of German history through Hitler's atrocities. Wehler wrote that Germany's elites defended their privileges not only through internal resistance to reform—that at some point would have overwhelmed them—but primarily by turning to a policy of conquest that would divert the people's attention, arouse nationalistic support, and expand German power. Wehler concluded that the power and values of these elites remained in place after World War I and made Nazi policies possible.

Historians Geoff Eley and David Blackbourn cautioned against accepting Wehler's approach. They argued that German politics and society were much more complex and suggested that the "capitalist mode of production" favored a new structure for politics in which the bourgeoisie did not accept a subordinate role to the aristocracy. In addition, they argued, the peasants were not automatically subjected to the control of the landowners, that the relationship was complex, and that the focus should be on the specifics of that association and on compromise.

"THAT RAMSHACKLE REALM": AUSTRIA-HUNGARY

Germany's major ally, Austria-Hungary, appeared to be an anachronism at the beginning of the twentieth century. Consisting of territories collected by the Hapsburg dynasty over the course of centuries, throughout the nineteenth century it opposed nationalism and constitutionalism because it favored limited governments and the independence of national minorities—ideals that threatened a multinational empire held together by an absolutistic emperor and a German-speaking ruling class.

In 1867, the Austrians and Hungarians agreed on the Ausgleich (Compromise) that created the dual monarchy of Austria-Hungary that sanctioned the Austrian Germans' rule in Austria and Magyar control of Hungary, both of which contained many nationalities demanding equal rights.

A Complicated Constitutional Structure

The 1867 Compromise established separate parliaments for Austria and Hungary, along with a complicated system of coordination. Austrian Emperor Francis Joseph was also king of Hungary and had to give his consent for all major

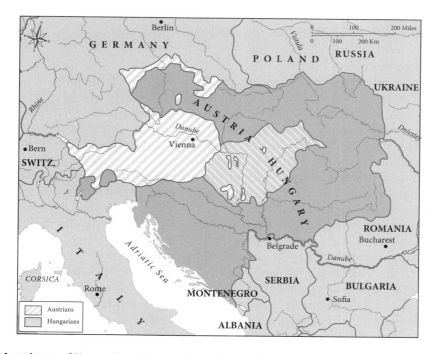

Austrians and Hungarians. This map shows the Austrian and Hungarian populations of Austria-Hungary in 1910. Other nationalities that composed the empire ruled by these two national groups included Poles, Czechs, Slovaks, Serbs, Ruthenes, Croats, Romanians, Italians, and Ladins. Bosnia-Herzegovina included a large Muslim population. Note the presence of Austrians in a strategic area of what would become Czechoslovakia after World War I and would cause a major crisis during the interwar period.

decisions in both countries. Austria had a bicameral legislature (the Reichsrat) consisting of a hereditary House of Lords and a House of Representatives elected after 1907 by universal male suffrage. In matters affecting both Austria and Hungary, the Lords elected twenty delegates and the representatives forty; this "Austrian delegations" and a similarly elected Hungarian delegations met separately to express the views of their countries and to enact limited legislation. The Hungarian parliament consisted of a Chamber of Magnates and a Chamber of Deputies elected under a restricted and complicated electoral system, to which must be added forty deputies from Croatia during discussion of Croatian matters.

In order to run affairs common to both halves of the empire, the emperor appointed three common ministers who served at his pleasure—finance, foreign affairs, and war; otherwise, the countries had separate governments except for the same person as monarch. Ten-year treaties between Austria and Hungary regulated economic affairs, each country's contribution to the common budget, and customs issues. Negotiation also determined the number of conscripts from the two countries who would be drafted into the army. Complex crown councils conducted the empire's everyday affairs, subject to the king-emperor's approval. Disputes among the many nationalities, the unwieldy parliamentary structure, and a centralized German-speaking bureaucracy that resisted reform and concessions to the subject nationalities ensured the emperor's power.

The Nationalities Problem

Austria and Hungary faced similar problems during the early twentieth century with regard to the subject nationalities. In Austria, the Czechs were 23 percent of the population and led the cultural and political opposition to German domination. The Austrian government attempted to meet some of the Czech opposition's demands, but the measures alienated the Austrian Germans, and the government had to promulgate them by decree. The emperor had scarce regard for Parliament. In January 1900 he appointed as minister president a civil servant who resorted to emergency decrees, deals, and corruption when the government could not attain a majority for its legislation: "Parliament had ceased to have any effective voice in the government of the country," and, furthermore, the system curtailed the influence of parties, such as the Christian Socials and the Social Democrats, whose support increased as the result of a growing economy.

In the first decade of the twentieth century, the nationality question worsened. In 1908 the Czechs boycotted ceremonies celebrating Francis Joseph's sixty years in power, a state of emergency had to be called in Prague, and the local government suspended. The Ukrainians became increasingly attracted to Russia, and a pro-Russian Pan-Slav movement held a great congress in Prague. Ethnic divisions also permeated the Social Democrats, whose rank-and-file viewed the dictatorship of the proletariat as a centralized state run by German-speaking Austrian workers, despite the feelings of party leader Viktor Adler. In 1905 Czech workers split the party and trade union movement on the basis of nationality.

The Catholic Church was similarly affected even though it officially repudiated nationalism. It was rich, taught religion in the schools, told peasants whom to vote for through the parish priest, and underwent a political revival because of its influence in parties concerned with social issues. In 1891 several Christian currents that were concerned with social questions had joined together under the leadership of Karl Lueger to form the Christian Socials. Lueger's enormous popularity, the organization's support of social legislation, his skillful manipulation of anti-Semitism, and his efficiency in implementing municipal services as mayor of Vienna made the party a force to be reckoned with as its German base allied with traditional clerical forces.

Hungary versus Austria

Hungary faced similar problems, but the situation was exacerbated by the complicated relationship between the two countries. The question of whether to retain, modify, or terminate the 1867 Compromise with Austria dominated Hungarian political discourse until the empire's dissolution in 1918. During these years, pro-Compromise politicians Count Kálmán Tisza, his son Count Istvan Tisza, and Count Gyula Andrássy tried to ensure that the popular misgivings over the Austrian arrangement had little representation in Parliament, governmental agents intervened in elections, and political leaders who challenged the Compromise were made to understand that Francis Joseph would reject any modification.

BIOGRAPHICAL SKETCHES

Karl Lueger
Mayor of Vienna

Karl Lueger would not be a center of debate if the young Adolf Hitler had not spent time in the Austro-Hungarian capital and stated that he learned from the anti-Semitic techniques of the longtime Vienna mayor. Lueger led the Christian Social Party during the early twentieth century, the first political party in the country with mass appeal. Perhaps the country's most popular politician, he transformed anti-Semitism so that it became the basis of his vast political power. Lueger attained so much political influence that no prime minister could come to power without his unofficial approval.

Historians argue over the character of Lueger's anti-Semitism. Some observers, including Jews at the time, believe that it was not racist but that Lueger employed it only as an instrument for achieving and retaining power. This version is summarized in a famous statement attributed to him: "*I decide who is a Jew!*" A second interpretation holds that his anti-Semitism had a biological basis and that it foreshadowed Hitler's racism. Supporters of this view point to the writings and speeches of followers who called for the partial extermination or eradication of the Jews and predicted a time when they would be killed and burned. A statement attributed to Lueger seems to lend credence to this rendering: "I'll only be happy after the last Jew has disappeared from Vienna." Emperor Francis Joseph and the Austrian Catholic hierarchy both feared the extreme reactions his anti-Semitism elicited.

continued

continued

Regardless of the historical debate, it seems clear that Lueger's politics made anti-Semitism a strong force in Austria. Regardless of Lueger's personal feelings about the Jews, his anti-Semitic techniques inspired Hitler's admiration, and the Fuehrer not only mentioned him in *Mein Kampf* and in his table conversation, but carried around a medal with his portrait. Joseph Goebbels, Nazi propaganda minister, used Lueger's figure in one of his most infamous propaganda films.

In addition to anti-Semitism, Lueger skillfully used his influence with women to perpetuate his political power. He never married, perhaps because he realized that marriage would reduce his sex appeal and the devotion of the legion of women who worked for his success. "Lueger's Amazons" canvassed Vienna raising funds for him, built up preelectoral interest, and got out the vote. His rhetoric was legendary, and his ability to whip up enthusiasm among all classes is reminiscent of fascism.

Lueger had an active sex life, cherished good food, and dressed well, all elements that increased his popular appeal. According to his longtime mistress, he loved to eat caviar and crabs and drank fine wines and champagnes. He also enjoyed simpler fare and could go on for pages about the virtues of dumplings. His mistress reported, however, that he embarrassed her by closely scrutinizing the restaurant bills. He dressed elegantly and valued jewelry, such as gold watch chains, cuff links, and stickpins, although he did not like to spend money on such items and relied on gifts. In his administration of municipal funds, on the contrary, he was scrupulously honest, opposed corruption, and gave away half his salary.

Born on October 24, 1844, to a family of humble origin, Karl Lueger studied the law and was elected mayor five times before Francis Joseph consented to his installation. After twelve years in office, the much-loved mayor died on March 10, 1910, of complications from diabetes and nephritis. A million people attended his funeral, the greatest Vienna had ever seen. The city paid the expenses for Lueger's last illness, his funeral, and his tomb in Vienna's Central Cemetery, where the Lueger Memorial Church is a commanding presence.

Nevertheless, the dispute threatened the empire's internal structure. The Austro-Hungarian army wanted a larger contingent from Hungary to reflect the increase in population. The Hungarians, in turn, demanded that the units be made more Hungarian through changes in the language of command, the soldiers' oath, and the insignia. Francis Joseph vehemently objected to these requests, and in 1906 the fight ended in a victory for the emperor, which increased confusion and resulted in greater interference in the electoral process and an intensification of tensions between Hungary and Austria in other areas regulated by the Compromise. Francis Joseph's successful opposition to changes in the Compromise in Parliament increased radical opposition to the political system in the country. Strikes and disorders proliferated and culminated in strikes on the land and a general strike in 1912.

The Nationalities Question in Hungary

Hungary did not go its separate way because of the serious challenge that Hungarian domination faced from the subject nationalities. The Hungarian government followed a policy of forced assimilation. It "Magyarizied" the civil service by requiring a degree from a Hungarian university, which could be earned only in the Magyar language; with few exceptions, Magyar was also the language of the primary schools. Only Hungarian speakers could enter the professions or even get menial jobs in the administration. State employees had to Magyarize their names, and the government did the same to the place names of areas inhabited by non-Hungarians. The assimilation policy succeeded only in preparing the ground for the later partition of Hungary.

Resistance to the Hungarians centered on the Romanians who were concentrated in Transylvania. The Romanians boycotted parliament, demanded full autonomy, circulated their grievances to all Europe, and established a vigorous cultural league with links to independent Romania, which they joined after World War I. The Slovaks and the Serbs united with the Romanians in calling for greater cultural autonomy, while the Croats frequently rioted. Self-determination might have been a productive way to respond to these problems, but the Hungarians responded by excluding prominent leaders of the subject nationalities from Parliament, arresting others, and intensifying their Magyarization campaign. The nationalities issue thus was even more explosive in Hungary than it was in Austria.

Economic Development and Its Effects

Had Hungary and Austria followed a more flexible policy toward the subject nationalities, the "ramshackle realm" might have survived. The empire was economically viable, and its development would have contributed to a positive resolution of its social problems. In both Austria and Hungary booms followed by busts followed by the loss of land by many Austrian peasants and subsequent emigration characterized the late nineteenth century. By 1900, the reduced population, technical improvements, and the cooperative movement brought economic renewal, while a new tariff encouraged industrialization. Almost 26 percent of the Austrian population earned its living through industry and mining, compared to 52 percent for agriculture; city populations expanded rapidly; and Vienna grew to 1.675 million people.

This economic progress favored the high and middle bourgeoisie, increased its political importance, and altered its composition. There was an influx of Jews, who concentrated in industry, the professions, finance, and the press. Anti-Semitism increased dramatically, especially among the petite bourgeoisie, who received the right to vote in 1882. Initially attracted to Georg von Schonerer's extremist anti-Semitic Germanic nationalist movement, they later switched to Karl Lueger's Christian Socials, only moderately anti-Semitic compared to the Nationalists.

The Christian Socials and the Social Democrats championed the growing number of factory workers, and between 1885 and 1887, the government adopted a series of social reforms that included limited working hours, protection for women and children, Sunday rest, factory inspections, and some sickness insurance. These measures were frequently evaded, however.

Social and economic change came slower to Hungary than to Austria. Economic activity increased during the early twentieth century, but slowly, so by

1914 Hungarian national wealth amounted to about half of Austria's, even though its population was only 20 percent less. Furthermore, Hungarian wealth was badly distributed among a few very rich families and a great number of poor people. Vast estates run by old families characterized the Hungarian countryside, with four thousand magnates owning 30 percent of the land. These magnates dominated Hungarian social and political life and supplied the country's minister presidents. The medium-to-large landholders (about ten thousand) were the bulk of the empire's supporters because the emperor had favored their acquisition of land following the 1848 revolution. However, most Hungarian peasants held very small plots, and rural life had undergone a decline after the 1880s when a depression in wheat prices prompted the introduction of machinery. In the early twentieth century, increasing industrialization siphoned off labor from the land to the cities and eventually mitigated the bad conditions.

The influx of labor into the urban areas depressed wages, working conditions, and living standards. A 1900 survey revealed that in the factories, men typically worked a twelve-hour day for very low wages, and women, paid proportionately less, nine to ten hours. In burgeoning Budapest, only about 6 percent of the people lived one or two to a room in 1910, while 10 percent resided ten or more to a room and others lived in caves, holes in the fields, and even in trees. Workers responded by joining unions and the Hungarian Social Democratic Party, which was not able to get many of its demands implemented because the government strongly opposed the party's internationalist ideology and its non-Magyar and Jewish leadership.

As in Austria, the growth of industry caused a large inflow of Jewish immigrants into the country. In 1900, Jews accounted for 8.5 percent of the total population but for 25 percent of Budapest's inhabitants. The newcomers achieved a near-dominant role in industry, trade, finance, the professions, the press, and the law. Jews were not well represented in Parliament, the civil service, or the army, but exercised considerable behind-the-scene influence on the government. The alliance of Jewish capitalists with Liberal party leader and Minister President Kálmán Tisza and other politicians who were anxious to spur rapid economic development produced a tolerant policy toward Jews and other religions, in contrast to Austria. In 1894 Hungary ended the Catholic Church's privileged position and declared all religions equal, required civil marriage, and recognized interfaith marriages.

Could Austria-Hungary Have Survived?

During the first decade of the twentieth century, the industrialization of Austria-Hungary became almost dizzy in its tempo. Between 1898 and 1913, industrial plants increased by 84 percent, employed workers by 76 percent, and the value of goods manufactured by 126 percent. Industry accounted for 27 percent of the national income. Factories in Austria grew by 40 percent, and workers who were employed by 49 percent. Real per capita income in both Austria and Hungary rose by about 40 percent. Austria-Hungary's commercial development suggests that its national and political problems, not its economic viability, account for its eventual destruction.

The tragic and long-reigning Emperor Francis Joseph occasionally took courageous stands but refused to renounce any part of his power or to reform the parliamentary system. He rejected meaningful autonomy for the subject nationalities and stubbornly followed the policies of centralization and absolutism handed down to him by his ancestors. Plans to restructure the empire by reaching agreement with other national minorities that would allow them to rule in their own areas, similar to the Hungarian Compromise, once the old emperor died were vague. The leader of this movement, heir presumptive Francis Ferdinand, a conservative with a liberal reputation because he had married outside a restricted noble circle, was rumored to have a plan to include Serbs and Croats in the governing groups; he seems unlikely to have made significant structural alterations even if had he not been assassinated on June 28, 1914.

IMPERIAL RUSSIA: "INSTITUTIONS ARE OF NO IMPORTANCE"

Russia suffered from mediocre leadership and outmoded institutions. The notion that leaders, rather than institutions, counted most in governing Russia became a mantra in the nineteenth and twentieth centuries. The failure of the autocracy to adapt to a changing world and the inability of Parliament to sink roots in the country conditioned Russia's modern history.

A Multinational Empire

In 1900 the Russian empire included one-sixth of the earth's landmass, stretching into Asia as far as Siberia. In central Asia the Russians dominated large and nationally diverse Muslim and Christian populations, some of whom resisted Russian domination by force of arms. In the West, they ruled over numerous European subjects, including Poles, Finns, Swedes, Baltic Germans, Romanians, Ukrainians, Letts, Lithuanians, and Estonians. With few exceptions, the Russians allowed the ethnic minorities no political autonomy, arousing resentment especially among the Poles, who revolted several times in the nineteenth century. Finland, linked to Russia through a personal union with the tsar, enjoyed some autonomy.

Religious problems exacerbated national ones. The Russian majority belonged to the Eastern Orthodox Church controlled by the tsars. The church performed governmental functions and received direct state subsidies. Other religious groups, Catholics, Lutherans, and Muslims, encouraged resistance to Russian rule and contributed to the growth of national feeling in the subject territories. The incorporation of Polish and other lands also brought large numbers of Jews into Russia, so that by 1897 they numbered 4 percent of the population. The Jews were forced to live in certain areas (the Pale) and were excluded from higher education and the professions, and restrictions were placed on their economic activities. Even if restrictions were gradually lifted, the Jews suffered from official anti-Semitism and pogroms that spurred emigration.

Russian economic weakness impeded the country's social progress and military potential. Tsar Peter the Great (1689–1725) had attempted to import Western technology, and periodic attempts of this kind set off disputes between the

Slavophiles—champions of traditional Russia who opposed foreign influences—and the Westernizers, who were ashamed at Russia's backwardness and wanted to import Western technology and a parliamentary government. Out of this contest, which lasted into the twentieth century, the intelligentsia emerged—well-educated persons who sought to modernize Russia according to creeds that ranged from moderate to revolutionary, from liberalism to socialism.

Insufficiency of Reform and Radicalization

Given the autocracy's complete control of the country, only the tsars could initiate reforms. They did so sporadically throughout the nineteenth century, instituting governing institutions but not a constitution. Probably the most important reforming tsar was Alexander II, who emancipated the serfs in 1861. However, emancipation produced such a complex situation that it prevented rapid progress on the land and impeded industrialization in the cities. The state compensated landlords for the loss of their lands but obliged the peasants to reimburse the treasury in annual installments for the next forty-nine years and created legal barriers to owning, selling, and leaving the land. This situation prevented the cities from importing the labor they needed and slowed Russian industrialization.

Contemporaneously, the failure to implement political reforms, such as parliamentary institutions, created resentment, alienated middle-class intellectuals, and radicalized the intelligentsia. The regime's opponents split into broad groupings: The Liberals, moderates who wanted a Parliament on Western European lines—and different shades of Socialists, who believed that parliaments were useless and wanted to overthrow the social and political order by violence. Russian authorities violently attacked both, alienating Liberals who were willing to accept a representative government and fostering terrorism.

Social discontent grew exponentially in the cities and on the land as the government's encouragement of industrialization to catch up to the West, unaccompanied by political reforms, contributed to urban disaffection. Finance Minister Count Sergei I. Witte instituted monetary reform, encouraged the building of railroads, extended tariff protection, and provided subsidies and guarantees to entrepreneurs. This policy stimulated the building of factories but resulted in the creation of an urban proletariat working under miserable conditions and to growing labor unrest. In the countryside, the peasants bitterly complained about the lack of land, but it was backward cultivation techniques, indebtedness as a result of emancipation, obstacles to freedom of movement, and the instability created by the village communes running the farms that accounted for the ills of Russian agriculture.

The Crumbling Autocracy

The absolute government of the tsars could not adapt to the complexities of modern life. Russia's last tsar, Nicholas II, refused to delegate decisions and was overwhelmed by insignificant trivia, such as approving the requests of pages for leaves of absence, that he could not devote appropriate attention to the major problems of his empire. The autocratic system also failed to produce

Sergei Witte had a distinguished political and domestic career. A reformer, he concentrated on building a railway network in Russia and labor reform. After the 1905 revolution, he became Russia's first "Prime Minister." Witte set the stage for the crucial reforms of Peter Stolypin. He is shown on the far left in this picture negotiating an end to the Russo-Japanese War in 1905 with the aid of Teddy Roosevelt in Portsmouth, New Hampshire.

high-quality rulers: Russians joked that they did not need a limited monarchy because Nicholas already was a limited monarch.

Ironically, the Russian autocratic system produced governmental anarchy. The tsar often named cabinet ministers who frequently pursued contradictory policies and warred with each another. This technique bolstered the tsar's power but made for inefficiency. Another serious governmental flaw: because ministers served at the tsar's pleasure, and the tsar controlled their salaries and privileges, they feared expressing their true opinions because they understood that they were the tsar's servants rather than his trusted advisers. Their obsequiousness toward the monarch and their poor salaries caused the public to hold them in low regard.

Despite some indication before his accession that he might change the autocratic system, Nicholas II proclaimed his intention to keep it intact. He continued his father's repressive policies, curtailed the rights of national minorities, and pursued an anti-Semitic policy. His refusal to change emboldened the opposition, helped as it was in the early twentieth century by the social changes fostered by industrialization. Liberals clamored louder than in the past for a constitution and representative government. They allied with *zemstvo* (elected local governmental officials) activists and professionals, found leaders in economist Peter B. Struve and historian Paul N. Miliukov, and in 1903 formed the Union of Liberation, the nucleus of the future Constitutional Democratic Party (Kadets). Socialist parties, such as the Russian Social Democratic Workers' Party (SDs)—a Marxist organization that demanded a revolution led by the industrial proletariat—grew in strength. This party split over whether there should be a transitional phase to socialism through the establishment of a bourgeois democracy (the Mensheviks, guided by Georgii V. Plekhanov), or whether a violent revolutionary elite should overthrow the government immediately (the Bolsheviks, led by Vladimir I. Lenin). Secret governmental agents attempted to combat the Marxists by infiltrating workers' associations and encouraging them to accept the ideas of Socialist revisionists, such as Eduard Bernstein. This strange experiment was known as police socialism, but it encouraged strikes and quickly ended. Another socialist organization, the Party of the Socialist Revolutionaries (SRs), appealed primarily to the peasants, demanded all land for the workers, and advocated terrorism.

The 1905 Revolution

Despite the confused political condition in which it found itself, Russia became embroiled in a disastrous war with Japan in 1904 and 1905. On January 9, 1905— "Bloody Sunday"—troops guarding the tsar's Winter Palace in Saint Petersburg fired on workers marching to redress grievances. The resulting massacre touched off mass demonstrations demanding a parliament, civil rights, and a reduction

The many problems of imperial Russia and the refusal of Emperor Nicholas II to concede meaningful political reform led to a revolution in January 1905 during the Russo-Japanese War that was a prelude to even more momentous events. Here is an illustration of the "Bloody Sunday" fighting at the Winter Palace that eventually led to the Bolshevik Revolution in 1917.

of the working day while a Soviet (council) of Workers' Deputies, consisting of Mensheviks, Bolsheviks, SRs, and revolutionary intellectuals, called a general strike that paralyzed the capital. As violence spread to the countryside, Nicholas was faced with the choice of instituting a military government or granting a constitution. On October 30, 1905, his promise of civil liberties and a democratically elected assembly defused Soviet calls for revolution and split the opposition. The Socialists demanded a republic and nationalization of the land, while the Liberals divided into the Octobrists, who thought the revolution had achieved enough, and the Kadets who demanded more liberties. However, the army remained loyal, and by the end of 1906 the government had quelled the disturbances.

The new constitution had a limited scope, and legislation creating the state Duma, the national representative body, instituted a complex voting system that granted the vote to males aged twenty-five years or over. Governmental ministers were responsible to the tsar, not the Duma, and the government did not need Parliament's approval for its actions. After February 1906 the Council of State—half of whose members were appointed by the tsar and half who were elected by privileged groups—had to give its assent, and no law could take effect without the tsar's permission.

Struggle in the Duma

The unsettled conditions after the war, land hunger, and universal male suffrage favored governmental opponents in elections and spelled the quick end of the first two dumas. Opposition groups in the first Duma elected in 1906 have been estimated at 55 percent, and the government proved unable to work with moderate groups. All parties demanded a cabinet responsible to Parliament, abolition of the Council of State, the cessation of extraordinary security measures, and expropriation of privately held lands for redistribution to the peasants. The government, led by Ivan L. Goremykin, rejected these provisions, and when the first Duma turned into a disorderly battleground, the tsar dissolved it in July 1906.

The energetic new prime minister, Peter A. Stolypin, implemented agricultural reforms and drafted a reform program for presentation to the new Duma. The elections increased the representation of opponents on both the left and the right, and when the new Duma rejected the government's program, Stolypin dissolved it. For the next elections, Stolypin and the tsar changed the criteria for representation by giving a greater voice to European Russia and to the propertied classes. The strategy worked. The third Duma met in November 1907, and while it was far from pliant, it had a working majority based on the Octobrists, a party dominated by the moderate nobility, commercial, and industrial interests. The third Duma passed major land, educational, judicial, administrative, and social legislation, lasted its full five-year term. and was regularly succeeded by the fourth Duma.

This increased stability did not resolve Russia's parliamentary weakness. Nicholas retained too much power, resorted to ruses to get his way, and regularly interfered in parliament's operations. The Kadets refused to support the government because the cabinet was not responsible to Parliament. This forced Stolypin to rely not only on the Octobrists, but on nationalist groups that favored the passage of objectionable legislation with regard to the national minorities. Moreover, Stolypin had problems with Nicholas, who was reluctant to work within the parliamentary system. The ascendance of Gregory Rasputin, a religious mystic with an unsavory reputation, increased Stolypin's difficulties at court. Rasputin convinced the empress that his special powers could stop the bleeding of her son and the heir to the throne, a hemophiliac, and wielded great political influence. When Stolypin complained to Nicholas, the tsar answered: "I agree with you . . . but it is better to have ten Rasputins than one of the Empress's hysterical tantrums." In 1911 Stolypin threatened to resign if legislation he presented favoring Ukrainian peasants over the Polish gentry that had been stalled by the Council of State did not go into effect. The tsar supported him, but only half-heartedly. The strained relations between the two men indicated that the prime minister was headed for dismissal when he was assassinated in September 1911.

By then, Nicholas regretted his institution of a parliamentary system. In the last years before World War I, constitutional reform in Russia seemed remote, and the tsar's excessive power caused increasing resentment. A historian observed: "First among the grave-diggers of Russia comes her last emperor."

Stolypin's Reforms

While Nicholas refused to concede a greater political voice to his people, he favored economic development that brought unparalleled advances. In November the government eliminated the redemption payments that the peasants still owed after their emancipation from serfdom. Over the next several years, Stolypin's government and the third Duma implemented crucial reforms that aimed at creating Western-style small peasant landholders, who would be free to buy and sell their land and to move about at will without the expropriation he considered unjust and inefficient, and at eliminating peasant support for the revolutionary parties. In order to achieve this goal, he set out to give individuals, instead of the village commune, legal title to the land and to allow peasants to move without passports and without forfeiting their holdings. In 1906 legislation instituted freedom of movement and established procedures by which peasants could obtain legal title to their land and consolidate scattered strips into single farms. By 1915 a quarter of the communal peasants had completed both steps.

This process brought greater inequality to the peasant villages than had previously been the case, but at least poorer peasants could sell their holdings and move to the cities with their capital and find work in the growing industrial sector. The governmental reforms raised the normal harvests for grains from 400 to 500 pounds per acre to 700 to 800, and the annual harvest increased from 54 million tons in 1900 to 97 million in 1913. The production of other crops saw similar increases, and the value of imported farm machinery rose from 28 million rubles in 1908 to 109 million in 1913.

Similar progress occurred in industry as the growth of cartels favored better use of capital and greater efficiency. Foreign investment flowed into Russia to finance industrialization, and native capital became progressively more important. Private entrepreneurs took their place beside the government as major investors in the country's modernization. Between 1909 and 1913, the pace of industrial increase outstripped Germany, France, and Britain. There were comparable increases in the commercial, banking, and trading sectors, and exports increased in value from 762 million rubles to over 1.5 billion between 1901 and 1913. The standard of living rose, and the largest Russian cities acquired modern services, such as electricity, water, and sewerage facilities.

Because Russia started from a lower base, it still trailed the industrially advanced European nations, but the pace of its growth on the eve of World War I pointed to the end of its economic backwardness.

Bibliographical Essay

An informative general history of Germany from the seventeenth century is W. M. Simon, *Germany: A Brief History* (New York, 1966) and Gordon A. Craig, *Germany, 1866–1945* (New York, 1978). Other informative, general histories with at least some coverage of the period discussed in this chapter include Martin Kitchen, *A History of Modern Germany, 1800–2000* (Malden, Mass., 2006); Stefan Berger, *Germany* (London, 2004), and Frank W. Thackeray, *Events that Changed Germany* (Westport, Conn., 2004), ten events, two of which occurred during the period under consideration. E. J. Feuchwanger, *Imperial Germany, 1850–1918* (London, 2001) is a thorough history, but also look at Michael Sturmer, *The German Empire: A Short History* (New York, 2002).

Since the issue of how the process of German unification affected later history is so important, see the excellent work by Otto Pflanze, *Bismarck and the Development of Germany,* 3 vols. (Princeton, N.J., 1990). The same might be said about the most important character in that story, Bismarck, who has been the subject of numerous biographies. On Bismarck, see Erich Eyck, *Bismarck and the German Empire* (London, 1950); a standard work, Theodore S. Hamerow, ed., *The Age of Bismarck: Documents and Interpretations* (New York, 1973); and the more recent *Bismarck* (Harlow, UK, 2000), a through work. Readers should not neglect the delightfully written biography by A. J. P. Taylor, even while taking some of his interpretations with a grain of salt: *Bismarck: The Man and the Statesman* (New York, 1967). Jonathan Steinberg's *Bismarck: A Life* (New York: Oxford University Press, 2011) can now be considered the standard biography.

For particular issues, see Gordon A. Craig, *Politics and Culture in Modern Germany: Essays from the New York Review of Books* (Palo Alto, Calif., 1999), and Ann Goldberg, *Honor, Politics and the Law in Imperial Germany, 1871–1914* (New York, 2010). See also Peter Fritzsche's *Reading Berlin 1900* (Cambridge, Mass., 1996), a discussion of the German capital's cultural influence; Peter Alter, *The German Question and Europe: A History* (London, 2000), which goes up to 1990; *Modern Germany: Society, Economy, and Politics in the Twentieth Century* (New York, 1987), which includes a chapter on Wilhelmine Germany; Matthew Jefferies, *Contesting the German Empire, 1871–1918* (Malden, Mass., 2008), which raises new questions; and James N. Retallack, *Imperial Germany, 1871–1918* (New York, 2008), a collection by different scholars on important topics. Reappraisals by different scholars may be found in Jack R. Dukes and Joachim Remak, *Another Germany: A Reconsideration of the Imperial Era* (Boulder, Colo., 1988).

The classic work by Arthur Rosenberg, containing the view that the blockage of reform set a long road toward the revolution that took place in 1918, was originally written in 1928 and translated into English in 1931: *The Birth of the German Republic 1871–1918* (New York, 1962). This book stands the test of time very well. The quote about the German emperor being the most powerful man in the world is on p. 33. Hans-Ulrich Wehler's interpretations may be found in English in *The German Empire 1871–1918* (Providence, R.I., and Oxford, UK, 1991, 1993). This book may be slow going because it is replete with information and insights but will amply reward a careful reading. The quotes on how aristocratic values were inculcated into middle-class boys are on pp. 125–26, and the unwillingness of the ruling circles to adjust to changing conditions is on p. 245. Wehler's views raise the issue of the German problem in Europe; on this broader question, consult Louis L. Snyder, *German Nationalism: The Tragedy of a People* (Port Washington, N.Y., 1969), and David Calleo, *The German Problem Reconsidered: Germany and the World Order, 1870 to the Present* (Cambridge, UK, 1978).

The best book on the changes in the German Right and the growing influence of radical nationalism is Geoff Eley's *Reshaping the German Right: Radical Nationalism and Political Change after Bismarck* (New Haven, Conn., 1980). Eley's introduction is an admirable summary of some important historiographical issues, and Eley discusses the developments and changes in important associations on the right, such as the Navy League and the Pan-German League, with acumen. It is his judgment on radical nationalism, pp. 352–53, that is cited. Eley represents a different general view from that expressed by Wehler, as may be seen in the introduction; consult also David Blackbourn and Goeff Eley, *The Peculiarities of German History: Bourgeois Society and Politics in the Nineteenth Century* (Oxford, UK, 1984). The classic work on the German army, including an excellent treatment of this period, is Gordon A. Craig, *The Politics of the Prussian Army 1640–1945* (New York, 1964). Another important book for the understanding of German politics during this era is J. C. G. Rohl, *Germany Without Bismarck* (Berkeley, Calif., 1967). Some other works dealing with the constitutional crises include J. Alden Nichols, *Germany After Bismarck. The Caprivi Era 1890–1894* (Cambridge, Mass., 1958). Ekkehard-Teja P. W. Wilke, *Political Decadence in Imperial Germany* (Urbana, Ill., 1976) deals with the bureaucratic-political aspects of the crisis. Feminism during this period is covered by Richard J. Evans, *The Feminist Movement in Germany 1894–1933* (London, 1976).

There is a debate on the exact nature of Wilhelm II's role in German history. James N. Retallack, *Germany in the Age of Kaiser Wilhelm II* (Basingstoke, UK, 1966) is primarily a biography of the most important personage during the era. On him, consult as well Michael Balfour, *The Kaiser and His Times* (Boston, 1964), a readable biography; Thomas A. Kohut, *Wilhelm II and the Germans* (New York, 1991), which emphasizes Wilhelm's interaction with his people, from which (p. 5) Bismarck's description of the emperor is taken; and John C. G. Rohl, ed., *Kaiser Wilhelm II: New Interpretations* (Cambridge, UK, 1982), essays on important aspects of Wilhelm's reign.

George Dunlap Crothers, *The German Elections of 1907* (New York, 1968), provides an interesting account of the campaign and argues that these elections resulted in an increase of national sentiment. His position that Bülow's resignation had the result of somehow "involving the chancellorship in a kind of responsibility to the Reichstag," however, is weak and contradictory. Katharine Anne Lerman, *The Chancellor as Courtier: Bernhard von Bülow and the Governance of Germany, 1900–1909* (New York: 1990) is a biography. Konrad H. Jarausch has written a thorough study of Imperial Germany's last prewar chancellor: *The Enigmatic Chancellor: Bethmann-Hollweg and the Hubris of Imperial Germany* (New Haven, Conn., 1973).

The classic account of the SPD during this period is Carl E. Schorske, *German Social Democracy 1905–1917* (Cambridge, Mass., 1955). An interesting debate revolves around the attitude of German revisionist Socialists to German imperialism, a question raised in other countries as well. On this issue, see Roger Fletcher, *Revisionism and Empire: Socialist Imperialism in Germany 1897–1914* (London, 1984). See also Nicholas Stargardt, *The German Idea of Militarism: Radical and Socialist Critics, 1866–1914* (New York, 1994). For a detailed analysis of the role of religion in German politics, see Helmut Walser Smith, *German Nationalism and Religious Conflict: Culture, Ideology, Politics 1870–1914* (Princeton, N.J., 1995). Center Party policy is examined by Ellen Lane Evans, *The German*

Center Party, 1870–1933: A Study in Political Catholicism (Carbondale, Ill., 1981). A local study is David Blackbourn, *Class, Religion and Local Politics in Wilhelmine Germany* (New Haven, Conn., 1980). Richard J. Evans, *The Coming of the Third Reich* (New York, 2004), part of a trilogy, seeks to explain the seeds of Nazism.

The term "that ramshackle realm" to describe the Hapsburg Empire was used by David Lloyd George. Robin Okey's *The Habsburg Monarchy* (New York, 2001) is a general history from the eighteenth century to its end. An excellent brief history is A .J. P. Taylor's *The Hapsburg Monarchy 1809–1918* (London, 1948), which has a convenient appendix with figures for the different nationalities. Mark Cornwall discusses problems in the early twentieth century in *The Last Years of Austria-Hungary: Essays in Political and Military History, 1908–1918* (Exeter, UK, 1990) and *The Last Years of Austria-Hungary: A Multi-National Experiment in Early Twentieth Century Europe* (Exeter, UK, 2002). Steven Beller's *Francis Joseph* (London and New York, 1996) is an excellent attempt to recount the country's complex modern history in a short work; the book includes a good bibliography, maps, and a chronology. Longer biographies are Joseph Redlich, *Emperor Francis Joseph of Austria: A Biography* (New York, 1929); Jean Paul Bled, *Franz Joseph* (Oxford, UK, 1992); and Alan Palmer, *Twilight of the Hapsburgs: Life and Times of Emperor Joseph* (London, 1994).

A book that should be consulted for the scene it sets for the period discussed here is William A. Jenks, *Austria Under the Iron Cross 1879–1893* (Charlottesville, Va., 1965), which provides a full-scale analysis of an important period just before the one discussed.

The Hapsburg Empire's political and social structure has been well studied in a series of older major works; more recent scholars seem to be interested in the breakup of the empire rather than its functioning. The books include C. A. Macartney's meticulously detailed study of Austria and its possessions from the eighteenth century that is essential for its treatment of the twentieth, *The Habsburg Empire 1790–1918* (London, 1969). Macartney also published a more manageable and readable study on the same period, *The House of Austria: The Later Phase 1790–1918* (Edinburgh, 1978), from which the quotes on Hungary's industrial development and the Reichsrat's ineffectiveness may be found (pp. 233 and 249), as well as some of the statistics cited. Another superior work dealing with the issues in this chapter is Arthur J. May, *The Hapsburg Monarchy 1867–1914* (Cambridge, Mass., 1965). Robert A. Kann's *The Multinational Empire: Nationalism and National Reform in the Hapsburg Monarchy 1814–1918,* 2 vols. (New York, 1970) takes the story to another level of detail, examining in depth each of the different nationalities and their concerns. The nationalities question is examined in Paula S. Fichtner, *The Habsburg Empire: From Dynasticism to Multinationalilsm* (n.p., 1997) and in *The Nationalities Question in the Habsburg Monarchy* (Minneapolis, Minn., 1993), by Solomon Wank. Harold J. Gordon, Jr., and Nancy M. Gordon, eds., *The Austrian Empire: Abortive Federation?* (Lexington, Mass., 1974), provides interpretations on the question of whether the Hapsburg Empire was really an attempt to bring together different nationalities in one supranational unit, a debate that began much earlier. Laurence Cole and Daniel L. Unowsky examine another important question: *The Limits of Loyalty: Imperial Symbolism, Popular Allegiances, and State Patriotism in the Late Habsburg Monarchy* (New York, 2007). Oscar Jaszi, *The Dissolution of the Hapsburg Monarchy* (Chicago, 1929), asked the same question and concluded that the empire's breakup resulted from a long, organic, internal process, not from external causes.

The statement on institutions not counting in Russia is alleged to have been made by Konstantin Pobedonostsev, adviser of Alexander III and Nicholas II. Books on Russia with good chapters on the prerevolutionary scene include Ezra Mendelsohn and Marshall Shatz, eds., *Imperial Russia: State, Society, Opposition* (De Kalb, Ill., 1988), a series of essays in honor of Marc Raeff. W. E. Mosse, *Alexander II and the Modernization of*

Russia (New York, 1962), gives an overview of Alexander's policies and their effects. *Russia and the Russians* (Cambridge, Mass., 2001) is a general history.

Revolutionary movements against the Russian government during the late nineteenth and early twentieth centuries are well covered. Adam B. Ulam's *In the Name of the People: Prophets and Conspirators in Prerevolutionary Russia* (New York, 1977) is a detailed history of conspiracies in prerevolutionary Russia and the same author's *Russia's Failed Revolutions: From the Decembrists to the Dissidents* (New York, 1981) includes good chapters on the 1905 revolution and the years up to 1914. Avraham Yarmolinsky discusses radical movements in *Road to Revolution: A Century of Russian Radicalism* (New York, 1962). An account of Alexander III's reactionary policies and the bureaucracy's role in their implementation is Heide W. Whelan, *Alexander III and the State Council* (New Brunswick, N.J., 1982). The Jewish question is discussed in *Beyond the Pale*, by Benjamin Nathans (Berkeley, Calif., 2004).

Two classic works that consider all aspects of the period under discussion are Bernard Pares, *A History of Russia* (New York, 1958), and Richard E. Pipes, *Russia Under the Old Regime* (New York, 1974).

A brief introduction to Russia is Michael Karpovich's *Imperial Russia, 1801–1917* (New York, 1932); readers should be aware that Karpovich leans toward the thesis that the Bolshevik Revolution was probably unnecessary because of the empire's rapid modernization. A detailed and balanced history of Russia by a noted historian is Hugh Seton-Watson, *The Russian Empire 1801–1917* (Oxford, UK, 1967); Seton-Watson also wrote a shorter work concentrating on the later years of the empire, again at a high level, *The Decline of Imperial Russia, 1855–1914* (New York, 1952), from which the judgment of Nicholas II is taken (p. 378). Excellent books of moderate length include Sergei Pushkarev, *The Emergence of Modern Russia 1801–1917* (New York, 1963), which gives the view of a Russian expert and has an extremely useful bibliography; the quotation of Nicholas II on Rasputin is on p. 262. Edward C. Thaden, *Russia Since 1801: The Making of a New Society* (New York, 1971) emphasizes the development of Russian society. J. N. Westwood, *Endurance and Endeavour: Russian History, 1812–1971* (Oxford, UK, 1973) is particularly good on the period discussed. The same author also published a social history, *Structures of Society: Imperial Russia's "People of Various Rank"* (DeKalb, Ill., 1994).

Hans Rogger, *Russia in the Age of Modernisation and Revolution 1881–1917* (New York, 1983), takes a thematic approach and is excellent in his discussion of institutions and different social groups. Other books with a similar emphasis include another excellent contribution by Bernard Pares, *Russia Between Reform and Revolution* (New York, 1962), and Jacob Walkin, *The Rise of Democracy in Pre-Revolutionary Russia* (New York, 1962). Richard E. Pipes, ed., *The Russian Intelligentsia* (New York, 1961), is a series of essays on the intelligentsia in general, with some specific contributions for the period discussed in this chapter. Roberta Thomson Manning discusses *The Crisis of the Old Order* (Princeton, N.J., 1982), and Elise Kimerling Wirtschafter examines *Social Identity in Imperial Russia* (DeKalb, Ill., 1997) while Peter Gatrell looks at industrial development before World War I, particularly the armaments industry, and tsarist policies: *Government, Industry, and Rearmament in Russia, 1900–1914* (New York, 1994).

The 1905 revolution is covered in a thorough and scholarly manner by Abraham Ascher, *The Revolution of 1905,* 2 vols. (Stanford, Calif., 1988–92). Laura Engelstein's *Moscow, 1905* (Stanford, Calif., 1982) is a specialized work on the Moscow uprising with an emphasis on the social and political background and worker organization. The best general analysis of rural conditions before 1917 is Geroid T. Robinson, *Rural Russia Under the Old Regime: A History of the Landlord-Peasant World and a Prologue to the Peasant Revolution of 1917* (Berkeley, Calif., 1967). Andrew M. Verner looks at the role of the tsar in the revolution and its effects, *The Crisis of the Russian Autocracy* (Princeton, N.J., 1990).

Books that consider the policies of specific individuals are also valuable in getting at the history of a period. Mary Schaeffer Conroy, *Peter Arkad'evich Stolypin* (Boulder, Colo., 1979) is an impartial analysis of Stolypin's policies; George Yaney, *The Urge to Mobilize: Agrarian Reform in Russia, 1861–1930* (Urbana, Ill., 1982), is an extensive discussion of Stolypin's agrarian reforms, their implementation, and their effects. Books that discuss the wider significance of Stolypin's reforms include Abraham Ascher, *P. A. Stolypin: The Search for Stability in Late Imperial Russia* (Stanford, Calif., 2001); Stephen F. Williams, *Liberal Reform in an Illiberal Regime* (Stanford, Calif., 2006) which discusses the creation of private property in Russia during this period; and Judith Pallot, *Land Reform in Russia, 1906–1917* (Oxford, UK, 1999), which examines how the peasants reacted. The constitutional/parliamentary aspect is studied by Leonid Ivan Strakhovsky and Florence Strakhovsky, *The Era of Stolypin* (Portland, Maine, 2009) and by Alexandra Shecket Korros, *A Reluctant Parliament: Stolypin, Nationalism, and the Politics of the Russian Imperial Council, 1906–1911* (Lanham, Md., 2002). Richard Pipes's, *Struve: Liberal on the Left, 1870–1905* (Cambridge, Mass., 1970) and *Struve: Liberal on the Right, 1905–1944* (Cambridge, Mass., 1980) are sympathetic biographies of the Kadet leader. Edward H. Judge tells the story of a famous interior minister, assassinated in 1904, who sought to maintain the autocracy but who wanted it to adapt to changing conditions: *Plehve: Repression and Reform in Imperial Russia 1902–1904* (Syracuse, N.Y., 1983). Howard D. Mehlinger and John M. Thompson published *Count Witte and the Tsarist Government in the 1905 Revolution* (Bloomington, Ind., 1972), an uncommonly complete work with a valuable appendix of different drafts of the fundamental laws issued at the time. Sidney Harcave's *Count Sergei Witte and the Twilight of Imperial Russia* (Armonk, N.Y., 2004), is a good biography. Biographies of Nicholas II are easily obtainable; Dominic Lieven, *Nicholas II: Twilight of the Empire* (New York, 1993), is a manageable one. Raymond K. Massie, *Nicholas and Alexander* (New York, 1967), is the readable story of Russia's royal couple.

CHAPTER 4

✍

Foreign Policies

CHAPTER OUTLINE
Britain: Managing Decline • World Policy (*Weltpolitik*) • France's Lost Provinces • Showdown in the Balkans • The Peace Emperor and the Balkan Cauldron • Italy Searches for Security

BIOGRAPHICAL SKETCHES
Francis Joseph of Hapsburg, Unlucky • Théophile Delcassé, Warrior Diplomat

The foreign policies of the European powers involved complex issues. Germany's economic advance spurred it to become a world power, like Britain. The Germans believed that a large colonial empire was necessary to achieve that aim, but most of the colonial areas already belonged to the British and the French. In Europe, Russia wanted to increase its influence in the Balkans and the Turkish Empire, but the dominant power in the Balkans was Austria-Hungary, Germany's major ally, and Germany was increasing its own influence in Turkey. A clash appeared likely even to contemporary observers.

BRITAIN: MANAGING DECLINE

At the beginning of the twentieth century, Britain ruled the largest empire ever seen. With an imperial population of 400 million, the country governed ten times as many people as its closest competitor France. Britain, however, had fallen behind Germany in the areas of industrial production that translated into economic and military strength. Britain was forced to alter its foreign policy in order to manage its relative decline and to confront Germany.

The German Challenge
The British Empire reached is peak in 1901 when South Africa came solidly under its control as a result of the Boer War. The poor British performance in that conflict,

European Empires, 1914 (Population in 000's)

	AFRICA	ASIA	AUSTRALIA AND PACIFIC	AMERICA AND N. ATLANTIC	TOTALS
Belgium	15,000.0	–	–	–	15,000.0
Denmark	–	–	–	125.8	125.8
France	26,681.2	14,773.0	81.1	450.9	40,986.2
Germany	11,428.4	168.9	636.5	–	12,041.6
Great Britain	37,990.2	323,865.9	6,551.5	10,006.8	378,504.4
Italy	1,373.2	–	–	–	1,373.2
Netherlands	–	38,000.0	–	140.6	38,140.5
Portugal	8,243.6	895.8	–	–	9,139.4
Spain	235.8	–	–	–	235.8
				Grand Total	495,547.0

*Adapted from *Statesman's Year-Book*, 1914.

Source: From C. E. Black and E. C. Helmreich, *Twentieth Century Europe*, 2nd ed. (New York: Knopf, 1961), p. 24.

however, revealed military weaknesses and produced a debate over the empire's future. Technical changes could not resolve the military problems because British hegemony had been based upon industrial leadership and in recent decades, other countries, especially Germany, had outpaced it.

The seriousness of the German industrial challenge may be summed up in one astounding statistic: modern steel production. Before German unification, Britain produced twice as much steel as all the German states; forty years later, Britain manufactured only half as much. Germany's economic development and military efficiency held out the prospect that it could fight two great powers simultaneously and still have a reasonable likelihood of victory. According to historian Paul M. Kennedy, "Germany was not only growing out of its European 'skin' but was also acquiring the early attributes of a world power—booming overseas trade, political influence abroad, colonial acquisitions and an expanding fleet. All this necessarily implied a *relative diminution* in Britain's own commercial/colonial/maritime position unless it in turn was able to export more, colonise more, and build more ships, so as to preserve the original relationship." Instead, Germany left Britain increasingly in the dust.

In the late 1890s, Germany embarked on a big navy program, an essential element of its drive to become a world power. Geography dictated that this buildup must take place in the North Sea, which automatically threatened Britain. Because it was an island, Britain could maintain a navy bigger than any of its rivals could afford in order to prevent an invasion, but only a small colonial army, while the continental powers had to split their economic resources between a large army and a navy. Before 1914, Germany's economic develop-

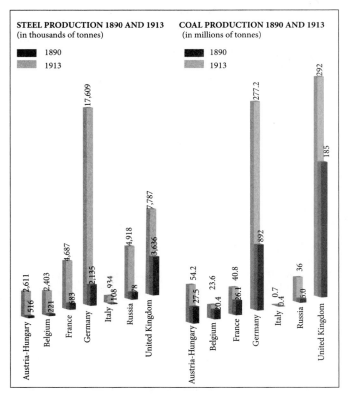

This graph shows the increases in production of steel and coal of the major European powers between 1890 and the eve of World War I. Note the German increases as compared with Britain.

ment held out the frightening prospect it could build a fleet that threatened the Royal Navy while retaining the capability of landing a superior army on the British Isles.

Technological advances worsened the situation. Navies took decades to build, and Britain possessed a lead in the number of ships that would be difficult to overtake. However, in 1906, the British launched the *Dreadnought*, a technological revolution in naval warfare. Pre-*Dreadnought* warships were now obsolete because big-gun dreadnought-class ships could easily sink them. The British faced the prospect of an evaporating lead as the Germans and others built dreadnought-class ships, stimulating an invasion psychosis in Britain that showed up in a war scare in 1909 and an insistence on the immediate construction of a large number of dreadnoughts; as a popular slogan of the year demanded: "We want eight, and we won't wait!" Dreadnoughts were extremely expensive to build, even for the Germans, but the British psychosis led to an overestimation of the dreadnoughts the Germans were building, and they went full steam ahead. The British estimated

Strategic materials produced by major powers. Note how Germany caught up with its rivals by 1900 and surpassed them by 1910.

		UNITED KINGDOM	FRANCE	GERMANY
Steel				
(thousands of metric tons)	1865	225	41	97
	1900	5,130	1,565	6,645
	1910	6,374	3,506	13,698
Pig Iron				
(thousands of metric tons)	1865	4,892	989	882
	1900	9,003	2,714	7,549
	1910	10,380	4,032	14,793
Coal				
(thousands of metric tons)	1860	80.0	8.1	12.3
	1900	225.2	32.7	109.3
	1910	292.0	40.9	277.3

*Adapted from S. B. Clough and C. W. Cole, *Economic History of Europe* (New York, 1941), pp. 538, 545.
SOURCE: C. E. Black and E. C. Helmreich, *Twentieth Century Europe*, 2nd ed. (New York: Knopf, 1961), p. 5.

The appearance of *Dreadnought* class battleships in 1906 revolutionized the arms race before World War I by making older battleships obsolete and giving Germany the possibility of catching up and surpassing Britain on the seas. This development, in turn, revolutionized diplomacy before 1914 by encouraging Britain to abandon its "splendid isolation" and join European allies. Here is a picture of the *Dreadnought* at sea in 1909.

that the Germans would have twenty-one by 1912, but the actual numbers were fifteen for the British and nine for the Germans. This furious naval arms race brought war closer.

Diplomatic Revolution

The arms race had revolutionary effects. The traditional British policy of "splendid isolation"—refusing to enter into permanent alliances because their island home was invulnerable to invasion—was now obsolete. Faced with an increasingly powerful Germany and their own relative decline, the British were forced to make agreements with continental powers, which were also faced with the possibility of German hegemony, a normal feature of their diplomacy.

The new British policy gave a new dynamism to foreign affairs. In 1902 the British reached an agreement with Japan in which the Japanese helped look after their Asian interests. This pact allowed them to transfer much of the Asian fleet to European waters to confront the growing German naval challenge. This arrangement strengthened the war party in Japan that advocated a war with its Asian rival Russia, a not-unwelcome outcome for the British, who considered the Russian expansionist dreams toward Britain's Mediterranean lifeline a dangerous threat. When the Russians lost the Russo-Japanese war (1904–05), Germany became the focus of British foreign policy. The British strengthened their ties with the French, who were at risk from a possible German attack. Britain agreed to French freedom of action in Morocco in return for a free hand in Egypt from the French, a deal that ignored German interests and contributed to German fears of isolation and to the series of international crises that preceded World War I.

The kaiser's blustering language and intimidations encouraged a belief that German expansion was unavoidable and that only the end of German economic prosperity could blunt the threat. In 1907, British naval war planners argued: "The country [Germany] has been launched on a road which has led to this enormous increase of material prosperity, and whether the authors of the policy would like to draw back now or not, they cannot do so. The expansion must go on until it meets a force stronger than itself, or until the policy directing the [German] State ceases to be of a sufficiently virile nature to stimulate growth and encourage prosperity."

Britain's new pro-French policy, framed in the context of preserving the European and world balance of power, was reinforced by military conventions with France. Even more than Britain, the French were vulnerable to the German threat because they shared a common border with the Germans. Germany's explosive economic growth produced great imperialistic ambitions, and geography dictated that to fulfill those ambitions, Germany had to threaten both the British and French homelands. This mortal threat united Britain and France, ancient enemies and declining powers, which understood that the defense of their homelands and colonial possessions was inextricably tied to their success in containing Germany.

WORLD POLICY (*WELTPOLITIK*)

The Germans had abandoned Bismarck's legacy in foreign affairs that he had elaborated following unification. Cognizant of French enmity and desire for

This map illustrates France's isolation by Bismarck.

retribution, Bismarck had attempted to nullify France's ability to wage a war of revenge by depriving it of allies. Bismarck especially feared an alliance between France and Russia, a two-front war that would force the Germans to split their army.

Collapse of Bismarck's System

By juggling the complex issues driving big-power diplomacy, Bismarck fulfilled his goal of isolating France. In 1879 Germany signed the Dual Alliance with Austria-Hungary in which each pledged to aid the other if attacked. In 1881 Bismarck concluded the Three Emperors' League joining Germany, Austria-Hungary, and Russia. In 1882, Germany, Austria-Hungary, and Italy signed the Triple Alliance, an agreement that was a result of Italy's search for allies. Bismarck also hoped for a British alliance. He fell short of this goal, but his efforts produced excellent relations with Britain because he agreed not to threaten Britain's hegemony at sea.

Bismarck's diplomatic system, however, contained deep flaws that quickly developed wide cracks after the kaiser fired him in 1890. Despite the Three Emperors' League, the Austrians had been clashing with the Russians in the Balkans and the Turkish-controlled Near East for centuries. The Russians were anxious to gain access to the Mediterranean Sea, which Turkish control of the Straits (Bosporus and Dardanelles) denied them. After Bismarck left the scene, the Germans favored the Austrians, which led the Russians to refuse to renew the

The Germans reacted to the breakdown of Bismarck's diplomatic system and the fear that they would have to fight against the French and the Russians simultaneously in case of a war by elaborating the famous "Schlieffen Plan." Here is its author, Alfred von Schlieffen, in his military uniform, sporting his medals.

Three Emperors' League in 1887. Likewise, the Austrian-Italian enmity hollowed out the Triple Alliance. After Italian unification, the Austrians still held Italian-speaking areas (the *Irredenta*) and mistreated the Italian minority there. This and other disputes actually brought the two allies close to war at different times.

Bismarck foresaw the likelihood of a Russian-French alliance if the link with Germany and Austria were broken, and in 1887 signed the Reinsurance Treaty with Russia, "reassuring" the Russians that if the Austrians attacked Russia, Germany would not come to Austria's aid. Bismarck did not consider this understanding a conflict with the Dual Alliance because that pact provided for German help to Austria only if another power attacked it, not if Austria attacked another country or provoked a conflict. The Reinsurance Treaty has been interpreted as Bismarck's attempt to moderate Austrian policy in the Balkans by warning it that if Austrian machinations there produced a conflict with Russia, Austria could not automatically count on German aid. However, his successors believed that a contradiction with Germany's commitments under the Dual Alliance did exist and let the treaty lapse in 1890. This decision signaled that Germany valued the Austrian alliance above the Russian connection and left the Russians free to link up with the French.

Over the next several years, the Russians and French negotiated a treaty and a military convention that left the Germans vulnerable to a two-front war.

The Schlieffen Plan

The Germans answered with the Schlieffen Plan. Instead of splitting their army into two equal parts to fight the French and Russians in the East and the West, they would concentrate most of their military might on the Western front to deliver a swift knockout blow against France. Having defeated the French, the German army would be shifted to the East and defeat Russia. This plan depended on an important factor without which it would not work: the different rates at which Germany, France, and Russia mobilized. Germany and France, modern industrial countries, mobilized rapidly, while industrially backward Russia did so slowly. The Germans would hold off the Russians in the East with small forces and make their right wing on the Western front invincible. To ensure its success, the Schlieffen Plan called for an invasion of France through Belgium (and the Netherlands, but this feature was dropped). The Germans would take the French by surprise because both countries had guaranteed Belgian neutrality in case of war; this combination would overwhelm the French, and the German army would deal with the Russians before they had fully mobilized.

A brilliant conception on paper, the scheme had unfortunate consequences. The plan obliged the Germans to attack France first if Russia ever became involved in a conflict, but what if France stayed out of a war involving Russia, Germany, and Austria-Hungary? In case of a Balkan war in which Russia became involved, Austria would need German help. Should the Germans agree to aid their allies, the Schlieffen Plan obliged them to attack France even if that country was not involved. Moreover, going through Belgium risked bringing in the British, who feared a big power occupying the European coast closest to their island homeland—or at least it would serve as a pretext to do so. Germany could not risk going to war against Russia while leaving France neutral and free to intervene once the German army was entangled in the East. The Germans did not have a contingency plan in which they would fight only Russia and not France, increasing the likelihood that a Balkan war would set off a general conflict in Europe.

Moreover, the Schlieffen Plan created a rigid mindset that favored war. Russia had embarked on a program of rapid industrial modernization that threatened to undercut the assumption that Russia would mobilize slowly. The Schlieffen Plan ran the risk of becoming obsolete very soon, contributing to a mindset among German officials that it was better to have a war sooner rather than later.

Several factors convinced many Germans that war was certain. They included the implications of social imperialism, the economic understanding between industrialists and large landowners already discussed, and the enormous growth of German industry. Many Germans assumed that a British decline would lead to Britain's colonial possessions being divided among the rising powers, for which they had to be prepared. Convinced that their impressive strength entitled them to a "place in the sun," already by 1897 the Germans embarked on *Weltpolitik* (World Policy). As Kaiser Wilhelm remarked: "Nothing must henceforth be settled in the world without the intervention of Germany and the German Emperor."

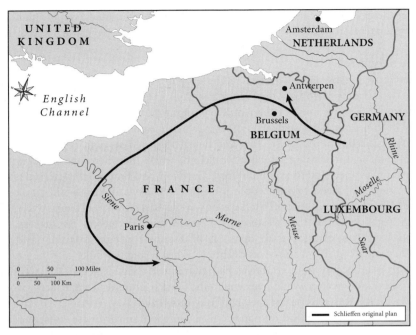

The Schlieffen Plan. This map shows the original plan, which was later modified so that the Germans would not invade the Netherlands or wheel around Paris. In addition, the right wing was weakened to bolster other fronts. The map demonstrates how the Germans planned to violate Belgium's neutrality, which the European powers—including Germany—recognized.

Making good on this promise, the Germans suddenly appeared as a force in China, Africa, and other parts of the world, where they clashed with the Russians and the British. In the Turkish Empire they built the Baghdad railway, a centerpiece of German influence, and sent advisers to train the Turkish army. Wilhelm offered German protection to the Muslims by posing as a defender of the weak against British and Russian imperialism. *Weltpolitik* also dictated construction of a big navy that incarnated the ideas of world policy, social imperialism, profits for industrialists, increased employment, and national pride. Historian Fritz Fischer contended that this mentality seized hold of the cultural and political elite and permeated German society.

Aggressive German posturing during the crises that led up to World War I spurred the other big powers to put into place a series of alliances to contrast with German power. German policy makers, in turn, interpreted these agreements as encirclement and as a desire to deprive Germany of its rightful position as the world's leading power. Germany increasingly felt that it could count only on a crumbling Austria-Hungary. Anxious to achieve world power status before time ran out, German statesmen played by the accepted diplomatic rules less and less, and German policy took on a blundering and upstart quality. The country's constitutional structure, which had few checks on policy makers who pursued reckless policies, worsened the foreign policy situation.

FRANCE'S LOST PROVINCES

Relations were especially bad with France, which continued to resent bitterly Germany's annexation of Alsace and Lorraine in 1871 after France lost the Franco-Prussian War.

The Poisoned Atmosphere

For the next 20 years Bismarck prevented the French from retaliating against Germany by keeping them isolated and deprived of allies. However, he also attempted to distract them by encouraging their successful efforts to win a large colonial empire in Africa and Asia. Bismarck was disinterested in colonies and hoped that a friendly policy would make France forget about going to war and perhaps even culminate in a Franco-German alliance. As he told the French ambassador, referring to his support for French colonial gains: "Renounce the Rhine and I will help you to secure everywhere else the satisfactions you desire."

The answer arrived from a French nationalist leader: "I have lost two children and you offer me twenty domestics." Despite a periodic warming of relations, French and German statesmen considered it just a matter of time before war broke out. In 1875 there was a war scare. Both countries increased military spending in 1886, 1887, and 1888. In 1892 demonstrations broke out when the German queen mother visited France, prompting Germany to implement the steps preliminary to mobilization.

France Emerges from Isolation

France fought Germany's growing power with an increasingly sophisticated diplomatic campaign. In 1894, it emerged from diplomatic isolation by concluding a mutual cooperation agreement with the Russians, the Entente Cordiale (Entente in French means understanding). Russia had had qualms about linking up with a republican regime with radical roots, but the Reinsurance Treaty's lapse left France as the only choice for an ally. At first, this alliance meant little in military terms, but in 1899 both countries transformed it into an active means of maintaining the European balance of power by tightening their diplomatic and military cooperation.

The person responsible for this new assertive French policy became foreign minister in 1898. Théophile Delcassé aimed to revive French influence by strengthening the Russian connection and by reaching agreements with Britain and Italy. He skillfully played on Italian resentment of Austrian policies and on the traditional Franco-Italian friendship. Although the Italians formally remained in the Triple Alliance, in 1902 both countries pledged not to attack each other in a treaty reminiscent of Bismarck's Reinsurance Treaty.

Delcassé's major goal, an agreement with Great Britain, caused him the greatest agony. Franco-British tensions caused by competing colonial interests remained high. In September 1898, a crisis erupted over Fashoda, in the Sudan, bringing the two countries close to war, and Delcassé had to exercise all his talents to avoid a rupture. The crisis, however, ended with an unexpected result: friendship. With the Germans increasing in strength on land and sea and threatening

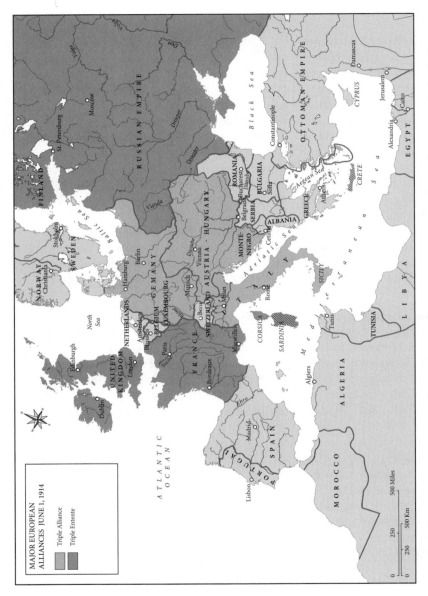

MAJOR EUROPEAN
ALLIANCES JUNE 1, 1914

Triple Alliance

Triple Entente

This map shows France's success in emerging from isolation, the danger to Germany of a two-front war, and why the Germans feared "encirclement."

BIOGRAPHICAL SKETCHES

Théophile Delcassé
Warrior Diplomat

An ardent patriot, Théophile Delcassé believed that the Alsace-Lorraine problem made a war between France and Germany certain. As the French foreign minister from 1898 to 1905, he worked to end the isolation into which Bismarck had thrust France by strengthening the alliances with Russia and Britain and favoring a rapprochement with Italy. His policies irritated the Germans and alarmed the French political establishment, which feared a war. Delcassé reached an agreement with the British and stood up against the Germans in Morocco, but the French cabinet feared that in doing so, he would provoke a war with Germany. In a cabinet meeting on June 6, 1905, the French cabinet forced Delcassé out of office. The affair strengthened the German reputation as bullies.

It seemed that Delcassé was through, but his policy eventually triumphed because French public opinion believed that the government ousted Delcassé because of German pressure. During the next few years, a Franco-British-Russian entente for which Delcassé had laid the basis became a reality. At this point, historical accounts of Delcassé's role usually stop, but his subsequent actions may have had an even greater impact.

A serious gap existed between the strong foreign policy that Delcassé advocated and the country's military prowess. Particularly worrisome was the state of the French navy, plagued by neglect, scandal, and a series of accidents culminating on March 12, 1907, in the explosion of a warship that killed 118 men. A parliamentary commission headed by Delcassé reported that the French built battleships too slowly, that they lacked sufficient war supplies and ammunition, and that the country possessed only one shipyard capable of repairing them. In June 1911, Delcassé took over as navy minister until January 1913.

Delcassé believed that if France were to win a war against Germany, it must hold the Mediterranean with a strong navy. Only with the safe transport of men and supplies from the colonies to the western front could France ensure that it would obtain numerical superiority against the German army. Delcassé constructed more and better ships faster, reorganized the naval command structure, improved training for crews, modernized shipyards, gained the trust of the Socialist-influenced shipyard workers, built an efficient support structure for the ships, improved naval ammunition, and founded an air arm.

In addition, Delcassé negotiated a crucial agreement with Britain by which the British navy protected the coast of northern France while the French concentrated their power in the Mediterranean. This understanding morally committed Britain to enter a conflict on the French side in case of war with Germany. In February 1913, the government appointed Delcassé ambassador to Russia. Delcassé convinced the Russians to increase their preparedness for a war against Germany, which in 1914 resulted in a more formidable enemy for the Germans than they had expected. During World War I, he served as minister of war. Following that conflict, he opposed the Versailles treaty because he believed that it guaranteed France neither reparations nor security. He retired from public life in 1919.

continued

continued

Born on March 1, 1852, into a modest family, Delcassé early adopted the ideas of Léon Gambetta, the father of the Third Republic, and gained notoriety as a journalist. Because his wife was sickly and his son died following his release from a German prisoner-of-war camp in World War I, sadness marked his personal life. Théophile Delcassé died on February 22, 1923, received a state funeral, and lies buried at Paris's Montmartre cemetery.

their homelands, the British and the French could not afford a war over colonies. They pulled back from the brink of war and, over the next several years, worked out their outstanding colonial problems, particularly in Africa. France recognized Britain's paramount interest in Egypt, and England did the same for France in Morocco. In 1904 an Anglo-French accord, the Entente Cordiale, foreshadowed the Triple Entente, solidified in 1907 when France's allies England and Russia concluded an agreement.

These French successes irritated Germany. In the diplomacy of imperialism, countries planning to take over an area negotiated with all powers that had interests in a region and compensated them. When he moved on Morocco, Delcassé neglected to negotiate with Germany—blunder or provocation? Germany reacted strongly, typically going beyond a mere defense of its interests. In this case, the Germans were also motivated by a wish to test the strength of the new friendship between France and Britain and to discover how it would hold up in a crisis.

Violating diplomatic protocol, the kaiser visited Tangier in March 1905 and informed the sultan that Germany supported Moroccan independence, touching off a crisis in which the Germans threatened war. At a cabinet meeting on June 6, 1905, Delcassé made his case for resisting German demands, but his colleagues judged France unprepared for a conflict while its Russian ally had recently been defeated in a war with Japan. The cabinet then forced Delcassé to resign, a great victory for the Germans. This triumph turned into a debacle when the British strongly supported the French at an international congress held in 1906 at Algeciras and the other European countries isolated Germany.

Escalating Nationalism

The 1905 Moroccan emergency preceded a series of grave crises that shook Europe before 1914. Because these crises usually ended in diplomatic duels between France and Germany, they increased the stridency of French nationalism, which became more influential and steeled for war. The dramatic increase of French chauvinism favored the rise of hard-liners, such as Raymond Poincaré—the premier and later president—who rebuffed German offers of a rapprochement. The hardening of French public opinion strengthened Germany's fear of "encirclement," and in 1913 Germany undertook the largest increase ever in its army. Convinced of the inevitability of armed conflict, French diplomats had woven a tight web around their traditional enemy.

SHOWDOWN IN THE BALKANS

In the meantime, tensions increased between Russia and Austria-Hungary in the Balkan Peninsula and brought the area to the boiling point. The decline of the Ottoman Empire encouraged the Russians to push harder for the right of passage of their warships through the Straits into the Mediterranean and to increase their influence by strongly supporting the Slavic inhabitants of the area. These policies clashed with those of Austria-Hungary, long dominant in the peninsula, but slipping and fearful that strong Russian backing would encourage the Slavs in their empire to secede and threaten its very existence. The situation was radicalized because the diplomatic agreements with France and Britain had brought the Russians powerful new allies, while German support for the Austrians increased because they were the only reliable German allies.

Increasing Conflict

Already by 1903 the situation in the Balkans was on its way to becoming critical. Nationalists staged a palace coup in Serbia, a Russian protégé and the strongest independent Balkan State. This development increased tensions in Bosnia-Herzegovina, which had been under Austrian military occupation since 1878 but was not legally Austro-Hungarian. Serb nationalists hoped to end the Austrian occupation and eventually to annex the two provinces. The Serbs demanded autonomy for Bosnia-Herzegovina, giving rise to a new diplomatic crisis.

The Russians hoped to use the affair for their own purposes. In September 1908, Russian Foreign Minister Alexander P. Izvolsky and his Austrian counterpart Lexa von Aehrenthal struck a secret deal: the Russians agreed to formal Austrian annexation of Bosnia-Herzegovina provided that an international conference approved and that the Austrians supported Russian demands on Turkey. Because of internal Turkish developments, however, Austria suddenly annexed Bosnia-Herzegovina without waiting for a conference. When other powers objected to this unilateral change, a major crisis ensued, and Austria moved toward mobilization. The Serbs looked for aid from their Russian protector, but Russia, still weak from defeat in the Japanese war and the 1905 revolution and intimidated by Germany, backed down.

The Bosnian crisis stimulated Slavic nationalism and increased Russian sympathy for the Balkan Slavs. Moreover, Serb nationalists founded the *Narodna Obrana,* or National Defense, society to promote Slavic interests in Bosnia-Herzegovina. Pan-Slavic congresses in 1908 (Prague) and in 1910 (Sofia, Bulgaria) emphasized Slavic kinship and called for national liberation from the Austrians and Turks. Encouraged by this increased activity, the new Russian foreign minister, Sergei D. Sazonov, capitalized on the Libyan War that Turkey fought with Italy in 1911–12 by forging Serbia, Montenegro, Bulgaria, and Greece into an anti-Turkish coalition. In September 1912, those countries attacked Turkey and drove it out of the Balkans in the First Balkan War. The Second Balkan War saw the coalition break up as the former allies fought each other. The result of these wars was a huge gain in territory for Serbia followed by an Austrian ultimatum threatening war if Serbia did not withdraw from territory giving it access to the sea (the area of Albania, formally recognized as independent in 1913). Serbia turned to a still-weak Russia, which backed down in order to avoid a war. The Austrians aimed to prevent Serbia's transformation into a powerful pole of attraction for dissatisfied Slavs in the Dual Monarchy, but the affair increased tensions among the great powers.

The 1912–13 events left Russia embittered and Europe at the brink of war. Russia had suffered two humiliations and could not continue to be humbled without losing its great power status. Serbia still hoped to bring all the Slavs who lived in Austria-Hungary together in one state with Russian support, a goal that threatened Austria-Hungary's existence because it would embolden the other nationalities to secede. Convinced that Serbia must be eliminated as an independent state, the Austrians understood that they could not accomplish this aim without German help because Russia was unlikely to accept another diplomatic humiliation and would go to war. The Germans feared both the collapse of their Austrian ally and the long-term Russian economic and military potential, so a showdown between Russia and Austria-Hungary over the Balkans seemed destined to touch off a war that would bring in their allies.

Emperor Francis Joseph professed to oppose war. He said in November 1912: "I don't want war. I have always been unlucky in wars," but the nationalities question had made a general conflict likely.

ITALY SEARCHES FOR SECURITY

Italy's economic deficiencies made it the weakest of the great powers and severely conditioned its foreign policy. During the early twentieth century, Italy's long-term prime minister, Giovanni Giolitti, followed a prudent foreign policy, and Italian diplomats aimed at achieving security for the country.

The Troubled Triple Alliance

Giolitti and his foreign minister Antonino Di San Giuliano feared that Austria's Balkan policy would drag Italy into war. Both of them made clear to their partners on several occasions that the Triple Alliance was a defensive pact and that on no account would their country enter a conflict provoked by an Austrian desire to suppress Serbia. Italy also had friendly relations with Britain—publicly declaring with the agreement of its allies when it signed the Triple Alliance that it was not directed against Britain—and pursuing friendly relations with France during the early years of the twentieth century.

While relations with France warmed, those with Austria-Hungary cooled primarily because of the poor treatment of the Italian minority in Austria and conflicting interests in the Balkans. By 1908 tensions were so high that the chief of staff of the Austrian Army advocated an attack on Italy when a massive earthquake in Sicily made the country particularly vulnerable. Italian diplomats told their colleagues that only fear of war with each other kept Austria and Italy in the same alliance.

Italy fought Turkey for Libya, the last part of North Africa not colonized by a Western power, in 1911, thus threatening the European diplomatic equilibrium. It was the first war in which air power was used. The Italians were criticized for their brutal treatment of Libyan rebels; such treatment was typical, in varying degrees, of Western imperialism. This picture shows the execution of rebels during or shortly after the conflict.

BIOGRAPHICAL SKETCHES

Francis Joseph Of Hapsburg
Unlucky

Francis Joseph's characterization of himself as unlucky in war applied to his entire life. In fact, the only happy time he had was probably during his childhood, which ended early and abruptly.

Francis Joseph was born on August 18, 1830, the oldest son of the archduke and heir to the throne of Francis Charles and the Archduchess Sophia. His uncle, Emperor Ferdinand I, was mentally unfit to govern, leaving a regency council to rule the Austrian Empire. In 1848 revolutions shook Western Europe, including the Austrian possessions. Vienna came under the control of revolutionaries who were put down only by the ruthlessness of Prince Felix Schwarzenberg. Schwarzenberg forced the incompetent Ferdinand's resignation, and when Francis Charles refused to become emperor, Francis Joseph acceded to the throne on December 2, 1848, at age 18.

Francis Joseph had no governing experience and relied on Schwarzenberg's advice. After the prince's death in 1852, the young emperor was on his own as Austrian power declined precipitously. The Austrians refused to join the Russians against the British and French in the Crimean War (1853–56). Because of former close relations, the Russians considered this failure a betrayal and never forgave

continued

continued

it. Between 1859 and 1866, Austria lost its Italian possessions, and an unfriendly Italy emerged on its borders. In 1866 Prussia drove the Austrians out of Germany, uniting that country under its suzerainty. In 1867, in order to keep Hungary in the empire, Francis Joseph agreed to an arrangement that made Hungary practically independent (the Dual Monarchy).

Bismarck favored friendly relations with Austria-Hungary, and the two countries signed a treaty in 1879. However, because of strategic considerations, he was primarily concerned with placating the Russians rather than the Austrians. After Wilhelm II fired Bismarck in 1890, Austro-German relations became closer because the kaiser gave less weight to the Russian connection and because the two emperors had close personal ties. Francis Joseph's lack of independence from the German emperor contributed to the eventual breakup of the Hapsburg Empire.

Francis Joseph's bad luck in foreign policy extended to his personal and political life. In 1854 he insisted on marrying a sixteen-year-old Bavarian princess Elizabeth (Sissy), against his mother's opposition. His wife and his mother quarreled, and Sissy became more eccentric over the years. The couple had one son, Rudolf, the heir to the throne, born in 1858. Rudolf, more liberal than his father, constantly quarreled with Francis Joseph about politics. In 1889 the unhappy Rudolf committed suicide with his mistress at Mayerling outside Vienna. In yet another tragic occurrence, an Anarchist assassinated Sissy in 1898.

These were not the sum of his misfortunes. Francis Joseph had been particularly close to his younger brother Maximilian, who became involved in an ill-fated French attempt to take over Mexico and claimed its throne. The Mexicans revolted and, despite Francis Joseph's attempts to save him, executed Maximilian on June 19, 1867. In 1896 his other brother, Charles Ludwig, died on a pilgrimage to the Holy Land after he drank disease-laden water. With the deaths of his brothers and his son, the succession passed to Charles Ludwig's son Francis Ferdinand. The new heir did not get along with the old emperor, not the least because he insisted on marrying Sophie Chotek. Sophie did not belong to the restricted noble circle in which royalty married, and their children were ineligible to inherit the throne. On June 28, 1914, assassins killed Francis Ferdinand and his wife, touching off World War I despite the emperor's reluctance. Luckily he died on November 21, 1916, before his empire and dynasty ended. Transformed over the decades after his death into an Austrian national hero, Francis Joseph proved luckier in death than in life.

The Libyan War

The only exception to Giolitti's unadventurous foreign policy was Italy's declaration of war on Turkey in 1911. Italy had long sought colonies and, during the early years of the century, had staked its claim on Libya, the last available area in North Africa. When it seemed that other powers might move into the area if Italy did not act soon, a vociferous Italian Nationalist campaign mobilized public opinion against Giolitti and pressured the prime minister into taking action. For Giolitti, however, the main motivation for war was to make Italy more secure by preventing a takeover of Libya by a great power, possibly Germany, that would install itself on the Mediterranean shore opposite Italy.

The Balkan Peninsula Before the Wars of 1912–1913. The map shows the borders of the small states and the amount of land held by Turkey. With the expulsion of Turkey, the small states fought among themselves for the territory formerly held by the Ottoman Empire, involved the Great Powers, and set the stage for World War I.

In the course of defeating Turkey, Italy gravely weakened it. The Europeans had avoided armed conflicts with Turkey because of fears that it might fall apart and touch off wars for parts of its vast empire. The Libyan War led directly to the Balkan wars of 1912 and 1913 when the Russians brought together the feuding

Balkan states and convinced them to attack Turkey. The wars increased tensions among the big powers and set the stage for World War I.

Bibliographical Essay

Many of the books cited in Chapter 3 have chapters on foreign policy. Good, basic texts on diplomatic history, with coverage of this period include René Albrecht-Carrié, *A Diplomatic History of Europe Since the Congress of Vienna* (New York, 1958), a standard work, and Norman Rich, *Great Power Diplomacy 1814–1914* (New York, 1992). A. J. P. Taylor's *The Struggle for Mastery in Europe 1848–1918* (Oxford, UK, 1954) is a classic. For an understanding of the diplomatic history leading up to the period under discussion, see William L. Langer, *European Alliances and Alignments 1871–1890* (New York, 1950). Patricia A. Weitsman's *Dangerous Alliances: Proponents of Peace, Weapons of War* (Stanford, Calif., 2004) gives a more up-to-date examination of the major alliances during this period.

On the central question of this era, the best work is Paul M. Kennedy, *The Rise of the Anglo-German Antagonism 1860–1914* (London, 1980). This book stands out for its comprehensiveness, insight, and balanced judgments. Kennedy's 1907 citation from the British Admiralty's war plans may be found on p. 310; the quotation on the implications of Germany's economic expansion is on p. 465. A little collection of essays, Donald Read, *Edwardian England* (New Brunswick, N.J., 1982), is excellent on all aspects of British life of the period, but there are two outstanding essays on the armament and foreign policy issues discussed in this chapter: Michael Howard, "The Edwardian Arms Race" (pp. 145–161), and, of note for the sophisticated interpretations of the wider foreign policy of the period, J. A. S. Grenville, "Foreign Policy and the Coming of War" (pp. 162–180).

For more specialized views of Britain's relative economic decline discussed in this chapter, consult Bernard Elbaum and William Lazonick, eds., *The Decline of the British Economy* (Oxford, UK, 1986); the work contains an informative essay on the steel industry before World War I. The collection edited by Derek H. Aldcroft and Harry W. Richardson, *The British Economy 1870–1939* (New York, 1969), also includes illuminating studies, as does Derek H. Aldcroft, ed., *The Development of British Industry and Foreign Competition 1875–1914* (Toronto, 1968). Trade rivalry, a frequently mentioned issue of uncertain impact on the relations between Britain and Germany, is discussed by Ross J. S. Hoffman, *Great Britain and the German Trade Rivalry 1875–1914* (New York, 1964). Look also at the book of essays and interviews by Richard English and Michael Kenny, *Rethinking British Decline* (New York, 2000). Newer books tend to concentrate on the period after World War I to the present, but they usually have material related to the early twentieth century.

On Germany, see Andrew R. Carlson, *German Foreign Policy, 1890–1914, and Colonial Policy to 1914: A Handbook and Annotated Bibliography* (Metuchen, N.J., 1970). The book contains much valuable technical information about foreign and colonial policy and the domestic influences on it. The kaiser's remark on *Weltpolitik* is on p. 16. Ludwig Dehio's classic *Germany and World Politics in the Twentieth Century* (New York, 1959) argues that Germany's wars were in the European tradition of a struggle for continental hegemony and that Germany was preparing to succeed Britain in the early twentieth century. Dehio's book criticizes Germany's foreign policy even while putting it in a wider context, but Gordon Craig, *From Bismarck to Adenauer: Aspects of German Statecraft* (Baltimore, 1958), discusses the personalities involved during this period (usually harshly) and argues that German diplomats proved unequal to the task required by Germany's situation. Peter Alter wrote a history of the German problem in Europe from 1800 to 1990: *The German Question and Europe: A History* (London, 2000). The way the Germans and French saw each other is the subject of Michael E. Nolan, *The Inverted Mirror: Mythologizing the Enemy in France and Germany, 1898–1914* (New York, 2005). Mark Hewitson challenges accepted views in *National Identity and Political Thought in Germany: Wilhelmine Depictions of the French Third Republic, 1890–1914* (New York, 2000).

For Austria, there is Samuel R. Williamson, *Austria-Hungary and the Origins of the First World War* (New York, 1991).

Good studies of different lengths exist on French foreign policy. Frederick L. Schuman's *War and Diplomacy in the French Republic* (New York, 1970) is an excellent and detailed study of how foreign policy was controlled in France, along with accounts of the various crises, the politics influencing them, and how they were handled. The quotations from Bismarck and Paul Déroulède, the nationalist, on Alsace and Lorraine, are cited on p. 21 of the 1923 Creighton lecture by G. P. Gooch, *Franco-German Relations 1871–1914* (New York, 1967), an excellent, brief, and clear account. Charles W. Porter published a specialized, readable, account of Delcassé's aims and action, *The Career of Théophile Delcassé* (Westport, Conn., 1975), at its best when describing how Delcassé built the French relationship with Britain during a difficult period. One of Delcassé's most important collaborators was the French ambassador to England, Paul Cambon (not to be confused with his brother Jules, ambassador to the United States), whose career can be followed in Keith Eubank's *Paul Cambon: Master Diplomatist* (Norman, Okla., 1960). On the Entente Cordiale, see Antoine Capet, *Britain, France, and the Entente Cordiale Since 1904* (New York, 2006), which contains several essays on the period discussed in this chapter, and an examination of the agreement and the British King: *Edward VII and the Entente Cordiale* (London, 2004), by Ian Dunlop. The growth of chauvinism in France during this period is described very well by Eugen Weber, *The Nationalist Revival in France, 1905–1914* (Berkeley, Calif., 1968).

The standard diplomatic history of French and Russian diplomacy at the end of the nineteenth century is Willliam L. Langer, *The Franco-Russian Alliance 1890–1894* (New York, 1967), but see the book by Fiona K. Tomaszewski, *A Great Russia: Russia and the Triple Entente* (Westport, Conn., 2002). Michael Hughes's *Diplomacy Before the Russian Revolution* (New York, 2000) examines relations between Britain and Russia. Alan Sharp and Glyn Stone produced a book on British-French rivalry, *Anglo-French Relations in the Twentieth Century* (New York, 2002). A history examining a similar topic over a hundred years is Philippe Chassaigne and M. L. Dockrill, *Anglo-French Relations, 1898–1998* (New York, 2002). George F. Kennen's *The Fateful Alliance; France, Russia, and the Coming of the First World War* (New York, 1984) is a work by a famous American diplomat. *United Government and Foreign Policy in Russia, 1910–1914* (Cambridge, Mass., 1992) is an overview.

Barbara Jelavich's *A Century of Russian Foreign Policy 1814–1914* (Philadelphia, 1964) is a good survey of the topic, while the same author's *Russia's Balkan Entanglements, 1806–1914* (New York, 1991) puts the question into historical context. For an understanding of the Turkish situation in relation to big-power imperialism, see Edward Mead Earle, *Turkey, the Great Powers, and the Baghdad Railway* (New York, 1966). Ronald Park Bobroff's *Roads to Glory* (London, 2006) examines Russia and the Straits question.

Two works that address Austrian foreign policy in a scholarly and well-documented manner are F. R. Bridge, *From Sadowa to Sarajevo: The Foreign Policy of Austria-Hungary, 1866–1914* (London, 1972), and the brief treatment by Barbara Jelavich, *The Hapsburg Empire in European Affairs, 1814–1918* (Chicago, 1969).

Italian foreign policy during this period has not received much specialized treatment in English, and the interpretations frequently tend to be colored by later developments or by unreasonable assumptions. Spencer M. Di Scala's *Vittorio Orlando:*

Italy (Makers of the Modern World series) (London, 2010) offers a different view of prewar Italian diplomacy. Among the more objective treatments of the subject, see William C. Askew's chapter in Lillian Parker Wallace and William C. Askew, eds., *Power, Public Opinion, and Diplomacy: Essays in Honor of Eber Malcolm Carroll by His Former Students* (New York, 1968), "The Austro-Italian Antagonism, 1896–1914"—an outstanding overview of the subject. Askew also wrote the diplomatic history of the Libyan War's origins and impact, *Europe and Italy's Acquisition of Libya 1911–1912* (Durham, N.C., 1942). R. J. B. Bosworth, *Italy, the Least of the Great Powers* (London, 1979), is marred by too close an identification of this period with later ones. R. A. Webster's *Industrial Imperialism in Italy, 1908–1915* (Berkeley, Calif., 1975) is an examination of Italian industrial development and its connection to imperialism.

CHAPTER 5

European Peripheries

CHAPTER OUTLINE

Scandinavia: An Ideal Unity • Different Roads: The Low Countries •
The Making of a Conservative: Switzerland • The Iberian States •
Southeastern Europe

BIOGRAPHICAL SKETCHES

Niels Henrik David Bohr, "Uncle Nick" • Émile Vandervelde,
Evolutionary Socialist

Although the smaller countries of Europe lacked the military power of the larger states, they had enormous influence on the continent's intellectuals, as the careers of Danish storyteller Hans Christian Andersen, the Swedish writer August Strindberg, and the Norwegian playwright Henrik Ibsen testify. Twentieth-century Scandinavia presented interesting new social democratic models of organizing modern society, while the Low Countries and Switzerland had a disproportionate impact in the economic and colonial areas. The Iberian states offered the lesson of once-great powers that languished in the modern age, only to conserve unsuspected energies that allowed them to flourish by the end of the century. The countries of southeastern Europe presented a different picture—restless, turbulent states whose resentments and ambitions critically affected the course of world history.

The states of the European peripheries thus presented a highly differentiated but important picture of the continent at the beginning of the twentieth century.

SCANDINAVIA: AN IDEAL UNITY

The independent Scandinavian states—Sweden, Norway, and Denmark—had been united in the Union of Kalmar from 1363 to 1434, but even after this union ended, the cultural interchange and the idea of political collaboration remained strong and still characterizes the area.

The small countries of Europe, sometimes neglected, had a major influence on the continent's history in the twentieth century.

Swedish Democracy

Modern democracy in Sweden has it origins in the eighteenth century, when an
era of strong, warlike kings ended with the death of Charles XII in 1718. An Age
of Freedom followed, in which a seesaw political struggle between the kings and
representative institutions occurred, and the Swedes adopted a constitution in
1809, Europe's oldest written document of its kind. The executive branch retained
considerable powers, but the Riksdag (Parliament) voted taxes and exercised joint
power with the king. The king appointed the government (Council of State), but
it was accountable to the Riksdag. The constitution opened up offices to all social
groups, but nobles still enjoyed tax advantages and the division of the Riksdag into
four estates (nobility, clergy, peasant, and burgesses) gave greater representation
to the privileged classes. By 1841, after the growth of an industrial middle class,
a shift in the balance of power to the legislative branch had occurred. In 1865,
the First Chamber, indirectly elected on a weighed vote dependent on income,
and the Second Chamber, elected directly with a property qualification for voters,
replaced the four estates, gave power to the urban middle class, but excluded the
city workers and rural laborers. In 1889 the Social Democratic Party was founded
and joined the Swedish trade unions in championing the demands of the growing
ranks of workers produced by increasing industrialization. This situation led to
more strikes during the early years of the new century and the government's passage of legislation regulating workers' safety, workers' compensation, diminished

social strife, and an extension of the vote following a 1905 electoral victory for leftist groups. A compromise combined male universal suffrage and proportional representation for the Second Chamber and a more complicated proportional system for the First Chamber. Clearly delineated parties emerged, with farmers, industrialists, and the upper-middle class composing the Right and Liberal groups (urban radicals, small farmers, tradesmen) and Social Democrats (factory workers and the lower-middle class) making up the Left, with both open to collaboration. In 1911 the Social Democrats renounced orthodox Marxism and cooperated with Liberals in the Riksdag, while conservatives accepted reforms they believed inevitable and helped enact them into law. In 1919, the Swedes extended voting privileges to women.

Swedish Economic Progress

Economic progress paralleled political developments. The industrial revolution had created vast demands for lumber, which Sweden possessed in abundance, and the timber industry powerfully stimulated the economy, helped as well by free trade legislation. In 1858 a Swedish industrialist perfected the Bessemer method and opened up the age of modern steel. The need to haul products over long

Alfred Nobel, inventor of dynamite, was a businessman and a man of peace. He established the famous Nobel Prizes in five categories that are the most prestigious in their fields. The prizes include the Peace Prize, awarded in Oslo because at the time of their institution Sweden and Norway were a single country, while the other prizes are awarded in Stockholm.

distances stimulated construction of a railway network, built through the cooperative efforts of the state and private enterprise. People assembled everywhere "in countless numbers to gaze on the splendour" of the railway. Alfred Nobel, who later instituted the prizes named after him, patented dynamite, Lars Magnus Ericsson invented the table telephone and founded a company with worldwide sales, Alexander Lagerman built a machine to mass produce matches, and Sven Wingquist developed the modern ball bearing. Notable progress also occurred in agriculture. The Swedes resisted the protectionist policies adopted by many countries to confront the crisis of cheap American and Russian grains flooding Western Europe and switched to the production of dairy products and sugar beets and the machinery necessary to process them.

In the early twentieth century, the Swedish economy boomed with new technology, such as the invention of methods for making brown paper from wood pulp and for working Swedish iron ore, rich in phosphates. Sweden emerged as an important player in the new industries of the second industrial revolution: electricity, the telephone, and related products. This expanding economic activity led to the development of new credit institutions that helped change Swedish life. This impressive economic activity changed the nature of Swedish emigration. It remained sizable, but the new emigrants were better educated and prosperous than in the past.

Norwegian Democracy

A combination of democratic reform, social advance, and industrial growth also characterized Norway. The greatest problem at the beginning of the twentieth century was a union with Sweden, imposed by the Great Powers in 1814, by which the Swedish monarch ruled both countries. However, Norway already had a constitution and a unique parliament, the Storthing, which combined the characteristics of a unicameral and a bicameral legislature. Voted in by a restricted number of electors, the Storthing elected one-third of its members to a separate house, the Lagthing, while the remaining members constituted the Odelsthing. By July 1884 the Storthing sitting together gained the right to name the government.

End of the Union with Sweden

Despite its domestic independence, Norwegians chafed at their subordination to Sweden in foreign policy and Swedish control of the consular service. Norway possessed the world's third-largest merchant marine, and Norwegian captains and businessmen resented having to turn to Swedish consuls to handle their business matters abroad. Resolution of the dispute failed in 1905, and in June the Norwegians dissolved the union. Norway made military preparations to resist possible Swedish action, but instead a referendum resulted in the union's official end and the selection of a Danish prince as the new king of an independent Norway.

Important political reforms followed. Election to the Storthing was made direct, and in 1919 proportional representation was instituted in national elections. Women gained the right to vote sooner than in other countries. The leader of the movement, Frederikke Marie Quam, had supported the dissolution of the Swedish union by securing the signature of hundreds of thousands of women.

In 1907 women with high incomes, who in 1901 had been given the vote in local elections, secured that right in national contests. In 1910 all women received the vote on an equal basis with men in local elections and in 1913 in national elections.

Novel Economic Experiments

A combination of private initiative and state activity brought unprecedented prosperity to the country in the decade following 1905. Railroad building reached a fever pitch after 1908, and new steamship lines improved communication between coastal areas. The old sailing fleet rapidly converted to steam, and in 1910 the Norwegian American Line entered the Atlantic route. The Norwegian fishing fleet was rapidly modernized, a telephone network was built, and facilities for the extraction of nitrogen from the air and modern hydroelectric plants materialized. The enormous development of electricity from Norwegian waterways made the country one of the earliest to be sensitive to ecological matters. Between 1906 and 1909, the Storthing passed the first modern concession laws restricting the purchase and use of forests.

Norwegians addressed traditional social concerns under the guidance of the Liberal (or Left) Party. Between 1909 and 1915, a wave of social legislation established or strengthened accident insurance for industrial workers, health insurance, and aid for mothers and illegitimate children. Legislation established mediation of labor disputes and a labor court to settle differences over contracts. In agriculture, the government encouraged land ownership, a policy that produced a stunning increase in the number of small farms, and established agricultural schools to introduce and maintain the highest standards.

Denmark's Anguished Politics

Once the most important Scandinavian country, Denmark's proximity to the big powers made its political and foreign affairs history more turbulent as it became embroiled in French Revolutionary affairs and in the wars for German unification.

The modern Danish constitution has its origins in the 1848 revolutions that forced the Danish king to issue the June Constitution that guaranteed freedom of the press and of religion and established a Rigsdag (Parliament). Composed of the lower house (the Folketing), elected by men aged thirty and older who were not on relief, and an upper chamber (the Landsting), indirectly elected by property owners at least forty years of age, the Parliament shared the legislative power with the king. In July 1866, however, a new, more conservative constitution that ensured the government a perpetual majority in the upper house came into force and precipitated a political struggle between the Left and Right for the next thirty years. In 1901 the conservative parties were defeated, and the king appointed a government that had the confidence of the majority party in the Folketing, opening up an era of parliamentary democracy.

In 1905, radical townspeople and poorer rural inhabitants founded the Radical Left Party, which supported the breakup up of large estates, the cession of land to landless peasants, and reduced military expenditures. This party, in alliance with the Social Democrats, emerged supreme in 1913 and remained a staple of Danish politics for the next fifty years. The coalition favored constitutional changes, and in June 1915 the constitution was liberalized and power was shared. Men and women over age twenty-five would elect the Folketing, while conservative control of the Landsting was assured by indirect elections and a higher age requirement.

Danish Economic and Social Change

Steady economic and social progress occurred in Denmark from the mid-nineteenth century with the application of steam-engine technology to the manufacturing sector, the growing ability of peasants to own their land free and clear, the end of trade monopolies once enjoyed by urban areas, and end of guild control of manufacturing. The government reduced tariffs and fees on seaborne traffic, measures that helped the Danish merchant fleet to convert to steam and stimulated its rapid growth. Industrial development encouraged construction of a railway network to connect vital parts of the country, and the development of iron and steel manufacturing, food processing, and porcelain production.

Growing industrialization brought with it an expanding proletariat, a Social Democratic Party, social legislation, and labor organizations. In 1903, laws facilitated entrance into higher schools. The tax system was modernized with the abolition of church tithes and the institution of general property, progressive income, and wealth taxes. Women won the right to vote in local elections in 1908. During the early twentieth century, strikes and lockouts agitated the country but labor unions and employers defined the conditions for strikes and agreed on procedural rules for resolving disputes that lasted until 1960. In 1907, the state began paying subsidies to trade unions for their unemployment funds and for poor relief. These compromises resulted in the doubling of real wages for Danish workers in the forty years before 1914.

The major innovations in the Danish economy came on the land. The cheap American and Russian grain that flooded Europe beginning in the 1870s threw European agriculture into crisis and forced most countries to impose high tariffs, but the Danes turned away from cereal growing and towards lucrative dairy and cattle production. The invention of appliances necessary for the working of dairy products encouraged farmers to band together and spurred creation of producers' and consumers' cooperatives that collaborated in the exportation of bacon and eggs to the English breakfast table. Specialized schools and the Folk High School Movement spread knowledge of the new agricultural techniques, and Danish cooperatives became a model for Europe.

The World Center of Quantum Physics

The Danish capacity for innovation during the early twentieth century is illustrated in the transformation of its capital, Copenhagen, into one of the world's most important centers of science. The Danish physicist, Niels Bohr, had gone to Manchester, England, to study with British physicists J. J. Thompson and Ernest Rutherford in 1911 and 1912. Bohr, a graduate of the University of Copenhagen,

The gates of the Carlsberg Brewery in Copenhagen, Denmark. It was on these grounds that Niels Bohr eventually took residence and where major advances in quantum physics were made—all financed with the proceeds from the sale of Carlsberg beer.

became intrigued with Rutherford's model of the atom and in 1913 published a fundamental paper on its quantum structure.

When Bohr returned to Copenhagen, the Royal Danish Academy of Science financed an institute for theoretical physics for him. The academy granted fellowships to physicists from all over the world to study atomic physics with Bohr. The roster of physicists who arrived in Copenhagen reads like a who's who of the giants of modern physics: Germans, Italians, Americans, Belgians, Swedes, Dutch, Japanese, Russians. Among them, Bohr's "children," the proudest boast was: "I used to work with Bohr."

Bohr's story has an interesting connection with Danish economics and cultural outlook because the Carlsberg Brewery made much of this scientific activity possible. The founder of the brewery willed the academy the income from the proceeds of the business. In the 1930s, with the death of the previous occupant of a mansion built for the brewery's founder on the grounds of his establishment, Bohr and his family took up residence in it. The sales of Carlsberg beer built Bohr's institute, paid for the fellowships to visiting scientists, and had a crucial role in the development of atomic theory that changed the world.

DIFFERENT ROADS: THE LOW COUNTRIES

Like the Scandinavian countries, the Low Countries—the Netherlands and Belgium—once had the same ruler. Unlike Scandinavia, language, culture, and religion caused serious problems and hardened divisions. The Dutch language pulled the Netherlands into the German cultural orbit, while French civilization attracted the French-speaking Belgians. Also living in Belgium were the Flemish, who were closer to the Dutch. Belgium was thus an ethnically divided land and has remained so. Religious differences accentuated the linguistic-cultural split in the Low Countries. In the sixteenth century Spain ruled both countries, but the Dutch revolted and established Calvinism as the predominant religion while Belgium remained predominantly Catholic. In 1815 the Congress of Vienna gave Belgium to the Kingdom of the Netherlands, but the Belgians successfully revolted in 1830. Between 1830 and 1839 the European powers recognized Belgium's independence and agreed to its neutralization.

BIOGRAPHICAL SKETCHES

Niels Henrik David Bohr
"Uncle Nick"

Niels Bohr, one of the most influential physicists of the twentieth century, was born in Copenhagen on October 7, 1885. His father taught physiology at the University of Copenhagen, where Niels and his younger brother Harald, a famous mathematician, both studied. Their mother Ellen Adler was the daughter of an assimilated Jewish politician. The Bohr family's intellectual activities gave the children a deep respect for learning, and Niels received a doctorate in physics in 1911.

Bohr won a Carlsberg foundation grant to study with J. J. Thompson in Cambridge, England, but left in March 1912 to work with Ernest Rutherford. During the next year, he published three fundamental papers, presenting the now-familiar model of the atom with electrons orbiting around the nucleus. He indicated that each successive orbit could contain more electrons than the inner ones and that atoms gave off radiation when electrons jumped to different orbits—the "quantum leap." Bohr applied the quantum theory to atomic structure, becoming a leader in the elaboration of the quantum mechanics that revolutionized physics in the 1920s and winning the Nobel Prize in 1922. Bohr's theories, including the "liquid drop" model of the atomic nucleus, proved essential for the explanation of fission and the development of the atomic bomb.

Bohr received a chair in theoretical physics at the University of Copenhagen in 1916 and began planning for his celebrated physics institute that opened in 1921. He remained its director until he died. With Bohr's institute, Copenhagen became the world center of quantum studies, hosting famous physicists from all over the world. "Bohr's Boys" reported him to be a slow thinker with a low-key style and a voice so soft it frequently could not be heard. At conferences brilliant young physicists would explain complicated theories that everybody immediately understood and applauded, except for Bohr. He would stubbornly request explanations of a simple point. Soon no one understood anything anymore, except for Bohr, who began to understand. In the end, what he got from the lecture was different from what everyone else had understood, and correct, while the lecturer was frequently wrong. In addition to physics, Bohr loved sports and westerns. His favorite films included *The Gun Fight at the Lazy Gee Ranch* and *The Lone Ranger and a Sioux Girl*. He would cajole his friends into going to the movies with him and ask constant questions about the plot during the show, annoying the audience. He developed a scientific theory of why the good guy always wins gunfights, tested it with his students using toy guns, and turned out to be right.

Bohr remained in Denmark when the Germans occupied the country during World War II. His favorite student Werner Heisenberg, in charge of the German atomic bomb project, visited him. The two had a long conversation that remains mysterious and controversial, but relations between the two scientists were cold from then on. When resistance operatives informed the part-Jewish Bohr that the Germans were about to arrest him, a Danish fisherman rowed him to the Swedish shore, where a British Mosquito bomber flew him to Britain. Bohr occupied the tail gunner's position and could communicate only by intercom. Over the North Sea the pilot asked how he was but could get no answer. Distressed, he rushed to the tail section after he landed—to find Bohr fast asleep.

Out of the Nazi clutches, Bohr participated in the building of the atomic bomb under the alias Nicholas Baker—"Uncle Nick." In 1944 he wrote to President Franklin Delano Roosevelt urging international cooperation for the control of nuclear weapons, and after the war became a powerful voice advocating peaceful uses for the atom. In 1957 he received the first Atoms for Peace Award given by the United States. On November 18, 1962, in his beloved Copenhagen, Niels Bohr died of a heart attack.

ECONOMIC PROGRESS

Dutch Economic Development

Splitting off from the more industrially advanced South stimulated the growth of industry in the Netherlands. Glass and porcelain manufacturing, cloth production, railways, shipbuilding, electricity, and chemicals all boomed, helped by the coal and oil reserves of the Dutch East Indies. Postal and currency reform, an extensive canal system, and the telegraph strengthened communications; Amsterdam, Rotterdam, and The Hague all expanded greatly. In agriculture, the Netherlands became the major producer of butter and margarine, while traditional sources of income, such as the diamond industry, flourished.

Political and religious problems made it difficult to address the growing problem of workers' discontent that accompanied industrialization. Originally the Dutch constitution reserved most power for the monarch, and in the constitutional debate, Liberals backed by Catholic groups fought against Calvinist conservatives linked to the Dutch Reformed Church. The crisis ended in a victory for Parliament in 1868 and in 1898, females were allowed to succeed to the throne in the person of William's daughter Wilhelmina.

The Influence of Dutch Socialism

Constitutional alterations allowed the Netherlands to confront the growing discontent caused by expansion of the factory system, low wages, and long working days that led to bad diet, poor sanitary conditions, low life expectancy, and alcoholism. In 1881, Ferdinand Domela Nieuwenhuis founded the Social Democratic Union (SDB) that favored revolution, but in 1894 the Dutch revisionists organized themselves into the Social Democratic Labor Party (SDAP) and defeated the Nieuwenhuis faction.

In the meantime, the Liberal-run government tried instituting social reforms to slow the growth of socialism. By 1901, Parliament had prohibited the employment of children under age twelve, limited women's working hours, implemented factory inspections, and made accident insurance mandatory for all workers. Between 1900 and 1905, the state established compulsory education and gave the local authorities the power to set minimum housing standards. Intervention in the medical field culminated in a 1912 law providing medical services to the poor.

These reforms left the Dutch Socialists unsatisfied, and when a conservative cabinet came to power in 1901, labor disturbances increased and culminated in a great rail strike in 1903. Fortunately, the period from 1903 to 1914 brought economic prosperity and moderate conservative businesspeople supported reform. In 1907, labor contracts brought employment under the purview of the States General; the fifty-eight-hour workweek for women and children arrived in 1910; between 1905 and 1913, secondary and university education was reformed; and in 1917 the stated mandated equal subsidies for public and private schools.

The voting system was also reformed. In 1917 Socialist-championed universal male suffrage arrived, along with proportional representation. Women won the right to be elected but, strangely, not the vote. However, in a struggle spearheaded by Wilhelmina Drucker and her Free Association of Women, women won full voting rights in 1922. Dutch women made important progress during the early twentieth century. In 1901 legislation ensured that a woman's property did not automatically become her husband's, and in 1909 women gained the right to file paternity suits.

The Dutch had an active foreign policy. They fought a long war against Indonesian rebels to maintain their control of the area, but in Europe they stood out for their peace efforts. They remained unofficially neutral and gained notoriety as the host of the First International Peace Conference, held at The Hague in 1899. This conference was a celebrated attempt to implement international law conventions. Dutch support of the Afrikaners (Dutch immigrant descendants in South Africa) during the Boer War won world attention. Because of their close cultural affinity and empathy for the Germans, Dutch diplomats talked about an alliance with them to avoid invasion in case of war and rebuffed a Belgian request to coordinate military measures in case of a German attack.

Divided Belgium

The progressive nature of Belgian politics and the region's intense and rapid industrialization following the 1830 revolution contrasted with the Netherlands. The country had a strong constitutional tradition but struggled with the reality of its division into two conflicting language and cultural groups and the power of the Catholic Church.

The Belgian Constitutional Tradition

The Belgian constitution of 1831 was a model for European Liberals. The document mandated a cabinet responsible to Parliament consisting of two houses—the Chamber of Representatives and the Senate—both directly elected.

In the early twentieth Century the Dutch worked hard to formulate international laws regarding the conduct of war, despite the excessive force they sometimes employed to maintain their colonial rule in Indonesia. Here is a street scene in The Hague, the Netherlands, probably in 1910, location of the first international peace conferences. Note the pedestrians dressed in Indonesian attire.

Although property qualifications limited the electorate, it was still the largest in terms of the proportion to the population. The constitution guaranteed fundamental liberties, including freedom of speech, the press, assembly, and association, and severely limited arbitrary state action. These were unusual features at the time. In practice, weak cabinets had difficulty confronting energetic kings, who successfully exercised greater authority than the constitution gave them, but the constitution's flexibility and a national consensus that the parliamentary system was the best means of resolving intractable problems made it a work in progress. For example, Belgium introduced compulsory universal male suffrage in 1893, although it was conditioned by plural voting dependent on property and education, which was rectified only in 1899. The record was poor when it came to the vote for women; women gained limited suffrage in 1921 and full voting rights in national elections only in 1948.

An Industrial Powerhouse

Belgium was the first country to which the industrial revolution spread—along with the steam engine and the railroad—in the early nineteenth century after its introduction in England. It very quickly became an industrial powerhouse diffusing the new technology. By 1900 Belgium ranked as one of the most heavily industrialized areas in Europe, building railroads and developing modern enterprises all over the world: "Belgian locomotives, railway tracks, tramlines, gas, electrical and coal-mining plant and steelworks combines could be found from Siam to Spain and from Russia to South America."

This rapid industrialization brought social problems in its wake: low wages, long working hours, strikes, and the growth of socialism. Unions and workers' cooperatives emerged, and in 1885 the Belgian Labor Party was founded. In 1893 the Socialists called a great general strike in support of universal male suffrage. Led by their noted leader Émile Vandervelde, they also demanded free education, shorter working hours for women and children, the legalization of trade unions, and an income tax. With Socialist encouragement, Belgium became a model for the European cooperative movement. Alongside the Socialists, a strong Christian Democratic movement demanded social justice in line with Pope Leo XIII's landmark 1891 encyclical *Rerum Novarum*. This activity spurred the passage of laws to protect workers, including the restriction of working hours for women and children, housing for workers, workers' insurance, and pensions.

Struggle with the Church
The development of the industrial sector did not resolve the deep divisions in Belgian society. Belgium suffered from a typical nineteenth-century malady that lasted well into the twentieth: the Catholic-Liberal schism. The governing Liberals favored a secular state, while the Catholics, conditioned by Pope Pius IX's hostility to liberalism, rejected the Liberal constitution. Combat between the two concepts took place mainly in education, culminating in the 1878 School War. The Liberals attempted to reverse a law that had established secular schools in the cities and Catholic ones in rural areas, both at state expense, by mandating nonchurch schools controlled by the state for all communes. For many Belgians, the legislation violated religious precepts and local autonomy, and they protested by transferring their children from the state schools to newly established Catholic institutions.

In 1884 the Catholics defeated the Liberals and retained control of the government until World War I. They mandated compulsory religious instruction in all schools and authorized local officials to provide subsidies to Catholic schools. This policy resulted in serious underfunding of non-Catholic schools in Catholic communes, while suppression of the ministry of education and the weakening of state oversight of education lowered standards. In 1910, the illiteracy rate was estimated at 10 percent, causing concern and prompting King Leopold II to intervene to check Catholic extremists.

The Flemish Problem
In addition to the serious challenge of the religious issue, the Flemish problem threatened to dismember the state. Dominated by the French-speaking Walloons, the Belgian government made French the official language of the country following independence. Local governmental officials and the primary schools used Flemish, but French was the language of the law, the army, and higher education. Flemish suffered from de facto discrimination because higher officials could not understand it, and Flemings had to learn a second language if they wished to go on to higher education and advance in the bureaucracy and political life.

BIOGRAPHICAL SKETCHES

Émile Vandervelde
Evolutionary Socialist

Despite many splits in the prewar European Socialist parties before 1914, the prevailing theory advocated the gradual achievement of socialism through parliamentary reforms. Émile Vandervelde, born in Ixelles, Belgium, on January 25, 1866, was a universally respected theoretician of this ideology, in addition to a skilled practitioner.

Having joined the Belgian Workers' Party in 1889, Vandervelde quickly assumed a leading role in the party. He received a doctorate in social sciences in 1891 and in 1894 won election to Parliament as a Socialist. He favored peasant cooperatives, contributed articles to the most influential European Socialist journals, and published several books expounding his Socialist ideas. He led the battle for universal male suffrage in Belgium, granted in 1914.

Vandervelde's writings and avid participation in international Socialist affairs made him one of the best-known leaders of his time. He won election as president of the Socialist (Second) International in 1900 and remained its head until 1918. This organization of Socialist parties was supposed to coordinate their action, but it collapsed when it failed to prevent World War I from breaking out. When the Germans invaded Belgium in 1914, Valdervelde joined the cabinet and remained in the government throughout the war. Following the conflict, he participated in the talks leading to the Versailles treaty and obtained the inclusion of a clause advocating the eight-hour workday and other measures favorable to labor. As minister of justice in 1919, he implemented a series of penal reforms and a law that greatly reduced alcoholism in the country. Throughout the postwar period, he remained an active and visible participant in international Socialist politics.

In 1925, Vandervelde became foreign minister in a Socialist-Catholic coalition government following the success of the Workers' Party in the elections of that year. As foreign minister, he helped negotiate the Locarno Pact of 1925, an agreement among Germany, France, Britain, Belgium, and Italy that promised a new era of peace. He resigned his post in 1927 when the opposition criticized him for his antimilitarism and for advocating the reduction of compulsory military service to six months. Vandervelde rejoined the Belgian cabinet from 1935 to 1936 as a minister without portfolio and from 1936 to 1937 as the minister of public health. On January 29, 1937, he resigned in protest against the government's neutral stance in the Spanish Civil War that pitted the Fascist and Nazi-backed rebellion of Generalissimo Francisco Franco against the legitimate government of the second Spanish republic.

Since 1924 Vandervelde had held a chair at the University of Brussels. After he left public life, he devoted his time to teaching law. Émile Vandervelde died in Brussels on December 27, 1938.

Besides the language issue, the Flemish areas of Belgium failed to keep pace with the country's economic development and were increasingly dominated by the French-speaking bourgeoisie. A study showed that fewer than 10 percent of Flemings knew French and that of Belgium's 382 high civil servants, only 22 were Flemish. Popular discontent after an 1866 incident in which the state executed two Flemings after a trial conducted in French, which they did not understand, led to a series of laws that were designed to improve the Flemish condition. This legislation was frequently not enforced, but with the extension of suffrage in 1893, the Flemish population gained more political clout because Liberals, Catholics, and Socialists vied for their votes. In 1898, Parliament decreed the legal equality of Flemings and Walloons.

Far from calming the waters, this success encouraged demands for ethnic favoritism in Flanders and bilingualism in government, which, in turn, led to the proliferation of French-speaking Walloon defensive associations bent on preserving their position. The Walloon-Flemish split defied resolution, and a Walloon politician informed the king of the "enormous and horrifying truth: there are no Belgians. . . . You are reigning over two different peoples." Events during World War I—ethnic unrest in the Belgian army and German attempts to exploit it—and following World War II confirmed that harsh judgment.

Belgian Foreign Affairs

Belgium's strategic position in Europe and its African possessions gave it an importance disproportionate to its small size, and its foreign policy stands out for the role of its kings. In 1885, King Leopold II successfully gained control of the

King Leopold II of Belgium, whose rule in the Belgian Congo was so vicious that it qualified as the first genocide of the twentieth century. He owned the Congo personally and made a vast fortune from it. Eventually the Belgian Parliament had to take away control from him because his brutal methods there aroused international indignation.

Congo Free State, a central African territory eighty times the size of Belgium. Even though the Congo belonged to him and not to the country, this vast mineral-rich area brought numerous economic benefits to the Belgians. Leopold's shameless use of slave labor and mass killings to enrich himself and enforce his rule gave rise to "the first great international human rights movement of the twentieth century" and forced the Belgian Parliament to intervene.

Another area in which the kings took an active role was in preparing for the danger of an invasion despite the country's neutralized status. Belgian monarchs unsuccessfully tried to convince Parliament that in case of war, the Germans might try to outflank the French by going through Belgium. In order to prevent Belgium from being quickly overrun, however, the Belgians either had to abandon their neutrality or reinforce their defenses. The first choice was impossible; the second unpopular. Only in 1913 did the Belgians agree to increase the size of the army and bolster their fortifications—too late. In 1914 the Belgian armed forces fought the German invasion bravely but unprepared and alone.

THE MAKING OF A CONSERVATIVE: SWITZERLAND

Besides Belgium, the other European neutral, Switzerland, also struggled to maintain its neutrality, recognized on March 20, 1815, in the face of periodic pressure from the great powers. The country adopted a novel organization of its armed forces, the "armed nation" by which its citizens received military training and took their rifles home with them. This and the rugged mountainous terrain was enough to discourage attacks by larger powers. Switzerland's trust in its citizens made it a darling of European radical movements, but with increasing prosperity came greater conservatism, unfriendliness to exiles, and a shrewd capacity to profit from neutrality. The country of democracy-obsessed, freedom-loving mountaineers emerged in the twentieth century as a haven for funds sent by unsavory rulers who were threatened by their subjects. By the end of the century, these distasteful aspects would characterize Switzerland for many foreigners.

Swiss Direct Democracy and Its Involution

The origins of Swiss direct democracy can be traced back to the thirteenth century, when leaders from Switzerland's forest, mountainous, and plateau areas banded together in common defense against the Holy Roman emperors. After securing their formal independence in 1648, the cantons set up a system to arbitrate differences among themselves and established a weak confederation with a Diet possessing few powers in order to maintain maximum local autonomy. After the centralizing efforts of the French Revolution, in which Switzerland was involved, the Swiss adopted the Pact of 1815 by which the cantons regained their sovereignty and the central state lost practically all its powers. During the nineteenth century, wars between Protestant radicals and Catholic conservatives ended with a Catholic defeat and the promulgation of a new constitution on September 12, 1848, that created a unique balance between federalism and centralism by the creation of a bicameral legislature consisting of the National Council elected by men aged twenty and older representing the nation as a whole and the Council of States, modeled on the American Senate, representing the cantons. In setting up the executive branch, however, the Swiss rejected the American presidential model because they believed it would foster monarchy or dictatorship. They opted for a seven-man executive, the Federal Council, voted in by the legislature. The legislature also elected a Supreme Federal Court.

In 1874, the Swiss introduced the popular initiative and the referendum, institutions that promoted the famous image of Swiss direct democracy. In fact, however, these institutions had a major impact on the country's political orientation by ensuring that major changes in policy would only occur very slowly if at all. The requirement that the people be consulted meant effective and frequent use of the referendum to block progressive measures. Swiss direct democracy paradoxically encouraged the country's drift in an increasingly conservative direction as Switzerland became more prosperous and sought to keep outsiders from sharing its wealth. The Swiss had continual problems with minorities, even before a large number of persons immigrated to the country later in the twentieth century, and in 1866 Switzerland was the last Western European country to grant civil rights to the Jews, primarily for trade reasons and under French pressure. The Swiss stubbornly refused to grant women the right to vote in federal matters, and, despite a strong suffrage movement, women received voting rights in some cantons only in the latter years of the twentieth century.

A positive aspect of the Swiss constitution was its suitability for a country that was composed of different linguistic groups and religions. Switzerland has three official languages, German, French, and Italian, with only 1 percent of the population speaking Romanche, the other national language. The population is evenly divided between Protestants and Catholics who once fiercely opposed each other.

Economic and Social Development

The Swiss economy followed general European trends. In agriculture, the Swiss offset the price decline that affected grains beginning in the 1870s by increasing production from pasture and dairy farming, especially cheese, and these activities remained lucrative into the twenty-first century. Cotton weaving and silk production prospered, and Switzerland maintained its domination of the watchmaking craft. The country participated in the industrial boom touched off by railway building, initially run by private enterprise and later taken over by the state. Locomotives, electric power plants, and different types of machinery headed a long list of exports that, along with tourism, helped pay for the resource-poor country's imports. Banking, the activity that would become synonymous with Switzerland, was not a major activity in the early twentieth century, but grew dramatically during and after the two world wars.

The rise of industry stimulated the rise of a Socialist party and demands for social legislation, which was initially enacted by the cantons and later by the federal government. In the late nineteenth and early twentieth centuries, legislation limited the workday, restricted women and child labor, and introduced factory inspections, health regulation, and industrial accident, unemployment and old age insurance.

The social and economic development of Switzerland, Scandinavia, and the Low Countries thus followed general West European trends, but in the South and Southeast it was a different story.

THE IBERIAN STATES

Spain and Portugal both confronted the twentieth century with a heavy legacy of greatness and decay.

Spain

Political Chaos in Spain

During the seventeenth century, Spain had dominated Europe and constructed a vast empire in the New World, but Spanish monarchs rapidly squandered the wealth, and the country became the "sick man" of Europe. During the next century, Spain remained divided between liberal and conservative forces, entrenched in different geographic areas that fought over whether the king or the legislature would have political power into the mid-twentieth century. A liberal constitution implemented in 1876 brought some stability, but in 1902 King Alfonso XIII implemented personal rule.

Social Disintegration

By the twentieth century, political and economic turbulence in Spain had resulted in large landholders greatly increasing their possessions while smaller holdings shrank. Pauperization of the rural population and massive emigration to the cities was widespread, and an oversupply of unskilled labor, depressed wages, and unemployment characterized them. Because of extreme poverty, the Spanish population was in no position to stimulate a demand for new products. Industrial growth consequently faltered, and Spain could not successfully absorb the increased population. Railroad building arrived late, investment remained in the hands of foreigners and wealthy Spaniards, and wealth was badly distributed. As modern problems exacerbated the old, the nobles, bourgeoisie, and large landowners maintained their economic and social domination through a tacit understanding between the Liberal and Conservative parties that alternated in government and did not adopt measures that might change the social situation. Spanish cabinets favored private entrepreneurs and passed social legislation only late and under the pressure of demonstrations. The political compromise brought a false political stability and allowed Alfonso XIII to make a sham of parliamentary institutions. Most important, it resulted in an abiding distrust of politics and forced opponents to act outside the discredited political system.

Leftist Violence and Rightist Reaction

This disenchantment produced disorder. The Anarchists dominated labor organizations and leftist politics into the 1930s, its labor federation counting four times as many members as its Socialist counterpart. In 1879 the typesetter Pablo Iglesias founded the Spanish Socialist Workers' Party, hoping to channel workers'

The Guardia Civil, military guardian of Spanish order, would be unleashed against government opponents during the frequent conflicts of the early twentieth century that beset the country. This picture from 1953 of a Guardia Civil horseman attacking a civilian illustrates why adversaries feared them.

demands into peaceful legal methods, but Anarchist violence and direct action had a greater appeal for the disaffected Spanish workers. Waves of strikes, bombings, and assassinations marred Spanish life, and voting rates remained low. Revolutionary syndicalism also attracted a peasant following—another anomalous and unusual development. In 1911, Anarchist unions united in a national labor federation, the CNT, whose membership outstripped the Socialist union, the UGT. The government did not propose reforms but employed the dreaded Guardia Civil to suppress disorders, suspended constitutional liberties, and called out the army instead of proposing reforms.

In June 1909, Catalonia erupted in revolt following Conservative Prime Minister Antonio Maura's request for military credits to suppress a revolt in Morocco. A major target was the Catholic Church, the prime factor in maintaining Spanish social conditions in a backward state. The church's political arm, Catholic Action, waged war on anarchism and on secular influence in all phases of Spanish life, reactionary Catholic capitalists sabotaged social initiatives fostered by their Liberal coreligionists, and the number of nuns and priests tripled in the fourteen years before 1900. The government suppressed the Catalonian outbreak and executed the anticlerical school reformer, antimilitarist, and former Anarchist Francisco Ferrer. The execution touched off a wave of protest all over Europe. Like the Dreyfus case in France, the Ferrer affair split Spanish society on the question of whether Spaniards should accept the status quo or fight to overthrow it. Moreover, Catalonia demanded regional autonomy and the Basque country demanded separation, increasing the fear of Spanish rightists.

Spanish neutrality during World War I, the tremendous demand for goods during the conflict, and the influx of foreign capital brought the possibility of change, but with a great acceleration in Spanish industrial growth came increased turmoil. In 1917 disturbances broke out, and a sharp economic downturn at the war's end provoked more disorders in an increasingly dangerous situation. The "tragic week" of June 1909 had brought the army back into the fore of Spanish politics after a hiatus of some years, and its presence increased ominously before and after World War I. The 1906 Moroccan revolt led to an increase in the army's resources and a conviction by the king and the conservatives that the military was the last bastion of order against a rising tide of violence and disorder. The army's strengthened role in Spanish society and the increased opposition to the government set the stage for civil war in the 1930s.

Portugal

Portuguese Upheavals

If anything, the state that shared the Iberian Peninsula with Spain suffered greater instability and political disorder. Portugal followed an evolution similar to that of Spain during the nineteenth century, with a great struggle between liberal and conservative forces and an even more complicated dynastic contest. In 1834 "Miguelism," the Portuguese counterpart of conservative Spanish "Carlism," (support for conservative pretenders to the throne) went down to defeat and a constitution established a two-house legislature—one elected by limited suffrage, the other appointed—that remained the basis of Portuguese constitutions until 1910.

Miguelism's defeat produced rule by upper and upper-middle class Liberals, the growth of Freemasonry, and an attack on the church. Church lands were sold but wound up in the hands of the wealthy, industrialization advanced slowly, and agriculture remained stagnant. During the 1890s, economic development accelerated but remained handicapped by the lack of raw materials, capital, and technicians. Furthermore, foreign capital, especially British, received favors and dominated the country. Fewer changes came to Portuguese society than to any other part of Europe, except perhaps the Balkans, and poor working conditions and the decline in the real wages of urban workers encouraged the rise of Socialist and Anarchist working-class organizations. As in Spain, political power alternated between conservative and liberal groups, a system called *rotativismo*, and the compromise remained in force until the rise of Portuguese republicanism.

The Portuguese Revolution

The Portuguese Republican program demanded political freedom, equality, separation of church and state, the right of association, the right to strike, and the repeal of regressive indirect taxes. Support for the Republican movement was concentrated in the larger towns, and it also enjoyed the support of a large radical nationalist secret society, the Carbonária. The government reacted to the Republican challenge by strengthening the crown's powers, but in 1900 the rotativist system began to break down with the defection of one of its leaders,

Joao Franco, who institution rule by decree. In 1908, the government suppressed a Republican-inspired army revolt, and the Carbonária assassinated King Carlos I and his heir in Lisbon. Carlos's inexperienced second son became king, and Portugal descended into chaos as cabinets rapidly succeeded each other, the monarchists split into warring groups, strikes increased dramatically, and radicals took over the republican movement. In October 1910, a military revolt overthrew the monarchy and established a republic.

The new Republican regime acted immediately; it adopted radical measures, curbed the power of the church, and announced new social policies favoring workers. On the whole, however, the middle class and the bureaucracy dominated the new republic and prevented it from implementing drastic measures on behalf of the population. The Republicans did little for women and, although they instituted a voting system approximating universal male suffrage in 1911, they cut the electorate in half in 1913. Republican fiscal policy tripled the already large Portuguese deficit and caused severe inflation. In 1912 the most serious wave of strikes in the country's history shook the country, protest demonstrations escalated, and radical army officers attempted to overthrow the government. The republic thus failed to resolve Portugal's economic backwardness, social problems, and political instability.

SOUTHEASTERN EUROPE

While turmoil in the Iberian Peninsula remained isolated, the political and territorial ambitions of the southeastern European states affected Europe and the world. Having gained their independence from the Ottoman Turks after centuries of domination, all the southeastern states hoped to gain territory from a rapidly declining Turkey and maneuvered between the dominant regional powers— Austria-Hungary and Russia. In these fights, the wild cards were Russian Pan-Slavism, the common Eastern Orthodox faith that all these states shared with the tsarist colossus, and Austria's German ally. This last factor meant that regional issues had the capacity to trigger a wider European war.

Romania

The Romanian King
The great powers helped carve independent states in the region from Turkish territory even while taking a generous helping of territory for themselves, and in 1858, they pressured the Ottomans into allowing the previously formed principalities of Moldavia and Wallachia to choose their own rulers. Proponents of Romanian unity selected the popular Alexandru Cuza as the ruler for both areas, and in 1861 Cuza united both principalities as Romania and issued a constitution.

Five years later a coup led by radical liberals removed Cuza and issued a constitution that lasted until World War II. Although the constitution created a bicameral legislature that had substantial powers on paper, it failed to achieve a Liberal regime because of the country's weak middle class and limited franchise through favoring the wealthy. Peasants, the vast majority of the population, elected only a

Extreme poverty characterized the situation of most Romanians in the early 20th century. The condition was especially dire and did not improve much until after World War I. Here is a picture of Romanian vendors in 1916.

few representatives to the Chamber of Deputies. Under these circumstances, the monarch had a preponderant role in the government until after World War I by allowing the alternation in power of liberal and conservative political parties that did not threaten the status quo.

Economics and Society

Romania's first king, Charles I, was a sophisticated member of Prussia's ruling family who ruled from 1866 until his death in 1914. He hoped to industrialize the country on the Western capitalist model through protective tariffs and subsidies for large and medium enterprises. These measures produced a concentration of capital and production in a relatively small number of industries, along with serious gaps and foreign domination of the important oil-refining sector. In 1914, along with lumber and food processing, oil refining accounted for almost 75 percent of the country's production.

Working conditions were very poor as immigration from the countryside into the cities ensured an oversupply of inadequately compensated labor and long working days ranging between twelve and sixteen hours. Wages stayed low, and enterprises preferred to hire women and children who were paid from 20 to 50 percent less than men. The weakness of the Romanian Socialist party ensured that no social legislation protected workers. Dissolved in 1899, the party struggled to rebuild itself in the early years of the twentieth century.

The peasantry formed the backbone of the Romanian population and economy, and agriculture still accounted for two-thirds of the country's production and for most of its exports in 1900. Reforms in the late nineteenth century had freed the peasants and granted them property rights, but the lack of sufficient land to make a living kept them in extreme poverty and bound to the landlords through rents paid in the form of labor services. Large landlords and the state owned 70 percent of the land, in contrast to Romania's neighbors Bulgaria and Serbia. These conditions and the peasants' exclusion from the government led to a serious revolt, in February 1907. The government quelled the uprising at the cost of 11,000 lives, after which it passed a series of ineffective reforms. Conditions on the land remained static until a wholesale reform was implemented after World War I.

The "Jewish Question"

Another serious social problem in Romania was the influx of Jews, primarily from Russia. By 1900, Jews accounted for over half Romania's urban population. Periodic anti-Semitic riots were a common feature because Romanians feared economic domination by the Jews, and Article 7 of the Romanian constitution restricted naturalization to Christians. This treatment of Romanian Jews prompted the intervention of French Jewish groups, which applied economic pressure and created difficulties when the government floated foreign loans. In 1879, under French and German compulsion, Romania modified Article 7, but it adopted implementing legislation that made it practically impossible for Jews to become citizens; Jews did not obtain full rights until after World War I.

Foreign Policy

Romanian recalcitrance on the Jewish question affected the country's international economic position, but King Charles's German heritage and control over foreign policy secretly brought Romania into the Triple Alliance because he aimed to secure a German guarantee of Romania's territorial integrity against potential Russian aggressiveness. There was a contradiction in Romania's adherence to the Triple Alliance because Austria-Hungary owned Transylvania, a Romanian-inhabited area coveted by Romanian nationalists. During the Balkan War of 1913, Romania attacked Bulgaria and won territorial concessions. The Balkan wars, the friendly French and Russian attitude, and Hungary's policies against its Romanian minority completed the country's alienation from the Triple Alliance, and the country entered World War I on the allied side after the death of King Charles.

Bulgaria

Bulgaria's Political Fragility

Bulgaria's past resembled Romania's. The Bulgarians lived under Muslim tutelage for five hundred years, maintaining their national identity and Orthodox faith. What was more remarkable, the Bulgarian peasants and nobles also survived Ottoman rule, and the typical Bulgarian peasant emerged from Turkish rule as a small proprietor who was able to support his family on his own land. A national revival occurred in the early and mid-1800s, and, as a result of a victorious Russian war with Turkey in 1878, a large independent Bulgaria reemerged. The new country included parts of Macedonia, a disputed region that destabilized the entire area.

In 1879 the Bulgarians adopted a liberal constitution that set up a complex unicameral legislature (the Subranie), enfranchised men over age twenty-one, invested power jointly in the executive and legislative branches, and granted wide individual rights to the citizens, but Liberal leader Stefan Stambolov, in league with the Russians, circumvented it. In 1894, Ferdinand fired Stambolov and ruled Bulgaria by manipulating the different liberal and conservative groups who were operating in the country. Before World War I, the Bulgarian parliamentary system failed to function according to the constitution, and neither the urban working class nor the peasantry looked to the established parties to address the grievances that arose from economic growth. In 1899, the peasants formed the Bulgarian Agrarian National Union, which advocated reforms and the establishment of a peasant republic.

Bulgarian governments favored industrialization through foreign loans, protectionism, an expanded transportation system, a solid banking system, direct intervention, and the promotion of new agricultural methods. Economic growth continued strong until 1912, with the number of industrial plants increasing from 36 to 345 between 1887 and 1911. This development was financed by an enormous increase in the national debt that by 1912 resulted in interest payments eating up 20 percent of the budget. The resulting high taxes and corruption led to resentment and revolts, especially in 1905 after the Russian Revolution of that year. In 1906 a rail strike and anti-Greek rioting over Macedonia shook the country. In 1907 the prime minister was assassinated, and in 1908 more rioting occurred, revealing the great fragility of Bulgarian institutions.

Foreign Dissatisfactions

Besides these internal problems, the Macedonian problem created serious domestic and international difficulties. The Internal Macedonian Revolutionary Organization, demanded the liberation of Macedonia from the Turks through violence and terrorism and its annexation to Bulgaria. The problem was complicated because Greece and Serbia also claimed parts of Macedonia, and partisans of the different countries clashed there. In 1912 the Bulgarians participated in the first Balkan War against Turkey but the resulting disagreement among the victorious powers over Macedonia encouraged the Bulgarians to attack Serbia in 1913. This provoked a counterattack by Serbia, Greece, Romania, and Turkey that resulted in a Bulgarian defeat. The war ended with Bulgaria in possession of only a small part of Macedonia—an outcome that incensed Bulgarian nationalists. More importantly, in attacking Serbia, Bulgaria had ignored Russian warnings, worsening the already tense relations between the two countries. Bulgarian foreign policy, shifted toward the Central Powers and it would join them during World War I.

Greece

Instability and Corruption

Like Bulgaria, Greece also suffered hundreds of years of Turkish domination and retained its national identity through its Eastern Orthodox faith. Following independence won between 1821 and 1833, Greece came under British influence and established a monarchy under a young German prince who ruled as Otto I.

His new state included under a million people and left the most prosperous Greeks within Ottoman borders. Greek peasants were mostly landless, and the banditry and disorder that afflicted rural areas induced many Greeks to flee the country. Two Greek constitutions floundered on primitive social conditions and corruption. After Otto was driven out, corruption, factionalism, and instability characterized the reign of the new Greek King George I. During the 1880s and 1890s, however, King George became convinced that rule by a parliamentary majority would lead to political coalitions and stability, and two politicians, Charilaos Trikoupis and his rival Theodore Deliyannis, alternated in power, but corruption and instability remained serious problems despite the passage of some reforms, especially by Trikoupis. Trikoupis improved education and the state administration, curbed banditry, and bolstered the armed forces. Cotton and woolen mills were constructed, railway building achieved modest success, a telegraph line was built, and the basis of the Greek merchant marine, one of the twentieth century's largest, was laid. The Greek economy, however, remained backward, and its few exports were mostly agricultural and highly subject to market fluctuations. Greece borrowed heavily to finance its industrial development and by 1893 was bankrupt in everything but name.

The "Great Idea"

Greek domestic and foreign affairs were closely linked. Following independence, the Greek state hoped to bring the "unredeemed" Greeks living in the Ottoman Empire into Greece, a policy known as the "Great Idea." At first the Greeks concentrated on Crete, which constantly revolted against the Turks, and in 1897 Greece went to war with Turkey with disastrous results.

In 1908 more Cretan unrest and an economic crisis produced a revolt by disgruntled army officers who were upset at restrictions on promotion and favoritism. In 1909 they formed a military league and threatened to march on Athens if the government did not accept their demands for military, economic, and tax reforms. When the government responded unsatisfactorily, the league threw its support to a politician from Crete who had not been compromised by the corrupt ruling elite—Eleftherios Venizelos. In December 1910, Venizelos won a large majority in Parliament but did not drastically alter the 1864 constitution.

The energetic Venizelos improved the civil service, established free and compulsory primary education, introduced a progressive income tax, and set minimum wages for women and children. Legislation recognized trade unions and banned company unions. Because of the reforms, in 1910 and 1911 the country ran a budget surplus after many years in the red. Venizelos oversaw the reorganization of the army and the navy by bringing in British and French experts. Military reconstruction and the political unity that Venizelos achieved account for the important Greek military successes during the Balkan wars, which advanced the Great Idea.

In 1912 Greece joined in the first Balkan War against Turkey, and in the second helped defeat Bulgaria and was rewarded with a substantial slice of the ancient Greek province of Macedonia. In 1913, the Great Powers recognized Greek sovereignty over Crete. Greece did not completely achieve its Great Idea of

THE BOILING POINT.

Although the Balkans were a peripheral part of Europe politically and economically, their international squabbles affected Europe and the world and would touch off World War I. Here is a cartoon from 1912 from *Punch* magazine that shows the large powers of Europe desperately trying to contain the "Balkan Cauldron" from exploding.

redeeming all Greeks, but the country did amazingly well and increased both its territory and population by 70 percent. These gains, however, put a large number of Slavs and Turks under Greek control, and in 1913 another event occurred that presaged trouble ahead: George I fell to an assassin. George I left a successor who lacked his flexibility and commitment to constitutional rule.

Serbia

Instability and Assassination

Serbia had even vaster ambitions for the conquest of unredeemed territory and a greater impact on Europe's future.

Under the Turks, the Serbs had maintained their Eastern Orthodox faith and a measure of local self-government. In 1878 an independent Serbia appeared as a country of small but politically subservient landholders, and in 1882 it became a full-fledged kingdom. In contrast to Western parliamentary states, in which the executive needed the confidence of the legislature, "in Serbia it seemed as though the parliament had to enjoy the confidence of the government." In 1889 a new constitution was promulgated (called the constitution of 1888, from the Julian calendar). The fruit of a compromise between the Radicals, who pushed for a full-fledged parliamentary regime, and King Milan Obrenovic, the new instrument increased the assembly's prerogatives and introduced the concept of sharing power between the executive and the legislature. However, politically burned out and shaken by personal problems, the king abdicated.

A regency council ruled for his son Alexander and ushered in increased confusion. The years from 1889 to 1892 witnessed a Radical ascendancy that encouraged the growth of disorder and banditry. Austria and Russia became involved in Serbia's internal affairs by supporting different plots and counterplots. Complicating the political situation, Alexander took as his mistress a woman of disrepute and, to make matters worse, married her. This marriage, his purging of officials who disapproved, her inability to have children, and rumors that her brother might succeed Alexander outraged the country. In 1901, the king promulgated yet another constitution contrary to the established procedure, but his main goals were to allow a female to succeed him should he have no male progeny, to make his wife regent in case of his death, and to acquire popular support for the monarchy. In 1902 and 1903, political opposition increased; between demonstrations and attempted coups, the army's disaffection became clear.

On June 10–11, 1903, army conspirators invaded the royal palace and brutally butchered Alexander, his wife, the prime minister, and other officials. They installed a rival dynasty under Peter Karadjordjevic. A Western European-type liberal, the new king promulgated a constitution that established a unicameral legislature, extended its powers over finances, strengthened civil rights, and provided for a strong executive. The new regime then set out to modernize the army and reform Serbian society and national life.

The disorders delayed Serbian economic development. Industrialization remained slow until 1906, when a tariff war with Austria-Hungary caused the economy to loosen its dependence on imports from its giant neighbor and stimulated industry. The government strengthened credit institutions and attracted foreign investment that went primarily into mining, railway building, meatpacking, and electrification. In 1910 some social legislation was passed to address the most egregious problems of the workers.

Destabilizing the Balkans

The 1903 revolution reoriented Serbian foreign policy. The Serbs believed that they had the historic mission of freeing the South Slavs from Austrian and Ottoman domination and unifying them under their leadership. These principles had the strong support of the Serbian people, and the conviction that Alexander had not furthered the mission was part of the reason for the army's revolt in 1903.

With the new regime, Serbia turned definitively against Austria-Hungary and toward Russia. The Serbian desire for economic independence from Austria and political opposition to Austria contributed to the tariff war of 1906 to 1911. The Bosnia-Herzegovina crisis from 1908 to 1909 further exacerbated relations between the two countries, provoking popular demonstrations against the Austrians and an enraged reaction by the Serbian government. The crisis escalated, and the Austrians threatened war. Nationalist feelings led to the founding of secret organizations that pledged to achieve South Slav unification by revolutionary action and by influencing Serbia's governmental policy—ideas with strong army support. The Balkan wars, in which Serbia made enormous gains, brought the issue of Greater Serbia to a new plateau by expelling the Turks from Europe and by making Austria-Hungary the focus of Serbian action to free the Slavic inhabited lands possessed by Austria-Hungary. Austrian statesmen understood that Serbian success in this endeavor would logically lead to the empire's breakup, and they determined to eliminate Serbia as a threat.

Bibliographical Essay

Wayne C. Thompson, *Nordic, Central, and Southeastern Europe, 2008* (Harper's Ferry, W.Va., 2008) is a general history of many of the regions covered in this chapter.

Modern Scandinavia as a whole—including the areas that were not independent and therefore not covered in this chapter—is analyzed in separate chapters of the massive Jorgen Bukdahl et al., eds., *Scandinavia Past and Present: Through Revolutions to Liberty* (Copenhagen, n.d.). The separate articles also consider the arts and humanities. Tony Griffiths, *Scandinavia,* 8th ed. (New York, 2004) is a concise general introduction that also discusses intellectuals. T. K. Derry's *A History of Scandinavia: Norway, Sweden, Denmark, Finland, and Iceland* (Minneapolis, Minn., 1979) is a standard work. H. Arnold Barton's *Essays on Scandinavia History* (Carbondale, Ill., 2009) gives a grounded background on the 18th and 19th centuries. Two books of essays that look at different aspects of Scandinavian economic and social experience are Susanna Fellman, *Creating Nordic Capitalism* (Basingstoke, UK, 2008) and Niels Finn Christiansen, *The Nordic Model of Welfare: A Historical Reappraisal* (Copenhagen, 2006).

On Sweden, general works with good coverage of the period discussed include Neil Kent, *A Concise History of Sweden* (Cambridge, UK, 2008), combining social, economic, and cultural history, and Byron J. Nordstrom, *The History of Sweden* (Westport, Conn., 2002), which discusses the emergence of the democratic system in the country. See also Franklin D. Scott, *Sweden: The Nation's History* (Minneapolis, Minn., 1977), subsequently republished with an epilogue by Steen Koblik. Andrew A. Stromberg, *A History of Sweden* (New York, 1970), is a more detailed, older work originally published in 1931 that is particularly useful for intellectual, constitutional, and social issues. Ingvar Andersson, *A History of Sweden,* 2nd ed. (New York, 1970), the translation of a work by a noted Swedish observer, is a particularly engrossing account; the citation on the Swedish railways is on p. 356. For readers seeking a more concise history, Irene Scobbie, *Sweden* (New York, 1972), is a good choice, emphasizing economic and social affairs. More specialized works on Sweden's economy include Eli Heckscher, *An Economic History of Sweden* (Cambridge, Mass., 1954), and Carl G. Gustavson, *The Small Giant: Sweden Enters the Industrial Era* (Athens, Ohio, 1986), an industrial history. Swedish politics over a hundred-year period are the topic of Leif Lewin, *Ideology and Strategy: A Century of Swedish Politics* (Cambridge, UK, 1988). Books on interesting topics include Jan-Erik Nylund et al., *Forest Tenure in Sweden: A Historical Perspective* (Uppsala, Sweden, 2007), which demonstrates Swedish interest in a topic mentioned in this chapter; and Eva Ahren, *Death, Modernity, and the Body: Sweden 1870–1940* (Rochester, N.Y., 2009), which discusses an unusual topic in the coming of modernity.

For Norway, see Hjalmar Hjorth Boyesen, *A History of Norway From the Earliest Times* (n.p., 2007). Karen Larsen published a full and interesting general account: *A History of Norway* (Princeton, N.J., 1948). For a very detailed and complete history that also pays attention to the arts, see Knut Gjerset, *History of the Norwegian People* (New York, 1969, published originally in 1932). T. K. Derry produced two good general works: *A History of Modern Norway, 1814–1972* (Oxford, UK, 1973), good not only on economic, political, and social affairs, but on Norwegian emigration, and the shorter but still useful *A Short History of Norway*, 2nd ed. (London, 1968). On the important Norwegian shipping industry, see *Norwegian Shipping* (Oslo, 2007), a history of technological innovation.

For Denmark, see Knud J. V. Jespersen's *A History of Denmark* (New York, 2004), a general history including material on the modern period. Stewart Oakley, *The Story of Denmark* (London, 1972), is an excellent source. Another useful work is W. Glyn Jones, *Denmark: A Modern History* (London, 1986). Both books go into ample detail on modern Danish history, with the first being more complete. On Niels Bohr, there is the volume edited by Stefan Rozenthal, *Niels Bohr: His Life and Work as Seen by His Friends and Colleagues* (Amsterdam, 1967). For information on his institute, see George Gamow, *Thirty Years that Shook Physics* (New York, 1966). The citations are from p. 51.

On Holland, there is the excellent, compact, and clear work by Gerald Newton, *The Netherlands: An Historical and Cultural Survey, 1795–1977* (London, 1977), which covers the modern period very well. Another good survey is Frank E. Huggett, *The Modern Netherlands* (New York, 1971). Mark T. Hooker, *The History of Holland* (Westport, Conn., 1999), is another survey. A very brief survey is A. J. Barnouw, *The Making of Modern Holland: A Short History* (London, 1948). Bartholomew Landheer, ed., *The Netherlands* (Berkeley, Calif., 1943), offers specialized essays on different aspects of Dutch affairs. Amry Vandenbosch, *Dutch Foreign Policy Since 1815: A Study in Small Power Politics* (The Hague, 1959), is a meticulous examination of the subject. J. W. Schot examines the role of technology beginning in the period discussed in this chapter: *Technology and the Making of the Netherlands* (Cambridge, Mass., 2010). Luxembourg, connected dynastically with the Netherlands, is the subject of James Newcomer's *The Grand Duchy of Luxembourg* (London, 1984).

E. H. Kossman wrote a very detailed parallel history of the Netherlands and Belgium, *The Low Countries 1780–1940* (Oxford, UK, 1978). Similar treatments are Paul Arblaster, *A History of the Low Countries* (New York, 2006) and J. C. H. Blom and Emiel Lamberts, *History of the Low Countries* (New York, 1999). *A House Divided* (Lanham, Md., 1997) discusses the Flemish problem in relation to the Catholics and Socialists in the 19th century. Margot Lyon, *Belgium* (London, 1971), is an excellent short history; Lyon quotes the statement about the king ruling two peoples on p. 58. Bernard A. Cook, *Belgium* (New York, 2002) is a general history. Stephen B. Wickman, ed., *Belgium: A Country Study* (Washington, D.C., 1985), primarily concerns the period after the one discussed in this chapter, but has an excellent introduction and chronology. Another way to understand Belgium during the years covered is through biographies of its monarchs. In this respect, consult Barbara Emerson, *Leopold II of the Belgians: King of Colonialism* (London, 1979), which also devotes considerable attention to his imperialistic activities. The older book by John de Courcy MacDonnell, *King Leopold II: His Rule in Belgium and the Congo* (New York, 1965, but originally published in 1905), is still useful for its wealth of detail. The best account of Leopold's rule in the Congo is Adam Hochschild's *King Leopold's Ghost: A Story of Greed, Terror, and Heroism in Colonial Africa* (Boston, 1999); the quote on the first international human rights organization is on p. 2. Martin Ewans discussed the topic and its ramifications in detail in *European Atrocity, African Catastrophe: Leopold II, the Congo Free State and Its Aftermath* (London, 2002). There is also a biography of Leopold's successor by Evelyn Graham, [pseud. for Lucas Netley], *Albert King of the Belgians* (New York, 1929).

The best manageable history of Switzerland, noted for its balanced viewpoints and its rich detail, is E. Bonjour, H. S. Offler, and G. R. Potter, *A Short History of Switzerland* (Oxford, UK, 1952). George Arthur Codding, *The Federal Government of Switzerland* (Boston, 1965), is an excellent examination of the Swiss government in relation to the land, people, and history. Other general histories that can be profitably consulted are

Wilhelm Oechsli, *History of Switzerland* (Cambridge, UK, 1922), and, for its particular outlook on Swiss direct democracy dating from the years covered in this chapter, Henry Demarest Lloyd, *A Sovereign People: A Study of Swiss Democracy* (New York, 1907). *Peace, Freedom, Security* (Bern, 2003) discusses Swiss defense policy over two centuries. Matthieu Leimgruber, *Solidarity Without the State?* (Cambridge, UK, 2008) examines the Swiss welfare system.

The historical literature on Spain is abundant, although readers will have to glean out the material covered in this chapter. Salvador de Madariaga's *Spain: A Modern History* (New York, 1967) is a classic account that exhaustively discusses the major themes of Spanish history. Mary Vincent's *Spain 1833–2002* (New York, 2007) is a general history that concentrates on politics and culture. Eléna de La Souchere, *An Explanation of Spain* (New York, 1964), is excellent for the clarity of its interpretations; the quotation on Spain in the text is taken from p. 106. Some particularly useful general histories are Raymond Carr, *Modern Spain 1875–1980* (Oxford, UK, 1980), a concise work with three excellent chapters on the period discussed and a valuable chronology and glossary that allow readers to keep developments clear; George Hills, *Spain* (New York, 1970), particularly valuable for chapters on the constitutional monarchy and the African war and its political effects; and Richard Herr, *Spain* (Englewood Cliffs, N.J., 1971), which contains a series of essays by a noted historian.

There is also good literature on specialized topics. These works include Adrian Shubert, *A Social History of Modern Spain* (London, 1990), which investigates important sectors of the economy and social development. Earl R. Beck's *A Time of Triumph and of Sorrow: Spanish Politics During the Reign of Alfonso XII, 1874–1885* (Carbondale, Ill., 1979) is an account of the reign of Alfonso XII arguing that the king failed in modernizing Spain because of the opposition of entrenched customs, traditions, and political groups. The church has been a focus of investigation in the historical literature, but a clear, concise, and balanced treatment of the institution with material on this period is Frances Lannon, *Privilege, Persecution, and Prophesy: The Catholic Church in Spain, 1875–1975* (Oxford, UK, 1987). Joan Connelly Ullman studied the Catalan revolt of 1909 in its historical and anticlerical dimensions in *The Tragic Week: A Study of Anti-Clericalism in Spain, 1875–1912* (Cambridge, Mass., 1968). Joseph McCabe, *The Martyrdom of Ferrer* (London, 1909), is a contemporary account illustrating the international echo of the affair. Carolyn P. Boyd, *Praetorian Politics in Liberal Spain* (Chapel Hill, N.C., 1979), examines the army's role in Spanish politics primarily after 1917, but includes two chapters on earlier years.

Portugal is not nearly as well covered in the literature as is its larger Iberian neighbor, but Stanley G. Payne's *A History of Spain and Portugal,* vol. 2 (Madison, Wisc., 1973), includes a comprehensive and clear account of Portuguese history of this period, in addition to Spanish affairs. A. H. de Oliveira Marques, *History of Portugal,* vol. 2 (New York, 1972), discusses the constitutional monarchy and the republic in detail, including the African colonies and their vicissitudes. H. V. Livermore, *A New History of Portugal* (Cambridge, UK, 1966), includes two chapters on the same topics. Douglas L. Wheeler, *Republican Portugal: A Political History, 1910–1926* (Madison, Wisc., 1978), is a history of Portugal from 1910 to 1926. V. de Bragança-Cunha, *Revolutionary Portugal* (London, 1937), an examination of Portuguese republicanism, pronounces the republic a disappointment. Two general books are worth looking at: M. D. D. Newitt, *Portugal in European and World History* (London, 2009), and Richard Alan Hodgson Robinson, *Contemporary Portugal* (London, 1979).

On the Southeastern European states, Romania is fortunate to count some impressive works. Keith Hitchins, *Rumania 1866–1947* (Oxford, UK, 1994), is a thorough, balanced, and well-informed work with a good bibliography. Hitchins also published *The Identity of Romania* (Bucharest, 2009). Lucian Boia concentrated on *Romania: Borderland of Europe* (London, 2001). The older book by R. W. Seton-Watson, *A History of the Romanians* (New York, 1963), is very detailed, well written, and clear. Valuable briefer accounts include Vlad Georgescu, *The Rumanians: A History* (Columbus, Ohio, 1984), and Georges Catellan, *A History of the Rumanians* (Boulder, Colo., 1989). On specialized topics, see the account of the crucial early years of independence, Gerald J. Bobango, *The Emergence of the Romanian National State* (New York, 1979). Philip Gabriel Eidelberg contends that the 1907 peasant revolt resulted from fights between political parties supporting or opposing industrialization: *The Great Rumanian Peasant Revolt of 1907: Origins of a Modern Jacquerie* (Leiden, the Netherlands, 1974).

Although there is material on post–World War I and Communist Bulgaria, Bulgaria has not attracted as much scholarly attention as Romania for the time period discussed in this chapter. Luckily, however, a clearly written, balanced, thorough, and scholarly work exists: Richard J. Crampton, *Bulgaria 1878–1918: A History* (New York, 1983), from which the quote on the effects of the Stambolov regime is taken (p. 158). The same author also wrote *A Short History of Modern Bulgaria* (Cambridge, UK, 1987), with a brief chapter on the period covered in this chapter, and *A Concise History of Bulgaria* (New York, 1997). An older work is useful for its thematic approach: George Clenton Logio, *Bulgaria: Past and Present* (Manchester, UK, 1936). For an example of Communist historiography on Bulgaria, see D. Kossev, H. Hristov, and D. Angelov, *A Short History of Bulgaria* (Sofia, 1963). John Macdonald's *Czar Ferdinand and His People* (New York, 1971, but reprinted from an older account of an unspecified date), is a romantic account.

As is the case of many areas with a glorious ancient past, modern Greece has suffered from some neglect. Richard Clogg's *A Short History of Modern Greece* (Cambridge, UK, 1979), however, is a very good study. C. M. Woodhouse, *Modern Greece: A Short History* (London, 1991), has several good chapters on the period covered here. Douglas Dakin, *The Unification of Greece 1770–1923* (London, 1972), goes into more detail, and Dionysios A. Zakythinos, *The Making of Modern Greece* (Oxford, UK, 1976), and John K. Campbell and Philip Sherrard, *Modern Greece* (London, 1968), emphasize social history. Less scholarly but informative treatments include Jane Perry, Clark Carey, and Andrew Galbraith Carey, *The Web of Modern Greek Politics* (New York, 1968); David Holden, *Greece Without Columns: The Making of the Modern Greeks* (London, 1972); and D. George Kousolulas, *Modern Greece: Profile of a Nation* (New York, 1974). Thomas W. Gallant, *Modern Greece* (London, 2001) is a survey. On the most remarkable Greek politician of this period, see Herbert Adams Gibbons, *Venizelos* (Boston, 1920). Theodore A. Couloumbis et al., *Greece in the Twentieth Century* (Portland, Ore., 2003) is a book of essays on important modern topics.

On Serbia, an essential starting point is Michael Boro Petrovich, *A History of Modern Serbia 1804–1918,* 2 vols. (New York, 1976), from which the quote on the 1869 constitution is drawn (vol. 2, p. 369). Stevan K. Pavlowitch, *Serbia; The History of an Idea* (New York, 2002), is a detailed survey; Alex N. Dragnich, *Serbia Through the Ages* (Boulder, Colo., 2004) is less detailed. The early twentieth century is covered by Wayne S. Vucinich, *Serbia Between East and West: The Events of 1903–1908* (New York, 1968). David MacKenzie, *The Serbs and Russian Pan-Slavism: 1875–1878* (Ithaca, N.Y., 1967), discusses the relationship between Russia and Serbia in the late nineteenth century, while his *Serbs and Russians* (Boulder, Colo., 1996) has more material on the period discussed in this chapter. Charles Jelavich's scholarly study *Tsarist Russia and Balkan Nationalism: Russian Influence in the Internal Affairs of Bulgaria and Serbia, 1879–1886* (Berkeley, Calif., 1962), examines Russian influence in Serbian (and Bulgarian) internal affairs and draws an implicit comparison to the post–World War II situation in the same region.

PART II

End of Hegemony

CHAPTER 6

World War I

CHAPTER OUTLINE

Imperialism and Diplomacy: From Crisis to Crisis • History of a History:
Causes of World War I • Combat! • The Home Fronts • The War Ends

BIOGRAPHICAL SKETCHES

Henry Gwyn Jeffreys Moseley, A Casualty of War • Erich Maria Remarque,
"But now, for the first time, people learned what it was really like"

At the height of their political and economic influence in 1914, Europeans
went to war lightheartedly. Film footage shows troops from the different
nations smiling and waving to ensure that they would be filmed for posterity.
The last major European war had ended a hundred years before, writers and poets
had glorified combat, and most expected that a modern war could not last long.

Instead, the Great War turned into a global conflict, lasting four years, killing
millions, bankrupting countries, and ending Europe's world hegemony.

IMPERIALISM AND DIPLOMACY:
FROM CRISIS TO CRISIS

In 1900 Europeans believed that imperialism had contributed to the prosperity
of the colonial powers by providing raw materials and markets. The desire of the
powers to increase their colonial possessions was a major cause of the war.

German Imperialism

Given Bismarck's disinterest in colonies, Germany possessed only a few African
territories and some islands in the Pacific. In the late 1890s, however, Germany
made a bid for more colonies as an aspect of its drive for world power, but found
the colonial world dominated by Britain and France, which Germany considered
declining powers. As a result, one school of historical scholarship to be discussed
later argued, German rulers wanted to acquire sufficient resources to guarantee

their country's "place in the sun"—not only colonies, but domination of the European continent. The German drive for power was the most important factor in the crises leading to World War I.

An Entangled Web

In 1904 Britain and France had sealed the Entente Cordiale by a colonial deal recognizing each other's interests in Egypt and Morocco. This bargain alienated Germany, which demanded an international conference to discuss colonies. Germany's bellicosity led to its diplomatic isolation at the 1906 Algeciras conference and prompted conversations between the British and French military staffs. In 1907, fearing that a war might break out with Austria-Hungary backed by Germany over the Balkans, the Russians resolved their imperial differences with the British and reached an understanding with them. Because the Russians already had an agreement with the French, the Triple Entente was born.

These developments confirmed the German fear of encirclement, and the Schlieffen Plan—the means by which the Germans hoped to win a two-front war—became an article of faith: "The German General Staff, indeed, the whole German officer corps (with negligible exceptions) regarded this plan as the infallible recipe for victory. This is all the more significant because the political leaders (before, during, and even after the war) also accepted this plan as sacrosanct or at any rate did not question it." The Schlieffen Plan came to dominate German foreign policy because it envisioned a German attack on France in case of a crisis involving Austria and Russia, even if the French were not directly involved, thus ensuring that a war in the Balkans would not remain localized. Moreover, the Germans had a sense of urgency about applying the plan because they calculated that Russian modernization would enable the Russians to mobilize as quickly as the Germans and make the Schlieffen Plan obsolete by 1917.

The Schlieffen Plan convinced the Germans that they could simultaneously defeat both France and Russia, but what would happen if the British intervened? It was likely that the British would intervene in any war to prevent France's destruction and Germany's domination of the continent and to protect Belgium. The Germans hoped for a British alliance or, at least, neutrality, offering to slow down the naval buildup that threatened British security, a condition that their *Weltpolitik* (world policy) made impossible. Nevertheless, they convinced themselves that the British would remain neutral if they could blame the Russians for a war that forced them to defend a superior Anglo-German civilization against the "inferior" Slavs. Consequently, according to historian Fritz Fischer, the Germans pushed the Austrians to maneuver the Russians into mobilizing first in order to justify a German attack on France, through Belgium, in the naive assumption that Russian mobilization would ensure British neutrality.

Diplomatic Crises

These considerations, combined with the German need to bolster Austria-Hungary, produced a series of diplomatic crises before 1914. In 1908 and 1909 it took an Austrian show of force that risked war to resolve the Bosnia-Herzegovina crisis. The Austrians consulted carefully with Germany. German Chief of Staff

Helmuth von Moltke offered his full support, while Wilhelm II noted in the margins of a military attaché's report: "Such a favorable opportunity for disciplining the unruly Serbs will not come again soon." On March 19, 1909, Austria sent Serbia an ultimatum demanding Serbian recognition of Austrian annexation of the two provinces. Three days later the Germans sent one to the Russians, demanding clear acceptance of the annexations and warning that the responsibility in case of refusal would fall exclusively on them. Not yet recovered from war and revolution, the Russians complied. Both Austrian and German officials lamented that diplomacy had deprived them of a golden opportunity to settle the Balkan question.

In 1911 the second Moroccan crisis flared when the French exploited local disturbances to extend their control of the area. The Germans reacted more vigorously than they had during the previous Moroccan crisis of 1905–06, perhaps because domestic public opinion had been upset with the kaiser's failure to make gains then. The Germans dispatched the gunboat *Panther* to the Moroccan port of Agadir—the "*Panther* leap." They demanded exorbitant compensation for recognizing the French protectorate: western Morocco or the entire French Congo. Afraid that French weakness would change the balance of power in Europe, the British strongly backed their ally, and David Lloyd George issued a stern warning the Germans. The kaiser frequently blustered and then retreated when war actually threatened, and he did so now.

"Wilhelm the Timid's" acceptance of worthless territory in the French Congo deluded all sectors of German society. It contributed to the German government's electoral losses in 1912 and, more ominously, to establishment of a conservative pressure group, the Army League, that took its place alongside the Navy League. Both these organizations aimed to mobilize the nation in favor of imperialism and more armaments. In 1912 the Germans expanded their peacetime army to 544,000 soldiers and, in 1913, to 661,000, forcing less populous France to increase the term of conscription to three years.

The Balkan wars of 1912–13 cast the German and French moves in an ominous light. Impressive Serbian territorial gains increased Austrian fears that the Serbs constituted a powerful pole of attraction for Slavs living in the Dual Monarchy and threatened its existence. On October 18, 1913, after securing a pledge of assistance from the Germans should the Russians intervene, Austria ordered the Serbs to evacuate territory on the Adriatic Sea that they had won during the conflict. The ultimatum carried an eight-day deadline, after which the Austrians would declare war. The Serbs conferred with their Russian allies, who once again counseled Serbia to back down. A disappointed Austrian Chief of Staff, Franz Conrad von Hoetzendorf had wanted war to eliminate the Serbian nuisance, but his German counterpart Moltke told him that "this was only a postponement and not a solution."

German Aims

In 1961, German historian Fritz Fischer published a controversial book citing German war aims as proof that the Germans were responsible for World War I. He argued that by 1914, the Germans were desperate to achieve their goal of

German Chancellor, Theobold Bethmann-Hollweg, shown here at the beginning of World War I in his military uniform, played an important part in the developments leading to the conflict and has been viewed as both a moderate wishing to avoid war and an aggressive leader whose actions during the final crisis favored it.

becoming a world power. However, despite growing German industrial and military power, the British and French succeeded in blocking them. Germany hoped to join Britain and the United States in the rank of world powers by reorganizing Europe according to its Mitteleuropa (Middle Europe) policy. The exact shape that Mitteleuropa would take was under constant discussion among representatives of powerful economic, social, and political groups, but as expressed in 1914 and later, Mitteleuropa meant that Germany would annex vast stretches of European territory and strategic areas and would create a customs union that would unite the entire continent economically. This discussion raged into the opening weeks of World War I when Chancellor Bethmann-Hollweg adopted the September Program, officially accepting Mitteleuropa as a German war aim. The program was stunningly ambitious in its complex whole of annexations, including economic, military, and political details that would have permanently destroyed France and eliminated Russia as a European power. At the same time, the Germans aimed at creating Mittleafrika from French and Belgian colonies, the African counterpart to Mitteleuropa, to guarantee a steady supply of raw materials for German industry.

Although the crises before 1914 were settled at the last minute, Germany's search for a place in the sun meant threatening Britain and destroying French and Russian power. At the same time, the Germans believed that time was running out on them because Russia was modernizing and Austria-Hungary would break up if it did not eliminate Serbia; Austria could not do so without fighting a war with Russia that required German support—and a two-front war.

HISTORY OF A HISTORY: THE CAUSES OF WORLD WAR I

On June 28, 1914, the Bosnian Serb nationalist Gavrilo Princip assassinated Francis Ferdinand, heir to the Austrian throne, and his wife on a visit to the Bosnian capital Sarajevo. The subsequent investigation of the crime revealed a conspiracy by the Black Hand, a Serbian terrorist organization, and the possible involvement of Serbian officials but never demonstrated direct governmental responsibility.

On the surface, the reason for war was the assassination of the archduke and the Austrian desire to eliminate Serbia as a threat. The Austrians obtained German support for a possible Russian reaction and for an ultimatum to Serbia, deliberately framing it so that if the Serbs accepted it, they would lose their sovereignty. On July 23, 1914, the Serbs received an ultimatum and two days to answer it. British Foreign Minister Edward Grey remarked that he had never seen such a "formidable document" sent to an independent state. The ultimatum demanded that the Serbians accept ten points, two of which, points 5 and 6, would have effectively ended Serbian independence. Point 5 would have required the Serbs to accept the collaboration of Austro-Hungarian officials in suppressing "the subversive movement directed against the territorial integrity of the Monarchy." This point was dangerous for Serbian sovereignty, but the Serbs agreed to it consistent with international law. However, they could not accept Point 6, which demanded that "delegates of the Austro-Hungarian Government will take part in the investigation" of the assassinations because acceptance would have severely limited Serbia's sovereignty. When Austria-Hungary declared war, the Russians mobilized, and the Germans implemented the Schlieffen Plan by attacking France through Belgium, which brought Britain into the war.

This explanation would make the outbreak of World War I the result of prewar diplomacy gone haywire, but the victors of World War I charged the Germans with war guilt. The origins of the war took on greater significance because of the German rejection of blame and the role it had in bringing Adolf Hitler to power in 1933. The causes of the World War I are still debated.

The Fay Hypothesis and Its Impact

American historian Sidney B. Fay best represents the school that attributed the outbreak of war to prewar conditions, which provided the tinder for it. His 1928 book *The Origins of the War* minutely examined the diplomacy and actions of the different powers and cataloged errors on the Austrian, British, French, Russian, and Serb sides, as well as the German. Fay cited the conflict's multiple causes—diplomatic entanglements and alliances, the arms race, the irresponsible conduct of newspapers, and surging nationalism. He rejected the notion that Germany deliberately provoked a war and maintained that Germany made belated efforts

Sir Edward Grey, British Foreign Secretary, in 1914. He has been accused of favoring the outbreak of World War I by failing to make clear to Germany that if it started a war Britain would intervene against it.

to avoid the conflict. According to Fay, Germany made a mistake in giving Austria a "blank check" in the form of unconditional support in case of war, a policy that allowed the Austrians to call the shots in the Balkans. Confident in the support of Germany, Austria used the blank check to pull Germany into the conflict in support of its policies. Fay concluded: "[T]he verdict of the Versailles Treaty that Germany and her allies were responsible for the War, in view of the evidence now available, is historically unsound. It should therefore be revised."

Fay's analysis confirmed the German thesis of the war's outbreak and had a major impact on the way in which many observers viewed the war's causes. His interpretation reinforced British misgivings soon after the war's end about how the Germans had been treated and added to the criticisms of the economic clauses of the 1919 Treaty of Versailles already made by British economist John Maynard Keynes. Furthermore, conditioned by balance-of-power ideas, the British suspected the French of wanting to dominate the continent following Germany's defeat; well protected by the English Channel, the British did not share French fears of a German resurgence. Confirmation from non-German historians that the conflict had resulted from general conditions, that Germany had been punished too harshly, and that its objections to the peace settlement were justified encouraged the British to support what they considered legitimate German requests for revision of the Versailles settlement that would normalize international relations, exorcise the specter of a new conflict, and restore the balance of power on the continent. This attitude would later contribute to a policy of appeasement that was a factor in the coming of World War II.

The Fischer Thesis

German historian Fritz Fischer contradicted the idea that the war was a result of ordinary prewar diplomacy in two books that used previously unknown archival material: In *Germany's Aims in the First World War* (1961, English translation 1964) and *War of Illusions: German Policies from 1911 to 1914* (1969), Fischer blamed the war on Germany because its goal of dominating the European continent forced Britain, France, and Russia to defend themselves. In the first book, Fischer concentrated on Germany's vast war aims and on German diplomatic manipulations during the final crisis. Far from Austria pulling Germany into the war, the Germans exploited the Austrians so that they could serve as the catalyst that forced the Russians to mobilize and the Germans to implement the Schlieffen Plan. The vociferous controversy that Fischer's book aroused forced him to write *War of Illusions,* detailing exactly how German policies led to the war.

All the European powers had resentments, contingency war plans, and objectives they wanted to achieve in case of war, but for Fischer, Germany had the strongest motives—the quest for world power and the conviction that it was fighting against time. German society agreed with the country's rulers: *Weltpolitik* required specific territorial and economic gains that could never be achieved peacefully. Reinforcing the appeal of world power, the undemocratic structure of German government made an expansionist policy necessary to divert the attention of the lower classes who were increasingly turning against the ruling class.

Fischer wrote that German officials decided for war in a council held on December 8, 1912. Soon thereafter, the kaiser approved a press campaign to prepare his people for war. Aiding this conditioning was the belief in empire as essential for a nation's economic success and Social Darwinism—proving the natural supremacy of some races over others through war as an element determining the survival of the fittest. This idea permeated European society and intellectuals, expressed it habitually and with great conviction; this attitude helps explain the genocides that occurred before, during, and after World War I. In 1900 the Englishman Karl Pearson admonished his countrymen that they had to prove themselves fit to survive: "The dependence of progress on the survival of the fitter race . . . gives the struggle for existence its redeeming features; it is the fiery crucible out of which comes the finest metal." Despite the lightheartedness regarding war, not all sectors of German society favored it. It was imperative for the German government to gain the Social Democratic Party's (SPD's) support in any conflict because of the party's influence over the masses—and because the SPD considered wars as conflicts between capitalists. German officials plotted to gain SPD support, according to Fischer, by portraying the Russians as repressive Asiatic aggressors against whom the German workers had to defend their hard-earned gains.

Fischer's work had vast implications. If the Germans had provoked the war, their complaints against the war guilt clause had no basis, and they were not absolved of the responsibility for Hitler. Fischer's account imparted a sense of continuity to German foreign policy and even domestic affairs, from before World

War I through the Nazi period, including the idea of racial imperialism. Fischer's work led to a historical debate and criticism of its interpretation of foreign and internal affairs, but it has strongly affected scholarship on the causes of World War I.

COMBAT!

The Germans implemented the Schlieffen Plan on August 6, 1914. The German railway system, developed under military tutelage, ran 550 trains daily to the western front, and 11,000 trains transported 3,120,000 soldiers. The trains of the other combatants did likewise. Historian A. J. P. Taylor labeled it "war by timetable."

Failure of the Schlieffen Plan

Schlieffen had envisioned an irresistible attack on France by the German right wing west through Belgium. In the meantime, the weaker German left wing in Alsace-Lorraine would be a tempting target for the French, who would force it to retreat and bring the French out of their fortresses in hot pursuit. The right wing would smash into France in the north, wheel around Paris, and attack the French army in the rear, out in the open, without the protection of its forts, and caught between the right and left wings. In order to function properly, the right wing had to be made invincible. Schlieffen's dying words were supposed to have been: "Don't weaken the right wing!"

Not surprisingly, the trenches took on the national characteristics of the soldiers who built them. This photo shows French soldiers on the Western front enjoying dinner during a lull in the fighting. Note the tablecloth and the flowers.

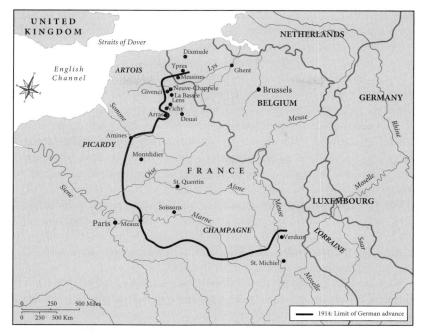

The Schlieffen Plan Misfires. This map shows the limit of the German advance in 1914 and the German inability to score a military breakthrough or to take the French capital.

Schlieffen's successor Moltke and the kaiser balked at the thought of French troops on German soil and strengthened the left wing by adding to it eight of the nine divisions that became available between 1905 and 1914, weakening the right wing. Schlieffen had also accepted the likelihood of a Russian invasion of Germany because the army on the eastern front would be weak, but because the Russian army could not mobilize quickly and could not attack in force, it would quickly be driven out after the expected rapid German victory on the western front. But the kaiser did not want Russian troops on German territory and reinforced the Russian front, again at the expense of the right wing in the West.

The weakened right wing proved unable to complete the task that Schlieffen had assigned to it. Belgian resistance slowed it down, and by the time it smashed into France, the forewarned French stopped it at the Battle of the Marne (September 5–12, 1914). The war of movement that was supposed to win victory in three or four months turned into one of position as both sides dug trenches that allowed them to resist withering enemy fire.

Trench Warfare

Both sides dug deep narrow trenches to present a difficult target for enemy artillery. In wet areas, the trenches had earthen ramparts reinforced by sandbags. In dry terrain, the trenches went deeper, some German trenches as deep as 30 feet. In snow-covered mountain areas, the trenches rose higher in winter and fell lower in the spring and summer as the snow melted. The armies dug several lines of parallel trenches. Two hundred yards or so behind the front line, there would be a support line, with reserve trenches 400 yards behind it, but no consistent pattern because the trenches shifted as armies retreated and advanced. Traverses—kinks designed to minimize artillery hits—periodically broke the straight lines of the trenches. Communication trenches, which allowed interaction among the soldiers, tired troops to go to the rear, and reserves to reach the front, ran at right angles to the main trenches. Saps projected from the main trenches into the "no man's land" between the lines of the different armies. Barbed wire, invented by American ranchers, surrounded the trenches, thinly at first but progressively denser. The trench system resembled a maze in which soldiers easily got lost. In the east the trench system was thinner because of the lower ratio of troops to space, and communication lines were frequently above ground.

The casualties were enormous, and the fighting cost Europe an entire generation of men. The war did not spare artists and scientists who could have given much to the world, including the poet Wilfred Owen, killed on the western front a week before the war ended, and Henry Mosely, an eminent physicist who died during a British offensive against Turkey in 1915.

Wartime propaganda portrayed the trenches almost as resort hotels, but reality differed. British troops rose at 4:30 A.M. and got ready to meet a possible dawn attack. If no attack came, they prepared breakfast, cleaned their weapons, made repairs, got shelled by enemy artillery, tried in vain to get the lice off themselves, brought up supplies, answered questions posed by bureaucrats, wrote letters, or slept. At night the men worked outside the trenches under enemy fire, conducted patrols, and launched raids.

Historian Paul Fussell described the trenches' national styles: "cynical" for the French, "amateur" for the British, and "clean, pedantic" for the Germans.

The machine gun drastically changed the nature of war, forcing troops to dig trenches for protection. Usually soldiers had to be fortified with alcohol to induce them to "go over the top" toward an almost certain death. This photograph graphically portrays why soldiers were so reluctant to leave the trenches during World War I.

This photo illustrates the horror of World War I. In the so-called "No Man's Land" between enemy trenches it was too dangerous to recover the remains of fallen soldiers. Their bodies eventually decayed and their skeletons remained fully clothed, to the point that it was possible to identify when they were killed by the changes that had taken place in the design of the uniforms since their deaths. The photograph shows dead French soldiers in one of the many No Man's Lands that characterized all the fronts of World War I.

The terrain determined the nature of the trenches. In the West, the Germans were frequently fortunate enough to occupy dry, high land. The British, engaged in a wet, rainy sector, waded in water up to their waists—one soldier remarking that the navy would come to their aid. Lice infested all the troops, and all attempts to get rid of them failed miserably. Rats rummaged everywhere, growing fat on the food the men ate and on their dead bodies. They became increasingly bold, attacking the men while they slept but were a source of amusement: soldiers dipped them into gasoline, set them afire and threw them over no man's land; enemy soldiers, believing an attack had begun, would fire on the suffering and wriggling animals.

BIOGRAPHICAL SKETCHES

Henry Gwyn Jeffreys Moseley
Casualty of War

Henry Moseley's story gives a taste of the tragedy and losses for humanity caused by World War I. Born on November 23, 1887, at Weymouth, England, Moseley grew up in a household with two scientists as parents. He received his secondary education at Eton, Britain's elite private school, and then attended Trinity College, Oxford, in 1906. He graduated in 1910 with a degree in the natural sciences.

From Oxford, Moseley went to the University of Manchester, where he collaborated with Britain's premier physicist Ernest Rutherford. In 1912 he left teaching for full-time research, and in 1913, using X-rays, he noted that there was no relation between the atomic weight of atoms and the wavelengths of the elements, but that there was one with the atomic number.

continued

continued

Moseley had made a fundamental discovery. Scientists had believed that the position of elements on the periodic table describing their chemical characteristics depended on their atomic weights, not their atomic number (the number of protons in the nucleus of an atom). This error had made it difficult to explain certain inconsistencies in the periodic table, but Moseley's work clarified them, predicted the position on the periodic table of yet-to-be identified elements, and enabled chemists to analyze the composition of materials in hours instead of years. Besides chemistry, Moseley's work had important implications for physics because his discovery had a close relationship to Niels Bohr's model of the atom, also elaborated in 1913. Moseley's research demonstrated that there could be no element lighter than hydrogen and that no element could exist between hydrogen (atomic number = 1) and helium (atomic number = 2). Scientists had postulated both possibilities.

In 1914 Moseley returned to Oxford, but World War I intervened, and he volunteered to join the Royal Engineers. Despite the efforts of Rutherford and other prominent scientists to protect him from danger, he insisted on doing combat duty. He participated in Winston Churchill's ill-fated operation at Gallipoli against the Turks and, on August 10, 1915, a sniper's bullet killed the young man who will always be remembered as the person who "numbered the elements."

Scientists agree that Moseley could have advanced the cause of science much more had he not become a casualty of war at age 27. His death contributed to the decision of the British government to exempt scientists from combat duty in World War II.

The troops feared "no man's land," a relatively narrow, deadly, area 200 to 300 yards wide on the western front, but sometimes only 25 yards. On the eastern front, the width of no man's land might be 3,000 to 4,000 yards. Because fire from the opposing army prevented the men from rescuing their wounded comrades, they died a horrible death from their wounds and lack of water. The best gift a friend could give comrades in that situation was a bullet in the head. Successive waves of offensives left thousands of dead bodies in no man's land to putrefy and turn into skeletons.

Under the circumstances, the men drank the hard liquor all armies generously provided. They would not normally go out of the trenches without being fortified with rum or cognac because it meant almost certain death. Soldiers could usually tell if an enemy offensive was imminent because the smell of alcohol on the breaths of enemy soldiers reached them or if they received an increased supply of alcohol when their side was planning an attack. A British soldier testified that rum won the war.

German Successes in the East

In the West neither side made much headway for four years, but the story was different in the East. Given the German engagement in the West, on the eastern front Austrians and Russians fought the big initial campaigns. The Austrians made headway in late August and early September but were pushed back by the Russians whose war industry overcame the early shortages of materiel.

The Russians invaded Germany, but the Germans, under generals Erich von Ludendorff, Paul von Hindenburg, and August von Mackensen, struck back, defeating the Russians in the battles of Tannenberg and of the Masurian Lakes. The Germans and Austrians linked up, but, given German involvement on two fronts, they were unable to knock the Russians out of the war.

A Widening War

The war widened considerably with Turkey's entrance in October and November 1914. The Germans had wielded considerable influence in the Ottoman Empire, reorganizing the Turkish army and building important projects, and the Turkish-Russian rivalry reasserted itself with the outbreak of war. When reflagged German ships fired on Russian cities, the Russians declared war, followed by Britain and France. The Turks attacked in the Caucasus but made little headway. In April 1915, alleging that the Armenians living in the empire helped the Russians, Ottoman authorities began roundups and deportations, accompanied by massacres, quickly leading to genocide.

European Stalemate. When World War I broke out the Schlieffen Plan proved unable to resolve Germany's two-front dilemma. The shaded areas show the extent of the different armies at different dates. Even after Germany defeated Russia, it did not obtain a breakthrough on the Western Front.

The war spread to North Africa when the Turks attacked Egypt. The campaign failed, but the Turks pinned down many British troops, preventing them from intervening on the western front. The British, Russians, and Turks also clashed in Asia, where their empires or spheres of influence bordered each other. In sub-Saharan Africa, the outmanned Germans lost most of their possessions to British, French, and South African attacks, but in some cases were still in the field when the war ended. The Germans lost their Pacific Ocean possessions to the Japanese, who entered the conflict on August 23, 1914.

Despite the conviction of Allied commanders that victory would come on the western front, the war there remained hopelessly stalemated in 1915, despite a series of great offensives that gained insignificant amounts of territory at the cost of hundreds of thousands of casualties. These failures led the Allies to consider other options. Some British planners, especially Winston Churchill, championed a strike against Turkey. Despite the objections of Sir John French and Joseph Joffre, British and French commanders on the western front, a force that included Australian troops sailed for the Dardanelles with the objective of taking the Turkish capital of Constantinople. Tenacious Turkish resistance defeated the attempt despite heroic fighting by the Australians at Gallipoli. Churchill resigned and did not reemerge as an influential leader until World War II.

The most important event of 1915 was Italian intervention. Italy had long regarded the change in the defensive nature of the Triple Alliance with alarm and had warned its allies several times that it would not follow them into an aggressive war. After the Austrian ultimatum to Serbia led to war, the Italians declared their neutrality and, under the terms of the alliance, requested compensation from the Austrians for the changes they had made in the Balkans. They hoped to gain the Italian-speaking area of Austria, the Irredenta, in return for their continued neutrality, but the Austrians refused until it was too late. The Entente, anxious to secure Italian intervention hoping that it might tip the scales in their favor, offered the Italians the Irredenta and other gains in case of victory. On April 26, 1915, Italian foreign minister Sidney Sonnino negotiated the Pact of London, which called for Italian entrance into the war within three months, and Italy declared war on Austria-Hungary on May 23, 1915, citing the Irredenta as the reason.

Italy's weight was not decisive, but it was influential because it opened up a major new front and tied down hundreds of thousands of enemy troops. The Italian front was the most difficult of the war—it was mountainous and stony, and the Austrians occupied all the mountain crests. The Italian war effort quickly bogged down as had the one on the Western front, and, like their allies, the Italians made little headway despite enormous casualties.

The Bleeding of Armies

Both the Allied and German commanders hoped to reach a decision on the western front in 1916, which instead was noted for its great battles, horrific human losses, and military futility. German General Erich von Falkenhayn opened the Battle of Verdun on February 21, hoping to achieve a breakthrough by bleeding the French dry. He chose a small area of the front and attacked it in a battle that holds the record for length because it ended only on December 15. Verdun cost

The Battle of Verdun was one of the bloodiest of the war. This pile of the bones of dead soldiers gives a graphic idea of the battle's ghastly cost.

both sides 700,000 casualties for no substantial gains. "It was France's supreme sacrifice and her supreme triumph, and to the splendor of her achievement all the world paid homage." French losses, however, drastically reduced the country's ability to contribute to a great offensive led by the new British commander, Sir Douglas Haig. The Battle of the Somme lasted from July to November 1916 and witnessed the first appearance of tanks, but it accomplished little beyond a million casualties on both sides. The Russians also launched an offensive that achieved few strategic results.

In the Balkans the Austrians had been unable to defeat the Serbs, and both camps maneuvered to secure the intervention of other Balkan states on their side. In 1914 the Russians had promised the Romanians large gains in Transylvania, and the death of their pro-German King Charles on October 14, combined with a massive Russian offensive that began in June 1916, convinced the Romanians to enter the conflict on the Allied side on August 27. The Allies had hoped to entice Bulgaria to intervene on their side with the assurance of important gains, but the Central Powers outbid them because Bulgaria's geographic position threatened Serbia. On September 6, 1915, Bulgaria signed an alliance with Germany and Austria and attacked Serbia, which fell under the control of the Central Powers. The Russian failure in the June 1916 campaign allowed the Central Powers to defeat Romania, most of which the Central Powers occupied by January 1917. This victory allowed them to take control of Romanian wheat and oil reserves that they desperately needed for their war effort. The Greeks also bargained with the Entente, but could not decide whether to intervene until the Allies forced the abdication of King Constantine and Venizelos brought his country into the war on June 26, 1917.

With Serbia and Romania controlled by the Central Powers, 1917 began on a bleak note for the Entente and worsened as it progressed. On the western front, the siege-battles continued throughout the year with huge losses and scant results. The continuous slaughter caused mutinies to break out between May and June in the French army affecting sixteen corps as soldiers refused to leave the trenches to fight the enemy. "If the Germans had a better information service, and had attacked at that moment, they would have inflicted upon the French army a defeat which would perhaps have been irreparable." Strikes also broke out in the country protesting war profiteering and high prices. The French named a new commander, Philippe Pétain, who had to implement army reforms and renounce offenses for a year.

In the East and the South, the situation was worse. War weariness and defeat brought about a revolution in Russia in March 1917, after which Tsar Nicholas II abdicated. Russia became a republic, and the country's new rulers vowed to remain in the war. They unleashed a new offensive that failed. The failure turned into a collapse when the Bolshevik Revolution took place in November 1917, the Russian army dissolved, and the Russians agreed to an armistice on December 15. On March 3, 1918, the Bolsheviks signed the Treaty of Brest-Litovsk and handed over large stretches of territory in Eastern Europe to German control. The Germans reorganized the territory, which included Russia's most productive areas, under their direct or indirect rule. The most important result of the Russian defection was that a large number of German troops were freed up for use on the western front.

The Germans also responded to the pleas of their Austrian allies to knock Italy out of the war. Repeated Italian offensives had failed to gain much territory but had brought Austria to the brink of collapse, and the Austrians doubted they could resist the next one. A powerful German force caught the Italians by surprise at Caporetto and broke through. For a period, the Italian retreat took on the aspects of a rout, but the Italians halted the attack on the Piave River and began a steady recovery. The Italian commander General Luigi Cadorna blamed the defeat on subversive Socialist propaganda, but the real reasons were war weariness, surprise, and his own harsh disciplinary measures, and he was replaced. The most important result of the German intervention, however, was its failure to knock Italy out of the conflict.

Weapons and Tactics

The industrialization of war accounted for the appalling slaughter of World War I and the failure of either side to break the military deadlock. Before World War I, most commentators believed that it would be impossible for society to support a long modern war because of the enormous costs in men and materiel.

Instead the belligerents replaced the incredible amount of war material swallowed up by the conflict, railroads delivered the material and troops to the front, the troops endured much more punishment than ever considered possible, and medical services proved adequate. The tremendous capability of modern industry may be illustrated by one statistic: during a German offensive on May 27, 1918, 6,000 guns fired 2 million artillery rounds in about four hours.

In addition, few understood the impact of new weapons. In the decade before 1914, the French developed an accurate, rapid-fire 75mm field gun that set the artillery standard for other European armies. Magazine rifles came into general use. Above all, the previously unwieldy machine gun was streamlined and became easy to manage, prompting European armies to equip their forces with it between 1905 and 1908, even though they did not know exactly how to utilize it. The Russo-Japanese War of 1904 to 1905 should have taught the Europeans the machine gun's potential. For example, French military observers reported:

> The [Russo-Japanese] war has shown the incontestable value of machine guns. . . . It was above all in the defensive that these weapons displayed their terrible effectiveness, particularly at the point when, with the two adversaries being a few hundred meters from each other, the men become nervous and aim too high, although their fire could be more effective if it were properly adjusted. In these circumstances machine guns, soulless devices without nerves, literally mow down the attackers.

But the military planners drew the wrong conclusions. They downplayed the enormous casualties caused by machine guns and commented that Japanese bayonet charges carried the day in spite of heavy losses. Despite their observations regarding the power of the defense, military observers concluded "that the Japanese performance had proved, up to the hilt, the moral and military superiority of *the offensive.*" European generals later sent millions of their soldiers to their death in futile offensives because they admired bayonet attacks, which, they thought, proved the moral superiority of the society whose soldiers employed bayonets and because these attacks coincided with their philosophical precepts. European military academies emphasized Bergson's élan vital, which they interpreted to mean that moral strength counted more than material conditions. The offensive embodied this concept. Instead, the machine gun tragically proved the military superiority of the material to the moral during World War I.

Besides the adoption of the machine gun, several other important changes occurred in European armies in the early years of the new century. Military experts realized that bright colors made good targets and recommended neutral colors for their uniforms, except for the French, to their regret. Powerful field glasses extended an army's vision. In theory the telephone should have enabled commanders to communicate more effectively with their troops, but in practice huge batteries were needed, and the wires were frequently cut. Mass battles and the inability to communicate except through runners contributed to the high casualty rate. Trucks made armies more mobile and allowed supplies to be brought right to the theater of operations that railroads could not reach.

The internal combustion engines also revolutionized aviation. Balloons had been flying since the eighteenth century, but in the twentieth century, the new

Military planners missed the significance that the machine gun would play in future wars. Here is a picture of British machine gunners wearing gas masks in action at the Battle of the Somme in 1916. It is estimated that 60,000 soldiers were lost on the first day of that July offensive.

The airplane played a romantic role during World War I in which the pilots were essentially transformed into the knights on horseback of old. However, the new weapon was not decisive. Here is American Ace Eddie Rickenbacker riding his trusty steed, an airplane.

engine made possible different types of dirigibles that were useful for warfare, pioneered by the French. In 1907 Prime Minister Georges Clemenceau and his war minister generated enormous enthusiasm for the new airship when they flew in a balloon. Germany trailed France but pulled ahead, thanks to the efforts of Count Ferdinand von Zeppelin, who pioneered a rigid design. From the military viewpoint, however, airships had major disadvantages: they were very expensive, needed complex ground support to take off and land, could easily be blown off course in adverse weather, were slow, made wonderful targets, and frequently exploded because they used hydrogen gas. The dirigible's disadvantages and the development of reliable engines made airplanes more attractive. Once again, the French led the way. In 1909 Louis Blériot's flight across the English channel and a weeklong air show at Rheims drove public enthusiasm for the airplane to fever pitch, the German emperor endorsed them, and the Italian pacifist Socialist leader Claudio Treves became an enthusiastic supporter of air power after he was taken up in a plane.

In World War I the airplane demonstrated its great potential for reconnaissance, but the difficulty of flying the machine severely limited the pilot's capability in this area. The pilot had to take along an observer to examine what was happening below and then had an arduous time communicating with the ground regarding the observations. Dogfights developed early but were also limited by the risk of pilots shooting off their own propellers. When the Germans invented a synchronized machine gun that fired through the propeller, they gained temporary control of the skies until the Allies got hold of a downed plane and copied the invention. Thereafter, air battles captured peoples' imaginations, but despite the visibility of air aces, such as Manfred von Richthofen—the "Red Baron," with eighty kills—the airplane did not alter the fortunes of war between 1914 and 1918.

Three weapons potentially had the ability to end the military stalemate, but the combatants used them prematurely. Properly used, poison gas might have changed the course of the war. First employed by the Germans at the Second Battle of Ypres (April–May 1915), the surprise use of poison gas opened up a large hole in the Allied lines as the troops holding the sector were incapacitated or fled. The Germans could have poured their forces through this gap, but the troops concluded it was a trick and stopped. From then on, both sides used poison gas, but both had more- or less effective gas masks. The tank met the same fate. Championed by Winston Churchill, this supersecret British weapon had the capacity to crash through enemy lines, but the British utilized it in insufficient numbers at the Battle of the Somme. Instead of being employed at night, making it more difficult for artillery to see them, and in large numbers, only forty-nine tanks saw action the first time they appeared, on September 16, 1916. Nine broke down, German artillery hit ten, and five did not advance. "My poor 'land battleships,'" lamented Winston Churchill; "they have been let off prematurely and on a petty scale." The Germans played the submarine card. The submarine had the potential of starving the British Isles and preventing fresh supplies and troops from reaching Allied lines in France, but its employment raised moral issues. Because submarines were considered sneaky, international law obliged them to surface before sinking merchant ships, announce themselves, and let the crew off safely. The British took advantage of the law to arm their merchantmen and blow the German submarines out of the water when they surfaced. As a result, submarines abandoned the rules, but then they encountered moral condemnation. When the Germans sank the *Lusitania* in 1915 with the loss of 1,198 civilians, including 139 Americans, the United States threatened war if the Germans did not desist. Unwilling to draw in such a powerful enemy, the Germans complied. In desperate straits by 1917, however, they reinstituted unrestricted submarine warfare and provoked American intervention. The Germans calculated that the Americans could not send enough soldiers to Europe to make a difference in the war, but thanks primarily to the convoy system, not a single American soldier who came over to fight the war was lost to the German submarine.

Political Changes

Even though the British believed that they could carry on business as usual, the belligerents had to organize their societies around the war effort. This made World War I the first total war and had an impact on all areas of civilian life.

In the Allied countries, politics changed. The political conflicts that marked prewar societies could no longer be tolerated in public, although antagonism continued behind the scenes. Politically, this harmony found expression in coalition governments, the enormous strengthening of the executive power, and the emergence of powerful personalities. France established the "sacred union" coalition, and in November 1917, Georges Clemenceau formed a strong cabinet in response to the army mutinies and political divisions that led France to victory and lasted until 1920. In England, the Asquith government created a coalition in May 1915. As in France, an inner cabinet group supervised military operations, and the government tightened its control over the production of munitions. The British had attempted to meet the war's manpower demands through a volunteer army that raised a million soldiers. By the end of 1915, volunteers no longer sufficed, and in January 1916, Parliament instituted conscription. In April, the British reacted harshly to the German-supported Easter Rebellion in Ireland by executing the rebellious leaders, but the shock and the mounting crisis produced a war cabinet headed by the energetic Lloyd George. In Italy on June 16, 1916, the nondescript Paolo Boselli headed a cabinet that replaced the existing government that had gotten Italy into the war. The trauma of the Caporetto defeat produced a new, more effective coalition cabinet headed by Vittorio Emanuele Orlando on October 25, 1917, to guide the country successfully through the last year of war. In all three countries, the military was a concern, but the governments kept it under control.

In the authoritarian countries, the monarchs made changes but refused to give their populations a greater political voice, which might have helped the war effort. In Germany, by 1917, the army effectively ran the country in the persons of generals Hindenburg and Ludendorff. Even though insistent demands for political reforms divided the country, the kaiser promised only abolition of the three-class voting system in Prussia. In Austria-Hungary the imperial government made no substantial concessions to the empire's different nationalities. The new emperor, Charles, who succeeded Francis Joseph after his death on November 21, 1916, issued a manifesto transforming the state into a federation of nationalities on October 16, 1918, but it was too late. The other autocratic state, Russia, stubbornly refused to concede significant reforms, which, along with its military failure, led to two revolutions in 1917.

THE HOME FRONTS

When hostilities first broke out, World War I enjoyed an enormous amount of popular support. Socialist ideology vociferously opposed war, but with the exception of the Russians and the Italians, the major European parties voted for funds to support the war. Parties, unions, and workers put their demands on the back burner for the war's duration even though past grievances were not resolved and new ones surfaced because of the economic strains.

Governmental relationships with industrialists were different as the combatants abandoned the gold standard, suspended gold payments, and ended the convertibility of currencies. The involution of trade and the difficulties producing armaments and supplies forced the belligerents to restructure their economies and confront the labor shortages that resulted from the great expansion of armies and the high number of casualties. All the warring countries imposed controls on wages, prices, raw materials, and freedom of movement.

Industrial Reorganization and the Civilian Population in Germany

In Germany the Prussian war ministry controlled the raw materials necessary for the manufacture of arms, and private industry produced them at enormous profits. By August 1916, the demand for war materiel became critical, and the army proposed the Hindenburg Program calling for compulsory labor service for the entire population, including women, and the utilization of all men ages fifteen to sixty in the armed forces or in arms manufacturing. All suitable factories were to be converted to war production, and, in a reversal of previous policy, enterprises that could not be so transformed were to be closed.

The dire need for workers would have drastically restricted freedom of movement for workers before it was modified, but the Germans still faced labor shortages. The Germans hoped to end the labor shortages by recruiting Polish and Belgian workers who had been left unemployed by the German occupation of their countries. When the Belgians, in particular, did not respond, in October 1916 German soldiers began rounding up Belgian workers for deportation to Germany, transporting them under harsh conditions and herding them into concentration camps until they could be distributed to industries. It was difficult for the Germans to force them to work, however, and protests by neutral countries ended the program in February 1917.

Unions initially supported their governments by renouncing wage increases, but because of excessive profits and inflation, real wages plunged. In Germany, cooperation between unions and employers' associations ended as the war dragged on and real wages declined sharply because of the inflation caused by steep increases in governmental expenditures. The Allied naval blockade created shortages of basic commodities, along with a decline in quality. Luxuries disappeared, and the supply of butter, potatoes, and vegetables dwindled. The consumption of eggs and fish declined by half, and coffee disappeared. The civilian population was malnourished, and their homes were poorly heated. These conditions increased mortality rates, with that of German women increasing in 1917 by 30 percent over the prewar period. The black market flourished, making a mockery of governmental statistics. Officially, the cost of living rose 200 percent in Germany, but black market prices for important commodities increased from 300 to 700 percent, while average wages for men went from 4.84 marks daily in March 1914 to 10.26 in September 1918, when a pound of butter on the black market cost 24 marks. Women fared even worse, their average daily wage rising only from 2.27 to 5.41 marks.

By 1917 sporadic protest strikes became extensive and turned into political instead of economic actions that involved the armed forces as the navy mutinied. In April 1917 the Independent Social Democrats split from the official Socialist party and demanded peace without annexations. In July, the Reichstag passed a resolution favoring such a peace. In September, however, the Supreme Army Command and leaders of heavy industry demonstrated that a large part of the German people still favored the war effort by founding the Patriotic Party, but these events illustrated the country's deep divisions.

Class Divisions in Britain

In Britain the prewar class divisions remained, but a grave crisis did not develop during the conflict because of the ability of the ruling class to compromise. The government met workers' demands more successfully than in Germany, and most labor leaders collaborated with it. The major labor problem was "dilution"—the employers' policy of replacing skilled workers who had gone to the front with unskilled labor. In February 1915, dilution and rapidly rising prices provoked a severe wildcat strike in the Clyde River valley, an important industrial complex producing iron, steel, and chemicals. The government settled the strike by imposing compulsory arbitration and pledging to limit employers' profits. The Munitions War Act gave the government wide latitude to restrict workers' freedom of movement, but it usually gave in to wage demands, and the unions temporarily obtained the right to define a skilled worker. In January 1916 the government instituted the conscription of single men. In order to meet the resulting shortage of skilled workers, the government determined who would be conscripted, and in April 1917, the unions could no longer define who was skilled.

The labor issue was just one aspect of the British government's escalating ability to control British life. As a result of a national debate on the quality and quantity of British arms, the government instituted controls over the armaments industry through the munitions ministry, originally under the energetic Lloyd George. When unrestricted submarine warfare begun by the Germans in 1917 threatened the food supply, the government instituted price-fixing to check rapidly rising prices and rationing to control distribution. By then, rationing had become a fixture of all belligerents.

In Britain and all belligerent countries, wages did not keep up with rising prices. The wages of skilled workers rose to a lesser degree than did those of unskilled workmen—less than 100 percent as compared to 100 percent to 125 percent between July 1914 and July 1918. Women, who moved in large numbers into traditionally male jobs such as armaments production, saw their wages rise in comparison by an average of 150 percent, but their wages did not reach parity with those of men.

Social Resentment

The conflict exacerbated the social struggle among the classes, to various degrees, in all the countries that participated in it. The frontline soldiers resented anyone who was exempted from military service or was stationed in the rear. Exemptions for essential skilled workers antagonized the unskilled workers. The peasants and urban workers, who were disproportionately represented in the armies and in the casualty lists, were especially resentful. The enormous losses—10 million dead soldiers, 20 million wounded—brought postwar bitterness between people who had fought in the trenches and those who had not, considered by the soldiers as deserters and war profiteers.

The rancor was not only in one direction. The peasants ate better than did the urban dwellers, who could not escape rationing, and withheld food in order to drive up prices. In the cities, declining real wages increased strife between the workers and capitalists, who profited inordinately from the war. The Liberals, who had formerly accepted badly distributed wealth in the belief that capitalism created enough riches for all and who looked forward to their more equitable distribution, watched the war eat up their countries' treasure and the police repress civil rights in the name of unity. After the conflict, many of them would turn to communism, which blamed the war on the capitalists.

The war's insatiable appetite for weapons, ammunition, artillery shells, trucks, airplanes, and ships set off what amounted to a new industrial revolution in both the established and emerging industrial powers. The engineering industry in Russia quadrupled between 1914 and 1916, and the production of chemicals doubled. This expansion enabled Russian industry to increase its production of shells by 2,000 percent, rifles by 1,100 percent, and artillery by 1,000 percent, but in all countries, the expansion set the stage for a postwar economic crisis and labor disorder when it came time to convert wartime industry to peacetime uses.

Women at War

Unprecedented industrial growth created a great demand for new labor, partially supplied by the entrance of more women into the labor market. Many women moved from domestic or other work activity to war-related work, where the proportion of women rose in various degrees in the combatant countries. The number of women in the British workforce increased approximately 1.5 million between 1914 and 1918. The number of French women employed in the metals industry went from about 17,700 in 1914 to 104,600 in mid-1916, and the

During World War I, women moved into jobs held by the men fighting on the front. This happened not only in the armaments industry but in other occupations as well. Of course the prejudices against women persisted. This illustration shows a woman taxi driver who has crashed and demolished five lampposts and was consequently given the nickname of "The Tank."

proportion of women working in the industrial labor force increased from 29.8 percent in 1914 to 37.1 percent in 1917. Despite this increase, social attitudes against women working in all the belligerent countries changed little. The Germans and Austrians preferred to use prisoners of war and foreign workers to meet the increased demand for labor. In countries, such as Italy and France, whose economies had large agricultural components, fewer women went into industry, but with their husbands away, women took over on the land and became heads of households, which altered traditional mentalities.

In most countries, the entrance of more women into the labor force decreased the differential between wages earned by women and men, but equal pay for women remained elusive. The female presence in labor unions and in strikes for higher pay and better working conditions increased. Many women considered work a temporary expedient and left their jobs after the war. Others resisted returning to less desirable activities and hoped to continue their jobs, but following the war, society was less welcoming and interpreted the desire of women who wanted to remain in the labor force as selfishness because they took jobs away from returning veterans.

After the conflict, most countries considered marriage a bar to working, with the British excluding married women from receiving benefits in 1922. Such measures effectively forced women to stop working once they married.

Besides joining the war effort by serving in the workforce, women contributed in other ways. In general, the belligerents expected women to act in traditional ways: help in recruiting, staying home to keep the birth rate up, encouraging the men to fight. The armies considered women valuable as nurses, cooks, drivers, and clerks. The British organized the Women's Army Auxiliary Corps (WAAC), which numbered 41,000 in 1918, many of whom served in France as cooks, and the navy and in the air force similarly utilized them. In Germany and Austria-Hungary, women had comparable roles.

Except for a Russian combat battalion in 1917 and for some Polish women fighting in the Austro-Hungarian army, women did not generally engage in combat. The sight of women in uniform (as in the WAAC), even in noncombat roles, aroused hostility. In part, this reaction was due to women freeing up men who served in noncombat positions for combat roles, partly because of class distinctions, and partly because of the perception that women were appropriating the role of men. Women in uniform were particularly susceptible to charges of immorality. The increased illegitimacy rate (from 9 percent to 14 percent in France from 1914 to 1918 and from 10 percent to 13 percent in Germany), as well as increased allegations of adultery as a cause for divorce, reinforced this perception.

Interpretations of the effect of World War I on gender relations differ—from an increasing division because men fought and women did not, to increasing solidarity as women served as nurses and in other auxiliary positions. In either case, the war did not alter the traditional perception of women's role in European society.

State and Society

Total wars, of the kind World War I was the first, demand that the entire society participate in the drive to outproduce and defeat the enemy. This necessity leads to the tremendous growth of state power because governments control and coordinate the economies and society itself.

Governments in the states at war passed emergency legislation that gave them sweeping emergency powers. Parliamentary elections were postponed, and, in practice, legislatures surrendered their right to criticize the government or to act as a check on it, although representative institutions in the democratic countries showed life when war-related crises occurred. Governments set goals for the production of war materiel, allocating resources, and regulating labor through many newly created ministries, commissions, and agencies and controlled the railways, the major means of transportation. They regulated wages and prices, provided welfare, and organized food supplies.

The combatants accepted censorship, once intolerable, as normal. Governmental propaganda urged the people to work hard and to support the governments and their allies. They utilized posters, the press, and the movies—but also parlor games, jigsaw puzzles, and toy soldiers. They published official books to reinforce their viewpoints (which took their name from the colors of their covers). Italian poet Gabriele D'Annunzio dropped propaganda leaflets from the sky for the first time. The belligerents used truths and half-truths to whip up the feelings of their people; some of the stories about German atrocities in Belgium were true, but others were not. Allied propaganda proved more effective than that of the Central Powers, as the campaign against German submarine warfare and attacks on people of German descent in various countries demonstrated. Churches generally supported their governments, as did the Catholic and Protestant churches in Germany. The German Protestants emphasized a war against Catholic France and Orthodox Russia. German Jews were attacked for purported war profiteering and draft dodging. Italian and French Catholics supported the war effort despite Pope Benedict XV's call for peace in January 1915.

The greatly expanded role of government during World War I created enormous difficulties in the postwar period, despite the attempt of some governments to reduce their presence in society, touching off the conflict over governmental interference that characterized twentieth-century Europe.

War and Science

Science benefitted from governmental support. The Germans organized the Raw Materials Section and other entities after September 1914. They hoped to develop substitutes for substances that were needed by the army but were denied them by the Allied blockade. Fritz Haber, the first person to synthesize ammonia from its elements, allowed the Germans to continue their war effort after the blockade cut off this compound necessary for explosives and worked on developing poison gas. Ironically, Haber, a Jew who won the 1918 Nobel Prize for chemistry, resigned his position as director of the Berlin-Dahlem Institute for Physical and Electrochemistry in 1933, following Hitler's anti-Semitic legislation and, heartbroken, left Germany. In Britain, the Zionist Chaim Weizmann made a great contribution to the British war effort with a new process for producing acetone, necessary for munitions, and was a factor in the Balfour Declaration of 1917 that envisioned Palestine as a possible Jewish homeland.

Considerable progress also occurred in medicine. The trenches made soldiers more susceptible to disease, including gangrene, tetanus, and trench fever (caused by lice excrement dug into the skin because of scratching), which the development of new antiseptic preparations and anesthetics helped. The Austrians discovered an early diagnostic procedure for typhus, a chronic disease of soldiers at war. The French perfected a vaccine against typhoid fever, and the British developed one against dysentery. Blood transfusions became normal during the war, and, because of this and other advances, soldiers were much more likely to survive their wounds than in previous wars.

These improvements contrasted with the little that scientists could do against a deadly disease aided by the conflict: Spanish influenza. Although not caused by the war, influenza may have been fostered by the overcrowded conditions in military camps and by the transfer of soldiers to all parts of the world. By 1918 influenza had developed into a pandemic that killed 21 million people, and estimates run as high as 100 million.

THE WAR ENDS

The Germans had attempted to use their submarine weapon effectively in 1915, but the threat of American intervention had dissuaded them. Discussions on reactivating the submarine campaign continued among German planners only because of the deadlock on land and the stalemate at sea, illustrated by the inconclusive Battle of Jutland (May 31–June 1, 1916). The military standoff and British implementation of a successful blockade of Germany led to a change in strategy.

American Intervention

By the end of 1916, the Germans calculated that they could win the war in five months if they instituted unrestricted submarine warfare by designating a zone in which any ship could be sunk without warning and by destroying 600,000 tons of Allied shipping a month. The campaign would prevent food and war material from being shipped to England and prevent the landing of an American Expeditionary Force in France should the United States make good its threat to enter the war because of the submarine campaign. In fact, the Germans exceeded their target but still failed to achieve their objective. A greatly increased British shipbuilding program made good and even exceeded the losses, and the new convoy system reduced the initially high damages to less than 1 percent. The development of depth charges and the use of airplanes against submarines also contained the submarine threat. The United States intervened with its enormous resources on April 6, 1917, making American shipbuilding capacity available to the British and a great number of new troops available for fighting.

Germany's inability to stop American troops and supplies from reaching Europe spelled defeat for the Central Powers. Although the war was generally expected to last into 1919, Germany's allies began to collapse in the fall of 1918. The Bulgarian and Turkish fronts collapsed. The Italians routed the Austrians at Vittorio Veneto, and, on November 4, the war in the South ended with an armistice. The Austro-Hungarian army dissolved, and with it, the empire. Emperor Charles abdicated, Austria and Hungary proclaimed themselves separate republics, and the different nationalities became independent or joined other countries.

On the western front, powerful German offensives in the spring and summer of 1918 failed. Large-scale Allied assaults followed (the Battles of the Argonne and Ypres). Ludendorff insisted that the government begin armistice negotiations as hopelessness triumphed among his troops and as war weariness and the bleak military situation paralyzed Germany. On November 3 naval crews mutinied at Kiel, and the disorders spread rapidly. Revolution broke out in Munich on November 7 and 8. On November 9, Wilhelm II abdicated and fled to Holland, while the Socialists announced the establishment of a German republic and requested an armistice. The fighting was over.

Strategic and Cultural Issues

American intervention and emergence from isolation had worldwide significance. Before 1914, Europe had dominated the world, but the military stalemate demonstrated that the Europeans could not settle their own affairs and had to depend on an outside force to do so.

BIOGRAPHICAL SKETCHES

Erich Maria Remarque
"But now, for the first time, people learned what it was really like"

The author of the most famous antimilitarist war novel *All Quiet on the Western Front* was born Erich Remark on June 22, 1898, in Lower Saxony, Germany, but reclaimed the French spelling of his name used by his ancestors. Because he was the child of an artisan family, the school system barred him from taking humanities courses, but he read widely. He joined with several other youths who were taken with art and literature in a club they called the Dream Circle, where he encountered an older poet and painter who became his mentor.

On November 21, 1916, the army drafted Remarque. At the front he carried a comrade wounded by shrapnel to safety, a soldier transformed into a character in *All Quiet*. A long-range British artillery shell severely wounded him behind the lines, and he became a pacifist during an extended hospital stay. The conflict over, Remarque worked for a magazine as the publicity director and editor, moved on to sports journalism, and wrote novels. He traveled widely and became addicted to hard drinking and beautiful women even after he married. On January 31, 1929, his third novel appeared: *All Quiet on the Western Front.*

According to Remarque, he wrote the novel during a six-week period at night after he returned home from the office. Unsatisfied with the work, he did not submit it for six months, and then the publisher turned it down because no one would be interested in a war novel ten years after the war. A new publisher agreed to bring it out, first serializing it as the biographical work of a nonprofessional writer. The novel confounded the publishing world, selling 1.5 million copies in its first German edition, going through numerous editions worldwide, and making its author rich.

Observers have maintained that despite his claim to have written the work in a hurry, Remarque planned *All Quiet on the Western Front* for years, perhaps while he lay wounded in the hospital. Since he saw little action, he asked friends to describe their wartime experiences and used people he knew as his characters. The manuscript apparently contained explicit pacifist portions that he modified at his publisher's insistence.

In 1930 a film made from the novel attained success everywhere but in Germany, where the Nazis opposed its antimilitarist tone. At its premiere in Berlin, Nazi head Joseph Goebbels and his followers released bevies of white mice, threw stink bombs and beer bottles, and shouted "Germany Awake!" Such tactics blocked its screening in Germany. In the early hours of January 29, 1933, with Adolf Hitler poised to become chancellor, a friend warned Remarque to flee Germany, and he fled across the Swiss border in his Lancia. His novels joined other proscribed books in Nazi bonfires. Ironically, when two storm troopers who were sent to guard his agent's house during the book burnings asked for reading material, they chose to read *All Quiet* and another Remarque novel.

With the royalties from *All Quiet*, Remarque had previously purchased a villa in the Italian part of Switzerland and had sent his money there. He began collecting art with the help of one of his lovers, and the paintings he purchased later were worth millions. When he was later invited to return to Germany, Remarque remarked: "What? Sixty-five million people would like to get away and I'm to go back of my own free will? Not on your life!" He led a pleasant life in the Swiss cafés, had a penchant for movie stars, and had a long affair with Marlene Dietrich. In April 1951 he fell in love with Paulette Goddard, the actress launched by Charlie Chaplin in his classic *Modern Times* and who was formerly married to him. Remarque and Goddard married on February 22, 1958. Remarque wrote twelve other novels but never duplicated the success of *All Quiet on the Western Front*. He died of heart failure on September 25, 1970, and is buried at his villa in Ronco, Switzerland.

In addition, in 1917 the conflict changed character. Imperialist ambitions caused the war, the hope of aggrandizement enticed other powers to enter it, and dreams of gain kept it going. But by 1917 the huge toll of the fighting convinced people that no gain could compensate them for the losses they had sustained. Enter the United States—which claimed to fight only for a principle, to make the world safe for democracy. Democracy would end war and was well worth the price, so World War I was reborn as the "war to end all wars." In 1917 as well, the Bolsheviks seized power in Russia. also claiming to fight for moral principles—to end capitalist exploitation, to transform the world, and to achieve social justice. From 1917 until 1989, communism and liberal democracy, represented by the Soviet Union and the United States, shared the world stage as protagonists.

The experience of the war's main characters, the soldiers, emerged in novels, memoirs, plays, poetry, and films. Perhaps the best-known novels are Erich Maria Remarque's *All Quiet on the Western Front,* from the German side, and Ernest Hemingway's *A Farewell to Arms,* based on his experiences as an ambulance driver in Italy. Robert Grave's *Goodbye to All That* stands as a classic. Former soldiers brought their wartime experiences in the trenches to the general public, and the concrete descriptions of the fighting contrasted with the pompous wartime propaganda.

One important area in which the traditional persevered was in the mourning in which all combatants engaged and that became a central theme. The anguish over the loss of so many loved ones graphically demonstrated the common cultural tradition of the continent. Throughout Europe, commissions searched for the millions of missing soldiers, established new cemeteries, collected bones, and built monuments to the dead. The millions in mourning shared common images, icons, and symbols. The response to the slaughter of World War I produced shock waves in European culture that could be heard into the 1980s, as the French film *Life and Nothing Else But* illustrates. Europeans pursued a suitable diction of bereavement and turned to traditional religious or romantic topics that that emphasized the common character of Europeans, defeated or victorious, and illustrated that the war had been a true civil conflict.

Bibliographical Essay

For more detail on the important economic and foreign policy issues facing the different powers before World War I, refer to the books cited for Chapters 2, 3, and 4.

There are a number of good general treatments of the causes of World War I. James Joll and Gordon Martel, *The Origins of the First World War* (Harlow, UK, 2007), is an excellent diplomatic history. Richard F. Hamilton and Holger H. Herweg, *The Origins of World War I* (New York, 2003), contains essays by distinguished scholars. Laurence Lafore, *The Long Fuse*, 2d ed. ((Philadelphia, 1971), is useful as an introduction, as is David Fromkin's engagingly written *Europe's Last Summer* (New York, 2004). Ian F. W. Beckett's *The Great War 1914–1918* (Harlow, UK, 2001) is as complete a history in one volume as anyone could wish; it examines social, political, and military elements of the conflict, while Miranda Carter's *George, Nicholas and Wilhelm* (New York, 2010) focuses on the three most important monarchs. Eric Dorn Brose's *A History of the Great War* (New York, 2010) is a general account, as is H. P. Wilmott, *World War I* (New York, 2003). William Kelleher's Storey's *The First World War* (Lanham, Maryland, 2012) is a global military history that includes an examination of environmental factors on the war, a discussion of non-European people, and an analysis of the conflict's global impact. As a magisterial treatment considering the issue in minute detail but keeping the whole in perspective, Luigi Albertini's *The Origins of the War of 1914,* 3 vols. (Oxford, 1952–1957), is unlikely to be surpassed.

The English-language translations of Fischer's books were published as *Germany's Aims in the First World War* (London, 1967) and *War of Illusions: German Policies from 1911 to 1914* (New York, 1975). In this latter work may be found the quotations regarding the widespread acceptance by German politicians and military commanders of the Schlieffen Plan, p. 389; of Moltke, p. 214; and the citations of Bethmann-Hollweg on the September Program, p. 536. The debate on the Fischer thesis may be followed in Fritz Fischer, *World Power or Decline: The Controversy over Germany's Aims in the First World War* (New York, 1974), and the excellent, brief John A. Moses, *The Politics of Illusion: The Fischer Controversy in German Historiography* (London, 1975). Woodruff Smith's *The Ideological Origins of Nazi Imperialism* (New York, 1986) is a balanced discussion of Fisher and the "social imperialism" thesis and the relationship of Wilhelmine foreign policy to Hitler's. The idea that the war came out of general conditions before World War I is best argued in Sidney B. Fay, *The Origins of the War* (New York, 1928). Fay's conclusion, quoted in the text, is taken from the second edition, revised, *After Sarajevo: The Origins of the World War,* vol. II (New York, 1966), p. 558. Harry Elmer Barnes, *The Genesis of the World War* (New York, 1970, originally published in 1926), is a more aggressive attempt to blame the war on the general situation, not on Germany. Niall Ferguson's *The Pity of War: Explaining World War I* (New York, 1999) is a revisionist view that sees the war as unnecessary. The historiographical debates are summed up in Annika Mombauer, *The Origins of the First World War* (New York, 2002), and in J. M. Winter and Antoine Prost, *The Great War in History* (New York, 2005).

Walter Laqueur and George L. Mosse, eds., *1914: The Coming of the First World War* (New York, 1966), contains excellent essays on different problems from the perspective of the large and small powers. George F. Kennan, *The Fateful Alliance: France, Russia, and the Coming of the First World War* (New York, 1984), is a thorough examination of the relationship between France and Russia, the counterpart to the Austro-German connection. There is not much in English on Italy's entrance into the war, but see the treatment in Spencer M. Di Scala, *Vittorio Orlando: Italy* (Makers of the Modern World series) (London, 2010), and William A. Renzi, *In the Shadow of the Sword* (New York, 1987). On the general diplomatic issues, see the older but still useful previously cited books by A. J. P. Taylor, *The Struggle for Mastery in Europe* (Oxford, UK, 1954); and René Albrecht-Carrié, *A Diplomatic History of Europe* (New York, 1958); and the more recent Norman Rich, *Great Power Diplomacy, 1814–1914* (New York, 1992). Imperialism is given a good general treatment, including an analysis of the economic and political factors and interpretations, in

Woodruff D. Smith, *European Imperialism in the 19th and 20th Centuries* (Chicago, 1982). Isaiah Friedman wrote a book on British policy in the Middle East during and after the war: *British Pan-Arab Policy, 1915–1922* (New Brunswick, N.J., 2010).

On the arms race before World War I, there is the excellent David G. Herrmann, *The Arming of Europe and the Making of the First World War* (Princeton, N.J., 1996), which compares the armies of all the great powers and their development from 1904 to the war's outbreak; the citations on the lessons learned from the Russo-Japanese War and the 1909 ultimatum are found on p. 68 and p. 126, respectively. Paul M. Kennedy, ed., *The War Plans of the Great Powers 1880–1914* (Boston, 1985), also discusses the thinking behind the plans.

There are many works on the military progress of the war, but Captain B. H. Liddell Hart's *The Real War 1914–1918* (Boston, 1930) remains a classic of its kind; the judgment on the Battle of Verdun is found on p. 215. John Keegan's *The First World War* (New York, 2000) is the most accessible military history in one volume. Michael Howard, *The Lessons of History* (New Haven, Conn., 1991), has several excellent essays on the prevailing mentality before World War I and on military affairs; the Karl Person citation is reported on p. 110. The quote on the French mutiny of 1917 is in the opening chapter of Gaetano Salvemini's *The Origins of Fascism in Italy* (New York, 1973), p. 14. While concerned with Italian Fascism, this book has a good treatment of the misconceptions regarding Caporetto. The full story of the French mutiny and its impact may be found in John Williams, *Mutiny 1917* (London, 1962). Martin Gilbert's *The First World War: A Complete History* (New York, 1994) is a blow-by-blow military history oriented toward the general reader but has surprising gaps; the Churchill citation on tanks is on p. 286. Robert B. Asprey's *The German High Command at War: Hindenburg and Ludendorff Conduct World War I* (New York, 1991) is an excellent account of how the Germans ran the war. The eastern front is covered in scholarly detail by Norman Stone, *The Eastern Front, 1914–1917* (New York, 1975). The best book in English on the Austro-Italian front is John R. Schindler, *Isonzo: the Forgotten Sacrifice of the Great War* (Westport, Conn., 2001); there is also Mark Thompson, *The White War: Life and Death on the Italian Front* (London, 2008). On the war in Africa, an unusual topic, see Edward Paice, *World War I: The African Front* (New York, 2008).

The horrors of trench warfare (and their "literary" repercussions) are detailed by Paul Fussell, *The Great War and Modern Memory* (New York, 1975), invaluable also because of his discussion of the conflict's literary impact. The quotes regarding the national style of the trenches is on p. 45. Marc Ferro, *The Great War 1914–1918* (London, 1973), emphasizes the social aspects of the fighting. Neil M. Heyman, *Daily Life During World War I* (Westport, Conn., 2002), focuses on life both in the trenches and at home. The conduct of the German occupiers of Belgium has long been debated; Larry Zuckerman's book *The Rape of Belgium: The Untold Story of World War I* (New York, 2004) presents evidence on the brutality of the occupation. On the Armenian genocide, see Tanaer Akcam, *A Shameful Act: The Armenian Genocide and the Question of Turkish Responsibility* (New York, 2006). Jennifer D. Keene, *World War I* (Westport, Conn., 2006), describes the lives of the American soldiers.

Developments in the home fronts may be followed in Gerd Hardach, *The First World War 1914–1918* (London, 1977), which is good in discussing international ramifications of the war in all fields, Britain and Germany, especially, and various other countries. Arthur Marwick, *The Deluge: British Society and the First World War* (New York, 1970), is a good general history of British society during the war, as is E. Sylvia Pankhurst, *The Home Front: A Mirror to Life in England During the First World War* (London, 1932), the reminiscences of a radical Englishwoman. Germany is covered in detail in two excellent works by Gerald D. Feldman, *Army, Industry, and Labor in Germany, 1914–1918*

(Princeton, N.J., 1966), and Robert B. Armeson, *Total Warfare and Compulsory Labor: A Study of The Military-Industrial Complex in Germany During World War I* (The Hague, 1964). Jean-Jacques Becker examines the French experience in *The Great War and the French People* (New York, 1986). On Austria-Hungary, see the essays in Robert A. Kann, Bela K. Kiraly, and Paula S. Fichtner, eds., *The Hapsburg Empire in World War I* (Boulder, Colo., 1977).

On women munitions workers in England, there is Angela Woollacott, *On Her Their Lives Depend: Munitions Workers in the Great War* (Berkeley, Calif., 1994), and the more general work by Arthur Marwick, *Women at War 1914–1918* (London, 1977).

Finally, two brief general works may be cited. Jack J. Roth, ed., *World War I* (New York, 1967), argues that World War I was a turning point, and A. J. P. Taylor, *From Sarajevo to Potsdam* (London, 1965), takes the story beyond the war.

On the cultural impact, see Fussell, cited earlier, and Jay Winter, *Sites of Memory, Sites of Mourning: The Great War in European Cultural History* (Cambridge, UK, 1995), which emphasizes the role of mourning and challenges some of the standard interpretations. Some of Fussell's themes are continued by Samuel Hynes, *A War Imagined: The First World War and English Culture* (London, 1991).

CHAPTER 7

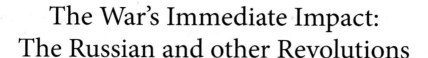

The War's Immediate Impact:
The Russian and other Revolutions

CHAPTER OUTLINE

War and the Russian Revolutions • The German Revolution • Revolution in Austria • The Hungarian Revolution • Continuous Rebellion: Artists and Scientists

BIOGRAPHICAL SKETCHES

Vladimir Ilych Ulyanov, A Sealed Train • Rosa Luxemburg, Marxist Martyr

World War I had enormous immediate and long-term repercussions for both the losers and the victors. In the authoritarian countries, revolutions broke out with the goal of establishing liberal or social democratic governments, and fierce struggles raged among the Liberals, Socialists, and Communists. In the parliamentary democracies, economic dislocations, resentment, and radical ideologies caused severe unrest.

WAR AND THE RUSSIAN REVOLUTIONS

In Russia the assassination of Francis Ferdinand and the ensuing diplomatic crisis had touched off popular demonstrations in favor of Serbia, and leading observers predicted a revolution if the tsar failed to protect that country. Nicholas hoped that a Russian victory would build national unity, bolster his popularity, and increase his personal authority.

Russian Military Deficiencies

The Russians had contingency plans only for a short war, and the tsarist regime proved too inflexible, inefficient, and authoritarian to confront the hardships of modern war. The Russians had some competent commanders, but the army suffered from the lack of a general plan of operations and a clear command structure. According to one general, the strategy was "order, counter-order, disorder."

165

In theory, Russia had an inexhaustible reserve of manpower, but Russian officials mobilized less than half the percentage of its population than did the Germans and less than a third of the French and had poorly trained reserves. When spectacular defeats decimated the standing army and the immediate reserves, untrained recruits replaced them.

The war ministry had no wartime production plan and placed orders in foreign countries, causing long delays in delivery, complicating the integration of weapons, and causing problems with the low quality of foreign purchases. The army ordered its soldiers to fire only ten bullets a day and, when they had no rifles, to wait until they could pick up those of their fallen comrades. The shortages of munitions, clothing, food, and medicine soon became critical and contributed to the spread of deadly diseases in the ranks. The scarcity of railways, trucks, telephones, and telegraphs hampered mobility and impeded communications. Eventually, Russian industry responded better to the enormous demand for war materiel, but too late. The increasing carnage caused by spectacular German victories broke the army. A million soldiers surrendered, and disorderly troops became bandits behind the lines.

Although Russian industry started off slowly in meeting the enormous demands of war and its production of war materiel greatly accelerated during the course of the conflict, it was too late to change the outcome. This poster illustrates a woman working in a war factory; it proclaims "All for the War!"

The February Revolution

Defeat, demoralization, and disorganization ultimately brought down the regime. In July 1915 pressure from critics, including some ministers, small businessmen, and dissident generals, forced the tsar to call the Duma into session. Two-thirds of the members of the Duma joined the Progressive bloc, made up of parties whose political orientation went from the moderate right to the moderate left, that demanded a cabinet that could win the people's support. Paul Miliukov, the leader of the Progressive bloc, asked about the war effort: "Is this stupidity or is it treason?" Ten governmental ministers came out in support of the bloc when Nicholas suddenly announced that he would leave St. Petersburg and assume personal command of the armies at the front.

Panic resulted because Nicholas's plan gave effective control of the capital to the empress and Rasputin. On September 2, 1916, the tsar dissolved the Duma; reaffirmed confidence in his loyal but ineffective prime minister, Ivan Goremykin; and tongue-lashed the rebel ministers. The two-day general strike that followed failed to convince Nicholas to reconvene the Duma, and he fired the Liberal ministers, replacing them with allies of Rasputin. The tsar also tightened police control, extended censorship, fanned anti-Semitism in order to gain popular support, and banned public meetings. When Nicholas left for the front, Empress Alexandra's influence increased dramatically. Rasputin determined the hiring and firing of governmental ministers, causing instability and confusion. Rasputin replaced Goremykin as prime minister with the even more incompetent Boris Stürmer, while the empress consistently misinformed Nicholas about the true situation at home and swayed military decisions by a continuous stream of letters.

The public turned against the tsar, openly criticizing him, discussing his abdication, and accusing the tsarina and Rasputin of sexual misconduct and pro-Germanism. Opposition to the monarchy became synonymous with patriotism, and conspirators talked about how to force the tsar's abdication, arrest the tsarina, and murder Rasputin. On December 16, 1916, young aristocrats lured Rasputin to one of their homes, where they poisoned, shot, and dumped him into a river until he finally died. They had hoped to change Nicholas's politics by this act, but the tsar strengthened his opposition to reform.

By early 1917, the Russian domestic situation had reached a crisis. An exceptionally cold winter exacerbated the food shortages that afflicted the capital. On March 8,[1] International Women's Day, women in St. Petersburg demonstrated for equal rights. Women strikers protesting the bread shortage joined them, and their men came out in support. The government called out the Cossacks, but they hesitated when ordered to fire on the crowds, and the rioting turned into protests against the tsar and the war. Nicholas ordered the military commanders to suppress the uprising, but the soldiers joined the demonstrators. Themselves peasants and workers, the troops went over to the crowd, fought with the police, and

---

[1]The dates used in this account are according to the New Style (Western calendar). As a result, the February Revolution occurred in March, and the October Revolution, discussed in the next section, took place in November.

mutinied. The soldiers occupied strategic points in the capital and transformed the disorders into a revolution. Insurgents raised red flags, commandeered motor vehicles, rushed from one part of the city to the other, attacked the police, and destroyed the symbols of imperial authority. Fifteen hundred people died in the fighting, and 6,000 were wounded. On March 12 the revolutionaries formed the Petrograd Soviet [Council] of Workers' Deputies, dominated by the moderate Socialists (Mensheviks and Social Revolutionaries), and three days later adopted the name Soviet of Workers' and Soldiers' Deputies because of the soldiers' role.

Unfortunately for the revolution, there were two centers of power, the Soviet and the Duma, both of which hesitated to assume command. The Soviet had authority over the revolutionaries but declined to accept formal governing responsibility. It feared that the people might turn on it if it tried to rule and wavered because the revolution had not spread from the capital to the rest of Russia. It also feared an attack from frontline troops headed by the tsar and believed that a government formed by the Duma would reassure the tsar and prevent counterrevolution.

Most of all, the Soviet got caught up in squabbles over doctrine. The idea that Russia must pass through an obligatory bourgeois revolution before it could

The February Revolution overthrew the Tsar and set up a de facto republic but did not end the story. The continued fighting provoked hardship and increasing disorder before the Bolsheviks carried out their coup d'etat in November 1917. This photograph from May 1917 shows Petrograd (St. Petersburg) residents burning coats of arms torn away from buildings.

institute socialism strengthened the idea that the Duma should form a government, but the Duma hesitated because it had little influence in the streets. The result was ironic: the Duma set up a provisional government that had legal power but no real authority; the Soviet, which had authority, did not want legal authority. Finally, the Soviet agreed to support the provisional government, but only if it implemented Soviet principles—rejecting formal command but preventing the provisional government from ruling.

This dual power resulted in paralysis, as illustrated by the Soviet's Order Number One. The order acknowledged the Soviet's authority but provided that the provisional government's military orders be obeyed only if they did not contradict the Soviet's. Order Number One established elected soldiers' committees in army units that undermined the authority of officers and encouraged the breakdown of army discipline, indirectly contributing to the Bolshevik takeover.

The Tsar Abdicates

When the disorders that threatened his throne began, Nicholas attempted to return to his capital, but the revolutionaries diverted his train from Petrograd to Pskov. His most senior advisers informed him that it was too late to put down the revolution and convinced him to abdicate. Nicholas first indicated his son as successor, then his younger brother Michael. This plan might have saved the monarchy but proved impossible to implement. Riots broke out when the tsar's action was announced, and, at any rate, Michael rejected the job. As a result of these developments, Russia became a de facto republic.

Following Nicholas's abdication, the revolution quickly got out of hand. The people rejoiced, then destroyed the symbols of tsarism and attacked the rich. The peasants took matters into their own hands and expropriated the gentry's property. The provisional government had not condoned this move, its inaction helping to account for the decline of its authority and the rise of the Bolsheviks. As violence and looting spread throughout the country, the intellectual demolition of the old regime began. Pamphlets and plays about the royal family's supposedly degenerate lifestyle proliferated. At the front, the officers lost control of their troops. The soldiers desired peace and to return home to participate with their fellow-peasants in the expropriation of land owned by the gentry. Between March and October 1917, a million Russian soldiers deserted. They accelerated the revolution that had already begun on the land. Bolstered by frontline troops, the peasants first forced the gentry to accept long lists of concessions, then confiscated their land and went on a rampage of killing and looting. Local peasant Soviets proliferated and legalized the land takeovers. The administrative structure of the old regime collapsed overnight.

The land and the cities erupted into full revolt. Workers struck for higher wages, the eight-hour workday, better working conditions, and equal pay and maternity leave for women. The spiraling inflation, layoffs, and employers' resistance induced many workers to join labor unions and to make political demands, including governmental control or nationalization of factories and elected factory committees to oversee all phases of production. Workers formed armed Red Guard units to protect the workplaces. As the situation became more chaotic, the moderate Socialist majority of the Soviet sought to oppose the demands of the radical workers. Because moderate Socialists also predominated in the labor unions, these institutions became frontline opponents of the Bolsheviks, who demanded radical changes. Their control of the factory committees and the Red Guards gave the Bolsheviks an enormous influence in the cities that they skillfully exploited in their drive to achieve power. Bolshevik popular support grew rapidly and was substantial by September 1917.

The provisional government proved helpless to confront the revolutionary situation. It endorsed full civil rights, universal, equal, secret, and direct suffrage, and called for a constituent assembly. Because of the different parties' maneuvering for position, voting for this body was finally held only on November 12—too late. A cabinet crisis occurred when Foreign Minister Miliukov avowed that the country would demand the annexation of Constantinople in case of an Allied victory. This declaration touched off a dispute with the Soviet, which advocated peace without annexations. Demonstrations against the government forced Miliukov to resign, and the government followed his example.

A new cabinet came to power. Its strongest member was War Minister Alexander Kerensky, a Socialist Revolutionary (SR), and it included representatives of the Soviet. This government supported continuation of the war and attempted

Seen here saluting his troops, Alexander Kerensky was the strongest and most visible political leader in Russia during the period after the Tsar's fall and the Bolshevik takeover. Many Russians blamed his ineptness for allowing Communism to take over their country. After his defeat he fled to the United States where he did research and lectured. He died in New York in 1970 at age 89.

to stop the breakdown of order. The Soviet representatives went along with both aims, alienating the rest of the body. The majority in the Soviet moved toward the left, while other political forces in the capital reacted by strongly supporting the bourgeoisie and the restoration of order. This polarization of the Russian political situation caused more confusion and helped the Bolsheviks, the only political force with a clear idea of its goals and the will to achieve them.

The October Revolution

Bolshevik chief Vladimir Ilych Lenin had returned to Russia from Swiss exile in a sealed train, courtesy of the Germans. The Germans brought him home because he favored immediate peace, but secured the train because he was a dangerous revolutionary who might infect German workers with his ideology.

Once home, Lenin enunciated the April Theses that he believed would lead to a second revolution. Like the Mensheviks, he had to grapple with Marxist ideology, which mandated that agricultural countries such as Russia would have to traverse a bourgeois phase because socialism could be implemented only by an industrial society. He neatly resolved this issue by maintaining that the February revolution had simultaneously implemented a bourgeois dictatorship and a revolutionary democratic dictatorship of the proletariat and peasantry, which had taken the guise of the provisional government and the Soviet. He then addressed the practical question: the Bolsheviks must proceed directly to the Socialist revolution, which he defined as the rule of the workers and the poor peasants. The Bolsheviks had to do so through the Soviet, Lenin believed, despite its domination by the moderate Mensheviks and SRs. The Bolsheviks should push the Soviet into seizing power and then transform it into a class-conscious (Bolshevik) institution. All production would then come under Soviet control, and all the land would be nationalized and subsequently collectivized. The peasants would not be allowed to hold land privately, except perhaps on a temporary basis.

In implementing these ideas, the Bolsheviks had a great advantage—they were backed by strong armed forces—revolutionary sailors at Kronstadt, the machine gunners of the Petrograd garrison, and the radical workers of the capital's Vyborg district. These shock troops champed at the bit, but Lenin had little popular support. This lack of popular support caused a problem illustrated by the "July days." In an attempt to change the fortunes of war, Kerensky launched an offensive that cost the Russians 400,000 casualties and a like number of deserters. These losses touched off popular demonstrations in the capital, followed by a military revolt by Bolshevik units. This mutiny was spontaneous, had little direction, and quickly failed. The government reacted by arresting key Bolshevik leaders, although Lenin escaped.

The government's show of force against the Bolsheviks, interpreted by the Soviet as a counterrevolution, backfired. Soviet protests led to a government reshuffling. Kerensky emerged as the prime minister with a moderate Socialist majority in the cabinet. He was at the height of his prestige because of his links to the Soviet and the Duma and because of the support he had among the people, the bourgeoisie, and the military leaders. These advantages prompted Kerensky to shift to the right in an attempt to restore calm and to strengthen the country's war effort. His government reduced Soviet influence, reinstated the death penalty for indiscipline at the front, diminished the authority of soldiers' committees, and restricted public gatherings. Kerensky also appointed General Lavr Kornilov, a political rightist and proponent of continuing the war against the Germans, as the commander in chief of the army.

BIOGRAPHICAL SKETCHES

Vladimir Ilych Ulyanov
A Sealed Train

The man who led the Bolsheviks to victory in Russia using the pseudonym Lenin was born on April 22, 1870, in Simbirsk. His father taught school and rose to the position of a provincial school inspector. His mother, Maria Aleksandrovna Blank, a doctor's daughter, devoted her life to her six children.

As a child, Lenin was unruly, noisy, and given to temper tantrums. He is alleged to have had a cruel streak, and his parents punished him more frequently than they did the other children. An intelligent boy, Lenin learned to read at age 5 and excelled in literature, history, and languages at school. He read Latin and Greek and could speak and read several modern languages, including German. In 1887, he graduated from secondary school with a gold medal for excellence in his studies.

Particularly attached to his older brother Alexander, Lenin participated in sports and played chess with him despite their personality differences. Alexander was reserved and studious and, as a child, had his toys broken by his raucous younger brother. The brothers and the other Ulyanov children learned to despise the reactionary social system of tsarist Russia and turned to subversive activities. When Lenin was 17, the police arrested and executed Alexander for plotting to murder Tsar Alexander III. This event was a turning point in the young Lenin's life and filled him with a visceral hatred of tsarism.

After secondary school, Lenin decided to study law at the University of Kazan, but the police arrested and banished him to his grandfather's home village for taking part in a demonstration protesting the lack of freedom. In the fall of 1888, he returned to Kazan but was not readmitted to the university. In September 1889 the family moved to Samara, and in the spring of 1890, Lenin was permitted to resume his studies as an external student at the University of St. Petersburg: He could study for his law degree, but not attend courses. Lenin completed his requirements in eighteen months, passing the final examination in November 1891. He then practiced law in Samara in 1892 and 1893, taking up the causes of poor clients and building up more hatred for the political and legal establishment.

During the time he spent in Samara, Lenin undertook a vast study of Marxist texts and gained a reputation as a formidable theoretician. In August 1893, he moved to the capital of St. Petersburg, continuing his activities as a defender of the poor and a Marxist thinker. During this time, he met his future wife and coworker, Nadezhda Konstantinovna Krupskaya, who taught school for factory workers. Two years later, he was exiled to Siberia, where he remained until 1900. He then left Russia to continue his activities abroad.

Lenin lived and breathed Marxism, attempting to convince people that revolutionary Marxism was still alive despite the assertions of revisionists that Marx had been wrong about the imminent coming of the revolution. His most influential publication from this early period is probably the pamphlet *What Is to Be Done?* (1902). Lenin wrote prodigiously, earning the nickname "the Old Man" at age 23 because of his intensity. He insisted that an elite vanguard dedicated only to the revolution should lead the workers' movement—and he practiced what he preached. It is said that he once rejected a lover because she was not a Social Democrat; she answered that he was "only a Social Democrat" and left him.

Lenin returned to Russia during the revolution of 1905 and left in 1907. When World War I broke out, he was in Switzerland. Lenin believed that war brought a great revolutionary opportunity, and he was right. A revolution occurred in Russia in March 1917, but the country did not withdraw from the war. Because Lenin advocated that the Russians abandon the imperialist conflict, the Germans gave him passage home, but in a sealed train so he could not contaminate their compatriots. Back in Russia, Lenin successfully guided the Bolshevik revolution to victory.

These changes led to the murky Kornilov affair that weakened Kerensky and smoothed the Bolsheviks' road to power. Kerensky and Kornilov hoped to use each other to bolster their own power, jockeyed for position, and got their signals crossed. Kornilov moved troops toward the capital in the mistaken belief that Kerensky had asked for protection from the Bolsheviks, but Kerensky feared being ousted and denounced Kornilov for attempting a coup d'etat. The Soviet reacted by mobilizing, an action that revealed its dependence on Bolshevik military might.

Kerensky's influence declined after the Kornilov affair because the right resented his treatment of Kornilov and the left suspected him of plotting with the general. The episode further radicalized the urban areas and contributed to the process by which the Bolsheviks took over the Soviet in Petrograd, which drove events to take a more radical turn in other major Russian cities during August and September. The Bolsheviks won over the executive bodies of the Soviets, and the Bolshevik leaders, who were arrested during July, were released. These Bolshevik leaders included Leon Trotsky, a subtle strategist, tireless activist, and a spellbinder of crowds.

City elections confirmed the Bolsheviks' increasing importance when the party won an absolute majority in Moscow. At the same time, the moderate Socialist Mensheviks and SRs collapsed. Factory workers had been going over to the Bolsheviks in the spring of 1917, and the trend intensified in the fall because the younger, more militant Bolshevik leaders appealed to them more than did the indecisive Mensheviks and SRs. By late July, Bolshevik party membership swelled to 250,000 members and by October, 350,000. A great increase in industrial strikes and an acceleration of the peasant revolution also took place. What accounted for the growth in Bolshevik popularity was their clear demands: radical social revolution, expropriation of property, peace, and power to the Soviets.

Kerensky continued to hold formal power but became increasingly isolated as the people ignored the government's decrees. The government marked time until a constituent assembly could be elected and produce an executive that had national support. Lenin, however, cut the Gordian knot by convincing his party to organize a revolution before the assembly could meet. He rejected the thesis of Bolshevik leaders who wanted to wait until the outcome of a Soviet congress, which was scheduled for late October, on the assumption that a Soviet government with a strong Bolshevik component would emerge from it. Reasoning that the Bolsheviks would be only one faction of the government, he demanded sole power for his party.

On November 7, 1917 (October 25, old style), a Bolshevik coup took place. Portrayed as a grand occasion in Sergei Eisenstein's classic film *October*, the event was instead described by observers as a small affair that people had almost come to expect. The Kerensky government offered only slight resistance at its seat, the Winter Palace. As Bolshevik troops careened in trucks to take control of the city's strategic areas and buildings, performances at theaters went on as scheduled, patrons drank coffee in cafés, and streetcar traffic was normal. The October Revolution "was in reality such a small event, being in effect no more than a military coup, that it passed unnoticed by the vast majority of the inhabitants of Petrograd."

Consolidation of Bolshevik Power

The next day, at the Soviet congress, the Bolsheviks announced the government's arrest (except for Kerensky, who had escaped). Some resistance now materialized, but Lenin deflated it with a manifesto promising peace, bread, and land. As the Bolsheviks moved to seize the machinery of government, the first signs of division appeared. Strikes broke out, especially among the civil servants who considered the new government illegal. Few believed that the new Bolshevik government would endure because Lenin's drive for complete control had divided the party and isolated it from the rest of the revolutionary movement.

Several factors worked in Lenin's favor. First was his determination to seize power and hold onto it from the bottom up. Lenin energized the Soviets at the local level, the factory organizations, and the soldiers' committees by giving them full support to destroy the existing power structure. This technique undermined local support for his most dangerous competitors, the SRs, and reduced backing for a constituent assembly by making the Soviets the organs of direct democracy. This method eradicated the old political system, a prelude to the building of a new state through a Bolshevik dictatorship. The Bolsheviks also gained the support of the ethnic nationalities by giving them the right to break away from Russia should they wish to do so. The Bolsheviks made a bid for the support of women by repealing laws favoring inequality with men, calling for equal pay for equal work, and supporting the liberation of women from household drudgery.

The Bolsheviks' opponents underestimated them by failing to organize a serious resistance on the assumption that the elections for the constituent assembly would be a national referendum that would end Bolshevik power. In fact, Lenin opposed the elections because he was convinced that the Bolsheviks would lose them. He argued that the direct democracy of the Soviets negated the need for a constituent assembly, but the Bolsheviks' previous propaganda and the national support for the body proved impossible to counter, and the Bolsheviks won only 24 percent of the seats. However, Lenin had no intention of surrendering power.

The Bolsheviks intimidated the assembly's officers, outlawed the Kadet party, and arrested Menshevik and SR leaders. When Bolshevik opponents organized a series of nonviolent demonstrations against these tactics, the Bolsheviks ordered the troops to fire on them and dissolved the constituent assembly after its first meeting in January 1918.

The people did not rise to save the assembly because Lenin pursued a successful campaign to weaken its popular support. Local Soviets approved takeovers of the gentry's holdings, thus satisfying the peasants' centuries-old hunger for land. Lenin encouraged the action of the revolutionaries as "looting the looters." The result was an orgy of despoliation, degradation, and murder perpetrated against the gentry, the bourgeoisie, and the Orthodox Church.

At the same time, Lenin constructed a police state that systematically terrorized its enemies. The Cheka, headed by Felix Dzerzhinsky, was the prime instrument of this campaign. Dzerzhinsky, who had spent half his life in tsarist prisons, created a vast police apparatus of 250,000 people and organized a network of prisons, concentration camps, and torture chambers. The murder of the ex-tsar and his family during the night of July 16–17, 1918, eliminated the threat of a restoration and signaled the beginning of this Red Terror. By then a "White" volunteer army had taken the field to overthrow the "Reds" in a civil war that lasted until 1921. The Allies sent in small detachments to protect their interests, and the Whites hoped that these soldiers would support their efforts, but they did little. The civil war, the Whites' propensity to return land to the gentry in the regions they liberated, and the urgency of organizing a Red Army to fight the Bolshevik enemies increased the terror. The Whites also conducted a vicious terror campaign. These events stiffened the resolve of the Bolsheviks to remain in power. The Cheka greatly extended its activities, and its victims, representing a cross section of Russian society, numbered in the hundreds of thousands.

Bolshevik Policies

Besides a confused domestic situation and civil war, the Bolsheviks still faced the German army. The Bolsheviks supported immediate peace with no annexations or indemnities, but when the Germans continued the conflict, many Bolshevik leaders advocated a revolutionary war on the grounds that the Russian peasants would fight to defend the gains they had made. Lenin disagreed and advocated an immediate separate peace because the Bolsheviks needed time to consolidate their revolution and feared that army remnants would overthrow them if peace were not concluded. The Bolshevik leadership rejected these arguments and adopted Trotsky's idea of withdrawing from the war without signing a peace treaty. The Germans ignored them, attacked, and moved forward 150 miles in five days, forcing the Bolsheviks to sign the peace of Brest-Litovsk on March 3, 1918. This treaty practically pushed Russia out of Europe, with the Russian republic losing 34 percent of its territory, 32 percent of its agricultural land, and 54 percent of its industry. The Ukraine, one of the richest areas of Russia, became a German puppet state.

The disastrous peace nevertheless allowed the Bolsheviks to translate their ideology into action. In 1918 they attempted to organize collective farms, but failed. Even worse, the irate peasants refused to sell their grain at prices fixed by the government because of the rampant inflation and the hope for greater profit. The government thereupon organized committees of poor peasants to seize the stocks of peasants with surplus grain but dropped this policy by the end of the year. The attempt caused great confusion and disorganization that caused a drastic decline in agricultural production. In 1921 and 1922, deaths from famine and disease surpassed the combined total casualties suffered in World War I and the civil war.

Industry was easier to dominate than agriculture because it employed far fewer people and was limited to the cities where the Bolsheviks had greater influence. The Bolsheviks pushed the workers to take over the factories but ran into such strong resistance from former owners and managers that the attempt severely handicapped production. During the summer of 1918, the Bolsheviks responded by nationalizing industry and centralizing its operations under a supreme economic council, a move that failed to eliminate the disorganization and inefficiency. By 1920 industrial production had dropped to 20 percent of the 1913 level. Other areas of the economy, including trade and banking, collapsed as well as the Bolsheviks nationalized them. The economic situation was so desperate that many areas of the country resorted to barter while revolts on the land and in the cities shook the regime.

The NEP

Given this disastrous situation, Lenin backtracked. In 1921, the Bolsheviks officially recognized the private enterprise that had spontaneously revived in various parts of the country and implemented trade liberalization. This New Economic Policy (NEP) had immediate benefits. It increased the volume of trade and reinvigorated agriculture, and state concessions to peasants who wanted to own their own farms greatly bolstered production. Peasant farms increased 65 percent over the prewar figure during the NEP period, but it was an important defeat for the Bolsheviks because the rich and poor reappeared. The NEP was a tactical withdrawal signifying that for the moment the Bolsheviks had renounced their attempt to implement socialism in the agricultural sector, the largest part of the economy. The Bolsheviks were more successful in the much smaller industrial sector, which remained under state control and slowly returned to the 1913 level of production by 1927.

In July 1918 the Bolsheviks announced a new constitution. This document formalized the system of government by Soviets. It created a federation of republics based on the Soviets, the Union of Soviet Socialist Republics (USSR), of which the Russian Socialist Federated Soviet Republic (RSFSR) was the largest. The constitution mandated that the Soviets meet twice a year in the All-Russian Congress of Soviets. This body, in turn, elected the All-Russian Central Executive Committee that voted for the Council of Commissars or government. All citizens aged 18 and older could vote, including women, but the vote was weighted in favor of city workers.

World War I had thoroughly revolutionized Russian politics and society. The monarchy had disappeared, and a Socialist federation had been created.

Most important, the Bolsheviks had demolished the country's entire social, economic, and political structure down to the smallest administrative level of local government. They hoped that the Socialist revolution would spread to the entire world, as Marx had predicted, but when this revolution failed to occur, Bolshevik policy reaffirmed Russian national interests. Nevertheless, in 1918 and 1919, the Bolshevik Revolution's success stood in stark contrast to the other revolutions provoked by the world war.

THE GERMAN REVOLUTION

The revolution that broke out in Germany during the last days of the war was more limited than the Bolshevik Revolution.

Disorders engulfed Germany as the Germans sued for peace. In October a massive strike demanded food, the abolition of martial law, and an end to the three-class Prussian system of voting that propped up conservative rule. The strike was not limited to the antiwar left and Bolshevik sympathizers but drew on the deep dissatisfaction of workers throughout the political spectrum.

End of the War in Germany

Sniffing imminent military disaster, Ludendorff called for the introduction of a parliamentary regime in October 1918. Such a change might get better peace terms from the Allies and would make civilian politicians responsible for the defeat. A new chancellor, Prince Max von Baden, established a parliamentary government that included representatives of the SPD because the prince was a liberal and because the conservative parties were excluded. On October 28 at the Kiel naval base, sailors defied orders to put to sea and mutinied. They raised the Red flag, elected sailors' councils, and demanded the kaiser's abdication. "Fear and hatred ruled the day in Germany." The disorders culminated in Berlin on November 9. The army withdrew its support from Emperor Wilhelm, forcing him to abdicate, and SPD leader Philipp Scheidemann proclaimed a republic. SPD leader Friedrich Ebert replaced Prince Max as chancellor and installed a cabinet consisting of three SPD and three USPD representatives and called for a constituent assembly.

The Struggle for Power

These events touched off a struggle for power between diverse revolutionary centers. The German revolution had been essentially spontaneous, but it took on a more radical character as it progressed. The previous state governments dissolved, and the resulting vacuum encouraged the rebels to elect workers' and soldiers' councils on the Russian soviet model and to proclaim world revolution. The SPD joined the revolution by participating in the election of the councils but was most concerned with preventing chaos and civil war. Consequently, moderates predominated in the revolutionary councils and dampened calls for the nationalization of property. The USPD (which had broken off from the SPD) and the Spartacists, Bolshevik sympathizers, tried to make the German Soviets the revolutionary instruments of government. The lines in Germany were clearly drawn between moderates favoring a parliamentary regime and radicals advocating the implementation of socialism by revolutionary councils.

Because neither side could immediately achieve its objective, they compromised. The constituent assembly would be postponed, the SPD hoping to regroup and the USPD aiming at a consolidation of rule by councils. The compromise turned out to be a defeat for the radicals. On November 12, Ebert eliminated martial law, censorship, and labor restrictions and decreed an amnesty. He promised an eight-hour working day; unemployment assistance; and secret equal voting rights for persons over age 20, including women. The government pledged to nationalize enterprises, consistent with continued production and the protection of property. Because these reforms satisfied the country's desire for democracy and the army's demobilization seemed to end the militarist problem, a large majority of the German people supported a parliamentary government rather than revolutionary socialism. In reality, the government's nationalization program encountered insuperable practical problems and a fear of Bolshevism, and on November 25 a conference of the prime ministers of the German states overwhelmingly voted against nationalization of the banks and in favor of a constituent assembly. The executive committee of the workers' councils objected that any decision on convening the constituent assembly should be delayed until a December 16 meeting of the Congress of Workers' and Soldiers' Councils, but it received a rude shock when the delegates endorsed a constituent assembly.

A sailors' revolt following the meeting was quickly repressed, causing the USPD to withdraw from the cabinet and producing a break between it and the Spartacists. The extreme left concluded that their radical program could be realized only by force before the constituent assembly convened, as had happened in Russia. Consequently, the Spartacists constituted themselves as the German Communist Party (KPD) on December 30, 1918. The KPD's most visible leader and most notable theoretician, Rosa Luxemburg, favored caution but published inflammatory statements in the party newspaper that had the opposite effect. The revolt began when the government dismissed the Berlin chief of police, supported by the Communists, but it lacked a strategic plan.

The government deputized SPD leader Gustav Noske to quell the revolt. He aimed to destroy the KPD, but the army was demobilized, so Noske turned to the Freikorps—restless, conservative, elite, intensely anti-Communist volunteer ex-soldiers who were committed to protecting Germany's eastern frontier against Russians and Poles. Freikorps units brutally suppressed the Spartacists and murdered Luxemburg and Liebknecht. By employing the Freikorps, the government set a precedent for later paramilitary action.

Foundation of the Weimar Republic

Balloting for the Constituent Assembly occurred on January 12, 1919, with women voting for the first time. The democratic parties won a majority: the SPD, the Center party, and the Democrats (the old Progressives). The election ended the German revolution despite the continuation of disorder over the next few years. In the winter and spring of 1919, there were several Communist uprisings, but the Friekorps suppressed them. Strikes and uprisings continued into the early 1920s because of the severe economic crisis. In March 1921 and October 1923, Communist revolutions were attempted and failed. The extreme right attempted two failed putsches that occurred under Wolfgang Kapp in March 1920 and Adolf Hitler in November 1923.

BIOGRAPHICAL SKETCHES

Rosa Luxemburg
Marxist Martyr

A prolific writer, Rosa Luxemburg earned a lasting reputation as a major Marxist theoretician. She was born in Russian-controlled Poland on March 5, 1871, to an assimilated Jewish family. Rosa's father ran a timber business and frequently traveled to Germany. He had been educated in Germany, and German culture predominated in the home. The family paid little attention to the active local Jewish community.

As a young woman, Luxemburg became attracted to socialism and took an active part in the Socialist debates in Poland. She established a reputation as an independent thinker and as a tenacious defender of her ideas. Both in her youth and in later years, she engaged in spirited fights with famous European Socialists, including the Russians Vladimir Lenin and Georgii Plekhanov and Austrian Socialist leader Viktor Adler. Besides her intellectual capacities, Luxemburg's appearance commanded respect from adversaries and colleagues. A fastidious woman, she wore expensive but plain clothes and never appeared in disarray. Because of time served in prison, Luxemburg suffered from ill health, and her hair turned white. She had a rigid personality, which contributed to her difficulties in getting along with people, especially her intellectual inferiors. Luxemburg disliked some people easily and quickly, not necessarily on ideological grounds. Addicted to walking, for example, she detested colleagues she considered physically lazy. Her German collaborator Clara Zetkin managed to work with her because she acknowledged Luxemburg's intellectual preeminence.

Upon graduation from the University of Zurich, Luxemburg moved to Berlin in May 1898, obtaining a residence permit by concluding a sham marriage with the son of a Polish friend living in Germany. In Berlin, she lived in an apartment that faithfully reproduced her meticulous personality —filled with old, well-preserved furniture, carpets, and favored gifts. She methodically marked everything, neatly stored her books, and carefully put away her manuscripts so they would be easy to find if she requested friends to do so.

Once established in Germany, Luxemburg rose to prominence in Socialist circles. In February 1914, the authorities tried her because she publicly called on German soldiers to refuse to fire on their French brethren in case of war. When the trial ended, she made a speech that became legendary in German Socialist annals, but, her appeals exhausted, the police arrested her in early 1915 and shipped her off to prison.

In the last weeks of the war and during the revolutionary crisis immediately following the conflict, Luxemburg and Karl Liebknecht led the Spartacists, a revolutionary Communist league. This organization sparked a revolution, and Luxemburg went along despite her misgivings. The Freikorps put down the

continued

continued

revolution in blood and arrested both leaders on January 15, 1919. The Communist leaders were brought in for questioning, but the soldiers had already made plans to kill them. The soldiers beat Luxemburg and took her to a waiting car where an officer shot her through the head. The killers dumped the body in a canal and gave out the story that a mob had kidnapped her. Luxemburg's body resurfaced on May 31. The murders of Luxemburg and Liebknecht, shot "while trying to escape," led to widespread protests in Germany and outside the country, but except for the left, the German press considered the killings a natural consequence of the attempted revolution.

On June 13, 1919, Luxemburg was buried alongside her fallen comrades who had been entombed earlier. Supporters dedicated a memorial to the fallen martyrs of 1919 on June 13, 1926, but the Nazis later demolished it. The East Germans rebuilt it after World War II.

On February 11, 1919, the Constituent Assembly, meeting in the city of Weimar, chose Friedrich Ebert as the republic's first president and on July 31 adopted a Liberal constitution. The Weimar Republic would last only twelve years. The German Socialists allowed the empire's authoritarian bureaucratic structure, its social structure, and its powerful army to remain intact, and these were the Achilles' heel of the new democratic republic.

REVOLUTION IN AUSTRIA

In Austria, the Social Democrats (SDs) played a role similar to that of their German counterparts in defeating attempts to revolutionize Austrian society. During the war, the SDs supported the war effort on the grounds that Russia was an autocracy, but with the Bolshevik Revolution, this rationale dissipated, and resentment against the war increased.

The Austrian Uprising

As Austria-Hungary spiraled toward defeat, an ethnic and social revolution loomed. Strikes broke out, and different subject minorities plotted to secede. On May 30, 1917, the government called Parliament back into session after a three-year break in order to defuse the discontent. Instead the Socialists recognized the right of Slavic peoples to self-determination and looked forward to a democratic republic, socialism, and union with Germany if the empire broke apart.

In January 1918, a wave of strikes hit the country, and a Socialist manifesto exhorted the workers to fight for peace without annexations. The strike movement spread to Hungary, and the first revolutionary workers' councils were established. The SDs, however, did not push for revolution because the Czechs were heading toward succession and the Germans appeared ready to invade. The strike ended with the government's acceptance of a set of workers' demands, but had important political consequences. It hastened the breakup of the empire by touching off mutinies in the armed forces and encouraged the Slavs to prohibit the export of food and strategic materials to Austria. This action prompted the SDs to demand

Socialist head Karl Renner was instrumental in preventing a social revolution in Austria and instituting reform in a democratic context, as was Friedrich Ebert, his German counterpart. He became the first Chancellor of the new Austrian Republic in 1918 and the first President of the Second Republic in December 1945.

a separate German Austrian parliamentary republic and, in concert with other Austrian parties, declared that the German Austrian deputies constituted a provisional national assembly. On October 24, 1918, the final Italian offensive that destroyed the Hapsburg armed forces began, and between October 28 and 31, the empire dissolved. The subject territories declared their independence, the Austrians issued a republican constitution, the emperor abdicated, and the Political Council of the provisional national assembly took control. Returning Austrian soldiers formed Red Guards, seized armories and food stores, and ran amok.

The Austrian revolution quickly turned into a social uprising. A new SD-led cabinet took power and raised a military force based on a preexisting Socialist network, the Volkswehr, composed primarily of factory workers returning home from the war. This force included soldiers who had witnessed the revolution in Russia and who were anxious to spread it to Austria.

The Revolution Winds Down

Like their German colleagues, the Austrian Socialists opposed a Bolshevik type revolution and faced a dilemma. The Entente maintained its blockade against

Austria as the war wound down and vowed to lift it only if peace and order were maintained. The SDs understood this policy to mean that the Allies opposed the spread of Bolshevism and supported the establishment of a bourgeois democracy. The Allies could starve any radical revolution into submission—a revolution that, at any rate, had little popular support outside Vienna. The peasants favored a republic only because of the hardships of a long war, but they rejected government-imposed price controls and condemned the nationalization of property.

The SDs concluded that the dictatorship of the proletariat demanded by radical Viennese workers would lead to a bloody civil war and emphasized reform in a democratic context. On February 16, 1919, they won 69 out of 150 seats in elections for the National Assembly. Led by Karl Renner, they became the dominant partners in a coalition cabinet with the progressive wing of the Catholic (Christian Social) party. The government implemented a series of social reforms, including unemployment relief, forcing employers to hire new workers in a set proportion to their existing personnel, and prohibiting them from dismissing employees. On December 17, 1919, a law established the eight-hour workday and on July 30, annual vacations. Other legislation instituted workers' committees in factories and other enterprises.

After these reforms, the passion for revolution cooled off because of fears of a Communist takeover and the bourgeoisie's recovery of confidence. An Austrian Communist party was founded on November 3, 1918, and the spring of 1919 brought the establishment of a Soviet republic in Hungary, a Hungarian request for Austrian support, and an SD refusal. The Hungarians fomented Austrian revolutions on April 18 and June 15, both put down by the Volkswehr.

By the summer of 1919, the Austrian revolution had run its course, with even the SD considered too far to the left. On October 17, 1920, the Catholics won a majority in the National Assembly and formed a new cabinet without the SDs. A currency crisis and the financial restrictions necessary to resolve it completed the return of the bourgeoisie to power. As in Germany, the Social Democrats succeeded in instituting important reforms but not in altering Austrian society.

THE HUNGARIAN REVOLUTION

The Hungarian part of the former Dual Monarchy followed a different course. Hungary was the only country to which the Bolshevik revolution spread, if only briefly.

Opposition to the War

In Hungary dissatisfaction, strikes, and sabotage increased as World War I dragged on. In the fall of 1917, supporters of the Bolshevik revolution organized workers' councils on the Russian Soviet model, and in January 1918, a massive strike movement hit Budapest when news of the Brest-Litovsk negotiations and the Austrian protest strikes arrived. The Hungarian Socialists endorsed the strike, but only on a limited basis. The government's backtracking on a series of promises favored the emergence of an extreme left and polarized the Socialist movement. In June a second major strike wave rocked the country, and a determined Communist group began taking shape.

Béla Kun and the Hungarian Communists

The Communist hard core consisted of a group of Moscow-trained Hungarian prisoners of war, led by former Social Democrat Béla Kun, who had participated in the Bolshevik revolution. The Communists returned to Hungary with Lenin's blessing with the goal of establishing a Hungarian republic of Workers' and Soldiers' Councils. Kun arrived in Budapest on November 7, 1918, and by November 24 had convinced opposition elements in the Social Democratic opposition to secede and form the Communist Party of Hungary. Kun built a centralized party organization on the Russian example and recruited members among the unemployed, the poor, and former prisoners of war.

In October 1918, opposition leader Mihály Károlyi formed a liberal democratic government with Social Democratic participation. By then Hungary had lost half its territory, the economic situation was desperate, and demands were made to set up a popular republic. Social Democratic membership in the cabinet limited the party's political choices and favored Kun's intransigent Communists as workers seized factories, peasants attacked landed estates, workers' councils replaced city administrations, and unruly soldiers roamed the streets. On March 19, 1919, the Entente sent Hungary an ultimatum requiring it to form a neutral zone on its eastern frontier and to withdraw its army behind it, further radicalizing the masses and resulting in a Socialist withdrawal from the government. The Socialists then reached an agreement with Kun and the Communists that effectively merged their two organizations. Thus, the Hungarian Soviet Republic came into existence because of Kun's Russian connections and Allied blundering.

The Hungarian Soviet Republic

The Hungarian Soviet Republic, born in April 1919, had a brief life of 133 days. Two fatal illusions and two ideological fallacies condemned it. The illusions were that the Russians would send help and that the Socialists and Communists would cooperate; the fallacies were that socialism could be installed rapidly in Hungary and that the revolution was part of a worldwide wave.

The Hungarian Soviet Republic's governmental structure consisted of an executive, the Revolutionary Governing Council (RGC), and, wielding the ultimate power, the Budapest Council of Workers' and Soldiers' Deputies. Both institutions had Socialist not Communist majorities. As time went on, the Socialists became more restless with the alliance, and the Communists proved unable to garner much mass support in the country. Despite their minority status in the government and the country, the Communists initially had great influence because of Kun's presence in the cabinet and because the RGC passed reform measures, including the eight-hour workday, higher wages, and lower rents.

Other, more specifically Communist, actions proved less successful or alienated the population: the abolition of conscription, a volunteer army composed exclusively of proletarians, and collectivization of the land. The Communists also failed to keep support in the cities because extremist Communists controlled the

Although Béla Kun's Communist regime in Hungary following World War I was relatively brief, its success and its policies alarmed Europe and he was overthrown. However, its historical impact was considerable and its memory remained strong. The photo shows a Soviet-era rendering of the Hungarian Revolution of 1919.

secret police and utilized terror against the Revolution's enemies through the "Lenin Boys"—leather-jacketed thugs and criminals—who specialized in break-ins and kidnapping. The Socialists ended the Lenin Boys' activities, won control of the police, and reversed Communist influence.

End of the Soviet Republic

On April 17, the Romanians attacked Hungary after Kun turned down yet another Allied ultimatum, and the Hungarian Soviet Republic descended into chaos as the population turned against the postwar disorder, Jewish Communist leaders, and a governmental anticlerical campaign. On June 24 the Socialists resigned from the RGC, resulting in a new wave of Communist violence. Czech and Romanian forces converged on Budapest, and on August 1, 1919, Kun resigned and fled the country.

The balance sheet of the Hungarian Soviet Republic was unimpressive. Its brief tenure did not alter Hungarian society, and the reaction to it paved the way for an authoritarian regime.

CONTINUOUS REBELLION: ARTISTS AND SCIENTISTS

World War I encouraged not only political and social but also cultural revolutions that had antecedents in prewar Europe; the conflict removed all restraints on them. In the case of science, the fundamental research conducted before the war came into full fruition during the 1920s, 1930s, and thereafter, culminating in the development of the atomic bomb and in nuclear energy.

Dada and Revolution

While in exile in Zurich, Lenin lived at Spiegelgasse number 12. Across the street, on February 5, 1916, a young German couple opened the Cabaret Voltaire, which had "the object of becoming a center of artistic entertainment. The Cabaret Voltaire will be run on the principle of daily meeting where visiting artists will perform their music and poetry." While the staid and cold Lenin studied and plotted revolution, Hugo Ball, a poet and theater director who had fled Berlin during World War I, played the piano while his future wife, Emmy Hennings, sang for the patrons. The new café began quietly as a literary adventure but quickly escalated into a boisterous nuisance that instigated many complaints by the public. It is easy to understand why: "Total pandemonium. The people around us are shouting, laughing, and gesticulating. Our replies are sighs of love, volleys of hiccups, poems, moos, and miaowing. . . . Tzara is wiggling his behind like the belly of an oriental dancer. Janco is playing an invisible violin and bowing and scraping." The sedate but now irate neighbors called the police, who shut down the cabaret but ignored Lenin. While Lenin read Marx, the Cabaret Voltaire gave birth to the extraordinary literary and artistic movement known as Dada.

The émigrés who flocked to the club included Tristan Tzara, the tiny but aggressive Romanian poet who invented the word *Dada* and electrified audiences with his iconoclastic readings; Dr. Richard Huelsenbeck, whose riding whip whistled in the air during his performances—"metaphorically—onto the public's behind: Shalabenshalabei-shalametzomai"—and the artists Hans Arp, Marcel Janco, and Max Oppenheimer. Dada fights, abuse, and audience provocations, copied from Italian Futurism, became their trademark and its iconoclasm an instant sensation. The proponents of Dada opened a gallery in Zurich in January 1917, where Ball read abstract sound poems that discarded traditional language, "devastated and ravaged by journalism." Arp tore up one of his drawings, let the pieces flutter to the ground, and glued them back together again in the chance arrangement in which the pieces had fallen: Dadaists contended that they had discovered in chance the "'mobilization of the unconsciousness."

The Dadaists mutinied against the nineteenth-century belief in progress, but in contrast to futurism, Dada was apolitical: a "state of mind," "a force of nothingness," above all "a protest against the civilization that had led to the war. . . . " The conflict proved the total bankruptcy of European civilization, and its adherents claimed that they wanted to destroy its moral and social assumptions through a savage anti-middle-class program. That strategy seemed to be working when, at the war's end, Dada spread like wildfire to revolutionary Germany, Italy, Hungary, and other countries where old political systems were breaking down. Dada was the counterpoint to political revolution, spreading rebellion against art and authority.

In 1918 Dada's center shifted to Paris, where prewar avant-garde movements and disgust at the war had prepared a fertile ground. In late 1919, Tristan Tzara arrived to wild acclaim to organize Dadaist activities in the French capital. André Breton, his main contact there, had been converted to Dadaism by his wartime experiences. In 1918 he founded the review *Littérature* in which disillusioned former French warrior intellectuals aimed to tear down the restraints of bourgeois society and attracted Tzara's attention. On January 23, 1920, the *Littérature*

Dada and Surrealism were the two revolutionary artistic movements that shook
Europe during and following World War I. In this 1932 photograph, the most famous
exponent of Dada, Tristan Tzara, is in the center, and Paul Breton, founder of Surrealism,
is on the left.

group organized the first Parisian Dada manifestation. By this time, ironically,
the bourgeois society that it vilified had accepted Dada, and Dada acknowledged
this critical acclaim. Consequently, Parisian exponents of Dada, including Breton,
condemned the movement for having become stagnant and orthodox and started
a new artistic movement.

Surrealism

Like Dadaism, surrealism demanded the destruction of art and a return to chaos
in order to recover the subconscious and believed that the automatic method of
writing could achieve that aim. While Dadaism stressed destruction, surrealism
declared that a new art would emerge from the unconscious, from the irrational, and from the uncontrolled regions of the mind. In this sense, the surrealists
accepted psychoanalytical notions and methods and discovered a second reality
fused with but different from ordinary reality. This conception influenced important novelists writing at the time, such as James Joyce and Franz Kafka, "who,
although they have nothing to do with surrealism as a doctrine, are surrealists in
the wider sense, like most of the progressive artists of the century."

Unlike Dada, a sense of wonder was linked to surrealism, and surrealism
appeared as a fundamentally optimistic movement. It represented a first attempt
to heal from the horrors of war and paralleled the winding down of revolutionary
activity in politics. Surrealist ideas may be seen in the paintings of Salvador Dali,
who introduced and mixed the most incongruous realistic items, such as a

donkey's dead body on a piano. Superficially, Dali's paintings are absurd, but they are really "the expression of a desire to bring unity and coherence . . . into the atomized world in which we live."

As the war receded, revolutionary artistic developments were gradually absorbed into the mainstream to become, along with death, destruction, and upheaval, the common European heritage of World War I.

Revolutionary Developments in Physics

The search for unity in the arts paralleled events in science. Since its first expression in 1900, the quantum theory had produced stranger and stranger notions of reality. In 1925 German scientist Werner Heisenberg elaborated the uncertainty or indeterminacy principle according to which the observer, far from being neutral, changed reality. Experimenters, for example, could not simultaneously determine both the velocity and position of an atom's electron because doing so would alter the variables involved. In the hidden subatomic world, the rules changed, nothing could be known for certain, and weird and contradictory states coexisted. This uncertainty resembled the unconscious that was so important in modern art. Just as the surrealists believed in a second reality, light had a dual nature, and scientists Werner Heisenberg and Niels Bohr contended that in the subatomic world, "there are two truths rather than one alone." In 1919, an important confirmation of Einstein's relativity theory arrived when an experiment conducted during a solar eclipse showed that gravity bent light. Relativity, which had "disintegrated common sense," was accepted, and Einstein became famous. After World War I, science kicked out the intellectual underpinnings of European society with even greater effect, perhaps, than art.

Bibliographical Essay

The historical literature on the Russian revolutions of 1917 is extraordinarily rich and generally includes discussions of the old regime; the reader, however, should beware of interpretations based on ideology. Interestingly enough, these viewpoints have varied not only according to ideology but also to periods. Moreover, it is likely that different perspectives will emerge on the entire Communist experience because of the Soviet Union's demise in 1991 and as previously closed archives are combed by historians.

Richard Pipes wrote two extraordinarily detailed and scholarly works that are basic to an understanding of events, *The Russian Revolution* (New York, 1990), and *Russia Under the Bolshevik Regime* (New York, 1993). Orlando Figes produced a detailed and well-documented but very accessible history, *A People's Tragedy: The Russian Revolution, 1891–1924* (New York, 1996); it is from this book that the quotations on the lack of a general plan for the Russian army in World War I (p. 259) and the description of Petrograd on October 25 (p. 484) are taken. The role of Russian peasants in the years up to and including the revolutions and later is examined by Aaron B. Retish, *Russia's Peasants in Revolution and Civil War: Citizenship, Identity, and the Creation of the Soviet State, 1914–1922* (Cambridge, UK, 2008). Alexander Rabinowitch published a good account of how *The Bolsheviks Came to Power: The Revolution of 1917 in Petrograd* (New York, 1978) and one on how they maintained power during the crucial first year, *The Bolsheviks in Power* (Bloomington, Ind., 2007). An idea of the different terrors may be found in

The Red Terror in Russia (London, 2008), by S. P. Mel'gunov, and *White Terror: Cossack Warlords of the Trans-Siberian* (New York, 2005) by Jamie Bisher. Sean McMeekin discusses the "looting" of Imperial Russia's riches by the Bolsheviks in *History's Greatest Heist* (New Haven, Conn., 2008). All these works pay great attention to social as well as political and intellectual matters. A classic eyewitness account is John Reed, *Ten Days That Shook the World* (New York, 1967); another eyewitness description is Nikolai N. Sukhanov, *The Russian Revolution, 1917: Eyewitness Account*, 2 vols. (New York, 1962). A brief but well-done overview of the revolution is Sheila Fitzpatrick's *The Russian Revolution* (Oxford, UK, 1982). Another good, short book is Theodore H. Von Laue, *Why Lenin? Why Stalin? A Reappraisal of the Russian Revolution, 1900–1930*, 2d ed. (Philadelphia, 1971).

Bruce W. Menning's *Bayonets Before Bullets: The Imperial Russian Army, 1861–1914* (Bloomington, Ind., 2000) is a general history, while the agony of the Russian army and its role with respect to the revolution is minutely examined by Allan K. Wildman, *The End of the Russian Imperial Army*, 2 vols. (Princeton, N.J., 1980–87). The standard work on Brest-Litovsk is John Wheeler-Bennett, *Brest-Litovsk: The Forgotten Peace, March 1918* (New York 1971).

Good studies of the working class in major Russian cities include S. A. Smith, *Red Petrograd: Revolution in the Factories, 1917–1918* (Cambridge, UK, 1983), a thorough examination of factory organization and the workers during the revolutionary period. David Mandel, *The Petrograd Workers and the Soviet Seizure of Power: From the July Days, 1917 to July 1918* (London, 1984), looks at the role of the workers between those dates. Diane Koenker does the same for Moscow in *Moscow Workers and the 1917 Revolution* (Princeton, N.J., 1981). The situation on the land is amply discussed in the previously cited books, but see also a work dedicated to the SRs and their fate, Oliver H. Radkey, *The Agrarian Foes of Bolshevism: Promise and Default of the Russian Socialist Revolutionaries, February to October, 1917* (New York, 1958). Robert Vincent Daniels, *The Conscience of the Revolution: Communist Opposition in Soviet Russia* (New York, 1960), examines the disputes on various issues within the Bolshevik party itself. On a different social class and its role, see Matthew Rendle, *Defenders of the Motherland: The Tsarist Elite in Revolutionary Russia* (New York, 2010). The civil war's course is considered in detail by David Footman, *Civil War in Russia* (New York, 1961).

Biographies of the major characters are plentiful and easily available, but two may be mentioned here: Robert Service, *Lenin: A Political Life*, 2 vols. (Bloomington, Ind., 1985–91), is a complete life, and the first volume of Issac Deutscher's classic biography, *The Prophet Armed: Trotsky, 1879–1921* (New York, 1955), covers the period considered in the text while *The Prophet Outcast* (New York, 1963) covers his later life. Robert Service takes a different view from many historians in his *Trotsky: A Biography* (Cambridge, Mass., 2009). Raymond K. Massie tells the story of what happened to the bodies of the royal family and their servants after their murder and explains how DNA evidence was used to identify their remains in a fascinating study, *The Romanovs: The Final Chapter* (London, 1995).

F. L. Carsten discusses the German, Austrian, and Hungarian revolutions in an excellent work, *Revolution in Central Europe 1918–1919* (Berkeley, Calif., 1972). Pierre Broue, *The German Revolution, 1917–1923* (n.p,, 2006) is a general work. The German Socialists and their action during the revolution of 1918 are examined in a well-argued and detailed work by A. J. Ryder, *The German Revolution of 1918: A Study of German Socialism in War and Revolt* (Cambridge, UK, 2008). The first volume of Richard J. Evans, *The Coming of the Third Reich* (New York, 2004) discusses Germany right after the end of World War I; the quote on the fear that prevailed is on p. 78. Richard A. Comfort,

Revolutionary Hamburg: Labor Politics in the Early Weimar Republic (Stanford, Calif., 1966), concentrates on labor politics in an important city. The most thorough work on Rosa Luxemburg and her influence is J. P. Nettl, *Rosa Luxemburg* (New York, 1975). Werner T. Angress, *Stillborn Revolution: The Communist Bid for Power in Germany, 1921–1923* (Princeton, N.J., 1963), analyzes Communist attempts to take power in Germany between 1921 and 1923.

Mark Cornwall discusses the Austro-Hungarian war effort and the end of the empire in his *The Undermining of Austria-Hungary* (New York, 2000). The Austro-Hungarian Empire's breakup is considered in detail in Z. A. B. Zeman, *The Break-Up of the Hapsburg Empire* (New York, 1977); Leo Valiani, *The End of Austria-Hungary* (London, 1973); and the second volume of Arthur J. May's *The Passing of the Hapsburg Monarchy 1914–1918* (Philadelphia, 1966). The chapter on Austria-Hungary in Sir Lewis Namier's *Vanished Supremacies: Essays on European History, 1812–1918* (London, 1958) can still be read for its remarkable insights. A manageable and surprisingly objective account of the revolution in Austria and the interplay of the various nationalities, by an important participant, is Otto Bauer, *The Austrian Revolution* (New York, 1970). John C. Swanson, *The Remnants of the Habsburg Monarchy* (Boulder, Colo., 2001) examines the end of the empire and the creation of the new states up to 1922.

Rudolf F. Tökés, *Béla Kun and the Hungarian Soviet Republic: The Origins and Role of the Communist Part of Hungary in the Revolutions of 1918–1919* (New York, 1967), is an excellent account of the roles of the Communists and Socialists during the Hungarian revolution and a good general history of that event; it is also valuable for its reproduction of documents and other appendixes. Tibor Hajdu, *The Hungarian Soviet Republic* (Budapest, 1979), is a good complement to the previous work because of its archival sources and treatment of social and cultural issues, although it takes a rather narrow approach. Howard Morley Sachar, *Dreamland: Europeans and Jews in the Aftermath of the Great* War (New York, 2002) has a chapter on Kun. A reprint of a 1924 work, Oscar Jaszi, *Revolution and Counter-Revolution in Hungary* (New York, 1969), is still useful for its detail.

Some books that analyze the themes with relation to the arts discussed in this chapter include Irving Howe, ed., *The Idea of the Modern* (New York, 1967), which primarily deals with literature. The reader will find interesting essays on Dadaism, surrealism, and other modern movements; the citations on surrealism and surrealist painting are on pp. 231 and 232. A good idea of Dadaism's nature can be gained by reading Tristan Tzara's *Seven Dada Manifestos and Lampisteries: Documents of the International Dada Movement* (London, 1977). Hans Richter published *Dada 1916–1966* (Munich, 1966), which includes art reproductions and documents; the quote on Huelsenbeck's performance is on p. 3, and the idea of the mobilization of the unconscious is on p. 7. Hugo Ball's diary, *Flight Out of Time: A Dada Diary* (New York, 1974), features an excellent introduction; the description of activities at the Cabaret Voltaire is on p. xxiii. Kenneth Coutts-Smith, *Dada* (London, 1970), is a brief overview that reprints the advertisement quoted in the text on p. 9 and uses the term "savage anarchism" on p. 22. Histories of Dadaism include Dietmar Elger and Uta Grosenick, *Dadaism* (Los Angeles, 2004), and Rudolf E. Kuenzli, *Dada* (London, 2006), a wider treatment. Ruth Hemus, *Dada's Women* (New Haven, Conn., 2009) assigns a more important role to women in Dadaism than was previously thought. J. H. Matthews, *An Introduction to Surrealism* (University Park, Penn., 1965), is an excellent starting point for understanding the movement, while Mary Ann Caws, *Surrealism* (London, 2004), is a general history. See also Nahma Sandrow, *Surrealism: Theater, Arts, Ideas* (New York, 1972), for the remark on Einstein's disintegration of common sense, p. 13. The discussion of Einstein,

Heisenberg, and quantum theory may be followed in Denis Brian, *Einstein: A Life* (New York, 1996); the citations regarding the uncertainty principle and its implications are on pp. 162 and 163 (see also Einstein's remark regarding quantum theory on p. 199). Galvin Parkinson describes the connections between physics thinking and art during the period in *Surrealism, Art, and Modern Science: Relativity, Quantum Mechanics, Epistemology* (New Haven, Conn., 2008).

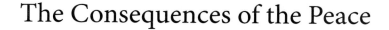

CHAPTER 8

The Consequences of the Peace

CHAPTER OUTLINE

The Paris Peace Conference • The Territorial Consequences • Economic Consequences • The Moral Consequences • The League of Nations

BIOGRAPHICAL SKETCHES

Georges Clemenceau, Tiger • Sidney Sonnino, Failed Diplomatist

The Paris Peace Conference that convened on January 18, 1919, to hammer out peace terms and ensure future peace, had as its model the Congress of Vienna, held in 1814 and 1815, at which "the boundaries of almost every state in Europe were remodeled; reparations were inflicted upon the dominant military power; colonial territories were redistributed; new international organizations were erected; and even schemes for the perpetuation of world peace were considered."

In fact, the Vienna precedent did not hold for several reasons. In Paris the representatives had to consider popular opinion, which demanded revenge against the Germans, and to confront a new factor, the overwhelming power of the United States, which had rescued the Allies and did not sympathize with their values.

THE PARIS PEACE CONFERENCE

In a speech to the U.S. Congress on January 8, 1918, American President Woodrow Wilson issued the Fourteen Points as the basis for ending the war and concluding a lasting peace. Open agreements "openly arrived at" must replace traditional diplomacy and secret treaties, he said, as he enunciated his points: freedom of the seas as defined by international law; elimination of trade barriers; arms reduction; and giving native colonial populations equal weight with imperial governments. His concrete proposals included the autonomous development of the nationalities of the Austro-Hungarian and Turkish empires; the formation of an association of nations to guarantee peace; and German withdrawal from Russian, Belgian,

French, Romanian, and Serbian territory. Very important for Wilson and the Europeans was the establishment of an independent Poland with access to the sea to ensure its economic viability; the return of Alsace and Lorraine to France; and the rectification of international borders, such as the Italian, along clearly recognized lines.

Contentious Issues

When American intervention and acceptance of the Fourteen Points by the Germans ended the war and Wilson toured the continent, the people received him with wild enthusiasm, but the Allies tried to water down the proposals that most affected their own national interests. They bargained with Wilson before the peace conference met and compromised his principles, especially with regard to British and French requests, to gain support for his cherished League of Nations. The British did not want their own freedom of action on the seas limited by international law because it would hamper them in wartime; they objected, and Wilson relented. Moreover, existing treaties negotiated after the war broke out limited Wilson's freedom of action and caused problems. Alsace-Lorraine had been promised to France, Constantinople to Russia, and the head of the Adriatic to Italy. No one disputed France's claim, Russia had forfeited its rights, and Wilson's opposition to Italian demands caused a crisis.

Boundary issues in Western Europe were child's play when compared to those in Eastern Europe, where frontiers based on national lines meant little because different nationalities had lived in mixed areas for centuries and where often a city was predominantly of one nationality and its hinterland of another. Nationality conflicted with strategic considerations, historical claims, centuries-old ethnic and racial hatreds, and contrasting Allied promises. The victorious powers could either sanction the expulsion of national minorities from areas in which they had lived for centuries or impose guarantees of minority rights on the small Eastern European states, which they did. However, the clauses they imposed in the peace treaties mandating respect for minority rights caused fierce resentment and opposition that sowed the seeds of dissension, war, and expulsion of the minorities. In addition, the great weakness of the Versailles system was the absence of Russia, which, when it recovered from the war's devastation, reasserted its ambitions in Eastern Europe.

In the Middle East, Africa, and Asia, the Allies coveted the German and Turkish colonial possessions, but thanks to Wilson's Fourteen Points annexation of the colonies was impossible. The problem was solved by a "mandate" system that allowed them to govern the areas under the authority of the newly created League of Nations in order to bring the native peoples closer to democracy and to prepare them for independence. The scheme classified the former German and Turkish possessions "A" mandates; colonies fairly close to independence, "B" mandates—unlikely to achieve independence anytime soon—and "C" mandates to be ruled as if they were part of the mother country. The mandate system did not resolve the problem of colonialism, and the mandates did not gain their freedom until the general decolonization movement after World War II. In principle, the league had widespread support but major difficulties in practice. The Allies distrusted the league's capacity to keep the peace and relied on alliances and on economic means, particularly reparations, to ensure that Germany would never again threaten them.

Reparations

In theory, reparations would force Germany to pay for the material devastation and financial costs of war that they had provoked. French Prime Minister Georges Clemenceau was most adamant in utilizing them not only as repayment for the enormous costs of the conflict but as a means of keeping Germany permanently weak. British Prime Minister David Lloyd George had a softer attitude, but he had gone on record that he would make the Germans pay "until the pips squeaked." This common goal gave some unity to British and French policy, but the French feared above all a future German attack, while the British, more secure behind the English Channel, were less anxious. The United States, even farther away, was less concerned about a German military revival.

BIOGRAPHICAL SKETCHES

Georges Clemenceau
Tiger

Georges Clemenceau was determined and opinioned from the time of his youth. Born in the Vendée, the poor region in the west of France, on September 28, 1841, he grew up as a solid Republican like his father. His views got him into trouble with Emperor Napoleon III's regime, and he spent a period of about two months in jail. Clemenceau studied to be a physician and went to New York after he got his degree. He admired the freedom he found in the United States and contemplated settling there. He found a job as a teacher in Stamford, Connecticut, and eventually married one of his students. In 1869, after seven years' residence in the United States, he returned to France to practice medicine in the Vendée.

In 1870 the Franco-Prussian War broke out. Napoleon III was quickly defeated, and a republic was established. Clemenceau moved to Paris, where he was elected to the Chamber of Deputies in February 1871 as a radical Republican. His aggressive debating and writing style earned him the nickname of "The Tiger." Accused of being paid off by the British in a scandal involving a French attempt to build a canal across the Isthmus of Panama, Clemenceau lost a reelection bid in 1893. He then turned full time to journalism, which he had practiced in the past. Clemenceau contributed daily articles to newspapers and in 1900 founded his own newspaper, *Le Bloc*. The newspaper defended Alfred Dreyfus, a Jewish military officer who was falsely accused of treason.

In 1902 Clemenceau returned to Parliament as a senator. In contrast to his earlier politics, he was now a nationalist. In 1907 he became prime minister in a cabinet that lasted until 1910 during which he fought bitterly with the French unions. His oratorical duels in Parliament with Socialist leader Jean Jaurès over social reforms became legendary. When World War I broke out, he edited a newspaper, *L'Homme Libre*, which criticized the government's conduct of the war.

continued

continued

His objections to Joseph Joffre as the commanding general of the French army and accusations of pacifism against important members of the government led to the suppression of his newspaper.

At the height of the French crisis during the war in November 1917, Clemenceau became prime minister at the head of a coalition government and minister for war. He brooked no criticism and had prominent politicians arrested for treason. Clemenceau successfully revived French morale and reinvigorated the flagging war effort. He persuaded the Allies to create a unified command under Marshal Ferdinand Foch in order to achieve victory. His view of war was cynical. "War," he said, "is a series of catastrophes that results in a victory."

At the Paris Peace Conference, Clemenceau—strongly anti-German from the time of his youth—took on both Woodrow Wilson, whom he considered too idealistic, and British Prime Minister David Lloyd George, who thought that Clemenceau's tough stance toward Germany would provoke another war. Clemenceau got Alsace-Lorraine restored to France, but his strategy to contain Germany failed.

Ironically, considering his charges that the Americans and the British were too lenient toward Germany, he lost the January 1920 presidential election because the French thought that the Versailles treaty was soft on the Germans and blamed him. After his loss, "The Tiger" retired from politics to write his memoirs and to warn of a renewed conflict with Germany. Georges Clemenceau died in Paris on November 24, 1929.

In addition, the Bolshevik revolution; the uprisings in Germany, Austria, and Hungary; and the disorders in the Allied states provided a dramatic backdrop to the Peace Conference. The Allies were furious with the Bolsheviks because they had pulled Russia out of the war with Germany, had published the secret treaties signed before World War I, and had repudiated the enormous debts the country owed the Western powers. The Germans argued that they should be treated well because they had established a democratic republic; the Austrians maintained that the Hapsburgs should be held responsible for the war, not they; and fighting continued to rage over the boundaries of the new states in East Europe.

These issues could not be resolved in the six months that the conference met, and negotiations continued long afterward. The territorial, economic, and military terms are embodied in five instruments signed between 1919 and 1920: the treaties of Versailles with Germany, June 28, 1919; St. Germain with Austria, September 10; Neuilly with Bulgaria, November 27; Trianon with Hungary on June 4, 1920; and Sèvres with Turkey, August 20, 1920. The allies presented a reparations bill of 132 billion gold marks to Germany on April 27, 1921, but disputes over reparations continued into 1924—and the bad blood for much longer.

THE TERRITORIAL CONSEQUENCES

The general principle that the new European frontiers should follow ethnic lines guided the victors, but they also considered strategic factors and the

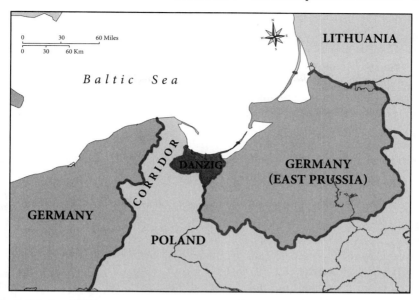

The Polish Corridor. This strip of land served as a pretext for the outbreak of World War II on September 1, 1939.

rectification of past injustices. The losers protested against the decisions and argued that vengeance drove them.

German Losses

The new German boundaries caused problems that were not resolved. In the West, Germany lost Alsace and Lorraine to France, a foregone conclusion that the Germans did not accept because they demanded a plebiscite. A plebiscite held in Schleswig resulted in the predominantly Danish northern part opting for Denmark. The Allies required Germany to cede some small strategic areas to Belgium.

The disposition of the left bank of the Rhine river strained the relations among the Allies. The French demand for paramount influence in the area to create a buffer against German invasions ran into stiff British and American opposition because they feared that it would create a new problem that would poison future European relations. Clemenceau accepted a compromise: a demilitarized Rhineland occupied by an Allied force for fifteen years and an Anglo-American pledge to sign a treaty with France guaranteeing aid to France in case of an unprovoked German attack, a promise the Americans did not fulfill. The French also backed off their demand to annex the strategic, coal-rich Saar basin, which they claimed as compensation for German destruction of French mines. France agreed to having the rights to the area's coal, sovereignty exercised by a League of Nations commission for fifteen years, and a plebiscite that in 1935 restored the Saar to Germany.

The Germans objected to these changes on their western borders, but were enraged by those in the East. An independent Poland with secure access to the sea was one of Wilson's basic points, but there were formidable practical problems. German statesmen considered the maintenance of Germany's eastern borders a condition of its continuation as a great power, and Poland's revival of Poland earned undying German enmity. Moreover, the Germans had systematically encouraged immigration into Polish-speaking areas for 150 years after the Polish partitions of the eighteenth century, resulting in an intermixture that made it impossible to draw clear-cut lines on the basis of nationality and inflamed tensions during the interwar period.

The nationality issue guaranteed that any solution to the problem of Polish access to the Baltic Sea would fail because no access to the sea meant economic "strangulation" for Poland. The Allies created a "Polish Corridor" that split East Prussia from the rest of Germany and put a sizable German minority into Poland. Danzig, a German city of 300,000 and the main port in the area, became a free city protected by the League of Nations within a Polish customs union. In 1939, World War II began in Danzig.

The Polish Corridor was only the tip of the eastern iceberg. Plebiscites were ordered in other German districts, leading to bloody confrontations with the German paramilitary Freikorps. The Germans objected to Polish annexation of Upper Silesia, an important industrial area, after they won a plebiscite on March 20, 1921, but after which the Poles with French support annexed the principal industrial and mining districts. In all, Germany ceded an area of 16,750 square miles to Poland with a population of 1 million Germans and 1.8 million Poles. German losses did not cripple the country or significantly reduce the country's industrial capacity, but they inflamed German emotions and set the stage for World War II.

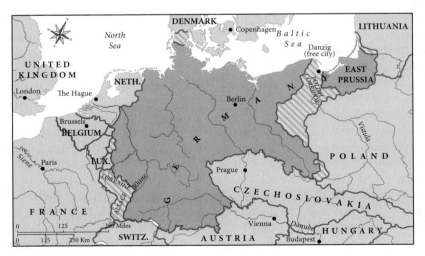

Germany's Losses. Shown here is the territory Germany lost after World War I. The country's core and its productive capacity, however, remained intact.

The Polish Problem and Russian Losses

Reconstituting Poland also caused many difficulties in settling the new state's boundaries with Russia. In principle the Russians accepted an independent Poland to include regions having an indisputable Polish ethnic majority, but in a large zone it was impossible to determine the ethnicity of the majority population. In December 1919, experts at the Paris Peace Conference drew a provisional eastern boundary that included incontrovertibly Polish areas, the Curzon line, that could be extended farther east with the determination of relevant facts. The Poles refused to accept this solution and insisted on boundaries based on the 1772 frontiers, when Poland was a large state. After the Russian refusal, the Poles with French support attacked them in April 1920 and won large gains because of the turmoil caused by the Russian civil war. At the Treaty of Riga, March 18, 1921, the Russians agreed to large territorial losses and the placement of a large number of Ukrainians and White Russians in Poland. This solution alienated the Russians and disregarded geography. The Poles estranged two temporarily weakened big powers that had common borders with them, thereby helping create the conditions for a new partition in 1939.

In addition to the territory the Russians lost to the Poles, Finland and the Baltic States (Estonia, Latvia, and Lithuania) won their independence from the Bolsheviks. More territory went to Romania. Because of the German military collapse, Russia recovered most of the territory lost at Brest-Litovsk, but, with the exception of Austria-Hungary, it was the biggest loser of World War I.

The Breakup of Austria-Hungary and Its Consequences

Former Austro-Hungarian lands accounted for all or a great portion of the territories acquired by Czechoslovakia, Poland, Yugoslavia, and Romania. This Balkanization of Eastern Europe caused bitter border disputes and increased nationalism, the incorporation of restless minorities by small states, and economic difficulties. The Poles incorporated eastern Galicia, along with 3.5 million Ukrainians, and claimed the rich coal mining area of Teschen that the Allies awarded to Czechoslovakia. The continual bad blood between the two countries resulted in Polish occupation of the area in 1938 during the infamous Czechoslovak crisis. In another complicated dispute, the Poles absorbed Vilnius, the ancient Lithuanian capital, on the basis of its slight Polish majority, producing a state of war until 1927 and acrimonious feuding thereafter.

Czechoslovakia also presented a major problem. The Allies took care to give it defensible frontiers, but this meant incorporating the mountainous Sudetenland inhabited by 3 million disgruntled Austrian Germans, who in 1938 became the focus of a crisis between Czechoslovakia and Germany. Luckily, Czechoslovakia inherited the old empire's industrial heartland, but this did not prevent it from incorporating Hungarian-inhabited areas on economic grounds.

The Hungarians were the most unfortunate of the East European losers. Like Austria, Hungary emerged as a separate state, but while most of the prewar German-speaking population was part of Austria, the peace settlement put large Hungarian minorities into the neighboring states, particularly Romania, causing Hungary to attempt to overthrow the Versailles system. Romania also

Russian Losses. The shaded areas of the map show the enormous amount of territory lost by Russia. These losses provoked the country to try to make them good once it got on its feet again. The Russians were very interested in regaining the Baltic States and areas of the new Poland that were inhabited by White Russians and Ukrainians.

The End of Austria-Hungary. After the war, major portions of former Austro-Hungarian territory went to Czechoslovakia, Poland, Romania, and Yugoslavia.

tried to annex a southern Hungarian district of mixed population (the Banat of Temesvar), but had to split the area with Serbia, which created bad relations between them. Finally, Bulgaria was forced to cede territory to Greece and lost its access to the Aegean Sea.

The peacemakers did not authorize the expulsion of national minorities as happened after World War II but instead forced the East European states to protect minorities by inserting clauses into the treaties with them and assigning enforcement to the League of Nations. Hostility to the minority clauses helped undermine the postwar settlement in Eastern Europe.

Southeastern Europe

In southeastern Europe, the Serbians had difficulty uniting the south Slavs in the new South Slave state it had dreamed about. On December 4, 1918, the Kingdom of Serbs, Croats, and Slovenes (later, Yugoslavia) was proclaimed. The new state faced serious domestic difficulties because the Croats and Slovenes were Roman Catholic and had a Western orientation while the dominant Serbs were Orthodox Christians with Eastern roots. These problems emerged as a never-resolved struggle between the Serbian demand for centralization and the federalism desired by the other Slav groups in the area. Centralization won out in a constituent assembly held in 1919, but the struggle continued until Yugoslavia's violent breakup in the 1990s.

Yugoslavia faced serious questions on the foreign front as well. President Woodrow Wilson supported Yugoslavia against Italian claims for the city of Fiume at the Paris Peace Conference, causing a rift with the Italians. The question dragged until January 27, 1924, when a treaty signed with Benito Mussolini of Italy ratified Italian annexation of the city, but this settlement failed to calm the Duce's determination to undermine the peace settlement or his hostility toward Yugoslavia.

Left to right: Prime Minister David Lloyd George of Britain, Prime Minister Vittorio Emanuele Orlando of Italy, Prime Minister Georges Clemenceau of France, and President Woodrow Wilson of the United States. Although Wilson was the most prominent participant at the Peace Conference, Clemenceau and Lloyd George managed to get what they wanted from him, frequently in violation of his ideals and of his famous Fourteen Points. Orlando, representing the weakest power and with a divided government behind him, received less than his people and political opponents demanded.

ECONOMIC CONSEQUENCES

When the Germans requested an armistice, they agreed to Wilson's point specifying that they would pay for the war damages caused to the Allied civilian populations, but the reparations question was the most troublesome at the peace conference and after.

The Allies and Reparations

No matter what their sympathies, American experts who studied reparations concentrated on a practical question: how could the world return quickly to a sound financial footing and restore the prewar trade regime? They suggested that $15 billion was a realistic sum based on the German capacity to pay, profoundly disappointing the British and French. Clemenceau and Lloyd George objected that such a low figure would cause their governments to fall and interrupt the peace conference until new elections could be held.

The dispute revolved around two central points—whether an amount should be fixed at Paris or later, and what expenses should be included in the reparations bill in order to calculate a definitive sum. Clemenceau and Lloyd George argued that it would be politically unwise to agree on a sum at the conference because the British and French people would consider any sum too low. The American delegation argued that a fixed figure would permit the Allies to receive a maximum amount from the Germans immediately, allow France and other countries that were partially dependent on German payments to balance their budgets right away, and encourage Germany to work out methods to meet a specific payments goal. On this issue, however, Wilson supported Lloyd George and Clemenceau.

The other rancorous reparations question involved the categories to be included in the calculations for reparations. Damage to civilians and their property had been the basis on which the belligerents had agreed to end the conflict, but the British, with French support, insisted that this amount include war costs because these costs ultimately had to be paid by the civilian population. This reasoning allowed the inclusion of anything remotely connected to the war. For example, the British included as a legitimate war cost the price of a mortgage taken out by an Australian shepherd on his house as a result of the disruption of trade caused by the war. An alarmed Wilson informed his colleagues that the Allies had offered peace on the basis of civilian damages only and that including war costs in the reparations bill would be unjust. The American president won his case, but then the British and the French argued for the addition of separation costs and war pensions, also stiffly opposed by the American delegation. The South African delegate Jan Smuts responded that while the costs of arming and supporting troops were military expenses, the funds spent on citizens and their families before and after their military service were civilian expenses. This reasoning convinced Wilson, who shouted down his American advisers when they objected to the faulty logic: "Logic! Logic! I don't give a damn for logic. I am going to include pensions!" This inclusion doubled the German bill to $30 billion.

BIOGRAPHICAL SKETCHES

Sidney Sonnino
Failed Diplomatist

Italy's foreign minister during World War I and at the Versailles Peace Conference was Sidney Sonnino. The son of a wealthy Jewish banker and a Welsh woman, Sonnino spent his early childhood in the family home in Alexandria, Egypt, and was reared in the Anglican faith of his mother. His unusual circumstances did not harm his political career in Giolittian Italy as much as his rigid personality. He served in local and national politics and became prime minister in 1906 and 1909, the country's first Protestant chief executive of Jewish descent. Sonnino passed through a conservative phase but developed a reputation as a reformer. Nonetheless, his tenure in office lasted only a total of two hundred days.

continued

continued

An early opponent of Italian colonial expansion in Africa, Sonnino was not much interested in colonial gains after World War I but hoped to win Italy a position as a major power in the Mediterranean. Named foreign minister in November 1914 following the death of neutralist Antonino Di San Guiliano, Sonnino negotiated Italy's entrance into World War I in 1915 through the Pact of London with the Allies. Following this agreement, he and Prime Minister Antonio Salandra successfully maneuvered to bring the country into the conflict despite the opposition of the majority of the people and their representatives. Under Sonnino's leadership, Italy missed the opportunity afforded by the United States's entrance into the war to jump on the moral bandwagon against the Central Powers, unlike Georges Clemenceau and David Lloyd George. Consequently, the country remained identified with the unfortunate maxim under which Salandra said it had entered the conflict, *Sacro Egoismo* [Sacred Egoism]. This slogan and Sonnino's diplomacy conveyed the impression that Italy had exploited the precarious Anglo-French situation of 1915 to exact its pound of flesh and was still determined to do so at Versailles. Sonnino's failure to correct this perception demonstrated an amazing lack of understanding of the altered world atmosphere following World War I.

The major problem for the Italians at Versailles was their demand for territory that American President Woodrow Wilson believed should go to Yugoslavia. Wilson argued on the basis of self-determination, while the Italians sought a secure frontier. The dispute with Wilson provoked the Italian delegation to leave Versailles and withdraw from the negotiations for a time. Wilson and the Italians then struggled for the hearts and minds of the Italian people.

When the government of Vittorio Emanuele Orlando resigned in June 1919, Sonnino withdrew from political life. Lamentably, the unresolved territorial dispute with Yugoslavia had poisoned the Italian political atmosphere. Resentment at being ill treated welled up in the country, and public opinion condemned the Allies and Italians who accepted the principle of self-determination. Many Italians identified self-determination with renunciation of the country's gains made at the cost of a great number of casualties and the enormous expenditure of economic wealth. These feelings fueled the rise of extremist movements, especially Benito Mussolini's Fascist party, which destabilized the country and came to power in 1922.

Besides his diplomatic and political activity, Sonnino excelled as a scholar. In Parliament, he wrote influential political articles and coauthored a famous sociological study on poverty in Sicily that made the country aware of the scope of the southern problem. He was also an avid student of Dante's poetry. Born in Pisa on March 11, 1847, Sidney Sonnino died in Rome on November 24, 1922. He is buried by the sea at his castle near Livorno.

This latter figure was the American delegation's estimate, but the British estimate was $120 billion, and the French refused to give one. When the experts failed to resolve their differences, Allied representatives worked out guidelines and charged a permanent reparations commission to come up with a figure and method of payment by May 1, 1921. In the meantime, they directed the Germans to come up with $5 billion immediately, hand over their merchant fleet to make good British losses, deliver large quantities of coal to France and Italy, and give a great number of farm animals to the Allies. Eventually the total that Germany had to pay was set at $56 billion (current dollars) over a forty-two-year period.

The Criticisms of John Maynard Keynes

Although some Allied experts considered this sum reasonable, economist John Maynard Keynes, a peace conference participant attached to the British Treasury, objected in a very influential book published in 1920. In *The Economic Consequences of the Peace,* Keynes argued that Germany would be unable to pay the stated amount and backed his argument with a series of impressive statistics. Other economic clauses of the Versailles peace treaty—tariff restrictions, confiscation of the merchant marine and railroad stock, and the delivery of German coal—ensured that Germany would be unable to pay the reparations imposed by the Allies, he wrote. The interest would mount faster than Germany's ability to pay, so that the debt would increase despite the payments, and thus the treaty obliged Germany "to hand over to the Allies the whole of her surplus production in perpetuity." Keynes's estimate for reparations was under $9 billion.

Keynes believed that the Allies had deliberately set out to demolish Germany by destroying the three foundations of its economic prosperity because they threatened the British: its overseas trade, which required the healthy merchant marine it had been forced to surrender; its ability to manufacture high-quality, reasonably priced manufactured goods, which challenged the British in their overseas and home markets; and its growing foreign investments, which competed with the Allied investments. The Allies had not reconstructed Europe's fragile economic prosperity, Keynes maintained, but had dealt it a deathblow by wrecking its most vibrant economy.

Whether or not Keynes was correct, his book had an extraordinary influence as economic events seemed to vindicate his opinions. The Germans defaulted on reparations payments in 1922, which led to French and Belgian occupation of the industrial Ruhr valley in March 1923. This occupation touched off hyperinflation in Germany that crippled the middle class and later contributed to the rise of Adolf Hitler. In late 1923, the Dawes Plan revised reparations downward, worked out a new payment schedule, and offered the Germans a loan. In 1929, the Young Plan reduced the total bill to $8 billion, close to Keynes's suggestion, to be paid over fifty-eight years at 5.5 percent interest. These plans calmed the economic waters and seemed to vindicate the British economist, but Keynes thought that they did not correct the economic distortions caused by reparations and suggested either the cancelation of reparations and war debts or the lowering of Allied tariff barriers so that the Germans could sell their goods and earn the funds necessary to pay reparations.

The Americans rebuffed cancelation of the war debts, and the Allies refused to grant unrestricted German access to their markets because of the competition that the efficient German industry presented for their firms. An artificial and serendipitous economy resulted: only American loans, seemingly for other purposes, allowed the Germans to pay reparations to the Allies, which permitted them to pay war debts, which, in turn, enabled the Americans to lend more to the Germans to pay reparations. When the Great Depression arrived, the Americans stopped lending money to the Germans, who defaulted on reparations, which caused the Allies to default on their war debts to the United States. By the early 1930s, countries were paying installments on neither sum.

Although the collapse of Europe's postwar economy seemed ultimately attributable to the factors denounced by Keynes, the British economist came in for serious criticism. Observers noted that Keynes's book poisoned American and British opinion against the Versailles treaty and encouraged German resistance to it. Keynes's contention that Germany lacked the capacity to pay the reparations assessed by the Allies has also been challenged. Some historians have revised the view of a prostrate Germany unable to reimburse a hard-nosed and vindictive France, replacing it with the picture of a recalcitrant country capable but unwilling to pay.

THE MORAL CONSEQUENCES

Despite the efforts of the statesmen at Paris, the peace settlement following World War I had more negative than positive results. Besides the economic issues, the word *reparations* itself condemned Germany and its allies for deliberately instigating the war. Following past conflicts, the victors frequently assessed indemnities on the losers, but these had no moral connotations; the Versailles treaty made German guilt explicit.

The "War Guilt" Clause

Article 231 of the Versailles treaty forced Germany and its allies to accept exclusive blame for the war, a condemnation that appeared as the first article in a section entitled "Reparation" that describes how Germany will make atonement through monetary and in-kind compensation. According to a moderate member of the American Peace Commission: "While the causes of the war may still be in dispute, we cannot reconcile ourselves to any theory but that Germany's aggression was responsible." The Allies forced the Germans to agree, but the Germans never accepted exclusive blame for the war, greatly resented the charge, and launched a campaign to prove their innocence. Eventually, writers in the Allied countries agreed with them. The "war guilt" clause fueled nationalistic desires for revenge, failed to sap Germany's might, and was a factor in Hitler's rise to power.

The Disarmament Clauses

Finally the Allies disarmed the Germans, limiting their army to a volunteer professional force of 100,000 and their navy to a coast guard without submarines, and denying them an air force. Because a general aversion to war had already begun among their own populations, the Allies justified these provisions by saying that German disarmament would "render possible the initiation of a general limitation of the armaments of all nations." Talks discussing disarmament between the wars took place in Geneva, but went nowhere. The Allied contention boomeranged because it provided Hitler with a pretext to rearm, since the other European countries had not fulfilled their pledge.

The Allies repeated their errors with Germany's defeated associates, inspiring in them a desire for vengeance without following through on effective

Former Viceroy for India and postwar Foreign Secretary, the British statesman Lord Curzon was responsible for drawing up an equitable boundary between Russia and Poland, the "Curzon Line."

enforcement. Reparations worsened the precarious Austrian and Hungarian economic situations, and the two countries pleaded that the Hapsburg monarchy, not the successor states, was responsible for the war. The Allies responded that they could not shirk responsibility by a technicality and fanned resentment by blaming their populations for not having resisted Hapsburg militarism.

The Specter of Anschluss

The Allies also handled the Austrian desire for union (Anschluss) with Germany poorly. The Austrians utilized Wilson's nationality principles to argue that they should be in the same nation with their German brethren. Had the Allies agreed, however, Germany would have become the paramount European power, so they flatly refused. In short order, the Germans became the champions of Anschluss and inserted an article into the Weimar constitution defining how Austrians would participate in German affairs before and after union. The Allies blocked this procedure but acted slowly, allowing Anschluss to develop into a major emotional issue that came back to haunt them.

THE LEAGUE OF NATIONS

The Allies responded to the desire for Anschluss by agreeing to alter Austria's international status if the Council of the League of Nations agreed. Since Britain

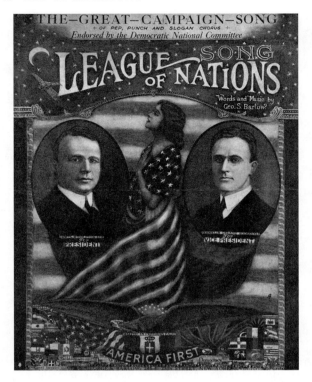

Brainchild of American President Woodrow Wilson and forerunner of the postwar United Nations, the League of Nations had serious flaws that doomed it to ultimate failure. The greatest lack was the refusal of the Americans to join the League. Shown here is a campaign song sponsored by the Democratic National Committee trying to solicit popular support for the new organization.

and France dominated the League of Nations, however, it ruled that Austria must remain a sovereign state, but only in late 1922. The decision did not settle the question because everyone recognized that the League of Nations was controlled by the victorious powers.

Structure of the League

President Wilson championed the creation of an international organization to prevent future conflicts. He called for an association of nations in his Fourteen Points, and the Paris Peace Conference named a commission headed by Wilson himself to draft a covenant that was adopted on April 28, 1919. The League of Nations came into being in January 1920. It is interesting to consider the league's structure because it both explains its weakness (and that of similar organizations like the United Nations) and because it was suggested as a model for European unification in the 1920s.

The League of Nations had a permanent secretariat located in Geneva. A council consisting of the big powers and four nations representing the small ones constituted the executive. All member states had one vote in the general assembly. The members agreed to submit their quarrels to inquiry or arbitration and, if unsatisfied, to refrain from war until after a cooling-down period of three months. They agreed to respect the territorial integrity of all members and, in case of aggression, to support each other. If members went to war with each other in contravention of the rules, the other members could impose sanctions and take military action—but the absence of a league military force made this impossible.

The question of giving the League of Nations an armed force was the subject of a crucial debate among the Allies. The French insisted on the establishment of an international military force under the league's command, but this meant the partial surrender of national sovereignty to the international organization. The United States and Britain, both geographically immune to a German threat, refused. The Americans returned to their isolationism, and the British suspected that France would dominate a League of Nations army. The U.S. Senate rejected the Versailles treaty, but with regard to the League of Nations, the senators refused the international commitments required by the league's covenant because they feared that the league would interfere in domestic affairs.

Consequences of the League's Weakness

The League of Nation's stillbirth had major consequences for world affairs. The league failed to resolve the disarmament question because of resistance by the big powers, which generally ignored it. It had jurisdiction over the clauses guaranteeing minority rights in Eastern Europe, but this emotional issue constantly embarrassed the organization, which had no effective authority in the matter. The League of Nations' minor diplomatic successes did not counterbalance its structural defects, and the powers continued to use traditional diplomacy to defend their interests.

During the 1920s, the French set up a new diplomatic order on the European continent. First, they torpedoed German membership in the League of Nations and attempted to make Poland a strong power as an eastern counterweight to Germany. As was already seen, this policy required supporting Polish claims against Germany and favoring its expansion against Bolshevik Russia. The French also signed alliances with the countries of Eastern Europe that had profited from the postwar settlement (Czechoslovakia, Romania, and Yugoslavia) in order to establish a front to Germany's east and a wall blocking Soviet influence in the West, in addition to defending the Versailles settlement. This policy had the major flaw of being based on weak countries that could never balance the military potential of Germany and the USSR while alienating both and driving them into each other's arms.

The League of Nations was consequently unable to keep the peace. Its real legacy was its establishment of a forum for discussion and its social policies, both of which foreshadowed the United Nations, and its inspiration of a plan for a European Union presented in 1930 (see chapter 17). Women leaders from different nations urged the league to broaden its horizons to nonpolitical issues by extending the principle of international cooperation to areas, such as health; labor; and the suppression of the arms, opium, and white slave traffic. The League of

Nations created specialized agencies to deal with these issues that became part of the United Nations structure after World War II.

At the Congress of Vienna, the French delegate had exploited allied differences to his country's advantage; influenced by this historical tidbit, the Allies prohibited German representatives from taking part in the Paris discussions. On May 7, 1919, they delivered a copy of the Versailles treaty to the German delegation and allowed the delegation to make only written comments. The Germans vehemently protested that the treaty did not keep faith with the Fourteen Points and that Germany could never fulfill its provisions. The Allies made some insignificant modifications and threatened to resume the war if Germany did not sign. On June 28, 1919, German representatives affixed their signature, but the Germans never accepted the peace.

Bibliographical Essay

The most complete and detailed work on the Paris Peace Conference that all serious students should consult is the classic by Arno J. Mayer, *Politics and Diplomacy of Peacemaking: Containment and Counterrevolution at Versailles, 1918–1919* (New York, 1967). Mayer emphasizes the relationship between internal and foreign politics and sees the conference as influenced by reactions to the Bolshevik revolution. The comparison with the Congress of Vienna was made by Charles K. Webster, quoted on p. 4 of Mayer's book. Harold Nicholson, *Peacemaking 1919* (London, 1943), is a classic work on the topic. Margaret MacMillan, *Paris 1919: Six Months that Changed the World* (New York, 2002), is a detailed work. Although the emphasis of historians has been placed on the Paris Peace Conference and the Treaty of Versailles, this is only part of the story because the conferences continued long afterward and a series of treaties were signed. A major new series on these events by London's Haus Publishing has resulted in the publication of 32 volumes, published between 2008 and 2011: "Makers of the Modern World: The Peace Conferences of 1919–23 and Their Aftermath." Erik Gosstein, *The First World War Peace Settlements 1919–1925* (Harlow, UK, 2002) is a one-volume treatment.

Good older and briefer books that are worth consulting are F. S. Marston, *The Peace Conference of 1919* (London, 1944), and Paul Birdsall, *Versailles Twenty Years After* (Hamden, Conn., 1962).

A superb source is the collection of articles illuminating a variety of problems and the complexities of peacemaking by the American delegates: Edward Mandell House and Charles Seymour, eds. *What Really Happened at Paris: The Story of the Peace Conference, 1918–1919, by American Delegates* (Westport, Conn.,1976); Wilson's exclamation about logic is on p. 272, and the citation on Germany's war guilt is on p. 288. Good books containing essays on the most varied themes at the conference include M. L. Cockrill and John Fisher, *The Paris Peace Conference, 1919: Peace Without Victory?* (New York, 2001); Conan Fisher and Alan Sharp, *After the Versailles Treaty: Enforcement, Compliance, Contested Identities* (New York, 2008); and a book dedicated to a distinguished scholar, Gaynor Johnson, *Peacemaking, Peacemakers and Diplomacy, 1880–1939: Essays in Honour of Professor Alan Sharp* (Newcastle, UK, 2010).

Given the enormous impact of the results of Versailles, the question of their impact in the future has been an object of great discussion. David Andelman's *A Shattered Peace* (Hoboken, N.J., 2008) discusses "the price we pay today," while Sally Marks examines the "illusions": *The Illusion of Peace: International Relations in Europe, 1918–1933* (New York, 2003).

Readers may better understand the postwar settlement by considering the policies, problems, and diplomacy of individual countries at the peace conference and after. Luckily, there are a number of good studies they may consult. Michael L. Dockrill and J. Douglas Goold, *Peace Without Promise: Britain and the Peace Conference, 1919–1923* (London, 1981), examines Britain's role; W. M. Jordan, *Great Britain, France, and the German Problem, 1918–1939: A Study of Anglo-French Relations in the Making and Maintenance of the Versailles Settlement* (London, 1971), discusses the major problems. A. Lentin, *Lloyd George and the Lost Peace: From Versailles to Hitler, 1919–1940* (New York, 2001), examines the role of an important participant from an interesting perspective. Seth P. Tillman analyzes the relationship between Americans and British in *Anglo-American Relations at the Paris Peace Conference of 1919* (Princeton, N.J., 1961). René Albrecht-Carrié's *Italy at the Paris Peace Conference* (New York, 1966), is the standard work on the subject. Spencer M. Di Scala, *Vittorio Orlando: Italy* (Makers of the Modern World series) (London, 2010) consulted little-known archival sources that shed more light on the Italian position. Dragan R. Zivojinovic analyzes one of the thorniest problems of the peace in *America, Italy and the Birth of Yugoslavia* (New York, 1972). Yugoslavia's policies are presented by Ivo J. Lederer, *Yugoslavia at the Paris Peace Conference: A Study in Frontiermaking* (New Haven, Conn., 1963). John M. Thompson argues that European affairs could not be resolved without considering Russia and discusses the Bolshevik problem in *Russia, Bolshevism, and the Versailles Peace* (Princeton, N.J., 1966). The Belgians are discussed by Sally Marks, *Innocent Abroad: Belgium and the Paris Peace Conference of 1919* (Chapel Hill, N.C., 1981). Kay Lundgren-Nielson wrote *The Polish Problem at the Paris Peace Conference* (Odense, Denmark, 1979). Another problem with fateful consequences is the subject of an excellent study by Francis Déak, *Hungary at the Paris Peace Conference: The Diplomatic History of the Treaty of Trianon* (New York, 1972). The complicated legacy of Hungary in terms of minorities, economics, and boundaries as a result of the Treaty of Trianon is spelled out in C. A. Macartney's *Hungary and Her Successors: The Treaty of Trianon and its Consequences, 1919–1937* (London, 1937). Hungary suffered most unjustly from the peace settlement; see the lectures delivered by former Hungarian Prime Minister Count Stephen Bethlen, *The Treaty of Trianon and European Peace* (New York, 1971). Romanian policy is analyzed in *Rumania at the Paris Peace Conference: A Study of the Diplomacy of Ioan I. C. Bratianu* (New York, 1962), by Sherman David Spector. The politics of the smaller powers is the subject of Stephen Bonsal, *Suitors and Suppliants: The Little Nations at Versailles* (New York, 1946).

The story of the Germans at the conference is told by Alma Luckau, *The German Delegation at the Paris Peace Conference* (New York, 1971). On the ramifications of the desire of Austria and Germany to unite, see Alfred D. Low, *The Anschluss Movement, 1918–1919, and the Paris Peace Conference* (Philadelphia, 1974).

On the disarmament question, see Lorna S. Jaffe, *The Decision to Disarm Germany* (Boston, 1985), and Gerda Richards Crosby, *Disarmament and Peace in British Politics, 1914–1919* (Cambridge, Mass., 1957), a succinct study of the issue. James F. Willis, *Prologue to Nuremburg* (Westport, Conn., 1982), analyzes the war criminal problem after World War I.

On colonial questions, see the work by George Louis Beer, American representative on the territorial section committee for Africa, *African Questions at the Paris Peace Conference* (New York, 1923). Consult also William Roger Louis, *Great Britain and Germany's Lost Colonies 1914–1919* (Oxford, UK, 1967). Quincy Wright presents a full discussion of the origins and development of the mandate system in *Mandates Under the League of Nations* (Westport, Conn., 1968).

On reparations, see how the clauses were arrived at in a book by the chief American representative on the Reparations Commission, Bernard M. Baruch, *The Making of the Reparation and Economic Sections of the Treaty* (New York, 1970). John Maynard Keynes's brilliant 1920 classic *The Economic Consequences of the Peace* has been reissued many times; there is a good Penguin edition with a readable introduction by Robert Lekachman that puts his ideas into context (New York, 1971); Keynes's statement on reparations quoted in the text is on p. 167. Keynes published a sequel to this book in which he considers events since the original publication of his work and fleshes out his ideas, *A Revision of the Treaty* (London, 1922). Don Markwell's *John Maynard Keynes and International Relations: Economic Paths to War and Peace* (New York, 2006) has interesting material on the period covered. An important rebuttal of Keynes is Etienne Mantoux, *The Carthaginian Peace or the Economic Consequences of Mr. Keynes* (Pittsburgh, 1965). British economic war aims and foundations of reparations are the subject of Robert E. Bunselmeyer, *The Cost of the War 1914–1919* (Hamden, Conn., 1975). A major issue at the peace conference was how much Germany could pay, analyzed in Harold G. Moulton and Constantine E. McGuire, *Germany's Capacity to Pay: A Study of the Reparation Problem* (New York, 1923). Reparations are also considered in Carl Bergmann, *The History of Reparations* (Boston, 1927), and by the revisionist Marc Tractenberg, *Reparations in World Politics* (New York, 1980).

There are many sources on the League of Nations. A good survey is F. S. Northedge, *The League of Nations: Its Life and Times, 1920–1946* (Leicester, UK, 1986), while F. P. Walters produced a longer account, *A History of the League of Nations* (London, 1960). For a view from a particular perspective, see the book by Alfred E. Zimmern, *The League of Nations and the Rule of Law, 1918–1935* (New York, 1969).

CHAPTER 9

⥺

Hard Landings: From Crisis to False Prosperity

CHAPTER OUTLINE

Britain: Back to 1914 • France's Quest for Security • Italy: From Red Biennium to Fascism • Weimar's Three Original Sins • The USSR: The Crisis of NEP

BIOGRAPHICAL SKETCHES

John Maynard Keynes, Savior of Capitalism • Benito Amilcare Andrea Mussolini, Young Rebel

In stating that the world must return to normal following the devastation of World War I, American President Warren G. Harding made a grammatical error by using the word *normalcy*. This word stuck, but the former belligerents had a very difficult time getting back on track because the costs of the conflict produced severe economic and social crises for victors and vanquished alike. Many soldiers who were used to fighting could not readjust to peaceful civilian lives and developed a strong bond—a "trenchocracy"—that contributed to the rise of fascism. Economic conditions worsened as the people in all countries demanded rapid demobilization. This demobilization created mass unemployment because millions of soldiers came onto the labor market when industry was shedding wartime jobs and converting to peacetime production, and the need to pay war debts and reparations contributed to inflation and hyperinflation.

BRITAIN: BACK TO 1914

In 1917 in Britain the ministry of reconstruction planned for an orderly demobilization and the reorganization of health services, housing, transportation, and relationships in the workplace in order to achieve greater equality.

Economic Problems

The planners had feared the unemployment that rapid demobilization would bring but could not resist the popular desire to see the soldiers return home.

Demobilization did not create as many problems as were feared at first because Britain had not suffered any destruction, British industry was poised to take advantage of the pent-up postwar demand for civilian goods, and an economic boom created plenty of jobs. But the boom proved short lived, and a downturn that occurred in 1920 turned into a depression in 1921.

By 1923, the economic crisis had killed hopes about improving the social conditions of the lower classes. Parliament watered down bills extending the length of secondary education, building subsidized housing, and reorganizing the electric and transportation industries. Health and transport ministries were created, but they lacked the clout to make a difference. Joint industrial bodies, called Whitley Councils, which were created to encourage collaboration between capital and labor, failed to change conditions in the country's major industries. The economic slump prompted the government to curtail activities even in areas where its action had been moderately successful, such as housing; caused breakdowns in social insurance; and led to the detested dole.

Political Questions and Ireland

In the political arena, Britain alternated between movement and stagnation. In 1918, the country held elections for the first time since 1910, with women aged 30 and older granted the right to vote. The Labour Party withdrew from the wartime coalition, and a Conservative-Liberal coalition won 484 seats. Lloyd George remained prime minister, but trouble loomed ahead because, although defeated, Labour was on its way to replacing the helplessly divided Liberals and, in the future, would regularly alternate with the Conservatives in power. Furthermore, the Lloyd George government was hamstrung by the prevailing economic belief in austerity during slowdowns, which caused unemployment to skyrocket.

Added to the weak economy, Britain's Irish dilemma threatened the stability of Lloyd George's cabinet. A home-rule provision had been put on hold during the war, but by 1918 resentment caused by executions following the Easter Rebellion had made it irrelevant. In the 1918 elections, Sinn Fein (Ourselves Alone), an Irish party supporting independence, won seventy-three seats, all but four outside Ulster. This party proclaimed an Irish parliament, declared independence on January 2, 1919, and created the Irish Republican Army (IRA). A guerrilla war, complete with terror, broke out, pitting the IRA against the Black and Tans, auxiliary British forces.

In December 1920 the British established parliaments in both northern and southern Ireland, with a council coordinating them. Ireland remained part of the United Kingdom. In May 1921, elections took place. Northern Ireland agreed with the British plan, but the southerners, under Eamon de Valera, Michael Collins, and Arthur Griffith, favored independence. Amid continuing violence, negotiations produced an Irish Free State as a dominion of the British Empire in December 1921. The Irish Parliament ratified this solution, but a civil war broke out between the "Regulars," who supported Parliament, and the "Irregulars." By 1923 the Irish government had suppressed the Irregulars, but sporadic acts of violence continued for many years.

Irish events and foreign policy problems brought Lloyd George down in October 1922. Conservative leader Bonar Law replaced him, and new elections resulted in a Conservative majority. In May 1923 Law resigned because of ill health and was replaced by Stanley Baldwin, his chancellor of the exchequer, and, in Winston Churchill's characterization, "a man of the utmost insignificance."

Rise of the Labour Party

The early 1920s brought a rise in the Labour Party's fortunes, stimulated by workers' unrest, the Liberal Party's decline, an internal reorganization, and a sharpened Socialist ideology. Labour's program, elaborated by Fabian Socialist Sidney Webb, *Labour and the New Social Order,* advocated a minimum standard for social services, full employment, higher taxation, a capital tax to shrink the national debt, and democratic control of industry that aimed at the nationalization of industry and land.

In 1922 Labour doubled its popular vote and in January 1924 got its opportunity after the Conservatives lost their majority in the December 6, 1923 elections. Labour received the second-largest number of seats, allied with the Liberals, and came to power under Ramsay MacDonald. Inexperience and dependence on Liberal votes weakened MacDonald, and he fell because of his friendliness to the Soviet Union and his refusal to prosecute a Communist journalist who was accused of political interference. During the intense electoral campaign of 1924, the forged "Zinoviev Letter" from Moscow, purporting to give British Communists instructions to work for a Communist revolution, might have affected the outcome in favor of the Conservatives. Baldwin returned to power and succeeded in passing some reforms.

BIOGRAPHICAL SKETCHES

John Maynard Keynes
Savior of Capitalism

Contradictions marked the life of John Maynard Keynes, the most famous economist of the twentieth century. Keynes worked at the British Treasury during World War I, where he labored to prevent his country's economic collapse under the strain of the conflict. A pacifist who disagreed with Britain's avowed aim of Germany's unconditional surrender, he prayed for an absolute financial crash, yet strove to prevent it. A practicing homosexual, he married ballerina Lydia Lopokova in 1925 in a happy union. An economic liberal, he successfully blended liberal values and state intervention. He despised capitalism, but his economic theories saved it.

Born on June 5, 1883, in Cambridge, England, Keynes grew up in an academic family. His father Neville was a scholar and administrator at the University of Cambridge. Florence, his mother, a minister's daughter, was an early female Cambridge graduate. Maynard enjoyed a happy childhood, attending Eton, the elite private school, where he achieved both academic and social success.

continued

continued

In 1902, Keynes entered Cambridge University, where he garnered even more success. He joined the Bloomsbury Circle, a famous group that included the most influential British intellectuals who dominated cultural life during the 1920s. He joined the civil service after graduation and wrote a treatise on Indian finance. He began teaching at Cambridge, joining the Treasury Department in 1915, where he became an influential personage. He accompanied David Lloyd George to Versailles, became disillusioned with the peace process, and published the book that made him famous, *The Economic Consequences of the Peace.*

Keynes returned to teaching at Cambridge in October 1919 and remained there until 1937. His light teaching load allowed him to devote himself to writing. Keynes gave eight lectures a year, the early drafts of books that attracted hundreds of listeners, and supervised a small number of students at his house on Fridays or Saturdays before dinner. On Monday evenings he presided over the Keynes Club in his drawing room, where members listened to his papers or others by distinguished guests. He financed his lifestyle through his journalism and investments, which he directed while having breakfast in bed. He gained and lost several small fortunes and fared poorly in the stock market crash of 1929.

Keynes freely gave the British government advice on public policy. He criticized its return to the gold standard in 1925 and fretted about the consistently high unemployment rate. When the Great Depression arrived in 1929, governments confronted the slump by restricting spending. Keynes denounced this policy and argued in favor of increasing both private and public spending. In a famous radio broadcast on January 15, 1931, he advised British homemakers that their patriotic duty lay in spending their money and in taking advantage of the cheap prices, not in saving. He likewise urged the government to undertake public works, at the cost of accepting deficit spending, in order to create employment. In 1936 his most influential work appeared: *The General Theory of Employment, Interest, and Money.*

Keynes stood previous liberal economic theory on its head by arguing in favor of state intervention in the economy through public works and subsidies when lowering interest rates did not work. In order to reverse severe economic downturns, governments must accept budget deficits. Keynes convinced his colleagues and governments of the correctness of his stance, and after World War II the Western democracies accepted them. This reversal of their previous economic beliefs helped capitalism adapt to the modern world.

Keynes participated in important economic decisions during and following World War II, but died soon after it ended on April 21, 1946, in Firle, Sussex, England.

Return to the Gold Standard

British reinstitution of the gold standard on April 28, 1925, in an attempt at a return to pre-1914 economics, was disastrous. The United States was economically dominant, and British industry could no longer successfully compete with more modern and aggressive foreign industry. Oil and electricity replaced coal, a major British revenue source, as fuel. Returns from British investments had fallen off considerably and could no longer pay for the gap created by high imports and low exports. With the return of the gold standard and reinstatement of the pre-war exchange rate with the dollar, the British pound became overvalued and hurt

British exports. British industrialists tried to reduce costs by lowering wages, which provoked strikes. In June 1925, mine owners announced lower wages and longer work hours. The T.U.C. (Trades Union Congress) General Council and the government opened talks, but on May 2, 1926, the government ended them. A general strike resulted but failed on May 13 when the government called out the army. The strike's failure on May 13 left a bitter taste for workers, who straggled back to work as new legislation weakened the unions. The government's victory was short-lived as Baldwin's popularity steadily declined, and he lost the next election held in May 1929. Even though it did not win a majority, Labour emerged as the largest party, and Ramsey MacDonald returned as prime minister. In October the New York stock market crashed, signaling the Great Depression. British export markets collapsed, and by the end of 1930, British unemployment reached 2.5 million.

British Foreign Policy in the 1920s

Paralleling domestic developments, British postwar foreign policy was nondescript. MacDonald encouraged the negotiations that produced the Dawes Plan, which seemed to resolve the thorny issue of reparations and supported the Geneva Protocol that promised to achieve security for France, resolve defaults, favor collective security, bolster the League of Nations, and promote a general European peace, but it was not ratified before his cabinet fell. MacDonald recognized the

Stanley Baldwin, British Prime Minister during the later 1920s, ran a humdrum administration that failed to confront the country's problems in any meaningful manner. Winston Churchill labeled him a man of the "utmost incompetence." Here he is speaking on the radio, a new instrument that permitted politicians of the era to speak to their citizens directly.

Soviet Union and aimed to resolve outstanding issues with it, but Baldwin did not continue this policy.

Baldwin's administration agreed to the 1925 Locarno Treaty, in which the Germans recognized their western borders with France and, along with Italy, guaranteed them. This treaty was important for the moral pledges made by the countries involved and for accepting Germany's entrance into the League of Nations, and it initiated a period of goodwill known as the "Spirit of Locarno." In 1927, however, Baldwin denounced the treaties that the Labour government had signed with the USSR because of Soviet subversive activities.

FRANCE'S QUEST FOR SECURITY

Not surprisingly France embarked on a painful quest to recover the confidence it had lost during the war, a quest made difficult by political instability.

The "Red Menace"

Bolshevik influence had a major impact on France. The French government's intervention in the Russian civil war and its refusal to consider legislation favorable to workers contributed to increased radicalism that culminated in a failed general strike in May 1920. This strike resulted in the firing of more than 20,000 workers and in workers' hostility for the next fifteen years.

Politically, the "Red Menace" had incalculable results. On December 30, 1920, the Socialist SFIO split because its congress at Tours voted to join the Third (or Communist) International controlled by the Bolshevik government. The majority of SFIO leaders founded the French Communist Party (PCF), and a minority continued in the old organization, severely weakening the Socialists who, despite the split, did not resolve the old question of whether they should pursue revolutionary or reformist policies. The continuing divisions among the Socialists hindered their political action in the 1920s and 1930s, while the PCF followed Russian Bolshevik directives.

In addition to the Socialist split, the Red Menace frightened the middle class into supporting the Bloc National (National Bloc), a coalition of right and center groups whose candidates ran on a conservative platform and supported demands to make Germany pay for the war. The Bloc National won the elections of November 1919 by such a large majority that the resulting Chamber of Deputies was called the "Blue Horizon" Chamber because so many of the former soldiers who were elected showed up wearing their blue uniforms. The chamber was so conservative that it rejected Clemenceau as president of the republic because it considered the Versailles treaty too lenient.

Politics and Economics

The Bloc National coalition followed a conservative course in economic affairs as well as in politics. It refused to raise the income tax rate, held down during the war, in order to pay for reconstruction and relied on short-term bonds that favored privileged bondholders. Although German reparations helped balance the budget and maintain the franc's value for a while, the French currency began a precipitous fall during 1923. Worth 20 U.S. cents in January 1919, it slipped to 4 cents in 1926, causing a severe inflation. Governmental policy also alienated the middle class that, during the war, had patriotically traded gold for war bonds paying 6 percent. In addition to the erosion caused by inflation during the 1920s, while gold kept its worth, the government reduced the interest rate to 4.5 percent.

In 1923 French Prime Minister Raymond Poincaré occupied the Ruhr Valley because the Germans defaulted on reparations and further alienated French public opinion by raising taxes 20 percent in order to pay for the operation. Combined with the National Bloc's determined pro-Catholic Church policy (the resumption of diplomatic relations with the Vatican and Joan of Arc's sanctification), the occupation galvanized Leftist parties into action. Radicals and Socialists were the primary components of the Cartel des Gauches (Cartel of the Left) that won a large majority in the 1924 elections.

The Cartel des Gauches had built-in weaknesses that doomed it to failure. On the one hand, its decisive victory stimulated the rise of extreme right nationalist groups in response, but on the other the cartel was badly split. The leftist rhetoric of the Radicals contrasted with their desire to protect existing privileges and caused friction with their Socialist allies. The leftist roots of the Radicals and their objection to the conservative policies of the rightist parties drove them to ally

Raymond Poincaré was an activist French President who played an important role in the lead- up to World War I. In 1923 he occupied the Ruhr Valley, which touched off German hyperinflation. In the later 1920s he stabilized the volatile French political and economic situation.

with the Socialists, but Socialist policies frightened them and they pulled back toward the center and the right. The Socialists demanded higher taxes on the rich, which they knew their allies opposed. These contradictions destabilized the cartel governments and set the stage for a reversal of alliances as the weak cartel cabinets proved unable to resolve the grave postwar financial crisis. Moreover, the Socialist demand for higher taxes on the wealthy caused the rich to dump governmental bonds and send their capital abroad, and the franc sank ever further. In 1925 six governments followed one another, and in 1926 the cartel disintegrated.

Poincaré returned as prime minister. He had learned his lesson from the Ruhr occupation disaster and turned foreign affairs over to Aristide Briand, who was willing to make up with Germany, and concentrated on domestic affairs. Poincaré skillfully balanced the cabinet between the Radicals and rightists, practiced budgetary restraint, kept labor in line, coaxed French money back home, and attracted foreign loans. He inspired confidence at a time when a worldwide economic recovery began and in 1928 stabilized the franc at one-fifth its prewar value. Stabilization at this low rate made French goods more competitive on the world market and stimulated exports, but it ruined holders of fixed-rate obligations, governmental bonds, and insurance policies, while landlords who had leased their property long term suffered severe losses.

Elections in April 1928 gave Poincaré's the National Union a comfortable majority. When ill health forced Poincaré to resign on July 27, 1929, France appeared confident and serene, but the 1930s demonstrated the extreme fragility of the structure that had been built during the previous decade.

A Real Peace?

During the 1920s, foreign affairs and a search for security were high on the French agenda. In the early postwar years, the French followed a harsh policy toward Germany that culminated in the occupation of the industrial Ruhr Valley in January 1923 when Germany defaulted on reparations. When the occupation touched off hyperinflation in Germany that threatened to ruin the European economic system, France found itself isolated and criticized even by the British and was forced to compromise. Negotiations eventually led to the Treaty of Locarno, which recognized France's border with Germany, and sent disputes to arbitration. The "Spirit of Locarno" seemed to bring real peace to Europe and security to France for the first time since World War I. French evacuation of the Rhineland five years before the term specified at Versailles, the Young Plan giving Germany better payment terms for reparations, and a plan for a federal European union culminated on August 28, 1928, in the Kellogg-Briand Pact, which outlawed war and called for a system of compulsory arbitration in case of disputes.

However, Germany refused to recognize its eastern borders with Poland and saw the French alliances in Eastern Europe as tightening the Versailles noose around it; France emphasized collective security against aggression and continued to conceive of the League of Nations in an anti-German light and, despite the Kellog-Briand Pact, began construction of the Maginot line in 1929 to repel an attack across the same borders that Germany had just guaranteed.

ITALY: FROM "RED BIENNIUM" TO FASCISM

Italy was not attacked in 1914 but entered the conflict ten months later out of fear that if the Central Powers won, they would dominate the continent; a longing to take over the Italian-speaking areas of the Austro-Hungarian Empire; and a desire to win new territory. During its period of neutrality, a debate raged between opposing political forces that wanted to keep the nation neutral and those who advocated intervention—neutralists and interventionists. The neutralists included Giovanni Giolitti, the major Liberal politician, the Catholics, and the Socialists, while the king and prime minister were interventionists. The neutralists either opposed war on principle or believed that it would be too much of a strain for the country; the interventionists hoped for glory and territory or wanted to defend democratic ideals.

The Troubled Postwar

Instead of ending, the national debate escalated after the war. Despite the Italians' best military effort, the dispute over Fiume and other areas at the Paris Peace Conference convinced many that that they had won a "mutilated victory." The disruptive economic and social effects of the war raised the level of the controversy. Although the conflict contributed greatly to the modernization of Italy's industrial base, industry had a difficult time adjusting to peacetime. The cost-of-living index soared to 268 in 1919 from a base of 100 in 1913, the lira dropped from 19.30 U.S. cents prewar to 4.97 U.S. cents in 1920, and the budget shot completely out of balance. The Socialists, who had opposed the war, saw membership in their labor union (the CGL) explode from 249,000 in 1918 to 1.2 million in 1919 and to 2.3 million in 1920. Man-days lost to strikes increased from 906,000 in 1918 to a record 14.1 million in 1919.

The country also suffered social unrest. Returning peasant soldiers, promised land to keep them fighting, invaded large estates and began working vacant land. In the cities, workers demanded an eight-hour workday and factory councils on the Soviet model that would have a dominant voice in management. Strikers attacked former soldiers who frequently had no other clothes to wear but their old uniforms. Future Communist Party founder Antonio Gramsci declared Italy ripe for Bolshevism.

The "Red Biennium"

At its 1919 Bologna Congress, a Bolshevik-influenced Italian Socialist Party (PSI) revoked its 1892 program and endorsed violence as a means of taking power, but it still emerged severely split. The majority Maximalists, led by Giacinto Menotti Serrati, rejected the extreme left's demand to abstain from elections and to organize a revolution, pushing the extreme left to break off in 1921 and found the Italian Communist Party (PCI, originally PCd'I). At the same time, Maximalist revolutionary rhetoric antagonized the moderate Socialists, paralyzed the party, and frightened the middle class, which sought salvation on the right.

In contrast to Britain and France, Italian resentment against the results of the Paris Peace Conference led to the triumph of the left, not the right, in Italy in the first postwar elections of 1919. The Socialists tripled their vote and became the largest party in the Chamber of Deputies with 156 seats. The next largest party, the new, left-leaning, and Catholic Italian Popular Party (PPI), led by sociologist priest, Don Luigi Sturzo, won 100 seats. A Socialist-Catholic alliance would have given Italy a stable majority, but these forces hated each other, and the Bolshevik-influenced Socialists would not cooperate with any other party. Making matters worse, proportional representation, implemented in 1919, permitted many miniscule groups to win representation in the Chamber of Deputies. The old Liberals, also badly divided, barely collaborated with the Catholics to give Italy a series of weak and highly unstable governments.

In this situation, Parliament turned to the country's senior statesman Giovanni Giolitti, who attempted to reestablish fiscal soundness by increasing levies on the rich, imposing a war profits tax, and registering stocks and bonds in owners' names so they could be taxed. This program alienated the bourgeoisie and the Catholic party, which, combined with lack of Socialist support, sabotaged it. In the meantime, increasing disorder in the country provoked a response. In August and September 1920, 600,000 workers occupied the factories and tried to continue production. Giolitti wisely refrained from using force, correctly believing that the movement would soon fall apart, which it did. Giolitti next tried to reduce Socialist representation in Parliament by calling new elections for May 1921, and when the elections failed to do so, he resigned on June 27. His departure worsened governmental instability, and rightist groups started taking matters into their own hands.

The Fascist Reaction

If the danger of a Bolshevik revolution in Italy had ever existed, historians agree that it dissipated after the failure of the factory occupations. In 1921 man-days lost to strikes dropped by more than half in industry and by over 90 percent on the land, and a backlash began. Former revolutionary Socialist Benito Mussolini established the Fascist movement in Milan on March 23, 1919. Mussolini had initially agreed with the Socialist party line and supported neutrality, but his belief in the war's revolutionary potential led him to advocate intervention, after which, in an emotional meeting, the party expelled him. Mussolini saw action in the war and after the conflict joined bands of ex-soldiers, nationalists, and futurists in attacking former neutralists. He emphasized a common bond among soldiers who had fought in the war and who hated those who had opposed it, especially Socialists and Bolsheviks. Mussolini's innovation was to proclaim his movement both Socialist and nationalist and to organize it into *Fasci di combattimento* [combat groups]—members of which were called "Fascisti"—consisting of war veterans, former revolutionary interventionists, Republicans, and dissident Socialists.

In 1919 the Fascists issued a program that made radical demands similar to those of the Socialists: universal suffrage, lowering the voting age to 18, the right of women to vote and hold office, abolition of the conservative Senate, the election of a constituent assembly, an eight-hour working day, a minimum wage, workers' participation in industrial management, lowering the retirement age from 65 to 55, nationalization of arms factories, a heavy graduated income tax, the confiscation of property belonging to religious congregations, the expropriation of 85 percent of war profits, and a republic. The Fascists, however, could not compete with the more established and better organized Socialist party and failed to elect anyone to the Chamber of Deputies in 1919.

This failure, Fascism's strong nationalist component, and the national backlash against the "Reds" combined to drive the Fascists to the right and to abandon the radical 1919 program. On the land, where anti-Socialist resentment predominated, the agrarian bourgeoisie financed armed Fascist action squads that destroyed property belonging to peasant leagues, leftist parties, and working-class institutions. Lacking central direction, the peasant labor organizations succumbed to the Fascist onslaught while the local authorities, alienated by the leftists, turned a blind eye. Hammered by the Fascist offensive, the Socialist party split in 1921, the left wing forming the Italian Communist Party, and in 1922, the Maximalists expelled the reformists, who established a separate competing party.

BIOGRAPHICAL SKETCHES

Benito Amilcare Andrea Mussolini
Young Rebel

Mussolini's background would not have led anyone to predict his political future as Il Duce of Fascism. His father Alessandro, a Socialist with anarchistic tendencies, named his son after Mexican revolutionary Benito Juarez and two Italian Anarchists, Amilcare Cipriani and Andrea Costa. Alessandro published articles in local Socialist newspapers and read sections of Marx's *Capital* and other Socialist literature to his children (Benito had a brother and a sister) and, like his son, was committed to violent revolution. Mussolini freely acknowledged his father's influence, stating that his fate would have been much different without him.

Alessandro, a blacksmith frequently out of work, spent a good deal of time at the pub and left the details of running the house to his wife, Rosa Maltoni, an elementary school teacher. Alessandro's unreliability intensified the family's poverty. Benito recalled daily meals of vegetable soup and turnips eaten out of a common dish, with some meat broth on Sundays. Benito, born on July 29, 1883, at Predappio, in the Romagna region of northeast Italy, uttered inarticulate sounds and hardly spoke until age 3. He was wild as a boy, roaming the fields at the head of a gang of young boys, fighting, and stealing fruit from trees. Periodically, he went off by himself, a habit he continued into adulthood. He liked music and played the violin, which always had a soothing effect on him, and his musical talent was transferred to one of his sons who became a jazz pianist.

Worried about her son, Rosa sent him to a Catholic boarding school. Mussolini bitterly resented the discipline and the class distinctions that forced him to eat bread teeming with ants with the poorest children. He had few friends, and the school asked him not to return when he stabbed a fellow student in the hand during a fight. Mussolini finished school nevertheless and in 1901 received his diploma as a teacher. In February 1902 his father's Socialist connections got him

continued

continued

a job as a substitute teacher for the second and third grades in a small town, but his contract was not renewed because of his scandalous love affair with a woman whose husband was away in the army—one of many liaisons. Faced with the prospect of returning to his hometown, and boredom, Mussolini left Italy for Switzerland on July 9, 1902.

The Swiss experience was decisive because Mussolini became a politician there. He took a job in construction, but the work was too hard, and he only lasted a week. He went to Lausanne and made contact with emigrant Italian Socialists, writing articles for their newspapers and giving lectures. His talents as a journalist and orator emerged during this period. Returning to Italy in late 1904, Mussolini had success as a newspaperman, wrote a novel *(The Cardinal's Mistress)*, and rose in the local Romagna party hierarchy because of his participation in the peasant struggles against big landowners. In 1911 he gained national notoriety because of his violent opposition to the Libyan War and for his denunciations of the reformists who headed the Socialist party. Mussolini was a firebrand who did not believe in voting but in violent revolution. At the party congress of 1912, he delivered a violent speech against the reformists. Mussolini belonged to a radical group that gained control of the organization, bullied his way into the editorship of the party's daily newspaper *Avanti!*, and used the newspaper as a platform to call for violent revolution. In June 1914 this revolution seemed to have arrived with violent disorders in the "Red" region of Emilia. However, the defeat of the movement by the army dashed Mussolini's hopes.

Mussolini changed. In the past he had called for revolution to attain socialism; now he revealed himself as more interested in violent revolution for its own sake. This attitude helps explain his abandonment of the party's official position at the beginning of World War I opposing Italian entrance into the conflict. Mussolini reversed himself because, among other reasons, he believed that the war would hasten a revolution. The Socialists expelled him from the party, and Mussolini founded a new movement called fascism.

The Fascist Dictatorship

The Socialist splits prevented them from stopping the Fascist drive to power, while the Liberals and Catholics underestimated the danger. On October 28, 1922, Fascist squads staged the March on Rome in the midst of a governmental crisis. The king refused to declare martial law because, he later said, he feared civil war. The monarch asked Mussolini to head a government even though the Fascists held only 35 of the 525 seats in the Chamber of Deputies. Mussolini formed a coalition cabinet in which Fascist members were a minority and received a vote of confidence on November 17. Italian non-Fascist politicians voted in favor of it, believing that it might be able to restore calm and assuming that they could vote Mussolini out of office at any time— a fatal error because Mussolini's squads controlled the streets.

In April 1924, Mussolini held elections under the "Acerbo law," which modified proportional representation in an effort to create political stability by making it easier to win a majority in Parliament. According to the new law, two-thirds of the seats in the Chamber of Deputies would go to the electoral coalition receiving the most votes, provided it was at least 25 percent of those cast, the remaining seats to be divided proportionately. Governmental interference and Fascist violence ensured that the Fascist-led coalition received almost 65 percent of the vote despite heavy opposition in the North, where the Fascists did not receive a majority.

The magnitude of the violence during the campaign prompted Giacomo Matteotti, a reformist Socialist deputy, to protest publicly and to demand new elections. On June 10, 1924, Matteotti disappeared and was later found beaten to death. The resulting crisis seriously threatened Mussolini as the country and even Fascists turned against him. The opposition boycotted Parliament hoping to force the king to intervene, but Victor Emanuel III was convinced that he would have to replace Mussolini with a Socialist prime minister, and he merely reshuffled the cabinet by putting trusted advisers in key posts.

As the crisis dragged on, extremist Fascists, concerned that they would be tried for their crimes if the government fell, pressured Mussolini to take action. On January 3, 1925, in the Chamber of Deputies Mussolini accepted moral responsibility for the Matteotti murder and defied his opponents to remove him. Mussolini's supporters then passed repressive legislation, made easy because of the boycott. Measures passed between January 1925 and the end of 1926 instituted governmental control of the press, gave the police new powers to arrest citizens, outlawed all parties except the Fascist, and jailed Fascist adversaries—many of whom fled into exile. Mussolini also reorganized the government's machinery by extending executive control over the legislature; solidifying his dominance of the

As soon as they assumed took over in Italy in 1922, the Fascists instituted a dictatorship, even though the actual contours of the fascist state assumed form only in the years following the assassination of Socialist leader Giacomo Matteotti in 1924. Here is an illustration of the Italian police conducting mass arrests of Communists in Trieste in 1923.

executive branch; purging the bureaucracy; and giving party institutions, such as the Fascist Grand Council, governmental functions. Mussolini had organized a one-party dictatorship complete with secret police in the heart of Western Europe, becoming both Il Duce (leader) of the party and of the country.

The rise of the Fascists signaled a dangerous new trend. Mussolini's opponents characterized his regime by inventing a new term: *totalitarian*. Although the monarchy, the church, and other traditional institutions of Italian society resisted and sometimes limited it, fascism replaced democracy with a revolutionary party that imposed a new form of mystical, expansionistic nationalism whose aim was to change the Italians into an organic, unified community of single-minded conquerors. Such tendencies had existed in Italian and European society before World War I, although it is unlikely that the Fascists would have come to power anywhere without the disruptions and dislocations caused by the conflict. In the 1920s, fascism appeared to European observers a peculiarly Italian phenomenon, but under the economic and social pressures of the Great Depression of the 1930s, it spawned similar movements throughout Europe—although each with their national variations. In 1933, Nazism, the movement that copied Mussolini's style most closely, came to power in Germany and altered Europe's destiny.

Fascist Policies in the 1920s

The first real test of the Fascist regime's stability came in the economic field. Mussolini benefited from the policies of earlier postwar cabinets that had begun to turn around Italy's dismal economic predicament. Following the normal postwar pattern, during the 1920s Mussolini favored less governmental intervention and restrained the workers, policies that brought him international praise. Between 1922 and 1925, a free trader, Alberto De Stefani, held the post of minister of finance. De Stefani's low tax, privatization policies, and continued aid to banks and industry, pleased large industrialists and the church. Combined with low wages and the low value of the lira, these measures allowed Italy to take advantage of a European recovery, and Italian exports and productivity jumped.

In 1925 the lira dropped precipitously because of international speculation and caused inflation, the erosion of real wages, and labor agitation. In 1926 Mussolini artificially pegged the lira at a high value and choked credit. The costly lira made Italian goods expensive, and exports fell. Large firms weathered the deflation crisis because the government, foreshadowing future policy, intervened to help them, but small firms and the workers suffered. In 1927 the government implemented a 20 percent wage reduction on the grounds that lower prices compensated workers for the cut, but by 1929 real wages had fallen considerably.

On the labor front, the Fascists had destroyed the independent unions shortly after they came to power, but there were Fascist labor unions whose leaders were genuinely committed to helping workers and who had helped Mussolini come to power. These labor unions counted on Mussolini's help to strengthen their movement, but the industrialists pressured Mussolini to immobilize it. Il Duce did so between 1923 and 1927. The government issued a "Labor Charter" in 1927, but this charter turned out to be a pious statement of principles. There was an internal debate over Fascist "corporativism"—restructuring the country's economy—an interesting intellectual concept that Mussolini also defeated.

In the 1920s, Mussolini also campaigned to make Italy self-sufficient, especially in foodstuffs. He launched the "Battle of the Grain" with great fanfare in 1925, succeeding in increasing grain production, but at an enormous cost to the treasury and to other crops more suited to Italian conditions. Fascist industrial polices favored heavy industry and modernization, and by 1929 the country had made economic progress at the expense of the weakest sections of society.

Mussolini's preoccupation with consolidating his power and economic development prevented him from following through on his pledge to pursue an active foreign policy during the 1920s. He resolved the Fiume dispute with Yugoslavia and in 1923 occupied the Greek island of Corfu in retaliation for the murder by Greek bandits of Italian officials marking the Albanian border for the League of Nations. This issue was settled quickly, however, after which Mussolini's foreign policy entered a quiescent phase. Nevertheless, Mussolini chafed at French dominance of the continent and harbored ambitions that would produce radical changes in Italian foreign policy in the 1930s.

WEIMAR'S THREE ORIGINAL SINS

During the 1920s Germany seemed to take the opposite road of Italy by implementing a democratic regime. The Weimar Republic retained the empire's federalist structure, with the states (Länder) represented in a Reichsrat. Unlike the prewar Bundesrat, however, the states could not veto legislation passed by the popularly elected Reichstag, which could override the Reichsrat's rejection of its bills by a two-thirds majority. In addition, the constitution imposed restrictions on the states' areas of competence and on Prussian representation. A president elected by the people rounded out the constitution's democratic structure.

The reality of Weimar, however, differed from the appearance. Three factors threatened its success: its structural continuity with the Empire, the legacy of Versailles, and hyperinflation.

Structural Continuity

While federalism had benefits, it also had disadvantages in the German postwar context. Prussia, whose size and importance had dominated the Empire, was weakened but not broken up into several administrative units as some reformers had suggested. However, the SPD-Center coalition that ran Prussia from 1920 to 1932 made that state a "bastion of Weimar democracy," and it was a great blow to democracy when Nazi leader Hermann Goering became Prussian president in 1932. Germany's regional character, with states having different social and political traditions, contributed to radically different politics and threats of secession in the Rhineland, Bavaria, and other areas. This disparity occasioned continual conflict between the central and state governments, and the danger posed by possible secession helped secure passage of the constitution's Article 48, which effectively gave the president the right to rule by decree under emergency conditions. This provision would contribute to Hitler's rise.

The perpetuation of other aspects of the Empire also weakened Weimar. The November revolution had retained the bureaucratic structure and personnel nurtured during the Empire. Judges punished violent action by rightists against the Republic leniently—such as when Hitler tried to overthrow the government in 1923—and reserved harsh treatment for leftist opponents. Like the bureaucracy, large German industry and large landholdings in the eastern part of the country survived practically intact, allowing both to resist the notion of trade unions as equal partners in economic discussions and in the formulation of policy. Even though organized labor and the SPD had important responsibilities in the country, industrialists, Junkers, and large sections of the population looked at them with a suspicion that conferred a vaguely illegitimate air on the Republic. Many Germans viewed Weimar as a consequence of defeat and as essential to bargain with the Allies, not the result of the people's desire for a republic. The middle class yearned for traditional values, which the war and inflation had swept away. Despite passage of a democratic constitution, historians, from Arthur Rosenberg to Fritz Fischer to Hans-Ulrich Wehler, concurred that Germany did not change in a fundamental way after World War I.

The Versailles Legacy

This outline puts the complex events of Weimar into perspective. By 1920 right-wing extremism had become a serious problem. Furious nationalists condemned the government for accepting the Versailles treaty even though it had no choice. In March, the government fled before a nationalist coup effort led by Wolfgang Kapp. The army refused to intervene, and only a Socialist strike ended the attempt. When radical workers tried to transform the movement into a revolution, however, the army suppressed them.

Elections on June 6, 1920, validated this shift to the right. Parties supporting Weimar lost votes when compared to the 1919 elections, the SPD dropping from 37.9 percent to 21.6, later settling at about 25 percent until the 1930s in large measure because it its inability to shed its Marxist ideology. Its Center party ally went from 19.7 to 13.6 percent after a split. A third important liberal component of the Weimar coalition, the German Democratic Party (DDP), which was primarily responsible for the constitution, went from 18.6 to 8.4 percent. In contrast, Weimar's most determined enemy, the German National People's Party, or Nationalists (DNVP), rose to 15.1 percent from 10.3. The Nationalists were the heirs of the prewar Conservatives . Reactionary and anti-Semitic, they had the support of the old ruling class—large landowners, army officers, and industrial and middle-class elements. Weimar's enemies on the left, the Communists, received 2 percent of the vote in 1920, but they engaged in obstructionist tactics that reinforced the right. The 1920 elections revealed a rightist national trend away from the parties supporting Weimar; between June 1920 and November 1922, minority cabinets ran the country.

In May 1921, the Allies set a final figure for reparations and threatened retaliation if the Germans did not pay. This threat increased disorder in the country.

In Weimar Germany persons who favored a policy of "fulfillment" of the terms of the Versailles Treaty were targeted for assassination. Such was the case of moderate liberal Walter Rathenau, a Jew and a German patriot who had put the country on a war footing during World War I. He was brutally assassinated on June 24, 1922, a few short months after becoming Foreign Minister.

The Minister for Reconstruction and later Foreign Minister Walter Rathenau, a Jewish industrialist, supported a policy of fulfillment on the grounds that French intransigence would alienate its Allies; enraged anti-Semitic Nationalists brutally murdered him on June 24, 1922. Public outrage against reparations would subside when economic conditions improved, but the reparations played an important role in the Nationalist and Nazi propaganda against Weimar.

In November 1922, a cabinet of experts came to power in order to deal with reparations, but on January 9, 1923, Germany's default caused France and Belgium to occupy the highly industrialized Ruhr Valley.

Hyperinflation

The German government responded by calling for passive resistance. Workers struck, and industrialists refused to cooperate with the occupiers. The government paid workers and reimbursed the industrialists, putting a severe strain on German finances. These events have frequently been cited as the major reason for the hyperinflation that followed, but this does not seem to be the case. All governments had relied more on borrowing than on taxation to finance the war, causing postwar inflation, but Germany had done so more than the others, assuming it would win and the losers would pay the debts. The financial effort to meet the Ruhr occupation tipped the scales into hyperinflation because it added to the enormous debt left over from the conflict. The story of the German hyperinflation can be summarized by a few figures. The exchange rate of the mark to the dollar stood at 76.7 in July 1921. When the Ruhr invasion began in January 1923, the rate was 17,972. By September 1923, it stood at 98.8 million, and at the mark's lowest point, November 1923, the exchange rate was 4.2 trillion to the dollar.

Hyperinflation devastated German society as the savings of the middle class were wiped out, and heavy debtors profited handsomely. Industrialists who had borrowed heavily to finance their activities paid off their debt in worthless currency. Streetcar conductors collected fares at the end of a trip because, in the interval, the mark lost even more value. A monthly streetcar ticket cost 12 million marks in August 1923. A woman who put her currency in a basket to buy bread forgot her money outside the bakery; she ran out and was shocked to discover that someone had dumped out the money and stolen the basket. Newspapers published a list of daily prices and multipliers for goods and services that necessitated complicated arithmetical operations for ordinary daily tasks. Taking a cab required multiplying the stated fare by 600,000, and buying a book meant multiplying the published price by 300,000. Workers rioted if they were not paid daily and used wheelbarrows to carry their wages home.

The hyperinflation accelerated the corrosion of the nation's traditional values that occurred during the war by contributing to sexual promiscuity and to the family's breakdown. Daughters scoffed at their mothers' advice that they should get an education, work, and get married only when a couple had attained economic security: "Earn money! Ridiculous! Our money isn't worth earning!" Women no longer had dowries necessary to set up a solid household, and the men coming back from the war had nothing to offer. If they had to wait for security, daughters argued, they would be too old to marry. Consequently, many women left their families, with their restrictive, obsolete, morals. "The first man who offered a chance [to get away from their families] was the one with whom they went away, either marrying him or not."

The loss of savings that families had built up over a lifetime also increased the despair of the postwar situation as hyperinflation and the economic crash made it difficult to put food on the table, added to the specter of starvation, and increased political disorder. On August 13, 1923, a great coalition cabinet, headed by Gustav Stresemann, tried to end the crisis by implementing fulfillment of the Versailles treaty, but did not immediately stop the disturbances. In October, workers' outrage revived left-wing radicalism in Saxony, Thuringia, and Hamburg. Industrialists reduced the gains previously won by workers and forced out several opponents from the cabinet demanding that the army be used to quell the unrest. In the South, Bavaria became a hotbed of rightist and anti-Semitic activity. In Munich in November 1923, Adolf Hitler attempted a revolution known as the Beer Hall *Putsch*. Badly organized, it failed miserably, but his subsequent trial and the publication of *Mein Kampf*, written in jail, made him a national figure.

These events shifted the political axis to the right. Angered by the government's bias against the left, the SPD toppled Stresemann's government. The ensuing crisis and elections weakened the Socialists, and a more conservative cabinet that included DNVP representatives took power. In 1925, the election of World War I hero Paul von Hindenburg as president accentuated the conservative trend.

Foreign Policy and Its Domestic Effects

The saving grace was that Stresemann remained in the cabinet as foreign minister. Stresermann's policy of fulfillment brought Germany out of diplomatic isolation so it could profit from a worldwide economic recovery between 1925 and 1929. Hyperinflation subsided with the substitution of the inflated currency by a new one backed by a "mortgage" on all German land and industry, the Dawes plan establishing a repayments schedule for reparations, and a foreign loan. By 1927 German production surpassed that of 1913, and, at Locarno, Germany accepted its western frontiers, thus recognizing Alsace-Lorraine as French. In September 1926, Germany was admitted to the League of Nations with a seat on the Council. Despite these hopeful developments and other signs of thawing, however, Germany still refused to accept its responsibility for the war and conducted an "innocence" campaign that was designed to demonstrate that it had not caused the war and to fight against reparations. In a September 18, 1927, speech President von Hindenburg formally rejected the notion of German culpability for the war. Simultaneously, Germany conspired with the USSR to develop new weapons that evaded the Versailles treaty's disarmament terms and helped lay the basis for the rapid rearmament under Hitler. The army seemed to become more integrated into the Republic, but its officers were antirepublican, nationalist influenced, and recalcitrant to civilian control.

With the easing of the economic crisis in the mid-1920s, these troubling aspects of the new Germany remained hidden. The internal peace and good economy brought political stability as right-wing violence and assassinations declined. In May 1928, the parties supporting the constitution won an electoral victory, and the extremist parties took only 30 percent of the vote. Socialist ministers joined the cabinet for the first time since 1923, and an SPD member became chancellor.

However, the moderate victory would be short lived. The anti-Weimar Nationalists had reluctantly participated in cabinets despite internal divisions, but their severe defeat in the 1928 elections made them accept antirepublican industrialist and newspaper magnate Alfred Hugenberg as their new leader and financier. Under Hugenberg's leadership, the party virulently opposed the Republic. Its opposition to the Young Plan, which in August 1929 lightened reparations and set a new payment schedule, embodied this policy. Believing that the plan would undermine Germany's will to resist the war guilt idea and to nullify the Versailles treaty, Hugenberg campaigned against the Young Plan in concert with other right-wing groups, including the Nazis, in a December 1929 referendum. Although the referendum failed miserably, this campaign brought the Nazis to the forefront of German politics.

Between 1925 and 1929, the Weimar republic enjoyed stability and economic progress along with the rest of Western Europe, but it never overcame its original sins. It failed to develop sturdy institutions on which it could rely in times of crisis and did not change the nation's social structure and mentality. With the strain of the Great Depression, the Weimar republic's fragile structure came down.

THE USSR: THE CRISIS OF THE NEP

In Soviet Russia, the New Economic Policy (NEP) turned out to be an important economic success that allowed agricultural production to regain its prewar level in 1926. Livestock production, for example, rose by 3 percent to 4 percent a year between 1924 and 1928—faster than before World War I. However, the NEP cost the Communists their ideological consistency by introducing a market economy into Soviet agriculture.

The NEP Debate

The NEP's economic success contradicted Communist theory by allowing the reemergence of capitalism on the land and economic differentiation within the peasantry, but because the Bolsheviks remained committed to state planning, industrialization, modernizing agriculture, and transforming society, a dispute emerged among the leaders. The majority on the Communist Party's most important organ, the Politburo, consisting of an alliance between Josef Stalin and Nikolai Bukharin, argued that Communist objectives could be achieved *through* rather than *against* the market by governmental guidance. However, Bukharin believed that socialism could be achieved by increasing the wealth of the peasants, so he therefore favored more economic differentiation on the land, tax reductions, and the allocation of more resources for consumer goods; Stalin viewed the increased standards of living as Socialist accumulation, available for the implementation of communism, and eventually turned against Bukharin. Lenin's death in 1924 weakened the NEP and set the stage for a battle for succession that Stalin would win. Against the majority opinion, the Bolshevik left, led by Trotsky, Lev Kamenev, and Grigorii Zinoviev, believed that the party had made too many concessions to petty bourgeois landowners by allowing private trade and favoring rich peasants. It argued in favor of proceeding full speed ahead with rapid industrialization, a policy that Stalin would eventually adopt.

The Peasant Challenge

Relations between peasants and the government were filled with tension. The socialized sector of agriculture accounted for only about 2 percent of production. Ninety percent of households belonged to peasant communes (*mirs*) that periodically redistributed land as they had before the revolution. The Bolshevik Revolution had broken up the large private estates, redistributed land in a more or less equitable manner, and supplied peasants with farm implements and draught animals, but otherwise agriculture continued as before.

The Bolsheviks rejected this result and saw the peasants as divided into four categories: rich peasants, or kulaks, who hired labor and therefore exploited it; middle peasants, who cultivated their own land; poor peasants, who owned very little land and hired themselves out for part of the season; and proletarians with no land who worked the land of others. This characterization led Communist ideologues to target the kulaks when the government decided to proceed with rapid industrialization and the creation of large collective farms and to turn the poorer peasants against the richer ones, with varying success. The Communists also targeted the middle peasants because owning land went against their ideal of common ownership of the means of production.

These considerations set the stage for suppression of the peasants because communism could not be implemented through the NEP. Good harvests lowered the price of grain, but governmental subsidies kept the cost of industrial goods high; peasants refused to buy these goods until the government reduced the price. The situation worsened with bad harvests, as in 1924. In theory, agricultural prices should have risen, but the government refused to pay more, and the kulaks withheld their products in the hope of selling them in the expanding private market. The government doubled the price of grain, but this development made a mockery of Communist theory. In 1927 shortages of consumer goods and speculation brought about a governmental crackdown on private enterprise just at the time when Politburo advocates for rapid industrialization won their case because the defeat of the Chinese revolution and a dispute with the British brought home the USSR's urgent need to defend the Bolshevik Revolution.

The End of THE NEP

Because of these domestic and foreign developments, the Leftists escalated their criticism that the moderate policies pursued under the NEP endangered the gains of the October revolution and won their case. They abandoned their conciliatory attitude toward the kulaks and prepared an assault against them; in December 1927 the XV party congress accepted the conversion of small farms into collectives as the party's main task.

The Bolsheviks immediately ran into resistance from the peasants. Between October and December 1927, the peasants sold only half as much grain to state collection agencies as they had before because the government's prices were too low and they preferred to store their grain instead of selling it for cash that they could not spend on industrial goods that were in short supply anyway. Whereas the party had accommodated the peasants in the past, this time it refused to increase prices for grain, insisted on its push for industrialization, and seized the peasants' products. As the peasants obstructed collections, the government tried them for hoarding and speculation and called on the poorer peasants for support. The government's actions ignited a debate in the party. The alliance between Nikolai Bukharin and Stalin collapsed; Bukharin opposed the policy while Stalin favored it, strengthening his own political position. The party raised taxation for the kulaks to intolerable levels, raised collection quotas, confiscated land, and escalated punishments for resisters by sending them to prison or internal exile. Fearful of being labeled kulaks, the most efficient and prosperous farmers reduced the amount of land they farmed and sold or slaughtered their animals. The results were a drastic decrease in production, severe food shortages, rationing in urban areas, intensified state control of the countryside, requisitioning, the closing of private shops, and the expansion of state farms.

During the civil war, the Bolsheviks had requisitioned grain and other agricultural products that were necessary to win, but the policies of 1928 and 1929 signified that the party was determined to collectivize the peasantry and forcibly implement communism on the land. The normalcy that the NEP had brought to Russia had been more apparent than real and, as happened in the rest of the European continent, the 1930s ushered in more repression than Russia had previously experienced.

Bibliographical Essay

Raymond J. Sontag, *A Broken World 1919–1939* (New York, 1971), considers the period discussed in this chapter and the next. Good general works on the first post-war decade include Charles S. Maier, *Recasting Bourgeois Europe: Stabilization in France, Germany and Italy in the Decade after World War I* (Princeton, N.J., 1975), which is concerned with the attempt to stabilize those countries. Zara S. Steiner, *The Lights that Failed* (New York, 2005), is a comprehensive history of the attempt to recon-struct Europe in the 1920s. Dan P. Silverman, *Reconstructing Europe after the Great War* (Cambridge, Mass., 1982), concentrates on economic issues. Dirk Berg-Schlosser and Jeremy Mitchell, *Authoritarianism and Democracy in Europe, 1919–1939* (New York, 2002), is a comparative analysis.

The most complete work on Britain after the war is Charles Loch Mowat, *Britain Between the Wars 1918–1940* (Chicago, 1963). A. J. P. Taylor, *English History 1914–1945* (Oxford, UK, 1965), has chapters on this period filled with details and insights. Roy Jenkins wrote *Baldwin* (London, 1995). On different aspects of the Baldwin period, see the essays collected by John Raymond, ed., *The Baldwin Age* (London, 1960). For an analysis of Ramsay MacDonald, see Benjamin Sacks, *J. Ramsay MacDonald in Thought and Action* (Albuquerque, N.M., 1952). On the ramifications of the Zinoviev Letter, see Gill Bennett, "A Most Extraordinary and Mysterious Business: the Zinoviev Letter," *Historians LRD*, N. 14 (London 1999). Two useful works on British foreign policy are Anne Orde, *Great Britain and International Security 1920–1926* (London, 1978), and David Carlton, *MacDonald versus Henderson: The Foreign Policy of the Second Labour Govern-ment* (New York, 1970). Keith Erick Neilson, *Britain, Soviet Russia and the Collapse of the Versailles Order, 1919–1939* (Cambridge, UK, 2006), argues that the intellectual inability to maintain the order established in 1919 contributed to the outbreak of World War II. *The Morbid Age: Britain Between the Wars* (London, 2009), by the distinguished historian Richard J. Overy, is an examination of intellectual life during the period.

France during the 1920s has not been a popular topic. Nathaniel Greene's brief *From Versailles to Vichy: The Third French Republic, 1919–1940* (New York, 1970), covers the entire interwar period. Another general history, Charles Sowerwine's *France Since 1870,* 2d ed. (New York, 2009), discusses culture and society and has a chapter on interwar France. Allan Mitchell, *A Stranger in Paris: Germany's Role in Republican France, 1870–1940* (New York, 2006), is a wide-ranging discussion of the relationship between the two countries. A good biography of the most important French statesman during this period is J. F. V. Keiger, *Raymond Poincaré* (Cambridge, UK, 1997); Keiger states that Poincaré was the only French politician to have exercised a decisive influence in both the first and second halves of the Third Republic. Stephen A. Schuker's *The End of French Predominance in Europe: The Financial Crisis of 1924 and the Adoption of the Dawes Plan* (Chapel Hill, N.C., 1976) presents a thorough analysis of both domestic and foreign affairs up to 1924. Piotr S. Wandycz, *France and Her Eastern Allies 1919–1925* (Westport, Conn., 1974), is a detailed look at French and Eastern European diplomacy of the period.

Spencer M. Di Scala, *Italy: From Revolution to Republic, 1700 to the Present,* 4th ed. (Boulder, Colo., 2009), includes a detailed treatment of twentieth-century Italian his-tory. H. James Burgwyn discusses the concept of the mutilated victory in *The Legend of the Mutilated Victory: Italy, the Great War, and the Paris Peace Conference* (Westport,

Conn., 1993). Books that focus on the "Red Biennium" in English are scarce, while those that concentrate on Italian Communist Party founder Antonio Gramsci are plentiful. See John Cammett's *Antonio Gramsci and the Origins of Italian Communism* (Stanford, Calif., 1967); Martin Clark, *Antonio Gramsci and the Revolution that Failed* (New Haven, Conn., 1977); and Richard Bellamy and Darrow Schecter, *Gramsci and the Italian State* (Manchester, UK, 1993). A classic work on the Red Biennium and the coming of Fascism was written by the (then) Communist Angelo Tasca, *The Rise of Italian Fascism, 1918–1922* (London, 1938). Historian Gaetano Salvemini wrote two polemical but classic accounts of the rise of Fascism: *The Origins of Fascism in Italy* (New York, 1973), previously cited, and *The Fascist Dictatorship in Italy* (London, 1928). Alexander De Grand published a parallel history of the Italian Socialist and Communist parties with good coverage of this period, *The Italian Left in the Twentieth Century: A History of the Socialist and Communist Parties* (Bloomington, Ind., 1989). The period of the Red Biennium and the rise of fascism has been examined by Donald Sassoon, *Mussolini and the Rise of Fascism* (London, 2007), and Dalia S. Elazar, *The Making of Fascism:Class, State, and Counter-Revolution, Italy 1919–1922* (Westport, Conn., 2001). Adrian Lyttelton, *The Seizure of Power: Fascism in Italy, 1919–1929* (New York, 1973), is a thorough work on the subject. Spencer M. Di Scala's *Renewing Italian Socialism: Nenni to Craxi* (New York, 1988) includes a chapter discussing the early exile movement, and his previously cited *Italy: From Revolution to Republic, 1700 to the Present*, 4th ed. (Boulder, Colo., 2009) has a comprehensive chapter on the rise of fascism.

Fascism's love affair with violence is discussed by David Forgacs, "Fascism, Violence and Modernity," in Jana Howlett and Rod Mengham, *The Violent Muse: Violence and the Artistic Imagination in Europe, 1910–1934* (Manchester, UK, 1994). Alexander De Grand's essay "Bolshevik and Fascist Attacks on the Liberal State, 1919–1922" in Frank J. Coppa, ed., *Studies in Modern Italian History: From the Risorgimento to the Republic* (New York, 1986), is a good account of agrarian fascism. Anthony Cardoza's *Agrarian Elites and Italian Fascism: The Province of Bologna, 1901–1926* (Princeton, N.J., 1982) links agrarian and commercial fascism. Cardoza also published a good brief biography of Mussolini: *Benito Mussolini: The First Fascist* (New York, 2006). Discussions of fascisms in different parts of the country include Paul Corner, *Fascism in Ferrara 1915–1925* (London, 1975), and Alice Kelikian, *Town and Country under Fascism: The Transformation of Brescia,1915–1926* (Oxford, UK, 1986). H. James Burgwyn, *Italian Foreign Policy in the Interwar Period 1918–1940* (Westport, Conn., 1997) is a good book on a neglected topic.

On economic issues, see Douglas Forsyth, *Monetary and Financial Policy and the Crisis of Liberal Italy* (New York, 1993), and on diplomacy, see Alan Cassels, *Mussolini's Early Diplomacy* (Princeton, N.J., 1970).

Good general histories of Weimar Germany include Detlev Peukert, *Weimar Germany: The Crisis of Classical Modernity* (New York, 1992), and Paul Bookbinder, *Weimar Germany: The Republic of the Reasonable* (Manchester, UK, 1996). Stephen J. Lee's *The Weimar Republic* (New York, 2010) is a wide-ranging introduction. A. J. Nicholls, *Weimar and the Rise of Hitler* (London, 1968), is an excellent short work. Richard Bessel and E. J. Feuchtwanger, *Social Change and Political Development in Weimar Germany* (London, 1981), collects a number of good essays on the social history of the period. Richard Bessel has also published a detailed history of the immediate aftermath of the war, *Germany After the First World War* (Oxford, UK, 1993). Two contemporary accounts of the Weimar republic that can still be read with profit are Elmer Luehr, *The New German Republic* (New York, 1929), and James W. Angell, *The Recovery of Germany* (Westport, Conn., 1972). Annika Mombauer, *The Origins of the First World War: Controversies and Consensus* (London, 2002) is an excellent account of the controversies swirling around the question of whether Germany was to blame for the outbreak of the war and of the official attempt to establish German "innocence."

On the German hyperinflation, the most complete and detailed work is Gerald D. Feldman's massive *The Great Disorder: Politics, Economics, and Society in the German Inflation, 1914–1924* (New York, 1993). Feldman also published a study of heavy industry and its antiworker politics, *Iron and Steel in the German Inflation 1916–1923* (Princeton, N.J., 1977). A good short work is Fritz K. Ringer, *The German Inflation of 1923* (New York, 1969), which includes a good introduction and interesting readings; the citations in the text are taken from p. 135. Adam Fergusson's *When Money Dies: The Nightmare of the Weimar Collapse* (London, 1975, 2d ed., 2010) is a readable account of inflation's consequences. Constantino Brescian-Turroni's *The Economics of* Inflation (London, 2003) examines the depreciation of German currency and the hyperinflation between 1914 and 1923. Bernd Widdig, *Culture and Inflation in Weimar Germany* (Berkeley, Calif., 2001), analyzes the traumatic effects and permanent scars on German culture. A German view of reparations and of the Versailles settlement in general can be gleaned from Hjalmar Schacht, the man credited with planning the end of the hyperinflation, *The End of Reparations* (London, 1931), while Leonard Gomes, *German Reparations, 1919–1932* (New York, 2010), is a complete survey.

The crucial role that American loans played in Weimar's economic recovery is analyzed by William C. McNeil, *American Money and the Weimar Republic* (New York, 1986).

On particular personalities, institutions, and parties, see David Felix, *Walter Rathenau and the Weimar Republic* (Baltimore, Md., 1971), which concentrates on the crucial issue of reparations. Gene Smith, *The Ends of Greatness* (New York, 1990), has a good general account of Rathenau's fate (and those of other World War I characters). Henry L. Bretton, *Stresemann and the Revision of Versailles* (Stanford, Calif., 1953), is a good treatment of Stresemann's attempt to change the Versailles settlement peacefully. More disturbing is Hans W. Gatzke, *Stresemann and the Rearmament of Germany* (Baltimore, Md., 1954), which reveals German attempts to evade the disarmament clauses of Versailles, especially in collusion with the Soviets. Lewis Hertzman, *DNVP: Right Wing Opposition in the Weimar Republic, 1918–1924* (Lincoln, Nebr., 1963), examines a pivotal political party; this book should be consulted in conjunction with John A. Leopold's *Alfred Hugenberg: The Radical Nationalist Campaign Against the Weimar Republic* (New Haven, Conn., 1977), which puts the Nationalist leader and his campaign against Weimar under a microscope. Hermann Beck, *The Fateful Alliance: German Conservatives and Nazis in 1933* (New York, 2008), examines the complex relationship between the two. Germany's attempt to regain the military attributes of a great power is discussed more fully by Gaines Post, Jr., *The Civil-Military Fabric of Weimar Foreign Policy* (Princeton, N.J., 1973). A more general discussion of foreign policy, reparations, and Versailles is Royal Jae Schmidt, *Versailles and the Ruhr: Seedbed of World War II* (The Hague, 1968), and F. L. Carsten provides a full treatment of army policy in *The Reichswehr and Politics 1918 to 1933* (Oxford, UK, 1966). John Wheeler-Bennett's *The Nemesis of Power* (New York, 2005) looks at the German army in politics between 1918 and 1945. The coverage of Weimar in the first volume of Richard J. Evans, *The Coming of the Third Reich* (New York, 2004), is excellent; the quote on Prussia is on p. 89.

On the USSR during the NEP period, see Sheila Fitzpatrick, ed., *Russia in the Era of NEP* (Bloomington, Ind., 1991), which includes essays on various aspects of the NEP; so does R. W. Davies, *From Tsarism to the New Economic Policy* (Ithaca, N.Y., 1991). Gregory L. Freeze, ed., *Russia: A History* (New York, 1997), contains an essay by Daniel Orlovsky on the experiment. Fitzpatrick's more general work, *The Russian Revolution* (New York, 2008) includes a chapter on the NEP. See also Vladimir I. Lenin, *The New Policies of Soviet*

Russia (Chicago, 1921), with writings of protagonists. The discussion of the NEP crisis is usually covered by works that discuss the later collectivization effort as well. Two excellent works that look at the period examined in this chapter, as well as the 1930s, are R. W. Davies, *The Socialist Offensive: The Collectivization of Soviet Agriculture, 1929–1930* (New York, 1980), and Steven F. Cohen's *Bukharin and the Bolshevik Revolution: A Political Biography, 1888–1938* (New York, 1973). Christopher Read's *The Making and Breaking of the Soviet System* (New York, 2001) is a comprehensive history of the period, including the implications of the NEP, the struggles that brought it to an end, and ensuing events.

PART III

An Age of Dictators

CHAPTER 10

✐

The Great Depression and the Liberal Democracies

Economic dislocations of the Great Depression's scope, intensity, and duration profoundly challenged Europeans to maintain or revamp their democratic traditions in the face of social and political disorder.

THE GREAT DEPRESSION

In October 1929 the U.S. stock market collapsed and touched off a Great Depression that stunned the leaders of the advanced industrial nations who believed that they had successfully overcome the dislocations caused by World War I.

The Long Wave

Despite the economic progress that characterized most of the 1920s, warning signals, such as the weak state of agriculture, were apparent. The rising grain prices during World War I had encouraged farmers to put more land into production, but the end of hostilities brought about a reduced demand and falling prices. The decline hit the small countries of Eastern Europe the earliest, and in the mid-1920s the strong peasants' parties forced governments to enact tariff barriers against imported agricultural goods—the first shots in an economic war that would engulf the world. A similar crisis affected coal, the basis of British prosperity since the industrial revolution and now being rapidly being displaced by oil.

Greater economic interdependence, symbolized by American loans to Germany and mistaken governmental policies, increased the severity and length of the 1930s economic downturn. The Germans paid reparations to the European allies partly with American funds, who used them to pay war debts to the Americans, who then had more money to lend to the Germans—and so on. When Wall Street crashed, American investors withdrew their loans, and the process stopped. European banks faltered, capped by the clamorous failure of the Kreditanstalt in Vienna in May 1931 that intensified the financial panic and led to more bank closings, industrial failures, and layoffs.

As for the governments, their insistence on the gold standard and balanced budgets when the crisis began made things worse by contributing to a deflationary spiral. When unemployment increases, people reduce their spending, and the decreased purchasing power reduces demand. Producers cannot sell their products and lay off more workers, which reduces demand, production, and prices even more. Severe deflation ignited social and political unrest, especially in the most highly industrialized countries where production fell about 37 percent and unemployment reached 25 percent.

The Great Depression increased the appeal of communism because it seemed to confirm the hypothesis of Karl Marx, who predicted that capitalism would collapse in a gigantic final crisis of overproduction that would cause the proletariat to revolt, overthrow capitalism, and implement socialism. Many leftists took the Soviet Union as a model, provoking a serious backlash even in countries with well-developed democratic traditions. In countries where democracy did not have a long tradition, the reaction against communism encouraged the rise of dictatorial regimes.

A Downward Spiral

Combined with the American stock market crash, trading difficulties had lethal effects. In June 1930, the United States adopted the Smoot-Hawley tariff that touched off a new round of protectionism that worsened the economic downturn. The crash wiped out the savings and jobs of millions of Americans and Europeans. The greatly diminished purchasing power caused production to drop and business confidence and investment to slip as the increased risk of business failures caused investors to sell stocks and call in mortgages and loans. With the tightening up of credit, Germany could no longer pay reparations, and the British and French defaulted on their war debts to the United States. High unemployment rates led countries to close their borders to imports to keep as many of their own citizens employed as possible. The decline of international trade caused more unemployment, which caused increased governmental expenses and decreased tax revenues. Governments had to provide benefits to more people but had a limited ability to raise taxes because people were less able to pay them. They borrowed to make up for the shortfall, but lenders demanded further cuts to ensure that they would be paid back, and more borrowing caused a run on currencies as citizens tried to exchange currency for gold.

In the past, agriculture had served as a buffer against economic disaster, but this time no relief arrived. The bountiful harvests of 1929 and later years worsened the agricultural crisis of the mid-1920s. Prices kept falling because major world producers of wheat and cereals lacked enough storage facilities, forcing them to

The Great Depression that followed the American Stock Market Crash of 1929 had its origins in the mistaken policies of the major countries. They followed restrictive economic policies and remained on the gold standard, thus worsening the recession that followed that event. This picture shows a protest march of the unemployed in London.

sell their products quickly, and the USSR increased wheat exports hoping that the revenues would help fund its policy of rapid industrialization.

Governmental Policies

After World War I, governments insisted on reinstituting the gold standard as a means of anchoring national currencies and preventing wild fluctuations in exchange rates that would result in inflation and social disorder. For example, in 1925, the British responded to balance-of payments deficits by contracting their economy in order to reinstitute the gold standard. Because they imported too many goods and paid for them in gold, however, the precious metal flowed out of the country, and British monetary authorities tried to reduce the outflow by restricting people's ability to buy goods.

The classic way of reducing consumer buying is to increase unemployment, but in times of severe crises, this policy can set off a dangerous downward spiral. The gold standard made it impossible to address balance-of-payments deficits by devaluing the currency, which reduces the price of a country's products on the world market and increases exports and, consequently, employment. According to Peter Temin, bad monetary policy, not structural causes, precipitated, prolonged, and deepened the Great Depression.

The gold standard was not the only reason for the severe downturn. In times of crisis, governments of the period cut expenses and raised interest rates, the exact opposite of what was needed, according to British economist John Maynard Keynes, who advocated increased governmental spending and lower interest rates to stimulate the economy during economic crises. Keynes wrote during the depression, but monetary officials did not accept his ideas until the post–World War II period. Governments, such as that of German Chancellor Heinrich Bruening, followed restrictive financial policies and adopted harsh budgets to decrease the deficit, and the Americans increased interest rates and shrank their economy. The British followed similar policies until 1931, when they pursued a policy of mild expansion that brought some relief.

BRITISH DEMOCRACY

During the Great Depression, the liberal democracies of northern Europe retained their democratic structures despite difficult and sometimes dramatic circumstances.

Britain Confronts the Crisis

In Britain, Ramsay MacDonald's second Labour government (May 1929–August 1931), in office when the Great Depression began, needed Liberal support to remain in power and forced him to confront the emergency with classic economic, not Socialist, solutions.

BIOGRAPHICAL SKETCHES

James Ramsay Macdonald
Labour's "Nonperson" Prime Minister

Born to Anne Ramsay out of wedlock in Lossiemouth, Scotland, on October 12, 1866, Ramsay MacDonald shared the stigma of an illegitimate birth with two other famous British Labour leaders, Keir Hardie and Ernest Bevin. Education was MacDonald's ticket to success. At age 15, his appointment as a "pupil teacher" took him out of the fields and gave him an excellent grounding in English literature, Latin, and Greek. This education—unusual for political leaders of his class—inclined him to leadership.

In 1885, MacDonald went to Bristol and then London, working in humble jobs. He joined the Fabian Society, inspired by Beatrice and Sidney Webb, who believed in achieving socialism gradually. MacDonald championed equal opportunities for women and married Margaret Gladstone, a leader in the struggle. A meeting of local workers congratulated "Mrs. J. R. Macdonald in having won the esteem of Comrade J. R. Macdonald which in due time matured into love and it further resolves that she is one in a thousand."

Margaret's private income gave MacDonald a measure of economic security and aided his rise to political prominence. MacDonald became the first secretary of the Labour Representation Committee, the forerunner of the Labour Party, in 1900. In 1906, he won election to Parliament, along with twenty-eight other members of the organization, and in 1911 became its parliamentary leader. A traditional

Socialist pacifist, in 1914 MacDonald opposed Britain's entrance into World War I because he believed that the conflict did not threaten the country. The Labour parliamentary delegation disagreed with him and voted war credits, prompting him to resign his leadership post. His popularity plummeted, and in 1918 he lost his seat.

Recovering from this defeat, MacDonald won reelection and led the Labour opposition. Following the 1923 elections, the Liberals supported MacDonald as prime minister in a coalition government. Despite some successes, his first term ended on a sour note on November 4, 1924, because of the botched prosecution of a Communist newspaper editor for his opinions. In the 1929 elections, Labour became the largest British party, allowing MacDonald to return as prime minis-ter. He named as minister of labor the first woman to hold cabinet rank, Margaret Bondfield. This governmental experience proved a failure because the cabinet did not resolve the problems of the depression. MacDonald resigned on August 24, 1931, but, believing a national government necessary to confront the crisis, agreed to head a cabinet that included Liberals and Conservatives. In reality, MacDonald had little real power, and Conservative Stanley Baldwin led the cabinet. MacDonald relinquished the prime minister's post on June 7, 1935, but stayed on until May 29, 1937. Exhausted and lonely, he departed for a South American tour and died of heart failure at sea on November 9 aboard the steamship *Reina del Pacifico*. His body was taken back to Scotland, cremated, and interred with that of his wife, who had died of blood poisoning in 1911.

Although MacDonald was the first Labour prime minister, the party treated him as an embarrassment and ignored him because it considered him a traitor for not implementing Socialist policies, for his decision to stay on as prime minister in 1931, and for being an impractical dreamer. In fact, MacDonald lacked a ma-jority to achieve a Labour program, and no other leader handled the depression satisfactorily. In treating him as a nonperson, the Labour Party and its historians disregarded the successful efforts that MacDonald made to construct a Labour Party organization and to win public acceptance as a replacement for the Liberal Party.

When unemployment shot up from 10 percent to 16 percent and the country's exports declined by one-half in two years, MacDonald had no choice but to extend the dole to an increasingly greater number of the unemployed—2.5 million by the end of 1930. As tax receipts fell precipitously because fewer people could afford to pay taxes, MacDonald and his unimaginative Chancellor of the Exchequer Philip Snowden could do no better than implement austerity. In July 1931, economic experts recommended sharp increases in taxation and drastic spending cuts for the country to qualify for new loans and to remain on the gold standard. They suggested a 10 percent cut in unemployment benefits and prohibiting the embat-tled unemployment insurance fund from borrowing more money. In August, the American J. P. Morgan Bank declared that it would not lend any more money to the Bank of England unless the Labour government went along with the cuts, which were bound to increase unemployment. MacDonald and Snowden saw no alternative because they feared that the pound would lose value if they did not comply. MacDonald brought the question before the cabinet, which split on the question and resigned.

The National Government

Instead of resigning when he consulted with the king, MacDonald unexpectedly secured a mandate for a national government from the monarch. He believed that the crisis required a unified, nonpartisan cabinet, but his own Labour Party objected and expelled him. MacDonald's new National Government cabinet included Conservative leader Stanley Baldwin, who quickly overshadowed the prime minister. It reduced relief and governmental salaries and attempted to balance the budget, measures that alleviated neither the financial nor the social crisis. Investors continued to dump pounds for gold, and salary reductions provoked antigovernment riots. Realizing that strikes and social disorder would intensify if it continued on its deflationary course, the government abandoned the gold standard.

Almost immediately the pound fell to 70 percent of its old exchange rate with the dollar—less than observers had expected. MacDonald then called for new elections to ask a mandate from the voters. On October 27, 1931, the elections gave the National Government a large majority of 497 seats, but the mandate went to the Conservatives, not MacDonald, by decimating the Labour Party and making MacDonald more dependent on Baldwin. Labour retreated to reorganize itself, but it would take power again only in 1945. The National Government cabinet, with Baldwin as its real star, enjoyed a large majority to take decisive action. Fortunately for Britain, abandonment of the gold standard by reason of popular discontent stimulated the British economy because the pound's devaluation made British goods cheaper on the world market.

The electoral campaign had been fought primarily over the question of whether the country should reverse its traditional free-trade policy and protect essential industries, and protection won out. In 1932 the government imposed a 10 percent general duty and intervened in the private industrial sector by fostering mergers and nationalization in areas such as cotton and steel production, eliminating weaker companies, and giving it the ability to control prices. It also nationalized London transport, subsidized shipbuilding and important agricultural products, and imposed import quotas, all of which helped stimulate growth. In 1934 the government embarked on a public works program and made grants to the country's most depressed areas, where, despite the country's economic improvement, unemployment remained distressingly high.

Political Challenges

Despite the economic crisis, the British political system proved remarkably stable and successfully confronted challenges from both the right and the left.

A native Fascist movement under Sir Oswald Moseley, a former Conservative Member of Parliament from an old distinguished family, as well as an ex-Socialist, took root. As a minor official in the MacDonald government, Moseley had presented a radical proposal for emergency action to the cabinet, but after its defeat, he turned sharply right, embraced fascism, and formed the raucous British Union of Fascists. This organization created a commotion in the country, but never won enough followers to make a difference in British politics.

On the left, one of the most important Labour party affiliates, the Independent Labour Party (ILP), seceded in 1932. ILP members included influential young leftist intellectuals who revolted against old-line trade union Socialists and founded the Socialist League. Influenced by Harald Laski, a political science professor at the London School of Economics, and John Strachey, scion of a celebrated literary family, and attracted by Marxism, they denounced fascism and the rightward drift of the Labour Party. They advocated a Popular Front alliance with the Communists, believing that the Labour Party should institute a temporary dictatorship to impose a Socialist revolution. The ILP had great cultural appeal in England, and in 1935, the publication of a new book that was favorable to the Soviet Union by Sidney and Beatrice Webb—*Soviet Russia: A New Civilization?*—boosted their cause. The ILP's influence, however, remained cultural, and the Labour Party remained firmly under the control of Clement Attlee, who succeeded George Lansbury in 1935, and Ernest Bevin, a trade union leader who distrusted intellectuals.

Unlike Labour, the Conservative Party under Stanley Baldwin weathered political uprisings with little difficulty. These revolts included Churchill's denunciation of the British dominions' drift toward de facto independence that resulted in Ireland effectively becoming a republic in 1937 and India's increasing shift toward the independence that occurred after World War II. More important, Churchill advocated resisting Hitler's demands and unsuccessfully opposed the appeasement policies of Baldwin, after he became prime minister in 1935, and of his successor Neville Chamberlain.

TROUBLED FRANCE

The 1930s were years of crisis for the other major European democratic power, France, which saw a rapid growth of nationalistic and quasi-fascist organizations after the victories of the Cartel des Gauches coalition of Radicals and Socialists in 1924 and 1932. The economic crisis of the 1930s and the seeming success of Fascist Italy and the growth of Nazism in Germany emboldened French Fascist-leaning organizations.

France and the Depression

Despite the growth and increased efficiency of French industry during the 1920s, France remained a country based on small business and an inflexible mentality. The Great Depression struck later than in other countries because of its self-sufficiency and large number of small companies and independent landowners. Investors trading their currencies for gold also preferred Paris as a refuge for their wealth, which gave the impression that France had immunity from the economic crisis. The French, leaders of the "gold bloc," stubbornly refused to go off the gold standard and followed deflationary policies longer than other countries. This policy caused a drop in industrial production of 27 percent between 1930 and 1932, rising unemployment, increased expenses, and revenue shortfalls.

The country's steadily worsening economic situation radicalized workers, peasants, and the middle class. The workers increasingly supported Socialist and Communist organizations. On the land, the peasants joined right-wing and leftist organizations that were hostile to the republic because of a fall in revenue of 40 percent between 1931 and 1934. The middle class, its security gone, favored right-wing groups advocating the government's overthrow. Owners of small businesses, themselves caught by the crisis, tenaciously resisted workers' demands for improved wages and working conditions. Popular support for the Third Republic seemed to evaporate.

Political Disorder

In this situation, the French political system failed. In 1929 and 1930 André Tardieu, the most energetic premier after Poincaré, proposed massive construction projects, electrification, industrial and agricultural renovation, and increased social insurance, but the right opposed him because it favored the lower classes, and the left feared political competition. Pierre Laval replaced Tardieu and followed a deflationary economic policy that gave rise to a new Cartel des Gauches that won the 1932 elections. The new union suffered from the same weakness as the old one—a fundamental incompatibility between the Socialists and the Radicals. The Socialists demanded a forty-hour workweek and nationalization of the armaments industry, but the Radicals opposed them, and the cartel then fell apart; six cabinets followed each other in rapid succession between June 1932 and February 1934.

In February 1934 the Stavisky scandal set off serious street disorders. It had been rumored that high governmental officials had protected Serge Stavisky, a financier who had been involved in many questionable dealings. When Stavisky died under mysterious circumstances, his victims protested because they believed that the police had killed him to cover up the involvement of his highly placed partners. Radical Prime Minister Édouard Daladier took a strong stand against the disturbances by firing the Paris police chief, and rightist groups sympathetic to Fascist Italy and Nazi Germany reacted by leading riots in Paris on February 6, 1934, that left 14 dead and 263 wounded. Daladier resigned—the first time in the Third Republic's history that a cabinet left office because of riots. A national union cabinet replaced Daladier and followed deflationary economic policies that failed to resolve the economic and political tensions.

The French leftists interpreted the disorders as a Fascist conspiracy to overthrow the republic, demonstrating and calling a general strike to protest the growing threat from the right. At this point, the Communists, who had previously rejected cooperation with the Socialists, decided to negotiate with them because of the rise of Hitler in Germany and the Nazi threat to the USSR. The talks produced a unity-of-action pact that brought closer relations between them, and the agreement was enlarged in 1935 with the adherence of the Radicals. In January 1936 the parties joined in a common program known as the Popular Front.

Right and Left: A Mortal Struggle

Challenging the left were fascistic groups that had an important cultural impact and would reach their zenith after the French defeat by the Nazis in 1940. The rightist leagues had absorbed the popular nationalism of Maurice Barrès and Charles Maurras (see Chapter 1), denouncing French political decadence and exhorting the nation to strive for excellence and heroism. Although they might cooperate as they did in the February 1934 riots, they did not speak with a unified

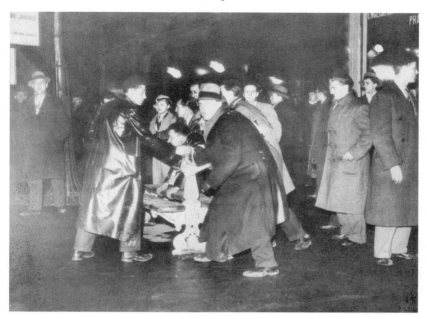

France was struck by corruption and disorders during the Great Depression. The riots in Paris that resulted from the financial embezzlements of Serge Stavisky in 1934 left many dead and wounded and resulted in the government's fall.

voice. The Action Française, the Camelots du Roi, and the Croix de Feu were ultra-nationalist, antiparliamentarian, and authoritarian, but were not in the Fascist tradition; the Jeunesses Patriotes, the Solidarieté Français, and later the Cagoulards admired Fascist Italy and Nazi Germany. In the 1930s French fascism was highly visible but failed to attract a mass following. Georges Valois's Le Faisceau collapsed in 1928. Marcel Bucard's Francistes, founded in 1933, received Italian subsidies but remained small. Jacques Doriot's Parti Populaire Français (French Popular Party, PPF), created after the Popular Front's electoral victory of 1936, was a partial exception. It grew rapidly for a time but declined even faster in 1938 and 1939 when apprehension that the leftists would take over France faded.

The Popular Front and Its Failure

The struggle between the right and the left became fiercer following the Popular Front's electoral campaign and victory in May 1936, which polarized the country as never before. The Socialists emerged as the largest French party, with 146 seats in the Chamber of Deputies, and the Radicals followed with 116. The most spectacular result, however, was the increase in Communist seats—from 10 to 72. For the first time, a Socialist leader, Léon Blum, became prime minister, increasing fears that the Popular Front would lead to a Communist dictatorship and confiscation of private property, and eliciting expressions of anti-Semitism because Blum was Jewish. The likelihood of a Communist dictatorship was slim because the Communists refused to enter the cabinet and restricted their support to parliamentary votes. The Radicals joined the cabinet, but they opposed the social and economic reforms advocated by their Socialist and Communist partners.

BIOGRAPHICAL SKETCHES

Léon Blum
Popular Front

The most important French politician of the 1930s, Léon Blum, was born in Paris on April 9, 1872, into a Jewish family from Alsace. Blum graduated with honors in law in 1894 from the Sorbonne and became a literary critic. Scandalized by the Dreyfus affair, Blum went into politics, joined the French Socialist Party in 1899, and helped Jaurès found the leading Socialist newspaper L'Humanité. Blum won election to the Chamber of Deputies in 1919.

Blum had a crucial role in French Socialism in the 1920s and 1930s. After the Bolshevik revolution in Russia, the Communists founded the Third International (Comintern) and circulated a list of twenty-one conditions. Parties that wanted to join the Comintern had to accept all of them for membership in the new organization, a demand that threw the postwar European Socialist parties into crisis. In France on December 20, 1920, a majority of the Socialist Party agreed to all the conditions. The Communist faction thus gained control of the party machinery, funds, and newspaper and changed the party's name. The Socialists had to rebuild their movement from its foundations, and Léon Blum guided the process.

Blum directed Socialist Party policy after its reconstitution. In 1924 he supported the Cartel des Gauches that won the elections of that year. In the 1928 elections, the Socialist Party won 104 seats. Blum's bid for reelection failed, but he was returned the next year.

Faced with the challenge of rising right-wing agitation at home and increasing Fascist aggression abroad, Blum elaborated a program in 1932 emphasizing the battle against unemployment. After the Stavisky riots of February 1934, Blum worked hard to build a left-wing coalition to fight fascism. Despite internal party opposition, he successfully formed the Popular Front electoral alliance with the Radicals and the Communists. In the national elections of April and May 1936, the Popular Front swept to victory with 376 seats in the Chamber of Deputies.

As the architect of the Popular Front, Blum became French premier in June 1936. His background as France's first Jewish and Socialist prime minister, his program, and his activism raised the hostility of the right. He forced industrialists to grant a forty-hour workweek, vacation time, and other concessions to the workers and nationalized the Bank of France and the munitions industry. In foreign policy, he responded positively to the Spanish government's request for aid against the Fascist-supported attempt to overthrow it, but then backtracked under pressure from the British and from members of his own cabinet to adopt a policy of nonintervention. However, the bitter hostility of French business to Blum's plans to confront the deepening depression doomed the government. When the Senate refused to grant him emergency powers to counter the economic crisis in June 1937, Blum resigned.

The heroic period of Blum's life was over. Blum served as vice premier in 1937 and briefly returned as prime minister from March 13 to April 10, 1938. After France's defeat by Germany in World War II, the Vichy government arrested and tried him with other leaders of the Third Republic in February 1942. It accused them of having caused France's collapse. The trial ended without a verdict because of the strong arguments of the defense and the outlandishness of the charges, but Blum remained in jail until the Germans shipped him to a concentration camp. Allied troops liberated him in May 1945, and Blum resumed his Socialist politics. He negotiated an important financial agreement with the United States in which the Americans forgave French debts and lent the country money for postwar reconstruction.

Blum headed a month-long cabinet in December 1946 and retired from public life after the fall of 1948 to his estate of Jouy-en-Josas. He died there on March 30, 1950.

Bad feelings between the Socialists and Communists divided the Popular Front coalition. The Communists had previously alienated the Socialists by labeling them "Social fascists." Moreover, the Socialists aimed at salvaging the Third Republic, while the Communists wanted its destruction. In 1934, Communist policy changed because of Stalin's fear that Hitler would invade the USSR, and in 1935 Stalin signed an alliance with France directed against a possible German attack. The agreement would become worthless if the right took over in France, so Stalin ordered the French Communists to reverse course, and they entered the Popular Front coalition.

The dramatic change in Communist tactics did not end the differences. The Communist trade union rejoined the Socialist-influenced CGT, from which it had split in 1920, but ideological problems quickly appeared between the old Socialist leadership, oriented toward economic reforms, such as a reduced workweek and paid vacations, and the revolutionary orientation of the Communists who were joining the union. Ideology also polarized the Socialist Party. Blum and other leftist Socialist Party leaders supported a Communist alliance after the February 1934 Stavisky riots, but Socialist leaders, such as general secretary Paul Faure, distrusted the Communists. The Socialists also split on foreign policy: Faure was a convinced pacifist, while Blum was willing to use force against Germany.

The Popular Front government took office on June 5, 1936, and trouble began immediately. A massive wave of sit-in strikes by workers demanding immediate reforms shook the country, with 2 million strikers participating in Paris alone. Blum coerced the employers into accepting measures known as the Matignon Accords, named after the prime minister's residence. These agreements granted workers a general wage increase, a forty-hour workweek, and paid vacations and provided for the reorganization and ultimate nationalization of the Bank of France. The workers claimed victory, but bitter members of the bourgeoisie sent their money out of the country to the tune of 30 billion gold francs. The slogan "Better Hitler Than Blum" summarized their view of the prime minister after this incident.

The government's hopes that the Matignon agreements would stimulate the economy quickly evaporated. The shorter workweek was an obstacle to this goal and was later lengthened. The improved social legislation raised costs and resulted in increased prices, stagnant production, and fewer exports. The nationalization of the Bank of France raised fresh fears of the confiscation of property and increased the outflow of capital. By March 1937 the economic crisis had intensified to the point that the government unsuccessfully requested decree powers to block the flow of currency out of the country. Blum resigned, and the Popular Front experiment officially ended in 1938 with the withdrawal of the Radicals from the coalition.

The Popular Front's failure may be attributed to a variety of causes. The workers were concerned with increasing their wages and reducing working hours, not finding solutions to the country's economic ills. The Communists did not believe in the Third Republic's capacity to reform itself. The Radicals, as usual, were not willing to make drastic changes. Finally, the bourgeoisie crippled the Popular Front by sending its money outside France, depriving the country of investments. In the end, the Popular Front exacerbated French divisions.

A series of weak governments followed Blum's resignation. In foreign affairs, they proved incapable of stopping Hitler from marching troops into the Rhineland or from taking over Austria. In domestic affairs, the economy improved after April 1938 after the franc's devaluation and after Parliament granted Radical Prime Minister Daladier the power to rule by decree.

In the 1930s the French republic was less able than other industrial democracies to confront the economic emergency and passed through unprecedented tumults, political upheaval, and loss of confidence. At the beginning of World War II, France found itself polarized and unequal to the task of defending the country against a resurgent Germany.

SCANDINAVIA: TOWARD SOCIAL DEMOCRACY

In the Scandinavian area, the most industrially developed country, Sweden, served as a model. The individual countries were faced with disorders, labor problems, inflation, and political instability after World War I, despite their neutrality. In general, single parties did not win absolute majorities, and the countries were ruled by coalitions.

Postwar Unrest and Reform

Neutrality during World War I brought Scandinavia economic benefits, but their uneven distribution allowed Bolshevism to make strong inroads. In Sweden, Norway, and Denmark, strikes and demonstrations demanded the creation of workers' and soldiers' soviets. The Norwegian Labour Party joined the Communist International, but the appeal of communism quickly faded for the Norwegians. In Finland, which achieved independence from Russia in 1917, the Finnish Communist Party remained an important presence. In Sweden, workers' sympathy for the Bolsheviks did not translate into political support. The Social Democrats, the largest Swedish party, were Marxists, but they backtracked when they discovered that they lost votes when they moved toward socialism and ended up as a moderate party with a strong social consciousness.

The Swedish government responded to postwar unrest with sweeping electoral reform. In 1922, reforms eliminated voting restrictions based on tax payments, gender, and property, making Parliament's conservative First Chamber more democratic. Other Scandinavian countries also responded to demands for reform: Denmark embarked on a program of social legislation and land reform that continued into the 1920s; Norway introduced the eight-hour workday (forty-eight-hour workweek); Finland allowed agricultural workers to buy the land they held at 1914 prices and conceded generous state loans that by 1930 permitted tenants to buy 90 percent of all the rented farms.

Like the rest of Europe, the Scandinavians fought postwar inflation by orthodox economic methods. They implemented deflationary policies that, by the 1920s, allowed them to reestablish the gold standard. These policies caused difficulties, but prosperity returned, as in the rest of Europe, during the decade. Norway witnessed a great expansion of its fishing industry, and the Norwegian fleet resumed its prewar position as the world's fourth largest. In Denmark, the gold standard produced greater disruption than in the rest of Scandinavia, with 30 percent unemployment and numerous strikes, but by 1928, good times had returned. An economic boom driven by exports to Britain followed Finland's successful struggle for independence. By 1928, Finland exported 56 percent more than it had in 1913, and the value of its industrial production increased by 33 percent.

Confronting the Depression

The Scandinavian countries coped better than the other democracies with the end of the 1920s prosperity and the depression of the 1930s. Governing coalitions based on Social Democrats emerged as the central Scandinavian political force. In Sweden and Denmark, governmental coalitions based on the Social Democrats presented programs to strengthen social legislation. In 1932 the Social Democrat–Agrarian coalition in Sweden confronted high industrial and

The Swedish modern style that had its origins during the Great Depression has exerted an enduring influence on modern design. Here is an example from 1956.

agricultural unemployment and strikes by acting on two fronts: economic policy and social welfare.

In economics, Sweden became one of the first countries to apply the theories of John Maynard Keynes, advocating more governmental spending, not less, during economic slowdowns. The Swedish government devalued the krona and stimulated the economy by increasing spending for public works and unemployment relief. Its policies doubled Swedish exports between 1932 and 1936. In the social sphere, Swedish housing cooperatives constructed affordable housing in partnership with the state and private industry and established their own bank. The housing program emphasized efficiency and utilitarian design in construction and decoration and made "Swedish modern" world famous. In keeping with the country's tradition of social welfare, the cooperatives planned housing with both working wives and husbands in mind, including labor-saving devices that they hoped would help reverse the declining birth rate. The Scandinavian countries also cooperated with each other in combating the depression by aggressively encouraging cooperatives and extending their influence at the national and international levels with the aim of combating international cartels, high prices, and capitalist excesses. Sweden encouraged the formation of mixed public-private firms to protect its national resources. These policies resulted in greater industrial efficiency and an unusually rapid Scandinavian recovery from the depression.

Swedish governmental intervention in daily life in the 1930s came about as the result of a compromise among the parties and was emulated in the other Scandinavian countries. The Swedish Social Democrats renounced socialism and emphasized welfare; the conservatives criticized and modified social legislation but did not block it. The Danish government embarked on a program of public works and direct intervention in the economy, and in 1933 the Danish parties reached a compromise similar to the Swedish understanding, the *Kanslergade* agreement. This agreement sanctioned the social reform policy advocated by Social Democrat leader Karl Kristian Steinche, according to whom social legislation was a right not a charity. Steinche's program "was a thorough tidying-up of Danish social legislation, which then remained unaltered for some forty years." In Norway the Labour party supported strengthening social legislation—unemployment insurance, protection of workers, employee consultations, and compensation for dismissal. Finland passed significant social legislation and encouraged a robust cooperative movement. Finnish women made important progress and actively participated in politics. Finland had been the first country to recognize the equality of men and women, and during the interwar years the Scandinavian countries enacted over a dozen laws strengthening the position of women. This legislation defined the status of unmarried mothers, freed children who were born out of wedlock from legal disabilities, and gave Scandinavian women the vote before other countries in Western Europe.

Foreign Affairs

Despite the successful Scandinavian response to postwar unrest and the economic downturn, several parties modeled on the Nazis appeared in Sweden, Denmark, and Norway, but even at the height of their influence, they received only

2.2 percent of the vote. The most important Scandinavian Fascist organization was Vikdun Quisling's National Unity Party in Norway. Quisling cooperated with the Nazis during the World War II occupation, and his name became a synonym for traitor. Finland, facing strong leftist labor agitation and disorder, witnessed a long period of illegal violence against the Communists but overcame the crisis.

The small Scandinavian countries had a greater influence in foreign affairs than was warranted by their small population. They supported the rule of international law, and one of them always occupied a nonpermanent seat on the Council of the League of Nations. The Scandinavians were most concerned about preserving their neutrality against the pretensions of the big powers. Finland faced the most serious problems because of a territorial dispute with Sweden, the existence of an influential Swedish minority, and the USSR's eye on Finnish territory. Denmark, which had received North Schleswig from Germany following World War I, feared the revived German claims to the area after the Nazis came to power. Militarily, only Sweden supported a strong armed force.

MARKING TIME: THE LOW COUNTRIES AND SWITZERLAND

The different experiences of Belgium and the Netherlands during the war marked their immediate postwar history. The Germans had occupied Belgium, causing a great deal of destruction and world sympathy. The Netherlands had remained neutral, and the Allies thought that it tilted toward Germany, a suspicion confirmed in their minds when, after the war, the Netherlands gave asylum to the former German kaiser and refused to hand him over for trial.

The Low Countries

Impact of the War
Belgium received a small amount of territory and reparations from Germany after the war, but not enough to pay for the country's reconstruction, which took until 1928 to complete. The Belgians devalued the franc, stimulated the economy, and returned to the gold standard in October 1926. In contrast to the Dutch, they also implemented significant social legislation after the war. Economically, the Dutch were better off after the war until 1939 and returned to the gold standard before Belgium in April 1925.

Postwar Politics
There were curious similarities and differences in the politics of the two countries. In the Netherlands, male universal suffrage and proportional representation produced a proliferation of political groups that did not occur in Belgium. In the Netherlands, governmental stability prevailed despite frequent cabinet changes because the same persons kept their old positions despite shifting governments. Religious parties dominated the country during the interwar years, with the Dutch Catholic Party seeking at all costs to maintain Catholic unity by avoiding severe conflict with its partners. This concern made it swallow the unpalatable Hendrick

Colijn, head of the Protestant Anti-Revolutionary Party (ARP), as the country's leader. In Belgium the opposite occurred. Although Catholics, Socialists, and Liberals continued to dominate Parliament, Belgian cabinets did not reflect this stability. Prospective prime ministers could not conciliate the disparate demands of party factions, and numerous cabinets followed each other.

The acute divisions between the Walloons and Flemings described in Chapter 5 continued to dominate Belgian politics during the interwar years, and the Flemish question flared up during the 1920s. The election of eleven members of the Flemish nationalist Front party to Parliament in 1929 made the government open to compromise. In 1932 it attempted to resolve the language problem by dividing the country into two separate linguistic regions and by imposing the use of the Flemish language in the public administration, schools, and courts of the Flemish regions, but relations between the Walloons and the Flemings remained tense despite these concessions.

The Depression's Impact

When the Great Depression hit the Low Countries in 1931, both the Belgians and the Dutch implemented deflationary measures in an unsuccessful attempt to counter it. Failure forced Belgium off the gold standard in March 1935, followed by the Netherlands in September 1936. In both countries, currency devaluation of over 20 percent, public works projects, and unemployment assistance brought some relief, but in both countries, the economic downturn favored the growth of fascist-type organizations on the Italian model. In Belgium, Léon Degrelle's ultra-Catholic Rexists, formed in 1935, advocated authoritarianism and corporativism (see Chapter 12). The Rexists received Italian support, won 12 percent of the vote and 22 parliamentary seats in the elections of 1936, but were defeated in 1937 by Prime Minister Paul van Zeeland. Besides the Rexist threat, groups sympathizing with fascism also appeared in the Flemish areas, but they were concerned with the ethnic question, as illustrated by Verdinaso, an organization that advocated a federation of the Low Countries. In the Netherlands the Dutch National Socialist movement won 8 percent of the vote in 1935 but lost half its electoral support in 1937.

Switzerland

Swiss Anxieties

In Switzerland, fascistic organizations made little headway despite unrest following the war and during the depression.

The Swiss had made money during the conflict by supplying war materiel to the belligerents, but this activity distorted the economy by stimulating war-related industries. Moreover, the country had mobilized to defend its neutrality, greatly increasing the national debt and setting the stage for postwar economic difficulties and unrest. The Swiss Social Democratic Party demanded reform and, after a threatened general strike in Zurich in November 1918 that the government repressed, a forty-eight-hour workweek and proportional representation for National Council elections were implemented.

Economic dislocations caused by the depression increased agitation and favored the rise of Fascist groups. In November 1932 demonstrations in Geneva left twelve demonstrators dead. Fascist organizations appeared in each of the different language areas, prompting a widespread governmental crackdown on extremist groups in May 1933. This repression reduced the danger posed by Fascist groups, but support for these groups had already dwindled because of German and Italian claims to Swiss territory. These threats rallied the Swiss, and in October 1933, the government was empowered to rule by decree in economic affairs, and the country adopted the banking secrecy laws for which it later became famous.

In foreign policy, the Swiss concentrated on their neutrality and security. They agonized over the question of whether joining the League of Nations meant relinquishing their neutrality, but ultimately joined the League, whose headquarters were located in Geneva, and the International Court of Justice at The Hague. With the rise of Nazism, Switzerland reiterated its commitment to absolute neutrality, and the League of Nations exempted it from certain obligations, but recent evidence has suggested that during World War II Swiss foreign policy was more pro-Nazi than neutral.

During the interwar years, Scandinavia, the Low Countries, and Switzerland confronted difficult economic times and witnessed the rise of groups advocating fascistic answers to the Great Depression, but they all maintained their democratic structures.

Bibliographical Essay

Peter Temin produced an excellent overview of the Great Depression, drawing its lessons for contemporary economic policy: *Lessons from the Great Depression* (Cambridge, Mass., 1989). His *Did Monetary Forces Cause the Great Depression?* (New York, 1976) is a more detailed work. Charles P. Kindleberger, *The World in Depression, 1929–1939*, rev. and enlarged ed. (Berkeley, Calif., 1986), is a standard general account, as is the readable Goronwy Rees, *The Great Slump: Capitalism in Crisis, 1929–1933* (New York, 1970). Ben Bernanke's *Essays on the Great Depression* (Princeton, N.J., 2000) is a technical work. Good general books that are quite thorough include Patricia Calvin, *The Great Depression in Europe, 1929–1939* (New York, 2000); Charles H. Feinstein, Peter Temin, and Gianni Toniolo, *The World Economy Between the World Wars* (Oxford, UK, 2008); Theo Balderston, *The World Economy and National Economies in the Interwar Slump* (New York, 2003), a book of essays; and Timothy J. Kehoe and Edward C. Prescott, *Great Depressions of the Twentieth Century* (Orlando, Fla., 2002). Patricia Calvin's, *The Failure of Economic Diplomacy* (New York, 1996), Thomas Emerson Hall's and J. David Ferguson's *The Great Depression* (Ann Arbor, Mich., 2001), and Nikolaus Wolf, *Europe's Great Depression* (London, 2010), focus on the international dimension.

For the economic history of specific countries during this period, consult Robert Skidelsky, *Politicians and the Slump: The Labour Government of 1929–1931* (London, 1967), for England, and *The Slump: Britain in the Great Depression* (Harlow, UK, 2010), by John Stevenson and Chris Cook. Developments in English political history may be followed in Charles Loch Mowat, *Britain Between the Wars 1918–1940* (Chicago, 1955), and economic affairs in H. W. Richardson, *Economic Recovery in Britain, 1932–9* (London, 1967). See also Stuart Ball, *Baldwin and the Conservative Party* (New Haven, Conn.,1988), and Noreen Branson and Margot Heinemann, *Britain in the 1930s* (New York, 1971). For Germany and the Great Depression, see Mark Weder, *Some Observations on the*

Great Depression in Germany (London, 2003), and Harold James, *The German Slump* (Oxford, UK, 1986).

France in the 1930s has received greater attention than Britain. David A. Irwin, *Did France Cause the Great Depression?* (Cambridge, Mass.,, 2010) asks whether the hoarding of gold by France caused the depression. Eugen Weber's *The Hollow Years: France in the 1930s* (New York, 1994) is an excellent treatment. Julian Jackson, *The Politics of Depression in France 1932–1936* (Cambridge, UK, 1985), pays particular attention to economic affairs. Philippe Bernard and Henri Dubief, *The Decline of the Third Republic, 1914–1938* (Cambridge, UK, 1985), is a scholarly summary of the major issues. On the Popular Front in general, see Julian Jackson, *The Popular Front in France* (Cambridge, UK, 1990). The French Socialists during the Popular Front era are examined by Nathaniel Greene, *Crisis and Decline: The French Socialist Party in the Popular Front Era* (Ithaca, N.Y., 1969). Peter J. Larmour's *The French Radical Party in the 1930s* (Stanford, Calif., 1964) is a thorough study of the party's structure, policies, and personnel. Susan B. Whitney, *Mobilizing Youth* (Durham, N.C., 2009), considers the Communist and Catholic youth movements. John Bulaitis, *Communism in Rural France* (New York, 2008), looks at the complex relationship between the French Communist Party and rural France during the Popular Front. Jessica Wardhaugh published a study of left- and right-wing organizations during the Popular Front: *In Pursuit of the People: Political Culture in France, 1934–9* (Basingstoke, UK, 2008). Books on the international dimensions of the Popular Front include Nicole Jordan, *The Popular Front and Central Europe* (New York 2005), and *Leon Blum, French Socialism and the Popular Front*, by Helmut Gruber (New York, 1986). Biographies of Léon Blum include Joel Colton, *Léon Blum: Humanist in Politics,* 2d ed. (New York, 1987), and Jean Lacouture, *Léon Blum* (New York 1982). James Joll's *Three Intellectuals in Politics* (New York, 1961) has a portrait of Blum and, as an added bonus, of Rathenau and Marinetti. Zeev Sternhell wrote a major work on the ideology of French fascism, *Neither Left nor Right* (Berkeley, Calif., 1986), while Robert Paxton, a distinguished historian of France, takes a different view and concentrates on fascism as practice rather than as ideology in *The Anatomy of Fascism* (New York, 2004).

On Scandinavia, see Marquis Childs, *Sweden: The Middle Way* (New Haven, Conn., 1963), which describes the cooperative movement in Sweden, and *Welfare Peripheries* (New York, 2007), by Steven King and John Steward, which has material on the Scandinavian countries. The quotation on Danish social legislation may be found in W. Glyn Jones, *Denmark: A Modern History* (London, 1986), p. 141. Another informative work is W. R. Mead, *Finland* (New York, 1968). Concise histories of the Scandinavian countries, usually beginning in ancient times, include Neil Kent, *A Concise History of Sweden* (Cambridge, UK, 2008); Byron J. Nordstrom, *The History of Sweden* (Westport, Conn., 2002); Hjalmar Hjorth Boyesen and Charles Francis Keary, *A History of Norway from the Earliest Times* (n.p., 2007); Knud J.V. Jespersen, *A History of Denmark* (New York, 2004); John H. Wuorinen, *A History of Finland* (New York, 1965), the most comprehensive book on Finland; D. G. Kirby's *Finland in the Twentieth Century* (Minneapolis, Minn., 1979), which concentrates on modern history, and his *A Concise History of Finland* (New York, 2006); and Jason Edward Lavery, *The History of Finland* (Westport, Conn., 2006), a book of essays.

Information on Scandinavian fascism, as well as fascism in the other countries discussed in this chapter, as well as in Italy and Germany, may be found in Stanley G. Payne's comprehensive *A History of Fascism 1914–1945* (Madison, Wis., 1995). Payne's book is important for its nuanced and balanced treatment of the issue of just what constituted Fascist movements. On a Danish organization, see Henrik Lundbak, *Danish Unity: A Political Party Between Fascism and Resistance 1936–1947* (Copenhagen, 2003).

Hans Rogger and Eugen Weber, eds., *The European Right: A Historical Profile* (Berkeley, Calif., 1966), contains excellent essays on the rightist movements, including those in some of the small countries. See also Martin Blinkhorn's book of essays on different countries, *Fascists and Conservatives: The Radical Right and the Establishment in Twentieth-Century Europe* (London, 2003).

E. H. Kossman's *The Low Countries 1780–1940* (Oxford, UK, 1978), previously cited, has a detailed discussion on developments in Belgium and the Netherlands during this period. Concise histories of the Low Countries are Paul Arblaster, *A History of the Low Countries* (Basingstoke, UK, 2006); J. C. H. Blom and Emiel Lamberts, *History of the Low Countries* (New York, 2006); Paul F. State, *A Brief History of the Netherlands* (New York, 2008); and Bernard A. Cook, *Belgium: A History* (New York, 2002). On Switzerland, there is John Wilson, *The History of Switzerland* (New York, 2007).

In addition, on individual countries, consult the works cited in Chapter 9, or, in the case of the smaller countries, Chapter 5, which usually include sections on this period.

CHAPTER 11

The Crisis of Democracy in Eastern and Southern Europe

CHAPTER OUTLINE

The Victors of the Versailles Settlement • The Versailles Settlement's Losers •
The Aegean and the Adriatic • Iberia

BIOGRAPHICAL SKETCHES

Josef Klemens Pilsudski, Polish Dictator • Thomas Garrigue Masaryk,
European Democrat

Most of the nations of Eastern and Southern Europe installed authoritarian regimes during the postwar period. There was nothing inevitable about this trend. Liberal traditions existed in both areas, but most Eastern European countries faced impossibly difficult situations following World War I. The new nations had to create an administrative and political structure while absorbing a great deal of territory and sizable minorities and confronting foreign threats. For most of the countries in the East and the South, the Great Depression was the last blow to democratic ideals.

THE VICTORS OF THE VERSAILLES SETTLEMENT

The Versailles settlement left the countries of Eastern Europe facing major border disputes, national minorities of 19 million out of a total population of 98 million, and poor economic circumstances. Eastern Europe quickly became polarized between groups advocating political systems according to ideological schemes of the right or left that promised greater economic justice and efficiency than democracy, and a similar trend emerged in the South.

In examining Eastern and Southern Europe following World War I, one can roughly group the countries into those that benefited from the postwar settlement and those that lost.

The Baltic States

The Baltic states—Lithuania, Latvia, and Estonia—had been part of the Russian Empire and won independence after World War I.

The weakest state, Lithuania, had a serious border dispute with Poland over Vilnius, which the Lithuanians claimed as their capital. Lithuania was overwhelmingly Catholic, while the majority of Estonians and Latvians were Lutheran. All the states contained significant minorities of Germans, Poles, Jews, and Russians, and, in the 1920s, Lithuania had a significant problem with anti-Semitism, while the German minority caused serious difficulties for Lithuania and Latvia.

The Baltic population was mostly peasant, and all three states had large agrarian parties that favored land reform that led to a strengthened agricultural sector between 1918 and 1931, while industries in all three countries lacked raw materials, capital, and markets.

Between June 1920 and August 1922, the Baltic states adopted democratic constitutions but were unable to achieve political stability, and right-wing dictatorships took over. In Lithuania in 1926, party infighting and political instability provoked a military coup on December 17 with the support of Nationalist leaders Antonas Smetona and Augustinas Voldemaras and of elements of the Christian Democratic bloc. Smetona dissolved Parliament and promulgated a constitution providing for a strong president. Voldemaras, head of a secret pro-Nazi paramilitary organization, Iron Wolf, challenged him, but Smetona cracked down on the German minority and Nazi organizations.

Right-wing regimes came to power in Estonia and Latvia in 1933 and 1934 as the result of the depression and parliamentary instability. In Estonia, Nazi-influenced nationalists won a referendum establishing a strong presidency. The Agrarian Party leader Konstantin Pats, installed as the temporary chief executive with emergency powers, liquidated Parliament. In Latvia, the Nazi-influenced Thunder Cross fought leftist groups that were accused of planning a Communist coup. Karlis Ulmanis, head of the Farmers' Union, assumed emergency power on May 15, 1934, outlawed political parties, dissolved Parliament, and arrested political opponents.

Smetona, Pats, and Ulmanis ran "largely nonideological arbitrary governments of a predominantly rural, conservative nationalist character, restrained by the leaders' self-imposed limitations and by the old social pluralism" until the absorption of the Baltic states into the USSR in 1939.

Poland's Reemergence

One of the biggest gainers from the war, Poland had major weaknesses. Victory over Soviet Russia in 1919 and 1920 put 6 million Ukrainians and Belorussians into the state, in addition to the Polish Corridor and 800,000 hostile Germans. This situation encouraged the formation of separatist movements and made it easy for the USSR and Nazi Germany to partition Poland in 1939.

Poland struggled to reunite the different parts of the country dominated by foreigners for 150 years, ruled by a hodgepodge of diverse laws, subject to different customs unions, and separated by different railway systems and political traditions. At the same time, Poland's enormous war debt and defense expenditures (one-third of its budget) to guard against a possibly resurgent Germany and Russia drained resources that were urgently needed for economic development.

The Rise of Pilsudski

Economic problems and political divisions touched off hyperinflation that sent the exchange rate of the Polish mark (the zloty was introduced later) with the dollar to 20 million in January 1924. On April 26 the Socialists resigned in protest from a coalition government that proposed measures that would reduce the real income of workers. The resulting crisis produced a coup d'état by Marshal Josef Pilsudski supported by the army.

Pilsudski, a strong personality with left-wing connections, had been a powerful contender for president following Polish independence. The assumption that he would win induced his right-wing opponents who controlled the Sejm (Parliament) to adopt a constitution modeled on that of the Third French Republic, with a very weak president. Pilsudski thereupon refused to run for president and retired as chief of the general staff. In the next three years, the inflation crisis forced the Sejm parties to give wide powers to a reforming cabinet led by Wladaslaw Grabski, but Parliament lost support because of its inability to revise the constitution, galloping inflation, strikes, rioting, and bloodshed, and Pilsudski took over.

Pilsudski had the support of Socialists, Radical Peasants, and Communists to implement social and economic reforms. Pilsudski declared that he was neither a leftist nor a rightist but favored social equilibrium. He governed through prime ministers and held elections but brooked no opposition. Over the years Pilsudski shifted to the right with the support of industrialists and large landowners. The strong peasant parties lost influence, and land reform was delayed. After Pilsudski's death in May 1935, strikes, violence on the land, and serious opposition in elections confronted his successors.

Polish Economic Stabilization

Pilsudski curbed inflation by ending cost-of-living increases for state employees, budget cuts, American loans, higher taxes, and scaling back costly social programs. The Polish state intensified its regulation and intervention in the economy, and Polish industry increased efficiency by organizing stronger cartels. In 1924 the government introduced a new gold-backed currency, the zloty. These policies resulted in a recovery beginning in 1928, but the good times ended with the Great Depression that dealt the overwhelmingly agricultural country a severe blow by decimating the value of its exports. The government worsened matters by stubbornly sticking to its deflationary policies and to the gold standard until April 1936. Abandonment of the gold standard and the introduction of centralized planning that was designed to industrialize the country improved economic conditions.

BIOGRAPHICAL SKETCHES

Josef Klemens Pilsudski
Polish Dictator

Between World War I and World War II, Marshal Josef Pilsudski was an Eastern European fixture. The hero of Polish independence, Pilsudski was looked upon by Polish Americans as their George Washington, and even now squares and roads in Poland bear his name.

Pilsudski's adventurous life, travel, and war experiences were similar to those of other Eastern European national leaders of the period. Pilsudski was born on December 5, 1867, at Zulow, near present-day Vilnius in Lithuania, at the time part of Russia. His parents, from old well-known and well-off families in the area, had twelve children. His mother was a Polish patriot who read Polish books that were banned by the Russians and instilled in her children a love of the Polish language. When Pilsudski attended high school, he was obliged to speak only in Russian, his defiance of which got him into trouble.

In June 1885, Pilsudski attended medical school, became marginally involved in the same conspiracy to assassinate Tsar Alexander III that cost Lenin's brother his life, and was sentenced to five years' exile in Siberia. After his release in April 1892, Pilsudski joined the Polish Socialist party (PPS) and wrote for its clandestine newspaper *Robotnik*. His articles dealt with Socialist themes and called for Polish independence from Russia. He traveled to London and Paris in 1896 to gain international support for his position but failed. On July 15, 1899, converted to Protestantism, he married Maria Juskiewicz, called "the beautiful lady": a Protestant, divorced, and with a daughter. The couple continued to publish *Robotnik* together until February 1900, when the police arrested them. Pilsudski, by now an essential member of the PPS, was freed in a plot by which Pilsudski pretended to be insane. Transferred from prison to a less secure hospital, he escaped.

By now, war was changing the political landscape of Europe, and Pilsudski saw in the conflicts an opportunity to win Polish independence. When the Russo-Japanese war broke out in 1904, Pilsudski traveled to Japan to offer a Polish legion to help the Japanese defeat the Russians. The Japanese refused the offer, but Russian losses contributed to the revolution of 1905 and to disturbances in Poland. Pilsudski took charge of creating a Polish armed force and, with the reestablishment of Russian control, turned to raids on governmental establishments to raise funds for his cause. His most famous exploit was a daring attack on a night train carrying tax money on September 19, 1908. Pilsudski also trained an armed force under cover of rifle associations, and in 1914 he commanded Polish soldiers fighting with the Austrians against the Russians. Pilsudski achieved the rank of brigadier general, but was arrested by the Germans when he refused to cooperate with them against the allies after Russia's defeat.

The Germans released him in November 1918, and he negotiated their withdrawal from Poland. After the war Pilsudski successfully created a large Poland, incorporating millions of Ukrainians and White Russians. This annexation brought him into conflict with the Bolsheviks, but he successfully defended the country against them in 1919 and 1920. Pilsudski had gained supreme control of Poland, but he respected the constitution and resigned as chief of state in December 1922.

continued

continued

However, unhappy with the workings of Parliament, he staged a coup d'état in May 1926. He established a dictatorship and served in several offices, including prime minister, from 1926 to 1928 and again in 1930. In foreign affairs, he followed a policy of friendship with both Russia and Germany, unaware that his annexationist policies had doomed his country.

In his last years, plagued by ill health, Pilsudski left the details of government to his trusted lieutenants. He died in Warsaw on May 12, 1935, spared the knowledge that his country would be dismembered when World War II began in 1939.

Poland after Pilsudski

On May 12, 1935, Marshal Pilsudski's death left "the dictatorship without a dictator." Different contenders competed for power, and the government veered from right to left and back again to confront growing opposition from the peasants and Socialists. The government feared communism and created the Camp of National Unity (OZN) to capitalize on the anti-Semitic and Nazi appeal illustrated by the success of the National Radicals (Naras) and other rightist groups that the regime had closed down. When the OZN leader called for a totalitarian Poland, alarmed governmental moderates restrained it in 1938, but by then domestic politics took a backseat to the approaching war.

BIOGRAPHICAL SKETCHES

Thomas Garrigue Masaryk
European Democrat

The career of Thomas Garrigue Masaryk demonstrates that strong democratic personalities operated in Eastern Europe between the wars, despite the problems of the region.

Thomas Masaryk was born in the Moravian town of Hodonin on March 7, 1850. His Slovak father worked on Emperor Francis Joseph's estates, while his mother, from a Germanized Moravian family, was a domestic servant. His mother insisted that he get a good education in order to avoid the manual labor of the parents. Masaryk attended a German school, since no Czech schools existed in Moravia at the time. While at this school, he came to doubt the prevailing anti-Semitism because of his contact with a Jewish student. In 1864, he worked with a locksmith and later with a blacksmith before he returned to school at Brno and then Vienna. He had the good fortune to meet a schoolmate whose father, later the chief of police in Vienna, befriended and employed him to tutor his son. In 1872, he began to study at the University of Vienna and received his doctor's degree in philosophy in 1876. In the hope of securing a university position, he published his first book, which criticized the existing social structure.

Masaryk moved to Leipzig, where he met the daughter of a Dane who had immigrated to America, Charlotte Garrigue, a former pupil of Franz Liszt who was studying at the conservatory. Together they read English philosophers and fell in love. Masaryk proposed and followed her to America, where they married on March 15, 1878. Happily married for fifty years, he added her name to his.

Masaryk began teaching at the University of Vienna in 1879 and, despite opposition from the archbishop of Prague to his philosophical writings, was named professor at the University of Prague. He chastised capitalism and wrote on the Czech Reformation and the Czech cultural revival of the nineteenth century. He examined the strains between Czechs and Austrians, which he had encountered as a student in Vienna. In 1889 Masaryk turned to politics and was not afraid to risk unpopularity. He unmasked two supposedly medieval Czech poems as forgeries and in 1899 fought the anti-Semitism aroused by the Hilsner case, in which a Jew was falsely accused of ritual murder. He considered anti-Semitism a superstition and a danger to the Czech people and hoped to eradicate it.

Elected to the Austrian Parliament, he denounced Austria-Hungary's alliance with Germany and its Balkan policies. With the outbreak of World War I, Masaryk fled to the West and cooperated with British, French, and Italian leaders. He advocated the breakup of Austria-Hungary on ethnic lines and the creation of an independent, democratic Czech-Slovak state. After the revolution of February 1917 in Russia, he organized the Czechoslovak Legion—formed by former prisoners of war. He left for the United States after the Bolshevik takeover, working with Czech and Slovak groups to obtain American support for Czechoslovak independence. At Pittsburgh he promised the Slovaks ample home rule, which turned out to be a source of later disputes.

In June 1918 Czechoslovakia came into being along the lines envisioned by Masaryk. The newly independent country rewarded him by electing him president on November 14, 1918, at age sixty-eight, reelecting him another three times. The people recognized him as a hero and as their liberator. Despite all the problems of the new multinational state, Masaryk tried to ensure that it would respect minority rights. He was one of the first statesmen to fear for Eastern Europe's future after the Nazis came to power in 1933. On December 14, 1935, he resigned as president and died on September 14, 1937. After World War II, his son Jan became foreign minister and died under mysterious circumstances just before the Communist takeover of his country.

Birth of Czechoslovakia

Poland's neighbor Czechoslovakia faced similar economic and political problems but had the advantage of having inherited the industrial heartland of the old empire. It also had great liabilities: bad blood between its two major ethnic components, Czechs and Slovaks, and large minorities that handed its neighbors convenient claims to part of its territory.

Czechoslovakia's success in the early years was due, in great measure, to the leaders of its independence movement, Thomas G. Masaryk and Edvard Benes, respectively, its first president and its longtime foreign minister. Fighting during the war destroyed the Czech economy and led to shortages, high postwar inflation, and unemployment. Disorder followed, with workers clamoring for a Bolshevik-type social revolution and the peasants seizing land.

Masaryk's government fought inflation by introducing a new currency, the Czechoslovak crown; by following deflationary policies, such as reducing the circulation of notes and imposing a high tax on the property of wealthy persons; and by encouraging foreign investment. The state took an activist role in the economy and acquired important parts of the country's infrastructure, including the railways and the electric, telephone, and telegraph industries, while cities took over municipal services. Parliament passed wide-ranging social legislation: the eight-hour workday; accident, sickness, and unemployment insurance; pensions for widows and children; and workers' participation in management and profits. It implemented land reform by breaking up large estates and by making funds available to peasants who wanted to buy land. It also invested in education; during the next twenty years, the number of elementary schools increased by 300 percent.

These measures revived the economy and diminished the appeal of Bolshevism, but strong social tensions and rioting returned with the hardships caused by the Great Depression. In 1934, the government helped farmers by establishing a grain monopoly that had the exclusive right to purchase and sell agricultural products and to regulate their importation and exportation. In industry, a 1935 law regulated the circumstances under which employers could close factories or lay off more than 10 percent of their workers, and in 1936, legislation expanded collective bargaining.

Dilemmas of Czech Democracy

The Czechoslovak experiment in democracy was the most successful in postwar Eastern Europe, but it faced serious problems. In 1920, the country adopted a constitution setting up a Parliament and guaranteeing liberty and equality, but the existence of numerous parties and proportional representation encouraged splintering. Five-party coalitions were the norm for cabinets, and they rarely had focused programs.

The major parties included the leftist Social Democrats and National Socialists (no relation to the Nazis), agrarian parties, and organizations representing the large German minority in the Sudetenland. In 1921, the Communist Party of Czechoslovakia (CPC) was founded and briefly became the second-largest party, but its subservience to Moscow, which opposed Czechoslovakia's existence, brought about its decline. On the extreme right, the Nazi Sudeten German Party, under Konrad Henlein, had 60 percent support from the large German minority in the Sudetenland. As the second-largest ethnic group after the Czechs and 23 percent of the population the Sudeten Germans were a mortal threat because they also inhabited the only defensible frontier against Germany and favored annexation to the Reich after Hitler came to power.

Besides the German problem, Czechoslovakia could not satisfy the contrasting demands of its different national minorities or fully integrate them into the democratic system. The Czechs, constituting only half the country's population, dominated political and economic life, which caused constant friction not only with the German, Polish, Hungarian, and Ruthenian (Ukrainian) minorities, but also with the Slovaks, who were supposedly their partners. The Slovaks chafed at Czech bureaucratic and political domination, and there were religious differences as well: Catholicism in Slovakia was more conservative than in the Czech areas, and the Slovaks resented the inroads that Protestantism had made among the Czechs. The real basis for Czech influence over the country, however, was economic. Slovakia was a predominantly agricultural economic backwater with an ill-educated population possessing few technical skills, while the Czech area was

Konrad Henlein, the Nazi leader of the Germans living in the Sudetenland, Czechoslovakia on May 13, 1938, shown here leaving Winston Churchill's house. The Sudetenland had never been a part of Germany and was ceded to the new Czechoslovak state after World War I because the Sudeten Mountains provided the new country with a defensible frontier against a possible German attack. Henlein's movement was important because if it succeeded in uniting with Germany it would in effect make the country a German satellite. Henlein illustrates both the major weakness of Czechoslovakia—ethnic minorities that resisted Czech rule—and Hitler's technique of utilizing Europe's German-speaking minorities to further his foreign policy aims.

highly industrialized. Resentment against the Czechs by the Catholic peasants of Slovakia threatened unity because the peasants supported the authoritarian Slovak People's Party that demanded autonomy and then separation. Following the Munich Conference that dismembered Czechoslovakia in September 1938, Slovakia gained full autonomy under Monsignor Joseph Tiso and declared its independence the following March. Czechoslovakia's nationalities problems gave foreigners the idea that the country was "a medley ruled by a minority" (*The Observer,* March 6, 1938) destined to fall apart.

The Aggrandizement of Romania

The national question that destroyed the Czechoslovak state also threatened Romania. The country doubled in size and population after World War I by annexing Transylvania and the Bukovina, formerly Austro-Hungarian, and Bessarabia from Russia. In order to safeguard their gains, the Romanians joined Czechoslovakia and Yugoslavia in the French-sponsored "Little Entente" alliance.

The gains brought all ethnic Romanians into the country, but also hostile minorities that amounted to 30 percent of its population: Hungarians (9 percent); the hated Jews (almost 5 percent); and sizable numbers of Germans, Ukrainians, and Bulgarians. Disputes over land reform, the press, education, and religion among these minorities immediately caused trouble. Finally, the enormous increase in the country's size disrupted the traditional prewar parties and politics.

King Ferdinand I introduced mass politics into Romania by granting universal male suffrage, and political instability resulted. The 1919 elections did not produce a majority, but two parties based on strong personalities dominated the political scene. The National Liberal Party, controlled by the Bratianu family, advocated strong administrative centralization, while the National Peasant Party (PNP), headed by Iuliu Maniu, championed land reform.

The threat of Bolshevism encouraged the passage of important agrarian reform legislation in June 1921 that increased the average size of farms, but dwarf holdings continued to proliferate and large estates did not disappear. Yields remained low, capital short, and living standards one of the worst in Europe. Furthermore, many large landowners were ethnic Hungarians who blocked reform by appealing to the League of Nations under the terms of treaties safeguarding minority rights; this process led to years of disputes and litigation.

The Royal Dictatorship

The National Liberals were in power between 1922 and 1928. They favored industry by passing antiunion measures and banning the Romanian Communist Party. The pace of industrial development quickened, but when the depression struck in 1930, industry still represented only 10 percent of the gross national product. National Liberal policies that had produced sporadic strikes in the 1920s escalated into violence during the depression, and the industrialists called on the army to intervene. A new king, Carol II, took over on June 8, 1930, and for the next several years he alternated among the main political parties to help him rule the country. In 1937, National Liberal influence declined, and King Carol entrusted the government to the extreme right anti-Semitic Christian National Party. Within a month, this party had outraged international public opinion by implementing a savage anti-Semitic policy, and Romanian bankers and industrialists, fearing economic retaliation from the international financial community, called upon Carol to intervene.

On February 10, 1938, the king imposed a dictatorship. He proclaimed martial law, issued a new constitution that gave him control of Parliament and the judiciary, dissolved all political parties, and established his own political organization, the National Renaissance Front. In economic policy he worked with a small group of bankers and industrialists to spur state investments and increase production.

Carol's was a conservative, not a Fascist, dictatorship marked by anticommunism and fierce nationalism. Carol particularly feared the anti-Semitic virulence that marked Romanian fascism because of its rapid spread after Mussolini's March

Cornelieu Zelea Codreanu was the most important Fascist theoretician in Eastern Europe. He was also a practical leader whose "Legion of the Archangel Michael" threatened the government. The Romanian security police murdered him while he was in their custody, along with his most important associates. The picture shows Romanian and German officials at his funeral in December 1940.

on Rome. The most successful Romanian Fascist organization was the Legion of the Archangel Michael, established in 1924 by Cornelieu Zelea Codreanu—called "the Captain." The legion presented a serious threat because it emphasized orthodox Christianity and Rumanian peasant values and had a strong peasant electoral base in addition to competent middle-class leadership. Adding to the danger was its powerful and violent paramilitary organization, the Iron Guard. Carol's government ordered the legion dissolved, setting off a deadly battle during which the Iron Guard assassinated the prime minister.

The king could not win a decisive victory. Every time the government dissolved the legion, it returned more sympathetic to the Nazis under an assumed name. In 1937 the movement won 15.5 percent of the vote, making it the country's third-largest political force. Carol tried to negotiate with Codreanu but failed. In April 1938, the police arrested "the Captain" and several thousand followers. Codreanu was sentenced to ten years in prison, but on November 30 the state security police murdered him along with thirteen associates. Codreanu's death made him a martyr, and the brutal battle continued with the Iron Guard assassinating another prime minister.

Yugoslav Factionalism

Yugoslavia (called the Kingdom of the Serbs, Croats, and Slovenes), another Versailles "winner," traveled a similar path. The new country concretized the Serb dream of creating a large south Slav state from the Slav-inhabited territory of the old Austro-Hungarian Empire, but national divisions favored a royal dictatorship.

Because of their desire for control, the Serbs could not conciliate the different Slavic groups, and they engaged in a struggle for control over the other nationalities, complicated by religious differences. The combatants included the Kosovo Albanians and the Bosnian Moslems who inflamed Balkan passions until the end of the twentieth century. The Serbs controlled the country's administrative machinery but proved unable to run a state three times the size of prewar Serbia. The main conflict was fought between the supporters of federalism and the supporters of centralization (which, in practice, meant Serb control) that would end in the breakup of Yugoslavia after the fall of communism.

The King Takes Over

The divisions among Slavic groups surfaced immediately after the war. Peasant leader Stephen Radic won the 1920 Croatian elections for a constituent assembly on a platform advocating federalism and a republic. In June 1921, however, the assembly adopted a constitution that established a strong central government favoring the Serbs. This constitution alienated the Croats and the Slovenes and

Croatian Fascist leader Ante Pavelic (left), shown here with German Foreign Minister Joachim von Ribbentrop in 1941, was a nationalist who hoped to break Croatia off from Yugoslavia. He spent some time in exile in Italy but relations with the Italians were poor and he turned to the Germans. During World War II he organized a Croatian State, a Nazi satellite. Pavelic's organization, the Ustase, committed so many brutal atrocities against Jews, Serbs, and Gypsies that they shocked even the Germans. Pavelic escaped after the Nazi defeat and spent a long exile in several countries, finally dying in Spain on December 28, 1959.

provoked terrorist activities. Parliament then passed repressive legislation, and several years of political confusion followed.

On June 20, 1928, a deputy sympathetic to the Serbs shot and killed Radic and his nephew in Parliament. On January 6, 1929, King Alexander dissolved Parliament and political parties, abolished the constitution, suppressed the press, and assumed complete power; the police imprisoned and tortured Croat leaders and other opponents.

Despite the confused political situation, during the 1920s Yugoslavia made economic progress. The decade saw the recovery of agriculture, railway building, and stabilization of the dinar. When the depression hit, however, credit collapsed, banks failed, and foreign loans dried up. The government was forced to buy up the 1932 wheat crop at above market prices, declare a moratorium on peasant debts, cut administrative salaries, and increase taxes. The slump heightened political tensions, and on October 9, 1934, Croat separatists assassinated King Alexander in Marseilles. A regency council ruled the country for his young son, but the government remained authoritarian.

The most virulent Croat separatist movement was the anti-Semitic Ustasha, whose agents killed Alexander. The organization's head, a lawyer from Zagreb named Ante Pavelic, fled the country and took refuge in Mussolini's Italy. Pavelic gained international prominence during World War II as the head of a puppet, German-controlled Croatia. He ran one of the most brutal regimes of the period and set up a concentration camp, known as the Auschwitz of the Balkans, that specialized in exterminating Serbs and Jews.

THE VERSAILLES SETTLEMENT'S LOSERS

By the end of the 1930s, dictators ruled three of the four Eastern European victors of World War I; the losers fared even worse.

Hungary's Rightist Regime

The biggest East European loser in World War I, Hungary, lost two-thirds of its territory and population. After the fall of Béla Kun's Communist regime, Admiral Mikós Horthy, former commander of the Austro-Hungarian navy, took over the country.

Horthy instituted a rightist regime. He restored the old social system by returning large landed estates, banks, industrial, and commercial concerns to their former owners and by giving jobs or land grants, in proportion to their social status, to 350,000 former members of the old landowning class who returned to Hungary after the war.

Hungary's decrease in size fueled anti-Semitism because Jews as a percentage of the population increased, and the success of Jewish professionals fueled resentment. The government harassed the Jews, restricted the number allowed to attend universities, and practically excluded them from the bureaucracy and other state jobs.

In political life Horthy wielded supreme power and ruled through cabinets headed by leaders of different political factions. In the 1920s, he appointed as prime minister Count István Bethlen, a moderate reactionary who made some room for liberty. In October 1932, he installed General Gyula Gombos, a radical rightist who sympathized with Mussolini and Hitler, as premier.

Officially the government condemned trade unions and social democracy but in practice tolerated both. Industrial activity increased, with national income from manufacturing rising from 21 percent to 28 percent while income from agriculture declined from 54 to 43 percent. In the rural areas only about a third of the peasantry had enough land to sustain themselves, and the rest led a miserable existence with starvation always part of the landscape. Between 1934 and 1937, the Hungarian economy became more dependent on Germany, but the increased activity smoothed Hungary's transformation into a semi-industrialized country by the late 1930s.

Hungarian Fascism
The Great Depression and its aftershocks spurred the development of fascism. The most successful of a great variety of Fascist organizations was Ferenc Szalasi's green-shirted Arrow Cross. Szalasi theorized a Hungarian-dominated East European federation but repudiated Nazi racial ideas and favored Jewish emigration. Horthy and his surrogates opposed the Arrow Cross, suppressed it several times, and attempted to steal its thunder by strengthening governmental power, ratcheting up their own anti-Jewish program, and creating a quasi-Fascist party. Nothing worked. In the 1939 elections, the middle class, workers, and peasants awarded the Arrow Cross 25 percent of the vote.

The Political Struggle in Austria
Austria never settled down after its defeat in World War I. Although the Social Democrats had blocked Bolshevism, many Austrians identified Socialists with Communists, and Austrian nationalists founded paramilitary groups—particularly the *Heimwehr*—to fight them. The disproportion between "Red" Vienna, with about half the country's population, and the conservative Catholic countryside complicated politics. When powerful Socialist groups gained control of working-class districts in the cities, the industrialists subsidized nationalist units, and bloody street fighting between nationalists and leftists followed.

Austrians were hopelessly divided by politics and a bad economy. Many favored a union with Germany (*Anschluss*), prohibited by the peace treaties; blamed the Socialists for signing the peace treaty; were terrified of Marxism; and rejected the republic. The postwar economic recovery stumbled. Between 1922 and 1926, only a large loan granted by the League of Nations under onerous conditions enabled Austria to survive. Between 1925 and 1929, unemployment averaged between 10 percent and 15 percent. In 1931, the French vetoed a proposed customs union with Germany, fueling resentment during the depths of the depression. In May 1931 a major bank in Vienna, the Kreditanstalt, collapsed and led to runs on banks in Germany and Eastern Europe.

Struggle with the Nazis
The depression radicalized Austrian politics. *Heimwehr* leader, E. R. von Starhemberg, had close links to Mussolini, who actively interfered in Austrian politics. In 1932, the Austrian Nazis won over 16 percent in local elections and

staged demonstrations against the government of anti-Nazi Christian Social leader Engelbert Dollfuss. Dollfuss opposed both Anschluss and Nazi racism, as did Mussolini (who at this time opposed Hitler), and suppressed the Nazis, which produced tensions with Hitler. In March 1933 Dollfuss instituted a dictatorship with *Heimwehr* support, creating a fatherland front and dissolving all other political organizations. This step provoked a Socialist uprising in Vienna in February 1934 that the government suffocated in blood, destroying the only domestic force capable of blocking a Nazi takeover.

In May, Dollfuss promulgated a new conservative Catholic constitution instead of the Fascist one he had promised Mussolini. Nevertheless, Mussolini considered Dollfuss a protégé, and he favored the Austrian leader because of his usefulness as a partner in his attempt to revise the Versailles settlement in Eastern Europe. What was most important, an independent Austria served as a buffer between Italy and Germany. This combination of ideology and reality explains Mussolini's action when the Austrian Nazis attempted a coup d'état on July 25, 1934. The *Putsch* failed, but the Nazis shot Dollfuss and left him to bleed to death. When it appeared that Hitler might intervene militarily, Mussolini rushed six divisions to the Austrian frontier, and Hitler backed off—the only time anyone called his bluff before World War II.

Dollfuss's lieutenant Kurt Schuschnigg succeeded Dollfuss, with *Heimwehr* leader Starhemberg serving as the vice chancellor. By 1936 the two had fallen out over Schuschnigg's anti-Nazi vigor, and the government dissolved the *Heimwehr*. Schuschnigg persisted in his efforts to crush the Nazis, but their popular support

The "losers" of World War I were led by Italy, a country that won the war but that remained unsatisfied with its results. This picture shows Benito Mussolini (center) with Englebert Dollfus (left), Austrian Chancellor who established a sort of "Catholic" Fascism, and Hungarian President Gyula Gomboss. Dollfuss died in an attempted Nazi coup in 1934, when relations between Mussolini and Hitler were still poor.

grew. By March 1938 the party counted proportionately more members than the German Nazis had before they took over Germany. Schuschnigg, however, blocked their road to power until Mussolini allied with Hitler and withdrew his opposition to Anschluss.

Bulgaria: From Defeat to Dictatorship

The losses suffered by Bulgaria did not compare with either Austria's or Hungary's, but they caused lasting bitterness and terrible consequences. Besides leaving an estimated 16 percent of Bulgarians outside the mother country, mostly under Greek control, Bulgaria lost access to the Aegean Sea and had to pay heavy reparations. Inflation, starvation, and revolt caused King Ferdinand to abdicate in favor of his son, Boris III, on October 1, 1919. The Agrarian party (BANU), led by Alexander Stamboliisky, won the most seats in new elections. The Communists came in second but were not a decisive factor during the interwar period.

Stamboliisky followed a radical program. On the land, he encouraged the formation of cooperatives and attempted to legislate equality by reducing larger holdings, a policy that increased the size of very small farms but that ultimately failed. The government revamped education by constructing new schools, changing the content of the curriculum, and making teachers accountable. Finally, Stamboliisky reformed the electoral system, which greatly benefited his party and successfully defeated a series of domestic opponents. He seemed headed for personal rule, but, ironically, his success contributed to his downfall.

During the interwar period, the Macedonian Revolutionary Organization (IMRO) conducted a brutal terrorist campaign to make Yugoslavian Macedonia part of Bulgaria. Stamboliisky, however, favored improved relations with Yugoslavia as a way of bringing Bulgaria out of its diplomatic isolation and in March 1923 reached agreement with it to combat terrorism. The pact united Stamboliisky's enemies against him. In June, they revolted, hunted him down, cut off his ears and hands, decapitated him, and sent his head to the capital in a box.

Following Stamboliisky's death, shifting, heterogeneous coalitions of nationalists, army elements, and bourgeois parties ruled Bulgaria, and the country seemed to fall apart. IMRO was a state within a state and continued its terrorist campaign. The economy was saddled with high reparations payments, hit by price declines for its crucial tobacco crop, and ruined by the gold standard that made Bulgarian exports too expensive on the world market. The economic decline brought political fragmentation, the growth of communism, and the army's return to politics.

In April 1935, the instability prompted King Boris to ban parties and to take power through civilian politicians and government-dominated elections. Notable features of Bulgaria were Boris's concession of the vote to married women and widows and the lack of a large role for anti-Semitism because the merchant class was Greek, not Jewish.

THE AEGEAN AND THE ADRIATIC

As in Eastern Europe, democracy did not survive in the South during the interwar period.

The Greek Labyrinth

Extreme instability, characterized by a bewildering array of coups, countercoups, failed coups, cabinet changes, and constitutional revisions, characterized Greece between the wars. Greece had made important gains in Thrace after World War I and, following Turkey's defeat, attempted to complete the Great Idea policy of incorporating all Greeks into the motherland by invading Asia Minor. The Turks under Kemal Ataturk routed them and then expelled the Greek minority, after which 1.5 million destitute refugees flooded into Greece—25 percent of its population.

The collapse of the Great Idea had important political, social, and economic consequences. A revolt of army colonels signaled the entry of the army into politics. It forced King Constantine to abdicate in favor of his son George. In April 1924, a republic was proclaimed, followed during the next four years by short-lived governments, attempted military coups, a dictatorship, and the restoration of parliamentary government; the fight was between Eleftherios Venizelos, who favored a republic, and supporters of the monarchy.

In 1928, Venizelos returned to power at the head of a large parliamentary majority. He expropriated large estates, protected small-scale industrialists and merchants, built schools, and instituted public works projects. Venizelos financed his reforms with international loans, but corruption scandals brought Venizelos down, and political instability forced him to flee the country. In November 1935, the army restored King George.

The Refugee Problem

The other consequence of the Great Idea's collapse was socioeconomic instability. On July 24, 1923, the Treaty of Lausanne provided for the compulsory exchange of populations with Turkey. Unable to handle the great influx of refugees, Greece negotiated large loans under League of Nations auspices in 1924 and 1927, handed over administration of the refugees to the Refugee Settlement Commission, and tried to give the refugees land. The government obtained land from the expropriation of large estates and from state holdings, so that by 1930 large landholdings practically ceased to exist and almost 146,000 refugee families had been settled on the land. These measures alleviated Greece's refugee problem. In addition, new crops, such as tobacco, were introduced, and the value of agricultural products doubled between 1922 and 1932.

Refugees who settled in the overcrowded cities had a harder time, but some had managed to bring money, jewelry, and other movable wealth with them. Aided by Greece's protectionist tariff, many of them established commercial and industrial enterprises. Industry, which contributed only marginally to the national income in 1918, accounted for 18 percent in 1940.

Depression and Dictatorship

With the collapse of agricultural prices during the depression, the refugee problem became explosive. Because they were not committed to the existing political structure, many joined the Communist Party (KKE), which grew rapidly as hundreds of strikes and demonstrations shook the country. The January 1936 elections were a draw between the monarchists and republicans, which gave the Communists the balance of power in the formation of coalition governments. However, the army refused to accept Communist participation in the government, which led King George to institute a dictatorship under General John Metaxas on August 4, 1936.

Metaxas was convinced that only the suppression of political parties and a strong government could save Greece, so he dissolved Parliament, eliminated press freedom, and jailed his opponents. Otherwise, Metaxas ran a fairly efficient and honest government. He regulated the economy and trade unions and banned strikes, but protected workers through compulsory arbitration of disputes and minimum wages. Metaxas talked about creating a third Greek civilization based on classical and Byzantine society. His administration adopted some of the Fascist trappings of power common to the age, including a youth movement (EON) that attracted a million members, but was not a Fascist.

Isolated Albania

Greece's neighbor to the northwest, Albania, was the least advanced part of Europe. It possessed few schools or roads, a tribal social organization in large parts of the country, and an armed populace. Deep regional divisions increased the strong divisions between remote Catholic tribes of the north who were seeking governmental largesse, Muslim landowners employing their influence to increase their holdings, and Eastern Orthodox southerners complaining about economic exploitation. The tensions between peasants and large landowners who owned over half the arable land was expressed in antagonism between the landowner-backed conservative Progressive Party and the Democratic, or Popular, Party, headed by an Eastern Orthodox Bishop, Harvard-educated Fan Noli.

International disputes had resulted in Albanian independence in 1913, but contending forces fought over it during World War I. After the conflict, disputes broke out with Greece and Yugoslavia, which claimed different areas of ethnic Albania. In 1921, the Allies awarded Kosovo to Yugoslavia despite documented Serbian atrocities. Albanian-inhabited territory that went to other countries caused trouble throughout the interwar period and up to the end of the twentieth century.

Instability and the Albanian Dictatorship

Albanian conditions fostered instability and revolts that probably no parliamentary system could have survived. In the 1920s, Fan Noli and Muslim leader Ahmed Zogu emerged as the most important personalities. In June 1924, a revolution put Noli at the helm with a program of radical agricultural, legal, and administrative reform that alienated the landowners without gaining the peasants' support. Backed by Yugoslavia and financed by the British (who hoped to find oil in Albania), Zogu took over as president on January 31, 1925. Zogu declared himself Zog I, king of the Albanians, on September 1, 1928. He had absolute power through a new constitution supported by large landowners and others favoring the status quo. Zog could at times be moderately progressive, as in 1937 when he attempted to force the unveiling of Muslim women, ban men from wearing national costumes, and discourage peasants from sleeping on the floor by promoting beds.

Zog maintained his rule through a system of paying pensions and salaries to tribal leaders—effective but expensive. Because the Yugoslavs could not afford to keep subsidizing him and the international financial community refused to consider loans, Zogu turned to the Italians. Albania's proximity to the Italian coast and Mussolini's desire to extend his influence in the Balkans made Italy the only large power with an important stake in the country. The Italians granted loans, set up a credit system and a currency, made investments, signed friendship pacts, and widened their influence over Albanian civilian and military life. However, Zog chafed under Italian tutelage, and Mussolini invaded the country in April 1939. Italy's King Victor Emanuel III thereupon became the king of Albania as well.

IBERIA

On the opposite end of Europe, the Iberian Peninsula also came under the control of dictators.

Failure of the Portuguese Republic

The Portuguese republic, established in 1910, promised progress and social justice but was characterized instead by anticlericalism, financial failure, factionalism, instability, and the army's interference in politics. Portugal entered World War I

Antonio Salazar, shown here in 1959. Salazar established a state that had Fascist elements but was authoritarian rather than totalitarian. He kept Portugal neutral during World War II and his regime lasted until September 1968 when a fall incapacitated him.

in 1915 on the Allied side; when the war ended, inflation, strikes, disorder, terrorism, and leftist demands for revolution followed. The military took over in June 1926 and sought loans that the international financial community would not give because of the country's disastrous economic situation. The military then called on a professor of political economy at the University of Coimbra, Antonio de Oliveira Salazar, to put Portuguese finances in order.

Salazar's "New State"

Salazar cut expenses, increased the efficiency of tax collection, and balanced the budget. These accomplishments made him the strong man of the regime. In May and June 1930, when the depression devastated Europe, Salazar stated that he would transform Portugal into a corporate republic based on Catholic thought and patriotic unity—the "New State"—and in 1933 issued Europe's first corporate constitution. Corporativism, an important component of Italian Fascism, was supposedly based on the peaceful collaboration of all classes and social and economic groups.

The constitution's major innovation was a consultative corporate chamber chosen by economic groups and cultural and professional societies. The government orchestrated elections and established the "National Union" to aid in this task. As in Italy, the regime banned strikes and lockouts and regulated relationships between workers and employers. The new organization did little to spur the economy, and static agriculture, slow industrial progress, and high illiteracy continued to characterize Portuguese society.

Salazar's regime was authoritarian rather than Fascist. In fact, the Fascists, organized in 1932 as the National Syndicalists or Blue Shirts, wanted to graft elements of Portuguese Catholicism onto a movement of the Italian type. Salazar condemned their emphasis on Fascist values, such as the cult of youth and direct action, and dissolved them on July 29, 1934. In foreign policy, Salazar supported Francisco Franco during the Spanish Civil War by allowing the Spanish rebels to use Portuguese facilities. Portugal remained neutral in World War II, although it favored the Allies after 1943. Salazar's careful foreign and domestic policies allowed the regime to survive until 1974.

Military Dictatorship in Spain

Another long-lived authoritarian regime emerged in Spain, albeit in a more dramatic and bloody fashion.

Spain was neutral during World War I, but the conflict still affected it. Industry grew rapidly because of the war-related demand from the Allies, but in 1917 a wave of strikes led by the Socialist trade union, the UGT, demanding social and economic reform hit the country. Continuing disorders between 1918 and 1920 and a revolt in Morocco discredited the parliamentary government and resulted in a military dictatorship under General Miquel Primo de Rivera on September 13, 1923. Primo de Rivera resolved to restore order, deal with Spain's financial chaos, win in Morocco, and save Spain from its politicians.

The dictatorship succeeded in all these goals except the last. Between 1920 and 1930, the percentage of the industrial labor force rose from 22 percent to

26.5 percent and the service sector from 20.8 percent to 28 percent, while agricultural labor declined from 57.2 percent to 45.5 percent; illiteracy fell; the number of university students doubled; and greater economic opportunities for women materialized. However, Primo de Rivera failed to create a political constituency, and his illness weakened his regime. In January 1930, the peseta's fall, rising unemployment, and an unbalanced budget convinced King Alfonso XIII to request his resignation.

Despite Spain's rapid progress, its economic and social development lagged far behind the advanced industrial countries, and Spanish society was unready for the Liberal leftist governments of the 1930s.

The Republic and the Polarization of Spanish Politics

Alfonso aimed at a gradual return to a parliamentary regime, but strong republican opposition materialized. Manuel Azaña's Republican Action Group, formed in 1925, combined with other republican societies on August 17, 1930, to create the umbrella Republican Committee and to set up a provisional government that included the Socialists. Disorders and a victory in the local elections of April 1931 encouraged the provisional government to demand the monarchy's end. When huge crowds supported the end of the monarchy and the army refused to back Alfonso, the king left the country without abdicating on April 14.

The provisional government proclaimed a republic and attacked the church. Over a hundred church buildings were torched without Azaña discouraging the destruction. The violence, burnings, killings, and atrocities caused resentment and demonstrated that the Republicans had lost control of public order.

A republican constitution, adopted in 1931, instituted a parliamentary form of government, guaranteed civil rights, and granted women the vote and equal rights in marriage and divorce. The constitution decreed the separation of church and state, but while it guaranteed freedom of conscience, it dissolved religious orders and confiscated their property. Between 1931 and 1933, Azaña undertook a vigorous reform program that brought mixed results. The state alienated Catholic parents by closing their schools, while the construction of new schools faltered. The lack of local compliance often negated labor legislation giving workers new benefits and a voice in management. The new land reform was complicated and underfunded and failed to resettle many families. Finally, the breakdown of public order made it difficult to implement the reform measures.

By late 1933, mounting unemployment, strikes, and strains in the republican coalition forced the Azaña government to resign. The left's radical policies encouraged more unity on the right and spurred the growth of the CEDA (Confederation of Autonomous Rightist Groups), headed by a university professor, José Maria Gil Robles, that, with the addition of several Catholic groups, grew into the largest Spanish party. In addition to the CEDA, the right included business groups; radical right monarchists, headed by Mussolini admirer José Calvo Sotelo; and the Fascist Falange, led by José Antonio Primo de Rivera—son of the former dictator.

The right staged a comeback in the 1933 elections, and the leftist parties responded by uniting in a Popular Front coalition on the French model in

Spain experienced political unrest during the early 1930s, with violent struggles between the right and the left. The elections of 1936 established a Popular Front government that implemented radical measures for which the country was unprepared and set the stage for a civil war during the 1930s that has been seen as a prelude to World War II. In this photograph, posters go up during the turbulent electoral campaign of 1936.

preparation for the upcoming elections of February 16, 1936. The balloting produced a big victory for the Popular Front, and Azaña returned as prime minister. Emboldened by the triumph, the left undertook radical land distribution that included sanctioning land seizures and expropriation through taxation. Between May and July 1936, strikes, demonstrations, arson, and killings directed mainly against the right escalated. This violent period culminated in the murder of Calvo Sotelo by leftist police officers.

The Spanish Civil War

These events produced a rightist military revolt in mid-July 1936. The conspirators envisioned a quick victory and a regime modeled on the Portuguese New State, but their plans went awry when they encountered major opposition in the areas that supported the Popular Front. The military effort bogged down and developed into a civil war. Both sides called for foreign help. Italy and Germany intervened in favor of Francisco Franco, leader of the nationalist forces, while Soviet-backed Communists dominated the left. The Civil War turned into an internecine struggle between the international Fascist and anti-Fascist forces.

The opponents of fascism formed the International Brigades and fought alongside the Spanish republicans, while the Italians and the Germans presented their thinly disguised military intervention as an anti-Communist crusade. The struggle—a milestone on the road to World War II—lasted until 1939 and caused a million casualties before Franco finally won.

In April 1937, Franco took over the Falange and turned it into the official state party, but watered it down at the same time that he gave his regime some of the Fascist trappings that were typical of 1930s authoritarian governments. More than Fascist, Franco's Spain has been interpreted as "a Catholic, corporative, and increasingly demobilized authoritarian regime."

Bibliographical Essay

The statement on the nature of the dictatorships in the Baltic states is taken from V. Stanley Vardys and Romuald J. Misiunas, eds., *The Baltic States in Peace and War 1917–1945* (University Park, Penn., 1978), an excellent collection of essays (pp. 77–78). The Information Department of the Royal Institute of International Affairs, *The Baltic States* (London, 1938), is packed with information on the economies, social situation, and politics of the Baltic states. John Hiden and Patrick Salmon, *The Baltic Nations and Europe*, rev. ed. (London, 1994), brings the story up to the present. There are several concise histories of the Baltic States; they include Kevin O'Connor, *The History of the Baltic States* (Westport, Conn., 2003), a narrative from ancient times, and Andres Kasekamp, *A History of the Baltic States* (New York, 2010), which deals with all three of the countries.

Economics in Eastern Europe between the wars is covered thoroughly by M. C. Kaser and E. A. Radice, eds., *The Economic History of Eastern Europe 1919–1975*, Vol. 1 (Oxford, UK, 1985). *A Low Dishonest Decade* (New York, 2002) by Paul N. Hehn considers the role of the great powers in economics and the origins of World War II. A book of essays that discusses more specialized business topics is Christopher Kobrak and Per H. Hansen, *European Business, Dictatorship, and Political Risk, 1920–1945* (New York, 2004). The most thorough general work on all Eastern Europe during this period remains Hugh Seton-Watson, *Eastern Europe Between the Wars 1918–1941*, 3rd ed. (New York, 1962). Anta Prazmowska's *Eastern Europe and the Origins of the Second World War* (New York, 2000) analyzes the complex dilemmas of the East European states. Alexander V. Prusin's *The Lands Between* (New York, 2010) has ample material on the period under consideration. The previously cited book by Zara Stein, *The Lights that Failed* (New York, 2005), is a thorough history of international affairs between the wars with much material on Eastern Europe.

Ferdynand Zweig, *Poland Between Two Wars: A Critical Study of Social and Economic Changes* (London, 1944), neglects the minority question but otherwise is a very good study of the social and economic situation. Economics is more fully discussed by J. Taylor, *The Economic Development of Poland 1919–1950* (Ithaca, N.Y., 1952). A good general history is Norman Davies, *Heart of Europe: A Short History of Poland* (Oxford, UK, 1984). Aleksander Gieysztor et al., *History of Poland*, 2nd ed. (Warsaw, 1979), is a thorough work on the entire sweep of Polish history, seen from the East. Bernadotte E. Schmitt, ed., *Poland* (Berkeley, Calif., 1947), contains perceptive essays on all aspects of modern Poland. On the important Polish Jewish community, consult Israel Gutman et al., eds., *The Jews of Poland Between Two World Wars* (Hanover, New Hampshire, 1989) *Anti-Semitism*; on the Catholic Church in Poland during the interwar period, see *Rome's Most Faithful Daughter* (Athens, Ohio, 2009) by Neal Pease.

Mark Cornwall et al., *Czechoslovakia in a Nationalist and Fascist Europe, 1918–1948* (New York, 2007), is a collection of essays on the dilemmas of democracy in the country during the interwar period. Josef Korbel, *Twentieth-Century Czechoslovakia: The Meanings of its History* (New York, 1977), is a clearly written account, sympathetic to the Czechs, that includes much information on the period discussed. William V. Wallace's *Czechoslovakia* (Boulder, Colo., 1976) is an excellent, more detailed work. Essays on particular themes and problems may be found in Victor S. Mamatey and Radomir Luza, *A History of the Czechoslovak Republic, 1918–1948* (Princeton, N.J., 1973). Georges Castellan's *A History of the Romanians* (New York, 1989) has a good chapter on the interwar period. David Mitrany's study on land reform, *The Land and the Peasant in Rumania: The War and Agrarian Reform, 1917–21* (New York, 1968), originally published in 1930, gives a complete picture. Dejan Djokic, *Elusive Compromise* (New York, 2007), is a history of interwar Yugoslavia. Stephen Clissold, ed., *A Short History of Yugoslavia: From Early Times to 1966* (Cambridge, UK, 1966), includes an excellent chapter on interwar Yugoslavia. On Hungary, the most scholarly work is C. A. Macartney, *A History of Hungary 1929–1945* (New York, 1956). Paul Ignotus, *Hungary* (New York, 1972), has the passion of a participant. Another participant in the events, Oscar Jaszi, wrote about an important transition, *Revolution and Counter-Revolution in Hungary* (New York, 1969).

The Fascist movements in Hungary and Romania are analyzed by Nicholas M. Nagy-Talavera, *The Green Shirts and the Others: A History of Fascism in Hungary and Romania* (Stanford, Calif., 1970). A good idea of the Austrian situation may be gained by looking at C. E. Edmondson, *The Heimwehr and Austrian Politics* (Athens, Ga., 1978); F. L. Carsten, *Fascist Movements in Austria from Schonerer to Hitler* (London, 1977); and Gordon Brooke-Shepherd, *Dollfuss* (London, 1961). A comparative study of the Heimwehr and the Nazis is offered by John T. Lauridson, *Nazism and the Radical Right in Austria 1918–1934* (Copenhagen, 2007). See also Gottfried-Karl Kindermann, *Hitler's Defeat in Austria, 1933–1934* (London, 1988). For details on Bulgaria during this period, consult R. J. Crampton, *A Short History of Modern Bulgaria* (Cambridge, UK, 1987).

For the rise of Fascist-type organizations during the latter part of the period discussed, see Béla Vago, *The Shadow of the Swastika: The Rise of Fascism and Anti-Semitism in the Danube Basin, 1936–1939* (London, 1975).

On Greece, see John Campbell and Philip Sherrard, *Modern Greece* (London, 1968). On the economic details, there is Mark Mazower, *Greece and the Inter-War Economic Crisis* (Oxford, UK, 1991); on Metaxas, consult J. V. Kofas, *Authoritarianism in Greece: The Metaxas Regime* (Boulder, Colo., 1983). Miranda Vickers, *The Albanians: A Modern History* (London, 1995), provides a succinct account of Albanian developments.

Portuguese events can be followed in T. Gallagher, *Portugal: A Twentieth-Century Interpretation* (Manchester, UK, 1983); R. A. H. Robinson, *Contemporary Portugal* (London, 1979); and Hugh Kay, *Salazar and Modern Portugal* (New York, 1960). On Portuguese corporativism, see H. J. Wirda, *Corporativism and Development: The Portuguese Experience* (Amherst, Mass., 1977). Much more has been written on Spain and the Spanish Civil War. The most comprehensive work on the republic is Stanley G. Payne, *Spain's First Democracy: The Second Republic, 1931–1936* (Madison, Wis., 1993), from which the statistics on Spain's economic progress are taken (p. 24). The best book on agrarian reform is Edward E. Malefakis, *Agrarian Reform and Peasant Revolution: Origins of The Civil War* (New Haven, Conn., 1970), while the resurgence of the right is discussed by Richard A. H. Robinson, *The Origins of Franco's Spain* (Plymouth, 1970). The quotation on Spain's political evolution under Franco comes from Payne, *Fascism*, previously cited (p. 267). Books on the Civil War are cited in the bibliography to Chapter 14.

On two important topics discussed in this chapter, see Matthew Feldman et al., *Clerical Fascism in Interwar Europe* (New York, 2008), a book of essays on the topic, and

Civil War and World War in Spain, Yugoslavia and Greece, 1936–1949 (New York, 2008), by Philip B. Minehan.

Much has been written on the Spanish Civil War and the conditions leading up to it. Hugh Thomas's *The Spanish Civil War* (New York, 2001) is a classic that has been brought up to date. Paul Preston wrote both a general history of the conflict, *The Spanish Civil War: Reaction, Revolution and Revenge* (New York, 2007), and the acclaimed *Franco: A Biography* (New York, 1994). Antony Beevor's *The Battle for Spain: The Spanish Civil War 1936–1939* (New York, 2006), a complete history, and *The Spanish Civil War* (New York, 2001) are good sources. Andrew Durgan's *The Spanish Civil War* (New York, 2007) has the added bonus of surveying the recent literature on the topic. Hilario M. Raguer Suñer and Gerald Howson's *Gunpowder and Incense* (New York, 2007) is a study of the Catholic Church's role in the Spanish Civil War.

CHAPTER 12

Mussolini's Fascism

CHAPTER OUTLINE
Fascist Practice • Fascist Ideology
BIOGRAPHICAL SKETCHES
Edmondo Rossoni, Fascist Labor • Margherita Sarfatti, "Dictator of the Figurative Arts"

Fascism's economic policies during the 1920s were similar to those described in Chapter 8 for other European countries, but the implementation of a dictatorship was a radical departure from Italian tradition. Mussolini's seizure of power convinced opponents that industrialists and big landowners were behind the takeover, but, although Mussolini did have support in both groups, Fascism was a highly complex phenomenon whose significance transcended economics. (Used with a capital letter, *Fascism* refers to Italy; *fascism* in lower case refers to the generic movement). Because of the contradictions within Fascism, it is important to examine both its practice and ideology.

FASCIST PRACTICE

Fascism's opponents described it as a jumble of ideas. The Fascists themselves claimed that they disdained the quibbling of intellectuals and favored "action," that theory did not interest them because they lived for the moment, and that their movement was based on youth. In fact, at age 39, Mussolini and was the youngest prime minister in Italian history, and the movement attracted the young. Fascism's formal systemization came only after the Fascists had been in power for a decade.

The Government
After Mussolini consolidated his regime in 1925, he got rid of the non-Fascists in his cabinet and replaced them with party stalwarts known for their support of the monarchy and their personal closeness to the king. He had previously opposed the

monarchy, and after the Matteotti affair, he thought it essential to mollify the king by reducing the influence of Fascist left-wingers who noisily advocated a second wave of revolution to sweep away existing Italian social and political institutions. Mussolini transformed the National Fascist Party (PNF) into a mass organization that ordinary Italians were obliged to join if they wanted to accomplish the tasks of everyday life. Membership in the PNF, in contrast to the Soviet Communist or German Nazi parties, meant little.

Mussolini blended traditional and new organizations, which consolidated his power and made his rule more attractive abroad. His compromises with existing Italian institutions allowed him to rule easier, but Mussolini never gained complete power over Italian society and frequently could not enforce important measures. Ironically, when the Duce tried to make Italy more Fascist, he ran into greater passive opposition.

Structure of the Dictatorship

In 1925 and 1926, the government took control of the independent press, suppressed opposition parties and associations, expelled opposition deputies from the Chamber of Deputies, and created a special tribunal to try crimes against Fascism. The regime also gave the police broad new powers to arrest persons merely on suspicion of conspiring against the political and social order. Lina Wertmüller's film *Love and Anarchy*, for example, tells the loosely based-on-truth story of an anarchist who was executed because he was plotting to kill Mussolini, although he never made the attempt. Officials received the right to cancel passports, to fire on people who were attempting to flee the country, and to deprive opponents of the regime who were living abroad of their citizenship and property.

Fascist legislation deprived Parliament of any power. In December 1925, parliamentary control over cabinets evaporated with the transformation of the prime minister into a head of government responsible only to the king. The Chamber of Deputies lost its power to select individual cabinet ministers, to be chosen in the future by the Duce subject to the king's approval. Mussolini's control of the agenda of the Chamber of Deputies eliminated Parliament's legislative initiative. In January 1926, the government removed Parliament's power over the state administration by implementing decisions after consultation with the Council of State. Later in 1926 and in 1928, the government instituted control over local affairs by substituting elected officials by appointees from Rome.

The Fascists merged party and state institutions, although this phenomenon did not go as far as in the USSR or in Nazi Germany. In 1927, the Fascist Grand Council (the Fascist Party executive) changed the method of electing the Chamber of Deputies by drawing up a slate of 400 persons who were recommended by employer, employee, and other associations and presenting the list to the voters, who either accepted or rejected it. The Grand Council later gained a voice in the succession to the throne and in naming an eventual successor to Mussolini. The Duce asserted his control of the Grand Council by calling it into session only rarely. Ironically, when Italy was being defeated during World War II, the Fascist Grand Council ousted Mussolini from power in 1943 by asking the king to resume command. The event demonstrated how, despite all the changes, Italian

This February 1922 photograph of Pope Pius XI shows the Pontiff at the time of the March on Rome that brought Mussolini to power. Pius's policies helped the Duce, and the 1929 Concordat, in the minds of many people, signified that the Church approved of the regime. Mussolini did not intend to relinquish power and quickly attacked the Church, but after his fall the Concordat gave the Church great power in the new Italian Republic.

institutions retained the capacity to strike back at the Fascists: unlike Nazi Germany or Soviet Russia, Italy retained a constitutional official who could dismiss the Duce.

Uneasy Peace with the Church

The powerful Catholic Church had an ambiguous role when it came to Fascism. Mussolini understood the church's great influence and tried to gain its support. On February 11, 1929, the Duce and the Vatican signed the Lateran Accords ending the dispute between the church and state that had resulted from confiscation of papal territory in 1861 and 1870 during Italian unification. The Lateran Accords created the independent state of Vatican City in Rome, paid the church a large sum as compensation for the annexed territories, regulated religious affairs in the country, and instituted salaries for the clergy. Because Italy paid the money in state bonds, the Catholic Church acquired a large stake in the stability of the Fascist regime. In the concordat that was part of the accords, the state relinquished control over matrimony to the church, allowed religious instruction in public secondary schools, and gave the church censorship powers over free expression in the Holy City. This agreement ended the possibility of divorce in the country (until 1970) and, by making Catholicism the official state religion, put other religious denominations in an inferior position. The Lateran Accords contributed to Mussolini's international prestige and were the last important step in the consolidation of Italian Fascism.

Immediately after signing the Lateran Accords, the Duce curbed the church's political and social influence over the country's youths by attacking Catholic Action. The campaign ended in 1931 with a victory for Mussolini. At least until the anti-Semitic laws of 1938, the church supported the regime in domestic and foreign policy. Mussolini had achieved stability at home and respect abroad.

Labor Policy

The normalization of the Fascist state after the postwar disturbances accounted for Mussolini's appeal to foreigners. Indeed, the Fascists attained this peace by suppressing the Socialist and other independent trade unions. Nevertheless, Fascism professed to be a strong friend of labor even while it opposed the excessive strikes and violence that had marked the Red Biennium. Fascist trade unionists had won a large following, but because the powerful industrialists had thrown their support to the Duce, the question after 1922 was how they would influence labor policy. The desire of Fascist labor leaders to empower workers conflicted with Mussolini's need to solidify his regime by reaching agreement with the employers. Fascism's contradictory aims touched off an internal debate between the Duce and the Fascist union leaders.

Edmondo Rossoni, the Fascist labor movement's strongest advocate, aimed to strengthen the General Confederation of Fascist Unions by absorbing the Socialist and Catholic labor unions. Rossoni, a former member of the Socialist International Workers of the World (IWW) in the United States and an experienced labor organizer, hoped to win recognition for his organization as the only representative of labor. On December 19, 1923, the employers established a privileged relationship with the Fascist unions but put off creating corporations—institutions in which both employers and employees would have representation. During the next two years, tensions escalated as the standard of living for workers declined and provoked strikes by both the Fascist and non-Fascist unions. Alarmed by labor's activism, the Duce ordered wage increases but resolved to tame the Fascist labor movement.

On October 2, 1925, representatives of the industrialists' association (the Confindustria) and the Fascist unions signed the Palazzo Vidoni pact recognizing each other as representatives of employers and employees. This agreement seemed favorable to the workers, but a series of measures over the next two years achieved Mussolini's aim. Because only Fascist unions could legally negotiate and enforce contracts, all previous contracts were voided, and the independent unions were disbanded in 1926 and 1927. At the same time, the Confindustria became Fascist, and its president and secretary entered the Fascist Grand Council. In 1926, legislation drawn up by Nationalist theoretician Alfredo Rocco prohibited both strikes and lockouts. In 1928, the government further weakened Rossoni's labor movement by splitting his Confederation of Fascist Unions into six organizations.

The Nationalists had merged with the Fascists in 1923 and hoped to foster national unity by reducing labor conflict through the formation of corporations, which Rocco's legislation mentioned for the first time. In order to gain labor support in a climate of increasing tension, in 1927 the government issued a declaration of workers' entitlement to good wages, working conditions, and social security, known as the Labor Charter. Private enterprise was the most efficient means of serving the country's interests, but state intervention in the economy was promised, if necessary. The Great Depression soon put the government's assurance to the test.

The Depression, Industry, and Autarky

The economic crisis struck Italy when the country had not completely digested the effects of the revaluation crisis discussed in Chapter 8. The government responded to the slump by decreasing salaries, rationalizing and expanding social security, and undertaking a vast public works program that included land reclamation, building new cities, road building, and rural electrification. It also discouraged the movement of the rural unemployed into the cities, although it did not achieve this goal.

BIOGRAPHICAL SKETCHES

Edmondo Rossoni
Fascist Labor

Edmondo Rossoni's career paralleled Benito Mussolini's, although Rossoni remained more faithful to his principles. Born in Tresigallo in the province of Ferrara on October 6, 1884, Rossoni joined the Italian Socialist Party at an early age. He became attracted to revolutionary syndicalism, a Socialist faction that preached the supremacy of workers and their unions and considered the general strike the prime weapon for implementing socialism. He took part in strikes on the land and in 1904 moved to Milan, the stronghold of the revolutionary syndicalists. His activities attracted the attention of the police, and in 1908 he fled the country. Rossoni went to France and Brazil before going to New York in 1910. In New York, he wrote for the revolutionary newspaper *Il Proletario* and joined the IWW. In 1913, he returned to Italy, again engaged in revolutionary activities, was arrested and released, and again left for New York City. When World War I began, he advocated Italian intervention, and in May 1916, he returned to Italy and volunteered for combat.

On June 9 and 10, 1918, Rossoni and his friends resurrected the Unione Italiana del Lavoro (Italian Union of Labor, UIL), which represented revolutionary syndicalists who had supported the war. The UIL adopted Rossoni's slogan: "Do not deny the nation; conquer it." The UIL advocated fighting for workers' control of production and distribution. In March 1919, the union occupied a large steel plant outside Milan, an action that Mussolini supported. In 1920 the UIL urged the expropriation of land that was not under direct cultivation, thus increasing its appeal for the landless peasants and the returning peasant-soldiers.

In January 1922, Rossoni agreed to head the Fascist unions, mistakenly believing that Mussolini would support workers' increased power through mixed unions with employers. Although the corporative state later included elements of these institutions, industrialists and landowners resisted Rossoni's demands, and the Duce withdrew his support. In November 1928 the government broke Rossoni's Fascist Confederation of Labor Unions into several separate organizations, signaling his definitive defeat and that of Fascist labor.

Rossoni had little power as undersecretary for the presidency of the Council of Ministers (1932–35) and minister of agriculture (1935–39). He was a member of the Fascist Grand Council and voted for a motion that removed Mussolini from power on July 24 and 25, 1943. This act earned Rossoni Mussolini's enmity, and he had to take refuge in the Vatican when the Germans occupied Italy in September 1943. In 1944, Mussolini's puppet Italian Social Republic held trials in Verona for the Grand Council members who had betrayed the Duce, and Rossoni received a death sentence in absentia. After the war, a court sentenced him to life imprisonment for his role in suppressing Italian liberty during the Fascist era, but Rossoni fled to Canada.

In 1947, the sentence revoked, Rossoni returned to Italy, where he lived peacefully until his death in Rome on June 8, 1965.

The slump produced long-range changes in industry and commerce. As the economic situation deteriorated, Mussolini turned for advice to a non-Fascist banking expert, Alberto Beneduce. After the creation of new agencies that were empowered to make loans to ailing companies proved insufficient to stem the crisis, the government founded the Institute for Industrial Reconstruction (IRI) to arrange for the long-term financing of failing firms. The idea was for IRI to buy up depressed companies in the portfolios of the banks and liquidate them; instead IRI acquired the commercial and industrial holdings of the major banks and achieved control of the companies and of the banks themselves. Although IRI was supposed to sell its holdings when recovery came, its acquisitions had become too big and valuable to do so. Moreover, as Mussolini embarked on a series of wars, the state wanted to keep basic industries in its hands.

These considerations led to the reorganization of essential economic sectors in which IRI companies were active, such as steel, communications, and ship-building. By 1937 IRI had evolved into a modern holding company under public control employing the most advanced private-sector techniques. Through IRI and other public companies, the Fascist state owned and managed a greater proportion of Italian industries than any other European state except the USSR.

In 1935, preparations for the Ethiopian War, the combined cost of the conflict, public works, and increased interest payments produced large budget deficits that forced Mussolini to devalue the lira in October 1936 to keep it in line with the dollar and the pound. Prices rose despite governmental controls, and unions obtained salary increases in 1936, 1937, and 1939. A general economic recovery, accompanied by increased industrial production, occurred during those years.

In 1936, Mussolini instituted a policy of autarky, or self-sufficiency, in response to League of Nations sanctions imposed after his invasion of Ethiopia. The policy, however, had its origins earlier in the Great Depression and in the collapse of free trade and intensified under the pressure of war. Mussolini instituted currency controls, austerity, the substitution of Italian products for imported ones where possible, and curbs of imported raw materials by large firms and state agencies. The government also became involved in developing new products and processes, in regulating all phases of manufacturing, and in searching for new sources of energy. Among the most important of these newly created state agencies was the Italian General Firm for Petroleum (AGIP). Both AGIP and IRI survived the fall of Fascism, IRI closing only in the year 2000 and AGIP becoming part of a large state hydrocarbon combine.

Fascist economic policies counted both successes and failures. The deficiencies came primarily in agriculture and the poor performance of real wages. The accomplishments included stimulation of important modern industries, such as electricity, steel, engineering, chemicals, and artificial fibers, so that Italy's profile began to resemble that of a modern European country. This success contributed to the economic miracle after World War II. Up to the time that Mussolini embarked on his warlike adventures, Fascism's policies and ideology appeared brilliant and, for many depression-era Europeans and Americans, a model to emulate.

In attempt to make Italy self-sufficient in food, the Mussolini government began a huge propaganda effort to encourage farmers to grow more wheat. The campaign succeeded in doing this, but the economic impact of the effort showed mixed results. The Duce was always hands-on in his propaganda efforts. This picture shows him giving a hand with the grain harvesting.

Agriculture

Fascism achieved less-impressive results in the agricultural field. Relations between the Fascist unions led by Rossoni and the landowners' organization were poor and, despite his rhetoric, Mussolini threw his weight against the peasants.

In 1925 the Duce announced the "Battle of the Grain," one of the regime's more spectacular and successful propaganda efforts. For reasons of prestige and self-defense in case of war, Mussolini aimed to make the country self-sufficient in foodstuffs by encouraging investment and improvements to increase grain production. The government hoped to achieve its goal by increasing the yield per acre without reducing the production of other crops. The campaign cut Italy's grain imports substantially, and Mussolini claimed victory. However, bringing more land into production and shifting production away from other crops, not more yield per unit, accounted for the increase and caused the production and export of more lucrative products, such as wine, to suffer. Moreover, the collapse of international food prices forced farmers to kill off more of their animals and to introduce tractors and modern chemical fertilizers. Many small landholders who had contracted debts to pay for their land fell behind on payments and lost it. This development reversed a previous trend toward small landholding. The plight of agricultural laborers remained poor and was worsened by legal measures preventing them from leaving the land for urban areas. In contrast, the large landholders, who enjoyed close ties with the government, consolidated their position because their wealth made them better able to adapt to the changes. Because of this situation, Italian farmers had a difficult time participating in the economic recovery of the late 1930s.

FASCIST IDEOLOGY

In the 1930s the Duce tried to give his movement a clear ideological formulation to contradict the claim of anti-Fascists that fascism had no ideology and that its intellectual structure was a façade for exploiting workers. Historians have been debating these issues ever since. Some writers, such as Zeev Sternhell and Emilio Gentile, have pointed out that the Fascists were not the only ones whose ideology demonstrated discrepancies when compared to practice.

Since the international movements that professed to be Fascist had disparate ideologies, historians have attempted to identify specific characteristics that marked so-called generic fascism even while using Italian Fascism as a model. There is agreement on certain characteristics, such as nationalism, the paramount role of the leader, and perhaps corporativism, but not on all the elements of what has become a very long list. Although during the early years of his regime Mussolini did not consider his movement suitable for export, later the Fascists paid more attention to the international dimensions of the movement and subsidized groups, such as the Cagoulards in France and the Rexists in Belgium. Despite these activities, the Italians did not devote a great deal of effort to spreading the Fascist gospel, and the influence it had abroad came primarily from spontaneous emulation.

The "Third Way"

In the 1930s, sophisticated thinkers, such as philosopher Giovanni Gentile and Nationalist theoretician Alfredo Rocco, with contributions from Mussolini, undertook the task of systematically explaining fascism to the rest of the world. Judging from the regime's actions, this ideological framework functioned primarily as window dressing for conservative economic and social policies, but to conclude that the ideology had no importance for the Fascists would be inaccurate. Moreover, the ideas expressed during the frequently passionate internal debates among Fascists are helpful for understanding the inner mechanisms of the movement, the inconsistencies of the regime, and Italian Fascism's attractiveness outside Italy.

In a comprehensive statement in the *Enciclopedia Italiana* (Italian Encyclopedia), written with Gentile in 1932, Mussolini condemned communism as an absurd delusion. He also denounced liberalism and democracy, which he lumped together with socialism because they emphasized the individual over the community. According to the Duce, these doctrines reduced society to a mere "sum of individuals" that generates communism and submerges the individual within the community. The Fascists believed that their movement represented an alternative to liberalism and communism, the "Third Way," because it recognized the community as supreme but left ample space to individual initiative. Unlike the other ideologies, Fascist ideology held that individuals were naturally *unequal* and emphasized heroism and sentiment. Fascism, its adherents claimed, combined the superiority of the state with enhancement of the individual without the false freedom of democracy or communism.

These statements and the Duce's revolutionary Socialist roots suggested to some historians that Fascism had leftist origins. In the 1960s, Italian historian Renzo De Felice argued that the development of Mussolini's ideology was a subject worthy of serious consideration. His contention set off a furious debate, with some leftist observers accusing him of being a veiled Fascist. Over the next thirty years, however, De Felice continued to develop his ideas, stating also that, for a certain period, Fascism had the consensus of the Italians. After De Felice, other historians described Fascism in a variety of ways that have contradicted the contention of leftists that the movement had no coherent philosophy. They viewed Fascism as a developmental dictatorship and as a leftist revision of Marx by revolutionary syndicalists (see Chapter 1).

The Corporate State

The Fascists adopted principles that were derived from the prewar Italian Nationalists, who merged with the Fascist party (PNF) in 1923. They projected the Marxist class struggle onto the international plane as the struggle between rich and proletarian nations, of which Italy was the chief representative. Italian Nationalists believed that the international class struggle between proletarian and rich nations would culminate in a revolutionary war led by Italy. The Italian Fascists embraced this idea and updated it into a fight between the "Have-Nots" and the "Haves." In order to prepare for the coming conflict, the Italians had to achieve internal unity, the Nationalists believed. This concept had important repercussions and contributed to a fundamental Fascist principle, the Corporate

State, that had an influence outside Italy. Alexander J. De Grand defined it as "a system of institutional arrangements by which capital and labor are integrated into obligatory, hierarchical, and functional units (corporations) recognized by the state, which become organs of self-government for issues relating to the specific category as well as the basis for participation with other corporatively organized interests in policy decisions affecting the whole society (corporative parliament)." This idea required the creation of concrete institutions (corporations) in which workers and employers would be represented and work out disputes between capital and labor by negotiation.

The Corporate State dates from 1926, when a law alluded to the corporations, but because of employers' opposition, the government did not institute them. With the Great Depression, Fascist unionists pressed for their formal introduction and clear definitions of their structure and function. Between 1930 and 1934, a vigorous debate on the corporations occurred in which important Fascist intellectuals viewed them as the concrete embodiment of the "Third Way." Leftist Fascist Ugo Spirito argued that the corporations should integrate the workers as full-scale partners in production, transform existing entrepreneurs into managers, and assume ownership of the firms. Spirito believed that making the corporations owners of the means of production would end the class struggle and fulfill Fascism's promises. These ideas got Spirito denounced as a Bolshevik, and conservative Fascists won the fight.

On February 5, 1934, legislation created twenty-two corporations in all sectors of production—agriculture, commerce, services, and industry. On the surface, this law embodied the ideas of the Revolutionary Syndicalists, who saw the future Socialist society as being organized by unions dominating different areas of production. It is important, however, to distinguish the theory of the corporations from the facts of their operation. Employee and employer organizations had equal representation in the corporations, or *sindacati*, despite the numerical superiority of workers. This was a clear discrimination against labor. In theory, the corporations brought together representatives of employers and employees to determine production and settle differences in the presence of delegates representing governmental interests, as the Nationalists had preached. In reality, the corporations had little power and normally ratified governmental proposals generated by the employers' associations.

Completing the Corporate State, a 1938 law abolished the Chamber of Deputies and substituted for it the Chamber of Fasces and Corporations, composed of Fascist Party officials and members of the National Council of Corporations. People became members of this new chamber by virtue of their office, eliminating the need for elections. The Corporate State thus modified the basis of representation from the individual to the productive members of society. This change supposedly fulfilled the Fascist view of economic self-government and national unity that had its origins in revolutionary syndicalism and Nationalism. In practice, a PNF-business alliance ran the country.

Mobilizing the Masses

In seeking to determine the characteristics of Fascist regimes, historians emphasize mobilization of the masses in support of the government and its goals and to give people a sense of nationalism, identity, and security. Italian Fascism provided a model for the rest of Europe with its organizations and strong symbolism. Fascists wore black shirts, used the Roman salute (outstretched arm, open palm, facing downward), adopted the ancient Roman Fasces (bundle of rods) as their symbol of discipline, and established a paramilitary militia—the squads—that beat up their enemies. According to historian Emilio Gentile, they founded a secular religion with its symbols and mythology. Fascists all over Europe followed their example.

The Fascists created organisms of mass mobilization in the 1920s, but these organisms increased in importance during the next decade as Mussolini embarked on a series of wars. The Fascists attempted to regiment the country's youths in order to create the new Fascist man and woman. The Opera Nazionale Balilla (ONB) organized boys and girls ages 6 to 21 in seven youth organizations. These young people wore uniforms, marched, and participated in common activities. To influence future intellectuals, university students were obliged to join the Gioventù Universitaria Fascista (GUF), but higher education remained relatively free from political interference despite the requirement that university professors sign loyalty oaths. The regime also substantially failed to fascistize secondary education despite a 1923 reform, but propagandized the primary schools very heavily by inculcating students with Fascist principles and overtly glorifying the Duce. The Opera Nazionale Dopolavoro (OND) rounded out the Fascist socialization network. This leisure-time organization arranged discounts for theaters and cinemas and provided vacations, tours, and sports events at reduced prices. The OND engaged millions of workers and was the regime's most successful establishment of this kind, but was of doubtful utility in making Fascists. Italian institutions served as models for similar organizations in Nazi Germany.

By the 1930s, even the Fascist Party emphasized socialization and mass mobilization, despite its retention of some of its revolutionary attributes. Fascist revolutionaries in the early, unruly PNF had caused Mussolini difficulties, and he was determined to tame them. In 1930 he reduced the PNF to a bland and unthreatening body. By the early 1930s, membership in the party was required for all activities, diluting the organization to the point that it meant very little to the average citizen. This development helps explain why the party did not come to Mussolini's aid when he fell in 1943.

Propaganda

The 1930s also witnessed the greater use of technological innovations for propaganda. The radio, favored by the regime but of slow diffusion in the 1920s, profited from the government's help during the next decade, although the number of sets still trailed far behind those in Britain, Germany, and the United States. Nonetheless, the radio carried Mussolini's speeches to all the main piazzas of Italy, and the population gathered there while loudspeakers blared out the Duce's most important speeches.

From its beginnings Italian Fascism billed itself as a movement of the youth. Another of its important characteristics was that it concentrated on mobilizing the masses. That is, citizens had to support the state actively, could not remain passive with regard to it and had actively to support its policies. These photographs illustrate a combination of the two principles. The State created a vast youth movement designed to whip up enthusiasm for Fascism and propagandize the young who represented the future of the State and the movement. The Italian Fascist youth movement served as a model for other countries during this period, especially Germany.

BIOGRAPHICAL SKETCHES

Margherita Sarfatti
"Dictator of the Figurative Arts"

Born into a comfortable Venetian Jewish family on April 8, 1883, Margherita Grassini Sarfatti was exposed to feminism and socialism while still a teenager. She published in Socialist and feminist newspapers, cofounding and writing for *La Difesa delle Lavoratrici* (Defense of Women Workers) with Anna Kuliscioff and Angelica Balabanoff, Russian émigrés who were prominent in the Italian Socialist movement. She moved to Milan, where she worked with young firebrand Benito Mussolini, then editor of the Socialist Party's daily newspaper. When Mussolini advocated Italian intervention in World War I and left the party, Sarfatti and her husband Cesare followed his lead and joined the fledgling Fascist movement.

A refined art critic, Sarfatti became art editor for Mussolini's new newspaper, *Il Popolo d'Italia* (The People of Italy). During the Duce's rise to power, she greatly influenced Mussolini's actions, and the two became lovers. Mussolini made her editor of his ideological journal, *Gerarchia* (Hierarchy), in 1921, and in 1926 she published a famous biography of Mussolini, *Dux*, for which the Duce wrote a preface. Sarfatti used her connections to write newspaper articles favorable to Mussolini that helped establish his reputation abroad, particularly in the United States. It was in the arts, however, that she exerted a paramount influence.

Sarfatti's link to the Duce as his mistress and confidante, her extensive political connections, and her artistic sophistication allowed her to mold Italian cultural life before the anti-Semitic laws were passed in 1938. Sarfatti greatly esteemed and favored modern art, which, largely because of her influence, won the regime's official sanction. Italian art of this era substantially escaped the stultifying trends that characterized the figurative arts in Soviet Russia and Nazi Germany.

Sarfatti promoted modernism in art and literature through her membership on governmental committees that determined the course of cultural affairs, by sponsoring individual painters and architects, and through the Novecento (Twentieth Century) movement. Besides Sarfatti, Novecento counted painter Mario Sironi—in addition to other former Futurists—among its adherents and published an influential journal. Novecento aimed at a revolutionary reconciling of traditional, particularly Roman, elements with international modernism in order to provide Fascist Italy with a new cultural dynamic. On February 14, 1926, at the height of Sarfatti's influence, Mussolini addressed the opening of a major Novecento exhibition and gave his views on the intimate relationship between art and politics.

In the 1930s, Sarfatti's star declined, although she continued to travel on cultural assignments to the United States and Europe. The Novecento style had set off disputes among Fascist Party officials, and by 1934 Sarfatti and the Duce were no longer lovers. She kept on writing extensively until passage of the anti-Semitic laws when the government suppressed her articles, which Sarfatti fiercely contested.

In 1939, Mussolini ordered that Sarfatti be given a passport so she could leave Italy. The "Jewish mother of Fascism" went to Argentina, then to France, and later to the United States, where she lived until World War II ended. Margherita Sarfatti then returned to Italy and continued to pursue her artistic interests until her death at her villa on Lake Como on October 30, 1961.

The cinema, a field in which the country had once excelled, languished behind foreign and especially American films, which dominated at the box office. In 1931, a new law encouraged domestic production under governmental supervision, and later the Cinecittà studios were built. These developments stimulated the film industry and set the conditions for future development, but it remained behind in its own market. Ironically, censorship seemed to have little effect, and this period was the seedtime of the postwar flowering of Italian directors. In addition, although officials discussed using film for propaganda, the movie industry made few such films. The regime preferred to use the weekly newsreel—in whose editing Mussolini personally participated—as its primary propaganda vehicle. In 1935 the press and propaganda affairs, radio, cinema, and other means of communication came under a new ministry of popular culture.

In literature and art, the regime exercised only a weak censorship and did not crack down except in cases of blatant opposition. The government never adopted an official artistic style, exercising indirect control over artists through a combination of labor unions, governmental purchases, and regional and national exhibitions. Architecture, heavily dependent on public construction projects, was most susceptible to governmental influence, but building design ranged from classical to the most modern international styles. In the art world, until the anti-Semitic campaigns of the late 1930s, Mussolini's Jewish mistress Margherita Sarfatti served as the regime's unofficial dictator of culture. Sarfatti championed modernistic trends in cultural life until she left Italy because of the racial laws.

Fascism and Women

Sarfatti's prominence illustrates the ambivalence of Fascism toward women. The Fascist outlook disdained females and femininity, assigned women a subordinate position, and emphasized a masculine life of action and danger, while women were supposed to stay home to bear and look after children.

In practice, the reality of women did not differ to a great degree from that in the democratic countries. During the 1920s, the Fascists praised women and argued for recognizing their rights and duties within the nation, as they did for men; created parallel institutions to mobilize them; and expanded maternity leave and other social security benefits. During the 1930s, the depression and the wars made the policy on this issue more congruent with the Fascist style. Since the Duce required more soldiers and a larger population to allow him to claim more territory, he encouraged women to stay home and have more babies, giving them medals if they had many children. To increase productivity and profits, the government tolerated single women working at low wages, but tried to force them into the home as they got older. Fascist propaganda discouraged viewing work or the professions as a means of liberation for women and passed legislation to curtail the number of women working in state and private offices in order to reduce the unemployment of men during the depression. Despite such measures, however, women represented over a quarter of the nation's workforce in the 1930s.

The Fascists tried to increase the birth rate through propaganda and by giving subsidies for workers who had larger families and other economic incentives similar to those taken in France. The government also imposed a tax on bachelors. The ironic result: the birth rate fell.

Ordinary Lives

In attempting to create a feeling of community, the Italian Fascists borrowed heavily from poet Gabriele D'Annunzio, who, during the occupation of Fiume in 1919, staged parades, invented bizarre cries, developed symbols, and dressed his followers in distinctive uniforms. The Duce improved upon these techniques, which the Nazis would later perfect, by haranguing crowds from the balcony of his office in the Palazzo Venezia.

In private life, the Fascists impinged on the lives of ordinary citizens the least of the three major totalitarian regimes. Aside from attending rallies, applauding the Duce's speeches, and submitting to a constant barrage of propaganda, the ordinary person found that the regime exercised little control over his or her life when compared to Nazi Germany and the USSR. The Fascists emphasized sports and exercise and compelled teenagers to work out in the piazzas on Saturdays (the *sabato fascista*). The regime pushed physical fitness in newsreels, where the Duce appeared working with a bare chest in the fields while his paunchy subordinates were put through their paces.

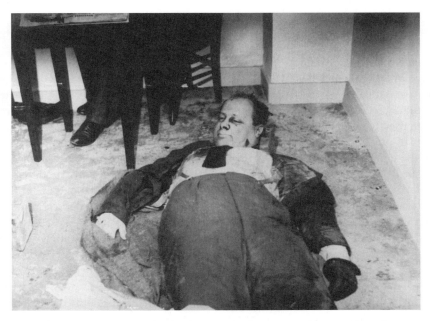

Although Mussolini was not as bloodthirsty as Hitler, his secret police acted brutally against his enemies abroad. In 1937 the OVRA incited a French Fascist organization to murder two of his opponents, Carlo and Nello Rosselli. Here is the body of Carlo, who had fought against the regime in the Spanish Civil War, shortly after his murder. The fact that brothers were Jews helped convince the Duce that the Jews opposed him and had a role in the institution of the anti-Semitic campaign. The murders served as the basis for Alberto Moravia's famous novel, *The Conformist*.

Overt political opponents of Mussolini could not operate in Italy and had to go into exile if they wished to participate in politics. There they were subject to surveillance by the OVRA, the Fascist secret police. OVRA operatives infiltrated exile organizations, fomented splits, and sometimes resorted to assassination. The most spectacular killings—the basis for Alberto Moravia's compelling novel *The Conformist*—occurred in France, where the Fascists engineered the murder of opponents Carlo and Nello Rosselli. In Italy, even prominent people who had opposed the Duce enjoyed relative personal freedom provided they renounced politics. The regime generally limited persecution to job discrimination and constant surveillance—with a few days in jail when Mussolini came to town. It was unwise for citizens to speak ill of the Duce in public. Mussolini's sayings appeared on the outside of buildings, and his stern image stared at students from their textbooks. The regime also attempted to change language, mandating Italian terms for foreign ones in current use (*coda di gallo* for cocktail) and the second person plural *voi* for the polite *Lei*. The regime praised a vigorous masculine lifestyle and persecuted known homosexuals, as illustrated in the film *A Special Day*. There was no official anti-Semitism in the movement.

The Anti-Semitic Laws

The Duce had compromised in order to remain in office, but in the 1930s he attempted to increase his personal power. Mussolini chafed at the king's constitutional supremacy, talked about establishing a republic, transferred potential rivals to lesser jobs, and became more nationalistic. Slogans like "Mussolini is always right" and "Believe, Obey, Fight" covered Italian buildings as his cult, *ducismo*, intensified. However, Mussolini perceived that Fascism was flagging and searched for a means of reviving its spirit. By the late 1930s, also because he had linked up with Hitler, he settled on anti-Semitism as a means of reinvigorating his movement and of strengthening the German alliance.

These factors help explain why Mussolini turned to a policy that had roots neither in Italian society nor in the Fascist movement: even if minor personages did favor anti-Semitism, they had little influence. Italian Jews numbered only about 45,000 and were well integrated into Italian society. Jewish Fascists had helped Mussolini come to power, and their numbers were proportionately greater in the Fascist movement than they were in the Italian population. Mussolini had publicly condemned and ridiculed Hitler's anti-Semitism and made Italy a refuge for German Jews. In 1937 and 1938, however, an anti-Semitic current, consisting of Fascist hierarchs who wanted to increase their influence by cementing Italian-German relations and of leftist Fascists who identified Jews variously with the bourgeoisie, liberals, Socialists, or Communists, formed in the Fascist Party. Mussolini initially refused to sanction an anti-Semitic campaign, but after May 1938, he changed his mind. Several factors seem to have motivated him: Hitler's visit to Italy that month, the existence of prominent Jewish anti-Fascists, a feeling that Italians fraternized with the local population in their African colonies and were not behaving as conquerors, and, above all, a sense that the Fascist movement was flagging and could be reinvigorated with a new goal.

In September 1938, the Fascists passed the racial laws prohibiting foreign Jews from entering Italy, banning Jews from the teaching profession, and excluding them from receiving an education in public secondary schools. More serious provisions followed in November, including a ban on intermarriage, exclusion from the army and public jobs, and a limit on Jewish economic activities. A host of confusing exceptions accompanied the laws, allowing many individuals to escape their worst effects, and concentration camps were not established.

Contrary to the Duce's expectations, a wave of disgust and passive resistance followed the enactment of the anti-Semitic legislation, despite acceptance by party hacks and some intellectuals. The Jewish community set up separate secondary schools, and state commissions continued to give the required examinations that conferred official state recognition of diplomas. Frequently, although Jews had to give up their professional licenses, employers continued to allow them to work. Many foreign Jews, who were supposed to leave within six months, remained in the country.

The laws harmed the country by provoking the emigration of prominent scientists, such as Enrico Fermi, whose wife was Jewish, and Emilio Segrè. Both men, Nobel Prize winners, and other Italian nuclear scientists did fundamental work on the development of the atomic bomb in the United States. Intellectuals in other fields immigrated to the United States, where they used their energies to turn the American government against Mussolini. The anti-Semitic campaign prompted significant segments of the population to turn against the regime, and popular rejection of the anti-Semitic campaign heralded the growing disenchantment with the regime.

In the late 1930s, internal opposition to Fascism was primarily passive. The exile movement plotted against the regime, but the Fascist secret police kept its activities in check. By 1940, however, increasing isolation from the nation marked Mussolini's Fascism.

Bibliographical Essay

There have been attempts to understand what elements make up the general phenomenon of Fascism. One of the most successful is that of Stanley G. Payne, *Fascism: Comparison and Definition* (Madison, Wis., 1980). George L. Mosse published *The Fascist Revolution: Toward A General Theory of Fascism* (New York, 1999). This book is mainly concerned with Germany but includes excellent essays on Italy and France. A controversial book that compares Italy with Germany and France is Ernst Nolte's *Three Faces of Fascism: Action* Française, *Italian Fascism, National Socialism* (New York, 1965). Roger Griffin's *The Nature of Fascism* (New York, 1993) is an examination of the phenomenon with a political science emphasis. Griffin's *Modernism and Fascism* (Basingstoke, UK, 2007) analyzes the relationship with modernization. Two books that summarize how Fascism has been interpreted include Renzo De Felice, *Interpretations of Fascism* (Cambridge, Mass., 1977), and A. James Gregor, *Interpretations of Fascism* (Morristown, N.J., 1974). Alexander De Grand, *Italian Fascism,* 3rd ed. (Lincoln, Nebr., 2000), and Alan Cassels, *Fascist Italy,* 2d ed. (Arlington Heights, Ill., 1985), are good brief treatments of the Fascist phenomenon. R. J. B. Bosworth, *The Italian Dictatorship* (New York, 1998), also focuses on interpretations.

On ideology, the best work is Emilio Gentile, *The Origins of Fascist Ideology, 1918–1925* (New York, 2005). Renzo De Felice's massive and controversial biography of

Mussolini is unavailable in English, but his brief interview, *Fascism: An Informal Introduction to Its Theory and Practice* (New Brunswick, N.J., 1976), edited by Michael Ledeen, is not to be missed. For an assessment of De Felice's impact, see the special issue of the *Italian Quarterly,* edited by Spencer M. Di Scala, *Renzo De Felice and the Problem of Italian Fascism,* 36: nos. 141–142 (Summer–Fall 1999). See also Borden W. Painter, "Renzo De Felice and the Controversy over Italian Fascism," *American Historical Review* 95, no. 2 (April 1990): 391–405. David D. Roberts, *Historicism and Fascism in Modern Italy* (Toronto, 2007) is a collection of articles by the author that examines the link between fascism and intellectuals. A. James Gregor takes the question head-on in *The Ideology of Fascism: The Rationale of Totalitarianism* (New York, 1969), and in *Italian Fascism and Developmental Dictatorship* (Princeton, N.J., 1979), and there is an excellent chapter in his *The Fascist Persuasion in Radical Politics* (Princeton, N.J., 1974). The idea of the Fascist mystique may be found in Adrian Lyttleton, ed., *Italian Fascisms from Pareto to Gentile* (New York, 1973). Important documents are published in Benito Mussolini, *Fascism: Doctrine and Institutions* (New York, 1968), while Roger Griffin's *Fascism* (New York, 1995) contains original writings. Palmiro Togliatti, *Lectures on Fascism* (New York, 1976), presents the Marxist viewpoint of the 1930s. The issue of origins is discussed in Zeev Sternhell's *The Birth of Fascist Ideology: From Cultural Rebellion to Political Revolution* (Princeton, N.J., 1994), cited in Chapter 1. A. James Gregor argues as well that fascism had a rational ideology and examines the contributions of different intellectuals to it in his *Mussolini's Intellectuals: Fascist Social and Political Thought* (Princeton, N.J., 2005).

Biographies are always important and especially so when it comes to Fascism. The best is still Ivone Kirkpatrick's *Mussolini: A Study in Power* (New York, 1964). The most noted biography in English, Denis Mack Smith's *Mussolini* (New York, 1982), has a polemical tone that reduces its value. Laura Fermi, *Mussolini* (Chicago, 1961), is readable but of little scholarly value. Paolo Monelli, *Mussolini: An Intimate Life* (New York, 1954), presents an interesting view of his personality. R. J. B. Bosworth, *Mussolini* (New York, 2002), has a section that traces his influence after his death. Peter Neville's *Mussolini* (New York, 2004) is a thorough work and Anthony L. Cardoza's *Benito Mussolini: The First Fascist* (New York, 2006) is an excellent short biograhy.

Good views of the Fascist regime may be found in the classic works of Gaetano Salvemini, an old enemy, *The Fascist Dictatorship in Italy* (New York, 1967), and *Under the Axe of Fascism* (New York, 1936). Adrian Lyttleton described the regime's consolidation in *The Seizure of Power* (New York, 1973). Philip Morgan, *Italian Fascism 1915–1945* (New York, 2004), is a concise general history. Doug Thompson, *State Control in Fascist Italy: Culture and Conformity, 1925–43* (Manchester, UK, 1991), discusses the transition from violent coercion during the early phase of fascism to nonviolent control of the country through legislation, mass organizations, and propaganda. On a similar theme, Emilio Gentile, *The Sacralization of Politics in Fascist Italy* (Cambridge, Mass., 1996), examines in detail the transformation of Fascism into a secular religion. Good treatments of how the regime mobilized the masses are Tracy Koon, *Believe, Obey, Fight: Political Socialization of Youth in Fascist Italy* (Chapel Hill, N.C., 1985), and Victoria De Grazia, *The Culture of Consent: Mass Organization of Leisure in Fascist Italy* (New York, 1981). On popular culture, consult Edward Tannenbaum's *The Fascist Experience: Italian Society and Culture, 1922–1945* (New York, 1972). The interpretation of cinema during this period has changed, thanks to Marcia Landy, who argued that the postwar cinema had its origins in the Fascist era, in *Fascism on Film* (Princeton, N.J., 1986), and to James Hay, *Popular Film Culture in Fascist Italy* (Bloomington, Ind., 1987), who sees a realistic culture in the films of the period. A book that argues that Italian cinema of this period reveals a fundamentally conservative view toward its role is Marga Cottino-Jones, *Women Desire, and Power in Italian Cinema* (New York, 2010). A good idea of radio's role can be gleaned from Philip Cannistraro, "The Radio in Fascist Italy," *Journal of European Studies* II, 2 (June 1972): 127–54. A excellent work on economics is the brief but incisive *Italian Fascism* (Harmondsworth, UK, 1974) by Giampiero Carocci. Fascist relationships with industry are explored by Roland Sarti, *Fascism and the Industrial Leadership in Italy, 1919–1940* (Berkeley, Calif., 1971). The complexity of censorship during the regime is analyzed by George Talbot, *Censorship in Fascist Italy, 1922–43* (New York, 2007).

The Corporate State is an issue that deserves greater attention but has been neglected; Carl T. Schmidt's *The Corporate State in Action* (New York, 1973), originally published in 1939, is now inadequate. The Fascist Party also has not received much attention in English, the only full-length study being Dante Germino's *The Italian Fascist Party in Power* (Minneapolis, Minn., 1959). On the idea of spreading Fascist doctrine and its implications, there is Michael Ledeen, *Universal Fascism: The Theory and Practice of the Fascist International, 1928–1936* (New York, 1972).

Fascism's view toward women received attention in Alexander De Grand, "Women under Italian Fascism," *The Historical Journal* 19 (1976): 647–88; Philip Cannistraro and Brian Sullivan, *Il Duce's Other Woman* (New York, 1993), a biography of Margherita Sarfatti and her influence on culture; Victoria De Grazia, *How Fascism Ruled Women: Italy, 1922–1945* (Berkeley, Calif., 1992); and Perry R. Willson, *The Clockwork Factory: Women and Work in Fascist Italy* (New York, 1994). Willson also published *Peasant Women and Politics in Fascist Italy: The Massaie Rurali Section of the PNF* (New York, 2002). See also Gigliola Gori, *Female Bodies and Italian Fascism: Submissive Women and Strong Mothers* (London, 2004). The term "The Jewish mother of Fascism," referring to Sarfatti, is the title of an article published in the Israeli newspaper *Ha'aretz* on June 17, 2008.

The relationship with the church is set in a wider context by Richard A. Webster, *The Cross and the Fasces* (Stanford, Calif., 1960). Two other books on the same important theme are J. F. Pollard, *The Vatican and Italian Fascism, 1929–1932* (Cambridge, UK, 1985), and, on the international reaction to the Lateran Accords, P. Kent, *The Pope and the Duce* (London, 1981). John F. Pollard, *The Vatican and Italian Fascism,1929–1932: A Study in Conflict* (New York, 2005), describes the relationship between the two after the signature of the Lateran Accords.

On the complicated issue of Fascism and the Jews, see Meir Michaelis, *Mussolini and the Jews: German-Italian Relations and the Jewish Question in Italy, 1922–1945* (Oxford, UK, 1978). A comparative view is emphasized in Ivo Herzer, ed., *The Italian Refuge* (Washington, D.C., 1989). Aaron Gilette's *Racial Theories in Fascist Italy* (New York, 2002) discusses early anti-Semitism and argues that racial theories did not reinvigorate the movement. Alexander Stille, *Benevolence and Betrayal* (New York, 2003), discusses the histories and fate of five Jewish families during the period. Michele Sarfatti takes a more revisionist, negative view about the Italian record, but in this author's opinion, has not proved his case. His book, originally in Italian, was translated as *The Jews in Mussolini's Italy: From Equality to Persecution* (Madison, Wis., 2006).

✒

CHAPTER 13

Stalin's Communism

CHAPTER OUTLINE
Communist Ideology • Communist Practice

BIOGRAPHICAL SKETCHES
Nikolai Ivanovich Bukharin, Communist Theoretician • Alexandra
Mikhaylovna Kollontai, "Red Rose of the Revolution"

Although the New Economic Policy (NEP) had yielded important practical results and had strong supporters, as pointed out in Chapter 9, by 1929 the stage was set for its termination. By the end of the decade, the Soviet Union had reached an impasse between Bolshevik ideology and the bourgeois practices that the NEP represented. Stalin had decided to go full-speed ahead to build communism and had begun his drive for absolute power, and the debate over the NEP became an important part of his campaign. Whether Stalin perverted Lenin's ideas and methods in constructing his dictatorship or was his worthy successor is still debated, but his rule embodied communism for the world from then on.

COMMUNIST IDEOLOGY

Unlike Italian Fascism, where practice preceded a coherent ideological statement, Soviet Communism claimed a long ideological pedigree and Lenin as Marx's successor.

Lenin's Concept of the Party
The Bolshevik Party's authoritarianism began with Lenin and culminated with Stalin. Lenin justified violence against the bourgeoisie and extended the principle to dissidents in 1921 when he put down internal party opposition and a mutiny of sailors at the Kronstadt naval base. Lenin contended that allowing the formation of factions within communism threatened party unity. He began with the

premise that, as the sole party of the working class, the Bolsheviks must educate the advance guard of the proletariat and organize the working masses. Consequently, Lenin attacked both the right and the left wings of Bolshevism, as Stalin would in the future.

Lenin criticized the right wing by contending that the revolutionary victory had deprived the unions of their primary task of defending the workers from capitalist exploitation. He denounced the leftist revolutionaries in *"Left Wing" Communism: An Infantile Disorder,* drafted in April 1920, because they objected to a centralized party structure. A truly revolutionary party delegated leadership to a few authoritative persons, he declared. The Bolsheviks had to be secure at the helm of the movement so it could destroy capitalism and attain recognition of the Soviet system as the revolutionary model for all countries. Lenin believed that allowing the formation of political currents in the party of the proletariat meant permitting backward groups of workers to cave in to the wiles of false Socialists who were planning to destroy communism.

Party congresses held in April 1920 and March 1921 debated these principles. With the defeat of capitalist intervention against the revolution (the Civil War), the Bolshevik Party had as its major tasks destroying the old social order, creating a new one, and building a Socialist state by means of an iron discipline. The party could not tolerate internal dissension; it could discuss policy, but then unanimity must follow because factions threatened unity.

Thus Lenin championed a single unified party in which minorities having different viewpoints would either conform or be silenced because party discipline, justified by the working class's superior interests, took precedence over freedom of expression. Lenin's concept of the party guided Communist Party organization and particularly inspired Stalin. (The older term *Bolshevik* gradually gave way to the more cosmopolitan *Communist* after the regime consolidated itself and began to export the revolution.) The Executive Committee of the Communist Party possessed the instruments to control central Soviet activities, and public authorities and party institutions absorbed state institutions. Within the Executive Committee, a political office (the Politburo) directed political affairs, but the party's command center was the Secretariat, the true decision-making organ of the Executive Committee and the Politburo. The Communist Party's combined political, economic, and social functions allowed it to impose its authority over every state institution and regulate the lives of its citizens. This centralized organization helped communism survive in Russia.

Josef Stalin headed the Workers' and Peasants' Inspection Commission, the party's most powerful control organism, and gradually accumulated other functions. As Stalin concentrated important tasks in his hands, his colleagues worried that he was gaining too much power. Lenin, however, did not act against Stalin and demurred only after he was too sick to have much influence.

Stalinism

Stalin's control of different party organs overwhelmed the strong tendencies toward collective leadership within early Bolshevism and allowed him to win the struggle for power by 1929. After Lenin's death on January 21, 1924, a committee that included Stalin succeeded him. Stalin presented himself as the dead leader's ideological successor in two works, *Foundations of Leninism* (1924) and *Problems of Leninism* (1926). In these books, Stalin defended Lenin's concept of party hegemony, condemning factions because they could not oppose an organization (the Communist Party) that personified the dictatorship of the proletariat and downplayed the possibility that party leaders might seize power with his argument that the Communist Party could guide the proletariat only by delegating the task of destroying world capitalism to some of its leaders.

Stalin's views set the stage for his absolute power and the internal purges of the 1930s, which he believed were nothing less than a necessary law of development for the prevention of party deviations. In sum, Stalin decreed the infallibility of the party, which had proved its worth by successfully making the revolution. He claimed for himself the right to liquidate all opposition because it endangered the social gains achieved by the working class.

Socialism in One Country

Stalin undoubtedly appears as a true Bolshevik, sincerely committed to implementing what he conceived as socialism; but his thinking also included a crucial international dimension. Concerned with the final victory of communism, Stalin believed that the capitalist countries would strike at the USSR when the opportunity arose. In the 1920s, he interpreted Russia's isolation as encirclement by the capitalist powers. He claimed that to defend the Communist revolution, Socialist encirclement had to replace capitalist encirclement. This concept meant that the nations surrounding the USSR must be transformed into Socialist countries, become Soviet allies, and dedicate their resources to protecting the Socialist fatherland, the USSR. Stalin viewed world revolution—spontaneous revolutions occurring in advanced capitalist countries because of industrialization—in neither traditional Marxist nor Leninist terms but in strictly territorial terms. Marx had argued that socialism grew out of increasing industrialization, and Lenin had expected that communism would quickly spread to the West. When successful Communist revolutions did not occur in the advanced Western countries, Soviet leaders concentrated on the need to defend communism in the USSR. Stalin hoped to do so by gaining control of neighboring countries. This view has produced the interpretation that Stalin viewed himself as both a true Bolshevik *and* as a classical Russian statesman: a National Bolshevik.

A consequence of this reasoning was the need to strengthen the USSR's power and influence. Russia had two important advantages in achieving this goal: The countries surrounding it were small and weak, and in the Western democracies, strong Communist parties favored close collaboration with the Socialist Fatherland. Stalin counted on Soviet diplomacy and the Third International's dominance of foreign Communist parties to exploit the differences among capitalist countries and to foster war among them. Such conflicts would exhaust capitalist nations and provide the USSR with opportunities for a revolutionary march into bordering areas. However, during the late 1920s and 1930s, Stalin had bungled events in Germany, and Hitler came to power. He then shifted his attitude toward France, encouraged the Popular Front, and sought a French alliance. These events demonstrated the flexibility on strategy that Stalin would demonstrate on numerous occasions in the future.

Agricultural Collectivization

Stalin's thesis had fundamental implications for Soviet domestic policy. Because Stalin assumed that war with the capitalist countries was unavoidable, the USSR had to expand its industrial capacity—vital for rearmament and the implementation of socialism; preparing for a major conflict with the capitalist powers required the creation of an immense, war-oriented heavy industry. This policy required the USSR's rapid transmutation from an importer of industrial products into a major world producer of heavy industrial goods. Without the country's transformation, both it and the revolution would be overwhelmed. This problem posed the urgent question of where the resources would come from to accomplish this ambitious goal. Because the USSR was a Communist country shunned by the capitalist industrial nations, it had to rely most heavily on its own assets.

At this point, Stalin, the Bolshevik, and Stalin, the Russian statesman, merged. He advocated rapid agricultural collectivization as a means of gathering wealth for the intensive industrialization effort he believed essential for the survival of communism, to guarantee grain deliveries at low prices, and to encourage the emigration of labor to the urban areas where industrialization would occur. Moreover, it made sense to combine the push for industrialization with a new offensive to implement socialism when Communist leaders decided to end the NEP that had represented a retreat for the Revolution. Already in the 1920s, Stalin had noted that merely encouraging the development of cooperatives in the countryside did not create socialism, and he favored their implantation with the help of peasant allies. When he referred to cooperatives, Stalin did not mean consumer or credit cooperatives favored by moderate Bolsheviks, but collectivization, which meant a radical departure from the NEP. Because the resistance of peasant landowners to collectivization would be tremendous, the state had to use force to implement it.

BIOGRAPHICAL SKETCHES

Nikolai Ivanovich Bukharin
Communist Theoretician

Probably the most attractive, humane, and flexible of the "Old Bolsheviks," Nikolai Bukharin was born in Moscow on October 9, 1888, the son of a schoolteacher. Bukharin entered political life early as an opponent of the tsarist regime. In 1906, still a university student, he joined the Russian Social Democratic Party's Bolshevik faction, rising to head the Moscow Bolshevik organization in 1908. In 1911 he left the country for the United States after being arrested for his political activity. Bukharin traveled to the West Coast; eventually, he settled in New York City, where he edited the revolutionary newspaper, *Novy Mir* in 1916. He established himself as a leading theoretician and returned to Europe to work on the party newspaper *Pravda* with Lenin. In August 1917, Bukharin was back in

Russia and later participated in the Bolshevik revolution. When Lenin advocated signing a separate peace with the Germans to end Russia's involvement in World War I, Bukharin disagreed and unsuccessfully sought to transform the conflict into a worldwide revolutionary war.

Before Stalin achieved absolute power, policy debates in the Bolshevik camp were common, without persons necessarily losing their influence or their lives because of their opposition to the ideas of other leaders. Although Lenin's line won out, Bukharin remained his good friend and a prominent member of the Bolshevik inner circle, holding important positions. He edited *Pravda* from 1918 until 1929 and *Bolshevik,* the party journal, between 1924 and 1929. Bukharin became a full member of the Politburo in 1924 and chair of the Communist International (Comintern) in 1926. During this period, he also published a number of major works, including *Economy of the Transitional Period* (1920), *The ABC of Communism* (1921), and *The Theory of Historical Materialism* (1921).

In the years following Lenin's death in 1924, a struggle occurred among the Bolsheviks for power that led to Stalin's supremacy. Because of the economic and social devastation caused by civil war and the attempt to impose communism in Russia, Lenin initiated the NEP. This policy allowed the economy to recover, but it delayed the implementation of communism. An ideological debate on whether to modify or end the NEP was part of the fight. Bukharin advocated gradual rather than rapid collectivization and industrialization, opposing Stalin, who favored the speedy accomplishment of both. The battle over this question and others ended in Stalin's triumph by 1929.

The end had begun for Bukharin. Accused of heading the "right deviation" faction, Bukharin lost his posts on the Politburo and the Central Committee and was expelled from the party. In 1934 he briefly edited another party newspaper, *Izvestia,* but was dismissed. Arrested in January 1937, Bukharin was a major victim in a show trial, known as the Trial of the Twenty-One, in March 1938. Accused of scheming to overthrow the state, Bukharin "confessed" and was shot on March 13, 1938.

The government also persecuted Bukharin's young wife Anna Larina. Arrested after her husband's trial, she spent twenty years in a Siberian labor camp but remained dedicated to her husband's memory. After her release, she worked to rehabilitate his reputation. She succeeded in 1988, when, under Mikhail Gorbachev, the Soviets sought to demonstrate that there was an alternate communism to Stalin's brand. The Soviets rehabilitated Bukharin and posthumously restored his party membership. In addition, the opening of Stalin's own archives revealed philosophical writings by Bukharin, poetry, and an autobiographical novel, *How It All Began,* published in 1994. Larina told her story and that of Bukharin in an award-winning 2001 documentary, *This I Cannot Forget.*

In 1926, Stalin declared: "Building socialism in the USSR means overcoming our own Soviet bourgeoisie by our forces in the course of a struggle." This struggle would occur primarily against the upper and middle strata of the peasantry, but it would transform the USSR into a world industrial power capable of confronting the capitalist countries, implement socialism, save the country, and create the premise for Soviet expansionism. By combining collectivization in agriculture with industrialization, Stalin linked Communist principles and economic development. He allied Lenin and Peter the Great.

COMMUNIST PRACTICE

The crisis of the NEP at the end of the 1920s provided Stalin with the opportunity to implement communism, industrialize the country, and increase his personal power. Stalin's alliance with Bukharin broke down in 1928 and he defeated Bukharin between February and April 1929, giving him control of the USSR.

Collectivization

Collectivization—the expropriation of peasants, the destruction of private property, and the creation of collective farms over which the state had complete control—set the stage for rapid industrialization. Collectivization had been encouraged earlier, but by 1928 collective farms had attracted only about 1 percent of the rural population. Most important, NEP had created a large reservoir of "middle" peasants who strongly resisted collectivization.

Given these facts, Stalin moved cautiously to create the political, psychological, and ideological preconditions for collectivization. Already in 1926 and 1927, Stalin exploited friction in foreign policy to argue that the USSR was in imminent threat of attack from the capitalists surrounding it. The next year witnessed the first show trial on a favorite theme: Russian counterrevolutionaries in league with foreign and counterrevolutionary capitalists in a conspiracy to wreck the Soviet economy. Then came the drastically reduced ability of state grain-purchasing agencies to purchase grain after the 1927–28 harvest at the desired prices. The government responded by closing the grain markets and a campaign of coercion—searches, confiscation of grain, and arrests—was followed by food rationing in February 1929. The peasants resisted, and disorders took place. The party moderates suggested resolving the conflict by offering higher prices, but Stalin argued that the needs of industrialization precluded any price increases, that the problem was not economic, and that the real issue was kulak opposition to the Soviet regime; the solution to this political opposition was a class war.

Given the importance of dogma in the Soviet context, Stalin justified his position from an ideological standpoint by recalling Lenin's description of the peasants as a vacillating class that would flock to collectivization when educated about its benefits and by concluding that peasant irresolution would end when the state demonstrated that only dire misfortune awaited them outside collectivization.

Stalin's collectivization campaign started in November 1929 with an article in the party newspaper *Pravda*. According to Stalin, Russian peasants had rushed to collectivization, opening a new historical chapter. If this accelerated collectivization continued, the USSR would become one of the world's largest grain producers. Combined with a five-year plan for industry, this development would rapidly produce a Socialist society. In fact, collectivization combined with swift industrialization would constitute a second revolution, from above.

Stalin's article depicted the USSR as being at a crossroads in the establishment of socialism, but it misrepresented reality. According to Stalin, collectivization had been so successful that the time for a final push had arrived. In reality, the state would achieve this aim by defining *kulak* (the supposedly well-off peasant) in such a manner that anyone would qualify and by treating the kulak in such a brutal fashion that no one would want to be considered one. Stalin's henchman and future foreign minister Vyacheslav Molotov put the matter succinctly: "We must deal the kulak such a blow that the middle peasant will snap to attention before us." By making an example of the kulak and his family of what would happen if anyone resisted, Stalin hoped to terrorize the peasants into accepting collectivization.

The subsequent development of the campaign seems to confirm this view. At the beginning the definition of *kulak* was ambiguous. The Communists applied the term to all who made the least objection to collectivization and proceeded to expropriate their property and to punish them. A commission that was charged with drawing up specific plans on how to collectivize the peasants originally suggested allowing the kulaks to join collectives and retain some small animals under certain restricted conditions, but Stalin overruled the idea. Stalin simply slated the kulaks for elimination as a class. Consequently, the state did not permit them access to collective farms under any circumstances, transferred ownership of their property to the collectives, and deported them and their families to distant areas under abominable conditions.

Besides socialism, the state aimed to achieve specific economic goals through confiscation and deportations. Slaughtering farm animals was a prime means of resisting collectivization, so harsh punishments and complete confiscation would prevent the killing of livestock and provide essential capital for the collectives. Expropriation also contributed to the enormous sums the USSR allocated to pay foreign technicians, attracted as a result of the lack of work in the West.

Stalin initiated the drive for collectivization because of his desire to institute Communism after the NEP had stalled the drive to do so, in his opinion, and to increase production. Collectivization became policy in 1929, and although many families were forced into collectives, resistance remained strong. This somewhat idyllic picture shows peasants having lunch together on a collective farm near Kiev in August 1936.

Furthermore, the five-year plan, which was adopted at the same time, mandated the building of large industrial plants. In order to protect the new factories from possible foreign invasion—in addition to industrializing different parts of the country—the state located them away from the western borders in undesirable areas. This wisdom of this policy was confirmed during World War II, but the sites attracted few volunteer workers and increased the demand for forced labor.

By the beginning of 1930, about half the USSR's families had been forced into collectives, which were required to hand over specific amounts of crops to the state (about 40 percent) and to accept low payments that had to be split among the members according to the work they did. Resistance became widespread. In January 1930, the Soviet secret police reported 402 mass demonstrations of peasants against collectivization and dekulakization and 1,048 in February and 6,528 in March. These uprisings caused agricultural production to nosedive and induced Stalin to backtrack. In March Stalin made some concessions to the peasants, such as allowing them to have individual garden plots. According to Stalin, the Communists implemented these changes because they were "Dizzy from Success," as expressed in the famous title of one of his articles. This pause in collectivization reduced the number of revolts, but the secret police noted that 2.5 million peasants participated in 14,000 revolts during the year. The peasants demanded that their property and that of the kulaks be restored, that churches be reopened, that deportees be allowed to return home, and even that the Bolsheviks give up power. The ones who suffered the most in these battles with the state were the women, whom the peasants sent ahead in the front lines in the vain hope of moderating the reaction of the police.

Having come so far, however, Stalin had little choice but to press ahead with his campaign after a brief interlude. The deportation of large numbers of peasants to remote regions where new factories were being built—and to other inhospitable areas with important raw materials—provided a large labor reserve. These unfortunate people did the most strenuous physical work at subsistence wages under police supervision, making a major contribution to the rapid industrialization of the Soviet Union. Besides peasants who served as unskilled labor, the government also arrested engineers and technicians who had been educated before the revolution, tried them, and sentenced them to work in the camps. The inmate population swelled from an estimated 30,000 in 1928 to approximately 2 million in 1931 and had to be organized under a separate Chief Administration of Corrective Labor Camps (GULAG), grippingly described by writer Alexander Solzhenitsyn. The inmates built roads, canals, and railroads and mined coal, gold, and other essential raw materials. Because prisoners had their sentences prolonged upon completion or otherwise remained within the camps' orbits, the camps were a means of systematizing vast amounts of slave labor. Combined with the government's imposition of an internal passport system, the arrangement was a Soviet version of serfdom that peasants called the "second serfdom."

Estimates of the number of people who were displaced during collectivization run to about 7 million, with half them being deported to labor camps or exile colonies in Siberia and other inhospitable areas. In the winter of 1932–33, the confusion and disruption of dekulakization and forced collectivization

This photograph shows the dark side of collectivization. Stalin ordered the expropriation of the "wealthy" peasants, the Kulaks, and their forcible integration into the collectives. A massive government campaign murdered or put them into forced labor camps after they resisted and hid their meager possessions. Here members of the Communist Youth are digging up bags of grain that Kulaks hid in a cemetery near Odessa.

precipitated a widespread famine, particularly in the grain-producing regions, such as the Ukraine, where estimates run to 3 million deaths in 1933. The peasants were convinced that the government caused the famine because they resisted collectivization, but from the government's viewpoint, the operation succeeded. By 1937, 93 percent of the households had been collectivized, the state had gained control over grain production and distribution, and a steady, low-cost supply of grain to industrial workers was assured.

Collectivization was not a spontaneous movement but a party and police-directed operation, with the cooperation of city dwellers, against rural Russia. Despite its efforts, the state failed to enlist substantial support from poor peasants, so shocked by the brutality that many did not participate in the expropriations.

The Five-Year Plan and the Personality Cult

The five-year plan to convert the USSR from an agricultural into a great industrial power was part and parcel of the collectivization and socialization effort. Formally adopted in April 1929, the plan called for an annual increase in industrial output of 20 percent. Stalin duly proclaimed the great success of the five-year plan in four years and implemented others. Indeed, if one looks at the bottom line, the USSR created industries that had hardly existed before, acquiring a substantial capacity to produce automobiles, aircraft, tractors and other agricultural machinery, textiles, and iron. It vaulted from a trailing to a leading position in coal and petroleum production. Total national output attributable to industry rose from 48 percent to 70 percent of the total between 1928 and 1932. This swift buildup of Soviet heavy industry permitted the doubling of the Soviet armed forces in less than ten years and made the USSR better able to resist Nazi Germany in 1941. Combined with the results of later five-year plans, the USSR increased its industrial production up to six times and eventually became the world's second-largest industrial power, behind the United States. At a time when the depression in the West decreased production and caused massive unemployment, the Soviet Union increased its industrial output and imported labor.

When observed closely, however, the five-year plan had wide implications beyond the numbers that are cited. Constant shifts in the production goals of heavy industry caused disruption and inefficiency in supplies and the production of materials necessary to meet those aims. Western economists have maintained that the Soviets could have accomplished similar impressive results without the millions of deaths or labor camps. Nor can it be argued that collectivization and the five-year plan furthered socialism, even according to Stalin's doubtful definition. Despite regimentation of the peasants in collective farms, by the end of the 1930s, Soviet society found itself more stratified than before, and with a depressed standard of living. Most of the population was overworked and hungry most of the time. Fifteen million persons lacked shelter. Peasants could be shot if they stole even insignificant amounts of grain from the collectives to help feed their children. The starving children of deported kulaks roamed the villages, with peasants afraid or unable to help them and with the state exploiting them as extra-cheap labor. At the same time, functionaries received important privileges from the government that permitted them to live relatively comfortably and distinguished them from ordinary people, with higher-level functionaries enjoying greater privileges.

This was only one area in which Socialist egalitarianism suffered a setback. Stalin reestablished ranks throughout Soviet society, replacing persons who had been purged and establishing a new Soviet citizenry that was completely committed to him. Stalin publicly glorified workers who produced more than their quotas or set new records by intensifying their pay differentials and by officially recognizing workers, such as Alexei Stakhanov, a coal miner who exceeded his quota by 1,400 percent. Stakhanov's example led to contests in which workers tried to outperform their quotas, which led to higher quotas that they resented. Stalin reestablished an aristocracy of merit through various orders—the Order of Lenin for special merit in Socialist construction, the Order of the Red Star for distinction in the defense sector, and the Red Banner of Labor. He reinstated officer ranks and insignia in the armed forces and uniforms for schoolchildren. The rewards included special privileges, such as lower rents, special consideration for the children of awardees in admission to schools, and free transportation on streetcars. Stalin promoted unknowns and young people and insisted on opening up careers to nonparty members on a par with party loyalists. The regime supported higher education to graduate technicians for industrialization, tripling the number of students and doubling those of working-class origins. In extending opportunities to all levels

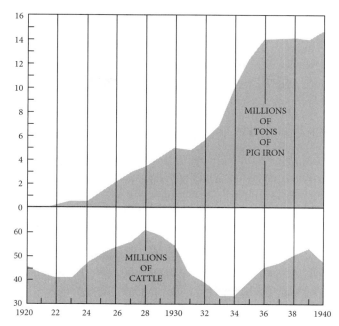

This chart illustrates how agriculture was made to serve the interests of industrialization during the Communist regime. The revolution, disorganization, and the civil war explain why Russia produced almost no pig iron in 1920. By the end of the decade, production had risen to pre-1914 levels, while the number of cattle grew significantly under the NEP. During collectivization, this number fell disastrously at the same time that pig iron production grew tremendously. By 1940, Russia produced more pig iron than Germany, Britain, or France. By the same year, however, numbers of cattle had risen only to the level of 1920.

This photograph illustrates the tremendous effort the USSR made during the Five-Year Plan to catch up to the West. Industrial production and unquestioning loyalty to Stalin combined with the constant threat of an attack from the capitalist world, which Stalin inflated, produced the brutal suppression of all possible enemies. They were the major instruments the Soviet dictator used to maintain his power. This is a picture of a Soviet metal plant in 1930.

of Soviet society, Stalin returned to the notion of a service nobility that had existed in prerevolutionary Russia.

Stalin's modifications made the state supreme. The state grew enormously by absorbing private property, building monumental new projects, multiplying central planning organs, and increasing centralization. High state functionaries constituted a new Soviet elite.

A Revolution in Culture

Rounding out these developments, a cultural revolution purged intellectuals and attacked historical figures whom Stalin did not believe fit in with his current thinking in an area—no matter how indirectly. Historical interpretation depended on what Stalin was thinking at the moment, and he took full advantage of cultural trends and authors for his own benefit. In the late 1920s and early 1930s, he favored leftist cultural movements, as represented by the Russian Association of Proletarian Writers, because he wanted to combat the right. In 1932, he dissolved the organization when his policy changed and set up a new writers' union that was charged with advocating the Soviet cause. In 1931, Maxim Gorky, Russia's greatest living writer, returned to live in Russia. Stalin celebrated him but, when the purges began, put him under virtual house arrest to prevent him from speaking out. When Gorky died in June 1936, rumors swirled that Stalin had him killed. From the mid-1930s, Soviet culture became decidedly conservative, with the state imposing Socialist realism in art, promoting the revival of traditional Russian folk culture, and slowing the campaign against religion. Stalin's supporters oversaw the rewriting of Bolshevik history to glorify his role, Cossacks sang traditional melodies for him in theaters, and the state printed his books in millions of copies.

The Bolshevik revolution had held out the promise of liberation for women, an ideal that faded under Stalin's rule. Few women were among the "new men" that Stalin groomed to replace the previous generation of leaders. Ideas of sexual freedom and free love, best represented by Alexandra Kollontai, evaporated. Communist theory held that the bourgeois family subjugated women, so in theory this family would disappear and the state would raise children, thus liberating women. In practice, it proved impossible to remove children from the family. Despite the Bolshevik conception of marriage as confining and bourgeois, a 1920s survey indicated that more than 90 percent of women believed in love and marriage instead of free sex, as did more than 80 percent of men. The disruptions and hardships caused by the revolution made both men and women less interested in free love and longing for traditional relationships.

This attitude was probably a reaction to the freedom in sexual matters that followed the revolution, when young Communists avoided even mentioning the word *love,* when marriage and family were considered restrictive, and collective love was thought of as revolutionary. However, this attitude frequently meant leaving women alone to raise children because the men left for other partners as soon as the women became pregnant and looked upon by men as finished. In short, men looked upon sex as a natural urge that women should fulfill.

BIOGRAPHICAL SKETCHES

Alexandra Mikhaylovna Kollontai
"Red Rose of the Revolution"

Born the daughter of a tsarist general, probably in April 1872, Alexandra Kollontai became widely known for her feminism and her endorsement of the widest possible sexual experiences for women. She participated in the Bolshevik Revolution with Lenin, became the first Soviet woman minister, and died a distinguished diplomat.

Rebellious and drawn to politics during her early teens, Alexandra Mikhaylovna Donontovich married her cousin at age 16, but the couple soon separated. She attended the University of Zurich, where she studied political science. Already attracted to socialism, on her return to Russia she actively participated in the movement, organizing workers and women. In 1908, the government exiled her for criticizing its Finnish policies. Abroad she continued her Socialist activities in several countries, leading strikes in Paris, organizing coal miners in Belgium, lecturing in Bologna, participating in political fights in Finland, and writing books on economic and social issues. In Switzerland she plotted with other Russian revolutionaries to overthrow their government. She also became a leading feminist who was concerned with society's proper recognition of motherhood.

When World War I broke out, she traveled extensively throughout Europe working for peace. In 1916, she visited eighty-one cities in the United States and lectured on socialism and pacifism. With the fall of the tsar in 1917, she returned to Russia, where the Kerensky government imprisoned her. Released, she won election to the Bolshevik Central Committee. On November 10, 1917, with her appointment as commissar (minister) of welfare, she became the first woman to hold cabinet rank. During her tenure, which ended on March 24, 1918, she helped write much of the legislation that regulated the status of women.

A well-known advocate of free love and the author of several famous books on the relationship between the sexes, Kollontai became the subject of many anecdotes. According to one of them, Kollontai had a passionate affair with a Bolshevik naval hero, during which they forgot about the revolution and went off to the Crimea. The Central Committee judged this action harshly, and its members demanded their execution. Lenin rose to speak and commented that death would be too good for them. He presented a motion condemning the lovers to faithfulness to each other for five years. The Central Committee, not known for its sense of humor, broke into laughter and dropped the matter, but Kollontai held this incident against Lenin well into the future.

In late 1922, Kollontai embarked on a distinguished diplomatic career. Named plenipotentiary representative to Norway in 1923, she became minister to that country when it recognized the Soviet Union in 1924. The appointment made her the world's first accredited woman envoy and aroused strong enthusiasm among women. Two years later, she became ambassador to Mexico, but the Americans refused to let her pass through the United States because they considered her a revolutionary. The Mexicans gossiped about her past loves and her supposedly fabulous jewelry collection. Kollontai returned to the more hospitable Norway after she suffered incidents of official disrespect. In 1930, she became minister to

continued

continued

Sweden, a country that had imprisoned her sixteen years earlier, with the Swedes graciously revoking the order exiling her. In 1943, she became Soviet ambassador to that country until she retired because of ill health two years later. During her tenure in Sweden, she conducted negotiations with the Finns that resulted in the end of the Russo-Finnish war in 1940. Rumor had it that she had negotiated to end the conflict between Russia and Nazi Germany, but she denied the allegation. Diplomats considered her one of the most brilliant practitioners of their profession and credited her with being "the diplomatic star of the Bolshevik world."

Alexandra Kollontai died on March 9, 1952.

Concerning divorce, a major demand of European leftists, a December 1917 decree permitted dissolution of the marriage bond for incompatibility if only one spouse requested it from the court—making Soviet Russia the first country to do so. The Bolsheviks also adopted advanced legislation on abortion; although they did not initially legalize it, they attempted to remedy the dangerous conditions under which abortions were performed. In 1920, legislation provided free abortions on demand if done by doctors in hospitals.

Stalin reversed this relative freedom in social relationships. In 1936, the government banned abortion as mentally and physically harmful to women and took measures to strengthen family life, including making divorce more difficult. A switch occurred from sexual freedom to a conservative policy with the banning of contraception and sex education. Women could not get safe abortions and resorted to illegal ones at the risk of their lives. Kollantai had already fallen out with the revolution, and Stalin had the adherents of her movement executed, although he found it inconvenient to eliminate Kollantai herself.

Leninist Antecedents

With regard to the initially tolerant cultural policy of the Bolshevik revolution, already under Lenin Bolshevik ideology favored state domination of cultural life. Because Marxists considered culture a manifestation of economics in which art reflected the social status of the artist, they had assumed that destruction of the bourgeoisie would produce revolutionary changes in culture. But this assumption raised the question of exactly how much freedom an artist should have, given the Bolshevik view that with the changes in property relations, mechanized collectivism would replace individualism. Communist theory thus eventually forced intellectuals to work within the guidelines established by the new ruling class and placed political constraints on them that suffocated the freedom that characterized the revolution's early years.

Leading this development, Lenin established the Commissariat of Enlightenment (*Narkompros*) that with its affiliated Proletarian Cultural (*Proletkult*) movement, blanketed the Soviet countryside with its local organizations. Despite his respect for earlier culture, Lenin feared that the bourgeoisie could use its cultural advantages against the workers and considered culture a propaganda weapon to be used against the bourgeoisie. His relatively relaxed Narkompros commissar, Anatoli Lunarcharskii, agreed and implemented the censorship that Lenin advocated. The artistic world quickly turned against the Bolsheviks, who were supported by novelist Maxim Gorky and the Russian Futurists and supported by party hacks. The Bolsheviks liquidated the daily and periodical press and assumed control of book publishing. In June 1922, a newly established cultural censorship office began bringing all the arts under its wing and arresting and exiling intellectuals it considered disgruntled or unorthodox. The regime also banned the importation of suspect foreign literature and newspapers and intensified its control of the schools and universities.

The Communists tried to win support through extensive use of the Agit-prop Theater. Actors traveled to the smallest towns and produced plays out of trains, streetcars, and trucks. The plays dealt with simplistic themes and featured stereotyped characters representing pure good or pure evil, as determined by their social status, their relationship with the regime, and their place in the Soviet ideological scheme. The audiences emotionally expressed their hatred for their enemies, frequently becoming uncontrollable.

As in Fascist Italy, the regime attempted to change language usage. Russians greeted each other as Comrade, avoided discredited words, invented euphemisms to signify arrest or execution, and showed a penchant for acronyms. As in other totalitarian countries, they used the schools to indoctrinate the young and encouraged students to rebel against the politically unreliable faculty. The government created youth organizations, such as the Pioneers, which included children younger than fifteen who could graduate into the Union of Communist Youth (*Komsomol*), which had a more overtly political and propagandistic function than did the Pioneers. Because ideology took precedence in the educational field, however, the Soviets did not achieve their goal of bringing universal literacy and education to Russia. Communist ideas on eliminating the family and the dislocation of Russian society contributed to the millions of homeless children who gathered in gangs and roamed the country rather than going to school. By the end of the 1920s, the literacy rate did not rise appreciably compared with tsarism's last years. In higher education, Soviet policy on affording the poor an equal opportunity changed because the need for more engineers and technicians for industrialization favored the heirs of the middle class; the number of women attending universities dropped as well, and ideology conditioned science.

Stalinism and Science

Stalin's word reigned in science as well as society at a time when science made spectacular advances. Hitler divided science into "Jewish" and "German," while Stalin considered it either "capitalist" or "proletarian." The renowned Russian physicist George Gamow wrote: "It became a crime for Russian scientists to 'fraternize' with scientists of the capitalistic countries, and those Russian scientists who were going abroad were supposed to learn the 'secrets' of capitalistic science without revealing the 'secrets' of proletarian science."

In his memoirs, Gamow tells how the Physico-Mathematical Institute of the Soviet Academy of Sciences set up a "jury of machine shop stewards" to judge physicists guilty of defending Einstein's relativity theory, condemning them to harsh punishments. Eventually the state prohibited scientists from traveling abroad, depriving them of the contact that is the lifeblood of scientific progress. It prevented the talented physicist Peter Kapitza from returning to Cambridge, where he had worked, and Russian scientists who were lucky enough to go abroad—including Gamow himself—refused to return.

In the most notorious case of state interference in science, Stalin backed Trofim Lysenko, who championed an early nineteenth-century theory of genetics regarding the inheritance of acquired traits because it allowed for the biological inheritance of the social alterations made by the Communist regime. Lysenko's opponents lost their positions, were jailed, or disappeared forever. Russian genetics did not recover until the 1960s.

The Purges

There was criticism against Stalin's policies toward high-level Communists, because of the old Bolshevik political culture based on collective leadership, and even attempts to sabotage them. In August 1932, a Moscow Communist official drafted an appeal condemning Stalin's collectivization and industrial policies and accusing him of setting up a dictatorship. The discord even affected Stalin's immediate family as his wife turned against him; in November, she reportedly killed herself, but there still is strong suspicion that Stalin shot her.

On December 2, 1934 party leader Sergei M. Kirov was assassinated. Stalin used the murder as a pretext to initiate a great wave of terror and to purge his own movement in a successful attempt to consolidate his power. There is strong evidence that Stalin himself was behind the assassination. This picture shows Stalin (on the right) and other high Communist officials carrying Kirov's bier to the Kremlin wall for internment.

The disfavor swirling around him convinced Stalin that a vast conspiracy against him existed. Historians have argued that he considered himself a hero of the revolution and a political genius and could not understand how others could believe that he had made serious mistakes. Considering himself Lenin's legitimate successor, he especially resented his unpopularity among the prestigious Old Bolsheviks with whom he had made the October Revolution in 1917. When the secret police confirmed the objections to his policies, Stalin acted slowly but deliberately and in great depth.

First, he justified the power of the state in contrast to Marxist theory that predicted that the state would wither away. In January 1933, he asserted that the revolutionary state could not disappear until it had obliterated the dying classes. He affirmed that counterrevolutionaries had infiltrated the Communist Party, which now had to be purged, and entrusted the purge to a specially created commission that he controlled, while gaining the loyalty of the police, increasing the privileges of those who supported him, and reducing the economic pressure on the civilian population in order to gain popularity. On December 2, 1934, the murder of Sergei M. Kirov, a popular rival of Stalin, touched off five years of purges. In 1956, Nikita Khrushchev indicated that Stalin and his secret police (NKVD) trumped up the conspiracy and had Kirov eliminated.

The terror proceeded in waves. Between January 1935 and the summer of 1936, a quiet terror lopped off the bottom rungs of the Soviet Communist Party with little publicity. In all regions of the USSR, black NKVD cars, called ravens and carrying secret police operatives, prowled the night, and Soviet citizens who considered themselves possibly vulnerable dared not sleep between 11:00 P.M. and 2:00 A.M., when the NKVD usually made its arrests. Arrests, exile, and banishment to labor camps followed expulsion from the organization. From May to December 1935, the party expelled an estimated 190,000 members as spies or suspected spies. Stalin exploited this phase of the purges to tighten his control of the secret police and to claim that a vast plot, directed by Trotsky and the Fascists, aimed to overthrow him and destroy the revolution. A Soviet agent assassinated Trotsky, who was in exile in Mexico. Because Stalin's goal was to overthrow the Bolshevik political culture that impeded his control of the country, he required his former comrades to "confess" publicly to their misdeeds. The police obtained these confessions through mental torture, promises of release, and threats against the defendants' families. In mid-1936, the show trials and executions of the Old Bolsheviks began with those of leftists Grigori Zinoviev and Lev Kamenev. Neither the left nor the right wings were safe, and the purges culminated in 1938 with the trial and execution of Bukharin and twenty others.

Along with the elimination of the Old Bolsheviks, Stalin's purge decimated the Red Army's command structure. Although Stalin played up the imminence of a conflict for internal ideological reasons and probably did not foresee a war with Hitler soon, the real reasons for the military purges remain obscure. Documents released after the fall of communism show that Stalin counted on a conflict between the capitalist powers that would exhaust them, after which the Soviets could expand westward. In 1939, Stalin reached an accommodation with Hitler that encouraged the Germans to begin a war with the Western powers. Stalin's calculation proved erroneous because, instead of a long debilitating struggle, the Germans quickly defeated France in 1940, but it helps explain why he did not worry about the immediate implications of weakening the Red Army. However, domestic reasons also help explain Stalin's actions. Mikhail Tukhachevsky, civil war hero and first-class military thinker, along with other army commanders, had served under Trotsky, were too independent and had protested against collectivization. Stalin claimed to see a German-inspired Trotskyist plot against him in the army and tried about a thousand high officers. The purge of the army command weakened the capacity of the armed forces to fight, as demonstrated in the war against Finland in 1939 and 1940, and encouraged Hitler to attack the Soviet Union in 1941. The army's defeat removed the last obstacle to Stalin's establishment of a totalitarian regime. It is estimated that between 1937 and 1938, the Great Purge resulted in the arrest of between 4.5 to 5.5 million. Of these, 800,000 to 900,000 were executed, and the rest ended up in slave labor camps with an average life expectancy of six months.

Stalin's Triumph

By the end of the 1930s, Stalin had destroyed Bolshevik political culture, established his personal rule, collectivized agriculture, and industrialized the country. He had replaced the old generation of leaders with a new one formed under the USSR, too young to remember prerevolutionary times, and that he had promoted and schooled. Unlike the situation in capitalist countries, no one lacked employment, and youngsters rapidly advanced to high-level jobs at a fast pace. However, Stalin also destroyed the ability of this new generation to build on the experience of the old. He communized and industrialized the USSR but failed to modernize it. By instilling in the Soviet population the habit of blindly obeying a highly centralized and rigid party and state structure, he ensured the later demise of Soviet communism.

Bibliographical Essay

Many works have been written on the events described in this chapter, and the reader will have little trouble finding sources. Some of the books cited in Chapter 9 and biographies of Stalin include discussions of the events considered here. Sheila Fitzpatrick, *The Russian Revolution* (New York, 2008), asks when the Russian Revolution ended and, in the process, provides an excellent short history of the entire event. For an examination of the debates on Stalin's rule, see Chris Ward, ed., *Stalin's Russia*, 2d ed. (New York, 1999). Robert C. Tucker, *Stalin in Power: The Revolution From Above 1928–1941* (New York, 1990), is one of the best books on the period, replete with sources and bibliography; the quote on building socialism in the USSR is on p. 58, and Molotov's statement on the kulaks is cited on p. 139. Robert Service's *Stalin: A Biography* (Cambridge, Mass., 2005) gives a more complex vision of the man and his polices than is usually the case. Simon Sebag Montefiore, *Stalin: The Court of the Red Tsar* (New York, 2004), describes the atmosphere and people surrounding him. Another interesting biography that can be profitably consulted is Dmitri Volkogonov, *Stalin: Triumph and Tragedy* (New York, 1991). Statistics of such enormous events are disputed but may be found in Tucker and in the works cited later. Richard Pipes's *Russia Under the Bolshevik Regime* (New York, 1993) ends earlier but is very good on Soviet society. Two books take a close look at everyday life in Stalin's USSR: Orlando Figes, *The Whisperers* (New York, 2007), and Sheila Fitzpatrick, *Everyday Stalinism (New York, 1999)*. On Soviet women, see Feiga Blekher, ed., *The Soviet Woman in the Family and in Society* (New York, 1979), which is a good collection of essays on the topic; the information about women who had children being considered finished is on p. 29. For a wider consideration of Russian women up to 1930, see Richard Stites, *The Women's Liberation Movement in Russia: Feminism, Nihilism, and Bolshevism, 1860–1930* (Princeton, N.J., 1978).

Alex Nove, *The Stalin Phenomenon* (London, 1993), emphasizes Stalin's achievements. Chris Ward, ed., *The Stalinist Dictatorship* (New York, 1998), looks at Stalinism from three different perspectives. Steven F. Cohen published an excellent biography of Stalin's most important rival of the period, already cited, *Bukharin and the Bolshevik Revolution* (New York, 1973).

R. W. Davies is best on the early period of collectivization, *The Socialist Offensive* (London, 1980), previously cited. Robert Conquest, *The Harvest of Sorrow: Soviet Collectivization and the Terror-Famine* (New York, 1986), graphically describes the terror of collectivization. Roberta Thompson Manning reexamines the causes that led to collectivization in *The Rise and Fall of "the Extraordinary Measures," January–June 1928* (Pittsburgh, 2001). Lynne Viola, *Peasant Rebels Under Stalin* (New York, 1999), discusses the peasants' resistance to collectivization, while Sheila Fitzpatrick describes the postcollectivization village in *Stalin's Peasants: Resistance and Survival in the Russian Village after Collectivization* (New York, 1994). The plight of the peasants during the period is also examined by Lynne Viola et al., *The War Against the Peasantry, 1927–1930* (New Haven, Conn., 2005). The Ukrainian famine is the focus of Andrea Graziosi's *Stalinism, Collectivization and the Great Famine* (Cambridge, Mass., 2009) and *Causes of the Holodomor*, by Frederic P. Miller et al., (n.p., 2009). Analyses of industrialization may be found in Donald Filtzer, *Soviet Workers and Stalinist Industrialization: The Formation of Modern Soviet Production Relations, 1928–1941* (London, 1986); R. W. Davies, Mark Harrison, and S. G. Wheatcroft, eds., *The Economic Transformation of the Soviet Union* (Cambridge, UK, 1994); and William G. Rosenberg, *Social Dimensions of Soviet Industrialization* (Bloomington, Ind., 1993). See also Hiroaki Kuromiya, *Stalin's Industrial Revolution: Politics and Workers, 1928–1932* (New York, 1988), and Michael Reiman, *The Birth of Stalinism: The U.S.S.R. on the Eve of the "Second Revolution"* (London, 1987). O. V. Khlevniuk gives the history of an essential institution in this and later periods of Soviet history: *The History of the Gulag: From Collectivization to the Great Terror* (New Haven, Conn., 2004).

For culture, consult the relevant chapters in Richard Pipes, *Russia Under the Bolshevik Regime* (New York, 1993). Richard Stites, *Russian Popular Culture: Entertainment and Society Since 1900* (Cambridge, UK, 1992), presents an introduction to Soviet entertainment and popular culture. Sheila Fitzpatrick analyzes cultural domination by the state in *The Commissariat of Enlightenment* (Cambridge, UK, 1970) and also published *The Cultural Front* (New York, 1992). Robert C. Tucker's *Stalin in Power: The Revolution from Above 1922–1941* (New York, 1990), previously cited, has some good insights on culture. George Gamow, *My World Line: An Informal Autobiography* (New York, 1970), is an autobiographical account centering primarily on his years in his native Russia; the excerpt regarding capitalistic and proletarian science is on p. 93.

Good works on the terror and the debate on its effects are Robert Conquest, *The Great Terror: A Reassessment* (London, 1990), and J. Arch Getty and Roberta Manning, *Stalinist Terror: New Perspectives* (Cambridge, UK, 1993). Anne Applebaum, author of *Gulag: A History* (New York, 2003), discusses the origins and development of the Soviet camps and concludes that they were an organic component of Soviet Communism. Hiroaki Kuromiya, *The Voices of the Dead: Stalin's Great Terror in the 1930s* (New Haven, Conn., 2007), tries to give faces to all the categories of victims and describes how they were arrested and died. Martin Amis, *Koba the Dread: Laughter and the Twenty Million* (New York, 2002), compares the Soviet camps to the Nazi ones.

CHAPTER 14

✦

The Nazi Assault on Weimar

CHAPTER OUTLINE
Weimar's Crumbling Support • Ascent of the Nazi Party • The Collapse of
Weimar • Installing the Dictatorship

BIOGRAPHICAL SKETCHES
Adolf Hitler, Down and Out in Vienna • Franz von Papen, Politico

In Germany, old mentalities, beliefs, and resentments remained strong despite
the change of political form from Empire to Liberal Republic. Bitterness pervaded the bureaucracy, industry, farmers, the bourgeoisie, and, most important,
the German people, who never fully accepted the Weimar Republic despite its
achievement of political stability and a measure of economic success between 1925
and 1929. As in 1919, they condemned Weimar for surrendering to the Allies,
accepting the Versailles treaty, and the hyperinflation.

WEIMAR'S CRUMBLING SUPPORT

The Great Depression facilitated the growth of extremist parties and paved the
way for Adolf Hitler and the Nazis.

The Radicalization of Agriculture and Big Business
The slump intensified the crisis of German agriculture that had been evident
since the 1920s. The Weimar government signed agreements with the new East
European countries in order to encourage industrial exports, and the country
paid the price by allowing the importation of cheap agricultural goods that caused
German farm prices to drop precipitously. With the depression, the agricultural
crisis merged with the economic slump, to which German farmers responded by
accentuating their rightist tendencies. The agricultural associations supported

radical organizations, such as the Nazis; demanded governmental relief; and advocated for preferential tariffs, quotas, and autarky. The Junkers, large landholders in the eastern part of the country who were hostile to Weimar, increased their political influence and successfully defended subsidies for big Prussian landowners (the *Osthilfe*).

The large industrialists also intensified their hostility to the republic during the depression. Big business detested everything Weimar stood for: social welfare policies, governmental intervention in labor-management affairs, and democratic politics. During the postwar period, the industrialists had greatly increased their concentration of wealth, making the opposition of business to the government more effective. When the government attempted to implement social measures to confront the depression, the industrialists insisted on cost-cutting procedures, such as reducing unemployment insurance. This fierce resistance presented the government with three unpalatable alternatives: replenish the unemployment fund from other governmental programs, raise taxes, or reduce payments to workers.

President Paul von Hindenburg, a stout Junker supporter, blocked the switching of funds from the *Osthilfe*, while the people vigorously opposed new taxes. Borrowing became harder because American bankers refused new loans unless the government balanced the budget. These circumstances forced Chancellor Mueller's coalition cabinet to reduce unemployment subsidies, which alienated the unions. In March 1930, the unions forced his resignation, an event that paralyzed parliamentary government and set the scene for Hitler's rise to power.

The Unemployed and the Welfare System

Besides increasing the opposition of the moneyed interests, the depression sapped popular support for the republic. Weimar's welfare organization and its humiliation of unemployed workers who were living in precarious conditions help explain this development.

To receive benefits, unemployed workers had to show up at the labor exchanges once a week. To ensure that workers would be available in case work materialized, workers could never come on the same day of the week or at the same hour as previous visits to collect their benefits. This process shamed and outraged desperate people and ensured that they could not organize their already disrupted lives. Unemployed workers spent long hours in overcrowded offices dealing with overburdened, irritable clerks. Tension, fights, demonstrations, arrests, beatings, and killings resulted. In one instance, a police officer told a civilian to move along. When he responded "Why, of course," the enraged officer asked what he meant by "of course," threw him into the paddy wagon, and took him to the police station where the police beat him up. Writer Christopher Isherwood summed up the general situation in Berlin: "Hate exploded suddenly, without warning, out of nowhere; at street-corners, in restaurants, cinemas, dance-halls, swimming baths; at midnight; after breakfast, in the middle of the afternoon."

Both Communist and Nazi political agitators converted exasperated workers into street fighters, but the Nazis excelled. While Communist ideology saw the middle class as "proletarianized" by the depression, the Nazis blamed the Versailles settlement, Jews, and Weimar traitors for their problems and gained a greater following among people who did not see themselves as losing social status.

ASCENT OF THE NAZI PARTY

The desperate circumstances of depression Germany and the declining support for the Weimar Republic translated into greater electoral support for extremist parties, especially the Nazis, with their simplistic explanations, fierce nationalism, charismatic leader, previous prediction of economic collapse, and clear remedies.

Hitler and the Nazis

The Nazi Party originated as the Munich-based German Workers' Party (DAP), founded by political unknown Anton Drexler. The organization glorified German workers, advocated their elevation to the middle class while favoring employers who did not abuse their privileged position, and featured strong anti-Semitism. In 1919, the DAP came to the army's attention, and the army dispatched one of its operatives, Adolf Hitler, to spy on it. Hitler converted to its ideas, left the army, and joined the organization.

Born in Braunau am Inn (near Linz), Austria, on April 20, 1889, Adolf Hitler was a lonely youth who had failed in his dream of becoming an artist. Poor but not destitute, he spent several years in Vienna imbibing nationalistic and anti-Semitic ideas, in addition to a distorted racial outlook based on pamphlets purporting to explain Darwinian ideas and to apply them to society. By the time he left for Munich, Germany, he had made no mark in Austria. When World War I broke out, he joined the German army, served with distinction, and was promoted to corporal. In 1918, he suffered temporary blindness by gas that is sometimes attributed to hysteria. He had a revelation that he would save Germany: "When I was confined to bed, the idea came to me that I would liberate Germany, that I would make it great. I knew immediately that it would be realized." Hitler felt that he was under divine protection: one day, while in the trenches eating his rations, a voice told him to move away. A few seconds later, a stray shell killed the group with whom he had been eating. Throughout his career Hitler never wavered in his faith that God guided him.

Hitler felt fulfilled in the army and accepted the assignment to investigate the DAP after the conflict. After he joined the party, he emerged from his former insignificance by exhibiting a great talent for oratory and bringing in funds through his fiery speeches and his ability to charm bourgeois observers, including the daughters of wealthy families. At his rallies, he sent speakers to warm up the audience, had a band play military marches, and strode in decisively at the proper psychological moment to the platform through columns of uniformed supporters looking neither to the right nor to the left but straight ahead. His speeches began haltingly as he sized up the audience. Then he heated up to the point that "every one of his words comes out charged with a powerful current of energy."

BIOGRAPHICAL SKETCHES

Adolf Hitler
Down and Out in Vienna

The history of the young Adolf Hitler gives no idea of his future career. Hitler's customs inspector father was restless and hot-tempered and moved several times before settling down in Leonding, a village outside Linz, Austria, in November 1898. Adolf attended the local elementary school, where he was an undistinguished student. He enjoyed reading stories of the American West written by popular author Karl May and recalled them later in life. In September 1900, he entered a secondary school that emphasized scientific over humanistic studies. He repeated the first year and frequently retook exams. His dream of becoming a great artist led to fights with his father, who wanted him to work at a steady job in the civil service.

Hitler's father died in January 1903. After 1905 Adolf convinced his doting mother that he should not go on to a technical school, and during the next two years, he led a comfortable life reading, painting, taking piano lessons, and daydreaming. He slept late and spent evenings at the opera listening to his favorite composer, Richard Wagner, and haranguing a friend about Wagner, art, architecture, and his own abilities. He contemptuously turned down all suggestions that he work, telling everyone that he intended to be a great artist.

Before his mother Klara died in December 1907 of breast cancer, Hitler went to Vienna and applied for admission to the Art academy, which promptly turned him down. Despite this blow to his pride, he became convinced that he would become a great architect. In Vienna, he roomed with a friend in town to study music. Thanks to a small inheritance, a small pension, and occasional contributions from his Aunt Johanna, he continued his leisurely existence. He ate poorly if at all and lived in a miserable room—but went to the opera. To the other merits he attributed to himself, he added writing and opera composition. He started plays and an opera but never got far. Aside from the opera, Hitler took no part in Vienna's lively cultural life. He is unlikely to have engaged in sex during his time in Vienna; in fact, sex seems to have repelled him. The politics of Mayor Karl Lueger impressed him, and, at some point, he became an anti-Semite and a biological racist. He had already been attracted to extreme nationalism in Linz.

In the summer of 1908, his money low and his friend gone, Hitler fell on hard times. By the autumn of 1909, he was homeless and slept in the open or in shelters. Reports have him unshaven, emaciated, infested with lice, wearing tattered clothes, and in the company of tramps. He moved to a hostel for the poor, where he could get a bed at night, a bath, some soup, and bread, but was expected to work during the day. Finally putting his artistic qualities to use, Hitler teamed up with another resident in a small business. He painted scenes of Vienna, while his partner sold them. He had Jewish partners in this endeavor and seems to have gotten along with them.

> The money the painting business brought in was little, but it enabled the future Fuehrer to survive. By February 1910, Hitler lived in a men's home, where conditions were tolerable. He discussed get-rich-quick schemes with his partner, but preferred to pontificate on political subjects to the other residents—Social Democratic decadence, the decay of the Austrian Empire, German greatness. Eventually, Hitler quarreled with his partner over money, and they went their separate ways. He remained an embittered, disconnected man who criticized his own paintings and chafed at society's rejection of him. He hated Vienna and dreamed of going to Munich to study art. His failure to register for military service in 1909 because he hated the empire provided another incentive to leave, but he stayed because after April 20, 1913, his twenty-fourth birthday, he became eligible to receive an inheritance from his father. When he received the money, he packed his belongings in a black suitcase and, to the good-byes of his fellow-residents at the men's home, left for Germany.

Hitler built up and dominated the DAP. In February 1920, he changed its name to the National Socialist German Workers' Party (NSDAP), Nazi for short, issued an anticapitalist and anti-Semitic program consisting of twenty-five points that expressed the grievances of the lower classes, and in 1921 demanded dictatorial powers over it. He instituted a paramilitary organization, the SA (*Sturmableitung*), or Storm Troopers, to prevent enemies from interfering with his inflammatory discourses. The SA specialized in the street fighting essential to the Nazi rise to power. Hitler emphasized uniforms, symbolism, and rallies to mobilize the masses. In November 1923, he attempted to seize the government but failed miserably. The results: a short jail term, during which he wrote *Mein Kampf*, and a conviction to follow the legal road to power taken in Italy by his hero Benito Mussolini.

After 1924, Weimar recovered economically, and Germany seemed on the road to European reintegration. Prosperity made Hitler's predictions of disaster because of the Versailles settlement seem absurd, and the Germans ignored his violent preaching. Nazi support dwindled, and, in the 1928 elections, the Nazis won only twelve seats in the Reichstag

Revival of the Nazi Party

The depression catapulted the NSDAP to the political forefront. The Nazi recovery was aided by changes in the Nationalist Party (DNVP) after its takeover by the ambitious and politically inept newspaper magnate Alfred Hugenberg. As a protest against reparations, Hugenberg challenged the government's acceptance of the Young Plan that reduced payments and, in order to increase his chances of success, organized a right-wing front that included the Nazis. Certain that he could control the Nazis, Hugenberg gave them full access to his newspapers and increased their visibility and respectability.

The Nazis transformed the campaign against the Young Plan into a sweeping condemnation of the Weimar Republic. Their denunciation of the Versailles treaty as the source of Germany's troubles increased their popular support as the depression deepened and panic spread. The middle class feared losing its economic status as had happened in the catastrophic hyperinflation, fueling resentment

The paramilitary SA or Storm Troopers were essential to the rise of the Nazi Party. They protected Hitler during his public appearances and engaged in the street fighting that eventually made the movement paramount in the country. Here is SA leader Ernst Roehm in his uniform. Hitler gave the order to dismantle the SA and to assassinate Roehm during the "Night of the Long Knives" because the Army felt threatened by the SA and Roehm was too revolutionary. Hitler made a pact guaranteeing that the Army would be the only armed force in the nation, but, as usual, he did not keep his word.

and increasing support for the Nazis. In addition, the Nazi alliance alienated the moderate nationalists and split the DNVP, a schism that gave the NSDAP supremacy on the right.

In the meantime, the ruling coalition broke up, and the parties failed to agree on a new government. The lack of a majority in the Reichstag triggered Article 48 of the Constitution, which effectively allowed the president to rule by decree if a parliamentary majority did not exist. Because no chancellor could rule if the president refused to sign the decree laws, the center of power shifted from the Reichstag to President Hindenburg and his narrow circle of advisers. The new chancellor sanctioned by Hindenburg, Heinrich Bruening, dissolved Parliament and scheduled early elections for September 1930 in the hope that a majority would emerge.

THE COLLAPSE OF WEIMAR

Combined with these political developments, the economy's continued plunge sealed Weimar's fate. By 1932 German industrial production had fallen by 44 percent, unemployment skyrocketed to 6 million or 40 percent, and the unemployment fund was bankrupt.

The Electoral Breakthrough

The Nazis ran emotional electoral campaigns that denounced the "November criminals" who supported the republic and the Jews who were supposedly responsible for Germany's troubles. They used powerful theater, including the pioneering use of the airplane—swooping down from the sky and making dramatic entrances into cities where Hitler addressed mass rallies. Hitler's rhetoric made short shrift of political moderates as he demanded the destruction of the Versailles treaty and the Weimar Republic. The economic catastrophe brought the Nazis new support from groups that would not ordinarily have voted for them, including unemployed workers, women, and young people who never had held a job. By July 1932, 30 percent of Berlin's workers were voting for the NSDAP, and they made up over half the membership of the capital's Storm Troopers.

The women's vote was particularly important because women participated in elections in larger numbers than before. Women voted for the Nazis less often than did men, but the Nazis did better among them than did the Communists, despite the KPD's (Communist Party of Germany) advanced platform on women's issues. Helping to explain this ironic consequence, the Nazis were not too far out of line with the general thinking in late Weimar Germany by believing that women should devote their energies to their homes, husbands, and children. However, because the Nazis argued that radicals and Jews dominated the women's movement, rejected women candidates for the Reichstag, and maintained that feminism enslaved women, why did they have so much success among women voters? There seem to be two major reasons: Most women accepted the view of German society that cast them in the role of wives and mothers, and they believed that Hitler would cut unemployment and put the family's primary breadwinners back on the payroll.

The economic situation helps explain the stunning Nazi victory in the 1930 elections. The Nazis increased their votes to more than 18 percent from 2.6 percent, and their seats in the Reichstag soared from 12 to 107. Of the other parties, only the KPD increased its percentage, but only from 10.6 to 13 percent. The Catholic Center Party remained stable at 15 percent, but the SPD lost votes, and the left as a whole declined 4 percent. What was most significant, the Liberals and the People's Party, mainstays of the Weimar coalition, lost about half their votes.

The Nazi increase came primarily from the center of the political spectrum and new voters. The unemployed, the never employed, small businessmen, farmers in distress, and civil servants who were worried about their jobs contributed heavily to the Nazi tide. The young accounted for a substantial proportion of the Nazi tally, and the 1930 Reichstag was the youngest ever.

Parliamentary Paralysis and Increasing Disorder

The outcome of the 1930 elections was a turning point. No parliamentary majority emerged, confirming Hindenburg and his circle as the arbiters of

ARBEITER

WÄHLT DEN FRONTSOLDATEN

HITLER!

The Nazis came to power not only through violence, but primarily through shrewd campaigning. While the economic situation was good they were not an important political factor, but their electoral support increased dramatically with the onset of the Great Depression. Here is a Nazi electoral poster: "Workers choose Hitler!"

German politics. Parliamentary business was paralyzed because the parties supporting Weimar had 40 percent of the seats, while Nazi and Communist opponents of the republic controlled 32 percent. The 1930 elections transformed the NSDAP into a mass party with roots in the urban and rural middle class, and violence increased as the SA recruited adherents by offering pay, excitement, and the prospect of beating up leftist opponents. Street brawls killed three hundred people in a single year. The government did not ban the SA until April 1932 when it was too late.

Encouraged by the party's growing popular support, Hitler challenged the popular Hindenburg in the March 1932 presidential election. He did not win, but he performed impressively by outpolling the Communist and Nationalist candidates and forcing Hindenburg into a run-off election. Because of the president's advanced age, Hitler's showing established him as the person to contend with in German politics.

Because the president had become the focus of power, intrigues aimed at influencing him dominated German politics. In May 1932, he forced Chancellor

Bruening to resign because he was dissatisfied with his strategy in the recent elections.

The Drive to Power

Hindenburg replaced Bruening with a conservative Catholic noble Franz von Papen, who had little support in the country but had the backing of General Kurt von Schleicher, who represented the army. Papen installed a "barons' cabinet" consisting of army officers, including Schleicher as defense minister, and senior civil servants. He attempted to get Hitler's support by making two goodwill gestures: lifting Bruening order outlawing the SA and dismissing the Social Democrat-led government of Prussia, which was hostile to the Nazis. Hitler responded by remaining intransigent and by stepping up SA violence. Papen now feared that the Reichstag would condemn his policies and obtained Hindenburg's consent to hold new elections in July 1932.

The Nazis emerged from the new balloting as the Reichstag's largest party, with over 37 percent of the vote and 207 members, but there was still no majority. Papen hoped to resolve the situation by bringing the Nazis into a cabinet—but Hitler turned him down. Papen then followed a policy of attempting to weaken the Nazis by holding frequent elections because he judged that Nazi support had peaked and that losses would make the party more malleable. In the elections of November 1932, the Nazi vote total dropped about 4 percent, probably signaling a backlash against Nazi violence, and created a crisis in the NSDAP.

Far from weakening Hitler's position, however, Papen's maneuvering set off a new round of intrigue. General von Schleicher turned against Papen because he feared that the chancellor would install an authoritarian regime and provoke a civil war. Schleicher sought to get Hindenburg to withdraw his support of Papen, but the president had taken a personal liking to the chancellor. Schleicher then informed the president that he, Schleicher, could put together a cabinet that would obtain a vote of confidence in the Reichstag. Because of the Nazi electoral decline, Schleicher hoped to split the Nazi Party by assuming that a substantial part of the Nazi Party would revolt against Hitler and support a cabinet that he would lead. This plan failed miserably.

Papen responded by going straight to Hitler to cut a deal. He had the backing of heavy industry and agricultural and banking interests, while Hindenburg's advisers tried to soften up the old general who personally opposed the Nazi leader. The army feared that Schleicher's intrigues might turn the president against it and abandoned him. Papen offered Hitler the vice chancellorship in a new government, but Hitler demanded that he become chancellor and Papen, vice chancellor. Papen agreed, and on January 30, 1933, Hitler became chancellor in a coalition cabinet that included only three Nazis. Papen and his supporters believed that they had boxed in the Nazi leader so he could not do much harm and that they could eventually remove him, but they were wrong.

BIOGRAPHICAL SKETCHES

Franz von Papen
Politico

A wily politician, Franz von Papen was born into a noble Catholic family on October 29, 1879, in the Westphalia region of Germany. He led a very agreeable life before marrying into a wealthy industrial family in 1905. His wife's connections provided him excellent links to big industrialists and rightist political circles during the waning years of the Weimar republic when Adolf Hitler came to power.

Papen's background favored him in his chosen military career even though he was inattentive to details, devious, and willing to take chances. In 1911 Papen was assigned to the general staff and, in January 1914, became military attaché at the German Embassy in Washington, D.C. The Americans shipped him back to Germany in 1916 because they charged that he had conspired to disrupt war production. Affidavits also stated that Papen had an open relationship with an American girl in New York and organized wild parties with secret agents and their girlfriends. Back in Germany, he fought on the western front, where he won the coveted Iron Cross (First Class). Transferred to the Middle East, he fought well and attempted to foment revolution among Muslims under British control.

After World War I, the progress of the Communists and Socialists alarmed him, and, as a Center Party member, he disagreed with Chancellor Heinrich Bruening's policy of alliance with the Social Democrats. His links with powerful industrialists and the army kept Papen in the political loop among rightist circles, although he devoted much time to farming and horse breeding on his family estates.

With Bruening's fall, General Kurt von Schleicher introduced Papen to President Paul von Hindenburg. The witty and urbane Papen charmed the aging president, who gave him a mandate to form a government. Papen's rightist Barons' cabinet had no majority in Parliament and no support among the people. Because Hitler had strong popular support, Papen thought to co-opt the Nazis by bringing Hitler into a Conservative governmental coalition. Papen believed that entangling the Nazi leader in practical politics would make Hitler more moderate. As Nazi influence increased in the country, Papen negotiated harder to lure Hitler into the government, also as a means of sabotaging his new rival, Schleicher. When Hitler refused to enter a cabinet except as chancellor, Papen struck a deal with him and convinced Hindenburg to appoint Hitler chancellor while he took the position of vice chancellor. Because the Nazis had only three cabinet posts, Papen believed their influence on governmental policies would be strictly limited. Papen hoped to counter Hitler's radicalism by the application of Christian principles and make him reasonable. He also thought that he had restored state authority based on ideals, which he admired, that had existed during the kaiser's time.

Papen stayed in Hitler's cabinet until July 1934. He bravely protested against Nazi terror in a speech on June 17, 1934, to no effect. On the Night of the Long Knives, June 30, the Nazis killed two of his assistants, and Papen himself narrowly escaped death. Papen nevertheless cooperated with Hitler. Appointed as ambassador to Austria, he helped undermine the Austrian regime and aided the German takeover in 1938. He served as ambassador to Turkey from 1939 to 1944. The Nuremberg tribunal acquitted Papen of war crimes, but in 1949 a German denazification court sentenced him to eight years' hard labor, which he did not serve. In 1953, he published a set of exculpatory memoirs.

Franz von Papen died on May 2, 1969, immortalized as the person who put Adolf Hitler in the driver's seat.

INSTALLING THE DICTATORSHIP

The Nazi revolution began once Hitler became chancellor. On February 23, 1933, the Reichstag building burned down. The arrest of a feeble-minded Dutch Communist seemed to confirm Nazi charges of a Communist conspiracy to take over the country.

The Elections of March 1933

In response to the burning of the Reichstag, Hindenburg declared a state of emergency under Article 48 of the Weimar Constitution, authorizing the government to implement necessary action to "restore public order and public security" by restricting the freedom of assembly, press, and expression. The decree provided the legal basis for Nazi terror during the campaign for elections scheduled for March 5, 1933. The Nazi police spied on private communications, conducted search and seizure operations with impunity, and arrested Nazi opponents without charging them with specific offenses. Despite the terror campaign and governmental interference in the voting, the Nazis won under 44 percent of the vote and had to rely on the DNVP's 8 percent for a parliamentary majority. The voting followed earlier patterns, with the Nazis receiving the greatest support from small urban centers, Protestant agricultural areas, the lower middle class, voters who had formerly abstained, and new voters and losing in the Catholic and working-class regions of the country.

Following the elections, on March 23, two-thirds of the Reichstag adopted the Enabling Act. This measure, voted by the Nazis, Nationalists, and Center Party members and opposed by the Social Democrats (the government had already imprisoned the Communists and some Socialists), gave Hitler power to promulgate laws for the next four years.

Results of the Enabling Act

The Enabling Act allowed Hitler to establish his dictatorship. On July 14, 1933, the government dissolved all parties except the Nazi Party and ended the separation of powers of the different branches of government. Hitler formalized this situation after Hindenburg's death on August 2, 1934, upon which he assumed the powers of the presidency, and German officials swore loyalty oaths personally to Hitler as Fuehrer (leader).

The Nazis also implemented a leveling process *(Gleichschaltung)* that subjugated the individual German states, the administration, and German society. Through terrorism, decrees, and political pressure, the Nazis eliminated the legal basis by which German states could offer resistance to the central government.

Many officials of Weimar were former officers of the German Empire, and their support for the Republic was questionable. President Paul von Hindenburg, for example, was the general who had led Germany during World War I. This lukewarm support from high and not-so-high authorities of the Republic, combined with the economic disaster of the Great Depression, undermined Weimar, and the rise of extremist movements and constitutional weaknesses finally did it in. Although Hindenburg did not like Hitler personally, he gave the go-ahead for him to become Chancellor. The photograph shows Hindenburg riding with Hitler shortly after naming him Chancellor in January 1933.

They did away with the *Reichsrat*, or upper house representing the states, and appointed officials to run them. The destruction of the rights of the individual states ended Germany's traditional federal makeup and established the central government's supremacy.

The only organization capable of opposing Hitler, the army, made a deal with Hitler: when the aged Hindenburg died, the army promised not to oppose Hitler's addition of the president's functions to those of chancellor; Hitler agreed to recognize the army as the strongest armed force in the nation. This promise meant eliminating the army's principal rival, the SA, led by Hitler's old friend Ernst Roehm. The Nazi drive to power had swollen the ranks of the organization, which insisted on revolutionizing German society and on invading the army's sphere of competence. On the Night of the Long Knives, June 30, 1934, Hitler kept his side of the bargain by brutally ordering the killing of Roehm and his top lieutenants; for good measure, other people who had crossed him, including Schleicher and Gregor Strasser, a Nazi leader who had considered a deal with Schleicher in 1932, were also killed.

The Nazis eliminated all opponents from the civil service, in addition to the Jews they had excluded in April 1933. They took control of the police and the judiciary and crushed the trade unions and professional organizations, creating economic and cultural organizations to supervise and mobilize the masses—the German Labor Front and the Reich Cultural Chamber.

Although the army acquiesced in Hitler's takeover, it was ambivalent toward the Nazi regime. Its leaders sympathized with some Nazi goals, such as restoring German power through rearmament and perhaps eventual expansion in the East, but resented Hitler's continued attempts to control the armed forces. Hitler removed General Werner von Blomberg, the minister of war, and Chief of Staff General Werner von Fritsch, but failed to establish complete control over the armed forces. In 1938, at the height of the Czech crisis, rumors flew that the army might try to remove him from power, and during World War II, it chafed at his interference in military affairs. In 1944, some army officers attempted to assassinate Hitler, allowing him to destroy his enemies and finally gain domination over the army.

Nazism's Rise in Retrospect
In attempting to explain the triumph of Nazism, historians have concentrated on two aspects: Hitler's personality and German conditions.

Kurt von Schleicher led the German Army during the Weimar period, but his political maneuverings unintentionally aided Hitler's rise to the Chancellorship. Hitler had the former Foreign Minister and Chancellor murdered, along with his wife, on the "Night of the Long Knives" that consolidated his power.

Hitler dominated Nazism to such an extent that many biographies analyzing his family background, youth, frustrations, sexual proclivities, psychological makeup, and talents continue to be published. This very informative literature provides clues about why he succeeded in taking over and ruling a sophisticated modern country. Most important, biographers have concentrated on the magnetic force of his personality, his talents as an orator, and his ability to create a myth of himself that kept together the party and the country. During the infancy of mass communication, when only newspapers, radio, and film were available, Hitler used the mass meeting to gain converts and win elections. He proved himself a master at staging dramatic events and winning over audiences according to the precepts he outlined in *Mein Kampf*. Hitler's personal popularity made his triumph and rule possible. Even in the last days of World War II, when Germany was reeling and the Nazi Party lost its support, Germans continued to support the Fuehrer.

Nevertheless, it seems unlikely that one man alone could have caused the collapse of the Weimar Republic, no matter how many "talents of tyranny" he possessed. The result of the March 1933 elections, in which the Nazis failed to secure a majority, demonstrated this fact. Most obviously, historians have pointed out the weaknesses of the Weimar Republic, its inability to establish legitimacy, and the catastrophic economic conditions that weakened it. According to this view, the Nazis had a great probability of success because they assaulted a vulnerable political construction during a time of great crisis, whereas they had failed when conditions were less desperate.

Despite Hitler's failure to win an electoral majority, the Nazis did become the largest party; this fact has led historians to analyze the electoral results of this voting. They have concluded that the Nazis had important backing beyond the lower middle class and socially marginal groups that had lost their status because of the depression and could count on significant support among farmers, shopkeepers, artisans who feared that they would lose their economic and social positions. Probably this empathy signaled discontent with the long-term trends of German economic and social development favoring industrialization and increased workers' rights. The Nazis also had support among upper-class constituencies, including students and civil servants who were fearful of Marxist gains and unhappy with their careers and future prospects. Despite its appeal to anti-Marxists, the Nazi Party had important backing among workers in small industry who were not well integrated into the large unions. The female vote for the Nazis possibly exceeded the male vote in the last free elections. In addition, the Nazi Party appealed in great measure to older people, but it also drew support from young people. Catholic voters and industrial workers were most recalcitrant to Nazi influence.

Bibliographical Essay

The Coming of the Third Reich (New York, 2004) by Richard J. Evans, previously cited, is the most complete work on the rise of Nazism. Karl Dietrich Bracher's *The German Dictatorship: Origins, Structure and Effects of National Socialism* (New York, 1970) is a classic work on the rise of Hitler and the intimate nature of his regime. Another excellent work is Martin Broszat, *Hitler and the Collapse of Weimar Germany* (New York, 1987).

A good document collection is Jeremy Noakes and Geoffrey Pridham, eds., *Documents on Nazism 1919–1945,* 2 vols. (Exeter, UK, 1989). Geoffrey Pridham, *Hitler's Rise to Power: The Nazi Movement in Bavaria, 1923–1933* (New York, 1973), emphasizes the context of the Weimar republic. Allan Todd discusses Hitler's coming to power in the context of the rise of the other European dictatorships discussed in this part: *The European Dictatorships* (Cambridge, UK, 2002).

Biographies of Hitler are crucial to an understanding of the man, and readers will find many works of different quality on the subject. Ian Kershaw's *Hitler,* 2 vols. (New York, 1999–2000), is the most comprehensive biography. The same author wrote *The "Hitler Myth": Image and Reality in the Third Reich* (New York, 1987), a study of Hitler's image. A classic work that is still worth reading is Alan Bullock, *Hitler: A Study in Tyranny* (New York, 1995). See also his *Hitler and Stalin: Parallel Lives* (London, 1991). Good and detailed biographies include Joachim Fest, *Hitler* (New York, 1973); John Toland, *Adolf Hitler* (Garden City, N.Y., 1976); and William Carr, *Hitler: A Study in Personality and Politics* (New York, 1979). More recent biographies include John Lukacs, *The Hitler of History* (New York, 1998). As may be expected, psychological biographies of Hitler have also been written to understand his actions. An early one, written for the OSS in 1943 but published much later, is Walter Langer, *The Mind of Adolf Hitler* (London, 1974). The citations on Hitler's revelation that he had divine support and on his speaking style are on pp. 37 and 52. Another classic work along these lines is Robert G. L. Waite, *The Psychopathic God: Adolf Hitler* (New York, 1977). Other relevant works include Rudolph Binion, *Hitler Among the Germans* (De Kalb, Ill., 1984). The psychiatrist Fritz Redlich, *Hitler: Diagnosis of a Destructive Prophet* (New York, 1998), concludes that although a variety of physical and psychological ailments afflicted Hitler, they do not explain his behavior.

Economic developments that helped provoke Weimar's end may be studied in Harold James, *The German Slump: Politics and Economics 1924–1936* (Oxford, UK, 1986). Goronwy Rees, *The Great Slump: Capitalism in Crisis, 1929–1933* (New York, 1970), previously cited,, is a general history with good material on Germany. Edward W. Bennett, *Germany and the Diplomacy of the Financial Crisis* (Cambridge, Mass., 1962), analyzes the Young Plan, along with the relationship of Germany to Europe and the United States. Henry Ashby Turner, Jr., examines the relationship between Hitler and big business, *German Big Business and the Rise of Hitler* (New York, 1985). See also the story of I. G. Farben by Peter Hayes, *Industry and Ideology: IG Farben in the Nazi Era* (Cambridge, UK, 1989).

A. J. Nicholls, *Weimar and the Rise of Hitler,* 2d ed. (New York, 1972), is a good, brief and still valuable general survey on the last days of the Weimar Republic. E. J. Feuchtwanger, *From Weimar to Hitler: Germany 1918–1933* (New York, 1993), is a complete and detailed history. R. T. Clark, *The Fall of the German Republic* (New York, 1964), is an older, still useful, work that focuses on politics. Richard Bessel and E. J. Feuchtwanger, *Social Change and Political Development in Weimar Germany* (Totowa, N.J., 1981), and Michael N. Dobkowski and Isidor Wallimann, eds., *The Social and Economic Collapse of the Weimar Republic* (Westport, Conn., 1983), contain a series of excellent essays on Weimar themes that help explain the republic's failures. For the role of an important politician, see William L. Patch, Jr., *Heinrich Bruening and the Dissolution of the Weimar Republic* (Cambridge, UK, 1998).

A series of books have analyzed the people who voted for the Nazis. Among the best are Thomas Childers, *The Nazi Voter: The Social Foundations of Fascism in Germany* (Chapel Hill, N.C., 1983), and, by the same author, *The Formation of the Nazi Constituency* (London, 1986). Richard Hamilton, *Who Voted for Hitler?* (Princeton, N.J., 1982), examines the support of both the upper and lower middle class. Robert Gellaty, *Backing Hitler* (Oxford, UK, 2001), examines the issue of "consent and coercion" in Hitler's coming to power and during his regime. Peter Fritzsche, *Germans into Nazis* (Cambridge, Mass., 1998) rejects the conventional explanations of why people voted for the Nazis and points to democratization. Local support is discussed in the excellent William Sheridan Allen, *The Nazi Seizure of Power: The Experience of a Single Town* (Harmondsworth, UK, 1989), and Rudolf Heberle, *From Democracy to Nazism: A Regional Case Study on Political Parties in Germany* (New York, 1970).

☙

CHAPTER 15

Hitler's Nazism

CHAPTER OUTLINE
Foundations of Nazism • Nazi Theory and Practice • Everyday Life

BIOGRAPHICAL SKETCHES
Gertrud Scholtz-Klink, Unrepentant! • Hermann Goering,
Nazi Chieftain

Hitler moved cautiously after he took over the state. Many Germans did not vote for him in 1933, and it is impossible to establish with certainty how many opposed his ideas. Nevertheless, as the Nazi regime established itself, it seems clear that most Germans believed in his ability to restore Germany to its former greatness.

FOUNDATIONS OF NAZISM

Nazism's underpinnings may be found already fully developed in *Mein Kampf,* which the Fuehrer penned while in prison for his failed 1923 Beer Hall Putsch. Biological racism was the centerpiece of the book, and Hitler tried to implement it.

Anti-Semitism
There is a distinction between Nazi anti-Semitism and the Nazi theory of racism. Although the Nazis believed in a superior race, the "Aryans," and inferior races, they reserved a special place for the Jews, who they saw as biologically inferior and warring on the Aryans in order to destroy the superior race. According to the Nazis, the Jews waged a subtle and disreputable campaign against the Aryans through divide-and-conquer techniques. Nazis viewed socialism, communism, capitalism, trade unions, feminism, and democratic ideas as Jewish conspiracies to split the "Aryan" community into antagonistic classes; they were inferior, evil, and cunning. Hitler believed that without the immediate implementation of urgent

Adolf Eichmann served in a number of capacities during the Third Reich. A major participant in the Holocaust, he coordinated the deportation of Jews to death camps and ghettoes in which they died of malnutrition and abuse. He fled to Argentina after the war but the Mossad tracked him down and brought him to Israel to stand trial for his crimes. Convicted by a civilian court, he was executed on May 31, 1962.

measures against the Jews, the fight would be lost. For the Nazis, the Jew served as the pervasive enemy and focus of hatred that totalitarian regimes require.

The Nuremberg Laws

When they came to power, the Nazis unleashed terror tactics against their leftist opponents and seized the occasion to include Jews in the attack. The Nazis initially tried to deprive Jews of the means to earn a living, not to extirpate them. In March 1933, violent demonstrations against Jewish businesses and professionals began, and on April 1, the Nazi Party organized a boycott of Jewish stores. Uniformed SA and SS thugs scared off customers and led noisy demonstrations while members of the Hitler Youth handed out leaflets. These efforts were not wholly successful, since non-Jews pointedly shopped in Jewish stores despite the intimidation. During the same month, a law to cleanse the civil service of Nazi opponents effectively removed most Jewish civil servants and excluded most Jews from the professions. Other measures in the spring and summer completed the work and established a quota for Jewish students. The Nazis hoped to force the Jews to emigrate and leave their property behind. Although 40,000 Jews emigrated in 1933, the effort failed; most of the 537,000 German Jews could not bear to leave their homeland, and the Nazi tactic of depriving them of funds made emigration more difficult.

On September 15, 1935, following a summer of boycotts and violence, the Nazis systematized their oppression of the Jews, and the police took a greater role in the persecution. The Nuremberg Laws deprived Jews of citizenship and prohibited sexual relations between Jews and non-Jews. Implementing legislation centralized Jewish matters under the Gestapo and the SD (Security Service). Adolf Eichmann became deputy chief of a new Jewish affairs section within the SD to reduce Jewish influence in German society and encourage emigration. With the passage of the laws, it became essential to define exactly who was a Jew. There was a difference of opinion between the party, which considered a Jew anyone with a drop of Jewish blood, and state officials, who argued for a distinction between pure and mixed Jews. Legislation in November 1935 defined a Jew as anyone with three or more Jewish grandparents, although under certain circumstances, a person could be considered a Jew with only two Jewish grandparents. Persons who did not qualify under the stated conditions or had only one Jewish grandparent comprised the *Mischlinge* (persons of mixed race), although arguments continued on a definition of this category as well.

Kristallnacht

The regime's desire to project a good image to the outside world during the Berlin Olympic Games made anti-Semitism less obvious during 1936 and 1937, but the pressure on Jews to sell their property cheaply to Aryans and leave the country intensified.

In November 1938, following the murder of a German diplomat in Paris by a Jew, the Nazis organized a widespread pogrom called *Kristallnacht* (the "Night of Broken Glass," November 9, 1938). Nazi thugs broke Jewish storefronts all over Germany and devastated Jewish homes, businesses, and synagogues. They arrested Jews en masse and herded many to the Dachau concentration camp. The government held all German Jews responsible for the murder and forced the Jewish community to pay for any losses and a heavy fine.

In early 1939, the state completed the measures that excluded Jews from all sectors of German business life. Employers could fire Jewish workers on short notice, and Jewish workers lost their rights to pensions and unemployment compensation as well. Courts shipped Jews off to concentration camps for minor infractions. Many Jews sold their property or businesses under duress to Aryans for a pittance, hoping to use the meager funds to emigrate, but few Jews made it out of the country before World War II.

Racial Imperialism

Although the Jews were the initial target, racism dominated the Nazi worldview. According to *Mein Kampf,* wherever there were Aryans, progress resulted; wherever there had been progress, there must have been Aryans who were responsible for it; wherever there was cultural decline, it resulted from the mixing of Aryan blood with those of inferior races. As evidence for the circular reasoning, Hitler claimed that Aryans could be identified by their physical characteristics, which were those of the ideal Nordic European —blond, fair-haired, blue-eyed, and slim. Ironically, the top Nazi leadership lacked these physical characteristics, except for the brain behind the SS state and SD head, Reinhard Heydrich, who perhaps had Jewish antecedents.

Hitler argued that Aryans always constituted a small proportion of the population of any given area. Therefore, their superior qualities were particularly subject to corruption through interbreeding, which led to the decline of culture and to the leveling off and end of progress. It is an error to believe that Hitler identified Germans and Aryans because Germans had themselves interbred and because Aryan blood had survived in other areas. Because of race mixing, it was necessary to purify Aryan blood and to prevent further defilement—hence, the Nazi racial laws that outlawed intermarriage with inferior races and euthanasia for persons with mental and physical handicaps, a program (discussed later) that foreshadowed the "final solution" of the Jewish problem.

Besides Jews, the Nazis vented their rage against the German Gypsies (Rom), both "pure" and "mixed." In Germany and in other countries, the Gypsies bore the stigma of being social outcasts. Under the 1935 Nuremberg laws, the Nazis

Once the Nazis came to power, they acted immediately to put their anti-Semitic policies into place. Besides instituting new laws against the Jews, they physically attacked them. On November 9, 1938, following the murder of a German diplomat in Paris, the Nazis destroyed Jewish property and conducted massive arrests of Jews. These events, known as Kristall-nacht, or the "Night of Broken Glass" were an early demonstration of the brutal anti-Semitic nature of the Nazi State. Here a man shovels broken glass from a Jewish shop destroyed the night before.

conducted research that was aimed at identifying Gypsies of mixed blood in order to register them and put them into camps where they would be unable to intermarry with other Germans. The Germans killed off a large percentage of Europe's Gypsy population in the extermination camps of World War II.

Hitler's racism had wide implications. Because the Aryans determined the progress of humanity, Hitler argued that they should dominate over other races and control their raw materials, land, and labor—in fact, had a duty to do so. He was convinced that Aryan control would ensure even the advance of the subject peoples: for example, the Slavs would achieve their greatest happiness working for the Germans. The Nazis established a hierarchy of races, and during World War II attempted to apply their racial doctrines in Eastern Europe: racial imperialism constituted the core of Nazism and mandated an aggressive foreign policy. They enslaved and eliminated millions of Poles, Russians, and other Slavs, in addition to Jews.

The Nazis did not intend to get rid of inferior people immediately but hoped to use their labor while implementing measures to increase the Aryan population that could occupy their land in the future. They were consistent in their folly, as witnessed by their campaign in Germany, to sterilize or eliminate Germans with mental and physical handicaps on the grounds that persons with such characteristics should not propagate undesirable characteristics to future generations. They persecuted gay people, shipping them to concentration camps, and, when convenient, used false charges of homosexuality to defeat their opponents.

"Life Unworthy of Life": The Nazi Euthanasia Program

Nazi brutality was a consequence not only of racial imperialism, but of the goal of creating a national community based on blood and race that had to be free of political undesirables, asocial elements, and persons with other genetic handicaps. Political undesirables included persons who actively opposed, or had opposed, Nazism; these persons either remained under a cloud of suspicion or ended up in concentration camps. "Asocials," persons whose behavior deviated from the norm, were similarly treated. In September 1933 and periodically thereafter, the police rounded up beggars, tramps, and homeless people and either put them to work or shipped them to concentration camps, where a black triangle identified them. Prostitutes, pimps, and other criminals met a similar fate. Because the Nazis considered criminal degeneracy to be biologically determined, legislation permitted the arrest of anyone deviating from national community standards and a physical examination to determine biological abnormalities. The law applied pseudoscientific biological principles to persons with genetic diseases, which might include active or former membership in the Communist Party, and sterilized them on the grounds of preventing them from passing on their undesirable characteristics. Estimates of people who were sterilized between 1934 and 1945 range from 320,000 to 350,000.

Besides sterilization, the Nazis instituted a program for the killing of mentally ill patients in asylums; these persons could include homosexuals or people who were consigned to asylums by police officers after traffic incidents who judged their behavior to be strange. In order to whip up feeling against mentally ill persons, Hitler ordered the making of propaganda films on the theme of mental illness for viewing by Nazi youth organizations and the public, and the Nazis conducted organized tours of asylums where they displayed patients who were the most ill.

Besides murdering the mentally ill, Hitler sanctioned the killing of severely ill and malformed children. This program allegedly began with a request to Hitler from the parents of an ill child and mushroomed into a large enterprise. In August 1939, the regime required doctors and midwives to register "idiot" children and those with Down's syndrome and a variety of other conditions, including physical deformities. This was the "T-4" program, named for its address in Berlin and organized by a physician, Dr. Leonardo Conti. The Nazi elimination campaign included physically handicapped persons who were considered to be present and future burdens on society. Nazi euthanasia was influenced by late nineteenth-century German thinkers who began with the concept of voluntary euthanasia and ended with the idea of the forced killing of what they considered "life unworthy of life." Economic arguments clinched the rationale for the campaign: "5,000 idiots costing 2,000 RMs [reichsmarks] each per annum = 100 million a year. With interest at 5% that corresponds to a capital reserve of 200 million. That should even mean something to those whose concept of figures has gone awry since the period of inflation." Capping the campaign, the Nazis informed Germans that, in only 120 years, the unfit would hopelessly outnumber the persons with valuable attributes.

The implementation of the T-4 program required the recruiting and training of a large number of professionals, such as doctors, nurses, and lawyers, and experimentation with the most efficient means of murdering patients. These methods varied from lethal injections to gas chambers, complete with the use of crematoria to get rid of the victims' bodies. The organizers took care to spread the responsibility for the killings so that everyone who committed them was equally guilty. Doctors sized up the victims before killing them and determined the cause of death from a standardized list of sixty-one diseases complete with symptoms. After cremating the victims, the doctors randomly collected the ashes and, in bureaucratic letters describing the illness and carefully noting the symptoms, informed the relatives of the deaths and offered to send the urns to them for interment. The euthanasia program was important in the training of personnel and in the determination the most efficient killing methods for later use in the extermination camps of World War II.

The deception linked to the euthanasia campaign did not work. In some cases, multiple urns arrived or a letter referred to a sick organ, such as the appendix, that the victim had had removed years earlier. Protests culminated in a public sermon against the program by Clemens August Graf von Galen, bishop of Muenster, on August 3, 1941, and discussion in diocesan churches. Following the sermon, Hitler agreed to a temporary halt for the duration of the war, although he specifically excluded children. Bishop Galen's sermon alone did not account for the pause in the euthanasia program, which has been explained by the increased demand for personnel in the extermination camps of the East. The Nazi euthanasia program

The Nazi euthanasia program—originally aimed at Germans—was stopped in Germany by internal opposition. Had Hitler won the war, he probably would have restarted it on a massive scale. As it was, it claimed hundreds of thousands of victims inside and outside of Germany and was a training ground for the Holocaust. Here is an exhibition held in January 2012 in Berlin commemorating the child victims of that program.

took at least 200,00 lives, including those within the occupied countries, during World War II.

NAZI THEORY AND PRACTICE

In theory the Nazi Party constituted a community of the elect that upheld moral values and aimed to regenerate political life. Consistent with the Communist and Fascist tendency to fuse party and state, in a law of December 1, 1933, the Fuehrer embodied the NSDAP's constitution, the repository of the German idea of the state.

The Party
The party was a public agency whose leaders assumed high-state functions. Their primary tasks: to explain National Socialism and transform the German people into a tight-knit community, goals that would permit the development to the fullest of the moral and heroic German man. German women instead, "mothers" of the people, had the duty of increasing the birth rate after a long period of decline as their special contribution to Nazi society. As one German official stated: "The German woman belongs in the kitchen!" Citizens could join the party, but only members of the German race could obtain

The SS was the core of the Nazi State and was the organization on which the future of Nazism was to be based. The organization had a major role in the Nazi euthanasia program and in the organization of the concentration camps. After a Nazi victory in World War II, they were to have the role of settling the East by returning to the soil and populating the region with racially pure Aryans. This picture shows an SS guard playing his trumpet at a rally. Note the skull and crossbones.

citizenship, so Jews could be neither German citizens nor party members. As the party's head, the Fuehrer concentrated all the powers of the state in his person, so state and party were one, and its task was to achieve racial purity.

The SS and the Nazi State

As Nazi practice developed, the SS (Security Guards), headed by Heinrich Himmler, increasingly tended to absorb the state, a development that had no real basis in Nazi theory. The SS penetrated and undermined existing institutions with the aim of creating an SS state. An observer wrote: "Fundamentally there was no sphere of public life upon which the SS did not make its competing demands: the economic, ideological, military, scientific and technical spheres, as well as those of agrarian and population policies, legislation and general administration."

The SS was the major instrument of Nazi racism. Himmler, with a degree in agronomy and a short stint as a chicken farmer, sought to apply to human genetics principles similar to animal breeding. Besides killing off subhumans so they could not pass on their undesirable traits, Himmler favored eliminating monogamy as a means of passing on desired Nordic features with less interference from society. He calculated that by applying Nazi genetic principles, only 120 years would be required to reestablish the authentic German look in the country. He waxed poetic about how the SS would return to the soil as peasant-warriors and entertained other romantic visions. Himmler prided himself on his own and on Germans' tenderness toward animals and condemned hunting as pure murder. It was ironic that such a person claimed to value honesty, boasting that the SS had very high standards and threatening to execute without mercy SS men who stole anything from the Jews they murdered. Even though the SS had a duty to eliminate the Jews as the chief enemy of the German race, he stated that "We have no right to enrich ourselves by so much as a fur, a watch, a mark, or a cigarette or anything else."

EVERYDAY LIFE

Most ordinary Germans accepted the Nazi regime and believed in National Socialism. Because most were not Jews, leftists, or members of religious sects that the Nazis targeted, such as the Jehovah's Witnesses, they had little contact with the authorities. The dreaded secret police, the Gestapo, could not have controlled the population if the regime did not have at least the tacit consent of the people.

Ordinary Germans

Germans during the Third Reich generally went about their own business and making a living. They knew that the Nazis persecuted Jews and political opponents, but the terror did not affect their own lives. There are even indications that a majority of Germans frowned on the violence and brutality of Kristallnacht and that public opinion, after hearing talk of gassings during World War II, criticized the practice. Germans told jokes about their leaders, including Hitler. Theoretically, the dissemination of such humor could result in severe punishments, but later surveys indicate that people did not expect to receive such punishment. Certainly, jokes, grumbling, and the like did not threaten the regime, nor did people intend them to do so. With the economy going well and with Germany respected internationally, most Germans felt satisfied. Most of them esteemed Hitler, even if they did not agree with all aspects of the regime.

Resisters who were ashamed of Nazism did appear in Germany, but generally restricted their activities to discussions. Perhaps the most famous, the Kreisau Circle of James Helmuth von Moltke, aimed to restore a decent German government once Hitler fell from power. This dangerous activity resulted in the execution of von Moltke, but no armed resistance or strong exile movement materialized.

On some social issues the Nazis demonstrated an ambivalent attitude. Some opposed bourgeois values, Hitler himself being the epitome of this outlook. In its relationship with most Germans, however, the party supported a bourgeois lifestyle. This approach won out with the enforcement of nineteenth-century behavioral norms and attitudes toward sex.

A similar ambivalent view emerged toward homosexuals. The number of homosexuals who were arrested and condemned to prison is unknown, although historians seem to accept 50,000 as a reasonable figure. Nazi authorities sent some of these prisoners to concentration camps, where they suffered about a 60 percent death rate, higher than the political prisoners. Nevertheless, with Nazi leaders estimating the number of gay people in Germany at 2 million, the arrests represented a limited number. In contrast to their views on race, the Nazis considered homosexuals curable because they supposedly had been seduced. Hitler himself had declared the homosexuality of his colleague Roehm a private matter, even if he used it against Roehm and the SA during the "Night of the Long Knives" and willingly exploited the charge against other enemies. After June 1934, the government stepped up the persecution of gays, but the campaign remained limited because, according to scholar Harry Oosterhuis, a widespread crackdown would have devastated the ranks of Nazi organizations.

BIOGRAPHICAL SKETCHES

Gertrud Scholtz-Klink
Unrepentant!

The daughter of a surveyor, the future chief of the Nazi Women's Group (NSF) was born Gertrud Treusch in Adelsheim (Baden), Germany, on February 9, 1902. In 1920 she married Friedrich Klink, future Nazi district leader of Offenburg.
She did social and propaganda work for the party, and in March 1930, her husband died of a heart attack during a demonstration. Spurred by a desire for revenge, her involvement with Nazism increased, and she took the lead in organizing the women of Baden in support of the Nazi cause. In 1932 she married Gunther Scholtz, a country doctor.

In 1931, the Nazis established the NSF as the central women's organization. Scholtz-Klink had been rising in the ranks of the Nazi women's movement and, following the Nazi takeover in 1933, she headed the National Women's Labor Corps. Her administrative talents, skill in cooperating with Catholic women, and Aryan appearance brought her to the attention of national Nazi leaders. Her close collaboration with Erich Hilgenfelt, director of national welfare, allowed her to overcome more accomplished rivals and led to persistent rumors that they were lovers. In February 1934, Adolf Hitler named Scholtz-Klink national women's leader of the Third Reich. German propaganda successfully portrayed her as one of the most important personalities in the Nazi leadership, and on a visit to England in 1939, the British press called her "the Perfect Nazi Woman." In 1940, two years after her divorce from Scholtz, she married an SS general. Before the marriage, an investigation of her background for four generations revealed that she did not have any Jewish blood.

Frequently seen in Hitler's company on public occasions, Scholtz-Klink had little influence on policy. Understanding that she would probably lose her position if she showed initiative, she was docile, downplayed ideology, and concentrated on everyday administration. She responded to allegations that she had no clout by stating that this was because Nazi leaders expressed their wishes orally. She claimed absolute independence for the Nazi women's movement because "No man ever represented us in the outside world. We spoke for ourselves." She insisted that she ran her organization in a democratic manner because, since it was a big happy family, the women ironed out their problems over tea. Even top Nazis were confused about her position in the state.

During the last days of World War II, Scholtz-Klink suffered depression and frequently failed to perform her official duties. Following Berlin's fall, the Russians captured her, but she escaped. She and her husband hid out in a small village as Heinrich and Maria Stuckebruck and worked as bakers. They were denazified under these false names in 1948 but were soon found out. A French court sentenced them to eighteen months in jail on April 14, 1948, for using false documents. In 1949, a German court sentenced Scholtz-Klink to eighteen months for having been the NSF leader, but commuted the sentence because she had already served the time. In 1950, an appeals court categorized both Scholtz-Klink and her husband as having been major criminals during the Nazi regime. The court condemned her to thirty months in a work camp, prohibited her from working as a teacher or journalist for ten years, and excluded her from political activity for life. Scholtz-Klink lived quietly until 1978, when she published her autobiography. Consisting primarily of speeches and articles written during the Third Reich, the book is an administrative report, rather than a reflection on her life. In interviews she praised the glory days, defended the Third Reich's most extreme policies, and reveled in her own role. More than forty years after its fall, Gertrud Scholtz-Klink remained an unbroken, enthusiastic, and unrepentant supporter of Nazism.

Nazi theory and practice toward women was also fundamentally ambiguous. Although the Nazis saw women as having their major role in the home, producing children, in 1931 they created the NSF. This was a centralized organization that was designed to regularize the auxiliary work—such as establishing soup kitchens, providing medical help to Nazi fighters, mending uniforms, and sewing flags and banners—provided by many local Nazi women's organizations. Between 1932 and 1933, the women's organization lost most of its important functions, especially as the vehicle attracting the young to the movement. In February 1934, the unimaginative Gertrud Scholtz-Klink became NSF head. The NSF did not easily reconcile itself to its loss of prestige and status but, given the primacy that the Nazis assigned to the male organizations and the competition that the NSF faced from women's organizations that were affiliated with the traditional religions, little could be done to restore its former reputation.

Ironically, the scant interest the Nazis had for women's organizations allowed these organizations greater freedom. In contrast to other parties that gave them greater importance but then limited their scope when they went off in directions the male leaders did not approve, the Nazi women's organizations could plan their activities with considerable flexibility. This liberty included interpreting the Fuehrer's thoughts, supervising mass marches and rallies, administering funds they collected, making speeches, and responding to rivals. The ideas of Nazi women may have been reactionary, but women expressed them in their own way, and, despite the official rhetoric, as Claudia Koonz pointed out, they never believed that they would return exclusively to homemaking and sought to open different areas of public life to their gender.

Cultural Aspects

In the cultural field, the Nazi government took over all areas of life. Education at all levels came under its control, and it imposed its racist thinking on intellectual discourse. A centralized Reich Chamber of Culture, established by Joseph Goebbels in September 1933, ran arts and leisure. Divided into subchambers for the different arts, this organization enrolled artists and professionals on a compulsory basis, weeded out what it considered dangerous elements and movements, and promoted "healthy" ones. The regime thus quickly took control of the country's writers, university professors, and other intellectuals and held it until 1945.

Submission also characterized German religious organizations. The Protestant churches objected more to Himmler's undermining of sexual mores in attempting to create a purified race than to the implementation of the more brutal features of Nazi racial policy. Hitler unified the Lutheran churches, traditionally close to the state, under a single authority controlled by the government and jailed opposition religious leaders. The Catholic Church, potentially less subservient to Nazi authority because it came under the pope's jurisdiction, feared subjugation to the Nazis and to the state's power. In July 1933, it signed a concordat with the state that prohibited priests from participating in politics and giving the regime a role in naming bishops. As in the Italian case, observers construed the concordat as moral approval for the regime, and Hitler apparently considered it significant in the struggle against the Jews. The extent to which Papal Nuncio Eugenio Pacelli, future Pope Pius XII, gave in to Hitler on these issues remains controversial. Although the Catholic hierarchy made some attempt to defend Jews who had converted, neither the Catholic nor the Protestant churches issued powerful rebukes against the Nazi racial policy, and the government did not hesitate to send any clergy or religious opponents to concentration camps.

The propaganda machine, which Goebbels created and ran, was instrumental in creating a consensus for the regime. The son of a Rhineland Catholic working-class family, Goebbels had a club foot that hampered him physically and psychologically. During Nazism's early days, his infirmity subjected the "little doctor" to ridicule from the muscular, well-built but unintelligent party specimens of the Aryan race. In 1926, Goebbels had demanded Hitler's expulsion from the party, but he grew to adore the Fuehrer and worked diligently to imbue the leader with a mystical quality. He orchestrated public spectacles favoring the regime, with the great marching columns, the flags, banners, searchlights, fanfares, and the coordinated shouting of slogans illustrated in Leni Riefenstahl's film *The Triumph of the Will.* Goebbels aimed to dissolve the individual into the mass and to induce the mindlessness that numbed the nation for the greater power of Hitler.

To organize leisure time, the Germans created the Strength Through Joy movement, modeled after the Italian *Dopolavoro.* This organization allowed workers to attend movies and live theater, to travel, and to participate in a host of activities. After World War II, German workers frequently cited the economic security of the Nazi era and their trips to the theater as the highlights of their lives.

Youths

The Nazis concentrated on indoctrinating and regimenting the country's young people aged 10 to 18 by incorporating them into the Hitler Youth, made compulsory between 1936 and 1939. Boys and girls aged 10 to 14 belonged to the German Young People and to the Young Girls League. Afterward, they graduated to the Hitler Youth and to the League of German Girls.

Boys and girls reveled in the camaraderie and feelings of power that came from membership in an association, uniforms, and a military atmosphere. Girls especially enjoyed the experience of time away from their stifling home lives. However, rebellious teenagers grew restive against the obligation to conform to the rules of the Nazi youth organizations. Hitler Youth leaders kept boys and girls strictly separate and prohibited them from smoking, drinking, having sex, or even from going out at night. Girls who dared wear makeup, high-heeled shoes, or short dresses had their heads shaved.

The rigidity and separation of the sexes that characterized the Nazi youth organizations encouraged the formation of rival groups that the regime frowned upon. Edelweiss Pirate groups consisted of boys and girls aged 14 to 18, mainly working class, who met during their leisure time with the avowed aim of escaping control by the Hitler Youth. They packed their gear during weekends, went to the countryside to camp together, and met with like-minded bands from other villages. They either avoided Hitler Youth patrols or attacked them, depending of the circumstances, according to the slogan: "Eternal War on the Hitler Youth." These adolescents experimented with subjects the Hitler Youth considered

Hitler wished to better the economic and social life of the Germans. This included fostering the development of an automobile ordinary Germans could afford, the "People's Car," or Volkswagen. A design of this car was sent to Pininfarina, the Italian automotive designer. He pronounced the design perfect, but suggested the addition of the rear side windows. Here is a photo of Hitler opening a Volkswagen factory on May 27, 1938.

taboo, especially sex, and the Nazi authorities viewed their exploits as delinquency.

The Swing Youth also sought to escape the conformity and rigidity of the Hitler Youth. This movement consisted of urban middle-class teenagers who rebelled against the bland music sanctioned by the regime, jitterbugging in city dance halls to the sound of jazz rhythms that the government frowned upon as "Negro" and foreign. These adolescents had more means and education than the Edelweiss Pirates; knew a smattering of a foreign language, usually English; and could afford to frequent dance halls, buy records, pay the fees to attend concerts given by foreign bands, and meet in homes big enough to hold large groups. Starting from traditional jazz music still played in Germany, they radicalized it and danced in ways the authorities considered sexually suggestive and sleazy. Although apolitical, the activities of the Swing Youth struck at the heart of the regime's philosophical core because its adherents had grown up during the Nazi regime and should have served as a showcase for it. The Nazis denounced the supposedly loose morals of the Swing Youth and discussed sending its leaders to concentration camps.

Reorganizing the Economy

Once in power the Nazis adopted new economic policies that spurred a recovery and prepared the country for war.

The Nazis quickly took on the powerful labor unions and their leftist political allies. In 1933 and 1934 they destroyed the labor unions through a terror campaign and by imposing strict controls on the labor force. They eliminated the possibility of striking and dismissed Socialist and Communist workers and shop stewards. Wages leveled off even as rearmament proceeded, but wages did not go up even when the economy improved dramatically because of the need to absorb large numbers of unemployed people, government-imposed controls, and the lack of unions.

In order to ensure their control over workers, the Nazis organized labor in the German Labor Front (DAF), led by Robert Ley, that industrial workers were obliged to join, and eliminated the influence of Nazi labor organizers. This arrangement symbolized the ideological unity of the Germans. Fearing too much concentration of power, employers and the government agreed that the DAF would not be the vehicle through which to settle the everyday issues of German industrial life. In November 1933, the employers joined the organization. Industry was considered to consist of industrial communities with a Fuehrer and followers. Consequently, industrial enterprises had to agree to councils that would advise administrators. Employers did not like this idea, but their return to profitability induced them to accept it.

In order to put people back to work and accelerate production for the coming war, the Nazis drew up a Four-Year Plan directed by *Luftwaffe* (air force) head Hermann Goering. The plan envisioned increasing governmental authority over workers, including the control of wages and production, and measures restricting job mobility. The government hesitated to implement these measures because of a labor shortage, and it anticipated workers' resistance. The authorities drafted workers for jobs on war-related enterprises in June 1938, but felt confident enough to institute wage and price controls only after the outbreak of war.

The government took pains to appear neutral in the relationship between labor and capital because a substantial number of workers had supported the Nazis and belonged to the party. The regime actively involved workers in its political accomplishments, subsidized leisure activities through the Strength Through Joy movement, and developed a "people's car," the Volkswagen, to increase the workers' personal mobility. Leisure activities included organized tourism, concerts by symphony orchestras at the factories, visits to theaters, participation in and attendance at sports events, and the creation of factory libraries (no subversive literature). Despite these activities, the workers lacked real power, and conflicts with their bosses smoldered under the surface.

BIOGRAPHICAL SKETCHES

Hermann Goering
Nazi Chieftain

Hermann Goering was probably the most visible and popular leader of the Third Reich besides Hitler. The son of a judge who had represented Bismarck in South West Africa, Goering had an aristocratic background that set him apart from the other prominent Nazi leaders.

Born on January 12, 1893, in Rosenheim, Germany, Goering fought in World War I as an infantry lieutenant and combat pilot. In 1918, he commanded Manfred von Richthofen's fighter squadron after the Red Baron's death, shooting down twenty-two enemy airplanes and winning two prestigious medals. After the war, he piloted planes for air shows in Denmark and Sweden, where he met his future wife. His love of adventure drew him to the Nazi party, and in 1923 he participated in the abortive Beer Hall putsch. Wounded, he fled to Sweden, where he had a mental breakdown and developed a life-long addiction to morphine. He returned to Germany in 1927 after an amnesty.

Goering's access to military, conservative, business, and aristocratic circles proved valuable for the Nazis, as did his organizational abilities. He was credited with the dramatic Nazi electoral victory of July 31, 1932, and was elected president of the Reichstag. When Hitler became chancellor in January 1933, Goering took over the Prussian Interior Ministry. Prussia, the biggest German state, played a crucial role in establishing effective Nazi control of the country. Goering purged the Prussian police force and, with Heinrich Himmler and Reinhard Heydrich, set up the first concentration camps. After passage of the March 1933 emergency decree, he eliminated the remnants of civil liberties in Prussia, imprisoned Nazi opponents, and destroyed the left-wing press. He also directed the "Night of the Long Knives," June 30, 1934, that destroyed his rival Ernst Roehm and the SA.

Goering amassed more power, offices, and wealth than any other Nazi chieftain. Appointed commander of the air force on March 1, 1935, he oversaw its rapid expansion. In 1936, he ran the Four-Year Plan that gave him effective control of the country's economic life. The Hermann Goering Works, established in 1937,

continued

continued

created a private industrial empire that employed 700,000 workers and allowed him to become fabulously wealthy. He lived in spectacular quarters in Berlin and in a hunting lodge outside the city, where he organized ostentatious parties and hunts. He collected art masterpieces and, during the war, stole many of them from all over Europe. However, Goering did not let his luxurious life interfere in the politics that had allowed him to attain it. He plotted against rivals who might have threatened him and worked out the details of Nazi actions against the Jews. He was so successful that in September 1939, Hitler named him his successor.

Goering had exaggerated pretensions to military greatness that proved his undoing during World War II. He made egregious errors that produced the German failure to defeat Britain from the air and contributed to the inability to defend Germany from Allied bombers. Hitler blamed him for these failures and came to hate him—more so because, compromised by the favors he had bestowed on him, he could not get rid of him. Aware of his sinking prestige, Goering withdrew into a world of denial. Just before Germany's final defeat, Goering misinterpreted Hitler's statement that he would stay in his bunker until the end and declared he would take over Germany. Hitler stripped him of his posts and had him arrested, but on May 9, 1945, the Americans captured him. The Nuremberg Tribunal found him guilty of war crimes and sentenced him to death. On October 5, 1946, two hours before his scheduled execution, Goering cheated the hangman by biting down on a cyanide capsule he had hidden in his mouth.

Nazism and Capitalism: Arms and Autobahns

Despite anticapitalist Nazi rhetoric and measures that appeared contrary to capitalist interests, the Nazis implanted capitalist policies to accelerate Germany's economic recovery and rearmament. The government attacked the high unemployment rate by launching a large road-building program—the *Autobahns*. When rearmament began full force after 1935, the government instituted a complex system of controls over the economy, including planning boards and governmental ventures into strategic industrial sectors that were necessary for arms production, including the massive Hermann Goering Steel Works. Large private enterprises, such as Krupp and I. G. Farben, profited handsomely from rearmament, but small businesses were unable to compete with the large private and state industries that enjoyed cozy arrangements with the Nazi Party. By spending enormous amounts on public works and rearmament, the Nazis eradicated the unemployment of the depression era, and governmental controls avoided inflation.

The Germans paid a heavy cost for governmental policies in the form of higher prices. Because the government reoriented the German economy away from consumer items and banned the importation of some goods, they paid higher prices for substitutes, wages failed to keep pace with production, and war-oriented state enterprises came with a high price tag. War preparations created a vicious economic circle: rearmament encouraged aggressiveness, which created a greater need for arms. Despite the great progress made by German industry, the country's war potential still fell short of the demands that Hitler made in preparation for the coming conflict. When World War II broke out, Germany was short of arms, food, fuel, and raw materials. The rapid conquests that were made during the early months of the war allowed Germany to make up the shortages, as Hitler had envisaged, but only temporarily.

The Nazis singled out agriculture as the inspiration for a romanticized and racist ideology and promised good times for this sector. Through the SS, the Nazis, in an ideal world, would return to the soil that they believed had nourished their race. This idea and promises of economic improvement had won the Nazis crucial support in rural areas, but they did not fulfill the Nazis' assurances. The government's halfhearted agricultural measures failed to stop the flight of the peasants from the land into the cities, whose population increased dramatically during the first five years of Nazi rule. Although the Nazis instituted a policy of restricting imports and firming up prices, rural income failed to keep pace with national income, and fewer people established farms during the Nazi era than during the Weimar period. Owners of small- and medium-sized farms sank deeper into debt, and peasants could not afford to make needed technological improvements. The Nazi emphasis on industry as a necessary facet of war preparedness makes it hardly surprising that governmental aid to farmers proved inadequate.

Social Ramifications

Nazi industrial policy had unintended effects that contradicted theory. The Nazis believed that women should remain at home producing more children for the master race, discouraging them from entering the labor market, politics, and the universities. The Nazis introduced measures, such as marriage credits, bonuses for children to combat earlier feminist demands for emancipation and to keep German women at home. With the booming economy and the resulting labor shortage caused by its rearmament policy, the government gradually reintegrated women into the workforce without admitting it. Women were paid less for their work than men and found it difficult to advance, but the number of women working outside the home increased from less than 4.25 million in 1933 to 5.2 million in 1938. Despite their ideology, the Nazis favored a trend that would accelerate during World War II and the postwar era.

Similarly, the Nazis advocated revolutionizing the existing society but implemented the idea only superficially. They claimed to aim at the creation of a people's community in which everyone would be equal under the leader; the people were national or "Volk" comrades. The Nazis scorned the existing society; derided the old bourgeoisie, capitalists, and intellectuals; glorified peasants and workers; and established a pervasive youth movement. The "people's community" had to act as one, especially on special holidays. On these occasions, the Nazis organized mass demonstrations with the emphasis on slogans epitomizing their ideals—"Blood and Soil" for the peasants, "Brawn and Brain" for the workers. Regimentation increased dramatically, and beginning in 1935, "labor soldiers"—workers—had to sign up at labor offices and be subject to the needs of rearmament.

The despised capitalists represented the old regime, but, contradicting this image, capitalists who cooperated with Nazism belonged to the "good" variety. The government favored charitable societies to aid less fortunate comrades and mobilized the population to raise money for the poor. On occasion, it used these events to humiliate the groups they despised, such as intellectuals. In 1937, the Nazis sent Leipzig professor and Nobel Prize-winning nuclear physicist Werner Heisenberg out onto the cold city streets to beg funds to aid the urban poor. Ironically enough, by knocking over class barriers, in the end National Socialism contributed to the modernization of German society, a goal that Nazi ideology professed to oppose.

Bibliographical Essay

Richard Evans's *The Third Reich in Power* (New York, 2006) is the most complete book on this period and beyond. A good general work that discusses the topics considered in this chapter is Martin Broszat, *The Hitler State: The Foundation and Development of the Internal Structure of the Third Reich* (London, 1981). More recently, there is Michael Burleigh, *The Third Reich: A New History* (New York, 2000).

The social impact of Nazism is examined by David Schoenbaum, *Hitler's Social Revolution: Class and Status in Nazi Germany, 1933–1939* (New York, 1997), who examines broken pledges to farmers and the lower middle class. William Allen Sheridan, *The Nazi Seizure of Power* (New York, 1984), discusses the events and social impact in a single town. David Crew, *Nazism and German Society: 1933–1945* (London, 1994), emphasizes interpretations. Timothy W. Mason concentrates on labor in *Social Policy in the Third Reich* (Providence, R.I., 1993) and in a series of essays (that also include Fascist Italy), *Nazism, Fascism, and the Working Class* (Cambridge, UK, 1995). Proving your Aryan blood was important; on this issue, see Eric Ehrenreich, *The Nazi Ancestral Proof* (Bloomington, Ind., 2007). Three works that explore the ordinary German's world during this period are Bernt Engelmann, *In Hitler's Germany: Everyday Life in the Third Reich* (London, 1988); Elaine Halleck, *Living in Nazi Germany* (San Diego, Calif., 2004); and Detlev Peukert, *Inside Nazi Germany: Conformity and Opposition in Everyday Life* (Harmondsworth, UK, 1989), which also discusses the issue of racism in everyday life. Eric A. Johnson's *Nazi Terror: The Gestapo, Jews, and Ordinary Germans* (New York, 1999), is an excellent detailed work on the everyday interactions of Germans, the Gestapo, and Jews. Volume 1 of Saul Friedlaender's *Nazi Germany and the Jews* (Cambridge, Mass., 1997) examines the period discussed in this chapter. Richard Bessel, ed., *Life in the Third Reich* (New York, 1987), discusses how Germans perceived the actions of their government during this period. Sarah Gordon published a nuanced book on *Hitler, Germans, and the "Jewish Question"* (Princeton, N.J., 1984). John Cornwell, *Hitler's Pope: The Secret History of Pius XII* (Harmondsworth, UK, 1999), is a controversial interpretation of Eugenio Pacelli's role during this period and as pope.

Elimination of the Jews in the Reich has been interpreted both as stemming from a design and as gradually evolving. Lucy Dawidowicz, *The War Against the Jews, 1933–1945* (Harmondsworth, UK, 1990), and Karl A. Schleunes, *The Twisted Road to Auschwitz: Nazi Policy Toward German Jews* (Urbana, Ill., 1990), take different positions on this subject. Robert Gellately's *The Gestapo and German Society: Enforcing Racial Policy, 1933–1945* (Oxford, UK, 1991) shows the public's reaction to the dreaded secret police and its operations.

Nazi women are discussed by Claudia Koonz, *Mothers in the Fatherland: Women, the Family, and Nazi Politics* (New York, 1987). Jill Stephenson examines the origins, development, and functions of women's groups associated with the party from the 1920s to 1945 in *The Nazi Organisation of Women* (London, 1981).

Biographies of Hitler's subordinates can also lead to an understanding of the Nazi phenomenon. Joachim C. Fest gathered a series of short sketches that serve as an excellent introduction to these subalterns: *The Face of the Third Reich: Portraits of the Nazi Leadership* (New York, 1970), from which the citation on the SS state and Himmler's statement on the duty of SS soldiers to be honest are taken (pp. 117 and 118). On Himmler, see Willi Frischauer, *Himmler: The Evil Genius of the Third Reich* (Boston, 1953), and Richard Breitman, *The Architect of Genocide: Himmler and the Final Solution* (Hanover, N.H., 1991). Another of Hitler's subordinates described Himmler's plans, Albert Speer, *The Slave State: Heinrich: Himmler's Masterplan for SS Supremacy* (London, 1981). Anthony Read, *The Devil's Disciples* (New York, 2004), is a book on Hitler's inner circle.

On the SS itself, consult Adrian Weale, *The SS: A New History* (London, 2010), a complete history from its rise to its fall. Gerard Reitlinger, *The SS: Alibi of a Nation* (New York, 1968), includes a discussion of the relationship with the SA, and Helmut Krausnick et al., *The Anatomy of the SS State* (London, 1982). Biographies of Hitler's other lieutenants include Ralf Georg Reuth, *Goebbels* (San Diego, Calif., 1994); Helmut Heiber, *Goebbels* (New York, 1972); and the earlier Curt Riess, *Joseph Goebbels* (Garden City, N.Y. 1948). Take a look also at *Joseph Goebbels* (New York, 2009). Leonard Moseley has written a comprehensive biography of Hermann Goering, *The Reich Marshal* (Garden City, N.Y., 1974); see also Richard J. Overy, *Goering: The Iron Man* (London, 1987). Joachim von Lang published an extensive biography of Hitler's influential secretary, *Martin Bormann* (Garden City, N.Y., 1974).

Books on more specialized issues include one on birth control and abortion: Atina Grossmann, *Reforming Sex* (New York, 1995). Michael Burleigh, *Death and Deliverance* (London, 2002), is an excellent work on the Nazi euthanasia program and some of its antecedents; the quotation on the cost of maintaining patients is on p. 99. Henry Friedlander makes the connection between Nazi policies on euthanasia and the final solution in *The Origins of Nazi Genocide: From Euthanasia to the Final Solution* (Chapel Hill, N.C., 1995). For some of the other groups discussed, see Richard Plant, *The Pink Triangle* (New York, 1986), for the Nazi attack on homosexuals; Sylvie Graffard and Michel Reynaud, *The Jehovah's Witnesses and the Nazis* (New York, 2001); M. V. Seeman et al., *The Holocaust and the Mentally Ill* (Armonk, N.Y., 2006); Suzanne E. Evans, *Forgotten Crimes: The Holocaust and People With Disabilities* (Chicago, 2004). On the Rom during this period, there is a chapter by Ian Hancock, "The Roots of Antigypsyism: To the Holocaust and After," in C. Jan Colijn and Marcia Sachs, eds., *Configuring the Holocaust* (Lanham, Md., 1997).

Dietrich Orlow, *The History of the Nazi Party,* 2 vols. (Pittsburgh, 1969–1973), analyzes the impact that the achievement of governmental power on the NSDAP. The army's role is analyzed by John W. Wheeler-Bennet, *The Nemesis of Power,* 2d ed. (London, 1980), the standard work, and Klaus-Jurgen Muller, *Army, Politics, and Society in Germany, 1933–1945* (New York, 1987). Ian Kershaw, *The "Hitler Myth": Image and Reality in the Third Reich* (Oxford, UK, 1989), previously cited, discusses public opinion during the Nazi period.

The debate about the extent to which the German people supported Hitler's policies against the Jews has always stirred historians. Two opposing views may be found in Daniel Goldhagen, *Hitler's Willing Executioners: Ordinary Germans and the Holocaust* (New York, 1996), and in the diary of a Jew who lived in the Third Reich, Victor Klemperer, *I Will Bear Witness: A Diary of the Nazi Years,* 2 vols. (New York, 1998). For an examination of Goldhagen's impact, see Geoff Eley, ed., *The Goldhagen Effect: History, Memory, Nazism—Facing the German Past* (Ann Arbor, Mich., 2000), and Robert R. Shandley, ed., *Unwilling Germans? The Goldhagen Debate* (Minneapolis, Minn., 1998).

On social issues, consult David Schoenbaum's *Hitler's Social Revolution: Class and Status in Nazi Germany 1933–1939* (London, 1966). A book of essays, Richard Bessel's *Life in the Third Reich* (Oxford, UK, 1987), previously cited, includes valuable treatments of important social issues. M. L. Thornton, *Nazism 1918–1945* (Oxford, UK, 1966), a general treatment of Nazism, has several useful chapters. Paul Brooker's *The Faces of Fraternalism* (Oxford, UK, 1991) examines consensus in Germany and Italy. See Chapter 12 for works on Italy.

On the churches, see Ernst Christian Helmreich, *The German Churches Under Hitler* (Detroit, 1979), and J. S. Conway, *The Nazi Persecution of the Churches* (London, 1968).

Good discussions of Nazi economic policies and their impact are in Avraham Barkai, *Nazi Economics: Ideology, Theory, and Policies* (New Haven, Conn., 1990), and Richard J. Overy, *The Nazi Economic Recovery, 1932–1938,* 2d ed. (Cambridge, UK, 1996).

Books emphasizing different interpretations of the Nazi phenomenon include Ian Kershaw, *The Nazi Dictatorship: Problems and Perspectives of Interpretations,* 3rd ed. (London, 1993). Thomas Childers and Jane Caplan, eds., *Reevaluating the Third Reich* (New York, 1993), is a series of excellent essays that discuss important themes regarding the history of the Third Reich and that illustrate some new thinking about Nazi Germany.

George L. Mosse has written many works on the ideas that eventually flowed into Nazism. Most relevant for this chapter is *Nationalism and Sexuality: Respectability and Abnormal Sexuality in Modern Europe* (New York, 1985). This book explains how such stereotypes as healthy, degenerate, normal, and abnormal could end up in the persecution of Jews, Gypsies, homosexuals, and the handicapped. Mosse also wrote *The Fascist Revolution: Toward A General Theory of Fascism* (New York, 1999), which is primarily concerned with Nazism but has interesting essays on Italy and France.

After the fall of Nazism, a debate took place on whether it had deep roots in German society and whether the country followed a "special path" that led to Hitler. This is known as the *Sonderweg* debate. For the ramifications of this debate, see Hans-Ulrich Wehler, *The German Empire, 1871–1918* (New York, 1985), and the essay "The German Identity and Historical Comparison," in Peter Baldwin, ed., *Reworking the Past* (Boston, 1987). See also Charles S. Maier, *The Unmasterable Past: History, Holocaust, and German National Identity* (Cambridge, Mass., 1988), and David Blackbourn and Geoff Eley, *The Peculiarities of German History: Bourgeois Society and Politics in Nineteenth-Century Germany* (New York, 1984).

CHAPTER 16

Interwar Society and Culture

CHAPTER OUTLINE

Society • Entertainment and High Culture • Technology and Society •
Pure Science: Revolution and Travail

BIOGRAPHICAL SKETCHES

Ettore Majorana, The Enduring Mystery • Lise Meitner,
The Role of Insight

World War I caused many changes in European society and culture. The sorrow caused by so many deaths dampened the European zest for living. Gigantic ossuaries containing soldiers' bones sprouted over the European landscape; hyperinflation destroyed the savings of Germans; fascism took over in Italy; war, boundary disputes, ethnic divisions, anti-Semitism, and incipient dictatorships disrupted East European life. Nevertheless, at least in the West, the middle class had come to expect leisure time and social welfare as a right. During the 1920s and the depression, European states passed legislation guaranteeing their citizens paid free time and other benefits, while technological changes improved the lives of ordinary people, and quantum mechanics revolutionized modern life and attitudes.

SOCIETY

World War I created a more subdued atmosphere in Europe, but the need for war supplies and labor improved the economic position of many people, and, on good days, British vacationers on the southern coast could hear the report of shells fired on the battlefield.

Private Lives

After 1918, the toned-down lifestyle of ordinary Europeans appeared in more subdued leisurely activities, such as reading books and daily newspapers, that became an ingrained habit by 1920 in Britain. Advertising came into its own, contributing most of the newspaper revenue and exercising an important impact on economics and society.

The results of the conflict revolutionized social habits during the 1920s and 1930s on the continent. In Germany hyperinflation removed the restraints from young bourgeois women to run off and get married without waiting for the financial security or the socially appropriate bridegroom that prewar attitudes demanded. Bolshevik Russia witnessed an extraordinary emancipation of women from the sexual mores of the prerevolutionary era. In Italy a new mood of confidence among workers marked the Red Biennium before Fascism's rise. In general, European family ties became looser.

In England, men and women mixed more easily than they had before the war, a trend that resulted in a national debate on the place of women in society. Observers argued about whether women were the intellectual equals of men. Feminist organizations demanded political rights.

Society condemned abortion and punished it severely, as was seen in France, which enforced its abortion laws more strictly than before 1914. Birth control laws forced abstinence on couples who wanted to limit their families—wives frequently opting for separate rooms and barred doors. Despite the obstacles to birth control, however, fertility rates declined.

Women in Western Europe improved their political and legal status and attained greater social freedom. In Germany and Scandinavia, they received the right to vote. In Britain, the first woman entered Parliament in 1919, and women were admitted to full membership in the professions and academic life—despite professorial protests. Throughout the 1920s, Western countries progressively repealed many legal disabilities that hampered women's progress, and women's growing freedom encouraged discussions of formerly taboo topics, such as homosexuality.

Fashion

Women's fashions reflected their emancipation, and commentators complained that women dressed too scantily: short skirts, sleeves above the elbows, floppy hats, skimpy lingerie. High heels, long associated with the theater and immorality, became common. Only rich women could afford silk stockings to go with them, and middle-class women contented themselves with wool or cotton stockings. The 1920s "flapper" made her entrance with bobbed hair and dancing to jazz rhythms. American music and African American singers, such as Josephine Baker in France, became models for a new life criticized by traditionalists. The upper and middle classes set the dance styles at first but later preferred restaurants and supper clubs and left the dance halls to their lower-middle-class brethren. In Britain new dance palaces dotted the postwar landscape, and skill in ballroom dancing seemed inversely proportional to social status. The emphasis on life, enjoyment, and youth was a reaction to the deaths caused by the recent conflict. Age lost its social status to youth and trim physiques, as reflected in the less formal fashions for both sexes. Men's beards disappeared, and English children earned points with their playmates by shouting "Beaver" when they spotted a man with a beard.

Perhaps African-American Josephine Baker best epitomizes the changes in women's roles during the Interwar period. She lived in France where she became the best-known entertainer there and was a friend of the most important artists and writers of the period. During World War II, she worked in the French Resistance and later supported the American Civil Rights movement in the 1950s and 1960s. She died in France on April 12, 1975, and was buried with French military honors.

Tourism and Sports

The desire to live life more fully brought a greater appetite for tourism and sports. Both had grown before World War I, and the expansion continued after the conflict. In 1930, a million Britons vacationed on the continent, producing a boom in the number of travel agencies and hotels. Unlike the pre-1914 period, tourists required passports to travel even to other European countries. In England the number of people taking vacations increased even during the depression; by the late 1930s, one in three Britons, 15 million, spent at least a week away from home. Workers came to regard paid vacations as necessary to confront the stresses of modern life, and contracts awarding them proliferated in the 1920s and 1930s.

The vogue for tourism and vacations stimulated the growth of the automotive industry, and in England, the number of motor vehicles increased from 500,000 in 1920 to 1.5 million in 1930 and to 3 million in 1939. Congestion resulted, and traffic regulations proliferated. Paris adopted parking rules in 1930, pedestrian crossings in 1931, and hand-operated electric traffic lights in 1932. The Italians invented the limited-access highway, but the French considered toll roads Fascist. In France victims of traffic accidents increased from 2,042 in 1930 to 5,000 in 1934, and car insurance was introduced to compensate them. City roads improved, but rural ones still presented considerable challenges. In 1929, the hearse carrying the

Europeans began taking vacations on a large scale before World War I. This trend continued and grew after the conflict. Despite economic setbacks, by the Interwar period vacations were a staple of European life. Here is a poster from the period touting a vacation on the Italian seaside.

body of French statesman Georges Clemenceau to Paris bogged down in the mud and had to be pulled out by teams of oxen.

Besides vacations, Europeans emphasized physical fitness, especially outdoor recreational activities such as walking and hiking. In Germany, "Pathfinder" groups—including Nobel-winning physicist Werner Heisenberg's—trekked on difficult excursions through the wild, something the more casual British called rambling; in Italy another Nobel Prize winner, nuclear physicist Enrico Fermi, missed no opportunity to ski, swim, and play tennis.

Along with this trend, participatory sports grew enormously among the lower-middle and working classes—particularly women. Camping, cycling, and rambling boomed. Dealers sold more than 500,000 bicycles annually in England in the mid-1930s, while the 3,500 cycling clubs attracted 60,000 members. The radio, associations, and party organizations encouraged physical fitness through sports. Dog and motorcycle racing especially appealed to the working class. Women demonstrated their newfound independence through sports, and the number of women's sports association exploded. During the 1920s and 1930s, sports clothing revealed more of their bodies because physical activity demanded shorter skirts, shorts, pants—and briefer bathing suits. In 1922 the Women's Amateur Athletic

Association was founded, and in 1928 women participated in the Olympic games for the first time.

ENTERTAINMENT AND HIGH CULTURE

Major changes in entertainment and culture, especially the cinema, took place during the 1920s and 1930s and established the basis for the extraordinary world-wide cultural impact that European filmmakers achieved following World War II. The nature of the changes depended on technological changes and the war's terrible legacy.

Motion Pictures

Cinema matured during the war and exploded in popularity during the 1920s and 1930s. Besides their entertainment value, movies had an important social function as a leveling experience. To be sure, the rich watched movies in more luxurious theaters than did ordinary people, but they enjoyed the same films, cheered the same movie stars, and cried with them when Rudolph Valentino, an actor who captured the imagination of all classes, died prematurely. Movies encouraged families to go out together instead of the men leaving their wives and children at home to go drinking. Families went to the movies to laugh at Charlie Chaplin, one of the first movie superstars, who spoofed politicians and social customs during the 1920s and 1930s. American films became popular, and more films were directed at women.

Besides attracting families, movie theaters were attractive places to meet people and, for couples in love, to enjoy the privacy conferred by the dark. Statistics confirm the cinema's growing popularity. By 1937, 20 million Britons watched a movie once a week, showing that the depression did not reduce the size of audiences as theater owners successfully introduced double features, cartoons, and newsreels for the price of admission. In 1935, France counted 4,000 theaters, with 3,300 of them wired for "talkies."

The Flowering and Decline of German Cinema

Trends in high culture affecting literature and the arts influenced the movies through film reviews, theoretical journals, and film associations. Although American films tended to dominate the market, Europeans established film as a contemporary art form and as a serious field of study.

Weimar Germany unexpectedly flourished as the major center of cinema after the war and for a time challenged American commercial superiority. Germany had lagged behind other western countries, but World War I sowed the seeds for the startling development of German film. Seeking to combat Allied film propaganda and to jump-start the depressed film industry, the German government created a large subsidized film company, called the UFA, in 1917. After the war, the government sold its shares to private concerns, but by then Germany possessed the largest film studios in Europe. The pessimistic postwar atmosphere and the end of censorship encouraged experimentation and increased the quality of German films. The cinematic style that prevailed in early postwar Germany was *expressionism,* a term already familiar in prewar painting and postwar literature. Filmmakers belonging to this school explored not objective reality but the subjective feelings of artists responding to existence. Their film technique included abstraction, perceptive distortion, and symbolism. In 1919 the film that became the symbol of German filmmaking appeared: *The Cabinet of Dr. Caligari,* which launched the great decade of German cinema. This film, loosely based on a sex slaying of the period, was an attack on authority. The incongruously juxtaposed and strangely proportioned structures conveyed an unnatural feeling of doom; the film's atmosphere reflected the dismal postwar situation and inspired the American horror movies of the 1930s.

After 1925, expressionism's gloomy outlook fit in poorly with the renewed German economic prosperity, and German film turned toward other cinematic styles, such as the *Kammerspielfilm* (intimate theater) that essentially rejected expressionism and street realism, which accepted the world as it existed. By the late 1920s, however, economics and politics contributed to the demise of the German film as international agreements stabilizing the country's finances damaged the film industry, particularly an abortive agreement between the UFA and American film companies. Nationalist media magnate Alfred Hugenberg took over the UFA, and German studios turned to producing more nationalistic films and documentaries.

Despite the Great Depression, motion pictures, which existed even before World War I, became a mass industry during the Interwar period because movie theaters were cheap and provided a getaway for the family and privacy for young lovers. Here is a still from Fritz Lang's classic 1927 film, *Metropolis.*

Hugenberg's ownership of the UFA facilitated domination of the film industry by Nazi Propaganda Minister Joseph Goebbels after 1933. The Nazis specialized in the use of newsreels and documentaries for propaganda, as demonstrated by Leni Riefenstahl's famous *The Triumph of the Will,* presenting the 1934 Nuremberg party congress as a mystical-religious experience. The Nazis left the movie industry in private hands but would not allow films to criticize society, killing the German cinema's spirit.

Experimentation and Repression: Soviet Film

Film-as-documentary followed a similar trajectory in the USSR and flourished in the 1920s. In 1919 the government nationalized the film industry and put it under a committee headed by Nadezhda Krupskaya, Lenin's wife, who founded a film school in Moscow. Because of the shortage of equipment and film in the early days of the revolution, the committee concentrated on newsreels and documentaries. In the 1920s, Dziga Vertov, an early practitioner and theoretician of the documentary, developed imaginative means of organizing film to suit his propaganda purposes and produced a series of documentaries that were collectively known as film truth; in the process, he made a major contribution to the art of the montage that accounted for much of the style of Soviet films.

A great film director who ranks with American D. W. Griffith as "one of the two pioneering geniuses of the modern cinema," Sergei Eisenstein, emerged from the Soviet school. Eisenstein's 1925 masterpiece, *Battleship Potemkin,* tells the story of the 1905 revolution against the tsar and ranks as one of the most influential films in history. Eisenstein created modern editing techniques that emotionally involved the viewer in the events that were depicted. *Potemkin* gave Russian cinema an international influence it has lacked since.

Eisenstein and the Russian cinema eventually ran afoul of political interference. Eisenstein increasingly fell into disfavor with Stalin, who disparaged *October,* another masterpiece. Stalin recognized the cinema's power to move the masses and in 1928 and 1929 imposed greater party control on film as on all the arts, discouraging experimentation and proclaiming Socialist realism the official Soviet style.

New Cinematic Forms

Of the other major European countries, France was the most consistent center of experimentation. Cubism, surrealism, Dadaism, impressionism (unrelated to the school of painting), and other avant-garde movements flourished. Films analyzed Freudian-type sexual repression, the psychological basis of provincial middle-class marriages, and the lives of ordinary people and workers. The French film industry introduced several important technical innovations, such as portable cameras. The "Second" avant-garde cinema, inspired by Dadaism and surrealism, produced films without subjects based on a series of "subconscious" images, such as Luis Buñuel's *Un chien andalou.* The French confronted the challenge of sound in the 1930s more successfully than did either the Germans or the Russians. The most famous filmmaker during this period was Jean Renoir, whose film *Grand Illusion* described the crumbling of dominant cultures caused by the war.

The golden age of the Italian cinema had ended with the outbreak of World War I and did not recover during the 1920s. By 1930, Italian studios made only thirty films yearly, a situation that preoccupied Benito Mussolini. Well aware of the cinema's power—Il Duce enjoyed editing newsreels—he acted. In 1935, he established the only film school outside the USSR and ordered the building of studios that rivaled the UFA—*Cinecittà*. A theoretical journal also appeared, and the government placed strict quotas on the importation of foreign films. The Italians continued to produce films of a propaganda-documentary nature, but, paradoxically, out of them would emerge the influential postwar style known as neorealism that used similar techniques, such as nonprofessional actors, shooting on location, and the newsreel style. The film school also produced some of the most famous Italian post-1945 directors, including Pietro Germi, Roberto Rossellini, and Michelangelo Antonioni. Innovations and new ideas came into Italy and, ironically, served as vehicles of intellectual opposition to Fascism. Once considered a dead interlude in Italy's film history, the interwar period marked a crucial time for the Italian cinema.

The British film industry was in crisis until 1927, when it recovered thanks to legislation establishing quotas for foreign films that reduced American competition and stimulated domestic production, so that by the 1930s, British-produced films trailed only American productions. The British specialized in biographical costume dramas, but also produced the mysteries of Alfred Hitchcock and excellent documentaries.

Literature

Literature and painting during the interwar years worked through the implications of ideas that had been announced at the century's dawn. Affected by developments in science, the old certainties, unity, and continuity of Western culture broke up. Literature in particular took on modern characteristics similar to those in science, with doubt and subjectivity permeating modern novels, poetry, and plays. Literature and art, like physics, became difficult for educated nonspecialists to understand, a development that had disturbing consequences.

Ambiguity in the arts produced exasperation among ordinary people. Laypeople considered pure science an esoteric activity, did not comprehend it, and left it to the scientists—but not the arts. Modernism, with its advocacy of constant change and shock tactics, alienated a public opinion traumatized by the devastation of World War I and its turbulent aftereffects. Utilizing the principles of modern science in a famous manifesto, Russian novelist Yevgeny Zamyatin condemned anyone who remained static, arguing that revolution is everywhere and will never end. The confiscation of modern paintings by the police and riots in France that greeted exhibitions of modern art symbolized the chasm between artists and the public. In Weimar Germany, the center of the new culture, the majority considered modernism decadent and an assault on German history, while artists objected that they were attempting to get at the social reality behind appearances. The adverse reaction to the worldview of modern artists and their attack on German society contributed to the rise of Nazism. When the Nazi regime imposed

The revolutionary developments in art before World War I and during the 1920s caused consternation among the public and resulted in a backlash. In the USSR, the government put an end to experimental artistic forms and instituted "Socialist Realism," and in Nazi Germany the regime's opposition to modernism translated into conformist art. This watercolor from the Nazi period is an example of this trend.

its own hackneyed art preferences or when it burned books, public opinion did not come to the intellectuals' defense. In the USSR during the Bolshevik revolution's early years, an explosion of modernistic movements and experimentation with new forms in all artistic fields occurred, but Bolshevism imposed conformity on intellectuals when their works criticized the regime; few people protested when the Communists shot, jailed, silenced, or drove the best writers to suicide. In 1932, the Communists formally imposed the Socialist realism that forced artists to idealize Soviet life in trite ways.

In the West, the earliest revolutionary reactions to World War I in the artistic world, Dadaism and surrealism (already discussed) had antecedents in Futurism and in the psychological theories of Sigmund Freud. This influence petered out after Marinetti founded an ineffectual Futurist political party in 1918 and then allied himself with Mussolini. The Russian Futurists made a similar error by supporting the new Soviet state; Lenin put up with the antics of its leader, poet Vladimir Mayakovsky, despite his hatred for his poetry, because of the movement's propaganda value to the regime, but Stalin showed less deference to Mayakovsky, which contributed to Mayakovsky's suicide in 1930.

In the West, Freud's psychoanalysis influenced the best interwar literature. French novelist Marcel Proust had begun his massive work, *Remembrance of Things Past* in 1908 and completed it after 1918. Proust sought to understand how reality emerges from unconscious memory, a clear connection with Freud's concerns. Along with the scientists describing the natural world, Freud had demonstrated that reality was not what it seemed. Artists asked, in effect, "What is reality?" Playwright Luigi Pirandello, a Nobel Prize winner, answered in his masterpieces: *Right You Are If You Think You Are, Henry IV,* and *Six Characters in Search of an Author.*

Freud's work had also demonstrated that persons acted not by reason alone but through the spur of the subconscious world. The surrealists emphasized this view as well by arguing that artists did not rely primarily on reason to create their work, but that emotion, feeling, or even accident played decisive roles. These ideas led to the stream-of-consciousness method of writing. The most famous practitioner of this technique, Irish writer James Joyce, produced his masterpiece *Ulysses* in this manner, but was hardly alone. Joyce, a teacher of English in Trieste, encouraged Italo Svevo to continue his work on the psychological novel that he had begun during the late nineteenth century. In 1923 Svevo published his masterpiece, *The Conscience of Zeno.* British feminist Virginia Woolf wrote *To the Lighthouse,* a novel analyzing the difficulties of human relationships and the breakdown of social values in the British upper middle class.

Painting and the Bauhaus Style

Painting witnessed similar attempts to evoke the subconscious. Giorgio De Chirico in Italy best represented the metaphysical school that shocked spectators. These painters juxtaposed real objects in an unreal manner—like ancient statuary and machinery—hoping to create magical effects to stimulate the unconscious mind. This school predated surrealist artists, such as Salvador Dalí, who aimed at liberating the subconscious from the rationalist straitjacket. Along with surrealist writers, these painters advocated an automatic technique that supposedly freed artists from rationalist interference.

This method affected the approach of Paul Klee, perhaps the interwar period's most famous painter. Klee began his paintings with no clearly defined idea but with a splash of color or lines drawn according to his feelings at the moment. He took these first feelings as indications of the subconscious mind at work that would determine the shape of the finished product. In a final act of creation, Klee entitled his works only after he had completed them. For Klee, an excellent violinist, this technique resembled musical creation—contemplation winning out over pictorial composition. In 1920, a celebrated exhibition of Klee's work opened in Munich. Shortly thereafter, he joined his friend Wassily Kandinsky at the Bauhaus, the most celebrated German cultural school of the period.

Architect Walter Gropius founded the Bauhaus in 1919. He aimed to fuse an art academy with the applied arts, believing that buildings could bring together the crafts and the arts in a new unity. Gropius applied this synthesis to all areas of artistic life, including the design of everyday objects used by ordinary people.

The Bauhaus style founded by architect Walter Gropius in 1919 aimed to fuse modern art with practical life. He founded a school that trained students to accomplish this aim and became the most famous institution of its kind in Interwar Germany but had to close because of economic conditions and political turmoil. Here is the Bauhaus building of 1925.

Bauhaus designers created new shapes for lamps, furniture, pottery, rugs, type fonts, and utensils. Production ranging from Marcel Breuer's chair to Gropius's 1925 Bauhaus building, the most famous structure of this period, to the paintings of Klee and Kandinsky consolidated the Bauhaus's reputation. Experimentation, freedom, inventiveness, and community marked the school's atmosphere— principles that infuriated artistic and political conservatives alike. Gropius attempted to keep the school out of politics, but the Bauhaus lost popularity at home as quickly as it gained fame abroad. In 1925, it left Weimar for Dessau, but in 1932, the victim of economic conditions and rightist political turmoil, the school moved to Berlin where it later closed.

Political Philosophy

As fascism and Nazism spread during the 1920s and 1930s, important political philosophers defended parliamentary democracy and rebutted the notion that the one-party state was the wave of the future. In the classic work *The Revolt of the Masses,* Spanish republican José Ortega y Gasset labeled fascism and communism new but regressive and made a compelling case for the reform and updating of parliaments that would bring the masses peace and social justice without subjecting them to the violence of totalitarian governments. A German thinker, Hans Kelsen, also pronounced parliamentary institutions fundamentally sound because they permitted groups to organize, scrutinize the management of public affairs, and implement democracy by resolving the social problems of modern times.

Flanking these political defenses of democracy were Catholic thinkers, such as Jacques Maritain, and liberal socialists who tried to update democratic socialism. Despite the prevailing political atmosphere favoring dictatorship, the ideas of these political scientists defending parliamentary democracy and democratic socialism assured the success of these models after World War II.

TECHNOLOGY AND SOCIETY

The 1920s and 1930s were decades of important technological changes that directly affected daily life as few in history have. For example, airplanes crossed the Atlantic and achieved unheard-of speeds of 400 miles per hour, anticipating the time when airplanes would carry millions of passengers across the oceans at a reasonable cost.

Diffusion of Technology

European governments invested funds to bring technology to the greatest number of their people by subsidizing rural electrification, despite the opposition of traditionalists who objected because it encouraged people to stay up too late at night partying. Despite concerns that governments were moving too quickly, extensive electrification during the interwar years gave people access to many important devices.

Telephones, familiar since the 1880s, became widespread, and when the telephone dial became widely available in the 1930s, people could finally call without operators. Most telephones were black, with only the rich being able to afford white ones that were the symbols of affluence.

The decline in the labor supply because of the large number of deaths during the war affected the diffusion of technology because the increased cost of labor and servants favored the introduction of labor-saving appliances, such as the washing machine. However, since the first washing machines were hand cranked, most people preferred using the washtub or the local stream to wash their clothes until the electric washing machine was introduced and became widely available. Along with washing machines, primitive refrigerators appeared.

The Radio and Its Impact

In the 1920s, the radio revolutionized political and social life by making it possible for leaders to influence millions of people instead of thousands. Mussolini and Hitler encouraged the diffusion of radio sets that brought their speeches into homes and to the masses gathered in the remotest town squares, but radios also spread rapidly in the democracies.

The explosive growth of the radio raised the question of how to administer programs, which led to novel forms of public involvement in society. In 1926, the British established a public corporation, the British Broadcasting Corporation (BBC), as an independently run public company financed by a yearly fee paid by radio owners, a model that spread to other countries and was frequently applied to television after World War II. The BBC established trends and transformed performers overnight into stars, as well as disseminating the latest news and

This is the BBC Broadcasting House in London, built in London in 1932 as the first dedicated broadcasting studio. Music and dance were popular areas for radio programming during the Interwar years, and the Broadcasting House's first transmission featured the BBC Dance Orchestra on March 15, 1932.

influencing everyday life. Daily French radio newscasts began in 1925, and by 1934 the Paris police had radio cars to help them control crime. The radio also transmitted American popular culture to Europe.

By the 1920s and 1930s, as the price dropped, the radio's economic impact increased. Between 1927 and 1939, the number of British set owners grew from 2 million to more than 9 million; the BBC counted 773 employees in 1927 and 5,000 in 1939. The radio favored rapid growth in advertising, sports, and gambling, making it possible to create football and other pools, both legal and illegal, because it quickly reported scores to a vast audience. These activities related to the radio resulted in more work for thousands of people. Millions tuned in to sports events, and sports commentaries became a regular part of broadcasting. The radio had a fundamental role in knitting together society and in increasing employment.

The Depression
The technological innovations of the interwar period, however, could not reverse the economic slump, which forced pullbacks in many areas of social life. French critics attributed the decline of dinner parties to increased poverty, not only to the growing use of cigarettes that caused burns on furniture. Less frivolously, public health problems increased, and, with growing unemployment and increased

prostitution, venereal diseases became more widespread. The alcoholism rate shot up: the average French adult drank a record of 250 liters of wine annually between 1930 and 1940. With increased drinking came a greater likelihood of contracting tuberculosis, which killed one-third of French men aged 35 to 50, and poverty intensified the virulence of more traditional diseases, such as typhoid and diphtheria. Fear of competition from immigrants prompted attacks against foreigners and Jews, and from 1932 to 1937, 500,000 foreigners left France.

PURE SCIENCE: REVOLUTION AND TRAVAIL

In pure science, the interwar years were the golden age of physics. Studying in cities, such as Copenhagen, Gottingen, Leipzig, Berlin, Cambridge, Rome, and Paris, physicists worked out the implications of the quantum theory that Max Planck had elaborated in 1900 and made fundamental progress in understanding the atomic nucleus. This knowledge eventually led to new weapons and energy sources that critically affected the modern world.

A New Revolution

Defeat in World War I did not end the primacy of German scientists, who continued to claim the lion's share of Nobel prizes. The Kaiser Wilhelm Institutes, founded by the former emperor to encourage science, were threatened by the loss of funding and by the hyperinflation. In response, German scholars employed modern methods of financing scientific research during the 1920s by giving research grants on the advice of committees and peer reviews of projects and seeking help from the Rockefeller Foundation. Crucially, the European tradition of collaboration among scientists of different countries survived the war, and the brightest physicists flocked to study with the best scientists, such as the Dane Niels Bohr in Copenhagen and Werner Heisenberg in Leipzig.

Research in the interwar period completed the revolutionary quantum theory, called quantum mechanics, by Heisenberg, Bohr, and other physicists. Between 1925 and 1927, the work of these physicists culminated in the uncertainty or indeterminacy principle enunciated by Heisenberg. Uncertainty meant that the velocity *or* the position of a subatomic particle could be determined at any one time, but not both; it demonstrated that the act of observation influenced the results of an experiment, a principle with enormous implications for other fields besides nuclear physics. At the subatomic level, statistical probabilities (separately worked out by Enrico Fermi and British scientist P. A. M. Dirac), not absolute values, best explained reality. In the visible world, the idea elevated uncertainty to a principle of nature for the real world. This concept coincided with the breakdown of European society and values brought about by World War I and corresponded to the chaos of life during the interwar period that affected the ordinary person. The certainties of the Newtonian worldview that had comforted Europeans since the eighteenth century and that had begun to crumble at the beginning of the twentieth ended during the 1920s and 1930s. Quantum mechanics and relativity set the state for the later development of the atomic bomb.

Important developments in the investigation of radioactivity that took place at the same time confirmed the hidden nature of reality theorized at the beginning of the century. In 1934, Madame Curie's daughter Iréne and her husband Frédéric Joliot discovered how to induce artificial radiation. In Rome, Enrico Fermi and his team systematically bombarded the different elements with neutrons, discovered by British scientist James Chadwick in 1932, as the best way to induce changes in the atomic nucleus. In the course of these experiments, the Rome team developed "slow neutrons" and probably split the atom. The Rome group failed to recognize this result, which was not given a theoretical explanation until 1939 by Austrian physicist Lise Meitner and her nephew Otto Frisch in a paper interpreting similar experimental results achieved by her old partner in Germany, Otto Hahn.

As a result of these developments, Fermi guided a project that produced the world's first controlled chain reaction on December 2, 1942, at the University of Chicago, a crucial event in the development of the atomic bomb and nuclear power plants.

BIOGRAPHICAL SKETCHES

Ettore Majorana
The Enduring Mystery

Ettore Majorana was perhaps the most brilliant of the brilliant physicists of the 1930s—certainly the most mysterious.

Born into a prominent Sicilian family, Majorana studied engineering at the University of Rome. In 1928, his friends encouraged him to switch to physics and study with Enrico Fermi. Majorana went to see Fermi, who had been working for some time on a new statistical method later named after him. Fermi showed Majorana a table of values that justified his method. Majorana returned the next day with a piece of paper and asked to see Fermi's table. He compared it to his results, pronounced Fermi's numbers correct, and consented to work with him.

Majorana revealed himself not only brilliant but eccentric. He kept to himself, published reluctantly, and refused to make his results known to the wider scientific community. A chain smoker, he neatly worked out complicated principles and formulas on his packs of Macedonia brand cigarettes, explained his ideas to his Rome colleagues, rejected their pleas to publish them, and casually flung the empty packs into the wastepaper basket. He published only nine articles, but anticipated many fundamental developments and principles that were elaborated as many as thirty years later. Fermi commented to a colleague: "You see, there are different categories of scientists in the world; there are second- and third-rate people who try hard but do not accomplish very much. There are first-rate people who make important, fundamental, discoveries for the development of science [Fermi considered himself one of them]. But then there are the geniuses, like Galileo and Newton. Ettore Majorana was one of those."

In order to bring Majorana out of his shell, Fermi secured a seven-month scholarship for him at Leipzig, where he impressed Werner Heisenberg. When he returned from Germany, Majorana became even stranger, refusing to leave his

continued

continued

apartment or even to shave, despite the urging of his friends. He spent his time thinking about physics, philosophy, and naval tactics. One of his favorite authors was fellow-Sicilian Luigi Pirandello, the playwright and distinguished novelist who speculated on the nature of reality. In November 1937, a committee named Majorana full professor at the University of Naples, based on his extraordinary merit, and he began teaching there.

On March 26, 1938, the head of his department received a puzzling telegram from Majorana from Palermo, telling him to disregard his previous letters and saying that a new letter would follow. A search of his hotel room revealed two suicide notes, but the later telegram and letter from Majorana said that he had changed his mind. That was the last time anyone heard from him.

An investigation produced sightings on the boat from Palermo to Naples, a witness who saw him in Naples, and a monk who identified him as asking if he could experiment with the monastic life. Benito Mussolini ordered the police to conduct a nationwide manhunt, and the Vatican scoured its monasteries. When he disappeared, Majorana had his passport and the equivalent of $10,000. Observers noted how the circumstances of his disappearance recalled a famous Pirandello novel. Almost thirty years later, stories surfaced about a person in Buenos Aires, Argentina, who called himself Ettore Majorana and wrote complicated formulas in neat handwriting on hotel napkins. Other sightings also occurred.

Writers and scientists have debated the Majorana case ever since. Suicide is probable, but why would Majorana recant his suicide letters and vanish with his passport and a large sum of money? Did he foresee the development of nuclear weapons and then disappear because he could no longer bear to work in the field, as some authors have speculated? Whatever the answer, one mild spring day in 1938, the world lost a person who might have been another Galileo or Newton.

BIOGRAPHICAL SKETCHES

Lise Meitner
The Role of Insight

As a shy young girl in Vienna, Lise Meitner, the first person to provide a theoretical explanation of the fission process that made the development of nuclear weapons possible, had an aptitude for mathematics and for physics. Her father, a Jewish lawyer with eight children, hired a private tutor to prepare his daughter to enter the University of Vienna, which rarely accepted females. In 1906, she received the first physics doctorate awarded to a woman by that institution.

In 1907, the young woman persuaded her parents to let her travel to Germany and attend Max Planck's lectures. There she met Otto Hahn, a chemist working at the Kaiser Wilhelm Institute, won a position as his assistant, and stayed for thirty years. The team achieved international recognition for its role in investigating the atomic nucleus, but could not end the irritating prejudices against Meitner because of her gender.

World War I fundamentally changed Meitner's world. During the conflict, she interrupted her work to serve as an X-ray technician at the front. Returning to her research after the war, she and Hahn discovered the ninety-first element of the periodic table (protactinium). Meitner became an assistant professor at the University of Berlin and headed a physics institute, but after 1933 Hitler's anti-Semitism threatened her career and her life, even though she had converted to Protestantism years before. In 1937, a courageous Max Planck objected to Hitler that famous scientists who were considered even one-quarter Jewish lost their positions. An enraged Fuehrer rejected Planck's appeal to let Jewish scientists keep their jobs; he thundered that they could not leave the Reich and would be detained pending charges. Meitner's Austrian citizenship protected her, but in 1938, Hitler annexed Austria, and she became subject to German anti-Jewish legislation. Denied an exit visa, she escaped Germany through the Netherlands into Sweden, where Niels Bohr had secured a position for her at the Nobel Institute of Theoretical Physics in Stockholm. In Sweden, Lise Meitner labored under poor conditions—but a flash of insight allowed her to make a great contribution to physics and history.

In 1934, Enrico Fermi had bombarded the uranium nucleus with neutrons, obtaining baffling results. According to the thinking at the time, the outcome should have been a new element heavier than uranium, an explanation that physicists continued to expound despite their uneasiness with it. On vacation at Christmastime in 1938, Meitner received a letter from Hahn in which he described chemical reactions resulting from bombardment of the uranium atom that he could not satisfactorily explain. The snow fell heavily as a radical idea suddenly struck Meitner. She paced in the snow and the cold as she considered it: the neutron bombardment had split the uranium atom, producing two different elements and releasing great amounts of energy according to Einstein's famous equation, $E = mc^2$! Unable to contain her excitement, Meitner summoned her nephew, physicist Otto Frisch, and worked out the details of the fission process that governs nuclear explosions.

Following World War II, the press hailed Meitner as the "mother of the atomic bomb," but she protested that she had always refused to work on the weapon. She spent the postwar years lecturing, teaching, continuing her research, and collecting a number of prestigious prizes and awards—except the big one. In 1946, the Nobel Committee awarded the Nobel Prize in physics to Otto Hahn and ignored Meitner. Meitner remained dignified until the end, and history does not record what she thought about this unfair denial, but she continued her friendship with Hahn even though he did not defend her. On October 27, 1968, a month before her ninetieth birthday, Lise Meitner died in a nursing home in Cambridge, England.

Science and Politics

The flash of insight that allowed Lise Meitner to explain nuclear fission came to her in Sweden, where she had fled from the Nazis. Meitner had worked in Germany for thirty years, but Hitler's persecution of the Jews and the dismissal of Jewish professors forced her and many German scientists of Jewish extraction to emigrate. The Nazis denounced Einstein and relativity as Jewish physics and non-Jewish Germans who accepted Einstein's conclusions as "white Jews." As one of these "white Jews," Werner Heisenberg stayed behind saying that he hoped to save German science as the Nazis replaced disgraced brilliant professors with third-rate hacks. Heisenberg emerged from suspicion to direct Germany's nuclear weapons program. In the meantime, anti-Semitic legislation drove Fermi—whose wife and several collaborators were Jewish—out of Italy. European émigré scientists joined American nuclear physicists in the Manhattan Project and built the atomic bomb.

The interwar period was a crucial turning point for scientists whose attempt to unlock the secrets of the subatomic world had appeared arcane. One reporter asked: "Professor Dirac solves all the problems of mathematical physics, but is unable to find a better way of figuring out Babe Ruth's batting average?" As searchers for basic truths, scientists had constituted a special kind of club that cut across national lines. The research they did during the 1920s and 1930s, however, would spell the difference between victory and defeat in the 1940s. From neglected ivory-tower intellectuals, physicists turned into warriors who were sworn to hold secrets instead of sharing information; the relationship that had linked them to a special mission vanished with the golden interwar years.

Bibliographical Essay

A. J. P. Taylor, *From Sarajevo to Potsdam* (London, 1965), is a brief, readable book that has interesting insights on culture and daily life during this period. James Walvin's excellent little book *Leisure and Society 1830–1950* (London and New York, 1978) has chapters on the interwar period. Robert Graves and Alan Hodge, *The Long Weekend: A Social History of Great Britain, 1918–1939* (New York, 1963), is a classic study of social developments in England between the wars. Charles Loch Mowat, *Britain Between the Wars: 1918–1940* (Chicago, 1963), while mainly concerned with economic and political history, also discusses social history, and A. J. P. Taylor, *English History 1914–1945* (New York, 1965), has important sections on social affairs. Matt Perry's *Bread and Work* (London, 2000) is about the experience of unemployment between 1918 and 1938. Eugen Weber, *The Hollow Years,* previously cited (New York, 1994), is an excellent social history of France during the 1930s that also discusses the war's effects and the 1920s. H. Stuart Hughes, *The Obstructed Path: French Social Thought in the Years of Desperation, 1930–1960* (New York, 1968), discusses social thought in France. Gary S. Cross devotes most of *Immigrant Workers in Industrial France: The Making of a New Laboring Class* (Philadelphia, 1983) to the period discussed in this chapter.

An interesting interpretation of cultural life during the Weimar Republic is Peter Gay, *Weimar Culture: The Outsider as Insider* (New York, 1968). For a detailed treatment of cultural affairs, see Walter Laqueur, *Weimar: A Cultural History* (New York, 1974). Connecting cultural refinement and society is Keith Bullivant, ed., *Culture and Society in the Weimar Republic* (Manchester, UK, 1977). On the plight of intellectuals, see the collected essays edited by Anthony Phelan, *The Weimar Dilemma: Intellectuals in the Weimar Republic* (Manchester, UK, 1985). John Willett, *The Weimar Years: A Culture Cut Short* (London, 1984), has good text and pictures. The Bauhaus from its beginnings to the cold war is discussed by Kathleen James, *Bauhaus Culture* (Minneapolis, Minn., 2006).

The mass media are treated by Ken Ward, *Mass Communications and the Modern Word* (Chicago, 1989), and Pierre Sorlin, *The Mass Media* (London, 1994). The best book on radio in England during this period is volume 2 of Asa Briggs's history of broadcasting in the United Kingdom, *The Golden Age of Wireless* (London, 1965). Aitor Anduaga published a book on the relationship among the British Empire, the radio, and atmospheric science between the wars: *Wireless and Empire* (Oxford, UK, 2009). There is not much in English on the radio outside of Britain, but see Philip Cannistraro, "The Radio in Fascist Italy," *Journal of European Studies* II, 2 (June 1972):127–54.

Sports and their influence are the subjects of three interesting books: Mike Huggins and Jack Williams, *Sport and the English* (London, 2006), and John Hargreaves,

Sport, Power and Culture: A Social and Historical Analysis of Popular Sports in Britain (New York, 1986), examine England, while France is the subject of Richard Holt's *Sport and Society in Modern France* (London, 1981).

A good general history of film is David A. Cook's *A History of Narrative Film,* 2d ed. (New York, 1990); the quotation on Eisenstein is on p. 142. The German film in its various aspects is discussed in Siegfried Kracauer, *From Caligari to Hitler: A Psychological History of the German Film* (Princeton, N.J., 1947), a fundamental work; David Welch, *Propaganda and the German Cinema 1933–1945* (Oxford, UK, 1983); and Erwin Leiser, *Nazi Cinema* (London, 1974). For French cinema, see Colin Crisp, *Classic French Cinema 1930–1960* (Bloomington, Ind., 1993). On Italian cinema, see the excellent general treatment by Pierre Leprohon, *The Italian Cinema* (New York, 1972), and the specialized works on the Fascist period: Marcia Landy, *Fascism in Film: The Italian Commercial Cinema, 1931–1943* (Princeton, N.J., 1986), and James Hay, *Popular Film Culture in Fascist Italy: The Passing of the Rex* (Bloomington, Ind., 1987). Roy Armes, *A Critical History of the British Cinema* (London, 1978), has several chapters on this period.

For a discussion of the political science aspects of the questions raised in this chapter, see the relevant chapters in Spencer M. Di Scala and Salvo Mastellone, *European Political Thought, 1815–1989* (Boulder, Colo., 1998).

A good introduction to the physics revolution of this period is Armin Hermann, *The New Physics: The Route into the Atomic Age* (Bonn, 1979), a collection of documents and photographs centered on Germany, and with a good chronology. Gino Segrè, *Faust in Copenhagen* (New York, 2007), is an examination of the "miracle year" 1932. An excellent book that stirred controversy when it appeared is Robert Jungk, *Brighter than a Thousand Suns: A Personal History of the Atomic Scientists* (New York, 1958). This work emphasizes the lives and research of the nuclear scientists and takes the story beyond the development of the atom bomb. On the most important physicists, see Abraham Pais, *Niels Bohr* (Oxford, UK, 1991), a biography by a physicist who knew him. David C. Cassidy, *Uncertainty: The Life and Science of Werner Heisenberg* (New York, 1992), is a massive but rewarding biography. Laura Fermi, *Atoms in the Family: My Life with Enrico Fermi* (Chicago, 1954), is a memoir by Enrico Fermi's wife. Emilio Segrè, *Enrico Fermi: Physicist* (Chicago, 1970), is a memoir by Fermi's Nobel Prize-winning student. Majorana has been the subject of increased interest; see, for example, Joao Magueijo, *A Brilliant Darkness* (New York, 2009). Deborah Crawford's short biography, *Lise Meitner, Atomic Pioneer* (New York, 1969), is a good portrait of the Austrian physicist who was the first woman to receive a doctorate in physics from the University of Vienna. Patricia Rife's *Lise Meitner and the Dawn of the Nuclear Age* (Boston, 2007) is a more complete biography. The quotation regarding Dirac is in Timothy Ferris, *The Whole Shebang: A State-of-the-Universe(s) Report* (New York, 1997), p. 209.

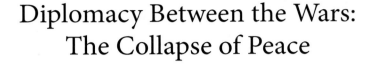

CHAPTER 17

Diplomacy Between the Wars: The Collapse of Peace

CHAPTER OUTLINE

The Continent in the 1920s • Correcting Versailles • The Hitler Revolution • From Crisis to Crisis • A New War

BIOGRAPHICAL SKETCHES

Gustav Stresemann, Fulfillment • Aristide Briand, Man of Peace, "Father of Europe"

International relations during the 1920s and 1930s may be seen either as a lull in what was a "Thirty Years War" from 1914 to 1945, in which the victors of World War I imposed a harsh peace on Germany that led to World War II, or as a period in which diplomats made substantial progress reintegrating Germany into Europe by modifying the harsher features of the Versailles treaty.

THE CONTINENT IN THE 1920s

European diplomats confronted an unprecedented situation following World War I. The German, Russian, and Austro-Hungarian empires had vanished. In the East, new and/or greatly enlarged states with sizable ethnic minorities created special strategic dilemmas because the minorities destabilized the new nations. The instability would provide Germany and the USSR—temporarily weakened but desirous of recouping lost territory—with an opportunity to subvert the postwar settlement.

The French Military Dilemma

The temporary weakness of Germany and Russia made France dominant on the continent. The French constructed a network of alliances linking the small East European states that had benefited from the war. In February 1921, the French signed a Polish alliance and sponsored the Little Entente among Czechoslovakia, Romania, and Yugoslavia in order to defend the status quo and to help contain a possible resurgent Germany. The agreements also created a *cordon sanitaire* around Soviet Russia to isolate and prevent it from exporting the Bolshevik revolution to the West.

However, French preponderance in the East proved untenable after the revival of Germany and Russia in the 1930s. French resources could not match German or Russian resources, while the British considered French policy aggressive and risky. Because of the distance from its Eastern allies and shifting power relationships, France's Eastern policy became more dubious by the late 1920s. The only realistic hope for the small French allies in a German war was for an immediate French attack on Germany from the West. As long as the Rhineland remained demilitarized, France maintained a military advantage, but when Hitler remilitarized it in 1936, the French became more reluctant to take military initiatives and became more defensive minded because of its stagnating population and the unwillingness to risk another war and losses such as those it sustained during World War I. The supposedly impregnable Maginot line was a symbol of France's emphasis on defense.

Moreover, Germany and the USSR opposed the Paris peace settlement of 1919 and secretly collaborated to evade the disarmament clauses of the Versailles treaty. The Russians allowed the Germans to test weapons on their territory, and in April 1922 the two countries signed the Treaty of Rapallo that settled the outstanding issues between the former enemies. Rapallo was the first step in the emergence of both countries from isolation.

Mussolini's Revisionism

During the 1920s, it was Benito Mussolini whose revisionism was most serious because of his feelings that Italy had been cheated at the Paris Peace Conference. In 1923, he temporarily seized the Greek island of Corfu following the murder of Italian experts marking the Albanian-Greek border. Il Duce focused on the Balkans and Eastern Europe, traditional areas of Italian interest, and helped create the premises for a future alliance with Hitler. Yugoslavia's ethnic divisions encouraged Mussolini to finance separatist and terrorist organizations there and to plot Yugoslavia's disintegration. In November 1927 Yugoslavia signed a treaty with France, but Mussolini continued to stir up trouble by sheltering Croat separatists. In March 1932, he signed the Rome Protocols with Austria and Hungary, both revisionist states, and exploited Fascist influence in a failed attempt to bring Romania into his camp. In October 1934, Croat terrorists assassinated the king of Yugoslavia and the French foreign minister in Marseilles, and il Duce's support for the Croats was criticized.

Hitler's takeover in Germany exacerbated the revisionist debate. The French fretted about an eventual Italian-German rapprochement and attempted to placate Mussolini. Hitler's rise created a potential ally whom Mussolini believed he could exploit to subvert the Paris peace settlement.

CORRECTING VERSAILLES

With the exception of Mussolini's attempts to revise the peace settlement, Europe in the 1920s seemed to have returned to normal. Bolshevism seemed to have been

War Minister André Maginot gave his name to the spectacular—and very expensive—line of defensive fortifications between France and Germany, some of which are seen here. The line was built with the intention of stopping a German attack without the gigantic loss of life that France had suffered during World War I. A major weakness was that the Maginot Line could not be constructed on the Franco-Belgian border for political reasons: it would place Belgium on the "German" side of the fighting in case of war, "abandoning" Belgium to the Germans. When World War II broke out, the Germans outflanked the line.

contained by sealing off the USSR from the West, and the economic situation seemed to have calmed down. The efforts of Allied and German diplomats to correct the shortcomings of the Versailles treaty also seemed to be having success.

The "Spirit of Locarno"

In January and February 1925, German Foreign Minister Gustav Stresemann proposed to the British and French a series of agreements regarding Germany's western frontier that amounted to German recognition of the peace settlement of 1919. Stresemann aimed to calm both the French and domestic German unrest by accepting the verdict of Versailles.

BIOGRAPHICAL SKETCHES

Gustav Stresemann
Fulfillment

The man who, along with Aristide Briand, achieved the most success in attempting to reintegrate Germany into Europe following World War I came from an unlikely background. His father, a retailer of bottled beer, found prosperity as a small businessman. Gustav, born in Berlin on May 10, 1878, his mother's favorite, reportedly suffered from loneliness. The child had reddish hair, bright blue eyes, and an inclination toward literary romanticism. At the University of Berlin, his dissertation on the Berlin bottled beer industry demonstrated a flair for combining the theoretical with the practical that never left him.

In 1901, Stresemann took a position in Dresden as assistant manager of the German Chocolate Manufacturers' Association and championed small business against heavy industry. Because small businesspeople relied on cheap imported raw materials, they fought for low tariffs against large business interests and big landowners who wanted high duties. Following this job, Stresemann led the Union of Industrialists, a manufacturers' organization that affiliated with the Central Union of German Industrialists after 1914. The contacts he formed in the business world proved particularly useful to him during the postwar period when he needed support for his policy of reconciliation with the West.

Stresemann's parliamentary debut came in 1907 with his election as a Reichstag deputy as a member of the National Liberal Party, which he headed after July 1917. Before and during World War I, Stresemann favored a strong nationalist and expansionist policy. The Central Union of Industrialists, with Stresemann in its wake, became a powerful supporter of the Pan-German League, advocating peace only if Germany achieved substantial gains. Stresemann also joined the Wednesday Society, a nonpartisan group that sought to keep support for the war high. After the war ended, however, Stresemann shifted gears, realizing that Germany must accept defeat and follow a more conciliatory course that others had already advocated. His previous hawkishness allowed him to win over many resentful diehards to the policy. Albert Einstein wrote: "During the War [sic], Stresemann was warlike enough to be able, later on, to hold the confidence of those whom he wanted to win over to his own wise and noble purposes."

Following the war, Stresemann founded the People's Party, a small organization but one of the mainstays of the Weimar Republic. Between August 14 and November 23, 1923, he headed a coalition government that stabilized the country after Hitler's attempted *putsch,* confronted the hyperinflation crisis, and ended the passive resistance to the occupying French and Belgian forces in the Ruhr. When the cabinet resigned, Stresemann retained the office of foreign minister. He resisted a closer alliance with the USSR, which was desired by the army and elements in the foreign ministry, and attempted a rapprochement with the French. Through a dual policy of revision and fulfillment of the Versailles treaty, he initiated the moves that resulted in the Locarno treaties and in 1926 shared the Nobel Peace Prize with the French statesman Aristide Briand. Stresemann also negotiated the Dawes and Young Plans and brought Germany into the League of Nations with its status as a great power intact.

Stresemann married Kathe Kleefeld in 1906, his serene family life contributing greatly to his success. Stiff and formal in public life, his bald head shining, in private Stresemann displayed a lighter side. He loved food, a glass of beer or wine with dinner, and a good cigar. He greatly enjoyed spending time with his family and friends, and he entertained journalists at frequent teas. At Locarno, he frequented a small café. His health was poor, and he languished from a kidney ailment. In his last years, he refused to stop working despite the rapid deterioration in his health, and his death in Berlin from a stroke on October 3, 1929 surprised no one.

Negotiations with the Allies went forward in the Swiss resort of Locarno, and the agreements were signed in London on December 1, 1925. Germany, France, and Belgium accepted their common borders, and Britain and Italy acted as guarantors. In a crucial achievement, Germany freely accepted the demilitarization of the Rhineland that the Versailles treaty had once imposed. In addition, Germany, France, Belgium, Poland, and Czechoslovakia also signed treaties that bound them to submit disputes to outside arbitration. The lack of a German pledge to respect the borders of its eastern neighbors was a disappointment, but treaties of mutual assistance among France, Poland, and Czechoslovakia within the Locarno framework partially compensated for this deficiency. Continuing negotiations achieved other significant successes. The Allies agreed that Germany could join the League of Nations with a permanent seat on the Council and, by the end of 1926, that Allied inspection to enforce German disarmament would end.

Besides the formal agreements, the Locarno spirit buoyed European hopes. A special relationship seemed to link Stresemann and his French counterpart, Aristide Briand. Joy at achieving the Locarno agreements brought Briand and his British counterpart Austen Chamberlain to tears. An enthusiastic Mussolini kissed Mrs. Chamberlain's hands while bands played. *The New York Times* announced that Germany and France had barred war forever. In August 1928, twenty-three countries signed the Kellogg-Briand Pact, renouncing war. However, complications increasingly spoiled the spirit. The Reichstag received the Locarno agreements with little enthusiasm. An international controversy erupted when Germany applied for admission to the League of Nations and when President von Hindenburg publicly denied German responsibility for the outbreak of World War I. Diplomatic disputes continued over some areas in Germany that the French continued to occupy, and by mid-1927, the friendly feelings of Briand and Stresemann evaporated. Furthermore, it soon became obvious that the Kellogg-Briand Pact lacked teeth. The Locarno era failed to survive Stresemann's death and the Great Depression.

BIOGRAPHICAL SKETCHES

Aristide Briande
Man of Peace, "Father of Europe"

Aristide Briand's father, for love of his wife Magdeleine, settled down in Nantes, in Brittany, where he established an inn and prospered. Two years after their marriage, on March 26, 1862, Magdeleine gave birth to a son, Aristide.

An unruly student with no desire to study, the young Aristide met the famous novelist Jules Verne while attending the Nantes lycée (high school). Verne liked and befriended him, basing the character "Briant" on him in his novel *A Long Vacation*. Verne described "Briant" as a lively teenager unwilling to study but given to occasional bursts of energy during which he outperformed all his fellow students. Briand studied law but preferred journalism. He wrote for a number of influential newspapers, and after he joined the Socialist Party, he collaborated with its leader Jean Jaurès to found *L'Humanité,* the most famous French newspaper on the left. In 1902, Briand ran for election to the Chamber of Deputies and won.

Briand hit his stride as a politician. When the French decided to separate church and state in 1905, Briand headed the commission that was charged with drawing up the implementing legislation. He so impressed his colleagues that Premier Jean Sarrien invited him to join his cabinet in 1906 as minister of education and religion to ensure proper enforcement of the law. Briand accepted, but, because Socialist policy did not allow party members to join governments, the party expelled him. This exhilarating period also brought great personal satisfaction because Briand met the love of his life, actress Berthe Cerny. Briand never formed his own party, but his skill in Parliament, rhetorical ability, and intelligence made him one of the most successful French politicians of the era. In 1909, he became prime minister, heading the first of eleven cabinets he eventually formed. A man of peace, he found himself leading the French government during World War I from October 1915 to March 1917, during which he participated in military planning and strengthened the country's military institutions. His tenure as wartime premier ended amid criticism when he favored a negotiated peace with Germany.

Briand returned to the fore as Europe's most active diplomat in the 1920s, alternating in the offices of prime minister and foreign minister. In collaboration with German Foreign Minister Gustav Stresemann, he negotiated the Locarno Pact, a complex series of mutual guarantee and arbitration treaties that were designed to normalize German relations. This achievement won him the Nobel Peace Prize in 1926, which he shared with Stresemann.

A famous cartoon of the period summed up the French diplomat's association with peace in the popular mind. It depicted world leaders, except for Briand, smashing the statue of Mars. In the vignette, Briand tries to talk the ancient Roman god of war into committing suicide. An enthusiastic Briand greeted Germany's admittance to the League of Nations in September 1926 with the words: "Away with rifles and cannon; make place for arbitration and peace." The next year, Briand approached U.S. Secretary of State Frank B. Kellogg with the idea of renouncing war in favor of arbitration, which led to the Kellogg-Briand Pact. In May 1930, Briand proposed to twenty-six nations the creation of a European Union based on federative principles and linked to the League of Nations. For the first time, the French Foreign Office took concrete steps to implement the initiative, but the plan died when the cabinet of which Briand was part resigned. For the French, the effort was enough to baptize Briand "the father of Europe," and he deserves a high place along with other influential French proponents of European unity.

In May 1931, Briand attempted and failed to win election as French president. On March 7, 1932, he died suddenly. He lies buried at Cocherel, where he periodically took refuge from his intense political and diplomatic labors.

Economic Issues

Strengthening the good feelings during the Locarno period was the apparent resolution of the reparations issue, one of the major obstacles to a lasting peace. After the occupation of the Ruhr, the Allies created a committee to examine relevant issues. Headed by Charles G. Dawes, director of the American Budget Bureau, the committee made a series of recommendations in early 1924. It proposed stabilizing the German currency (ruined by hyperinflation) by pegging it to the British pound, a new schedule of reparations payments starting at 1,000 million gold marks and rising to 2,500 million after five years, and a foreign loan to back the new currency and help raise the amount needed for the first payment. A reparations agency including Allied representatives would oversee the details of payment and eventual variations.

The Dawes Plan achieved success. The French accepted it and withdrew from the Ruhr, while Germany made regular payments, demonstrating that reparations were not incompatible with Europe's economic recovery. In 1927 and 1928, the height of the Locarno era, a new committee, which was set up in 1929 and headed by American banker Owen D. Young, recommended reducing reparations by about a quarter and suggested a rising rate of annual payments that would definitively end reparations in 1988. The countries involved agreed, and Germany made the first payment under the new arrangement in May 1930.

German acceptance, however, did not come easily. Financial officials objected to the plan and wrestled with the German cabinet before finally agreeing to it, but a referendum on the plan aroused hostile feelings among the opponents of reparations and brought the Nazis greater recognition in the country as a result of their participation in the voting. Nevertheless, just before the Great Depression, Europe seemed to have achieved economic stability despite persistent problems. Germany had successfully replaced its currency, Britain had stabilized the pound sterling in 1925, and France, the franc in 1926. In 1924, French industrial production surpassed that of 1913, and in 1926, German production exceeded its prewar level. Moreover, trade increased substantially between France and Germany. Unclear at the time was the degree to which European economic progress depended on American loans. American capital flowing to Germany stimulated production and helped the Germans pay their reparations bill, which in turn allowed the Allies to pay their war debts to the Americans. When American money dried up because of the stock market crash in October 1929, the Americans called in their loans, and the system collapsed, but would it have done so without the shock of the ensuing depression?

Economic stabilization mirrored social stabilization. Following the war, revolution had shaken the continent, but, with the exception of Russia, the old social order had substantially survived. Europe's calm encouraged new efforts at cooperation as an antidote to conflict. In May 1930, Briand proposed restructuring Europe as a federal union. Its organization would be similar to the League of Nations, with an assembly representing all the states, a body representing the large countries, and a Secretariat. The proposal included a common market. The new European federal union would coordinate action with the League of Nations, which illustrated the high hopes that Europeans placed in the international organization.

THE HITLER REVOLUTION

Although the settlements of the 1920s had important defects, the flaws would not have necessarily been fatal without the political and economic destabilization caused by the depression, including Hitler's rise to power.

The Austrian Debacle

As was previously discussed, strong sectors of German and Austrian public opinion favored the union of Austria and Germany, known as the Anschluss.

The Allies, however, had forbidden any form of unity and in 1931 vetoed a customs union to combat the depression.

Austrian Chancellor Engelbert Dollfuss jealously guarded his country's independence. A rightist Catholic and Mussolini protégé, Dollfuss, in February 1934, destroyed his Social Democratic opposition, which left the Austrian Nazis as the main paramilitary force. On July 25, the Nazis attempted to overthrow the government. The *putsch* failed, but Dollfuss bled to death in the attempt. Hitler threatened to invade the country, but Mussolini dispatched several divisions to Italy's border with Austria and denounced the Fuehrer as "a horrible sexual degenerate, a dangerous fool." Hitler quickly backed down.

Il Duce recognized that German absorption of Austria would have put a dangerous power on its border. Furthermore, Italy had annexed the South Tyrol, an area populated by a restive Austrian minority that Mussolini sought to Italianize, and Germany's Austrian ambitions presented a clear enough danger that forced il Duce to act.

After Italian forces blocked the Anschluss, Britain, France, and Italy discussed ways of curbing future German aggression. Mussolini believed he deserved a reward for his action against Hitler. Over the next several months, however, he concluded that the British expected him to defend Austria without any compensation. Should he be relegated to the position of permanently defending Austria, it would spell the end of his ambitions in Eastern Europe and Africa. By 1935, he hoped to conquer Ethiopia in order to create an empire and to avenge a humiliating defeat that Italy had suffered in 1896 but could not do so while stationing forces on the Austrian border to stop Hitler. Despite Austria's importance for Italy, Mussolini informed the Germans that only Austria stood between them. This attitude signaled a basic reorientation of Italian foreign policy by loosening the ties that linked Italy to Britain and France and exploiting the threat posed by Hitler to induce them to agree to his demands.

Africa and Europe: Breakup of the Wartime Alliance

By January 1935, the French had become convinced that an agreement with the Duce was necessary to defend against Hitler. Prime Minister Pierre Laval met Mussolini in Rome and discussed a deal on the Ethiopian question, which had become critical because of a December 1934 military confrontation on the poorly demarcated border between Ethiopia and Italian Somaliland. The conflict produced an Ethiopian appeal to the League of Nations, and Mussolini accelerated his timetable to take over the country before the Ethiopians could modernize their army or gain world sympathy. He was prepared to make concessions to the French in return for their diplomatic backing and agreed to a greater role for the League of Nations in the Austrian question and to renouncing Italian rights in Tunisia. France made minor colonial adjustments in Africa, but the core of the agreement seems to have been a French promise of a free hand in Ethiopia. Exactly what this free hand meant has been disputed ever since. Both men preferred to keep things vague, but it seems likely that il Duce received French backing for his African plans. Mussolini also sought British acquiescence but failed to achieve it.

On March 16, 1935, Hitler denounced the disarmament clauses of the Versailles treaty. In discussing the Allied response, the British favored conciliating Hitler, but Mussolini argued that only a show of force would bring the Germans into line. At the Stresa Conference in April 1935, Mussolini demanded binding commitments and concerted action by the Western powers against aggressive German moves. The French agreed with him but went along with the British, who opposed strong action. Far from retaliating, the British negotiated a naval agreement with Hitler that sanctioned his building of a fleet up to 35 percent of theirs. In effect, this agreement endorsed Hitler's violation of the Versailles disarmament clauses.

The British attitude assured that no decisive step resulted from the Stresa consultations, an outcome that convinced Mussolini that the Western democracies were pusillanimous. Worse, the conference relegated Italian ambitions in Africa to talks among experts, where British opposition to Italy's African venture surfaced. In a contradictory move, however, the British agreed that the final communiqué would remain silent on the issue, suggesting to the Italians that Britain would not oppose Italy's African adventure.

The Stresa conference's failure and the Anglo-German naval agreement had major consequences. The Italians could not understand why the British opposed them in Africa while insisting that they protect Austria and concluding an agreement with Hitler that violated the Versailles treaty. The dispute between the British and Mussolini escalated during the Ethiopian affair and alienated Italy from the victorious World War I alliance.

The Ethiopian War and the Discredit of the League of Nations

As an Italian invasion of Ethiopia loomed in the fall of 1935, the British proposed that the League of Nations invoke collective security if the Italians attacked Ethiopia. On October 3, 1935, Italian troops entered the country. The league imposed sanctions on Italy but left petroleum off the list, the only commodity that could stop the Italian war effort. Sanctions caused the Italians hardship but transformed the Fascist adventure into a national crusade and boosted Mussolini's popularity. Sanctions were a test to determine if the League of Nations could be utilized against Germany in the future, but their failure destroyed the organization's reputation and irremediably weakened it. Consequently, the League of Nations would not be a significant factor in the crises that led to World War II.

For the big powers, the major focus of the dispute was Europe, not Africa. Italy's involvement in Ethiopia left Austria vulnerable to Germany and encouraged the British and French to halt the African conflict quickly. Discussions among Britain, France, and Italy culminated in the Hoare-Laval proposals, which offered the Italians major economic and territorial concessions in Ethiopia. The deal fell through because of leaks and the so-called Peace Poll that indicated popular support in Britain for the League of Nations and opposition to the dictators. Contemporaneously, Mussolini's archenemy Anthony Eden became British foreign minister, and the leftist Popular Front government came to power in France, producing further complications. At this crucial juncture, a new crisis diverted attention from the Ethiopian conflict.

Remilitarization of the Rhineland

The Treaty of Versailles had prohibited the Germans from keeping troops in or fortifying the Rhineland, but on March 7, 1936, Hitler remilitarized it, violating the treaty by sending troops into the area. This move clearly threatened France, but, led by a caretaker government, it did nothing. The British also did not react strongly. Many Europeans, convinced that the Germans had been treated too harshly after the war, accepted the fait accompli.

Astonished at the soft British reaction against Germany compared to the hard line taken against him over Ethiopia, Mussolini concluded that London plotted a general German agreement with a redistribution of colonies, leaving Italy out in the cold. On the other hand, Hitler's spectacular move helped Italy by taking the wind out of the drive for oil sanctions, which the British championed. These developments confirmed il Duce's alienation from the Western democracies, convinced him of their weakness, and demonstrated that the two dictators could benefit by cooperating.

In the meantime, the Italians rapidly conquered Ethiopia, although guerrilla activities continued until World War II. On May 9, 1936, they proclaimed the empire.

The Spanish Civil War and Its Impact

Following the Duce's victory in Ethiopia, the British and French sought to placate the Italians, hoping to gain Mussolini's support for the diplomatic containment of Germany. The British induced the League of Nations to remove the sanctions and reduced tensions in other ways. Despite serious differences with the democracies, il Duce had not irredeemably thrown in his lot with Hitler, but German revival had proved useful to him. However, the Spanish Civil War made a rapprochement less likely.

In July 1936, rightist forces, headed by General Francisco Franco, revolted against the Spanish Republican government. Despite initial hesitation, Mussolini dispatched forces to aid the rebels. Instead, the Spanish conflict escalated and ended only in 1939, becoming an ideological war that antifascists viewed as an opportunity to stop international fascism. Volunteers from all over the world fought on the Republican side and dealt the fascists an embarrassing defeat at the Battle of Guadalajara. With his prestige at stake, il Duce sent more troops and material to Spain. Mussolini had not coordinated his action with the Germans, but the Spanish war brought the dictators closer together as Hitler sent soldiers to Spain and the two collaborated. Hitler pledged to support Italian primacy in the Mediterranean, and on November 1, Mussolini baptized the new cooperative attitude between Germany and Italy the "Axis." In the same month, Germany and Japan signed the Anti-Comintern pact against the Soviet Union, with Italy joining later. In September 1937, Mussolini paid Hitler a friendly visit.

Besides producing a closer relationship between Hitler and Mussolini, the Spanish Civil War worsened relationships with the democracies. The British and the French advocated nonintervention by the big powers. The Germans and Italians agreed but violated their commitments. The Soviets sent military aid to the Spanish government, greatly increasing their influence over the Republican war effort. Moreover, Soviet predominance raised the specter of a Communist Spain, which weakened the British and French resolve and strengthened the Republican opponents. Furthermore, the German military performance had important repercussions. The Nazis tested new and fearful air power tactics—Pablo Picasso's *Guernica* captures the brutality of bombing helpless civilians in the city that gave the painting its name.

FROM CRISIS TO CRISIS

In 1938, the focus of diplomatic activity shifted from Spain to Eastern Europe as Hitler felt strong enough to escalate his challenge to the Allies.

The Austrian Crisis

Following the failed Nazi coup of 1934, Kurt Schuschnigg replaced Dollfuss as chancellor, but the increasingly close association between the Duce and the Fuehrer made Mussolini less inclined to oppose Hitler's Austrian policy. Already in July 1936, Schuschnigg had caved in to German pressure to accept several pro-Nazi Austrians into his cabinet, and the Duce had gone along with this arrangement.

On February 12, 1938, Hitler summoned Schuschnigg to his mountain headquarters in Berchtesgaden, berated him, and threatened to invade if he did not agree to Austria's Nazification. Schuschnigg consented, but once back in Vienna, he attempted to strengthen his hand against the Fuehrer by ordering a plebiscite on the Anschluss. A furious Hitler prepared to invade. Only a show of force by Italy could have stopped Germany from swallowing Austria, but the Duce refused to intervene. Schuschnigg called off the plebiscite, and Austrian Nazi leader and interior minister Arthur Seyss-Inquart invited German troops into the country.

The Austrians joyfully greeted the German soldiers, leading the Western powers to conclude that the Anschluss enjoyed majority support, but the absorption of Austria was a defeat for them and for Mussolini. The enlarged Reich increased German power, and Mussolini accepted the presence of a great power on his border that could threaten Italy's independence. This fact made it less likely that he would end his association with Hitler.

Czechoslovakia's Strategic Dilemma

Within a few months of the Anschluss, Hitler provoked a crisis over Czechoslovakia, exploiting the 3 million formerly Austrian Germans within its borders. A country of 10 million people with an efficient army and a strong armaments industry, Czechoslovakia could not defeat Germany in case of war, but could offer stiff resistance. President Beneš and Foreign Minister Thomas Masaryk had sought security by allying with France in 1924. There was no British pact, but the Czechs counted on British involvement in case of a conflict with Germany because of Britain's commitment to the French. Unfortunately for them, the British feared being drawn into a conflagration in Eastern Europe and, when a crisis broke out between Germany and Czechoslovakia in 1938, encouraged the French to accept the German demands.

The Czech Crisis

The Anschluss set the stage for the Czech crisis by absorbing Austria and creating a common German-Czech border. Hitler incited the Sudeten German minority, led by Nazi Konrad Heinlein, to make extreme demands on the Czech government. France and the USSR indicated they would aid Czechoslovakia, but the British, reluctant to be dragged into a conflict, pressured the Czechs to agree to concessions.

During the summer and fall of 1938, Hitler berated the Czechs for mistreating the Sudeten minority. In September, President Benes agreed to autonomy for the Germans, but the Nazis did not desist. British Prime Minister Neville Chamberlain cautioned Hitler that Britain and France would fight should his Czechoslovak policy lead to war, but his warning failed to dissuade the Fuehrer.

At Hitler's urging, the Sudeten Germans took to the streets, prompting Chamberlain to fly to Berchtesgaden for consultations on September 15. The two leaders agreed that Czechoslovakia should cede the Sudetenland to Germany. The loss of this mountainous, heavily fortified area rendered Czechoslovakia militarily helpless, but the British accepted this consequence because they believed it would produce peace. France, a possible obstacle because its treaty with Czechoslovakia committed it to war under such circumstances, backed off when the British intimated that they would not support the French in case of war. A stunned Benes could only acquiesce.

Just when the crisis seemed resolved, Hitler suddenly changed his mind. Alleging escalating Czech atrocities, he demanded more land, a plebiscite, and the immediate entrance of German troops into Czechoslovakia. A second meeting between Chamberlain and Hitler failed to settle the differences. The Fuehrer seemed determined to have a conflict, which prompted the Czechs to mobilize, the French to gear up for war, and the British to ready their fleet. As a last resort, however, the British appealed to Mussolini to intervene, and the powers agreed to a conference.

The Munich Conference

On September 29, 1938, Hitler, Mussolini, Chamberlain, and French Prime Minister Édouard Daladier, "The Bulldog," met at the infamous Munich conference without the Czechs or the Russians. At this meeting, the four statesmen agreed on the details of Czechoslovakia's dismemberment and saved the peace for a year. The Soviets offered to aid Czechoslovakia, but Poland and Romania objected to Soviet troops crossing their territory.

After the Munich Conference, the Poles seized the rich area of Teschen, Benes resigned, and Czechoslovakia reorganized itself into a feeble federation. The British and French guaranteed the new borders, but Hitler had no good reason to take them seriously. The Western democracies had in effect put the country into Germany's sphere of influence, and the Fuehrer soon dispensed with the formalities of Czech sovereignty. Slovakia broke off in March 1939 and became a German satellite. Hitler summoned the new Czech president, Emil Hácha, and subjected him to a violent tirade. German troops marched on Prague, and Hitler threatened to bomb the city if the president did not acknowledge a German protectorate. Hitler

Czechoslovakia's Strategic Predicament. The areas that Hitler claimed and eventually got were Czechoslovakia's strategic border, the Sudetenland, protected by mountains. By giving the Germans Czechoslovakia's strategic border, shaded in the map, the British and French rendered it militarily defenseless. The German minority living in this area had not been part of united Germany but of Austria-Hungary.

also allowed the Hungarians to take Ruthenia, a piece of the hapless state that they had long claimed. The British and French backed out of their pledge to preserve the borders of the rump state because it no longer existed.

A NEW WAR

After the Munich conference, Chamberlain announced: "Peace in our time." The conference had turned Europe away from the brink of war at the last minute, but a new crisis brewed.

Poland's Strategic Dilemma

The independent Poland that appeared after World War I faced the strategic dilemma of being located between an aggressive Germany and Russia and of lacking defensible frontiers. Even worse, the Polish Corridor contained a large German minority, and Poland had annexed large tracts of Soviet territory inhabited by former Russian subjects, primarily Ukrainians, that the USSR wanted to regain.

Polish political leaders based their foreign policy during the 1920s on a French alliance, but during the 1930s, France appeared weaker while German and

On September 29, 1938, the leaders of the big powers met at Munich at the behest of Mussolini to try to save the peace during the Czechoslovak crisis. They met without either the Czechs or the Russians being represented and agreed to resolve their differences by giving in to most of Hitler's demands. The Conference saved the peace, but at the cost of a French betrayal of its commitments to Czechoslovakia. In this photograph, from left to right, British Prime Minister Neville Chamberlain, French Prime Minister Édouard Deladier, Hitler, and Mussolini, pose for the camera. The man in uniform on the extreme right is Count Galeazzo Ciano, Mussolini's son-in-law and Italian Foreign Minister.

Russian power increased. With Hitler's takeover of Austria and Czechoslovakia, Poland's military situation deteriorated. The Poles had a longer border with German-controlled territory and, even if Hitler and Stalin clashed, the fighting would take place on Polish territory because Germany and the USSR lacked a common border. Furthermore, because of the distances involved, Western military support would not reach Poland in time to make a difference.

The Polish Crisis

After his successes in Austria and Czechoslovakia, Hitler raised the unresolved questions of the German minority and the Polish Corridor. In October 1938, he demanded the return of the former German port of Danzig, a road across the Polish Corridor connecting East Prussia with the rest of Germany, and Polish adherence to the Anti-Comintern Pact. After March 1939, Hitler made new demands, and on April 6, Chamberlain responded by guaranteeing Poland's borders; the French followed suit.

Probably the sudden British-French guarantee can be explained by Hitler's absorption of Prague in violation of the Munich agreements, after which they understood that the Fuehrer could not be appeased. Presenting Hitler with the

Poland's Quandary. Poland was caught between the claims of Germany and the USSR. Here the Polish Corridor and the territory desired and eventually annexed by the Soviet Union are shaded.

certainty of war to dissuade him from attacking Poland seems a likely explanation for the guarantee, although the British advised the Poles to negotiate with the Germans in a last-ditch effort to save the peace. The Poles refused, fearing that the British might withdraw their guarantee should they see an opening to maintain peace by yielding Polish territory.

The Nazi-Soviet Nonaggression Pact

The British-French guarantee thrust the USSR to the forefront of European diplomacy. Should war with Poland and the Allies break out, the Allies needed the Soviets in order to present Germany with a credible military threat on two fronts. Poland might be defeated, but the Germans would face a long war with the French and the Russians. If the Fuehrer ensured Russian neutrality, however, he could overrun Poland and then turn his attention to the Western front, or perhaps the West would not to go to war under circumstances in which it could not save Poland.

For the Allies as well, the USSR's attitude was crucial. To have any chance of saving Poland, they needed Soviet help. However, they were at a disadvantage in the negotiations during which the Soviets bargained with them and with the Germans. Stalin distrusted the Allies because of their anticommunism; moreover, the British and French had guaranteed Poland's borders and could not offer the Soviets what they wanted: the land Russia had lost to Poland after World War I. Even if their enmity made Nazis and Communists improbable friends, a deal

From the strategic viewpoint, modern Poland was doomed from the beginning, just as it was in the eighteenth century, because it was a large weak state with no defensible borders caught between hostile big powers. After World War I, the Poles alienated both Germany and Russia, and later it became impossible for the country to have friendly relations with either Nazi Germany or Soviet Russia without becoming the satellite of one or the other. In this photograph, a smiling Stalin seems satisfied with his pact with Hitler plotting the partition of Poland and the absorption of the Baltic States by the USSR. The Nazi-Soviet Non-Aggression Pact set the stage for World War II.

would give the USSR the territory it desired and, by pushing Soviet borders farther west, would create a buffer against an eventual German attack. For Stalin, there was the added prospect that Germany and the Western powers would wear each other down.

In order to get an agreement quickly, Hitler dispatched Foreign Minister Joachim von Ribbentrop to Moscow on August 23, 1939. Ribbentrop and the Soviets quickly agreed to a nonaggression treaty. The Soviets and Nazis pledged enduring friendship, promising not to attack each other or to join any third party that might attack their respective countries. Secret clauses split up Poland and left for later consideration whether a rump state would remain on the map. Germany recognized Latvia, Estonia, and Finland as belonging in the Soviet sphere of influence and declared its disinterest in Bessarabia, which Russia had lost to Romania after World War I. In return, Germany got Lithuania. By assuring that the USSR would remain neutral in a war with the Western democracies, the Nazi-Soviet Nonaggression Pact set the stage for war.

The Outbreak of War
Following up its pledge to guarantee Poland's borders, London signed a pact with Warsaw committing itself to war if the Germans attacked. In a last-ditch effort to save the peace, the British asked Mussolini to arrange a conference, but the Duce

Danzig, the German-inhabited free city in the "Polish Corridor" that had been a major bone of contention during the Polish crisis, heard the first shots of World War II, fired from a German warship, on September 1, 1939. This photograph shows a street in the historical city, now briefly German, decorated with swastikas. The city was mostly destroyed during the conflict.

refused, although he kept his country out of the imminent conflict by inform-ing Germany that Italy was unprepared for war. The Japanese also refused to get involved. On September 1, 1939, German armies invaded Poland. Britain sent an ultimatum to Germany, and France also declared war.

World War II had begun only twenty years after the First World War ended, but on a different basis from the previous world conflict. The Germans had a tradition of expanding in the East, but Hitler based his *Lebensraum* on extreme racism that mandated the subservience and destruction of so-called inferior races, such as the Jews, Gypsies, and Slavs who lived in the area. While World War

Mussolini and Hitler dominated the international scene in the 1930s. They had similar foreign policy aims in that both opposed the post-World War I Versailles Settlement and wished to overthrow it. Hitler's goals, however, were much more ambitious than those of the Duce, who aimed primarily at a Mediterranean and colonial empire. Although this picture portrays Mussolini and Hitler as being solidly with each other, Mussolini distrusted Hitler and had doubts about joining him in World War II until mid-1940.

I had been a struggle against German domination, the new war was a fight for survival.

Bibliographical Essay

Two books that examine significant foreign policy issues during the 1920s are Piotr S. Wandycz, *France and Her Eastern Allies 1919–1925* (Westport, Conn., 1962), and Robert Machray, *The Little Entente* (New York, 1970). A good general account of the interwar years is Raymond J. Sontag, *A Broken World, 1919–1939* (New York, 1971). Patrick O. Cohrs, *The Unfinished Peace After World War I* (New York, 2006), is a thorough history of the attempt to stabilize Europe between 1919 and the rise of Hitler and includes the U.S. role.

Stephanie Salzmann emphasizes an important but neglected topic mentioned in this chapter in *Great Britain, Germany, and the Soviet Union: Rapallo and After, 1922–1934* (London, 2003). Jon Jacobson, *Locarno Diplomacy: Germany and the West 1925–1929* (Princeton, N.J., 1972), is a thorough examination of Locarno, while Anne Orde, *Great Britain and International Security 1920–1926* (London, 1978), describes the British perspective. Orde also published *British Policy and European Reconstruction After the*

First World War (Cambridge, UK, 2002). William J. Newman's *The Balance of Power in the Interwar Years, 1919–1939* (New York, 1968) is a clear discussion of the European balance during the years concerned through an examination of the Locarno agreement and its implications for wider policy. Stresemann's aims are examined by Henry L. Bretton, *Stresemann and the Revision of Versailles: A Fight for Reason* (Stanford, Conn., 1953). Hans W. Gatzke, ed., *European Diplomacy Between Two Wars, 1919–1939* (Chicago, 1972), contains a series of essays on major issues pertinent to the coming of war. Gordon A. Craig and Gilbert A. Felix, *The Diplomats 1919–1939,* 2 vols. (Princeton, N.J., 1953), is a classic treatment of interwar diplomacy. Winston Churchill's *The Gathering Storm* (Boston, 1948) is a protagonist's account that sets forward the case against appeasement while summarizing the dissolution of the postwar settlement.

The most comprehensive work on Mussolini's interwar diplomacy and goals is H. James Burgwyn, *Italian Foreign Policy in the Interwar Period 1918–1940* (Westport, 1997). MacGregor Knox, *Common Destiny: Dictatorship, Foreign Policy, and War in Fascist Italy and Nazi Germany* (Cambridge, UK, 2000), is an analysis of the Fascist and Nazi dictatorships and their foreign policies. Denis Mack Smith, *Mussolini's Roman Empire* (New York, 1976), covering the same period, is more impressionistic. John Gooch weighs in on a unusual topic: *Mussolini and His Generals: The Armed Forces and Fascist Foreign Policy* (New York, 2007); Gaetano Salvemini, an old enemy of Mussolini, sees the Duce as an important protagonist in the coming of World War II in *Prelude to World War II* (New York, 1954), a standard account. Older examinations of Mussolini's foreign policy that still have value include Elizabeth Wiskemann, *The Rome-Berlin Axis* (London, 1969); Mario Toscano, *The Origins of the Pact of Steel* (Baltimore, Md., 1967); and Maxwell H. H. Macartney and Paul Cremona, *Italy's Foreign and Colonial Policy, 1914–1937* (London, 1938). On the Ethiopian War, see George Baer, *The Coming of the Italian-Ethiopian War* (Cambridge, Mass., 1967). Franklin D. Laurens discusses the French position in *France and the Italo-Ethiopian Crisis, 1935–1936* (The Hague, 1968), while William I. Shorrock examines the general issue of Italian Fascism in French diplomacy in his *From Ally to Enemy* (Kent, Ohio, 1988). On the Spanish Civil War, John Coverdale, *Italian Intervention in the Spanish Civil War* (Princeton, N.J., 1975), debunks some of the myths about the ineffectiveness of Mussolini's participation in the conflict.

Felix John Vondracek's *The Foreign Policy of Czechoslovakia 1918–1935* (New York, 1968) is a thorough examination. Polish and Russian foreign policy up to the final crisis is analyzed by Bohdan B. Budurowycz, *Polish-Soviet Relations 1932–1932* (New York, 1963).

Hitler's foreign policy has been the subject of many works. See Christian Leitz, *Nazi Foreign Policy, 1933–1941: The Road to Global War* (New York, 2004). Consult Klaus Hildebrand, *The Foreign Policy of the Third Reich* (Berkeley, Calif., 1983). Gerhard Weinberg, *The Foreign Policy of Hitler's Germany: Starting World War II, 1937–1939,* 2 vols. (Chicago, 1994), argues that Hitler wanted war over Czechoslovakia, indeed, that he planned a series of conflicts. An earlier book by the same author describes how the coming of Hitler to power was a diplomatic revolution: *The Foreign Policy of Hitler* (Chicago, 1970). Williamson Murray rebuts commentators who argue that the allies profited by Munich, which allowed them to go to war a year later when they were supposedly better prepared. See *The Change in the Balance of Power, 1938–1939* (Princeton, N.J., 1984). E. M. Robertson discusses the relationship between Hitler's foreign policy and military planning in *Hitler's Pre-War Policy and Military Plans* (New York, 1963). Keith Eubank studies the problem of appeasement in *Munich* (Norman, Okla., 1963) and the coming of World War II in *The Origins of World War II,* 3rd ed. (Arlington Heights, Ill., 2004). On the question of appeasement, two works that examine the issue in detail are *Hitler, Chamberlain and Appeasement* (Cambridge, UK, 2002) by Frank McDonough, and *Public Opinion and the End of Appeasement in Britain and France* (Farnham, UK, 2010) by Daniel Hucker. Appeasement is inextricably involved with the question of whether or not the Western democracies were militarily prepared to fight successfully against Hitler. Discussions of this issue may be found in Gaines Post, *Dilemmas of Appeasement: British Deterrence and Defense* (Ithaca, NY, 1993), and Robert J. Young, *In Command of France: French Foreign Policy and Military Planning, 1933–1940* (Cambridge, Mass., 1978). Young also wrote *France and the Origins of the Second World War* (New York, 1996), a study of why France chose to enter a war for which it was so badly prepared. Donald Cameron Watt, *Too Serious a Business: European Armed Forces and the Approach to the Second World War* (New York, 1975), is a readable analysis of the European armed forces and the coming of World War II.

The role of the League of Nations is the subject of two books: Ruth B. Henig, *The League of Nations* (London, 2010), in the Makers of the Modern World series published by Haus, and Peter J. Yearwood's *Guarantee of Peace: The League of Nations in British Policy, 1914–1925* (New York, 2009).

Geoffrey Roberts examines the crucial relationship between the USSR and Nazi Germany from 1933 in *The Soviet Union and the Origins of the Second World War: Russo-German Relations and the Road to War, 1933–1941* (New York, 1995). Simon Newman dedicated a study to the all-important guarantee to Poland, *March 1939: The British Guarantee to Poland* (Oxford, UK, 1976). Poland's predicament during the interwar period is examined in Richard M. Wate, *Bitter Glory: Poland and its Fate,* 1918 to 1939 (New York, 1998).

The book that reopened the question of the origins of the war is A. J. P. Taylor, *The Origins of the Second World War* (New York, 1961). E. M. Robertson, *The Origins of the Second World War: Historical Interpretations* (London, 1971), is a collection of articles that includes attention to Taylor. The debate itself may be followed in a series of works, including Wm. Roger Louis, ed., *The Origins of the Second World War: A. J. P. Taylor and His Critics* (New York, 1972), and Gordon Martel, *The Origins of the Second World War Reconsidered,* 2d ed. (London, 1999). Over the years, Taylor's book has led to extensive examinations by other authors of Hitler's motives and tactics. Andreas Hillgruber's *Germany and Two World Wars* (Cambridge, Mass., 1981) concludes that Hitler aimed at world power. Norman Rich, *Hitler's War Aims* (New York, 1974), argues that Hitler's racist ideology spurred him toward great territorial expansion. A detailed history of how the war actually broke out is Donald Cameron Watt's *How War Came: The Immediate Origins of the Second World War, 1938–1939* (New York, 1989). P. M. H. Bell, *The Origins of the Second World War in Europe,* 2d ed. (New York, 1997), does a good job of putting everything into perspective.

〜

CHAPTER 18

The German Tide Over Europe

CHAPTER OUTLINE

Confrontation • German Successes • The Home Fronts

BIOGRAPHICAL SKETCHES

Heinz Wilhelm Guderian, Panzer General • Maurice Gustave Gamelin,
Historical Footnote

With the beginning of World War II on September 1, 1939, the great struggle between Germany and Russia for supremacy in Eastern Europe, and perhaps the world, began anew, although ostensibly on a different basis: ideology.

After World War I, a class ideology dominated Russia, and a racist one, Germany. The accidents of history help explain Russia's choice, while historical continuity is more appropriate for Germany—but below the surface, history and national ambition guided their policies. Confronted with a German invasion in 1941, Stalin appealed to his people to defend "Mother Russia," and the Nazis invoked European civilization against the Asiatic hordes. After World War II, the Soviets exploited Communist ideology as a façade for their control of Eastern Europe, but the events of 1989, when communism collapsed, illustrated the fragility of ideology compared to national realities.

CONFRONTATION

Even though the major European powers expected a conflict when World War II broke out, they were less prepared for a war than in 1914.

The Allies

After World War I, British planners assumed that the country would not have to fight a major war for ten years, an assumption they abandoned in 1932, but only in theory. In February 1936, the British decided on a five-year rearmament program, but financial considerations and the government's reluctance to interfere with civilian production limited rearmament.

The need to protect its empire also limited Britain's ability to confront a European conflict. The doctrine of limited liability placed the major burden of fighting the Germans on the French. In 1938, 74 out of 138 British battalions served abroad. The lack of conscription limited the growth of the British army, making it much smaller than those of the other major powers. In early 1939, the government decided to raise thirty-two divisions within a year of the outbreak of war, and in April it announced conscription, but when the war began, only four British divisions departed for the continent.

Similar considerations affected the British navy and air force. The British had the strongest navy in Europe, but Britain's worldwide role made it less able to confront the combined German, Italian, and Japanese fleets. A building program, adopted in 1936, that would have doubled British cruisers and aircraft carriers and significantly increased the number of other ships, came too late to make a difference in 1939. In the air, the British hoped that a strong force would deter a German attack; between 1934 and 1938, they concentrated on building bombers, but in 1938 changed their emphasis to building fighters that were better able to protect British civilians. The quality of the planes increased dramatically with the introduction of the Hurricanes and Spitfires. Luckily, the secret British work on radar made it possible to intercept enemy bombers some distance away.

Unlike the British army, regular soldiers made up only the core of the French army, which was based on conscription. The French had periodically reduced the term of service but increased it to two years in 1935 to compensate for the low birthrate. After their active duty, these solders went into the reserves, which allowed the French to field eighty-four divisions when the war broke out. This force was better armed than its rapid defeat in May–June 1940 suggested. In the autumn of 1936, the French began an ambitious rearmament program to increase their tank forces and antitank capabilities. Much of the rearmament plan was completed, but the defense-mindedness of its generals hampered the army. Wanting to avoid the huge World War I-style offensives, they built the Maginot Line, a series of impregnable fortifications that, they hoped, would save their manpower and wait for reinforcements while the Allied fleets strangled Germany, as they had in World War I. The French generals expected a replay of the previous conflict in which the defense would be supreme.

The other French armed services were mixed. High quality and modern construction characterized the French navy, except for several old battleships. In combination with the British navy, the French fleet was a powerful force, in stark contrast to the air force, which consisted mainly of old planes. In 1933, the French instituted a new program to refit their air force, but planning and industrial difficulties hampered modernization. When war began, the French had just three hundred modern warplanes of a poorer quality than their German counterparts.

The Axis

Germany's rapid rearmament from the disarmed state imposed by the Versailles treaty stands out as an amazing achievement, but its stunning military achievements between 1939 and 1942 gave a false impression. After Hitler announced conscription and rearmament in March 1935, the German army rapidly expanded from 7 to 21 divisions and by 1939 could field 103 divisions.

This quick expansion caused serious problems in recruiting, in training an adequate officer corps, and in producing the tanks that were needed to outfit the new armored (Panzer) divisions. In 1939 German equipment did not fulfill officers' expectations, deficiencies that help explain the caution of the German generals, who feared that Hitler's reckless foreign policy would embroil them in a war. Hitler's success in the Rhineland and the Czechoslovak crises, however, allowed him to brush the generals aside and take control of the command structure of the armed forces by establishing the High Command of the Armed Forces (*Oberkommando der Wehrmacht, OKW*).

The excellent performance of the German armed forces under these conditions says as much about the weakness of their opponents as it does about German military skill. Despite the strong influence of the traditional tactics of using tanks for infantry support, the Germans emphasized concentrated employment of tank divisions, along with close, dive-bomber support (*Blitzkrieg*), pioneered by General Heinz Guderian.

The Germans concentrated on their air force, the flower in the Nazi military lapel. In 1932, the air force possessed only a small number of military planes, and the aircraft industry had dwindled to just over 3,000 workers. Under Hitler crony Hermann Goering, the German air force began a spectacular expansion in 1933. Between 1936 and 1938, the number of workers in the German aircraft

Although the Germans were famous for their tank operations during World War II, their early tanks performed poorly. The Germans had a greater edge in the quality and design of their airplanes, and during the war developed models that were much more advanced than those of the Allies. However, by concentrating on ever more advanced weapons that could not be developed and put into production quickly enough they did not make a difference in the fighting. Here is a picture of a German "Komet," a rocket-propelled fighter that appeared in combat in May 1944, outperforming all other planes but with a very short powered flying time. It was credited with fewer than ten kills.

industry rose to more than 125,000, and production reached an annual average of over 5,000 planes. Even though the Germans had problems obtaining enough raw materials, deciding on which models to produce, and agreeing on the proportion of bombers and fighters, and never reached their ambitious targets, in 1939 the German air force was the strongest in Europe.

The Germans also embarked on an enormous naval building program, but the navy received low priority compared with the other services. By September 1939, the German navy boasted only two battle cruisers, three pocket battle-ships, and six cruisers among its capital ships, although the powerful battleships *Bismarck* and *Tirpitz* neared completion. The navy had only fifty-six submarines, of which twenty-six were capable of operating in the Atlantic Ocean. In 1939, Admiral Erich Raeder and Hitler agreed on "Plan Z," which would have given Germany a world-class fleet over the next several years, but war's outbreak in 1939 scuttled the ambitious naval plan.

Despite rearmament, Germany was not ready for a long conflict in 1939. Hitler consistently stated that a war would not break out before 1943 or 1944, and its early arrival caught the armed forces at a disadvantage. The country was militarily and economically prepared for short wars but had to import strategic raw materials in a long one, making it vulnerable to a blockade.

The Italian armed forces were the least prepared to fight a major war. The successes that they had achieved in Ethiopia and Spain during the 1930s drained their limited resources and made it less likely that they could sustain a full-blown European conflict. Furthermore, Fascist direction of war preparations was incompetent and bumbling. In theory, Fascism provided for central direction, with Mussolini holding the three cabinet military posts—the army, navy, and air force—in addition to being prime minister. Il Duce could not keep up with the work and did not coordinate his actions with the general staff. The different services did not have coherent military doctrines and did not work out consistent strategic plans for the likely war scenarios.

This confused situation had disastrous effects. The Italian army had a structure similar to the French army, but in order to increase the army's maneu-verability in 1937, the Chief of Staff reduced the size of a division from three to two regiments. The reorganization began in late 1938, creating confusion, but that was not the only problem. Armaments were poor. Italian commanders had proposed forming a number of armored divisions, but by 1940 had not proceeded very far. Only a few medium tanks reached the armed forces, the main armed vehicle remaining a lightly armored tankette. The production of heavy artillery in 1939 stalled at about seventy pieces a month. Most of the army's artillery and its rifle, the Model 91, were of World War I vintage. Even Fascism's prize service, the air force, under Fascist hierarch Italo Balbo, was woefully unprepared for war, despite its prestige during the interwar period and the excellent models on the drawing boards. Mussolini claimed 8,500 planes, but the air force began the war with only 1,000 obsolete planes and did not coordinate its action with the army. The most efficient service was the navy, whose strength compared well with the British and the French fleets in the Mediterranean and could have dominated the central part of that sea. Unfortunately, the navy lacked fuel and did not have radar.

Compounding these issues, il Duce had never been able to gain control over the armed forces, which remained loyal to the king, the soldiers disliked their German allies, and there was a culture of disobedience to Fascist orders.

THE USSR

Given its military and geographic situation, the USSR's best course was neutrality in a European conflict, despite possessing Europe's largest armed force with a peacetime strength of almost a million soldiers in 1939. Estimates of its tanks range from 3,000 to 10,000, but several models proved unsatisfactory until production of the T-34 medium tank in 1940. From their military operations during the Spanish Civil War, the Soviets favored the organization of their tanks to support the infantry. When the German defeat of France proved the superiority of concentrating tank divisions in highly mobile attacks, the Soviets began reorganizing their tank forces on the German model and were in the process of this reorganization when the Germans attacked them with devastating results. Military doctrine was another problem. Because the Soviets assumed that any new conflict would be a class war and uprisings would take place behind enemy lines, they also believed that the Red Army would take the offensive; instead the German attack forced the Soviets to go on the defensive.

The Soviet air force was large but had a large number of obsolete planes, and serious problems afflicted the main bomber. As war approached, the Soviets began

Unlike the Germans, the Russians concentrated on producing reliable weapons rather than focusing on exotic ones. Here is the Soviet T-34 medium tank, the most effective and most common tank of World War II. It continued to be produced until 1958 and widely exported throughout the world. The picture shows a World War II era T-34 during a victory parade in October 2004. The flag is the one the Russians hoisted above the German Reichstag in 1945.

to deploy modern aircraft and, during the conflict, followed an intelligent policy of producing few but serviceable models in great quantity—a strategy that eventually overwhelmed German air superiority.

Two other major problems that affected Soviet military performance were poor training for recruits and damage done to the officer corps by the purges. The resulting weakness emerged dramatically in armed clashes with the Japanese in 1938 and 1939 and in a war against the Finns that began on November 30, 1939. The Russian difficulty in defeating the Finns encouraged Hitler to believe that he would win an easy victory over the USSR.

GERMAN SUCCESSES

Hitler's rapid victories in 1939 and 1940 allowed Germany to capture and utilize the resources of the defeated countries. Military observers expected Germany to defeat Poland in short order, and Hitler's pact with Stalin made the task easier. Two days after Warsaw's fall on September 27, 1939, the Nazis and Soviets formally divided the country between them. During the assault on Poland, the Germans fought a holding action against the French and British in the West, with the Allies missing the opportunity to help the Poles by launching a major offensive during what they called the "phony" war.

In April 1940, the Germans invaded Denmark and Norway. On May 10, they launched an offensive against France through Belgium, the Netherlands, and Luxembourg and defeated France in a month. Hitler then attempted to knock Britain out of the war through a massive air campaign that continued until June 1941. He failed to accomplish his goal, but the British remained isolated in their island fortress and could not take offensive action on the continent. Hitler then turned his attention against the USSR, which had been his prime target to achieve *Lebansraum* (living space) in the East. On June 22, 1941, German troops invaded Russia in the expectation of a quick victory

The Nazi-Soviet Assault on Poland and the Baltic

With the defeat of Poland, the Soviets and Nazis renegotiated their non-aggression pact. Germany gained a larger amount of Polish territory in return for letting the Russians take Lithuania. One quarter of a million Polish Jews escaped into Soviet territory, although many died on the way or were turned back by Soviet soldiers.

As the Nazis wreaked havoc in Poland, the Soviets deported hundreds of thousands of civilians to labor camps in the USSR and systematically murdered the Polish officers and specialists they captured. The most spectacular atrocity, known as the Katyn forest massacre, was part of Stalin's long-term objective to Sovietize Poland. Although the Germans later discovered mass graves, the Soviets denied responsibility until Premier Mikhail Gorbachev admitted it on April 13, 1990. Once they had achieved their immediate aims in Eastern Europe, the Nazis and Communists signed a treaty on February 11, 1940. In return for German manufactured goods, the Russians assured Germany the steady stream of strategic raw materials it needed for its military machine.

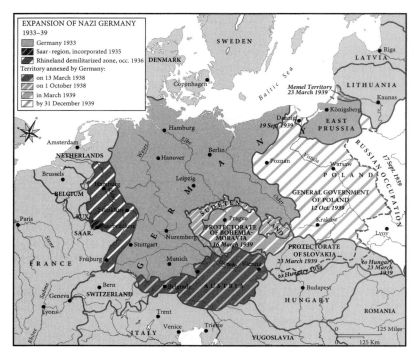

Expansion of Nazi Germany 1933–39.

The Germans had great success at the beginning of World War II thanks to their greater military preparation and tactics based on speed of action, concentration of their forces on vulnerable points of the enemy's defenses, and a skillful combination of land and air attacks—the "blitzkrieg." The most clamorous example of the effectiveness of these tactics was the rapid defeat of France. Here is General Erwin Rommel, one of the most brilliant practitioners of the new military method, and his staff planning their advance through France in May 1940.

Hitler Turns West

Before he could attack Russia, Hitler had to secure his western front. Following Poland's defeat, Hitler aimed to destroy the British and French armies by going through neutral Belgium and Holland, a plan the military establishment did not favor. Hitler endorsed a blueprint for the French campaign, prepared by Generals Erich von Manstein and Gerd von Runstedt, by which the Germans would draw the Franco-British forces north to save Holland and Belgium while they attacked in force through the Ardennes forest, cutting their enemies off and defeating them.

At the same time, driven by Admiral Raeder's desire for naval bases in Norway to confront the British, Hitler authorized an intrepid scheme to take over that country. In April 1940, utilizing the element of surprise, the Germans seized control of Norway and Denmark. A bumbling British effort to dislodge them failed miserably. Unfortunately for the Germans, the surface fleet sustained heavy losses in the conquest of Norway, ending any hope of defeating the British navy in an invasion of Britain itself. The Norwegian campaign was a warning to Sweden if it had any ideas about cutting off the vast quantities of high-grade iron ore it supplied to Germany. In the future, Sweden adjusted its neutrality to the demands of its aggressive neighbor and to the fortunes of war.

In Britain, the Norwegian debacle increased popular dissatisfaction with the government, which lost support in Parliament. Chamberlain lost control of his own Conservative Party and resigned. Led by its female deputies, the Labour Party favored a national coalition government headed by Winston Churchill, who had been tainted by the Norwegian disaster but had made his reputation in opposing appeasement and in pressing for resistance to Hitler. The new prime minister electrified Britain on May 13, 1940, offering his people nothing "but blood, toil, tears, and sweat" and by defining British policy as "Victory—victory at all costs."

France Falls

In the meantime, the Germans implemented their invasion of France using Heinz Guderian's *Blitzkrieg* tactics, perfected in Poland, of concentrating their armor to create an irresistible mobile mass supported by dive-bombers and in constant touch by radio. The French and British had a large number of tanks, and the French machines were superior to the German, but they failed to exploit the tank's speed or ability to roll over the most stubborn resistance.

The Germans unleashed their offensive on May 10, 1940, by attacking Holland and bombing Rotterdam, killing hundreds of civilians to terrorize the Dutch people. The Dutch army surrendered on May 15, and Queen Wilhelmina fled to London to set up a government in exile. On May 18, Belgium capitulated. When the British and French moved their best mobile forces far to the north to confront the German invasion of the Low Countries, the Germans attacked France through the Ardennes forest, splitting the Allied forces into northern and southern chunks. French commander Maurice Gamelin committed his reserves to the northern theater, leaving none to confront the deteriorating military situation. The Allies lacked an effective command structure, making it difficult to coordinate their actions as the Germans split the Allied armies. The Allies tried to stop the German advance by bombing the bridges, but their air forces proved unequal to the task. By May 20 and 21, the Germans had reached the channel coast.

BIOGRAPHICAL SKETCHES

Heinz Wilhelm Guderian
Panzer General

Heinz Guderian exemplifies the strength and weakness of German society during the Hitler era. Most Germans were not evil or committed Nazis but, frequently, talented people who lent their expertise to the regime without bothering about the consequences.

Born on June 17, 1888, in Culm (now in Poland), the son of an army officer, Guderian was educated in military schools. In 1908, he joined a ranger battalion commanded by his father, who in 1911 sent him to study wireless communications, an important component of his future military strategy. Guderian, who was a very serious student, exhibited an acerbic sense of humor that made him enemies. As a young lieutenant during World War I, he wrote a scathing report about his commander, displaying another character trait that would get him into trouble.

Guderian made a brilliant career in Germany's postwar *Reichswehr*, serving as the youngest staff officer on the general staff. An expert in tanks and motorized warfare, he took command of motorized (mostly supply) units. Because the Versailles treaty prohibited the German army from possessing tanks, the Germans secretly developed them in Russia with Soviet cooperation. Guderian participated in this activity and in 1937 published a seminal tract on tank warfare: *Achtung Panzer!* He called for the reorganization of the army around armored divisions, a proposal that upset traditional army commanders who favored the infantry, but one that Hitler supported by ordering the creation of three tank divisions. There followed the rapid promotion to general, full control of the army's armored units, and prestigious assignments leading German troops into Austria and Czechoslovakia.

During World War II, Guderian led an army corps in Poland, but his most famous victory came in France. Guderian fully implemented his *Blitzkrieg* tactics by disobeying the orders of his superiors, who, afraid of outflanking movements by the enemy, constantly ordered him to stop and wait for the infantry when his tanks outran it. Guderian remarked that it was more difficult to fight his superiors than the French. Aided not by better machines but by radio communication among his tanks and perfectly trained crews—his innovations—Guderian pushed his tank forces as far as they could go, broke through French lines, and delivered a spectacular victory. During the Russian invasion, Guderian commanded a Panzer army, but constant fighting with his commanding officer led to his removal and reassignment in February 1943. Put in charge of reorganizing German tank units and increasing the production of armored vehicles, he achieved great success. After the failure of a conspiracy by army officers to kill Hitler on July 20, 1944, he accepted the Fuehrer's nomination as the army chief of staff. Guderian loyally served until March 1945, when Hitler dismissed him because of military disagreements.

At the war's end, the Americans found no evidence of war crimes, but questions surfaced about Guderian's failure to support the July 20 conspiracy, acceptance of the post of army chief of staff, indifference to slave laborers in German arms factories, and fidelity to Hitler. Even after the conflict, he did not criticize Hitler or take a strong position on the persecution of the Jews.

After the war, Guderian participated in an American historical project on the German general staff, wrote several cold war tracts, and published *Panzer Leader*, a best-seller translated into ten languages. He died on May 17, 1954, and was lowered into his grave to the sound of West German frontier police firing a salute. His name remains identified with armored warfare, but he left an emblematic legacy symbolized by a 1960s proposal, rejected, to name a German army barracks after him.

The question for the Allies became what to do with the two chunks of their armies; for the Germans, how to destroy them. The British decided to evacuate the British Expeditionary Force (BEF) and as many French soldiers as possible from the northern theater so the army could be re-formed in Britain. On May 25, the Dunkirk evacuation began utilizing governmental vessels and private craft of all kinds. They saved about 340,000 men, including 120,000 French soldiers.

The German success in France almost destroyed the British Expeditionary Force operating in that country. In order to save their troops and surviving French soldiers the British mounted a massive evacuation effort from Dunkirk on May 25, 1940, using large ships but also small craft of all types. Most of the soldiers were saved so they could fight later. Here is a picture of Allied troops boarding a ship during the evacuation.

The overconfident Germans rested their victorious forces and prepared to move against French troops in the south, leaving the job of finishing off the soldiers trapped at Dunkirk to Goering's Luftwaffe. Weather and the British air force thwarted the Germans, and by the time they realized that a large number of troops were escaping, it was too late. On June 14, with the French army in an advanced state of disintegration, the Germans entered Paris.

The internal malaise that contributed to France's fall can be traced back to the beginning of the twentieth century: the profound social divisions among the classes; the political divisions that led some groups to support the USSR and others, Nazi Germany; the lack of significant reforms to address the complaints of different social strata; and the defense-mindedness.

In the military sphere, Hitler became overconfident. His spectacular success in France despite opposition from the generals had major repercussions in the conduct of the war by increasing his suspicion of the army and convincing him of his own military genius. He took greater direction of the conflict's military side and implemented his frequently mistaken decisions against the advice of his generals.

BIOGRAPHICAL SKETCHES

Maurice Gustave Gamelin
Historical Footnote

General Maurice Gamelin, commander in chief of Anglo-French forces at the beginning of World War II, served as a fitting foil to Heinz Guderian. From comparable backgrounds, both men had roughly similar careers, but a fatal timidity transformed Gamelin from a prominent general into a historical footnote.

Born in Paris on September 20, 1872, the son of a high army official, Gamelin attended the prestigious French military academy of Saint Cyr and served in North Africa from 1883 to 1897. Cultivated and brilliant, he impressed his superior officers and in 1906 published *Étude philosophique sur l'art de la guerre (Philosophical Studies on the Art of War)*, a tract that revealed a good military mind. Two future commanders of the western front during World War I, Generals Ferdinand Foch and, especially, Joseph Joffre, strongly supported him and advanced his career.

During World War I, Gamelin participated in the most famous battles of the conflict and demonstrated talent as an administrator and tactician. Skilled in politics in addition to war, Gamelin achieved promotion to brigadier general on December 8, 1916. After the war, Gamelin headed the French military mission to Brazil and, in September 1924, took command of French troops in Syria, successfully restoring his country's shaky military position there. In February 1929, he assumed command of an army corps and the next year became the second highest officer on the French general staff. Within two years, he had replaced General Maxime Weygand as its chief. Through his political acumen and subsequent promotions, Gamelin became virtual head of the French army by 1935.

As an influential adviser to French governments and known to be admired by the British, Gamelin exercised more sway on French foreign policy than did other generals in the great democracies. Consequently, he bears a substantially greater responsibility for French indecisiveness toward Hitler in the 1930s. Especially critical was his abandonment of Czechoslovakia, despite that country's long alliance with France, and his personal promise of aid in case of a German threat.

Most seriously, his ineptitude helped set the stage for France's spectacular defeat by Germany despite the rough military equality between the two countries in armaments, training, and military tradition. Before the war, Gamelin did not seriously consider or implement modern doctrines that his military attachés reported were under discussion by foreign armies, particularly the use of tanks. As the commander of Allied forces from September 1939 to May 1940, he proved incompetent. He failed to deliver on a promise to the Poles to launch a powerful attack against the Germans while their army was engaged in Poland, a strategy with a good probability of success. Fearful of retaliation, Gamelin kept his forces on the defensive behind the Maginot Line. He established his headquarters far from the front, isolating himself and hindering good communication with his troops. He proved incapable of controlling the rivalries among his subordinates and issued commands in a hesitating manner, suggesting, rather than ordering, action. His most famous directive begins: "Having no wish to intervene in the battle currently underway. . . ." Gamelin also made a major error during the German offensive by committing most of his reserves in the wrong place. On May 19, 1940, the government dismissed him—too late to repair the damage and spare France its greatest defeat in modern times.

In February 1942, the Vichy government tried Gamelin and important politicians as responsible for the French disaster but recessed the trial. The Germans arrested him in April, but he went free in May 1945. From then on, Gamelin defended his role in the war but died in Paris on April 18, 1958, unsuccessful to the end.

Italian Intervention

With France defeated and Britain beleaguered, isolated, and on the brink of defeat, many Europeans believed that the war was almost over. This attitude encouraged Mussolini to enter the conflict.

Il Duce had kept Italy out of the war despite the "Pact of Steel" signed with the Germans on May 22, 1939. He had made it clear that Italy would be unprepared to fight a major war until 1943 and was unhappy when Germany touched off the conflict. Mussolini's son-in-law, Foreign Minister Galeazzo Ciano, took the lead in this effort by sending the Germans a long list of supplies that the Italians needed in order to join the Germans. Ciano and his friends fretted about the Italian position in a German-dominated Europe, although Mussolini himself seemed untroubled at the prospect. The Duce could not conceive of the war continuing for long after the French defeat and, after his initial doubts, worried that he could not get into the fray fast enough to claim French territory and build an empire in the Mediterranean. To his generals, who timidly pointed out the country's lack of preparation, he remarked that he required only a few thousand dead in order to sit at the peace table. On June 10, 1940, he declared war, not only militarily unprepared but without having made definite military plans.

The quick German defeat of France in May-June 1940 was one of the great shocks of World War II. The French had a great military tradition and, despite their defeat during the Franco-Prussian war of 1870, had a long history of defeating Germans in war. Hitler danced with joy at the news of his army's great success. After the Germans occupied the proud French capital, they staged a victory parade at the Arc de Triomphe, one of the most famous Parisian landmarks.

Britain Resists

Mussolini had made a monumental miscalculation. The British vowed to resist a anticipated German invasion by all possible means. They planned to use poison gas against the invaders; prepared to destroy bridges and other essential structures; and, if occupied, to continue the struggle from Canada. They attacked and destroyed most of the French fleet off North Africa on July 3, 1940, when it refused to surrender because of the fear that it would fall into German hands. They sought arms from the neutral Americans, who in June sent rifles, machine guns, artillery pieces, and ammunition. On September 2, 1940, the two countries concluded an agreement by which the Americans transferred fifty destroyers to the British in return for ninety-nine-year leases on a series of British bases close to their shores. This deal represented a step toward future American intervention.

Because of the overwhelming British superiority at sea, the air war took center stage. The Battle of Britain began in earnest in July and August 1940. The British and Germans lost a large number of airplanes, but Hitler made a fundamental error by ordering the Luftwaffe to change its targeting from fighter bases to London.

On September 17, Hitler postponed his invasion plans, cancelling them in October. The blitz followed as the Germans intensified their bombing of London and industrial centers in an attempt to break British morale. In May 1941, with Britain undefeated and German plans to attack Russia well advanced, the blitz ended, but the targeting of civilian areas had become a normal part of warfare and culminated in the carpet bombing of German cities and in the atomic bombing of Japan.

Italian Failures

While the Germans were preparing to attack the USSR, Italian intervention widened the war to the Mediterranean and Africa and diverted the Germans into areas where they did not want to be involved. Mussolini was jealous of Hitler's successes and dreamed of invading Yugoslavia and Greece. When German troops appeared in Romania in preparation for the Russian attack, Mussolini believed that Hitler was moving forward in southeastern Europe without regard for Italian interests. The Duce resolved that the next time he acted, he would not inform the Fuehrer, and in late October 1940, badly prepared, ill equipped, and badly led, the Italians invaded Greece while Mussolini informed Hitler only at the last moment. The Greeks threw them back and moved into Albania, and the Germans had to rescue the Italians by invading Greece and Yugoslavia.

The Italians did poorly not only in the Balkans, but in Africa. They initially advanced in North Africa, but the British defeated them in early 1941. This disaster forced the Germans to send an army under General Erwin Rommel to bolster their allies. In East Africa, which the Italians could not supply, they lost their newly acquired Ethiopian Empire and their old colonies.

The Assault on the USSR

In the East, Hitler hoped that early spectacular victories against Soviet forces would cause the Soviet state to collapse and give him the control of the East of which he dreamed. On June 22, 1941, three German army groups, known as north, center, and south, attacked the USSR. The Germans seized large stretches of Soviet territory, including the Polish lands they had taken, and inflicted a large number of casualties. By mid-July the Germans had taken 600,000 prisoners in the central portion of the front alone, had seized the Baltic states, moved into the Ukraine, and besieged Leningrad (now St. Petersburg). The German generals talked about the war in terms of mopping-up operations, and Hitler began claiming Germany's new borders and defining his plans for the territories to be incorporated.

Soviet Resistance

This optimistic scenario turned out to be unrealistic. The defeated Red Army retreated but did not collapse, nor did the Soviet state. Brutal German tactics helped attain these results. The Germans murdered captured Soviet political officers, slaughtered or starved prisoners of war, and liquidated tens of thousands of civilians and Jews. Aware of the fate that awaited them should they lose the struggle, the Russians fought harder than ever. Partisan activities tied down thousands of German troops. The Soviet government mobilized the economic and human resources of the country to fight the enemy.

The Germans had planned a brief war and consequently lacked reserves of men and equipment to win. By late July the German army stopped to rest its men, overhaul equipment, and fix damaged transportation facilities. Its long supply lines proved a major handicap, as they had for previous invading armies. As the Soviet government drew up plans to leave Moscow, the Germans failed to attain their objectives—to reach Murmansk and the Caucasus or to take Leningrad or Moscow—and failed to knock Russia out of the war before winter. The German invasion would soon take on the proportions of a military disaster.

Hitler had believed that the Germans would quickly annihilate the USSR and had earmarked Russian raw materials for the buildup of the navy and air force for the invasion of Britain. In September 1941, he reversed those orders and told German industry to concentrate on the production of weapons for the army so it could keep fighting the Soviets. The sacrifices of the Russian people made a major contribution to the ultimate Allied victory.

THE HOME FRONTS

The enormous amount of war materiel that was needed to fight World War II necessitated a more efficient mobilization of the home fronts than had been the case from 1914 to 1918. In theory the centralized administrations of the dictatorships should have made them more efficient than the democracies, but while the USSR mobilized its economy and citizens in an astonishingly successful but brutal manner, Britain rallied its population more effectively than did Nazi Germany.

Home Front: Britain

Total mobilization for war brought major changes to British society, helped, ironically, by the intense German aerial bombardment. British authorities issued gas masks that people carried around in cardboard boxes, ordered blackouts, and prevented motorists from turning on their headlights. They evacuated young children from endangered cities, along with their mothers and teachers. This step should have meant moving 4 million people, along with 2 million who left voluntarily, but only half the mandated evacuees left. The evacuation went smoothly only to encounter significant problems at the destination points. In the countryside, the evacuees found abominable weather and social conditions, since many children of the urban poor wound up staying with poor rural families who could not supply their needs, while the children of the richer classes were placed with wealthy families. This fact exposed the perversities of the British class system and would have an impact on British social policy after the war. Another problem was that the localities from which the evacuees came had the financial responsibility for paying expenses to the receiving areas, but the funds either arrived late or never; this put a tremendous burden on rural towns. In the cities, the children who remained found that their schools were frequently closed until November or later and that there was no governmental supply of free milk or food. In addition, the authorities reserved city hospitals for casualties that the "phony" war never produced and cut off access to them by the poor, including pregnant women. The evacuation during the "phony" war and a second one while the bombs fell during the Battle of Britain and the blitz revealed the conditions of the urban poor and spurred the government to take action to improve the living standards of distressed people both during and after the war. One observer wrote: "The Luftwaffe was a powerful missionary for the welfare state."

Besides the social impact of the evacuations, the "war socialism" resulting from the organization of the country for combat had major repercussions on the nation's future social and economic development. The British people supported the war against Nazism and did not allow the social discord of the 1914–1918 conflict to resurface. Governmental agencies elaborated an equitable and practical rationing system that was generally accepted as fair. The Labour Party sent the authoritative Ernest Bevin to participate in the cabinet as labor minister. Thanks to him, workers, including a large number of women, united to achieve the government's production goals.

The government's innovative financial policy kept social antagonism to a minimum. It did not attempt to contain inflation by using its wartime powers to depress wages but allowed them to rise with the aim of keeping the gap between national income and expenditures as narrow as possible. This policy allowed for some inflation but kept it at a minimum and had the important social consequence of evening out the imbalance in the sources of wealth. In fact, income from wages grew by 18 percent while earnings from property fell 15 percent and those from salaries fell 21 percent. The workers judged tax increases to be fair, and the taxes from labor paid for a greater percentage of expenditures than in World War I. The equitable economic regime helped the British government mobilize English society for war more effectively than did Nazi Germany.

Home Front: Germany

Because of its army's early successes, which allowed Germany to loot its victims and employ a large number of slave laborers, German citizens lived a relatively comfortable life, and the state faced less severe economic hardships than did Britain. Hitler deliberately followed this policy because of his conviction that during World War I, the hardships suffered by the German people because of the Allied blockade and the demands of war had led to disaffection and to the uprising that had defeated Germany.

The Germans instituted more generous rationing than did the other belligerents; allowed the production of consumer goods to remain high until 1942, when they ordered industry to concentrate on war-related items; and exempted an exceptionally high proportion of men from military service. Unlike the British or the Russians, the government did not mobilize women to work in the factories on a large scale until 1944, on the grounds that women should stay at home to tend their children and because of the large number of slave laborers who took the place of the men serving in the armed forces. Indeed, the government's generous subsidies to servicemen's families encouraged women to leave their jobs.

The Nazis were also less efficient than the British and Americans in mobilizing science for war. Nazi planners concentrated on developing weapons, such as the V-1 and V-2 and the jet fighter, but the use of slave laborers exposed the V-2 rocket project to frequent sabotage. They failed to recognize the importance of developing a nuclear weapon or to devote the necessary resources to it (perhaps because of Werner Heisenberg's influence), and the jet fighter arrived too late to affect the war's course.

Slave labor probably ended up damaging the war effort. Slave laborers were in poor physical condition, required guards, lacked motivation, and sabotaged the war effort when they could. Probably their greatest contribution to Germany's war effort was to free a greater proportion of men for service in the armed forces than was the case in other countries. Because they received no salaries or pensions, were overworked, underfed, and easily replaced upon death, slave laborers supplemented the profits of German companies, an issue that returned to haunt German industry during the 1990s. Slave laborers permitted Germans to live relatively well at the upper reaches of a racial hierarchy and, divided into racial categories that determined the severity of their maltreatment, provided a foretaste of Hitler's hopes and plans for Europe. However, they presented one overwhelming social hazard: possible sexual activity. The Nazis banned sexual relations, even touching, between the slave laborers and German women, and meted out ruthless punishment for infractions. Some Germans felt uncomfortable with the pervasive presence of slave laborers, but the majority profited or turned their eyes away.

The Germans tasted not only the future that Hitler held out for Europe, but the one he held for them. After the war began, Hitler ordered an intensification of the euthanasia program—the killing of selected categories of Germans whom the government considered useless. An October 1939 decree mandated the systematic removal and murder of patients with incurable physical and mental infirmities, of ailing elderly people in institutions, and of babies born with severe handicaps. Pervasive rumors placed severely wounded veterans of the current conflict on the list, although the government backtracked. Relatives and some institutions resisted the elimination of sick Germans, and scattered rioting occurred. In August 1941 the bishop of Munster, Clemens August von Galen, publicly protested, and the government temporarily backed off the most extreme aspects of its program. By then, the program had disposed of between 100,000 and 200,000 Germans and had important results with respect to the Jewish question. The euthanasia program required the collaboration of doctors, other medical personnel, and experts of all kinds, which favored the development of a core of workers specializing in methods of mass murder in the concentration camps.

The casualties of war created a novel problem. Because the Nazis feared that German women would marry men from stock they considered racially inferior, they planned ways of increasing the Aryan population during the postwar period without this inconvenience. The Nazis recognized the illegitimate children of SS members and of German soldiers with Germanic women of the occupied countries, extending subsidies to the mothers. They seized children from occupied Eastern Europe if they had the proper racial characteristics and raised them as Germans. For the future, SS head Himmler and other Nazi leaders advocated multiple wives for men, so they could breed more progeny, and proposed the procurement of wives from the United States and other areas of significant past German emigration. In the conquered East, Himmler planned for a large number of Germans to return to the soil as farmers and to have large families. These Germans would lord it over the local population that was to be kept poor.

The war witnessed an exponential growth of SS power in German society. Favored by Albert Speer, industrial tsar and Hitler's favorite architect, SS enterprises expanded rapidly at the expense of private industry, and its armed units, the Waffen SS, at the army's cost. Had the Nazis won the war, the SS would have become the major industrial power in a German-dominated postwar Europe. The Nazis also planned to continue the strict wartime regulation of private industry.

Flanking the SS, the Nazi Party intensified its presence in German society during the war. Hitler's secretary Martin Bormann expanded the party's power despite the decline of popular support owing to increasing realization that Germany would lose. Intensification of the Allied bombing campaign forced more people to depend for clothing and other necessities on social relief agencies, especially the party welfare organization. Welfare activities and the country's desperate efforts to raise more soldiers kept the party viable in the war's final years.

Hammered by the most devastating conventional bombing in history in the latter part of the conflict, German civilian morale dropped but induced passivity rather than rebellion. No matter how bad the bombing, the German people feared even more a Russian invasion and the fate of their country once the nature of its war crimes became general knowledge. The Germans grumbled but remained faithful to their Fuehrer, and his soldiers fought bravely for him until the end.

Home Front: Italy

Unlike Hitler, Benito Mussolini, could not count on the loyalty of his people, who had grown continually disaffected from the regime that brought them into the war unprepared. Opposition to Italian entrance into the conflict ranged from the highest levels of government to the ordinary citizen. The formerly pro-German Foreign Minister Ciano exclaimed in his diary for June 10, 1940: "May God help Italy!" Forced to fight, ordinary Italians would have preferred the Germans as enemies.

The National Fascist Party, long utilized to mobilize the masses, could not convince Italians to put their hearts into the conflict. Italian opinion became even more hostile to the Duce when he sent soldiers to fight in Russia, where they suffered high casualties for no vital interests. This campaign and the military defeats the Italian armed forces suffered sapped what little support il Duce had.

The Fascists made a greater attempt than the Nazis to mobilize women in an effort to support troops on the front. The regime removed its quotas on working women in June 1940, just before the country declared war, hoping that they could fill in for the men who were conscripted into the army. By 1943, when Mussolini was overthrown, women figured prominently in both private and public enterprises. By then, hunger stalked the country, and mass protests began. March 1943 witnessed widespread strikes in the important industrial center of Turin—the first in Axis Europe—with workers shouting "peace and bread." The largest target, Fiat, quickly agreed to pay overtime and to grant cost-of-living increases. Politically, the failure of the police and party authorities to intervene demonstrated that il Duce's authority had evaporated. Many of the strikers were women, a sign that the regime had lost their support. A strong Italian resistance movement took root, and women were prominent among the opponents of the Fascists and their Nazi allies even though the regime retained some support among women. In the last days of the war, 6,000 women answered the call to join a women's armed force in a last, desperate attempt to fight the Allies and anti-Fascist partisans.

These developments demonstrated the folly of Mussolini's participation in the war. Although it had made good progress during the Fascist era, Italian industry could not compete with the other combatants in the production of war materiel, a weakness compounded by the country's lack of raw materials. For example, the Italians manufactured 667 tanks in 1942, compared to the USSR's 25,000, and only 350 in 1943.

The war arrived at the Italian homeland with severe bombardments of the northern industrial cities of Milan and Turin in March 1943. Strikes, the loss of North Africa, and the invasion of Sicily by the Allies followed. Faced by the certainty of defeat, Fascist leaders rebelled against the Duce, and on July 25, the Fascist Grand Council voted a motion of no confidence in Mussolini and asked King Victor Emmanuel III to take charge of the country. The monarch had Mussolini arrested, prompting popular demonstrations that eliminated the vestiges of the Fascist regime. Hitler rescued his partner and placed him at the head of a satellite state in northern Italy. The story of Mussolini's last few months as titular head of the Italian Social Republic makes a degrading final chapter to a high-stakes gambler's amazing career.

Home Front: The USSR

At first it seemed that the Ukrainians and Russians would welcome the Germans, but they quickly discovered that Nazi racism and brutality outdid the horrors of Bolshevism and made them support their leaders despite the loss of over 20 million lives and the terrible misery caused by the war. Communist modernization during the 1930s had gotten the Soviet people used to working under abominable conditions and allowed Stalin to mobilize the country. Visitors' reports described shabbily dressed and severely overworked workers enjoying no privileges or breaks in their routine, toiling between twelve and sixteen hours a day. The state canceled all leaves and holidays for the war's duration, added three hours of compulsory overtime to the workday, put much of the Soviet workforce under military law, and sent habitual latecomers and slackers to labor camps.

Of all the combatants, the Soviet government succeeded best in militarizing society. It called up all men aged 18 to 50 and kept industrial and agricultural production high through the mass mobilization of women, who accounted for 40 percent of the industrial workforce in 1940 and over 50 percent in 1943; on the farms, women topped 85 percent. In 1944, over 80 percent of tractor drivers were women. After 1941, the Soviets called up women without children who were not working in critical industries to serve as fighter and bomber pilots, communication and transportation specialists, machine gunners, snipers, infantry, tank commanders, and anti-aircraft gunners, so that about 8 percent of the Soviet armed forces consisted of women. Women received 4 percent of the military medals and 1 percent of the highest decoration, the Hero of the Soviet Union, which indicate that their efforts were underrewarded. Besides appealing to nationalism, the government made workers who excelled at their jobs into national heroes and rewarded productive workers with extra food and fuel. Conversely, if workers failed to meet expectations, the government withheld food.

During the conflict, ideology faded as an incentive for hard work, despite the omnipresent propaganda and secret police. Nationalism and hatred of the Germans took the place of ideology. When the Germans invaded, they seized the Soviet industrial, mineral, and agricultural heartland. As a result, the Soviet supply of coal, iron, and steel fell by 75 percent, strategic raw materials by 66 percent, electricity by 40 percent, and meat and grain production by 50 percent. Nevertheless, between 1941 and the time the United States could gear up its vast industrial potential, the USSR carried the major burden of the war against the Nazis.

The Soviets accomplished this feat by evacuating entire industries to the Urals, Central Asia, and Siberia in the last five months of 1941. These industries included over 1,500 iron, steel, engineering, and other war-related industrial concerns, and the 16 million people and technicians who were needed to run them. What they

When the Germans invaded the USSR in June 1940 it seemed that the Russian people would welcome them. Once they experienced the Nazi occupation, however, they strongly supported their Fatherland despite great hardship, spurred by Stalin's appeals to nationalism. This photograph shows Russian women digging anti-tank traps outside Moscow.

could not relocate, they destroyed. The Soviets also built new industries, concentrating on giant plants that were needed to supply their forces with weapons. By 1942 the eastern regions produced 75 percent of Soviet arms and practically all the country's coal and steel. In an effort to get as much materiel as possible to their soldiers rapidly, the Soviets constructed tanks, airplanes, and artillery in only a few basic models of good quality, outproducing the Germans, despite more limited resources. In 1943, for example, 8 million tons of Soviet steel and 90 million tons of coal were transformed into 48,000 pieces of heavy artillery and 24,000 tanks. The Germans used 30 million tons of steel and 340 million tons of coal to make 24,000 guns and 17,000 tanks. After 1943 the production gap widened in favor of the Soviets.

Bibliographical Essay

The reader will find a flood of material on World War II, and no attempt to be exhaustive has been made here. P. M. H. Bell's *The Origins of the Second World War in Europe*, 3rd ed. (New York, 2007), is excellent on the situation of the different powers just before the outbreak of the conflict. Readers who are interested in the origins of the conflict now have a good choice, with books that include R. J. Overy, *The Origins of the Second World War* (New York, 2008), who looks at the issue of the short war; Jonathan Wright, *Germany and the Origins of the Second World War* (New York, 2007); and Victor Rothwell, *Origins of the Second World War* (New York, 2001). For considerations on the controversial book by A. J. P. Taylor on the problem, already cited, see Gordon Martel, *The Origins of the Second World War Reconsidered: A.J.P. Taylor and the Historians* (New York, 2002).

The best one-volume work on the fighting in Europe is Gerhard L. Weinberg, *A World at Arms: A Global History of World War II* (New York, 2005). This detailed, perceptive, and comprehensive work discusses all military aspects of the war in different parts of the world. Peter Calvocoressi and Guy Wint, *Total War: Causes and Courses of the Second World War* (New York, 1974), is excellent, also goes into detail on Europe, and has a large section on the Pacific. Both books are indispensable for an understanding of how the war developed. James L. Stokesbury, *A Short History of World War II* (New York, 1980), is a good representative of a numerous and growing class of books. *Europe at War: 1939–1945* (London, 2006) concentrates on the Nazi and Soviet regimes at war, reminding readers of the brutality of the Soviets as well as the Nazis. S. P. MacKenzie, *The Second World War in Europe* (New York, 2009), is a brief treatment. Lee Baker, *The Second World War on the Eastern Front* (New York, 2009), concentrates on the engagement between the USSR and Germany. Readers should be reminded of a classic— Gordon Wright, *The Ordeal of Total War 1939–1945* (New York, 1968), which analyzes the conflict from all aspects and includes information in one handy source.

Adrian Ball, *The Last Day of the Old World* (Westport, Conn., 1978), follows developments hour by hour on the last day of peace. John Lukacs, *The Last European War: September 1939/December 1945* (New York, 1976), contrasts people's everyday lives with the movement of armies and high politics during the conflict. Alan S. Milward, *War, Economy and Society* (Harmondsworth, UK, 1987), discusses the conflict's economic and social aspects. Richard J. Overy, in *War and Economy in the Third Reich* (Oxford, UK, 1995), does not believe that Hitler planned a brief war.

Anyone who is serious about understanding World War II should include a reading of Winston Churchill's classic account, *The Second World War*, 6 vols. (Boston, 1948–54). There are many good biographies of Churchill, including, among the best, Martin Gilbert, *Churchill: A Life* (New York, 1991); William Manchester, *The Last Lion: Winston Spencer Churchill* (New York, 1988); and John Lukas, *Churchill: Visionary, Statesman,*

Historian (New Haven, Conn., 2002). The appearance of revisionist accounts of Churchill's policies demonstrates that the subject is still lively. See John Charmley, *Churchill and the End of Glory* (New York, 1993), which argues that Churchill should have considered a compromise with Germany, and Robert Rhodes James, *Churchill: A Study in Failure* (New York, 1970), which faults Churchill's style. Roger Parkinson, *Blood, Toil, Tears and Sweat: The War History from Dunkirk to Alemein, Based on the War Cabinet Papers of 1940 to 1942* (New York, 1973), details the war from 1940 to 1942 from the British government's perspective. E. S. Turner's *The Phony War* (New York, 1961) is a social history of Britain during the period.

Specific books on the Battle of Britain include Francis K. Mason, *Battle Over Britain: A History of the German Air Assaults on Great Britain* (London, 1969), and Peter Townsend, *Duel of Eagles* (London, 1971). R. J. Overy's *The Battle of Britain: The Myth and the Reality* (New York, 2001) is a thorough scholarly coverage of the event. See Michael Korda's book on the same subject, *With Wings Like Eagles* (New York, 2009). The battle is well covered in more general histories of air operations during World War II. Philip Ziegler, *London at War* (New York, 1995), looks at the city up to the war's end.

Robert Mallett produced a closely argued book on *Mussolini and the Origins of the Second World War, 1933–1940* (New York, 2003). MacGregor Knox's *Mussolini Unleashed, 1938–1941* (Cambridge, UK, 1982) is a controversial book that discusses Italy's entrance into the war and the Duce's plans. The poor performance of the Italian armed forces should be considered in context. See James Sadkovich, "Understanding Defeat," *Journal of Contemporary History* 24 (1989): 27–61, and his *The Italian Navy in World War II* (Westport, Conn., 1994). See also Knox's *Hitler's Italian Allies: Royal Armed Forces, Fascist Regime, and the War of 1940–43* (New York, 2000). On the Russian women combatants, see the essay in Nancy Loring Goldman, ed., *Female Soldiers—Combatants or Noncombatants?* (Westport, Conn., 1982).

For the defeat of France, see Guy Chapman, *Why France Fell: The Defeat of the French Army in 1940* (New York, 1968), which gives a thorough account of why the French army was not successfully reconstituted before the war and of the fighting. Alistair Horne, *To Lose a Battle: France 1940* (Boston, 1969), is well written and complete. Other good works on the French collapse and its causes are A. Gunsberg, *Divided and Conquered: The French High Command and the Defeat of the West* (Westport, Conn., 1979); Brian Bond, *France and Belgium 1939–1940* (London, 1975); and William L. Shirer, *The Collapse of the Third Republic* (New York, 1969). Robert Jackson, *The Fall of France*; May–June 1940 (London, 1975), describes the French defense-mindedness and its contribution to the country's defeat. Ernest R. May, *Strange Victory: Hitler's Conquest of France* (New York, 2000), rejects the standard view and considers France's military collapse to be the result of intelligence failures. Julian Jackson's *The Fall of France: The Nazi Invasion of 1940* (New York, 2003) incorporates the latest research on the subject. Gregory Blaxland, *Destination Dunkirk* (London, 1973), recounts the events leading up to the famous withdrawal from France, while *Dunkirk: Fight to the Last Man* (Cambridge, Mass., 2006), by Hugh Sebag-Montefiore, is a more recent account. Kenneth Macksey wrote a good biography of the German general who was most famous for his use of armor during this period: *Guderian: Panzer General* (London, 1975).

Richard J. Evans, *The Third Reich at War* (New York, 2009), is the most comprehensive account of Germany during the war years. Walter Ansel, *Hitler Confronts England* (Durham, N.C., 1960), reconstructs the project to assault England. Peter Fleming, *Operation Sea Lion: The Projected Invasion of England in 1940* (New York, 1957), is a thorough account of the German preparations for invasion and British countermeasures. *Hitler's War Aims* (New York, 1973–74), by Norman Rich, includes views of works on German-occupied Europe. The campaign in northern Europe is chronicled by Earl F. Ziemke,

The German Northern Theater of Operations 1940–1945 (Washington, D.C., 1960). There is a good chapter on Finland in World War II in John H. Wuorinen, *A History of Finland* (New York, 1965). The Polish campaign is covered by Nicholas Bethell, *The War Hitler Won* (New York, 1972); the paucity of books in English on this subject has been partially alleviated by books on the Nazi-Soviet collaboration to destroy the country: *Poland Betrayed* (Barnsley, UK, 2009), by D. G. Williamson, and by a book on the German military campaign, Alexander B. Rossino, *Hitler Strikes Poland* (Lawrence, Kans., 2003). Allen Paul wrote a good account of the Katyn massacre: *Katyn: The Untold Story of Stalin's Polish Massacre* (New York, 1991). Allen Paul's *Katyn: Stalin's Massacre and the Triumph of Truth* (De Kalb, Ill., 2010) looks at the Soviet attempt to hide the facts. Michael Hope focuses on *Polish Deportees in the Soviet Union* (London, 2000). The Russian role in the East during this period is examined by Jan T. Gross, *Revolution from Abroad: The Soviet Conquest of Poland's Western Ukraine and Western Belorussia* (Princeton, N.J., 1988), and there are several interesting essays on various subjects dealing with the Baltic states, which fell into the Soviet sphere, in V. Stanley Vardis and Romuald J. Misiunas, eds., *The Baltic States in Peace and War 1917–1945* (University Park, Pa., 1978). For the East in general, see Robert Cecil, *Hitler's Decision to Invade Russia 1941* (London, 1975), and Gerhard L. Weinberg, *Germany and the Soviet Union, 1939–1941* (Leyden, 1972).

For discussions of the home fronts during the war, particularly Britain, consult Harold L. Smith, ed., *War and Social Change: British Society in the Second World War* (Manchester, UK, 1986). Leonard Moseley, *Backs to the Wall: London Under Fire, 1939–1945* (New York, 1971), emphasizes the social history of London. A. J. P. Taylor's *British History 1914–1945* (New York, 1965) has important sections on the same issue; the quotation about the Luftwaffe helping bring about the welfare state is on p. 455. Alan Milward discusses Germany at war in *The German Economy at War* (London, 1965). Goetz Aly focuses on the plunder of Europe for the benefit of Germans in *Hitler's Beneficiaries: Plunder, Racial War, and the Nazi Welfare State* (New York, 2007). An important aspect of the home front in Germany is treated in detail by Edward L. Homze, *Foreign Labor in Nazi Germany* (Princeton, N.J., 1967). For information about the Soviets, see John Barber and Mark Harrison, *The Soviet Home Front 1941–1945* (New York, 1991), and Mark Harrison, *Soviet Planning in Peace and War 1938–1945* (New York, 1985).

An interesting perspective on the influence of the smaller states during the conflict is offered by Annette Baker Fox, *The Power of Small States: Diplomacy in World War II* (Chicago, 1959), which covers Finland, Norway, Sweden, Spain, and Turkey. Several important books have been published on the European neutrals during World War II. They include Neville Wylie, *European Neutrals and Non-Belligerents During the Second World War* (New York, 2002), and, by the same author, *Switzerland: A Neutral of Distinction?* (n.p., 2002); Jerrold M. Packard, *Neither Friend nor Foe: The European Neutrals in World War II* (New York, 1992); and Christian Leitz, *Sympathy for the Devil: Neutral Europe and Nazi Germany in World War II* (New York, 2001).

CHAPTER 19

Inside Hitler's Europe: Military Occupation and Genocide

By early 1942, the Axis occupied most of Europe, and the process of reorganizing the continent according to Hitler's "New Order" had begun: a territorial and economic reordering for Germany's benefit and an alteration of Europe's racial composition.

SHORT- AND LONG-TERM AIMS

In line with Hitler's "living space" concept, the Nazi blueprint for reorganization of the conquered lands included unimagined brutality.

Territorial Designs

The Nazis slated substantial parts of the occupied regions for incorporation into the Reich, including most of Poland and occupied Soviet territory. In the West, the Nazis planned to incorporate Nordic areas, along with strategic sectors, including Norway, Denmark, Holland, Luxembourg, most of Belgium, and parts of France, and integrate the Nordic population into the Reich while killing off the Jews and other so-called inferior races.

The Nazis reserved their most brutal treatment for the inhabitants of Eastern Europe, exterminating or using them as slave labor. The Germans either immediately killed the Jews in the conquered regions or sent them to labor or death camps. The Nazis planned to reduce the non-Jewish population substantially through systematic murder—Himmler suggested a figure of 30 million for the Slavs—leaving the survivors to work in menial jobs for the Germans.

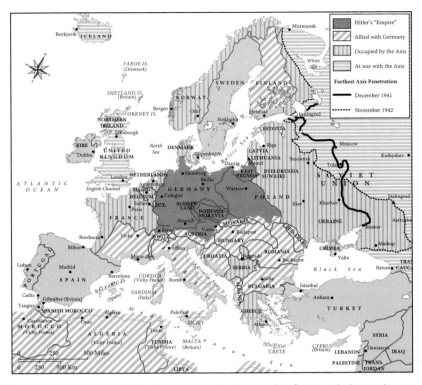

1942: German Europe. In 1942, German-occupied Europe briefly exceeded even the size of Napoleon's empire. German plans for the occupied areas varied depending on racial criteria, being particularly brutal in the East. The Germans encountered growing resistance everywhere as time passed.

They aimed to keep the number of subject peoples low by separating men and women and utilizing mass sterilization techniques and by ensuring their permanent subjugation through the mass murder of intellectuals and denying them all schooling. Hitler believed that the subject populations should "know just enough to understand road signs, so as not to get themselves run over by our vehicles. For them the word 'liberty' must mean the right to wash on holidays." Once the German inhabitants had increased sufficiently and no longer required extra labor, the Nazis would exterminate or expel the native populations from the areas of German colonization.

Economic Goals

The Nazis planned to restructure Europe economically by dividing the continent into an industrialized zone, consisting of a greatly enlarged Germany, and an agricultural one. One would produce arms and heavy machinery, the other would dedicate itself to farming and supplying raw materials for the Reich. In this way, the Nazis grotesquely claimed, Germany would provide Europe with centralized economic planning, a guaranteed export market, and a regulated labor supply that would eliminate waste and unemployment and establish a rational international planning mechanism.

In 1942, SS leader Himmler worked out a long-range Eastern plan for the next twenty-five years that described the details of Europe's Nazi future. He envisioned the construction of centrally located fortified areas garrisoned by peasant-soldiers, with the mission of defending the conquered regions and of colonizing the areas through increased birth rates. At the frontiers of the new German conquests, military settlements, modeled on the marches of the Middle Ages, would stand guard. These soldier peasant-colonists would rule over an impoverished, landless local population.

MILITARY OCCUPATION IN THE EAST

The areas of German military occupation suffered diverse fates. In the East, the Germans implemented harsh measures that resulted in millions of civilian deaths. In the West, the occupation was less harsh because the Germans wanted to gain the support of the Nordic populations, there was a smaller Jewish population, and the conquered countries could supply crucial industrial products. Moreover, the Germans worked through existing civil administrations and puppet governments that resulted in more moderate occupation administrations than in the East.

The brutal Nazi occupation of Czechoslovakia brought retaliation. In May of 1942, SS chief Reinhard Heydrich was assassinated. The assassination occasioned a vicious crackdown in the country. The town of Lidice was razed to the ground with its population either killed or sent to concentration camps, 10,000 arrests, and 1,500 deaths. These tactics were typical of the German occupation.

Northeastern Europe

The occupied areas of the Soviet Union and Poland suffered the most. Both had large Jewish populations, the Nazis considered the Slavs an inferior race to be killed or used for slave labor, and the USSR was Bolshevik. In both countries, the Germans immediately murdered millions of people, hoping to kill Jews and to decapitate the despised Communist ruling elite.

In the USSR on July 18, 1941, the Central Committee of the Communist Party gave the order for partisan warfare against the German invaders. On May 30, 1942, the Soviets formed the Central Partisan Staff, which centralized partisan activities during 1943. The Soviets armed hundreds of thousands of partisans in the occupied parts of the USSR and in eastern Poland and coordinated their actions with those of the regular armed forces. Jewish fighters had a significant part in these activities.

The Germans annexed large sections of Poland, killing, starving, or deporting the inhabitants to concentration camps or to Germany as slave laborers. They killed the Jews, expropriated Polish property, and sent to the Reich any children they believed possessed Aryan racial characteristics. The SS employed special police units to murder Jews and intellectuals—the *Einsatzgruppen* later used in the USSR. They sent millions of Poles to the Government General, an area of prewar Poland under their direct control but not incorporated into Germany and used as a dumping ground for deportees. The Nazis also introduced their program of murdering sick people. The Poles resisted this brutal occupation through military and passive means, attacking the occupying forces and performing important intelligence services for the Allies and the Polish government in exile.

The German army initially administered the eastern conquests, but in Poland, Hitler transferred authority to civilian administrators because he wanted the occupied territories to supply large quantities of raw materials, food, and industrial products. The Germans milked the considerable industrial potential of the protectorate of Bohemia and Moravia, the nucleus of the defunct Czechoslovakia. They ruled indirectly through Czech collaborators, some of whom hoped that cooperation would spare the population the more brutal aspects of German occupation, but in May 1942, Czech and Slovak resisters assassinated Reinhard Heydrich, SS chief of German administration. The Germans immediately killed 1,500 Czechs, then murdered or sent to concentration camps the entire population of the village of Lidice and then razed the village to the ground, and then made 10,000 arrests that practically wiped out the resistance.

Southeastern Europe

Southeastern Europe presented a more complex picture than did Poland and Czechoslovakia, including as it did such diverse countries as Greece and Yugoslavia, victims of Axis aggression, and Germany's allies Hungary, Romania, and Bulgaria.

After the defeat of Greece, the Germans and Italians divided the country into separate occupation zones. The Germans ruled through a Greek collaborationist government. Greek fighters, split between Communist partisans and anti-Communists, resisted the occupiers with varying effectiveness as the German army plundered the country, reneged on promises to supply food, stripped the country of its assets, and demanded exorbitant occupation costs. The result: wild inflation and a famine that killed 250,000 Greeks and that had social and political repercussions after World War II. The Germans destroyed the Jewish community of Salonika, one of the oldest in Europe, and killed more than 85 percent of the Jewish population of Greece. These developments shocked the Italians, who protested German plundering of the country and protected Jews in their zone of occupation.

Yugoslavia presented an even more confusing situation. The Germans invaded the country after a military revolt established a regime that was unfriendly to the Nazis. The Axis then occupied and dismembered the country, giving free rein to intense ethnic divisions. Germany and Italy annexed parts of the country, while Hungary and Bulgaria seized other areas. In the zones incorporated into the Reich, the Germans instituted measures favoring the inhabitants of German ancestry and then expelled and tried to murder the rest. The German army administered Serbia with a brutality second only to their administration of the East. In the remaining part of Yugoslavia, the Axis established an independent Croatia under Ante Pavelic, head of the Fascist *Ustasha*, who closely allied himself to the Germans. At Jasenovac, the "Auschwitz of the Balkans," the Croatians exterminated Jews, Serbs, Gypsies, and Muslims. A fierce guerilla war broke out in which Serb bands attacked the Croatians and the Germans. At the same time, Communist partisans under Tito fought against the occupiers and engaged in a civil war with the anti-Communist Serb nationalist fighters of Draza Mihailovic.

In the rest of southeastern Europe, there was an uneasy relationship between Germany and its allies.

The Hungarians were primarily interested in regaining territory lost to Romania after World War I, but resented Nazi support for the German minority in Hungary and attempts to take over Hungarian economic assets. The Germans viewed Hungary as useful in fighting the Russians, but Hungarian recalcitrance in handing over the Jews for liquidation angered them. In 1943, Hungarian losses in the USSR produced an anti-German government. The regent, Admiral Horthy, considered a separate peace with the Allies and resisted Hitler's demands for greater cooperation, and in 1944 the Germans occupied the country and installed a subservient government. The SS seized control of the Hungarian economy and slaughtered the Hungarian Jews. Horthy attempted to surrender to the Allies, but his efforts exacerbated the atrocities perpetrated by Hungarian collaborators.

The Germans valued Hungary's rival, Romania, for its oil reserves and for the large contingent of troops it sent to fight against the USSR. In 1940, Germany had forced Romania to surrender territory to Hungary, but Romanian policy makers calculated that if they sided with the Germans against the Soviets, they could retrieve these lands and retake territory lost to the Russians under the Nazi-Soviet Nonaggression Pact. Romania curried favor with Germany by sending troops to the Soviet front and by collaborating in the so-called Final Solution against the despised Jews. These hopes vanished with the destruction of their forces by the Russians. In August 1944, with the Soviets invading, Romania formally ended the German alliance, switched sides, and joined the Soviets in fighting the Germans. This timely action allowed the country to retain its prewar borders after the postwar settlement, but postwar Romania was dominated by the Soviets.

In August 1944 the German position in Bulgaria also deteriorated. Because of its sensitive geographic location close to Russia and the danger that a Bulgarian collapse would represent, the Germans exerted minimal pressure on Bulgaria to conform to its policies, such as handing over the Jews. The Bulgarians did not surrender Bulgarian Jews but did hand over Jews in their occupied areas. The Bulgarians profited from their military cooperation with the Germans by making gains in Greece, Yugoslavia, and Romania, but the Red Army overran the country after Romania's collapse and brought it into the Soviet orbit.

MILITARY OCCUPATION IN THE WEST

Even after France's stunning defeat, the possibilities that the French could revolt, continue the war from their colonies, or direct their fleet to assist the British gave the Germans reasons to avoid treating France too harshly. In addition, there were tendencies in France that were willing to accept a new, subordinate, position in a German-dominated Europe.

Defeated France and Its Divisions

After their victory, the Germans annexed Alsace and Lorraine, expelled the non-Aryan population, and occupied about 75 percent of France, including the entire coastline and the capital. They left the southeastern quarter of the country unoccupied but ruled by a collaborationist government headquartered at Vichy, a town famed for its mineral water. Prewar Premier Pierre Laval ran the government, and World War I hero Marshal Philippe Pétain served as the head of state. Laval cooperated with the Germans while seeking to gain advantage from the vestiges of French power and hoping to exploit the situation if the war worsened for the Germans. Hitler, a fanatic Francophobe, aimed to keep France quiet during the conflict so he could exploit its resources and industrial potential. Some semblance of independence for Vichy allowed the Germans to rule a large population at a minimal cost through the preexisting administrative structure.

The French defeat exacerbated the deep domestic divergences that had characterized the country during the twentieth century. Some leaders like General Charles de Gaulle favored continued resistance, while Pétain and Laval hoped that cooperation would spare the country the worst horrors of the Nazi occupation. Pétain rallied the country through his belief that after a temporary period of hardship, there would be a peace treaty and revival. Convinced that Britain could not hold out for long, Pétain's supporters favored a place for France in what would be the new Nazi, European order. They attributed the fall of France to the liberal principles of the Third Republic and wanted to restructure the country along conservative lines.

Vichy France brought to the fore the splits in French society of the previous hundred years. Prewar Prime Minister Pierre Laval, shown here sitting behind his desk, incarnated these divisions. Laval and other Vichy leaders thought that France still had an important role to play in what they believed would be a German-dominated future Europe. This idea gave rise to a strange policy of collaboration with the Nazis and an attempt to assert French rights within the new order. Laval was executed after the war.

The National Revolution

Many of Pétain's supporters were military leaders who considered the army the highest expression of fundamental French values. With German permission, they formed an armistice army of 100,000 soldiers, from which liberal officers were excluded, a force that could not threaten German control but was adequate to buttress conservative social values. They attributed the French defeat in 1940 to the Third Republic's liberal political and secular values and to the principles of the French Revolution of 1789: "Liberty, Equality, Fraternity," against which they presented their "National Revolution" and "Work, Family, Fatherland."

The Vichy rulers considered a radical change in social values as the key to French revival: the National Revolution guided by a stern, benevolent father chastising his children for their own good in return for obedience and loyalty. This theory implied that social groups had a specific place and function in French society and that agitators who disturbed this hierarchy must be weeded out. The Vichy government consequently proscribed intellectuals, foreign elements, and Jews; Vichy prefects complied with the German demands to hand over foreign Jews for deportation and vigorously applied their own government's anti-Jewish measures. The Vichy regime thus adopted the core of the fascist notion of the nation as an organic entity whose social groups worked in unison for the Fatherland's greatness.

Women and the Family

Because of Vichy's emphasis on France as a large family, the regime took particular care to spell out the role of men and women by defining their roles. Fathers had a duty to be the breadwinners and decision makers, and mothers must dedicate themselves to motherhood, children, and home. Vichy legislation reinforced the family's cohesion even while taking into account the large number of separations caused by soldiers who were still prisoners of war. A September 1942 law reaffirmed the authority of the man as the head of the family but accepted previous legislation that allowed mothers to make decisions in case of the fathers' absence. The concept of the man as head remained in French legislation until 1970, and as late as 1965, the husband had a legal veto on his wife taking a job. Since rejecting motherhood was evil, in February 1942, Vichy adopted stronger measures against abortion than those that passed in the 1920s (legal restrictions on abortion remained in France until 1975). A December 1942 law made a woman who left the home criminally liable, and adultery with the wife of a prisoner of war could be prosecuted as a crime against society. In 1943 the government abrogated a tacit understanding against the death penalty for women by executing a midwife for providing abortions. Vichy law also targeted fathers who did not provide for their families, convicting 4,000 transgressors a year between 1942 and 1944. In April 1941, Vichy reversed legislation passed in the 1930s easing restrictions on divorce.

Consistent with its view of women, Vichy discouraged women from working outside the home, an attitude reinforced after the 1940 defeat, demobilization, and increased unemployment. The government adopted harsh measures to prevent married women from working, but the French people received them with hostility. The officials responded that they had to implement temporary expedients to share the work, but the issue soon became moot. The Germans needed the products of French industry to support the war effort, which increased the demand and encouraged the growth of new industries, such as aluminum, the output of which surpassed prewar production. These relatively well-paying new jobs went to men, rather than women, who took poorly paying public jobs that men avoided.

Friction increased when the Germans demanded that women workers go to Germany, and the church and other organizations protested against the German insistence that single women work in the Reich. Despite these objections, Frenchwomen accounted for 2 percent of foreign females working in Germany in 1944.

Growth of Resistance

The forced incorporation of French women into the Reich's labor force contributed to a growing resistance movement. Initial French toleration for Vichy evaporated with increasing German reprisals for acts of resistance, the roundup of Jews, the expulsion of French citizens from parts of their own country, the deportations to labor camps, and the refusal to release French prisoners of war. Both passive and

As the Nazi occupation of different European countries lengthened it became more unbearable and generated more resistance. Here is a 1944 poster from Vichy France that shows both this growing resistance and the attempts to stop it. The poster shows pictures of condemned resisters and says: "Liberators? Liberation for an army of crime!"

active resistance increased after November 1942 when the Germans occupied the entire country. The French responded with silence when a German came into the room, mimicked German habits, hid resisters, allowed their houses to be used for intelligence activities, issued false documents, and refused to spend coins containing metals needed by the Germans. From these activities, many persons passed to sabotage and military action, tying down thousands of German troops and slowing the transfer of others to the front.

This pattern of opposition was repeated in the other occupied Western countries. Despite Hitler's invitation to the Nordic populations of Norway, Denmark, Luxembourg, Holland, and most of Belgium to join the "master race" after the cleansing of impure elements, they opposed him. In Norway, Vidkun Quisling ran the country for the benefit of the Germans, but his name became synonymous with *traitor*. The Norwegian resistance blew up the Vermork High Concentration Plant for the production of heavy water, depriving the Germans of a crucial resource for nuclear research and obliged them to station thirteen divisions and a large number of SS and naval personnel to police the country. In Denmark the Germans allowed the government to remain in power and initially ruled through it. The country provided food and important bases for the Nazi war effort until 1943, when Hitler ordered a change in the moderate German policy, provoking active resistance, the rescue of the country's Jewish population, and the dramatic flight of nuclear scientist Niels Bohr to England and later to the United States to work on the atomic bomb. The Danes then sabotaged German efforts to use Danish resources and later could field a significant number of resistance fighters.

The Dutch queen and government fled with her government to continue the fight against the German military administration in Holland, soon replaced by civilian authorities who attempted to assimilate the Germanic Dutch population into the Reich. The German policy of exploiting Dutch resources and liquidating the Jews provoked major strikes in February 1941, but the Nazis succeeded in wiping out most of the Dutch Jewish community. Few Jews lived in Luxembourg, but the Germans deported the foreign population in anticipation of annexation, policies that stimulated opposition. In Belgium the Germans succeeded in exploiting industry for their own purposes, but less than 30 percent of the Belgian Jews perished, thanks to the efforts of German commander Alexander von Falkenhausen's attenuation of measures to kill the Jews and starve the population; he was arrested for his effort. The Belgian king remained in the country but provided no leadership. Nevertheless, the majority of Belgians passively opposed the occupation, and by the end of the war, it is estimated that 120,000 of them were fighting in regular units against the Germans.

By 1943, opposition to the brutal German occupation had developed into armed resistance that tied up thousands of German troops and hampered their movements against the Allies. The Resistance compensated Western Europeans in some measure for the quick victory of the Germans and restored national pride. In the West many Resistance leaders became convinced that Europeans should never again fight against themselves and revived ideas of unity that were based on reciprocal respect for the different nationalities that would be important after the war.

THE HOLOCAUST

The Holocaust has come to mean the Nazi attempt to exterminate the Jewish people, but it was much wider. *Shoah*, or catastrophe, is a more appropriate term when referring to the destruction of European Jews, and it is important to remember that the slaughter in and out of the concentration camps included a large number of different victims: Jews, Gypsies (Roma or Sinti), Slavs, Russian prisoners of war, and other unfortunates from all the countries of occupied Europe.

The Holocaust Debate

In interpreting the Holocaust, historians have argued about when the Nazis decided to kill all members of the Jewish people. Because Hitler proclaimed his rage against the Jews most famously in the first volume of *Mein Kampf*, published in 1925, the attempt to eradicate all Jews during the World War II can be seen as a fulfillment of Hitler's intentions all along. Adding to the strength of this argument is a prophesy that Hitler made before the conflict that should another world war break out, the Jews would be annihilated. During the Holocaust, Hitler constantly stated that this prophecy was coming true. To most observers, it seemed obvious that the Nazis always intended to eliminate the Jews and that they attempted to put this policy into effect when they had the power to do so. These are the "intentionalists."

Opposed to them, the "functionalists" (or "structuralists") argue that Hitler did not seek to eliminate the German Jews (about 570,000) when he came to power, only to pauperize and expel them. This policy of expulsion, they maintain, continued well into 1941. The Nazis planned to resettle Eastern Europe according to their living space ideas, which meant expelling the inhabitants of Poland and the Jews farther to the East into the cold wastes of the Soviet Union. They planned to expel the Jews first, but when the Russian campaign bogged down, they could not fulfill their plans and turned to exterminating them. Contradicting this argument is the reality that the Germans began exterminating Jews immediately upon invading Russia, but the functionalist rebuttal points to the entire Nazi structure as evolving the final solution through "the system's automatic mechanisms for 'cumulative radicalization.'" The Nazis supposedly did so through various unplanned stages that represented Nazi thinking on how to resolve the so-called Jewish question at the time of their implementation.

The important difference between the intentionalists and the functionalists thus appears to be that the first school attributes the Holocaust to premeditation while the second emphasizes the evolution of Nazi practice. Neither side in this

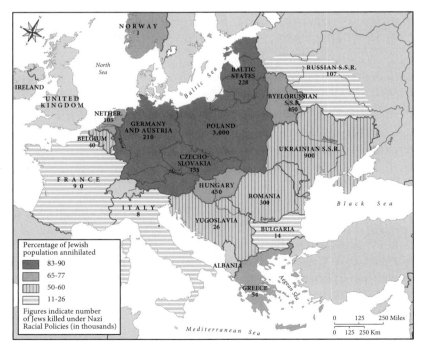

Jewish Population Killed During the Holocaust. This map provides estimates of the percentages of European Jews exterminated by the Germans during World War II.

There has been a historical debate about whether the Nazis planned to eliminate the Jews from the beginning of the movement or whether they decided on the "Final Solution of the Jewish Problem" after World War II began and they found themselves controlling a vast Jewish population. Whatever the answer, final agreement is supposed to have come at a conference of Hitler and Nazi officials at the Wannsee Conference on January 20, 1942. Here is the villa in which the meeting took place.

historical debate absolves the Germans for implementing the Final Solution to the Jewish question.

The Final Solution

The inhabitants of occupied Eastern Europe, slated for permanent German colonization, suffered most during World War II. Hitler talked about eliminating large segments of the Czechoslovak population, and, even before war broke out, SS and army heads discussed how the Polish intelligentsia would be killed along with the Jews. Hitler set up a research agency under ideologist Alfred Rosenberg to study the Jewish (and Communist) question in Poland and in the occupied Russian areas, and Rosenberg drew up plans for the disposition of the eastern territories and Russia that served as a cloak for SS mass murder operations.

SS chief Himmler took the lead in exterminating the Jews. He first supported expulsion of the Jews to Madagascar, an island off the East African coast, which proved impossible, then expulsion to the East, which proved impossible because of the lack of transportation facilities. In May 1940, Himmler proposed dumping 8 million "racially inferior" people into the General Government in the former Poland, an area that had not been annexed, which would serve as a source of labor. This policy brought complaints from German officials there who pushed for their extermination. Nazi thinking rapidly evolved away from eventually annihilating the Jews through expulsion and forced labor to eradicating them before the war ended. On January 20, 1942, Nazi officials held a conference at a villa on the Wannsee, a beautiful lake west of Berlin. Apparently Hitler had decided on the Final Solution several weeks before: immediate and complete eradication of the Jewish race by means of industrialized murder in death camps. The participants represented the SS, the Nazi Party, and the civil service. Heinrich Himmler and Reinhard Heydrich wanted to make certain that the entire apparatus of the German state understood that Hitler's plan to destroy the Jews worked smoothly and participated in the operation.

BIOGRAPHICAL SKETCHES

Heinrich Himmler
"Architect of Genocide"

When the Gestapo investigated Werner Heisenberg, the famous German nuclear scientist, on suspicion of anti-Nazi activities, his mother appealed for help to the mother of Heinrich Himmler, the leader of the SS and the German police. Himmler listened to his mother, and the SS cleared Heisenberg.

The irony of supposed soft-heartedness coexisting with fiendish brutality in the polite figure of the Final Solution's chief of operations emerges in other reported incidents. Shaken after witnessing the execution of a hundred people by the *Einsatzgruppen,* Himmler expressed concern about the emotional effects on the executioners, mostly married men, of shooting women and children. In order to help them, he favored more "humane" killing methods to achieve Hitler's aim of destroying the Jews and other groups, such as employing poison gas.

Himmler had not had a particularly brilliant career. Born into a Catholic family on October 7, 1900, in Munich, Himmler set his sights on becoming a farmer and studied agronomy. He seems to have believed in the application of animal breeding to human society. He served in the army at the end of World War I, and after the conflict, right-wing causes attracted him. By 1923, he had entered Adolf Hitler's orbit and participated in the *Putsch* of that year. Recognizing his loyalty and his outstanding organizational qualities, Hitler appointed Himmler head of the SS in 1929. From a small body of 300 men, Himmler expanded his organization to 50,000 by 1933. The SA's destruction after June 30, 1934, opened greater horizons for Himmler and the SS. Himmler controlled the Gestapo (the secret police), the SD (the SS's security service), and the concentration camps, and on June 17, 1936, became chief of the German police.

When World War II erupted, Himmler ran the camps that served as the main tools for Hitler's extermination policy. He saw the task of killing Jews as a duty and a glorious page in German history. He considered it a moral crusade and guarded against corruption. In October 1943, he admonished SS leaders not to enrich

continued

continued

themselves "even just with a fur or a watch or a Mark or a cigarette!" This principle, however, did not apply to the SS Empire, which he greatly expanded. Himmler established a huge industrial base and an enormous armed force, the *Waffen SS* (armed SS units), that rivaled the army. Within the Third Reich, his power also increased immensely during the conflict. In 1943, he became minister of the interior and, following the failed attempt to assassinate Hitler on July 20, 1944, took charge of the investigation and arrests of the conspirators. During the same year, he became the second most powerful figure in the Reich by achieving power over the Reserve Army and the People's militia.

"Loyal Heinrich" remained true to Hitler, but not quite until the end. Anticipating that Germany would lose the war, in October 1944 he tried to save his skin and position by secretly offering twenty-five German divisions to the Allies to fight communism, a ridiculous proposition. During the war's last days, he put out peace feelers through a Swedish intermediary, demonstrating a strong unwillingness to die with his Fuehrer. In the course of these talks, he released a small number of concentration camp inmates but regarded the others as hostages. When Hitler discovered his activities, as one of the last acts of his life in the bunker, he expelled Himmler from the party and removed him from all his offices.

Himmler had his files destroyed, disguised himself, and tried to flee the Reich using the papers of a victim of Nazism. Captured by the British on May 23, 1945, he bit down on a hidden cyanide capsule when a doctor attempted to examine his mouth; fifteen minutes later, he died. British doctors made casts of his face, removed part of his brain for study, and buried him in a secret grave. "The bastard's beat us!" exclaimed a British officer.

The *Einsatzgruppen*

In anticipation of the Russian invasion, the SS established four *Einsatzgruppen* consisting of 500 to 700 people each—special mobile police units trained for the task of killing German enemies in the occupied territories. Composed of Waffen SS, Gestapo, SD, police, and other personnel, these units took their orders directly from Himmler and, before his death, Reinhard Heydrich. These two leaders, who received their orders from Hitler, personally briefed the leaders of the special units on several occasions in June 1941. Their main task: to eliminate Jews, Gypsies, and political commissars in the occupied areas. They conducted massive roundups or forced Jewish leaders to assemble members of their communities, after which they shot and buried them in ditches that the victims had previously been forced to dig. Although most of their victims were Jews, the *Einsatzgruppen* also killed Russian prisoners of war and anyone they considered partisans or German opponents.

For the *Einsatzgruppen,* anyone who was a Jew was a partisan or a Bolshevik, and vice versa. Hitler had specified that pacifying the occupied areas meant shooting anyone who looked askance at the Germans. Consequently, the *Einsatzgruppen* butchered men, women, children, and elderly people. The murderers also confiscated the victims' property, not stopping at their clothing. At one famous operation, Babi Yar, on September 29 and 30, 1941, they killed 33,770 Jews. The killings took place primarily in the Ukraine and in the Baltic states, frequently with the assistance of Lithuanian and Ukrainian nationalists, and especially the *Wehrmacht*.

From a bureaucratic viewpoint, the *Einsatzgruppen* operated independently from the army, as the high command took pains to emphasize. However, the *Wehrmacht* and the SS collaborated closely to aid the *Einsatzgruppen's* work and even participated in it. Army commanders entreated their soldiers to act without pity in the struggle to liberate the Germans from the clutches of Jews and Bolsheviks, to avenge them, and to carry Volkish ideology eastward. Without the army's active cooperation, it would have been more difficult for the *Einsatzgruppen* to destroy the estimated 600,000 to 1.5 million human beings they are believed to have killed.

Despite the massive *Einsatzgruppen* operations, eliminating entire races and groups required the industrialization of murder, as exemplified by the concentration camps where most Nazi victims died.

The Concentration Camps

Originally established at Dachau in March 1933 to intern political enemies and intimidate the German population, the camps soon brimmed with prisoners of all kinds. There were two categories of camps. In the labor camps, inmates toiled for the German war effort and for giant German industrial concerns, such as I. G. Farben. Inmates worked until they died or until they could no longer toil for the Reich and were murdered. The normal survival rate in the labor camps was a few months.

The German victory over Poland, with its 3 million Jews, altered the scale and purpose of the camps. Poland became the major killing ground and home to six large death camps, including Auschwitz, and numerous satellite camps where Jews from all over Europe were exterminated. The death camps employed modern industrial methods to eliminate anyone who was judged incapable of working for Germany, regardless of age or gender. Camp officials deprived inmates of all their possessions upon arrival and selected those who were to die immediately, depending on their age and general health conditions. In order to get them to follow instructions, they lied to the new arrivals, sending them to showers that were really gas chambers. Children were gassed immediately, along with their mothers, if they objected to being separated. After their deaths, the camp officials had the victims' hair and gold teeth collected. The punctilious Germans carefully divided the booty among different agencies, with the SS profiting economically from the camps. The economic objective helps explain why the SS chose campsites close to cities, although not in easily accessible areas, and built good transportation facilities.

The camps had three major divisions: headquarters, an SS residential area, and the prisoners' compound. Luxury generally marked the headquarters and residential areas. At Buchenwald, the SS stocked a game preserve and fed the animals a richer diet than the inmates. In 1943 the SS also established a brothel there. Concentration camp prisoners lived in crowded, unhealthful, wooden or masonry barracks surrounded by barbed wire, electrified fences, and watch towers. The barracks might be several stories high and consist of two or four wings, including a day room and sleeping quarters. The small beds, divided into tiers, consisted of straw mattresses. The prisoners stored their canteens and spoons in wooden boxes. A typical barracks included a washroom and open toilets that the prisoners had to clean under humiliating circumstances. The camps also included a hospital, which sick prisoners usually did not leave alive and where SS doctors conducted outrageous medical experiments. Finally, in a large open space surrounded by a high wall stood the furnaces, with their enormous smokestacks, that consumed the inmates' bodies.

The camps were tightly organized. At the top of the hierarchy, the camp commandant and his staff had complete authority. The administrative officer handled day-to-day administration, working with the officer in charge and the roll-call officer, who had direct command over the prisoners through the block leaders. The block leaders, famed for their brutality, commanded individual barracks. A labor service officer determined inmate tasks and work organization, frequently holding in his hands the life and death of individual prisoners. SS Death Head units provided the guards, who were armed with weapons and with special dogs that were trained to attack the inmates. The camps included a political department run by the Gestapo. This hierarchical organization was reflected in the lives of the prisoners. Each barracks had a senior block inmate, approved by the camp administration, responsible to the block leader for everything that went on in the barracks and who had responsibility for keeping order and for disbursing rations. Prisoners, known as capos, ran the labor details. In most cases, egged on by their SS guards, prisoners who had some authority over their fellow inmates were known for their brutality.

BIOGRAPHICAL SKETCHES

Primo Levi, 174517

Primo Levi seemed destined for an ordinary though good career, but World War II intervened. Born on July 31, 1919, as a Jew living in Turin, he represented a minority of a minority because most Italian Jews lived in Rome or Milan. Levi, who traced his ancestry to Jews expelled from Spain in 1492, proved an outstanding student and attended the University of Turin despite the 1938 racial laws. In 1941, he received a chemistry degree. Some of his chemical texts were in German; his knowledge of the language and his chemical expertise would save his life.

The overthrow of Fascism and creation of a German puppet state in northern Italy prompted Levi and some friends to take to the mountains and join the resistance in 1943. Captured in December, he was sent to Auschwitz in February 1944, where he was assigned to a labor detail building a synthetic rubber factory. It is unlikely that Levi would have lived had it not become known that he was a skilled chemist who knew German. His reassignment to a camp laboratory with better rations and easier working conditions enabled him to survive.

Released at the war's end, Levi returned to Italy, a voyage described in *The Reawakening* (*La tregua*, or "The Truce," 1958, later made into a film). Back home, he resumed his career as an industrial chemist, working at a paint factory in his native Turin. Despite his profession, he felt the need to write. As he told an interviewer:

"After Auschwitz, I had an absolute need to write. Not only as a moral duty, but as a psychological need." In 1947, he published his famous *Se questo è un uomo* (published in English as *Survival in Auschwitz*). This book has become the classic account of life in the Nazi concentration camps.

Levi's masterpiece describes the creation of a full-blown society among the death camp prisoners and the relationship of that culture to the camp authorities in a detached, almost scientific, manner. Far from being a cold work, however, *Survival in Auschwitz* demonstrates in a graphic but matter-of-fact tone the total failure of the Nazis to achieve their objective—to dehumanize even more than to kill the inmates. Despite their suffering under intolerable conditions, the inmates expressed their full humanity, their strengths and their foibles, virtues and defects. In his work Levi fused the scientist-observer, philosopher, and poet. After writing *Survival in Auschwitz*, he published other important works on the camps and in 1974 retired to write full time.

At 10:00 A.M. on April 11, 1987, the concierge of the late nineteenth-century building in which Levi and his family had lived for three generations delivered the mail. Levi thanked her and closed the door of his third-floor apartment. Outside the apartment was a spiral staircase, an elevator enclosed by a cage, and an open space down to the ground floor. Moments after the mail delivery, Levi's body tumbled to the ground, crushing his head when he landed. The police ruled his death a suicide.

Despite the official ruling, a debate raged about whether Levi killed himself or fell accidentally. Levi constantly fought depression, and his son pointed to his conviction that the best people had died in Auschwitz and that only the worst survived. A friend stated that his death should be backdated to 1945 and that he killed himself when his writing was done. In 1962, Levi wrote about a recurrent dream: "I am in the Lager once more, and nothing is true outside the Lager." The chief rabbi of Rome disclosed that Levi had called him minutes before he died and said his terminally ill mother reminded him of the bodies at Auschwitz: He could not go on with life. Those who believed in an accidental death pointed to the lack of a note and to the difficulty of committing suicide in the physical circumstances of the building.

Whatever the answer, Levi's experiences in Auschwitz never left him. He lies buried in a Jewish cemetery near Turin under a headstone engraved: Primo Levi—174517—1919–1987. That was the number that the Nazis tattooed on his arm.

Resistance in the Camps

Under these circumstances, resistance in the camps was very difficult, but it existed. Prisoners attempted to organize themselves in the best way possible in an attempt to survive physical destruction and lift their spirits. The SS tried to plant informers among the inmates but rarely succeeded. The inmates' resistance focused on two areas: they constructed a pervasive intelligence network, so they knew almost immediately what the SS planned, and they became skilled at sabotage.

Contrary to the conception that inmates went meekly to their fates, concentration camp inmates not only resisted their tormentors, but attempted to escape and revolted against them. Successful escapes were difficult because the surrounding population was generally hostile and feared ending up in the camps if they helped escaping prisoners. In the last years of the war, revolts occurred at Treblinka, Sobibor, and Auschwitz.

As much as possible, the prisoners also wrote descriptions of their ordeal. In 1947, Eugen Kogon published a detailed description of the camps, *The Theory and Practice of Hell*, and an Italian Jew, Primo Levi, published *Survival at Auschwitz* and several other classic works on the universe of the concentration camp, describing the psychology of the prisoners and the administrators and the daily operations of the camp.

Ghettoization

Besides the camps, the Germans employed ghettos to eliminate Jews. They obliged Jews to live in certain parts of the most important cities, then walled off the ghettos, systematically subjected the inhabitants to atrocities, and carefully restricted essential supplies. Overcrowding and maltreatment resulted in epidemics that killed hundreds of thousands. When the Nazis decided on the Final Solution, they methodically moved the ghetto inhabitants to extermination

During World War II, the Allies probably did not realize the full extent of the Holocaust, despite the many signs that pointed to mass killings, and did very little to stop it. Only in the later stages of the conflict did they see the consequences, and only later still did its full impact sink in. This May 1945 photograph shows American soldiers observing the consequences of the Nazi murders of Jews, Slavs, Gypsies, and political prisoners in a concentration camp around the city of Ohrdruf in Germany.

camps, lying to the ghetto populations that they would enjoy better conditions in the East.

Many ghettos existed in Eastern Europe, but the most infamous was the Warsaw Ghetto, created on October 2, 1940, in the slums of the Polish capital and holding a population of 500,000 at its height. The average person subsisted on only 184 calories per day, and hunger and epidemics decimated the population. The Germans used a supposedly self-governing Jewish organization, the *Judenrat*, the ghetto police, and collaborators to rule the area. In late 1941 and early 1942, reliable reports arrived at the ghetto about the Nazi gassing of Jews. This news and continual German atrocities prompted Jewish leaders to establish relations with the Polish resistance outside the ghetto and to plan a revolt.

The uprising began on April 19, 1943, when German troops entered the ghetto, and lasted a month as the resisters employed Molotov cocktails, handmade grenades, and weapons taken from fallen German soldiers against the attackers. The Warsaw Ghetto rebellion represented the zenith of Jewish resistance to the Nazis and was remarkable for military reasons and because the entire population of the Ghetto participated.

The West

Jews in a large Western country like France had a better chance of survival than did those in smaller countries, like Holland, even though France had a long and inglorious tradition of anti-Semitism; decades later, shameful cases of anti-Semitism during the conflict continued to emerge, and trials took place into the 1980s. Ironically, France's nationalistic pride mitigated the Jewish condition to some extent as Vichy handed over foreign Jews but balked at surrendering French and denaturalized Jews, stubbornly seeking to implement its own anti-Semitic measures. Many Jews survived by joining the Resistance or fleeing to the safety of the Italian zone.

The Phenomenon of Rescue

Despite intense pressure from the Germans, the Italians protected the Jews in their occupation zones in France, Yugoslavia, and Greece and were unique in protecting foreign Jews, not only the few Italian Jews present there.

In southern France, the Vichy government demanded that the Italians hand over Jews and sent its police into their zone to round them up, but the Italians asserted their complete legal authority as the occupying power and ordered the Vichy police to halt their activities. Laval complained to the Germans, who appealed to Mussolini to order his generals to arrest Jews on the grounds that they constituted a security risk. Il Duce then appointed a special police official to resolve the problem, but he appointed an Italian Jew as an adviser and avoided the German officials. The Italians then moved Jews to the interior, putting up the poorest in requisitioned hotels. In France about 50,000 Jews fled to the Italian zone. In the Italian occupation zones of the Balkans, Italian soldiers and diplomats followed similar policies and instituted bureaucratic obstacles, preventing the handing over of Jews to Germans and Croats that caused Jews all over the Balkans to flood into Italian-occupied areas.

While the Italian effort was unique because soldiers and diplomats obstructed the Final Solution, other rescue efforts should not be underestimated. The controversial Pope Pius XII has been harshly criticized for refusing publicly to denounce the Holocaust, but he ordered priests and nuns to open church buildings and monasteries to shelter Jews. In Hungary, diplomats from the neutral nations bonded together to rescue the Jews of Budapest. Swedish representative Raoul Wallenberg and his collaborators from other countries saved thousands. While most ordinary Europeans may have remained passive to the plight of Hitler's victims or to have behaved badly, many ordinary people risked their lives to hide and protect them. Despite the gloomy picture presented in occupied Europe in this respect, rescue was a significant humanitarian phenomenon whose importance has increasingly been recognized.

GENOCIDE

Of the 40 million to 55 million victims of World War II, about half were civilians. This figure resulted from the Nazis' attempts at not only physical destruction, but also cultural and social destruction,.The Polish lawyer Raphael Lemkin, who invented the term in 1943, wrote in his preface to *Axis Rule in Occupied Europe*:

> Genocide is effected through a synchronized attack on different aspects of life of the captive peoples: in the political field (by destroying institutions of self-government and imposing a German pattern of administration, and through colonization by Germans); in the social field (by disrupting the social cohesion of the nation involved and killing or removing elements such as the intelligentsia, which provide spiritual leadership . . .); in the cultural field (by prohibiting or destroying cultural institutions and cultural activities . . .); in the economic field (by shifting the wealth to Germans and by prohibiting the exercise of trades and occupation by people who do not promote germanism "without reservation"); in the biological field (by a policy of depopulation and promoting procreation by Germans in the occupied countries); in the field of physical existence (by introducing a starvation rationing system for non-Germans and by mass killing, mainly of Jews, Poles, Slovenes, and Russians); in the religious field (by interfering with the activities of the Church, which in many countries provides not only spiritual but also national leadership); in the field of morality (by attempts to create an atmosphere of moral debasement . . .).

The Techniques of Genocide

During World War II, the Germans implemented genocide on a wider scale than ever before. They attempted to eliminate races and national and cultural groups, trying at the same time to impose their own national patterns.

Depopulation

In accomplishing their aims, the Germans followed an organic program that was not limited to the elimination of undesirable groups by means of concentration camps and ghettos, but pursued vigorous depopulation policies to reduce populations who were not related to the Germans by blood. This policy was intended to make room for future German generations and for Germans living in different parts of Europe where political agreements or other factors called for their transfer.

The German government instituted measures to decrease births among the defeated populace, combining them with steps favoring an increased German birthrate. Nazi doctors conducted sterilization experiments on concentration camp inmates. In the parts of Poland incorporated into the Reich, German officials required Polish couples to request special permission to marry—and then refused authorization. They physically separated men and women by deporting them for forced labor to different areas and by other means. They lowered rations for Poles because undernourishment reduces the birthrate and the chances that offspring will survive. At the same time, German families in Poland having at least three children received special subsidies. In Norway and Holland, populated by Germanic peoples, the Reich commissioners provided aid for the illegitimate children of German soldiers who were born to Norwegian and Dutch women.

Debilitation
The occupiers employed physical means to debilitate the races they earmarked for immediate or eventual eradication, providing them with little food of poor quality. The German rationing system allocated 93 percent of their prewar caloric intake to Germans and only 20 percent to Jews. With reference to quality, the percentages of meat rations that were earmarked to different national groups was as follows: Germans, 100; Czechs, 86; Dutch, 71; Poles (incorporated Poland), 78; Lithuanians, 57; French, 51; Belgians, 40; Poles (unincorporated Poland), 36; Serbs, 36; Slovenes, 29; Jews, 0. Similar proportions prevailed concerning other foods that are essential for good health, with Germans on top and Jews on the bottom. This policy greatly increased the death and illness rates for the subject populations. In Warsaw, anemia jumped 113 percent for Poles and 435 percent for Jews. The occupiers complemented their food rationing policy by withholding or requisitioning essential materials, such as medicine and, during the coldest parts of the winter, fuel and blankets.

The Germans sought to ensure the permanent impoverishment of the subservient populations and the economic superiority of Germanic elements by seeking to destroy the livelihood of the conquered peoples. In the parts of Poland that they incorporated, the Germans confiscated the property and bank accounts of Poles, allowing access only to German depositors of Polish banks who submitted a certificate of their national origin. They required licenses to exercise trades and issued them only to Germans. They closed cooperatives and associations that had been principal vehicles for improving the standards of living of Poles.

Denationalization
The Germans sought to obliterate the national identities of the people living in the areas they conquered by destroying their cultural and political heritage. They destroyed Jewish libraries and synagogues and burned Talmudic scrolls and other sacred items. In Poland, the Germans wrecked national monuments

and demolished or confiscated the contents of libraries and museums. They devastated churches and attacked the clergy in order to destroy the Polish national religion and gave top priority to murdering the nation's intellectuals who might serve as future leaders.

In the eastern incorporated territories, German policy was to remove the inhabitants and replace them with *Volksdeutsche,* Germans who had lived elsewhere in Europe. These settlers received the property of the deported inhabitants and other economic inducements. Members of the subservient population could not access higher education.

In areas of Germanic populations that were destined for incorporation into the Reich, the Germans killed the Jews, expelled the foreign population, and gave special privileges to persons of German origin who cooperated with them. The authorities imposed German culture, instituted special agencies to control high culture through special agencies, and required licenses for artists and writers. They ordered changes in names of people, communities, enterprises, and signs to German forms. They forbade the teaching of the primary language of a conquered area, replacing it with German; inculcated National Socialist principles starting at age 6; and enticed children into Nazi organizations. German became the official language of the courts, and German law codes either replaced or modified local laws. Finally, the Germans banned local political organizations and supplanted them with local Nazi parties enjoying special legal privileges.

Had the Nazis won the war, the brutal application of this comprehensive program would have completely altered the face of Europe.

Bibliographical Essay

On the conduct of the war by German soldiers, see Omer Bartov, *The Eastern Front 1941–1945: German Troops and the Barbarization of Warfare* (New York, 1985). Richard Rhodes's *Masters of Death: The Einsatzgruppen and the Invention of the Holocaust* (New York, 2002), which shows Hitler's wider intentions. See as well, Wendy Lower, *Nazi Empire-Building and the Holocaust in Ukraine* (Chapel Hill, N.C., 2005). Heather Anne Pringle, *The Master Plan: Himmler's Scholars and the Holocaust* (New York, 2006), is the story of the SS chief's plan to create a new racially pure Europe.

For information on the organization of the German army and how it fought, see Tim Ripley, *The Wehrmacht* (London, 2003), and David Stone, *Hitler's Army* (London, 2009). For an analysis of the Nazi occupation, see Mark Mazower's *Hitler's Empire: How the Nazis Ruled Europe* (New York, 2008). The mistreatment of occupied Eastern Europe is treated by Alexander Dallin, *German Rule in Russia 1941–1945* (London, 1957). Hitler's remark on keeping the subject populations ignorant is quoted by Peter Cavalcoressi and Guy Wint, *Total War* (New York, 1974), previously cited, p. 212. Theo Schulte discusses the army in *The German Army and Nazi Politics in Occupied Russia* (Oxford, UK, 1989). Poland is discussed by Richard C. Lukas, *The Forgotten Holocaust: The Poles Under German Occupation, 1939–1944* (Lexington, Ky., 1986), and Stefan Korbonski and F. B. Czarnomski, *Fighting Warsaw: The Story of the Polish Underground State, 1939–1945* (New York, 2004). There are five essays on Czechoslovakia during the World War II period in Victor S. Mamatey and Radomir Luza, eds., *A History of the Czechoslovak Republic, 1918–1948* (Princeton, N.J., 1973); C. A. MacDonald and Jan Kaplan published a study on *Prague in the Shadow of the Swastika: A History of the German Occupation* (n.p., 2001). On Vichy France, see Robert Paxton, *Parades and Politics at Vichy: The French Officer Corps*

Under Marshal Pétain (Princeton, N.J., 1966), an examination of the French officer corps, and *Vichy France: Old Guard and New Order* (New York, 2001). Julian Jackson, *France: The Dark Years, 1940–1944* (New York, 2001), is a thorough analysis of France under the German occupation and its effects on the country; see also *Marianne in Chains: Everyday Life in the French Heartland Under the German Occupation* (New York, 2003), by Robert Gildea. With regard to "undesirables" in Vichy, Shannon L. Fogg published *The Politics of Everyday Life in Vichy France* (Cambridge, UK, 2008). The debate on the Vichy experience continued long after the war. See Éric Conan and Henry Rousso, *Vichy: An Ever-Present Past* (Hanover, N.H., 1998); Richard Golsan, *Vichy's Afterlife: History and Counterhistory in Postwar France* (Lincoln, Nebr., 2000); and Michael Curtis, *Verdict on Vichy* (London, 2004). On Vichy's foreign affairs, see Adrienne Doris Hytier, *Two Years of French Foreign Policy: Vichy 1940–1942* (Westport, Conn., 1974). On the relationship with Britain, see R. T. Thomas, *Britain and Vichy: The Dilemma of Anglo-French Relations, 1940–42* (New York, 1979). P. M. H. Bell, *A Certain Eventuality: Britain and the Fall of France* (n.p., 1974), analyzes relations between Britain and France before and after the defeat. Eleanor M. Gates, *End of the Affair: The Collapse of the Anglo-French Alliance, 1939–1940* (London, 1981), is an account of the breakdown of the Anglo-French alliance. On the question of collaboration, there is Philippe Burrin, *France Under the Germans: Collaboration and Compromise* (New York, 1996). Bertram M. Gordon also examines France in *Collaborationism in France During the Second World War* (Ithaca, N.Y., 1980). On the resistance to the German occupation, see the results of an international conference held in 2007: Jun Glasgow et al., *Partisan and Anti-Partisan Warfare in German-Occupied Europe 1939–1945* (Basingstoke, UK, 2010). On the behavior of business under the German occupation, there is Joachim Lund, *Working for the New Order* (Copenhagen, 2006).

Mark Mazower wrote an excellent and readable work on the Axis occupation of Greece, *Inside Hitler's Greece* (New Haven, Conn., 1993). The Italian occupation is examined, controversially, by Davide Rodogno, *Fascism's European Empire* (Cambridge, UK, 2006), and by H. James Burgwyn, *Empire on the Adriatic: Mussolini's Conquest of Yugoslavia 1941–1943* (New York, 2005). Dietrich Orlow's *The Nazis in the Balkans: A Case Study in Totalitarian Politics* (Pittsburgh, 1968) examines the role of an important agency operating in the area. Ilija Jukic, *The Fall of Yugoslavia* (New York, 1974), gives good, firsthand information. Walter R. Roberts, *Tito, Mihailovic and the Allies* (New Brunswick, N.J., 1973), examines the resistance and its divisions in Yugoslavia.

The reader will find many good books on the Holocaust; a good introduction is Doris L. Bergen, *War and Genocide: A Concise History of the Holocaust* (Lanham, Md., 2003). The most thorough and complete work is the excellent Raul Hilberg, *The Destruction of the European Jews*, 3 vols., rev. and definitive edition (New York, 1985). This book goes into all the details about the roundup of the Jews, the organization of the concentration camps and ghettos, the disposition of the victims and their property, and the number and modalities of Jewish deportation from all the European countries. Shorter general histories include Neil Tonge, *The Holocaust* (New York, 2009). *A Mosaic of Victims* (New York, 1990), edited by Michael Berenbaum, discusses the non-Jewish victims of the Nazis. Raphael Lemkin, *Axis Rule in Occupied Europe: Laws of Occupation, Analysis of Government, Proposals for Redress* (New York, 1973), observes the administrative and legal position of occupied Europe, attempts to put it within the context of accepted international law, and suggests legal remedies; the book, originally published in 1944, also has a wealth of difficult-to-find documents. Gotz Aly's *"Final Solution": Nazi Population Policy and the Murder of the European Jews* (New York, 1999) analyzes developments leading to the Nazi genocide. David A. Hackett, ed., *The Buchenwald Report* (Boulder, Colo., 1995), provides brief accounts by victims about their treatment and the organization of one of the most infamous concentration camps. Eugen Kogon, *The Theory and Practice of Hell: The German Concentration Camps and the System Behind Them* (New York, 1975), is an early but accurate account (original publication date in English, 1950) describing the setup of the concentration camp system. Auschwitz is described by Yisrael Gutman and Michael Berenbaum, *Anatomy of the Auschwitz Death Camp* (Indianapolis, Ind., 1994). *The Business of Genocide: The SS, Slave Labor, and the Concentration Camps* (Chapel Hill, N.C., 2002), by Michael Thad Allen, examines the modern management aspects of the concentration camps. James Caplan and Nikolaus Wachsmann produced a book of essays providing new scholarship on the concentration camp system: *Concentration Camps in Nazi Germany: The New Histories* (New York, 2010). Lucy S. Dawidowicz, *The War Against the Jews 1933–1945* (New York, 1975), attempts to answer the questions of how a modern state could bring itself to institute the Holocaust and how its people could have followed it. George M. Kren and Leon Rappaport examine *The Holocaust and the Crisis of Human Behavior* (New York, 1994). Richard Breitman, *The Architect of Genocide: Himmler and the Final Solution* (New York, 1991), examines Himmler's role in the Holocaust.

Women are treated by Vera Laska, *Women in the Resistance and in the Holocaust* (Westport, Conn., 1983), which describes sterilization and other experiments; Lenore J. Weitzman and Dalia Ofer, *Women in the Holocaust* (New Haven, Conn., 1998), which discusses the conditions for women in the camps; Carol Ann Rittner and John R. Roth, eds., *Different Voices: Women and the Holocaust* (New York, 1993), which contains essays by survivors and observers; and Roger A. Ritvo and Diane M. Plotkin, *Sisters of Sorrow: Voices of Care in the Holocaust* (Austin, Tex., 1998).

Two interesting books on how and why the Holocaust was actually begun are Philippe Burrin, *Hitler and the Jews: The Genesis of the Holocaust* (London, 1994), dating the decision to late 1941, and, especially, Christopher Browning, *The Path to Genocide: Essays on the Launching of the Final Solution* (New York, 1995), which does a good job of discussing the intentionalist and functionalist theories and the debate's evolution; the quotation on cumulative radicalization of the Nazi system is on p. 87. *Ordinary Men* (New York, 1992) is an attempt by Browning to analyze the composition of some of the killing groups and their mentality. Browning also published *Nazi Policy, Jewish Labor, German Killers* (New York, 2000), on the evolution of Nazi methods from 1939 to 1941. The question of the willingness of Germans to kill Jews is discussed in the controversial Daniel Goldhagen, *Hitler's Willing Executioners: Ordinary Germans and the Holocaust* (New York, 1997); see Chapter 15 for books discussing the debate on Goldhagen's work. Henry Friedlaender, *The Origins of Nazi Genocide: Ordinary Germans and the Holocaust* (Chapel Hill, N.C., 1995), traces events from euthanasia to the final solution. Saul Friedlaender wrote *Nazi Germany and the Jews* (New York, 1998).

Controversy surrounds the question of whether the pope at the time, Pius XII, should have spoken out forcefully against the Holocaust. This issue has brought up the question of anti-Semitism in the Catholic Church. The most outspoken and controversial books are John Cornwell, *Hitler's Pope: The Secret History of Pius XII* (New York, 1999), and Daniel Jonah Goldhagen, *Moral Reckoning: The Role of the Catholic Church in the Holocaust and Its Unfulfilled Duty of Repair* (New York, 2002). More balanced treatments may be found in Susan Zuccotti, *Under His Very Windows: The Vatican and the Holocaust in Italy* (New Haven, Conn., 2000) and Michael Phayer, *The Catholic Church and the Holocaust, 1930–1963* (Bloomington, Ind., 2000). Ronald J. Rychlak, *Hitler, the War, and the Pope* (Columbus, Mo., 2000) maintains that Pius acted wisely in being circumspect but signaling to the faithful that they should help people in need.

On Jewish resistance, Reuben Ainztein's, *Jewish Resistance in Nazi-Occupied Eastern Europe: With a Historical Survey of the Jew as Fighter and Soldier in the Diaspora*

(London, 1974) is a comprehensive work. On the wider topic, see Yuri Suhl, *They Fought Back: The Story of Jewish Resistance in Europe* (New York, 1978). There are a number of good books on the Warsaw Ghetto. Israel Gutman's *The Warsaw Ghetto Uprising* (Boston, 1994) is a good account.

On rescue, Martin Gilbert's *The Righteous: the Unsung Heroes of the Holocaust* (New York, 2003) is a general history. For the little-known story of how Italian soldiers and diplomats protected Jews in Greece, Yugoslavia, and France, see Jonathan Steinberg's *All or Nothing: The Axis and the Holocaust 1941–1943* (London, 1990). Documents related to these events, with commentaries, are published in Léon Poliakov and Jacques Sabille, *Jews Under the Italian Occupation* (Paris, 1954); see also Susan Zuccotti's *The Italians and the Holocaust* (New York, 1987) and Charles T. O'Reilly, *The Jews of Italy, 1938–1945* (Jefferson, Mo., 2007). Tela Zasloff, *A Rescurer's Story* (Madison, Wis., 2003), is an example of a rescue in Vichy France. Karen Gray Ruelle and Deborah Durland De Saix, *The Grand Mosque of Paris* (New York, 2008), tells how Muslims saved Jews during the Holocaust. Suzanne Vromen, *Hidden Children of the Holocaust* (New York, 2008), describes how Belgian nuns rescued young Jews. The Bulgarian case is examined by Frederick B. Chary, *The Bulgarian Jews and the Final Solution 1940–1944* (Pittsburgh, 1972). The case of Wallenberg is the most famous also because he disappeared when the Russians took over Hungary. See John Bierman, *Righteous Gentile: The Story of Raoul Wallenberg, Missing Hero of the Holocaust* (New York, 1981); Andrew Handler, *A Man for all Generations—Raoul Wallenberg and the Hungarian Apparatus, 1944–1945* (Westport, Conn., 1996); and Alan Gersten, *A Conspiracy of Indifference: The Raoul Wallenbeg Story* (Philadelphia, 2001).

How the War Was Won

Their early victories allowed the Germans to exploit Europe's resources and productive capacities, and between 1940 and 1942, the Nazis enjoyed an aura of invincibility and important bases from which they would be difficult to dislodge, while their opponents had no convenient staging areas for war operations. However, the fortunes of the war slowly shifted against the Germans because the Americans joined the British and the Soviets. On December 7, 1941, the Japanese bombed Pearl Harbor, and the Germans and Italians declared war on the United States.

WEAPONS

During World War II, the Allies emphasized the large-scale production of reliable weapons rather than seeking to perfect ever more advanced ones, as did the Germans.

Armies and Armor

For land armies, the rifle remained the fundamental weapon. The major innovations were ammunition clips and rapid-fire submachine guns. Machine guns became lighter but remained fundamentally the same. With reference to another basic weapon, the belligerents (except Germany) entered the war with artillery manufactured during World War I, but innovations that combined heavy artillery with rapid-fire ability made it necessary to shift to more modern guns. Heavier artillery forced armies to mount them on vehicles, giving rise to self-propelled artillery. The Russians adapted rockets to artillery uses, employing a bank of them, the *katyusha*. The design of shells accounted for the most important change in the evolution of the artillery because changes allowed them to penetrate thicker armor and to explode in the proximity of targets without direct hits.

Tanks developed into reliable vehicles and conferred great mobility to the battles of World War II. Ironically, the Germans did not enjoy qualitative superiority at first; the Mark III and IV were disappointments, and they utilized Czech-built T-38 medium tanks that they had taken after the Munich crisis to great effect during the early days of the war. The French had better tanks than the Germans but used them poorly. The Russian T-34 was clearly superior to the German Mark III and IV and equal to the later Mark V and VI. The Americans intervened with the heavily armored and reliable Shermans that also replaced earlier British armor, but they were inferior to later German models. The tank initially gave the offensive the edge over the defense through its ability to roll over machine guns, but the Germans in North Africa discovered that they could stop them with the use of anti-aircraft weapons. Handheld tank-killing rockets could also destroy tanks, but subsequent changes in the tank meant that neither offense nor defense had a clear superiority.

Another weapon that was commonly employed in World War I, poison gas, was not used in World War II despite ominous developments in its effectiveness. Both sides possessed it, and the Allies threatened massive retaliation against the Germans should they employ it, especially on the eastern front where its use appeared most probable. Given the scarcity of gas masks and the subjection of Germany to mammoth air raids, German leaders heeded the warning—luckily, because the Germans had invented nerve gas, against which no defense existed, and Hitler mistakenly assumed that the Allies also had it. There was some attempt to develop biological weapons, especially anthrax, but they were not a significant factor in the war.

War in the Air

Greater changes occurred in the air than on land, even with regard to personnel. With the exception of the USSR, where women saw significant action in the army in addition to the air force, female service in the air corps captured the public's imagination in the Allied countries. By 1939, single-winged warplanes had substantially replaced biplanes, and American development of long-range fighters revolutionized the air war by permitting these fighters to escort bombers to strike enemy territory. Twin-engine bombers continued to be used for combat support, but the four-engine airplane set the standard for the long-range bomber carrying large loads.

Allied strategic bombing of Germany spurred the development of famous four-engine bombers, such as the American B-17 Flying Fortress and the B-29 that dropped the first atomic weapons on Japan. The Germans had begun the tradition of heavily bombing cities and civilian populations during the Spanish Civil War, but the British and Americans mastered the technique. They implemented the ideas of prewar theorists who had argued that air power alone could break the will of populations to continue fighting and spur them to revolt. Allied carpet bombing claimed many victims; the bombing of Dresden, for example, created ferocious firestorms and is estimated to have killed 70,000 people. The bombing of Germany did not induce the Germans to revolt and force their government to surrender, but it severely damaged the production of war materiel and the ability to keep armed forces in the field. The Germans ultimately proved less efficient than the Allies in the air war because, impressed by the achievements of their dive-bombers in the opening months of the war, they concentrated on perfecting them, which proved to be a dead end, instead of developing more potent four-engine bombers.

On the other hand, the Germans excelled in advanced air weapons that did not affect the course of the war but were important for the future. The V-1 "flying bomb," utilizing a jet engine and capable of being dropped from airplanes, foreshadowed the cruise missile. Because its low speed made it vulnerable to being shot down by fighters, the Germans developed the V-2, a true rocket and ancestor of the ballistic missile against which no defense existed. Despite its late employment, its early stage of perfection, and Allied bombing against research and assembly bases, it killed 15,000 persons. The Germans' use of slave labor on this project, however, subjected the weapon to sabotage. The Germans had in the works the V-4, a rocket capable of reaching the United States. Luckily for the Allies, the Germans had previously interrupted earlier research on missiles because they believed the war would be a brief one.

The Germans made progress in the development of jet fighters, but too late to affect the course of the conflict. In 1943, they flew a jet fighter and a jet bomber that was more advanced than any similar weapon the Allies had. Because Allied bombing had become so efficient, the Germans had to scatter their aircraft production facilities, which delayed the deployment of the jet aircraft. Disputes over how the aircraft should be used, the inability to train pilots, and the capture of a manufacturing plant prevented the Germans from exploiting their technical advantage.

Naval Warfare

On the sea, there were fewer changes in weaponry, and battleships and submarines remained essentially the same as those of the World War I. The Germans built powerful battleships, such as the *Bismarck,* that raided the Atlantic and gained great notoriety, but had a minimal effect on the war. For the Germans, the real challenge in World War II was to destroy the shipping that carried American supplies and troops to Europe, and as in World War I, their most potent weapon was the submarine. With the exception of Admiral Karl Doentiz, German leaders failed to give submarines high priority, building fewer of them than was required to fulfill their mission and employing mistaken tactics. Even so, it is doubtful that the submarine could have been successful because it still traveled too slowly under water and had to surface and move significant distances to find targets, making it vulnerable. The convoy system proved as effective as it had been in World War I, even against improved German "wolf pack" tactics that pitted groups of submarines against convoys. The slow American response to the German strategy resulted in

As the war began turning against the Germans, they developed more advanced weapons, such as the V-2 rocket. Although the new weapons came too late to affect the war's outcome, they were important for the future. As the war came to a close, the Americans scrambled to bring German scientists as to the United States in order to keep them out of Soviet hands and to take advantage of their expertise. Werner von Braun, developer of the V-2, helped develop the Intermediate Range Ballistic Missile (IRBM) during the Cold War and the Saturn booster that was essential in the successful effort to land Americans on the moon in July 1969.

the loss of a significant number of American ships to submarines, but eventually the Allies responded with improved convoy schemes and high-frequency direction finders that defeated the submarine menace.

The most important innovation in naval warfare was the development of radar, which gave the Allies great advantages over the Germans and Italians. In another electronic area, radio communication among the fighting forces became commonplace, making the interception of messages and the breaking of secret codes an essential element of warfare on land, air, and sea. A war within the war took place in which the belligerents tried to break each other's codes and then struggled to keep the development secret so they could continue to learn of the other's plans and operations. In a field related to naval warfare, the need to land in occupied Europe spurred the development of amphibious craft capable of landing troops and tanks from naval transports. These craft played a crucial part in Asia as well.

Atomic Weapons

The most radical development for the future of the world, however, was the successful production of nuclear weapons—the culmination the progress made in understanding the nucleus made in the 1930s. The idea that splitting the atom would yield enormous amounts of energy was implicit in Einstein's 1905 relativity theory, but whether the theory could be used to develop a bomb was a question. Einstein doubted it until he was confronted with the work of Enrico Fermi and Hungarian physicist Leo Szilard. Einstein then wrote to President Franklin D. Roosevelt, and the Americans, spurred by the fear that the Nazis would develop the bomb first, began an expensive but successful crash project to develop nuclear weapons. Also aware of the possibilities, the Germans sponsored nuclear research as well, but they underestimated the possibility of producing such weapons in time to make a difference in the war. The American bomb came too late to use against Germany but was used against Japan.

Wartime Propaganda

Finally, propaganda—print, film, and radio—was utilized during the conflict, but, at least until the later stages, it probably had more effect on the home front than against the enemy. Radio broadcasts inducing enemy soldiers to give up usually produced a good laugh, as did propaganda leaflets. Toward the end of the war, the Americans dropped leaflets with passes promising safety to German troops if they surrendered. Although the soldiers used them, it is doubtful that they persuaded anybody. Probably the most effective propaganda weapon in the war was the truth about the war's course. BBC broadcasts gave hope to people in occupied areas and encouraged them to resist. The United States was particularly successful in getting Americans to buy war bonds to support the war effort.

WARTIME PRODUCTION

Napoleon Bonaparte stated that armies marched on their bellies. Modern armies, however, march thanks to economics because in the twentieth century, machines achieved domination over the battlefield, and soldiers depended on the weapons and supplies produced by their workers at home.

Axis Inferiority

In the field of production, the Axis was decidedly inferior to the allies, especially in the long run. Hitler's successful dismantling of Czechoslovakia in 1938 brought him control of that country's considerable reserve of armaments and its industrial plant. The time that elapsed between the Munich Pact and the outbreak of war did not permit the British and the French to fill the gap in armaments opened by the German rearmament program, but the inability of the Germans to win the war quickly and the entrance of the United States into the conflict meant that the Axis lost the arms race.

The manufacture of weapons that the armies needed to fight World War II required about twenty essential materials and a host of other natural products ranging from petroleum and coal for fuel; to lead for ammunition; to cotton, mercury, and glycerin for explosives; to antimony, nickel, and manganese for steel; to copper for electric wire. With the exception of coal, Germany produced none of them in substantial amounts. The Germans did succeed in obtaining indispensable primary materials, either from their conquests or from their allies, and in producing some substitutes, but not enough. Germany's major ally, Italy, had to import almost everything it needed and was a drain on Axis resources. In contrast, the USSR had large reserves of raw materials despite its vast territorial losses in the west, Britain could import key materials from its empire and the United States, and the Americans constituted an "arsenal of democracy." The United States produced about 66 percent of the world's petroleum and 50 percent of its cotton and copper and, with the exception of a handful, had a sufficient supply of the other necessary minerals.

In addition, the Germans turned out to be much less efficient in producing war materiel than the Allies. The Soviets ploughed ahead, used to their command economy, while the Americans relied on informality to spur industrialists—but both undertook the greatest war effort yet known—while Germany produced military equipment well below its capacity to do so. Hitler issued orders, but a vast bureaucratic and corrupt party network overwhelmed them. Moreover, unlike the United States, the German armed forces determined the kind of weapons to be produced. The Germans prided themselves on a tradition of skilled craftsmanship and looked down on American mass production techniques. They produced high-quality weapons and numerous models that had to be constantly modified and slowed production.

The Germans failed to exploit the economies of scale until Hitler appointed his favorite architect Albert Speer as the armaments minister. Speer introduced the mass production methods that proved so effective for the Allies, reducing the number of models and concentrating on bigger manufacturing plants. German efficiency finally approximated that of the Allies, but too late. The fierce Allied bombing campaign made it impossible to continue production of war materiel undisturbed, and the Germans had to move and camouflage their factories. The Germans' reliance on poorly paid and unmotivated foreign workers and slave laborers also hampered their war effort. Furthermore, the continuous bombing sapped the will of German workers and prompted the Gestapo and the SS to intervene against them. The security services harassed industrialists, whom they could send to concentration camps. Threats and coercion proved poor motivators. Thus, the Americans outclassed the highly skilled German industrial workforce and entrepreneurs who looked down upon them as producers of shoddy goods.

BIOGRAPHICAL SKETCHES

Erwin Rommel
The Desert Fox

Adolf Hitler named Erwin Rommel a field marshal, at the young age of 50, because of Rommel's exploits against the British in North Africa. Sent to bolster the faltering Italians, Rommel soon had the British on the run despite his inferiority in armaments. His style contrasted vividly with that of his desert enemy, the meticulous Eighth Army commander General Bernard Montgomery. By contrast, Rommel was daring, impulsive, and imaginative. In 1941 and 1942, he developed such a great reputation among his enemies that the British launched an extraordinary propaganda campaign to convince their soldiers that he was not a magician but an ordinary German general.

Rommel served as an infantry officer on the western front during World War I, winning medals for bravery and receiving his country's highest decoration on the Italian front in 1917. His tactics foreshadowed the Blitzkrieg employed during World War II and his development into the perfect fighting animal.

Ironically, Rommel in war contrasted with his tranquil, middle-class—even dull—existence during peacetime. He was born on November 15, 1891, in Heidenheim, near Ulm, in southwestern Germany. His mother, the daughter of an important local official, and his father, a mathematics teacher, ensured practicality in his life. After planning to study engineering, Rommel joined the army in July 1910. In 1911, while studying to be an officer, he met Lucie Maria Mollin, the daughter of a Prussian landowner and his future wife. They married in 1916 and had their only child Manfred in 1928. Aside from her, he was uninterested in women.

After World War I, Rommel settled down to the normal life of a German career officer. He wrote *Infantry Attacks*, which became a training manual for the army and brought him to Hitler's attention. By 1938, he commanded the Fuehrer's bodyguard, but, despite his closeness to Hitler, he kept out of politics throughout his life.

During the German Blitzkrieg against France in May 1940, Rommel headed a Panzer army, demonstrating the dash and intuition that made him and his Afrika Korps legendary in the North African desert fighting between February 1941 and March 1943. He fought at the head of his troops, often risking his life; he ate the same rations and slept in the open with them. After he left North Africa, Rommel undertook a series of important assignments in the last phases of the war. He designed Axis—the successful operation to take over Italy after it surrendered. By November 1943, he was engaged in the building of the Atlantic Wall, consisting of concrete blockhouses and other obstacles, 4 million mines, and the so-called Rommel Asparagus—anti-aircraft barriers—to prevent an Allied landing. The Allied success prompted him to tell Hitler that Germany should ask for peace.

Given Hitler's refusal, Rommel looked favorably on the possibility of the Fuehrer's overthrow. Not involved with the July 20 plot to kill Hitler, he nonetheless was the conspirators' choice for temporary president of Germany after Hitler's planned assassination. When the plot failed, Hitler also took his revenge on Rommel. On October 14, 1944, while recovering from wounds inflicted when a British plane strafed his car, two generals brought Hitler's ultimatum: commit suicide (a hero's funeral and safety for his family) or go on trial (execution and retaliation against his family). Rommel left with them in a green car, took poison, and died.

Four days later, a day of national mourning, Rommel's body lay in state, with his coffin covered by an enormous Swastika flag, a general at each corner of his bier, his many decorations prominently displayed on a velvet cushion, and his family forced to take part in the charade. The funeral oration written by Hitler ended the sham with a lie: "His heart belonged to the Fuehrer."

American Production Techniques

The United States performed an economic miracle; despite a weak tradition of military production, workers initially opposed to war, and industrialists unhappy about taking orders from the government, the Americans produced more than all the Axis powers combined by the end of 1942; in four years they doubled their industrial capacity. The United States produced two-thirds of the equipment used by the Allies during World War II—297,000 airplanes, 86,000 tanks, 193,000 artillery pieces, 8,800 ships, 87,000 amphibious assault vessels, and 2 million trucks.

American industry, government, and labor worked together in an imaginative way. The government listened to the suggestions of entrepreneurs and gave them practically free rein to institute unusual ideas instead of giving them orders. Unconventional contracts left production details and methods up to the industrialists. The Americans regulated the economy as little as possible, implementing only absolutely necessary wartime controls. The industrialists responded with flexibility and commitment. They swiftly converted peacetime industries to wartime uses, built gigantic factories bigger than those in the Soviet Union, and perfected mass production methods and applied them in such unorthodox fields as shipbuilding and the manufacture of complex modern aircraft. In the process, American manufacturers made a fortune, but a workforce just emerging from high unemployment also shared the wealth through higher wages that outpaced the high inflation rate. High wages drew the workers from the impoverished South to the booming North and attracted women to take jobs in the armaments factories. "Rosie the Riveter" became an American staple and a symbol of American production. Social disruption, juvenile delinquency, shortages, and racial tension accompanied this progress, but a productive workforce was effectively mobilized to make the equipment that won the battles.

BATTLES

The European war encompassed three broad fronts: southern, eastern, and western.

The South

The Allies focused on the South first, where Italy was the weak link. The Italians' inability to supply their isolated East African colonies led to their rapid loss, but in North Africa, their lack of modern tanks made the Italians succumb to the

Besides the size of its armed forces, the greatest American contribution of World War II was the country's military production capacity. It is estimated, for example, that the Americans provided the USSR with about 10 billion dollars worth of war materiel. If it had not been for American production techniques and workers, the course of the war would have been very different. Here Douglas Aircraft Corporation workers in Long Beach, California, greet the 3,000th C-47 "Skytrain" transport airplane to come off the assembly line of their factory just before it heads off to the war zone.

British despite their superior numbers. The brilliant general Erwin Rommel and his Afrika Korps arrived in Libya to rescue them and in April 1941 pushed the British back into Egypt despite his inferiority in men and equipment.

The rest of the year witnessed back-and-forth battles between the British and Axis forces. Operation Battleaxe, designed to wipe out Rommel, failed when Rommel drew the British Matilda tanks into traps, destroying them with anti-aircraft guns and proving that it was possible to resist armored vehicles. After Battleaxe, Operation Crusader also failed in November, despite British numerical superiority on the ground and in the air. In 1942, both the Allied and Axis forces received reinforcements, but the Axis inferiority in tanks did not prevent Rommel from unleashing an offensive that nearly won him Egypt. By October 23 and 24, however, Montgomery's Eighth Army had recovered and unleashed an offensive at El Alamein. On November 4, the Germans fled before an irresistible British advance. On November 8, when American and British troops landed in northwestern Africa, the battle heated up.

BIOGRAPHICAL SKETCHES

Bernard Law Montgomery
Hero of El Alamein

Erwin Rommel's antagonist, Bernard Montgomery, presented a different picture than "the Desert Fox." In his personal life, Montgomery was flamboyant; in public relations, skilled; in his public pronouncements, arrogant. As a general, however, he moved deliberately and only when he had superior means.

Montgomery had a miserable childhood because of his mother, with whom he was always in a state of war that he always lost. The fourth of nine children, Montgomery had a cool relationship with his siblings, with the partial exception of his younger sister Una. Relations with his saintly father Henry, who came from a long line of clergymen, were good. Henry became Episcopal bishop of Tasmania (Australia) when Bernard, born in London on November 17, 1887, was not yet 2. Bernard grew up in Tasmania with a well-earned reputation for bad behavior.

The family returned to England in late 1901, and in 1907, Montgomery entered the Royal military college at Sandhurst. He was an indifferent student, and an officer told him he was useless. He fought on the western front during World War I, learning, as Rommel did, from his early combat experience. Montgomery concluded that a successful general had to have a plan and to implement it with certainty. He lived and breathed the army and paid attention to nothing else. This focus gave him a reputation as an eccentric, but one who steadily moved up through the ranks.

After the war, Montgomery served in a series of positions and in different overseas posts. In 1926, he decided to marry and began looking for a wife as if he was conducting a campaign. He met a war widow with two children and—surprisingly for a person so much in control of everything—fell in love. Unusual for a husband, he took command of the household, arranging for its orderly functioning down to the grocery shopping. His wife Betty Carver allowed him to do so, but while he reigned, she got her way on the major issues. After ten years of a happy marriage, however, tragedy struck when an insect bit his wife on the leg. Infection spread, and on October 19, 1937, she died. He never married again and could still write emotionally about the incident in 1961.

Montgomery commanded a division in France at the outbreak of World War II. After Dunkirk, he received important commissions in Britain and helped plan important aspects of a 1942 raid on Dieppe, a French port that could have served as a landing area when the British returned to the continent. With the operation's failure, a debate began on his military qualities, despite his disavowal of the raid and his transfer to Africa.

Montgomery rebuilt the demoralized Eighth Army, fighting a losing war against a legend. He became a legend himself by beating Rommel. He had a different style of fighting than did Rommel, but he also was a master at establishing rapport with the troops. Montgomery had the gift of communicating with individual soldiers, who willingly died for him. Long before, Montgomery had become convinced that a successful general had to learn where the enemy was weak and then hurl overwhelmingly superior forces against that point. Using this strategy, he waited until he had accumulated greater resources than his enemy did and won the breakthrough victory at El Alamein.

continued

continued

Following his service in North Africa, Montgomery fought in Italy, participated in the planning for D-Day, and held crucial commands in Western Europe.
The polemical field marshal criticized his American allies and received blame for
faulty planning in a number of operations, especially Arnhem. After the war, he
became the military commander of Germany, commander of the Imperial General
Staff (CIGS), and the deputy supreme commander of NATO. Montgomery retired in
1958, controversial as always, and wrote his memoirs. On March 24, 1976, "Monty"
died, in the world's imagination still the hero of El Alamein.

The Fight for North Africa

With the North African landing (Operation Torch), the Germans and Italians
decided to make a stand in Tunisia and sent reinforcements to the country. The
Axis forces that were employed in the Tunisian campaign were unavailable for
combat elsewhere and weakened the Germans in the Soviet Union at a crucial
time. The Americans did poorly, taking 2,000 casualties at the Battle of Kassarine
Pass, but their losses helped them make adjustments in their training that transformed them into an effective fighting force. The Allies had hoped for a quick
victory, but it was April before the Axis had been defeated in North Africa;
however, in the final battles, 275,000 Axis troops surrendered to the Allies.

At the Casablanca Conference between Churchill and Roosevelt from January
14 to 23, 1943, the two leaders recognized that Axis resistance in North Africa had
made an Allied invasion of France impossible in 1943 and postponed it until 1944.
In a major step toward that objective, U.S. general George Marshall successfully
insisted on the creation of a staff to begin preparations for the French invasion.
The Allies also agreed on the invasion of Sicily by July.

The Italian Surrender

The successful Sicilian invasion, Husky, began on July 10, 1943. The Italian situation had been unstable because the population blamed Mussolini for the string of
Italian defeats. The disaffection had spread to the highest levels of the government
and the Fascist Party. After the fall of Sicily, Fascists who believed the war had been
lost scheduled a meeting of the Fascist Grand Council. The council turned against
Mussolini at a long meeting held on July 24 and 25, voting to return power to the
king. When Mussolini went to discuss the situation with Victor Emanuel, the king
removed him from office, named a military government under Marshal Pietro
Badoglio, and had il Duce arrested.

Badoglio announced that "the war continues," but he opened negotiations
with the Allies. The ruse did not fool Hitler who, in anticipation of Mussolini's
overthrow and an Italian attempt to switch sides, had sent a number of crack divisions into the country. The Badoglio government botched the armistice talks with
the Allies and bungled the military preparations for turning against the Germans.
As a result, plans for the participation of American troops in the operation were
canceled, and, worse, the government left the armed forces without orders and
fled with the king to the Allied-occupied part of Italy. The Germans disarmed the

Italian units and took Rome after a brief battle. The Germans also moved into the Italian-occupied zones in the Balkans and in France. In a daring operation, they liberated Mussolini and brought him to the north, where he led a puppet regime called the Italian Social Republic (or the Salò Republic).

Operations on the Italian mainland went poorly for the Allies. The German troops they had allowed to escape from Sicily continued the battle, taking advantage of the rugged Italian terrain. An Allied amphibious operation in September 1943 at Salerno, near Naples, stalled despite its establishment of a beachhead. Montgomery's Eighth Army crossed the Straits of Messina onto the Italian boot but made slow headway, as did the Americans. Nevertheless, the Allies had returned to the European heartland and diverted a great number of German troops from the crucial eastern front.

The East

In Eastern Europe, the tide of war turned against Germany in 1942. As the winter ended, Hitler planned a new offensive despite the Germans' weakened state caused by the transfer of forces and supplies to Tunisia.

The Germans planned to undertake their major efforts on the southern flank, where they had the best chance of a breakthrough in areas rich in minerals that they required for the war. At the same time, however, they projected taking Leningrad in the north, assuming that they would win and then could move a large number of troops to Leningrad. In June, the Germans launched attacks aimed at taking the Caucasus oil fields, but the offensive failed as Stalin relied more than he previously had on the professionals in his military and Hitler took exactly the reverse action by interfering more than before. By late summer, activities on the southern flank of the eastern front soon concentrated on the strategic city of Stalingrad, whose importance the Germans had initially failed to consider.

Stalingrad, January 26, 1943. In addition to the strategic value of this city, it had great symbolic worth for being named after the Soviet dictator and because Hitler vowed to capture it. The battle was a disaster for the Germans as Hitler forbade even a tactical retreat and the Axis armies suffered tens of thousands dead or taken prisoner. In the photograph, Red Army soldiers advance among the city's ruins.

Stalingrad

The loss of Stalingrad, a major industrial center, would have been a blow to the Soviet war effort, and in German hands could block all trade on the Volga. Besides its strategic value, Stalingrad had the great symbolic significance of being named for the Soviet dictator. As the battle unfolded, Hitler continually swore that he would take the city, while the Russians resolved to hold it at any cost. By September 3, the battle for Stalingrad was in full swing, and fighting devastated the city. The Germans made slow headway, entering the city that the Soviets defended block by block and house by house (the film *Enemy at the Gates* gives a good idea of the ferocity involved in the fighting). Hitler promised that he would take it, but the Germans failed to see the larger picture and their own potential weaknesses, which Georgi Zhukov, V. I. Chuikov, and A. I. Eremenko—the Soviet generals defending Stalingrad— exploited. Between September and November, the Soviets quietly assembled massive forces for a surprise counterattack against the Germans' Romanian allies and on November 19 unleashed a huge infantry and tank offensive that broke through and surrounded the German army besieging Stalingrad. The Germans could have either elected to break out of the pocket, as the generals wanted, or to resist until reinforcements arrived, as Hitler ordered. The Germans could not send enough soldiers and supplies to relieve the encircled troops, and the operation failed. In lifting the siege of Stalingrad, the Russians took over 90,000 German prisoners, while 150,000 others died either from combat or the cold. The Romanian, Italian, and Hungarian losses weakened the German hold over those countries. The German loss at Stalingrad dealt a devastating moral blow to Germany and gave the Allies a tremendous lift.

Progress of the Russian Fighting

In the north, the Germans also failed to take Leningrad, and in January 1943, the Soviets broke the siege. In the central part of the front, the German drive to take Moscow failed as well. Fighting on the Soviet fronts progressed with victories and defeats on both sides, but while the Soviets could replace men and materiel, the Germans found it increasingly difficult to do so. In July and August 1943, the Russians won the battle of Kursk, breaking the German ability to mount offensives in the east. In June and July 1944, at the same time that the Americans and British came ashore at Normandy, successful Russian offensives began sowing panic in the German ranks, and many soldiers surrendered. The central portion of the German lines collapsed, and the Russians began their march toward Warsaw. By the fall, the Finns withdrew from the war, and the Soviets extended their military and political influence westward.

The German army commanders implemented defensive tactics that slowed the Soviet advance but were hampered by Hitler's opposition to retreat, forcing the army to take greater losses of men and equipment than would otherwise have been the case.

The West

Faced with an improving but still difficult situation, Stalin continued to insist that the Anglo-Americans immediately establish a second front to take the pressure off the Soviets. He suspected that the western Allies delayed this move in order

On D-Day, June 6, 1944, American troops landed on the Normandy coast of France and began their assault of the German-dominated European continent. Historians debate whether the Normandy invasion or the Battle of Kursk in which the Russians defeated the Germans in July/August 1943 was the turning point of World War II, but either way the tide had turned against Hitler. This photograph shows American marines landing on one of the four Normandy beachheads on June 7, 1944.

to weaken him, but the military situation precluded the possibility of a second front until 1944. The western Allies had to assemble a great invasion force on the British Isles that was capable of dislodging the Germans from their heavily fortified positions on the European coastline by bringing men and equipment from the faraway United States.

D-Day

Led by U.S. General Dwight D. Eisenhower and Montgomery, the Allies launched the invasion of France on D-Day, June 6, 1944. The invasion force successfully established bridgeheads in Normandy and landed a huge army in the following weeks.

Several factors explain the Allied success in this arduous breach of the German Atlantic Wall. They included the crushing Allied air superiority and, on the German side, a dispute about exactly where the Allies planned a landing and how to confront it. Thus, the Germans had only one Panzer division near the zone where the Allies landed. The German commander Erwin Rommel had pleaded in vain with his colleagues to station strong mobile forces closer to where the invasion actually occurred, and the debate about how they would meet the invaders ended in a compromise that worked poorly. In this case as well, Hitler constantly interfered with the generals and hampered German military operations. Rounding out the picture and ultimately accounting for the German defeat was the inability of the Germans to match Allied resources in tanks and aircraft.

The Battle of the Bulge

Given the advance of the Allied armies in the West, Hitler decided to risk everything on a last throw of the dice. He planned an offensive against the Americans with thirty reformed divisions and six hundred tanks. He counted on a heavy American defeat to break the will of Americans at home to continue the war. While he envisioned a break in the Allied coalition, even if it did not come, a victory in the West would allow him to shift his troops again to the East to defeat the advancing Soviets.

On December 16, 1944, with bad weather grounding the Allied air forces, the Germans threw 200,000 men against a sector of the front held by 80,000 Americans—the Battle of the Bulge. This attack achieved surprise and caused the American defenders to waver. The Germans achieved a temporary success, but the American lines held, and they soon passed to the counterattack. Hitler's last, desperate plans to recoup his position failed and worsened the German situation because the Germans had exhausted their last reserves and their best equipment.

The Strategic Bombing Campaign

As a major part of their strategy to defeat the Germans, the Anglo-Americans conducted increasingly heavy strategic bombing of Germany. The effectiveness of this campaign has been debated because in 1942 and 1943, strategic bombing did not have great effects either on German civilian morale or on production, which actually increased because of Speer's reorganization of German industry.

In 1944, the Americans introduced long-range fighters that were capable of escorting bombers to distant targets. This development, along with refined navigational aids, radar-evading devices, and improved night capabilities, allowed the Allies to area and carpet-bomb more cities and disrupt production to a greater degree than had been possible before. Raids included hundreds of bombers, thousands of tons of ordnance, and tens of thousands of civilian casualties. Whether bombing civilians was the best use of air power or whether it might have shortened the war by concentrating on military targets is still disputed.

RESISTANCE

The German occupation stimulated both collaboration and resistance. Collaborators were motivated by self-interest or by a belief that given the new European order, cooperation was better for their countries. As German exploitation and atrocities increased, resistance movements appeared that saved the honor of the conquered countries and gave them the self-confidence to rebuild after the liberation even though the number of those who actively resisted is still in dispute. The European Resistance can be considered a combination of patriotic, class, and civil warfare.

Divisions

Despite the common goal of fighting the occupiers, divisions regarding the future organization of their countries and the desire for revenge against collaborators remained strong, and the Resistance movements in Western and Eastern Europe took on the aspects of a civil war. In Italy, the fight between the Fascists and the partisans is graphically illustrated in the film *The Night of the Shooting Stars*. In Yugoslavia, a civil war openly raged during the German occupation, and in Greece, following the occupation. In Poland, the underground movement barely tolerated Jewish resisters and hardly cooperated with them. After the conflict, the Communists in Eastern Europe eliminated the non-Communist resisters.

In the Balkans, Yugoslav Communist leader Josip Broz, called Tito, conducted an all-out war against the Germans and Cetniks, Serb partisans, skillfully cooperating with the different nationalities and gaining Allied support. When the Germans withdrew, he took control of Yugoslavia without the help of the Red Army and achieved a measure of independence from the USSR.

In Greece, the Communist-controlled ELAS and the monarchist EDES Resistance organizations competed against each other. After the war, the British supported the monarchists against the Communists in a brutal civil war that led the Americans to declare that they would contain communism (the Truman Doctrine). With Greece solidly in the Western zone of influence, the Communists lost, but in neighboring Albania, Communist resistance leader Enver Hoxha took control and ruled the country until his death in 1986.

Different Phases

The course of resistance may be divided into stages, although not all of them occurred at the same time in different countries. Humor frequently marked the beginnings of the process. In Paris, the following story circulated: Hitler had discovered an old rabbi whose family had handed down the secret of parting the seas so that people could cross them in safety. Hoping to send his army across the channel to attack Britain, the Fuehrer promised the rabbi that thousands of Jews could go free if he revealed the secret. The rabbi quickly agreed. A special little wand waved over the seas caused them to part. Hitler asked where the wand was. The answer: "In the British museum."

Other modest actions, such as scraps of information passed to opponents of the occupying power, solidarity toward its victims, telling others of brutal behavior, or helping someone escape a roundup, preceded the organizational phase that was usually provoked by brutal acts of repression. Finally came the entrance into battle—hiding Allied airmen, stealing secret information, assassinating Nazi officials, fomenting strikes, sabotaging and attacking military installations, and joining partisan bands. The British conducted operations in concert with the Resistance movements through their Special Operations Executive (SOE), the Americans through the Office of Strategic Services (OSS). Many Resistance leaders hoped that their opposition would culminate in uprisings against the occupier and in political and social revolutions, although the western Allies rejected them.

Toward the end of the war in the West, the Resistance movements in France and Italy, organized by secret committees, constructed important military formations. In France, armed resistance took on a new dimension in early 1944 when the different Resistance forces joined in the *Forces Français de l' Intérieur* (French Forces of the Interior, FFI). Guerrilla bands usually numbered about fifty, but toward the end of the conflict fielded thousands of fighters. They engaged in pitched battles with the Germans and obstructed the movement of troops to important battles. Eisenhower believed that they were worth fifteen divisions.

The Italian Communists played a crucial role in the Resistance, aided by their underground experience in fighting Fascism. The Italian Resistance opposed the Nazis and Fascists in occupied northern Italy following creation of the Salò Republic. The political organization of the Italian Resistance took the form of committees of national liberation consisting of six-party coalitions that included the mass parties—Communists, Socialists, and Christian Democrats. This coalition formed governments recognized by the Allies after the war.

The Italian Communists and Socialists aimed at a revolution, but, ironically, the Communists were most apt to compromise the revolutionary ideal. Because Stalin knew that Italy would be in the Western sphere of influence following the war, he insisted that the Communists come to power by legal means, through elections. Upon his return from the Soviet Union, Communist leader Palmiro Togliatti announced at Salerno on March 24, 1944, that the Communists would cooperate with the conservatives and monarchists to rid the country of the Germans. At the same time, guerrilla bands carried out daring raids, some of them described in Elio Vittorini's masterpiece *Men and Non-Men* and in the works of Beppe Fenoglio. The most famous was an action that killed thirty-three German soldiers in Rome that provoked the brutal execution of 335 civilians. The guerilla bands helped clear northern cities and forced a retreating German column to hand over Mussolini, after which they executed him and his mistress Claretta Petacci. They also executed major Fascist hierarchs and minor officials and continued their actions after the war in the hopes of eliminating potential political enemies; estimates of persons who were murdered after the war because of revenge or politics, primarily by Communists, range up to 100,000. The Italian Resistance, however, claimed to have created the ideological basis for a new republic set up after the war.

In Poland a large underground army had the support of the population and collected arms for a planned rural insurrection. It gathered intelligence on German military movements, tactics, and secret weapons and forwarded the information to London. The underground army perished during the last days of the war when it was called upon by the Red Army to rise in Warsaw. The Soviets then halted their advance while the Germans eliminated the rebels and destroyed the city. The Soviet goal: to facilitate the establishment of a pliable Communist regime in postwar Poland.

Different Groups

The Resistance movements included diverse groups. Jews figured prominently in the national Resistance movements and developed their own tradition of opposition. In addition to the spectacular Warsaw Ghetto uprising of April 1943, Jewish partisans operated independently of other groups in the forests of Poland,

During the latter part of World War II, resistance to the German occupation became widespread even though the number of people involved in the Resistance has been debated. Throughout Europe the probability of a Nazi defeat emboldened people to fight Nazism and contributed to its overthrow. Women made a notable contribution to the Resistance movements all over Europe as indicated in this picture of a woman Resistance fighter in France.

Lithuania, and the Ukraine even though they frequently faced anti-Semitism among the Christian partisans.

Women participated in Resistance movements in both the East and the West. They took part in operations, as novels such as *L'Agnese va a morire* [Agnese Goes to Her Death] illustrate. In the West, women excelled in operating printing presses and distributing clandestine material. Different French accounts emphasize their capacity as liaison officers, fomenters of demonstrations and strikes, and agitators against the forced deportation of laborers—dangerous activities in occupied Europe. Many women resisters belonged to the middle- and lower-middle classes, the strongest repositories of national feeling and resistance.

Workers did not distinguish themselves early as resisters because of their need for employment, but became strong opponents when confronted with increases in the draft and in forced labor. They tended to support Communist groups, but in France the so-called Worker Priest movement strengthened the church's presence among them.

Opposition in Germany

In Germany, passive rather than active resistance had existed since Hitler had come to power, but was confined to restricted circles because any kind of opposition led to execution. A desire to save persecuted Jews and to get the Catholic Church to intervene forcefully against the Nazis motivated some people, such as Margerete Sommer. Other opponents formed discussion groups. The most significant of these groups was Helmut von Moltke's Kreisau Circle, which discussed Germany's future should Hitler be overthrown. As German losses mounted in Russia, opposition increased. In Munich, university students established the White Rose organization, which distributed leaflets calling for opposition to the Nazis. In 1943, the Nazis executed the leaders of this group, including sister and brother Sophie and Hans Scholl.

The German Catholics had been among the political groups that supported Hitler the least, but after Hitler's accession, the Vatican preferred to leave opposition to the German bishops on the grounds that they knew more about local conditions. During the war, Pope Pius XII did not openly condemn the Germans, believing that he risked Nazi military action against the church and that conditions would worsen if he did so. Although church authorities, priests, and nuns helped persecuted Jews with the pope's knowledge, Pius's failure publicly to denounce German genocide produced furious debate after the war.

The German military hierarchy was uneasy with Hitler for different reasons, but the Fuehrer constantly outmaneuvered the generals. As the situation became increasingly desperate during World War II, some of his opponents, such as Colonel Claus von Stauffenberg, chief of staff of the reserve army, came together in a conspiracy to assassinate him and overthrow the regime. On July 20, 1944, Stauffenberg successfully planted a bomb close to Hitler in a conference room. The Fuehrer miraculously survived the blast, retained the army's loyalty, and struck back savagely. He ordered the traitors brutally tortured and murdered and eliminated what opposition remained in the armed forces and in the country.

Despite their variety and complexity, the significance of the European Resistance movements may be summarized in a few points. The movements demonstrated the depth of a prostrate continent's opposition to German conquest and suggested that the Germans would have had a difficult time implementing their ultimate aims even if they had won. They brought right and left together to fight a common enemy, but also highlighted civil strife. They positioned the Communists politically for a major role in the politics and society of postwar Western Europe and provided a fig leaf for Soviet expansion in the East. The Resistance contributed to the Allied victory, restored the hope and self-assurance of European nations who were crushed by defeat and dictatorship, and rekindled confidence in a united Europe that would prevent future wars.

THE FUTURE

As the defeat of Nazi Germany loomed, the Allied leaders met to plan their military strategy and Europe's future.

Conferences

The British and Americans met to discuss their military options at conferences in Quebec, Moscow, Cairo, and Teheran in 1943.

The British insisted on military priority for operations in Italy and the Eastern Mediterranean; the Americans demanded precedence for a cross-channel invasion by May 1944, proposing that battle-hardened divisions be withdrawn from the Mediterranean to support the invasion. Churchill feared that the invasion would fail, leading to another Dunkirk or a stalemate similar to the one that had occurred in World War I. The Americans disagreed and had the resources to try again in case of failure. They worried that the Russians would defeat Germany quickly and establish their hegemony in areas overrun by the Red Army, possibly including regions of Western Europe. In late 1943, Stalin settled the question at the Teheran Conference by insisting on the invasion of northwest Europe while stiff German military resistance preventing Stalin's implementation of any plans he may have had for rapid westward expansion calmed immediate American fears. Planning for Overlord, the Normandy invasion of June 1944, went into high gear under General Dwight D. Eisenhower.

The political issues among the Allies proved knottier to resolve. At the Moscow Conference in October 1943, the Allies agreed on trying German war criminals and on the disarmament and denazification of Germany itself. But the participants reached no agreement on Germany's future borders or whether the country should be dismembered. The Americans focused on Allied agreement on the unconditional surrender of Germany, the establishment of a postwar international organization to safeguard the peace, and recognition of China as a major power. The Soviets raised the problem of future borders, but the Americans were reluctant to make commitments while the war raged. The British went along with Soviets' insistence that their partners agree that their western border include territory annexed as a result of their 1939 pact with the Nazis, on the grounds that that the Red Army would conquer the East anyway and would make concessions in the West in return and that the proposed boundary coincided roughly with one drawn up in 1919 by British Foreign Secretary Lord Curzon. The British were also willing to allow the Soviets wide latitude in setting postwar boundaries in the entire East. The Western Allies were anxious to secure the USSR's commitment to military strategy in the Pacific, and Stalin agreed to attack Japan following Germany's defeat.

The Teheran Conference (November 28, 1943–January 12, 1944) ratified the border decisions taken at earlier meetings. The Russians would get large areas of prewar Poland, compensating Poland with German territory. In practice, the Western Allies also acquiesced to the expulsion of the German population of Eastern Europe, which would make Poland and the states that emerged from the conflict ethnically homogeneous.

Yalta and Potsdam—and the Cold War

The consensus on Eastern Europe that was ratified at Teheran went a long way toward implementation at the Yalta Conference, held February 4 through 11, 1945. The Russians promised to allow free elections, but this pledge conflicted with their

Of the World War II conferences, Yalta, held February 4–11, 1945 remains the most
controversial. Although the "Big Three" settled the fate of postwar Germany and
compromised on setting up the United Nations, they essentially divided Europe into
a Western and a Soviet sphere of influence. This picture shows the British, American,
and Russian leaders in a convivial moment. From left to right, Winston Churchill, a
visibly ill Franklin D. Roosevelt, and Joseph Stalin. Roosevelt died on April 12, 1945.

desire to retain control of the region for security purposes. Because the Communists did not win power legally after the war, the Soviets imposed regimes that
were favorable to them, alienated Western opinion, contributed to the beginning
of the cold war, and gave them a bad reputation among the American public. At
the same conference, the participants compromised on the structure of the United
Nations, which had been causing difficulties. From the Soviet geopolitical viewpoint, the arrangement in the East counterbalanced Allied supremacy in Western
Europe and Greece. The Yalta Conference also divided Germany into occupation
zones, including one for the French carved out of the American and British occupation areas.

At the end of February 1945, Western public opinion hardened against the
USSR following a Soviet-sponsored coup in Romania, the arrest of non-Communist Polish underground leaders, and the refusal to hold free elections. The Potsdam Conference, held in July 1945, hammered out the last details with regard to
reparations and the new Polish borders and set the first international trials of war
criminals. Harry S. Truman, who had succeeded to the presidency following Roosevelt's death, secured a definitive agreement from the Russians to enter the war
against Japan on August 15, which was projected to last until 1947 until the atomic
bomb was used. Most ominously, an Allied control council set up at Yalta proved
unworkable. The Soviets moved toward the establishment of a de facto govern-

On May 8, 1945, World War II came to an end in Europe with the German surrender. The continent was devastated. This picture shows a street scene in Berlin. German officials forced Nazi Party members to clear the once-impassible street of rubble.

ment in their zone, eventually precipitating the creation of two German states that would reunite only after the end of the cold war.

End of the War in Europe

On April 29, 1945, with Soviet soldiers entering Berlin, Hitler married his mistress Eva Braun in the depths of his Reich Chancellery. The couple, Hitler's staff, and his loyal followers drank champagne, ate sandwiches, and reminisced about the past. Later Hitler retired with his secretary to dictate his last will and political testament, including naming a government to succeed him. On the same day, he had had his dog poisoned. After lunch on April 30 and chats with his staff, Hitler and Eva Braun retired to his study. Ten minutes later, they were both dead—Braun from poison and Hitler from a gunshot wound. Their associates took the bodies to be burned with some gas set aside for the purpose. It was not enough, and Soviet soldiers had no difficulty identifying the remains.

On May 8, the Germans surrendered unconditionally. The war in Europe had left 55 million to 60 million dead.

IDEOLOGY: NATIONALISM'S HANDMAIDEN?

The civilian deaths caused by World War II outnumbered those of any previous war or revolution. Competing ideologies help account for the brutality demonstrated by the combatants during the conflict, but this is not the full explanation.

Nazism and Nationalism

Nazism aimed at the racial restructuring of Europe and to make Germany supreme in Europe. The wholesale destruction of the Jews, the attempt to exploit Slavic slave laborers for the benefit of future German generations while eliminating them from history, and the efforts to murder the cultures of other nationalities were revolutionary goals. Although Imperial Germany shared the characteristic of nationalism and considered Germans superior to other European "races," it did not plan their destruction.

Italian Fascism, the regime that initially served as a model for Hitler, was openly nationalistic but not racist until 1938. It was a reaction to a parliamentary regime that was considered weak domestically and neither warlike nor successful in the scramble for colonies. The Fascists pledged to reverse this situation; to construct a strong state where a fragile one had existed; to make the country's voice heard in Europe where it had been ignored; to win colonies that had been denied to it; and, finally, to transform Italians into warriors where they had been too peaceful. That the Fascists failed miserably in all their goals only highlights their nationalistic objectives.

Communism and Russian Nationalism

Communist ideology posited class domination instead of racial control. In practice, however, nationalism triumphed in Russia, and the foreign policy of the USSR came to resemble that of the old tsarist Russian Empire. The Russians were supreme over the other republics of the USSR, and the Communist state expanded toward the west in order to create a buffer zone around itself, as had the Russian Empire. Both sought aggrandizement in Asia. Like the tsars, the Communists participated in the partition of Poland and incorporated the Baltic States. Communists alleged that capitalism wanted to destroy them and that they had to take measures to defend themselves; the tsars did their utmost to kept Western influence from contaminating the country, as did the Soviets, and pursued a similar expansionist policy. Making due allowance for the difference in technology, both regimes used similar means to maintain internal control, although the Communists were harsher and more destructive.

Like the Nazis, the Communist leaders justified themselves as people with a mission to fulfill. At the same time, the Russian motherland drew benefits from this mission. The Communists absorbed vast amounts of territory and derived economic advantages from their satellite states. They supported, morally and financially, vast flanking organizations in the Western states and manipulated them for the benefit of the USSR's foreign or domestic policies. They slaughtered the elites of other nationalities and suppressed their culture, as did the Nazis; to call those cultures bourgeois mattered little. After the war, the Communist countries exploited Marxist ideology to expel and subjugate German and other ethnic minorities and confiscate their property. Ironically, while the Nazis exploited other nationalities and passed some of the material benefits to their people, Soviet Communism transmitted fewer advantages to its citizens.

Nationalism and Democracy

Finally, what of democratic ideologies? Nationalism is not an overt part of democracy, but it was present nonetheless. After World War I, the two greatest imperial powers, Britain and France, took the lion's share of German and Turkish colonies on the grounds that they had to teach the natives about democracy. It took them decades to give up their mandates, in effect, colonies taken from the losers in World War I, and they did not do so willingly. Both countries exploited the natural resources of their empires even though economic forces spurred the British to move toward a commonwealth. Both democracies suppressed revolts in colonies against the conquerors. Winston Churchill fought against his countrymen to hold on to India, made deals with Stalin over spheres of influence, championed continued British supremacy in the Mediterranean, and wanted to retain discredited monarchies in Italy and Greece because he thought they suited British interests. The United States is not immune from similar charges and interfered in the political workings of foreign countries after World War II.

In Western Europe, recognition of the destructive role that extreme nationalism played in the twentieth century produced a strong movement favoring unification. This idea had been discussed before, was lost in the war, but reemerged powerfully during the darkest days of the conflict. A common political structure that allowed full expression of national differences, the proponents of a united Europe argued, was the only way to exorcise the scourge of nationalistic wars from the continent. What better time to begin the process than after the most destructive conflict in history had taught all the European nations a lesson they resolved not to forget?

Bibliographical Essay

Readers should refer to the previous chapter for other books on World War II.

Richard Overy, *Why the Allies Won* (New York, 1995), is an excellent work stressing the production of war materiel and other reasons accounting for the Allied victory. Besides the works cited in previous chapters, the famous military analyst B. H. Liddell Hart published the very readable and clear *History of the Second World War* (New York, 1970). The same author also published *The Other Side of the Hill: Germany's Generals, Their Rise and Fall, with Their Own Account of Military Events* (London, 1951), an enlarged edition of *The German Generals Talk*, originally published in 1948. Gerhard L. Weinberg, *A World at Arms* (New York, 1994), previously cited, is the best one-volume work on the fighting of World War II. Norman Davies also wrote a general history: *No Simple Victory: World War II in Europe, 1939–1945* (New York, 2008). Ralf Blank et al. published a book on German wartime society during the war: *Germany and the Second World War* (New York, 2008).

In contrast to the long works already cited, there is an excellent very brief book that considers all aspects of the war, including intelligence and weapons, and that can be used for further research into the different issues: Anthony Wood, *War in Europe 1939–1945* (London, 1987). A good account of the war's overall course is Chester Wilmot, *The Struggle for Europe* (Westport, Conn., 1972).

For the North African campaigns, see Robin Neillands, *Eighth Army: From the Western Desert to the Alps* (London, 2004). On the commanders, see Ronald Lewin, *Rommel as Military Commander* (Princeton, N.J., 1968), and Charles Douglas-Home,

Rommel (London, 1973). On Montgomery as a soldier, consult Alun Chalfont, *Montgomery of Alamein* (London, 1976); Nigel Hamilton's massive biography *Montgomery of Alamein, 1887–1942* (London, 2001); and Hamilton's *Monty: Final Years of the Field Marshal, 1944–1976* (New York, 1987). On Italy's surrender and the consequences, see Elena Aga Rossi, *A Nation Collapses* (Cambridge, UK, 2000). The relationship between Mussolini and Hitler during this period is examined by F. W. Deakin, *The Brutal Friendship: Mussolini, Hitler, and the Fall of Italian Fascism* (London, 1962).

For specific books on the fighting in the East, see Alan Clark, *Barbarossa: The Russo-German Conflict* (Harmondsworth, UK, 1985); Rold Dieter Muller and Gerd R. Uebershar, *Hitler's War in the East* (Providence, R.I., 1997); Paul Schmidt, *Hitler's War on Russia* (London, 1964); Earl Frederick Ziemke, *Moscow to Stalingrad: Decision in the East* (Washington, D.C., 1987); and John Ericson, *The Road to Stalingrad* (London, 1993). On the most important fighting in the European theater, see Stephen E. Ambrose's excellent account of *D-Day, June 6, 1944: The Climactic Battle of World War II* (New York, 1994). The Battle of the Bulge is analyzed in two books: Trevor N. Dupuy, David L. Bongard, and Richard C. Anderson, Jr., *Hitler's Last Gamble* (New York, 1994), and Jacques Nobecourt, *Hitler's Last Gamble: The Battle of the Bulge, December 1944–January 1945* (New York, 1967). The best book on the atomic bomb is Richard Rhodes, *The Making of the Atomic Bomb* (New York, 1986), a comprehensive work that traces the story back to the earliest developments.

Many books have been written on the air war, but among the best comprehensive overall treatments is Richard Overy's *The Air War 1939–1945* (New York, 1980). An official history in four volumes, *Strategic Air Offensive Against Germany 1939–1945* (East Sussex, UK, 2006), by Charles Webster and Noble Frankland, also gives a good account. Good works on more specialized aspects of the air war include Mark K. Wells, *Courage and Air Warfare: The Allied Aircrew Experience in the Second World War* (London, 1995), an account of the selection and experiences of Allied air crews; David MacIssac, *Strategic Bombing in World War II* (New York, 1976), which discusses the doctrine and organization of strategic bombing; and Anthony Verrier, *The Bomber Offensive* (New York, 1968), the story of bombing from the beginning until the end of the war. An idea of what it was like to be on the receiving end of the bombs may be gleaned from Earl R. Beck's *Under the Bombs: The German Home Front 1942–1945* (Lexington, Ky., 1986). For the German side, see Werner Baumback, *The Life and Death of the Luftwaffe* (New York, 1960). Many treatments also exist about the war at sea, but a good overall picture can still be obtained from Samuel E. Morison, *History of the United States Naval Operations in World War II. Volume One: The Battle of the Atlantic* (Boston, 1947); and for the British side, Stephen W. Roskill, *The War at Sea, 1939–1945* (Ukfield, UK, 2004). See also Jurgen Rohmer, *War At Sea, 1939–1945* (Annapolis, Md., 1996). On the submarine struggle, see Clay Blair, *Hitler's U-Boat War* (New York, 1996), and Peter Padfield, *War Beneath the Sea, 1939–1945* (London, 1997).

Many books on the Resistance movements in different countries and the attitude and operations of the Allies have been written, but Henri Michel's *The Shadow War: European Resistance 1939–1945* (New York, 1972) is outstanding on the general structure, purposes, and organization of the movements. Other general treatments are Jorgen Haestrup, *European Resistance Movements (1939–1945)* (Westport, Conn., 1981), and, by the same author, *Europe Ablaze: An Analysis of the History of the European Resistance Movements* (Odense, 1978). Also, see Stephen Hawes and Ralph White, eds., *Resistance in Europe 1939–1945: A Complete History* (Harmondsworth, UK, 1976). *The Intellectual Resistance in Europe* (Cambridge, Mass., 1981), by James D. Wilkinson, discusses French, Italian, and German intellectuals. For the resistance in France, see Matthew Cobb, *The*

Resistance: The French Fight against the Nazis (London, 2009); *In Search of the Maquis* (Oxford, UK, 1994) and *Resistance in Vichy France: A Study of Ideas and Motivation in the Southern Zone, 1940–1942* (New York, 1983) both by H. Roderick Kedward; and H. R. Kedward and Roger Austin, eds., *Vichy France and the Resistance: Culture and Ideology* (London, 1985). Everyday life is examined by Denis Peschanski et al., *Collaboration and Resistance: Images of Life in Vichy France, 1940–1944* (New York, 2000) and *Between Resistance and Collaboration* (New York, 2000), which describes the impact of occupation. For Eastern Europe, there is *War in a Twilight World* (New York, 2010), essays edited by Juiliette Pattinson and Ben Shepherd. On Yugoslavia, see Marcia Christoff Kuropovna's *Shadows on the Mountain* (New York, 2009); *Tito's Partisans 1941–45* (Oxford, UK, 2003) by V. Vuksic; and Walter R. Roberts's *Tito, Mihailovic and the Allies 1941–1945* (Durham, N.C., 1987). For Italy, there is a classic by Charles Delzell, *Mussolini's Enemies: The Italian Anti-Fascist Resistance* (Princeton, N.J., 1961), and books by Tom Behan, *The Italian Resistance* (New York, 2009), and Philip E. Cooke, *The Legacy of the Italian Resistance* (New York, 2011), which takes important cultural factors into consideration. For the complicated situation following the Italian surrender, see David W. Ellwood, *Italy 1943–1945* (Leicester, UK, 1985). On the Jewish Resistance, see *Caged* (Sydney, 2000), by David Landau. On the other side, there is Colin D. Heaton, *German Anti-Partisan Warfare in Europe, 1939–1945* (Atglen, Pa., 2001). On Germany, there is the standard work by Peter Hoffman, *The History of the German Resistance 1933–1945* (Cambridge, Mass., 1977), and books by Ruth Bernadette Melon, *Journey to the White Rose in Germany* (Indianapolis, Ind., 2007), and John J. Michalczyk, *Confront* (New York, 2004), a book of essays; but more than resistance, the literature shows that the opposition consisted of limited circles. The lack of effective resistance to Hitler is a point made by Joachim Fest in his history of the plot to assassinate Hitler: *Plotting Hitler's Death: The Story of the German Resistance* (New York, 1996). On this subject, see also Roger Moorhouse's *Killing Hitler* (London, 2006). Klemens von Klemperer's *The German Resistance Against Hitler* (Oxford, UK, 1994) looks at the failure to find support abroad. Michael Geyer and John Boyer, *Resistance Against the Third Reich* (Chicago, 1994), includes wide-ranging essays.

Religious opposition to the Nazis is an interesting subject in the context of the German Resistance. The role of women resisters is discussed by Theodore N. Thomas, *Women Against Hitler: Christian Resistance in the Third Reich* (Westport, Conn., 1994), and Michael Phayer, *Cries in the Night: Women Who Challenged the Holocaust* (Kansas City, Mo., 1990). John E. Morley analyzes Vatican policy in *Vatican Diplomacy and the Jews During the Holocaust* (New York, 1980). Gordon Zahn wrote a perceptive study on *German Catholics and Hitler's Wars* (Notre Dame, Ind., 1989).

A complete understanding of the role of women in the Resistance awaits further research. Two good works on the subject are Margaret Collins Weitz, *Sisters in the Resistance: How Women Fought to Free France, 1940–1945* (New York, 1995), which discusses the French Resistance, and Jane Slaughter's *Women in the Italian Resistance* (Denver, 1997). Chris Corrin published *Women in a Violent World: Feminist Analyses and Resistance Across Europe* (Edinburgh, 1996). The Polish Resistance is analyzed by Stefan Korbonski, *Fighting Warsaw: The Story of the Polish Underground State* (New York, 1956); an organizer of the Polish Resistance and later its commander, T. Bor-Komorowski, wrote his memoirs, *The Secret Army* (New York, 1951). On the Greek Resistance, see Stefanos Sarafis, *ELAS: Greek Resistance Army* (Atlantic Highlands, N.J., 1980). For more information on Greece and Yugoslavia from the Allied side, consult *British Policy Towards Wartime Resistance in Yugoslavia and Greece* (London, 1975), a collection of important papers and interesting discussions.

On the diplomacy among the Allies and the conferences discussed in this chapter, see Martin Kitchen, *British Policy Towards the Soviet Union During the Second World War* (New York, 1986). Mark A. Stoler gives a detailed account of American military policy in the coalition between 1941 and 1943 and American differences with the British in *The Politics of the Second Front: American Military Planning and Diplomacy in Coalition Warfare, 1941–1943* (Westport, Conn., 1977). On the difficult relationship between the British and DeGaulle, see François Kersandy, *Churchill and DeGaulle* (New York, 1982). Herbert Feis's *Churchill, Roosevelt, Stalin* (Princeton, N.J., 1957) analyzes the relationships among the three leaders, as well as the conferences. Keith Sainsbury, *The Turning Point: Roosevelt, Stalin, Churchill and Chiang-Kai-Shek, 1943* (Oxford, UK, 1985), is the best account of the Moscow, Cairo, and Teheran conferences and the discussions among Roosevelt, Churchill, and Stalin. On the 1943 Teheran summit, see also Paul D. Mayle, *Eureka Summit: Agreement in Principle and the Big Three at Tehran, 1943* (Newark, N.J., 1987). On the pivotal Yalta Conference, see Fraser J. Harbutt, *Yalta 1945* (New York, 2010), and Russell D. Buhite, *Decisions at Yalta: An Appraisal of Summit Diplomacy* (Wilmington, Del., 1986); Diane

Shaver Clemens, *Yalta* (New York, 1970); and the essays by prominent scholars in John L. Snell et al. *The Meaning of Yalta* (Baton Rouge, La., 1956). Herbert Feis published a standard account of the Potsdam Conference, *Between War and Peace: The Potsdam Conference* (Princeton, N.J., 1960).

PART IV

Dual Europe

CHAPTER 21

↙

Making Postwar Europe

CHAPTER OUTLINE

Closing the Books on World War II? • Soviet Dominance in the East •
The West: American Influence • The Cold War

BIOGRAPHICAL SKETCHES

Klement Gottwald, Stalinist • Josip Broz Tito,
Communist Nationalist

The atrocities committed during the Second World War led to trials of major
Nazi figures for their criminal behavior. The problem of trying defeated leaders after a war presented major political and legal issues, and similar suggestions
made after World War I had not been implemented.

CLOSING THE BOOKS ON WORLD WAR II?

Joseph Stalin advocated executing between 50,000 and 100,000 German officers
after the war, and the Americans and British agreed that Nazi leaders should be
tried for their crimes against humanity. After some discussion, U.S. Secretary of
War Henry Stimson drafted a plan for the trials to be held in the Nuremberg, the
site of massive prewar Nazi rallies, and trials there would be a fitting symbol of
Nazism's final defeat. Legally, the trials were based on discussions at the Tehran,
Yalta, and Potsdam conferences, the adoption of the Inter-Allied Resolution of
German War Crimes in 1942, the London Charter of August 8, 1945, and other
documents.

What are generally considered the "Nuremberg Trials" refer to the proceedings of the International Military Tribunal conducted by American, British, and
Soviet prosecutors between November 20, 1945, and October 1, 1946. This tribunal condemned most of the twenty-two defendants, major surviving Nazis, and
sentenced them to death or imprisonment. However, there was a series of twelve

trials before military tribunals lasting until 1949, after which trials in German courts continued as war criminals were apprehended.

The Nuremberg trials have been condemned as "victor's justice," in which the winners judged the defeated. In addition to viewing the trials as a "lynching party," on the part of the winners, criticism ranges from the use of a double standard (Allied leaders, particularly the Soviets, were not tried for committing similar atrocities) to the application of ex post facto laws that were tailored to condemn the defendants; from the unprecedented nature of the trials to allowing the admissibility of normally inadmissible evidence; and from producing false evidence to concealing crucial evidence. The debate over the legality of the trials is unlikely to be resolved, but the trials were important from a political viewpoint because of the moral condemnation of the Nazis who were considered to have brought a new barbarism to the world.

The U.S. role in the trials demonstrates how the Americans took an active role in Europe after 1945—unlike their withdrawal from the continent after 1918. It is interesting that the Americans mistakenly believed that they could restore the balance of power and reestablish the traditional European equilibrium in about two years. It is difficult to understand this optimism because Europe lay prostrate, and the signs pointed to a difficult recovery. All the European powers had been defeated except Great Britain, which had been ruined economically. The Soviets extended their control in the East more vigorously than had been foreseen and had an important influence in strategic Western countries through their control of the communist parties. A cold war erupted within two years, and Europe split into two hostile camps dominated by the Soviet Union and the United States. Historian John Lewis Gaddis pointed to a fundamental difference between them: the USSR imposed a brutal regime on Eastern Europe, while the West Europeans, fearing Soviet expansion, invited the Americans into their affairs. In short, the majority of West Europeans consented to the American presence, while the East Europeans came to consider themselves oppressed and exploited by the USSR. Over the next five decades, rule by consent proved more stable than rule by force.

SOVIET DOMINANCE IN THE EAST

Following their triumph over Germany, Winston Churchill proposed to Stalin a division of Eastern Europe and the Balkans into areas in which each power would have a certain percentage of control in the different countries. This idea proved unrealistic, and the exhausted British soon surrendered their role in Europe to the United States, the only power strong enough to confront growing Soviet influence in Europe and the world.

Communists and Coalitions: Stalin's Popular Front Tactics

Stalin utilized flexible tactics to take control of Eastern Europe. Because the Communists had considerable popular support owing to the USSR's role in defeating the Nazis, Stalin mistakenly believed that free elections would produce Communist governments, but he used the Red Army when it was clear that the Communists would not win a consensus. Between 1945 and 1948, Stalin endorsed the popular front strategy—the cooperation of Communist and non-Communist parties—as a method of bringing the Communist parties to power legally because he could not simply suppress the non-Communist parties for fear of upheaval and Western protests.

Soviet Hegemony in Poland

In Poland, the Communists hoped to exploit the Polish Socialists to gain popular support and sole power, but Stalin was ready to use the Red Army if the attempt failed. In January 1943, the Polish Workers' Party, under Communist leader Wladislaw Gomulka, initiated talks with the London exile government and the Polish Socialists aiming at instituting a collaboration among anti-Nazi resisters, but they floundered because of the Soviet desire to keep the huge gains made under the Nazi-Soviet Nonaggression Pact of 1939 and because of Communist hegemony over Polish popular front organizations. In July 1944 the Red Army entered Poland, instituted radical social changes, and sponsored the Polish Committee for National Liberation through which it hoped to install a popular front government by inviting non-Communist parties to participate in a cabinet. The Polish Socialist Party and the more diffident Peasant Party accepted, the latter being particularly important because radical agrarian and factory reforms had provoked armed resistance by non-Communist forces.

Stalin dealt with international opposition by recognizing the Polish Committee for National Liberation as Poland's provisional government in January 1945. The United States and Britain insisted on a process by which they and the London exile government would be involved in broadening representation in the Polish government. In March 1945 the Soviets arrested non-Communist leaders and stalled the Allied foreign ministers who were charged with supervising the proceedings. Nevertheless, these ministers approved a popular front government after Stalin endorsed it, despite the intervention of the Red Army in favor of Polish Communist forces.

In August 1945 a new anti-Communist peasant party was founded, and factory elections revealed the preference of workers for Socialist candidates who were not subservient to the Communists. Stalin reacted by pressuring pro-Moscow leaders in the Socialist Party to join with the Communists in the electoral campaign of January 1947, and on election day, the police arrested 12,000 persons, disqualified 246 peasant candidates, and arrested 149 other candidates. Eighteen prominent peasant leaders were assassinated, and representatives of non-Communist parties were not allowed to participate in the vote counting. The result: 328 seats for the pro-Moscow parties and 62 for the non-Communist parties. Next, Gomulka and Moscow called for merging the Socialist and Communist parties, despite rank-and-file Socialist opposition to the fusion that signaled the end of their party, but arrests, trials, and executions eliminated the opposition. In December 1948, the United Polish Workers' Party officially came into being and completed the Soviet takeover.

The Political Struggle in Czechoslovakia

In Czechoslovakia the outlook for the Communists seemed particularly bright because an active Communist Party had existed before the war, an influential Communist-dominated resistance movement had emerged, and Communists and most non-Communists differed little on future social policy. Czech unions and politicians agreed that industry should be nationalized, and in October 1945, the government took over all businesses employing more than 150 workers and instituted radical land reform supported by their hero President Edvard Beneš. The question in Czechoslovakia was to what extent the country should be subservient to Soviet interests. Czech Communist leader Klement Gottwald favored a legal road to power because the Communists had won 38 percent of the vote in the May 1946 elections and, in concert with their Socialist allies, had a majority. But while they held the most important posts in the government and were firmly entrenched in the local administration, the bureaucracy, the army, and the police, the Communist leaders feared that growing tension with their non-Communist partners could threaten their position.

By the spring of 1947, this anxiety escalated because of international factors. The French and Italian Communists had renounced revolution in favor of governmental collaboration with non-Communist forces, but had subsequently been excluded from the cabinets. In June, the Americans announced the Marshall Plan, under which American aid would be funneled to war-torn Europe. The Soviets responded by establishing a new international organization of Communist parties, the Communist Information Bureau (Cominform), to guide Western Communist organizations in their bid for power. In the East, this event signaled a change in the Soviet policy favoring popular fronts to a bias in favor of force. This idea sounded the death knell for Gottwald's gradualist approach.

In July, the Czech government accepted American aid, but Stalin called in Gottwald and forced a reversal. This development came during a shift in the country away from the Communists, most obvious among the Czech Socialists. In September 1947, the pro-Moscow Socialist leader, Zdenek Fierlinger, had signed a new unity-of-action pact with the Communists without consulting the Socialist Party executive body, causing his ouster as party president in November. The struggle between Communists and anti-Communists, which the Communists and their trade union allies lost, continued into February 1948. In order to stave off a final Communist defeat, Gottwald employed delaying tactics, and several coalition partners resigned in protest on February 20.

BIOGRAPHICAL SKETCHES

Klement Gottwald
Stalinist

Klement Gottwald, the instrument of Stalin's policy in postwar Czechoslovakia, was born in a small village in Moravia on November 23, 1896. He came from a peasant family, but at age 12, he went to Vienna as an apprentice woodworker. In 1915, the Austro-Hungarian Army drafted him. He fought on both the Italian and Russian fronts and deserted before the conflict ended.

After the war, Gottwald joined the Czechoslovak Social Democratic Party. During this period, the Bolsheviks issued the Twenty-One Demands that Socialist parties deciding to transform themselves into Communist organizations had to accept. These conditions caused splits in the European Socialist parties. In 1921, Gottwald followed the left wing out of the Socialist organization and helped found the Czechoslovak Communist Party. He edited several party newspapers and occupied high positions in the Czech and international Communist movements. In 1925, he won election to the Central Committee, the Czechoslovak Communist Party's ruling body, and, between 1928 and 1943, served on the Executive Committee of the Comintern—the international organization of Communist parties that were subservient to Moscow. In 1935, he became its secretary. Elected a deputy to the Czechoslovak National Assembly in 1929, Gottwald ran for president of the republic in a joint session of that body in 1934 against the popular Thomas Masaryk, but lost handily. In the same year, Czech authorities sought to arrest him for his revolutionary activities, but he fled to the USSR. He returned to Czechoslovakia but left again in 1938 when the Munich agreement established German supremacy in the country.

In Moscow, Gottwald edited a newspaper calling for the liberation of his country and, during World War II, transmitted radio messages to the Czechoslovaks urging their resistance against the Germans. He also prepared himself for a crucial postwar role by organizing a group in the Soviet capital consisting of exiled Czechoslovak Communists.

In April 1945, Gottwald returned to Czechoslovakia as deputy premier in a coalition government. The Communists received a plurality of votes in the May 1946 elections, allowing Gottwald to claim the prime minister's post. He combined this office with his position as Communist Party chairman. Between 1946 and February 1948, Gottwald was a crucial player in the political maneuvering that was designed to strengthen the Communists and, when it appeared certain they would lose the 1948 elections, in the coup d'état that brought them sole power. When President Edvard Beneš resigned in June 1948, rather than sign a newly drafted constitution establishing the basis of Communist rule, Gottwald succeeded him in office.

Gottwald ran Czechoslovakia as a Stalinist. In 1948 and 1949, when the Soviets split with Yugoslavia and Stalin determined to eradicate Titoism, Czechoslovakia was swept up in the whirlwind despite Gottwald's initial recalcitrance. Tito had little influence in Czechoslovakia, but the Soviets discovered an absurd plot linking Titoism, Trotskyism, and support for Israel. They identified the leader as Rudolf Slansky, the Czechoslovak Communist Party's Jewish general secretary. Gottwald agreed to Slansky's demotion, but Soviet advisers in Czechoslovakia wanted Slansky to be tried. Gottwald resisted until Stalin intervened through a personal representative. He then gave in, and on November 20, 1952, the first show trials began. They ended with the execution of eleven prominent Communist leaders.

On Stalin's death, Gottwald traveled to Moscow for his funeral. He caught pneumonia on the trip and died in Prague on March 14, 1953. In his parliamentary debut in 1929, Gottwald had pledged to the non-Communist deputies and the supporters of Czech democracy that he would "break your necks." He had the satisfaction of having fulfilled his promise.

The Coup d'État

The resignations were a major tactical error. Gottwald labeled them a reactionary coup attempt and, fearing that without Socialist support they would lose the imminent elections and, bolstered by the aggressive new Cominform policy, prepared to take power by force. On February 24, 1948, armed Communist squads supported by the police beat up and arrested their opponents and attacked the Socialists. Gottwald established a new government composed of Communists and pro-Moscow Socialists and called for new elections. President Beneš did not react against the unfolding takeover because he feared a civil war. On March 10, the most prominent non-Communist in the government, Jan Masaryk, son of Czechoslovakia's founder, jumped or was pushed out a window. In April, Fierlinger and a Socialist rump merged with the Communists. On June 10, Beneš resigned as president, and Gottwald replaced him. Beneš's death in September deprived the country of its most significant non-Communist political figure. The Communist takeover distressed Western opinion, ushered in forty years of Communist rule, and was a major factor in the beginning of the cold war.

Jan Masayrk, the son of Czechoslovakia's first president, was Foreign Minister in the Czech government in exile during World War II and remained in the post after the conflict. On March 10, 1948, during the Communist coup d'etat in that country, he was found dead in the courtyard of the Foreign Ministry building below his bathroom window. In the West it was believed that he had been assassinated by the Communists by being pushed. Investigations in later years have given credit to the view that he fell or committed suicide. The Cold War had been a long time in the making, but the Czechoslovak coup and the alleged Communist murder of Masayrk convinced Westerners that their freedom was under serious attack and that they must prepare for a possible war.

The Former Nazi Satellites: Romania, Hungary, and Bulgaria

The status of Romania, Hungary, and Bulgaria as defeated Axis satellites made it easier for the Soviets to achieve domination and, because of potential international complications, more complex. In these countries, the victors established Allied Control Commissions (ACCs) with American, Soviet, and British representatives to supervise their postwar development. Because the Western allies ignored the Soviet representative on the ACC in defeated Italy, the Soviets did the same in Eastern Europe but still had to tread lightly when utilizing the Red Army. In Romania and Hungary, Communist opponents hoped to prevent a Soviet takeover by encouraging the ACCs to intervene because Allied representatives on these commissions could refuse to recognize governments that did not have wide representation. To get around this obstacle, the pro-Moscow Communists broadened the ruling coalitions but kept effective control of the governments by filling the most important cabinet posts with the support of the Red Army. After the governments received recognition from the ACCs, the Communists set up dictatorships.

In Bulgaria the Communists quickly established their dominance in popular front organizations, thanks to their own resistance activities and the Red Army. By September 1944, they gained popular support by implementing radical land reforms and by establishing new peasant cooperatives in the overwhelmingly rural country. The Communists conducted a violent campaign against the bourgeoisie, confiscating their property. Given Bulgaria's proximity to Russia, the strength of the Communist movement, and the Red Army, no substantial opposition was possible against the Communists.

Romania presented a more complex picture because the monarchy was an independent center of power. King Michael had overthrown the pro-Nazi ruler in August 1944. Several non-Communist parties maneuvered for power against the Communists, but Churchill's recognition of Romania as being in the Soviet sphere of influence, the Red Army occupation, and Stalin's insistence on a friendly government that would recognize the cession of territory to Russia brought the country under Soviet domination. In fact, when Romanian Communist leader Gheorghe Gheorghiu-Dej promised Stalin that his party could gain control of the government but failed, the Red Army forced the king to appoint a Communist-dominated cabinet. The ACC refused to certify it, but did so after some adjustments. Following ACC recognition, the Communists merged with the Socialists, split and defeated the non-Communist parties, and established dominance over the trade unions and the youth and women's organizations by bringing them into the Romanian popular front organization. Balloting on November 19 gave this National Democratic Front 80 percent of the vote in rigged elections. The last acts in the Communist takeover of the country were the forced abdication of the king on December 30, 1947, and the proclamation of a Romanian republic.

Romania's neighbor Hungary followed a similar pattern with Soviet interference even more blatant. In November 1945 elections, the non-Communist Smallholders won 57 percent of the vote to the Communists' 17 percent, but the Soviet occupiers installed a coalition government in which the key Interior Ministry went to a Communist. With Red Army support, the Interior Ministry ordered the police to attack the Smallholders and forced a Hungarian Socialist merger with the Communists. These steps resulted in a meager 22.5 percent of the vote going to the Communists in the August 1947 elections, who, even with the support of political allies, lacked a majority in parliament. However, the opposition's fragmentation, Communist control of the police, and Red Army support allowed them to arrest and deport their opponents to forced labor camps. In 1948, Hungary was transformed into a Communist state, with the nationalization of industry and the Communists taking over the presidency and the government.

A Special Case: Yugoslavia

Hungary's neighbor Yugoslavia followed a different path. Tito had successfully fought Axis occupiers and non-Communist partisans and ended the war in control of his country, with the Red Army playing little part. Tito employed the coalition tactics favored by Stalin only on the local level and rejected collaboration with non-Communist political forces. He consolidated his power by giving land to the peasants, effectively giving 80 percent of the land to peasants who had previously possessed none, but forcing the peasants to join new cooperatives and edging toward the Soviet model of land tenure in July 1946. Tito hoped to export his model of revolution to Eastern Europe and favored gaining control of national governments by pressure exercised from below through Communist control of mass organizations. He also advocated Communist intervention in the Greek Civil War and the establishment of a Balkan federation with Bulgaria and Albania, but Stalin frowned on Tito's foreign policy and revolutionary model because they created international complications for Moscow.

By 1947, when Stalin's popular front tactics faltered in Czechoslovakia and the Americans responded to Soviet actions in a more aggressive manner than in the past, the Russian dictator adopted a friendlier attitude toward the Yugoslav model of revolution at the founding congress of the Cominform. However, Tito's insistence on pushing his Balkan Federation project and his dispatch of troops into Albania in January 1948 to aid the Greek Communists fighting in the Civil War prompted Stalin to dictate several conditions to ensure Yugoslav submission to the USSR. The Yugoslavs refused and opened a schism in the Communist world. Soviet leader Nikita Khrushchev revealed in a secret report on Stalin in 1956 that Stalin stated: "I will shake my little finger—and there will be no more Tito." However, he could not get rid of Tito, and after Stalin died, political realities inspired the Soviets to make amends to the Yugoslav leader.

BIOGRAPHICAL SKETCHES

Josip Broz Tito
Communist Nationalist

Because of his ability to win the partisan war against the Germans and his internal opponents without the Red Army's help, Josip Broz defied Stalin, became a significant world figure, kept his raucous country together, and became a myth.

Born the son of a Croatian blacksmith and a Slovene mother on May 25, 1892, in Croatia, Broz became an apprentice locksmith in 1907. In 1915, as a soldier in the Austro-Hungarian army, he was captured by the Russians. In 1918, he joined the Red Army and fought in the Russian Civil War that broke out following the Bolshevik Revolution. Returning to Croatia in 1920, he joined the Communist Party and in 1927 became secretary for the Zagreb city organization. He spent five years in jail from 1929 to 1934, after which he went to Moscow and worked for the Comintern. In 1936, he returned to Yugoslavia, and from 1937, he reorganized and led the Communist Party.

After the invasion of Yugoslavia by the Germans and Italians in 1941, Broz led the Communist partisans and adopted the pseudonym Tito. He had many enemies among the non-Communist resisters, and the Yugoslav government in exile opposed him, but Tito simultaneously fought both domestic opponents and invaders. His masterful guerrilla tactics and his idea for the construction of a federated Yugoslavia after the war brought him strong non-Communist support. The British and Americans provided him with help in 1944 that counterbalanced Soviet influence. The Croats, Slovenes, and other non-Serb components of Yugoslavia that had always objected to Serb domination rallied to him. In November 1944, with the liberation of Belgrade, he merged his organization with the royal government and, in March 1945, headed a new federal executive. Despite these maneuvers, Tito already controlled Yugoslavia. In the elections of November 1945, only candidates from the Communist-dominated National Liberation Front were allowed to run for office. The opposition abstained, but Tito gained 80 percent support. Following this triumph, Tito deposed the king and proclaimed a republic.

Next Tito erected a Communist dictatorship, his strength in the country permitting him to defy Stalin and international opinion. He limited the activities of Soviet agents, executed his enemies, imprisoned the archbishop of Zagreb, established a secret police, nationalized industry, and implemented economic planning. He followed Communist policies independent of Stalin, prompting the Cominform to expel Yugoslavia. After Stalin's death, Yugoslavia's relationship with the USSR ranged from friendly to antagonistic. Although Tito received encouragement from the West, he irritated the United States by attempting to organize a common policy among nonaligned nations that were independent of both superpowers.

Later Tito altered important aspects of Yugoslav communism, according to changing conditions, by experimenting with workers' self-management and reforms that were intended to raise his people's standard of living. He allowed some dissent, including publication of *Praxis*, an influential journal criticizing the Communist regimes. Despite the sentencing of dissenter Milovan Djilas to a seven-year term because he wrote that communism had produced a privileged new class, Yugoslavia qualified as the most liberal Communist country in Europe.

Tito's greatest success was preventing Yugoslavia from breaking up during his lifetime. Reelected president from 1953 on, in 1971 Tito instituted a collective presidency that was designed to establish a firm basis for the federation after he died. He also favored a measure of autonomy to reduce growing ethnic tensions. Increasingly, however, Yugoslavia suffered from growing debt and inflation, secessionist tensions, and inefficient industry. It became clear that only Tito held the federation together. After he died a national hero on May 4, 1980, and by the end of the decade, Yugoslavia fell apart in a series of bloody civil wars.

Social Change in Eastern Europe

Soviet communism in Eastern Europe brought fundamental social change. The implementation of social and economic reforms was accompanied by the punishment of categories of persons who had collaborated with the Axis and of national minorities—a major difference with the West in which guilt was individual. In the East, governments, not courts, meted out punishment. In Hungary, for example, the campaign against the pro-Nazi Arrow Cross included the feudal elements of society and a redistribution of their land. Many of these feudal components were ethnic Germans, and the campaign served the goals of both revenge and social revolution.

Polish social reforms did not slavishly follow the Soviet model. The government strengthened small property holders and eliminated large landholdings, but collectivization never succeeded. Poland had made territorial gains against Germany to compensate for its losses to Russia. In these new possessions, the government brutally expelled the Germans and replaced them with peasants who had lost their land in the part of Poland that was ceded to the USSR. The Poles also expelled the Ukrainian minority. In industry, the government nationalized factories that employed more than forty people but aimed at a mixed economy. As a rule, the state took over key industries, German holdings, and the possessions of citizens killed during the Holocaust. At the end of 1947, however, the private sector still accounted for 63 percent of production.

Like the Poles, the Czechoslovaks expelled the German minority, with the November 20, 1945, approval of the Allied Control Commission, and resettled their own population on the lands. The number of Germans who were transferred out of Eastern Europe under unspeakable conditions has been variously estimated at between 6.5 million and 14 million, with perhaps a million deaths. The expulsions satisfied demands both for nationalist revenge and social reform. Romania, for example, confiscated land belonging to the German minority and deported Germans to the USSR for forced labor. It combined these measures with the expropriation of farms owned by families whom the government considered collaborators, and of holdings of ten hectares or more if the owners had not themselves worked it. Such measures were enormously popular all over Eastern Europe and helped entrench the new Communist regimes.

THE WEST: AMERICAN INFLUENCE

In Western Europe, the United States favored mild, not radical, social reform and encouraged rather than imposed it. The Americans feared the strong Communist parties in strategic France and Italy, but used covert and financial means to prevent them from taking over. The United States opposed the extension of Communist influence in the West for fear that it would become embroiled in a new war with the industries and energies of Western Europe ranged against it.

From Resistance to the Welfare State

Unlike in the East, reconstruction in the West began with the failure of revenge and ideology. After the war, partisans meted out summary justice to collaborators, killing an estimated 30,000 in France and perhaps up to 100,000 in Italy before calm returned and the courts took over. In Italy, Communist Party head Palmiro Togliatti as justice minister ended the purge. In Germany, major Nazi chiefs were tried for crimes against humanity at Nuremberg between November 1945 and October 1946, and denazification procedures began.

Resistance fighters complained about the failure of purges in the West, but some of their ideals headed toward long-term fulfillment. Many had dreamed of a federal European union, which seemed doomed immediately following the war but revived thanks to economic developments. They favored a society in which social justice would prevail with the help of governments, and postwar Europe witnessed a general acceptance of the welfare state and governmental intervention in everyday life. In 1942 in Britain, the Beveridge Report called for a comprehensive social security system to protect the weakest members of society by extending medical and health care and by passing comprehensive social legislation for low-income groups. After 1945, Britain and the other Western European states implemented social insurance systems that protected their populations from the cradle to the grave.

Along with the welfare state came economic planning, but not based on governmental coercion, as in the East. This economic planning coincided with the need to repair the war damage. As a rule, West European countries avoided nationalization, but in some cases, governments nationalized essential sectors or enterprises that were necessary for national prosperity or whose owners had collaborated with the Nazis. British Labourites favored widespread nationalization; the Norwegians, private ownership within government-designed plans; and the Italians, the public holding-company concept pioneered by the Fascists. Governments charged committees with the task of issuing guidelines on how reconstruction should occur. Resistance principles and the need to manage American aid efficiently strengthened the idea of planning in national debates about the extent to which the government should force industries to follow its guidelines. In general, persuasion won out over compulsion, particularly in formerly totalitarian Germany and Italy.

War Damage

The planners faced a formidable task because of the tremendous damage caused by World War II. Compared to prewar yields, agriculture had been halved, and industrial output had declined by two-thirds. Europe depended on American food supplies to avoid famine. Except for Germany, the belligerents had lost fewer fighting men than in World War I, but the civilian toll had been incomparably higher. The deaths of civilians meant great losses for industry of skilled manpower that was essential for reconstruction. The fighting had destroyed or severely degraded transportation and communication facilities that were vital to economic recovery—railways, bridges, and shipping. Large cities lay in ruins, with tens of millions of people left homeless. Twenty percent of France's houses were uninhabitable. In central Italy, electricity worked only 3 percent of the time. Because of the swift pace of the Allied advance, northern Europe had fared better, but had still suffered severe damage. Norway had lost half its merchant fleet, and the Germans had followed a scorched earth policy in parts of the country. Little physical damage had occurred in Denmark, but the country was bankrupt. Belgium, more fortunate, had been spared the worst destruction and was owed credits by the Allies for valuable resources, such as uranium supplied by the Belgian Congo during the conflict. The Netherlands lost a third of its housing stock, and valuable farmlands had been flooded.

Both defeated Germany and victorious Britain emerged from the war in poor shape. Germany had suffered physical destruction on a scale unknown in any other Western European country. The Allies had destroyed 40 percent of the housing in Germany's largest urban areas and rendered some cities practically uninhabitable. Coal production had all but stopped, and German industrial output stood at 30 percent of its prewar level. Britain had escaped physical damage, with the exception of areas that were subject to air attack, but the cost of the conflict had bankrupted it and finished it as a great power. Britain ended the war with a quarter of its merchant fleet sunk and with little capital available for investment to repair the damage and modernize its antiquated industries.

Moreover, Europe stared hyperinflation in the face. Because of reconstruction and the demand for civilian goods, an economic boom arrived, with the certain prospect of a bust. The shortage of goods in relation to demand favored a flourishing black market on the continent and a tremendous rise in prices. The value of the French, Italian, and German currencies dropped precipitously in relation to the dollar. In Germany, cigarettes threatened to replace money as an exchange instrument, and they were commonly used as a standard of value in other countries. The political uncertainties faced in these nations exacerbated the economic distress. Workers demanded higher wages to keep up with inflation and increased welfare payments and found radical political forces to support them. The governments hoped to keep employment levels high because deteriorating social conditions might lead to social and political upheavals, as they had after World War I. Western governments averted revolutionary disorders only through strong action, new investments, and American economic aid.

American Aid and Economic Stabilization

European governments aimed to prevent the 1946 boom from turning into a crash. The British fought the crisis by means of a stringent rationing system. In Italy, the classic economic medicine of Luigi Einaudi saved the Italian currency. In Germany, the old money was exchanged for a new currency. Belgium, shaken by the crisis of the monarchy; the Netherlands; and Scandinavia all reached a domestic consensus that allowed them to keep inflation within reasonable bounds.

Besides stemming inflation, the Europeans aimed at making economic growth orderly and steady. This goal necessitated an increase in exports so they could regain their former world trading position, but they could not do so under the prevailing conditions. The Europeans required raw materials and new machinery, which they could not import because their depreciated currencies could not pay for them. As a result, European economic recovery proceeded at a slow pace, with industry and agriculture stuck at less than 90 percent of its 1938 figure and exports at less than 60 percent in 1947.

Continuation of this situation prevented the normalization of the international trading system and intimately involved U.S. interests. The lack of improvement or deterioration of European economic circumstances threatened the stability of key countries like Italy and France and increased the likelihood of a Communist takeover. The Americans also counted on Europe as a market for their own products and feared returning to the post–World War I conditions that favored the outbreak of World War II. The Americans extended an estimated 12 billion dollars' worth of aid through the United Nations Relief and Recovery Agency, grants to individual countries, and other aid, but these measures proved insufficient to get Europe back on its feet. They attempted to foster free trade through the Bretton Woods agreement of 1944, which established fixed currency exchange rates, and financed the World Bank and the International Monetary Fund (IMF) to aid war-devastated countries and to redress balance-of-payments problems. These measures proved insufficient because the Europeans could not finance the modernization of their industries that would return international trade to normal.

The Marshall Plan

The fear of communism's spread had become real for the new administration of President Harry S. Truman. A civil war raged in Greece, and the Soviet takeover of Eastern Europe had prompted the famous "Iron Curtain" speech of Winston Churchill that focused on communism's rapid advance. During World War II, Treasury Secretary Henry J. Morgenthau, Jr., had proposed a plan to split Germany into two independent states and an international zone, with strategic areas going to France, the USSR, and Poland. Germany's heavy industry would be dismantled, and it would be transformed into an agricultural and pastoral state in order to prevent it from waging war ever again. With the growth of the Communist threat and the beginning of the cold war, this plan was generally recognized as being unworkable and was given a death blow by former President Herbert Hoover, who argued in March 1947 that it could not be implemented because the United States would have to move millions of Germans out of Germany and that Europe would never recover economically without the revival of Germany.

Given this realization and the slow European economic recovery despite billions in American aid, Secretary of State George C. Marshall and his collaborators developed an economic recovery plan that aimed not just at reconstruction, but at modernizing European industry, including Germany's, instilling confidence, and restoring the conditions for normal international trade. Marshall announced the plan at a speech in Harvard Yard on June 5, 1947, in which he emphasized that the modern economic system of the division of labor was in danger of breaking down and that there could be no political stability or peace without the world's return to "normal economic health."

It remained for the United States and the countries that were willing to participate in the "Marshall Plan" (officially, the European Recovery Program) to establish a concrete mechanism to deliver the aid. This was done in 1948 by the creation of the Economic Cooperation Administration and the Organization for European Economic Cooperation (OEEC, later OECD) that coordinated the financial aid. The OEEC included fifteen European countries in addition to Europe and the

United States. The offer to join was extended to the East Europeans as well, but Stalin vetoed the desire of Czechoslovakia and Poland to collaborate, but the Soviets rejected all interference in their sphere of influence.

The Marshall Plan funneled about $13 billion to its recipients and was both an economic and a political success. From an economic viewpoint, the countries receiving the aid already had a solid industrial base but found themselves in severe temporary difficulties because of the war. The plan helped Western European industry return to its prewar production level by 1948 and to surpass that level by 200 percent by 1952, after the plan ended (various forms of American aid continued, however). From a political viewpoint, the Marshall Plan probably helped stabilize the continent, and its collateral institutions favored European integration that pointed the way to the European Union. The Marshall Plan has been criticized by revisionists as a form of American economic imperialism, but the weight of historical opinion is that it was a great success in reviving Europe.

The Defeat of Communism in France and Italy

The failure of communism to come to power in both France and Italy was influenced by the economic recovery in both countries. In 1946 the French Communist Party (PCF) was one of three major parties in the Constituent Assemblies that created the Fourth French Republic, held key posts in the cabinets, and wielded considerable local authority under their hard-line leader Maurice Thorez. General Charles de Gaulle's spectacular resignation as the head of the government (the provisional president) on January 20, 1946, because of his opposition to a weak presidency, strengthened the Communists who hoped to dominate the government. However, the French Socialists refused to go along with the Communists in excluding the moderate, anti-Communist, Catholic right-center Popular Republican Movement (MRP), led by Resistance leader Georges Bidault, from the governing coalition.

In France the Communist-Socialist-Catholic bloc proved unstable, as it did in Italy, and the government was paralyzed by the inability of the parties to agree on policy. In May 1947, the French resolved the political dilemma by excluding the Communists from the cabinet on the grounds that they fomented strikes and unrest. In fact, the French Communists had assumed a more aggressive line following criticism at the founding congress of the Cominform. After their exclusion from the government, the Communists called for a revolutionary nationwide strike, accompanied by violence and sabotage that brought the country to a standstill. The government's firm action in calling out the army and threatening workers with economic sanctions, combined with the lack of support for a revolution, forced the Communists and the unions to back off.

The focus shifted to Italy, where the situation was even more critical. On June 2, 1946, the first elections in which women participated had done away with the monarchy. A constituent assembly issued a new constitution representing a compromise among the Catholics, Socialists, and Communists and established a parliamentary regime on the lines of pre-Fascist Italy. Like France, an uneasy coalition of Christian Democrats (DC), Communists (PCI), and Socialists (PSI) had the major say in the governments following World War II, but unlike in France,

Of all the Communist parties in the West, the Italian Communist Party (PCI) was the largest and best organized and would remain so for decades. Unlike its French counterpart, the PCI's shrewd leaders adapted to different conditions, allowing it to have a major role in Italian society and bringing it close to power in the years following World War II. This is its longtime Secretary in 1949. Palmiro Togliatti, in exile in Moscow during the Fascist period and had been a close collaborator of Stalin. He died on August 21, 1964 in Yalta.

Socialist leader Pietro Nenni had long been closely allied with the Communists. In May 1947, following a visit to the United States and in view of the upcoming elections for the first postwar parliament under the new constitution, DC Prime Minister Alcide De Gasperi dropped the Communists and Socialists from the cabinet. The left reacted angrily, and the ensuing electoral campaign was the most turbulent and closely watched of the era. The Communists and Socialists, allied in the Popular Front, confidently believed that they would win, but the Italians feared the establishment of a new dictatorship. This fear, along with opposition to the Popular Front by the church and the Americans, help account for the Popular Front's decisive defeat on April 18, 1948. The front received only 31 percent of the vote, while the DC won a majority of seats in parliament, the only party or coalition to accomplish such a feat before 1994. De Gasperi wisely chose to rule with the support of smaller secular allies.

The strength of Italian communism created a quandary for the country in the future. Because so many votes were locked up in a left that could not come to power because of non-Communist and American opposition, the Christian Democrats—the fulcrum of the non-Communist alliance—ruled for forty-five years. The impossibility of a political alternation in power promoted widespread corruption because the Italians could not "vote the scoundrels out."

The reverses of French and Italian communism brought relative peace and political stability to Western Europe, and their defeats contributed to the decline of the Communist parties in the smaller countries of Northern Europe. The German situation, however, had a greater impact on the cold war.

THE COLD WAR

As more documentation becomes available after the cold war's end in 1989, historians will undoubtedly gain a new perspective on the events of 1945 to 1948. The long-term view may favor interpretation of the cold war as a parenthesis in European and world history: an anomaly that resulted from a set of circumstances that evolved in an unforeseen direction because of the personalities involved and that probably will not recur. This interpretation does not mean that there were no permanent elements in the picture. Nuclear weapons, for example, had a fundamental role in the cold war's evolution and will probably greatly influence the world's future. Other circumstances that seemed immutable because of the length of time they existed, however, turned out to be transient.

The Division of Germany

When World War II ended, it left Europe in an anomalous situation that few predicted would last for over five decades. The post–World War I settlement, no matter how defective, held out the hope that Germany would eventually regain its rightful place as an essential member of the European concert. In the post–World War II bipolar world, the superpowers failed to settle the German problem, and Germany remained divided and took on an air of permanence, but not because the Americans and Russians had intended it that way.

In 1945, Germany was divided into four occupation zones, but despite earlier talk, the Western Allies did not intend to dismember it because they understood the importance of the country for a stable continent. By early 1946. the three Western occupation zones were developing as an economic unit, and the Western Allies allowed the Germans to begin rebuilding their industrial and commercial base and favored the rebuilding of representative political institutions. The Soviets, instead, demanded reparations and systematically despoiled and deindustrialized their occupation area, in addition to seeking revenge through mass rapes and massive looting. In 1947, the announcement of the Marshall Plan, the closing of the American zone to Soviet depredations, and Allied disagreement with the Soviets over German peace terms made relations between the two superpowers difficult. With little hope for a German settlement, the Americans and British merged the economies of their zones (Bizonia) and set production goals. In February 1948, the Allies agreed to a reconstituted German political authority in the West, and the Soviets countered with moves toward a separate state in the East.

George Kennan, American chargé d'ffaires in Moscow, coherently explained the Soviet postwar position to American officials in a "long telegram" on February 22, 1946, that served as the basis for the hard line taken by the United States against the USSR in the decades following World War II. Kennan has been seen as the inspirer of the "containment" policy, although he maintained that he did not intend this result. Kennan died on March 17, 2005, at age 101.

The Berlin Airlift

Economic developments forced the German crisis to peak. The black market and inflation had destroyed Germany's currency and threatened to wipe out the middle and working classes. After seeking an agreement with the Soviet authorities on German currency reform, the Western Allies exchanged the old reichsmarks (RM) for new deutsch marks (DM) at the rate of ten to one. This step restored confidence in the currency, but the circulation of DM in Berlin caused major problems for the Soviets as anxious Easterners traded their money, labeled the foul mark, for the new Western currency. By the end of 1948, the eastern mark had dropped to one-fifth the value of the DM, and currency reform threatened to make Berlin a showcase of West German economic prosperity in the heart of the Soviet zone because the German capital, which also had been divided into four zones, lay deep in the Soviet occupation zone. To counter this development, the Soviets began blocking Western access to the city on April 1, 1948.

This challenge touched off the gravest crisis of the cold war before the 1962 Cuban missile crisis. The Americans and British rejected the temptation to send an armed convoy to the city because it might have set off a clash and airlifted all

The Cold War began soon after the end of World War II as the United States contested the USSR's attempts to dominate Germany and Eastern Europe. The dispute led the Soviets to block the land route to the former German capital, thus threatening to starve out the city. The Allies responded by supplying Berlin by air and the massive airlift became the defining event of the early postwar era. Here Berliners greet a plane bringing vital supplies to their besieged city.

the supplies necessary to ensure West Berlin's survival for almost a year, up to 13,000 tons a day. The Soviets backed off from taking military action against the planes because it might have led to war. On May 12, 1949, their blockade having failed, the Soviets ended it, and the establishment of two separate states in Germany became a certainty.

Stalin's German Strategy

Ironically, Stalin did not favor a permanent division of Germany but would have accepted reunification because he hoped that the Communists would win power legally, after which he could throw all Germany's resources onto the scale against the Americans. Indications are that by June 1945, he had formulated a plan to extend Communist control over a reunified Germany by using popular front methods, as he explained to leaders of the German Communist Party (KPD). In the Soviet zone, the KPD and the German Social Democratic Party (SPD) merged, creating the Socialist Unity Party (SED) under Communist control. This party would appeal to Marxist sympathizers and Social Democrats in the Western zones, he hoped, eventually winning political control of the entire country. This technique was a necessary variation on Communist coalition tactics in the East, where the Red Army had control. In the American-dominated West, the Communists would have to achieve power through popular support, as they hoped to do in Italy and France. This idea failed because the American democratic tradition and style favored democratic governments for Germany and the other European states, and the United States understood the great threat that the popular front formula presented to democracy in the West. Moreover, the Americans reacted strongly to the threat of Soviet takeovers of European countries.

America Adopts a Hard Line: Kennan and Truman

On February 9, 1946, Stalin announced a new Five-Year Plan for the USSR. In the context of widespread Soviet spy activities, the intensification of Soviet nuclear research, and American suspicion that Russian support for a reunified Germany aimed at absorbing all of it, alarmed American officials viewed Stalin's address as a declaration of war. On February 21, a Joint Chiefs of Staff document stated that "from a military point of view, the consolidation and development of the power of Russia is the greatest threat to the United States in the foreseeable future." In Moscow, the American chargé d'affaires, George Kennan, wrote an 8,000-word reply to a government request asking why the Soviets had refused to join the World Bank and the IMF—the "long telegram." Kennan favored a policy of "containment," that is, stopping Soviet expansion rather than war. He argued that the Russians had always considered themselves surrounded by enemies and now used appealing Marxist ideology and a tightly controlled Communist network to subvert any group with a grievance in order to bring the non-Communist nations into the Soviet orbit. Kennan urged the government to educate the American public about Communist goals and explain clearly to other countries the kind of world the United States hoped to create.

This document did not advocate extending military and economic aid to countries that were threatened by communism or exclude negotiations with the USSR, but American officials saw it as recommending a hard line. The Joint Chiefs of Staff had already proposed that military aid be extended to friendly countries. Kennan's views complemented this attitude, governmental officials circulated the telegram widely, and it was published in different versions in *Time* and *Foreign Affairs*. On March 5, 1946, Winston Churchill maintained, in a famous speech at Westminster College in Fulton Missouri, that an Iron Curtain had descended across Europe "from Stettin in the Baltic to Trieste in the Adriatic." Soviet control and police states had been established in Eastern Europe, Churchill said, and now threatened Italy.

President Truman endorsed Churchill's address and acted decisively. The Americans were concerned about Soviet moves in Iran, Korea, and China but, most of all, in Europe, where Stalin had Sovietized the East and badgered Turkey by demanding a role in the Straits. In Greece, a civil war raised the specter that the Communists would take over yet another country. The British had prevented a Communist takeover in 1944, but were exhausted and turned over responsibility for preventing a Communist victory to the United States. In March 1947, Truman made a commitment that went far beyond Greece by pledging support for countries that were fighting subjection by "armed minorities or by outside pressures." This Truman Doctrine ended the hesitation and debate that had characterized American foreign policy by recognizing that the world was interdependent and that American interests mandated support for democracies. The country had accepted the Soviet challenge, which, given the atomic bomb, made the world a much more dangerous place.

Evolution of Nuclear Weapons

American intentions during the early postwar years can be judged by considering how the Americans handled their atomic monopoly. The Americans developed the atomic bomb out of fear that the Germans would get it first and used it for the purpose of shortening the war. The war won, the United States demobilized its conventional forces and neglected its atomic arsenal. When the United States proclaimed the Truman Doctrine, for example, it possessed only fourteen nuclear weapons. During the Berlin blockade, it had only fifty unassembled bombs and only thirty B-29 planes capable of delivering the weapons, not enough to win a war with the USSR.

If the United States had intended to impose its will on the USSR, it would have produced enough nuclear weapons to win a war before the Soviets developed a nuclear capability, but instead they allowed their nuclear arsenal to fall into disarray for several reasons. American democratic tradition mandated that Americans did not start wars or launch surprise attacks. In addition, as part of the democratic process, pressure from nuclear scientists and public opinion motivated American officials to make an offer to relinquish the nuclear monopoly if a strong international agency could be established to control them.

The Soviets disagreed because such an agency would have meant giving up their right to build their own bomb. Soviet scientists understood the principles of constructing atomic weapons, and spy operations made the task easier for them, especially at the crucial initial stages. For Stalin, the important question was how to conduct himself during the brief period in which the United States possessed the bomb and he did not. Theoretically, the Americans could force the Soviets to bend to their will by threatening to use the bomb, but no such credible threat ever materialized. Soviet espionage kept Stalin informed about the small number of atomic weapons the Americans possessed, and this knowledge allowed Stalin to proceed with relative tranquility in authorizing such hazardous operations as the Czech coup, the Berlin blockade, and the invasion of South Korea by the North.

It is instructive to look at Soviet intentions by examining the USSR's research program with regard to nuclear weapons. The Soviets did not stop with the atomic bomb, tested in 1949, but, in a bid for supremacy, quickly initiated work on the hydrogen bomb, for which the atomic bomb served as a trigger. The development of fusion weapons had been debated in the United States since 1942, but American scientists not only had not gone ahead but had not informed President Truman that the possibility existed. The successful testing of an atomic bomb by the Soviets and the understanding that they had the capacity to develop the "Super" (a hydrogen bomb) spurred the Americans to move forward on fusion weapons, which both countries developed at approximately the same time.

The invention of the atomic bomb changed the nature of war and international politics. Despite dangerous crises during the cold war, the two superpowers refrained from using nuclear weapons because they realized that their use could end the world and relied heavily on "proxy wars" such as the Korean conflict. The two types of bombs used against Japan, "Fat Man" and "Little Boy," photographed here, were quickly surpassed by the fusion bombs that dwarfed the bombs the United States used in 1945.

The Paradoxical Impact of the Bomb

As nuclear weapons became more powerful and easier to produce, an ironic thing happened. Rational statesmen would not use them because these weapons had the capacity to destroy the world. Thus, as the number and destructiveness of nuclear weapons increased exponentially, the United States was forced to increase its conventional forces to confront the vastly superior number of troops the Soviets could deploy, so that it would not be forced to rely on the bomb. The weapons contributed to the globalization of the cold war as the two superpowers confronted each other on stages less dangerous than Europe, such as in Korea from 1950 to 1953.

The Korean War made Europeans anxious to ensure a continued American presence on the continent where the American nuclear umbrella protected them. The nuclear stalemate froze into place the anomalous condition of Germany and Europe because there, the superpowers confronted each other directly and any

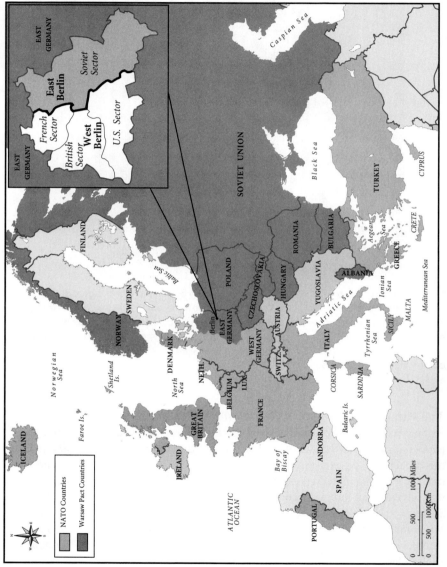

Divided Europe, showing the NATO and Warsaw Pact members.

conflict threatened to go nuclear. The amount of destruction that would result in an attempt by either side to alter the existing situation was inconceivable. But the avoidance of a European conflagration carried a price—the continued division of the continent over a lengthy period. The abnormal became normal.

The Two Blocs

In the long run, the USSR could not sustain this condition because it could not sustain prolonged competition with the West, and it turned out to be less efficient, in all respects, than its democratic rivals. Thus, the cold war will likely prove to have been a parenthesis in human history. It is improbable that anyone will again combine such overwhelming power at home and abroad at similarly critical times as did Stalin. At the end of the twentieth century, Europe and the world headed away from the bipolar condition of the post–World War II period, and the lack of a Stalin at a superpower's controls does not augur well for new cold wars.

Paradoxically, Soviet exploitation of satellite countries helps explain the USSR's inability to sustain competition with the West. Communist exploitation ruined the economies of Eastern Europe, including the USSR, and did tremendous ecological damage. The command economy imposed by the Soviet Union proved a failure in all respects, making dubious economic progress at a horrendous cost in human lives and misery. The Communist regimes fostered education and provided an economic floor for everyone, but at the cost of depressing living standards as a whole and of creating a new class system. "Actually existing communism" mistreated its populations to such a great extent that the social contract that allows societies to function broke down and over the decades caused many revolts.

In a sense, the preponderant American influence in Western Europe also constituted an empire, but in this case, despite tensions and strains that occasionally boiled over, the European "subjects" accepted it. Most West Europeans were terrified that they might meet the fate of the eastern part of the continent and were anxious to have the Americans stay. Communism failed the test of popular support in the West even where its appeal was the greatest, Italy and France. The PCI, the largest Communist party in Western Europe, boasted an intelligent leadership and drew political clout from its advocacy of reform and from protests against corruption. It even slowly distanced itself from Soviet communism, but it never came to power. In France, Thorez's leadership remained stubbornly pro-Moscow, and the PCF declined into insignificance.

While Europeans criticized American policies, including their hostility to the idea of Communist parties participating in cabinets, most of them understood that the Americans would not trample on their basic freedoms. The Americans intervened in the internal affairs of the major Western European states indirectly, mainly by threatening to ostracize them from the Western family of nations should they choose a totalitarian form of government. American policy opposed communism in the name of democracy, but it also opposed extreme rightists. The United States encouraged economic prosperity as a means of bolstering democratic attitudes, insisting on free trade and on European economic, political, and military collaboration. After World War II, the contrasts between West European economic development and East European stagnation and between West European freedom and oppression in East Europe were too blatant to be ignored. In contrast to the Soviet bloc, the West Europeans felt comfortable—perhaps too comfortable—with entrusting the Americans with their military security, while, ironically, the Americans exhorted them to take a greater role in their own defense.

Bibliographical Essay

The facts of the Nuremberg trials have been told many times. A general history was published by Paul Roland, *The Nuremberg Trials: The Nazis and Their Crimes Against Humanity* (London, 2010). The trials can also be followed in Joseph Persico, *Infamy on Trial* (New York, 1994). Since the trials, important books have seen the light on their impact and implications. The most valuable of these books frequently include books of essays in which scholars examine different aspects of the problem. Books of essays include G. Mettraux, *Perspectives on the Nuremberg Trial* (New York, 2008), one of the most detailed and complete considerations; Beth A. Griech-Polelle *The Nuremberg War Crimes Trial and Its Policy Consequences Today* (Baden-Baden, 2009); and Mitchel G. Bard, *The Nuremberg Trials* (San Diego, Calif., 2002). An interesting book on how intelligence gathering contributed to the trials is Michael Salter, *US Intelligence, The Holocaust, and the Nuremberg Trials* (Boston, 2009). For the other side of the coin, see Donald M. McKale, *Nazis After Hitler: How Perpetrators of the Holocaust Cheated Justice and Truth* (Lanham, Md., 2012).

A good general book on Europe's condition immediately following the war is Hugh Thomas, *Armed Truce: The Beginnings of the Cold War 1945–46* (New York, 1987). This well-written and detailed work examines all the major Eastern and Western European countries during the period and presents an excellent view of Soviet and American policy. The quote from the Joint Chiefs of Staff memorandum on giving aid to friendly nations to fight communism is on pp. 484–85. Lloyd C. Gardiner, *Spheres of Influence* (New York, 1994), discusses international relations up to Yalta, and the story can also be followed in Philip E. Mosely, *The Kremlin and World Politics: Studies in Soviet Politics and Action* (New York, 1960).

The tension in American foreign policy between preparing for war and containment is examined by Nicholas Thompson, *The Hawk and the Dove: Paul Nitze, George Kennan, and the History of the Cold War* (New York, 2009).

Balazs Apor et al. have written *The Sovietization of Eastern Europe: New Perspectives on the Postwar Period* (Washington, D.C., 2008); see as well Norman Naimark and L. Gibianskii, *The Establishment of Communist Regimes in Eastern Europe, 1944–1949* (Boulder, Colo., 1997). Liesbeth van der Grift examines how the Communists in East Germany and Romania won over the security apparatus in these countries in *Securing the Communist State: The Reconstruction of Coercive Institutions in the Soviet Zone of Germany and Romania* (Lanham, Md., 2012). A good, detailed book on Eastern European events is Hugh Seton-Watson, *The East European Revolution* (New York, 1956, and later editions). Joseph Rothschild and Nancy M. Wingfield published a general history, *Return to Diversity: A Political History of East Central Europe Since World War II* (New York, 2000). Lynn Etheridge Davis, *The Cold War Begins: Soviet-American Conflict over Eastern Europe* (Princeton, N.J., 1974), is a well-documented and well-argued work on the Eastern European origins of the cold war. Adam B. Ulam's *Expansion and Coexistence, The History of Soviet Foreign Policy 1917–1967* (New York, 1968) is still useful. There are good chapters on Stalin's postwar policies in Adam B. Ulam, *Stalin: The Man and His Era* (Boston, 1989), and in Dimitri Volkogonov, *Stalin: Triumph and Tragedy* (New York, 1988). Geoffrey Swain and Nigel Swain, *Eastern Europe Since 1945* (New York, 1993), argue that Stalin had no blueprint to take over Eastern Europe at the end of the war.

For Poland following the war, consult R. F. Starr, *Poland 1944–1962* (Baton Rouge, La., 1962); Norman Davies, *God's Playground: A History of Poland* (Oxford, UK, 1981);

J. Coutouvidis and J. Reynolds, *Poland, 1939–47* (Leicester, UK, 1986); and M. K. Dzi-ewanowski, *The Communist Party of Poland: An Outline of History* (Cambridge, Mass., 1959). On Czechoslovakia, see K. Kaplan, *The Short March: The Communist Takeover in Czechoslovakia 1945–1948* (London, 1981); P. Zinner, *Communist Strategy and Tactics in Czechoslovakia 1918–1948* (London, 1963); J. Bloomfield, *Passive Revolution: Politics and the Czechoslovak Working Class* (London, 1970); and Claire Sterling, *The Masaryk Case* (Boston, 1982). On the expulsion of the Germans, see Alfred de Zayas, *Nemesis at Pots-dam: The Anglo-Americans and the Expulsion of the Germans*, 2d ed. (London, 1979); Freda Utley, *The High Cost of Vengeance* (Chicago, 1949); and Alfred Maurice de Zayas, *A Terrible Revenge: The Ethnic Cleansing of the East European Germans, 1944–1950* (New York, 1994).

For Hungary, see Miklós Molnar, *A Short History of the Hungarian Communist Party* (Boulder, Colo., 1978). Details of the Communist takeover may be found in Paul Ignotus, *Hungary* (New York, 1972). For Romania, see Reuben Markham, *Rumania Under the Soviet Yoke* (New York, 1949); Ghita Ionescu, *Communism in Rumania 1944–1962* (London, 1964); Stephen Fischer-Galati, *The New Rumania* (Cambridge, Mass., 1967); and Robert King, *A History of the Rumanian Communist Party* (Stanford, Calif., 1980). Bulgarian events are analyzed by Oren Nissan, *Bulgarian Communism: The Road to Power 1934–1944* (New York, 1974), and *Revolution Administered: Agrarianism and Communism in Bulgaria* (Baltimore, Md., 1973).

On Yugoslavia, an excellent source is Milovan Djilas, *Conversations with Stalin* (New York, 1962). Walter R. Roberts discusses the relationship among Tito, his non-Com-munist rivals, and the Allies in *Tito, Mihailovic, and the Allies* (New Brunswick, N.J., 1973). On Tito's life, see Fitzroy Maclean, *The Heretic: The Life and Times of Josip Broz-Tito* (New York, 1957), and on his fight with Stalin, consult Leigh White, *Balkan Caesar: Tito Versus Stalin* (New York, 1951). Richard West, *Tito and the Rise and Fall of Yugoslavia* (New York, 1995) is a broad-ranging work. The memoirs of Enver Hoxha are useful not only for Albanian events but for portraits of other Eastern European Communist protagonists: *The Artful Albanian: Memoirs of Enver Hoxha* (London, 1986). Norman M. Naimark gives a detailed and compre-hensive history of Soviet policies in their zone and relations with the West in *The Russians in Germany: A History of the Soviet Zone of Occupation, 1945–1949* (Cambridge, Mass., 1995).

The Berlin airlift story is told by Jonathan Sutherland and Diane Canwell, *Berlin Airlift: The Salvation of a City* (Gretna, Scotland, 2008) and Bob Clarke's *The Berlin Airlift: 10 Tons for Templehof* (Stroud, UK, 2007). See also Eric Morris, *Blockade: Berlin and the Cold War* (London, 1973); A. Tusa and J. Tusa, *The Berlin Blockade* (London, 1988); Michael D. Haydock, *City Under Siege: The Berlin Blockade and Airlift, 1948–1949* (Washington, 1999); and Thomas Parrish, *Berlin in the Balance, 1945–1949: The Blockade, The Airlift, the First Major Battle of the Cold War* (Reading, Mass., 1998).

On Germany after the war, J. H. Backer, *The Decision to Divide Germany* (Durham, N.C., 1978), provides an account of events leading to the division. Giles MacDonogh presents histories of the occupation and the immediate years following the war in *After the Reich: The Brutal History of the Allied Occupation* (New York, 2007) and *After the Reich: From Liberation: From the Liberation of Vienna to the Berlin Airlift* (London, 2007). Norman Naimark published a history of the Russian occupation and the Soviet zone: *The Russians in Germany* (Cambridge, Mass., 1995). On denazification in the West, see Tom Bower, *The Pledge Betrayed: America and Britain and the Denazification of Postwar Germany* (Garden City, N.Y., 1982).

For the revenge following World War II, see the essays in Istvan Deak et al., *The Poli-tics of Retribution in Europe: World War II and its Aftermath* (Princeton, N.J., 2000).

Communist Party policies in France and Italy are examined by François Fejto, *The French Communist Party and the Crisis of International Communism* (Cambridge, Mass., 1967), while Simon Serfaty and Lawrence Gray, eds., *The Italian Communist Party: Yester-*

day, Today, and Tomorrow (Westport, Conn., 1980), include a good section on the early postwar period. On Christian Democracy, see Mario Einaudi and François Gaguel, *Christian Democracy in Italy and France* (Notre Dame, Ind., 1952), and Richard Webster, *Christian Democracy in Italy, 1860–1960* (London, 1961). James Miller's *The United States and Italy 1940–1950* (Chapel Hill, N.C., 1986) and John Lamberton Harper's *America and the Reconstruction of Italy, 1945–1948* (Cambridge, UK, 1986) give good details on America's involvement with Italy during the early postwar period. See also Elena Aga Rossi and Victor Zaslavsky, *Stalin and Togliatti: Italy and the Origins of the Cold War* (Stanford, Calif., 2010), and Robert Ventresca, *From Fascism to Democracy: Culture and Politics in the Italian Election of 1948* (Toronto, 2004).

John L. Gaddis discusses different aspects of the cold war in several fundamental books that are particularly relevant to this chapter. *The United States and the Origins of the Cold War 1941–1947* (New York, 1972) discusses the beginnings, and his *We Now Know: Rethinking Cold War History* (Oxford, UK, 1997) is important for interpretations of the cold war's developments over the decades and its end. The chapters on Germany and the role of nuclear weapons are especially useful. See also his *The Cold War: A New History* (New York, 2005). On three important moments in the American reaction against the Soviets, see John Gimbel, *The Origins of the Marshall Plan* (Stanford, Calif., 1976); Fraser Harbutt, *The Iron Curtain: Churchill, America, and the Origins of the Cold War* (New York, 1986); and George F. Kennan, *Memoirs: 1925–1950* (Boston, 1967). John Gaddis published a biography of Kennan, *George F. Kennan: An American Life* (New York: 2011) and a history of containment during the cold war: *Strategies of Containment*, rev. ed. (New York, 2005). Walter LaFeber gives a solid general interpretation in *America, Russia, and the Cold War*, 5th ed. (New York, 1985). British and French policies during the early cold war are examined by Anne Deighton, *The Impossible Peace: Britain, the Division of Germany and the Origins of the Cold War* (New York, 1993), and John W. Young, *France, the Cold War and the Western Alliance, 1944–49* (Leicester, UK, 1990). Books analyzing the Marshall Plan include Greg Behrman, *The Most Noble Adventure: The Marshall Plan and How America Helped Rebuild Europe* (New York, 2008), and Nicolaus Mills, *Winning the Peace: The Marshall Plan and America's Coming of Age as a Superpower* (Hoboken, N.J., 2008). A reflection on the impact of the plan is Martin Schain's *The Marshall Plan: Fifty Years Later* (New York, 2001).

On the role of nuclear weapons, see Gregg Herken, *The Winning Weapon: The Atomic Bomb in the Cold War, 1945–1950* (New York, 1980). David Holloway chronicles Russian activity in the nuclear field in *Stalin and the Bomb: The Soviet Union and Atomic Energy, 1939–1956* (New Haven, Conn., 1994). Insights into the thinking of the American scientific community—including its divisions—and the political establishment may be found in Edward Teller's *Memoirs: A Twentieth-Century Journey in Science and Politics* (Cambridge, Mass., 2001) (with Judith Shoolery).

⤶

CHAPTER 22

Economic Integration
and Political Stabilization
in the West

CHAPTER OUTLINE

Defense Mechanisms • Economic Integration • The Community:
New Europe's Core • Associated Countries

BIOGRAPHICAL SKETCHES

Jean Monnet, Cognac and Europe • Konrad Adenauer,
Senior Statesman

Following World War II, the West Europeans and Americans worked for economic development and political stabilization in the context of a divided and militarily vulnerable Europe, no German peace treaty, and internal Communist threats. The first step was to ensure Western Europe's independence in light of possible Soviet aggression.

DEFENSE MECHANISMS

In 1947 and 1948, Britain, France, and the Low Countries signed a series of treaties that were aimed at preventing future German dominance because they did not trust the United Nations (UN), formed in 1944 to succeed the League of Nations and paralyzed by the Soviet veto in the UN Security Council when it seemed likely that the Communists would win the civil war in Greece. Given the disparity of conventional forces between the USSR and Europe, the United States would have had to use nuclear weapons in case of a Soviet attack. Because the Westerners wanted other options besides recourse to the atomic bomb, they signed the military alliance known as the North Atlantic Treaty Organization (NATO) in April 1949.

NATO

NATO was a loose defensive alliance consisting of the United States, Canada, and ten European nations (France, Italy, Britain, Belgium, the Netherlands,

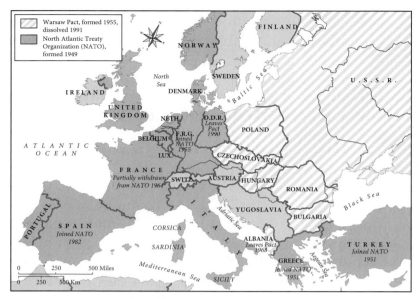

Europe Divided. This map shows the two military camps in Europe following World War II. Different members joined NATO over the years, the most important being Germany in 1955. France partially withdrew from the alliance in 1964. The Warsaw Pact joining Communist East Europe dissolved between 1990 and 1991.

Luxembourg, Norway, Denmark, Iceland, and Portugal) and was enlarged over the years. Each country contributed forces according to their means, and NATO did not prohibit them from using their committed forces for other purposes. NATO's major importance was as the symbol of American commitment to the European continent and as a warning to the USSR that NATO and the Americans would intervene in a war against Soviet aggression that would eventually escalate into a nuclear war, given the West's inferiority in Soviet conventional forces. The Atlantic Alliance also served notice that the Americans would not permit a political take-over of Western European nations by Communist parties.

German Rearmament and European Military Organizations
From the beginning, it was clear that the West had to allow Germany to rearm, a prospect viewed by many Europeans and some Germans with alarm. Between 1950 and 1953 during the Korean War, the United States pushed for speedier German rearmament within NATO, something that West German Chancellor Konrad Adenauer supported as a step toward West Germany's full independence. Distressed at the prospect of a rearmed Germany, the Russians proposed reunification of the country as a neutralized state, but the effort failed because the USSR allowed Poland and East Germany (the German Democratic Republic or GDR) to keep the Oder-Neisse line as their border and because the Soviets refused to allow free elections in the GDR. In this situation, the French proposed to create an integrated European army that would include German units: the European Defense Community (EDC).

The Failure of European Military Initiatives

The EDC's primary significance was that it would have deprived the Germans of a separate army under their own command because it required the entire German army to be part of the defense community, while other participating countries had to contribute only some units. The proposal ran into British and Scandinavian opposition because these countries feared the loss of sovereignty, and in August 1954, the French parliament killed the EDC.

The EDC's collapse induced British Prime Minister Anthony Eden to propose immediate German membership in NATO. The British argued that Germany could not act unilaterally within NATO's integrated military structure, and the French had no choice but to go along. In 1955, the leaders of the United States and the USSR met at the Geneva Summit, and a temporary thaw that alarmed European leaders resulted because the Europeans feared an American withdrawal from the continent. This consideration and a call for the stationing of British troops in Germany, in line with the framework of the West European Union, paved the way for Germany's entrance into NATO in 1955.

ECONOMIC INTEGRATION

During the resistance, the idea of a European federation as the means of overcoming Europe's nationalistic divisions was a powerful ideal. After the war, the realization that Europe could not compete with the superpowers strengthened the desire for unity, but the British favored loose, intergovernmental arrangements and opposed close political and economic integration because of their Commonwealth ties and special relationship with the United States. Continental statesmen, such as French Foreign Minister Robert Schumann and Italian Prime Minister Alcide De Gasperi, however, adopted a pragmatic approach to European unity by favoring strong but gradual economic integration that they hoped would eventually lead to political unification.

The Council of Europe

In contrast to their later recalcitrance, the British played a crucial role early in the development of European unity. In 1943 Winston Churchill advocated a Council of Europe as the concrete embodiment of a united Europe. In 1946 he reiterated his position, and European federalists organized a congress at the Hague in May 1948 at which representatives from sixteen countries called for political and economic unity and a European court. The Labour government (and Churchill) backed off and announced that they did not want membership in a united Europe but only an association with it. Foreign Minister Ernest Bevin warned against the dangers of integration that would bring interference in British domestic affairs by supranational agencies, economic control by continental countries, and a decline in Britain's standing. Nonetheless, the Hague Conference had enough support among the British people that in May 1949 the Labour government joined a new institution created there, the ten-nation Council of Europe.

European federalists, anxious to secure Britain's participation, agreed to a flawed council that was best exemplified by the contradictions of its two most important governing bodies. The Committee of Ministers, consisting of the foreign ministers of the member states or their representatives, met twice a year, represented the national interests of the member states, and opposed further attempts at political unity; the Consultative Assembly, named by the parliaments of member states, favored integration but could only make recommendations. Despite these shortcomings, representatives in the Consultative Assembly cooperated according to political persuasion, rather than national association, emphasizing common problems and solutions, and adopted many important resolutions, particularly those pertaining to civil rights and economic affairs. It encouraged collaboration in agriculture, transportation, culture, and the environment. By the 1980s the council had expanded to include most of West Europe, and in the 1990s Russia and several other Eastern European states joined it.

Marshall Plan Institutions

The Americans provided an important stimulus for economic integration by insisting that Marshall Plan aid be distributed in the most efficient manner possible. In April 1948, Marshall Plan recipients founded the Organization for European Economic Cooperation (OEEC) to distribute American aid, performing very well and establishing important associated agencies, such as the European Payments Union (EPU), to settle financial affairs related to European trade and contributing to the liberalization of commerce. Individual countries rarely turned down the OEEC's recommendations, which were backed by the full weight of Western Europe's collective expertise. In 1960, the successful OEEC was transformed into the Organization for Economic Cooperation and Development (OECD), an agency concerned with the worldwide problems of industrial democracies that included non-Europeans.

The European Coal and Steel Community

The OEEC demonstrated that mutual collaboration could work over the short run, but the European Coal and Steel Community (ECSC) confronted the problems of long-term development and integration of crucial sectors. The brainchild of French Foreign Minister Robert Schuman and economist Jean Monnet, the ECSC put German and French steel production under a common authority and provided for membership for other European nations. Announced in May 1950, the plan had political in addition to economic objectives. Schuman intended to create a strong bond between the rapidly growing West Germany and France by eliminating trade barriers in all sectors but beginning with one crucial industry. In April 1952, the ECSC, consisting of France, West Germany, Italy, and the Benelux countries, came into existence. Britain refused to join.

The ECSC had important implications for the principle of a united Europe. Its executive body, the High Authority, charged with enforcing decisions, was not dominated by any one state, which made it the first supranational body with the power to implement policy in a crucial economic sector. The High Authority made its share of mistakes, but its operations convinced many Europeans that the road to political unity would gradually emerge from economic collaboration. This feeling made economic integration more acceptable, and in 1957

This cartoon from 1950 shows Western Europe crossing over a body of water on several stepping stones and heading toward "Recovery." The stones are labeled for the various postwar institutions, including NATO, the Marshall Plan, and the pooling of the coal and steel industries, i.e., the European Coal and Steel Community. The ECSC was an important forerunner of the European Economic Community.

the six ECSC countries signed the Treaty of Rome that brought the European Economic Community (EEC) into existence.

The European Economic Community

The European Economic Community (EEC) had a working model illustrating how economic collaboration might work and encouraging Europeans to undertake the formidable task of integrating a diverse continent: Benelux (Belgium, the Netherlands, and Luxembourg). However, in November 1954 the idea of a united Europe had passed through one of its periodic crises when Monnet announced his intention to resign from the High Authority because Europeans favored proposals made by the European Political Community (EPC) for the rapid political unification of Western Europe and economic integration. Monnet considered those plans too ambitious and had made a proposal for the pooling of European atomic energy efforts that had been rejected.

Shocked by Monnet's resignation, ECSC foreign ministers met at Messina (Sicily) in June 1955 and commissioned Belgian Foreign Minister Paul-Henri

Western European Economic Institutions

INSTITUTION	PURPOSE
Council of Europe	The embodiment of Europe through the *Committee of Ministers* (foreign ministers or their representatives) and the *Consultative Assembly* (representatives named by member states).
Organization for European Economic Cooperation (OEEC) and Organization for European Economic Cooperation and Development (OECD)	To distribute the American Marshall Plan aid and, after 1960, to examine worldwide problems of industrial democracies.
European Payments Union (EPU)	To settle financial affairs related to European trade.
European Coal and Steel Community (ECSC)	To foster European economic integration beginning with a crucial sector: steel. Decisions to be made by a supranational High Authority (members: France, Germany, Italy, Belgium, Luxembourg, and the Netherlands).
European Economic Community (EEC, later, with new members, the name was changed to the European Community (EC) and the European Union (EU)	To create a common market by gradually lowering and eventually eliminating tariff barriers among members and looking forward to an eventual political union. Political institutions include the Commission (the executive, with nine appointed members, France, Germany, and Italy appointing two each and the Benelux countries appointing one each) and the European Parliament, elected in the different member states.
European Free Trade Association (EFTA)	To create a free-trade area among the members (Britain, Norway, Sweden, Denmark, Switzerland, Austria, and Portugal).
General Agreement on Tariff and Trade (GATT)	To stabilize trade by seeking agreements on tariffs.

Spaak to report on the feasibility of creating a European Atomic Commission, as suggested by Monnet, and a Common Market. Spaak, a proponent of a united Europe, produced a report recommending the integration of the atomic energy sector *and* the complete economic integration of ECSC member states through the establishment of a common market, endorsed by the foreign ministers at Venice in May 1956. Britain had dropped out of the talks in November 1955, but France, its attention forced back to Europe by the Suez Crisis, supported the idea. In fact, international considerations hastened the desire for unity. Stalin's death on March 5, 1953, forced Western Europeans to think about a new world in which a USSR that appeared less threatening might convince the Americans to reduce their commitment to Europe, in which case the Europeans would be forced to rely on themselves. The 1956 Suez Crisis, in which the Americans forced the British and French to back down in their confrontation with Egypt after that country took over control of the Suez Canal, showed Europeans that the Americans would not automatically support them and that only by acting in concert could the Europeans hope to protect their vital interests.

On March 25, 1957, West Germany, Italy, and the Benelux countries, known as the Six, signed the Treaty of Rome, embodying the report, and in January 1958, the EEC and Euratom, an agency for atomic research, began operations.

The European Economic Community was the most successfully spectacular economic experiment of the postwar period. The EEC integrated the major European economies, a development that spurred tremendous economic growth and made other European countries anxious to join. Here are representatives of the original founders signing the EEC treaties in Rome on March 27, 1957: France, Germany, Italy, Belgium, the Netherlands, and Luxembourg.

The EEC's Objectives

The EEC aimed at removing trade restrictions; allowing free movement of labor and capital; and establishing common trade, investment, and social welfare policies. The Six could accomplish this tall order only gradually because the EEC had to make allowances for the enormous differences among its member states, a task that required time and flexibility. In order to overcome this difficulty, the EEC adopted clauses that permitted divergences because of special national circumstances. Agriculture was a particularly delicate area that would be handled according to both EEC principles and national interests, and it proved to be the most recalcitrant problem.

Agriculture presented a difficult long-term problem because in Western Europe, particularly in France and West Germany, small farming with high fixed costs had developed over the centuries. The volatile farmers were prone to violent action and had great political influence. Confronted with stiff competition from imported food and fodder, they were susceptible to the siren song of right-wing demagogues. Politicians remembered how German farmers supported the Nazis in the late 1920s and were instrumental in their rise. The story in France, where right-wing movements also appealed to small farmers, presented a similar danger.

Consequently, Western politicians were anxious to keep farmers happy, despite the economic inefficiency of their farms, in an effort to avoid political destabilization. In France, for example, farmers frequently attacked and overturned trucks bringing in cheap wine from Italy, another EEC member, and manifested through violent demonstrations their displeasure at proposed reforms that would change their way of life. In order to preserve peace, therefore, national governments and later the EEC subsidized farmers producing excess commodities, such as butter. These subsidies were the price of domestic peace, but agricultural problems caused continued wrangling among the EEC members, touched off frequent crises, and blocked the EEC's development.

BIOGRAPHICAL SKETCHES

Jean Monnet
Cognac and Europe

Jean Monnet was born in the French town of Cognac on November 9, 1888. In some ways typical of the narrow-minded mentality of the French countryside, Cognac also had an international flavor thanks to the influence of its famous brandy. People who were interested in importing cognac came to bargain, while local salesmen fanned out over the world to find markets. These activities stimulated the growth of the local business and fostered a mentality of discussion, negotiation, and compromise.

This world of business and international cooperation gave Jean Monnet his start. His father owned a cognac business, and Monnet began as a salesman. Monnet apparently aspired to nothing more than taking over the family business. He traveled to Britain, Scandinavia, Russia, Egypt, and North America, areas that fascinated him. In 1912, scheduled to travel to Canada, he narrowly missed booking passage on the *Titanic*.

In August 1914, World War I broke out, but Monnet was unable to fight because of a kidney ailment. The war had made the sharing of resources among the Allies crucial, but stubborn nationalistic pretensions of French statesmen complicated the process. Monnet presented practical solutions to the French prime minister himself, a typical move for a man who did not back away from taking on a difficult task. He negotiated a deal with the Hudson Bay Company with which, in 1911, he had worked out an agreement naming his concern its sole cognac supplier in western Canada. His unassuming ways and effectiveness became his hallmark and a major reason for his success in reaching agreements during this period and later, when he established the basis for a united Europe.

Following the conflict, Monnet served as deputy secretary-general of the League of Nations. In 1923, he returned to head the family cognac business, now on the verge of bankruptcy because of postwar dislocations. He refused to collect large commissions that he had earned from the Hudson Bay Company during wartime and instead asked it for a loan to save his company. Monnet put the business on a profitable basis and turned it over to a cousin—although he kept his shares and remained involved in the business for the rest of his life—and went to work in the banking sector. He became a millionaire, but lost his fortune during the depression. During World War II, he went to the United States and worked to arrange for the transfer of American arms to the Allies.

After the war, Monnet tackled an intractable problem: bringing the different European countries together in a United States of Europe. Never a politician, he worked behind the scenes and left the glory to others, which explains why his concept for the European Coal and Steel Community was called the Schuman Plan after the French foreign minister. Monnet reasoned that he could start the process toward European unity by persuading governments to give up a piece of their sovereignty—the coal and steel sector—that could bind the European nations together in a web of common interests. Monnet ("Mr. Europe") believed that if the ECSC succeeded, cooperation would extend to other areas of economic activity, and political unity would follow. The negotiations among countries that had been rivals for centuries proved extremely difficult, but Monnet successfully brought them to a conclusion. U.S. Assistant Secretary of State George W. Ball described Monnet's method as the equivalent of Blitzkrieg tactics in war—concentrate all available power on a narrow sector and break through. The troops could then spread out at their leisure and win the war. Monnet's narrow sector was coal and steel, and a united Europe was the objective.

Monnet's funeral, on March 20, 1979, symbolized the progress that Europe had made toward unity. During the Catholic service, classic pieces from each of the European Community's member states were played, but the strains of "The Battle Hymn of the Republic" joined them. That song epitomized Monnet's model for a unified Europe, the United States of America.

The need to shape the diverse political elements of the different countries into an organic governing structure presented the most complex challenge for the EEC's framers. The Rome Treaty established the Commission as the EEC's supranational executive body. Member governments appointed nine commissioners, with France, Italy, and West Germany entitled to two each and the smaller Benelux countries to one each. The Commission administered the EEC's daily affairs but had limited powers because it shared executive power with the Council of Ministers. The Council of Ministers had a complex voting system that allowed individual countries to hold up implementation of a policy if they disagreed with it. The treaty's framers did this consciously, believing that action based on consent would be more effective than coercion.

The Parliamentary Assembly, which soon changed its name to the European Parliament (EP), was the EEC's popular component. Elected in the different member countries, the EP represented a host of different interest groups. It was designed as a consultative and recommending body but had the power to dismiss the Commission on a two-thirds vote. An appointed Court of Justice rounded out the EEC governing structure. Composed of seven judges, this tribunal judged disputes between the member states. Implementation of its verdicts depended on the individual states, but the even-handedness of the court's decisions gained it so much prestige that no single state could resist its judgments.

The EEC's Success

The EEC's first years brought enormous economic achievements. The first scheduled tariff reductions occurred on January 1, 1959, and other cuts regularly followed. A Customs Union charged with creating a homogeneous economic area came into effect on July 1, 1968, eighteen months ahead of schedule. Business-people were confident that the Common Market and other measures mandated by the Treaty of Rome would occur, and trade among EEC members surged 50 percent from 1958 to 1960. High growth, roughly stable prices, and good bal-ance-of-payments regimes characterized the member nations. The EEC became a powerhouse on the world economic scene, extending its activities to the lesser-developed countries and to world-trade negotiations. In 1967, the Commission negotiated for the EEC on tariffs during the so-called Dillon and Kennedy Rounds of GATT (General Agreement on Tariffs and Trade). The desire of other countries to join or associate with the EEC was the most striking sign of its success. In the early 1960s, Britain abandoned the rival EFTA that it had established and applied for admission. In 1962, Greece associated with it, and in 1964 Turkey, seventeen African countries, and Madagascar reached association agreements.

This dynamism allowed the EEC to survive political crises in the 1960s, due primarily to the policies of General Charles de Gaulle, who wanted the commu-nity to be more independent of the United States. The crises sparked by de Gaulle included his veto of British application for membership in 1963, his unhappiness with the EEC's Common Agricultural Policy (CAP), his desire to use the EEC to assert European autonomy with regard to the United States, and his dramatic attempt to limit the Commission's powers. An election in 1965, however, dem-onstrated the limited domestic appeal of de Gaulle's EEC policy, and the general moved toward compromise before his resignation following disturbances in 1968. De Gaulle's exit, however, did not immediately produce major changes in France's negative attitude toward British membership. Under his successor, Georges Pom-pidou, the British question caused continual tension, but in 1970 the Six com-promised on an agricultural policy and a new budget. Euphoria followed, with agreement on the extension of political cooperation and rapid progress on the European Monetary Union (EMU).

Foreign Affairs and Enlargement

In fact, the new decade brought a crisis because of shifts in the balance of power among the member states, national politics, changing economics, and the oil crisis. The West German economy surged, transforming the Federal Republic of Germany into the EEC's driving force. Social Democrat Willy Brandt became chancellor and implemented a bold new foreign policy, *Ostpolitik*, which aimed at normal-izing West Germany's relations with the East European countries. In 1967, the executive bodies of the EEC, ECSC, and Euratom merged, creating the Economic Community (EC). Over the next several years, Brandt attempted to utilize the EC to further *Ostpolitik*. Friction resulted, complicated by issues related to a mon-etary union. Animosity replaced the amicable relationship between France and Germany, which had been established by de Gaulle and former West German Chancellor Konrad Adenauer. British membership remained another bone of con-tention among the EC members.

British Prime Minister Edward Heath pushed for British entry despite a firestorm of opposition in his own country. When negotiations came to a suc-cessful conclusion, Pompidou announced a French referendum on enlargement.

In truth the French leader had modified his opposition, and his move aimed at undermining lingering Gaullist sentiment against British entry, but the referendum encouraged EC opponents in England to redouble their opposition and prompted referendums on the question in Norway, Denmark, and Ireland, also applicants for admission. Heath avoided a referendum that he feared might go against him. In Norway, the EC went down to defeat, while the balloting in Denmark and Ireland gave positive results. On January 1, 1973, Britain, Denmark, and Ireland joined the EC.

Crisis and Survival

In October 1972, Pompidou hosted EC leaders in Paris. The leaders announced an ambitious new agenda, including their intention to transform the EC into the European Union (EU) by the end of the decade. An impressive list of initiatives accompanied this declaration, most rendered moot by the events of a turbulent decade. In May 1971, a serious monetary crisis occurred, caused by a decline in U.S. interest rates and the subsequent flight of investors from dollars into German marks. The Americans complained about *Ostpolitik* and the cost of maintaining troops in Europe at a time of financial difficulty. Brandt proposed concessions, which Pompidou opposed. In August, President Richard Nixon imposed trade restrictions and declared that the dollar would no longer be tied to the value of gold. In Europe, a slump followed, and disruption of the "snake," a system that kept European currencies fluctuating in relation to each other within a narrow band of 2.5 percent. The other major result was inflation, exacerbated by the Arab oil boycott prompted by the Middle East Yom Kippur war of October 1973 and the resultant dramatic rise in petroleum prices. Divisions deepened among the EC members and between the EC and Washington.

By 1973 the EC seemed mired in a deep crisis, but the situation suddenly changed. In 1974 Pompidou died unexpectedly, Brandt resigned because of a scandal, and Heath was voted out of office. The new British Prime Minister, Harold Wilson, opposed British membership and sought to renegotiate the terms of British entry. British influence within the EC plummeted, while France and Germany reestablished an axis under their new pro-EC chiefs, Valéry Giscard d'Estaing and Helmut Schmidt. Their leadership enabled the EC to survive the economic emergency of the 1970s and foreshadowed a robust revival in the 1980s.

The complex maneuvering within the EC stemmed from Western Europe's diverse and sometimes bewildering political universe. Parliamentary systems of government with many parties struggling for power characterized the democratic West. Except for England, this arrangement made complicated coalition politics the norm. In Northern Europe fewer parties competed than in the South, which also labored under the disadvantages of economic underdevelopment, more intense political infighting, and long-term dictatorships in Spain and Portugal. During the 1950s, 1960s, and 1970s, Western Europe's political forces battled over how to accommodate the social change that accompanied modernization and prosperity. France altered its political system, and Italy struggled with the question of allowing Socialists and Communists into the ruling coalition—running the risk of a military coup in the process. Britain passed through a period of instability. In Greece a

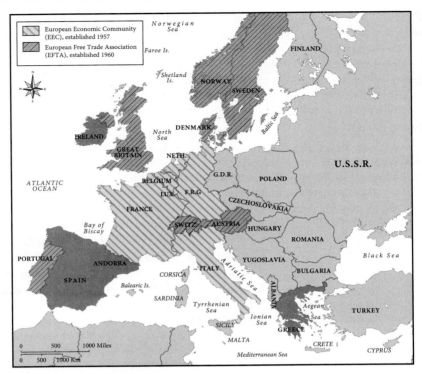

New Economic Organizations. The European Economic Community (EEC) became the new core of Europe, while the European Free Trade Association (EFTA) discussed in Chapter 23, was unsuccessful. Note the geographical dispersion of the EFTA countries and the territorial contiguity of the EEC.

military regime took power in 1967. Luckily, European political cooperation and economic integration favored a smoother transition than would otherwise have been the case.

THE COMMUNITY: NEW EUROPE'S CORE

The EEC's core members—the Federal Republic of Germany, France, and Italy—all achieved a measure of stability that permitted them to make enormous economic strides and to confront the turbulence of the 1970s. Their increasing strength allowed France and Germany to take important foreign policy initiatives. Italy was the most troubled, its political fragility reducing its foreign policy role.

The Federal Republic of Germany and the Achievement of Stability

The Federal Republic's Basic Law (constitution) took effect on May 24, 1949. The West Germans avoided the term *constitution* to emphasize their continuing commitment to reunification. Past German constitutional history and the goal of correcting political deficiencies that had been revealed during the Weimar period guided the Basic Law's framers. For this reason, the new government, based in Bonn, had a president and a parliament that looked quite different from their Weimar predecessors.

The lower house of parliament, the Bundestag, not the people, elected the president for a five-year term. The office had only nominal powers, with real power residing with the chancellor and cabinet. In order to prevent dangerous periods without a government, as had happened in Weimar, the Bundestag could not vote a chancellor out of office without designating a successor. This "constructive no confidence" was bolstered by another mechanism favoring stability. If the chancellor asked for a vote of confidence and did not receive it, he or she could ask the president to dissolve the chamber. The prospect of new elections and perhaps losing their seats made members of the Bundestag more cautious about bringing down governments than their Reichstag predecessors had been.

The overwhelming concern for stability appeared in electoral mechanisms. When electing the Bundestag, West German citizens voted for a candidate and for a party on the same ballot. In the first case, the person who received the most votes won. In the second, the parties chose the persons to sit in the Bundestag. Seats were allocated to parties based on proportional representation, but in order to avoid the political splintering characteristic of Weimar, a party had to win at least 5 percent of the vote. The Basic Law recognized the Bundestag as the primary law-making body but also instituted an upper house, the Bundesrat, representing individual states, to check its power.

Konrad Adenauer and the Christian Democratic Union

These devices stabilized German politics. From September 1949 to October 1963, Konrad Adenauer and his Christian Democratic Union (CDU)—Catholic, but with considerable Protestant support—were in power. Helping their victory were women, who, as in France and Italy, were more likely to vote Christian Democratic than men, and who helped account for CDU electoral victories between 1949 and the mid-1950s. Despite criticism of Adenauer's so-called chancellor democracy, he posed no danger for German democratic government, and in later years his support declined. In 1957 his party won an absolute majority, but in 1961 he was forced to enter a coalition with the small Free Democratic Party (FDP). In 1962 the defense minister, Franz-Josef Strauss, attacked a leading newsmagazine for an article exposing the weakness of German forces participating in a NATO exercise. Adenauer strongly supported Strauss, head of the powerful Christian Social Union (CSU), but the FDP forced Adenauer to accept retirement. Ludwig Erhard, father of the economic miracle, replaced him, but he proved to be unlucky. The economy stalled, and his foreign policy problems with the United States, Israel, and the Arabs prompted the FDP to force him out of office in December 1966.

The CDU's extraordinary longevity in power had important repercussions among the leftist opposition and contributed to German political stability. Concluding that it had little chance of coming to power if it clung to its Marxist ideology, the Social Democratic Party (SPD) officially abandoned Marxism and espoused welfare liberalism at Bad Godesberg in 1959.

BIOGRAPHICAL SKETCHES

Konrad Adenauer
Senior Statesman

Konrad Adenauer's life spanned German history from Bismarck's Reich to Hitler's, but his career came to full fruition after World War II. Then, as an old man of 72, he led his country's economic and moral recovery and won for it renewed respect as one of Europe's prominent nations.

Konrad Adenauer was born into a poor Catholic family on January 5, 1876. His father, also named Konrad, fought in the wars of German unification and received a battlefield commission. He left the army because the woman he loved did not bring him a dowry, which was necessary for an officer's social status in the Prussian army; afterward he worked as a clerk in a district court.

His son, born in the great Rhineland City of Cologne, studied law on a scholarship. Adenauer imbibed the Rhineland's political and social climate, more liberal than Prussia's, which helps account for his conviction that Germany was an integral part of the West and should be fully integrated into it.

A morose, highly religious, and unflappable man noted for his ironic sense of humor, Adenauer married Emma Weyer, an attractive young woman from an affluent family, in January 1904. His political career also took off. A member of the Catholic Center Party, he won election to the city council on March 7, 1906. Adenauer's sober debating style, command of the facts, and dedication to work brought him to prominence. During World War I, with Germany under a blockade, he took charge of Cologne's food supplies and made certain that its citizens had enough to eat. During the summer of 1917, when his chauffeur fell asleep at the wheel, Adenauer was involved in an accident that broke his nose and cheekbones, crushed his jaw, and knocked out several teeth, giving him his strange physical appearance in later life. While he was recovering, two city councilors visited him, assured themselves that his mental facilities were intact, and asked him to run for mayor.

Elected on October 18, 1917, Adenauer ran Cologne like an autocrat, but very successfully. He achieved national prominence, and in 1926 the Center Party considered him as a possible chancellor. His personal life also changed with Emma's death on October 16, 1916, and his marriage to Auguste (Gussi) Zinzer, eighteen years younger, on September 25, 1919.

Adenauer stayed on as mayor until the Nazis removed him in March 1933. He narrowly escaped death on the Night of the Long Knives, June 30, 1934. During the rest of the Nazi period, he remained inactive politically, which did not prevent the Gestapo from arresting him after the failed July 1944 assassination attempt against Hitler. As the Nazis prepared to send him to Buchenwald, Adenauer luckily escaped, was recaptured, and then released.

The Americans reinstalled him as mayor of Cologne, but the British military authorities removed him and banned him from political activity. Adenauer interpreted the British action as Labour support for the German Social Democrats and distrusted the British thereafter. His removal as mayor, however, allowed him to focus on national instead of local politics. Adenauer participated in the creation of a new Catholic party, the Christian Democratic Union (CDU), and by 1948, at age 72, he had achieved firm control of the new organization. Against all predictions, he led the CDU to victory in the crucial elections of August 1949 and established a coalition government. Responding to sensitivity about his age, Adenauer suggested that he could serve as chancellor for two years. He stayed for fourteen years, presiding over West Germany's economic miracle, rearmament, European integration, and return to full sovereignty. In 1963, at age 87, he was edged out of power and remained bitter against his own party. He was bored in retirement. On April 19, 1967, death finally claimed Adenauer, a father of the new Europe and the greatest German chancellor since Bismarck.

The Social Democratic Party and Ostpolitik

In 1963, the mayor of West Berlin, Willy Brandt, took over as Socialist leader and injected a new dynamism into the party. Erhard's fall gave him the opportunity to negotiate the Grand Coalition, an SPD, CDU, CSU cabinet. With this agreement, the Socialists participated in the government for the first time since the 1930s, with Brandt serving as vice chancellor. What is more significant, the Grand Coalition foreshadowed a Socialist government. Brandt called for a new West German foreign policy seeking improved relations between the Federal Republic, the Soviet Union, East Germany, and Eastern Europe—*Ostpolitik*. Brandt's initiative proved extremely popular because many West Germans had relatives living in the East and yearned for greater contact with them. In October 1969, Brandt won the office of chancellor, allowing him to implement his foreign policy ideas and proving that in West Germany there could be a normal alternation of political power.

Brandt's *Ostpolitik* produced tensions within the EEC and with the Americans, but it did improve relations with the East. West Germany signed treaties with the USSR and Poland in 1970 and, most important, a landmark agreement with East Germany in 1972. By 1973, relations had improved to such an extent that both the Federal Republic and the GDR entered the UN. *Ostpolitik* signaled not only reduced tensions with the East but, equally important, German resumption of an autonomous role in European affairs.

West German Economic Success

West Germany's dazzling economic success, based on state action and labor peace, underpinned this expanded role. The Federal Bank and the ministries of Finance and Economics cooperated in making economic policy. Determined to avoid inflation of the kind that had brought down the Weimar Republic, these institutions imposed a hard money policy and instantaneously reacted against the slightest whiff of inflation, frequently irritating West Germany's economic partners. German officials made unpopular but correct decisions, closing inefficient plants and temporarily increasing unemployment to fight inflation.

Labor's cooperation was crucial for the country's economic revitalization. Its highly centralized structure discouraged strikes and reinforced governmental policies. The major German unions belonged to the German Federation of Trade Unions (DGB), and all went along when a wage agreement was reached in an industry. Workers who were unhappy with settlements would not strike because they received no support from the DGB unions. The resulting labor peace benefited employers and production, and workers could be certain that no labor category (except immigrant workers) would be left behind as the country progressed.

These policies, the capacity of the German people, and West Germany's natural resources made the country the economic powerhouse of Europe.

The Federal Republic's startling material success ironically contributed to an increasing malaise among the country's intellectuals and youths, who had no ideals to believe in. As the 1960s progressed, opposition to the Vietnam War, the disarmament movement, and environmental concerns energized them, as occurred in other West European countries. German youths who did not remember the physical destruction of World War II believed that economic progress had been made at the cost of stifling spiritual values. Brandt's Grand Coalition also had a negative role because, with the former leftist opposition now firmly entrenched in the establishment, young people had no way to express their alienation within the political system. Many turned to the Marxism that had been rejected by the SPD but that the philosophers of the Frankfurt Institute had revived. As in Italy, the most extreme elements considered themselves Maoists—violent revolutionaries influenced by Chinese leader Mao Zedong—rejecting both Soviet communism and the fashionable Eurocommunism of Western European Communist parties. Political unrest and demonstrations culminated in riots in May 1968, and the government took countermeasures. Then a serious terrorist movement led by the notorious Red Army Faction shook the country in the 1970s. Germans fretted about the ability of their democracy to survive, but as in the rest of Western Europe, terrorism was defeated, and many revolutionaries of 1968 channeled their energies into more conventional politics.

Instability in France

Unlike the Germans, the French restored their traditional political structure in 1946 after a more ambitious governmental reorganization plan went down to defeat. The Fourth Republic closely resembled the Third, with short-lived governments following each other in rapid succession. If the Fourth Republic was politically unstable, however, it made important economic innovations. It continued the nationalization of major economic sectors initiated by the provisional government in the war years of 1944 and 1945 and instituted economic planning. Governmental commissions and experts set general guidelines, production, and investment targets and successfully enforced them because the government controlled enough of the French economy to persuade the industrialists to go along. Industry benefited more than workers from planning. Unlike West Germany, the French labor movement was split into Communist, Socialist, and Catholic unions that called numerous strikes. Unrest was also endemic in the rural areas, where governmental policies favoring mechanization and the consolidation of small landholdings into larger ones caused resentment. The peasants fled the land for the cities, putting pressure on the educational, health, and political structures of the urban areas. The cost of reconstruction and France's desire to maintain its world position stimulated unrest by straining the budget. The franc had to be devalued and taxes increased, but no significant reform of the antiquated tax system accompanied these measures. The results were inflation, strikes, and an increase in French Communist strength.

Charles De Gaulle, leader of the Free French during World War II, left politics in 1946 because party leaders refused to create a strong presidency. He returned to power in 1958 after a military revolt caused by the widening war in Algeria and because the French Army supported him. De Gaulle founded the Fifth Republic, which stabilized the country. He then worked to increase France's influence in the world through an active foreign policy and advocacy of a "Europe of the Fatherlands" that irritated the Americans. This photograph shows De Gaulle making a speech in favor of his new constitution on August 23, 1958.

What finally ended the Fourth Republic, however, was a revolution against French colonialism in Algeria, brilliantly portrayed in Gillo Pontecorvo's film *The Battle of Algiers*. The French had a strong emotional attachment to Algeria because it was an old colony with a large French population. The unstable French political system broke down when popular opposition to the war increased as a result of the dispatch of draftees to fight the war. In 1958, French army chiefs seized power in Algeria and called for the return of General Charles de Gaulle. The revolt spread, forcing parliament to give in. De Gaulle demanded and received the right to rule by decree for six months and to propose constitutional reforms directly to the people in the form of a referendum.

Charles de Gaulle and the Fifth Republic
In 1946, de Gaulle left politics because the parties refused his demand for a strong executive. In 1958, this provision was a prominent part of his proposed constitution.

His plan called for a strong president with the right to name the prime minister, dissolve parliament under certain conditions, and rule during emergencies. The constitution originally called for the president to be elected by parliament and other high officials, but a 1962 amendment allowed for direct popular election of the president, further strengthening the prestige of the office. Parliament consisted of a popularly elected National Assembly and an indirectly elected Senate that would check the lower house. The premier needed the National Assembly's confidence to rule. In order to minimize debate over the constitutionality of laws, a Constitutional Council examined important legislation before it went into effect. The constitution also restructured overseas France. In October 1958, a popular referendum accepted the constitution that established the Fifth Republic. De Gaulle made the referendum a durable feature of the new republic, but, despite this element of direct democracy and the problem of cohabitation (a president of one party, a prime minister of a different one), the Fifth Republic proved remarkably stable.

This stability allowed de Gaulle and his successors to follow dynamic domestic and foreign policies. De Gaulle pursued modernization through economic planning. The French economy continued its impressive growth, although at a slower pace than the German and the Italian. Like his predecessors, de Gaulle favored big industry, a policy against which peasants and workers continued to protest. Growing restiveness fueled the growth of the leftist political opposition, but the more moderate Socialist Party overtook the Communists during the Gaullist era as the strongest party on the left. In 1967, the leftist candidate François Mitterrand exposed de Gaulle's political vulnerability by forcing him into a runoff election for president.

The 1968 Disorders in France

In March 1968, disorders exploded among university students led by Daniel Cohn-Bendit ("Danny the Red") and culminated in May. The students demanded the implementation of long-delayed educational reforms and facilitation for employment after graduation. Workers joined them because they had not participated fully in the country's economic prosperity and demanded a forty-hour workweek, retirement at age 60, and a guaranteed wage. De Gaulle first ensured the army's loyalty, then promised educational reforms and a 35 percent increase in minimum wages. This latter pledge contributed to the rapid deflation of the demonstrations, soon replaced by spontaneous pro-government demonstrations. De Gaulle dissolved parliament, handily won new elections, and proposed new reforms to the country though a referendum. His easy victory over the demonstrators, however, made him overconfident. DeGaulle announced that he would quit if the country did not support him, and when he lost the vote by a small margin, he resigned on April 27, 1969.

Despite the fear of instability, De Gaulle's successors Pompidou and Giscard d'Estaing established stable governments, and the Fifth Republic proved that it could take political change in stride. Pompidou died suddenly in April 1974, and Giscard, an independent republican, won the presidential election and finished out his term in 1981. These two presidents ruled during the oil crisis and strong inflation that confronted Europe with serious problems and the strenghening the leftist opposition. Giscard implemented measures favoring the workers, but these measures proved inadequate, and in 1981 Mitterrand was elected president.

French Foreign Policy

De Gaulle's return signaled a new dynamism in French foreign policy. Although DeGaulle favored European unity, he believed that each country should maintain full autonomy in what he called "Europe of the Fatherlands." He thought that France should have the leading role in this revitalized and independent Europe and, through Europe, the world. He refused to follow the American lead in certain circumstances and seized the initiative in European matters by strengthening France's ties with Adenauer and shunning the British as too different and pro-American. In 1963, this policy culminated in a treaty of cooperation between France and West Germany.

De Gaulle had a difficult relationship with the Americans. In the 1960s, he gradually withdrew from NATO because he opposed American domination, although France retained close ties with the Atlantic Alliance. Because de Gaulle argued that the United States would not risk a nuclear holocaust on behalf of the Europeans, he forged ahead with an independent French nuclear strike force, the *force de frappe*. De Gaulle also contested U.S. policy in Vietnam, rejected claims that France's membership in the Southeast Asia Treaty Organization (SEATO) implied any military commitment, and ceased to participate actively in the alliance. To the Americans' chagrin, he improved relations with the USSR and recognized Communist China.

The Kennedy administration feared that de Gaulle might find emulators in other European countries and scrambled to blunt his influence, but de Gaulle was firmly committed to the West. He supported the United States during the 1962 Cuban missile crisis and assisted in the negotiations to find a solution to the Vietnam War. In Europe, his strong positions had many supporters, and his openness toward the eastern bloc favored a reduction of tensions.

Italian Political Paralysis

De Gaulle's ideas found a favorable echo among some Italian leaders who hoped to bring the country out of its political paralysis.

The postwar Italian constitution that went into effect on January 1, 1948, restored the parliamentary system on the pre-Fascist model. In order to avoid another dictatorship, the framers reduced the powers of the executive, but political divisions prevented them from adopting safeguards to prevent instability as the West Germans had done. A president elected by parliament for seven years had nominal powers, although frequent political stalemates conferred greater powers on the office than was provided for in the constitution. The cabinet required a majority vote of confidence in both the Chamber of Deputies and the Senate. These bodies, elected by popular vote, including women for the first time, had little to distinguish them. A party did not have to win a minimum percentage for representation in parliament, and after 1948 none received a majority. Easy representation favored the proliferation of small parties and caused political instability because cabinets depended on coalitions of four or more parties whose internal policies were determined by combinations of many currents within them. Until the extraordinary conditions that confronted the country in 1992 and 1993, it proved impossible to alter this "pure" proportional representation because of the historical memory of the Acerbo law that had changed proportional representation and contributed to Mussolini's dictatorship.

Another factor made a difficult problem worse. The Italian Communist Party (PCI) attracted a large number of votes, eventually winning about a third of the total. Because of the cold war, Italian fear of a Communist takeover, American opposition to Communist participation in a cabinet, and Italy's strategic importance to NATO, the party could not participate in governmental coalitions. In addition, until 1960, the Italian Socialist Party (PSI) was closely allied with the Communists. Since Communist (and Socialist, until 1962) votes could not be utilized in forming governmental coalitions, the largest non-Communist party, the Christian Democratic (DC), ruled in conjunction with small parties. The result: In Italy there could be no alternation of power because the largest opposition party that might have served as the nucleus of a new governing coalition was frozen out of the government. Consequently, the DC remained in power continuously

President John F. Kennedy imparted a new momentum to American foreign policy, of which support for a Center-Left government in Italy was only one example. He aimed to contrast De Gaulle's "Europe of the Fatherlands" and supported the Center-Left as a model for the future.

for over forty years. This predicament favored corruption and, in turn, increased pressure for changes that could not occur and that increased the probability that opponents would seek political solutions outside the system. The PCI sought a way out of the dilemma by augmenting internal democratization, loosening its ties with the Soviet Union, and searching for an accommodation with the DC, but the changes came too slowly and alienated many young people who believed that the Communists had sold out to the establishment and who turned to terrorism.

Although the DC continued in power, it lost votes throughout the 1950s. By the end of the decade, support for its centrist coalition (Liberals, Republican, and Social Democrats in addition to DC) had declined to the point that the coalition required either rightist neo-Fascist (Italian Social Movement, MSI) or leftist PSI help to remain in power. Internal fights on this issue took place among DC factions, and serious riots occurred in 1960 when a Christian Democrat accepted MSI votes for his cabinet.

The Kennedy Administration and the Opening to the Left

The disorders excluded an opening to the right, but important DC leaders and some smaller parties tenaciously opposed an opening to the left with the Socialists. The Eisenhower administration supported these opponents, but President John F. Kennedy favored the opening to the left through his adviser Arthur M. Schlesinger, Jr., in order to broaden the governing coalition, end opposition to reform, secure more labor support for the government, weaken de Gaulle's appeal, and sap the Communists' electoral strength. Kennedy considered the center left as a possible political model for a post–de Gaulle France, a post-Adenauer Germany, and for Latin America.

Despite Kennedy's support, the center left came to fruition slowly because of staunch opposition in the U.S. State Department and on the Italian right and extreme left. In 1964, an organic center-left cabinet took office under DC leader Aldo Moro, but a governmental crisis later induced the Socialists to drop demands for their most important reforms because Socialist leader Pietro Nenni feared that a military coup d'état was in the wings if he did not agree to participate in a government without insisting on a strong reform program. The Socialists' willingness to drop their demands short-circuited the coup, but the PSI was stuck in governments that offered no realistic hope of reform, giving the Communists an opening to charge that the Socialists had betrayed Marxist principles and eroding the Socialist electoral base.

Disorder and Terrorism

In 1967, disenchantment with the political system spilled into the streets, with students occupying the universities and demanding radical educational and social reforms that could not be implemented because of the political stalemate. Workers, whose low salaries had financed the Italian economic miracle, joined them in demonstrations that culminated in May 1968 and in the "hot autumn" of 1969 when a massive wave of strikes swept the country. Despite concessions and the passage of a model labor law, the strikes continued for years. The increased expenses and budget deficits that were intensified by the exorbitant increase in the cost of social programs and petroleum imports touched off fifteen years of double-digit inflation. Unrest generated terrorism, heralded by a bomb placed in a Milanese bank that killed fifteen people. Armed terrorist groups of the left and the right roamed the country planting bombs and kneecapping executives; this wave of terror culminated in the kidnapping and murder of former Prime Minister Aldo Moro in 1978 by the Red Brigades.

Eurocommunism

PCI leader Enrico Berlinguer tried to calm the dangerous political situation by proposing a pact between communism and Catholicism, the "historic compromise." The Italian Communists claimed to drop the concept of the dictatorship of the proletariat and to accept coming to power through democratic means. Berlinguer founded "Eurocommunism," joint action independent of Moscow by European Communist parties; this idea and his acceptance of NATO riveted the world's attention on the Italian Communists. In 1978, the Italian Communists supported the government coalition in order to stabilize Italian politics, but the administration of President Jimmy Carter publicly announced its opposition. At the same time, Moro's kidnapping threw the country into a crisis. PCI aid for the governing coalition was the high point of its influence, but extreme leftists accused it of selling out. When the PCI proved unable to reform the political system, its popularity dropped, and it lost vote share even after it distanced itself from the ruling coalition. When Berlinguer died prematurely on June 11, 1984, the party lost its most competent leader. Even after the police broke the terrorist threat to the state, Italian politics limped along with the DC dominating governing coalitions until the cold war's end, and a widespread corruption scandal after 1992 altered the Italian political scene.

The Italian Economic Miracle

If paralysis characterized Italian politics, dynamism marked the country's economic development, guided by the Bank of Italy's steady hand. Italy's export-led growth rate ranked among the highest in the world in the 1950s and 1960s. The tremendous economic expansion transformed the country from a backward agricultural nation into a leading world industrial power. Led by state industry, large private companies such as Fiat, and highly efficient small industrial concerns, Italy's gross domestic product surpassed Britain's and caught up to France's (if the underground economy was counted). Per capita production and wage figures approached those of the most advanced European countries, Italians ceased to emigrate, and the country developed a shortage of skilled labor beginning in the 1980s. The country soon confronted the reverse dilemma that was common to Western Europeans: immigrants flocking to Italy hoping for a better life.

The country's political problems, however, hampered its economic development. Strikes paralyzed production, and labor legislation that was passed in response to political unrest proved too liberal and encouraged absenteeism. The government's attempts to solve the problem of the underdeveloped South, with its high unemployment and its Mafia influence, failed, and the North pulled further ahead. Southerners and rural inhabitants streamed into northern cities, causing overcrowding, land speculation, environmental decay, pollution, a strain on social services, bad relations with the urban population, and tensions between the North and South. Disorders forced successive governments to permit easier access to universities, but the infrastructure could not handle the increase; overcrowding, the lack of professors, and inefficiency produced strife that lasted for decades. Public services remained inefficient because of the excessive bureaucracy, and progress toward autonomous regions and decentralization was slow.

The Benelux Countries—Political and Economic Progress

Of the Benelux countries, Belgium ran the greatest risk of political instability after World War II. The Belgians criticized the monarchy because of King Leopold III's surrender to the Germans during the war, and only Leopold's abdication in favor of his son Baudouin in 1951 saved it. This left three major issues—Flanders, the schools, and the Congo. Parliament dealt with Flanders in legislation passed in 1962, 1970, and 1980, establishing linguistic and cultural parity between Flemings and Walloons, but the problem remained intractable. With regard to the schools, a 1959 education law establishing the equality of subsidies for church and state institutions provoked protest, but it removed the disabilities under which the secular schools had long labored. In colonial affairs, the Congo's demand for independence threatened Belgian residents and economic interests there, and when the Congo became independent in 1960, the resulting disorder caused an international crisis.

On the positive side, Belgium was highly industrialized and enjoyed a strategic geographic position and excellent transportation facilities. These factors and its support for a European union established Brussels as the center of the European government.

The Netherlands reestablished a monarchical government smoothly under Queen Wilhelmina, but economic recovery came slower than in Belgium, although some firms, such as Shell and Philips (electronics), remained among the largest in Europe. The discovery of natural gas deposits in the North Sea increased the supply of natural resources and bolstered the economy. In the 1970s, the Dutch became notable for their advanced social outlook and their tolerance for unconventional lifestyles, but social welfare policies put a strain on the economy and increased taxes.

Luxembourg responded to the decline of its steel industry by encouraging the influx of large banking enterprises. The Grand Duchy became a haven for firms seeking favorable financial treatment and became Europe's third largest banking area.

The three countries created an economic union that came into being on January 1, 1948. Benelux favored the gradual establishment of free trade among its members and the construction of a common external tariff. In November 1960, the three agreed to end tariff restrictions, diminish tax differences, permit the free movement of labor, and institute common trade and payments policies. They also created common institutions and decision-making procedures that served as a model for the EEC.

ASSOCIATED COUNTRIES

As the EEC expanded beyond its six core members, it ran into the problem of considering for membership countries that were economically less advanced and ruled by undemocratic regimes. In such cases, it used its economic clout to encourage democracy.

The Greek Dictatorship

The Greek case best illustrated this policy. Following the civil war in which communism was defeated, American aid helped stabilize Greece, and the country joined NATO in 1952. In 1962, Greece successfully negotiated an association with the EEC, but the stationing of NATO troops in Greece and the West's lack of support for the country's claims to Cyprus kept politics volatile. Cyprus, an island off the Turkish coast with a mostly Greek population, was claimed by both Greece and Turkey. At the same time, feuding between Greek politicians and King Constantine II produced continuous crises. These struggles resulted in a military coup in 1967 by Greek colonels using a NATO contingency plan.

The Greek military regime stifled democracy and pursued a nationalistic policy on Cyprus. Its aggressiveness brought Greece and Turkey close to war and later precipitated a Turkish invasion and the partition of the island between the Greeks and Turks. The colonels' repressive activities turned both the United States and the West Europeans against them. The EC suspended its association agreement with Athens, and this economic and political pressure contributed to the collapse of the regime in 1974, after which the EC reinstated the agreement. The new democratic government applied for full membership in the EC, but the Commission turned it down on economic grounds in January 1976. The Council of Ministers, however, supported the Greek request both as a reward for the country's reentering the democratic fold and as an encouragement to remain there.

The Turkish Question

The case of another associate member, Turkey, was not so clear-cut. Between the wars, Kemal Ataturk attempted to transform Muslim Turkey into a modern secular Europeanized state. Threatened by the USSR after World War II, Turkey joined NATO in 1952. Extensive U.S. aid stimulated economic growth and modernization that brought in its wake the migration of a large number of peasants into the cities and abroad, social problems, and heavy indebtedness to the West. The resulting political turmoil produced an oppressive government in 1953 and a military regime between 1960 and 1961. Continued turbulence brought about a fresh military takeover in 1980, followed by the restoration of civilian rule and new disorders. The EC once again attempted to exploit its economic clout to force political reform. In the late 1980s, it blocked protocols to the Turkish association agreement on the grounds of human rights violations. Turkey was constantly turned down for membership until 1999, when it was finally promised admission, although exactly when was unclear. The EC alleged human rights transgressions, political instability, and economic weakness as reasons, but the Turks alleged discrimination on religious grounds.

The Turkish case raised a crucial question. As the EC became more successful and diverse countries applied for membership, how would it accommodate applicants that were increasingly different from the community's European founders?

Bibliographical Essay

On NATO, Lawrence S. Kaplan's *NATO 1948* (Lanham, Md., 2007) examines the alliance's birth and the American decision to abandon its traditional military isolation. John C. Milloy, *The North Atlantic Treaty Organization, 1948–1957: Community or Alliance?* (Ithaca, N.Y., 2006), is an examination of NATO's formative years. William Park's *Defending the West: A History of NATO* (Boulder, Colo., 1986) is a good, brief history, emphasizing the role of nuclear weapons. André Beaufre, *NATO and Europe* (New York, 1960), gives a good history from the European perspective into the 1960s, while Klaus Knorr, ed., *NATO and American Security* (Princeton, N.J., 1959), provides the American vision. Morton A. Kaplan, *The Rationale for NATO* (Washington, D.C., 1973), gives an interpretive history of NATO's development in a world context. James L. Richardson, *Germany and the Atlantic Alliance: The Interaction of Strategy and Politics* (Cambridge, Mass., 1966), presents the German context and a comprehensive examination of strategy and politics. Two works provide the cold war perspective: John J. McCloy, *The Atlantic Alliance: Its Origins and Its Future* (New York, 1969), three lectures by the former U.S. military governor and high commissioner for Germany, and Lawrence S. Kaplan, ed., *NATO and the Policy of Containment* (Lexington, Mass., 1968), a collection of different views. Andreas Wenger et al., *Transforming NATO in the Cold War* (New York, 2007), brings the alliance into the 1960s. Stanley R. Sloan, *NATO, the European Union, and the Atlantic Community* (Lanham, Md., 2002) discusses NATO's later development.

On the founders of a united Europe, see Sherrill Wells, *Pioneers of European Integration and Peace, 1945–1963* (Boston, 2007). Emile Benoit, *Europe at Sixes and Sevens: The Common Market, the Free Trade Association, and the United States* (New York, 1961), is a good general history. W. O. Henderson, *The Genesis of the Common Market* (Chicago, 1962), takes the long view of the efforts toward European economic unity, going back to the late eighteenth century. Ian Davidson, *Britain and the Making of Modern Europe* (New York, 1971), analyzes the British position.

European integration has been much studied. Mark Gilbert's *European Integration: A Concise History* (Lanham, Md., 2012), a revised and updated edition of a book the author published in 2003 gives a balanced overview of the subject.   Derek W. Urwin's *The Community of Europe* (London, 1995) is a history of the subject since 1945. John Gillingham, *European Integration, 1950–2003: Superstate or New Market Economy?* (New York, 2003), asks an interesting question. For nontechnical works, see Melvyn B. Krauss, ed., *The Economics of Integration* (London, 1973), a collection of readings on selected topics.. F. Roy Willis, ed., *European Integration* (New York, 1975), takes a wide perspective on integration. Leon N. Lindberg, *The Political Dynamics of European Integration* (Stanford, Calif., 1963), investigates some features of the EEC's experience during its first four years. Leon Hurwitz, ed., *Contemporary Perspectives on European Integration* (Westport, Conn., 1980), presents the issues of integration at various levels, including political, governmental, and legal. G. R. Denton, ed., *Economics and Integration in Europe* (London, 1969), is a collection of papers examining various problems of economic integration in the EEC and EFTA. Paul Taylor's *The Limits of European Integration* (New York, 1983) emphasizes the limits placed on cooperation by the various member governments, while Allan M. Williams looks at the contradictions of integration in *The European Community* (Cambridge, Mass., 1994). Stephen George, *Politics and Policy in the European Community*, 2d ed. (New York, 1991), discusses the interplay between politics in the various countries and the struggle for European integration. Richard T. Griffiths,

Europe's First Constitution: the European Political Community, 1952–1954 (London, 2000), examines a significant aspect of European unity.

A. E. Walsh and John Paxton, *The Structure and Development of the Common Market* (London, 1968), presents a clear history of the EEC's beginnings and development. Stuart de la Mahotiére, *Towards One Europe* (Harmondsworth, UK, 1970), synthesizes the efforts at unity in the major areas of European endeavor. John Calmann, ed., *The Common Market* (London, 1967), is a very brief work on the basic issues confronting the early EEC. Desmond Dinan, *Ever Closer Union?* (Boulder, Colo., 1994), is a comprehensive work that discusses the problems and achievements of the movement to unite Europe. P. D. Dagtoglou, ed., *Basic Problems of the European Community* (Oxford, UK, 1975), presents contributions by different observers on institutional problems. J. Warren Nystrom and Peter Malof, *The Common Market: The European Community in Action* (New York, 1962), gives good profiles of the EEC and EFTA in a short work. Steven Joshua Warnecke, ed., *The European Community in the 1970s* (New York, 1972), provides papers on the crucial issues of the decade. Frances Nicholson and Roger East examine the early enlargement of united Europe: *From the Six to the Twelve* (Chicago, 1987). Roy H. Ginsberg, *The European Union in International Politics: Baptism by Fire* (Lanham, Md., 2001), gives the long-term picture, while Daniela Preda and Daniele Pasquinucci, *The Road Europe Travelled Along; the Evolution of the EEC/EU Institutions and Policies* (New York, 2010) sums it up.

Stephen George, ed., *Britain and the European Economic Community: The Politics of Semi-Detachment* (Oxford, UK, 1992), examines the reasons for Britain's diffidence toward Europe. On the ambiguous position of Britain toward a united Europe, consult N. Piers Ludlow, *Dealing with Britain: The Six and the First UK Application to the EEC* (New York, 1997); D. A. Gowland and Arthur Turner, *Reluctant Europeans; Britain and European Integration, 1945–1998* (New York, 2000); and Robert F. Dewey, *British National Identity and Opposition to Membership in Europe, 1961–63: The Anti-Marketeers* (New York, 2009). On the all-important question of a common agricultural police, see M. D. M. Franklin, *Joining the CAP: The Agricultural Negotiations for British Accession to the European Economic Community, 1961–1973* (New York, 2010). Richard Bailey, *The European Community in the World* (London, 1973), is an account of the EEC's impact on Britain's world position. Pascaline Winand, *Eisenhower, Kennedy, and the United States of Europe* (New York, 1993), discusses the American role. Arnold J. Zurcher, *The Struggle to Unite Europe, 1940–1958* (New York, 1958), puts the EEC in the context of a pan-European movement.

Armin Gruenbacker, *The Making of German Democracy: West Germany During the Adenauer Era, 1945–1955* (New York, 2010), examines the immediate postwar era. Alfred Grosser, *Western Germany* (London, 1955), is a brief treatment from division to rearmament. Fritz Erler, *Democracy in Germany* (Cambridge, Mass., 1965), is a series of lectures on the establishment of democracy in postwar Germany, including an analysis of the military and the SPD's role. Hans J. Morgenthau, ed., *Germany and the Future of Europe* (Chicago, 1951), presents a series of essays on Germany's institutions and future. Alistair Horne's *Return to Power: A Report on the New Germany* (New York, 1956) reports on West Germany's growth in the 1950s. Mark E. Spicka, *Selling the Economic Miracle: Reconstruction and Politics in West Germany, 1949–1957* (New York, 2007), links economics and politics. Richard Hiscocks, *The Adenauer Era* (Philadelphia, 1966), gives an appraisal of the Adenauer period, while Terence Prittie's *Konrad Adenauer 1876–1967* (Chicago, 1971) is a good biography. Marion Donhoff, *Foe into Friend: The Makers of the New Germany from Konrad Adenauer to Helmut Schmidt* (London, 1982), profiles the most important West German leaders of the postwar period. Karl W. Deutsch and Lewis J. Edinger, *Germany Rejoins the Powers: Mass Opinion, Interest Groups, and Elites in Contemporary German Foreign Policy* (Stanford, Calif., 1969), discusses the domestic influences on German foreign policy. *Ostpolitik* is examined by Julia Von Dannenbert, *The Foundations of Ostpolitik*

(New York, 2008); for a wider consideration, see William E. Griffith in *The Ostpolitik of the Federal Republic of Germany* (Cambridge, Mass., 1978). Pertti Ahonen, *After the Expulsion* (New York, 2003), is an examination of West German relations with Eastern Europe between 1945 and 1990. Charles Burdick, Hans-Adolf Jacobsen, and Winfred Kurszus, eds., *Contemporary Germany: Politics and Culture* (Boulder, Colo., 1984), is a collection of essays on politics, economics, and the arts.

For France, see *The Fourth Republic, 1944–1958* (Cambridge, UK, 2008), a general history by Jean-Pierre Rioux. Consult also Robert Gildea, *France Since 1945* (Oxford, UK, 1997), a handy, concise general history. Gordon Wright's *The Reshaping of French Democracy* (New York, 1970) describes the process of setting up the Fourth Republic and its early years up to 1947. Adam Steinhouse, *Workers' Participation in Post-Liberation France* (Lanham, Md., 2001), examines unions and the state. Irwin M. Wall, *The United States and the Making of Postwar France, 1945–1954* (Cambridge, UK, 1991), analyzes the American role. François Goguel, *France Under the Fourth Republic* (Ithaca, N.Y., 1952), is a good account of politics, economics, and constitutional issues. Philip M. Williams, *Wars, Plots and Scandals in Post-War France* (Cambridge, UK, 1970), deals with political scandals in the Fourth Republic and the Algerian War. Jean Lacouture, *Pierre Mendès-France* (New York, 1984), is a chronicle of the Fourth Republic through its most notable politician. Herbert Tint, *French Foreign Policy Since the Second World War* (New York, 1972), is a comprehensive account. C. L. Sulzberger's *The Test: De Gaulle and Algeria* (London, 1962) is the story of the Algerian crisis and the coming of de Gaulle. French communism is the subject of M. Adereth's *The French Communist Party: A Critical History (1920–1984), From Comintern to "The Colours of France"* (Manchester, UK, 1984), half of which is devoted to the postwar period. Anne Kriegel, *The French Communists: Profile of a People* (Chicago, 1968), emphasizes personnel and organization. The French Catholic movement is examined by R. E. M. Irving, *Christian Democracy in France* (Hoboken, N.J., 2010), a book from the origins of Christian Democracy to the Fifth Republic.

Nicholas Atkin wrote a general history of the republic that De Gaulle established, *The Fifth French Republic* (New York, 2005). Dorothy Pickles gives a clear explanation of the Fifth Republic's institutions and politics in *The Fifth French Republic: Institutions and Politics*, 3rd ed. (New York, 1966). David Scott Bell published two studies of politics under the presidentialism of the Fifth Republic from different angles: *Presidential Power in Fifth Republic France* (New York, 2000) and *Parties and Democracy in France: Parties Under Presidentialism* (Brookfield, Vt., 2000). Serge Berstain's *The Republic of De Gaulle, 1958–1969* (Cambridge, UK, 1993) is an analysis of the political, social, and economic changes during the period. In some ways, the Fifth Republic was synonymous with de Gaulle's life. There are many biographies, but consult the massive Jean Lacouture, *De Gaulle*, 2 vols. (New York, 1990–1992), and the more manageable but still comprehensive *The Last Great Frenchman: A Life of General de Gaulle* (New York, 1993) by Charles Williams. Julian Jackson, *Charles De Gaulle* (London, 2003), is by a noted scholar in the field. Jonathan Fenby's *The General* (New York, 2010) focuses on his saving of France. Jean Charlot instead focused on the Gaullist party and associated groups in *The Gaullist Phenomenon: The Gaullist Movement in the Fifth Republic* (New York, 1971). Daniel Singer, *Prelude to Revolution: France in May, 1968* (London, 1970), and Bernard E. Brown, *In Paris* (Morristown, N.J., 1974), are analyses of the French revolts of 1968. Daniel Cohn-Bendit and Gabriel Cohn-Bendit, *Obsolete Communism: The Left Wing Alternative* (New York, 1968), presents the ideas behind the 1968 revolt.

Philip Alexandre, *The Duel* (New York, 1972), is an account of the complex relationship between de Gaulle and Pompidou. J. R. Frears, *France in the Giscard Presidency* (London, 1982), gives an overview of Giscard's tenure. Sally Baumann-Reynolds, *François Mitterrand* (Westport, Conn., 1995), describes Mitterrand's life up to his election as French president.

On foreign policy issues, consult Anna Locher et al., *Globalizing De Gaulle* (Lanham, Md., 2010). Simon Serfaty, *France, de Gaulle and Europe* (Baltimore, Md., 1968), is a general description of the European policies of the Fourth and Fifth Republics. On de Gaulle and NATO, see Frédéric Bozo, *Two Strategies for Europe: De Gaulle, the United States, and the Atlantic Alliance* (Lanham, Md., 2000). Edward L. Morse, *Foreign Policy and Interdependence in Gaullist France* (Princeton, N.J., 1973), is an analysis of de Gaulle's foreign policy. Philip H. Gordon, *France, West Germany, and the Western Alliance* (Boulder, Colo., 1995), examines the relationship between the continent's two major powers from 1949. Wilfred L. Kohl's *French Nuclear Diplomacy* (Princeton, N.J., 1971) is a study of the origins and development of France's nuclear strike force.

Modern Italy has not been as well covered in English as have the other Western European countries. A general treatment may be found in the chapters on the postwar period in Spencer M. Di Scala, *Italy: From Revolution to Republic*, 4th ed. (Boulder, Colo., 2009). Roy Palmer Domenico published a good, concise book covering the major issues in postwar Italy: *Remaking Italy in the Twentieth Century* (Lanham, Md., 2002). Most of the important issues at the war's end are discussed in Stuart J. Woolf, *The Rebirth of Italy, 1943–1950* (London, 1972), a collection of essays. Another good collection of essays is Frank J. Coppa and Margherita Repetto-Alaia, *The Formation of the Italian Republic: Proceedings of the International Symposium on Postwar Italy* (New York, 1993). Elisa Carillo published a good biography of De Gasperi, *De Gasperi: The Long Apprenticeship* (Notre Dame, Ind., 1965). The American role in Italy is discussed by James Edward Miller, *The United States and Italy 1940–1950* (Chapel Hill, N.C., 1986), and John Lamberton Harper, *America and the Reconstruction of Italy, 1945–1948* (Cambridge, UK, 1986). The older H. Stuart Hughes, *The United States and Italy* (Cambridge, Mass., 1979), is readable and still useful.

Italian economic development is treated in a clear manner by Shepard B. Clough, *The Economic History of Italy* (New York, 1964), and by Vera Zamagni, *The Economic History of Italy, 1860–1990* (New York, 1993). Luigi De Rosa published *Italian Economic Development Since the Second World War* (Rome, 2008). Insights on economic planning may be gleaned from Joseph La Palombara, *The Politics of Planning* (Syracuse, 1966). John Clarke Adams and Paolo Barile, *The Government of Republican Italy* (Boston, 1966), is a detailed account, while David Hine's *Governing Italy: The Politics of Bargained Pluralism* (Oxford, UK, 1993) explains how the political system worked in practice. The country's complex politics may be followed in Norman Kogan, *A Political History of Italy: The Postwar Years* (New York, 1983). Frederic Spotts and Theodore Weiser, *Italy: A Difficult Democracy* (Cambridge, UK, 1986), is a good summary of Italian politics. Sidney Tarrow, *Democracy and Disorder: Protest and Politics in Italy 1965–1975* (New York, 1989), links unrest in Italy to similar movements in Europe and believes it strengthened Italian democracy.

Unfortunately, English-language scholars have not paid much attention to the Christian Democrats. The best books are the older Mario Einaudi and François Gaguel, *Christian Democracy in Italy and France* (Notre Dame, Ind., 1952), and Richard J. Webster, *Christian Democracy in Italy, 1860–1960* (London, 1961). Robert Leonardi and Douglas A. Wertman published *Italian Christian Democracy: The Politics of Dominance* (New York, 1989). See also the books cited in Chapter 27. Alexander de Grand wrote a general history of the left, *The Italian Left in the Twentieth Century: A History of the Socialist and Communist Parties* (Bloomington, Ind., 1989). On Italian communism, see Donald Blackmer, *Unity in Diversity: Italian Communism and the Communist World* (Cambridge, Mass., 1968); Donald Blackmer and Sidney Tarrow, *Communism in Italy and France* (Princeton, 1975); and Sidney Tarrow, *Peasant Communism in Southern Italy* (New Haven, Conn., 1967). The PCI's different nature is the subject of Giorgio Napolitano and Eric Hobsbawm, *The Italian Road to Socialism* (Westport, Conn., 1977). Stephen Hellman discusses the historic compromise in Turin in *Italian Communism in Transition: The Rise and Fall of the Historic*

Compromise in Turin (New York, 1988). The changes in Italian communism have been the subject of several books. See Donald Sassoon, *The Strategy of the Italian Communist Party from the Resistance to the Historic Compromise* (New York, 1981); Leonard Weinberg, *The Transformation of Italian Communism* (New Brunswick, N.J., 1995); and John Baker, *Italian Communism: The Road to Legitimacy and Autonomy* (Washington, D.C., 1989). For the Communists and religion in the Catholic country, see David I. Kertzer, *Comrades and Christians: Religion and Struggle in Communist Italy* (Cambridge, UK, 1980). Italian socialism has been analyzed by Spencer M. Di Scala, *Renewing Italian Socialism: Nenni to Craxi* (New York, 1988). The book discusses the American role in the opening to the left. The idea of the center-left as a model for other European and even Latin American countries is discussed in a taped interview of Arthur Schlesinger, Jr., with the author on June 25, 1985. The American ambassador to Italy who advised President Jimmy Carter on excluding the Communists from the ruling coalition published his memoirs: Richard N. Gardner, *Mission Italy: On the Front Lines of the Cold War* (Lanham, Md., 2005).

The Italian labor movement is examined by Maurice Neufeld, *Italy: School for Awakening Countries* (Ithaca, N.Y., 1961), and Joan Barkan, *Visions of Emancipation* (New York, 1984). Union strategy can be understood from Peter Lange, George Ross, and Maurizio Vannicelli, *Unions, Change, and Crisis* (London, 1982).

For the Benelux countries, see the book of essays by Robert J. Thornton et al., *Benelux: Integration and Individuality* (Bethlehem, Pa., 2008), and F. Gunther Eyck, *The Benelux Countries: An Historical Survey* (Princeton, N.J., 1959). On Belgium, there is John Fitzmaurice, *The Politics of Belgium: Crisis and Compromise in a Plural Society* (New York, 1983), a good discussion of economics, society, and government, in addition to politics. E. Ramon Arango, *Leopold III and the Belgian Royal Question* (Baltimore, Md., 1961), is a good analysis of the question that shook Belgium in the immediate postwar period. For the Dutch, consult Max Schuchart, *The Netherlands* (London, 1972), and Gerald Newton, *The Netherlands: An Historical and Cultural Survey* (London, 1978); both have good sections on the modern period. Richard T. Griffiths, ed., *The Economy and Politics of the Netherlands Since 1945* (The Hague, 1980), is a good survey of those topics. Helen Colijn, *Of Dutch Ways* (New York, 1980), concentrates on modern Dutch life. James Newcomer, *The Grand Duchy of Luxembourg* (New York, 1984), covers the period up to the 1980s.

On Greece, Evanthis Hatzivassiliou, *Greece and the Cold War: Front-Line State, 1952–1967* (New York, 2006), covers Greece from its accession to NATO to the taking of power by the colonels. Robert V. Keeley, *The Colonels' Coup and the American Embassy* (University Park, Pa., 2010) is an American diplomat's view. For the Greek colonels and their regime, see C. M. Woodhouse, *The Rise and Fall of the Greek Colonels* (New York, 1985). A good history of Turkey during this period is Feroz Ahmad, *The Making of Modern Turkey* (New York, 2002). Heinz Kramer, *A Changing Turkey* (Washington, D.C., 2000), is a comprehensive examination of Turkey's changing situation and its challenge for Europe and for the United States. Comparative histories of the Mediterranean dictatorships and their transformation into democracies are cited in the bibliography for Chapter 23.

✍

Failure of EFTA and Expansion of the European Community

CHAPTER OUTLINE
EFTA • Characteristics of the Seven • The Disappearing Periphery
BIOGRAPHICAL SKETCHES
James Harold Wilson, Reluctant European • Kurt Waldheim,
Austria in the Dock

B ritain kept out of the EEC because it disagreed with its political, not its economic, goals. It wanted to keep its special relationship with the United States and the Commonwealth and feared that surrendering any of its sovereignty might encourage the EEC to dictate policy to it. Despite attempts to reconcile the differences, talks broke down in December 1958. Britain then took the lead in establishing the European Free Trade Association (EFTA) on May 3, 1960.

EFTA

EFTA aimed at creating a free-trade area, not a common tariff or political unity, by 1970. Austria, Denmark, Sweden, Norway, Switzerland, and Portugal joined Britain. The "Outer Seven" had a smaller population than did the EEC, but, with 90 million inhabitants, still constituted a formidable trading bloc.

Failure of the EFTA Model
Although EFTA reached its goal of reducing tariffs, economics scuttled it. As the EEC approached its goal of establishing a Common Market, worried EFTA members feared being cut out of the vast market that was in the process of formation. British, Austrian, and Swiss trade with the EEC, for example, was more important than trade with EFTA. In addition, the geographic disparity between EFTA countries made trade among them more difficult, and the EFTA connection proved too loose. The imposition of a British surtax of 15 percent on EFTA imports in 1964 meant that EFTA products did not have an advantage in the British market

and sometimes were worse off than non-EFTA imports. Some members, such as Denmark, recognized the inherent weaknesses of EFTA and were anxious to come to terms with the EEC.

Furthermore, the British assumption that they had a special relationship with the United States proved erroneous. The United States did not favor EFTA because it produced an economic rift among the NATO allies, and it established closer links to the EEC that threatened to leave Britain in the cold. Taken together with the results of the Suez crisis in the late 1950s that weakened ties between the two countries, Britain reoriented itself toward Europe.

These factors demonstrated that EFTA could not serve as a model for Europe's future, and in 1961, less than two years after EFTA's establishment, Britain announced that it would apply for EEC membership. Long negotiations and the opposition of important sectors of the British public delayed membership, but Britain, along with Denmark, joined in January 1973. Other EFTA members successfully applied as well, and by 1995 EFTA was just a ghost of itself.

Present and Former EFTA members. This map shows EFTA at its greatest extent and the way it is now. The countries that are crosshatched are former EFTA members that have joined the European Union; the darker shaded countries are the remaining members.

CHARACTERISTICS OF THE SEVEN

The original EFTA countries were widely disparate. Britain and its Commonwealth dominated it, while the Scandinavian states represented a strong bloc, and both had a strong commitment to implement social welfare policies. Austria and Switzerland had modern economies but were small, socially conservative, and neutral. Portugal had a backward economy and was still ruled by the dictator Antonio Salazar.

British Social Policy

The United Kingdom (England, Scotland, Wales, and Ulster) accounted for the predominant share of EFTA's wealth and population, and its long economic decline relative to the other West European countries accelerated after World War II when political and social turbulence increased. In 1942 a report by Sir William Beveridge endorsed a welfare state to provide all citizens with a minimum standard of living, full employment, health insurance, and a decent education. The question of how to implement these goals set off a national debate that confronted the Labour Party following its victory in the elections of July 1945.

The comprehensive and expensive social welfare program passed by Clement Attlee's new government brought about a decline in the pound's value. At the same time, a crisis in Iran over British domination of oil production and the Korean

The European Free Trade Association (EFTA) was championed by Great Britain on May 3, 1960 as a counterweight to the EEC. It proved a failure and Britain left the association and joined the Common Market. However, EFTA continued to exist as a shadow of its former self. The photograph shows the Swiss Minister of Economics (right) conversing with the EFTA Secretary General at a ministerial meeting at EFTA headquarters in Geneva on November 23, 2010.

War forced him to increase British armaments and adopt an austerity budget. These developments caused differences in the Labour Party with proponents of an advanced social agenda that contributed to Labour's loss in the October 1951 elections that returned Churchill and the Conservatives to power. However, the Conservatives did not dismantle Labour's social legislation, and an upturn in the economy helped them stay in charge. The British economy's revival confirmed the Conservatives in their opposition to joining the EEC.

The Struggle for EEC Membership

After 1957, this attitude changed because of the Suez crisis, the success of the EEC, and the increasing difficulty of trading with EEC countries as the EEC adopted policies favoring their members. The British applied for membership, but the road was difficult. The EEC members objected to British requests for concessions to shield their agriculture and to safeguard their Commonwealth ties, and the Labour Party strongly opposed British accession for the traditional reason that it would reduce British independence and because it was alarmed that Christian Democrat-dominated Europe might sabotage their social programs. When de Gaulle abruptly ended negotiations, the British established EFTA in 1960 without, however, abandoning their attempts to join the EEC. In 1964, the process was further delayed after Labour won the elections under Harold Wilson, a Socialist who opposed the EEC and focused on modernization and planning. Wilson had some political success, which encouraged him to hold new elections in 1970, but the Conservatives, under pro-EEC leader Edward Heath, won a surprise victory. Heath negotiated British entry into the Common Market.

BIOGRAPHICAL SKETCHES

James Harold Wilson
Reluctant European

The man who conducted the crucial 1975 referendum confirming Britain's membership in the European Community, Prime Minister Harold Wilson, was born in Huddersfield, England, on March 11, 1916. The son of a manager employed by a dyestuffs company, Wilson attended Oxford University on a scholarship. Wilson, a Socialist, collaborated with Sir William Beveridge on his famous 1942 report advocating the establishment of a welfare state. During World War II, he was the director of economics and statistics at the Ministry of Fuel and Power. In 1945, Wilson won election to the House of Commons as a member of the Labour Party. He joined the cabinet as president of the Board of Trade in 1947 and dismantled wartime controls over the economy. Wilson resigned in 1951 to protest changes in the National Health Service necessary to pay for British participation in the Korean War.

Wilson became the spokesman for Labour's left wing and distinguished himself challenging Labour Party leader Hugh Gaitskell's opposition to unilateral nuclear disarmament. On this and other issues, especially the EEC, however, Wilson demonstrated himself a pragmatist who could change his mind. In 1963 Gaitskell died,

continued

continued

and Wilson took over as party leader. The next year he became prime minister after a Labour win in the national election. Wilson served two terms as prime minister, from 1964 to 1970 and from 1974 to 1976.

Although he had been unsure about the EEC during its conception, Harold Wilson emerged as its implacable foe. During the early 1960s, the Labour Party, divided into feuding factions, united on opposition to Britain's entry into the EEC. Its foe, the Conservative Party, had applied for EEC membership on July 31, 1961. The issue stirred heated controversy not only on its merits, but because the French objected to England's membership and humiliated the British negotiators. When in a famous speech to the 1962 party conference, Gaitskell declared that by joining the EEC the British would forfeit a thousand years of history, Wilson cheered.

Wilson based his opposition to the EEC on several points. Most important, the EEC's supranational organization threatened the sovereignty of the British Parliament, which would no longer be able to make laws for the country in an unfettered manner. This constraint would block British action on a principle that Wilson considered fundamental. A committed Socialist, he favored planning as a way to protect workers' rights and to increase the nation's industrial efficiency. Wilson argued that the EEC, by contrast, opposed planning, except insofar as it would enhance free competition. For the EEC, he believed, planning meant creating a more favorable atmosphere for capitalism; for him, it signified state intervention on behalf of national, not private, interests. British closeness to the Commonwealth rounded out his anti-EEC arguments.

By 1966, however, Wilson's attitude had softened. The decline in Britain's financial position and world influence had continued implacably despite Wilson's attempts to reverse them. In 1965, a white supremacist government in Rhodesia (now Zimbabwe) had unilaterally declared its independence of Britain, and his efforts to topple it through economic sanctions failed. A domestic economic crisis forced the prime minister to take drastic measures. Moreover, influential Labour Party members had come to support the EEC as essential for Britain's future, and in 1967 Britain reapplied for membership. In June 1970, Wilson lost an election but returned as prime minister after the general election of February 1974. He declared his intention of renegotiating the terms of British membership in the EEC and in 1975 won a vital referendum on the issue.

In 1976, Wilson suddenly resigned among rumors that the CIA and British security forces had forced him out of office. Wilson was knighted, kept his seat in the Commons, and was made a life peer in 1983. He died in his sleep of cancer, in London on May 24, 1995.

British Decline

Heath faced a series of new challenges after his election. The oil crisis forced him to freeze wages and prices and to reduce the workweek to three days. Inflation spiraled out of control; unemployment increased drastically; and Heath, who had promised to curb the power of unions, confronted escalating labor opposition. Finally, members of Heath's own party, unhappy with Britain's entry into the Common Market, rebelled against him. These events favored a Labour win in the February 1974 election. Wilson returned to office in June 1975, but now favored membership in the EEC and held a referendum that confirmed Britain's desire to remain in the EEC.

These events brought about major changes in the British political scene. Margaret Thatcher replaced Heath as Conservative leader, the first woman to head a major British party. Thatcher, a grocer's daughter sensitive to middle-class values, promised to reduce greatly the state's role in British society and the economy and pledged to tame the unions. Her rise portended a sea change should she come to power. This seemed more likely because Wilson failed to stem inflation and rising interest rates and resigned in March 1976. His successor James Callaghan did no better. In the late 1970s, the government's economic remedies failed, the unions instead of the state seemed in control, street demonstrations occurred, and the country appeared to be falling apart. Serious separatist movements gained ground in Scotland and Wales, gravely weakening the Labour government when a referendum rejected legislation granting Scotland and Wales substantial autonomy. The British faltered in their bid to end terrorism in Northern Ireland, despite the dispatch of soldiers, and their violation of civil rights there brought international criticism. Growing outrage against the power of unions and the British decline set the stage for Thatcher's victory in 1979.

The Scandinavian Countries

Of the Scandinavian countries, the largest, Sweden, had kept out of World War II and had benefited from its favorable trading position. Following the war, Sweden maintained its neutralist policy. It did not join NATO and frequently served as a valuable mediator between the East and the West in cases such as the Vietnam War. Sweden's mixed economy balanced public interest and private enterprise, and its advanced social welfare system combined comprehensive educational, health, and old-age and child care programs. Social welfare, however, consumed a high proportion of the national income and became progressively more burdensome as the population aged and as immigrants were integrated into the country.

The high taxes required to pay for the welfare system caused debate, but the Social Democratic Party, which dominated politics for most of the postwar years, protected it and followed high employment policies. In 1971, Sweden replaced its bicameral parliament with a unicameral one, and coalitions of smaller parties ruled the country between 1976 and 1982. In 1986, the assassination of the prominent Social Democrat leader Olaf Palme briefly raised a question about the future of Swedish politics, but no evidence ever surfaced linking the killing to political affairs, and the country remained stable.

Swedish neighbor Norway's recovery from World War II was based on the rebuilding of its merchant fleet and a 1952 economic plan. Into the 1960s, about half the value of foreign payments came from shipping, with forest products, mining, and electrochemical production accounting for a large share of exports. Scandinavian characteristics of a mixed economy, an advanced social welfare system, and stable politics distinguished Norway as well. The Labor Party had a majority in Parliament until 1961, followed in power by a coalition consisting of conservatives and liberals, and then alternation of the two political forces. Norway was a constitutional

Although the Scandinavian countries had a low crime rate, a spectacular crime occurred in 1986. Olaf Palme, leader of the Swedish Social Democratic Party from 1969, generally walked the streets without a bodyguard, and he was assassinated on February 28. His frequent criticism of American (and Soviet) policies created suspicion that one of those powers was involved. A small-time drug addict was later convicted of the murder but later set free on appeal. The assassination is still unsolved.

monarchy like the other Scandinavian states, and Parliament retained the supremacy it gained in 1864. Membership in the EEC was a major political issue, and in a 1972 referendum, the country decided not to join.

Denmark shared with the other Scandinavian states a constitutional government, a mixed economy, an advanced social welfare state, and a long history of stable government by Social Democrats who ruled until 1982. The Danes implemented a major constitutional change in 1953, adopting a unicameral legislature and granting representation to Greenland and the Faeroe Islands. From an economic viewpoint, a major change was the increase in the manufacturing base. By the 1960s, industry contributed more to the national income than did agriculture. As in the rest of Scandinavia, the welfare system came with a high price tag that touched off political debate. The oil shock of the 1970s caused a recession that exacerbated the problems of the Danish economy—a very high budget deficit that required austerity measures. Large debts and high taxes remained unresolved problems.

Their history, homogeneity, stable government, and similar political systems and economic policies prompted a feeling of kinship among the Scandinavian peoples. They attempted a high degree of political, economic, and even military collaboration culminating in the Nordic Council, an organization dedicated to economic cooperation but that took political stands on important issues. In the postwar world, the Scandinavian countries distinguished themselves as United Nations (UN) supporters and contributors to that organization's peacekeeping efforts.

Austria: Looking Toward the EEC

Austria would have preferred to join the Common Market instead of EFTA, but the USSR blocked its application as a violation of neutrality. Like Germany, Austria had been occupied by the four victorious powers following World War II, but by 1955, the USSR and the Western powers had signed a treaty with Austria and pulled out of the country.

Austria had a smooth postwar political transition, with Socialist veteran Karl Renner reinstating the 1920 constitution. Elections were held in November 1945, and in January 1946, the occupation powers formally recognized Austria as a state. The Socialist and People's (Christian Democratic) parties had almost equal appeal for the electorate, while the Communists had only slight support. Between 1947 and 1966, a Socialist-People's Party coalition governed the country. In 1966 the Catholics ruled but were replaced in 1970 by a government headed by Socialist Bruno Kreisky. The Socialists renounced Marxism and gave the party a new image. Their favorable policy toward Catholic schools induced the Vatican to stop habitually endorsing the People's Party after 1971, strengthening the Socialists, who remained in power until the 1980s; thereafter, coalitions maintained governmental stability. Austria kept its political balance despite charges during the 1986 presidential campaign that Kurt Waldheim, former UN secretary general, had been involved in World War II anti-Jewish war crimes as a member of the German army. After his election, an investigation criticized him for doing nothing despite being well informed about the crimes, and he announced that he would not run for a second term.

Austria made significant social and economic progress during the postwar period, recognizing the rights of women and minorities. Most of its trade was with the EEC countries, and tourism became an important economic factor. The Austrians challenged the USSR's veto of their EEC membership and in 1972 gained associate status despite Soviet protests. In foreign affairs, Austria remained formally neutral during the cold war, signed an important treaty with Italy regulating the Austrian minority in that country, and joined the UN.

BIOGRAPHICAL SKETCHES

Kurt Waldheim
Austria in the Dock

The saga of Kurt Waldheim illustrates how the memory of World War II could roil Europe many years after the conflict ended. Kurt Waldheim was born in Sankt Andra-Worden, near Vienna, on December 21, 1918, the son of a civil servant. He served in the Austrian army in 1937 and 1938. Since Austria had been incorporated into Germany in 1938, the German army drafted Waldheim when World War II broke out. He completed his law degree in 1944 at the University of Vienna after his discharge from the army.

In 1945, Waldheim entered the Austrian diplomatic service and had a distinguished career. He served with the Austrian delegation at the Austrian State Treaty

continued

continued

negotiations from 1945 to 1947, in the Austrian legation in Paris from 1948 to 1951, and as ambassador to Canada from 1956 to 1960. He was minister for foreign affairs from 1968 to 1970 and ran for president in 1971.

Waldheim had established a close association with the UN in 1955. This relationship culminated with his appointment as secretary general in January 1972. Elected to a second term, he failed to win a third and joined Georgetown University as a research professor in 1982. During his tenure at the UN, Waldheim worked on a number of difficult crises, including Vietnam, the Middle East, the Iran hostage crisis, the Iran-Iraq war, and a war between India and Pakistan.

In 1986, Waldheim ran as the People's Party candidate for the presidency of Austria, but a scandal broke out when reports in the American media alleged that during his World War II military service as a translator and intelligence officer in the Balkans, he had been involved in the mass deportation of Jews from Salonika to concentration camps and in the murder of Yugoslav partisans and British commandos. The campaign against him, led by the World Jewish Congress, demonstrated that he had not been completely open about his war record, but he maintained that he did not know about the atrocities.

Waldheim won the election, but the furor damaged Austria's reputation. In 1987, the United States put the new president on a watch list of suspected Nazis and barred him from entering the country. In 1988, an international commission of historians maintained that Waldheim was informed about the atrocities taking place in the Balkans and did not attempt to stop them. In an interview the same year, the Austrian president praised those who had resisted the Nazis, admitted that he wanted to survive by following orders, and pleaded for the world's understanding for his position at the time.

Waldheim's presidency ushered in a traumatic period for Austria. World leaders shunned the president and isolated his country. The press focused on Austria as a participant in Nazi war crimes instead of as a victim—the light in which the Austrians had successfully presented themselves in the past. A debate between the generations began, with the young asking why and how the average Austrian, whom Waldheim reflected, could have followed orders resulting in war crimes without asking questions or resisting. Many older people resented the criticism, arguing that the youths were not present and could not understand the atmosphere at the time. The discussion forced Austria into a painful examination of its recent past of the kind Germany had confronted two decades earlier and stimulated an investigation of cover-ups in other European countries.

The flood of negative world opinion and the diplomatic isolation of his country convinced Waldheim not to run for a second term in 1992, but it also caused an upsurge of nationalism. In addition to the debate about its past, this period in Austria marked the rise of a far-right leader named Jörg Haider. Haider took over the small Freedom Party, gave it a rightward shove, and within a few years led it into the governing coalition.

Kurt Waldheim died in Vienna on June 14, 2007, at age 88.

Recalcitrant Switzerland

Another neutral country, Switzerland, maintained its traditional status even to the extent of refusing to join the UN and other international organizations, although meetings of those institutions frequently convened on Swiss soil. Following the war, Switzerland negotiated an agreement with the Allies for the return of Nazi assets concealed in Swiss banks. With their strict secrecy, Swiss banks had been and have continued to be a traditional haven for funds from abroad and a source of great wealth. In the 1990s, the banks became a major source of embarrassment when it was revealed that they exploited their secrecy to withhold the assets of Holocaust victims from their heirs and utilized the funds for their own purposes. The banks denied the charges, but by 1999 investigators had found more than 40,000 bank accounts belonging to Holocaust victims. Swiss actions in refusing to help Jews fleeing Nazi persecution during the 1930s and 1940s also came into question. The Swiss eventually reached an agreement with survivors or their heirs in order to rebut criticism, but the American and world press condemned their actions.

A hard line against social and political liberalization, especially with regard to women and immigrants, by utilizing the popular referendum distinguished the Swiss. In 1959 a referendum rejected legislation allowing women to vote in federal elections, to hold office, and to be appointed to high federal positions. In the 1980s, the equality of women at work and in the home was recognized, but individual cantons could still determine if women could vote. The last canton granted that right only in 1990. Switzerland also received negative publicity because of its treatment of immigrant workers. Fearing that the influx of foreign workers from Catholic Italy and Spain needed by industry would alter the country's religious balance, the Swiss limited the number of workers who could legally enter the country. Many immigrants had limited civil rights and were subject to long delays before they could call their families to live with them or obtain social benefits. As non-West European immigrants replaced the Italians and the Spanish, the Swiss directed their hostility toward them.

Switzerland was one of the world's richest countries. Besides the banks, watches, and tourism that made it famous, large chemical, machinery, pharmaceutical, and arms concerns made their home in the country. Trade with the EEC increased, and Switzerland became an associate member in 1972. Social security made life comfortable for citizens, and the four linguistic groups continued to live in harmony. These groups tended to reach political compromises within the four parties that dominated Swiss politics after 1959. If anything, Switzerland was too stable.

Portuguese Revival

Another EFTA member, Portugal presented a different picture. After longtime dictator Salazar succumbed to a stroke in 1968, his successor promised liberalization, but his failure to keep his pledge caused a revolution in 1974. Two years of chaos were followed in 1976 by moderation and coalition politics. A radical constitution, passed in 1975, underwent considerable revision in a moderate direction in 1982. Socialist Mário Soares, determined to bring stability and economic progress, headed a coalition government in 1984 that returned to the private sector industries that had been previously nationalized. His policies set the stage for an economic boom that lifted the country out of its status as the poorest in Western

Europe and gained him not only Portuguese but also Europe-wide recognition for his efforts.

Portugal joined EFTA because of the country's strong British connection but was oriented toward the EEC. Several factors prevented Portugal from linking up with the EEC: survival of the Salazar dictatorship, structural economic shortcomings exacerbated by inflation during the oil crisis, and the threat of a Communist takeover after the dictatorship's overthrow. In the 1970s and 1980s, the country's democratic progress and the resolution of differences with the community regarding agriculture facilitated an understanding with the EC (the EEC changed its name to the European Communities, or EC, in 1967, although it was commonly known as the European Community) and brought full membership in 1986. The EC extended aid that promoted modernization and impressive economic gains. Along with the entrance of Spain the same year, the long isolation of the Iberian Peninsula from the rest of Western Europe ended.

THE DISAPPEARING PERIPHERY

From the end of World War II until the 1970s and 1980s, several states could be considered as being on Western Europe's political, diplomatic, economic, or geographic periphery, but economic and political changes tended to bring those countries into an increasingly close association with the EC.

Changing Spain

In 1946, the UN voted to keep Franco's Spain permanently out of the organization and urged its members to withdraw their diplomatic missions; the Americans excluded Spain from receiving Marshall Plan aid and from the Atlantic Alliance. With the beginning of the cold war, however, American and Western European attitudes gradually changed because Spain's strategic geographic position made it a valuable asset against the Soviets. A 1953 agreement allowed American bases in Spain in return for economic and military aid. Thereafter, Spain gradually emerged from isolation, entering the UN, important European organizations, and NATO.

Remarkable political and economic changes favoring reintegration into Europe began during the latter part of the Franco regime as its three props—the army, church, and party—weakened. The army changed character as younger officers from different classes injected a different outlook into an institution that was once dominated by a social elite that was loyal to Franco. In the Spanish church, support diminished as changes in the Vatican liberalized Catholicism and as Opus Dei, a powerful secular Catholic society that Franco favored, failed to maintain its position against more liberal rivals. Finally, the ruling political party lost what little coherence it had.

Constitutional changes paralleled these developments. In 1966 a new liberal constitution instituted direct election of part of the Cortes and allowed married women to vote. Even though Franco made certain that he stayed in control, some liberal elements appeared in the country during the latter part of his rule, including legal recognition of marriages between Catholics and Protestants, legislation establishing freedom of conscience, and the lifting of the centuries-old ban on

After Francisco Franco's death in 1975, democracy rapidly returned to Spain thanks to the support of the European Community and of the royal house. In 1981 King Juan Carlos successfully faced down an attempted coup d'etat by the Guardia Civil and later ruled as a constitutional monarch. This picture of the King and his wife, Queen Sofia, at a gathering at New York University dates from December 6, 1983.

Jews. In 1969 Franco named Prince Juan Carlos of Bourbon as his successor, and the prince, who assumed power after Franco's death, played a major role in the reestablishment of Spanish democracy.

The Return of Spanish Democracy

After Franco died on November 20, 1975, a Basque terrorist (ETA) offensive, determined democratic opposition, and international condemnation induced Juan Carlos to appoint a moderate reformer as prime minister, who in 1976 replaced the old Cortes with an elected Congress and Senate and allowed parties (except for the Communists until 1977) to operate freely. In June, the first democratic election since 1936 produced a ruling center-left coalition. The new Congress adopted a democratic constitution that the Spanish people accepted in a referendum and proceeded toward the administrative decentralization of the country.

Spain's new democracy was challenged by rising inflation and unemployment provoked by the oil price hikes, and in 1980 civil guards seized the parliament building and threatened to overthrow the government. King Juan Carlos firmly opposed them, and the military remained loyal. In 1982, Socialist Workers' Party head Felipe González led his party to a surprise electoral victory and remained in office for over a decade. Economic progress, fostered by private investment and EC aid, contributed to impressive growth despite high unemployment rates. Social policy also brought Spain closer to the European norm, with women gaining the right to work, open bank accounts, and take jobs without their husbands' permission.

Spain passed a divorce law in 1981 and legalized abortion in 1985. The country's political stability and economic and social progress fostered its reintegration with Europe.

Irish Troubles

Ireland's turbulent history, hostility to Britain because of centuries of British occupation, and backward social and economic conditions, like those in Spain, tended to isolate it from mainstream Europe. Ireland proclaimed itself a republic on April 18, 1949, but its poor relations with Britain and the high-profile terrorist activities of the Irish Republican Army (IRA), which were designed to force British abandonment of the North (Ulster), tainted its international reputation. Nationalist leader Eamon de Valera, who strongly favored incorporation of the Protestant-dominated state of Northern Ireland, served as prime minister six times and as president from 1959 to 1973. In February 1962, however, the IRA said it would end its terrorist campaign, and high-level meetings between republican and Ulster officials resulted.

These positive developments did not prevent a more serious wave of terrorism in Northern Ireland beginning in the late 1960s. Leaders of the Irish Republic publicly supported reunion by peaceful means, but terrorists used southern Ireland as a base for their activities, and in 1972 the Republic had to create special courts to try them because ordinary Irish courts acquitted them. For the next twenty-five years, talks between the Irish Republic, Ulster, and Britain failed to bring peace. Leaders of the Irish Republic hoped to change conditions there so union would become more attractive to the northern Irish Protestants who feared being overwhelmed by a Catholic, agricultural, conservative South. In the meantime, terrorist campaigns conducted by the Provisional IRA, the massive British military presence in Ulster, and the question of unification roiled Irish politics.

The economy and the social outlook of the Irish Republic were among the bleakest in Western Europe, with the economy remaining predominantly agricultural and trade, finance, and currency continuing to be intimately linked with Britain. Irish application for EEC membership encountered the same de Gaulle veto as the British did, and in 1971, acceptance along with Britain. The EEC extended loans to Ireland to help it confront its economic difficulties. By the century's end, these credits, technology, and globalization touched off impressive economic advances and a flow of return immigration. From a social perspective, the Republic continued to trail the rest of Western Europe, particularly because of the Catholic Church's influence. In the 1980s, the church successfully opposed abortion and divorce and resisted legislation allowing contraception.

Finland: Political Stability and Economic Development

Finland was more in tune with European developments even if, after World War II, the close proximity and influence of the Soviet Union impaired its ability to integrate with Western Europe. The treaty with the USSR forced the Finns to give up 12 percent of their territory and to pay heavy reparations. The Soviets insisted on a friendship and security treaty tying the countries closer and blocked Finland from joining the EEC on the grounds that membership would violate its neutral status, but allowed association with EFTA in 1961. The strength of the Finnish Communist Party into the early 1960s gave the Soviets significant economic and political clout. However, the Soviets hesitated to alienate neutral Sweden, Finland's Scandinavian brother, for fear of pushing it to join the Western defense system, and the Finns skillfully avoided diplomatic isolation. The USSR's weakness in the 1980s and 1990s allowed Finland to strengthen its Western ties and to join the European Union (EU), successor of the EC, in 1995.

Despite the presence of a Communist Party commanding approximately 20 percent of the vote, postwar Finnish politics were stable. The Finnish Communists participated in a coalition cabinet from 1945 to 1948. Like their Eastern European brethren, they attempted to acquire control of the all-important Interior Ministry but failed. Subsequently, the Communist share of the vote declined, and after 1958 a leftist-centrist coalition dominated Finnish politics until the 1980s, with conservative influence increasing during the latter part of the decade. Finland's political stability enabled it to make significant economic progress. It possessed both "green" and "white" gold—forests and waterpower—which it skillfully exploited. During the 1950s, the country reinvested a third of its gross national product in its agricultural and industrial plant, a policy that produced prosperity and rapid economic expansion despite considerable hardship.

Emerging Iceland

Iceland, a small, island of 180,000 next to Greenland, ended its long union with Denmark in 1944. Its isolation decreased when it joined NATO. Iceland contributed no military forces, but the Atlantic Alliance established important bases there. Iceland's climate forced it to import food and raw materials, but its economy rested on fishing, which it fiercely defended. After independence, the country concentrated its investments in housing, fishing, agriculture, and communications. Iceland joined EFTA in 1970 and benefited from an industrialization fund and special tariff treatment to foster industry. Trade, NATO bases, rapidly increasing tourist activity, and globalization increased Iceland's interaction with the outside world and reduced its insularity.

Accelerating contact, democratization, and economic integration characterized the Western European periphery in the postwar era, so that by the 1990s it had all but disappeared.

Bibliographical Essay

Bela Belassa looks at the experience of the EEC and EFTA after ten years and at the time of Britain's entrance into the Common Market in *European Economic Integration* (New York, 1975). *EFTA 1960–2000* (Brussels, 2000) is a general consideration during the years covered. Victoria Curzon, *The Essentials of European Integration* (New York, 1974), is a study of the EFTA experience. Books cited in Chapter 22 on the EEC will generally have a discussion of EFTA.

Good general histories of England that discuss the postwar period include David Thompson, *England in the Twentieth Century*, 2d ed. (Harmondsworth, UK, 1983), and Alfred F. Havighurst, *Britain in Transition: The Twentieth Century*, 4th ed. (Chicago, 1985). Kenneth O. Morgan's *The People's Peace: British History, 1945–1989* (London, 1990) is a detailed history of Britain from 1945 to 1990. David Childs, *Britain Since 1945*

(London, 2006), is a political history. Arthur Marwich's *British Society Since 1945* (New York, 2003) is a new edition of a classic work.

The British were forced to confront their declining world role following World War II. F. S. Northedge, *British Foreign Policy: The Process of Readjustment, 1945–1961* (London, 1962), emphasizes changes after 1945. Donley T. Studlar, *Great Britain: Decline or Renewal?* (Boulder, Colo., 1996), discusses social, economic, and political policy and Britain's changing role in the world. Max Beloff, *The Future of British Foreign Policy* (London, 1969), illustrates principles that should guide British foreign policy.

Works that give a good idea of the policies of Labour during the 1945–51 period include Kenneth O. Morgan, *Labour in Power 1945–1951* (Oxford, UK, 1984); Henry Pelling, *The Labour Governments 1945–51* (New York, 1951); and Michael Sissons and Philip French, eds., *Age of Austerity, 1945–51* (London, 1963), a book of collected essays on the period. The politics of later periods are analyzed by Mary Proudfoot, *British Politics and Government 1951–1970* (London, 1974), a treatment of the various governments and their policies; Paul Foot, *The Politics of Harold Wilson* (Harmondsworth, UK, 1968); and Bernard Donoughue, *Prime Minister: The Conduct of Policy Under Harold Wilson and James Callaghan* (London, 1987), which deals with the policies of two important British leaders. Raymond Plant et al., *The Struggle of Labour's Soul* (New York, 2004), examines the party's political thought after 1945.

British leaders have been fortunate to find competent biographers. Kenneth Harris wrote *Attlee* (New York, 1982). John Campbell's *Aneurin Bevan: A Biography* (New York, 1987) is a full-scale study of the venerable Socialist leader. Harold Macmillan has found several biographers. Consult Nigel Fisher, *Harold Macmillan* (New York, 1982). Kenneth O. Morgan published the detailed *Callaghan: A Life* (Oxford, UK, 1997); Paul J. Deveney concentrates on *Callaghan's Journey to Downing Street* (New York, 2010). Alan Bullock's *The Life and Times of Ernest Bevin* (London, 1983) is a detailed examination of the British foreign secretary from 1945 to 1951.

Foreign policy had a more important role in Britain than in the other European countries. Joseph Frankel, *British Foreign Policy 1945–1973* (London, 1975), provides a good overview. C. M. Woodhouse, *British Foreign Policy Since the Second World War* (New York, 1960), is a general treatment of the topic. Mark Phythian wrote *The Labour Party, War and International Relations, 1945–2006* (New York, 2007). Ritchie Obendale, *The English-Speaking Alliance: Britain, the United States, the Dominions, and the Cold War, 1945–1951* (London, 1985), is the story of Britain and United States in the cold war up to 1951. Eugene J. Meehan, *The British Left Wing and Foreign Policy: A Study of the Influence of Ideology* (New Brunswick, N.J., 1960), seeks to demonstrate how ideology influences foreign policy. A detailed analysis of Britain and the Suez crisis is Leon D. Epstein, *British Politics in the Suez Crisis* (Urbana, Ill.,1964). George Cunningham, ed., *Britain and the World in the Seventies* (London, 1970), is a collection of essays on British attitudes toward different parts of the world. Donald McClean, *British Foreign Policy Since Suez* (London, 1970), discusses British relations with the West, the Third World, and the Communist powers. On Britain's relationship with continental Europe, see Roger Broad, *Labour's European Dilemmas: From Bevin to Blair* (New York, 2001), and Andrew Mullen, *The British Left's "Great Debate" on Europe* (London, 2007).

The literature on the Scandinavian countries is not proportional to their importance. Refer to Chapter 5 for titles, but add Franklin Daniel Scott, *Sweden: The Nation's History* (Carbondale, Ill., 1988), a general treatment. Leif Lewin, *Ideology and Strategy: A Century of Swedish Politics* (Cambridge, UK, 1988), surveys Swedish politics during the past hundred years. Henry Milner, *Sweden: Social Democracy in Practice* (New York, 1989), describes the welfare state. Desmond Lacjan et al., *Challenges to the Swedish Welfare State* (Washington, D.C., 1995), a book of essays, and Dimitris Tsarouhas, *Social Democracy in Sweden: The Threat from a Globalised World* (London, 2008), discuss why the welfare state has survived. Samuel Abrahamson, *Sweden's Foreign Policy* (Washington, D.C., 1957), examines a crucial aspect of Swedish history. T. K. Derry, *A History of Modern Norway* (Oxford, UK, 1973), takes the Norwegian story up to 1972. On modern Denmark, two books with good information are Stewart Oakley, *The Story of Denmark* (London, 1972), and W. Glyn Jones, *Denmark: A Modern History* (London, 1986). A book packed with information on Finland is Eric Solsten and Sandra W. Medlitz, eds., *Finland: A Country Study*, 2d ed. (Washington, D.C., 1990). D. G. Kirby, *Finland in the Twentieth Century* (Minneapolis, Minn., 1979), is strong on the postwar period. L. A. Puntila, *The Political History of Finland 1809–1966* (London, 1975), is a general survey.

Jill Lewis, *Workers and Politics in Occupied Austria* (New York, 2007), investigates Austrian economics during the Allied occupation. Richard Hiscocks, *The Rebirth of Austria* (London, 1953), is a history of the early postwar period. Donald R. Withnah and Edgar L. Ericson, *The American Occupation of Austria: Planning and Early Years* (Westport, Conn., 1985), discusses the relationship between Americans and Austrians. Sven Allard, *Russia and the Austrian State Treaty: A Case Study of Soviet Policy in Europe* (University Park, Pa., 1970), is the story of Austria after the war through the eyes of a Swedish diplomat. Postwar Austria was distinguished by its position between the West and the East. On this topic, see William B. Bader, *Austria Between East and West 1945–1955* (Stanford, Calif.,1966). Thomas O. Schlesinger, *Austrian Neutrality in Postwar Europe: The Domestic Roots of a Foreign Policy* (Vienna, 1972), deals with domestic considerations in Austrian foreign policy. Kurt L. Shell treats an important topic in his *The Transformation of Austrian Socialism* (Albany, N.Y., 1982).

On the topic of Swiss society, see Armin Gretler and P. E. Mandl, *Values, Trends, and Alternatives in Swiss Society* (New York, 1973). Essays on the theme of whether Switzerland will have to change are found in Theo Chopard, *Switzerland Present and Future* (Bern, 1963). Barbara A. Salazar, *The Holocaust—Recovery of Assets from World War II: A Chronology (May 1995 to the Present)* (Washington, D.C., 2000) is a good introduction to the problem of recovering Jewish assets. Raul Teitelbaum and Moshe Sanbar, *Holocaust Gold: From the Victims to Switzerland* (Tel Aviv, 2001), follows the "trail of the Nazi plunder." Isabel Vincent, *Hitler's Silent Partners: Swiss Banks, Nazi Gold, and the Pursuit of Justice* (New York, 1997), is representative of the criticism of Switzerland's wartime role, and, finally, on another aspect of the problem, there is Charles Weiss, *Closing the Books: Jewish Insurance Claims from the Holocaust* (New York, 2008).

Mediterranean dictatorships and their transformation into democracies have been a source of study. Nikos Poulantzos, *The Crisis of the Dictatorship* (London, 1976), is a comparative study of the decline of dictatorship in Greece, Portugal, and Spain, as is Geoffrey Pridham, *The New Mediterranean Democracies: Spain, Greece and Portugal* (London, 1984).

The emphasis on Spain has been on the latter years of the Franco regime, the transition to democracy, and the country's rejoining of Europe, although two good general histories of modern Spain are Raymond Carr, *Modern Spain, 1875–1980* (New York, 1981), and Christopher Ross, *Spain 1812–1996* (New York, 2000). Jean Grugel, *Franco's Spain* (New York, 1997), provides an overview of the regime. Stanley G. Payne, *The Franco Regime: 1936–1975* (Madison, Wis., 1987), and Raymond Carr and Juan Pablo Fusi Aizpurua, *Spain: Dictatorship to Democracy* (London, 1981), are both good on the last years of Franco. Paul Preston published the comprehensive *Franco: A Biography* (New York, 1994). Robert Graham, *Spain: A Nation Comes of Age* (New York, 1984), deals with the transformation of Francoism and the coming of democracy.

Pamela Beth Radcliffe's *Making Democratic Citizens in Spain: Civil Society and the Popular Origins of the Transition, 1960-78* (New York, 2012) discusses ordinary men and women in the transition to democracy. Diego Muro and Gregorio Alonso, *The Politics and Memory of Democratic Transition: The Spanish Model* (Hoboken, N.J., 2010), is a good account of the changes. E. Ramon Arango, *Spain: From Repression to Renewal* (Boulder, Colo., 1985), is good on economics and society. Arango's *Spain: Democracy Regained* (Boulder, Colo., 1995) is an updated edition. David Gilmour, *The Transformation of Spain: From Franco to the Constitutional Monarchy* (London, 1985), emphasizes the transition to the monarchy. José Maravall, *The Transition to Democracy in Spain* (New York, 1982), is a good brief treatment. Paul Preston, *The Triumph of Democracy in Spain* (London, 1986), tells how democracy won. Samuel D. Easton, *The Forces of Freedom in Spain, 1974–1979* (Stanford, Calif., 1981), discusses the forces responsible for the maintenance of Spanish freedom. David S. Bell, ed., *Democratic Politics in Spain: Spanish Politics after Franco* (New York, 1983), is a collection of essays on political forces. Richard Gillespie, Fernando Rodrigo, and Jonathan Story, eds., *Democratic Spain: Reshaping External Relations in a Changing World* (London, 1995), is a series of essays describing democratic Spain's relations with the world. The reintegration of Spain into Europe between 1962 and its entrance into the EEC in 1985 is the subject of Julio Crespo MacLennan et al., *Spain and the Process of European Integration, 1957–85: Political Change and Europeanism* (Basingstoke, UK, 2000).

On the development of "the troubles" in Ireland, see Thomas Hennessey, *The Evolution of the Troubles, 1970–72* (Dublin, 2007). Alan F. Parkinson, *1972 and the Ulster Troubles: "A Very Bad Year"* (Dublin, 2010), examines the events of a crucial year and their impact. Brian M. Walker, *A Political History of the Two Irelands: From Partition to Peace* (New York, 2012) analyzes the "Troubles" and the coming of peace.The IRA is discussed by Ed Maloney, *A Secret History of the IRA* (New York, 2002), and Nicholas Van der Bijl examines the role of the British army in Northern Ireland between 1969 and 2007 in *Operation Banner* (Barnsley, UK, 2009).

Portugal has had similar treatment as Spain. See Ronald H. Chilcote, *The Portuguese Revolution: State and Class in the Transition to Democracy* (Lanham, Md., 2010). Antonio de Figueiredo, *Portugal: Fifty Years of Dictatorship* (New York, 1976), gives the history of Portugal and Portuguese Africa from 1926 to 1976. Hugh Kay, *Salazar and Modern Portugal* (London, 1970), attempts to view the Salazar regime dispassionately. Lawrence S. Graham and Harry M. Marker, eds., *Contemporary Portugal: The Revolution and its Antecedents* (Austin, Tex., 1979), is a wide-ranging collection of essays. Thomas C. Bruneau, *Politics and Nationhood: Post-Revolutionary Portugal* (New York, 1984), also talks about the revolution and its background, including modernization. Phil Mailer, *Portugal: The Impossible Revolution* (London, 1977), is an eyewitness account. Hugo Gil Ferreira and Michael W. Marshall, *Portugal's Revolution: Ten Years On* (Cambridge, UK, 1986), is a good history of the country from 1974 to 1984. Douglas Porch, *The Portuguese Armed Forces and the Revolution* (Stanford, Calif., 1977), analyzes "the army in politics and politics in the army." Jorge Braga de Macedo and Simon Serfaty edited *Portugal Since the Revolution* (Boulder, Colo., 1981), a study of economics and politics. Kenneth Maxwell's *The Making of Portuguese Democracy* (New York, 1995) is a comprehensive work.

For economic changes on the Iberian peninsula, consult E. N. Baklanoff, *The Economic Transformation of Spain and Portugal* (New York, 1978).

Donald E. Nuechterlein, *Iceland: Reluctant Ally* (Westport, Conn., 1975), is a history from 1940. See also Gunnar Karlsson, *The History of Iceland* (Minneapolis, Minn., 2000).

CHAPTER 24

✐

Decolonization

CHAPTER OUTLINE

Origins of Decolonization • Death by War • Failed Transformations

BIOGRAPHICAL SKETCHES

Frantz Fanon, Language, Peasants,
and Revolution

World War II set off the process by which the Western European states lost their empires, even if the origins went back further. The losers were stripped of their possessions, as was Germany following World War I, but the victors also lost theirs because the ideologies of the postwar world were unfriendly to imperialism. As violent struggles for liberation followed, the colonial powers resisted and then understood that they would be economically and politically better off without their colonies. Consequently, decolonization, in addition to political stabilization and rapid economic growth, marked the post–World War II era in Western Europe.

ORIGINS OF DECOLONIZATION

European countries considered colonial empires to be a source of national greatness; essential for economic survival, growth, and prestige; and a sign of their superiority over native peoples they sought to "civilize." When the twentieth century opened, European leaders assumed that their colonial rule would last for centuries, but the end of that World War I left colonialism with an unsavory reputation that had led to genocide and hundreds of thousands of victims, especially in German Southwest Africa and the Belgian Congo. The criticism of intellectuals before World War I had increased opposition to imperialism in the European Socialist parties, and the slaughter that took place during the conflict convinced ordinary Europeans that colonies were not worth the cost of obtaining them. Given this attitude, European governments masked their imperialist ambitions after 1918 under the cloak of mandates that gave German and Turkish colonies to the victorious allies, particularly to Britain and France, in order to teach the native populations about democracy before they could have their independence. During the interwar period, none of the mandates received independence, and they all had to fight for it after World War II.

World War II radically changed the situation. The British and the French attempted to reorganize their possessions on the basis of greater cooperation with the colonies. They failed because they kept effective control and because growing nationalist movements insisted on complete independence. As the conflicts escalated, the Europeans discovered that colonies were unnecessary for national prestige or economic prosperity. Moreover, fighting against the independence movements proved costly, caused domestic turbulence, and shifted the focus of

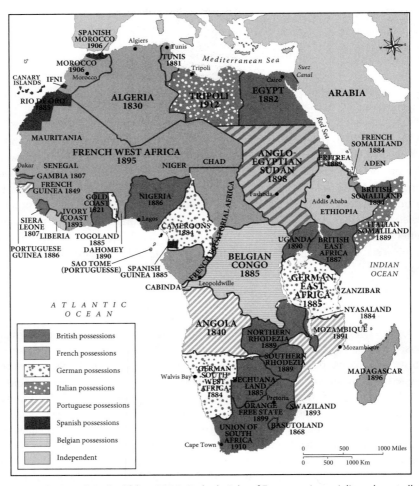

European Possessions in Africa, 1914. At the height of European imperialism almost all of Africa was under European control.

governments away from more pressing questions. The issue that caused the most soul-searching among the West Europeans was not economics, but an emotional involvement with the colonies and the long-standing European communities that had emigrated to them, but this problem was worked out, and the age of colonialism ended.

World War II and Its Implications

After World War II, the colonial powers lacked the strength to reestablish their rule firmly enough to defeat nationalist movements in Africa and Asia. In Asia the conquest of European colonies by the Japanese demonstrated the weakness of the colonial powers and touched off independence movements. In Africa the process was more complex than in Asia because most of the continent had been at the tribal stage of development and lacked modern economic and political infrastructures. Colonial interests had determined the boundaries of the various African countries, which included ethnic tribes that hated each other in the same state. These factors help explain why in Africa the decolonization process had a long development and was more turbulent than in other areas.

World War II showed colonial peoples that the imperialist powers were not invincible. Moreover, African troops took part in the wars fought against white soldiers in Africa and in Europe and proved their equals, and following the war, the Dutch lost their Asian Empire and the Vietnamese defeated the French in Indochina. These events demonstrated to the subject peoples that the colonialists could be defeated.

The Cold War

Another crucial result of the conflict that stimulated decolonization was the cold war. Both the United States and the Soviet Union opposed colonialism, as did their historical traditions. Although it can be argued that both countries created empires of a kind after World War II, these were different from the European colonial empires of the nineteenth and early twentieth centuries. The United States urged its allies to give up their colonies, frequently using diplomatic and economic pressure against them, and the USSR supported independence movements with advice, arms, and funds. In fighting the cold war, both superpowers were anxious to secure the moral support of neutral Third World countries, and this factor aided nationalists who were struggling for independence.

Besides superpower politics, the United Nations contributed to decolonization by assuming supervision over the mandates of the defunct League of Nations, by declaring that all peoples had a right to freedom, and by providing a world forum from which newly independent nations could support the independence of other colonial areas.

Economics and Society

When the Europeans had established their empires, their governments obliged the colonies to be financially self-sufficient and not burden the colonial powers, and the Great Depression froze the availability of funds for colonial development. During and after World War II, the great demand for scarce natural resources that were needed first for the fighting and later for reconstruction swelled the coffers of the colonial administrations.

The rapid economic growth and the increased powers of taxation available to West European governments increased the resources that were available for colonial development, while the welfare-state encouraged efforts to alleviate the social conditions of the poor. In the colonies, this attitude encouraged increased spending on education, health, unemployment insurance, pensions, and social services.

The availability of funds spurred investment in economic modernization and development in the colonies as Europeans realized that colonies with modern economic systems would be more useful to them than colonies that just supplied raw materials. Consequently Britain and France poured enormous amounts of money into their colonies to build dams for hydroelectric energy that would provide power for industrialization, roads, railways, and ports to facilitate the transportation of products. Most of the colonies, however, remained largely agricultural, and the Europeans expanded veterinary services; favored the introduction of machinery; instituted instruction on the use of new techniques; and encouraged the consolidation of small plots and the formation of cooperatives and the improvement of soil fertility, seed, and stock.

State involvement in these projects convinced the educated elite in the colonies that some form of socialism was necessary for future development once they achieved independence. This belief made them more susceptible to Soviet influence and willing to take up arms in their quest for freedom. Furthermore, development projects required a major investment in education, and the colonial governments did their best to expand education on all levels, including higher education. It is not surprising that the creation of a larger educated class, along with accelerated economic development, stimulated demands for independence.

In the past, colonial administrators had affection for the colonies, knew the history of the area, established a rapport with the population, and tended to settle their families there permanently, but postwar economic development created more overt social friction. The shortage of skilled personnel to undertake the massive projects meant that the best jobs went to Europeans who had no commitment to the colonies and who wanted to return home. The Europeans lived in the colonies for brief periods, enjoyed extensive privileges, earned high salaries that drained the projects' budgets, and behaved arrogantly. They were necessary for the successful completion of industrial enterprises, but they alienated the native populations and intensified the demand for independence.

Politics and Nationalism

At the same time, important political changes encouraged autonomy. Neither the British nor the French could maintain the authoritarian system of rule they had established at the height of their power. Although they attempted to export their own democratic models of government to the colonies, these models rarely worked well owing to traditions and the attitudes of native populations, but they gave the native populations invaluable experience that favored independence.

British and French schemes for increasing representation and gradual self-government were contradictory. Settlers in the British colonies feared that representation according to population would end their political, economic, and social privileges and would eventually produce rule by Africans. The British government accommodated them by setting up multiracial representative systems in which persons were represented by their status in society, not by majorities, violating British constitutional principles and angering the Western-educated colonial leaders. The French had similar problems, established assemblies, and then restricted their powers.

These contradictions encouraged the native elites to support complete independence rather than cooperation. Many African intellectual nationalists who had been educated abroad were influenced by the ideas of African American leaders, such as William Du Bois and Marcus Garvey, who advocated African control of Africa. In the French colonies, intellectuals insisted on the autonomy of their own cultures, the premise of freedom, and spread their ideas of sovereignty among the rest of the population; eventually they won over the majority of peasants and villagers to independence.

African intellectuals, claiming to represent the people, organized congresses that instigated strikes, boycotts, and civil disobedience. By the 1950s, these congress movements generated political parties that, thanks to their discipline and coherence, seized control of the independence movements. Experience gained in the representative institutions established by the colonial powers, combined with a heightened political consciousness, gave new impetus to the movements for self-government. Party propaganda activities favored resistance and violence, and new leaders who articulated their desire for independence to international audiences came to the forefront.

DEATH BY WAR

During the early postwar period, two colonial empires, the Italian and the Dutch, came to an end.

Italian Colonialism

Having been finally united only in 1870, Italy had come into the colonial game late. The country's weakness, combined with its ambition, led to a tragic colonial history. It managed to take over only poor areas with few natural resources, Eritrea and Italian Somaliland in East Africa and Libya in North Africa. The colonial experience cost the Italians dearly. The Italians suffered a severe defeat in 1896 in Ethiopia, fought a hard war against Turkey for Libya in 1911, and were bogged down in a guerrilla conflict there for the next twenty years. The Italian colonies had very few products to trade and were unsuited for industrial investment. (Oil was not discovered in Libya until after World War II.) In fact, the Italians spent a fortune building roads and public works with funds that could have been better used in Italy. In the early days of Italian colonialism, Italian industry was weak, and industrialists, Socialists, and northern workers believed that the government should concentrate on investing in the Italian industrial infrastructure, rather than pursue imperialistic adventures, while Italian imperialism drew its support primarily from the impoverished South that hoped for glory and an outlet for its excess population under the Italian flag. In fact, few Italians settled in the colonies, despite the government's encouragement of their emigration. In 1938 Libya, with an area five times that of Italy, counted fewer than 90,000 Italians. The East African territories had an Italian population of only about 6,000.

In 1935 and 1936, Mussolini conquered Ethiopia, richer in natural resources than Italy's other colonies, but revenge for the 1896 defeat and dreams of imperial glory had as much to do with the war as economics. The Ethiopian adventure had a disastrous impact on Italy's international image and foreign policy, and the country spent a fortune on the war and on public works. The few years the Italians held Ethiopia brought them only huge expenses and a guerrilla conflict.

Italian Losses after World War II

Cut off from the possibility of receiving supplies, Italy's East African possessions quickly fell to British attacks during World War II, after which Ethiopia regained its independence and the Allies allowed it to annex Eritrea, which was not returned to Italy. This Ethiopian-dominated union produced conflict, the consequent breakaway of Eritrea, and endemic warfare; the Italians followed these by events with great interest, since the Eritrean Liberation Front (ELF) had its headquarters in Rome. Italian Somaliland also gained its independence after a UN Trusteeship under Italy ended in 1960, when it joined with British Somaliland to form Somalia. This area, one of the world's poorest and most troubled, required Italian economic intervention to alleviate starvation. The Italians gave aid on a regular basis, and the Italian government had close, if controversial, relations with various Somali leaders. In the 1990s, the United States and Western European countries sent their forces in the vain hope of preventing further economic and political disasters. Differences on how to proceed caused friction between the United States and Italy, a disaster for the United States ("Blackhawk down"), and the sea around it became a center of piracy in the new century. Significant Somali emigration to Italy occurred, but presented less of a problem than the emigration of former British, French, and Dutch colonials to the former colonial homelands.

In North Africa, Italy lost Libya, which became independent under King Idris. Large reserves of petroleum were discovered in Libya, presenting companies from energy-poor Italy with a great opportunity to exploit the fields in cooperation with the Libyans, and Italy became the largest investor in the area. Petroleum brought great wealth to Libya and afforded the Italians an opportunity for trade and for building public works, both of which increased dramatically. In this way, Libya became economically more valuable for Italy after independence than before, even after the irrational and nationalist Colonel Moammar Kadafy established a long-lasting dictatorship in 1969. Economic relations continued strong even following Kadafy's expulsion of Italian settlers and his sponsorship of terrorism that brought him world condemnation. Despite their rocky relationship, the Italians remained indulgent toward their former colony, an attitude that caused problems with the United States. The Italians, however, felt they had a special relationship with the Libyans that went beyond economics.

The loss of Italy's colonies initially caused consternation in the country, but Italy benefited from the loss as the Italians remained involved with their former colonies but were no longer drained of significant resources.

End of the Dutch Empire

The Dutch Empire dated from the seventeenth century and was primarily situated in East Asia; its jewel was Indonesia, which consisted of approximately 13,000 islands and a population of 70 million. The East Indies supplied oil, tin, rubber, coal, tobacco, sugar, coffee, and other valuable products that contributed to the well-being of the Netherlands. The Dutch population of Indonesia numbered about 240,000 and was engaged mainly in business enterprises and in civil service. The Dutch ruled through a decentralized system in conjunction with a native bureaucracy that found the highest positions closed to it.

In 1942, the Japanese occupied Indonesia, opened up to native Indonesians positions that had previously been closed to them, and encouraged nationalism against the former imperial rulers. The Japanese conquest broke the continuity of Dutch rule, shattered the previous administrative system, and fostered independence. In 1945 a bloody national revolution broke out against the Dutch and ended with Indonesian independence in 1949. The national revolution resulted in considerable tension with the United States, who supported the rebels, and caused the Dutch to consider not joining NATO. In short, the Indonesian struggle impinged on the most vital interests of the Netherlands.

The loss of the East Indies was an economic blow to the Netherlands because Indonesian raw materials were in demand and brought foreign exchange and wealth, but the end of the war stopped the outflow of funds that drained the Dutch economy. After Indonesia's loss, the friction with the United States ended, and the Dutch concentrated on their domestic economy. New collaborative efforts with Belgium and West Germany fostered the development of nuclear power, and the discovery of natural gas reserves off their coast compensated the energy-short country for the loss. Following independence, the Dutch continued to be involved with former colonials, particularly by allowing the entrance of immigrants who were attracted by the high living standard in the Netherlands.

The Italian and Dutch colonial empires were the first to be liquidated as a result of World War II, but the Belgians, French, and British attempted to make adjustments to their empires that would allow them to survive in a New World in which they were fast becoming anachronisms.

FAILED TRANSFORMATIONS

Belgium, Britain, and France made changes in their colonial empires that they hoped would adapt them to the postwar world, but they failed.

The Belgian Congo

Eighty times larger than Belgium, the Congo's Belgian population numbered approximately 18,000 in 1940 and about 89,000 in 1958. The Congo possessed great natural wealth, including diamonds, uranium, rubber, copper, tobacco, and cotton, among other products. The Belgians hoped to transform the Congo into a partner by reforming their administration. Eventually the Congo sent the highest percentage of Africans to primary schools, but only a handful to the universities. The Belgians never intended to create a native elite that could take over if they left the Congo, a tragic and costly error.

The Belgian government tried to deflect native desires for independence by offering economic and social gains, but this policy did not work well. After 1945, taking advantage of the unsettled postwar situation in Belgium, the Congolese demanded a greater political voice in governance. Belgian political problems after World War II

Patrice Lumumba became the first Prime Minister of the former Congo in 1960 after he had helped it gain independence from Belgium. Strong economic interests opposed him and civil strife resulted. In January 1961 he was executed by firing squad with the complicity of the Belgians.

increased the deep divisions that had existed with regard to colonialism in the country, and in 1954, a new coalition with Socialist participation announced new reforms for the Congo, including more civil rights, increased educational opportunities, and a transition to independence. Instead of ending the debate, this approach intensified the rhetoric of Belgian anti-imperialists, who were encouraged by the seeming end of British and French colonialism. In 1959 rioting shook the Congo, and the Belgians, reluctant to be drawn into a war of the kind that was taking place in Algeria, moved full-speed ahead toward independence. On June 30, 1960, the Congo received its independence, with disastrous results, primarily because of the lack of a native ruling class, the desire of Belgian business interests to keep control of their wealth, and the embroilment of the Congo in cold war politics.

On July 5, 1960, the Congolese army mutinied against its Belgian officers and attacked Europeans. A week later, the mineral-rich state of Katanga seceded with the support of Belgian business interests and with the help of Belgian troops and European mercenaries, depriving the newly independent state of many of its assets. Prime Minister Patrice Lumumba asked for UN intervention, or he would call for Soviet aid. The UN agreed, but balked at Lumumba's request that UN troops be used to help subdue Katanga. When the diamond-rich state of South Kasai seceded, the country descended into chaos, with the main rivals being Lumumba, supported by advisers, and General Joseph Mobutu, bolstered by Western governments and backed by the CIA. On September 14, Mobutu seized control in a military coup and arrested Lumumba. The former prime minister escaped but was captured and shot in January 1961 in Katanga with Belgian officers present. The fighting in the Congo over five years of turmoil has been estimated to have cost 100,000 lives, and it ended with Mobutu's triumph. With the help of the West, Mobutu ran one of the worst regimes on the African continent between 1965 and 1996.

The Belgians retained important investments in the Congo (renamed Zaire, then renamed several times) and good relations with its former colony returned. In Belgium, the Congo fiasco caused a flood of Belgian citizens returning home, forcing the government to increase taxes and adopt austerity budgets that led to protests. However, while the loss of the Congo produced temporary dislocations and necessitated adjustments, it did not hamper Belgian economic development.

Failure of the French Union

The decolonization process produced the most tumult in France. The French had poured more resources into their colonies than the other imperialist powers in an effort to mesh the colonial and French economies, and the colonies were a source of pride that partially compensated for France's defeat by the Germans. However, in the colonies, their efforts failed to win the support of the native populations but created restricted elites that were committed to French culture.

Algeria had been a French colony since the 1830s. Since many French nationals had emigrated to Algeria, lived there for generations, and refused to leave, the French government did its best to hold onto it. After World War II, a revolt developed into a full-fledged war into which the French poured hundreds of thousands of troops and threatened the country's stability. In 1958 an Army revolt resulted in recalling Charles De Gaulle to the government to run the country. In this photograph, French troops in full battle dress conduct house-to-house searches in the Casbah of Algiers on May 30, 1956.

The French attempted to retain control of their colonies and mandates by creating the French Union in 1946, made up of France and its overseas possessions, which were divided into different categories: overseas departments (Algeria and a handful of other territories), overseas territories, or associated states. A parliamentary structure that included a metropolitan assembly that gave the colonies representation governed the union, but this arrangement was designed to centralize the empire and keep control in French hands.

The French Union failed in its aim of tying the colonies closer to France. As nationalist movements demanded independence, a number of wars broke out. The French withdrew from the Middle Eastern mandates Syria and Lebanon, surrendered Tunis and Morocco, lost colonies in India, and battled nationalists in sub-Saharan Africa. In 1947, a revolution took place on the island of Madagascar, suppressed by the French after a year of bitter fighting; the estimated cost in lives varies but was probably between 30,000 and 40,000. The French also tried to reconquer their colony of Vietnam, but failed. In 1954 the Vietnamese Communists inflicted a severe defeat on them at Dien Bien Phu, forcing a humiliating withdrawal from Indochina and Asia. At the same time, a war for independence broke out in Algeria, the oldest colony, and the government sent 20,000 troops that grew to 500,000 by 1962.

The War in Algeria

The Algerian War destabilized the Fourth Republic by favoring instability and protest. Unlike Indochina, conscripts were sent to fight in Algeria, creating resentment among the French. As the conflict escalated, so did the dispute between important sectors of the French population that opposed the war and French settlers in Algeria, who enjoyed a privileged economic and political position there; the colonial civil service, which had a high proportion of settlers; and the army on the spot. As the war increased in ferocity, the French poured in more troops and alienated international opinion when the French army resorted to torture and other atrocities to defeat the rebels. The conflict also produced a major revolutionary thinker, Frantz Fanon, whose book, *The Wretched of the Earth*, was a fiery indictment of racism and colonialism that had a great impact on the way the West viewed imperialism. At the same time, the French economy expanded, and industrialists who were interested in modernizing the country became convinced that colonialism was outdated and that hanging on to Algeria hampered France's effort to confront increasing economic and political globalization.

In 1958, the inability of the Fourth Republic to conclude the conflict led to an army revolt in Algeria and the return of Charles de Gaulle to power. De Gaulle was primarily interested in restoring France's image and military strength in Europe and increasingly viewed the Algerian conflict as an impediment to his plans to restore French grandeur. When more troops failed to end the rebellion, terrorism spread to France, and de Gaulle reestablished control of the governmental apparatus in Algeria, de Gaulle signaled his willingness to negotiate with the rebels. This move led to the formation of an opposition front in Algeria, divisions in France, and de Gaulle's assumption of emergency powers, but in a January 1961 plebiscite, the French people backed his policy of conciliation.

In April French generals, acting in the name of the Secret Armed Organization (OAS), seized control of several Algerian cities, including the capital. De Gaulle reacted vigorously, making a powerful speech against the military rebellion and call-ing up reserves. The French army, navy, and air force remained steadfast, and loyal units retook Algiers. Negotiations with Algerian rebels followed, and the OAS began a terror campaign of shootings and bombings in Algeria and France. In March 1962, with an accord reached, the two sides ceased fire. The settlement provided for a ref-erendum on Algerian independence, preferential tariff and economic agreements, mutual exploitation of Algerian oil fields, and a military base for France; it gave guarantees to the settlers and allowed them three years to choose either French or Algerian citizenship. Once again, the OAS resorted to terrorism, but the campaign failed. By 1963, 900,000 out of an estimated 1 million settlers returned to France, and although this great number of returning *pied noirs* (blackfeet) caused social and political problems, the country reabsorbed them without difficulty.

The French Community

By this time, de Gaulle had already liquidated the remainder of the French Union by replacing it with the French Community. In 1958, he gave the African colo-nies the choice of accepting the new constitution of the Fifth Republic, in which case they would have complete control of their domestic affairs, and secession. The states that agreed to join the French Community would keep their favora-ble tariff position and economic aid. If they rejected membership, France would terminate aid and association in the tariff system. All the former colonies except Guinea voted to join the new community, but in the following years, several states seceded, and the French Community gradually lost its cohesion. Neverthe-less, many former members retained some association with France, particularly through the language, received French economic aid, and looked predominantly to France in foreign affairs; the French retained a strong military presence in the 1970s and 1980s.

BIOGRAPHICAL SKETCHES

Frantz Fanon
Language, Peasants, and Revolution

The struggles of decolonization produced African and Asian rev-olutionary leaders who were educated in Europe or were other-wise familiar with its revolutionary culture, particularly Marxism. In this respect, Frantz Fanon, whose influence continued long after his untimely death, was an exception because he came from a medical background.

Fanon was born in Martinique, a French island in the Caribbean Sea, to a mid-dle-class family, on July 20, 1925. In 1943, he volunteered to fight the Nazis with the Free French and after World War II received a scholarship to study psychiatry in Lyon. While still in France, he married and began writing on the effects of colonization. His most famous work of this period is *Black Skin, White Masks*, published in 1952.

Drawing on his own experience, Fanon argued that the relationship between the colonizer and the colonized is warped. Although he thought of himself as

continued

continued

French, he encountered French racism, which bewildered him but, at the same time, made him understand the process of how racism alienates black men while tying them to the white world. The black man is colonized by language, which makes him accept the attitudes of the French (or the colonizer). Because French culture identifies blackness with evil, the black man puts on a white mask to fit into white society. He thus internalizes cultural ideas that supposedly view equality as independent from appearance. This process creates a schism that divides him from himself. Racism, therefore, prevents the black man from achieving psychological health.

During the Algerian War, Fanon reached his full maturity as a revolutionary thinker. He served as chief of psychiatry in an Algerian hospital (Blida-Joinville) beginning in 1953, where he heard shocking stories about the conflict. Alienated from the French, he threw in his lot with the Algerians. He affirmed that he could not continue to carry out his psychiatric duties in a colonial environment that alienated the colonized peoples in their own land. The colonial administration, he said, provoked the war by seeking to rob the Algerians of their personality and intelligence.

In 1956 Fanon resigned his post at the hospital, went to Tunisia, and linked up with the Algerian National Liberation Front (FLN). He saw patients and wrote about the movement in French and Algerian publications and in other writings published posthumously, such as *Toward the African Revolution*. As the FLN representative to Ghana, he directed supplies from the south to Algerian rebel groups. While in Ghana, Fanon developed the leukemia that killed him. He wrote *The Wretched of the Earth*, his most fervent denunciation of colonialism and his most significant political work, in only ten months.

Published in 1961, *The Wretched of the Earth* develops some of the themes expressed in *Black Skin, White Masks*. In order to overcome the duality of black-bad, white-good, Fanon believed that violence and complete revolution were necessary. Violence destroys the past and liberates people from it. He argued that in Africa the peasants should be the ones in the vanguard of the revolution, not the urban bourgeoisie, who, tainted by conditions installed by imperialism, could only make incomplete revolutions. This view illustrated the influence on Fanon of the FLN, a movement based on the rural classes. Fanon's emphasis on the peasantry and on the role of language has had an important influence on scholars who seek to understand the phenomenon of colonialism and its impact.

Fanon came to the United States to be treated for his cancer. He died on December 6, 1961, at the age of 36 in Bethesda, Maryland. His body was returned to Algeria, where the FLN buried him with honors.

Evolution of the British Commonwealth

Despite the appropriation of large sums for colonial improvement, the British Commonwealth, formed in the 1920s, rapidly changed as a result of World War II. The factors determining this transformation were nationalist movements demanding independence, the decline of Britain as a world power, and the rise of the United States. The newly independent states had regional and individual concerns that were frequently remote from Commonwealth issues, and their priorities were generally linked to American, not British, policy. The British

The British hoped to salvage their empire by transforming it into a cooperative community after World War I. This attempt, while noble, did not work and after 1945 the countries of the Commonwealth drifted apart and even went to war against each other. Here is a poster created between 1939 and 1944 that graphically illustrates the failed ideal of unity.

Commonwealth was an increasingly loose association whose individual nations even went to war with each other.

During the interwar years, the British handed over more administrative functions to the native elites, but with a view toward securing greater control in the colonies in the face of growing opposition. With an eye toward holding on to the empire, the British appropriated more funds for colonial improvement during World War II, but doing so did not preserve the Commonwealth. In India, the "crown jewel" of the empire, independence movements had been active since the beginning of the twentieth century and found their leader in Mahatma Gandhi, the advocate of nonviolence. Despite the Indian military contribution to Allied victory in World War II, there was considerable opposition to India's entrance into the conflict and several revolts, and an Indian force even fought against the Allies. Indian demands for independence culminated in June 1947, when the British announced the partition of India to accommodate a Muslim state known as Pakistan. On August 14 and 15, Pakistan and India became independent. In October, the new countries went to war over possession of the state of Kashmir, with several wars following. Burma and Ceylon (Sri Lanka) gained their independence in 1948. In 1971, Bangladesh seceded from Pakistan, causing a new crisis, and Pakistan withdrew from the Commonwealth.

In Africa, the British faced a serious revolt in Kenya known as the Mau Mau rebellion. This revolt was organized in 1951 when nationalists vowed to drive the British and British settlers, who had the power and most of the land, from the country. On October 20, 1952, the British declared a state of emergency and dispatched troops to subdue the revolt. Atrocities occurred on both sides during the uprising in which the British held prisoners in camps under brutal conditions and probably cost around 50,000 lives. The emergency ended on November 10, 1959, and Kenya became independent on December 12, 1963.

The Reorientation of British Opinion

Between 1957 and 1967, most of the British possessions received their independence. Contributing factors included the Suez crisis that exposed British weakness; a desire to please the Americans, who were known to oppose colonialism; the growing strength of African nationalism; fear of Algeria-like uprisings; and doubt about the colonies' economic value to Britain. Economic problems induced the British to reduce the scope of governmental departments directing Commonwealth affairs, and Britain reoriented itself toward the continent as more colonies became sovereign states when the national debate concentrated on Britain's relationship with the Common Market.

Economic changes strengthened the European link as British trade shifted from the Commonwealth countries to the EEC. In 1950 British exports to the Commonwealth and Ireland exceeded those to all other countries, and British imports from the Commonwealth were only slightly inferior to those from other countries; by 1971 trade with Commonwealth members amounted to only a quarter of the total. This meant that Commonwealth trade was only slightly higher than trade with the Six and much less than British trade with Western Europe as a whole. By 1971 as well, the Sterling Area, once considered the financial prerequisite for the Commonwealth, was less important than Europe in maintaining London as a world financial powerhouse.

Problems with immigrants contributed to British detachment from its former colonies. In the 1960s, the number of immigrants from Asia and Africa grew rapidly, and racial tensions increased. Protests led to restrictive legislation that was carefully crafted to avoid charges of racial discrimination. The 1962 Commonwealth Immigration Act established a system of entry vouchers for immigrants who did not possess United Kingdom passports. In 1968, the British, fearing a new flood of Asian immigrants from Kenya who held British passports, regulated the entry of British passport holders, cutting the number of such eligible migrants in half. In 1971, the government presented a bill establishing complex procedures that tightened immigration controls for people of color while easing them for white citizens of the dominions. Because the bill would have instituted the principle of immigration restriction by race, British liberal sentiment rebelled, and in 1972 the proposal was defeated.

As racial tensions increased, they further weakened the British commitment to the Commonwealth. When constituted in the 1920s, the Commonwealth, as opposed to the empire, consisted of the mostly white, English-language dominions. In 1971 it included thirty-one full members and a like number of associated states. By 1991, it included fifty members with little in common.

The decolonization process did not have the major repercussions on British politics that it had in France. The Conservatives were more attached to the empire than were the Labourites, but neither allowed the colonies to dominate their politics, despite the emotional attachment of both to the former colonies, and several factors made for a smoother transition than in the French case. British civil servants carried out their government's orders more unquestioningly than did their French counterparts, small independent British farmers had less influence, and British business feared destruction of their property in case of violence. It is interesting that British investment in some colonies was greater following independence than preceding it. The British viewed the end of their empire as a return to "Little England" and accepted it as a necessary adjustment to the modern world in which Britain would have to focus on its own problems, rather than holding on to a disparate empire that had lost its significance.

The Last Empire

Portugal held on to its imperial mission the longest. The impoverished country possessed huge colonies in Africa, Angola and Mozambique; a number of islands; and scattered territories in Asia as a legacy of the country's golden age in the fifteenth century.

Because of Portuguese weakness, before World War I most of Angola and Mozambique were not under effective Portuguese control for long periods. Poor conditions, due primarily to the use of forced labor on plantations run by British-controlled companies, prompted frequent international protests that prompted the Portuguese to pass reform legislation in 1926. Because the empire had an important place in his hopes of reviving Portugal, Salazar modernized communications, transportation facilities, and education. Educational progress remained relatively slow, but the Portuguese followed a progressive racial policy and considered colonial society a multiracial one.

Portugal did not contemplate giving up the colonies despite the decolonization wind following World War II. Nationalist uprisings began in Angola in 1961 and in Mozambique and Guinea-Bissau in 1964. In the 1970s, the uprisings took on huge dimensions, and the Portuguese poured in 200,000 troops to quell the revolutions, an enormous number, given Portugal's small population. The revolutions increased cold war tensions because Communist Cuba sent troops to support the rebels. Despite the losses in lives and the expenditure of half their budget and internal opposition to the war, the Portuguese tenaciously fought to retain their colonies.

Following the Portuguese revolution that began on April 25, 1974 and the return to democracy, the country's new leaders dismantled the empire. The African colonies received their independence between 1974 and 1975, and in 1976, the Azores obtained autonomy. In 1986, Portugal agreed to return its last remaining possession, Macao, to China in 1999. During these years, Portugal linked its economic fortunes to the EC, rather than to the colonies, encouraging the modernization that brought it into the European mainstream.

The Portuguese realized what the other Western Europeans had learned: colonialism did not pay.

Bibliographical Essay

Many of the books cited for the previous chapter have sections on the effects of decolonization in the home countries.

The question of how many victims European imperialism made has become an important to topic. For discussions of this question, see the essays in A. Dirk Moses, *Empire, Colony, Genocide: Conquest, Occupation, and Subaltern Resistance in World History* (New York, 2008), and Jeremy Sarkin-Hughes, *Germany's Genocide of the Herero* (Woodbridge, UK, 2011); see also Sara Friedrichsmeyer et al., *The Imperialist Imagination: German Colonialism and Its Legacy* (Ann Arbor, Mich.,1998).

Claudio G. Segrè, *Fourth Shore: The Italian Colonization of Libya* (Chicago, 1974), describes the myth of Libya in modern Italy and the loss of the colony. See also, by the same author, *Italian Development Policy in Libya: Colonialism as a National Luxury* (n.p., 1982), and Ali Abdullatif Ahmida, *The Making of Modern Libya: State Formation, Colonialization, and Resistance* (Albany, N.Y., 2009). Miles Kahler, *Decolonization in Britain and France: The Domestic Consequences of International Relations* (Princeton, N.J., 1984), is a good description and comparison of the French and British experience. Bartholomew Landheer, *The Netherlands* (Berkeley, Calif., 1943), contains several essays on the Dutch colonies.

The Congo is examined by Georges Brausch, *Belgian Administration in the Congo* (London, 1961), and Roger Anstey, *King Leopold's Legacy* (London, 1966). Colin Leguin, *Congo Disaster* (Gloucester, UK, 1972), is a history of Belgian rule and the story of what happened after independence, while Robert B. Edgerton, *The Troubled Heart of Africa: A History of the Congo* (New York, 2002), links the tragic events surrounding independence to the present. Edgar O'Ballance, *The Congo-Zaire Experience, 1960–98* (New York, 2000), focuses on the period discussed by this chapter. Ludo de Witte's *The Assassination of Lumumba* (New York, 2001) is a history of the revolt.

The history of French colonialism after World War II is not well treated in English. For a good background, consult S. H. Roberts, *History of French Colonial Policy, 1870–1925*, 2 vols. (London, 1929). On the general question, see Raymond F. Betts, *France and Decolonization* (New York, 1991); Tony Chafer, *The End of Empire in French West Africa: France's Successful Decolonization?* (New York, 2002); and *Colonial Power and National Identity* (Stockholm, 2008), by Marie Demker. Todd Shepard's *The Invention of Decolonization: The Algerian War and the Remaking of France* (New York, 2006) describes the war's effect on French life. Good works on the war include J. Talbott, *The War Without a Name: France in Algeria, 1954–1962* (New York, 1980), and Alistair Horne, *A Savage War of Peace: Algeria 1954–1962* (London, 1987). Matthew James Connelly's *A Diplomatic Revolution: Algeria's Fight for Independence and the Origins of the Post–Cold War Era* (New York, 2002) is good on the war and its aftermath. For French opposition to the Algerian War, there is Martin Evans, *The Memory of Resistance* (New York, 1997). On other parts of the French Empire, see J. D. Hargreaves, *West Africa: The Former French States* (Englewood Cliffs, N.J., 1967), and Thomas L. Hodgkin and Ruth Shachter, *French-Speaking West Africa in Transition* (New York, 1961). For the conflicts associated with French decolonization, there is Anthony Clayton, *The Wars of French Decolonization* (New York, 1991).

Undoubtedly, the reader will find most material on this subject related to the British Empire and Commonwealth. Lawrence James, *The Rise and Fall of the British Empire* (New York, 1996), gives great attention to the period after World War II. Colin Cross, *The Fall of the British Empire 1918–1968* (New York, 1969), is a detailed account. D. A. Low, *Eclipse of Empire* (Cambridge, UK, 1991), is a study of the end of the British Empire on the various continents. C. A. Bayly and T. N. Harper, *Forgotten Wars: The End of Britain's Asian Empire* (New York, 2007), follows the wars accompanying British decolonization.

Peter F. Clarke examines *The Last Thousand Days of the British Empire: The Demise of a Superpower 1944–47* (London, 2008). Martin Lynn describes *The British Empire in the 1950s* (Basingstoke, UK, 2006). James Morris, *Farewell the Trumpets: An Imperial Retreat* (New York, 1978), is about the process of how the empire ended. Essays discussing the end of the empire and the Suez affair are collected in William Roger Louis, *Ends of British Imperialism: The Scramble for Empire, Suez and Decolonization* (New York, 2006). Richard Aldous and Sabine Lee, eds., *Harold Macmillan and Britain's World Role* (New York, 1996), a collection of essays discussing aspects of the topic, includes a study of the end of the British Empire in Africa. Niall Ferguson attempts to draw general conclusions in *Empire: The Rise and Demise of the British World Order and the Lessons for Global Power* (New York, 2003).

There are good studies of how the British Empire slowly transitioned into the Commonwealth. J. B. Watson, *Empire to Commonwealth, 1919 to 1970* (London, 1971), is a good account of this change. W. David McIntyre, *The Commonwealth of Nations: Origins and Impact, 1869–1971* (Minneapolis, Minn., 1977), is one of the best works on the topic. Nicholas Mansergh, *The Commonwealth Experience* (New York, 1969), concentrates on Commonwealth relations. J. D. B. Miller, *Survey of Commonwealth Affairs: Problems of Expansion and Attrition* (London, 1974), gives a taste of the problems associated with expansion and contraction. The changes in British culture and its implications within and outside Britain are discussed by Stuart Ward, *British Culture and the End of Empire* (New York, 2001).

Angola and Portuguese rule is examined by George J. Bender, *Angola Under the Portuguese: The Myth and the Reality* (London, 1978). Don Barnett and Ray Harvey discuss the rebellion in *The Revolution in Angola: MPLA, Life Histories and Documents* (Indianapolis, Ind., 1972). Neil F. Bruce discusses the loss of empire in *Portugal: The Last Empire* (New York, 1975). The essays in Stewart Lloyd-Jones and Antonio Costa Pinto, *The Last Empire: Thirty Years of Portuguese Decolonization* (Portland, Ore., 2003), discuss the journey of Portugal after 1974 from the colonies to European community.

Two books on growing African nationalism during the period are Thomas L. Hodgkin, *Nationalism in Colonial Africa* (New York, 1957), and J. S. Coleman, *Nigeria: A Background to Nationalism* (Berkeley, Calif., 1958). Robert H. Taylor collected essays that discuss similar themes in both Africa and Asia: *The Idea of Freedom in Asia and Africa* (Stanford, Calif., 2002).

CHAPTER 25

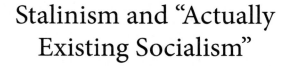

Stalinism and "Actually Existing Socialism"

CHAPTER OUTLINE

Guiding Principles • The East European Revolution • Stalinism in
Eastern Europe • "Actually Existing Socialism"
in the USSR

BIOGRAPHICAL SKETCHES

Georgi Dimitrov, Master in Ideology • Ana Rabinovici
Pauker, Communist Nonperson

Stalin controlled the process of Sovietizing Eastern Europe, keeping the interests of the USSR paramount. In theory, the USSR's role of guide for other countries seemed reasonable because it was the first country to implement communism, but the line between ideology and Russian national interest was a blurry one.

The USSR ruled in Eastern Europe because of its massive military presence and its skillful exploitation of communism's ideological appeal following the Nazi defeat. Communism lacked majority support in Eastern Europe, and, despite social reforms, Soviet military domination and a powerful police and party apparatus kept communism in power for the next forty-five years despite political instability and revolt.

GUIDING PRINCIPLES

In reconstructing their societies, East European Communists followed the Soviet model, a difficult task because some countries were more underdeveloped than Russia had been in 1917 while others had more advanced economic and social systems. The less-industrialized group (Bulgaria, Romania, and Albania) found the rate of industrial development projected by the Communists too fast, while ideology dictated that the second group, the German Democratic Republic and Czechoslovakia and, to a lesser extent, Poland and Hungary, had to repeat the steps previously followed by the USSR. In short, the Soviet model dislocated the

Eastern Europe, 1938–1948.

economic and social equilibrium of Eastern Europe, making force necessary to impose communism.

People's Democracies

Communist Eastern European states called themselves People's Democracies or People's Republics, loaded ideological terms. According to the leading East European Communist theoretician, Bulgaria's Georgi Dimitrov, communism advanced through this new type of state that emerged after the working class destroyed governments that were controlled by capitalists and great landowners and transformed the state into an instrument of the class struggle; the People's Democracies guarded against the return of bourgeois rule and would implement true communism. Dimitrov believed that only an alliance with the USSR could ensure the independence of the People's Democracies in the struggle against international capitalism and, therefore, had to repress opponents of the USSR and adopt constitutions that were modeled on the 1936 Soviet Constitution.

Dimitrov's Bulgaria proclaimed itself a People's Republic on December 4, 1947, followed by Romania on April 13, 1948; Czechoslovakia on May 9, 1948; Hungary on August 20, 1949; East Germany on November 16, 1950; and Poland on July 22, 1952. Yugoslavia had already declared itself a Federal People's Republic on November 29, 1945. Albania, closely linked to Yugoslavia, adopted a constitution patterned on Yugoslavia's on December 4, 1947. With the decline of Yugoslavia's influence after its expulsion from the Stalinist camp on June 28, 1948, however, Albania issued a Soviet-style constitution on July 4, 1950.

BIOGRAPHICAL SKETCHES

Georgi Dimitrov
Master of Ideology

The man who would become the chief ideologist of Eastern European communism had a long history as a revolutionary thinker and activist. Georgi Dimitrov was born in the Bulgarian village of Kovachevtsi on June 18, 1882. He left school and went to the capital of Sofia to learn a trade as a printer. While still a teenager, he participated in the foundation of a trade union and in 1902 joined the Bulgarian Social Democratic Party. By 1903, Dimitrov headed the left-wing faction, and in 1909, he became a member of the Central Committee. Previously elected to the Sofia City Council, he won election to the National Assembly (Subranie) in 1913 and remained a deputy for ten years. In 1918, the government imprisoned him briefly for his antiwar activities. The following year, he was instrumental in founding the Bulgarian Communist Party (BCP), and in 1921 in Moscow, he won election to the Executive Committee of the Communist International (Comintern). He attempted to overthrow the Bulgarian government in 1923 and 1925.

Dimitrov had to leave the country following these abortive revolts, for which the Bulgarian government sentenced him to death. He traveled to Moscow, Paris, Prague, Vienna, and Berlin. In the German capital, he headed an underground network, and the Nazis accused him of starting the Reichstag fire of February 27, 1933, an event that Hitler exploited to seize power. His trial in Leipzig before the Supreme Court created an international sensation because of his skillful defense and courage, during which the court had to rebuke the minister president of Prussia, Hermann Goering. Dimitrov won worldwide admiration, and Germans quipped: "There is only one man left in Germany, and he is a Bulgarian." On November 23, 1933, the court acquitted him, and he left Germany in February 1934 after a prisoner exchange.

Dimitrov went to the USSR, where his rise as an ideological star of international communism began. He became secretary of the Comintern in 1935, remaining in this post until its dissolution in 1943. He was the chief theoretician of the popular-front strategy as the best way to bolster the Western democracies against the rising tide of fascism. In 1935 at the Comintern's Seventh Congress, he came up with the classic Communist definition of fascism as a terrorist dictatorship of the most reactionary part of finance capitalism. In the late 1930s, he entered into a dialogue with Chinese Communist leader Mao Zedong on how to use popular-front tactics against the Japanese. In June 1942, Dimitrov founded the Fatherland Front, a Communist-led coalition to fight the Germans, which seized control of Bulgaria on September 9, 1944.

He returned to Bulgaria in 1945 and in 1946 added the title of prime minister to his post as general secretary of the BCP. Dimitrov then imposed a Stalinist regime on the country. He eliminated the bourgeoisie, nationalized industry and the banks, and seized private property. He imposed collectivization but could not completely eliminate peasant resistance. In December 1947, he successfully pushed for the adoption of a Soviet-style constitution, and over the next two years, he destroyed independent organizations in Bulgaria through a terror campaign he extended to the BCP.

Dimitrov's imposition of Stalinism did not distinguish him from other East European leaders. The interest he continues to hold for students of communism is due to his ability to provide a sophisticated intellectual basis for Stalinism in Eastern Europe. His greatest contribution toward this end came in his elaboration of the role of the People's Democracies at the Fifth Congress of the BCP in December 1948. According to Dimitrov, the People's Democracies were the fundamental forms of "actually existing socialism" and the means to achieve communism.

Dimitrov fell ill and died in Moscow on July 2, 1949.

The Communist Parties and the States

The concept of the party complemented the idea of the People's Democracies. The party, supposedly the repository of the supreme authority of the working class and of the state, was at the same time infallible and unconditioned by constitutions. Following the destruction of the bourgeoisie, the Communist parties took control of Eastern European social democratic and popular organizations in 1948. However, according to a paradoxical principle of Stalin, the class struggle now intensified because if failures had occurred in the construction of socialism (this word was used to mean achieving conditions that would lead to communism) and the Communist parties were infallible, the failures must be the fault of individual Communist leaders who must be purged—hence the periodic purges that shook the Eastern European Communist states and the Soviet Union.

THE EAST EUROPEAN REVOLUTION

Since the economic development of the USSR served as a model for the People's Democracies, three major principles characterized their progress toward communism: collectivization, industrialization, and a command economy.

Revolution on the Land

East European Communists immediately set a social revolution into motion. Some aspects of this revolution, such as land reform, corresponded with long-standing demands, but the Communist side of the changes, especially collectivization, received less support or encountered resistance, depending on the country.

On April 15, 1945, Bulgaria passed a law collectivizing agriculture. The government forcibly consolidated peasant holdings into large farms owned and run by the state. New legislation, passed on June 9, 1946, limited the amount of land that farmers could own, combined state and expropriated land into a State Land Fund, and settled people on this land. In November 1948, the government restricted the amount of private land that could be held on the collectives to between two and fifty acres and limited the amount of livestock that peasants could hold. Nevertheless, the Bulgarian tradition of individual landholdings was difficult to break, and by the end of 1948, the collectives held only about 6 percent of the land.

In Romania on March 20, 1945, the king signed legislation passed by the Communist government expropriating private property over 124 acres and confiscating all farm machinery and livestock. In March 1949, the country began the process of collectivization and in 1962 pronounced it complete. In Hungary on March 15, 1945, the expropriation of land proclaimed by the Red Army began. This measure aimed at eliminating the great estates and redistributing the land to the poor, thus doing away with the large landowning classes and obtaining the support of the peasants. Anyone possessing more than 1,420 acres, traitors, former Horthy supporters, the church, and other institutions lost their land without any effective compensation (promised but not given). The state took a large share of the confiscated land, while the peasants received small plots that did not yield enough to feed their families. The Albanian Communists passed an agricultural reform law on August 29, 1945, supposedly aimed at breaking up the large estates and redistributing the land to the peasants. In fact, the government aimed at collectivization, which it officially announced on April 17, 1947. In Poland, property over 250 acres, and later over 125 acres, was expropriated, but the collectivization effort failed. In July 1956, the government called off its collectivization efforts. In East Germany, the Soviets broke up the large estates in 1945. Both East Germany and Czechoslovakia seized and redistributed the lands of persons who were compromised with the previous regimes.

In short, between 1944 and 1948, all the Communist regimes in the East had passed measures nationalizing the land and industry, thus establishing state control of the economy. However, the process was not uniform and varied in pace and scope, depending on the country, and sometimes did not achieve its aim of establishing communism. In Romania and Poland, for example, the collectivization effort faltered, and in Bulgaria, where individual land ownership was widespread, nationalization laws had little effect.

Revolution in Industry

The GDR and Czechoslovakia were the industrial powerhouses of Eastern Europe. In East Germany, most big enterprises were nationalized following World War II by both the Russians and German Communists on the basis that they had supported the Nazi war machine. In July and August 1946, the USSR seized the property of war criminals and announced the expropriation of large business concerns in its zone. On February 14 of the following year, basic industry was nationalized, and on January 1, 1949, East Germany implemented Soviet-style economic planning to build the industry necessary for socialism. It followed up this action with a full-fledged Five-Year Plan on January 1, 1950.

Czechoslovakia nationalized heavy industry and other large firms on October 24, 1945, before the Communists took power. The government instituted planning on January 1, 1947. The nationalization process, however, accelerated dramatically after the Communist coup of February 1948. An April 26, 1948, law nationalized all businesses employing more than forty-nine people. On April 28, the government nationalized the construction industry and most of the other sectors of the economy. In August, it announced that it had nationalized 93 percent of all the industries.

Nationalization and planning affected more than the most heavily industrialized East European states. The Communist regimes of the lesser industrialized countries confiscated the property of persons who were accused of supporting the former regimes and then nationalized other sectors of the economy. By 1949, with the partial exception of Poland, they had completed the process. Seven East European states (not including Yugoslavia) controlled an average of about 95 percent of industrial production. Between 1946 and 1950, the regimes had all established state planning bodies on the Soviet model to control industry and guide further industrialization. They also nationalized banks and commercial enterprises and took charge of foreign trade by creating Soviet-style entities that controlled a very high percentage of that trade—approaching 100 percent in some of the countries.

Revolution in the Economy

All these changes may be summarized by saying that the Eastern European countries implemented the Soviet economic model (that is, abolition of the free market), the adoption of central planning, and concentration of investment in heavy industry. Despite attempts at reform and, in some countries, the emergence of an underground economy, the East European regimes followed these principles for the next forty years of Soviet domination. Central planning and all that it implied proved inefficient and deleterious and contributed to the demise of communism in the 1980s.

Instead of consumer demand determining which products to produce and the product price, in Eastern Europe and the USSR, central planning offices made those decisions. The central planning offices on the Soviet model were set up in the East between 1946 and 1950, while state run foreign trade companies, also inspired by the Soviet example, appeared in all the Eastern Communist countries between 1946 and 1956. Central planning created a host of problems. Despite all their efforts, it was impossible for planners to know exactly what kind of products— and of what quality, type, size, shape, and so forth—consumers needed or wanted. They were also unable to keep up with the changing demand, a task that proved impossible with the passage of time. Attempting to plan exactly what to produce led to serious economic and social dislocations. It created imbalances in the number of goods that were produced and dangerous distortions of the economies of the individual East European states and the USSR. For example, a country would produce too much of one product and not enough of another, or it might produce too much of the wrong type of good—too many boots, for example, and not enough shoes, or too many shoes of a particular type and not enough of another. The planners could not keep up with the details of what to produce; they would call for the production of a certain number of shoes, but proved unable to specify what kind of the myriad types modern industry was able to manufacture. Moreover, because planners, not the market, set the price of goods, prices could not be lowered in order to sell goods that were least in demand or raised to slow the demand of the most desired goods. When requested to supply a certain number of goods, manufacturers produced the type that was the easiest to make—not necessarily the cheapest or the best—because the profit motive no longer existed.

These shortcomings resulted in chronic shortages of specific types of goods that consumers wanted. In fact, the centrally planned economies of Eastern Europe resulted in extreme shortages of goods and services and massive corruption. Waiting and standing in line became a fixture of life in the East and the butt of jokes. One story went as follows: A consumer bought a new car and was informed that he had to wait ten years for delivery. He then asked if the car would be delivered in the morning or in the afternoon. When asked what difference it would make, he answered: "Because the plumber is coming in the morning!"

Compounding the shortages created by a rigidly centralized economy, the Soviets and Eastern European regimes invested a large proportion of their wealth in heavy industry, dictated by Marxist-Leninist doctrine, and too little in consumer items. After Stalin's death in 1953, the proportions shifted somewhat, but the investment in consumer goods remained paltry compared to that in the West.

As economic theory and practice, "actually existing socialism" proved a failure, and it was unlikely to have survived as long as it did except for Soviet power.

Revolution in Society

In addition to the changes on the land, in industry, and in the economy, "actually existing socialism" revolutionized society. The Communist states attempted to impose Marxist values, such as materialism; removed religious studies from school curricula; favored atheism; and curtailed the activities of the churches. Communist Poland, for example, attacked the Catholic Church against the wishes of its people. In 1946 the pope excommunicated Communist party members, and on September 26, 1953, the Poles arrested the country's cardinal primate, charging him with conspiring against the state. The Hungarians had done the same to their cardinal on December 27, 1948. Attacks on religion were not limited to Catholics. In 1948 and 1949, Bulgaria unleashed a campaign against the Eastern Orthodox Church and Protestant denominations, while the Romanians campaigned against the Uniate Church (which had broken off from the Eastern Orthodox Church in 1698 and recognized the pope as its leader). The Bulgarians also pushed for the emigration of Jews, Gypsies, Turks, and Armenians.

Along with religion, the Communist regimes assaulted another major force in East European society—nationalism. They replaced national holidays with ones that had significance for communism, renamed streets, and adopted Communist symbols along with their national symbols. Hand in hand with deemphasizing national identity went exaltation of the Soviet Union. Soviet films, books, and visiting artists proliferated, while Western cultural manifestations were discouraged. In Czechoslovakia, books published before May 5, 1948, were banned. Another policy of "actually existing socialism" was the destruction of the numerous East European mass organizations that had existed before the Communists came to power, including church, secular, and political associations. The regimes then replaced them with a relatively small number of government-controlled bodies, including official youth, labor, and women's organizations. However, the governments were unable permanently to suppress these movements and ideas, and, after the fall of communism, they returned with a vengeance.

The East European regimes were more successful in the areas of health, welfare, and education. Despite complaints about the delivery of these services and disparities among the sectors of society that received them, East Europeans came to take for granted a high degree of government-sponsored social services. Although their assumption that disparities would automatically disappear because "actually existing socialism" had supposedly achieved a classless society proved mistaken, the achievements of the Communist regimes in social welfare represent an important legacy.

STALINISM IN EASTERN EUROPE

Ideology supposedly held the East European states together, but Stalin dictated policy in the area.

The Purges

After Tito thwarted Stalin's attempt to dominate Yugoslavia, the Soviet leader moved to eliminate all opposition that may have arisen in the Communist parties. As Stalin prepared to impose his policies on the postwar USSR and Eastern Europe, he feared possible mass opposition led by prominent Eastern Communist leaders who might put the interests of their countries first, and they became the prime candidates for elimination. The late 1940s and 1950s witnessed widespread purges that removed leaders who had been loyal to Moscow and, moreover, struck hard at the most disparate social groups in unpredictable ways.

Titoism as the Official Reason for Repression

Stalin had mistakenly believed that he could eliminate Tito quickly and was determined not to repeat his error in Soviet-controlled Eastern Europe. During a meeting of the Cominform, communism's international organ, his representative Andrei Zhdanov claimed that the Russians had indisputable proof that the Yugoslav leadership was riddled with Western spies. This was the origin of Titoism as the pretext for eradicating anyone the Russians believed could jeopardize Soviet control. "Titoism" came to mean nationalism, spying for the West, and betrayal of the Communist cause. With the guidance of Soviet agents, numerous arrests, trials, and executions rapidly followed in Albania, Romania, Hungary, Bulgaria, East Germany, Poland, and Czechoslovakia.

Janos Kadar was one of the most prominent victims of the postwar purges in Eastern Europe. He was lucky to have survived and was called back to rule Hungary after the Hungarian Revolution of 1956. Perhaps because of his own history and because the Russians feared another revolution, Hungary under Kadar was allowed a fairly liberal economic system.

The Victims

Janos Kadar, who would lead Hungary after 1956, described how he was tortured:

> They had begun to beat Kadar. They had smeared his body with mercury to prevent his pores from breathing. He had been writhing on the floor when a newcomer had arrived. . . . Kadar was raised from the ground. Vladimir stepped close. Two henchmen pried Kadar's teeth apart, and the colonel, negligently, as if this were the most natural thing in the world, urinated into his mouth.

Who were the victims? Persons who were contaminated by having spent time in the West, even in exile or fighting in the Spanish Civil War, made up one important category. Bourgeois social origins or having a Western spouse practically guaranteed that a person would run afoul of the inquisitors. The feeling that one might possibly turn against the Soviets in the future brought torture, trial, and condemnation.

Victims confessed to absurd crimes for a variety of reasons. Many did so because their families were threatened with torture. Others swore that they had committed crimes because officials assured them that they would not be executed once they had admitted guilt and had abjectly participated in a public trial. Others falsely confessed because interrogators convinced them that they were rendering a service to communism.

BIOGRAPHICAL SKETCHES

Ana Rabinovici Pauker
Communist Nonperson

The career of Ana Pauker demonstrates how it was possible to go rapidly from nothing to high office in Communist Eastern Europe and then back.

Ana Pauker was born in Moldavia, Romania, in 1893. Sources differ about whether she was the daughter of a rabbi or a Jewish ritual butcher. Like many Socialist women before her, she spent time in Zurich studying medicine. During World War I, she taught at a Jewish primary school in the Romanian capital of Bucharest. She joined the Romanian Communist Party in 1921. In 1924, when Romanian authorities outlawed the party, she dedicated herself to clandestine activities and achieved a position of leadership in the organization. The police arrested her in 1936 for illegal activities, and she received a ten-year sentence.

In 1940, the Romanians and Soviets engaged in a prisoner exchange, and Pauker went to the USSR. While in that country, she was a member of the Comintern's Executive Committee until 1943. In that year, the Soviets dissolved the Comintern in deference to the Americans and British, always suspicious of the Soviet-dominated organization that directed the activities of international communism. Pauker spent the war years in the Soviet Union organizing a division of the Red Army consisting of Romanian prisoners of war. As the conflict wound down, she served as a liaison between the Soviet occupying forces and the Romanian Communist Party. Returning to Romania during the summer of 1944 with the Red Army, Pauker rose to the top echelons of the Communist Party, becoming a member of its Central Committee, and devoted herself to rebuilding it. Many years of hard opposition had severely weakened that organization, and Pauker later stated that, when she returned, the Communists counted fewer than a thousand members.

In Romania, Pauker was a "Muscovite," one of the Communists who had spent the war years in the USSR and who were Soviet supporters, as opposed to being local or national Communists. The Muscovites did not receive any cabinet posts when the Communists entered a Romanian coalition government after November 1944 that included two local Communists. Stalin opposed this government because it was a true coalition and its interior minister opposed communism. He pressured the Romanians, who replaced the cabinet, but in January 1945, the Communists started a bid for control of the country through a front organization known as the National Democratic Front. This organization called for radical land reform and persecution of Romanians it labeled reactionaries and criminals of war. The National Democratic Front presented itself as the only organization that was capable of convincing Stalin to transfer to the Romanians territory he still controlled and drew its strength from Soviet support. Soviet diplomatic pressure, street riots, and strikes, followed by direct Soviet intervention, forced the king to install a government that was subservient to the USSR on March 6, 1945.

The Communists completed their takeover of Romania during the next two years. Pauker participated in the process and became minister of foreign affairs on November 5, 1947. In 1949 she added the post of vice prime minister, but factional divisions between locals and Muscovites were already splitting the Romanian

continued

continued

Communists. In 1952, the local Communist Gheorghe Gheorghiu-Dej joined forces with a Muscovite leader, a former Pauker ally. After winning the power struggle, Gheorghiu-Dej purged the party of his rivals and eliminated foreign elements, such as ethnic Hungarians and Jews.

Ana Pauker, a Jew and a Gheorghiu-Dej opponent, lost her posts in the government in the purge. Luckily, she escaped a show trial and execution, but not obscurity. She lived out the rest of her life as a petty bureaucrat in limbo, as a nonperson, even the date of her death being uncertain. Depending on the source, she may have died in 1953, in June 1960, or at some other unknown time.

Show Trials

Upon obtaining a signed confession, prosecutors sent off nine copies of the document and an official report to local leaders and to Stalin, who personally monitored the process while Soviet agents instructed local officials on how to extract confessions and on conducting show trials. Defendants, judges, and prosecutors were all expected to follow prepared scripts, and sometimes the defendants, experienced operatives that they had been, guided the judge's performance when he erred.

Former Secretary of the Czechoslovak Communist Party Rudolf Slansky, a dedicated Communist veteran, was put on trial in November 1952 at the high point of the show trials in Czechoslovakia, charged with treason and sabotage. His guilty verdict showed that having been a life-long loyal Communist did not guarantee one's survival. He was executed and his ashes mixed with building materials to make roads. He is shown here at the May Day festivities in 1947.

In September 1949, former Hungarian Interior Minister Laslo Rajk went on trial on charges of having spied for Horthy, betraying his Communist comrades during the Spanish Civil War, spying for the United States and France, and plotting with Tito to restore capitalism. Rajk, a devoted veteran who had participated in all the important Communist causes since the 1930s, admitted his guilt and was executed. In Bulgaria, onetime holder of prestigious governmental positions under the Communist government, Traicho Kostov, confessed but then recanted. Abruptly the radio broadcast of his trial and simultaneous translations for foreign journalists terminated. The trial continued without him, and he was executed. In November 1952, in Czechoslovakia, the high point of the show trials arrived. Rudolf Slansky, secretary general of the Czechoslovak Communist Party, and thirteen codefendants faced charges of being "Trotskyist-Zionist-Titoist-bourgeois-nationalist traitors, spies and saboteurs, enemies of the Czechoslovak nation, of its people's democratic order, and of socialism." Found guilty, eleven were executed, their ashes were mixed with paving material to make roads, and their property was sold off cheaply to other party members.

Although anti-Semitism did not appear to be an important factor during the early trials, it soon became prominent. Eleven of the fourteen defendants in the Slansky trial were Jewish. The Romanians expelled Foreign Minister Ana Pauker from the party's Central Committee. In Poland, the purges appeared in a milder guise because of the tenacious opposition to them and because of the well-known Polish propensity to stand up against overwhelming odds. Wladyslaw Gomulka, the most prominent Polish leader, was put under house arrest, and other Communist leaders endured years of imprisonment.

The Purges and Society

Stalin's adherents in Eastern Europe purged the societies in their respective countries, not just the politicians, by targeting real, imagined, and potential enemies. Officials encouraged or forced denunciations from ordinary people for vaguely defined crimes. All groups were subject to persecution, but the purges struck particularly people who had belonged to social categories the Communists abhorred before they came to power, such as the middle class.

Purge mechanisms wormed their way into everyday life. Possessing a desired item exposed one to arrest and elimination. Links with Western organizations, including the Boy Scouts, presented a serious danger. The inquisitors required associations, departments, and production units to fill quotas of victims to be handed over to the police and allowed them to make their own choices. Faced with such decisions, committees turned over people for irrelevant reasons: because they were Jews, because they ruined things for others by working too hard, because they did not fit in with the group. The secret police used the Stalinist tactic of dispatching vans during the early morning hours to arrest the victims. An inordinately large proportion of the East European population landed in prison as the arrests expanded to include priests, nuns, cardinals, school officials, army officers, and personalities in the cultural field. The purges completed Soviet control of the satellites and had disastrous economic and moral effects.

Repression and Economic Development

The purges coincided with implementation of five-year plans for the construction of socialism. The Eastern European states instituted centralized planning, promoted rapid industrialization, and collectivized agriculture. Forced industrialization brought lower living standards and passive resistance, which the purges addressed. Victims could be blamed when things went wrong and the fault placed on spies, saboteurs, and traitors. The purges terrorized workers into fulfilling their production quotas, kept the parties in line, and coerced many peasants to accept collectivization.

Communist economics caused widespread long-term devastation. The five-year plans inaugurated large projects with insufficient capital and inadequate labor resources that made their goals unobtainable. A large number of people who could have been constructively employed in modernization were busily engaged in overseeing the purges and the many bureaucratic tasks they required. The temptation and tradition of exploiting inefficient prisoner labor proved too much for East European planners who lacked modern machinery. The purging of social categories who were considered anti-Communist required that qualified professionals be put to work in menial jobs. In an absurd reversal of roles, incompetent political hacks or young people with insufficient training determined which projects should go forward and directed the more capable people, who were utilized as workers. These techniques did long-lasting damage to the East European mentality and environment.

Despite Communist ruthlessness, opposition to collectivization and communization remained strong. Polish peasants successfully impeded it. The Bulgarian and Romanian Communist regimes never eliminated peasant resistance. Opposition to collectivization was an important factor in the 1956 Hungarian Revolution, and Communist economics spurred disorders in East Germany and Poland during the 1950s.

During the 1950s, the East European countries showed rapid economic growth and an annual increase in the national income of between 6 percent and 8 percent. This development was due primarily to early reforms and forced industrialization. "Actually existing socialism" could not sustain these growth rates, and during the 1960s they fell despite attempts to reform communism after Stalin's death.

Hollowing Out the Communist Parties

The East European persecutions struck the rank-and-file in addition to the party leaders. The police rounded up hundreds of party members to provide witnesses against the alleged crimes of the leaders and purged members on the possibility that they might deviate from Stalin's policies in the future. Probably one party member in four suffered some kind of abuse, and many more Communists died at the hands of their comrades in the Communist states than during the anti-Communist persecutions in Eastern Europe before World War II. The decline in party membership in the satellite states as a result of the purges varied from 25 percent to 40 percent.

The purges completed the subordination of the East European Communist parties to Soviet control and rendered them meaningless. Secret police agents penetrated the party machinery to ferret out spies and traitors. Given the low incidence of real betrayal, the police trumped up charges against their targets. The resulting witch-hunts fostered the growth of doublespeak and doublethink, described by George Orwell in his celebrated novel *1984*—simultaneously speaking sense and nonsense and holding contradictory beliefs.

Communist Parties and the State After the Purges

In the long run, hollowing out the Communist parties severely weakened the Soviet bloc. The parties permeated government, economics, and society. They ran the planned economy and the army. They managed the elected legislatures and named deputies as a reward for party work with a complete disregard for elections. As a consequence, the legislatures met infrequently and counted for nothing. Judges, lawyers, and court personnel had to belong to the party. Judges attended lessons on party ideology and applied it as law, which discriminated against citizens of the former middle class and other class enemies and denied full educational opportunities to their children.

The parties, shorn of their best elements by the purges, managed Eastern European society and monopolized the best jobs. They rigorously controlled education, journalism, and the arts; exercised strict censorship over the mass media and writers; dominated professional associations; ran the factories and the offices and even altered weather reports to ensure sunny May Days. Through the secret police and spies, the parties kept tabs on ordinary people and their own members to ensure conformity. Loyal party members, the "nomenklatura," enjoyed extensive privileges that were unavailable to ordinary citizens, creating intense resentment among the ordinary people.

End of a Mission

At the Twentieth Congress of the Communist Party of the Soviet Union (CPSU) in 1956, the Soviets denounced Stalin's crimes and admitted the damage that his policies had done to communism, but did not blame communism as an ideology. This congress probably ensured communism's eventual demise because confirmation of the entity of the crimes threw doubt on the ideology.

When party members who had been purged were released from prison camps after Stalin's death in 1953, the truth became inescapable: Communist comrades had murdered, imprisoned, and tortured loyal party members on the basis of outrageous lies. The knowledge that the East European regimes had cooperated with Stalin reduced popular support for them and shook the faith of the parties in their mission. By the time communism fell in the 1980s, Communist Party members had long ceased to regard their cause as sacred and considered the party simply a vehicle for privileges and career advancement.

"ACTUALLY EXISTING SOCIALISM" IN THE USSR

It is not surprising that "actually existing socialism" in the USSR resembled communism in the satellite countries, particularly the purges. Stalin insisted on them because, during World War II, he had deemphasized ideology, stressed patriotism, and set into motion a liberalization process to win the Soviet people's support in fighting the Nazis that he feared might destroy his regime.

Postwar Purges

After the war, Stalin was very suspicious because of the glimpse his soldiers had gained of the Western world during their occupation service, even in war-torn Germany, and feared that fraternization with Allied soldiers and officers might cause them to compare Soviet and Western conditions, become dissatisfied, and revolt. As a result, the Soviet government limited contact with the Allies, initiated a propaganda campaign against false bourgeois values, and cracked down on returning prisoners of war and Russian administrators who had served in East Germany.

After President Roosevelt's death in 1945, Stalin argued that a progressive era in the history of capitalism had ended and that capitalism had reverted to its reactionary character. Consequently, capitalism, and its champion the United States, reemerged as communism's main nemesis, and he revived pre–World War II propaganda themes in preparation for a new purge. In 1946, Stalin centralized control over the Communist Party. Between 1940 and 1945, party membership had increased by a third, and, along with wartime conditions and less control from Moscow, had allowed local party secretaries to build up independent power bases. The party became more technocratic, nationalistic, and closed minded as young adherents with no memory of the Bolshevik Revolution and little knowledge of Marxist doctrine replaced older members. Greater centralization allowed the party to enforce procedures that had not been implemented during the war years, to accept fewer members, and to limit opportunities for advancement.

Following World War II, the Soviet Union made an enormous effort to reconstruct its industry and infrastructure. The government concentrated on heavy industry at the cost of consumer goods. It built housing but was never able to resolve the overcrowding that accompanied it to its end. Above are new apartment houses in Kiev, in the Ukraine, in 1955.

At the same time, a purge removed an average of 28 percent of the local secretaries in 1946 alone, although less violently than in the 1930s. The Leningrad Affair, during which all five secretaries in Leningrad had been removed by July 1949, became a symbol of the postwar purge.

The new purge affected the army. Service abroad subjected soldiers to a high probability of being removed. An estimated 20 percent of Russian administrators who had served in East Germany were arrested, a higher number of civilian and military officials were dismissed or demoted, and political personnel interfered with the work of military commanders. A large number of civilians were deported, particularly in the three Baltic states and in formerly German-occupied areas of the country.

Ideology and Nationalism in Soviet Society and Culture

In February 1946, Stalin believed that a war with capitalism might break out, and an intense propaganda campaign to prepare the Soviet population for a possible conflict followed. Headed by Stalinist lieutenant Andrei Zhdanov, the campaign blended Communist and national themes by exalting the Soviet way of life above Western values. It criticized Soviet magazines for denigrating Soviet achievements and lauding Western bourgeois values. Writers were criticized and punished if their works did not adequately praise Soviet accomplishments. Thus, the Soviets claimed most of the world's inventions, and Stalin or his representatives targeted scientists and scholars in all fields whose research did not fit in with the current Marxism-Leninism. The victims of these attacks were expelled from their professional associations, making it difficult for them to earn a living in a state where the government directed intellectual activity.

A vast security apparatus, dominated by secret police head Lavrenti P. Beria, controlled and enforced these activities. The secret police reported directly to Stalin and became the most important institution in the postwar USSR by terrorizing society, ensuring that Western political or cultural ideas would not pollute Soviet society, and implementing Stalin's most cherished policies—collectivization, industrialization, nuclear weapons research, and labor legislation. It fielded its own army to fight recalcitrant peasants and partisans; possessed its own economic empire, including factories and railways; and disposed of a large labor supply in its concentration camps.

Women in the Postwar USSR

The status of Soviet women was mixed. During World War II, the home front had become increasingly female, with the percentage of women working in agriculture and the industrial sector ranging as high as 70 percent and 56 percent, respectively. When the war ended, women were sent back to the home whenever possible, and their presence in the workforce declined to 47 percent in 1950. This development had both psychological and economic costs. Because of war losses, 30 percent of Russian households were composed of single women who needed to work. With the female population exceeding the male population by 20 million by 1959, loneliness became a feature of Soviet life, as did the preference for sons, more valuable because of their scarcity.

The state hoped to remedy the population decline by making divorce more difficult, glorifying motherhood, and punishing childless couples. Divorce proceedings were so long, expensive, and bureaucratic that it became practically impossible to dissolve marriages. In order to encourage matrimony, common-law marriages were abolished, and unmarried mothers were prohibited from bringing suits against the presumed fathers of their children. Also, the state increased subsidies for families with children and honored women who bore more than seven offspring. Couples without children were taxed, and marriage with foreigners was banned. Liberalization in the area of women's rights came only after Stalin's death, with abortion allowed once more in 1955 and divorce by mutual consent permitted after 1968.

Industrial Reconstruction

In order to rebuild the Soviet infrastructure after World War II, Stalin tapped the labor of prison camp inmates and of 2 million German prisoners of war. Up to 1956, German labor and reparations from former enemies supplied an estimated 10 percent of the state's fixed investments in heavy industry and agriculture.

Stalin's investment of a large proportion of the USSR's resources in heavy industry appeared in the five-year plan of March 1946 that set targets for increasing electricity output by 70 percent above the prewar levels and iron and steel production by 35 percent. Amazingly, Soviet workers toiling long hours for low pay and enduring inflexible party discipline managed to make it a success. Increased efficiency in the undamaged factories east of the Ural Mountains and the less devastating effects of the purges compared to those of the 1930s help account for this accomplishment. By 1950, industrial production had increased 40 percent above the 1940 level.

Costs of Postwar Reconstruction

The rapid industrial revival came at a heavy price. The production of consumer goods in 1945 dropped to about 40 percent of the 1940 figure, which was already very low, and failed to progress at a substantial pace thereafter. With little to buy, workers could not spend their meager earnings and lived under unbearable conditions. Half the urban dwellings and a quarter of rural housing had been destroyed in the occupied areas, causing millions to continue to live in caves, dugouts, and other temporary quarters. Families all over the country lived many to a room, and the housing shortage persisted until the end of communism.

Agriculture also paid the price for industrial reconstruction. The country suffered a severe shortage of bread as Stalin announced high steel production targets, and rationing continued until 1947. The need to repair wartime devastation and continued passive resistance to collectivization hampered agricultural production. The government faced the dilemma of increasing production by downplaying ideology or to continue to implement Communist principles at the cost of low production.

Stalin chose the latter. Governmental planners increased taxation and demanded a high proportion of the yields from collectivized farms at very low prices. If the crops produced by the collectivized farms increased, the state demanded more at the same low prices. This pernicious cycle killed the peasants' incentive to increase yields and, as a result, in 1953 agricultural production per head remained at the pre-1917 levels.

The inability to resolve the agricultural question was a major failing of Soviet central planners and contributed to the eventual demise of communism. Even after Stalin's death, the experiment with "actually existing socialism" was riddled with too many economic flaws to succeed.

Bibliographical Essay

Hugh Seton-Watson discusses developments in Eastern European in the 1950s in *The East European Revolution* (New York, 1956), a standard work; he tells a good story, connecting Sovietization to the end of the war. The best history of Eastern Europe during this period and up to the fall of communism is R. J. Crampton, *Eastern Europe in the Twentieth Century—and After*, 2d ed., (London and New York, 1997); the citation about Kadar's torture is on p. 264, and the charges in the Czech purges are on p. 262. Readers should also consult the appropriate chapters in Crampton's history of Bulgaria, previously cited.

Vladimir Tismaneanu, *Stalinism Revisited: The Establishment of Communist Regimes in East-Central Europe* (New York, 2009), discusses the entire period of Stalin's takeover of the region. F. Fejto, *A History of the People's Democracies: Eastern Europe Since Stalin* (Harmondsworth, UK, 1974) is a classic work. Several other good works that consider Eastern Europe during this period as a whole include Geoffrey Swain and Nigel Swain, *Eastern Europe Since 1945* (New York, 2009); J. Tomaszewski, *The Socialist Regimes of East Central Europe* (London, 1989); and Fernando Claudin, *The Communist Movement: From Comintern to Cominform* (London, 1975). Robert Service, *Comrades! A History of World Communism* (Cambridge, Mass., 2007), covers the period discussed in this chapter.

For particular countries, see Patrick Major and Jonathan Osmond, *The Workers' and Peasants' State: Communism and Society in East Germany Under Ulbricht, 1945–1971* (New York, 2002), and Gary Bruce, *Resistance with the People* (Boulder, Colo., 2001), for East Germany. For Bulgaria, see N. Oren, *Bulgarian Communism: The Road to Power, 1934–1944* (New York, 1971), and J. D. Bell, *The Bulgarian Communist Party* (Stanford, Calif., 1986). Vassellin Dimitrov, *Stalin's Cold War* (New York, 2008), discusses communism in Bulgaria and the cold war. Romania is discussed by Vladimir Tismaneanu, *Stalinism for all Seasons: A Political History of Romanian Communism* (Berkeley, Calif., 2003); Michael Shafir, *Romania: Politics, Economics, and Society* (London, 1985); G. Ionescu, *Communism in Romania, 1944–1962* (Oxford, UK, 1964); R. R. King, *A History of the Romanian Communist Party* (Stanford, Calif., 1980); and S. Fischer-Galati, *Twentieth Century Romania* (New York, 1970). N. Pano, *The People's Republic of Albania* (Baltimore, Md., 1968), discusses the Albanian situation.

On Poland, see Michael Fleming, *Communism, Nationalism, and Ethnicity in Poland, 1944–50* (New York, 2010), which examines the beginning of Communist rule and nationalism. Ronald C. Monticone, *The Catholic Church in Communist Poland, 1945–1985* (Boulder, Colo., 1986), and Marian S. Mazgai, *Church and State in Communist Poland: A History, 1944–1989* (Jefferson, N.C., 2010) both discuss relations between the church and state beyond the Communist period. See also J. Coutauvidis and J. Reynolds, Poland, 1939–1947 (Leicester, UK, 1986), and Teresa Toranska, *Them: Stalin's Polish Puppets* (New York, 1987). Hungary is examined by S. M. Max, *The United States, Great Britain, and the Sovietization of Hungary* (New York, 1985), and W. McCragg, *History of the Revolutionary Workers' Movement in Hungary* (Budapest, 1972). Peter Kenez, *Hungary From the Nazis to the Soviets* (New York, 2008), is a detailed work on the establishment of the Communist regime.

On Czechoslovakia, see Bradley F. Abrams, *The Struggle for the Soul of the Nation: Czech Culture and the Rise of Communism* (Lanham, Md., 2004), and Jiri Pelikan, ed., *The Czechoslovak Political Trials, 1950–1954* (London, 1970). On Yugoslavia, see Ivo Banac, *With Stalin against Tito* (Ithaca, N.Y., 1980). *Contemporary Yugoslavia: Twenty Years of Socialist Experiment* (Berkeley, Calif., 1969), edited by Wayne S. Vucinich et al., contains some still-useful essays. Neil Barnett's *Tito* (London, 2006) is a good introduction to the Yugoslav Communist leader.

The show trials as a phenomenon are analyzed by Bela Szasz, *Volunteers for the Gallows: Anatomy of a Show-Trial* (London, 1971), and G. H. Hodos, *Show Trials: Stalinist Purges in Eastern Europe, 1948–54* (New York, 1987). On Russian culture during this period, see Isaiah Berlin, *The Soviet Mind: Russian Culture Under Communism* (Washington, D.C., 2004) (edited by Henry Hardy).

In addition to the biographies of Stalin previously listed, conditions in postwar Russia are discussed by Robert Conquest, *Power and Policy in the USSR* (New York, 1961). R. W. Pethybridge's *A History of Postwar Russia* (New York, 1966), is excellent and manageable.

CHAPTER 26

De-Stalinization and Destabilization

CHAPTER OUTLINE
Stalin's Successors • Destabilization in Eastern Europe • Khrushchev's
Dilemma • Restricted Decentralization

BIOGRAPHICAL SKETCHES
Nikita Sergeievich Khrushchev, Peasant Wit •
Alexander Dubček, Brief Spring

In March 1953, a new era began for the Soviet Union when Joseph Stalin suddenly died and a period of instability began.

STALIN'S SUCCESSORS

Because Stalin did not designate a successor, an intense struggle among his heirs
that had important repercussions followed his death.

Stalin's Strange Death
In 1952 and 1953, signs pointed to a new Stalinist purge tinged with anti-
Semitism. In October 1952 a party congress gave the secret police greater power,
and a purge of prominent party bosses seemed probable. In January 1953, the
controlled press reported the "Doctors' Plot," a conspiracy in which nine doctors,
seven of whom were Jewish, had allegedly killed notable Soviet leaders. This was
the signal for a new purge, but on March 6, 1953, the government announced that
Stalin had suffered a stroke and died the day before. The purge never materialized,
and speculation of foul play has been rife ever since.

Struggle for Succession
Who would be Stalin's successor and what future Soviet policies would follow took
about four years to resolve. A period of collective leadership and a struggle for

Stalin lying in state, March 12, 1953. The dictator's death opened up the door to a fight for succession and the haphazard partial liberalization of the USSR. The contenders for the succession are present in this photograph. On the far left is Nikita Khrushchev; just to the left of the bier is Georgi Malenkov.

power followed Stalin's death in which the major rivals were Georgi Malenkov and Nikita Khrushchev.

Born in 1903, Malenkov graduated from engineering school in 1925. He had served as secretary of the Bolshevik Students' Association and in a variety of high posts in the party, including Stalin's personal secretariat, and had attracted favorable attention. Nikita Khrushchev, nine years Malenkov's senior, joined the Communist Party in 1918, became first secretary of the Ukrainian Communist Party in 1938, and like Malenkov was closely associated with Stalin's rule. In 1953 Malenkov became premier until 1955. He held but lost the more important party leadership position to Khrushchev in September 1953.

Khrushchev's power base was in the party, while Malenkov's was in the state institutions. Malenkov seemed to have the edge because of the apparent decline in the party's influence in recent years, but this decrease turned out to be an illusion. His and powerful ally, secret police chief Lavrenti Beria, favored a liberalization policy. Beria, however, was rapidly losing his influence, and disorders in East Germany in 1953 weakened him further. Beria was arrested and executed in December 1953, after which the secret police was purged and Malenkov's strength eroded.

Khrushchev's Rise

The debate in Soviet society following Stalin's death revolved around whether his policies should be revised. Malenkov favored a "New Course" by putting greater emphasis on the production of consumer goods, while his opponents wanted to continue to concentrate on heavy industry.

Malenkov's policies allowed his enemies to gain the support of entrenched interest groups, such as the army, who were opposed to altering the percentage of investment in the different industrial sectors. In agriculture, both rivals admitted the state's failure: too much central planning, forcing peasants to hand over produce at rock-bottom prices, and high taxation. Both agreed that farmers should have more freedom, but reforms encouraging local initiatives reduced the state's role and strengthened the party's presence on the land and, thus, Khrushchev's role. Furthermore, Khrushchev, the country's recognized agricultural expert, was skilled in farm policy. Malenkov opposed Khrushchev's land policy, but from 1953 to 1958, agricultural production increased by half while prices paid by the state rose threefold. These developments strengthened Khrushchev.

BIOGRAPHICAL SKETCHES

Nikita Sergeievich Khrushchev
Peasant Wit

Jovial Soviet ruler Nikita Khrushchev's demeanor strongly contrasted with that of the dour and brutal Joseph Stalin. Khrushchev gave the impression of a peasant with a clownish personality, but this attitude masked a shrewd political operator. He gained the attention of world leaders for his liberalization of Soviet policy, his homey comments, his sense of humor, and his unorthodox behavior. He sought to improve living conditions to spread communism. As he explained: "Would it be bad if we spread our Marxist-Leninist teachings with a piece of butter? I say that, with a good bread spread like that, Marxism-Leninism would be even more tasty." On one occasion, while visiting the United Nations, he removed his shoe and banged it on the desk to show disapproval.

Khrushchev came from a poor peasant background. His grandfather, freed from serfdom in the reform of 1861, owned the mud hut in Kallinova (Ukraine) where Nikita Khrushchev was born on April 17, 1894. His father, hopelessly in debt, worked the land in the summer but left his family during the winters to toil in the coal mines of the Donets Basin. In 1909, the family moved to an industrial town where the teenage Khrushchev worked in factories owned by foreign capitalists. The experience made him a convinced Communist. Khrushchev married in 1915 and had two children, but his wife died in the 1921–22 famine. In 1924 he married the remarkable Nina Petrovna, who smoothed out his rough edges and became a respected world figure alongside her husband.

Little in Khrushchev's steady but slow political advancement as a loyal supporter of Stalin prepared the world for his future political success and de-Stalinization policies. Khrushchev joined the Communist Party in 1918 and served in the Red Army as a mechanic. He had to wait until 1925 for his first important party job—secretary of a small provincial district. In September 1929, he landed an assignment at the Moscow Industrial Academy. By 1934, he had become party boss of the capital and, in 1938, Stalin's representative in the Ukraine. In the Ukraine, he implemented Stalin's purges, following policies similar to those for which he denounced Stalin in 1956. As his reward, Khrushchev was named a full member of the Politburo of the Central Committee, the party's policy-making executive.

After September 1939, Khrushchev headed the civilian administration of Soviet-occupied Poland. He deported a million Poles and Sovietized the region. When the Germans invaded the USSR in June 1941, Khrushchev enforced the government's iron discipline on the army and helped organize the partisan resistance. After the war, he directed the Ukraine's re-Sovietization and recollectivization, cementing his reputation as an agricultural expert.

After defeating Georgi Malenkov for the succession to Stalin between 1953 and 1955, Khrushchev implemented a policy of relative freedom in the USSR, al-

continued

continued

though he never intended to democratize it, and a thaw in foreign policy. He moderated communism's most drastic aspects and even made fun of the bureaucracy. He told the story that during the Bolshevik Revolution workers had to fill out stupid questionnaires. One employee who feared that admitting his belief in God would damage his career replied: "At home I believe in God; at the office—I do not!" Khrushchev, however, always remained a staunch defender of communism at home and abroad. When an American spy plane was shot down over Russia in 1960, he told reporters that his parents punished a cat that had stolen some cream by shaking it by the scruff of the neck. "Wouldn't it be better," he said, "to take the American imperialists by the scruff of the neck [and] give them a good shaking?"

Khrushchev's liberalization of Soviet politics contributed to the atmosphere that allowed him to retire peacefully to write his memoirs instead of being executed after his removal from office in October 1964. He died in Moscow on September 11, 1971.

By February 1955, Khrushchev had won the power struggle. Malenkov was demoted, accused of failures in agricultural and industrial policies and of past sins, such as having had a role in the 1948–49 purges. Malenkov's defense minister, Nikolai Bulganin, succeeded him as premier, but the real power resided with Khrushchev. In 1957, Malenkov was accused of participating in a failed plot to remove Khrushchev and Bulganin, was removed from his post, and was expelled from the party. In March 1958, Khrushchev replaced him, achieving absolute power by combining the positions of head of state and party.

DESTABILIZATION IN EASTERN EUROPE

The struggle for power in the USSR produced instability in Eastern Europe. Stalin had installed hard-liners who opposed de-Stalinization because it caused major headaches for them. As part of his campaign, for example, Khrushchev made peace with Yugoslavia, embarrassing East European leaders because Stalin had utilized "Titoism" as an reason for the postwar purges that had solidified Communist control in the satellite states and that had shaped their political and social development. By admitting their error with regard to Tito, Khrushchev delegitimated the rule of their East European allies.

Consequently, East European leaders resisted the attempt of Stalin's heirs to loosen political control over their people and to slow the drive toward communism. They could not openly defy the Soviets, but they feared the reaction of their peoples if they loosened controls. New leaders who supported the changes waited in the wings to lead the forces that were opposed to the fast pace of communization. The Soviets, unwilling to risk their hegemony in the region, followed an uncertain policy that, added to the resistance of the East European Stalinists, failed to relieve the tensions that were unsettling the region. Furthermore, anti-Russian sentiment and deteriorating economic conditions fueled dissatisfaction that would require Soviet military intervention to quell, allowing the East European Stalinists to claim that de-Stalinization brought destabilization.

Strains in East European Society

In May and June 1953, trouble arose in Bulgaria, Czechoslovakia, and Hungary when the governments increased work norms, decreased wages, and relaxed the repressive apparatus after Stalin's death. In Bulgaria, the tobacco workers struck to protest low salaries and high work quotas. On May 31, the Czechoslovak regime announced "currency reform" that raised food prices and resulted in a 12 percent decrease in workers' wages. Industrial workers struck and destroyed Communist symbols. Next, demonstrations erupted in Hungary.

The most serious disorders occurred in East Germany, where the contrast between Malenkov's promise of a rising standard of living and East German attempts to expand industrial production by increasing work norms and by decreasing wages produced violent protests that culminated in the events of June 1953. The origins of the rebellion went back to July 1952 when the East German Communist Party (SED) announced that it would increase nationalization, concentrate on building up heavy industry, collectivize more land, and increase police powers.

The East German Disorders

The East Germans reacted by fleeing to the West, primarily through Berlin. The flow of refugees reached nearly 300,000 in 1953. The refugees belonged to the most productive sectors of society, such as small businesspeople, tradesmen, and manufacturers who feared the effects of nationalization; peasants fleeing collectivization; and professionals evading party domination. The East German authorities could not halt the outflow and, in April 1953, appealed to Moscow for help. The Soviets refused pleas for economic aid and suggested liberalizing East German policies in line with Malenkov's New Course: reducing the drive for communization and emphasizing consumer goods as opposed to heavy industry.

In addition to finding himself with little support from his Soviet patrons, longtime German Stalinist leader Walter Ulbricht came under attack from party reformists who favored liberalization. By June 1953, it seemed that he had lost the struggle because the SED admitted its past mistakes, backed off attacks on the churches, promised less intervention in cultural affairs, and endorsed increased commercial relations with West Germany. The party promised more investment in consumer goods, less produce from farmers, reduced taxation levels, and help to private firms.

However, the party had imposed increased work standards in May, and when it failed to rescind them, Berlin construction workers, joined by industrial workers, marched on union headquarters on June 16. The government canceled the new work norms, but the demonstrators demanded that the government hold free elections and resign, and by June 17, 400,000 strikers were demonstrating. The strikers attacked, pillaged, and burned party offices and destroyed party symbols.

The Russians initially seemed disinclined to intervene, but the severity of the disorders forced them to do so. Soviet tanks and soldiers attacked the cities, killing hundreds of people. After restoring order, the Soviets were obliged to help their German comrades politically and economically. They renounced reparations owed by the East Germans, provided loans, turned over Soviet-controlled enterprises, and reduced the occupation costs they charged to East Germany.

In the period after 1945 the Communist world was rent by major protests. In June 1953 serious unrest hit East Germany. Stalinist leader Walter Ulbricht's policies provoked the disorders but, despite the existence of liberalizing forces, his reformist opponents were unable to calm the situation. The Soviets intervened, ironically winding up restoring Ulbricht. In this photograph, Soviet tanks swerve into action against the demonstrators.

Ironically, Walter Ulbricht, whose intransigence had provoked the disorders, emerged strengthened. He claimed that his opposition to the reforms had proved correct because they and the relaxed controls had encouraged the workers to rebel. Ulbricht reestablished control and purged the SED and the unions of his opponents. In April 1954, the party reaffirmed the measures to achieve communism that it had adopted in 1952, although in practice it slowed down implementation and did not reinstitute the work norm increases of May 1953. Malenkov's New Course had failed in East Germany, ironically, thanks to Soviet military intervention.

Khrushchev's Secret Speech and His De-Stalinization Policies
By February 1955, Khrushchev had replaced Malenkov as the USSR's prime leader, partly because of the German disorders and partly because of support for his greater emphasis on heavy industry. Khrushchev did not want to reinstate Stalinism but sought to counterbalance a return to traditional Communist economics in the industrial field by allowing greater political flexibility and by exploring a different basis for the eastern bloc through a new economic and military partnership. He also supported popular leaders over Stalinists, particularly in Poland and Hungary.

Khrushchev's de-Stalinization policies had enormous implications. In June 1955, Khrushchev tried to heal the rift with Yugoslavia by traveling to Belgrade.

This Soviet admission of fault alienated the East European Communist leaders, who owed their status to Stalin and the fight against Tito. The rapprochement of Khrushchev and Tito presented them with a dilemma. They were accustomed to following Moscow's lead, but did not favor de-Stalinization, which, however, had strong support in their countries and in the USSR. This support became obvious after February 1956 when Khrushchev made a powerful "secret" speech to the Twentieth Congress of the Communist Party of the Soviet Union (later made public by the U.S. State Department). In the speech, Khrushchev denounced Stalin's policies and the way Stalin retained power by murdering innocent people, by stifling opposition, and by glorifying himself as the personification of Marxism— the "personality cult." This speech was also remarkable because it revealed the enormous extent of Stalin's crimes.

Khrushchev followed up his attack on Stalin with action. De-Stalinization efforts, already under way, intensified. Khrushchev closed concentration and labor camps and restored legal procedures that had fallen into abeyance. The influence of the secret police diminished, and more debate was allowed. An atmosphere of relative freedom, diversity, and intellectual discourse appeared in the USSR. Even though Boris Pasternak's novel *Dr. Zhivago* could not be published in Russia because it criticized the Communist system and its author was forbidden from accepting the Nobel Prize, publication of Aleksander Solzhenitsyn's classic description of labor camp life in 1962, *One Day in the Life of Ivan Denisovich*, symbolized Khrushchev's liberalization.

These startling developments caused strong tensions in the East European Communist parties and, in Poland and Hungary, serious disorders.

De-Stalinization in Poland
Strong national resentment against the Russians, who had dominated Poland for over 150 years, and different religious faiths combined with economics to worsen the Polish situation. Communist economic policies caused real wages to drop by a third between 1945 and 1955. Catholicism permeated Polish society, history, literature, and art and contrasted strongly with Communist atheism. Unable to criticize Moscow openly, a large part of the Polish intelligentsia adopted a pro-Catholic attitude as a means of fighting communism. These views emerged in the study of Polish history, dominated by Catholicism, and in the strong resentment against the government's detaining of Cardinal Stefan Wyszynski in 1953. In addition, the national Communist and World War II resistance hero Gomulka remained popular despite his having been purged. Gomulka was a Communist loyalist but also a patriot.

The opposition to Russian domination took on a new form during the de-Stalinization campaign. The Poles discussed not how to eliminate communism but how to improve it. Intellectual fermentation appeared in new journals, discussion groups, and theater societies. De-Stalinization allowed literary works to be published relatively free of censorship and Western cultural ideas to be disseminated. This intellectual excitement favored sporadic uprisings. In February 1956, when party leader Boleslaw Bierut died a rumored suicide, his successors decided to respond to the ferment by carrying de-Stalinization further. They encouraged legislative opposition, declared an amnesty for political detainees, and printed Khrushchev's secret speech. This increased freedom quickly turned to violence.

On June 28, 1956, severe disorders erupted among railway workers in Poznan. These workers demanded improved economic conditions, freedom for Cardinal Wyszynski, and expulsion of the Russians. The police fired on them and killed fifty marchers. This occurrence shocked the party and the nation so much that in July, the party made some economic and political concessions, including readmitting Gomulka into its ranks. The concessions fell flat. Newly created workers' councils demanded that Gomulka be acknowledged as the party leader; Khrushchev agreed to Gomulka's return to power, and on October 21 the party elected Gomulka its head. Gomulka worked to end the disorders by releasing Wyszynski, making concessions to the church, abandoning attempts to collectivize the land, and giving up on the idea of eliminating the rural bourgeoisie. Gomulka's policies worked, but they blocked the so-called Polish October from developing into a full-fledged revolution; the church emerged as the major competitor to the Communist Party.

Following Khrushchev's denunciation of Stalin's crimes at the 20th Congress of the Communist Party of the Soviet Union there was a push for "Destalinization" that met resistance from the satellite leaders that Stalin had put in charge. In Poland, where anti-Russian sentiment had a long and strong history, unrest broke out in June 1956. The Soviets managed to block a full-fledged revolution by agreeing to the return to power of Wladyslaw Gomulka, a loyal Communist but a reformer who promised concessions to the Catholic Church and ended attempts at collectivization of the land.

However, if Poland did not revolt, it had demonstrated that poor economic conditions caused by Communist policies could combine powerfully with national pride and a rich cultural heritage to destabilize the Soviet Empire.

Discontent in Hungary

In Hungary the factors destabilizing Poland existed in exasperated form. Communists had created an inefficient state bureaucracy, had ruined agriculture by rapidly collectivizing farmland, and had allowed the blatant exploitation of natural resources and labor on behalf of the Soviet Union. The classic policy of favoring heavy industry to the detriment of consumer goods had aggravated economic conditions. The Communist regime had also offended Hungarian nationalism, which was particularly strong, by removing from army uniforms Hungarian symbols dating from the 1848 revolution and replacing them with the red star of communism. Furthermore, party officials who had spent years in Moscow were particularly arrogant.

These issues had produced ominously deep divisions within the Hungarian Communist Party between old-line Stalinists and national Communists led by Imre Nagy. As in Poland, history played an important part: The subjugation of Hungary to the USSR reminded Hungarians that the Russians had extinguished their revolution in 1849 and returned them to Austrian suzerainty. By the 1950s, Hungarians considered the government of Stalinist Prime Minister and party head Mátyás Rákosi to be an abomination whose survival depended on Russian arms and on the dreaded Hungarian secret police (AVH).

Crisis of the Old Regime

By 1953 social unrest and Malenkov's New Course spelled a crisis for the Rákosi regime. Moscow tried to force Rákosi to give up one of his posts to Nagy, who was slated to take over as prime minister in June 1953. Nagy was not associated with Hungary's ferocious purges and had criticized the fast pace of Hungary's communization. As prime minister, he immediately fired some of the country's most notorious Stalinists and made a series of promises to grant more civil rights, emphasize consumer goods, rehabilitate persons who had been unfairly purged, release political prisoners, adopt a more moderate stance toward religion, increase food supplies, and slow the pace of collectivization.

These policies encouraged Rákosi to call on his party allies to help him topple the prime minister, whose position had been weakened by Khrushchev's victory over Malenkov. Nagy attempted to broaden his support by appealing to non-Communist organizations, but this attempt aroused Moscow's suspicion, and Rakosi won the battle.

After his return to power, Rákosi found himself obliged to implement de-Stalinization and shifted between severity and softness. He allowed some expression of national feeling, instituted measures that gave the illusion of liberty, and then pulled back. He permitted the rehabilitation of Rajk, executed for anti-Communist activities, but because Rákosi owed his own rise to Rajk's demise, this move discredited him. He allowed foundation of the Petöfi circle, named after a poet who died fighting the Russians in 1849. This circle was a debating society that

Destalinzation also produced unrest in Hungary, where students touched off a widespread revolution in 1956. The Soviets allowed a Communist reformer, Imre Nagy, to come to power, but when he would not automatically follow the Soviet line, the Soviet army invaded.
In the picture, Nagy is making a radio address, probably at gunpoint, in which he did not deny asking for Warsaw Pact intervention. Nagy was later tried and executed. He was rehabilitated in 1989 as the Communist world was collapsing.

discussed the major questions of the time that established the intellectual foundations of the Hungarian revolution.

International events also worked against Rákosi. In a 1955 conference at Bangdung (Indonesia), the USSR endorsed self-determination for all countries and withdrew from Austria on condition that it be neutral in the cold war. Many Hungarians believed that since Hungary bordered on Austria, Hungary should also be neutral and free from Soviet interference. Finally, Marshal Tito, who backed Nagy, exploited his improved relations with the Russians to incite them against Rákosi. By late 1955 and 1956, Hungarians called for Nagy's return.

The Hungarian Revolution

The Soviets forced Rákosi to resign on July 18, 1956, but replaced him with an associate whom the Hungarians rejected. On October 6, 250,000 Hungarians demonstrated in Budapest. The party restored Nagy's party membership, but demonstrating students demanded that he become prime minister. On October 23, they marched to Petöfi's words: "We will never again be slaves" and tore down a huge statue of Stalin. The next day the secret police and the Red Army fought Hungarian freedom fighters armed by the Hungarian military.

The Soviets quickly allowed Nagy to return as premier, but unlike Gomulka, he failed to resolve the situation. He disappointed the Hungarians in a radio speech by not denying that he had requested Red Army aid (he may have given the talk at gunpoint), and his new cabinet was no improvement over Rákosi's. The leaders of the revolutionary councils that had formed to fight the Communists and that had gained control of the country demanded a coalition cabinet and multiparty democracy. Nagy gave in and abolished the one-party system. The structure of the Communist state dissolved, new parties formed, and pre-1945 parties reorganized themselves. High-level Soviet emissaries accepted the coalition government and promised to withdraw Soviet forces, but insisted that Hungary remain a Socialist state within the Warsaw Pact.

The Soviets could not risk letting the Hungarian example influence other parts of the Soviet world. They feared losing Eastern Europe as a buffer against a possible Western attack, and their hard-line Chinese allies pressed them to intervene. The Chinese argued, in Marxist-Leninist terms, that history could not regress—communism could not disappear from a country once established. Finally, the Anglo-French invasion of Egypt after the seizure of the Suez Canal and the objections of the United States convinced Khrushchev that the West would not intervene in Hungary.

On November 1 the Soviets invaded. The Red Army killed about 3,000 fighters and executed about 2,500 other Hungarians after the revolution, including Nagy. About 200,000 Hungarians fled the country, and many others were deported. Because the refugees included many valued professionals and workers on whom the Hungarian economy depended, the revolution deprived the Hungarian economy of important elements.

The Hungarian revolution demonstrated the Soviet system's instability, which was caused by Soviet domination and poor economic conditions, both flowing from Communist ideology. Most ominously, the swift collapse of the Communist power structure during the Hungarian Revolution and the opposition of the young people who had grown up under the system revealed the weakness of communism. In the West, a serious exodus from the Communist parties took place after the revolution.

KHRUSHCHEV'S DILEMMA

Khrushchev faced a difficult dilemma after the 1956 disorders. He still hoped to make consensus, rather than force, the bond holding the Communist world together, but the national interests and ideological authority of the USSR limited his attempt to decentralize the Communist world. The Soviets continued to fear that the granting of autonomy might lead to the end of Eastern European communism. Khrushchev was shrewd enough, even after 1956, to recognize that the USSR could not exercise full control over the Communist regimes. He allowed the East Europeans some freedom in developing an autonomous brand of communism, but he and his successors kept their military options open.

Comecon

In the economic arena Khrushchev's hope of reviving the Soviet bloc was made concrete by his attempt to integrate the East European economies into a unified whole by reforming the Council for Mutual Economic Assistance (CMEA or

Comecon), founded in 1949 as the Communist response to the Marshall Plan. The Soviets saw Comecon as an economic mechanism to coordinate the planning and industrial development of Eastern Europe, but the evolution of the Communist regimes into an economic bloc was hardly comparable to Western development. Consequently, Khrushchev's attempt to transform Comecon into the supranational planning body of the Communist world in 1962 failed when he proposed that the Communist countries agree to the principle of an international Socialist division of labor with a powerful supranational committee directing coordination ended in failure.

The East Europeans killed Khrushchev's scheme because it would have relegated some countries, such as Romania, to the permanent status of supplying raw materials, while as good Communists they favored rapid industrialization. In addition, they considered the proposed supranational planning body a thinly disguised tool of Soviet economic domination. Economic cooperation and coordination among the Comecon countries did increase between 1962 and 1970, but trade among them declined as a percentage of the total, in stark contrast to the great increase in trade with Western Europe.

The Warsaw Pact

Another element of Khrushchev's attempt to strengthen Communist cooperation was military. The Soviet Union had bilateral military agreements with all the Soviet satellite states, whose armies closely resembled their Soviet counterparts down to their uniforms and their acceptance of Russian military leadership and doctrine. Initially the Russians distrusted multilateral agreements on the NATO model, preferring to keep a highly centralized grip on the East European armies, but in 1955 the Soviets responded to the German Federal Republic's entrance into NATO by establishing the Warsaw Treaty Organization (WTO or the Warsaw Pact).

More than a military organization, Moscow conceived of the Warsaw Pact as a diplomatic instrument uniting the countries of East Europe because a centralized military organization run by the Russians seemed more efficient. Khrushchev sought to reinvigorate the Warsaw Pact by giving the East European allies a greater voice in military affairs, but continuing tension between military efficiency and ideological collaboration doomed the attempt. The Soviets created new bodies to facilitate consultations, but they met infrequently or not at all. It was not until 1961 that increased political consultation occurred more frequently and that the Soviets attempted to improve the military quality of the allied armies. The Berlin crisis of that year, during which the East Germans built a wall across Berlin to stem the tide of refugees; American mobilization of reserve units; and increasing competition with the Chinese Communists encouraged the change.

Even though meetings of the Warsaw Pact countries increased substantially after 1961, Romania and other countries challenged Soviet leadership in foreign affairs, and political collaboration slackened. Khrushchev's idea of using the alliance as a means of reviving Communist unity failed, and the Warsaw Pact increasingly functioned as a cover for the Soviets to invade WTO countries that rebelled, such as Czechoslovakia in 1968.

Foreign Policy Difficulties

Even in foreign policy, the outlook for the USSR worsened as competition between the Russians and Chinese for leadership of the Communist world created rival camps. Khrushchev favored a policy of peaceful coexistence with the West, while the Chinese denounced Soviet revisionism and advocated world revolution. Some East European countries exploited the rift to make overtures to the West, while others instituted friendly relations with the Chinese.

The bastion of Chinese influence in the region was Albania, dependent on Yugoslavia before its leader Enver Hoxha capitalized on the Soviet-Yugoslav split to join Stalin's camp and to consolidate his power. With Khrushchev's rise and the Soviet rapprochement with Yugoslavia, Hoxha denounced de-Stalinization, expelled the Russians, turned for protection and economic aid to the Chinese, and implemented Chinese-influenced policies.

The Albanian example encouraged another Communist maverick, Romania, to defy the Russians. In 1958, the Romanians joined with the Chinese in calling for the removal of armed forces from foreign territory in a context that pointedly applied to Russia. Incensed by Chinese Communist meddling in his own backyard, Khrushchev attempted to organize a conference to denounce the Chinese and reaffirm the USSR's role as the undisputed leader of international communism, but the attempt floundered largely because of Romania.

Khrushchev also had difficulties with the West. Unable to stem the continued exodus of East Germans to the West through Berlin, during the summer of 1961 the Communists constructed a wall to prevent them from crossing over. The concrete wall, complete with barbed wire and sentry posts, stretched for twenty-eight miles through the heart of the former German capital. Over the years, the wall stood as an appalling symbol of communism on a par with the "iron curtain." Hundreds of East Germans died trying to flee between 1961 and 1989.

These failures coincided with the 1962 defeat of Khrushchev's attempts to install missiles in Cuba and the ensuing world crisis. For years the Soviets had chafed at the American stationing of intermediate range ballistic missiles (IRBMs) in Turkey, where they could reach major USSR population centers. Khrushchev took advantage of Fidel Castro's takeover in Cuba in 1960 to send missiles to the island only ninety miles off the Florida coast and to bring major American cities within range of a Soviet nuclear missile attack. Khrushchev saw this act as counterbalancing the American threat from Turkey, but when American reconnaissance planes discovered the missile installations, the Americans viewed it as altering the global balance of power. The resulting crisis, which erupted in October 1962, was the most serious of the cold war. President John F. Kennedy ordered a naval quarantine of Cuba, and Russian ships heading to the island with the missiles turned back to avoid a confrontation with the Americans. This result took the edge off the crisis but seriously damaged Soviet prestige.

In 1963, both blocs tried to repair relations with each other by signing a nuclear test ban treaty and implementing a détente, but this renewal of peaceful intentions destabilized the East even more. As the West Germans instituted their *Ostpolitik* policy aiming at better relations with the East, the political thaw and

The fact that East Berlin had a common border with West Berlin severely damaged the Communist bloc, because East Berliners could easily see the difference between Western economic development and that of the Communist world. In addition, because it was easy to cross over into the West, East Germany lost valuable skilled professionals who could easily escape. Starting in August 1961, the Communists built a wall that traversed the former German capital and cut off East Berlin in order to prevent its inhabitants from fleeing to the West. Some three million citizens had already fled, causing the regime major economic problems. The wall was outfitted with towers whose guards shot to kill any escapees and became an enduring symbol of Communist repression.

increasing trade with the West induced Poland and Romania to consider joining Western economic organizations, while Romania explored normalization of its West German relations.

By 1964, Khrushchev had failed to revitalize the Communist world, had not eliminated Chinese competition, had blundered into the missile crisis, and had damaged the Soviet position in Eastern Europe. His foreign policy problems, combined with failures in his attempts at agricultural, economic, and administrative reform, led to his ouster in October 1964.

Leonid Brezhnev and Aleksei Kosygin replaced Khrushchev. They followed similar policies but had no greater luck than their predecessor. They hoped to regain the initiative in Eastern Europe from the West by restructuring the Warsaw Pact and by calling for a European Security Conference, but divisions among the East Europeans and Romanian opposition caused both attempts to fail.

RESTRICTED DECENTRALIZATION

The October 1956 revolts made necessary a new conception of Communist unity, the framework for which had been supplied in June by Italian Communist Party leader Palmiro Togliatti and his concept of polycentrism. According to Togliatti, there were many roads to socialism, depending on national circumstances. Individual countries might not follow the Russian model toward socialism, the Italian Communist leader said, the evolution toward which might not even be led by Communist parties.

Polycentrism became popular following the East European disturbances because it theoretically established equality among Communists but retained a common ideology; however, the idea diminished the USSR's moral authority. In a November 1957 conference held in Moscow, the Soviets reaffirmed their leading role and made a veiled reference to the possibility of military intervention in other Communist states if necessary, but polycentrism encouraged Communist regimes to follow different policies with Soviet approval or acquiescence. In 1968, however, the Soviets became alarmed at the changes taking place in Czechoslovakia and invaded the country. The invasion demonstrated that even if the Soviets were willing to allow some autonomy, the interests of the Soviet Union remained paramount.

Autonomy and Stagnation in Eastern Europe

During the 1960s, the East European states had limited autonomy to follow different policies, but this situation led to stagnation rather than progress. Ironically, the Soviet example encouraged economic reforms in some Eastern European states during the 1960s. Khrushchev followed up his initial de-Stalinization campaign with a more vigorous one in 1961, when he again denounced Stalin and intensified his drive for economic reforms as the Communist world faced a deepening recession. There was a debate over more administrative decentralization and the introduction of market principles, such as supply and demand, incentives, and greater attention to profitability, identified with the ideas of Professor Yevsei Liberman. While these policies had little practical influence in the USSR, between 1962 and 1968 reformers in some Eastern European countries took them seriously.

In Yugoslavia, Communist reformers had long suggested similar changes and in 1962 won the battle. Tito abolished economic planning and implemented comprehensive reform in 1965. New legislation introduced market socialism that allowed for some private employment, virtually dismantled price controls, and permitted companies to deal directly with foreign enterprises. "The Reform" was intended to create a framework whereby Yugoslavia could integrate itself into the world economy, with the government allowing foreign investment up to 49 percent of a company's capital and, in 1967, the exportation of profits earned by foreigners.

The Yugoslavs, however, failed to follow up this economic progress with political liberalization. A new constitution in 1963 brought institutional change, symbolized by the appearance of a dissident Marxist magazine, *Praxis*, but the perennial question of Serb domination of Yugoslavia went unresolved. The richer areas of Croatia and Slovenia resented Serb political domination and being forced to subsidize the poorer regions of the country, while in Kosovo, Albanian nationalism increased. These national tensions presaged the breakup of Yugoslavia after Tito's death.

Romania resembled Yugoslavia in its autonomous foreign policy. Khrushchev's proposed restructuring of Comecon alienated the Romanians because it relegated their country to the role of supplying the Communist bloc with raw materials. In 1964 the Romanians defied the Russians by attempting the full-scale industrialization of their country, a policy that would have a disastrous environmental impact, and declaring Romania's practical independence from the Soviet Communist Party. From then on, Romania was only a nominal member of the Warsaw Pact and of Comecon and formally adopted a neutral position in the Soviet-Chinese struggle. In 1965, its leader Nicolae Ceausescu objected to Soviet attempts to restructure the Warsaw Pact, criticized Moscow for interfering in the internal affairs of other state, reestablished relations with Israel after the Six-Day War, and reaffirmed Romanian identity in the schools and in the administration. The Albanians went further, becoming hostile to the USSR and allying with China.

In contrast to Yugoslavia and Albania, Bulgaria and East Germany remained loyal to the Soviets. Bulgaria lacked the economic resources and raw materials to consider policies that might alienate Russia. Its longtime leader Todor Zhivkov feared that economic reform might lead to political upheaval and supported Khrushchev and his successors; his slavish obedience to the Soviet Union apparently provoked an attempted military coup in 1965. Unlike Bulgaria, the GDR was one of the most economically advanced countries in the eastern bloc, which allowed it to consider economic reform. In 1963, it implemented the New Economic System to encourage decentralization, but this reform had little practical effect because of the country's political dependence on the USSR. East Germany depended on the Soviets to support it against West Germany, especially after building the Berlin wall in 1961, and to counter the threat of domestic political upheaval. By 1965, East German reformers had been defeated, and the GDR's ambitious aim of overtaking the Federal Republic was unobtainable.

Poland occupied a middle position in its relationship to the USSR in the 1960s. The return of Gomulka ended Stalinism and collectivization and brought greater cultural autonomy from the USSR, but his moderate reform communism stagnated. Gomulka remained an authoritarian and a staunch Communist at heart and had no intention of restructuring the country. No substantial reform measures followed his initial ones, and when traditional Polish anti-Russian feeling reasserted itself, he called in the police. When his authority was threatened in the 1960s he tried to keep his standing in the party by applying anti-Semitic measures. By the beginning of 1968, Polish students and police battled frequently. The old fear of Germany accounted for what popularity the USSR still possessed, but better relations as a result of West Germany's *Ostpolitik* policy did much to alleviate suspicion. As disorders snaked through Polish society, the Soviets tolerated the turmoil only because of their other problems in Eastern Europe.

The New Economic Mechanism

Surprisingly, Hungary had a different development than what may have been expected after the revolution of 1956. The Soviets installed János Kadar who reestablished Communist power. In 1959, he recollectivized the farms, although in a moderate manner that allowed for more private enterprise than before. In 1961 Kadar began a political and economic relaxation that allowed Hungary to undergo the greatest transformation of any Eastern European country. He ended Stalinism by reforming the criminal code, releasing the prisoners arrested after 1956, eliminating measures against class enemies, and liberalizing the political system. By 1967, contests for political office were possible, and the Hungarian parliament took a more active role in government.

The most dramatic changes occurred in economics. On January 1, 1968, Kadar introduced the New Economic Mechanism (NEM). This plan aimed at reforming the Hungarian economy so that it could become part of the international trading system. The NEM reduced the role of the state and the party in economic activity and implemented measures to encourage private enterprise. Central planning was greatly reduced, the pricing mechanism was restructured, and companies competed for market share. Kadar still depended on the Russians for military protection, but the Soviets, unwilling to provoke a new Hungarian revolution, allowed him to implement the most radical economic restructuring of an East European economy that had ever taken place.

Stalinism in Czechoslovakia

In Czechoslovakia conditions were much bleaker than in Hungary. The country's leader Antonin Novotny had been deeply implicated in the purges of the 1950s and resisted de-Stalinization. By 1963, some Stalinists had been removed from power, and censorship against intellectuals was relaxed, but Novotny found himself under fire for his opposition to de-Stalinization and was pressured by the Slovak Communists, who resented Czech domination.

In 1962 Czechoslovakia's strong economic performance faltered, and the Five-Year Plan had to be replaced by a new Seven-Year Plan that failed. Novotny was forced to establish a commission, headed by reformer Ota Sik, that downgraded central planning boards and encouraged a limited market economy. This change was partially implemented in 1965, but encountered governmental sabotage. The poor economy ignited social resentment at the same time that the government was forced to relax censorship, which increased criticism of the regime and produced an intense cultural debate that changed the nature of Czechoslovak politics.

The Prague Spring

The debate focused on the nature of communism. If the dictatorship of the proletariat had eliminated class differences and moved Czechoslovakia into the Socialist stage of development, what was the role of the Communist Party? Why, if Czechoslovakia faced no internal danger from a bourgeoisie that no longer existed, did the state repress different groups in society instead of reconciling their demands? The party had failed totally in this task, the intellectuals charged. They pointed to the many social problems the party had failed to resolve, such as housing, and noted that instead of mediating among groups, the government repressed them in a totalitarian fashion.

In 1967 Novotny readied a crackdown on the intellectuals who criticized his regime, but the erosion of the government's moral authority had gone so far that he could not use Communist cultural organizations for this purpose. This difficulty coincided with his loss of Slovak Communist support because of his opposition to their national aspirations, and open warfare broke out between Novotny and Slovak leader Alexander Dubček at a Central Committee meeting in October. Student demonstrations protesting poor economic conditions and battles with the police in the streets highlighted Novotny's weakness. Worse still, Brezhnev believed that the Czechoslovaks should resolve their own problems and refused to rescue him. In January 1968 the Czechoslovaks removed Novotny as first secretary and replaced him with Dubček.

Dubček's career had marked him as a good party bureaucrat, but he accepted the changes in a liberal direction demanded by the Czechoslovak people. In April 1968, the party issued the Action Program, which established "socialism with a human face." This program declared that the country's democratic traditions would guide Czechoslovakia's course within a now mature socialism that mandated a smaller role for governmental planning agencies and more freedom of action for industry and agriculture. It promised full individual rights, including freedom of speech, freedom of association, and freedom from arbitrary arrest. In foreign policy, it called for economic equality between Czechoslovakia and the USSR and the departure of Soviet advisers, but not withdrawal from the Warsaw Pact. On the national issue, it conceded that the Slovaks could have their own legislative and executive organs. On the question of the party, however, the program hedged by stating that it should be more responsive to the people but should keep its leading role.

Between April and August 1968, Dubček implemented many of these principles. Previously banned and new associations achieved a notable public presence. Religious life revived, and the major churches opened a dialogue with the state. The government took steps to concede some form of autonomy to other national minorities besides the Slovaks but discouraged demands for the creation of independent political parties because liberalization was raising the alarm in other East European states. The cabinet greeted serious talk of drastic economic reforms with caution because of opposition by workers who feared the loss of their jobs. Instead, it created new workers' institutions on the Yugoslav model as the populace increasingly abandoned the official Communist ones. Most important, on August 10 it published draft statutes that would have democratized the Communist Party, regulated its action, and separated party and state organs.

BIOGRAPHICAL SKETCHES

Alexander Dubček
Brief Spring

Alexander Dubček just missed becoming an American citizen because, in the spring of 1921, his family left the United States. His father Stefan had migrated from Slovakia in 1910 and had worked in a piano factory in Chicago but did not find the city to his liking. Stefan returned to his native village of Uhrovec, in western Slovakia, with his pregnant wife Pavlina and his son Julius. On November 27, 1921, his second son Alexander was born.

Convinced Communists, Stefan and his wife answered the Bolshevik call for workers and, in the spring of 1925, left for a village in Kirghizia, a remote area of the Soviet Union, to help build communism. The young Alexander grew up there and in industrial Gorky, where his parents migrated before returning to Czechoslovakia in the spring of 1938.

During World War II, Dubček worked in an arms factory. He established a Communist cell, stole arms, and directed acts of sabotage against the regime of German ally Monsignor Josef Tiso. In 1944, Dubček joined the partisans. The Germans killed his brother and sent his father to the Mauthausen concentration camp. Ironically, Antonin Novotny, whom Alexander Dubček would replace as Communist leader of Czechoslovakia during the Prague Spring, was in the same concentration camp as a *kapo* receiving special treatment and earned the enmity of father and son for his cooperation with the Nazis.

On September 15, 1945, Dubček married Anna Ondrisova, a partisan he had first met as a child in the USSR and who would be his lifelong companion. He worked hard to collectivize agriculture and nationalize the economy of his native Slovakia, acquiring the reputation of being an uncompromising bureaucrat. In 1951, he began work for the Slovak Communist Party's Central Committee and in 1953 was promoted to regional secretary in an area of central Slovakia where he specialized in agricultural problems.

Dubček was a skilled hunter, tracking down and killing a bear that damaged crops and attacked children.

Dubček was not known as a supporter of the show trials or of the government's assault on bourgeois-nationalism, a term the Czech Communists used when they suppressed Slovak requests for equality with them. There had been bad blood between the Slovaks and the Czechs since Czechoslovakia's foundation— tensions that broke up the country after communism's fall. In 1955, the party sent Dubček to the Higher Political College in Moscow, where he studied Marxist ideology, economics, and management techniques. Although he held several important party posts on his return to Czech-dominated Slovakia, Dubček became more sensitive than in the past to the issue of Slovakian rights and to the problems of communism to which he had paid scant attention. Contrary to his previous inclinations, between 1964 and 1967 he favored reform. His prominence as a reformer contributed to his choice as party leader in the attempt to establish "socialism with a human face." His kidnapping by the KGB on August 21, 1968, when Warsaw Pact forces invaded Czechoslovakia, and his announcement in a tearful television address that the Prague Spring was over, solidified his status as a national hero.

Dubček remained party leader after the invasion that destroyed the Czechoslovak reform movement, but was expelled from the organization in April 1969 and demoted to the rank of a forestry official. The people, however, continued to revere him. When communism in Czechoslovakia ended in late 1989, large crowds turned out to hear him wherever he went. On December 28, 1989, the Federal Assembly elected him its chair, an office he held until June 1992. From that post, he helped guide the country back to democracy. He worked on his memoirs and had not quite finished them when his BMW was involved in a fatal accident on September 1, 1992,. On November 7, 1992, the man forever identified with the brief Prague Spring died of his injuries.

The Brezhnev Doctrine

The Soviet Union and its East European allies, fearful that the Czechoslovak contagion would infect them, reacted on July 16, when Russian, Polish, Hungarian, East German, and Bulgarian leaders demanded an end to the reform movement. The Communist parties of these five countries sent a letter explaining the reasons: "The developments in your country have aroused profound anxiety among us. The reactionaries' offensive, supported by imperialism, against your party and the foundations of the Czechoslovak Socialist Republic's social system, we are deeply convinced, threatens to push your country off the path of socialism and, consequently, imperils the interests of the entire socialist system."

Dubček defended his policies on television and, in late July and early August, consulted with Brezhnev in two uncomfortable meetings during which he hoped to avoid an invasion. By mid-August, however, it was clear that he had failed. On August 20 and 21, 1968, the Red Army, bolstered by Polish, East German, Bulgarian, and Hungarian units, invaded Czechoslovakia and ended the Prague Spring. The Brezhnev Doctrine became the watchword of the Communist world: Any threat to communism in a single country imposed a duty on the other Communist states to intervene militarily against that country. Unlike the Hungarians in 1956, the Czechoslovaks did not resist the invasion by force of arms, but for the first time in a Communist state, a collaborationist leader did not emerge, and the Soviets had to leave Dubček in place until April 1969, when they finally found a

The Soviets intervened to stop reform in Czechoslovakia in August 1968. If any more proof was needed that communism could not allow reform, the invasion made it clear to the people of Eastern Europe and of the world. In this photograph, children play around a destroyed Soviet tank in Prague, but the Czechs could do little against the well-armed Warsaw Pact forces totaling 250,000 soldiers. The violence with which the Prague Spring was quashed demonstrated the bankruptcy of communism.

replacement. Nevertheless, Brezhnev imposed a brutal control over the country and restored Communist Party domination.

The Czechoslovak invasion showed that communism was bankrupt. The Czechoslovaks had portrayed the Prague Spring as an advanced elaboration of communism, not its elimination, nor did they threaten the Warsaw Pact, at least not in the short term. In the Soviet and the East European regimes, it now appeared obvious that any kind of communism besides the Russian was a mortal threat to be repressed by force.

Bibliographical Essay

Using KGB documents, Jonathan Brent and Vladimir Naumov, *Stalin's Last Crime: The Plot Against the Jewish Doctors, 1948–1953* (New York, 2003), claim that Stalin had three aims in the Doctors' Plot—to purge his government, end a potential threat posed by Jews whose major loyalty was to Israel, and prepare a war with the United States. They also believe that Stalin was murdered. See also Joshua Rubenstein and Vladimir Naumov, *Stalin's Secret Pogrom: The Postwar Inquisition of the Jewish Anti-Fascist Committee* (New Haven, Conn., 2001). Vladimir Zubok and Constantne Pleshakov, *Inside the Kremlin's Cold War* (Cambridge, Mass., 1996) takes the story from Stalin's death to Khrushchev. Edward Crankshaw, *Russia Without Stalin: The Emerging Pattern* (New York, 1956), gives a good picture of the USSR after the dictator's death. S. Bialer, *Stalin's Successors: Leadership, Stability, and Change in the Soviet Union* (New York, 1980), analyzes the general issue of succession.

Abraham Brumberg, ed., *Russia Under Khrushchev: An Anthology from Problems of Communism* (New York, 1962), examines different aspects of the country under the new leader. Nikita Khrushchev's speech denouncing Stalin's crimes was published in an annotated version as *The Crisis of the Stalin Era* (New York, 1962). Michael R. Beschloss, *The Crisis Years: Kennedy and Khrushchev* (New York, 1991), discusses world policy during this crucial period. Robert M. Slusser's *Berlin Crisis of 1961: Soviet-American Relations and the Struggle for Power in the Kremlin, June–November 1961* (Baltimore, Md, 1961) is a good history. For the various crises involving the United States, see A. A. Fursenko and Timothy J. Naftali, *Khrushchev's Cold War: The Inside Story of an American Adversary* (New York, 2006), which uses newly opened archival sources; W. R. Smyser, *Kennedy and the Berlin Crisis* (Lanham, Md.,2009), by an American diplomat of the period; and Max Frankel, *High Noon in the Cold War: Kennedy, Khrushchev, and the Cold War* (New York, 2004), which discusses Khrushchev's objectives.

For fuller treatments of Khrushchev himself, see William Taubman, *Khrushchev: The Man and His Era* (New York, 2003), a complete biography, and Taubman's book with Khrushchev's son, *Nikita Khrushchev* (New Haven, Conn., 2000). Consult also Fedor Burlatsky, *Khrushchev and the First Russian Spring* (New York, 1991), and Edward Crankshaw, *Khrushchev: A Career* (New York, 1966). See also Roy Medvedev, *Khrushchev* (Garden City, N.Y., 1982). William Taubman, *Khrushchev: The Man and His Era* (New York, 2003), sees Khrushchev as insecure, accounting for his blustering. The author believes that Khrushchev's many internal enemies led him to seek a victory against the Americans in Cuba. Finally, on the end of Khrushchev's power, see William Hyland and Richard Wallace Shyrock, *The Fall of Khrushchev* (White Plains, N.Y., 1968).

François Fejto, *History of the People's Democracies* (London, 1971), already cited, examines Eastern Europe after Stalin. Another good general overview is Hubert Ripka, *Eastern Europe in the Post-War World* (New York, 1961). J. F. Brown wrote *The New Eastern Europe: The Khrushchev Era and After* (New York, 1966). Carola Stern published a useful political biography of the German Stalinist leader: *Ulbricht: A Political Biography* (New York, 1965). Catherine Epstein published a general history of the German Communists of this period: *The Last Revolutionaries* (Cambridge, Mass., 2003). International reaction to East Germany is examined by William Glenn Gray, *Germany's Cold War* (Chapel Hill, N.C., 2003). Relations between East Germany and Poland are discussed in Sheldon R. Anderson, *A Cold War in the Soviet Bloc: Polish-East German Relations: 1945–1962* (Boulder, Colo., 2001).

Poland and Gomulka have been treated by Nicholas Bethell, *Gomulka: His Poland, His Communism* (New York, 1969). The 1956 events in Poland are described by Konrad Syrop, *Spring in October: The Story of the Polish Revolution, 1956* (New York, 1957). Hanna Diskin published a book on an important topic: *The Seeds of Triumph: Church and State in Gomulka's Poland* (Budapest, 2001). For Hungary, see Ferenc Vali, *Rift and Revolt in Hungary* (Cambridge, Mass., 1961), and Béla Király and Paul Jonas, eds., *The Hungarian Revolution of 1956 in Retrospect* (Boulder, Colo., 1978). See also Litván György and János M. Bak, *The Hungarian Revolution of 1956: Reform, Revolt, and Repression* (New York, 1996), and Béla Király and Barbara Lotze, *The First War Between Socialist States: The Revolution of 1956 and Its Impact* (New York, 1984). For documents on the uprising, see Melvin J. Lasky, ed., *The Hungarian Revolution: A White Book* (New York, 1957). The fiftieth anniversary of the revolution brought interesting books of essays reflecting on the events and their repercussions. See M. Janos Rainer et al., *The 1956 Hungarian Revolution and the Soviet Bloc Countries: Reactions and Repercussions* (Budapest, 2007); Terry Cox, *Challenging Communism in Europe: 1956 and Its Legacy* (New York, 2008); and Lee Congdon et al., *1956, the Hungarian Revolution and War for Independence* (Boulder, Colo., 2006). On Nagy and his legacy, see Karl P. Benziger, *Imre Nagy, Martyr of the Nation: Contested History, Legitimacy, and Popular Memory in Hungary* (Lanham, Md, 2011). For Khrushchev's policies in Eastern Europe following the 1956 disorders, consult the opening chapters of Robert L. Hutchings, *Soviet-East European Relations: Consolidation and Conflict, 1968–1980* (Madison, Wisc., 1983).

Ghita Ionescu analyzes Romania in *Communism in Rumania, 1944–1962* (London, 1964). See also Kenneth Jowitt, *Revolutionary Breakthroughs and National Development: The Case of Romania, 1944–1965* (Berkeley, Calif., 1971). Katherine Verdery examined the country under Ceauçescu: *National Ideology Under Socialism: Identity and Cultural Politics in Ceauçescu's Romania* (Berkeley, Calif., 1991). For Albania, the country most influenced by China, see William E. Griffith, *Albania and the Sino-Soviet Rift* (Cambridge, Mass., 1963), and James S. O'Donnel, *A Coming of Age: Albania Under Enver Hoxha* (Boulder, Colo., 1999). For Bulgaria, consult John D. Bell, *The Bulgarian Communist Party from Bloagev to Zhvikov* (Stanford, Calif., 1986). For Yugoslavia, see Hilde Katrine Haug, *Creating a Socialist Yugoslavia* (London, 2010). For Yugoslav economic developments, see Dennison Rusinow, *The Yugoslav Experiment, 1948–1974* (Berkeley, Calif., 1977), and on the nationalist tensions, see Sabrina Petra Ramet, *Nationalism and Federalism in Yugoslavia, 1962–1991* (Bloomington, Ind., 1992).

The problems of the Czechoslovak economy and the proposed reforms during the crucial years discussed in this chapter may be understood from Ota Sik's book, *Czechoslovakia: The Bureaucratic Economy* (White Plains, N.Y., 1972). On later events in Czechoslovakia, see Galia Golan, *Reform Rule in Czechoslovakia: The Dubček Era 1968–1969* (Cambridge, UK, 2008), and, by the same author, *The Czechoslovak Reform Movement: Communism in Crisis, 1962–1968* (Cambridge, UK, 1971). See also H. Gordon Skilling, *Czechoslovakia's Interrupted Revolution* (Princeton, N.J., 1976); Philip Windsor and Adam Roberts, *Czechoslovakia 1968: Reform, Repression, and Resistance* (New York, 1969); and Milan Simecka, *The Restoration of Order: The Normalization of Czechoslovakia* (London, 1984). Kieran Williams, *The Prague Spring and Its Aftermath: Czechoslovak Politics,*

1968–1970 (New York, 1997), takes a wider view. G. Bischof et al., *The Prague Spring and the Warsaw Pact Invasion of Czechoslovakia in 1968* (Lanham, Md., 2010), is a reflection through essays on the major themes of the event. The thinking of the Soviets is analyzed by Jiri Valenta, *Soviet Intervention in Czechoslovakia, 1968: Anatomy of a Decision* (Baltimore, Md., 1979). Results in Eastern Europe may be seen from E. J. Czerusinski and Jaroslaw Piekalkiewicz, *The Soviet Invasion of Czechoslovakia: Its Effects on Eastern Europe* (New York, 1972). The essays in Gunter Bischof et al., eds., analyze the cold war context in *The Prague Spring and the Warsaw Pact Invasion of Czechoslovakia in 1968* (Lanham, Md., 2010). Finally, a good analysis of the leader of the Prague Spring is William Shawcross's *Dubček* (New York, 1971).

CHAPTER 27

✍

The Shifting Economic Framework and Political Change in the West

CHAPTER OUTLINE

Economic Quandaries • The Thatcher Era in Britain • Mitterrand's "Unintended
Revolution" • Italy's Triple Revolution • Keeping the Balance in Germany

BIOGRAPHICAL SKETCHES

Margaret Hilda Roberts Thatcher, No Interpreter Needed •
François Maurice Adrien Marie Mitterrand, "A Very Good Dancer"

Between the 1970s and 1990s, new economic, political, and social trends independent of the cold war threatened the welfare state that had grown enormously after World War II. Drastic changes affected the world economy and the economic system of Europe's four largest democracies. Decolonization spelled the end of cheap natural resources, such as the oil located in the Middle East, which wrested control of the reserves from Western oil companies. Third World countries, such as Taiwan and South Korea, became efficient producers of modern goods and challenged European supremacy. Growing globalization allowed capital to be transferred quickly to different countries; factories were set up to exploit cheap labor, and the products were then sold in the affluent West. Globalization presented Western Europe with the difficult challenge of how to maintain employment and its high living standard.

The response was to increase efficiency by restoring free markets as far as possible, reducing social services, and privatizing governmental holdings. This fundamental alteration in the attitude of West Europeans, however, required years of struggle because the interest groups that had painfully acquired the benefits of the welfare state did not surrender them easily.

ECONOMIC QUANDARIES

Already in the 1970s, generous benefits of the European welfare state signaled a crisis by driving up taxes, while once-productive state-owned enterprises increasingly came under the influence of interest groups and became notoriously inefficient. The crunch came when oil prices escalated rapidly, forcing the West to spend a greater proportion of its wealth for energy. In October 1973, the Organization of Petroleum Exporting Countries (OPEC) imposed an oil boycott because the United States supported Israel during the Yom Kippur War between Arabs and Israelis that caught the Western industrialized world unprepared at a time when the escalating expenses of the welfare state had become increasingly onerous, pay raises had become unsustainable, taxes had become unbearable, and strikes had become more damaging.

Currency Adjustments

During the Yom Kippur War, OPEC quadrupled the price of oil and imposed an embargo on the United States and other countries that supported Israel. To meet the energy shortage, Western European countries imposed restrictions on the use of cars, heat, and energy in general. The combination of sharp price hikes and severe shortages caused cutbacks in economic production, unemployment, and a steep rise in inflation. The crisis altered the currency relationships that had been in effect since July 1944 when the Bretton Woods agreement had fixed exchange rates based on the dollar so they now "floated" according to the strength of the different countries' economies.

"Stagflation"

The Western economies had alternated between inflation and unemployment; that is, if inflation increased, the central bankers would restrict credit and raise interest rates. These measures increased unemployment by taking money out of the economy and bringing down inflation. With inflation under control, a high employment policy could then be reinstituted. After 1973 the industrialized West faced both high inflation (because of the rise in oil prices) and high unemployment—stagflation—as deflationary policies deepened the recession and high oil prices increased inflation. Excess capacity, poor productivity, and competition by more efficient developing countries and Japan also negatively affected economic growth.

Stagflation persisted into the 1980s, with inflation and unemployment rising to unseen levels. In the OECD-member countries prices rose an average 3.7 percent between 1961 and 1971, but in 1974, the average was 13.2 percent, with British inflation soaring to 25 percent in 1975. This rapid inflation, the fourfold increase in unemployment between 1974 and 1984, and labor unrest threatened to destabilize Western Europe.

Economic Crisis and Political Reorientation

European officials decided that reducing inflation and increasing efficiency took precedence over reducing unemployment. This policy meant allowing employers to lay off workers, close inefficient plants, change labor practices, and implement technological changes that reduced employment. The welfare state, a prime source of spending, had to be trimmed. Eventually, West European leaders believed, putting their fiscal houses in order would increase employment, but in the meantime unemployment rates would rise to previously unthinkable heights.

The pain necessary to correct the economic situation required a major political reorientation in the four largest West European democracies: Britain, France, Germany, and Italy. The earliest and most drastic alterations occurred in Britain, Europe's "sick man."

THE THATCHER ERA IN BRITAIN

Britain was hard hit by the 1973 oil shock. British industry went on a three-day workweek schedule, inflation hit 15 percent, and workers increased pressure on the government to maintain their jobs and salaries. The flash point was a struggle between the coal miners and Conservative Prime Minister Edward Heath. Heath lost the election held in February 1974, and in March, a minority Labour cabinet, headed by former Prime Minister Harold Wilson, replaced him.

Wilson caved in to the miners' demands for pay increases, and unemployment rose until, in September 1976, British sterling faced an acute crisis. The British appealed to the International Monetary Fund (IMF) for an emergency

By the 1970s and 1980s Britain was in a steep decline and many Britons believed that Labour Party policies favoring the welfare state, and Conservative Party acquiescence, had accelerated the process. Keith Joseph, a nobleman and founder of the Centre for Policy Studies, was the intellectual stimulus behind a new conservative thought that aimed to rehabilitate the free market.

loan, and the IMF demanded a reduction in expenditures as a condition for granting it. The workers challenged the government's attempts to implement the IMF conditions, and the struggle culminated in the 1979 "Winter of Discontent"—six weeks of strikes.

Important changes in British political culture to confront the country's crisis, however, were already under way in the Conservative Party.

The "Minister of Thought"

The pro-welfare state policies of the Conservative Party resembled those of the Labour Party. Following Heath's electoral defeat of February 1974, however, a shift occurred under the leadership of Keith Joseph, a nobleman attentive to the problems of the poor who won election to Parliament as a Conservative in 1956. During the crisis of 1973 and 1974, Joseph concluded that the interventionist state after World War II was trying to do too much and that the political culture according to which the state could solve all problems had to be changed.

The Conservative leadership flatly rejected this idea, so Joseph turned to a think tank in which conservative economists had a strong influence, the Institute for Economic Affairs (IEA). Later he established his own organization, the Centre for Policy Studies (CPA), which aimed at slowly changing the political culture of England to gain support for a market economy and won him the nickname of "the mad monk." His vice chair was a Conservative Member of Parliament: Margaret Thatcher. Joseph's elaboration of the centre's program in the late 1970s and its implementation by Thatcher in the 1980s, according to Daniel Yergin and Joseph Stanislaw, "would do much to set the global agenda for the 1990s."

Keith Joseph argued that the Conservative Party had been blindly supporting the socialistic Labour bandwagon for thirty years and had led to the country's and the Conservative Party's ruin because it induced postwar British governments to abandon the concept of sound money in exchange for chasing the illusion of full employment. The government printed too much money, which led to inflation, not full employment. Joseph's ideas heralded monetarism, the idea that sound money determines the strength of the economy in all its aspects. This principle sums up the policies of the Thatcher government, although the practice was much more complex.

The "Iron Lady"

Sir Keith Joseph would not become prime minister even if the Conservatives won a majority because he had made remarks that the British press condemned as racist, but Margaret Thatcher, daughter of a successful shopkeeper from the small town of Grantham, was a different story. A staunch anti-Socialist elected to Parliament in 1959, she rose to prominence in the Conservative Party. In February 1975, when Edward Heath was ousted as party leader, his heir apparent was too embarrassed to declare himself ready to take Heath's place, and Keith Joseph was unwilling to run. The time was right for Thatcher, who won election as the Conservative Party leader. The question was this: could a woman win a national election and become prime minister?

Thatcher forcefully denounced consensus politics, government-stimulated full employment, and public spending. She believed that the Conservatives must appeal directly to the working class—the people who had suffered most from the Labour Party's mistaken policies—rather than slavishly following Labour's lead. The Conservatives would champion workers against unions, taxpayers against tax collectors, tenants against landlords—ordinary citizens against the overbearing and intrusive state. She ran the election campaign of May 1979 on this sweeping platform and won.

BIOGRAPHICAL SKETCHES

Margaret Hilda Roberts Thatcher
No Interpreter Needed

The catalyst that, according to historian Paul Johnson, set a revolution in movement during the last twenty years of the twentieth century was born in the town of Grantham on October 13, 1925. In her autobiography, Margaret Thatcher notes that observers attributed her economic philosophy to her father's influence. In fact, she writes, her father, a grocer who rose to become mayor, was both a pragmatist and a theorist. Even before she studied the classical economists, she gleaned on a small scale the vast operations of the international market from the workings of her father's grocery store. She also concluded that governments impeded rather than helped free market operations. Thus, thanks to what she considered her practical experience, she was equipped at a very young age "with the ideal mental outlook and the tools of analysis for reconstructing an economy ravaged by state socialism."

After attending secondary school, Thatcher went to Oxford on a scholarship, where she headed the student Conservative Association and graduated with a degree in chemistry. While employed as a research chemist for the next four years, she studied for a law degree and later practiced tax law. She married businessman Denis Thatcher in 1951 and, on August 15, 1953, gave birth to twins.

Thatcher ran for a seat in the House of Commons in 1950 and 1951 and was elected in 1959. In 1970, she became education minister and rose in the party. Thatcher decided to run for the post of Conservative Party leader when Edward Heath's apparent successor unexpectedly withdrew from the race. She informed Heath of her decision, and he responded, without looking up: "You'll lose. Good day to you." Heath turned out to be wrong, and Thatcher took over the party in 1975.

Thatcher won the national elections of May 1979, and became Britain's first woman prime minister. She shocked the political world by speaking her mind and keeping her word in attempting to reverse forty years of governmental intervention in society. "Who rules Britain?" she asked when she took on the country's powerful unions. She insisted that she was implementing policies that the British people really desired and spoke bluntly to them. As she put it, because she led the same life as ordinary folk, "I did not feel I needed an interpreter to address people who spoke the same language."

Thatcher was outspoken and uncompromising. She favored open markets and the privatization of public industries and said so. By 1992, two-thirds of British public industry had been privatized—sold for $30 billion—and Britain had again become competitive. The symbols of Thatcher's success were British Steel and

British Airways, both transformed and privatized, saving the treasury billions of dollars in subsidies. Abroad, Thatcher's success inspired other countries to emulate her economic policies as best they could, depending on their political circumstances. At home, voters made her the only British prime minister of the twentieth century to win three general elections in a row. By the time she left office after eleven years on November 28, 1990, her once-controversial policies no longer shocked most people, and she herself had become an institution. "People seem to think," she remarked, "she isn't so bad, is she, this Maggie?"

On June 30, 1992, the "Iron Lady" was named Baroness Thatcher of Kesteven and entered the House of Lords. Despite her new, exalted position, she did not hesitate to speak her mind when it suited her, even embarrassing the Conservatives. As she grew older, her health declined, and she suffered a series of small strokes. Finally, in late March 2002, her office announced that the 76-year-old Lady Thatcher would retire from politics in order to avoid taxing her health. Her turbulent career was finally over, but not her popularity. On March 18, 2011, the *Mail Online* reported that Buckingham Palace had decided to give her a state funeral when she died, the first prime minister since Winston Churchill to be given that honor. The only worry was that there would not be enough troops available to line the procession route.

"The Lady's Not for Turning"

Once in office, Thatcher announced that her government would count on private enterprise to restore competiveness to British industry and drive down the inflation rate by trimming bloated public expenses. Her budget called for a reduction in the rates of some direct taxes and a rise in indirect taxes, particularly the Value Added Tax (VAT). This common European tax, roughly equivalent to the American sales tax, is added to every stage of production, is finally paid by the consumer, and affects the poor and middle class more than the rich. The aim was to increase the money supply by reducing the impact of several taxes on capital and by removing controls on salaries, prices, and currency exchange. The budget also cut the planned spending level of the previous Labour government. Finally, the cabinet increased interest rates and imposed restrictions on pay increases for public-sector workers.

Despite these measures, Britain's international economic position continued to deteriorate as factory output declined, unemployment rose, and changes in the exchange rate put the country at a competitive disadvantage. A new oil shock in 1979 and automatic pay increases in the public sector drove up inflation. These developments forced the government to modify its program in 1980. The government introduced a North Sea oil tax (petroleum discoveries in the North Sea were transforming Britain and some of its neighbors into significant oil producers), increased the contributions that employees were required to make to the national insurance system, and decreased the cost of borrowing money.

As the recession deepened, Thatcher rejected the Keynesian economics of previous administrations: during recessions they had cut taxes, putting more money in the hands of consumers so they could spend more and spur production. Thatcher refused to reduce taxes by changing the tax brackets, which in inflationary situations increased personal taxes.

This policy was supposed to favor a decline in the inflation rate and lower interest rates at the cost of higher unemployment, but did not immediately do so. This seeming failure made her extremely unpopular. Polls showed that people thought her arrogant and uncaring and showed only a 23 percent approval rating. It would not have been surprising if she dropped her controversial policies and adopt the consensus politics of her predecessors, but in a famous line she said: "The lady's not for turning."

The Falklands War

Thatcher frequently said that the unexpected always happened, and it did. At the depths of her unpopularity, on April 2, 1982, Argentina occupied the Falkland Islands. A military dictatorship, criticized internationally for its human rights violations, ran the country, which had long claimed the Falkland Islands, barren rocks in the South Atlantic 200 miles off its coast and ruled by Britain for almost 150 years. The islands were 8,000 miles away from Britain, and, given the logistical difficulties, the consensus was that Thatcher would accept the Argentinian action. However, she sent a task force to the Falklands, where, with American intelligence help, the British defeated the Argentinians. The British retook the islands, and the odious military junta was driven from power.

In Britain, the war resulted in a reversal of Thatcher's political fortunes. Her popularity skyrocketed when she announced that the country was no longer in retreat. Riding the crest of the wave, she called new elections for June 1983. The Conservatives won by a landslide, receiving a 144-seat majority in the House of Commons. The Labour Party won only 28 percent of the vote (Labour also lost votes because of the establishment of the new Social Democratic Party [SDP] that, however, proved ephemeral), its lowest percentage since 1918. The stunning victory set the stage for the so-called Thatcher Revolution.

Battle with the Miners

The Falklands War and the electoral triumph gave Thatcher the strength to face the aggressive British coal miners who had defeated many British cabinets. Thatcher believed it essential to break the miners' power because it represented everything she believed was wrong with the British economy and because the unions were a major obstacle to her policy of changing the country's direction. The British mines had been nationalized in 1947, were losing billions of dollars, and desperately required reorganization. However, the National Union of Miners led by Arthur Scargill fought modernization because it would cost jobs.

In March 1984 the coal miners called a strike that continued for a year. They had the sympathy of European workers and received financial help from European Social Democrats and international Communist organizations. Disorders accompanied the strike and the police arrested thousands of demonstrators, but, in contrast to earlier strikes, the miners lost. The government's victory spelled the end of an era in which labor was protected at a heavy financial cost for British society, and Thatcher was in a better position to implement measures to make British industry more flexible and competitive even at the cost of layoffs.

The coal miners strike in 1984 presented a major challenge to Margaret Thatcher's conservative economic policies. The British coal mines, under government ownership since 1947, had been losing billions of dollars and the union resisted reorganization and modernization because it would mean the loss of jobs. Despite support for the miners from European social democratic movements, Thatcher, who had recently won an important electoral victory, held fast and won big.

Privatization

The victory over the miners made it politically possible to realize the real goal of the Thatcher Revolution: the selling of state industry to private investors. Thatcher argued that state-run companies knew no better than private ones how to meet demand in the marketplace and that they frequently established monopolies that lost money for the state, provided cushy jobs for employees, and did not meet the consumer's wishes. The reasoning was so radical that the government had to approach the question cautiously, but after its victories in 1983 and 1984, it proceeded far beyond its original plans.

Several important issues needed to be studied. How would the state proceed in spinning off the companies? The shares had to be priced attractively to induce the public to buy them, which required knowing what no one knew—how much they were worth. The government began a good-faith effort to discover the value of the companies and a television advertising campaign to encourage investors to buy shares in expectation of a profit. Moreover, a fair price was essential because of the money the sales would bring into the treasury, which would help the tax reductions that Thatcher hoped to implement. These considerations raised another question: if the state companies were in poor shape, who would buy them? To fix this problem, the government fixed the companies, which required slashing the workforce. The government also needed to take measures to ensure that enterprises dealing in strategic areas would not fall under foreign control.

Over the next decade, many state companies in crucial areas were privatized, including telephones, airports, oil, gas, steel, coal, and railways. Privatization proved the most successful innovation of the Thatcher era, and it was emulated by many other countries and enunciated as a principle by the European Union.

The Thatcher Revolution

When measured by specific economic indexes, the Thatcher administration fell short of its stated goals. It failed to reduce public spending as a percentage of national income, but a treasury estimate put it at 5 percent less in 1982 and 1983 than the spending planned by the Labour government in 1979. Welfare spending actually increased, although it was combined with several cost-cutting measures. On the whole, the Thatcher cabinets increased spending on the National Health Service, whose average annual growth was 3 percent. Even here, however, the administration increased efficiency in order to cut bureaucratic costs. In education, the ratio of teachers to students improved, but this improvement was due to the falling school-age population. In housing, the government built fewer houses and instituted a number of efficiency measures. Most important, it encouraged public housing tenants to buy their apartments, sometimes at discounts of up to 50 percent when compared to market prices, transforming many tenants into homeowners.

Critics of the Thatcher administration noted that the personal tax burden rose from 1978 to 1979 and from 1983 to 1984, instead of falling as promised. But real income increased, primarily because of the fall in the inflation rate from 21.9 percent in May 1980 to 3.7 percent in May 1983. Even so, the standard of living fell for the unemployed, whose number continued to escalate, despite governmental measures to improve their condition and initially productivity increased only modestly.

Thatcher's policies needed time to work, and by 1993, the British economy was growing steadily. By then, Thatcher had left office, but her successors followed similar methods. In April 1997, the government reported unemployment at 6.1 percent, compared with double-digit levels in Germany, Italy, and France. Economic growth rose 2.6 percent, more than in the other major European countries, and foreign corporations clamored to enter the country to take advantage of low tax rates and skilled, reasonably priced labor. Thatcher succeeded in changing the prevailing industrial climate in Britain and in creating a new respect for private enterprise.

Thatcher's Fall

Thatcher went on to win a third election in 1987, confirming that "Thatcherism was not an aberration but a change of direction." However, she became more strident in her opinions and less charitable even to her old political allies. Her style increasingly made her unpopular in her own party even as she ran into domestic and foreign problems. In a radical effort to change local taxation, Thatcher supported an extremely unpopular poll tax. Characteristically for her, she refused to back off when the criticism became heated. In foreign affairs, she believed that the European Union (EU) treated Britain poorly, which prompted her to demand reductions in British contributions to the EU budget. What was more significant, she saw the EU developing into a vast bureaucratic monster in Brussels and objected to the projected single European currency because, she believed, it would lead to German domination of Europe. Worry rose in the country's financial circles, members of her own party came to view her opposition to the EU as crudely nationalistic, and objections to her domineering political style built up in the Conservative Party.

In November 1990, her former foreign minister, whom she had treated poorly, resigned his party and governmental posts in a speech that spelled out the conflict between them. The incident caused a fight for party leader. When Thatcher did not win a majority on the first ballot, she resigned.

John Major replaced her as party leader and prime minister. He led the Conservative Party to victory in 1992, largely on the merits of his predecessor. During the campaign, he pledged to continue the general lines of her policies, but his own blandness, eighteen years of Conservative power, and developments in the Labour Party convinced the British that the Thatcher Revolution had run out of steam.

Labour's Revival

Labour had reorganized itself in the opposition under the leadership of a young dynamic leader, Tony Blair. In a further indication that Margaret Thatcher's philosophy had become institutionalized, he appealed to the middle classes, owners of small businesses, the self-employed, and workers in terms that Thatcher might have used. Blair promised to implement tax relief and tight fiscal discipline, pledged to reduce the bureaucracy, and proclaimed "New" Labour the party of "law and order." Labour's love affair with socialism was over, Blair told his supporters on October 26, 1996: "Forget the past. No more bosses versus workers. You are on the same side." Even Labour's reluctance to enter the single currency area in 1999 mirrored Conservative policy toward the EU. As the electoral campaign progressed, *New York Times* columnist Anthony Lewis commented, "It seems increasingly difficult to tell the two major parties apart" (February 3, 1997). There would be no wholesale reversal of Thatcher's policies by the Labour Party.

On May 1, 1997, Labour won a huge victory but remained on a course similar to that pioneered by Thatcher, including reducing administrative costs at the National Health Service, strengthening the image of Britain as a country that was friendly to private enterprise, and reducing taxes for big business. New Labour made its biggest innovations in other areas. With 101 women in its contingent of 419 members of Parliament, it demonstrated its openness to women. Blair appointed 5 women and 1 known homosexual to his cabinet, and in October 1999, his government removed the hereditary right of peers to sit in the House of Lords. Blair also displayed sensitivity to the Irish problem, and on June 2, said he regretted Britain's role in the Potato Famine of the 1840s. This blend of Blair and Thatcher marked Britain's entrance into the new millennium.

MITTERRAND'S "UNINTENDED REVOLUTION"

France followed a less consistent course than Britain but eventually adopted similar policies. French Prime Minister Raymond Barre responded to the oil shock by instituting an austerity policy, including a wage-price freeze that brought positive results but also higher unemployment and lower wages. Complaints about these results, worsened by a second oil crisis in 1979, brought a resurgence of the left under Socialist François Mitterrand, whose rise resulted in the practical disappearance of the Moscow-influenced French Communists.

BIOGRAPHICAL SKETCHES

François Maurice Adrien Marie Mitterrand
"A Very Good Dancer"

Jarnac, the town in southwest France where François Mitterrand was born on October 26, 1916, is the white vinegar capital of France and is located only a few miles from Cognac. Mitterrand's father Joseph worked as a railway stationmaster until age fifty-four, when he went into the business of making vinegar. His mother, the devout but open-minded Yvonne Lorrain, heavily influenced him and counteracted the right-wing milieu of the French province. Mitterrand attended a Catholic school and was a fervent believer as a youth. He went to Paris, where he received a law degree in 1937 and in 1938 began work on a doctorate in public law. During the turbulent 1930s, Mitterrand participated in street demonstrations and belonged for a brief time to the Croix de Feu, a rightwing nationalist organization. In Paris, he met his first passionate love, Marie-Louise Terrasse, to whom he became engaged but who left him when he was a prisoner of war. Later a television personality, she remarked in an interview: "François was a very good dancer"—a comment that might also apply to his politics.

Mitterrand fought against the Germans during World War II, was wounded on June 14, 1940, and was sent to Germany as a prisoner of war. He escaped and returned to Paris, where he worked as a civil servant for the Vichy regime from April 1942 to late 1943. Whether Mitterrand truly believed in Vichy or labored to keep body and soul together remains in dispute. He admired Vichy's head, World War I national hero Philippe Pétain, and received the regime's highest civilian award in 1943. By then, however, Mitterrand had secretly become a resister, establishing a network of former prisoners of war and deportees. He went to Algiers to meet General Charles de Gaulle, leader of the Free French, where the two took an immediate dislike to each other. Upon returning to France, Mitterrand married Danielle Gouze—from a Socialist family and active in the Resistance—on October 28, 1944.

When the war ended, Mitterrand entered politics and served in eleven cabinets during the time of the Fourth Republic. He was an outspoken supporter of the French war in Algeria, and, when de Gaulle returned to power in 1958, Mitterrand rejected the general's plan for a Fifth Republic. He lost his parliamentary seat in the elections of that year.

Mitterrand's politics shifted progressively to the left in the following years. He ran for president in 1965, losing the election to de Gaulle by a closer margin than most people expected. His instinct told him that the left could not come to power unless it unified, and he spent the next several years in delicate negotiations to unite Socialist and radical clubs and to revive the Socialist movement. Although anti-Communist, Mitterrand advocated cooperation with the Communist Party in order to win power, correctly believing that he could deal with it later. On May 10, 1981, he won the presidential election and was reelected in 1988, remaining in office for fourteen years.

Flexibility marked Mitterrand's tenure. A convinced Socialist, he switched from state intervention to policies reminiscent of classical economics when his original policies failed. A haughty leader (his critics called him God), he adhered strictly to the constitution and ensured stability during several periods of so-called cohabitation when the right won the parliamentary elections. In foreign affairs, where the French president has the most influence, Mitterrand collaborated with France's archenemy Germany to put European unity on a solid basis. He also enriched Paris with notable monuments. Observers considered him the worthy heir of the French Jacobins and of the Popular Front of the 1930s.

Shortly after his election as president in 1981, Mitterrand was diagnosed with prostate cancer that had already metastasized. He died of the disease on January 8, 1996, in Paris and is buried in the family tomb at Jarnac.

Mitterrand's Policy Shifts

Mitterrand united the badly divided left, won the presidency in 1981, and instituted a course that was diametrically opposed to that of Thatcher in Britain: he strengthened the government's role in the economy by nationalizing major industrial groups and big private banks. He also raised the minimum wage, pensions, and housing subsidies by substantial amounts; reduced the workweek by an hour; and increased vacations from four to five weeks. The result: increased inflation, escalating deficits, and falling production. Capital flowed out of France, and unemployment mounted to 16 percent. Mitterrand hoped that nationalized industry would function as a locomotive for the economy, but it did not, and the subsidies increased the deficits and encouraged inefficiency. France's international trade suffered, and the franc had to be devalued three times in succession.

These developments forced Mitterrand to reverse course in 1983 and to adopt economic policies similar to those of Thatcher in Britain. He tightened social spending, levied an emergency 1 percent tax on incomes, and raised prices on a broad range of products. However, this austerity policy touched off strikes and disturbances and ran up against French political realities. In June 1984, the Communists, who had joined the governmental coalition, dropped out because of plans to reorganize failing industries. The parliamentary elections of 1986 produced a victory for the Center Right headed by Gaullist leader Jacques Chirac, who became prime minister.

Mitterrand and Cohabitation

The victory ushered in a period of "cohabitation" in which the president and the prime minister came from different parties. The risk of cohabitation had long been considered a flaw in the constitution of the Fifth Republic because both the president and premier had governmental functions. What would happen if a president elected by the people and a prime minister who commanded a majority in Parliament clashed on policy? Such a quarrel, if severe enough, might touch off a constitutional crisis and threaten France's stability. Mitterrand, however, made certain not to challenge Chirac's domestic policies even if he disagreed with them. By his restraint, Mitterrand helped define the role of the presidency in the Fifth Republic and consolidate its constitutional structure between a presidential and a parliamentary republic. In the first, the president has strong executive functions, while in the second, the president's powers are largely ceremonial, and the prime minister is the real executive. The Fifth Republic, with both a powerful premier and a strong president, is a mixed model that different countries considered adopting when altering their constitutional structures.

Mitterrand versus Chirac

Chirac's Center Right reversed many of Mitterrand's measures by denationalizing the parts of the economy that Mitterrand had nationalized, undoing the electoral reforms he had implemented, and allowing employers to lay off employees. In 1986 Chirac ran into serious problems when proposed legislation raising fees and entrance standards into the universities was interpreted as an attack on French principles of equality. Students staged demonstrations against the proposals and forced the government to back down. National Front leader Jean Le Pen also helped compromise the Center Right by blaming immigrants for the high crime rate and for France's other problems, charges that found support among discontented lower-middle-class elements who were threatened by immigration. These events brought a rise in Mitterrand's popularity, and Mitterrand defeated Chirac for president in 1988.

"Ni-Ni"

Mitterrand had learned his lesson. He did not attempt radical changes during his second term, whose slogan was "Ni-Ni"—neither privatization nor nationalization. This shift toward pragmatic politics has been described as producing an "unintended revolution." Supposedly, the Socialist stint in power had convinced the party that nationalization would not resolve France's economic problems. This realization, along with the electoral disappearance of the Communists, favored neglecting ideology in favor of policies that were closer to those of conservative economic principles that would encourage modern technology, even though these ideas influenced Mitterrand's France less than they influenced Thatcher's Britain. Mitterrand's prime ministers, who included Edith Cresson, France's first woman in the post, were moderates.

Failure of the Right

In 1993, Chirac's Center-Right coalition again won the parliamentary elections, and two years later, Chirac was elected president. Chirac promised fundamental changes to reduce the country's double-digit unemployment and the heavy burden of the welfare state, but constant protests defeated this attempt. Social security ran a deficit of 10 billion dollars, a figure destined to rise over the next twenty years as the population aged. Fully 36 percent of French wages came from social security benefits, compared to 10 percent in the United States. This burden helped drive many French and international corporations out of the country, and in 1995 the French unemployment rate stood at 12.8 percent.

All attempts to improve the economic situation by cutting benefits provoked strikes as employee categories from truck drivers to doctors defended and even extended them. Chirac's popularity and that of his prime minister, Alain Juppé, plummeted while social problems related to immigration escalated. Le Pen's anti-immigrant National Front gained visibility because the French feared that the technological revolution was leaving them behind despite the success of high-tech French products, such as the Airbus and modern fighter airplanes.

The European march toward unity alarmed the French as the EU progressed toward a single currency, the euro. Both Mitterrand and Chirac strongly supported French adoption of the common currency, and the country's prestige required that it meet the stringent economic conditions and qualify by 1999 for what was called the first round of the European Monetary Union (EMU). The government gambled that the French would support austerity measures to achieve that goal, but support for the EU eroded, and Chirac called early elections before support for his policies could deteriorate further. Chirac completely misjudged the political climate.

Return of the Socialists

In May 1997, the voters gave a majority to the Socialists, whose leader Lionel Jospin campaigned against austerity, ushering in a new period of "cohabitation." Jospin promised to create 700,000 jobs and to reduce the workweek to thirty-five hours. Once in power, the new Socialist administration announced a governmental program to hire 350,000 persons and mandated the shorter workweek after the turn of the century. French business leaders objected, insisting that the measure would raise labor costs and discourage new hiring. Jospin's proposals did not even satisfy the unemployed, who were impatient with the pace of the program and who protested loudly. The government responded by raising unemployment and welfare benefits. While France qualified for the common European currency in 1999 and did make progress toward economic responsibility, the French political culture would not accept the kind of changes that Britain had adopted.

French Foreign Policy

In foreign policy, the principal issue for France was German reunification following the fall of communism in 1989. Mitterrand accepted it. His successor Chirac, however, drew international criticism by resuming nuclear weapons tests and favoring the deportation of illegal immigrants. In the spring of 2000, he called Jospin on the carpet when the latter attempted to give French foreign policy a greater pro-Israel tilt and the Palestinians demonstrated violently against the prime minister during a visit. In foreign policy as in domestic, "cohabitation" caused the French to move in different directions.

ITALY'S TRIPLE REVOLUTION

Italian politics was more fractured than French politics, but in the 1980s and 1990s, three important changes occurred in Italy that altered the country's political and economic landscape: the metamorphosis of the Italian Communist Party (PCI), an economic transformation, and a radical change in the political system.

The "Historic Compromise"

Italy faced serious problems: the student revolution of 1968, riots in the South, and the so-called Hot Autumn of 1969. On December 12, 1969, terrorist bombs killed thirteen people in Milan, inaugurating fifteen years of terrorism by rightists and leftists. In addition, the 1973 oil crisis was much harder on energy-poor Italy, forcing the governments of this period to impose draconian conservation measures to combat a 70 percent increase in the price of petroleum that touched off fifteen years of double-digit inflation and social unrest.

These developments, combined with the overthrow in Chile of Social Democratic President Salvador Allende, which led the Italian Communists to fear a coup d'état if they came to power with a weak majority, prompted PCI Secretary Enrico Berlinguer in October 1973 to offer the Christian Democrats a "historic compromise," an alliance between Italy's two largest parties that could thwart any coup attempt. This proposal capped the long Italian Communist evolution away from Soviet control, and electoral support for the Communists jumped. However, the influential extraparliamentary left that had emerged from the 1968 movement accused the PCI of having been absorbed by the capitalist political structure. By 1977, Italy faced the most serious terrorist threat of any West European country from organizations, such as the Red Brigades, that believed in change through violence.

As the Communist vote total approached that of the DC (*Democristiani*, or Christian Democrats), the PCI, excluded from the ruling coalition, was now

Italian Communist leader Enrico Berlinguer had the most fertile political mind of the western Communist chiefs and proposed both the westernization of communism through "Eurocommunism" and a new Italian government based on a "historic compromise" with the Christian Democrats. Berlinguer continued the policy of gradually separating the Italian Communist Party from Moscow's tutelage, but his early death ended a brilliant career and the hopes of Italy's Communists to become the country's largest party.

necessary to convince workers to accept economic sacrifices and help stabilize the country. The Communists agreed to join a national solidarity coalition, but Communist participation in the ruling coalition as junior partners damaged the party. The Communists did not determine policy because they supported the government in Parliament and did not have representatives in the cabinet, but the voters still blamed them to some extent for the unpopular austerity measures that the government adopted. The PCI sought representation in the cabinet to have some control over policy, but failed to get it because many Italians considered the party still dependent on Moscow and the Americans objected. In January 1979, a badly bruised PCI withdrew from the ruling coalition.

Breaking the Political Equilibrium

The organization that stood to lose the most from the Historic Compromise was the Socialist Party (PSI), caught between the Catholics and the Communists. After the 1976 elections, the PSI share of the vote remained stuck at its historic low of 9.6 percent; young Socialist leaders revolted and in July elected Bettino Craxi party secretary. Craxi aimed to break the political equilibrium by which the Christian Democrats held the most important posts in the government, while the Communists dominated the opposition but followed a consensus policy in Parliament. Craxi discredited the PCI's democratic credentials in an effort to reverse the Italian anomaly of a large Communist Party and a small Socialist Party—the opposite of other West European countries. Craxi nominated Socialists for key institutional positions and put himself forward as prime minister, demanding that there should be a Socialist alternation with the Christian Democrats in the country's highest office because of the pivotal Socialist position in the ruling coalition. The 1983 elections produced a small Socialist increase but a large DC loss and set the stage for a Craxi cabinet.

By this time, terrorism had been defeated, and Prime Minister Craxi turned his attention to Italy's seemingly intractable economic problems. He aimed to lower the inflation rate from 15 percent in 1983 to 10 percent in 1984 and to reduce the large budget deficit from 16 percent to less than 15 percent through less governmental spending and increased revenues. Craxi's government proposed limiting pay raises to no more than the inflation rate, slowing wage indexation, and discouraging price increases. The government also promised to reform unemployment benefits, aid the South, increase employment, and reform the welfare state. The Communists rejected Craxi's plan and fomented strikes and demonstrations to bring the government down. They failed but, despite a slowing of the inflation rate, forced a national referendum on wage indexation. They lost the battle and local elections held at the same time and began a long electoral slide.

Craxi's victory on economic policy signaled a change in the country's style. Italian absenteeism, strikes, low productivity, tax evasion, bloated state industry, and large social service deficits had become legendary during the previous fifteen years. These problems did not suddenly disappear, but Italians felt that they could eventually be solved. Between 1985 and 1986, absenteeism declined, and time lost because of strikes diminished. Governmental measures encouraged industrial reconversion, increased productivity and privatization, and resulted in higher profits. These developments slowed inflation, and Italian growth rates rose to an average of 2.5 percent between 1983 and 1987, compared to less than 1 percent during the previous four years. However, the Italians failed to correct the historic distortions of their economic system: the large underground component, the wide gap between the North and the South, and the patronage system that seriously affected efficiency.

The Corruption Scandals

Craxi remained in power a record of four years. When he resigned, the Christian Democrats regained the office of prime minister, and Craxi agreed to support them until the current legislature's term ended provided that, following new elections, he would become prime minister for the entire duration of the new legislature (five years, barring early elections). Instead, a political upheaval occurred.

The Italian political system had become corrupt because it had been gridlocked and under DC control for forty-five years. Bribes were necessary to get anything accomplished, even at the lowest level, while at the highest political level, a public finance law proved inadequate for the needs of modern political parties, so these parties took kickbacks (tangenti) when contracts were negotiated for public works. The Communists, who were out of power, got a smaller share and financed themselves by receiving a percentage from companies that traded with the Communist countries.

In 1992, a corruption scandal broke in Milan that quickly spread to the entire country. With the end of the cold war, it had become possible to overthrow the old power structure, and some judges who had come out of the 1968 movement took the initiative. The immediate targets were Craxi and the Socialists, followed by the Christian Democrats. Communist corruption was harder to prove because the party had a tight organization and more committed followers who claimed that they took bribes for themselves and not for the party. Italian magistrates also utilized tactics that were originally designed to combat terrorism that would have been unacceptable in other Western countries—arresting people on hearsay testimony and keeping them in jail until they implicated accomplices. Besides Italy, in the late 1990s widespread corruption scandals erupted in France and Germany, and corruption emerged as an important aspect of West European politics.

The "Second Republic"

As a result of *Tangentopoli* (Kickback City), the Italian parties that had constituted the ruling coalitions since the end of World War II disappeared, and the political system underwent drastic alterations. The old system of proportional representation that allowed representation of very small parties ended. Although 25 percent of the parliamentary seats were still distributed proportionately, reforms instituted a winner-take-all system for the rest. The idea was to encourage parties to coalesce into rival coalitions for the elections. At the local level, reforms inaugurated a new electoral procedure that guaranteed mayors a majority in the city councils and long-term stability, in contrast to the past.

At the national level, the number of parties proliferated, but the largest joined electoral coalitions that offered voters a clearer choice. In 1994 a Center-Right coalition under media magnate Silvio Berlusconi won the elections. Included in his coalition was a party with neo-Fascist roots: *Alleanza Nazionale* (AN). With Berlusconi's victory, political forces that were associated with neo-Fascism entered the mainstream and the government of a major European country for the first time. The Berlusconi government fell after only several months in power when it tried to implement an austerity program against stiff leftist opposition and when another group, the separatist Northern League, pulled out of the coalition. This ability of parties to abandon coalitions they had promised to support during elections pointed to an important problem with the new system.

The Italian president set up a government composed of technocrats, and in 1996, early elections gave a narrow victory to the Center-Left or "Olive Tree" coalition. Although the core of the left coalition were the former Communists of the *Partito Democratico della Sinistra* (PDS), the coalition included many smaller parties that made the cabinets unstable. A similar problem afflicted Berlusconi's "Liberty Pole" coalition. His new *Forza Italia* (FI) party grew, but he squabbled with Gianfranco Fini, head of *Alleanza Nazionale,* and Umberto Bossi of the Northern League. The political forces agreed that the electoral system had to be reformed, but the attempts to do so ended in failure, and corruption worsened.

Economic Reforms

Despite Italy's political turmoil, the country met the stringent conditions imposed by the EU for the new common European currency. This fresh economic miracle occurred under the leadership of Olive Tree Prime Minister Romano Prodi, an economist and former Christian Democrat who implemented a rigorous austerity program that brought the budget deficit down from 7 percent to less than 3 percent. The cabinet's privatization policy continued the process of selling off Italy's major state-controlled companies in the oil, telephone, energy, banking, transportation, and other sectors to private investors. After Prodi left office as the result of divisions within the coalition, a former Communist, Massimo D'Alema, was sworn in as prime minister on October 21, 1998, the first time this happened in a major West European country.

D'Alema continued Prodi's policies, cutting social benefits and addressing the serious issue of pensions, alienating Italy's powerful unions that were allied with the coalition. The circumstances of Prodi's fall, D'Alema's political difficulties with his coalition partners when he supported the NATO bombing of Serbia because of Serb atrocities in Kosovo, and workers' opposition to his austerity policy led to his fall. Although constitutional changes during the 1990s made the political system more stable than it had been before, it was not as stable as those of its Western partners.

KEEPING THE BALANCE IN GERMANY

In Germany the Christian Democrats controlled the government until the mid-1960s, but were dependent on the small Free Democratic Party (FDP) for their majority. Unlike Italy, the opposition Socialists were fully integrated into the political system and could alternate in power with them. A 5 percent barrier that kept the very small parties out of Parliament made the West German political system flexible and stable.

Problems of Prosperity

In Germany in the late 1960s, West German exports boomed, and the mark became the strongest European currency. In theory, a strong currency is supposed to reduce trade surpluses by making imports cheaper, but this did not work in West Germany because the high quality of its products kept the demand high. Consequently, the 1973 oil crisis had less of an impact on West Germany than on other West European countries. West Germany imported large quantities of oil, but it paid for the petroleum by greatly increasing exports, especially to the Middle East, and by attracting Arab investment, and the country's trade surplus rose to near record levels in 1978. Consequently, the West German budget did not show a substantial deficit, nor did the inflation rate substantially increase.

This situation brought pressure from West Germany's trading partners to keep its markets open and caused the trade deficit to rise over the next several years. In order to contain this deficit, the West Germans built more nuclear plants to reduce their oil imports. This policy brought about the rise of the Greens, a new, environmentalist, political force. This turmoil, combined with opposition to the more flexible policy of the Social Democrats toward Eastern Europe (*Ostpolitik*), produced a backlash favoring the rise of neo-Nazi organizations.

A Delicate Equilibrium

However, the precautions taken by the framers of the West German constitution against the possible return of instability and the revival of Nazism kept the German political system in balance. The 5 percent barrier that parties had to overcome in order to win representation in Parliament reduced the influence of extremist parties.

Consequently, the neo-Nazi parties that periodically appeared on the German political horizon were contained. In the mid-1960s, the National Democratic Party of Germany (NPD) won seats in several regional legislatures and attracted international attention. In 1966 the Christian Democratic Union (CDU) contracted a temporary alliance with the Social Democrats, and the NPD's rise was attributed to CDU supporters who were outraged by this Great Coalition and others who were angry at the 1968 student revolt. In the 1969 national elections, the NPD came close to being represented in the Bundestag, but the economy improved, and its support declined to less than 1 percent. In the 1980s, another neo-Nazi organization, the Republicans, gained notable local support, primarily because of objections to credits extended to the East German government. The Republicans spouted anti-Semitic, anti-immigrant, and ultranationalist principles, but a desire to protest and not a wish to revive Nazism seems to have accounted for their considerable support in local elections and in the 1989 European Parliament vote. With Chancellor Helmut Kohl's espousal of German reunification after the fall of communism, their support dwindled.

Extreme leftist organizations caused less concern after the defeat of the Baader-Meinhoff terrorist group that grew out of the turmoil of the 1960s. The Communist Party was outlawed during the cold war, but even when the ban was lifted, it did not attract much support. The Green Party achieved some success, but it had to moderate its policies to do so.

The Christian Democrats

The moderately conservative CDU was actually a dual party, pooling its resources with the more conservative Christian Social Union (CSU), a Bavarian party headed by Franz Josef Strauss until 1980. The CDU-CSU attracted a middle-class membership; workers and women were underrepresented, although the percentage of women began increasing in the 1960s. Catholics represented an overwhelming 75 percent of the party in 1971, but the party made an effort to avoid being based on one creed, and by 1991, the percentage of Catholics had declined to 59 percent.

In 1973, the CDU elected Helmut Kohl chairman and, under him, followed a course influenced by classical economics but a more moderate one than that of Margaret Thatcher. The 1978 CDU program supported the free market economy and urged control of welfare expenditures. This philosophy appealed to the Free Democrats (FDP), a small liberal party, and in 1982 FDP votes allowed the Catholics to regain control of the government after a period of Social Democratic ascendancy. The CDU's moderate policies had strong support in West Germany until the end of the century, when a serious corruption scandal threw it into crisis.

Transformation of the Social Democrats

The CDU's rival, the Social Democratic Party (SPD), underwent major changes after World War II. In 1959 it formally renounced Marxism, dropping the nationalization of industry to control economic forces and emphasized freedom, democracy, and pluralism. Young people who were attracted to the left and who would participate in the 1968 disorders disagreed and demanded that the party commit itself to eliminating the private enterprise system. Despite bitter internal arguments, the appeal that pragmatism had for West German voters and the need to entice the FDP away from the CDU and win a majority favored the moderates. Moreover, the nature of the SPD changed as the proportion of blue-collar members declined and as more affluent workers joined it.

Because neither the CDU nor its rival the SPD received 50 percent of the vote in 1969, the FDP once again emerged as the power broker. The FDP was a middle-class organization of highly educated Protestants, professionals, teachers, high civil servants, salaried employees, and owners of small- and medium-sized businesses and regularly overcame the 5 percent hurdle for representation in Parliament. The party supported the free enterprise system, civil rights, and minimal governmental intervention in the economy, but favored governmental aid for the poorer sectors of society. The FDP allied either with the CDU or the SPD, depending on the internal balance of power and frequently determined the course of German politics.

The SPD at the Helm

In 1966, the CDU and the SPD established the Great Coalition cabinet, part of a strategy advocated by SPD leader Willy Brandt as a means for his party to lead a future government. By 1969, the Great Coalition had run its course, and Brandt successfully obtained FDP support for a cabinet that he would head and that would include FDP members. The FDP served as a brake on SPD policy, blocking Brandt from implementing a series of radical measures demanded by his left wing. Brandt's major triumph came in foreign policy, where his *Ostpolitik* seeking friendlier relations with the Communist East ended with treaties with the USSR (1970); Poland (1972); and, with greater difficulty, the German Democratic Republic (1973). During the negotiations, the Federal Republic had to make numerous concessions that paid off in the long run but aroused domestic hostility to Brandt that eroded his popularity in some quarters.

In general, however, West German voters appreciated Brandt's realistic approach to the problem of East Germany and Eastern Europe, and Brandt won the national elections of 1972. The next two years were rocky for the chancellor as the SPD left wing denounced him for failing to implement their demands, and its right wing and the FDP criticized what they considered his pro-Communist sympathies. In May 1974, revelations emerged that one of his close advisers was an East German spy, and an exhausted Brandt resigned.

This picture shows Ludwig Erhard, father of the German economic miracle and Chancellor between 1963 and 1966, with his trademark cigar conversing with Willy Brandt, author of West Germany's *Ostpolitik* policy of rapprochement with the East. Brandt won the 1972 elections and became Chancellor the same year. West German politics remained stable in the years before reunification with the transformation of the SPD into a moderate force.

Brandt's successor Helmut Schmidt faced major economic challenges. In 1982 a rise in German unemployment and a business crisis brought the differences between the SPD and the more conservative FDP to a head. The FDP wanted cuts in welfare spending that the SPD could not accept. The FDP left the coalition with the Socialists and allied with the Christian Democrats. The CDU won the 1983 elections, and its leader Helmut Kohl became chancellor. Kohl followed up this victory with another one in 1987. His moderate conservative policies appealed to the German electorate, and since the German economy was strong, the voters supported him. In addition, the Greens, the only radical group that managed to organize itself into an influential party, became more moderate in the 1990s and inserted themselves into a delicately balanced political system that tended to moderate extreme elements in West German society. After the fall of communism in 1989, Kohl's popularity increased and Kohl presided over reunification with East Germany.

MEETING THE CHALLENGE

When it became clear during the 1970s that Europe could no longer afford to continue to fund the welfare state at the high levels of expenditures then current and that heavy-handed governmental intervention in the economy had eroded European competitiveness, important changes occurred in West Europe's four largest democracies. Thatcher's policies played a crucial role in this evolution. A wave of privatization hit Europe, and by 2000 privatization—a new word meaning that state-run enterprises would be reformed and be sold to private investors, even if it meant layoffs—had taken hold of Europe. The state still had a more important role in West European society than in the United States, but there was a commitment to reduce its intervention in the economy despite opposition from labor unions, workers, and interest groups that benefited from the high level of spending for social services. The net result was a pragmatic compromise that increased West European economic competitiveness, at least for the rest of the twentieth century. However, Europeans continued to enjoy a level of social services that was unknown to Americans: long vacations, socialized medicine, generous maternity leaves, and free education from nursery school to the university.

The high level and costs of these services suggested that the welfare state would be subject to even more cuts in the twenty-first century even if individual states faced great resistance in implementing them. The EU recognized the problem and struggled to put into place procedures to guide its member states in the process of change and to ensure prosperity, low inflation, social justice, and competitiveness in an increasingly competitive world.

Bibliographical Essay

Derek W. Urwin, A Political History of Western Europe Since 1945, 5th ed. (London, 1997), covers the period discussed in this chapter, as does M. D. Hancock et al., eds., *Politics in Western Europe* (London, 1993). Y. Meny's *Government and Politics in Western Europe* (London, 1993) is a general history of the larger European states during the period.

David Childs, *Britain Since 1945: A Political History* (New York, 2006), discusses the general political history of Britain, while Arthur Marwick examines *British Society Since*

1945 (New York, 2003). Daniel Yergin and Joseph Stanislaw, *The Commanding Heights: The Battle Between Government and the Marketplace That Is Remaking the Modern World* (New York, 1998), is a detailed discussion of the effects that Thatcher's policies had in other countries; the quotation regarding Thatcher's setting of a global agenda is on p. 93, and the one regarding Thatcher's policies as a change of direction is on p. 123. A good understanding of the Socialist era's end in England and Margaret Thatcher's triumph may be gained by reading Peter Jenkins, *Mrs. Thatcher's Revolution: The Ending of the Socialist Era* (Cambridge, Mass., 1988). Peter Riddell, *The Thatcher Government* (Oxford, UK, 1983), a brief work, provides a good overview of the all-important early days of the so-called revolution. Covering approximately the same period is Martin Holmes, *The First Thatcher Government, 1979–83* (London, 1985). D. Kavanagh, *Thatcherism and British Politics* (Oxford, UK, 1990), emphasizes the end of consensus politics. Anthony Harrison, *The Control of Public Expenditure* (New Brunswick, N.J., 1989) discusses an important topic. A through biography of Thatcher is John Campbell, *Margaret Thatcher, Volume 1: The Grocer's Daughter* (London, 2007), and Margaret *Thatcher, Volume 2: The Iron Lady* (London, 2003). Thatcher's legacy is examined in Stanislao G. Pugliese, *The Political Legacy of Margaret Thatcher* (London, 2003); Earl A. Reiton, *The Thatcher Revolution: Margaret Thatcher, John Major, Tony Blair, and the Transformation of Modern Britain 1979–2001* (Lanham, Md., 2002); and Louisa Hadley and Elizabeth Ho, *Thatcher and After: Margaret Thatcher and her Afterlife in Contemporary Culture* (New York, 2010). John Campbell gives a balanced picture of Thatcher in *The Iron Lady: Magaret Thatcher, from Grocer's Daughter to Prime Minister (New York, 2012)*.

For France, Tyler Edward Stovall, *France Since the Second World War* (New York, 2002), has chapters covering the period discussed in this chapter; John Ardagh, *France Today* (London, 1988), is a good general history. J. R. Frears, *France in the Giscard Presidency* (London, 1981), is good on Giscard and valuable for its treatment of French institutions and Giscard's European policy. R. W. Johnson discusses the all-important leftist role in *The Long March of the French Left* (London, 1981). On Mitterrand, see Sally Baumann-Reynolds, *François Mitterrand: The Making of a Socialist Prince in Republican France* (Westport, Conn., 1995), a concise, informative book. Ronald Tiersky, *François Mitterrand: The Last French President* (New York, 2000), is a full-fledged biography. George Ross, Stanley Hoffmann, and Sylvia Malzacher, eds., *The Mitterrand Experiment* (Oxford, UK, 1987), is a series of essays analyzing continuity and change in France. S. Mazey and N. Nenman, eds., *Mitterrand's France* (London, 1987), covers the same period. For a history and analysis of Le Pen's extremist movement, see Harvey G. Simmons, *The French National Front: The Extremist Challenge to Democracy* (Boulder, Colo.,1996).

General histories on Italy during this period include Patrick McCarthy, *Italy Since 1945* (Oxford, UK, 2000), and Paul Ginsborg, *A History of Contemporary Italy* (London, 2003). Spencer M. Di Scala, *Italy: From Revolution to Republic*, 4th ed. (Boulder, Colo., 2009), has several chapters on economics and politics during the period discussed. Frederic Spotts and Theodor Weiser, *Italy: A Difficult Democracy* (Cambridge, UK, 1986), tells a good story in a manageable length. Donald Sassoon, *Contemporary Italy: Politics, Economy, and Society Since 1945* (London, 1986), focuses on postwar Italy. Norman Kogan, *A Political History of Italy* (New York, 1983), takes the longer view. David Hine, *Governing Italy: The Politics of Bargained Pluralism* (Oxford, UK, 1993), discusses institutions. Union strategy is examined by Peter Lange, George Ross, and Maurizio Vannicelli, *Unions, Change and Crisis: French and Italian Union Strategy and the Political Economy, 1945–1980* (London, 1982). Alexander De Grand published a parallel history of the Italian Socialist and Communist parties: *The Italian Left in the Twentieth Century: The History of the Socialist and Communist Parties* (Bloomington, Ind.,1989). On Italian Socialism, see Spencer M. Di Scala, *Renewing Italian Socialism: Nenni to Craxi* (New York, 1988), and his *Italian Socialism Between Politics and History* (Amherst, Mass., 1996), which includes an essay on the scandals that began in 1992. On Italian communism, there are Donald Blackmer and Sidney Tarrow, *Communism in Italy and France* (Princeton, N.J., 1975), and Donald Blackmer and Annie Kriegel, *The International Role of the Communist Parties of Italy and France* (Cambridge, Mass., 1975). There are no satisfactory general works in English on the Christian Democrats during this period. Paul Ginsborg published Silvio Berlusconi: *Television, Power and Patrimony* (New York, 2004). The other literature on Berlusconi in English tends to be more polemical.

Works that deal with German reunification are presented in the bibliography of the last chapter of this book, where that event is discussed more fully. General books on Germany that include at least parts of this period are Martin Kitchen, *A History of Modern Germany, 1800–2000* (Malden, Mass., 2006); D. L. Bark and D. R. Gress, *A History of West Germany*, 2 vols. (London, 1989), and I. Derbyshire, *Politics in Germany* (Edinburgh, 1991). Michael. Balfour, *West Germany: A Contemporary History* (London, 1982), is an excellent work. Peter Pulzer's *German Politics 1945–1995* (Oxford, UK, 1995) is an informative, brief introduction to the subject. See also Henry Ashby Turner, *Germany from Partition to Reunification* (New Haven, Conn., 1992).

Peter J. Katzenstein, *Politics and Policy in West Germany: The Growth of a Semi-Sovereign State* (Philadelphia, 1987), is good on economic policy. Peter H. Merkl, ed., *The Federal Republic of Germany at Forty* (New York, 1989), is a collection of essays on the most important West German themes. The CDU's policy toward women is examined by Sarah Elise Wiliarty, *The CDU and the Politics of Gender: Bringing Women to the Party* (New York, 2010).

Two biographies of Willy Brandt are Barbara Marshall, *Willy Brandt: A Political Biography* (Basingstoke, UK, 2004), and Viola Herms Drath, *Willy Brandt, Prisoner of His Past* (Lantham, Md., 2005). Terrence Prittie, *Willy Brandt: Portrait of a Statesman* (New York, 1974), is a biography that emphasizes his Ostpolitik policy. The same policy is examined by Anne Hoffmann, *The Emergence of Détente in Europe: Brandt, Kennedy, and the Formation of Ostpolitik* (New York, 2007), and by Julia Von Dannenberg, *The Foundations of Ostpolitik: The Making of the Moscow Treaty Between West Germany and the USSR* (New York, 2008). A book of essays on Ostpolitik and its influence was edited by Carole Fink et al., *Ostpolitik, 1969–1974: European and Global Responses* (New York, 2009).

A. James McAdams, *Germany Divided: From the Wall to Reunification* (Princeton, N.J., 1993), has good chapters on the relationship between the two Germanies during the period. For information on the left, see W. Graf, *The German Left: Socialism and Social Democracy in the German Federal Republic* (Cambridge, UK, 1976).

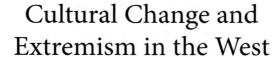

CHAPTER 28

Cultural Change and Extremism in the West

CHAPTER OUTLINE

Expanding Opportunities and Growing Protest •
Discontent in the West • The 1968 Revolts •
Terrorism and Society • Growth of Feminism •
Return to Normalcy • The Greens

BIOGRAPHICAL SKETCHES

Mara Cagol, Cofounder, Red Brigades • Simone Lucie
Ernestine Marie Bertrand de Beauvoir,
Philosopher-Feminist

The successful recovery of Western Europe from the physical destruction and psychological ravages of World War II might have brought great satisfaction to the older generation that had gone through the horrific period between September 1939 and May 1945 and its aftermath. However, spiritual dissatisfaction and unrest characterized the new generation who had grown up under the new prosperity. When this restless new generation, influenced by foreign and particularly American ideas, came of age, they revolutionized Western society.

EXPANDING OPPORTUNITIES AND GROWING PROTEST

Economic growth and welfare-state principles encouraged Western European countries to expand opportunities in education, including the university, to the youths of all classes. This ideal proceeded at varied rates in different countries. In the 1950s and 1960s, women were less likely to attend prestigious secondary schools or universities and generally stayed in traditional female fields, such as teaching. European schools at all levels were rigid, rigorous, centralized, and stratified with respect to their faculty. These factors and chronic overcrowding in French and Italian universities resulted in disorderly protests in 1967 and explosions

628

of rage in 1968. Students denounced the educational system as elitist. French students objected to the school system and to educational reforms passed in 1967 strengthening the natural sciences. University students in the different countries established strong links with one another, a major factor explaining the rapidity with which protest spread in the 1960s. The experiences of American students greatly influenced European universities as well, especially the Free Speech Movement headed by Mario Savio at the Berkeley campus of the University California. European students were fascinated and encouraged by this movement.

An important demand of European student protestors during the 1968 revolts was greater access for all social classes to the schools and universities, and the unrest spread to secondary educational institutions. In response to the disorders, the European governments allowed greater access to the universities but frequently failed to increase the resources needed for the new students. This policy led to a decline in educational quality, which produced more protests. The governments also agreed to demands to add new subjects to the curriculum. Typical of these subjects was sociology, a subject that contributed to the rise of more radical movements. In France, for example, sociology students, more concerned with analyzing society and its problems, were in the forefront of the protests, and in Italy, the terrorist leaders of the 1970s Red Brigades came from the same discipline.

DISCONTENT IN THE WEST

Although unrest in the West coincided with that in the East and a new generation supported both, the movements were different. In the East they were directed at a more rigid system that suffocated personal initiative, punished all dissent, perpetuated poverty, and opposed all change. Despite the inflexible aspects of Western European society, it was infinitely more prosperous, permissive, and open to social change than the East.

The 1968 Revolts

Ironically, the revolts that swept the youths in the West arose from prosperity. The youths became much drawn to the plight of Third World countries after the rise of the "New Left" in the United States during the early 1960s. This movement was convinced that capitalism must be overthrown, considered Stalinism and Leninism its opponents in the fight for freedom, and hoped to bring the masses in on the political decision-making process. The immediate aim of the American student movement was the struggle for civil rights and opposition to the Vietnam War. These were also the aims of the student movements in the different countries of Western Europe. Linked to them were artistic movements giving them their own culture, particularly the music of the British sensation The Beatles, the Doors, and other groups. The "Cultural Revolution" then taking place in China also had a great influence on students during this period.

The two Western countries in which the May 1968 student revolutions were the most serious were France and Italy. In France, student demonstrations were touched off by a plan to reform the universities by emphasizing science and technology

"Danny the Red" on May 30, 1968. He studied at the University of Nanterre, where he joined an anarchist group and participated in demonstrations aimed at gaining more sexual freedom and advocating Marxist principles. The university tried to expel him, but student protests prevented it from doing so. From Nanterre the unrest spread to Paris where students and workers rioted against De Gaulle and forced him to retire from politics. Opponents pointed to Cohn-Bendit's "foreign" origins because his father was a German Jew and his mother a French Jew and he had opted for German citizenship. Although the Gaullists made a comeback, Cohn-Bendit became a legend. Expelled to Germany, he joined the Green movement and became known as "Danny the Green."

in order to help industry. The plan would have made French universities much more selective and difficult to gain entrance to. French students immediately revolted and occupied the Sorbonne University, and their leader Daniel Cohn-Bendit ("Danny the Red," both because of his politics and the color of his hair) became a legend. In their actions, the students gained the support of the French workers, who claimed to be the worst paid in Europe. Cohn-Bendit argued that French students and workers were linked because they were both oppressed.

The 1968 demonstrations in France eventually petered out. The country turned against them, and while their actions eventually led to the resignation of President De Gaulle, this came about because he chose to resign when he did not win a large-enough vote in a referendum seeking changes in the government.

In Italy as well, the revolution united students and workers. Serious demonstrations had been occurring in the country since 1967, but worsened after the "French May." On January 24, 1966, students occupied the School of Sociology at the University of Trent, the first such occupation in Italy, and repeated the occupation in October in protest against poor conditions and proposed changes in the curriculum. When Florence was flooded in November 1966, the occupation ended as Italian students rushed to Florence to help save artworks and with the cleanup. This event brought many students from different parts of Italy together where they could exchange ideas. In November increases in tuition and changes brought about the occupation of the School of Architecture in Turin and the Catholic University in Milan, and the police were called in. In Milan 30,000 students demonstrated and fought with the police as disorders quickly spread all over the country. By May 1968, led primarily by Mario Capanna, students had occupied all the universities in the country.

The Italian authorities initially underestimated the demonstrators, considering them the spoiled children of the rich, but then the disorders spread to the workers who made common cause with them. United students and workers demanded equal pay, less work, and more benefits. As time went on, the demands became more radical, and the workers turned to sabotage. The workers gained a great number of benefits as the result of this movement, which continued into 1969 and beyond, including higher salaries, a say in running the factories, better health benefits, and, in 1969, passage of a Workers' Constitution (the work of Socialist Giacomo Brodolini) that gave Italian workers more rights and benefits than in any other Western European country. The radicalism of the Italian 1968 set off a fight with Italian rightist movements and the most serious terrorism of any other European state.

Terrorism and Society

The 1968 disorders set off a new type of terrorism in Western Europe. In the past, terrorism had been the method utilized by ethnic groups seeking freedom from what terrorists considered occupation forces—the IRA against the British, the Basque ETA against Spain. During the late 1960s and the 1970s, however, the most serious terrorism appeared in two European states that did not have such issues and that had made enormous economic progress after World War II: Italy and the Federal Republic of Germany.

In Italy, a long revolutionary tradition and the rapid change from an agricultural to an industrial society, in addition to the events of 1968, fueled terrorism. The ineffectiveness of the state in coping with the vast social changes that came with the great internal migration of people from rural to urban centers, overcrowding in the schools, an oppressive bureaucracy, and an inability to reform politics contributed to the disorders of 1967 and 1968 and to the labor unrest of the so-called Hot Autumn of 1969. In that year, a bomb in a Milanese bank killed thirteen people. This bombing was attributed at first to anarchists, but it soon became clear that it was the work of rightist extremists, perhaps rogue groups in the secret services, who hoped to blame the left and provoke a rightist reaction— the strategy of tension. In addition to the rightists, a fringe of the 1968 movement turned to terrorism, eventually killing or wounding 1,200 people. Dozens of terrorist groups operated during the 1970s, the most famous of which were the Red Brigades inspired by Mara Cagol and Renato Curcio. The support that the leftist terrorists had in some sectors of Italian society made them formidable. This support was based on their criticisms of capitalism, which they saw as dominated economically by Western multinational companies. Because the Italian Communists were so close to the political establishment, radicals had nowhere to go and acted outside the system. In fact, Italian politicians called upon the Communists to help get the country over the terrorist crisis, even though the terrorists were influenced by earlier Communist ideas of violence. Former Prime Minister Aldo Moro engineered an agreement by which the Communists joined the ruling coalition, but the Red Brigades kidnapped and killed him. This event undercut much of the support for the Red Brigades, which, combined with more efficient police work, had ended the most serious threat to a Western government by 1982.

BIOGRAPHICAL SKETCHES

Mara Cagol
Cofounder, Red Brigades

Mara (Margherita) Cagol came from a comfortable middle-class family from Trent in Northern Italy. Her mother was a pharmacist, and her father managed a perfume store. Mara was born on April 8, 1945. Along with her sisters Milena and Lucia, she received a Catholic education and studied accounting and classical guitar. In 1964 she matriculated at the University of Trent, joined the student movement, and met Renato Curcio with whom she fell in love. At Trent, the new faculty of sociology was influential in the rise of Italian terrorism.

Curcio and his friends published a Marxist-inspired review, *Lavoro Politico,* to which Cagol contributed. In 1969 she defended her thesis, received the highest grade possible, and ended the discussion by raising her left hand in a closed fist, the typical Communist salute. She received a fellowship to study sociology in Milan. Curcio moved there, and the two married and founded the "Metropolitan Political Collective." The group began political work in the city's factories, where they met persons who in 1970 founded the Red Brigades. Curcio wrote of his wife that she supported the creation of an armed group as much as he did, if not more. The group raised police suspicion and went underground. Soon the pair moved to Turin, where they had decided to infiltrate the Fiat factories there.

In 1974, the Red Brigades conducted its first major operation by kidnapping a judge, Mario Sossi, "interrogating" him over a month's captivity, and releasing him. At this point, the organization did not kill its victims, but on September 8, Curcio and another founder of the group, Alberto Franceschini, were arrested. Cagol worked out an audacious plan to liberate him. The action took place on February 18, 1975, in a bold attack on the jail where he was being held and succeeded brilliantly. In a letter to her mother, Cagol explained why she had taken up arms against the system: "This police state is supported by force of arms and whoever wants to fight it has to put themselves on the same plane." In April the Red Brigades kidnapped an industrialist with the intention of holding him for ransom in order to finance their terrorist operations. While Curcio was away, the Carabinieri came upon the hideout, and a ferocious firefight occurred in which several Carabinieri were killed or severely wounded, and Cagol was killed. Later the legend arose that she had been murdered after having been captured, but the evidence for this story rests only on the supposition of an unknown collaborator of hers who escaped.

In commemoration of her death, Curcio said: "Let a thousand arms extend themselves to pick up her rifle! As our last greeting we say: 'Mara, a flower has bloomed, and the Red Brigades will continue to cultivate this flower until victory! Armed struggle for communism!'"

In fact, until 1982, when the period of major Red Brigades activity ended, they kneecapped (a new word that entered the English language) and murdered hundreds of people, including, most spectacularly, former Prime Minister Aldo Moro. Besides those actions, Mara Cagol's memory lives on in song and on You Tube.

In the German Federal Republic, the 1968 revolution had been less disruptive than in Italy, but radicals, alienated by the increasing co-optation of the German Socialists by the political system, also turned to terrorism, the major problem facing Brandt's successor Helmut Schmidt. German terrorists, such as the Baader-Meinhof group, kidnapped and/or killed a number of high-level officials. Like Italian terrorism, the German variety had its roots in the 1968 student revolution and in the past immobility of German society, including the treatment of women, who accounted for a high proportion of the leadership in both movements. Although the terrorists might have received aid from East European sources, the phenomenon was linked more to what they saw as the immobility of Western society than to the cold war. German and Italian terrorists had strong connections to one another through the wealthy Italian publisher Giangiacomo Feltrinelli, who helped finance both groups, as well as with Arab terrorism. The police of both countries cooperated closely to defeat them and by 1980 had substantially vanquished West German terrorism. West German police methods raised serious questions, but on the whole, democracy in the Federal Republic or in Italy was never in question during the terrorist emergency.

A German policeman putting up a wanted poster for members of the Red Army Faction, a 1970s terrorist group led by Ulrike Meinhof and Andreas Baader and having links to Italian terrorists. They terrorized the country by kidnapping and murdering officials and robbing banks to finance themselves. After their capture they both committed suicide in jail, leading to allegations that they were murdered.

The German Red Army Faction, headed by Andreas Baader and Ulrike Meinhof, specialized in murdering officials and in bank robberies to finance themselves. Their most spectacular exploit came in 1977 when they kidnapped and killed Hanns-Martin Schleyer, president of the German Employers' Association. When the German police broke the movement by capturing its leaders, the leaders committed suicide in prison; persistent rumors held that they were murdered.

West European terrorism interfered a great deal with ordinary life. Travel in and between cities became more difficult as the police blocked off sensitive areas and crime scenes. Bombs went off on trains, in the stations, and in banks. Governmental officials moved around in armor-plated cars with bodyguards, as did the rich, fearful of being kidnapped and held for ransom. Terrorist activities and increasing crime rates made Europeans reluctant to go out at night. Once bustling cities became deserted after working hours. Muggings, purse snatching, and petty crimes reduced the quality of life. These events coincided with a strong reaction against the bourgeoisie in the 1970s. Women could no longer wear fancy evening gowns to cultural events because demonstrators threw rotten tomatoes at them. Student demonstrations, strikes, and protests proliferated.

Growth of Feminism

It was in this context that women were also radicalized. Although feminism had a long history in Europe, the 1970s gave a new and more radical impetus to the movement. Economic prosperity had brought more women into the workplace after World War II. As occurred after World War I, many women who had participated in the wartime economy returned to the home following the conflict, but this time more West European women received political rights. In France and Italy, for example, women could finally vote. Moreover, laborsaving devices, such as washing machines and refrigerators, became commonplace, and the number of hours women worked in the home fell at the same time that expanding industry and the growing service sector created a greater demand for female labor. In West Germany, in particular, many women were forced into the workplace to support themselves because so many men had been killed during World War II. Immediately after the war, they faced a difficult time owing to the high unemployment rate and to their lack of training, but during the 1950s, the German boom began, and women became a steadily increasing part of the labor force. By 1962 women represented about a third of the workforce, a figure that rose to 37 percent in 1976. The majority of European working women were married, had minor children, and worked in agriculture or textiles. The service sector was also an important outlet for them but restricted their rise to the managerial level. Women earned only about half of what men did, and, although in theory men and women were equal, the law codified discrimination.

French writer Simone de Beauvoir denounced these conditions in her influential 1949 book *The Second Sex*. The cofounder with Jean-Paul Sartre of a school of philosophy called existentialism, she examined the state of women over the centuries and concluded that the complex relationship between men and women made women dependent on men and was akin to the one between master and slave. De Beauvoir concluded that humanity would no longer be split only "when we abolish the slavery of half of humanity, together with the whole system that it implies."

The theories that de Beauvoir espoused in her writings seemed to move toward practical application in the 1970s. Women had been deeply involved in the 1968 student movement and in the upheavals following it, including labor agitation and terrorism. Furthermore, the stagflation of the 1970s made it more difficult for women to manage family economics, raised the specter of unemployment, and threatened to erase the gains that Western women had made during the postwar era. Because by the 1970s most families needed two wage earners to get by, the souring economic situation spurred more women to participate in party politics and trade union activities. Parties and unions were male dominated and not as sensitive to women's rights as they were to those of men. Women quickly discovered that conventional ideas of equality did not correspond to their requirements.

Participation in the social struggles of the period raised the collective consciousness of women and, besides general issues, focused them on questions related to their gender. Women demanded the end of the patriarchal family, equal pay for equal work, and the opening of top positions to them. They proceeded from the open discussion of sexual issues to demands for free abortions and birth control to sexual liberation. They organized politically, published journals, prodded parties, and demonstrated in the streets.

These activities won notable successes, particularly in the more restrictive Catholic countries. In France, women obtained the right to abortion in 1975. Legislation passed in 1975 and 1978 created equality with men in divorce, property, and jobs. Women accounted for an increasingly higher proportion of university students, including schools that formerly had been all male, and of the workforce. By the 1980s, women accounted for a higher percentage of the French workforce than in Britain. In politics, Frenchwomen were still at a considerable disadvantage, but a 1983 law obliged parties to include at least 20 percent women candidates for local elections. In 1981, François Mitterrand included six women in his government, a new record, and in 1991, Edith Cresson became France's first woman prime minister.

BIOGRAPHICAL SKETCHES

Simone Lucie Ernestine Marie Bertrand De Beauvoir
Philosopher-Feminist

The life of Simone de Beauvoir encapsulates the cultural, political, and sentimental journey of a European intellectual of the middle to late twentieth century.

Born in Paris on January 9, 1908, of a devout Catholic mother and a skeptical father forced by circumstances to become a lawyer, de Beauvoir rejected the religion and the bourgeois values of her family. She attended private secondary schools and studied philosophy at the Sorbonne. In 1929, she met philosopher Jean-Paul Sartre, the founder of existentialism, and joined his group. The two became lovers, staying together until his death in 1980, although de Beauvoir refused to marry him. De Beauvoir proclaimed herself Sartre's disciple, but recent research by scholars using early diaries and letters has led them to surmise that

continued

continued

her work influenced him. She also edited Sartre's seminal work, *Being and Nothingness*. In 1943, de Beauvoir published her first book, *She Came to Stay*, a fictionalized description of her complex relationship with Sartre and other women in his circle.

In 1931 de Beauvoir began teaching and was a professor at the Sorbonne between 1941 and 1943. There is no evidence of her active involvement in resisting the German occupation during World War II, but in 1945 she published *The Blood of Others* (made into a film by "New Wave" director Claude Chabrol in 1982), dealing with the issues raised by the Resistance. Following the war, she joined Sartre in founding *Les Temps modernes* (*Modern Times*, named after the Charlie Chaplin film), a review in which she published articles announcing her most important work. De Beauvoir traveled to many countries, including China and the Soviet Union. In 1947, she visited the United States, where she fell in love with writer Nelson Algren. Algren asked her to marry him, but she refused to leave Sartre. In 1948, she published a book criticizing the United States and capitalism. She had Marxist leanings, wrote a book about China, and supported the Vietnamese and Algerians in their struggle to gain independence from the French.

In 1949, de Beauvoir published her best-known and fundamental feminist work, *The Second Sex*. In it she argues that women are "made," not "born," meaning that male society casts women as insubstantial and inferior; they are "the other," defined by men as those who are not male. Some observers believe that her considerations constitute the intellectual origins of modern feminism and the beginning of gender studies. The Catholic church banned this book along with some of her other works. In the late 1960s, de Beauvoir became fully involved in feminist activism fighting for women's rights.

By the 1950s, de Beauvoir had established herself as a prolific and influential writer. In 1954, she published her most celebrated novel, *The Mandarins*. The central characters in this work are transparent stand-ins for de Beauvoir, Sartre, and Algren. In addition to examining the relationship among the three, the work is a criticism of leftist intellectuals and an incitement for them to become involved in political affairs. The book won France's most prestigious literary prize, the Prix Goncourt. During a period spanning forty years, de Beauvoir remained fully engaged in philosophical discussion and writing. During the 1960s and 1970s, she published four volumes of memoirs in an existentialist vein. This philosophy no doubt accounted for her increasing interest in aging and death. Her reflections resulted in works condemning the treatment of the elderly, and, in 1964, *A Very Easy Death*, the story of her own mother's demise. Following Sartre's end, she wrote an account of his lingering death, *Adieux: A Farewell to Sartre*. This work alienated Sartre's adopted daughter and resulted in bitter quarrels between them.

De Beauvoir's dependence on alcohol and amphetamines contributed to her own death, which came in Paris on April 14, 1986. She lies buried in a grave with Sartre, with whom she spent fifty-one years of her life.

Similar developments occurred in Italy. In 1975 a sweeping reform of family law removed the father's previous authority over the family, including over his wife, and children born out of wedlock received rights equal to those of legitimate children. Italian women received the right to free abortions in 1978, although Catholic doctors could refuse to perform them. Italian women also became more prominent in politics, with the Socialist Party establishing a set proportion of women to be included in its governing bodies.

After the 1970s, feminism became a staple of European society despite the increasing conservatism of the next two decades.

Return to Normalcy

In the 1980s and 1990s, a return to normality set in. The most dangerous terrorist movements, the Italian and the German, went down to defeat. Although large-scale political demonstrations and protests against the curbing of welfare-state benefits occurred, governments were more determined to resist them. The governments supported the right of employers to modernize, even if it meant layoffs and higher unemployment. They hoped that inflation would abate, and, in fact, the inflation rate gradually slowed. Europe slowly adapted to higher oil prices, and production increased, albeit at a slower rate than in previous decades. Per capita production and income in the most advanced European nations approached those of the United States. The EU began addressing the problems of lesser-developed countries, such as Spain, Greece, Ireland, and Portugal, and more economically disadvantaged regions within the advanced countries.

During the 1980s and 1990s, the daily routine of Europeans gradually returned to normal even though crime remained at a higher level than in the 1960s. The once-despised bourgeoisie returned to the fore more strongly than ever. Those who had wealth flaunted it once more, driving expensive Mercedes-Benzes and BMWs, living in upscale neighborhoods, and wearing designer clothing. The Gucci name became synonymous with conspicuous consumption. Despite the revolutionary 1960s and 1970s, the ruling elite of Western Europe changed little. The managers of Europe's large public and private corporations, the high state bureaucracy, and governmental representatives still graduated from select secondary schools and institutions of higher education that gave them entrée to the best jobs in their respective countries. Members of the lower-middle and middle classes could rise to important posts in European governments and businesses, but they were few, and those who did generally adopted the lifestyles of the traditional elite. Although the standard of living for West Europeans rose dramatically between World War II and the century's end, entry into the ruling elite remained an extremely difficult proposition.

The Greens

Of all the groups that emerged from the 1968 disorders, the Greens probably were the most successful, especially in West Germany, where they shook up the political system in the last years before reunification despite the small number of adherents. The Greens emerged from the environmentalism within the 1968 movement, where it had been a small but influential factor. The major force galvanizing them was opposition to nuclear power. The Greens opposed building more nuclear plants and this, along with other environmental concerns, stimulated the creation of several Green regional groups that participated in local elections in 1977. In 1980, these groups gathered together to hammer out a common

Petra Kelly, co-founder of the German Green Party, on February 6, 1983, with her companion Gert Bastian. Kelly is the person who put the German Greens and ecological movement on the map. She was born in Germany and brought to the United States in 1959 aged twelve after her mother married an American Army officer. She studied in the United States and participated in several political campaigns before her return to Europe in 1971 where she worked for the European Commission until 1983. She wrote several books and received the Right Livelihood Award in 1982 for her political and charitable work and for her advocacy of peace and non-violence. On October 1, 1992, she was shot by her companion, who committed suicide, according to German police. However, rumors that they were both murdered still persist.

program, producing left, center, and right factions. The most prominent Green and leader of the left faction was Petra Kelly, an opponent of the Vietnam War who was born in Germany and raised in the United States after her mother married an American officer. At Kelly's urging, the Green platform went beyond ecological issues, demanding the dismantling of nuclear power plants, social justice, the end of capitalism, the cutting up of large enterprises into smaller units, and production based on need rather than profit. The Greens demanded an end to discrimination against homosexuals, equal responsibility for child rearing, and a ban on cigarette and liquor advertisements and took positions on a whole array of social issues. They emphasized grassroots democracy and advocated nonviolent methods to achieve their aims. They did not believe that action outside Parliament could be successful and endorsed working within the political system. In foreign affairs, the Green platform demanded the end of NATO and the Warsaw Pact.

In the 1983 and 1987 national elections, the German Greens surpassed the 5 percent barrier and won representation in Parliament; interest in them increased when a nuclear disaster occurred at Chernobyl (USSR) in the spring of 1986. Green voters generally were young, hailed from middle- and upper-class civil service households, and were students and young professionals. A third of their votes came from women, a smaller proportion than they hoped for.

After these victories, the disappointments set in. The intense internal disputes led West German voters to fear that their ballots would be wasted because the infighting might cause the Greens to fall below the 5 percent barrier. In the 1980s, the two major factions were Kelly's Fundis (fundamentalists) and the Realos (realists), led by Joschka Fischer (a future foreign minister and vice chancellor between 1998 and 2005) and Otto Schily. The Fundis opposed political coalitions with other parties, including the SPD, and advocated working alone to implement their ideas of social change. The Realos considered the Fundis ineffective utopians and hoped to achieve their goals gradually, by means of political coalitions, particularly with the SPD.

In 1988, a long series of scandals and errors deprived the Fundis of their majority on the Executive Committee, and the Realos emerged supreme. In the 1990 elections, the intense ideological battles caused the Greens to slip below the 5 percent vote share required for representation in the *Bundestag*. This defeat, however, did not eliminate the Green presence in West Germany, and Green principles spread to other European countries. Green parties appeared in Sweden, Switzerland, Italy, Austria, Belgium, and Finland, and the West German Greens would make a comeback in future elections.

In Italy, the 1968 revolutionaries probably had their most important impact when many of them entered the justice system and used it to topple the old parties during the 1990s in a series of corruption scandals. As they aged, the 1968ers played out their most important role by joining the existing political systems and working against them from within.

Bibliographical Essay

For works on the social situation in the different European countries during this period, see the Bibliographical Essay for chapter 29. Daniel Singer, *Prelude to Revolution: France in May 1968* (Cambridge, Mass., 2002), and Serge Hambourg, Thomas E. Crow, et al., *Protest in Paris 1968* (Hanover, N.H., 2006) give an idea of conditions in France.

For the unrest in Italy, see Sidney Tarrow, *Democracy and Disorder: Politics and Protest in Italy 1965–1975* (New York, 1989), and Stuart J. Hilwign, *Italy and 1968: Youthful Unrest and Democratic Culture* (New York, 2009). Richard Drake, *Apostles and Agitators: Italy's Marxist Revolutionary Tradition* (Cambridge, Mass., 2003), and Drake, *The Revolutionary Mystique and Terrorism in Contemporary Italy* (Bloomington, Ind., 1989), links Italian terrorism to a long tradition. On the Moro case, see by the same author, *The Aldo Moro Murder Case* (Cambridge, Mass., 1995). The Italian situation in the 1970s is covered by Robert Lumley, *States of Emergency: Cultures of Revolt in Italy from 1968 to 1978* (New York, 1990), and by Phil Edwards, *More Work! Less Pay! Rebellion and Repression in Italy 1972–7* (New York, 2009). For an example of the Italian terrorist milieu, see Giorgio [pseud.], *Memoirs of an Italian Terrorist* (New York, 2003). The Red Brigades are considered by Robert C. Meade, *The Red Brigades* (New York, 1990), and Raimondo Catanzaro, *The Red Brigades and Left-Wing Terrorism in Italy* (New York, 1991), but the best book on the subject is Alessandro Orsini's *The Anatomy of the Red Brigades: The Religious Mindset of Modern Terrorists* (Ithaca, N.Y., 2011). Orsini traces the origins of the murderous ideology of the Red Brigades to religious Puritanism and to Italian communism.

For terrorism in Germany, there are Konrad Kellen, *The Impact of Terrorism on the Federal Republic of Germany, 1968–1982* (Santa Monica, Calif., 1987). On the Baader-Meinhof gang, see David L. Wisowaty, *The Baader-Meinhof Group, 1968–1972* (n.p., 1975);

Jillian Becker, Hitler's Children: The Story of the Baader-Meinhof Terrorist Gang (London, 1977), and, on Meinhof, Sarah Colvin, *Ulrike Meinhof and West German Terrorism* (Rochester, N.Y., 2009).

On feminism during this period, see Gisela T. Kaplan, *Contemporary Western European Feminism* (New York, 1992), and two biographies of Simone de Beauvoir: Carole Seymour-Jones, *A Dangerous Liaison: A Revelatory New Biography of Simone de Beauvoir and Jean-Paul Sartre* (New York, 2009), and Lori Jo Marso and Patricia Moynagh, *Simone de Beauvoir's Political Thinking* (Urbana, Ill., 2006).

On individual German parties, see the excellent analysis of Gerald Braunthal, *Parties and Politics in Postwar Germany* (Boulder, Colo., 1996). Andrei S. Markovits and Philip S. Gorski cover the story up to the Greens in *The German Left: Red, Green and Beyond* (New York, 1993). A thorough study of the German Greens and their impact is E. Gene Frankland and Donald Schoonmaker, *Between Protest and Power: The Green Party in Germany* (Boulder, Colo., 1992). On different aspects of the Greens, see Kris Deschouwer and Edward Page, *The Greens in Power* (Oxford, UK, 2006), and Sabine Von Dirke, *All Power to the Imagination: The West German Counterculture from the Student Movement to the Greens* (Lincoln, Nebr., 1997).

CHAPTER 29

⚖

Continuity and Change

CHAPTER OUTLINE
Scandinavian Social Democracy • Central Europe • The Lesser-Developed
Countries • European Union: The Acceleration of History

BIOGRAPHICAL SKETCHES
Joerg Haider, Embarrassment or Admonition? •
Andreas Papandreou, Democratic Fighter

The smaller European countries confronted challenges similar to ones faced
by the larger countries: escalating expenses for welfare state benefits and
increasing competition from rapidly developing countries.

SCANDINAVIAN SOCIAL DEMOCRACY

Sweden, Norway, Denmark, and Finland all had unicameral (single-body) legislatures that determined their governments' makeup. Proportional representation
ensured small political parties a voice in the parliaments, and coalition cabinets
ruled by consensus with Social Democratic parties generally having the largest role.

Dilemmas of the Welfare State
By the 1990s, the Scandinavian nations had to confront the realities that threatened the welfare system, especially the aging of the population and a lower birthrate that meant that fewer workers were paying into the social security system with
more aging pensioners to support. The immigrants who flooded into Scandinavia
and all Western Europe in the late 1980s and 1990s only partially offset this problem because of the expensive services required to help them. Furthermore, the
growing drug abuse problem among the young and the increased utilization of the
health and child care systems contributed to the strain on the budgets. These problems created a quandary: Citizens objected to the high taxes needed to finance
high-quality social programs but resisted cutting them. Toward the end of the

century, for example, Sweden spent almost half its gross domestic product (GDP) on welfare programs.

Challenges and Development of the Scandinavian Economies

Nevertheless, the Scandinavian economies, among the richest in the world, had fewer difficulties confronting these issues than did their larger neighbors. In Sweden, wealth was based on its engineering, electrical, electronic, and plastics industries; its forestry sector; and its pharmaceutical and biotechnology components. Its cars and appliances were valued the world over. But Sweden also faced economic challenges, notably the decline in the demand for steel, paper, and pulp. The country recovered slowly from the 1973 oil crisis, and between 1991 and 1993, a deep recession affected it. In 1995 the country joined the European Union (EU) as Swedish industry and engineering propelled Scandinavia into the forefront of the world's economies.

Norway was particularly fortunate because of the discovery of oil and gas in the North Sea, and by 1991, petroleum products amounted to 49 percent of its exports. This unexpected source of wealth subsidized its weaker economic sectors, contributed to lower unemployment, and helped it meet its increasingly onerous social security payments. However, the decline in oil prices in the late 1980s created severe problems that in 1998 led to an effective devaluation of Norway's currency. In 1999, oil prices rose steeply, promising to redress the economic problems, but the country remained vulnerable to fluctuations in oil prices.

North Sea oil was also a boon for Denmark, supplying half of Denmark's energy needs. This good fortune helped the country's economy recover from the crisis of the 1980s; however, such a large proportion of its population received benefits that it had to make some reductions because of the high per capita deficit. By the early 1990s, the Danes had put their economic house in order, but at the cost of 10 percent unemployment. At the century's end, Denmark was in a strong fiscal position, but the increased needs of the more technologically oriented Danish economy raised questions about whether North Sea oil could continue to supply such a large proportion of the country's energy requirements.

Finland followed the general Scandinavian trend. The 1991–93 recession caused skyrocketing unemployment, and the collapse of communism cut Finnish exports to the East. Budget cuts reduced the inflation rate to about 1 percent in 1999, and the Finnish economy staged a recovery. The Finnish economy grew at a 5 percent rate in 1998 and at a 4 percent rate in 1999, while unemployment dropped to less than 10 percent. Elections in 1999 brought Conservative gains, but a Rainbow Coalition, including Social Democrats, Conservatives, and Greens, continued to rule. In 1995 Finland joined the EU and in 1998 became the only Nordic country to join the common European currency (European Monetary Union, EMU) during the first round.

Between the 1970s and 1990s, important structural changes occurred in the economies of all four Scandinavian countries. The percentage of the population who were engaged in agriculture and forestry declined, reaching 3.2 percent in Sweden in 1990. Nevertheless, the economic value of agricultural sector products remained strong, particularly in Denmark and Sweden. A decrease occurred in manufacturing, and a very rapid increase in the service sectors of all four states accompanied the trend toward a smaller agricultural population. By 1990, over 60 percent of the active population in all these states worked in service activities, and the Scandinavian economies seemed well poised to keep up with modern trends, especially in high tech. For example, Swedish (Ericsson) and Finnish (Nokia) cell phones captured a huge share of the wireless communication market. However, these countries were also vulnerable to the rapid changes that took place in this economic sector at the beginning of the new century.

CENTRAL EUROPE

In contrast to the Scandinavian countries, the small states of Europe's central area presented a less uniform and more problematic development between the 1970s and the 1990s.

Finland's economy received a big boost from Nokia's cell phone operations. This Finnish company entered the cell phone business early, its car phone service dating from 1971, and became the largest producer of mobile phones in the world. It was a major developer of the GSM network, the world's largest in the world, and has operations and employees the world over. The photograph shows Nokia's flagship store in New York City, which opened on September 28, 2006.

Belgium: New Solutions, New Challenges

Belgium had relative success in calming the ethnic division between its Walloon and Flemish populations. In the 1990s, the country set up a complex federal system in an effort to end the ethnic problems. The Belgians devolved power to local elected assemblies that were based on linguistic groupings, while Brussels retained control of finances, defense, foreign policy, justice, and welfare.

As a result of the oil crisis and the decline of its traditional textile industry, Belgium suffered high unemployment and inflation in the 1980s. A Center-Right cabinet cut the budget, imposed wage restrictions, and limited benefits. The economy recovered, but the government's austerity measures increased unemployment and provoked street demonstrations. In 1991 a worldwide recession hit the Belgians hard. The government implemented a plan to increase efficiency, and by 1995 the economy recovered. The country brought its high budget under control by 1998 and qualified for the stringent requirements for the new European currency.

In the late 1990s, high welfare benefits and an influx of non-European immigrants presented new problems. The attraction Belgium had for new immigrants reflected the high living standard the country maintained despite its economic difficulties. The country faced the serious problems of an inefficient police force, crime, and political corruption that caused riots and threatened the government's stability.

Dutch Social Experimentation

Belgium's Dutch partners in the Benelux association seemed sedate by comparison. Having no need to restructure their country, the Dutch concentrated on perfecting their social security system between the 1970s and the 1990s, even though they were affected by the recessions of the 1980s and early 1990s and by problems with new immigrants from their old Indonesian colony and other Third World areas that strained relations with the growing number of Muslims. The Netherlands had one of Europe's most advanced welfare states that confronted such new issues as legalizing some drugs, establishing guidelines for euthanasia, allowing homosexuals to adopt children, and considering the legalization of gay marriages. These policies reflected the declining appeal of religious values and parties.

In fact, the Protestant and Catholic parties did not maintain their separateness and combined to form the Christian Democratic Appeal (CDA). The CDA became the fulcrum of governing coalitions until 1994. In that year, Labor Party leader Wim Kok formed the "purple coalition" with several smaller Center-Left groups. The Netherlands faced the same dilemma as other countries: balancing demands for reduced taxes with those to maintain social services.

Austria in the Spotlight

Farther south, Austria's thriving economy required adjustment as a result of the 1970s oil crisis. As in the other European countries, these measures included privatization and tax cuts to favor the free market and spur the modernization of Austrian industry. Nevertheless, the Austrians became sensitive to environmental issues following several highly publicized chemical spills. These concerns brought the Austrian Greens electoral success and representation in Parliament.

The collapse of Austrian trade with the Balkans because of warfare there was off-set by increasing exports to the reunited Germany and to post-Communist East Europe and did not affect the country's high living standard. Instead, the major concern was the country's international reputation.

In 1986, the Kurt Waldheim case broke out into the open. It was revealed that Waldheim, a former United Nations (UN) Secretary General who had served as a German officer in the Balkans during World War II, had knowledge about Nazi atrocities but had done nothing. Waldheim's election as president revived old questions about anti-Semitism.

BIOGRAPHICAL SKETCHES

Joerg Haider
Embarrassment or Admonition?

In the last years of the twentieth century, the flood of immi-grants into Western Europe, weariness with traditional par-ties, and unhappiness with high taxation rates contributed to the increased prominence of far-right parties. The rise of the Freedom Party in Austria under the leadership of Joerg Haider caused the most concern.

Haider was born on January 26, 1950, in Bad Goisern in upper Austria. His mother, a teacher, and his shoemaker father joined Nazi Party youth organizations in 1929, remained loyal Nazis during World War II, and were socially isolated after the conflict. As an ex-Nazi, Haider's mother could not teach in the schools, and the couple felt unfairly treated. Haider suffered from his family's situation, and, in some respects, it defined him.

Despite some portliness at a young age, Haider later projected the image of a physically fit, trim, tanned person who enjoyed fast cars and was sometimes called the "Yuppie Fascist." He excelled at sports, joining the right-wing Austrian Sports Union, led by former Nazis, in which he learned to fence and formed some of his ideas. At age 16, Haider entered and won a debating contest with a talk entitled "Are We Austrians German?" Given the association of Austria and Germany during the Nazi era, the question of whether the Austrians have a separate identity from the Germans was an important issue in the country. Haider, an ardent admirer of Germany, maintained that Austrians have no such identity.

From the age of 20, Haider held various positions in the Austrian Freedom Party. Formed in 1956, the Freedom Party was a lineal descendant of organizations with Nazi ties that advocated pan-Germanism; its first important leaders had for-merly been prominent Nazis.

Haider rose to the party's leadership in 1986, when it had only 5 percent of the vote in national elections. He served in Parliament from 1979 through 1983, reenter-ing it in 1992. He became governor of the province of Carinthia but resigned in 1991 over the negative reaction to his remark that the Nazis had carried out "an orderly employment policy" that the current Austrian government could not match. His de-fense of the Nazi past and his anti-immigration rhetoric propelled him to political prominence. In 1990 and 1995, Haider told gatherings of SS veterans that he appreci-ated their efforts and was glad that decent people in the world had "the courage of

continued

continued

their convictions." He called concentration camps penal colonies and opposed the Austrian government's plans to compensate 30,000 victims of Nazism. He accused immigrants of bringing crime into the country and proposed denying them the right to enter Austria if the unemployment rate was over 5 percent, expelling foreign workers, and keeping the proportion of immigrant children in schools below 30 percent. He also advocated a policy of segregation and fought bilingualism.

The Freedom Party prospered under Haider's leadership, going from a 5 percent share of the vote when he became its head in 1986 to over 27 percent in October 1999. This victory resulted in a governmental coalition with the People's Party in February 2000 that excluded the long-ruling Social Democrats from power. The EU imposed sanctions on Austria in an attempt to isolate it diplomatically, but the sanctions backfired. In the meantime, Haider resigned as official leader of the Freedom Party and regained his post as governor of Carinthia, where he engaged in an abortive attempt to carry his message to neighboring Italy.

In April 2005, as the result of the declining popularity of the Freedom Party, Haider engineered a split and founded a new organization that narrowly received representation in Parliament. The increasing divisiveness this controversial politician caused ended suddenly when he died as the result of an auto accident on October 11, 2008, but not the controversy. It was revealed that Haider had died driving twice the speed limit while his blood alcohol was three times above the legal limit, on his way back from a gay bar to celebrate his mother's ninetieth birthday. Allegations after his death seemed to confirm that he led a double life and had had gay lovers. In addition, other evidence surfaced that he took more than $50 million from Saddam Hussein and Muammar Gaddafi. The Mossad, the Israeli secret service, had been watching him closely because of his growing influence on Austrian and perhaps European politics. Even though the Austrian police denied the allegation, rumors quickly spread that it had murdered him and staged the accident.

Adding to this concern, elections held in 1999 ended the long-term governing pattern of Social Democratic coalition cabinets. Rightist parties, the appearance of controversial personalities, and an influx of new immigrants complicated Austrian politics.

In the 1990s, the fall of communism and the breakup of Yugoslavia caused an influx of refugees from the East, attracted by Austria's growing economy and close geographic proximity. With the new refugees came conflict and the rise of anti-immigrant sentiment that contributed to the rise of the Freedom Party that surpassed the Social Democrats and emerged as the country's second largest party. Led by Joerg Haider, this party distinguished itself by its controversial leader's praise of some of Hitler's policies, in addition to its strongly anti-immigrant posture. The electoral decline of the Social Democrats changed the parliamentary arithmetic, producing a coalition cabinet consisting of the Christian Democratic Austrian People's Party and the Freedom Party.

This development touched off widespread criticism from the international community, and the EU took the unprecedented step of snubbing the new government's representatives. Instead of dissuading the Austrians, however, the international outcry galvanized public opinion in the country against outside interference.

Despite demonstrations in Vienna protesting the Freedom Party's entrance into the governing coalition, the party was sworn in. Haider tried to calm the reaction by resigning as party leader, but he retained his predominant position behind the scenes until his death in October 2008.

Switzerland: International Outrage and Internal Debate

The intensified public concern over World War II issues also produced major embarrassments for Switzerland and damaged its reputation. Swiss banks had long refused to release to the heirs of Holocaust victims the funds that their relatives had deposited in order to salvage them from the Nazis. The banks demanded the death certificates of the depositors—murdered concentration camp inmates. A class-action suit instituted in the United States discovered 54,000 such dormant accounts, but the question went beyond that. Documents demonstrated that, during World War II, Switzerland had turned away thousands of Jews who were fleeing Nazi persecution (a 2002 report put the number at 20,000), consigning them to certain death. An international panel of historians maintained that the Swiss had effectively contributed to the Holocaust, and a U.S. government report stated that the Swiss had conducted a flourishing trade with Nazi Germany, had laundered gold looted from the treasuries of countries the Nazis had overrun and from individual victims, and had allowed Germany to purchase weapons to fight the Allies. These revelations set off an internal debate on the role of Swiss neutrality during World War II, and in August 1998, the Swiss established a fund of $1.25 billion to compensate victims of the Nazi period.

On December 9, 1998, the Swiss parliament elected Ruth Dreifuss the first woman to serve as president. Dreifuss, only the second woman ever to serve at the cabinet level, was also a Jew. Her election to the largely ceremonial post pleased the Jewish community, although Dreifuss emphasized it as a victory for women in a country in which women had only recently received full voting privileges. The euphoria was short-lived, because in June 1999 Swiss voters soundly rejected a government plan that she strongly backed to give women paid maternity leave, legislation designed to bring Switzerland up to European standards.

From the economic viewpoint, the Swiss continued to enjoy one of the world's highest standards of living. Bank mergers prepared the country's most famous industry for increased globalization, while the banks attempted to counter hostile criticism of their operations. New legislation aimed to prevent money laundering and the use of bank secrecy laws by criminals to cloak their ill-gotten profits.

THE LESSER-DEVELOPED COUNTRIES

Although Western Europe made enormous economic progress after World War II, some countries were left behind. Toward the end of the twentieth century, with the aid of the EEC and the EU, they began catching up.

The South: Assisted Progress

Three southern European states—Spain, Portugal, and Greece—threw off their dictatorial regimes between the 1970s and the 1990s. They were long characterized

Felipe Gonzalez in 1979, when he was Secretary of the Spanish Socialist Workers Party. Gonzalez went on to become Prime Minister of a re-energized Spain promising a modernization that many leftists believed violated Socialist principles. Elected in 1982, he remained in power for fourteen years, winning three general elections and implementing many needed reforms.

by economic backwardness, by clientelistic political systems in which favors were traded for political influence, and by the powerful conservative influence of the churches: the Catholics in Spain and Portugal and the Orthodox in Greece. Agriculture remained a more important component and employed a larger percentage of the population in all three countries than it did in the rest of Europe, while industry was underdeveloped and included a large public component.

Politically, the Communists played an important role in bringing down the dictatorships, but their influence rapidly declined, and rule by more centrist Socialist parties was the norm. Unfortunately, corruption scandals weakened all three Socialist parties in the face of strong conservative challenges, but the extreme right dwindled and no longer was a threat to the new democracies. Despite their previous turbulent history, in Spain, Portugal, and Greece, a surprising political stability prevailed and a smooth alternation of power between leftist and rightist parties occurred. All three countries faced the issue of modernization and adopted free-market policies to various degrees. Finally, all received financial aid from the EU to bring their economies up to West European standards.

Economic Development and Political Alternation in Spain

In Spain, Felipe González's Socialists aimed to modernize Spanish industry by selling off or closing obsolete governmental firms and by encouraging private enterprise. By the late 1980s, Spain achieved a 5 percent growth rate, but leftists criticized him for following policies similar to those of Margaret Thatcher in Britain. Workers increasingly opposed him and in 1988 staged serious strikes. The Achilles' heel for the González administration turned out to be Spain's high unemployment rate, which hovered between 20 percent and 23 percent. Disputes about how to resolve this problem occurred in the Socialist Party between free-market advocates and proponents of state intervention. By the 1990s, the impetus given the Spanish economy by entrance into the EU slowed down. In 1993, González survived a new election but had to depend on several small parties for a majority. When one of these parties withdrew its support because of González's plans to liberalize abortion, the prime minister called for new elections in the hope of winning a majority.

This maneuver failed. In 1996, José Maria Aznar's Center-Right Popular Party (PP) won a close victory but was forced to rule with the Catalan National Party, a conservative organization favoring greater decentralization. Aznar's pro-business administration favored privatization and supported agriculture in Spain's southern provinces, creating 2 million jobs between 1996 and 2000. Unemployment fell from 23 percent to 15 percent.

In March 2000, Aznar's party turned in a stronger performance than in 1996, won an absolute majority in Parliament, and this time did not need any coalition partners. Aznar's Socialist rivals lost 17 seats in Parliament, and their Communist allies lost more than half their seats in the election. Spain entered the new century with a vibrant economy and a stable political system that had become accustomed to alternation of the left and right in power.

Portugal's Progress toward Modernization

Political stability and alternation also marked Portugal's quest for modernization. President Mário Soares skillfully prevented extremists of the left and right from radicalizing Portugal after its transition to a democratic state. The Center-Right Social Democrats (PSD) won a majority in 1987 and in 1991. Prime Minister Anibal Cavaco Silva reduced protectionism and favored privatization and, along with political stabilization and low wages, attracted massive economic aid from the EU and foreign investment that promised to transform the country.

An economic recession in the early 1990s brought a political reaction, and the Socialist Party (PS) won the 1995 elections. The new Prime Minister Antonio Guterres concentrated on strengthening the market economy. In large measure, this policy succeeded. Portuguese exports to the large European countries expanded, and growth rates recovered to the 4 percent range while inflation remained low. Nevertheless, Portugal still depended heavily on EU grants to continue its spectacular development. Significantly, it received this aid because its GDP was still 90 percent below the EU average, and in 2000 a slowdown in the economy caused unhappiness with Socialist policies. The country still had a long way to go to achieve full

EU integration, and not just from the economic viewpoint. A referendum to liberalize abortion laws, opposed by the Catholic church, and one to increase decentralization both lost. These results demonstrated that Portuguese culture had not caught up with that of the most advanced European countries.

Andreas Papandreou and Greek Socialism

On the southeastern tier, Greece had significant difficulties following the overthrow of the military regime in 1974 and followed European trends to a lesser degree than did the Iberian states. The country's most visible politician, Socialist Party (PASOK) leader Andreas Papandreou, dominated the Greek scene almost until his death in June 1996 and advocated more radical policies than his Iberian Socialist counterparts. Papandreou, who came to power after 1981, attacked NATO and advocated ejecting U.S. bases. His proposal that the government take over the property of the Greek Orthodox church raised a firestorm, although it eventually ended in a compromise. Counter to the prevailing European climate, Papandreou believed in nationalization to keep unemployment down and favored spending a larger share of the country's income on social services. These policies damaged the Greek economy as governmental managers ran nationalized enterprises into the ground and the government continued paying wages to workers who did not produce. The result was Europe's weakest economy, 12 percent inflation, the continent's worst budget deficit, fleeing foreign investment, and a contracting GDP. Added to the economic problems, Papandreou turned politics into a frenzied farce by divorcing his wife of nearly forty years, having an affair with a much younger woman, and attempting to transfer his political mantle to her.

Papandreou's controversial policies weakened PASOK, resulting in the transfer of power to the opposition New Democracy (ND) Party after the elections of 1989 and 1991. The Greek situation hardly improved during ND's tenure because the wily Papandreou had implemented structural changes that hampered its rule. In 1993, a split in ND allowed PASOK to return to power, and in September 1996, following Papandreou's death, the more moderate Costas Simitis succeeded him.

Problems of Greek Modernization

Prime Minister Simitis reversed course by instituting austerity policies and by implementing Thatcherite measures. He aimed to cut inflation and the public debt, reduce unemployment, privatize state companies, and fight tax evasion in the hope that these measures would allow Greece to qualify for the common European currency by 2001. Simitis's policies incited numerous strikes and protests, but instead of standing by when workers tried to disrupt production, the government now sent in the police. The cabinet also attempted to attract foreign investors by granting tax relief and by promising to privatize nationalized industries. By 1997, investors began returning, but the slow pace of privatization hampered this trend—the state still owned key industries and 70 percent of banking. However, massive EU funds poured into the country to build infrastructure, such as airports and roads, which stimulated the economy. Simitis's policies resulted in the halving of inflation, the dramatic decline of interest rates, a shrinking deficit, and a growth rate that by 1997 had reached 3.5 percent.

BIOGRAPHICAL SKETCHES

Andreas Papandreou
Democratic Fighter

At his funeral elegy, the family of Andreas Papandreou noted his emphasis on familiar but ignored principles, such as democracy, justice, and equality—constant themes in the life of the most charismatic postwar Greek leader.

Born on the island of Chios on February 5, 1919, Andreas Papandreou followed the example of his father George, who became prime minister. Papandreou attended the University of Athens Law School and, as a young man, opposed the dictatorship of General John Metaxas, who took over the country in August 1936. Arrested and tortured by the regime in 1939, he was released and went into exile in the United States in 1940.

In the United States, Papandreou attended Harvard University, where he earned a master's degree and a doctorate in economics. He served in the U.S. Navy during World War II and was naturalized as an American citizen in 1944. Papandreou had a brilliant academic career in the United States, serving as a professor at some of its most distinguished universities, including Harvard, the University of Minnesota, Northwestern, and the University of California, Berkeley. He won prestigious awards, including Fulbright and Guggenheim scholarships.

In 1964, Papandreou gave up his American citizenship and reentered Greek politics. Elected to the Greek Parliament in 1965, he aided his father and became a government minister. In 1967, the Greek colonels, led by George Papadopoulos, seized control of the country. They arrested and exiled Papandreou, who again entered academic life, teaching at the University of Stockholm (1968–69) and at York University in Canada (1969–74).

In Stockholm in November 1968, Papandreou founded the Panhellenic Liberation Movement (PAK) to coordinate the Greek democratic resistance. Its program called for the dictatorship's overthrow and for the establishment in Greece of "Popular Sovereignty, Democratic Process, and Social Justice." After the dictatorship's fall, Papandreou returned to his homeland in August 1974 and founded a political party, PASOK. This organization won about 13 percent of the vote in the elections of 1974, increasing its consensus to 25 percent three years later when Papandreou emerged as the main opposition leader. For the 1981 elections, he ran on an anti-Western and reformist platform, pledging to take Greece out of NATO and the European Economic Community. His party won a landslide victory, and Papandreou became Greece's first Socialist prime minister. Despite his campaign rhetoric and the worry it caused the United States, Papandreou did not pull Greece out of Western institutions, and his reform program fell short of expectations. Nevertheless, he won another electoral victory in June 1985.

Papandreou's second administration was marked by financial and personal scandals and by ill health. In 1988, he underwent open-heart surgery. He had an affair with a considerably younger woman, an Olympic Airline hostess, Dimitra Liana, and in 1989 he divorced his American wife of thirty-eight years and married Liana. Parliament indicted him on embezzlement charges the same year, accusing him of participating in a scheme to skim off interest owed to state companies for the benefit of his party. During the same year, he lost the elections to the New Democracy party.

continued

continued

Found innocent of all charges in 1992, Papandreou bounced back by winning the October 1993 general elections, but his bad health slowed him down considerably. Hospitalized for lung and kidney ailments on November 20, 1995, he resigned as prime minister from his hospital bed on January 15, 1996. Papandreou enjoyed a brief recovery and returned home in March, but he was loath to give up politics. He was working on a speech to PASOK's Fourth Congress an hour before he died of heart failure in his sleep at 2:30 A.M. on June 23, 1996, in Athens. A symbol of democracy, Papandreou was Greece's most charismatic prime minister since Eleutherios Venizelos in the early part of the century.

But clouds darkened this rosy picture. Most of the growth came from the great inflow of EU funds. Unhappy labor leaders stressed that unemployment nearly doubled, from 6 percent to 11 percent. Nevertheless, the recovery of the Greek economy made Simitis's goal of joining the common European currency bloc appear within striking distance, and on March 9, 2000, Greece applied for membership. On January 1, 2001, the country formally qualified for the new currency, the euro, which was due to be introduced on January 1, 2002 (in November 2004 it emerged that Greece had falsified the data that qualified it to join the euro zone). These developments set off a stock market boom in the spring of 1999, and the Athens Stock Exchange became one of the world's hottest markets. Ordinary Greeks sold their land, sheep, and tractors to invest in stocks. Encouraged and hoping to take advantage of this trend, Simitis scheduled new elections. Then the market collapsed. Investors' anger against the Socialist government intensified, and PASOK's fortunes plummeted. Polls suggested that PASOK's rival, ND, headed by Costas Karamanlis, the son of a revered politician, might win the elections. In April 2000, however, PASOK won the elections by an incredibly thin margin.

Problems other than political also beset Greece. Like Portugal, Spain, and Ireland, Greece struggled against the overbearing influence of its national church. A disconcerting event emphasized the gulf that separated Greece from the prevailing European secular mentality on the same day that the country formally applied for EMU membership: A court banned a novel that was considered blasphemous in the country's six northern regions. The ruling embarrassed the Greeks, brought criticism from the governing Socialists, and reopened the question of church and state.

Greek Foreign Policy

In addition, Greek foreign policy caused concern. Relations with Turkey remained poor, because of Cyprus and because of Greek sympathy for the separatist Turkish Kurds. Greece began a military buildup it could ill afford, although relations improved after earthquakes struck both countries. Following the thaw, Greece withdrew its veto of Turkey's application for EU membership. Besides the Turkish quarrel, Greece objected to the former Yugoslav republic of Macedonia's taking that name and followed up with a trade embargo that hurt the Greeks as much as the Macedonians In addition, Greece had outstanding questions with Albania regarding the ethnic Albanian minority in the country. Finally, embarrassing demonstrations occurred in the country against its NATO allies during the bombing of Greek Orthodox Serbia in 1999.

Fresh Winds in Ireland

At the opposite end of Europe, Ireland struggled to modernize and needed to resolve the long-standing dispute over Northern Ireland (Ulster).

During the late 1990s, Ireland enjoyed an economic boom whose major symbol was return immigration. In 1998, Ireland met the requirements for the projected new European currency, its national debt fell by 7 percent, salaries rose, interest rates remained low, and the unemployment rate decreased. In 1999, the Irish GDP increased by 8 percent. According to a UN report, however, Ireland had the largest percentage of poor people in the industrialized world.

The Irish Republic still lagged behind the economic standards of Western Europe and struggled with social problems that had gone a long way toward resolution in the rest of Europe. Despite progress on the Ulster problem, this issue and the traditionally problematic relationship with Britain troubled the rest of Europe. The surprise election of a woman and Labour Party candidate, Mary Robinson, as president in 1990 failed to resolve some of the most glaring social issues or to reduce the church's power. Only in 1995 did Parliament approve the dissemination of information on the availability of abortions in other countries—and then only because the case of a 14-year-old girl who had been raped and sought an abortion in

The Northern Irish "troubles" began in 1969 and defied all attempts to settle them until the end of the century. Nevertheless, the road to implementing an agreement to bring peace to the area, signed on April 10, 1998, was rocky. Here is a picture of riots in Belfast sometime between 1970 and 1977 that shows the extent of the destruction in that city—unprecedented in Western Europe after World War II.

England received international attention. During the same year, Parliament approved a divorce law for couples who had been estranged for several years, but the law came into effect only in 1997 following a series of court fights.

Slow Progress on Northern Ireland

The Northern Ireland question raised hopes, but no real solution by the century's close. The major advance occurred on April 10, 1998, Good Friday. Prodded by U.S. President Bill Clinton and former Senate majority leader George Mitchell, British Prime Minister Tony Blair, Irish Prime Minister Bertie Ahern, and Gerry Adams, the leader of Sinn Fein (the political arm of the Irish Republican Army, or IRA) agreed to the disarmament of the contending parties and the election of a Northern Ireland Assembly. The election occurred on June 25, but, despite Adams's efforts, the IRA refused to surrender its weapons. In February 2000, Great Britain suspended the Assembly. Britain was criticized for this action, and Adams tried to restart the process. The prospects for the Good Friday agreement seemed poor but improved over the next several years as the IRA moved toward disarmament.

EUROPEAN UNION: THE ACCELERATION OF HISTORY

In the 1990s, the movement for European unity seemed to be going very well in contrast to the 1970s, when the future for such a union appeared bleak.

Agricultural Issues

The complex workings of the Common Agricultural Policy (CAP), previously examined, caused Britain's payments to the EC to soar from 60 million pounds in 1973 to 947 million pounds in 1979 and Thatcher to argue that the assessment of the EC on Britain for the EC's budget was unfair. Thatcher aimed to get a fair deal for Britain and to reform the wasteful CAP mechanism that threatened to fracture the EC. In June 1984, the EC reduced Britain's budgetary contribution and CAP spending and augmented the EC's income by increasing the percentage of the Value Added Tax (VAT, a kind of sales tax) that members earmarked for the EC.

These initiatives coincided with several other positive developments—direct election of the European Parliament by populations of the member states and greater activism on the part of the European Commission.

Declaration of the European Union

The seeming success of Thatcherism in England in the early 1980s focused attention on free-market policies and helped induce the European Commission to make efficiency and competitiveness top priorities. The commission skillfully pushed for implementation of a tariff-free single market among EC members, a policy that was strongly supported by business in the effort to meet American and Japanese technological challenges. In the 1980s as well, a series of foreign policy differences between Europe and the United States strengthened the European resolve to reform organizations of the European Community to increase Europe's political clout.

Capping off these initiatives, the Institutional Affairs Committee of the European Parliament replaced the agreements setting up the European communities

(Common Market, Euratom, and the European Coal and Steel Community) with a single instrument establishing the European Union. On February 14, 1984, the European Parliament passed the draft treaty by a huge majority, clearing the way for the EU. On December 31, 1992, the single European market became a reality with the end of all tariff restrictions among the member states.

The Maastricht Treaty

In 1988 European Commission President Jacques Delors prepared a three-stage plan for implementing a single currency for the EU: the coordination of a monetary policy and the removal of impediments to the movement of capital, the alignment of European currencies with respect to each other, and the single currency. In July 1990, the member states worked out the steps by which a common currency would be implemented, an agreement approved in the Dutch city of Maastricht in December 1991. On January 1, 1994, EU members agreed on the formation of the European Central Bank (ECB) to coordinate the monetary policy for the EU countries. In December 1995, at a meeting in Madrid, the EU leaders adopted the term *euro* for the common currency and agreed that they would decide in 1998 which countries met the Maastricht criteria for participation.

In order to qualify for the single currency, the budget deficits of member states had to be no more than 3 percent and the debt no more than 60 percent of

In 1991 in the Dutch city of Maastricht, members of the European Union approved creation of a common currency, later called the euro. In order to accomplish this goal, the EU set strict austerity standards that alienated many Europeans. After the euro appeared on January 1, 2002, it became one of the world's major currencies. Because the Europeans failed to adopt measures allowing the EU to coordinate the economic policies of the different member states, however, the euro entered a profound crisis in 2010 and 2011, prompting some demands that the old national currencies be restored. Above, a 1992 poster urges the French to reject Maastricht, along with President Mitterand, who supported the agreement.

the GDP. The members had to have low interest rates, and their currencies had to have a stable exchange rate. Who qualified for the first round of the EMU would be decided at the end of 1998, and on January 1, 1999, the common currency would take effect. National currencies of the countries that had qualified for membership would circulate for three more years until the euro actually appeared as the currency on January 1, 2002.

Impact of the Maastricht Treaty

In order to meet the Maastricht criteria, the EU member states had to implement strong deflationary measures that would increase both taxes and unemployment. There would be less deficit spending, fewer governmental subsidies, and reduced spending for social welfare programs. These austerity measures touched off strong protests and affected those countries that required a popular referendum for acceptance rather than only parliamentary ratification. On June 2, 1992, Denmark rejected the treaty. Two weeks later, the Irish narrowly voted in favor. In France, President Mitterrand risked a referendum, rather than opt for parliamentary ratification, in the hope that a popular vote would strengthen the EU. The French voted in favor of the treaty, but only by a slim 51 percent to 49 percent margin.

The Danish defeat and continuing opposition to the Maastricht arrangement forced the EU to make concessions. In October, the Danish government listed several policies that the country did not want to implement at that time, and the EU emphasized that it favored a kind of federalism that would not submerge the individual states and allowed Denmark to opt out of several commitments. As a result, the Danes ratified the treaty on May 18, 1993.

Ratification of the Maastricht treaty by the EU members cleared the way for institution of the euro. Denmark, Sweden, and Britain opted out of it for the time being. The strict economic criteria presented difficulties for countries that wanted to qualify for membership in the euro bloc on the first round. Italy stunned Europe by meeting the criteria. Belgium had similar problems but also qualified. In France, the issue caused the defeat of the Center-Right when Chirac called early elections, which he lost, and even Germany had some difficulty. Greece did not qualify and had to wait until 2001. On January 1, 2002, the euro appeared, and twelve national currencies disappeared (except for a brief grace period when the currencies and the euro circulated together). The new currency symbolized the economic and political changes that swept the European continent in the last two decades of the twentieth century.

Bibliographical Essay

B. Fullerton and R. Knowles, *Scandinavia* (London, 1991), is a good general history and supplements T. K. Derry's *A History of Scandinavia* (London, 1979). Consult also the general histories cited for the earlier chapters.

Eric S. Einhorn discusses welfare in *Modern Welfare States: Politics and Policies in Social Democratic Scandinavia* (Westport, Conn., 2003). There has been a lot of interest in the Scandinavian "model" of the welfare state. See Noralv Veggeland, *Paths of Public Innovation in the Global Age: Lessons from Scandinavia* (Northampton, Mass., 2007), and Heikki Ervasti et al., *Nordic Social Attitudes in a European Perspective* (Northampton,

Mass., 2008). On the same topic, see also Robert R. Friedman et al., *Modern Welfare States: A Comparative View of Trends and Prospects* (New York, 1987). For individual states, see Christoffer Green-Pedersen, *The Politics of Justification: Party Competition and Welfare State Retrenchment in Denmark and the Netherlands from 1982 to 1998* (Amsterdam, 2002); Karen Fog Olwig and Karsten Paerregaard, *The Question of Integration, Exclusion and the Danish Welfare State* (Newcastle upon Tyne, UK, 2011); and Kenneth E. Miller, *Denmark: A Troubled Welfare State* (Boulder, Colo., 1991). Johan P. Olsen examines the welfare state's political impact in Norway in *Organized Democracy: Political Institutions in a Welfare State, The Case of Norway* (New York, 1983), while Knut Halvorsen et al. describe the Norwegian welfare state and the impact of North Sea oil in *Work, Oil and Welfare: The Welfare State in Norway* (Oslo, 2008). Henry Milner, *Sweden: Social Democracy in Practice* (Oxford, UK, 1989), analyzes the country's social democratic system and Richard B. Freeman et al., discuss *Reforming the Welfare State: Recovery and Beyond in Sweden* (Chicago, 2010). Finnish politics are examined by D. Arter, *Politics and Policy-Making in Finland* (Brighton, UK, 1987).

On the central area, see Wayne C Thompson, *Nordic, Central, and Southeastern Europe 2009* (Harper's Ferry, W.Va., 2009), which includes discussions of the other regions considered in this chapter. See John Fitzmaurice, *The Politics of Belgium: Crisis and Compromise in a Plural Society* (London, 1983), which places an emphasis on federalism. The politics of the Netherlands are discussed by Ken Gladdish, *Governing from the Center: Politics and Policy-Making in the Netherlands* (DeKalb, Ill., 1991). John Fitzmaurice defends Austria's controversial history in *Austrian Politics and Society Today* (Basingstoke, UK, 1991). Austrian politics can be followed in Melanie A. Sully, *Political Parties and Elections in Austria* (London, 1981). On Haider, see Ruth Wodak and Anton Pelinka, *The Haider Phenomenon* (New Brunswick, N.J., 2002), and Jay Rosellini, *Haider, Jelinek, and the Austrian Culture Wars* (n.p., 2009). On Switzerland, see Wolf Linden, *Swiss Democracy: Possible Solutions to Conflict in Multicultural Societies* (New York, 1998). Several books have been written on the Nazi gold question. They include Jean Ziegler, *The Swiss, the Gold, and the Dead: How Swiss Bankers Helped Finance the Nazi War Machine* (New York, 1999); Isabel Vincent, *Hitler's Silent Partners: Swiss Banks, Nazi Gold, and the Pursuit of Justice* (New York, 1997); and Stuart E. Eizenstat, *Imperfect Justice: Looted Assets, Slave Labor, and the Unfinished Business of World War II* (New York, 2003).

Books discussing the consolidation of democracy in southern Europe include U. Liebert and M. Cotta, eds., *Parliament and Democratic Consolidation in Southern Europe* (London, 1990), and G. Pridham, ed., *Securing Democracy: Political Parties and Democratic Consolidation in Southern Europe* (London, 1990). Cristina Palomares examines the immediate post-Franco period in Spain: *The Quest for Survival* (Portland, Ore., 2004). Barry Jordan, ed., *Contemporary Spanish Cultural Studies* (New York, 2000), is a series of essays on social themes in contemporary Spain. David Borningham, *A Concise History of Portugal* (New York, 1993), covers Portugal up to the EC period while Ronald H. Chilcote analyzes the revolution in Portugal and the country's later development in his book *The Portuguese Revolution: State and Class in the Transition to Democracy* (Lanham, Md., 2012). On the economic development of the southern tier countries and the all-important EC, see Amparo Almarcha Barbado, ed., *Spain and EC Membership Evaluated* (London, 1993); José da Silva Lopes, ed., *Portugal and EC Membership Evaluated* (London, 1993); and Panos Kazakos and P. C. Ioakinides, eds., *Greece and EC Membership Evaluated* (London, 1994). For Greece, there is David Close's *Greece Since 1945: Politics, Economics, Society* (New York, 2002).

Dermot Keogh, *Twentieth-Century Ireland: Nation and State* (New York, 1994), is very informative on modern Ireland. For the economic issues, see John O'Dowd, ed., *Ireland, Europe and 1992* (Dublin, 1989). On the "Troubles," see Caroline Kennedy-Pipe,

The Origins of the Present Troubles in Northern Ireland (Harlow, UK, 1997) and Graham Dawson, *Making Peace with the Past? Memory, Trauma, and the Irish Troubles* (New York, 2012). For an analysis of Irish politics and economics during the boom and the bust that occurred after 2007, and the role of the EU, see Peadar Kirby and Mary P. Murphy, *Towards a Second Republic: Irish Politics and the Celtic Tiger* (New York, 2012). Gerald McCann has published an economic history of North and South: *Ireland's Economic History: Crisis and Uneven Development in the North and South* (New York, 2012).

In addition to the books that have already been cited on the EU, see Derek W. Urwin, *The Community of Europe*, 2nd ed. (New York, 1995), essays that the second edition brings up to the 1991 Treaty of Maastricht. Albert M. Sbragia, ed., *Europolitics* (Washington, D.C., 1992), collects essays on policy making and institutions in the new Europe. Clive Archer and Fiona Butler, *The European Union*, 2nd ed. (New York, 1996), is good on institutions and on explaining the budget process. See also Dean J. Kotlowski, *The European Union: From Jean Monnet to the Euro* (Athens, Ohio, 2000). Economics and integration, all-important issues, are discussed in the following works: M. J. Artis and N. Lee, eds., *The Economics of the European Union* (Oxford, UK, 1994); Nigel M. Healey, ed., *The Economics of the New Europe: From Community to Union* (London, 1995); William Wallace, *Regional Integration: The West European Experience* (Washington, D.C., 1994); and Mark Blacksell and Allan M. Williams, eds., *The European Challenge: Geography and Development in the European Community* (Oxford, UK, 1994). John Pinder's *European Community: The Building of a Union* (Oxford, UK, 1991) is a good retrospective look at the issues raised by European unity. Erik Jones, *The Politics of Economic and Monetary Union: Integration and Idiosyncrasy* (Lanham, Md., 2002), is a discussion of the single currency.

CHAPTER 30

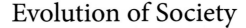

Evolution of Society

CHAPTER OUTLINE

Postwar Society • The Changing Family • Immigration

BIOGRAPHICAL SKETCHES

John XXIII, "The Good Pope" • Boris Pasternak, *Doctor Zhivago*

A t the end of World War II, Western European society underwent major
alterations that led to greater urbanization, economic improvements for the
lower and middle classes, and fundamental changes in the status of women.

POSTWAR SOCIETY

The Western governments gave top priority to repairing their infrastructure,
rebuilding bombed-out cities, constructing new housing, and implementing
welfare-state principles to help the lower classes overcome their economic disadvantages.

Housing

In West Germany, the Western country most affected by war and where a great
number of German refugees from the East had to be resettled, the Federal Republic's replacement of housing stock and infrastructure stimulated the economy.
Governmental programs contributed to the building of an estimated half million
housing units between 1955 and the early 1970s. In 1949, the proportion of public
housing approached 70 percent of new housing, but it declined in later years as
private enterprise recovered. The government built new housing, instituted rent
controls, and provided tax incentives.

West German unions and employers also built housing, and new neighborhoods commingled middle- and working-class Germans. The enormous increase
in the West German gross domestic product (GDP), 9.5 percent annually up to
1955 and 6.5 percent a year until 1960, facilitated the replacement of housing stock.

In Germany and Italy, public funds helped restore historic areas that were destroyed during the war. In Italy, the insufficiency of government-constructed housing and the absence of a well-conceived urban plan encouraged rampant housing speculation and environmental damage. The British performance in building new housing fell short of the German despite the more limited extent of the destruction.

The extent of the effort can be seen by the following statistics. In France, the war had either destroyed or made uninhabitable a million housing units, but the French built 7 million new units between 1945 and 1971, 5 million of them with the government's assistance. The West Germans built 9 new units per 1,000 population in 1963 and the Italians, 8, but the Swedes, with a long policy of social intervention, bested both by building 10. The Swedes further developed their heritage of a modern design inherited from the 1930s, and the Italians entered the field with astounding success. The new units brought modern living to their inhabitants—a minimum of four rooms, separate kitchens, bathrooms, living rooms, and bedrooms. The units came equipped with running water, central heating, gas, and electricity and partially relieved women of the onerous physical work related to the home. In the West, the square footage of the average dwelling doubled compared to prewar housing.

Changing Demography

The populations living in these houses changed as well. For the Germans and Russians, World War II had an important demographic impact. The conflict had killed millions of soldiers, resulting in a large postwar surplus of widows and unmarried women. France and Italy suffered less loss of life. The French and British birthrates increased after World War II. Overpopulated Italy instituted programs to induce people to emigrate to places as far away as Australia. More significant, a large number of southern Italians emigrated to the booming North in the greatest internal migration of postwar Europe, while others emigrated to Switzerland, West Germany, and France. A large wave of emigration from Portugal also occurred, and Portuguese immigrants became the largest ethnic community in France.

Work and Leisure

In Western Europe, workers reestablished their unions and fought for improved working conditions. They won a shorter workweek, and, during the 1950s, wages rose while the average hours worked declined. In Britain the average workweek dropped from 50 hours in 1939 to 44 in 1961; in West Germany the average annual hours worked declined from 2,316 in 1950 to 1,804 in 1973, and hourly wages in manufacturing increased by 53 percent between 1962 and 1969. Automobile sales skyrocketed. In 1950 the West Germans owned only a quarter as many cars as the British, but by 1970, they owned 14 million automobiles. The density of car ownership evened out among the four largest West European countries and approached that of the United States—as did the traffic jams.

Increased prosperity resulted in more leisure time. Besides the traditional activities—theater, films, and cafés—television greatly impacted West Europe. First in Britain and later on the continent, television broadcasts permeated the

Following World War II, Europe became motorized with the production of small cars whose cost was within the reach of the masses. The mass production of automobiles provided good livings for workers and stimulated the European economies. Here is a picture of the Fiat 600, the four-passenger car that motorized Italy. A smiling but somewhat uncomfortable Interior Minister Mario Scelba is testing it out. European cars were small but well suited to narrow streets and got high gas mileage because gasoline was heavily taxed and very expensive.

airways. National networks for which citizens paid a subscription brought television to the masses. In general, advertisements had a lesser role than in the United States. In Italy, the government regulated television advertising, mandating that ads be grouped together and shown at a certain hour. *Carosello*, the popular program that did so, served as a reference point after which the children went to bed.

Television initially favored more social interaction as people who could not afford the new instrument gathered around the sets of those who could, as had been the case in the early days of radio. As prosperity accelerated and the number of television sets proliferated, however, watching television increased social isolation. Television homogenized language, and the use of dialects declined. It instantly made personalities famous. It spread styles, fashions, and music and changed lifestyles. Personalities and politicians had to look good. Political debates and spot advertising changed the nature of politics, reducing the role of mass open-air meetings. Television news reported events occurring a world away, brought sports into the home, and attracted workers who could not afford more costly forms of entertainment.

"Swinging" London was the center of the 1960s cultural revolution with its changing views of sex, music, and fashion. In the picture, Carnaby Street in the Soho district of London, the center of "hip" European fashion during the period.

Increasing urbanization, industrialization, and greater employment encouraged vacations. During the 1950s, the number of persons who took long holidays was relatively limited compared to the 1960s, when the masses started going on vacation. Automobiles were a primary means of movement, but the trains became crowded during the summer as European vacations extended to five weeks. The first great waves brought vacationers from northern to southern Europe. Scandinavian, German, and British tourists traveling on vacation packages met on Mediterranean beaches in a frenetic search for the sun—and love affairs with southern Europeans. The number of Britons going abroad for vacations doubled between 1950 and 1962 to 4 million. Camping became popular, especially for the French. The rush to the sea left French, British, and Italian cities deserted in August as factories closed down. The vacation drama hit the movies. In 1953, French director Jacques Tati's *Les vacances de Monsieur Hulot* made audiences smile, and during the 1970s the misadventures of Italian tourist Fantozzi made them laugh.

The dancing craze that began during the 1920s expanded after World War II. In Britain, an estimated 5 million went dancing once a week, and a like number watched dancing competitions on television during the mid-1960s—and millions took dancing lessons.

The Arts and Society

In the Europe of the 1960s, the arts flourished, and subsidies made them more affordable than in the United States. Students could afford operas at Milan's La Scala, Vienna's Staadtsoper, and Paris's Opéra, especially if they chose a balcony (or second balcony) seat. In Milan's famed La Scala, the most expensive seat still cost less than $10. Symphonic and chamber music was readily available and inexpensive. One could attend free concerts in churches from Prague to Florence. European museums generally charged a modest admission, and students enjoyed special rates. Anyone could walk into a church and view medieval and Renaissance artistic masterpieces. In the evening, governmental subsidies made possible cheap subscriptions to the theater or to cinema clubs. Libraries presented a harder problem because of their restricted hours and the difficulty of taking out books, but secondary schools were free and universities practically so. The major barrier to higher education for poorer families was the families' inability to afford the lost income from their children.

Twenty years after World War II, modernity began exercising a greater attraction for European youths than did classical art forms. Surprisingly, London, once a staid old matron, became the Mecca for young people in the 1960s. European youths danced to the newest musical phenomenon, the Beatles. London's Carnaby Street dictated fashion. Mini-skirted girls shocked their elders, and not just because of the manner in which they were dressed. The use of contraceptives ("the pill") became widespread, and, with the fear of pregnancy evaporating, young women were less afraid to engage in sexual activity and married women could plan their families. The 1960s sexual revolution had its most visible manifestations first in Scandinavia and among the youths of "swinging" London. It spread to all segments of the West European population, and spectacular sex scandals rocked Western European governments.

The youth culture of the 1960s permeated daily life. In clothes, a new, casual style triumphed: blue jeans and colored, tie-dyed, T-shirts. American music set the standard for youths, especially jazz and Elvis Presley's rock and roll, before the "British invasion" led by the Beatles and the Rolling Stones swept the United States. Non-English-speaking peoples baptized the Beatles the "Yé-Yé," from one of their first hits. The youth culture spread into the Communist East, where the demand for blue jeans and Western music became overwhelming.

Travel

Young middle-class Europeans flocked to London to learn English and join the new youth culture, but travel in general became a hallmark of West European life. In 1965, air travel was still relatively uncommon in Europe, and the train reigned supreme. The distances were short—approximately a thousand miles separated southern Italy from Brussels. A tourist could travel at night; book a cucchette, a bunk that folded down from the compartment walls (six in a second-class compartment); and usually arrive at one's destination by the morning. Youth hostels provided inexpensive accommodations for students in the West, and travel in Eastern Europe was cheap. Travelers brought new tastes, fashions, and goods home with them: Italian shoes and coffee machines, French clothes and wines, and demands for foreign foods that stimulated the opening of ethnic restaurants in different European countries.

In the Communist East, railway travel was more difficult, and there were few products to bring home. Prague's beauty and exciting cultural atmosphere before the 1968 Soviet invasion made it a favored destination even if trains from Austria to Czechoslovakia stopped for hours as guards checked passports, searched trains, and looked for currency that tourists attempted to smuggle into the country to cash it in at a higher exchange rate than allowed by the government. Upon exiting the country, the delays were even longer as the police minutely searched trains for possible escapees. Westerners touring the East found that people offered them exorbitant prices for articles such as nylons and blue jeans.

Entry into West Berlin for the tourist was most convenient by airplane because the city was deep in East Germany. Flying into Templehof airport, visitors skirted the tops of buildings and flew by the windows of apartments situated practically along the runway. Once in West Berlin, tourists could visit East Berlin in what was an unforgettable experience. The normal means of getting beyond the wall, an ugly gray concrete construction that in some places incorporated apartment buildings, was by subway. In East Berlin stations, the fearsome East German police closely examined passports. Emerging from the subway station, visitors from the West in the 1960s were greeted by a desolating vista: bombed-out ruins left over from World War II and rows of dingy housing. Tourists who smuggled currency into the country hoping to buy items cheaply discovered that there was nothing to buy. However, the museums were spectacular, and the restaurants were fairly decent and inexpensive. Returning to the western part of the divided city, the tourists were usually grateful for the hustle and the bustle, the bright lights, and the honky-tonk atmosphere of West Berlin's *Kurfurstendam*.

Daily Life in the City

What was daily life like in an increasingly urbanized Europe in the 1960s? In 1965 the northern Italian city of Milan—a large city that resembled Europe rather than Italy—manufactured steel and cars, and publishing and nuclear research coexisted in the periphery. Milan housed a fashion industry that rivaled Paris and would soon overtake it. A rich bourgeoisie lived a high lifestyle that alienated the lower classes, which gravitated toward the Socialist and Communist parties that were influential in municipal governments. In the early 1960s, the workers lacked the confidence to challenge the bourgeoisie, even though their economic clout had increased. In 1967 and 1968, thanks to improving economic conditions and the coming of age of a younger, better-educated generation, students and workers would revolt in a spectacular manner.

In 1965, a streetcar driver, an envied and well-paid worker, earned 90,000 lire a month, about $145 at the then-current exchange rate. He worked a 44-hour week, 8 hours a day, Monday to Friday and half a day on Saturday. His children went to school for a half day on Saturdays. He typically lived in a rent-controlled apartment with rent at about $30 a month. He and many Europeans preferred to live in the city and considered the suburbs an abomination. Most likely, he drove a Fiat 600, the car that motorized Italy as the Volkswagen Beetle did West Germany, and somehow afforded gasoline at four times the American price. On his way to work, he might buy a newspaper that, at eight cents, cost less than its American counterpart but more than an espresso coffee. He could look forward to outings on weekends, except that the traffic was already approaching intolerable proportions. His interest and that of his family in religion was declining, although less than in the 1970s. Instead of church, the family preferred to go away on weekends. In driving to the lake country for a weekend outing, drivers had to fight the smog that blocked visibility and caused massive multicar pileups. In the city itself, the smog was sometimes so thick that pedestrians crashed into buildings. Should residents decide to stay home, they could watch television or attend one of the many relatively inexpensive cultural activities that European cities offered. The cheap paperback book was coming into vogue, but people were more likely to follow Europe's most popular sport, soccer, at the large San Siro stadium.

Europeans ate out a good deal because the restaurants were relatively inexpensive. They flocked to French or Italian restaurants, with Indian and Indonesian establishments opening up in Britain and the Netherlands and later overspreading the continent along with Chinese restaurants. French cuisine was world renowned. Northern Italians ate rice in many forms, while southerners preferred pasta, but every region had its own distinctive food. Continental Europeans refused to drink tap water and swore by the health benefits of bottled mineral water. In alcoholic beverages, the medieval pattern prevailed. Southern Europeans normally drank wine with their meals, France having the highest per capita consumption of alcohol and Italy coming in second. Northern Europeans preferred beer, the English even drinking it warm. German, Belgian, and Czech beer was renowned. Northern and Eastern Europeans consumed large quantities of hard liquor, reputedly compensating for the weather or politics or both. Russians and Poles drank vodka, and the Czechs preferred slivovitz. The French drank cognac; the Greeks, ouzo; and the Italians, grappa—and they all imported scotch.

Politics made up a large part of the ordinary European's conversation in those heady days, usually complaining bitterly about politicians, bureaucrats, southern immigrants, and deteriorating urban conditions. As massive migration from the poor agricultural South to the industrial North accelerated, cities were increasingly unable to cope with the demands for services. The different customs and habits of migrants who left for more prosperous countries in need of labor, such as Switzerland and West Germany, discovered discrimination. Algerians, French colonial subjects, went to France, while Turks—with traditional ties to Germany— immigrated to the Federal Republic. These migrations stirred up old feelings of racial hatred, exacerbated in the 1980s and 1990s when North African and East European migrants rushed into the prosperous West in greater numbers during poorer economic times. By the end of the century, West European countries included large minorities professing Islam and Eastern Orthodoxy that presented Protestant and Catholic Europeans with major challenges in their schools and communities.

In the 1960s, the culinary tastes of these immigrants had not had a major influence, and Europeans still prepared foods in the traditional manner. Wives cooked food from scratch because there were few canned goods and because Europeans distrusted them anyway. Housewives stopped at several small shops on a daily trek to buy food for the family, storing it in refrigerators that were small by American standards. Bread in Milan cost little because the government still subsidized it (10 lire, less than 2 cents, for a *michetta,* or roll). Beef, commonly imported from France, was very expensive in Milan and eaten much less than in France, Britain, or Germany. Oysters were plentiful in Paris. Chicken was more affordable, but European men avoided it because American chicken was stuffed with hormones, and they feared it would make them effeminate. Europeans ate more fruits and vegetables than Americans did. Normally, Italians avoided dessert and ate fruit and drank an espresso at the end of a meal, following it up with special drinks to aid the digestion. Other Europeans were more likely to consume desserts, with Vienna being famous for such desserts as *Sacher Torte*. In the 1960s, Italian housewives paid the utility bills directly to company employees who showed up at their homes. Later, as women entered the job market in greater numbers, they paid bills at the post office for a small fee or could arrange to have the bank deduct the amount directly from their accounts. In France and northern Europe, bills could be paid by checks sent through the mail.

In the 1960s, Europeans still dressed formally, with men wearing jackets and ties to work and when they went out. Air conditioning remained a rarity, and many Europeans were convinced that it caused health problems. By the late 1960s, more women joined the workforce and attended universities. Many of them were afraid to smoke on the streets for fear of being taken for prostitutes, whose image of standing on street corners smoking cigarettes persisted. Legalized, government-supervised houses of prostitution had been outlawed in 1954 in Italy, the only European country that allowed them. European society still tolerated married men, but not women, having steady liaisons outside marriage. Catholic Spain and Italy still did not have divorce in the 1960s. However, couples still split up and lived with other partners, causing complex legal problems and social problems, as illustrated in filmmaker Pietro Germi's satirical *Divorce Italian Style* that suggested murder as a way out of an unhappy marriage.

Change in the Catholic World: Vatican II

On October 9, 1958, Pope Pius XII died. Aloof and ascetic, Pius was a conservative who opposed change. After his death, the cardinals elected Angelo Cardinal Roncalli, an experienced, well-traveled prelate who had held posts in the Vatican's diplomatic service and who served as archbishop of Venice. Elected pope at age 76, Roncalli took the name of John XXIII and demonstrated himself to be an innovative pontiff who was unafraid of breaking with tradition.

BIOGRAPHICAL SKETCHES

John XXIII
"The Good Pope"

Angelo Giuseppe Roncalli was born into a family of poor share-croppers at Sotto il Monte, near Bergamo in northern Italy, on November 25, 1881. He studied for the priesthood at the local seminary. After his ordination in 1904, he became secretary to the bishop of Bergamo, a progressive who wanted to reconnect the church with modern society by collaborating with labor and women's organizations. Father Roncalli had a major role in his work until 1915, when the bishop died. During World War I, he served on the front lines as a medic and chaplain and rose to the rank of lieutenant. After the conflict, the church called him to Rome to teach and to serve in the Congregation of the Faith. However, his fast-track career suddenly stalled after 1925 when, after his promotion to bishop, the church sent him as its emissary to Bulgaria. This post, which the Vatican had not filled for 600 years, was the equivalent of exile. Years later as pope, Roncalli discovered that the Vatican had sidetracked him on suspicion of modernism, a heresy condemned in 1905.

Roncalli used his Bulgarian sojourn to reach out to the Eastern Orthodox religion, as he did to the Muslims after his assignment to Turkey in 1934. During World War II, he used his position in Istanbul to rescue Jews fleeing from Nazism by issuing visas to Palestine and false baptismal certificates. Jewish officials credited him with saving thousands of Jews. His next posting, in early 1945, was as Papal Nuncio to Paris. Pope Pius XII assigned him there because the French objected to the previous Nuncio's Vichy ties and, because Roncalli was an unknown, could not object to him. After a successful stay in Paris, he became a cardinal and patriarch of Venice in 1953. On October 28, 1958, following Pope Pius XII's death, the College of Cardinals unexpectedly elected Roncalli Pope on the twelfth ballot. At almost 77 years of age, he supposedly was a transitional pope pending the elevation of favorite Giovanni Battista Montini (future Paul VI) to cardinal and then to pope.

Under the title of John XXIII, the new pope elaborated a distinctive style by communicating directly with world leaders and ordinary people. He visited prisons and hospitals and often left the Vatican, where past popes had isolated themselves. He treated the world to a new kind of pontiff, one who smoked occasionally, enjoyed good food, and had a sense of humor. Asked how many persons worked in the Vatican, for example, he responded: "About half." Far from being a transitional figure, he set about modernizing the church. He called a council and nudged it and the recalcitrant curia in a liberal direction. He issued encyclicals endorsing state intervention to further social justice and individual rights and calling for cooperation among people of good will, even those, like the Communists, that the church considered mistaken. In five short years, John became the best loved and most popular pope of the twentieth century.

When "the Good Pope" died on June 3, 1963, of complications from stomach cancer, the entire world mourned. Participants in Vatican II, still in session, attempted to have him declared a saint by acclamation, but the move ran afoul of church politics. Pope Paul VI ruled that John's claim would have to go through the usual lengthy process by which the church makes saints. John XXIII's case continued going forward despite three changes in the procedure, and he seemed likely to become only the third pope proclaimed a saint since the institution of formal procedures in 1588. Besides his saintly life, he is reputed to have performed several miracles, and changes in the rules for sainthood mandated an increased emphasis on the candidate's historical role. Popular support for declaring Angelo Giuseppe Roncalli a saint also remained strong over the years, and his tomb under St. Peter's basilica continued to be the destination of pilgrims who knelt to pray for his blessing.

Pope John was determined to make accommodations between Catholicism and the modern world, a policy he called *aggiornamento* (updating). The mechanism he chose was the Church Council, which last met at the Vatican in 1870. After much preparatory work, Vatican II opened in Rome on October 11, 1962, and lasted for three years. The council made important changes, the most visible one authorizing celebration of the mass in the language of a country instead of in

A September 1, 1962, meeting of the Second Vatican Council in St. Peter's Basilica in Rome. Pope John XXIII called the Council to modernize Church doctrine so it would be better able to confront the modern world. It revolutionized the Catholic Church but created resentment that has still not completely abated.

Latin. The council's innovations aimed at increasing lay participation in church affairs, emphasizing dogma as a unifying element. The council adopted a more ecumenical approach to Christianity, showing a greater willingness to engage in a dialogue with non-Catholics, and favoring greater power for church councils.

Besides calling the Church Council, Pope John issued important encyclicals in his effort to harmonize church dogma and modern society. In *Mater et magistra*, May 15, 1961, he endorsed the welfare state as essential for the common good. This message confirmed the state's role in furnishing social security as a means of utilizing the world's God-given wealth for everybody's good. On April 11, 1963, in *Pacem in terris,* John sought to reconcile the modern world, individualism, and technology with God's will. It spelled out the rights of people, including the right to worship God according to one's conscience, and stressed the enhanced role of women in modern society.

Because of his work in modernizing church attitudes and his warm personality, John was one of the world's most popular and beloved figures when he died on June 3, 1963. He had accomplished much during his brief pontificate, but there was still much left to do. His successor, Paul VI, a liberal, continued John's work. Paul emphasized social justice and defended the church's traditional positions on birth control, the ordination of women, and celibacy and, like John, he sought a better relationship with the Communist regimes. Paul was the first pope to travel outside Italy in more than 150 years to carry the church's message of world peace, and he augmented the role that persons from the Third World had in the church.

After Paul's death in 1978, it seemed that the church would continue on the path set for it by Pope John when the College of Cardinals elected another liberal, John Paul I. This pope, however, died after only a month and was replaced by the conservative John Paul II. As a Pole, John Paul II was less willing to compromise with the regimes of Eastern Europe and took more traditional positions within the church.

East European Society

The East, with which Popes John XXIII and Paul VI hoped to start a dialogue, underwent important changes during the 1960s and 1970s. In the USSR, as in the West, the population trend was from rural to urban areas. New cities sprouted up around new industrial plants, and more Russians migrated to different parts of the Soviet Union, raising fears among minority populations that the result would be a predominance of the culture and language of the newly arrived Russians. The minority attempted to strengthen their cultures despite crackdowns by the central government against "bourgeois nationalism," a policy that failed and illustrated the continuing appeal of nationalism.

It became increasingly difficult for the Soviets to maintain their emphasis on heavy industry instead of consumer goods. The USSR had suffered through the privations of the 1930s, World War II, and the cold war, and pressure for the production of more consumer goods mounted following Stalin's death. In November 1958, Khrushchev published a Seven-Year Plan that aimed at greater equilibrium between consumer products and heavy industry, but the USSR never succeeded in satisfying consumer demand despite a projected construction of 15 million more units and despite population trends. While childhood mortality decreased, Soviet women had fewer children in the hope of increasing the family's living standard. The same trend occurred in Eastern Europe, where Hungary had one of the lowest birthrates in the world. Because modern birth control techniques were less accessible in the East, more women resorted to abortion as a birth control method.

In some cases, communism achieved its goal and encouraged the creation of a new middle class. The Communist world developed an excellent system of higher education, particularly in the sciences and engineering. With a large university-educated population and a new generation of Communists at the helm came a greater emphasis on physical comfort. The triumph of Malenkov and Khrushchev, a reduction in the role of the secret police, improved relations with the West, and a cultural thaw reflected this change.

The cultural thaw appeared with novels published by Ilya Ehrenburg in 1954 and by Vladimir Dudintsev in 1956. These writers called for more intellectual freedom, which arrived with agonizing slowness. In 1958, Boris Pasternak's novel *Doctor Zhivago* had to be published in the West because it displeased the Soviet rulers. When Pasternak won the Nobel Prize for literature, the Soviet government made it clear that Pasternak would not be allowed to return if he went to Stockholm to pick up the prize. Pasternak did not go, but his novel won fame in the West and circulated in the USSR only in clandestine editions. He became an unwilling hero to intellectuals in the East.

BIOGRAPHICAL SKETCHES

Boris Pasternak
Doctor Zhivago

Boris Pasternak, born on February 10, 1890, into an intellectual Jewish family, gained fame with poetry published in 1914.
He supported the Bolshevik revolution and participated in the
heady atmosphere that followed. Later he remained loyal to the
revolution even while criticizing Stalin. The dictator, it is said,
left him alone because he was convinced that Pasternak was a genius.

In 1946, Pasternak became disillusioned with politics because of an anti-
intellectual campaign and began writing the novel that would bring him world
fame: *Doctor Zhivago*, an autobiographical work set against the backdrop of
recent Russian history. When Pasternak presented his manuscript for publication
to the Soviet Union of Writers, it was rejected on the grounds that it libeled the
Soviet Union. The novel circulated underground for several years in a typed Samizdat version until it was smuggled out of the USSR by philosopher Isaiah Berlin.
After finding its way to Italy and being rejected by the famous Italian novelist Italo
Calvino, it was published by Italian publisher Giangiacomo Feltrinelli in 1957. The
novel was a blockbuster, was translated into twenty-nine languages, sold millions
of copies, and was made into a successful film. In 1958 Pasternak was awarded
the Nobel Prize in literature, which he first enthusiastically accepted and then
refused when Soviet authorities pressured him because they considered the novel
an insult to the USSR. Years later it emerged that the American and British secret
services provided a Russian-language version of the novel to the Nobel Prize Committee to embarrass the Soviets. From that point on, Pasternak was harassed in his
homeland, constantly threatened with expulsion, and only international pressure
saved him from exile or prison. The Italian Communist Party rewarded Feltrinelli by
asking for his party membership card back.

Doctor Zhivago plays out against the vast backdrop of Russian history between
1905 and the end of World War II. It is a realistic but hopeful work in which the
author weaves the tangled lives of a large number of characters into the historical events. In the film, the most memorable character besides Zhivago is his mistress Lara, said to have been modeled on Pasternak's real-life mistress Olga Invin-
skaya. Pasternak died on May 30, 1960, of lung cancer; twenty-eight years later,
his novel was published in his homeland.

In 1962 another Russian novel stirred the Eastern world, Alexander Solzhenitsyn's *One Day in the Life of Ivan Denisovich*. This brief book graphically described
life in the Soviet labor camps. Over the years, Solzhenitsyn published other novels
that were critical of Soviet life, including a massive description of the Soviet camp
system, the *Gulag Archipelago*. These works brought the ire of the Soviet rulers,
and he left for exile in Vermont. Younger writers continued the tradition of dissent
in the Soviet Union, and social trends made it more difficult to control the intellectual activity that would have decisive political implications.

THE CHANGING FAMILY

Despite the tendency of the Western European family to endure, it underwent profound changes between 1945 and 2000 particularly because of new contraceptive methods and the welfare state.

Birth Control

During the 1960s, two contraceptive devices found wide circulation in Western Europe: the contraceptive pill and the intrauterine device (IUD), while in the East, abortion was more widespread as a birth control method. The new contraceptives found quick acceptance among West European women, so that, to cite just one statistic, 74 percent of Frenchwomen who did not want to conceive used oral contraceptives and IUDs by the end of the 1980s. In addition, sterilization techniques had become safe and widespread and appealed particularly to women in Britain, Belgium, and the Netherlands. Widespread birth control appeared first in the Scandinavian countries and rapidly spread to the entire continent, including the Catholic South, and birthrates plummeted. The number of live births per woman in Europe in 1964 was 2.5 to 3, but by 1975 had fallen to 2. By 1988, it varied between 1.4 and 1.6 in the economically most advanced countries. In southern European countries, such as Italy and Spain, where birthrates were once higher, the fall was even more precipitous. By the end of the century, the European countries were concerned about their ability to maintain their population levels and labor forces without immigrants.

Family Life

The ease and popularity of birth control had a major impact on family life. Women could choose how many children to have and, perhaps more important, with whom to have them. This change coincided with lower infant mortality rates, feeding formulas that allowed husbands and grandparents to care for infants, and longer life spans. The European infant mortality rate fell from 5 percent in 1955 (higher in southern Europe) to 2.5 percent in 1965. By 1989 it had dropped to 0.6 percent in Sweden, with other countries following suit. Lower infant mortality signified that women could ensure reproduction by having fewer, healthier children with a greater likelihood of survival. Added to their dramatically increased life spans (from 40 years of age in 1930 to 80 in 1987 for Frenchwomen) and the diffusion of laborsaving devices for the home, more women could enter the workforce and remain there for a longer time than before. Increased life spans also meant that grandparents were available to take care of minor children while the mothers worked. By 1985, the percentage of married working women under age 50 had reached 87 percent in five of the ten EC member states.

The Welfare State and the Family

The welfare state had a great impact on family structure. Because of their traditional role as caregivers, a significant proportion of European women took public jobs as opposed to private ones. Occupations as teachers, hospital workers, and nursery school attendants provided greater flexibility than the private sector, allowing women to combine motherhood, domestic activity, and work outside the home. By the 1990s, for example, Swedish women held two-thirds of the jobs in the public sector. Thus, women both provided and consumed many of the services of the welfare state.

But the welfare state gave women much more than employment. Because of its financial and educational support for children and single-parent households, it allowed them to make the choice of leaving marriages if they failed. In addition, it brought about changes in attitudes and created conditions that allowed women to choose not to get married at all but still to have children. In the mid-1960s, a survey asked respondents about the probability that they would divorce if conditions in the marriage were unsatisfactory. That probability ranged from 6 percent to 18 percent, but in 1975 a similar poll reached a high of 50 percent in Sweden. It is not surprising that the percentage of divorces rose rapidly and that the time required to obtain them declined.

Single-parent households increased, and the average size of the nuclear family declined. The number of single-parent households reached a high in the 1980s in Denmark: 20 percent. Similarly, the proportion of unmarried persons living together increased, and the marriage rate decreased. At the beginning of the 1980s, Sweden had the highest rate of unmarried couples: 15 percent. These trends affected the number of children born to unmarried couples. In the large European countries, such births hovered around 7 percent during the mid-1960s but rose dramatically, reaching 15 percent to 20 percent and in France in 1990, 25 percent.

The welfare state encouraged these trends by aiding the new families. It paid the hospital and doctors' bills for the births, built nursery schools for the children, and eliminated the concept of illegitimacy by mandating equal treatment for children who were born to married and unmarried couples. The welfare state enabled many women to free themselves from economic dependence on their fathers and husbands, while observers worried about the new dependence of women on it.

Besides the profound alterations in family structure, postwar European society saw the beginning of a mass phenomenon that promised to impact the continent's social structure and its cultural traditions: immigration.

IMMIGRATION

Long a continent of emigrants, Europe was not used to immigration. In the past, France had been the focus of immigrants, but in the postwar decades, Switzerland and West Germany and then all the Western countries attracted a large number of workers from East Europe, Africa, and Asia.

The New Immigrants

In the 1990s, attracted by Western Europe's wealth, a flood of non-Europeans entered the EU countries, including Africans, Pakistanis, Indians, Chinese,

Bangladeshis, Kurds, Filipinos, and others. The economic disasters caused by the Communist regimes and the collapse of communism opened the Eastern European floodgates, with Albanians, Romanians, and Poles spilling into the West. The breakup of Yugoslavia and the ensuing warfare drove Slovenians and Croats into Austria and Italy. The poverty of the Eastern European populations caused clashes inside the host countries. Historically, immigrants took menial jobs that the natives were unwilling to do, and this remained true. In one automobile factory outside Paris, estimates put the number of foreigners holding unskilled assembly-line jobs at 80 percent in the 1970s. Foreign workers were the worst paid and most neglected segment of the labor force. In France riots periodically occurred in the impoverished *banlieues,* or outskirts, of French cities where poor immigrants lived and helped account for the increased support for Jean Marie Le Pen's National Front; the same held true in Austria, with Haider's Freedom Party. In Britain and the Netherlands, there was a clash of European and Muslim family and cultural values.

In the 1960s, industrialists gladly imported foreign workers, but when the European economies slowed during the 1970s, the governments sought to reduce the influx of foreign workers and offered them incentives to leave. Most foreigners stayed because years of work in the host countries had gotten them used to new ways of life and the advantages of the welfare state. Despite the best governmental

Beginning in the 1990s and into the new century Europe experienced a flood of legal and illegal immigration that only promised to increase. Europeans feared that their culture, including Christianity, would be overwhelmed and substantially changed by the new immigrants. This fear caused resentment while the immigrants protested at what they saw as discrimination and poor treatment. Many immigrants were unemployed and lived by expedients. In the photograph, British policemen in London arrest illegal immigrants on October 17, 2010.

efforts to discourage permanent immigration, immigrants and their families made up, on average, an estimated 5 percent of Europe's population by 1997. Germany had the highest proportion of immigrants, 9 percent, while corresponding figures for France and Britain were 5.7 and 3.8 percent, respectively.

Competition from immigrants caused resentment among the Europeans. Lower salaries for foreigners aroused fears among European workers that immigrants would take their jobs even if they did work that the European workers would not accept. Other anxieties included the swamping of their own culture by unfamiliar cultures they had been at war with for centuries and their belief that immigrants caused an increase in crime. Political events, such as German reunification, often complicated the relationship with immigrants. In Germany, competition between Turks and former East Germans who suffered high unemployment produced racist incidents. There was also resentment because many East European immigrants took advantage of Germany's liberal political asylum laws. In Germany, applications for asylum for political persecution in immigrants' home countries skyrocketed from 121,000 in 1989 to 438,000 in 1992, prompting the restriction of this right in 1993. The new immigration stirred up old racist feelings in Germany, France, and other European countries.

The Problem of Integration

By the late 1990s, unemployment and ill will had complicated Germany's relationship with the new immigrants and with the old ones of the 1960s and 1970s. The children of immigrants who had settled in Germany twenty to thirty years earlier could not become German citizens even though they were born in the country because German law clung to the concept of citizenship as a right acquired by ancestry, as defined in legislation passed in 1913. Children who were born in Germany of foreign parents had few ties to their parents' homeland, felt cut off from it, believed they were Germans, and resented being denied citizenship. The question touched off virulent debates in Germany between the major political parties and aroused resentment, especially among the Turks, Germany's largest ethnic group. The daughter of a Turkish immigrant said: "They call us the Deutschlanders. There you are not a real Turk, and here you are not a complete German." (*New York Times*, November 30, 1997). On January 1, 2000, a new law came into force that gave the children of foreigners who were born after that date the possibility of applying for citizenship until age 23, provided that one parent had lived in Germany for a long time.

In 1997, France granted the right of automatic citizenship to the French-born children of foreigners, provided they had lived in France for five years since age 11. The French, however, made immigrants from its former colonies of Algeria, Tunisia, and Morocco feel extremely unwelcome. The immigrants' Muslim religion and the accusation that they were heavily involved in drugs and other crimes made their lot particularly difficult despite France's traditional hospitality to foreigners and the country's successful integration of previous Portuguese and Italian immigrants. According to a supporter of the National Front, "Islam is a foreign culture and it is impossible for it to blend in" (*New York Times*, March 23, 1999). As an example of the problems, the mayor of Strasbourg (home of the European

Parliament) complained about the large foreign population. He complained that they were 14 percent of the population, accounted for 75 percent of the welfare cases in the region where the city is located, and had a 25 percent youth unemployment rate. In the 1995 presidential elections, extreme rightist leader Le Pen received almost 26 percent of this region's vote, and in 2002 he defeated the Socialist presidential candidate and qualified for the run-off election against Jacques Chirac.

In Italy, traditionally a land of emigrants, the new immigration caused tensions as prosperity transformed the peninsula into a promised land for immigrants. Director Gianni Amelio's acclaimed film, *Lamerica*, about Albanian immigrants, focused on this irony. By 1999, the number of legal immigrants living in Italy totaled more than 1.2 million. Albanians, Somalis, Moroccans, Filipinos, Peruvians, Sri Lankians, Ethiopians, and Chinese took jobs in industry, domestic labor, and agriculture. Many became small-time entrepreneurs at the law's margins. Chinese laborers moved into the leather goods industry in Florence, occasionally touching off protests in the city, and occupied important areas in Rome and Milan. Romanians, Ukrainians, and Poles entered the construction and restaurant industries. The difficulty of finding laborers to do these jobs made these immigrants necessary for the economy, although in the North, unsympathetic organizations, such as the Lombard League, issued racist pronouncements and called for tougher measures against illegal immigration. After 2000, waves of illegal immigrants from North Africa landed on the island of Lampedusa and at other points of the long, difficult-to-guard coastline, attracted by a lenient visa policy in a country that served as the gateway into the EU.

At the end of the twentieth century, integrating different cultures posed perhaps the greatest social challenge that modern Europe ever confronted. Troubling incidents that took place illustrated the magnitude of the gulf between Muslim and European values. In Britain and other countries, many Muslim immigrants followed a traditional custom of arranged marriages for their daughters to men in their home countries. These women, born and raised in Europe and attending European schools, frequently refused to follow their fathers' orders, fled, or became engaged to European men. Some families kidnapped them, forcibly sending them back to their countries of origin, or sometimes hired bounty hunters to hunt them down and kill them. In other cases, neo-Nazi groups (skinheads) attacked blacks and other minorities who streamed into their countries.

Along with changes in family structure, the new phenomenon of mass immigration promised to bring about the greatest alterations that European society and culture had seen for centuries. Europe needed these immigrants to help finance the welfare state and maintain production, but, as the children of immigrants grew up, would they become members of their countries' communities and become integrated into the culture of the host country? Or would they, as some observers charged, be unable to integrate, plot to implement Muslim Sharia law, and join terrorist organizations?

Bibliographical Essay

On reconstruction following the war, see David W. Ellwood, *Rebuilding Europe: Western Europe, America, and Postwar Reconstruction* (London, 1992). A general book on changes in postwar Europe during the period covered in this chapter is Max-Stephan

Schulze, *Western Europe: Economic and Social Change Since 1945* (New York, 1998). Frank Biess and Robert G. Moeller, *Histories of the Aftermath: The Legacies of the Second War in Europe* (New York, 2010), contains essays on the postwar world; Rudiger Dornbusch et al., *Postwar Economic Reconstruction and Lessons for the East Today* (Cambridge, Mass., 2000), a book of essays, looks at the relationship of postwar to post-Communist Europe. John Killick, *The United States and European Reconstruction, 1945–1960* (Edinburgh, 1997) examines the U.S. role. Andrea Bonoldi and Andreas Leonardi, *Recovery and Development in the European Periphery (1945–1960)* (Bologna, 2009), includes essays on the reconstruction of local areas. The role of government is treated by A. Graham, ed., *Government and Economics in the Postwar World* (London, 1990). Herman Lelieveldt and Sebastiaan Princen look at the nuts and bolts of how the EU operates and at controversial issues in EU politics in *The Politics of the European Union* (New York, 2011). A good general work on the European economy that includes this period is D. H. Aldcroft, *The European Economy 1914–1990*, 3rd ed. (London, 1993). Social issues and the economy are considered together by G. Ambrosius and W. H. Hubbard, *A Social and Economic History of Twentieth-Century Europe* (Cambridge, Mass., 1989). Angus Maddison published a study of capitalism's effects in the long term: *Dynamic Forces in Capitalist Development: A Long-Run Comparative View* (Oxford, UK, 1991). Arthur Marwick, *Class in the Twentieth Century* (Brighton, UK, 1986), is a good general study of the topic. Robert T. Anderson, *Modern Europe: An Anthropological Perspective* (Pacific Palisades, Calif., 1973), is a concise book with interesting information on many European countries.

Good treatments of social issues during the period covered include Richard Bessel and Dirk Schumann, *Life After Death: Approaches to a Cultural and Social History of Europe During the 1940s and 1950s* (Cambridge, Mass., 2002); Margaret Scotford Archer and Salvador Giner, eds., *Contemporary Europe: Class, Status and Power* (New York, 1971), a collection of essays that include most countries. Paul Thompson and Natascha Burchart, eds., *Our Common History: The Transformation of Europe* (Atlantic Heights, N.J., 1982), is a book with valuable essays on different social categories, the family, women, and life histories. Peter J. Hall, ed., *Europe 2000* (New York, 1977), is of a manageable length and discusses social change and future outlooks. Linda Hantrais, *Social Policy in the European Union* (New York, 1995), looks at the present and future of the EU's actions in various social fields. Silja Haeusermann discusses the welfare state in France, Germany, and other European states in *Welfare State Reform in Continental Europe: Modernization in Hard Times* (New York, 2010). Robert Weiner published *Change in Eastern Europe* (Westport, Conn., 1994).

A number of books on individual countries have strong sections on social history, the family, and women. For France, see John Ardagh, *France in the 1980s* (Harmondsworth, UK, 1982); *France Today* (Harmondsworth, UK, 1990); and *The New French Revolution: A Social and Economic Survey of France 1945–1967* (Harmondsworth, UK, 1968). Irwin M. Wall's *The United States and the Making of Post-War France 1945–1954* (Cambridge, UK, 1991) includes a discussion of social history. See also J. L. S. Girling, *France: Political and Social Change* (New York, 1998), and Michael Kelly, *The Cultural and Intellectual Rebuilding of France After the Second World War* (New York, 2004). Several authors have considered the idea of France suffering a social stalemate. See Michael Crozier, *The Stalled Society* (New York, 1974), and Jane Marceau. *Class and Status in France: Economic Change and Social Immobility, 1945–1975* (Oxford, UK, 1977). Henri Mendras and Alistair Cole, *Social Change in Modern France* (Cambridge, UK, 1991), take a different view. See also Henri Mendras, *Social Change in the Fifth Republic: Towards a Cultural Anthropology of the Fifth Republic* (Cambridge, UK, 1991), and Nicholas Atkin, *The Fifth French Republic* (Basingstoke, UK, 2005). Patrick J. McCarthy, ed., *The French Socialists in Power* (New York,

1986), includes a social component. A. G. Hargreaves, *Immigration in Post-War France: A Documentary Anthology* (London, 1987), gives a good idea of immigration issues. Two books discuss the rise of the radical right in Europe: Antonis A.Ellinas, *The Media and the Far Right in Western Europe: Playing the Nationalist Card* (New York, 2010), and David Art, *Inside the Radical Right: The Development of Anti-Immigrant Parties in Western Europe* (New York, 2011).

On Germany, Giles MacDonogh, *After the Reich: The Brutal Allied Occupation* (New York, 2007), is a book with surprising facts. Konrad Hugo Jarausch, *After Hitler: Reciviliz-ing Germans, 1945–1995* (New York, 2006), describes the cultural recovery of Germany. John Ardagh, *Germany and the Germans*, 3rd ed. (London, 1995), is a good introduction to contemporary German society. David Childs and Jeffrey Thompson, *West Germany: German Society* (New York, 1981), considers broad categories, including women, and overall is a good treatment of social issues. Kendall L. Baker, Russell J. Dalton, and Kai Hildebrandt, *Germany Transformed: Political Culture and the New Politics* (Cambridge, Mass., 1981), includes considerations on public opinion. Ralf Dahrendorf's *Society and Democracy in Germany* (Aldershot, UK, 1992) is a critical study by a well-known political philosopher. Ian Connor, *Refugees and Expellees in Postwar Germany* (Manchester, UK, 2007), describes the integration of German refugees who were expelled from other areas of Europe. The German labor movement is surveyed by H. Grebing and Mary Saran, *The History of the German Labour Movement: A Survey* (London, 1985). Peter J. Katzenstein's *Policy and Politics in West Germany: The Growth of a Semi-Sovereign State* (Philadelphia, 1987) is actually quite good not only for labor, but for social and economic issues. Another work in a similar mold is the one edited by Peter H. Merkl, *The Federal Republic of Germany at Forty* (New York, 1989). For the German economy, there is H. J. Braun, *The German Economy in the Twentieth Century* (London, 1990). On Germany, also see R. Willett, *The Americanization of Germany 1945–1949* (London, 1989).

On Italy, Spencer M. Di Scala, *Italy: From Revolution to Republic*, 4th ed. (Boulder, Colo., 2009), contains sections on social and cultural history. Paul Ginsborg, *A History of Contemporary Italy: Society and Politics, 1943–1988* (Harmondsworth, UK, 1990), con-centrates on social history. Ginsborg's *Italy and Its Discontents: Family, Civil Society, State, 1980–2001* (New York, 2003) brings his research up to the beginning of the new century. Patrick McCarthy, ed., *Italy Since 1945* (New York, 2000), presents wide-ranging essays on Italian society and economics. Vera Zamagni, *The Economic History of Italy 1860–1990* (Oxford, UK, 1997), includes sections on post–World War II. James L. Newell, *The Politics of Italy: Governance in a Normal Country* (New York, 2010) puts the sometimes confusing politics of Italy into its historical and institutional contexts. On Italy's social structure and its relation to power in the country, see S. S. Acquaviva and M. Santuccio, *Social Structure in Italy: Crisis of a System* (London, 1976). John Foot published a book examin-ing the memory of disastrous events in recent Italian history— *Italy's Divided Memory* (New York, 2009)—and another one on Milan: *Milan Since the Miracle* (Oxford, UK, 2001). Christopher Duggan and Christopher Wagstaff investigate conditions during the cold war, during which Italy was a battleground: *Italy in the Cold War: Politics, Culture, and Society, 1948–58* (Washington, D.C., 1995).

Works on British social history include Arthur Marwick, *British Society Since 1945* (London, 1996), and John H. Goldthorpe, *Social Mobility and Class Structure in Modern Britain*, 2nd ed. (Oxford, UK, 1987). David Kynaston, *Austerity Britain, 1945–51* (New York, 2008); Peter Hennessy, *Having It So Good: Britain in the Fifties* (London, 2006); and Domi-nic Sandbrook, *White Heat: A History of Britain in the Swinging Sixties* (London, 2006) are separate volumes of British social history from the end of the war through the 1960s. A. N. Wilson, *Our Times: The Age of Elizabeth II* (New York, 2010), and Andrew Rosen, *The Transformation of British Life 1950–2000* (New York, 2003), cover later years. The British family is considered by David Kynaston, *Family Britain, 1951–1957* (New York, 2010). British classes are examined in Rosemary Cromton, *Class and Stratification*, 2nd ed. (Cambridge, UK, 1998), and by Richard Scase, *Class* (Minneapolis, Minn., 1992). A similar theme is discussed by John Scott, *Who Rules Britain?* (Cambridge, UK, 1991). Pauline Gregg looks at *The Welfare State: An Economic and Social History of Great Britain from 1945 to the Present Day* (Amherst, Mass., 1969). For the most famous scandal of the 1960s as an example of changing values, see W. Young, *The Profumo Affair: Aspects of Conservatism* (Harmondsworth, UK, 1963).

For social aspects of some other important European countries, see M. Donald Hancock, *Sweden: The Politics of Postindustrial Change* (New York, 1972). On Holland, see Johan Goudsblom, *Dutch Society* (New York, 1968). For Spain, see John Hooper, *The Spaniards: A Portrait of the New Spain* (Harmondsworth, UK, 1987). On Portugal, José Cutileiro's *A Portuguese Rural Society* (Oxford, UK, 1971) is very instructive.

Frank J. Coppa's *The Modern Papacy Since 1789* (New York, 1998) contains good chapters on the period discussed.

The most comprehensive work on European women is Georges Duby and Michelle Perrot, eds., *A History of Women in the West*, 5 vols. (Cambridge, Mass., 1992–1994). Volume 5, edited by Françoise Thébaud, deals with the twentieth century and many of the issues discussed in this and earlier chapters. Other works on women include Janet Zollinger Giele and Audrey Chapman Smock, eds., *Women, Roles and Status in Eight Countries* (New York, 1977), and Paula Snyder, *The European Women's Almanac* (London, 1992). See also Judith Adler Hellman, *Journeys Among Women: Feminism in Five Italian Cities* (New York, 1988). On the welfare state and the changing family, see Robert Erikson et al., eds., *The Scandinavian Model: Welfare States and Welfare Research* (Armonk, N.Y., 1987). J. Jenson, E. Hagen, and C. Reddy, eds., *Feminization of the Labour Force: Paradoxes and Promises* (Cambridge, UK, 1988), contains provocative essays. Important statistics can be found in G. Esping-Andersen, *The Three Worlds of Welfare Capitalism* (Cambridge, UK, 1990). For a fuller discussion of some of the issues discussed in this chapter, see Gisela Bock and Pat Thane, eds., *Maternity and Gender Politics: Women and the Rise of the European Welfare States* (London, 1991). Sarah Elise Wiliarty has published a book looking at the gender politics of a major German party: *The CDU and the Politics of Gender: Bringing Women to the Party* (New York, 2010). On schooling, see Fritz K. Ringer, *Education and Society in Modern Europe* (Bloomington, Ind., 1979), and Torsten Husén, *Higher Education and Social Stratification: An International Comparative Study* (Paris, 1987).

On immigration, the literature is large and is bound to grow larger. See Craig Alexander Parsons and Timothy Michael Smeeding for a comprehensive treatment: *Immigration and the Transformation of Europe* (Cambridge, UK, 2006). Alessandra Venturini concentrates on the South and economic issues: *Postwar Migration Patterns in Southern Europe, 1950–2000: An Economic Analysis* (Cambridge, UK, 2007). Rafaela M. Dancygier has published *Immigration and Conflict in Europe* (New York, 2010), which considers economic and conflicts dealing with immigration in different European countries. Integration is discussed by Robert Miles and Dietrich Thraenhardt, *Migration and Integration: The Dynamics of Inclusion and Exclusion* (London, 1995). Marc Morjé Howard analyzes the problems of citizenship in *The Politics of Citizenship in Europe* (Cambridge, UK, 2009). Gerard Delanty et al. discuss another important issue, *Identity, Belonging and Migration* (Liverpool, UK, 2008). For the passion that Muslim immigration to Europe stimulates, see the controversial book by Bruce Bawer, *While Europe Slept: How Radical Islam Is Destroying the West from Within* (New York, 2006). Bawer, an American living in Europe, criticizes European liberals for failing to see what he considers the mortal danger that Islam poses to Europe. For a balanced work, see Ian Baruma, *Murder in Amster-*

dam (New York, 2006), which discusses "the limits of tolerance" that Europeans are now facing.

For information on social issues during more recent periods, consult such publications as *The Economist,* the *New York Times,* and reports issued by organizations like the OECD.

CHAPTER 31

❧

Cultural Dimensions

CHAPTER OUTLINE

Science and Technology • European Culture • Euromarxism

BIOGRAPHICAL SKETCHES

Jean-Paul Sartre, Model of an Intellectual • Arcangela Felice
Assunta Wertmüller von Elgg Spanol
von Braucich, Outrageous!

In addition to alterations in society, rapid changes occurred in all fields of culture. World War II dethroned Europe as the world's cultural leader, but the continent was still a leader in science and culture.

SCIENCE AND TECHNOLOGY

After 1945 the experience gained by the Americans in "big science" during the Manhattan Project that built the bomb ensured the Americans' lead in new fields, such as particle physics.

Big Science

After World War II, research on particle physics seemed out of the reach of the Europeans who had once dominated it because individual countries could not afford the expensive particle accelerators that were required for advanced research in the field, as well as large teams, costly equipment, intensive administrative support, and big budgets. Moreover, the Allies were wary about European research on physics because they feared its use in developing nuclear weapons and were reluctant to share scientific knowledge with European scientists.

Foundation of CERN

European scientists responded by proposing the establishment of a European research center that would pool resources and concentrate on work of a "pure scientific and fundamental character." Edoardo Amaldi, an Italian physicist who had worked with Enrico Fermi, and French physicist Pierre Auger were influential in creating CERN (European Council for Nuclear Research), established between 1952 and 1954, which fulfilled the dream of close cooperation among European countries.

CERN demonstrated what European collaboration could achieve. By 1956 CERN members included twelve countries, and CERN's staff ballooned from 144 persons in 1955 to 3,788 in 1975. It constructed powerful accelerators, conducted fundamental research, and restored Europe as a scientific powerhouse. Several CERN scientists won Nobel prizes and, by 1982, 56 percent of the publications in high-energy physics originated in Europe compared to 35 percent for the United States. In 1997, after the U.S. Congress killed the Superconducting Supercollider, which would have been the world's largest accelerator, the United States agreed to cooperate with CERN to build the world's largest machine for the detection of sub-nuclear particles (Large Hadron Collider, LHC). The LHC came online in 2008–09 and quickly began yielding fundamental information about our world.

In related areas, European physicists made fundamental contributions to the compact disc that revolutionized audio, video, and computers. In 1969, a physicist with Philips, a Dutch company, conceived of the compact disc, and in 1970, Philips produced a glass disc prototype. In 1978, Philips released the first video disc player. However, Europe trailed the United States in quickly incorporating new research into products and getting them to market.

The CERN laboratories in Switzerland and France (as shown by the border marks on the right). The large circle shows a tunnel for physics experiments; it is 27 kilometers in circumference. The vastness of the laboratories illustrates the heavy investment the Europeans have made in physics research and helps explain why they are in the forefront in this field. In July 2012, for example, European scientists claimed to have discovered the fundamental and elusive particle known as the Higgs boson.

In the East, the USSR took an early lead in the space race by launching the first artificial earth satellite, "sputnik," in 1957, and sending the first man into orbit on April 12, 1961. The United States won the "space race" by landing a human on the moon on July 20, 1969, but the Russians led in efforts to put a space station into orbit and in keeping cosmonauts in space for long periods. Even after the end of communism, the Russian space agency continued its work and cooperated with the American and European space agencies in research and in building an advanced space station.

The Preeminence of Biological Research

In the late twentieth century, the premier role that physics had enjoyed in science shifted to the biological sciences. Breakthroughs included the discovery of the double helix structure of the DNA molecule by British scientist Francis Crick and American researcher James Watson, and the appeal that biology had for the public brought increased governmental support, while the end of the cold war resulted in reduced financial support for physics.

The United States and Europe led in biological research. French doctors pioneered in the discovery and treatment of AIDS, with Luc Montagnier claiming to have discovered the disease. The French also produced an abortion pill. European scientists focused on cancer research and treatment, with a group in Milan demonstrating that lumpectomies could be as effective in fighting breast cancer as more radical techniques. In 1996, a consortium of EU scientists developed a promising technology that held out hope that paralyzed people would walk again. The British cloned a complex mammal, Dolly the sheep, and were leaders in biotechnical research.

Computers and the Internet

Europe initially lagged behind the United States in the use of home computers and the Internet, to the development of which CERN made a major contribution, but both soon approached American levels. Websites proliferated, Internet-driven sales increased, scams surged, and the computer became a standard feature of European offices in the private and public sectors.

In industry, computers found wide application with computer-aided design and computer-aided manufacturing techniques. Computers allowed new, modern models of small efficient firms and industry to flourish, especially in such sectors as fashion. Cottage industries based on computers became an important segment of the European economy and promised to help develop economically less-advantaged regions. In addition, European countries, particularly Sweden and Finland, became leaders in the wireless electronics industry.

New Technologies

Because of its heavy dependence on fossil fuels, Europe explored new sources of power. The French generated about half their electricity from nuclear power, but the resistance of many countries to nuclear plants because of accidents in the USSR and the United States, and later in Japan, and the objections of strong environmental movements encouraged the growth of renewable energy sources, such as wind power. From Sweden to Spain, high-tech windmills appeared on the horizon as Europe surpassed the United States in the production of energy from the wind using, in contrast to the Americans, the cottage industry model. In 1997, Europe's wind industry employed 20,000 people, and its capacity was two and a half times that of the United States. In 2010, it was estimated that 9.1 percent of the EU's total energy capacity came from wind power, up from 2.2 percent in 2000, and estimates put the total electricity produced by wind at 14 percent to 17 percent in 2020. Europe led in the production of solar (photovoltaic) energy; the electricity produced increased from slightly more than 10,000 Megawatts at the end of 2008 to 15,800 at the end of 2009, giving it 78 percent of the world's new photovoltaic power, to over 29,000 Megawatts in 2010.

In addition to these new sectors, European manufacturers held their own in traditional industries, such as automaking. German cars remained in worldwide demand, and European firms set up factories everywhere, from Latin America to Eastern Europe, in different areas of manufacturing. In other high-tech areas, including airplane and helicopter development, European consortia challenged the American giants, and this competition promised to increase in the future.

EUROPEAN CULTURE

The arts in Western Europe had a less difficult time recovering from the Nazi onslaught than did science and technology. Indeed, the war itself, the resistance to the Nazis, and the initially bleak postwar outlook stimulated artistic production.

Italian Literature

An outpouring of original artistic activity appeared in Italy, particularly in the form of novels and films. Baptized *neorealism*, this artistic style focused on the sufferings of the poor, presenting a "slice of life." The background for this style already existed in the works of the realistic (*verista*) writers of the late nineteenth and early twentieth centuries and in the novels of Alberto Moravia, who had published anti-Fascist novels and works describing Roman life and the horrors of war. Novelists, such as Elio Vittorini, Beppe Fenoglio, and Renata Viganò, described partisan operations against the Germans during the Resistance.

Following the 1950s, world-class Italian novelists continued to produce excellent works: Italo Calvino's most famous novels explored fantasy worlds, and Giuseppe di Lampedusa explored the Risorgimento movement for unification. Primo Levi and Giorgio Bassani published novels examining the Holocaust that became worldwide bestsellers. Some critics consider Elsa Morante's *History: A Novel*, a sweeping condemnation of war and capitalism, among the best novels of the century. Andrea Camilleri's mystery novels were best sellers in all the world's major languages.

Two poets also won the Nobel Prize, Salvatore Quasimodo (1959) and Eugenio Montale (1975), as did Dario Fo, a comic actor and dramatist, in 1997.

French Philosophy

While the Italians excelled in literature, the French were most famous for their influence on philosophy and for their nontraditional "new novel" (*nouveau roman*).

Existentialist philosophy concentrated on the bleakness and the desperation of life. Jean-Paul Sartre, founder of this school, published his seminal *Being and Nothingness* in 1943. Existentialism taught that there was no God and that persons created themselves by their own actions. People had free choice, which made what they did valuable, but they had complete responsibility for their choices. Sartre and his partner Simone de Beauvoir railed against the bourgeoisie, which helps explain existentialism's popularity immediately after the war and its influence on French culture. However, by the 1950s, intellectuals began turning away from existentialism because of its pervasive gloominess and because of its lack of emphasis on morals.

By the 1960s, another philosophical movement had replaced existentialism. According to structuralism, different kinds of structures determine the thought and action expressed by human beings. Members of this school applied its principles to different areas of human endeavor. The most influential writers were Claude Levi-Strauss, who applied structuralist concepts to primitive societies; Michel Foucault, who examined their role in philosophy; and Roland Barthes, who employed them to study language.

Structuralism greatly influenced the "new novelists," who deemphasized the usual structure of the novel: plot, narrative, and character depiction. New novelists Alain Robbe-Grillet, Nathalie Sarraute, Claude Simon, and Michel Butor wrote in a difficult style that alienated readers but that delighted intellectuals.

BIOGRAPHICAL SKETCHES

Jean-Paul Sartre
Model of an Intellectual

Sitting with his friends in the left bank cafés of Paris, discussing philosophy and smoking a pipe or a cigarette, Jean-Paul Sartre set the model of a European intellectual. He towered over the post-Liberation Parisian intellectual scene in a way few persons have ever dominated the French capital. He achieved this position through his enormous production in many literary fields, his philosophical insights, his free living, and his political activity.

Born in Paris on June 21, 1905, Sartre suffered the loss of his naval officer father while still young. His mother Anne-Marie Schweitzer was the niece of famed humanitarian Albert Schweitzer. When she remarried in 1917, she and her young son moved out of her father's home in Paris to the provincial town of La Rochelle. Sartre returned to Paris to attend the university, where he met his lifelong companion Simone de Beauvoir. He graduated in 1929, after which he served in the army as a meteorologist until 1931. Released from service, Sartre began a teaching career in the secondary schools and continued his philosophical studies in Berlin. He was drafted into the army at the outbreak of World War II and was captured by the Germans. In 1941, he returned to Paris and resumed teaching. He participated in resistance activities and collaborated with some of the best-known journals, including *Combat*.

Influenced by German philosophy, Sartre had produced startling works of fiction before the war. In 1938 he published *Nausea*, an existential novel that expressed the notion of life's purposelessness. *The Wall*, a collection of short stories, included a well-known story that gives the collection its title. In it, the main character considers that he does not exist and becomes embroiled with the extreme right.

During the Resistance, two of his important plays saw the light, *The Flies* (1943) and *No Exit* (1944). The first, set in ancient Greece, explored the theme of responsibility; the second took place in hell, where a traitor, a lesbian, and a nymphomaniac were condemned to live in the same room.

In 1943 Sartre published his seminal philosophical work, *Being and Nothingness*, the enduring basis of his reputation. In this and in subsequent books, he explained the philosophy of existentialism, according to which humans are free but alone: There is no God, the only purposes are those that people set for themselves, and freedom is terrifying. In 1945 Sartre gave up teaching for full-time writing. He founded *Les Temps Modernes*, a monthly journal that had a great cultural influence. His literary production continued to be enormous until his death: plays, novels, social and literary criticism, and philosophical works. In 1964, protesting against the bourgeoisie, he refused the Nobel Prize for literature.

Sartre vocally participated in the cultural and political battles that were agitating Europe. Like many French intellectuals who were disconcerted by the war, he strongly rejected bourgeois values. A Communist, he sought to reconcile existentialism and Marxism but never entered the party. He objected to open criticism of Stalinism and in 1951 broke with old friend Albert Camus, one of France's best novelists, over this issue. Even after Stalin's death in 1953, Sartre was ambivalent about Soviet Russia, but in 1956 and 1968, he defended the Hungarians and Czechoslovaks following the Soviet invasions of their countries. He opposed the Algerian war, prompting French nationalist terrorists to bomb his apartment. He fought American intervention in Vietnam and headed an international war crimes tribunal to judge American military action. In 1968 he supported the revolting students and in 1974 visited German terrorist Andreas Baader in jail.

Despite failing eyesight in old age, Sartre completed three volumes of a projected four on the life of nineteenth-century French novelist Gustave Flaubert using Marxist and Freudian themes. Before he could finish this work, he died in Paris on April 15, 1980, of a lung ailment. Sartre is buried with his companion Simone de Beauvoir.

German Literature and British Drama

Postwar German writers sought to understand what had happened to Germany during the Nazi era. Two German novelists, Heinrich Böll and Günther Grass, won the Nobel Prize. Grass's most famous work, *The Tin Drum,* denounced middle-class moral failings before and during the war in the story of a boy who refused to grow up. Böll's *Group Portrait with Woman* and *The Clown* condemned the middle class's materialistic values. Drama also flourished in Germany, but the continent's most influential playwright Berthold Brecht lived in East Germany.

In Britain in the late 1950s, a group, known as the angry young men, criticized the affluent and wasteful society emerging in the West in a series of scathing plays. The most influential member of this group, John Osborne, depicted a useless existence in *Look Back in Anger*. Samuel Beckett's *Waiting for Godot* examined a similar theme: Two tramps awaiting the arrival of a person who never comes end up waiting for its own sake. Beckett lived in France, as did Eugene Ionesco, who also wrote unusual plays. Critics baptized their works "theater of the absurd." Film, however, overshadowed literature as a form of art and mass consumption.

Vittorio De Sica was perhaps the most famed director of the Italian school of filmmaking called neorealism. His films include the acclaimed *The Bicycle Thief.* De Sica had been a famous actor before World War II and, after the success of his films during the Neo-Realistic period, went on to direct famous films such as *The Garden of the Finzi-Continis.* He is pictured here on July 14, 1955, in Edinburgh, Scotland, serving as Honorary President of the Edinburgh film festival.

Cinema

In cinema, Italian neorealism came into its own. *Obsession*, the 1942 masterpiece of up-and-coming director Luchino Visconti, and Roberto Rossellini's *Rome, Open City*, shot in Rome in 1944 and graphically depicting the city's resistance to the Germans, were the first classics of the genre. Vittorio De Sica's classics *The Bicycle Thief, Shoeshine*, and *Paisà*, continued the neorealistic portrayal of the difficult lives that ordinary people faced. Neorealist directors used ordinary people as actors and shot the films outside, making a virtue out of the lack of resources that plagued postwar Italy.

Neorealism declined in the 1950s, but for the next fifteen years, Italian directors dominated the cinematic scene, helped, as in France, by governmental subsidies. Perhaps most important was Federico Fellini, who directed critically acclaimed films about the aimlessness of modern life. *La Dolce Vita* criticized the meaningless life produced by growing wealth and gave the English language a new word: *paparazzi*. Fellini's most successful film was probably the autobiographical *Eight and a Half*, a theme to which he returned in *Amarcord* (I Remember). Michelangelo Antonioni's *L'avventura* and *Red Desert* paid little attention to plot in showing how alienation afflicted modern society. Italian directors went on to make films that reflected the political and social traumas of European history and current events—Fascism, war, Nazism, occupation, the Resistance, and terrorism. Bernardo Bertolucci's *The Conformist*, taken from a novel by Moravia, depicted the evils of Fascism, while Visconti's *The Dammed* illustrated those of Nazism. The Taviani brothers' *The Night of the Shooting Stars* examined the dilemmas of the Resistance. *To Each His Own, Investigation of a Citizen above Suspicion, Excellent Cadavers,* and *Bread and Chocolate* commented on the Mafia, crime, terrorism, and immigration. Lina Wertmuller, one of the world's most distinguished women directors, explored issues having to do with Fascism, concentration camps, the bourgeoisie, and the impact that different social customs had on people when they collided.

The other great filmmakers of the early postwar period were the French, who came to the forefront in the 1960s. The "new wave" (*Nouvelle Vague*), as the French cinematic style of the period was known, was influenced by a cinematic journal, the *Cahiers du Cinéma,* around which were gathered the most influential French directors. The new wave considered the director an author and the unique driving force behind the films. Whereas in the past French intellectuals would have written novels, they now concentrated on making movies, believing that this form of mass entertainment could also be a serious art form. Jean Luc Godard, Alain Resnais, Claude Chabrol, and François Truffaut were the most famous directors associated with the new wave cinema. A woman, Agnes Varda, was an early influence. In 1956, Roger Vadim's description of reckless youths in *And God Created Woman* achieved commercial success and stimulated the production of other movies. In 1959, Alain Resnais's *Hiroshima mon amour* won even greater artistic and commercial success. Truffaut's autobiographical film, *The 400 Blows,* and *Jules and Jim,* a story about a love triangle, probably had the widest circulation outside France. The desire to portray the less orderly parts of the human condition seemed to characterize the new wave and accounted for its enormous appeal.

French directors specialized in portraying problems of contemporary life. Louis Malle's *Lacombe Lucien* explored the issue of collaboration during the war, while *A Murmur of the Heart* examined the forbidden topic of incest. Godard's *Alphaville* was concerned with increasing mechanization and alienation in modern society, and *Breathless* discussed freedom. Luis Buñuel's *The Discreet Charm of the Bourgeoisie* made savage fun of the middle class, while some of Buñel's other films attacked religion. These films coincided with the French philosophical movements assaulting the bourgeoisie.

BIOGRAPHICAL SKETCHES

Arcangela Felice Assunta Wertmüller von Elgg Spanol von Braucich
Outrageous!

Lina Wertmüller was born on August 14, 1928, in Rome, of Italian and Swiss aristocratic parentage. A youthful rebel, she contested her father's wish that she become a lawyer. She also revolted against authority, which got her

continued

continued

expelled from fifteen different secondary schools. In 1951, she took directing courses in a famous theater school, afterward directing puppet shows—including Kafka for children—and wrote for and directed radio and television specials before turning to film.

Wertmüller entered the cinema world through her friendship with famous film actor Marcello Mastroianni, who introduced her to director Federico Fellini. She worked as Fellini's assistant on his classic *Eight and a Half,* and in 1965 made her own first full-length film. She wrote the story and the screenplay and directed the prize-winning *The Lizards*, an elegant, ironic examination of young boys in the Italian South. After directing other full-length movies and made-for-TV films, Wertmüller produced her best work in the 1970s and became an international celebrity.

The Seduction of Mimi, perhaps her most famous film, appeared in 1972. The story is about a Sicilian, Mimi, who emigrates to Turin to work in the steel industry and falls in love with an emancipated northern woman. The escapades of the couple in Turin and Sicily provide a comic but all-too-serious examination of sexual tension, the class struggle, and the clash between two cultures. Critics saw in this movie a statement of Wertmüller's fundamental methodology: a grotesque satire of the lower classes, although, as usual in her work, contradictions and controversy about it abounds. Ironically, feminists and antifeminists both love and hate her films, as do liberals and conservatives.

Wertmüller won the best director award for *Mimi* at the 1972 Cannes Film Festival and in 1973 directed *Love and Anarchy*. The film is about Tunin, who plans to kill Mussolini to avenge the murder of an Anarchist friend by the Fascists (the execution of an Anarchist for plotting to murder Il Duce actually occurred). He goes to a brothel to receive vital information, falls in love with a prostitute, misses his chance to murder Mussolini, shoots up the brothel, and is himself killed by the Fascists.

Wertmüller's next international sensation, *Swept Away* (1974), reversed the roles of proletariat and bourgeoisie. The story is a funny but disturbing parable of sex and politics. *Seven Beauties* (1975), which netted her the first nomination of a woman for best director at the Oscars, is the outrageous tale of Pasqualino, who murders his sister's lover. Arrested, he successfully fakes insanity and is sent to an insane asylum. When he rapes a female inmate, the authorities order him to choose between a concentration camp and the army. Pasqualino joins up, but deserts. He winds up in a German concentration camp and survives by seducing the female commandant, a woman whose physical features are exaggeratedly grotesque. Wertmüller made many more films, but none received the acclaim of these four, which gained a cult following. She scored her best success after the 1970s with the 1994 *Ciao Professore!*, a delicate story about a northern schoolteacher in the South.

In the years since she made her most famous films, critics have continued to argue about her work. Feminists debate whether Wertmüller is feminist or sexist. There is agreement that her films investigate forbidden subjects in order to analyze gender politics. Wertmüller has said that equality is impossible as long as society forces women into traditional roles—and that is the point of her movies. Some feminists, however, emphasize that her female characters are unsympathetic and that she uses grotesque and outrageous images to portray women but not men.

As is frequently the case with important artists, controversy over her work goes on.

Among the most powerful films made by postwar European directors were those that examined the deeper meanings of life. Swedish director Ingmar Bergman excelled in this genre. His classic films include *The Seventh Seal,* in which a medieval knight plays a game with Death and learns the value of life. *The Virgin Spring* is a haunting story in which a father avenges the rape of his young daughter—an examination of evil. Bergman's artistic production made him one of the most successful filmmakers in history. The German film industry that led the world commercially and artistically following the First World War had less success after the Second World War. In West Germany, Margarethe von Trotta's films explored the Nazi past and contemporary feminist issues. Her best-known film, *Marianne and Julianne,* tells the story of two sisters, one of whom becomes a terrorist and the other a journalist. Along with von Trotta, the films of Rainer Werner Fassbinder, Werner Herzog, Volker Schloendorff, and Wim Wenders achieved international success. Although in the 1970s these directors came to be considered a West German new wave, German cinema was less notable than the other major national schools.

The European cinema produced important films during the 1980s and 1990s, but lost its preeminent position to the American action film, which, if less artistically accomplished, dominated the film industry. The European cinema proved unable to compete at the box office, even in Europe itself, and went into a steep decline in the last two decades of the twentieth century.

Ferment in Eastern Europe

The arts in Eastern Europe flourished to a lesser extent than in the West because of restrictions imposed by the Communist regimes, and cultural movements emerged during periods of political thaws only to be repressed when these thaws ended.

The political liberalization culminating in the Prague Spring of 1968 made Czechoslovakia a cinematic center of international renown. Important films that were produced during that period included *Closely Watched Trains,* directed by Jiri Mensel, and Elmar Klos and Jan Kadar's *Shop on Main Street.* These films, set in Nazi-occupied Europe, mixed wry humor with tragedy. A more direct criticism of communism can be discerned in Milos Forman's *The Firemen's Ball.* Film also flowered to a certain extent in Hungary during Kadar's regime, but, in general, political conditions precluded the consistent development of the East European cinema. Important filmmakers, such as Forman and the Pole Roman Polanski, fled to the West.

With few exceptions, such as *Ballad of a Soldier* and *Moscow Does Not Believe in Tears,* censorship stifled the great Russian cinematic tradition that hailed back to Eisenstein. The same could be said for literature, where creative works secretly circulated in typescript.. This process had an important role in keeping artistic traditions and opposition alive, and some of the novels surfaced in the West, most famously Boris Pasternak's *Dr. Zhivago.* The most famous Soviet writers, such as Alexander Solzhenitsyn, wound up in exile or were shunned in their homeland.

Artists and scientists who criticized the governments of the Communist regimes and stayed in the East were persecuted. In Czechoslovakia, members of Charter 77, an opposition group requesting reform, were arrested. This organization included notable writers, such as playwright Václav Havel and novelist Milan Kundera. The Soviets persecuted Andrei Sakharov, father of the Russian hydrogen bomb, when he criticized Soviet policies. The attempts to repress cultural movements, however, ultimately failed when the resisters received international support. Charter 77, for example, would play a critical part in the fall of Czechoslovak communism, and Havel would become Czech president.

Music and Painting

Painting, music, and architecture declined in importance during the postwar years compared to the beginning of the twentieth century. Abstract art went in different directions, and pop art, representing common objects of mass consumption, flourished in the 1960s. In the 1970s painters reacted to abstractionism by working with strong colors, emphasizing light, and making a strong return to representational art—superrealism. Very important was the application of art to everyday industrial products, such as telephones, televisions, and radios, and to the new

The Americanization of Europe. After World War II, Europe, West and East, seemed to go wild for American fashion, products, and culture. The "invasion" far surpassed a similar development following World War I. The trend affected the continent to such a degree that it brought loud protests from European officials, particularly the French. This picture of a waiter serving Coca-Colas to customers at a famous outdoor café and restaurant in Paris illustrates how the objections fell on deaf ears.

medium of plastic. European industrial concerns favored this development, which boosted the popularity of their products and increased exports.

Serious modern music became less important as the youth culture swept Europe and emphasized popular music, such as rock and roll. The Beatles and other rock groups played a major role in the glorification of youth, armed with enormous buying power because of the unprecedented prosperity. Rock music and rap closed the twentieth century, with English being its dominant language. Swedish and Danish rock groups singing in English and American groups dominated the airwaves and television.

Television

American television programs, from dramatic programs to sitcoms to soap operas, ruled television, although Brazilian soap operas and Japanese cartoons made inroads in the last decade of the century, and brought criticism from European intellectuals. Except for the British, Europeans produced very few programs—except for variety shows—that reached wide audiences. Traditionally dominated by state TV, private stations proliferated during the 1990s and found it cheaper to transmit American programs than to produce their own shows. Worried officials made sporadic, unsuccessful efforts to halt American domination of European television but failed. American news in the shape of CNN also invaded Europe during the 1990s and reached households via cable and the Internet, while MTV greatly influenced European youths.

Americanization

The pervasiveness of American television programs was only one aspect of the Americanization of Europe. Immediately following World War II, the Americans attempted to spread their values in a campaign to eradicate Nazi culture, prevent resistance to U.S. occupation, rebut the Soviet model, and bolster American exports. In France and other countries, the Americans negotiated agreements establishing a quota for American films to be shown in the country. In 1948, the proportion of American films that were shown in France reached 50 percent. In addition to being profitable for the Americans, these films reinforced American values.

Despite their grumbling, postwar Europeans willingly accepted the American way of life, primarily because of the high standard of living Americans enjoyed. Western Europeans equated Americanization with modernization and imported American manufacturing techniques and products. American products, from Coca-Cola to toothpaste, were manufactured and sold all over Europe, and Europeans embraced American icons, such as Mickey Mouse, which was translated, distributed in large numbers of comic books, and shown on television. Europeans were anxious to learn English, and the Germans, the Dutch, and the Scandinavians excelled at it. The Fulbright program for the exchange of scholars brought European students and professors to the United States and Americans to Europe so each could learn about the others' way of life. The U.S. government established leadership grants, by which European political leaders could visit the United States to observe American society firsthand, and American colleges established year-abroad programs.

Even after deliberate American efforts to export culture declined, Europeans imported essential elements of the American lifestyle with a passion. Besides films, jazz, blue jeans, rock and roll, hamburgers, fast food, even American coffee invaded Europe. Americanization impacted European languages. French officials condemned terms, such as *le boom* and *le weekend,* and tried to legislate English out of French—to no avail. In the last years of the century, Europeans went online, where they used American terms to chat (*chattare,* in Italian, *chatter* in French) with their friends all over the world. The Internet age doomed attempts to keep European languages "pure."

Relations with the United States

Ironically, as cultural Americanization accelerated, the European relationship with the United States seemed to become more strained. The growing economic power and confidence of Europe and the success of the EU helped account for this trend. Europeans resented what they viewed as American political and economic interference, an issue that grew in importance as the twentieth century ended. The resentment could be discerned in the union of the Italian Communists and the Catholic church against the Gulf War, in the protests of Greek crowds against the NATO bombing of Serbia over the Kosovo affair, in the discord over the Arab-Israeli dispute, and in the conflict over the 2003 Iraqi War. The EU and the United States argued over trade issues and about who should head major world financial institutions. After 9/11 Americans differed with Europe over how to deal with international terrorism, and the American refusal to ratify the Kyoto agreement on greenhouse gasses angered the Europeans.

EUROMARXISM

European philosophy and political thought in the West were intimately bound up with Marxism, but not in cold war terms. "Euromarxism" had its centers in France, Germany, and Italy and was characterized by criticism of the bourgeoisie, the Americans, and Moscow Communism.

French Marxism

After World War II, French philosophers addressed the problem of being through the lens of existentialist philosopher Jean-Paul Sartre even though he broke with the French Communist Party. Sartre had enormous influence in Europe, especially after his 1960 book *Critique of Dialectical Reason,* and gave French Marxism great intellectual vitality despite his criticism of the Communist Party.

Another French Marxist, Maurice Merleau-Ponty, interpreted Marxism as reflection and research, not as static theory. On the one hand, he seemed to rebut Marx by rejecting the premise that any law governs the course of history, but on the other hand, he fervently believed in the revolution and defended the proletariat's cause. He rejected the capitalist system and was inspired by Marxist logic, according to which Western representative institutions were controlled by American imperialism, but condemned Stalinist purge trials, Russian gulags, the bureaucratic nature of the Communist Party of the Soviet Union, and Soviet doctrinal immobility.

French structuralism also influenced Marxism after the 1960s. From a Marxist perspective, it considered the dilemma of existential loneliness in a capitalist society as that of the human consciousness within a bourgeois structure. This construction is the sum total of the laws and relationships that are imposed on people and that condition their behavior. This philosophical conception influenced the thought of Louis Althusser and Michel Foucault, both of whom were alienated from Western bourgeois society.

German Marxism and Criticism of Western Society

The German Marxists denounced Western society, concentrated on the philosophical contradictions of contemporary capitalism, and condemned official communism.

The major German postwar Marxist philosophers were members of the Frankfurt Institute, whose longtime director, Theodor W. Adorno, questioned all philosophical and political standards. In his *Negative Dialectic,* Adorno attacked the West's authoritarian technological system and argued that capitalist society subjected people to its economic structure and weakened all dissenting forces. The bourgeoisie's social and philosophical system, he maintained, was concerned only with the proper functioning of social mechanisms, not values.

Adorno's colleague Max Horkheimer focused on the workers' movement and the German proletariat and their evolution. He charged that they no longer served as society's conscience and were no longer revolutionary. He assigned these tasks to philosophy, and more generally to culture, putting him far from dogmatic Marxism. Horkheimer considered Bolshevism a degeneration of the true Communist revolution but also criticized bourgeois society and considered Western civilization to be in crisis.

Another influential thinker, Jürgen Habermas, used sociological methods to delegitimate the modern state. He criticized public opinion, put technological society on trial, rejected liberalism, and devalued the concept of political participation. His criticism of Western society was profound, although he proved unable to identify the type of society that could provide a valid form of government.

The "Frankfort School" presented a critical analysis of a Western society that was intimately linked to American capitalism but did not impose acceptance of the forms of government that existed in Eastern Europe, and this factor allowed it to influence the revolutionary movements of 1968 and of the 1970s in Europe.

Italian Marxism: The Influence of Antonio Gramsci

In Italy, publication of the *Notebooks,* which Italian Communist Party founder Antonio Gramsci had written during the 1920s in a Fascist prison, described a Marxist humanism. According to Italian Marxists, Gramsci successfully integrated the historical traditions of democracy and Italian culture. Italian Communist intellectuals affirmed that the Italian Communist Party had respected electoral methods and that with a PCI victory, Italy's parliamentary democracy would be modified only by giving the party new significance. Because it implemented idealistic values, such as social justice, and because its support rested on both northern industrial workers and southern peasants, so-called Gramscism was interpreted as a major challenge to the capitalist order.

At the same time, using Gramsci, the Italian Communist Party challenged the Soviets. In 1971, at the Moscow meeting of the twenty-fourth Congress of the Communist Party of the Soviet Union, Enrico Berlinguer claimed the right of all Communist parties to follow their own policy, distinct from that of the Soviets. Nominated PCI secretary in March 1972, Berlinguer launched the idea of a historic compromise among leftist, secular, and Catholic forces. In 1975, influenced by Gramsci's tradition, he defended his proposal in the context of Italian parliamentary democracy. Italian Communist intellectuals presented Gramsci as the theoretician of the democratic road to power, as opposed to the Soviet model. Gramsci thus proved to be very useful to the Italians and East European Marxists and was the grandfather of the Eurocommunism that held center stage in the 1970s.

Flexibility of the West

Paradoxically, the Western European Marxist opposition strengthened parliamentary democracy because the Western multiparty system overcame political conflicts without repression. Western society adapted to the criticisms of leftists and favored the transformation of social classes through such mechanisms as the welfare state. This development forced a revision of Marxism because increasing wealth had fostered the growth of the middle class. By rejecting Moscow and Washington, Euromarxism prepared leftists for the new world that followed the fall of communism at the end of the millennium.

Bibliographical Essay

On the evolution of postwar European physics, see John Krige, *American Hegemony and the Postwar Reconstruction of Science in Europe* (Cambridge, Mass., 2006), which details the influence of the United States. The relevant sections of Helge Kragh, *Quantum Generations: A History of Physics in the Twentieth Century* (Princeton, N.J., 1999), are excellent. The development of CERN is chronicled in Armin Hermann, John Krige, Dominique Pestre, and Ulrike Mersits, eds., *History of CERN*, 3 vols. (New York, 1987–1990) and CERN, *Celebrating CERN: 50 Years at the Forefront of Science* (Geneva, 2004). The story and promise of the Large Hadron Collider is told in Amir D. Aczel, *Present at the Creation* (New York, 2010).

The number of general surveys on postwar intellectual trends is limited. See Roland N. Stromberg. *After Everything: Western Intellectual History After 1945* (New York, 1975). On general cultural issues, there are two interesting books by Arthur Marwick: *The Sixties: Cultural Revolution in Britain, France, Italy, and the United States* (New York, 1999) and *Culture and the Question of Americanization* (n.p., 1990). James A. Winders wrote *European Culture Since 1848: From Modern to Postmodern and Beyond* (New York, 2001), a detailed and informative work. For new telecommunications technologies, see Giorgio Natalicchi, *Wiring Europe: Reshaping the European Telecommunications Regime* (Lanham, Md., 2001). On Eastern Europe, there is Glenda Sluga, *Culture and Society in Eastern Europe Since 1945* (London, 2003), and Kevin McDermott and Matthew Stibbe, *Revolution and Resistance in Eastern Europe: Challenges to Communist Rule* (New York, 2006).

On the impact of Americanization, see the essays in Sabrina P. Ramet and Gordana P. Crnković, *Kazaaam! Splat! Ploof! The American Impact on European Popular Culture Since 1945* (Lanham, Md., 2003). More complete works include Alexander Stephan, *The Americanization of Europe: Culture, Diplomacy, and anti-Americanism After 1945* (New York, 2006), and, by the same author concentrating on Germany: *Americanization and*

Anti-Americanization: The German Encounter with American Culture After 1945 (New York, 2005). Dissonances between American and European values have led some observers to argue that basic differences divide the United States and Europe. See Robert Kagan, *Of Paradise and Power: America and Europe in the New World Order* (New York, 2003). See also the essays in Sabrina P. Ramet and Christine Ingebritsen, *Coming in from the Cold War: Changes in U.S.–European Interactions Since 1980* (Lanham, Md., 2002).

Postwar literature is discussed by Leon S. Roudiez, *French Fiction Today: A New Direction* (New Brunswick, N.J., 1972); John Gatt-Rutter, *Writers and Politics in Modern Italy* (London, 1978); and Peter Demetz, *Postwar German Literature* (New York, 1970). See also Santo L. Aricò, ed., *Contemporary Women Writers in Italy: A Modern Renaissance* (Amherst, Mass., 1990), and a book of essays on various aspects of postwar Italian literature: Linda Risso and Monica Boria, *Politics and Culture in Post-War Italy* (Newcastle, UK, 2006).

On the broader intellectual issues, see Mark Lilla, *New French Thought: Political Philosophy* (Princeton, N.J., 1994), which looks at political ideas. Tony Judt, *Past Imperfect: French Intellectuals, 1944–1956* (Berkeley, Calif., 1992), is critical of French intellectuals. Mark Poster has several useful books on the themes discussed in this chapter: *Existential Marxism in Postwar France: From Sartre to Althusser* (Princeton, N.J., 1977); *Sartre's Marxism* (London, 1979); and *Foucault, Marxism, and History: Mode of Production Versus Mode of Information* (Cambridge, UK, 1984). Sean Coombes published *The Early Sartre and Marxism* (New York, 2008). Edith Kurzweil discusses another important movement in *The Age of Structuralism: Levi-Strauss to Foucault* (New Brunswick, N.J., 1980), while Lee M. Rademacher wrote *Structuralism vs. Humanism in the Formation of the Political Self: The Philosophy and Politics of Jean-Paul Sartre and Louis Althusser* (Lewiston, N.Y., 2002). On modernism in general, there is Andreas Huyssen, *After the Great Divide: Modernism, Mass Culture, Post Modernism* (Basingstoke, UK, 1988). A survey of European political thought that includes discussions of the postwar period is Spencer M. Di Scala and Salvo Mastellone, *European Political Thought, 1815–1989* (Boulder, Colo., 1998).

The role of film is discussed by Wendy E. Everett, *European Identity in Cinema* (Portland, Ore., 2005), and in Alan Roy Armes, *The Ambiguous Image: Narrative Style in Modern European Cinema* (London, 1976). Alan Williams's *Republic of Images: A History of French Filmmaking* (Cambridge, Mass., 1992) deals with the same subject. The role of memory and occupation on French and European film is examined by Leah Dianne Hewitt, *Remembering the Occupation in French Film: National Identity in Postwar Europe* (New York, 2008). On one of the most famous French schools of filmmaking, see James Monaco, *The New Wave: Truffaut, Godard, Chabrol, Rohmer, Rivette* (1976). On the French cinema as a whole, see André Bazin, *French Cinema from the Liberation to the New Wave* (New York, 2000), and, by Phil Powrie, *French Cinema in the 1980s: Nostalgia and the Crisis of Masculinity* (Oxford, UK, 1997), and *French Cinema in the 1990s: Continuity and Difference* (Oxford, UK, 1999).

For Italy, there is Carlo Celli and Marga Cottino-Jones, *A New Guide to Italian Cinema* (New York, 2006). The previously cited older book by Pierre Leprohon, *Italian Cinema* (London, 1972), is still useful, and there is Peter Bondanella, *Italian Cinema from Neorealism to the Present* (New York, 1990). John J. Michalczyk believes that neorealism had a fundamental influence on Italian cinema: *The Italian Political Filmmakers* (London, 1986). Other works discussing the influence of Italian postwar cinema include Laura E. Ruberto and Kristi M. Wilson, *Italian Neorealism and Global Cinema* (Detroit, 2007), and Angelo Restivo, *The Cinema of Economic Miracles: Visuality and Modernization in the Italian Art Film* (Durham, N.C., 2002). Carlo Testa links Italian cinema to European literature in *Italian Cinema and Modern European Literatures, 1945–2000* (New York, 2005). Giuliana Bruno and Maria Nadotti's *Off Screen: Women and Film in Italy* (London, 1988) discusses the postwar period. Matthew Hibbard gives a global history of the Italian media, including cinema, in *The Media in Italy: Press, Cinema and Broadcasting from Unification to Digital* (Maidenhead, UK, 2007).

On European design, see the critical assessments in R. Craig Miller et al., *European Design Since 1985: Shaping the New Century* (London, 2009). Other works on the same subject include Philippe Garver, and Deyan Sudjic, *Style and Design* (New York, 1986), and Piero Sartozo, *Italian Revolution: Design in Italian Society in the Eighties* (Milan, 1982).

CHAPTER 32

Stagnation and Failed Reform in the East

CHAPTER OUTLINE

Stagnation in the Soviet Union • The East European Regimes •
Beginning the End: Poland • Mikhail Gorbachev's Failed Revolution

BIOGRAPHICAL SKETCHES

Andrei Dmitrievich Sakharov, "Our Regime Resembles
a Cancer Cell" • Nicolae Ceausescu, Gigantomania

L eonid Brezhnev replaced Nikita Khrushchev as first secretary and Aleksei Kosygin replaced Leonid Brezhnev as premier on October 14, 1964, but until November 1982, Brezhnev held real power. Frightened by Khrushchev's reform efforts, Brezhnev maintained the status quo in the USSR and, through the "Brezhnev Doctrine" by which the USSR could intervene militarily to defend socialism, in the satellite states.

STAGNATION IN THE SOVIET UNION

Khrushchev had attempted to decentralize the Soviet Union, but in 1965 Brezhnev abolished the regional administration and established control of the economy in an indirect manner. Sales and profits replaced outputs as measures of success, but governmental agencies retained overwhelming power. A centralized administration ignored growing demands for consumer goods and continued to pour resources into heavy industry, military hardware, and the army, favoring inefficiency, corruption, and shoddy, expensive consumer goods. Communist Party officials continued to enjoy special privileges, and ordinary citizens coped with inadequate social services and severe overcrowding in housing.

Increasing Dissent

Cultural repression increased and eventually amounted to re-Stalinization. Soviet officials discouraged criticism of Stalin, highlighted the heroic aspects of his era,

and banned references to the so-called personality cult. In 1966 the state prosecuted two writers, Andrei Siniavsky and Yuri Daniel, who had published fictional
works that were critical of the Soviet Union abroad. The trial was well publicized
in the USSR and abroad, and the guilty verdict led to protests that emphasized
the discrepancy between the beautiful words of Communist documents and the
brutal practices of officials who violated Soviet law. The protestors demanded due
process and "gave Soviet dissent a new dimension, inducing some individuals to
adopt bolder methods of protest"; the result was a cycle of more arrests, trials, and
demonstrations. Most important, international opinion focused on dissent and
the Soviet violation of human rights as dissidents organized and linked up with
international groups.

In 1970 dissidents formed the Committee for Human Rights and affiliated
with the international League of Human Rights in 1974, when human rights advocates organized a Soviet chapter of Amnesty International, and in 1976 with the
foundation of the Moscow Helsinki Watch Group after an international agreement
signed in 1975 during a period of détente. The Helsinki Accords requested citizens
of signatory nations to help make certain that the human rights specified in that
document were respected, so the USSR could not afford to crush dissident organizations in a world where information could no longer be suppressed.

During his eighteen years in power, Leonid Brezhnev allowed the Soviet Union to stagnate
economically. There was continued concentration on heavy industry, in addition to
widespread inefficiency, and corruption. It seemed as if the USSR had given up on economic
reform even while the dissent and cultural protest that helped bring the Communist State
down increased. In his private life, Brezhnev loved collecting fancy Western cars as his
people suffered. Here an impish Brezhnev gazes at actress Jill St. John during a pool party
given by President Richard Nixon at his San Clemente, California, home on June 25, 1973.
Nixon is seen on the right.

However, the Soviets violated the agreement in the case of the most prominent dissidents of the period, physicist Andrei Sakharov and his wife Elena Bonner. Sakharov, "father of the Soviet hydrogen bomb," abandoned his role as an unquestioning cold war scientist and objected to the return to Stalinist tactics. In 1968, he published a countercurrent journal in *Samizdat* (underground copies of forbidden works reproduced clandestinely in limited quantities using a typewriter and carbon paper, primitive printing presses, or even by hand) versions that reached a progressively more disenchanted Soviet intellectual elite. Sakharov had believed that, over time, the East would become more democratic, with the Communist Party guiding this evolution, but later concluded that communism could not change, sympathized with Western values, and championed human rights. Because Sakharov refused to leave the Soviet Union, the government sent him into internal exile in the provincial city of Gorky, where he became an international symbol of resistance. Dissent quickly spread to other scientists and to social scientists in the country's leading institutes.

The Soviets sent troops into Afghanistan to bolster the Communist regime there but soon bogged down. Despite the arrival of large numbers of reinforcements they were unable to defeat the rebels. The conflict caused increased domestic protest and was an important contributing factor to the downfall of the USSR. Eventually the Soviets withdrew without accomplishing their aim. Here elated Russian soldiers show their joy at leaving Afghanistan on May 15, 1988.

In foreign policy, events turned sour for the Soviets as well. The Soviets had responded to the request of the Communist government of Afghanistan to send troops to suppress a rebellion, but instead of a quick victory, Soviet troops became bogged down in a guerrilla war that became a debacle. Like the United States earlier in Vietnam, protests against the war occurred in the Soviet Union and progressively worsened. Unable to defeat the Afghan rebels and facing escalating disorder at home, the Soviets eventually pulled out of Afghanistan, but at great cost to their prestige and to their internal system of control.

In addition to the political crisis, the Soviet economic system was in shambles by the mid-1980s, with growth rates precipitating and per capita GDP reaching a high of only 40 percent of the American figure and the spreading of the crisis to the satellites.

The East European Regimes

The East European situation quickly spun out of control. The 1968 invasion of Czechoslovakia and the threats of Soviet military repression should the people attempt to alter communism caused the regimes to increase repression, but their fear of revolt prompted them to try to compensate their citizens for the greater political restrictions by increasing the standard of living: "consumer communism." However, this policy meant that they had to import the technology to modernize their economies from the capitalist West, which led to increased Western trade and heavy borrowing from Western banks to compensate for their lack of capital. Political and economic détente stimulated the process, but in 1973 the oil crisis struck. Bank credits could be obtained only at high interest rates, and trade shrank at the same time that higher oil prices induced the Soviets to charge more for their petroleum.

BIOGRAPHICAL SKETCHES

Andrei Dmitrievich Sakharov
"Our Regime Resembles a Cancer Cell"

The "father of the Soviet hydrogen bomb" whose criticism helped topple the Communist regime was born on May 21, 1921. His father, a physics teacher, home-schooled him until he entered the seventh grade. In 1938, Sakharov began studying physics at Moscow State University. Physically unfit for combat, he worked in a laboratory of a munitions factory during World War II. In 1943, he married a lab technician, Klavdia Vikhireva, and they had three children.

Sakharov pursued graduate studies at the Physics Institute of the USSR with Igor Tamm, a physicist who shared the 1958 Nobel Prize in physics. When Tamm went to work on the hydrogen bomb, he took his best students with him, including Sakharov. Sakharov changed the design on which physicists were working, and the Soviets detonated a successful hydrogen bomb in 1953. At the same time, Sakharov and Tamm proposed a model for a controlled fusion reactor to develop unlimited amounts of energy. The government awarded Sakharov several medals for his work.

In 1958, in response to the Americans' development of a so-called clean bomb that would produce only a small amount of fallout, Sakharov published an article demonstrating that "clean" weapons would still kill a significant number of people over the years. Later he dated his moral crusade against nuclear weapons and his increasing political awareness from the experience of writing this paper. He encouraged Soviet leaders to end nuclear tests and to accept an American proposal for a limited ban on testing, signed in Moscow in 1963. Although he continued to work on the development of nuclear weapons for a while longer, he turned to pure research in the fall of 1963. Sakharov made important contributions to the study of antimatter and gravitation and, in 1974, predicted the creation of a worldwide information system—in effect, the Internet.

Sakharov also became more politically active. In 1967, he wrote a memorandum urging Soviet acceptance of a moratorium on developing antiballistic systems but was refused permission to make it public. In May 1968, he wrote "Reflections on Progress, Peaceful Coexistence, and Intellectual Freedom," an essay that first circulated in a clandestine *samizdat* version and then saw the light in July in a Dutch newspaper and the *New York Times*. The essay warned of nuclear war and other dangers, urged an end to the cold war, denounced Soviet totalitarianism, favored human rights, and called for the radical reformation of the USSR.

Sakharov's essay gained him worldwide attention, but the Soviet government viciously campaigned against him. Sakharov became even more involved in politics and in the growing Soviet human rights movement. In 1970, he and two other dissidents founded the Moscow Human Rights Committee. He met Elena Bonner, who would be his constant companion and whom he married in 1972 (his first wife died of cancer in March 1969). His international reputation grew, and he received the Nobel Peace Prize in 1975. The government prohibited him from traveling to Oslo to receive it and, in 1980, after his strong protest against Soviet intervention in Afghanistan, the government exiled Sakharov to Gorky. There he was isolated and kept under police surveillance but smuggled his writings out. He protested against his treatment by going on hunger strikes several times, bringing him increased international support. In December 1986, Gorbachev lifted his exile. Sakharov became a prominent opposition leader, demanding radical political changes and democratic reforms, ran for election to the new Soviet Parliament, and worked on a new constitution.

On December 14, 1989, Sakharov, who had a history of serious heart trouble, died suddenly of a heart attack in Moscow.

These developments greatly increased the costs of energy and produced a severe debt crisis. By the 1980s, the amounts owed to the West had increased by a factor of fifteen. The East European regimes had to choose among default, more borrowing, or exporting goods their citizens desperately needed. They chose more borrowing and, ultimately, increased trade with the West undermined them.

The Lesser-Developed East European Countries

Within this general context, the economic and political situations of the East European countries varied considerably. The two nations with the most independent foreign policies, Romania and Albania, had the most repressive regimes and the weakest economies. In Romania, Nicolae Ceausescu followed a friendly policy toward China and the United States, but internally, Romania—dominated by the notorious secret police, the *Securitate*—was the most repressive society in Eastern Europe. Romania had the highest proportion of secret police agents to the population, required any Romanian who had a conversation with a foreigner to report it within twenty-four hours, and imposed the registration of all typewriters because they might be used to spread underground literature. Ceausescu trusted no one outside his family, so he appointed his relatives and those of his wife to important posts, enriching them and himself in the process. His grandiose schemes, such as acquiring a large capacity to refine oil at a time of oscillating prices, produced economic and ecological disasters, but Ceausescu borrowed heavily from the West and went into debt to further his plans.

Ceausescu left Romania a legacy of ruin and devastation that would haunt the country after he fell. He demolished an entire Bucharest neighborhood to build his gigantic presidential palace—second in size only to the Pentagon. His Boulevard of the Victory destroyed the city's center, and he ordered the destruction of 6,000 villages and the construction of large, shoddy concrete apartment blocs on their locations. In order to pay for his projects, Romania exported about 90 percent of its agricultural production. Shops consequently were empty: Hungry Romanians lined up before dawn for whatever food was available and stared at foreign businesspeople eating at restaurants that accepted only foreign currencies. Personal property also had to be registered with the state, and the possession of precious metals or stones, as in family jewelry, was illegal because these items were declared state property.

Albania resembled Romania. It was China's beachhead in Europe, infuriating the USSR, although it also went out of its way to provoke the United States. Its Stalinist dictator Enver Hoxha dominated the country through the *Sigurimi*, the secret police, and suppressed religion. The Albanian economy's continued poor economic performance prompted Hoxha to institute a thoroughgoing purge of the bureaucracy, the armed forces, and proponents of a softer line. By the mid-1970s, Albanian relations with China chilled, because that country did not deliver promised economic aid and because of the Chinese rapprochement with the United States. Hoxha isolated Albania from the world and thoroughly ruined its economy. He collectivized agriculture, which, despite its real potential, became inefficient. He constructed a few huge, uneconomical metallurgical plants, fostered population growth that the country could ill afford by encouraging large families and forbidding birth control and abortion. As a result, Albania had the largest rate of population growth in Europe with declining resources to support it.

BIOGRAPHICAL SKETCHES

Nicolae Ceausescu
Gigantomania

Several features marked Nicolae Ceausescu's rule in Romania. Romania was a poor country, but Ceausescu planned giant, expensive projects that destroyed historic buildings and areas. Romania was weak militarily, but he defied his patron, the Soviet Union. When the tide turned against oppressive Communist governments, he refused to end his repression.

Nicolae Ceausescu was born on January 26, 1918, in the Romanian area of Wallachia. He joined the Communist youth movement in the 1930s and was imprisoned in 1936 and in 1940. While he was in prison, his cellmate, the future leader of Communist Romania, Gheorghe Gheorghiu-Dej, befriended him. The two escaped from prison in August 1944. After the Communist takeover of Romania, Ceausescu served as deputy minister of agriculture in 1948 and, in 1950, deputy minister of the armed forces with the rank of major general. Under Gheorghiu-Dej, who became head of Romania in 1952, Ceausescu was appointed to important posts and rose to the second-highest position in the Communist power structure. When Gheorghiu-Dej died of cancer in March 1965, Ceausescu replaced him as first secretary of the Communist Party and became head of state two years later.

Ceausescu openly charted an independent course in foreign affairs, which meant defying the Soviet Union. He effectively ended Romania's participation in the Warsaw Pact and condemned the Soviet invasions of both Czechoslovakia and Afghanistan. He combined these actions with friendship toward China and the West. His friendliness to the West won him a good press in the United States.

At home, Ceausescu favored industrialization over agriculture. However, his intransigence, personality cult, and desire to build a Socialist dynasty spurred him to follow a repressive policy that ignored the periodic Soviet attempts to reform the Communist world. Romania remained a highly centralized country that rigidly controlled its population through the hated *Securitate,* the secret police. Ceausescu's policy of favoring births caused great hardship, especially after he ordered the export of Romania's agricultural and industrial production. This policy, implemented in response to the escalation of Romania's foreign debt because of mismanagement, impoverished the country and caused drastic energy, food, and medical shortages. Families became less able to support children, and women resorted to illegal abortions, from which many died. Despite the country's poverty, Ceausescu ordered the destruction of thousands of villages and their replacement with shoddily built cement apartment houses—and then ran out of cement. During the 1980s, he demolished churches and historic buildings in central Bucharest, about one-fifth of the area, to make room for his building projects.

In contrast to ordinary Romanian citizens, Ceausescu and his family lived lavishly and drove Western luxury cars. He ordered the building of a gigantic presidential palace and gave plush jobs to family members. His wife Elena, a poorly educated woman who had dropped out of school and who loved titles and honorary degrees, was awarded a Ph.D. and named head of Romania's best chemical research laboratory. With the declining health of her husband in the 1980s, she rose to the country's second-highest political position while their son Nicu also gained more influence.

With the Timisoara revolt in December 1989, Ceausescu refused to give in and ordered the army to fire on the demonstrators, but the army turned against him. Ceausescu and his wife fled the capital in a helicopter. The army captured them and, in order to prevent the couple from becoming a rallying point for the *Securitate,* quickly tried them on charges of mass murder and executed them on December 25, 1989. In one of the most dramatic images of the collapse of communism, their bodies were displayed on television in images flashed across the world.

Like Romania and Albania, Bulgaria and Yugoslavia had anomalous positions within the Soviet orbit, but in different ways. Under longtime leader Todor Zhvikov, unquestioning subservience to the USSR characterized Bulgaria. This attitude brought some economic gains, allowing the Bulgarians to attempt some economic and constitutional reforms, but these reforms failed to produce a higher standard of living or more freedom. Abroad, the Bulgarians engaged in a series of dubious operations on behalf of the Soviets, including cooperating in an attempt to assassinate Pope John Paul II.

The Communists had hoped to transform Bulgaria from an agricultural country into a modern industrialized society but failed. In 1945, about three-quarters of the population lived in agricultural villages, but Communist policies favored large-scale movements to urban areas and more education. Ironically, greater educational opportunity contributed to an increasingly skeptical view of the regime and a desire for material goods that it could not fulfill. These developments increased dissent that Zhvikov found increasingly difficult to control despite his crackdown on Bulgarian Communist Party members and nonmembers who supported the dissenters. These measures included expulsion from the party, the loss of jobs, and public condemnation.

If subordination to the USSR characterized Bulgaria, independence distinguished Yugoslavia. An aging Tito held together a disparate country created after World War I and marked by fierce ethnic divisions. Communism could not eliminate the divisions, which Communist economics worsened. Economic reforms in the 1960s produced mounting international debts and alienated the Croats, who, according to Croatian experts, transferred 45 percent of their income to the federal bank in Belgrade, leading to charges that the traditionally hated Serbs exploited them. The dispute encouraged historical and cultural writings that increased Croatian nationalistic fervor against the Serbs.

More ominous for Yugoslavia's future, the divisions permeated the party, emerging as ideological disputes on decentralization that were based on thinly disguised nationalism. The Serbs had a predominant role in the Yugoslav Federation and defended centralization as an important tenet of communism. The Croats argued the merits of decentralization and demanded freedom from Serb interference. In November 1971, students in Zagreb staged protests that had powerful nationalist and separatist overtones. Tito repressed them and purged the Communist parties of the Yugoslav states by attacking nationalists and proponents of decentralization indiscriminately. Despite this repression, the government barely contained nationalism in such areas as ethnically Albanian Kosovo. Between 1974 and 1976, Tito attempted to resolve internal disagreements, but he was the only glue holding the federation together, and he was in his 80s.

Besides ethnic divisions, increasing dissent undermined Yugoslav communism. In 1957, Milovan Djilas, a participant in the resistance and a loyal party member, published *The New Class: Analysis of the Communist System*. Djilas's sociological research highlighted the social division between the ruling class and the masses. Communism had generated a party bureaucracy that had become "a privileged social stratum," he maintained. This new class exploited the Communist Party by proclaiming itself the champion of the working class while searching for new ways to consolidate its position, authority, and privileges. This book earned Djilas a seven-year jail term, but in 1969, he expanded his criticism in *The Unperfect Society: Beyond the New Class*. Djilas's censure of the party had international significance because it condemned communism and reinforced dissent in the Communist world.

Playwright Václev Havel was among the founders of "Charter 77," an organization that resisted the Czechoslovak Communist regime. He later led Civic Forum during the "Velvet Revolution" that occurred in 1989 and presaged the end of the Soviet Empire. Here he is on the right, leaning over a table and arguing with the Czechoslovak Prime Minister on November 26, 1989. Havel went on to become the President of Czechoslovakia and, after its breakup, of the Czech Republic. He died on December 18, 2011 at age 75.

The More Industrialized Countries

The more industrialized satellites faced a greater crisis than the lesser-developed ones. In Czechoslovakia, Gustav Husák purged the party, the government, and local administrations of the pre-1968 reformers. Communist Party membership declined by a third, and a great number of intellectuals lost their jobs. The purge backfired because it discredited the party and reduced its popular support. During the 1960s party members had attempted to reform the system, but the 1970s opposition came from outside the Communist Party because its opponents viewed it as a foreign imposition and aimed at the elimination of communism, not reform.

The regime responded by offering more consumer goods, a policy that Moscow endorsed because it feared another revolt, improving the standard of living in the 1970s. Wages rose and consumers found more goods to buy, but this increased material well-being did not prevent the rise of an opposition movement that would eventually triumph: Charter 77. On January 1, 1977, this group demanded that the government heed individual rights guaranteed by the Czechoslovak constitution. Among Charter 77's founders was Václav Havel, playwright and future post-Communist Czech president. With a membership of intellectuals numbering at most a thousand, Charter 77 did not envision itself as a mass movement but as one that defied the government on moral grounds. This was another concrete manifestation of a new phenomenon that gained popularity in the Communist world: citizens demanding that constitutions and the ideals they expressed no longer remain dead letters.

In Hungary, which had also suffered a massive Soviet invasion, a slowdown in the reforms undertaken after the 1956 revolution occurred in the 1970s. The ambitious economic program that had relaxed the rules of Marxist economics and introduced market forces, the New Economic Mechanism (NEM), produced social tensions, inflation, and disparities in wealth by the early 1970s. These developments alienated party ideologues who preached Communist equality and who opposed a new elite based on wealth rather than position. In late 1972, these conservatives diluted the NEM through a series of measures that granted general wage increases, restricted profits, and tightened governmental control. By 1974, they had succeeded in dismissing the main NEM proponent and prominent intellectuals from their jobs.

Even though Hungarian agriculture was unusually healthy, the oil hikes of the 1970s hit the country hard, boosting energy costs, while the price of the raw materials the country exported in order to pay its debts fell. These changes discredited the conservatives, and in 1977 the Hungarians reinstated the NEM, but the combination of relative economic prosperity and communism contributed to escalating social tensions. A new class representing about 1 percent of the population and consisting of high party officials and the upper ranks of the civil service—military, police, trade unions, and state-run economic institutions—ran the country for its own benefit. Prominent scientists, experts, and artists rounded out this arrogant and corrupt new bourgeoisie that claimed a privileged lifestyle and alienated the population, most of whom lived close to the poverty line.

The most industrialized East European country, the German Democratic Republic, greatly suffered from the oil shock and its aftermath. Because of the rapprochement with West Germany, that country passed along hidden subsidies to it, but they could not resolve the crisis. While economically healthier than the other Soviet client states, the GDR manufactured inferior products and could not recover by generating revenue through increasing exports, and foreign indebtedness grew tenfold during the 1970s.

Although it had once been the most productive part of Germany, postwar Communist rule reduced the GDR's per capita rate of production to only half the Federal Republic's. In the once-vibrant chemicals and machine tools sectors, for example, the lack of investment made East German products uncompetitive, causing a serious drop in exports. East German computers were inferior and too expensive, despite increased investments in the area. Mistaken investment decisions meant that the state-run economy was unable to satisfy the demands of GDR citizens, professionals, managers, scientists, and technicians and caused acute dissatisfaction. Because the Communist system did not reward initiative, the most talented people fled the country. When the international climate loosened up in the 1980s, many East German professionals applied for exit visas, stimulated by trips to West Germany and the differences between the gloomy East and the vibrant economy and full shops of the West. West German sources put the number of people who wanted to leave at a third of the GDR. The Communist leadership, however, dug in and waited for the storm to pass, as it had so often done. Only West German subsidies of between 6 million and 7 million marks annually helped keep the GDR afloat.

In foreign affairs, East Germany remained sensitive to the international maneuverings of the USSR and the United States, ironically causing tension with the USSR. Hard-line leader Walter Ulbricht had opposed the USSR's welcoming of Willy Brandt's *Ostpolitik* and détente and would not renounce his demand that Germany be reunified as a Communist country. These views prompted the Soviets to remove him from effective power in May 1971, replacing him with Erich Honecker, the person who had overseen the building of the Berlin Wall. Honecker believed in the GDR as a separate entity and supported policies that he hoped would permanently ensure that result. These policies included agreements by which the Federal Republic recognized the GDR and East German entrance into the United Nations in 1973.

In domestic affairs, détente had a crucial impact. Freer travel resulted in 2 million persons visiting the West and a greater number of requests for permission to leave the country. Exposure to the non-Communist world caused the East German position to deteriorate. Most of the persons who left had no intention of returning, causing the government to crack down harder on dissatisfied intellectuals and to revoke the citizenship of prominent persons who were traveling abroad. The inability of the East German economy to sustain massive emigration increased the GDR's dependence on Soviet support.

BEGINNING THE END: POLAND

During the 1970s and 1980s, the Polish situation reached a crisis that eroded the entire Communist system and produced outright defiance against the Soviets.

Fall of Gomulka

By the 1960s, Wladyslaw Gomulka, hero of 1956, had run out of the goodwill he enjoyed when he assumed power. Gomulka was a committed old-fashioned Communist—puritanical, frugal, and ideologically rigid. He favored party strength above efficiency and cracked down on freedom of expression, workers' spontaneous attempts to organize themselves, and "revisionists." In 1967, he touched off an anti-Zionist campaign when, contrary to Soviet policy, Poles sympathized with Israel during the Arab-Israeli war. In 1968 Polish students demonstrated in favor of the Prague Spring, but Gomulka repressed them and sent army units to participate in the Soviet invasion of that country. Brezhnev appreciated his loyalty, but Poles resented friendliness with their country's traditional enemy.

The decline in Gomulka's popularity masked his substantial foreign policy gains. On December 7, 1970, West Germany accepted the Oder-Neisse line as Poland's western frontier—that is, it recognized the losses of core territory that Germany had sustained in World War II. Ironically, instead of strengthening the regime, this event weakened Gomulka because it reduced fears of a German invasion, thus lessening Polish military dependence on the USSR. This attitude and economic blunders were lethal for Gomulka's regime.

Following traditional Communist doctrine, Gomulka favored centralization and invested Polish resources in heavy industry at the expense of consumer items. These policies, combined with low productivity, low consumption, and a large labor pool, severely hampered the Polish economy. The government exported food to buy industrial equipment but paid farmers low prices that discouraged production. Counting on the domestic goodwill gained by the Oder-Neisse agreement, Gomulka abruptly increased food prices and industrial wages on December 13, 1970. This move backfired as workers poured into the streets to protest their reduced real wages. The centers of the resistance to the government's policy were the Baltic port cities of Gdansk, Gdynia, and Szczecin—which would lead the opposition during the next decade. The army quelled the workers' insurrection, but at the cost of Gomulka's authority. On December 18, the party seized the occasion of his mild stroke and replaced him with Edward Gierek. Gierek revoked the December 13 decree; for the first time, the Poles had removed a Communist ruler and secured the reversal of a governmental policy.

Failure of the Polish Economy

Gierek's economic reforms consisted of introducing the consumer, or "goulash," communism that prevailed in the other East European countries. Gierek favored the increased importation of consumer goods, augmented investment in the consumer sector, and reorganized manufacturing. Initially, this policy seemed spectacularly successful and produced a spurt in real wages and the growth rate, but ultimately it failed because the government did not restructure the economy. Gierek continued to emphasize heavy industry even as he encouraged the production of consumer goods. He attempted to pay for Western products in part by stimulating agricultural production, and in order to accomplish this goal, increased the farmers' access to welfare-state benefits. This policy worsened the economic collapse that awaited just around the corner.

In order to pay for his policies, Gierek secured large credits from the USSR, so he could import Russian oil and grain, and borrowed large sums from Western banks—overflowing with funds from Arabs investing skyrocketing oil revenues—to pay for Western imports. He planned to finance the loans by exporting Polish products to the West, but Poland could not do so without the basic restructuring that the regime rejected. Moreover, the sharp oil rises of the 1970s led to severe price increases for imported Western goods and a recession that depressed the demand for Polish exports, such as coal. Polish products paid for a steadily decreasing proportion of the imports that were necessary to buy domestic peace. Between 1971 and 1975, Poland's indebtedness zoomed from $700 million to $6 billion, forcing Poland to borrow even more from Western banks just to pay the interest.

The economic situation produced major political repercussions. Gierek's initial success had induced the government to make exaggerated assurances that proved impossible to keep, and the promises fueled social discontent because ordinary Poles compared their impoverished state with the privileges enjoyed by Communist Party officials; for example, the housing situation remained in a crisis, and the health system faltered under the influx of new peasant clients whom the government had admitted in order to stimulate agricultural production. Poles resented the system's shortcomings when compared with the health benefits provided to the police, for whom the government instituted a separate hospital building program. As in other Communist countries, the difference between struggling citizens and pampered party members fostered cynicism and opposition, but the government repressed all opposition.

Discontent exploded when the debt emergency reached such enormous proportions that it forced Gierek to follow in Gomulka's footsteps: on June 24, 1976, the government suddenly announced drastic price increases. The workers responded with massive rioting, the police arrested and beat up the demonstrators, and the government backed down and rescinded the increases. Gierek had shown that he could quell demonstrations but demonstrated how the regime's authority rested on brute force.

The 1976 disturbances elevated the country's political temperature. Gierek had attempted to start a dialogue with the Polish Catholic church to avoid a possible linkup with dissatisfied intellectuals, but failed. Intellectuals formed the Committee for Workers' Defense (KOR), reorganized in 1977 as a social self-defense committee. This organization set the stage for a new workers' movement that moved aggressively from self-defense to the offensive as it spread over the country. Anti-Communist Workers' committees proved very embarrassing for a workers' government, but the events of the past years had sapped popular support for the Communists, destroyed the chances for a consensus, and illustrated how the government's authority rested on force—a position that Polish intellectuals vigorously sustained.

The election of a Polish-born Pope, John Paul II, and his visit to Poland were defining moments in the strengthening of the protest movement headed by the Solidarity labor union. Despite the crackdown attempted by the Polish Communist regime, Solidarity survived with the help of the Church and of international public opinion. During John Paul's visit to Poland the Communist authorities did not dare to intervene and left the organization of the Pope's itinerary to Church officials. The photograph shows a Solidarity demonstration during the Pope's visit.

The Church

This Polish Spring was a more dangerous challenge to Communist rule than its 1960s Czechoslovak counterpart because of its connection to the Roman Catholic church. The church had cautiously but tenaciously contested the Communists since the 1950s under its popular primate, Cardinal Stefan Wyszynski. In the 1970s, another more assertive Catholic leader symbolized the church's opposition: Karol Wojtyla, archbishop of Cracow. Formerly a professor at the Catholic University of Lublin, Wojtyla equated Marxism with exploitation. He focused attention on Polish society's resistance to communism, his ideas resonating with Catholic and atheist intellectuals as well. On October 16, 1978, came the spectacular news that the College of Cardinals in Rome had elected Wojtyla Pope after the untimely death of Pope John Paul I. This event electrified the Poles, who considered the new pope a national leader with greater legitimacy than the Communists.

In June 1979, Wojtyla visited Poland for nine days in his new capacity as Pope John Paul II. Large, devoted crowds cheered him enthusiastically. The government wisely adopted a low profile, even leaving crowd control and the pope's itinerary to the church authorities. The pope's sojourn in his native country highlighted the contrast between Polish enthusiasm for the church and the disdain for the Communist state. For a few days, governmental authority vanished, and the ebullience of the throngs greeting the pope emphasized the extent to which Communist rule depended on force. The church's enhanced position in Polish society further weakened the government and made it more difficult to confront the economic crisis.

In July the government again tried to raise prices—this time gradually. The attempt provoked more numerous and more serious strikes than in the past as the strikers linked up with other social groups. The Lenin shipyard workers of Gdansk, who went out on August 14, were the most aggressive and best organized. The workers formed interfactory strike committees to coordinate their action and cooperated with members of KOR who sabotaged the government's attempts to block the spread of information to other parts of the country. Workers in other regions formed committees, and a massive strike wave overspread the country as the strikers issued a program consisting of twenty-one demands, the most important of which was the insistence on free trade unions. Other demands included the lifting of censorship, no work on Saturdays, equal access to better welfare services, and permission to broadcast the mass.

Gierek gave in on August 30, when the government granted workers unprecedented rights to organize independently of the party's control, recognized the right to strike, and accepted other requests. However, over the next year and a half, major problems surfaced—economic difficulties, internal quarrels between hardliners and moderates among workers and Communists, fear of a Soviet invasion, and the church's cautious attitude.

The Rise of Solidarity

In September 1979, representatives of the interfactory strike committees elected a national committee to coordinate policy, called "Solidarity" to symbolize the workers' common purposes. The leader was Lech Walesa, an electrician at the Lenin shipyard. Solidarity's establishment as the genuine representative of the Polish workers was the final blow in discrediting the Polish Communist Party, and on September 6, Gierek relinquished his post as first secretary to Stanislaw Kania.

Kania tried to revive the party by dismissing its most tarnished leaders and by coming to terms with Solidarity, but he sparred with Solidarity over the next two months. Solidarity complained about the government foot-dragging in implementing the August 30 agreement, increased police repression, and the failure to recognize the union as a legal entity. The government objected to Solidarity's exclusion of Communist Party members from positions of control and its refusal to acknowledge the party's leadership role.

Nevertheless, Walesa and Kania were anxious to reach a compromise because of possible Soviet intervention as the Communist Party imploded, and as the threat of a Russian invasion loomed, the church pleaded for moderation. Concerned about their image, the Soviets hesitated to invade and for the moment pursued a subtler course. They let it be known that they would not invade if the Poles themselves could enforce law and order—encouraging a coup d'état that would presumably stabilize the country. Worsening Kania's fears of an attack was Walesa's lack of full control over his followers. Prominent Solidarity leaders demanded drastic action against the government and the police, but Soviet troop movements near the Polish border in December, followed by Warsaw Pact maneuvers on Polish soil, sobered them. In January 1981, Kania and Walesa compromised on some of the issues that separated them, but a new problem arose: Rural Solidarity.

Rural Solidarity represented about half of Poland's small peasant farmers. It requested official recognition as a trade union, but its composition presented a grave problem for the government. In Poland, farmers were not collectivized, and the government refused to recognize a "bourgeois" group of private farm owners as a trade union. Accordingly, in February 1981, a court recognized Rural Solidarity as an association only, meaning that it could neither strike nor engage in collective bargaining. The court's decision caused animated debates, and the police broke up meetings and attacked activists. Solidarity demanded an investigation and threatened a general strike for March 30 if the government refused. The two sides reached a last-minute compromise, and Rural Solidarity received recognition on May 1.

The Coup d'État

Solidarity's first congress, held in Gdansk in September 1981, worried the Soviet and East European regimes. The meeting adopted a radical tone as the delegates favored a national referendum on workers' self-management and threatened to organize it themselves if the state refused. The delegates demanded elimination of Communist Party privileges and the strengthening of Polish culture. By offering aid to Communist workers in other East European nations, Solidarity threatened the stability of the entire Communist world, making an invasion more likely. These events induced Kania to resign on October 18.

Defense Minister General Wojciech Jaruzelski replaced him. Kania had appointed Jaruzelski prime minister on February 9, 1981; Jaruzelski represented the army, the only Communist institution that still held the country's respect. Jaruzelski, considered a moderate, secured Soviet backing but not Solidarity's because the union was determined to destroy the political system and end Moscow's veiled threat of invasion. Jaruzelski declared martial law on December 13 and 14, 1981, and used the army and the police to establish control over the country. There was only scattered resistance, and the Polish parliament dissolved Solidarity.

Solidarity, however, survived underground, continuing its challenge of the Polish and other Communist regimes. Solidarity contested Communist claims to have instituted the dictatorship of the proletariat and contended that the regimes were authoritarian administrations that oppressed workers through a sophisticated ideology backed by force. The union argued that events in Czechoslovakia 1968 and Poland in 1981 demonstrated that hopes of changing Communist ideology were doomed and that the continual economic crises, the incessant revolts, and the persistently low standards of living caused the chronic instability. Only deep-seated reforms in the Soviet Union could change things, and, all of a sudden, this seemed to be possible.

MIKHAIL GORBACHEV'S FAILED REVOLUTION

The rigid Soviet political system made it difficult for a person with imagination to undertake thoroughgoing reforms. By the 1980s, however, conditions had become so desperate that a Soviet leader, Mikhail Gorbachev, undertook the task.

An Accelerating Descent
The Soviet Union's decline accelerated during the last years of Brezhnev's rule. By 1980, the Soviet economy had stopped growing, industrial production fell, and only income from the export of raw materials and increased domestic sales of vodka sustained the economy. In modern technological sectors, such as computer technology, the Soviet Union fell hopelessly behind the West, and only a disproportionate investment in military hardware kept the space and missile programs competitive.

Severe shortages plagued the economy. Distribution difficulties and the need to increase the quality and quantity of food created chaos in the agricultural sector, and the USSR became dependent on grain imports from the United States. Increasingly, the USSR exported raw materials in order to import technology. Living standards declined, while time spent waiting in lines for scarce commodities increased. Finally, when world oil prices fell, a major prop sustaining the Soviet economy disappeared.

The altered relationship between the USSR and its satellites also caused an economic strain. During the 1950s and 1960s, the USSR exchanged raw materials for manufactured goods from the East European countries in a mutually satisfactory arrangement. Raw materials, especially the plentiful petroleum found in the USSR, were relatively inexpensive, and East European manufactured goods were of reasonable quality. By the 1970s and 1980s, however, the inability of the East Europeans to keep up with technological and qualitative changes made their products shoddy, while Soviet oil and raw materials shot up in value. This development meant that the Soviets were trading valuable commodities for questionable industrial products and that they could receive a better deal from the West. The Soviet Union made valuable economic deals with Western countries, but its economic relationship with the satellites became unprofitable.

The Role of Ideology

Besides international economic factors, ideology played an important role in the USSR's economic decline. The Soviets stubbornly retained a command economy that centralized planning and attempted to control production, distribution, and pricing. However, the centralized party apparatus and the lack of a market made it impossible for the planners to make judicious decisions about investment and production. The planners did not know how much or what to produce and had no idea about what to charge for products. When they did make policy determinations, they frequently found it impossible to enforce them because local managers ignored central planning that only made matters worse. Communist ideology also prevented changes in collectivized agriculture, and wheat rotted in the fields as the Soviets imported it.

Corruption and inefficiency riddled the economy, and the state could not stop them. Despite the concern of younger leaders about Russia's growing backwardness and their desire to experiment with market mechanisms on the Western model, the Soviet elite remained stubbornly orthodox. The older leaders lived in the past and refused to give up on a system that had supposedly modernized Russia and despised younger leaders who had been born after the heroic struggles to establish communism and who favored the hated bourgeois West as a new model for economic development.

The diplomatic breakthroughs of the 1970s—the German, Helsinki, and SALT (Strategic Arms Limitation Talks) agreements—reduced confrontation with the West and gave the USSR some economic breathing space. Reduced tensions allowed the USSR to lighten its military burden, much heavier in relative terms than that of the West, and encouraged the Eastern regimes to go on the borrowing binge that temporarily propped them up. However, German recognition of Polish and East German borders and the Helsinki pact guaranteeing respect for human rights boomeranged against the Communist regimes. In 1979, the Soviets invaded Afghanistan to rescue the Communist government there, but the invasion deteriorated into a costly guerrilla war and an unending series of military disasters. Soviet losses raised the level of opposition, already strong because of economic difficulties and political repression, and touched off the last crisis of the regime.

Transitions

On November 10, 1982, the ailing Brezhnev died. KGB head Yuri V. Andropov succeeded him two days later. Andropov began a campaign against corruption in order to rescue the Soviet economy, believing that restoring Communist discipline would generate enthusiasm. In July 1983, the government announced limited decentralization in order to improve the quality of Soviet products. Whether these limited reforms would have worked is doubtful because eventually Andropov would have faced a choice of reverting to Stalinism, progressing to the kind of reforms Gorbachev later attempted, or giving up as Brezhnev had done. During his time in power, Andropov promoted Michail Gorbachev and other younger leaders—inspired by Lenin's ideals and less corrupt than the older generation—to positions of power. These younger leaders staunchly believed in Lenin's ideals and were less corrupted by the power and privileges conferred by membership in the Communist Party than were the older generation of leaders. However, the downing of Korean Airlines Flight 007 by Soviet fighters when it strayed over Soviet air space and the killing of 269 innocent passengers demonstrated the Soviets' continued capability for brutal action.

Andropov, age 68 at his accession and suffering from acute kidney problems, died on February 9, 1984. The Soviets installed Konstantin Chernenko as general secretary on February 13. Chernenko's accession could be interpreted as a retreat from Andropov's reform mindedness, but at age 71 Chernenko was sicker than Andropov, and it is possible that the Soviet leadership expected a brief tenure and that he represented a compromise by which Gorbachev would become general secretary after a short transition. Chernenko, in fact, died on March 10, 1985, clearing the way for the party to elect Gorbachev, aged 54, as the general secretary on the next day.

Mikhail Gorbachev

Gorbachev grew up on a collective farm, studied law, married a student of philosophy who served as his adviser, and began his career as a local official. He became Andropov's second in command and, as general secretary, announced that he would follow Andropov's lead in rooting out corruption from Soviet society and in reestablishing discipline among the workers. At first Gorbachev seemed to offer nothing new and spent his first year as general secretary consolidating his power. He purged the numerous Brezhnev holdovers and replaced them with his own appointees. By February 1986, when the twenty-seventh Congress met, 40 percent of the party's Central Committee had been renewed. Gorbachev's address foreshadowed future radical reforms in the hope of halting the Soviet economic and moral decline.

Gorbachev made a clean break with Brezhnev's eighteen-year reign and tried to revive Lenin as a founding father of communism and to insert his own ideas into the Leninist tradition. He continued the ritual denunciation of Western imperialism but deemphasized international affairs that were understood as spreading communism to other countries. Because of the need for constructive interaction among the peoples and states of the world, and because others would judge the USSR by the manner in which it resolved its own problems, he stated that reform must take precedence. Gorbachev argued that the Soviet Union had reached a turning point in its history because the stagnation gripping Soviet society had been compounded by a strange psychology and summarized the Soviet dilemma: "How to improve things without changing anything took the upper hand . . . But that cannot be done, comrades." Either the Soviet system renewed itself or it would perish.

This revolutionary renewal was communism's main challenge, according to Gorbachev. What was to be done? Gorbachev proposed economic acceleration. He explained that while capitalist economies relied on the increase of their growth rates in simple terms, an increase over time, Communist acceleration meant a

The creation of the labor union Solidarity and its establishment as the representative of the Polish workers challenged the Polish, and, ultimately, the Soviet regime. It was a major development in the fall of international Communism and set off the events that brought the USSR to an end. Here its leader, Lech Walesa, is carried on the shoulders of jubilant followers. Solidarity won its fight with the government, and Walesa went on to win election as president of a non-Communist Poland in 1990.

perpetually increasing growth rate—2 percent one year, 4 percent the next, 6 percent the next, and so forth. This ideal would give a dynamic quality to the Soviet economy, and society, that would dramatically improve Soviet life.

Gorbachev left the question of exactly how communism could achieve acceleration unclear and emphasized the fight against corruption. He advocated a campaign against alcoholism and more labor discipline—Andropov's program. The campaign against alcoholism collapsed with the increase of illegally produced alcohol that, as an irritating side effect, depleted the country's sugar supply. In practice, labor discipline translated into a government-encouraged program of twenty-four-hour factory shifts, a plan that was abandoned because Soviet society could not adapt to the change. The highly visible arrests of prominent personalities for corruption also backfired because it confirmed Russians in their conviction that the party was hopelessly dishonest.

By 1987 these failures presented Gorbachev with several unappealing options: institute Stalinist-type measures to coerce the workers into producing more goods, introduce market conditions that would impose discipline among workers by accepting unemployment, or adopt the Brezhnev model (that is, give up). As a committed Communist, Gorbachev rejected all these choices in favor of a more radical, articulated program with greater risks.

Perestroika and Glasnost

The principles enunciated by Gorbachev in early 1987 had their origins in a group of advisers around sociologist Tatiana Zaslavskaia. Zaslavskaia believed that Soviet policies, from Stalin to Brezhnev, stultified the natural enthusiasm of workers to produce to their utmost under Communist conditions. This increased production could happen only if workers identified with their jobs and monitored their own performance according to their professional capabilities, dignity, and pride. Although Zaslavskaia remained vague on how exactly this could be done, she hinted that workers would have to receive rewards according to their capacities but did not go as far as accepting the idea of unemployment.

Another important spur to change was the explosion at the Chernobyl nuclear plant in the Ukraine on April 16, 1986. The accident killed 31 people and forced another 300,000 to evacuate, revealing the Communist regime's gross mismanagement of the economy and the environment. Although the accident was severe enough to send nuclear fallout over practically all of Western Europe, it was not until after the West Europeans reported it that the Soviets admitted that a serious accident had occurred. This failure smacked of the usual Soviet techniques of excessive secrecy and cover-ups. Once the news came out, however, it was not possible to return to the old standard operating procedures. The Soviet media began reporting on events that had been ignored in the past—opposition to the government, controversial opinions, accidents, crime, and drug addiction. Almost overnight, the media opened up, and publications and films appeared that never would have seen the light in the past.

These developments encouraged Gorbachev to develop a comprehensive vision of the future. In a widely circulated book, *Perestroika: New Thinking for Our Country and the World*, he painted a remarkable picture of what turned out to be the last attempt to reform communism from top to bottom. After providing an honest assessment of the problems faced by communism in the 1980s, Gorbachev downplayed the opposition of capitalists and other factors and cited the "mistaken premises and subjective decisions" of Communist leaders. Over the decades, the errors of the Communist leadership compounded the difficulties; caused them to accumulate; and produced the current inertia, conservatism, and stagnation. In order to overcome these problems, Gorbachev decided on the new policies of *perestroika* (restructuring) and *glasnost* (openness).

For Gorbachev, perestroika meant that individuals must become intimately involved with changing the economic system. In the past, citizens had been struck down for criticizing governmental policy, and debate had not been tolerated. Now criticism, self-criticism, discussion, and debate were essential to overcome the difficulties of communism. Indeed, perestroika imposed glasnost, the democratization "of all aspects of Soviet society." Gorbachev admitted that these concepts ran counter to the experiences of the Soviet citizen, but he argued that repression had resulted from the party's errors, not communism.

Gorbachev presented perestroika as originating from Lenin. He painted an alluring picture of Lenin as an ardent democrat who never faltered in his vision and then justified his own theories as being an updated expression of Communist democracy's long history. Gorbachev argued that Lenin believed in democracy as the necessary means for workers to gain power and wrote that the deeper the reforms that had to be implemented, the greater the people's participation must be: "This means that if we have set out for a radical and all-round structuring, we must also unfold the entire potential of democracy." •

Gorbachev's book also announced a revolution in foreign affairs. He criticized the East European regimes and informed them that they could no longer count on Soviet military force to save them from their own people. The Communist parties in the troubled people's democracies had made major miscalculations and, like the USSR, needed to institute a policy of restructuring and openness. However, he would not impose these policies because a new relationship between the Soviet Union and the East European countries had come into being, one based not on force but on fraternal cooperation and absolute independence.

Practice

It took Gorbachev several years to implement his plans. A number of reasons explain this hesitation. The failure of his campaigns against alcohol and for more labor discipline required him to turn to more radical means to implement reform. Gorbachev realized that most Communist officials did not intend to give up their privileges and opposed his ideas, so he could not move decisively until he had consolidated his power. Finally, the accelerating economic decline of the USSR made it less able to meet the military challenge launched by President Ronald Reagan, known as the Strategic Defense Initiative (or "Star Wars").

In practice, perestroika did not reverse the USSR's economic slide. The implementation of restructuring was half-hearted. Gorbachev did not want to abandon communism for a free-market system, and half-measures did more harm than good. In 1987, for example, local managers received more authority to make decisions, but central planning still determined salaries and prices. In 1988, cooperatives, small businesses, and new businesses received more rights, but because they had difficulty obtaining resources, most of which went to state-run concerns, they turned to the black market. This policy created more shortages and emboldened the criminal element present in Soviet society that was destined to have a much greater impact in post-Soviet Russia.

In the industrial sector, corruption was rife, and workers and officials sabotaged perestroika. Even though wages were low, the Soviet system provided workers with employment and social services. The workers feared unemployment, which grew rapidly despite the government's denials. Unemployment would supposedly help restore discipline and efficiency to the workplace, but it demoralized the workers and helped sabotage Gorbachev's reforms.

In the crucial agricultural sector, the bureaucracy did not respond to Gorbachev's directives for several reasons. It was rigid, corrupt, and arrogant, and half-measures were not strong enough to reverse its culture. Many bureaucrats considered Gorbachev a beginner with little experience and sabotaged his policies. A successful reform of agriculture might have translated into strong national support for Gorbachev, given the chronic shortages in the sector, but this did not happen, and consumer complaints continued.

Besides economics, perestroika had political implications, such as allowing more than one candidate for election to the same office. Here Gorbachev had more

Mikhail Gorbachev hoped that restructuring and openness would revitalize communism and the Soviet Union after decades of economic stagnation. His ambitious reform program had industrial and agricultural components. In this picture, Gorbachev and his popular wife Raisa mingle with supporters in June 1989, in contrast to the late Leonid Breshnev and other Soviet leaders who did not mix it up with the people. Gorbachev's reform program failed and communism collapsed.

success. A real electoral contest took place for the new USSR Congress of People's Deputies that convened in May 1989, the first truly representative body since the Constituent Assembly of January 1918. In March 1990, Gorbachev also ended the Communist Party's political monopoly. However, these measures did not mean that Gorbachev aimed at establishing a Western liberal parliamentary model in the USSR. For example, his creation of a more independent Supreme Soviet in 1988, hailed in the West, had more to do with building an alternative power base to support him in the struggle against the existing party and state apparatus.

Perestroika's complement, glasnost, was supposed to provide ordinary citizens with the information and freedom to discuss issues openly and to judge their leaders. After his initial hesitation to be truthful about Chernobyl, Gorbachev rehabilitated Stalin's victims; liberated political prisoners, including Sakharov and his wife; and tolerated the protests of veterans and their relatives against the disastrous Afghan war. He allowed glasnost to be applied to history, which became important because the government revealed questionable past policies. Officials acknowledged Soviet responsibility for the massacre of Polish officers in the Katyn

Forest in 1940 and admitted that the Soviets had signed a secret protocol as part of the nonaggression pact with Hitler in 1939 that allowed them to annex the Baltic states. This admission later encouraged those republics to secede.

Gorbachev's reforms failed to save the USSR. Perestroika and glasnost had a corrosive effect on a system that had already rotted away. Perestroika helped destroy the existing productive system, while glasnost exposed the horrors of Soviet politics from Stalin to Brezhnev and contributed to the events that ended the USSR. Gorbachev believed that his "new thinking" would renew the Soviet Union and that perestroika and glasnost would spark revolutionary spontaneity and restructure Soviet society and production from below, but they were incapable of transforming passive Soviet citizens into active ones. The dilemma of the Soviet Union was that the old methods of control no longer worked, but without them, the Soviet system could not survive.

Bibliographical Essay

Boris Meissner, ed., gives a general picture of social development in the USSR up to the point discussed in this chapter in *Social Change in the Soviet Union: Russia's Path Towards an Industrial Society* (Notre Dame, Ind., 1972). Leonard Schapiro and Joseph Godson, editors of *The Soviet Worker: From Lenin to Andropov* (New York, 1984), 2d ed., collected excellent essays on their subject. Marshal S. Shatz, *Soviet Dissent in Historical Perspective* (Cambridge, UK, 1980), is a well-argued work; the quotation on Soviet dissent being given a new dimension is on p. 122. H. Stuart Hughes, *Sophisticated Rebels: The Political Culture of European Dissent, 1968–1987* (Cambridge, Mass., 1988), has several chapters on dissent in Eastern Europe.

Two excellent books provide coverage of Eastern Europe from the 1970s to the 1990s. They are R. J. Crampton, *Eastern Europe in the Twentieth Century—and After*, 2d ed. (London, 1997), previously cited, and Joseph Rothschild and Nancy M. Wingfield, *Return to Diversity: A Political History of East Central Europe Since World War II*, 3rd ed. (New York, 2000), which concentrates on politics since World War II. Sabine Hering edited a book of essays on social care in Communist Eastern Europe: *Social Care Under State Socialism (1945–1989): Ambitions, Ambiguities, and Mismanagement* (Farmington Hills, Mich., 2009). Paul Hollander's *Political Will and Personal Belief* (New Haven, Conn., 1999) describes the decline of ideals among Communist officials in Czechoslovakia and Hungary.

Lothar Kettenacker, *Germany Since 1945* (New York, 1997), gives a parallel history of East and West Germany up to reunification; on the same idea, see J. Weber, *Germany, 1945–1990* (New York, 2004). Mary Fulbrook, *Anatomy of a Dictatorship: Inside the GDR 1949–1989* (New York, 1998), discusses the nature of the East German regime. Gary Bruce's *Resistance with the People: Repression and Resistance in Eastern Germany 1945–1955* (Lanham, Md., 2003) makes use of new documents. Technology is an important aspect of Raymond G. Stokes, *Constructing Socialism: Technology and Change in East Germany 1945–1990* (Baltimore, Md., 2000). M. E. Sarotte, *Dealing with the Devil* (Chapel Hill, N.C., 2001), describes East German reaction to Ostpolitik between 1969 and 1973.

Specialized works on individual countries that cover this period include *A Society in the Making: Hungarian Social and Societal Policy* (Harmondsworth, UK, 1975), an examination of Hungarian social policy by Zsuzsa Ferge. Hungarian agriculture is examined in a collection of essays edited by Marida Hollos and Bela C. Maday, *Hungarian Peasants* (New York, 1983). Jaroslav Krejci examines *Social Change and Stratification in Postwar Czechoslovakia* (London, 1972). Lee Congdon et al. describe *The Ideas of the Hungarian Revolution, Suppressed and Victorious, 1956–1999* (Boulder, Colo., 2006).

Poland has received much attention. See Wladyslaw Majkowski, *People's Poland: Patterns of Social Inequality and Conflict* (Westport, Conn., 1985), which examines social inequalities. David Lane and George Kolankiewicz, eds., *Social Groups in Polish Society* (London, 1973), provides insightful essays on the different classes. Dennis Clark Pirages, *Modernization and Political-Tension Management: A Socialist Society in Perspective-Case Study of Poland* (New York, 1972), discusses the most important issues of the period. For the role of Solidarity, see Andrzej Paczkowski et al., *From Solidarity to Martial Law* (New York, 2006); Kristi S. Long, *We All Fought for Freedom: Women in Poland's Solidarity Movement* (Boulder, Colo., 1996), on women's experience. For the role of the West, there is Helene Sjursen, *The United States, Western Europe and the Polish Crisis* (New York, 2003). On the army's role, see George Sanford, *Military Rule in Poland: The Rebuilding of Communist Power* (New York, 1986).

Bogdan Denis Denitch, *The Legitimation of a Revolution: The Yugoslav Case* (New Haven, Conn., 1976), is a thorough discussion of the Yugoslav model. Slobodan Stankovic, *The End of the Tito Era: Yugoslavia's Dilemmas* (Stanford, Calif., 1981), also discusses Yugoslavia. Alex N. Dragnich describes *Yugoslavia's Disintegration and the Struggle for Truth* (New York, 1995).

For Romania, see Dennis Deletant, *Romania Under Communist Rule,* rev. 2d ed. (Portland, Oreg., 1999); Daniel N. Nelson, *Romania in the 1980s* (Boulder, Colo., 1981); and Katherine Verdery, *National Ideology Under Socialism: Identity and Cultural Politics in Ceausescu's Romania* (Berkeley, Calif., 1991). Silvia Kerim described Ceausescu's destruction of Bucharest in *Parfumeria: Ceausescu's Destruction of "Little Paris"* (Bucharest, 2000). For Bulgaria, see John D. Bell, *The Bulgarian Communist Party from Blagoev to Zhivkov* (Stanford, Calif., 1986); for Albania, see James S. O'Donnell, *A Coming of Age: Albania Under Enver Hoxha* (Boulder, Colo., 1999).

On the Polish events, see Lawrence Weschler, *The Passion of Poland* (New York, 1982); Jan Josef Lipski, *KOR: A History of the Workers' Defense Committee in Poland 1976–1985* (Berkeley, Calif., 1985); Timothy Garton Ash, *The Polish Revolution: Solidarity 1980–82* (New York, 1984); and David Ost, *Solidarity and the Politics of Anti-Politics: Opposition and Reform in Poland Since 1968* (Philadelphia, 1990). Solidarity is also discussed in detail by Roman Laba, *The Roots of Solidarity: A Political Sociology of Poland's Working Class* (Princeton, N.J., 1991), and Lawrence Goodwyn, *Breaking the Barrier: The Rise of Solidarity in Poland* (New York, 1991). Idesbald Goddeeris edited a book examining how trade unions in the West supported its nascent and struggling Polish counterpart: *Solidarity with Solidarity: Western European Trade Unions and the Polish Crisis, 1980–1982* (Lanham, Md., 2010). For Pope John Paul II, see Tadeusz Szyma et al., *John Paul II and His Travels Around Poland* (Warsaw, 2002).

For the dissent that took place in the USSR during this time, see Yuri Feofanov, *The Siniavskii-Daniel Trial: A Thirty Year Perspective* (n.p., n.d.). One of the repressive means that the USSR used was to put dissidents into insane asylums. On this technique, see Theresa C. Smith and Thomas A. Oleszczk, *No Asylum: State Psychiatric Repression in the Former USSR* (New York, 1996). As may be imagined, there is plenty of material on Sakharov. Two biographies are Jay Bergman, *Meeting the Demands of Reason: The Life and Thought of Andrei Sakharov* (Ithaca, N.Y., 2009), and Richard Lourie, *Sakharov: A Biography* (Waltham, Mass., 2002). Sakharov published *Memoirs* (New York, 1990).

Vladimir Solovev and Elena Klepikova discuss the immediate background to the Gorbachev era in *Behind the High Kremlin Walls* (New York, 1986). Ed A. Hewett examines the Soviet economy from Khrushchev to Gorbachev in *Reforming the Soviet Economy: Equality versus Efficiency* (Washington, D.C., 1988). Peter H. Juvilier and Hiroshi Kimura look at the early period of his rule in *The Gorbachev Regime: Consolidation to Reform* (New Brunswick, N.J. 2009). David Lane's *Soviet Society Under Perestroika* (Boston, 1990) is a thorough examination of the subject. Archie Brown discusses *Seven Years that Changed the World: Perestroika in Perspective* (New York, 2007). Walter Laqueur focuses on glasnost in *The Long Road to Freedom: Russia and Glasnost* (New York, 1989), while Joseph Gibbs concentrates on the effect on the media: *Gorbachev's Glasnost* (College Station, Tex., 1999). The role of labor policy and the collapse of Gorbachev's reform are analyzed by Donald Filtzer in *Soviet Workers and the Collapse of Perestroika: The Soviet Labour Process and Gorbachev's Reforms* (Cambridge, UK, 1994). Jonathan Harris wrote about how Gorbachev took on the bureaucracy in *Subverting the System: Gorbachev's Reform of the Party's Apparat, 1986–1991* (Lanham, Md., 2004). Foreign relations with the West is analyzed in two books: David H. Shumaker, *Gorbachev and the German Question* (Westport, Conn., 1995), which examines relations with West Germany between 1985 and 1990, and Norman A. Graebner et al., *Reagan, Bush, Gorbachev: Revisiting the End of the Cold War* (Westport, Conn., 2008), which sees the end of the USSR as an unintended consequence of Gorbachev's reforms.

The well-researched biography of Gorbachev, Archie Brown, *The Gorbachev Factor* (New York, 1996), examines his style as well as his politics, while Mark Sandle's *Gorbachev: Man of the Twentieth Century?* (London, 2008) offers a different interpretation. Gorbachev himself spoke out on his policies. Besides his work on Perestroika mentioned in the text, see his *Memoirs* (New York, 1996) and his conversations with an old friend, *Conversations with Gorbachev on Perestroika, the Prague Spring, and the Crossroads of Socialism* (New York, 2002).

✍

CHAPTER 33

The Collapse of Communism

CHAPTER OUTLINE

Why the Dominoes Fell • The Process of Collapse I: Implosion •
The Process of Collapse II: Explosion • The Process of
Collapse III: Russia versus the Soviet Union

BIOGRAPHICAL SKETCHES

Václav Havel, Velvet Revolution • Boris Nikolayevich
Yeltsin, Maverick

In the fall of 1989 most of the Communist regimes of East Europe dissolved, and non-Communist governments replaced them, and in 1991 the Soviet Union disappeared. A generation who were used to thinking that the cold war and Europe's division would last forever gazed upon these events in amazement. The Communist world crumbled in only two years, the culmination of a long and complex process.

WHY THE DOMINOES FELL

During the 1980s, important changes that had shaped developments in Eastern Europe had occurred, as so often in the past, in the West. New, more aggressive leaders who were less willing to tolerate communism—U.S. President Ronald Reagan and British Prime Minister Margaret Thatcher—challenged the USSR during the most serious crisis in its history.

Arms Reductions

President Reagan pushed forward with his Strategic Defense Initiative (SDI or "Star Wars"), spending enormous amounts on weapons research to destroy incoming ballistic missiles. The Soviets tried to convince the Americans to end SDI by toning down the arms race that had occurred in the previous years, but, despite a 1985 agreement on intermediate-range missiles, the Americans refused to drop the program.

Its weak economy prevented the USSR from matching the resources that the Americans poured into the Star Wars program, and Gorbachev believed that the USSR's development and future role as a great power lay in repairing the Soviet Union's economy. The economic vibrancy of Europe and Japan and the spectacular success of small countries like South Korea demonstrated that countries could be extremely successful economically and have influence without being armed to the teeth. Both considerations influenced Gorbachev effectively to withdraw from the arms race.

Gorbachev and Eastern Europe

The economic decline of the USSR also characterized the satellites. During the 1980s, the standards of living and real wages in the satellite states had decreased precipitously. The drop of 17 percent and 15 percent, respectively, in Polish and Hungarian real wages in the 1980s was typical. This rapid decrease demonstrated that communism had structural problems that could not be fixed quickly and would sooner or later provoke disorders in the client states. The USSR would then be forced to repeat the usual pattern of repression and increased contributions of resources to rescue the East European countries. Given its own economic disarray and the falling value of the USSR's major export, oil, the USSR could no longer afford to do either.

In short, the satellites were an intolerable drain on the Soviet economy and hampered Gorbachev's hopes for modernization and economic parity with the West. In forty-five years, the East European regimes had proved themselves incapable of governing with the support of their own people, but now Gorbachev needed the West Europeans and their economic know-how and wanted to cooperate with them on the basis that they all belonged to a "common European home." The West Europeans could never fully cooperate with the USSR if it continued its military domination of Eastern Europe and threatened the West.

At the same time, the strategic assumption, dating from the Bolshevik revolution, that the USSR needed a buffer zone to confront a possible attack by the Western capitalist powers was obsolete by the 1980s. Missiles were the determining factor in any future European war, and buffers were useless. Conversely, the Soviets could not invade the West because their opponents were too strong, so forward positions had lost their value. In short, aggressive wars had become less likely, and defense was best handled through negotiation.

The Abandonment of Eastern Europe

Gorbachev refused to tie a modernizing Soviet Union to the old, hated East European leaders who opposed change. He informed them and their people that communism did not imply rigid uniformity, and the Soviet model became a thing of the past. Gorbachev endorsed democracy and promised to respect whatever road the East Europeans chose, making it clear that the Soviets would no longer intervene to rescue their leaders from their own people, thus abdicating as the policemen of Eastern Europe, or subsidize their economies.

In this way Gorbachev sealed the fate of the leaders in the Soviet satellites who had opposed structural economic reforms, had made their countries uncompetitive, and had proved incapable of winning popular support. The proliferation of information

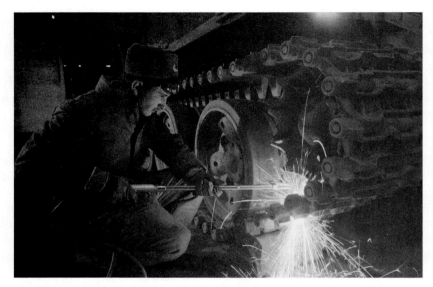

As the Soviet Empire in Eastern Europe collapsed, the Russians withdrew their forces from the areas they had controlled for so long. The withdrawal was phased, but the army did not have enough time to take all of its equipment home. In this picture, a Soviet soldier disassembles a tank on December 5, 1991, before the troops left East Germany for home.

sources and modern means of communication made comparison with other economic systems easy, and the East Europeans concluded that communism had failed. The main culprit was television. East Germans and Czechoslovaks watched West German TV; the Albanians, Italian TV; and the Bulgarians, Turkish TV. The East Europeans could see for themselves the differences in standards of living, and ads for modern products whetted their desire for the material goods they lacked. The fax machine would play an important role in the Polish events that brought down the regime. With the easing of travel restrictions, more East Europeans, especially East Germans, visited the West and returned with videocassettes, audiotapes, and Western values that no government could block.

The Western way of life appealed to East European young people, despite their governments' barrage against capitalism and "fascism" that the young people thought of as boring propaganda. Youths liked freedom of expression, and, with Gorbachev, it was possible to discuss once-prohibited topics.

Increasing Dissatisfaction

These once-prohibited subjects included religion, and the last days of the Soviet Empire witnessed a rise in the popularity of different faiths. Another important topic was history. Because the Communists had distorted the history of the Eastern Europe states to conform to Communist ideology, the young yearned for an accurate account of the past by seeking out eyewitnesses or participants in events that preceded the Soviet era. Meaningful anniversaries, such as those of the revolutions of 1848 and 1956 in Hungary, the anniversary of a resister's death in Czechoslovakia, or the feast day of a saint, sparked anti-Soviet manifestations.

Eastern Europe and the USSR also had green movements that damaged the regimes' reputation. The Communists had abused nature to a degree unheard of in the West through rapid industrialization and mammoth projects that poisoned the rivers and the atmosphere. The Chernobyl disaster was only the most visible sign of shameful incompetence that devastated large areas of the Soviet Union and Eastern Europe as dozens of unsafe nuclear power plants continued to operate. In one Bulgarian city, the breast cancer rate rose from 965 per hundred thousand in 1975 to 17,386 per hundred thousand in ten years. In large areas of Eastern Europe, children had intolerably high levels of lead in their blood, food was contaminated with heavy metals, miscarriage rates were high, and life expectancy was significantly below West European standards.

In the Czechoslovakian industrial and coal region of Bohemia, acid rain and strip mining destroyed the fields and forests. During the 1980s, a Czechoslovak report stated that 60 percent of the forests were dying. In Hungary, the figure was

After the Soviets withdrew from Eastern Europe the extent of the environmental disaster caused by Communist industrial policy became clear. Communist regimes had favored heavy industry for ideological and strategic reasons without giving a thought to the damage it would do to the environment or taking any measures to abate it. This picture shows the heavy industrial smoke and soot caused by a Romanian factory burning hydrocarbons to manufacture inks and paints and needed by the tire industry.

30 percent, and in Bulgaria, 34 percent. In Poland, 95 percent of the river water was found unfit for human consumption; the figures were 80 percent for Romania and 70 percent for Czechoslovakia. In the infamous "black town" of Copsa Mica in Romania, soot from a nearby chemical plant coated everything so that it appeared dipped in ink. In 1991 a study indicated that East Germany poured more sulfur into the air than any other country and that to bring it up to West German standards would require $125 billion. Other studies warned of the death of the Black Sea if current pollution rates continued. These environmental catastrophes touched off demonstrations and protests and were the most visible failure of Communist rule.

THE PROCESS OF COLLAPSE I: IMPLOSION

The process that ended communism was accompanied by remarkably little violence, although some did occur. In general, the countries that were most highly industrialized or had strong national traditions broke away from communism with the least disruption.

The Polish Breakthrough

Poland's banning of Solidarity and imposition of martial law failed to reestablish the government's authority, and Solidarity's appeal for the people remained a powerful attraction despite its dissolution. Jaruzelski hoped for a truce and, between 1982 and 1984, ended martial law and declared an amnesty, but in October 1984, the police kidnapped and murdered Father Jerzy Populielusko, a popular priest who was a critic of the government. Populielusko's murder increased opposition, exacerbated tensions with the Catholic Church, and heightened tensions with the Polish people.

Solidarity condemned the government when it pressed for price increases and called for a boycott of parliamentary elections. The frustrated government arrested Lech Walesa and then dropped the charges and tried conciliation with no result. In 1988, the union called new strikes and protests against yet another attempt to raise prices. Solidarity won a big victory when the Parliament voted no confidence in the government, and a new reformist cabinet headed by Mieczyslaw Rakowski was formed. Rakowski also became first secretary of the Communist Party and made considerable changes in the party leadership. In 1989 the revamped party opened direct talks with Solidarity through roundtable discussions, with the church playing a major role behind the scenes by supporting Solidarity and favoring democracy

In early April, the talks concluded with a breathtaking series of agreements that included the legalization of Solidarity, full rights to the Catholic Church, and a bicameral legislature. In June, new elections were held, in which half the seats were contested, practically all of which Solidarity won. The government had no choice by to accept this grave defeat.

When the Parliament convened in July, it elected Jaruzelski president as a guarantee to the Soviet Union and to the Polish army, but everyone understood that he owed his election to Solidarity. The Soviets made no move to intervene. Despite this compromise, however, Solidarity held fast on the composition of a new government, and two months later, the different political forces reached agreement on a new cabinet guided by Solidarity militant Tadeusz Mazowiecki.

Once in power, Mazowiecki dismantled the Communist system by abrogating the party's leading role and by restoring the free market. Poland then declared itself a republic that was non-Communist.

The Hungarian Establishment Gives In

Unlike Poland, the Communist Party in Hungary (officially, the Hungarian Socialist Workers' Party) took a leading role in making similar changes. The Hungarian opposition staged massive demonstrations that marked important anniversaries and protested the government's domestic and foreign policies. In 1985 the party leadership allowed limited contests in parliamentary elections, but because Hungary's foreign policy had provoked a Soviet invasion in 1956, the Hungarians were careful to combine domestic freedom with their commitments to the USSR. Within the party, the reformists won a seesaw battle with the conservatives.

In 1988 this victory set the scene for movement away from communism, which had become extremely unpopular because of the privileges enjoyed by the Communist elite. The standard of living for ordinary Hungarians continued to decline, especially for older people on pensions and for young people who were entering the workforce. For example, a pair of women's boots cost $64, and the average monthly wage was $140. After their victory in 1988, the Communist reformists strengthened market forces and permitted the political opposition to organize itself, and in 1989, the Hungarian party renounced its guiding role in politics and society and allowed the establishment of a multiparty system. The party gave in to popular pressure and allowed a reexamination of the 1956 uprising and acknowledged its illegal repression, implying that the governments that had ruled from 1956 to 1989 lacked legitimacy. The party agreed that the cabinet should be responsible to Parliament, not to the Party, and opened negotiations with the opposition to discuss further constitutional reforms.

In June 1989, the government took the extraordinary symbolic step of rehabilitating Imre Nagy and reinterred his remains in an honored grave, and large crowds of Hungarians and international representatives attended the emotional ceremony. In September the Communist party split, and Communist organizations—the youth movement, workers' militia, and factory cells—dissolved. The ongoing roundtable talks instituted free elections, direct election of the president, and a constitutional court, and the state renamed itself the Hungarian Republic.

Absorption of the GDR

Hungarian events put pressure on the next domino: the GDR. East German leader Erich Honecker opposed economic and political reforms on the Gorbachev model, which his people favored. Although the GDR was in better shape than the other Soviet satellites, its massive debt (about $12 billion in 1981) prevented its recovery without reforms or support from the USSR. But Honecker rejected reform, and, on a trip to East Germany in October 1989, Gorbachev publicly warned Honecker to adapt to the new situation as East Germans cheered him.

Honecker's resistance eventually brought him down. The Hungarians offered asylum to GDR citizens and opened their border with Austria, prompting hundreds of thousands of East Germans to travel to Hungary and then cross into the

West, exacerbating the traditional hemorrhage of East Germany's skilled workers. Honecker's rejection of demands to enter into roundtable discussions similar to those of Poland and Hungary lost him the support of the USSR, his people, and his party, and in early October 1989, the fortieth anniversary of the GDR's founding, events precipitated. Massive demonstrations occurred in Berlin, Dresden, and Leipzig. As Honecker prepared a bloodbath by sending in the police, the Communist Party (SED), members of the Politburo, and Gorbachev stopped him.

Honecker resigned and was replaced by a former protégé. Egon Krenz, determined to save the GDR, found that he had arrived too late. On November 8, the entire Politburo resigned, and on November 9, the Berlin Wall was opened, and the East Germans poured into West Berlin. The party promised economic and political reform; instituted a new government that opened roundtable talks with an opposition organization, *Neues Forum;* and scheduled free elections for March 1990. However, at this point, the pressure for reunification with the Western part of Germany became irresistible, with the Federal Republic's Chancellor Helmut Kohl skillfully guiding the reunification campaign. Making excellent use of West Germany's economic superiority, Kohl promised to exchange the worthless East German currency on a one-to-one basis with the valuable West German mark, an offer the East Germans could not resist. In the March elections, the pro-unity parties won a decisive victory, and on October 3, 1990, Germany formally reunited. The question of Soviet troops stationed in the former GDR was resolved by negotiating a gradual withdrawal.

German reunification brought many difficulties. The former GDR's state-run economy was obsolete, and the Federal Republic had to confront a flood of half a

With the end of communism came the end of its symbols. East German citizens, mostly young people, gathered at the Berlin Wall in November 1989 and tore it down piece by piece. This picture shows the ignominious end of what had become the most recognizable Communist symbol of repression.

Reunited Germany. During the Cold War, it was common to hear that Germany would never be reunited. This was not only because the Soviets would never allow it but because, looking back on the history of the twentieth century, Germany's neighbors and Europe feared the power of a reunited state. Instead, with the end of communism, reunification came with breathtaking speed. Europeans assumed that the efficient Germans would quickly resolve the economic and social problems connected with piecing together the West with the formerly Communist East, which lacked not only a modern infrastructure but a modern entrepreneurial mentality. In the short run, reunification presented formidable problems, but Europeans still were wary of possible German dominance.

million East Germans within a year. Only financial assistance from Bonn temporarily prevented East German companies from closing and causing massive unemployment. As it was, unemployment and underemployment soared to an effective rate of over 20 percent in 1990, particularly affecting women, compared with a 2.5 percent unemployment rate in the West. Reunification initially caused mutual resentment. Most East Germans were not sufficiently trained for work in the West and resented the economic difficulties they faced with a lower level of social security than they had become used to in the East, while the West Germans considered the East Germans lazy and resented the money they had to pay for relief and to bring the former East Germany up to Western standards.

The "Velvet Revolution"

At first, Czechoslovakia seemed unaffected by the dramatic developments in the Communist world. In the 1980s, only the activities of Charter 77 and, increasingly, the Roman Catholic Church contested the oppressive regime. In 1987 Miloš Jakeš replaced Husák, but changes did not come until 1989.

The opposition's technique was to demonstrate during important anniversaries that could be interpreted as anti-Soviet events and that would rattle the regime. Such anniversaries-with-demonstrations in 1989 were the twentieth anniversary of the death of Jan Palach, a youth who had burned himself to protest the Soviet invasion; the twenty-first anniversary of the Soviet invasion in August; and the seventy-first anniversary of the foundation of an independent Czechoslovakia in October. Demonstrations by scientists and environmentalists also occurred, while yet another form of antigovernment activity was the signing of petitions that opposed the government's policies.

The regime fought back by arresting Václav Havel and other Charter 77 members and by attacking protesters during rallies, but these moves failed. Havel and

The "Velvet Revolution" is the name given to the Czechoslovak revolution against the Communist regime, one of the most rigid and obstinate in Eastern Europe. Once the weakness of the regime was exposed and it was clear that Soviet military help was not forthcoming, the regime could not withstand the wrath of the people. This picture shows one of the widespread demonstrations against the government in Prague that made up the revolution between November 23 and December 10, 1989.

other dissidents circulated a petition for the democratization of Czechoslovakia that received 40,000 signatures. Journalists petitioned for the release of colleagues who had been arrested and formed an independent association. Catholic Church officials spoke out against the regime, and religious ceremonies attracted crowds that supported the opposition. In the midst of this great flood of popular condemnation, there suddenly appeared signs of a softening of the police's harsh stance and some talk of concessions. Rumors flew about a conspiracy of reformist Czechoslovak Communists and Gorbachev emissaries to replace Jakeš. In late November, large-scale demonstrations broke out after unconfirmed reports of the death of a student, and the government opened talks with two new opposition groups representing the Czech and the Slovak parts of the state: Civic Forum and Public Against Violence.

At this point, changes occurred with breathtaking speed. On November 24, the government and entire party leadership resigned: Czechoslovak communism just crumbled. A transition government appeared, but the Civic Forum and public opinion were in no mood to accept any compromise that would permit Communists to lead a new cabinet. At the same time, news arrived from Moscow that the countries that had participated in the 1968 invasion would repudiate their action, destroying the legitimacy of the postinvasion administrations as had happened in Hungary. On December 10, a new government that included a majority of non-Communists took power. In addition, President Husák resigned, and Havel was elected to replace him. At the beginning of 1990, the government dismantled the Communist system, released political prisoners, and encouraged exiles to return. It made plans to reintroduce the free market and transformed Czechoslovakia into a federative republic. The process of disengaging from communism had gone so smoothly that the world referred to it as the Velvet Revolution.

BIOGRAPHICAL SKETCHES

Václav Havel
Velvet Revolution

Václav Havel illustrates the problems of former bourgeois and intellectuals in the Communist states. He was born into a wealthy family in Prague on October 5, 1936, but the Havels lost their possessions and businesses after the Communist takeover in 1948. Because Havel was a member of the bourgeoisie, the Communist regime made it difficult for him to get an education and forced him to leave school at age 15. Although he worked hard as a lab technician, he attended night school to complete his education and eventually went to the Prague Academy of Arts. After army service, he took a job as a stagehand in the capital.

Havel began writing early but attracted attention with the production of plays in the 1960s:*The Garden Party* (1963), *The Memorandum* (1965), and *Increased Difficulty of Concentration* (1968). During the Prague Spring, several of his plays opened in the United States, and he traveled there. After the Soviet invasion of August 1968, his work was banned, although he continued to write and circulate his writings clandestinely.

Havel resisted the Stalinist-inspired regime that ruled Czechoslovakia following the invasion. He became one of the country's most famous dissidents and helped found human rights organizations, the most famous of which was Charter

continued

continued

77, which united different opposition factions. The catalyst for its formation was the arrest by the government of a rock band, the Plastic People of the Universe, in March 1976. The aim of Charter 77, so called because its declaration was dated January 1, 1977, was "resisting the lie" (that is, not to remain silent against the regime's repressive actions). Thanks to the efforts of Havel and his comrades, many more people adhered to the principles enunciated in the declaration. The government jailed Havel for his activities from January to April 1977, and in October of the same year, he received a suspended sentence for his dissident activities. In October 1979, Havel was again arrested, but by then, he had international support. The government released him because he had a severe medical condition and because it was unwilling to face the international criticism if Havel died in prison. However, jail and governmental persecution failed to stop Havel's activities favoring democracy and human rights.

In January 1989, Havel was again arrested for his activities in antigovernment demonstrations, but by now the Communist government was in its last year of life. In the midst of nationwide demonstrations in November, Havel participated in the founding of the Civic Forum, a coalition of groups opposing the government. It was under Havel's leadership that Civic Forum engineered the downfall of the Communist government with a minimum of violence—the so-called Velvet Revolution.

On December 29, 1989, Václav Havel became president of Czechoslovakia. He traveled to Europe and the United States, where he addressed a joint session of Congress, and, as he continued to do, answered questions from students. In the meantime, old tensions between the Czechs and Slovaks drove them toward separation despite Havel's attempts to prevent the breakup. On July 3, 1992, Havel failed to win a second term when Slovak deputies in the Federal Assembly did not vote for him. On January 1, the Czechs and Slovaks established separate republics—an action known as the Velvet Divorce. On January 26, Havel won election as president of the Czech Republic.

Havel's enormous personal prestige greatly benefited his country. Despite health problems, Havel traveled widely and was instrumental in the acceptance of his country into NATO and in the discussions for entrance into the EU. On another issue, after World War II the Czechs had brutally expelled the Sudeten Germans and confiscated their property. Sudeten German organizations demanded the repeal of the decrees implementing the measures, still in effect, on the grounds of incompatibility with EU membership. Havel's moderation helped to confront this major international question that threatened relations with Germany. Havel, a heavy smoker who suffered from lung cancer, died on December 18, 2011.

End of Communist Rule in Bulgaria

In Bulgaria, Zhivkov had attempted a series of reforms that would bring market socialism to the country, but they were unsuccessful, and the Bulgarian economy remained known for its shoddy products. After 1985 Gorbachev's reforms in the USSR sparked protests in Bulgaria that Zhivkov could not control.

The government attempted to strengthen its hold by ramping up Bulgarian nationalism by such means as a campaign to Bulgarianize the Turkish minority by attacking its Muslim religious practices, forcing name changes, and proscribing the Turkish language. The Turkish minority resisted and found support among the Bulgarian majority, and the attempt stimulated the organization of more opposition groups supporting Gorbachev's reforms. Widespread strikes and agitation followed, prompting the Bulgarian Communist Party (BCP) to remove Zhivkov from power on November 10, 1989.

Under the weight of the collapsing Communist world, this move had little effect. Massive demonstrations resulted in a new cabinet that ended the party's dominant role and sanctioned political diversity. In December several opposition groups united under an umbrella group called the Union of Democratic Forces (UDF), led by Zhelyu Zhelev, and in early 1990 roundtable discussions began. The negotiations produced agreements on free elections and a constituent assembly. In preparation for the voting, the BCP changed its name to the Bulgarian Socialist Party (BSP), keeping its infrastructure intact. This advantage allowed it to win a majority in the election but not to permit it to rule. Demonstrations forced a BSP cabinet to resign in November and its replacement by a government that guided the delicate process of writing a new constitution that was published in July 1991. The Bulgarian situation continued to be unsteady, but the Communists no longer ruled.

THE PROCESS OF COLLAPSE II: EXPLOSION

Bulgaria represented an intermediate stage in the transition of the former satellites to postcommunism and independence. In Romania, Yugoslavia, and Albania the process was a violent one.

The Fall of Ceausescu

Romania under Ceausescu and his wife went from bad to worse during the 1980s. Sporadic outbursts of violence became more serious at the end of the decade and spread to Transylvania when the government began a campaign against the ethnic Hungarians there. The disorders did not initially threaten Ceausescu's power because the "Conducator" (Leader) beefed up the dreaded *Securitate* (secret police) and increased his reliance on relatives to help him rule. It was difficult to keep Romania isolated, however, because Ceausescu's policies won him international condemnation, and he had no domestic support.

Ceausescu had ruined the Romanian economy by attempting to transform Romania into a major exporter of refined petroleum and engaging in massive borrowing and huge building projects. In order to reverse the effects of these errors, he instituted an austerity program that resulted in food shortages, fuel rationing, and a cut in electricity. In social policy, his plans to increase Romania's population from 23 million in 1966 to 30 million by 2000 drove him to declare the fetus state property and to prohibit sex education, contraception, and abortion. The government investigated women who had not had children and imposed a special tax on them that ranged up to 10 percent of their salaries. At first, the birthrate doubled, but inadequate natal care endangered both women and children. The infant mortality rate skyrocketed to 83 per thousand (compared to less than 10 per thousand for West European women). Women were so desperate not to have children that

Not all the revolutions against the Soviet regimes in Eastern Europe were bloodless. Romanian dictator Nicolae Ceaucescu fought against the revolution against communism and the battle between his supporters and the people is estimated to have caused thousands of deaths. Ceaucescu was captured and executed with his wife on December 25, 1989, to prevent further resistance by the former regime. The bodies were shown on television, from which this picture of the executed dictator is taken.

they resorted to illegal abortions, and Western sources estimated that 60 percent of all pregnancies ended in miscarriage or abortion.

Ceausescu rejected the changes that Gorbachev's policies had set in motion and hoped to lead the forces that were opposed to them. In December 1989, disturbances began in Timisoara, the Hungarian part of Romania, where ethnic tensions ran high. The disturbances were touched off by the case of László Tőkés, a Protestant pastor who had come under police pressure to leave his parish because of antigovernment activities. Tőkés refused and gained widespread support that turned into antigovernmental demonstrations demanding the end of communism and free elections. On December 16, the army was called out and fired on the people, killing hundreds and perhaps thousands of unarmed civilians. The Timisoara revolts had the support of all sectors of the population—blue- and white-collar workers, university and secondary school students, intellectuals, peasants who flocked into the city to fight the government, and the different ethnic groups—and spread to the capital Bucharest on December 21. Ceausescu called out the army again, but this time the soldiers joined the demonstrators.

A full-fledged revolution then broke out, with gun battles between the army and the *Securitate* raging in the capital and in other cities over the next two days, a brief, bloody civil war claiming thousands of lives. Ceausescu and his wife were captured on Christmas Day and, after a summary trial, were shot, and their bodies were exhibited on television.

By now, reformist Communists had formed the National Salvation Front (NSF), and its head, Ion Iliescu, an old Communist and a former Ceausescu protégé, became president of the country. A transition cabinet took power and abolished the hated *Securitate*. In May 1990, the NSF won new elections by utilizing the old Communist bureaucracy and apparatus that still remained intact. Their continued strength indicated that the ex-Communists remained a powerful force that the country could not shake loose and provoked new protests in Timisoara and elsewhere. Iliescu's policies caused concern, for example, in his use of miners from outside Bucharest to put down striking students in June 1990. Elections in 1992 saw the NSF's support drop and a political trend toward an umbrella organization of democratic forces. Romania's revolution had produced a multiparty system, but Iliescu still held the presidency.

The Breakup of Yugoslavia

Ethnic divisions in Romania did not threaten the country's unity, but in Yugoslavia they exploded and provoked a series of bloody conflicts. The ethnic and religious divisions that had plagued Yugoslavia since its foundation in 1919 emerged in different forms when economic conditions and a series of scandals provoked rioting and strikes against the government in 1988. The Croats and the Slovenes believed that communism favored the centralizing Serbs, while the Serbs argued that the Yugoslav Federation worked against their interests and in favor of their richer associates. Ideological disputes over decentralization masked these national and religious tensions between the Catholic Croats; the Muslims in Bosnia, Herzegovina, and Kosovo; and the Eastern Orthodox Serbs. The inability to resolve these issues made it impossible to amalgamate the different groups into a working whole.

With Tito's death in 1980, the presidency that he had held revolved among representatives of the different areas, further weakening the center. In 1989, Slobodan Milosevic was elected the president of Serbia. A strong populist and Serbian

Ethnic Groups in Yugoslavia, 1991

ETHNIC GROUP	PERCENTAGE
Serbians	36
Croatians	20
Bosnians (Muslim)	9
Slovenes	8
Albanians	8
Macedonians	6
Montenegrins	3
Hungarians	2
Others	8

SOURCE: From Dennis Sherman and Joyce Salisbury, *The West in the World* (Boston: McGraw-Hill, 2001), p. 839.

nationalist, Milosevic became prominent in April 1987 when he declared that the Serbs in Kosovo should retain their rights in the primarily ethnic Albanian region after they had accused the Albanians of atrocities. In September, Milosevic eliminated the influence of moderate "Titoists" who had downplayed Serbian claims to Kosovo. He then purged the staffs of important newspapers that had provided a balanced coverage of disputes between the Serbs and Albanians in Kosovo. During the next year, Milosevic's supporters gained the upper hand in several Yugoslav states through demonstrations that went under the collective name of the

The Breakup of Yugoslavia. The Balkans, the area that caused the most trouble in Europe at the beginning of the twentieth century, also caused the most at the end. Hoping to form a united country, Serb nationalists lit the spark that touched off World War I. At the end of that conflict, they created a state whose ethnic components were always at odds and threatened to tear it apart. During World War II, the Axis broke Yugoslavia into different parts. During the postwar era, the political genius of Tito kept the country together, but it began falling apart soon after his death. By the end of the century, bloody ethnic and religious wars raged in the area, bringing unspeakable atrocities and international complications in their wake.

"anti-bureaucratic revolution" (bureaucrats who supposedly did not reflect the will of the people), and his victories set the stage for an escalation of the Kosovo question.

Tito had shrewdly granted Kosovo wide powers, but the Serb residents of the area constantly complained about maltreatment by the majority Albanians. In 1988 and 1989, when unrest broke out in the province, Milosevic increased his legal control and sent in troops. In September 1989, Serbia officially incorporated Kosovo, setting off protests by its Albanian inhabitants. In the meantime, problems with Croatia and Slovenia increased, and the regions moved toward greater autonomy as they suspected Milosevic's motives and Serb expansionism. The Kosovo crisis helped communism to survive in Serbia, under a different name and in alliance with Serb nationalism, despite its renunciation in the breakaway regions. During the next several months, the major institutions that were attempting to preserve unity, including the Federal Bank, the Yugoslav Communist League, and the Federal Presidency, broke down either because of scandal or political maneuvering.

In late 1989 and early 1990, both Slovenia and Croatia declared full independence, dismantled the Communist system, and installed non-Communist parties in their governments. These two states and Serbia announced new constitutions signaling the de facto demise of the Yugoslav Federation. Trouble also brewed between the Serbs living in other parts of the federation who had Milosevic's support and the states in which they constituted a once-powerful minority.

With Slovenia and Croatia constituting their own military forces while Serbia dominated the Yugoslav army, the stage was set for a bloody struggle. On June 25, Croatia and Slovenia declared full independence from the federation. The next day the Yugoslav army attacked, but failed to subdue the two fledgling states. Yugoslav forces abandoned Slovenia and eventually agreed to a truce in Croatia. By then, however, the fighting had spread to other parts of the former Yugoslavia where Milosevic's forces practiced their odious ethnic cleansing—the mass murder of minorities and the raping of their women. At the close of the century, the situation remained volatile despite the international community's attempts to calm it, and Yugoslavia was in the process of breaking up into five independent states.

The Last Bastion

Unlike Yugoslavia, during the 1970s and 1980s Albania remained isolated despite some broadening of its international relations and trade. Its politics continued to be bizarre, with the probable murder of a prime minister at the hands of his Communist comrades during a meeting. In April 1985, longtime leader Hoxha died, but his replacement followed his line. The Albanian Labor Party (Communist) opposed the events that Gorbachev's accession had unleashed and hoped to remain unaffected by them, but in late 1989 and early 1990, riots and the army intervened to end them.

These disorders forced the ruling party to make some concessions, but they provoked more rioting in the capital, Tirana, and other cities during the summer, fall, and winter. Albanians fled the country in droves, flooding foreign embassies and storming leaky boats to make the short but dangerous trip to the Adriatic coast of Italy. In December 1990, the government responded to rioting students by adopting a new constitution that allowed multiparty democracy and sweeping economic changes. These changes remained largely a dead letter because of the continued strength of the Communist Party, renamed the Socialist Party of Albania. In elections held in March 1991, ex-Communists won a victory and delayed Albania's move toward democracy. The meaning of that term, at any rate, was doubtful, given the country's extreme poverty and severe food shortages. Disorders proliferated, and large parts of the country slipped from the government's control. New elections in March 1992 gave the victory to the country's democratic forces led by Sali Berisha, and the Communists were dislodged from power with Berisha as president and the installation of a non-Communist cabinet.

Despite this political progress, Albanian conditions remained appalling. In January 1996, new disorders, provoked by confidence schemes, necessitated the intervention of a European force led by Italy to stem the tide of violence, provide humanitarian relief, and set the scene for new elections. The force left in 1997, but Albania still remained dependent on foreign help for survival.

The withdrawal of the USSR from Eastern Europe had enormous ramifications. The countries with stronger economic and national traditions managed to exit the long Communist experiment with a minimum of violence. The countries that had weaker economies and, ironically, that had been less dependent on the Soviet Union struggled to enter the new order successfully.

THE PROCESS OF COLLAPSE III: RUSSIA VERSUS THE SOVIET UNION

Changes in Soviet policy allowed the East Europeans to destroy communism in their countries; although inconceivable and unintended, the progress of perestroika also destroyed the USSR.

The Progress of Democratization

Between 1987 and 1989, perestroika and glasnost ruptured the structure that held the USSR together and, although unintended, caused its collapse. The consequences of allowing citizens to question the Communist establishment, to form opposition parties, and to engage in free elections ended the legally decreed guiding role of the Communist Party of the Soviet Union (CPSU). The party's members abandoned it en masse and brought about a political struggle between the people and the party, which lost because it no longer had force to back it up.

The Soviet Union lacked a democratic tradition, which meant that two significant factors determined the outcome of the battle. Mikhail Gorbachev held his posts thanks to election by the party leadership, not the people. Because of the introduction of freely contested elections, this lack made him vulnerable in a struggle with leaders who were directly elected by them. In the fight that was brewing, the major questions were whether the party, the army, and other entrenched interests would stand idly by while popular intervention destroyed their power and privileges and whether Gorbachev would eventually turn to force to save himself.

Gorbachev's major rival in a context in which elections were important was Boris Yeltsin, a Communist official from Sverdlovsk whom Gorbachev had previously humiliated because of their differences. Outside the party, however, Yeltsin and his friends, the democrats, favored introduction in Russia and the USSR of a Western-style, multiparty liberal democracy and market economy. The democrats originated in July 1989 when perestroika and glasnost favored demands for new freedoms for intellectuals, the freedom to strike, workers' demands for improved conditions, and a desire for independence within the Baltic states (Lithuania, Latvia, and Estonia). In March 1989, elections had been held for a new USSR Congress of People's Deputies (parliament), and Yeltsin and his supporters won by a landslide. When the Congress met in May and June, a pro-democracy faction calling itself the Interregional Group (IRG) emerged. Gorbachev opposed this move because of the group's program of rapid change.

BIOGRAPHICAL SKETCHES

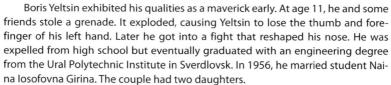

Boris Nikolayevich Yeltsin
Maverick

Boris Yeltsin, who presided over the dissolution of the Soviet Union, was born in the Sverdlovsk region of the USSR on February 1, 1931. His mother was a seamstress and his father a peasant convicted of anti-Soviet crimes during the Stalinist era who spent three years in a labor camp and then went into construction.

Boris Yeltsin exhibited his qualities as a maverick early. At age 11, he and some friends stole a grenade. It exploded, causing Yeltsin to lose the thumb and forefinger of his left hand. Later he got into a fight that reshaped his nose. He was expelled from high school but eventually graduated with an engineering degree from the Ural Polytechnic Institute in Sverdlovsk. In 1956, he married student Naina Iosofovna Girina. The couple had two daughters.

Yeltsin joined the Communist Party only in 1961, quickly rising in its ranks after he began full-time party work in 1968. He became a member of the party's Central Committee in 1981 and later backed Gorbachev's reforms. In 1985, Gorbachev made him secretary for construction and later first secretary of the Moscow City Party Committee—equivalent to mayor.

In supporting Gorbachev's new course, Yeltsin pledged to end excessive bureaucracy and corruption in the city. He ordered the arrest of hundreds of corrupt officials and called for the end of privileges for party members. Yeltsin mingled with ordinary citizens, riding buses and suddenly showing up at factories and stores in order to note the deficiencies of city services and to get them corrected with a minimum of red tape. His bluntness earned him many enemies, but the Communist maverick did not seem to care.

By 1987, Yeltsin had become impatient with the pace of Gorbachev's reforms and said so publicly in an outspoken speech to the Central Committee on October 21. He criticized the party hierarchy and resigned his posts in the organization. In retaliation, Gorbachev removed him as mayor, but the move backfired because people began questioning Gorbachev's commitment to perestroika. Yeltsin's removal produced popular demonstrations in his favor, and Yeltsin refused to keep quiet despite his firing. The official press ignored him, but he attracted international attention through explosive interviews given to foreign reporters. Elected to the Supreme Soviet of the Russian Federative Republic by a landslide, he resigned

continued

continued

from the Communist Party upon his election as its speaker. On June 12, 1991, he became the first elected president of the Russian Federation. In August he was the prime mover in defeating a Communist coup and, in December, the Soviet Union's dissolution.

Contrary to expectations, Yeltsin's two terms as Russian president after the collapse of communism were failures. Yeltsin tried to move Russia toward a free-market economy too quickly, creating havoc and causing the rapid decline of the ruble. In December 1994, he sent troops to quell rebel Chechnya, but they were unable to do so. He clashed with the United States in 1995 over Western intervention in the Balkans. He brought in American "spin doctors" and pollsters to win the 1996 presidential election. He had heart problems and many other ailments that took him out of public life for long periods. His behavior became bizarre: He drank heavily, danced with miniskirted young women, fired four prime ministers in eighteen months, and would not end an audience with Pope John Paul II (he shouted, "Holy Father, we haven't finished yet"). His last days in office were rife with charges of corruption against him and his family.

Ever the maverick, Yeltsin shocked the world by announcing on December 31, 1999, that he was resigning and appointing his politically unknown prime minister as acting president. He bowed out with an apology for "our unfulfilled dreams" and for being unable to make the leap from "the gloomy and stagnant totalitarian past to a bright, prosperous and civilized future at just one go." Yeltsin died on April 23, 2007.

In late July, the IRG formally organized itself and announced its program. It hoped to lead the transition from totalitarianism to democracy by instituting a multiparty system, granting freedom for citizens to establish organizations and associations, and abolishing the CPSU's monopoly on power. The program called for a market economy that, in practice, meant the radical decentralization of state property and economic independence for the individual republics and regions making up the USSR. In fact, the democrats were most powerful in the core republics of the USSR, as may be seen by its composition. Most IRG deputies, 286 of 388, came from the Russian Republic (officially, the Russian Soviet Federated Socialist Republic, RSFSR), while the second largest number, 48, came from the Ukraine. The desire of the IRG for autonomy blossomed into independence under the pressure of events and broke up the Soviet Union.

Struggle for Power

The RSFSR included two-thirds of the USSR's population and was its largest state. In the three-way power struggle among the Communist conservatives, Gorbachev and his supporters (the "center"), and Yeltsin's democratic left, the focus was the control of Russia. Yeltsin won this battle thanks to the support of the Russian populace. Alarmed at where his own policies were leading, Gorbachev shifted to the right in order to fight Yeltsin, but did not resort to military means when it became clear that only force could suppress the democracy movement and save the USSR.

Besides Russia, other parts of the Soviet Union had important roles in its demise in 1991. Gorbachev's policies unleashed nationalist fervor and anger against the USSR in the Baltic republics, which had been independent between World Wars I and II had been absorbed by the USSR as the result of Stalin's 1939 deal with Hitler. With glasnost, the release of a secret protocol to the nonaggression pact that spelled out the terms of the deal put the legitimacy of the Soviet annexation in doubt. Below the surface, resentment smoldered because of Stalin's mass deportations after World War II and the Soviet attempt to flood the Baltic states with Russian speakers in order to dilute their national compositions. In his attempt to win acceptance for perestroika, Gorbachev had set up popular fronts to support it in the Baltic (and other) republics, but these fronts instead favored increased nationalism. In the summer of 1987 in Estonia, the first signs of protest against the forced incorporation of the Baltic states had appeared, grew and grew steadily, and culminated on August 23, 1989, when citizens formed a human chain across all three republics. By 1988, popular fronts favoring secession had formed in all three countries, and similar events occurred in Russia and the Ukraine.

The Soviet Union threatened to break apart in the Caucasus and Central Asia as well. Ethnic tensions exploded between the Armenians and the Azerbaijani in 1988 and 1989 over border issues that left hundreds dead and forced Moscow to dispatch troops. After shootings that killed an estimated 300 people in January 1990, the Azerbaijan Supreme Soviet called for the withdrawal of Soviet soldiers. In April 1989, Soviet troops killed 30 and wounded 200 in putting down a peaceful demonstration in the Georgian capital of Tbilisi, and in July thousands of marchers demanded an end to Russian domination. Rioting necessitating military intervention also took place in Tajikistan in February 1990.

In August 1989, Gorbachev tried to weaken Russian nationalism by suggesting that the RSFSR be split up into five separate areas, or proto-states, but succeeded only in strengthening it. Yeltsin hoped to capture control of Russia through popular elections and implement the democratic program of the IRG (as outlined by the IRG, which had transformed itself into an umbrella organization for democratic forces called Democratic Russia). In March 1989 Yeltsin won election to the USSR Congress of People's Deputies with 90 percent of the vote, and the next year won 84 percent of the vote as a deputy to the RSFSR Congress (parliament), despite dirty tricks by the KGB and plots to kill him. On May 29, 1990, Yeltsin was then elected president of that body.

At a press conference, Yeltsin stated that Russia must become sovereign and have its own domestic legislation and foreign policies. He promised that Russia would recognize a free Lithuania, which had recently declared its independence and which Gorbachev denied. Asked what would be the role of the union, Yeltsin's answer was defense and security, but many Yeltsin supporters favored bringing all military, KGB, and other armed forces on Russian territory under Russian, not union, control. Two weeks later, parliament voted to favor Russian sovereignty, and in July the Ukraine and Belarus did the same. Eventually, fifteen independent republics emerged from the USSR.

The battle for the Soviet Union was not yet over because Gorbachev had the option of using military force. In January 1991, Gorbachev ordered military actions in the Baltic republics that resulted in a number of deaths. Yeltsin saw these events as preparation for a coup against him, defended the republics, appealed to Russian

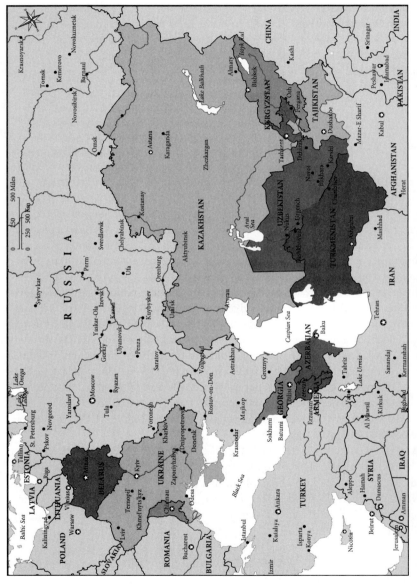

The loose "Confederation of Independent States" replaced the USSR on December 8, 1991. It has very little political or economic importance.

soldiers stationed in the Baltic not to shoot, and suggested that Russia should have its own army. The struggle moved in an ominous direction because while Gorbachev had control of the military and police apparatus, polls indicated that 90 percent of the population favored Yeltsin. In a televised debate, Yeltsin accused Gorbachev of refusing to grant Russian independence and requested his resignation. In late February, massive pro-Yeltsin demonstrations took place, and in March Yeltsin delivered a major pro-democracy speech that brought out a great number of supporters. On March 28 a showdown took place between Yeltsin and Gorbachev when 50,000 heavily armed troops surrounded 500,000 peaceful pro-democracy demonstrators in Moscow who had defied a ban on demonstrations. The people asked the troops: "If they order you to shoot, will you?" Gorbachev pulled back.

In June 1991, Yeltsin ran for president of Russia. Gorbachev attempted to stop him by encouraging the fielding of many candidates to make it impossible for Yeltsin to achieve the 50 percent vote required for a first-ballot victory, but Yeltsin won over 57 percent of the vote. Gorbachev had lost the battle and agreed that a treaty uniting the different republics on a new basis should be negotiated and signed on August 20, 1991.

On Christmas Day 1991, the Union of Soviet Socialist Republics ceased its existence and the new Russian flag flew over the dome of the Kremlin.

The Coup d'État

The Communist conservatives had been watching the battle between Gorbachev and Yeltsin with increasing unease and, alarmed at developments, began plotting a coup d'état. The plotters represented the army, the KGB, state industry, and a large wing of the Communist Party that was anxious to preserve its privileges. Their reasons included a desire to save the USSR, resentment against the explosive growth of the black market, anger with Gorbachev for his cavalier treatment of the party and his dismantling of the principle of collective Communist leadership, and his supposed sellout to the West. They claimed to be restoring order and suppressing crime, which had escalated with the breakdown of political authority. On August 19, 1991, the gang of eight, as the plotters were known, acted.

The conspirators sequestered Gorbachev in his vacation home and tried to take the so-called White House, the Moscow seat of the Russian parliament. Yeltsin mobilized the pro-democracy forces, which came out against the army units that had been called out. Some of these units refused to attack, although the reasons remain unclear. The failed arrival of supporting military units, the bad weather, the refusal to shoot at the pro-democracy crowd—especially the women, who took an important role—have all been given as explanations. Many mysteries besides this one surround the failed coup, including Gorbachev's precise role. Poor organization seems to have been the prime reason for the coup's failure.

Yeltsin, the symbol of democracy, organized the resistance and, in the enduring image of the event, stood on a tank and told a crowd of 150,000 people that the coup was unconstitutional and that its leaders were traitors. On August 20, tens of thousands of people responded to Yeltsin's call for a general strike, defying the coup organizers, while international support arrived in the form of the freezing of EU aid. The next day the coup collapsed. On August 22, Gorbachev returned to Moscow while thousands surrounded KGB headquarters and toppled the large statue of its founder. On August 24, Gorbachev resigned as general secretary, and the Communist Party's political activity was curtailed.

End of the Soviet Union

With the failure of the coup came the official end of the Soviet Union and the banning of the Communist Party. At the end of August, several republics moved toward independence. The Baltic states declared their independence on September 6. On December 1, 1991, the Ukraine, a core republic, left the Soviet Union with a 90 percent vote. The USSR had become a hollow shell. On December 8, a loose union, the Commonwealth of Independent States (CIS), replaced it. By December 25 twelve former Soviet republics had become independent. On Christmas Day 1991, Gorbachev resigned as president of the USSR, which formally ceased its existence, and the Red flag was lowered over the Kremlin. The long Communist experiment that began in November 1917 was over.

Bibliographical Essay

On the relationship of the USSR and developments in Eastern Europe during this period, see Kevin McDermott and Matthew Stibbe, *Revolution and Resistance in Eastern Europe* (Oxford, UK, 2006); Karen Dawisha, *Eastern Europe, Gorbachev, and Reform* (New

York, 1990); and J. C. Sharman, *Repression and Resistance in Communist Europe* (London, 2003). *Globalization and the State in Central and Eastern Europe* (London, 2008), by Jan Drahokoupil, discusses the role of direct investment in the area. Mary E. King's *The New York Times on Emerging Democracies in Easter Europe* (Washington, D.C., 2010) provides a general view. Thomas Allan Emmert and Charles W. Ingrao published *Conflict in South-Eastern Europe at the end of the Twentieth Century* (New York, 2006). Archie Brown wrote a general work, *The Rise and Fall of Communism* (New York, 2009).

Books on the Eastern European revolutions of 1989 and 1990 include Konstantin Pleshakov, *There is No Freedom Without Bread* (New York, 2009), which also examines the years leading up to that year; Ivo Banac, ed., *Eastern Europe in Revolution* (Ithaca, N.Y., 1992); and J. F. Brown, *Surge to Freedom* (Durham, N.C., 1991). See also Gale Stokes, *The Walls Came Tumbling Down: The Collapse of Communism in Eastern Europe* (New York, 1993).

Daniel Chirot, ed., *The Crisis of Leninism and the Decline of the Left: The Revolutions of 1989* (Seattle, Wash., 1991), gives excellent insights on the revolutions that ended communism. Timothy Garton Ash, *The Magic Lantern: The Revolution of '89 Witnessed in Warsaw, Budapest, Berlin and Prague* (New York, 1990), is an eyewitness account of the revolutions in several East European capitals by a scholar.

On Poland, see Lech Walesa, *The Struggle and the Triumph: An Autobiography* (New York, 1992), and Frances Millard, *The Anatomy of the New Poland: Post-Communist Politics in its First Phase* (Brookfield, Vt., 1994). On Solidarity, see Timothy Garton Ash, *The Polish Revolution: Solidarity* (New York, 1984). See also the book of essays by Lee Trepanier et al., *The Solidarity Movement and Perspectives on the Last Decade of the Cold War* (Krakow, 2010). On the role of women, see Shana Penn, *Solidarity's Secret: The Women Who Defeated Communism in Poland* (Ann Arbor, Mich., 2005). The networks of the Polish opposition are examined by Maryjane Osa, *Solidarity and Contention* (Minneapolis, Minn., 2003). On the role of Pope John Paul II, see his own *Pope John Paul II: Reaching Out Across Borders* (Upper Saddle River, N.J., 2003) and Robert Pledge, *Pope John Paul II: His Remarkable Journey* (New York, 2005).

Harald Wydra wrote *Communism and the Emergence of Democracy* (Cambridge, UK, 2007), which examines Poland, Hungary, and Czechoslovakia. Hungary is discussed by Rudolf L. Tökés, *Hungary's Negotiated Revolution: Economic Reform, Social Change, and Political Succession, 1957–1990* (Cambridge, UK, 1996), and János Kordai, *The Road to a Free Economy: Shifting from a Socialist System: The Entangled Hungary* (New York, 1990). See also Ansel Braun and Zoltan Barany, eds., *Dilemmas of Transition: The Hungarian Experience* (Lanham, Md., 1999). Klaus Offe looks at the GDR and Eastern Europe in *Variations of Transition* (Oxford, UK, 1996). For the people's part in the fall, see Jonathan Grix, *The Role of the Masses in the Collapse of the GDR* (New York, 2000). Charles Maier describes the end of the GDR in *Dissolution* (Princeton, N.J., 1999). On the reunification with West Germany, see David Childs, *The Fall of the GDR: Germany's Road to Unity* (New York, 2000). The fall of the Czechoslovak regime is analyzed by Bernard Wheaton and Zdenek Kavan, *The Velvet Revolution: Czechoslovakia, 1988–1991* (Boulder, Colo., 1992); see also Jiri Musil, *The End of Czechoslovakia* (New York, 1995). Iliana Zloch-Christy examines *Bulgaria in a Time of Change: Economic and Political Dimensions* (Brookfield, Vt., 1996).

On the Romanian revolution and its aftermath, consult George Galloway and Bob Wylie, *Downfall: The Ceausescus and the Romanian Revolution* (London, 1991); Tom Gallagher, *Romania After Ceausescu: The Politics of Intolerance* (Edinburgh, 1995); and Henry F. Carey, *Politics and Society in Post-Communist Romania* (Boulder, Colo., 2001). Yugoslavia's collapse is analyzed by Leonard J. Cohen, *Broken Bonds: The Disintegration of Yugoslavia* (Boulder, Colo., 1995), and Susan L. Woodward, *The Balkan Tragedy: Chaos and Dissolution After the Cold War* (Washington, D.C. 1995). For more details, see also Timothy Judah, *The Serbs, History, Myth and the Destruction of Yugoslavia* (New Haven,

Conn., 1998); Christopher Merrill, *Only the Nails Remain: Scenes from the Balkan Wars* (Lanham, Md.,, 2001); and Cvijeto Job, *Yugoslavia's Ruin: The Bloody Lessons of Nationalism: A Patriot's Warning* (Lanham, Md., 2002), which is part memoir, part analysis. Paul Mojzes uses models of genocide to describe the events that occurred during the breakup of Yugoslavia in his book, *Balkan Genocides: Holocaust and Ethnic Cleansing in the Twentieth Century* (Lanham, Md., 2011). See also Lenard J. Cohen and Jasna Dragovic-Soso, *State Collapse in South-Eastern Europe: New Perspectives on Yugoslavia's Disintegration* (West Lafayette, Ind., 2008). Miranda Vickers and James Pettifer look at Albanian developments in *Albania: From Anarchy to a Balkan Identity* (New York, 1997). Elez Biberaj, *Albania in Transition: The Rocky Road to Democracy* (Boulder, Colo., 1999), analyzes developments in the small Balkan state.

On the Soviet Union's most important protagonists during this period, see the biography by Zhores A. Medvedev, *Gorbachev* (New York, 1986), in addition to the one by Archie Brown, *The Gorbachev Factor* (New York, 1990), previously cited. Leon Aron, *Yeltsin: A Revolutionary Life* (New York, 2000), is a good biography. George W. Breslauer analyzes *Gorbachev and Yeltsin as Leaders* (Cambridge, UK, 2002). The best account of the struggle between Gorbachev and Yeltsin is John B. Dunlop's *The Rise of Russia and the Fall of the Soviet Empire* (Princeton, N.J., 1993); The demonstrator's question to a soldier cited in the text is on p. 34.

On the changes in the USSR, see the conversational book by Roy Medvedev and Giulietto Chiesa, *Time of Change: An Insider's View of Russia's Transformation* (New York, 1989). See also Shepard Sherbell's *Soviets: Pictures from the End of the USSR* (New Haven, Conn., 2001), a photographic record.

A number of good books on the end of the Soviet Union have been published. See David Pryce-Jones, *The Strange Death of the Soviet Empire* (New York, 1995). Longer accounts include David Remnick, *Lenin's Tomb: The Last Days of the Soviet Empire* (New York, 1993), and Jack F. Matlock, Jr., ambassador to the USSR, *Autopsy on an Empire: The American Ambassador's Account of the Collapse of the Soviet Union* (New York, 1995). There is also an account by Gorbachev's press spokesman, Andrei S. Grachev, *Final Days: The Inside Story of the Collapse of the Soviet Union* (Boulder, Colo., 1995). The Ukraine's road to independence is told by Taras Kuzio et al., *Ukraine: Perestroika to Independence* (London, 1999). The Baltic events that were so important to the USSR's demise are summarized by Anatol Lieven, *The Baltic Revolution: Estonia, Latvia, Lithuania and the Path to Independence* (New Haven, Conn., 1993). On this area, see also Walter C. Clemens, Jr., *The Baltic Transformed: Complexity Theory and European Security* (Lanham, Md., 2001).

For the international dimension to the story of the USSR's collapse, consult Jack F. Matlock, *Reagan and Gorbachev: How the Cold War Ended* (New York, 2004). But the reader will find plenty of material on this theme. Metta Spencer has published *The Russian Quest for Peace and Democracy* (Lanham, Md., 2010), examining contacts between Soviet intellectuals and Western peace activists that helped bring an end to the Soviet and East European regimes.

🖋

Europe in a Global Age: Problems and Prospects

The global era that Europe confronted at the end of the twentieth century started in 1900. The world revolved around the big European powers in politics, finance, culture, and science. British capital financed projects the world over, and Europeans set the tone in the arts and in the sciences. Ships plied the seas carrying European goods to all parts of the world, and European navies commanded respect when they showed the flag.

By the end of the twentieth century, Europe found itself in the midst of a new and vaster global age. From the military viewpoint, it was a minor power, but its attractiveness in economics, the arts, and science still allowed it to influence the world through "soft power." At the end of the twentieth century, the conflicts that had destroyed Europe seemed to have been resolved; competing ideologies and military barriers no longer divided it; the effects of communism were disappearing; and, at the beginning of the third millennium, Europeans enjoyed a standard of living they had never known before. However, Europeans struggled to come to terms with old and new problems.

THE NEW GERMANY

In 1900, the speed and force of Germany's growth most concerned European diplomats, and after World War II, fear of Germany's potential strength and cold war tensions seemed as if they would keep the country divided for the foreseeable future. When Germany reunited on October 3, 1990, Europeans worried about whether it could be contained because its economic power still overshadowed that of its neighbors.

Political Stability

The Federal Republic of Germany had proved so stable that its political system served as a model for other European states, but after 1990, the question was whether that stability would continue or whether instability would follow and lead to a crisis similar to the one that had brought Hitler to power in 1933. In the decade following reunification, however, political power regularly shifted between two broad coalitions in which large parties teamed up with smaller groups to achieve parliamentary majorities. The mechanisms that the German constitution had put into place to prevent the frequent fall of governments worked, far-right and neo-Nazi organizations failed to gain enough votes to be represented in parliament, and the country debated its Nazi past and attempted to atone for it. New German generations matured in a democratic cultural, educational, and political atmosphere, and Germany seemed to have left its authoritarian past behind.

Return of the Social Democrats

In the election of September 27, 1998, Social Democrat Gerhard Schröder defeated Christian Democratic Chancellor Helmut Kohl despite Kohl's record of sixteen years and his successful guidance of the reunification process. In Kohl's last years as chancellor, Germany had been plagued by economic problems that included the highest unemployment rate since 1933 (12 percent). Despite his long stretch in power, Kohl had been unable to reform the tax system, to confront the increasing inflexibility of German industry, or to stand up to the demands of the labor unions. German industry became less competitive in the global marketplace, and observers questioned its ability to ensure the country's elevated standard of living in the future.

Schröder gave the Greens important posts, included more women in the cabinet, and projected the image of a more sensitive and concerned leader. The partnership with the often-chaotic Greens demonstrated his vitality and concern for the environment, and Schröder tackled the problem of high unemployment by announcing an alliance for jobs and negotiations among unions, employers, and politicians. Schröder agreed to close Germany's nuclear power plants and to raise gasoline taxes as a means of reducing air pollution and of raising funds to decrease high individual tax rates. He also pledged to revoke several anti-immigrant provisions adopted by the previous government and, in March 1999, introduced a bill to admit the Nazis' persecution of homosexuals and to consider annulling the convictions of gays under Nazi legislation.

In practical politics, however, Schröder's cost-cutting policy alienated the traditional SPD base. When these voters stayed home in regional elections, the CDU made significant gains. In Germany, as in Britain and Italy, the left faced the same dilemma: Economics dictated cutting expenditures, which led to unemployment and disappointment among its own voters.

Schröder's election demonstrated the vigor and democracy of the German system, but in 1999 both again came into question. A corruption scandal struck Kohl and the CDU, one that raised fears in the international press for the survival of the CDU and the specter of a de facto one-party system in Germany. The commentators had Hitler's Germany in mind, but the CDU restructured itself, and the fears diminished.

The Question of Racism

Although the political system seemed solid, another question troubled observers: Racism remained a worrying aspect in democratic Germany despite the country's long effort to come to terms with its past. In West Germany, racism had been directed at foreign laborers. In the GDR, repression drove the question underground, but, following reunification, East Germany became the focus of racist activities. Waves of anti-Semitic incidents and attacks on foreigners and handicapped people occurred as the rage against 25 percent unemployment, years of suppression, and immigrants who they believed took their jobs came into the open. The incidents declined because of governmental action but surged again after 1996 and spread to the West.

Furthermore, troubling occurrences surfaced in the German army; videotapes showing troops training in Eastern Germany giving Nazi salutes and making disparaging remarks about Jews and people in the Balkans where they were about to be deployed came to light. The German authorities admitted that a neo-Nazi had given a lecture at an elite military academy and that SS veterans, including convicted war criminals, were receiving governmental pensions. On the Internet neo-Nazis proclaiming foreigner-free zones heightened alarm among officials. These events caused doubts just as the German armed forces prepared to go into combat for the first time since World War II in the sensitive Balkans. In related incidents involving foreigners, some German local administrations expelled Bosnian refugees who had escaped from the deadly Balkan wars. The expulsions were deliberately high profile because the authorities meant to frighten other immigrants and had the support of public opinion. Writer Günter Grass, Nobel Prize laureate for literature, labeled his fellow Germans "closet racists." Despite the German government's efforts, Germany continued to receive special attention on matters related to race.

The Problem of East Germany

Resentments also broke out because of reunification. Europeans expected the West Germans to bring East Germany up to Western levels very quickly. In the ten years following unification, the West poured over $900 billion into the East through tax breaks, aid for businesses, subsidies, and support payments. It gave East Germany modern malls, roads, communications, and railways, but the East remained bankrupt as unemployment hit 25 percent and productivity remained at half the level of that of West German workers. These conditions produced the rapid deterioration of the relationship between Easterners and Westerners. The East Germans resented the high-rolling West Germans taking over or closing inefficient industries, putting former state property on the block, paying East Germans wages that were only 75 percent of West German wages, and the end of social services that had existed under communism. The West Germans resented paying the bill for reunification through higher taxes and receiving nothing in return because of the "lazy" East Germans who contributed only 10 percent of the GDP and only 8 percent of the taxes.

The German Shadow over Europe

This setback for vaunted German efficiency did little to attenuate the unease of the country's neighbors. In 1997, the Germans and Czechs signed an accord in which the Germans apologized for the Nazi invasion of former Czechoslovakia, while the Czechs professed regret for their expulsion of 2.5 million Sudeten Germans in 1945. As part of the deal, the Germans promised to support Czech efforts to join NATO and the EU. Kohl emphasized the neighborly relations between the two countries, but, significantly, the agreement came only after two years of wrangling over language and even then brought vociferous protests from both Sudeten German and Czech groups. One Czech legislator stated that the agreement was just another step in the future total control of his country by Germany. Resentment at the harsh treatment and the ouster of the Sudeten Germans flared up as an issue when Günter Grass published a novel on the question. The German economy so overshadowed that of its neighbors that the Czechs feared that economics would accomplish what German arms had failed to do. The suspicion that the new Germany still aroused was illustrated by a former national security adviser to President Jimmy Carter who favored widening NATO because adding Poland, the Czech Republic, and Hungary to the alliance would make Germany less threatening as far as its neighbors were concerned. Enmeshing Germany in international organizations with multilateral decision-making machinery seemed to be the best means of assuaging the fear of possible German hegemony. At the same time, the increasingly confident young Germans were throwing off the shame of the Nazi era, believing that they should not be held responsible for the past.

In fact, even Germany's larger partners fretted that Germany's economic strength might allow it to dominate the continent through the EU. The British were especially sensitive to this danger, particularly after the Germans and French established a close collaboration. The mechanisms of mutual collaboration provided a buffer against possible German domination because EU institutions gave the smaller European countries a considerable voice in decision making. In 2010, the euro crisis that hit Europe brought increasing criticism that Germany was throwing around its economic power.

THE NEW RUSSIA

While German influence grew in Europe, the opposite happened to Russia. Boris Yeltsin's performance at Russia's helm for ten years after 1991 was a disappointment. The Russian economy nose-dived, Yeltsin used military force against his domestic enemies and separatists, he and his family became embroiled in a web of corruption, and Russian democracy remained fragile.

Failure of Yeltsin's Reforms

Following Western advice, Yeltsin immediately introduced private property and the free market into Russia. His finance minister and later prime minister, Yegor Gaidar, eliminated subsidies and price controls in January 1992 and privatized the economy by issuing vouchers giving part ownership in Russian industry to the country's citizens.

The government's program failed to accomplish the transition to capitalism smoothly, partly owing to the West's failure to provide enough financial aid and partly because of massive corruption. The economy's inability to boost production while demand for consumer goods increased caused prices to skyrocket. The black market expanded, and, with the decline of state power, criminals battled for the control of markets and murdered their competitors. International police agencies warned about the formation of a powerful Russian Mafia and believed that it had linked up with the Italian organization and had reached New York. The Russian national bank illegally diverted over $1 billion in loans from the International Monetary Fund (IMF) in 1993. By the beginning of 1993, prices had increased twentyfold. Powerful Communist Party members and Yeltsin's family profited from their privileged positions to gain control of privatized state firms. Because of the chaos, employers, including the state, paid wages months behind schedule if at all. Russian scientists, among the most competent, sold their skills abroad, raising the specter that they would build nuclear weapons for rogue states. The Russian military declined, and nuclear and biological weapons facilities were inadequately secured.

The Impact on Russian Society

Russian economic chaos had deleterious effects on Russian society as rampant inflation ate up the wages of pensioners and workers and impoverished much of the population. Families sold their heirlooms for a pittance to eat and keep warm.

These conditions contributed to a scourge afflicting post–cold war Europe: Russian (and East European) women, attracted by supposed work opportunities abroad, wound up as prostitutes in foreign countries. New diseases appeared, including a potent form of tuberculosis that resisted antibiotics and that heightened fears that the strain would spread to other parts of Europe. The West had to rush financial aid to block possible contamination because Moscow did not have the resources to fight the disease. AIDS spread through Russian society. The mortality rate for men aged 40 to 49 increased 77 percent between 1990 and 1995. Faced with a bleak future, Russians had fewer children, with the birthrate dropping to the third lowest in Europe. On the other side of the equation, a small class of fabulously wealthy tycoons emerged from the anarchy of the economic collapse. These new rich flaunted their ill-gotten gains—expensive Western cars, money, and well-dressed women on their arms—and caused resentment among the impoverished population.

Political Instability

The deteriorating economic situation affected Yeltsin's politics. Because the Parliament had been elected in 1990, Communists who disagreed with Yeltsin's desire to institute a market economy obstructed his policies. They insisted on increased social welfare payments and continued subsidies to state concerns, which Yeltsin opposed. Besides his goal of establishing a market system, Yeltsin greatly feared the loss of IMF aid that the country desperately needed. The argument reached an impasse, and the Parliament appealed to the long-suffering people to attack the Kremlin. On October 4, 1993, Yeltsin responded by ordering the army to shell the White House (the Russian Parliament building). Over a hundred people died during the disorders.

Yeltsin next tried to change the political system. After the parliamentary crisis, he issued a new constitution for the voters' approval in a referendum. The constitution greatly increased the president's powers, an innovation that Yeltsin hoped would ensure stability. The voters approved the referendum but set the stage for more turmoil by failing to give Yeltsin's reformist supporters a majority in Parliament. The rise of a right-wing party and a good Communist performance during these elections encouraged the Parliament to bring an impeachment proceeding against Yeltsin that finally failed only in 1999. Luckily for Yeltsin, he retained the upper hand because his enemies were divided. Over the next few years, Yeltsin clung to power despite many health crises and a series of political emergencies. These developments raised strong doubts that he could win reelection in 1996, but he did win because of the fear of disorder and the strong backing of the Americans, who opposed chaos or a possible Communist return to power.

Yeltsin caused consternation because of his habit of dismissing prime ministers and their governments wholesale and because of his erratic personality. In December 1992, Yeltsin appointed Viktor Chernomyrdin prime minister. Chernomyrdin, head of the former state natural gas monopoly, had become the largest shareholder in Gazprom, the new privatized monopoly. He appealed to the new tycoons who were powerful in post-Communist Russia. Chernomyrdin favored slowing down the process of liberalization so the Russian people could adjust to the market, but, when he was accused of corruption, Yeltsin fired him in March 1998. The president then appointed a young reformer who lasted only five months, reappointed Chernomyrdin to confront a dangerous financial crisis in Russia in August 1998, but fired him after eighteen days. This instability contributed to the fall of the ruble, which dropped 9 percent in one day, and to the globalization of the Russian economic crisis when Russia imposed a ninety-day moratorium on the repayment of foreign debts. Russians scrambled to buy dollars as a hedge against inflation, and television carried images of citizens fighting in long lines while waiting for their banks to open. Luckily Russia's largest creditors and Western governments intervened to contain the crisis. Despite the chaos, Yeltsin appointed and fired two prime ministers over the next ten months.

Complicating the picture were Yeltsin's health and bizarre behavior. Yeltsin had a serious heart operation and periodically dropped out of public view with no explanation for significant periods. His heavy drinking caused diplomatic incidents; at a meeting scheduled with Irish leaders at Shannon airport, Yeltsin was too drunk to get off the plane and had to be flown home. Finally, toward the end of his tenure, Yeltsin appointed Vladimir Putin, a political unknown who had worked for the KGB, as prime minister.

Russia and NATO

Russia's political instability and military decline had important repercussions in foreign affairs because Russia inherited nuclear weapons from the USSR that were capable of destroying the world, and some of them were on the territory of the weak states that had seceded from the USSR. The Russians wisely cooperated with the West in ensuring the destruction of many warheads, but a potentially more divisive problem was the expansion of NATO. Several former members of the defunct Warsaw Pact applied for NATO membership as an insurance policy against a possible Russian revival. The United States approved and argued that expansion would help preserve the peace while not posing a threat to Russia, but the Russians objected vigorously. In 1999, its fiftieth anniversary, NATO admitted Poland, the Czech Republic, and Hungary and looked forward to the entrance of Romania and Slovenia. This move and Russian military action against Chechnya in 1994 to prevent its secession increased discord between the West and Russia.

BIOGRAPHICAL SKETCHES

Vladimir Vladimirovich Putin
Dark Horse and White Poodle

The person who succeeded Boris Yeltsin as president of the Russian Federative Republic, Vladimir Putin, was born on October 7, 1952, in St. Petersburg (formerly Leningrad), where his parents had him baptized in the Eastern Orthodox faith despite official Soviet displeasure. "Putka," his nickname as a youth, had two brothers, both of whom died very young. At age 11, Putin took up a Russian form of self-defense called sambo, winning championships in that sport and in judo. He once proclaimed that martial arts were his favorite activity. As a dedicated sportsman, Putin shunned smoking and drank little.

Putin studied law at the Leningrad State University, graduating in 1975. His wife Lyudmila earned a degree from the same university. She was a student of philology, worked as a schoolteacher and a stewardess, and is fluent in Spanish, French, and German. Putin speaks English and German. They have two daughters and a white poodle but she has disappeared from public view while rumors of her husband's affairs with younger women proliferate.

Following graduation, Putin joined the KGB, the Soviet security service, spending several years in Germany as a spy. In 1990, he became adviser to the chair of the St. Petersburg City Council and from 1991 to 1996 held various positions in the St. Petersburg mayor's office.

In 1996, Putin moved to Moscow, where his rapid rise began. He worked in Boris Yeltsin's presidential administration, joining the group of Yeltsin insiders known as "the family." Liberal reformer and former Prime Minister Anatoly Chubais recommended Putin for deputy chief of staff, an office he achieved in March 1997. In July 1998, Putin took over as director of the Russian Federal Security Service, the KGB's successor. Despite his quiet manner and low profile, Putin impressed Yeltsin and combined several other jobs with that of director. He acquired the reputation of being the power behind the throne and continued to cultivate his contacts with liberal reformers. During this period of economic and political instability, On August 9, 1999, Yeltsin surprised everyone by nominating Putin prime minister.

continued

continued

Putin acted forcefully against Chechen Islamic fundamentalists who had previously humiliated Russian troops in Chechnya by ordering Russian soldiers to expel Chechen militants who had penetrated into neighboring Dagestan and sending them into Chechnya to root out the rebels whom he accused of terrorist bombings in Russian cities.

When Yeltsin suddenly resigned on December 31, 1999, Putin became acting president. This post put him in a favored position to win the presidential election of March 6, 2000. In his campaign, Putin said he favored a market economy, but one suited to Russian conditions. He criticized not only the Soviet past but post-Communist leaders for their errors and indicated that he would take a more gradual road to market reforms because Russians, unlike Americans or Britons, were used to a strong state.

Putin demonstrated himself a remarkably durable politician. He ended the parliamentary dominance that the Communists once enjoyed in post-Soviet Russia and jailed Russian tycoons who had grabbed large sectors of the Russian economy and were exercising too much political power. His policies stabilized the volatile Russian economic situation, helped enormously by the soaring price of oil—which Russia possesses in abundance. In foreign policy, Putin increased cooperation with the United States after the terrorist attacks on the World Trade Center and the Pentagon on September 11, 2001. He did not object to the Americans using bases in former Soviet republics for their Afghanistan operations, and in May 2002, Russia became an associate member of NATO.

However, Putin's regime in Russia has put the viability of democracy in doubt. Putin's tactics in jailing important tycoons have been criticized as undemocratic and motivated by a wish to crush all opposition. Putin has been accused of masterminding the murder of journalists who have criticized him. In addition, in order to get around term limits on the president, he favored the election of a political subordinate and took the position of prime minister. In 2012, he ran again for president and won with 64 percent of the vote in an election that provoked protests in Russia and international concern. New legislation had also lengthened the term for president to six years and had given him the option of running for a fourth term, giving him the possibility of remaining in power until 2024. In foreign policy, Russia under his leadership became more obstreperous and sought to reassert its dominance over independent states that were once part of the USSR.

The Rise of Putin

With Putin's installation as prime minister, the Chechen war flared up again as the Russians charged the Chechens with terrorism as part of their campaign for independence from Russia. This time the Russian military effort was more efficient. Russia also defended its old ally Serbia from Western criticism and NATO attacks in the wars associated with the breakup of the Yugoslav Federation. In 1999, the Russians condemned NATO bombing of Serbia during the Kosovo crisis and demanded a role in the peacekeeping operations in that province. Word also came that Russia had begun building a new mobile intercontinental ballistic missile (ICBM) and modernizing its nuclear submarines.

In December 1999, elections resulted in the weakening of the Communists in the Duma (parliament) so they could no longer block the formation of governments.

Putin's forceful actions in Chechnya and his appeal to Russian nationalism had worked, and a close Yeltsin adviser described the outcome as a revolution. Observers considered this election a dry run for the presidential ballot due in 2000, but they had not reckoned with the mercurial president. On December 31, 1999, Yeltsin suddenly resigned and anointed Putin on television as the man who could unite Russia and renew its greatness in the twenty-first century. Putin succeeded Yeltsin as acting president and granted him immunity from prosecution from possible corruption charges.

Putin's new job put him in an excellent position to win the March 2000 presidential elections, which he did handily. In his first remarks as president-elect, Putin pledged to work for a strong state capable of enforcing the law. In June 2000, he put forward a plan to strengthen central control over Russia's provinces and to repair the languishing economy. Russian tycoons who feared a new dictatorship criticized him, but the plan quickly received preliminary approval from the Duma. As part of his program, Putin promised more reform and continued efforts to establish a strong market economy. In foreign policy, he committed himself to destroying excess nuclear weapons and asked for American aid to get rid of Russia's stockpile of chemical weapons as required by the chemical weapons treaty signed in 1997.

Putin went on to win a second term and became prime minister after a protégé of his won the presidency. Although he strengthened the country and brought law and order, democracy suffered. He attacked some of the rich oligarchs who criticized him, brought them up on largely bogus charges, and imprisoned them for long terms. His government cracked down on journalists who reported unfavorably on his policies. Murders, kidnappings, and threats proliferated. In the most famous case, he was accused of ordering the murder of journalist Anna Politkovskaya in 2006 because she had denounced his actions in Chechnya and accused him of being a threat to Russian democracy. The Russian justice system, pressured by the government, was unable to resolve the case. On May 7, 2012 he became President again.

Economic Stabilization

The Russian economy that had turned down sharply in August 1998 caused a contraction of 4.6 percent in the Russian GDP. Official figures put inflation at over 84 percent and unemployment at 22 percent. Foreign investment fled the country, and Russian international debt skyrocketed. In late 1999, however, the economy registered substantial improvement because of the rise of petroleum prices and the reduction of imports because of the devalued ruble. The GDP stopped its free fall and showed some gains, while inflation stabilized at around 30 percent.

Twenty years after the Soviet Union's dissolution, Russia struggled to become a stable democratic state with a free market. Yeltsin's chaotic administration fell far short of its aims, but Putin reiterated them. Despite the chaos, the decline in economic and social conditions, "There has been no famine, large-scale civil war or collapse . . . ; neither has there been severe industrial unrest, let alone the 'social explosion' repeatedly predicted by the Russian opposition and seriously anticipated in the West." This was no small accomplishment, but as Putin's restraints on democracy became more severe, the future of democracy in Russia remained clouded.

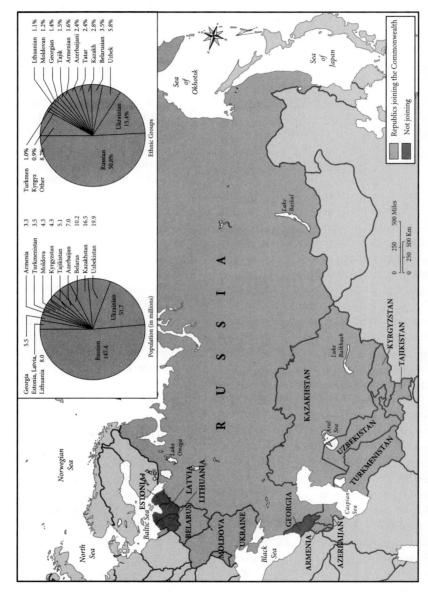

End of the Soviet Union. This map shows the states that emerged as independent after the Soviet Union's end, along with the Russian Federation. There were still problems among the different ethnic groups in the areas and the different states struggled to remain viable.

756

THE BALKAN AND SOUTHEASTERN
EUROPEAN HOT SPOTS

While Russia struggled to come to terms with postcommunism, a number of hot spots threatened the continent's peaceful development.

The Breakup of Yugoslavia

The most dangerous situation was the breakup of Yugoslavia. Slobodan Milosevic failed to subdue Slovenia and Croatia. In March 1992 Bosnia's declaration of its independence created a new problem: The Bosnian Serb minority (over a quarter of the population) refused to live in a Muslim-dominated state and rebelled. Milosevic sent in the Yugoslav army, which attempted to create a nationally homogeneous zone by murdering non-Serbs, occupying their towns, and gang-raping their women. The new Balkan war killed over 200,000 people.

The Europeans voted sanctions, but policy differences paralyzed further action as the Yugoslav army continued its rampage and took UN soldiers hostage. At this point, the United States took the lead, and NATO dispatched planes to bomb the Bosnian Serbs. Military pressure led to peace talks held at Dayton, Ohio, in 1995. The Dayton accords provided for the Bosnian Serbs to live in their own area and required them to join a loose Bosnian federation instead of uniting with Serbia, but American and NATO troops enforced the fragile agreement.

Former Yugoslav President Slobodan Milosevic on January 1, 2002, on trial before the International Criminal Tribunal at The Hague for war crimes, crimes against humanity, and genocide. Milosevic ordered the Yugoslav Army to attack Bosnian Muslims and invade Kosovo in the disorders that followed the breakup of Yugoslavia. The army, composed mostly of Serbs, looted, raped, and murdered thousands of people in their attempt at the "ethnic cleansing" of Bosnia. The wars caused hundreds of thousands of deaths and the displacement of innocent people. Milosevic died of a hear attack in his cell on March 11, 2006, before a guilty verdict could be rendered. He is still a hero to many Serbs.

By 1998, Milosevic attacked the Albanians in Kosovo, who made up 90 percent of the population. This province had great historical significance for the Serbs because of a defeat the Serbs had suffered there during the Middle Ages that led to the Muslim occupation of the Balkans. The Serb campaign against the Kosovo Liberation Army (KLA, a guerrilla group) displaced over 200,000 civilians and prompted the Contact Group (which included the United States and Russia) to hold talks with the warring parties in Rambouillet, France. Milosevic rejected an agreement and mounted a campaign in Kosovo that caused about 1.5 million Kosovars to flee their homes and head for neighboring Albania, Macedonia, and Montenegro. Serb paramilitary forces killed at least 11,000 civilians and destabilized the area.

On March 25, 1999, NATO initiated a massive bombing campaign against Yugoslav troops and Serbian military targets and infrastructure and imposed economic sanctions. These moves were aimed at protecting the Kosovars and forcing the Serbs to abandon their campaign, a policy that succeeded despite opposition to NATO's involvement in Italy and Greece and Russian objections. Elections in Serbia ended Milosevic's tenure, and Milosevic was eventually put on trial for war crimes by an international court in The Hague and died during the proceedings.

Nationality Problems in Slovakia
In neighboring Slovakia, post-Communist leaders attempted to exploit nationalism to increase their power. After separation from the Czechs, Vladimir Meciar,

The End of Czechoslovakia. After the fall of communism, Czechoslovakia split up. As the industrial heartland of the old Austro-Hungarian Empire, the Czech area had great economic potential. The rural Slovak Republic, however, soon ran into economic and political difficulties that the European Union attempted to address. The problems in this area illustrated the return to the surface of old issues after communism's end.

who had pushed for a division from the Czechs, ran the Slovak Republic. He ruled with an iron hand and was corrupt—selling off state-owned factories at bargain prices to party members. This policy caused enormous damage to the Slovakian economy, and by 1998 bankruptcy threatened the health and educational systems. Facing new elections in September 1998, Meciar attempted to win by following an antagonistic policy toward the Czechs and by attempting to whip up feeling against the large Hungarian minority but lost.

A four-party coalition cabinet of moderates, former Communists, and Hungarians headed by Mikulas Dzurinda followed Meciar and reversed his policies. The new government applied for membership in the EU and NATO, institutions that were antidotes to the old nationalism. The EU and the World Bank nudged the country toward democracy, called for greater efforts to improve relations with the Gypsy minority, and came through with loans to restart industry and aid the ailing banking system. In May 2004, Slovakia became part of the EU on January 1, 2009, adopted the common European currency, the euro, and the economy improved.

Bulgarian Economic Difficulties

Bulgaria did little to privatize its economy after the fall of communism, and the former Communist BSP and the more democratic UDF both condoned corruption. The Bulgarian economy and banking system collapsed as a result. Bulgarian salaries averaged $30 a month, among the lowest in Europe, and 90 percent of the population sank below the poverty line. These conditions caused massive protests, and new elections in April forced the discredited Socialists (former Communists) out of power.

In 1998, a new UDF (Union of Democratic Forces) government administered economic shock therapy by privatizing the banks and state enterprises, liberalizing the market, and passing an austerity budget. It ended the printing of money and pegged its currency to the German mark. The medicine had beneficial effects as inflation dropped from 670 percent in 1997 to 1 percent a month in 1998, and to zero in 1999. The GDP increased 4 percent, the budget registered a surplus, and a third of the state enterprises and 90 percent of agriculture were privatized. The EU provided economic assistance, and in 1995 Bulgaria applied for membership, was admitted in January 2007, and hoped to join the euro zone in 2013 or 2014. Once closely allied with the USSR, Bulgaria followed an increasingly pro-West foreign policy.

The Romanian Dilemma

In Romania, Ion Iliescu, a former member of the Communist Party's Central Committee, ruled for seven dismal years. Although Romania was potentially one of the richest countries in the area, the Romanian standard of living plunged, the government failed to modernize industry, and foreign investment shunned the country while Iliescu followed policies associated with communism. Iliescu ruled by ensuring workers jobs in the obsolete state sector, and Romania paid dearly for pursuing this course.

In 1996, the election of anti-Communist professor Emil Constantinescu as president brought big hopes for change, but squabbles among the parties of the ruling coalition created political instability that sabotaged economic reform. The expected negative reaction of workers to an austerity budget and the closing of state enterprises caused politicians to hesitate, despite the IMF's warnings that the government had to raise taxes, improve tax collection, and halt the rising budget deficit. Romania's failure to undertake structural reform or correct widespread corruption and inefficiency resulted in an economic slowdown. In 1999, unemployment rose to 11 percent, and inflation reached 50 percent. The GDP fell 5 percent, and state-owned banks neared collapse. These conditions and the closing of some state-owned firms touched off strikes that further weakened the economy and made structural reform more difficult. In addition, Romania seemed prone to ecological disasters. By 2000, the country showed little sign of improving its economic or political prospects, and a stable relationship with the large Hungarian minority was the only bright aspect in a very poor performance. However, the EU extended massive financial aid to the country, and Romania joined the EU in the enlargement round of 2007. Romania hoped to join the euro zone at the latest by 2012, but was in no condition to meet this date.

A Desperate Case

Romania had important natural resources that might eventually help the country rebound, but Albania, with few natural resources and damaged by the Hoxha regime, seemed a desperate case. An Italian-led force had to be dispatched to make the country secure for the June 1997 elections that gave victory to Socialist Party leader Fatos Nano. The previous leader Sali Berisha boycotted the new parliament and stirred up popular unrest.

Corrupt politicians and policemen who protected gangsters trafficking in cigarettes, drugs, arms, and women created a tightly interwoven network of politics, crime, and money laundering. The Albanian state remained hopelessly polarized between Nano and Berisha, who fought for privileges while political paralysis, rampant crime, antiquated industries, disorders, and corruption devastated the feeble economy. The World Bank declared Albania the most corrupt European country, and in 1997 the Albanian GDP dropped 7 percent, recovered somewhat in 1998, and dipped again in 1999. Unemployment hit 30 percent, and the extremely unstable situation caused professional and poor Albanians alike to flee the country, especially to Italy. In addition, the 1999 Kosovo crisis put the additional strain of 500,000 refugees on the country.

Beginning in 1999, however, the EU stepped in and, during the next few years, extended economic aid to the country in various agreements. The economic and political situation stabilized. On April 28, 2009, Albania formally applied for entrance into the EU and was recognized as a potential candidate country, but political instability continued to jeopardize its chances and the economy remained in poor condition.

UNFINISHED BUSINESS

Some of the issues that Eastern Europe needed to address also posed problems for the West.

Umberto Bossi in 1992. Bossi, head of the Northern League, epitomizes anti-immigrant sentiment in Italy. Bossi's movement began as a revolt of the North against the central government in Rome that he charged was overtaxing the industrious North for the benefit of lazy and corrupt southerners. Bossi made the same charges against immigrants, even though it was the Northern industrialists who needed their labor and favored their immigration into Italy. As the immigration problem became more widespread with thousands of illegal aliens landing on the Italian coasts, however, more Italians accepted his message. Bossi had political influence because the League is concentrated in densely populated Lombardy that sends a large, compact bloc of deputies to parliament. They joined in a coalition with Silvio Berlusconi, who dominated Italian politics in the eighteen years after 1994. In 2012 a corruption scandal removed him from power in the League and younger, more respectable, leaders took over.

Corruption, the "European vice," contaminated the West as well as the East. In Italy in 1992, revelations regarding the scope of corruption and the involvement of state companies brought down all the parties that had ruled the country since World War II and resulted in major alterations of the political system. The main reasons for corruption in Italy were the need to finance political parties, to counter the kickbacks received by the Italian Communists from companies trading with the Soviet bloc, and to get around the antiquated bureaucracy. Corruption scandals also exploded in Germany and France involving former Chancellor Kohl, French President Chirac, and former Prime Minister Alain Juppé. Despite new legislation, fraud remained a fact of political life in Europe, encouraged by inefficient bureaucracies and inadequate public funding of political activities.

Organized Crime

A related issue was the proliferation of organized crime. In Italy, the Mafia had spread from Sicily to the North after World War II. Similar criminal organizations operated in northern Europe, the East, and Russia. These organizations cooperated in the drug trade, traffic in women, and money laundering, spurring European police agencies to tighten their collaboration and the FBI to open offices in Eastern Europe.

The major problem with combating organized crime in democratic societies is how to combine crime-fighting techniques with civil rights. European public opinion historically was less sensitive than American public opinion to civil rights. The British regularly violated the civil rights of persons they suspected of IRA connections. Italy held mass Mafia trials, with defendants confined to steel cages in the middle of the courtroom, and accepted hearsay evidence. European states issued identity cards and required citizens to carry them. The police conducted random searches of people and cars. With the need to fight crime, terrorism, and illegal immigration, such techniques had public support and did not seem apt to disappear soon.

Immigration

The growth of immigration from Third World countries and Eastern Europe presented the West with new challenges. How would the new immigrants fit in with the culture of the host countries?

The Europeans first feared that immigrants would alter Europe's culture and religion and then that they would establish Islam. The high birthrate of the immigrants and the low European birthrate created fears that the Europeans would be swamped and that their way of life would disappear. European officials discussed how they would handle the influx of Muslim children into the schools while mosques sprouted in their cities and Christian churches closed.

Besides cultural and religious fears, many Europeans accused the immigrants of being drawn to crime. The fear of losing jobs made right-wing parties, some of them extreme, more attractive to Westerners. Various xenophobic organizations appeared in Germany, even though they remained small. In France, Le Pen's noisy National Front scored victories in the 1998 regional elections but appeared well contained until Le Pen qualified for a run-off election against President Chirac in May 2002 and later was succeeded by his daughter. In Italy, the disappearance of traditional parties favored organizations that had not been part of the previous political system. Gianfranco Fini's National Alliance (AN) allied with Silvio Berlusconi's Liberty Pole and briefly joined the cabinet in 1994. AN, however, had renounced a good deal of its neo-Fascist past and tried to stake out a position as a democratic force on the right, but Umberto Bossi's anti-immigrant Northern League gained an influential position in Italian politics by allying with Silvio Berlusconi's more mainstream Liberty Pole that won the 2001 and later elections. Even more disturbing news came from Austria, where Haider's anti-immigrant Freedom Party won an important part in the government in February 2000. Negative EU and other international reactions to this event isolated Austria and prompted Haider to resign, but the party stayed in the cabinet. When the EU realized that its snubbing of the new government united most Austrians against its interference, it concluded that the wiser course was to back off so the issue could deflate. In 2002, an anti-immigrant group in the Netherlands approached power, but its influence declined drastically after its leader was assassinated.

However, at the beginning of the twenty-first century, xenophobic movements did not come to power. In France, moderate rightist Chirac defeated Le Pen, and European officials and British Prime Minister Tony Blair warned Europeans not to go too far to the right and stressed the need for governments to take strong action against illegal immigration. Nevertheless, the issue that concerned ordinary Europeans the most was the accelerating pace of immigration from the poor countries into a Europe that had become rich, was in need of labor, and had a declining birthrate. Immigrants were attracted by possible jobs and by generous welfare state benefits. Between 1990 and 2010, it is estimated that 26 million immigrants flooded into the European Union. Europe needed professionals, and the population decline in Europe meant that millions of jobs went unfilled, but the vast majority of immigrants were an underclass who were untrained to step into them. In addition, they were at the margins of society, put a strain on the welfare system, and caused serious riots, for example, in France. With each political and economic crisis, the number of immigrants increased, particularly in Mediterranean countries with long coastlines, such as Italy and Spain. In addition, the desire of many of these immigrants to travel to other EU countries caused problems that threatened institutions that allow Europeans freedom of travel within the EU, such as the Schengen agreement. In short, if Europeans did not deal wisely with immigration, it threatened to destabilize the whole continent.

BIOGRAPHICAL SKETCHES

Anthony Charles Lynton Blair
"The Modernizer"

With the rise of center-right political formations in Europe during the late twentieth century, British Prime Minister Tony Blair found himself in the anomalous position of speaking for the European left despite his taming of the Labour Party.

Tony Blair was born on May 6, 1953, in Edinburgh, Scotland. He had a privileged childhood. His father, a lecturer in law, sent him to an elite college and then, in 1972, to Oxford to study law. As a student, Blair joined a rock band called the Ugly Rumors, playing bass guitar and singing the lead. After graduation, he went briefly to Paris, where he tended bar and worked as an insurance clerk. He decided to become a labor lawyer and apprenticed with a London law firm in 1976 after his return to London. He met his future wife, lawyer Cherie Booth, during this period. The two were of different religions; he was an Anglican and she, a Catholic. Blair converted to Catholicism after he left office. His wife has strong views on women's issues and insisted that he take a leave of absence from his job as prime minister to help her when their last child was born.

continued

continued

Blair became interested in politics at age 11, when his father suffered a stroke and shifted his own political ambitions to his children. He joined the Labour Party and won election to Parliament in 1983. Blair came of political age at the height of Margaret Thatcher's popularity, when Labour had lost three general elections and seemed finished. Blair's opportunity to rise in the organization arrived after Labour's 1987 defeat when leader Neil Kinnock tried to reform the Labour Party. He became party leader in 1994.

Blair was convinced that the Labour Party could survive only by eliminating its radical image and moving toward the center. He publicly conceded that Thatcher had been correct in her analysis of Britain's ills and that Labour should adopt similar principles in order to win, arguing that "principle without power is futile." He aimed to revitalize Labour by transforming it into a more moderate party.

Blair advocated a blend of liberal and conservative policies: improved education; vocational instruction for teenagers; an end to long-term welfare; an emphasis on law and order and family values; support for a market economy; elimination of the hereditary aspect of the House of Lords; and support for an English bill of rights, devolution, and a pro-Europe policy. His priorities included loosening the traditionally close relations between the party and the trade unions and reducing the unions' ability to influence Labour policy. In 1995, he eliminated "Clause IV" from the Labour Constitution. This "Communist" provision, dear to the hearts of the unions and Labour radicals, advocated "common ownership of the means of production, distribution, and exchange." Blair's reforms, geared toward nudging the organization from the left to the political center, earned him the nickname of "the Modernizer," but he described the renovated party as New Labour.

Blair's changes increased Labour's popularity, and, running as New Labour, he won the 1997 elections. At age 43, Blair became the youngest prime minister since 1812. Fighting for his domestic platform allowed him handily to win new elections in 2002. Besides his moderation in domestic affairs, in foreign policy Blair followed a pro-EU course and maintained good relations with European center-right leaders, such as Spain's José Maria Aznar and Italy's Silvio Berlusconi. After the September 11, 2001, attack on New York's World Trade Center, he emerged as the most effective spokesperson in the campaign against terrorism. Blair's critics accused him of surrendering Britain's independence to the Americans, while Labour's left wing kept up its attack on his domestic policies. His strong support of the Iraq invasion and the circumstances around it damaged his credibility, and Blair came under increasing fire until his resignation as prime minister on June 27, 2007, after which he dedicated himself to bringing peace to the Middle East.

The Woman Question

In addition to these questions, there was the unfinished business of women's status. In France, women made up only 6 percent of the National Assembly. In five other EU countries, the total approached 30 percent, and in Norway and Sweden, 40 percent. French historian Mariette Sineau labeled the situation an embarrassment for the entire political system. In Germany, the CDU named Angela Merkel, an East German physicist as its head to replace Kohl and to repair the damage caused by the corruption scandal. In Italy, former EU Commissioner Emma Bonino made a strong mark in politics by increasing women's visibility in politics and by raising the total vote of the small Radical Party. The Swiss Italian Carla del

Ponte was instrumental in bringing Slobodan Milosevic and his associates to trial for human rights violations during the Balkan wars.

Despite progress made over the years, women's salaries still trailed behind those of men. European women were poorly represented in many occupations and at the highest levels of business and government. Despite the growth of the welfare state, women had not achieved their aim—as proclaimed in a slogan of the 1970s—of "a child, if I want one, when I want one, and how I want one." In Eastern Europe, the position of women worsened with the breakdown of communism. Many women went to the West, frequently illegally, to provide the domestic labor in great demand there, leaving their husbands and children for long periods. Many others, promised jobs, were forced into prostitution—a phenomenon that taxed the resources of Western police forces.

In addition to these limitations in the progress of women, religious considerations blocked women's emancipation. Catholicism and Protestant fundamentalism were unfriendly to women's liberation. Islam, well on its way to becoming a major European religion, was even more restrictive toward women.

Religious Developments

At the beginning of the twentieth century, European intellectuals predicted that religion would disappear by the century's end, but religious influence in politics was still strong at the beginning of the twenty-first century.

Ironically, political clout, not piety or principle, accounted for the importance of religion. Catholic Italy, once heavily influenced by the Vatican, adopted liberal abortion laws, easily available contraception, and had a very low birthrate. Poland, devoted to the pope, had to be admonished by him to retain Catholic values. France, the church's "eldest daughter," debated the church's place in society during the pope's trip in September 1996. Catholic and Protestant churches closed in France, Italy, Germany, Britain, and northern Europe. In the Netherlands, many of the buildings were converted into mosques, serving the growing Muslim population, or into stores. The pope remained personally popular, drawing immense crowds wherever he traveled and retaining the capacity to influence the political dialogue in areas from Poland to Castro's Cuba.

The Eastern Orthodox Church, severely suppressed by the Communists, revived and attempted to restrict the rights of minority religions in Russia, including those of Catholics and Protestants. A 1997 bill passed by Parliament would have limited the freedom of religions not registered by the state fifteen years before, under the atheist USSR. The legislation provoked an outcry in Rome and in Washington, where the U.S. Senate threatened to cut off aid to Russia if the legislation passed. Boris Yeltsin vetoed the measure, but the affair illustrated the depth of feeling the Eastern Orthodox religion still engendered. In June 2000 Orthodox Greece proposed eliminating religious affiliation from identity cards only to have opponents of the measure charge the Jews with initiating the idea and deface Jewish cemeteries.

Other looming problems involved the Muslim faith of the immigrants who moved in increasing numbers to Europe, where Islam had been the enemy since the eighth century. In Italy, Catholic church officials openly questioned the compatibility of Islam with the country's traditional Catholicism, and they were not alone. The growth in the Muslim population also alarmed the Jews. In Russia, suffering provoked anti-Semitic outbursts, and in Western Europe, the continuing crisis in the Middle East provoked anti-Semitic incidents.

Protestantism seemed to lose its capacity to arouse violent emotions except in Northern Ireland, where militants exploited it to fight the Catholic minority. The mixed Protestant-Catholic cabinet, which had been established under the 1998 Good Friday agreement, was suspended by Britain in February 2000 when the IRA refused to give up its weapons. On June 2, however, it resumed deliberations after the Irish Republicans agreed gradually to rid themselves of their arms. This time the deal ran into problems from Protestant elements that were persuaded to rejoin the cabinet only with difficulty. After joining, they vowed to pursue tactics that would sabotage its workings, and a bomb went off in central London. Speculation attributed the explosion to renegade IRA members who were opposed to the Good Friday agreement, but the agreement held.

New Issues

In the past, issues such as separatism had been handled primarily with force and conciliation, but this situation changed during the latter years of the twentieth century. Britain agreed to self-governing assemblies in Scotland and Wales, endorsing a policy of devolution that affected other countries. In Italy, the Northern League campaigned for the independence of the North, which would have split the country and abandoned the poorer South to its own devices. It ended up in the political mainstream, but the regions would gain significant power. The evolution of the EU also spurred this process because the EU acted as a buffer with the national governments that were losing power to Europe.

THE EUROPEAN UNION'S MARCH

After the end of communism in Europe, the EU was the best hope for European nations to compete in a global marketplace and to acquire political clout. Despite the strict economic criteria adopted at Maastricht, applications for admission increased. The EU faced difficulties during the late 1990s, but the fifteen years before the Great Recession that began in 2008 was one of its most successful periods.

Economic Progress

At the beginning of 1999, the common currency of Europe, the euro, took effect smoothly, although some states, notably Britain, did not join it. Banks converted to the euro for their electronic operations, and shops posted prices of goods in their own currencies and in euros. The European Central Bank and the single currency gave Europe important tools to implement a common financial policy. Financially, the euro did not replace the dollar as the reserve currency, but after falling in its first year, it began a dramatic rise against the U.S. currency in early 2003. Most important, the European currency established itself as a mainstay in the world of finance after it went into everyday circulation on January 1, 2002.

Unfortunately, the euro's appearance stimulated at least a temporary inflation in some EU countries, and the inability of weaker European economies to devalue in order to meet the problems created by the 2008 recession caused a serious sovereign debt crisis beginning in 2010.

Foreign and Military Policy

The EU showed movement in other areas as well. Maastricht mandated a common European foreign and military policy, but the EU did not do so. The Kosovo crisis, however, uncovered sharp disagreements that made the coordination of EU foreign policies more urgent. At a summit in Cologne in June 1999, the EU appointed Spain's Javier Solana its high representative for foreign affairs. Solana had wide experience in foreign affairs and defense matters as secretary-general of NATO. In addition, Romano Prodi, the new president of the European Commission (EC), gave Chris Patten, the former British governor of Hong Kong, the job of overseeing the EU's foreign relations and assigned commissioners specific tasks in this area. In another important decision, the Europeans agreed to establish a 60,000-member rapid-reaction force by 2003 for deployment in areas where NATO was not involved.

Nevertheless, Europe split on the 2003 American invasion of Iraq. France and Germany, supported by Russia, opposed an attack in the UN, while Britain, Spain, and Italy supported the Americans. When East European countries who were aspiring to become members of the EU supported the American position, French President Jacques Chirac issued an arrogant statement implying that he would veto their applications. He did not, but the Iraq crisis demonstrated that the EU countries still had a long way to go in working out common foreign policy positions.

Preparing for Enlargement

Significant developments occurred in the relative positions of the European Parliament (EP) and the EC. In January 1999, the EP ordered an investigation into charges of corruption in the EC. A committee found that the EC members had engaged in fraud and mismanagement, and in March the entire EC resigned. A new EC president took over, former Italian premier Romano Prodi. A strong supporter of European enlargement, Prodi was determined to reform the EC and to set into motion a procedure that would revise the EU treaties to prepare the EU for the enlargement that he favored. Prodi charged the new commissioners with revising the EC's functions and preparing an intergovernmental conference to guide the process of revision. He also strengthened the office of EC president by securing a pledge from the commissioners to resign if he requested them to do so.

Prodi then proceeded on enlargement. In 1993, the EU had mandated certain conditions for aspiring members: a free market, a working democracy, a fair judicial system, and harmonization of national laws with EU legislation. In 1997, the EU had named Poland, Hungary, the Czech Republic, Slovenia, Estonia, and Cyprus as the most qualified candidates for membership and scheduled negotiations with them. It postponed consideration of Bulgaria, Romania, Slovakia, Lithuania, and Latvia and placed them on a slow track. It also budgeted funds to help all eleven countries prepare for membership. In late 1999, the EU speeded up

At the end of the twentieth century, the European Union was riding high and attracted other countries that wanted to join, including the former Soviet satellites in Eastern Europe. Romano Prodi, European Commission President from 1999 to 2004, supported a stronger Europe, increased the powers of the Commission President, and spurred enlargement of the European Union by favoring the candidacies of ten new members. He was criticized as moving too fast in letting other countries into the Union, a charge that critics reiterated during the euro crisis of the early 21st century. Prodi was Commission President when the euro came into existence in January 2002. This photograph of Prodi was taken on May 2, 2002.

the process by inviting the five slow-track countries to begin negotiations for entry in 2000 and granted Turkey the rank of a candidate for membership. At a European Council meeting in Athens on April 16, 2003, Prodi signed the Treaty of Accession admitting ten new countries—Poland, Hungary, the Czech Republic, Estonia, Latvia, Lithuania, Malta, Slovenia, Slovakia, and Cyprus—with a total population of 75 million into the EU as of May 1, 2004. The treaty also paved the way for the accession of Bulgaria and Romania by 2007. These developments promised to revolutionize the EU but raised the question of whether it was expanding too rapidly. In June 2003, a European Convention that had been meeting for sixteen months issued a draft constitution. Signed on October 29, 2004, the constitution was rejected by French and Dutch voters in the spring of 2005 and was a serious blow to the concept of European political unity even though the Treaty of Lisbon that entered into force on December 1, 2009, replaced it.

The European Parliament

In 1999, member states completed ratification of a treaty strengthening the European Parliament, which had been negotiated in Amsterdam in 1997. The EP gained the power to approve EC members and the president, making it more like a national parliament. The June 10–13 elections reinforced this trend as parties campaigned as groups favoring similar ideologies: Socialists, Greens, Liberals, and Conservatives.

The EU made significant progress, but it proved unable to resolve its serious agricultural problem. The common agricultural policy (CAP) gobbled up half the EU budget, and for years there had been a consensus that it had to be reformed, but little practical action was taken because members whose agricultural sectors benefited the most from EU subsidies resisted change. If not resolved, the agricultural question promised to severely damage the prospects of unity.

The EU's successes over the years outweighed its failures, and everyone recognized it as even more vital to the well-being of Europe after the collapse of communism and the intensification of globalization. Europeans remained committed to the idea of unity, but unification escaped them. However, they understood that they could not survive the economic and technological challenge of the modern world without acting together as a bloc, and this realization was important in facing the sovereign debt crisis that occurred in 2010.

Globalization

The increased unity toward which Europe was heading at the beginning of the twenty-first century was essential for its survival. Thanks to increasing globalization and the ease of communication, capital and labor were crossing national boundaries with greater ease, and competition with lesser-developed countries with cheaper skilled labor was more intense. Like the Americans, European companies manufactured goods outside the EU—enjoying tax breaks and paying less for labor—and imported them into their home countries at a greater profit. This development put enormous pressure on jobs, creating the specter of unemployment. As governments supported companies' demands to reduce employee benefits, institute more flexible regulations, make it easier to fire workers, increase part-time employment, and cut social services, workers and their allies objected. Tensions remained high because of these reasons and escalating immigration into the EU.

The tensions exploded especially among young people, who joined organizations resisting what they claimed was the economic insecurity, increasing exploitation in the West and in the Third World, and environmental damage. They took to the streets at meetings of high-profile international governmental organizations like the G-8 (the world's richest countries plus Russia) and the IMF. While most demonstrators were not violent, small groups were. Violence erupted, with anti-global demonstrators destroying parts of the host cities, and the police responded in kind. Protesters were wounded, arrested, or shot and killed in Italy, Spain, and the Czech Republic. This trend of violent protest at high-level meetings seemed set to continue in the future, and leaders openly speculated whether such gatherings could still be held. The unemployment, economic decline, and a slow recovery from the Great Recession of 2008 did not set off major violence, but the sovereign debt crisis of 2010 threatened to do so because of austerity programs that countries like Greece were forced to implement in order to receive funds to bail them out. Exactly how this crisis would work itself out remained unclear after the first decade of the twenty-first century.

THE LARGER EAST EUROPEAN ECONOMIES AND THE EU

Whenever a country applied for membership, the EU investigated whether it possessed a functioning democracy and a market economy. These principles, backed up by financial aid, had positive effects in Eastern Europe. The process could go slowly, but in Poland, Hungary, and the Czech Republic, the goal of qualifying for membership in the EU was a major stimulus to change.

Normalization in Poland

In Poland the potential for instability during the post-Communist years was great, but the Poles did not seek revenge for the forty years of Communist dictatorship and chose democracy. In 1990, Walesa became president but lost his bid for reelection in 1995. As workers in heavy industry and agriculture, Solidarity supporters suffered when Poland introduced the free market. The greatest paradox was when the economic liberalization brought the shutdown of the Lenin shipyard where the successful revolution against communism began. Rapid privatization caused hardships, but by 1997 the private sector accounted for 64 percent of the GDP. The economy turned around, and Poland achieved annual growth rates of between 4 percent and 5.5 percent, among the highest in the world.

In September 1997 new elections ousted from power the former Communists who had won a 1993 landslide election. The next month, Solidarity stalwart Jerzy Buzek, a Protestant, took over as prime minister. Buzek promised to step up privatization by selling restructured state companies and by raising the proportion of the Polish economy in private hands to 80 percent within four years. Buzek, strongly supported by France and Germany, continued Poland's drive to enter the EU. This policy caused apprehension among farmers, who demanded subsidies, and among workers, who struck against the prevailing low wages. In 1998, the Sejm stated that the Communist Party bore full responsibility for the crimes committed during Communist rule, but refused to punish Jaruzelski and his supporters for their actions during the martial law period.

Religion continued to be a greater factor in Polish life than in most other European countries. In 1998, Parliament ratified a concordat with the Vatican that confirmed the Roman Catholic Church's special position in Polish society. Pope John Paul II encouraged Poland's desire to join NATO and the EU, but he protested against liberalized abortion laws. In June, the pope traveled to his homeland again on a wistful journey. Enormous crowds greeted the pontiff, eager to see him on what they believed would be his last visit. Poland's close identification with the Roman Catholic Church, however, strained relations with the Jewish community and Israel. Nuns had implanted crosses at Auschwitz and at the sites of other concentration camps in remembrance of the people who died there, but Jews objected because they had been the primary victims. In May 1999, legislation banning building near such historic sites effectively prohibited such actions.

Hungarian Progress

Hungary's progress also allowed it to join NATO and aspire to EU membership with the first wave of new applicants. The Hungarian Socialists (former Communists) won free elections in 1994 and ruled democratically until May 1998 when new elections allowed the right-center Federation of Young Democrats-Hungarian Civic Party (FIDESZ) to replace them. Thirty-four-year-old FIDESZ leader Viktor Orban became prime minister with the support of smaller parties.

Hungary faced a nettlesome national question because the Hungarian minority, dispersed among Slovakia, Romania, and Serbia, was the largest in Eastern Europe and had been a major destabilizing factor between the wars. The Orban government faced the question squarely. Relations with Slovakia improved with the change of administration there in 1998. The Kosovo crisis alarmed the Hungarian government over the plight of Hungarians living in the Serbian province of Vojvodina because of Hungary's support for the NATO bombing mission, but the anticipated trouble did not materialize. Orban criticized Romania, the country with the largest Hungarian minority, but pledged to undertake negotiations to settle outstanding issues.

Hungary's entry into NATO put the seal of approval on its successful democratic evolution that allowed it to implement market reforms with a minimum of disruption. Hungary achieved annual growth rates of 4 percent to 5 percent and a declining inflation rate. An EU working group on new members declared the Hungarian and Polish market economies the most robust among new applicants for membership. Hungary qualified for accession in 2004 with Poland.

The most serious problems Hungary faced were corruption, crime, and discrimination against minorities. In 1999, scandals forced the resignation of several high governmental officials and disgraced over a hundred of the country's top politicians. On the streets, members of powerful organized criminal gangs car-bombed and murdered each other. Under EU pressure, the government pledged to crack down on these activities and on state corruption, but remained dissatisfied with the scope of the actions that the cabinet took and exhorted Hungary to make greater efforts to protect the Roma (Gypsy) minority. Its weaknesses made Hungary economically vulnerable and it was one of the countries that suffered the most from the Great Recession of 2008. In addition, the government took a turn that made observers fear for the continuation of its democratic system.

Difficulties in the Czech Republic

The Czech Republic's strong industrial base, the easy success of the Velvet Revolution, the election of the popular Václav Havel as president, the government's stability, and the rapid march toward a market economy misled observers into believing that the Czech Republic would easily adapt to Western European economic norms. Between the fall of communism and 1997 Prime Minister Václav Klaus, an economist and head of the Civic Democratic Party, took his country on a fast ride to capitalism by issuing Czech citizens vouchers that gave them part ownership in several thousand state companies—tangible property that they could sell. Privatization seemed to work as if by a miracle, and it took several years to realize that the privatized companies continued to be overstaffed, inefficient, and underproductive. By late 1997, the Czech economy had tanked and led to the devaluation of the currency, bank failures, and a drop in the stock market. At the same time, Prime Minister Klaus resigned after revelations that his party had accepted illegal financial contributions.

New elections in June 1998 gave Milos Zeman's opposition Czech Social Democratic Party the largest proportion of the vote, but not a majority. Zeman reached an uneasy accommodation with Klaus's party in order to address the economic situation by pledging to continue to implement a market economy at a slower pace so as to minimize the negative social repercussions. The failure of the effort brought protests and a call by heroes of the Velvet Revolution for the government's resignation.

In addition to the economic dilemmas, racial incidents marred the country's image. The incidences of hate crimes, including murders, escalated against the Roma minority. One Czech town even built a wall to separate the Gypsies from the rest of the population, provoking protests from the EU and Western governments, and relations with the Gypsies remained tense even after the barrier was removed. In another high-profile racial incident, a Sudanese university student was murdered in Prague, which provoked outrage.

Despite these problems, the Czech Republic's democratic progress brought quick acceptance of its application to join NATO. The Czechs applied for accession to the EU, but the EU insisted on greater protection for the Roma minority, a serious effort to end corruption, and greater restructuring of the economic sector. Its application was successful in 2004.

Of all the East European states, Poland, Hungary, and the Czech Republic made the most successful efforts to integrate their economic and political systems with the rest of Europe. They installed working democracies and, under EU pressure and assistance, tried to resolve their lingering problems.

WHAT IS EUROPE?

At the beginning of the twenty-first century, the question "What is Europe?" was still a relevant one. There was little debate about what constituted Europe, unlike in ancient times, even if there were questions about how a united Europe could be made operative in order to allow it to survive as an important protagonist in the modern world. Just how expeditiously and efficiently Europe would be created remained a question, but Europeans identified closely with the continent, the EU was increasingly independent from views from the United States in politics and economics, although not in military affairs. At a meeting in Helsinki in December 1999, European leaders looked forward within a decade to a reformed and enlarged EU of half a billion people.

That dream did not come true, but no one could deny that the Europeans had made enormous strides in amalgamating their economies and significant progress toward political collaboration. Given the strife and wars of the European past, Europe's success in remaking itself was nothing short of miraculous, but Europe had difficulty "making" Europeans whose loyalty to Europe as a whole was a strong as their allegiance to their own countries. This problem could be seen in a number of areas. The euro crisis, which began in 2010 in the wake of the Great Recession, claimed Greece as its first victim and then spread to Ireland, Portugal, Spain and Italy. The EU acted to bail out Greece and the others, and there was talk about establishing a mechanism to help other weak economies that would find themselves in the same position. The EU had faced serious problems before and had resolved them successfully, but it acted painfully slowly in resolving the particularly intractable crisis that threatened the common European currency. Hard feelings grew when northern Europeans—Germans in particular—resisted helping Greece because they accused the Greeks of being profligate and rebelled, criticized southern Europeans, and objected that they did not want their hard-earned savings to go to them. This view did not consider that the Greeks had purchased German exports that added to German prosperity or that German banks held large amounts of Greek debt and were threatened by a Greek bankruptcy. This attitude threatened the political viability of Chancellor Angela Merkel. The Germans eventually realized that the bailouts were in their own interest, but by then, views of this kind had spread to other countries and had expanded to include Southern Europe to such an extent that the proposal to name an Italian to be governor of the European Central Bank was criticized by the German press *because* he was an Italian.

By 2012 the euro crisis had swept away and replaced the ruling governments of Italy, France, Spain, Greece, Portugal, Ireland, and the Netherlands, and threatened to unseat Chancellor Angela Merkel and her party in the German federal elections planned for 2013. In the United Kingdom, the Conservative party lost important by-elections and some Conservative leaders called for David Cameron to be removed as party chief and prime minster in order to reduce the chances of their party's defeat in the next general election in 2015. The recession that began in 2008 and the euro crisis hit Eastern Europe even harder than Western Europe, with the output of most countries in the area dropping by 5 percent. The crisis had dire political effects as well. Hungary, once an economic superstar but one of the worst hit by the recession, gave the center right FIDESZ party a two-thirds majority in 2010. FIDESZ used this majority to adopt a new, more restrictive, constitution that went into effect on January 1, 2012. Legislation gave the government increased power over the news media, the courts, judges, and the central bank. These measures caused protests in the country and drew criticism from the United States and Europe. The EU brought legal action and used economic pressure against Hungary in order to change the legislation that it considered most anti-democratic and in conflict with European law. The danger of authoritarianism in the countries of Europe with the weakest democratic traditions was a worrying side effect of the economic crisis.

The integration of immigrants, particularly Muslims, posed an even more serious obstacle in the making of Europeans than the rise of far-right parties because it

The German Chancellor Angela Merkel. Merkel, from East Germany, a scientist before entering politics in 1989, became Chancellor in 2005. In remarks greeted by loud applause from the audience, she stated in October 2010 that multiculturalism in Germany had "utterly failed." French President Nicolas Sarkozy and British Prime Minister David Cameron later made similar statements. Studies found that in Germany, Europe's largest and most powerful country, 60 percent would "restrict the practice of Islam"; 30 percent believed that the nation had been "overrun by foreigners" who came to Germany primarily for its generous social benefits; 17 percent thought Jews had "too much influence"; and 13 percent would welcome a "fuehrer," a term explicitly associated with Hitler. These findings indicate the extent to which immigration presents a serious problem for Europe in the twenty-first century.

was one of the most important reasons for the increased support for those organizations. As Muslim immigration escalated, observers speculated that Islam would become the biggest European religion and that immigrants plotted to make Sharia law dominant in Europe. The terrorist threat was cited, but the more serious charge was that there was a plot by Muslim militants to take over the continent by stealth and through immigration and by increasing the Muslim population. The refusal of many Muslim immigrants to integrate and their insistence on hanging on to their beliefs, encouraging intermarriage and discouraging marriage with Europeans, and forcing daughters to marry husbands from ancestral lands, and their alleged plans to take over different European countries through elections when they had become a majority were supposedly all elements of the plot. Incidents in several Western European countries in which Muslim family members threatened or murdered daughters who had relationships with Western men reinforced this belief.

This kind of thinking was initially formless and restricted mainly to the unsophisticated "man in the street," but by the first decade of the twenty-first century, it had spread to more influential circles. Anti-immigrant parties had already been formed in the previous century, but they spread to influential, mainstream circles during the new century. In 2010 Thilo Sarrazin, a German Social Democrat and member of the board of the Bundesbank, published a book in which he endorsed the view that Muslim immigrants were contributing to a decline in intelligence in Germany and threatened the country's future. This genetic interpretation recalled the specter of the German past, and scholars eventually discredited it, but the book received widespread approval and support, even among the educated middle class and mainstream political parties, and created an international stir. Shortly after she condemned the book, Chancellor Angela Merkel announced to a Christian Democratic audience that multiculturalism in Germany was dead. In Italy and the Netherlands, the governments depended on anti-immigrant parties for a majority, and the trend spread to Finland. Switzerland banned the building of minarets. Even in countries that were long used to immigration, such as France, economic and social conditions confined Muslim immigrants and their children to the *banlieues* (suburbs), where they were discriminated against and harassed and high unemployment prevailed—and where serious riots broke out. In Britain, Prime Minister David Cameron echoed Merkel by stating that multiculturalism had failed and suggested that it had encouraged extremism and terrorism in Britain. In 2012 in France, the anti-immigrant National Front Party led by Jean-Marie Le Pen's daughter Marine took 18 percent of the vote in the first ballot for president, and in Greece the neo-Nazi "Golden Dawn" party that advocated the expulsion of immigrants, won enough votes to enter parliament for the first time.

Muslim immigrants were not the only ones who caused Europe serious problems. Refugees from the poverty and wars of the Arab world and sub-Saharan Africa arrived in droves, mainly in Italy and Spain, creating short- and long-term problems. Since immigrants from Tunisia aimed to immigrate to France, Italy issued short-term visas to allow them to get there, but the French rejected them, and the Danes considered similar actions that threatened the Schengen agreement allowing free travel among the states of the EU. In addition, although Europe needed immigrants to take up vacant professional and other positions, these immigrants were not educationally prepared to do so. Europe was confronted with the problem of educating thse immigrants, a process that strained the already overloaded educational system in some countries and that would take years and perhaps generations to resolve. Europe also needed immigrants to work and sustain its generous welfare states, but the kind of immigration into the EU put a greater strain on the welfare states that might one day have become intolerable. The EU faced the same problem with regard to internal immigration within the EU, with a flood of destitute people leaving the poorer East European countries like the Ukraine, Albania, and Romania for the richer West European ones like Germany and Italy. At the same time, poor immigrants arrived from Asia as well.

In 2005, the immigrant population of the different West European countries was estimated to vary between 4.3 percent and 23 percent, but it was increasing fast, with Italy's rising from 4.3 percent to 7.1 percent in 2010. With a declin-

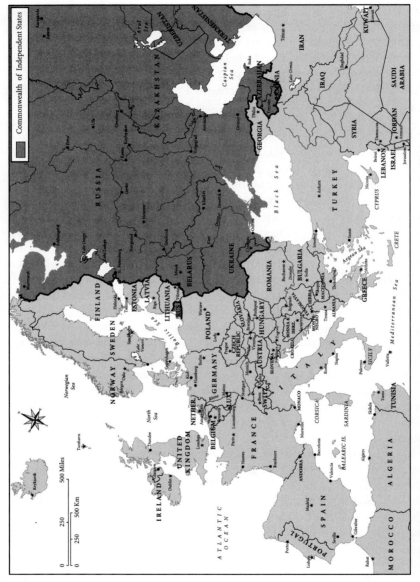

A New Map for a New Century. As the twenty-first century began, the map of Europe had been largely redrawn in Eastern Europe and the Balkans.

The worrying signs regarding the reaction of Europeans to the massive influx from the lesser-developed world of legal and illegal immigrants did not cause only fear and resentment. European governments set up centers to welcome them and to minister to their needs, at least temporarily. Many Europeans greeted them with kindness and hoped that their governments would be able to peacefully integrate immigrants and their descendants. The riots in the Paris "banlieues" in 2005, for example, were followed by a rally against violence attended by many families and called "Banlieues Respects." Here is a picture of the demonstration, held in the center of Paris, on November 11, 2005. The placard says: "Stop the Violence!"

ing birthrate and an aging population, immigration was the most important demographic problem facing Europe. If an acceptable solution to "making Europeans" cannot be found, it is difficult to see how "making Europe" is possible in the long run.

Bibliographical Essay

The concept of soft power, the ability to lead through the attraction of culture and institutions, rather than military force, is developed by Joseph S. Nye, Jr., in his book, *Soft Power: The Means to Success in World Politics* (New York, 2004).

Philip Zelikow and Condoleezza Rice cogently discuss German reunification in *Germany Reunified and Europe Transformed* (Cambridge, Mass., 1993). See also Peter H. Merkl, *German Unification in the European Context* (University Park, Pa., 1993), and Angela Leonard and Nigel Bushnell, *Germany Divided and Reunited 1945–91* (London,

2009). United Germany's growing influence in Eastern Europe is considered by Ann L. Phillips, *Power and Influence After the Cold War: Germany in East-Central Europe* (Lanham, Md., 2000). Peter Pulzer, *German Politics 1945–1995* (New York, 1997), discusses politics and governance in the first five years of the new Germany. Several books already cited have good chapters on reunification and put the process into a historical context. See A. James McAdams, *Germany Divided: From the Wall to Reunification* (Princeton, N.J., 1993). The same issue with particular emphasis on the parties is also discussed in the later chapters of Gerard Braunthal, *Parties and Politics in Modern Germany* (Boulder, Colo., 1996). M. E. Sarotte discusses the events in the twenty years following the fall of the wall: *1989: The Struggle to Create Post-Cold War Europe* (Princeton, N.J., 2009), and Harald Uhlig examines the continued decline of East Germany after reunification in *The Slow Decline of East Germany* (Cambridge, Mass., 2008). Simon Green et al., take a different approach to German politics in *The Politics of the New Germany* (London, 2008). Andrei S. Markovits and Philip S. Gorski, *The German Left: Red, Green and Beyond* (New York, 1993), has a chapter on the East German Greens.

G. D. G. Murrell, British ambassador to Russia, published *Russia's Transition to Democracy: An Internal Political History, 1989–1996* (Brighton, UK, 1997); the balance sheet quote is on p. 1 of this work. G. Lapidus, ed., *The New Russia: Troubled Transition* (Boulder, Colo., 1995), and R. Sackwa, *Russian Politics and Society* (London, 1993), are very useful, and Michael L. Bressler's *Understanding Contemporary Russia* (Boulder, Colo., 2009) is a general work. Julie M. Newton and William J. Tompson explore *Institutions, Ideas and Leadership in Russian Politics* (New York, 2010). The details of bringing the market to Russia are explained in Anders Aslund, *How Russia Became a Market Economy* (Washington, D.C., 1995), and Marshall I. Goldman, *Lost Opportunity: Why Economic Reforms in Russia Have Not Worked* (New York, 1994). Peter Rutland, *Business and the State in Contemporary Russia* (Boulder, Colo., 2000), is an analysis of the business elite and its role, but look at Alena V. Ledeneva, *How Russia Really Works: The Informal Practices that Shaped Post-Soviet Politics and Business* (Ithaca, N.Y., 2006). See also Peter Reddaway and Dmitri Glinski, *The Tragedy of Russia's Reforms: Market Bolshevism Against Democracy* (Washington, D.C., 2001).

Timo Piirainen, *Towards a New Social Order in Russia: Transforming Structures in Everyday Life* (Aldershot, UK, 1997), is an excellent account of how rapid political, social, and economic change affected ordinary Russians. Also on the issue of the transition and social policy, see the essays gathered in Ethan B. Kapatein and Michael Mandelbaum, eds., *Sustaining the Transition: The Social Safety Net in Postcommunist Europe* (New York, 1997).

Much has been written on the precarious state of Russian democracy under Putin. Among the books are Graeme B. Robertson, *The Politics of Protest in Hybrid Regimes: Managing Dissent in Post-Communist Russia* (New York, 2011); Stephen White, *Russia's New Politics: The Management of a Post-Communist Society* (New York, 2000); and Lilli Shevtosova, *Russia Lost in Transition: The Yeltsin and Putin Legacies* (Washington, D.C., 2007). Books analyzing Putin's regime include Peter Baker and Susan Glasser, *Kremlin Rising: Vladimir Putin's Russia and the End of Revolution* (New York, 2005), and Thomas Ambrosio, *Authoritarian Backlash: Russian Resistance to Democratization in the Former Soviet Union* (Burlington, Vt., 2009). For the direct testimony of a victim, see Anna Politkovskaia, *Putin's Russia: Life in a Failing Democracy* (New York, 2005), and *A Russian Diary: A Journalist's Final Account of Life, Corruption, and Death in Putin's Russia* (New York, 2007). On foreign policy in the Putin era, see Michael Stuermer, *Putin and the Rise of Russia* (New York, 2009); Eugene B. Rumer, *Russian Foreign Policy Beyond Putin* (New York, 2007); and R. Craig Nation, *Russia, the United States, and the Caucasus* (Carlisle, Pa., 2007).

Eastern European politics after the end of communism are treated in J. F. Brown, *Hopes and Shadows: Eastern Europe After Communism* (Durham, N.C., 1994). Robert Weiner's *Change in Eastern Europe* (Westport, Conn., 1994) manages to pack an amazing amount of information and interpretation into a brief work. Michael Kennen and Gur Ofer, *Trials of Transition: Economic Reform in the Former Communist Bloc* (Boulder, Colo., 1992), emphasizes economics. Derek S. Hutcheson and Elena A. Korosteleva look at *The Quality of Democracy in Post-Communist Europe* (New York, 2006). Sten Berglund, Tomas Hellen, and Frank H. Aarebrot, eds., *The Handbook of Political Change in Eastern Europe* (Cheltenham, UK, 1998), is concerned with the transition to and the consolidation of democracy in the post-Communist world.

Poland is considered by Walter Connor et al., eds., *The Polish Road From Socialism* (Armonk, N.Y., 1992). See also William Dan Perdue, *Paradox of Change: The Rise and Fall of Solidarity in the New Poland* (Westport, Conn., 1995). John Edgar Jackson et al. look at *The Political Economy of Poland's Transition: New Firms and Reform Governments* (New York, 2005). Gavin Rae examines *Poland's Return to Capitalism: From the Socialist Bloc to the Soviet Union* (London, 2008). The essays in Lavinia Stan, *Romania in Transition* (Aldershot, UK, 1997), assess the economic and political situation in that country after 1989 in a manageable form. For a general discussion of events down to the period covered, see Maureen P. Larsen, *Economic and Political Developments in Poland* (Hauppauge, N.Y., 2011).

Several good books exist on the disintegration of Yugoslavia. In addition to the works cited in chapter 32, see Laura Silber and Allan Little, *Yugoslavia: Death of a Nation* (New York, 1994). On Yugoslavia, see also Joyce P. Kaufman, *NATO and the Former Yugoslavia: Crisis, Conflict, and the Atlantic Alliance* (Lanham, Md., 2002), and Paul R. Williams and Michael P. Scharf, *Peace with Justice? War Crimes and Accountability in the Former Yugoslavia* (Lanham, Md., 2002). There are many descriptions of the atrocities in the Balkans related to the breakup of Yugoslavia, but Tom Gallagher provides a comprehensive account in *The Balkans After the Cold War: From Tyranny to Tragedy* (New York, 2003). See also the previously cited book by Paul Mojzes, *Balkan Genocides* (Lanham, Md., 2011). On the American role, see Lester Brune, *The United States and the Balkan Crisis, 1990–2005: Conflict in Bosnia and Kosovo* (Claremont, Calif., 2005). The Albanian situation is examined in Paullin Kola, *The Myth of Greater Albania* (New York, 2003).

R. J. Crampton, *Eastern Europe in the Twentieth Century*, 2d ed. (London, 1997), already cited, has a good chapter summarizing East European events after communism. Scholars have been particularly interested in the direction of the post-Communist world. See the following works on several important issues: Jane Leftwich Curry and Joan Barth Urban, eds., *The Left Transformed: Social Democrats and Neo-Leninists in East Central Europe, Russia, and Ukraine* (Lanham, Md., 2003), which examines the different paths taken by the former Communist parties; Pál Kolst, ed., *National Integration and Violent Conflict in Post-Soviet Societies: The Cases of Estonia and Moldova* (Lanham, Md., 2002), useful for a general conclusion; Stephen Growley and David Ost, eds., *Workers After Workers' States: Labor and Politics in Postcommunist Eastern Europe* (Lanham, Md., 2001); and Timothy A. Byrne's look at Catholicism, *Transnational Catholicism in Post-Communist Europe* (Lanham, Md., 2001). For a general consideration of events in Eastern Europe, see David Lane, ed., *The Legacy of State Socialism and the Future of Transformation* (Lanham, Md., 2002). Sabrina P. Ramet, ed., *Central and Southeast European Poltics since 1989* (New York, 2010) brings together essays that examine the collapse of communism and the rise of democracy in the area under consideration. Andrew Roberts, *The Quality of Democracy in Eastern Europe: Public Preferences and Policy Reforms* (Cambridge, UK, 2010) concludes that, despite appearances, the East Europeans quickly developed democracies of relatively good quality.

George Ross, *Jacques Delors and European Integration* (New York, 1995), is an analysis of the important French proponent of the EU. Paolo Cecchini, *1992: The Benefits of a Single Market* (Aldershot, UK, 1990), is important because it illustrates the costs of a nonunited Europe. Books on important themes related to the EU include John Van

Oudenaren, *Uniting Europe: European Integration and the Post-Cold War World* (Lanham, Md., 2000), and Doug Imig and Sidney Tarrow, eds., *Contentious Europeans: Protest and Politics in an Integrating Europe* (Lanham, Md., 2001). On the euro, see Erik Jones, *The Politics of Economic and Monetary Union: Integration and Idiosyncrasy* (Lanham, Md., 2002), and Amy Verdun, ed., *The Euro: European Integration Theory and Economic and Monetary Union* (Lanham, Md., 2002). On the EP, see Bernard Steunenberg and Jacques Thomassen, eds., *The European Parliament: Moving Toward Democracy in the EU* (Lanham, Md., 2002). On the evolution of NATO in the face of the dramatic events in Europe since the 1980s, consult Sean Kay, *NATO and the Future of European Security* (Lanham, Md., 1998).

The Italian corruption crisis and its effects are discussed by Mark Gilbert, *The Italian Revolution: The End of Politics, Italian Style?* (Boulder, Colo., 1995). Stanton H. Burnett and Luca Mantovani in *The Italian Guillotine: Operation Clean Hands and the Overthrow of Italy's First Republic* (Lanham, Md., 1998), already cited, portray Italian events as a coup d'état by judges that came out of the 1968 movement. The collection edited by Patrick McCarthy, *Italy Since 1945* (New York, 2000), attempts a wider view. The essays collected by Stephen Gundle and Simon Parker, eds., *The New Italian Republic: From the Fall of the Berlin Wall to Berlusconi* (London, 1996), is an early assessment of the period following the fall of the old parties. Roy Palmer Domenico's general history, *Remaking Italy in the Twentieth Century* (New York, 2002), has a chapter on the events discussed. Le Pen's challenge to French democracy is examined by Harvey G. Simmons, *The French National Front: The Extremist Challenge to Democracy* (Boulder, Colo., 1996).

There is an increasing literature on the new immigration. Books that readers will find useful include *Contested Citizenship: Immigration and Diversity in Europe* (Minneapolis, Minn., 2005), essays that discuss the effect of immigration on the changing concept of citizenship. Craig Parsons and Timothy M. Smeeding present a comprehensive analysis of the changes being wrought by so many new immigrants in *Immigration and the Transformation of Europe* (Cambridge, UK, 2006). Joel S. Fetzer and J. Christopher Soper published *Muslims and the State in Britain, France, and Germany* (Cambridge, UK, 2004). Conflict with the Muslims is examined in a book of essays: Michael Emerson and Oliver Roy, *Ethno-Religious Conflict in Europe: Typologies of Radicalisation in Europe's Muslim Communities* (Brussels, 2009). On the question of tolerance, see Pamela Kilpadi, *Islam and Tolerance in Wider Europe* (Budapest, 2007), and Raphael Israeli, *Muslim Anti-Semitism in Christian Europe* (New Brunswick, N.J., 2009). An example of one of the most virulent attacks on the Muslims in Europe was, paradoxically, written by an American expatriate: Bruce Bawer, *While Europe Slept: How Radical Islam Is Destroying the West from Within* (New York, 2006). On Angela Merkel's remarks regarding the "failure" of multiculturalism, and the statistics cited, see her remarks of October 17, 2010 as reported by The Christian Science Monitor, at http://www.csmonitor.com/World/Global-News/2010/1017/Germany-s-Angela-Merkel-Multiculturalism-has-utterly-failed (accessed 12/31/11).

For a positive assessment of Europe, see Steven Hill, *Europe's Promise: Why the European Way Is the Best Hope in an Insecure Age* (Berkeley, Calif., 2010). Also useful for reflection on the European future are Tommaso Padoa Schioppa, ed., *Europe After 1992: Three Essays* (Princeton, N.J., 1992), and Joseph Nye, Robert Keohane, and Stanley Hoffman, eds., *After the Cold War: International Institutions and State Strategies in Europe* (Cambridge, Mass., 1993).

IMAGE SOURCES AND CREDITS

Introduction: © Burstein Collection / CORBIS.

Chapter 1: pg. 8 © Bettmann / CORBIS; pg. 11 Courtesy of the Library of Congress; pg. 23 © Alinari Archives / CORBIS.

Chapter 2: pg. 36 Hulton Archive / Getty Images.

Chapter 3: pg. 55 Courtesy of the Library of Congress; pg. 71 Courtesy of the Library of Congress; pg. 72 © Bettmann / CORBIS.

Chapter 4: pg. 83 Courtesy of the Library of Congress; pg. 86 © Bettmann / CORBIS; pg. 91 akg-images / Jean-Pierre Verney; pg. 95 (top) © Hulton-Deutsch Collection / CORBIS; pg. 95 (bottom) Courtesy of the Library of Congress.

Chapter 5: pg. 107 © Christophe Boisvieux / Corbis; pg. 111 © Kirn Vintage Stock / Corbis; pg. 114 © Bettmann / CORBIS; pg. 118 © Bettmann / CORBIS; pg. 121 © No Credit Given / National Geographic Society / Corbis; pg. 125 © Bettmann / CORBIS.

Chapter 6: pg. 136 © Bettmann / CORBIS; pg. 138 © Hulton-Deutsch Collection / CORBIS; pg. 140 © Hulton-Deutsch Collection / CORBIS; pg. 142 © Bettmann / CORBIS; pg. 143 © Bettmann / CORBIS; pg. 147 © CORBIS; pg. 150 Courtesy of the Library of Congress; pg. 156 © Lebrecht / Lebrecht Music & Arts / Corbis; pg. 160 The Granger Collection.

Chapter 7: pg. 166 © CORBIS; pg. 168 © CORBIS; pg. 170 © Hulton-Deutsch Collection / CORBIS; pg. 179 Courtesy of the Library of Congress; pg. 181 © Hulton-Deutsch Collection / CORBIS; pg. 186 © Stefano Bianchetti / CORBIS.

Chapter 8: pg. 200 Courtesy of the Library of Congress; pg. 205 © E.O. Hoppé / CORBIS; pg. 206 © Bettmann / CORBIS.

Chapter 9: pg. 215 © BBC / Corbis; pg. 217 © Bettmann / CORBIS; pg. 223 © Stefano Bianchetti / Corbis; pg. 227 © Hulton-Deutsch Collection / CORBIS.

Chapter 10: pg. 241 © Hulton-Deutsch Collection / CORBIS; pg. 242 Courtesy of the Library of Congress; pg. 247 © Bettmann / CORBIS; pg. 251 © G. Jackson / Arcaid / Corbis.

Chapter 11: pg. 265 © Hulton-Deutsch Collection / CORBIS; pg. 267 © CORBIS; pg. 268 © Hulton-Deutsch Collection / CORBIS; pg. 271 © Hulton-Deutsch Collection / CORBIS; pg. 275 © Bettmann / CORBIS; pg. 278 © Bettmann / CORBIS.

Chapter 12: pg. 284 © Hulton-Deutsch Collection / CORBIS; pg. 288 © Hulton-Deutsch Collection / CORBIS; pg. 293 (top) akg-images / Interfoto; pg. 293 (bottom) © Bettmann / Corbis; pg. 296 © Hulton-Deutsch Collection / CORBIS.

Chapter 13: pg. 304 © Bettmann / CORBIS; pg. 307 © Bettmann / CORBIS; pg. 309 © Bettmann / CORBIS; pg. 311 Courtesy of the Library of Congress; pg. 316 © Bettmann / CORBIS.

Chapter 14: pg. 326 © Austrian Archives / CORBIS; pg. 328 © Lebrecht Authors / Lebrecht Music & Arts / Corbis; pg. 332 © Hulton-Deutsch Collection / CORBIS; pg. 333 © Hulton-Deutsch Collection / CORBIS.

Chapter 15: pg. 338 © Bettmann / CORBIS; pg. 340 Courtesy of the Library of Congress; pg. 343 © MAURIZIO GAMBARINI / epa / Corbis; pg. 344 © Bettmann / CORBIS; pg. 349 © Hulton-Deutsch Collection / CORBIS; pg. 351 Courtesy of the Library of Congress.

Chapter 16: pg. 362 akg-images; pg. 365 © Stapleton Collection / Corbis; pg. 367 © Dave G. Houser / Corbis; pg. 369 © Richard Bryant / Arcaid / Corbis.

Chapter 17: pg. 378 © Charles & Josette Lenars / CORBIS; pg. 389 © CORBIS; pg. 391 © CORBIS; pg. 392 © Bettmann / CORBIS; pg. 393 © Bettmann / CORBIS.

Chapter 18: pg. 400 © GLEB GARANICH / Reuters / Corbis; pg. 402 © CORBIS; pg. 405 © Hulton-Deutsch Collection / CORBIS; pg. 408 © Bettmann / Corbis; pg. 415 © Dmitri Baltermants / The Dmitri Baltermants Collection / Corbis.

Chapter 19: pg. 421 © CORBIS; pg. 425 © Bettmann / CORBIS; pg. 427 © Leonard de Selva / CORBIS; pg. 430 © Bettmann / CORBIS; pg. 436 © Bettmann / Corbis.

Chapter 20: pg. 447 © CORBIS; pg. 455 © Bettmann / CORBIS; pg. 461 © Hulton-Deutsch Collection / CORBIS; pg. 464 Courtesy of the Library of Congress.

Chapter 21: pg. 476 © Lebrecht Authors / Lebrecht Music & Arts / Corbis; pg. 478 Courtesy of the Library of Congress; pg. 487 Courtesy of the Library of Congress; pg. 489 Courtesy of the Library of Congress; pg. 490 Getty Images; pg. 493 © CORBIS.

Chapter 22: pg. 503 Courtesy of the Library of Congress; pg. 505 © Bettmann / CORBIS; pg. 506 Courtesy of the Library of Congress; pg. 515 © Bettmann / CORBIS; pg. 518 © Ted Spiegel / CORBIS.

Chapter 23: pg. 530 © SALVATORE DI NOLFI / epa / Corbis; pg. 534 © Ingrid Rossi / Sygma / Corbis; pg. 535 Courtesy of the Library of Congress; pg. 539 © Bettmann / CORBIS.

Chapter 24: pg. 552 © - / BELGA / epa / Corbi; pg. 553 © Bettmann / CORBIS; pg. 557 © Swim Ink 2, LLC / CORBIS.

Chapter 25: pg. 570 © Hulton-Deutsch Collection / CORBIS; pg. 571 © CORBIS; pg. 572 © Bettmann / CORBIS; pg. 576 © Bettmann / CORBIS.

Chapter 26: pg. 582 © Hulton-Deutsch Collection / CORBIS; pg. 583 Courtesy of the Library of Congress; pg. 586 © Bettmann / CORBIS; pg. 588 © Hulton-Deutsch Collection / CORBIS; pg. 590 © Tibor Hollos / epa / Corbis; pg. 594 © Bettmann / CORBIS; pg. 600 © Bettmann / CORBIS.

Chapter 27: pg. 606 © Hulton-Deutsch Collection / CORBIS; pg. 611 © Annie Griffiths Belt / Corbis; pg. 618 © Fabian Cevallos / Sygma /Corbis; pg. 624 akg-images.

Chapter 28: pg. 630 © Jack Burlot / Apis / Sygma / Corbis; pg. 633 © Regis Bossu / Sygma / Corbis; pg. 638 © Regis Bossu / Sygma / Corbis.

Chapter 29: pg. 643 © James Leynse / Corbis; pg. 648 © Hulton-Deutsch Collection / CORBIS; pg. 651 © Raymond Reuter / Sygma / Corbis; pg. 653 © John Garrett / CORBIS; pg. 655 © Julia Waterlow / Eye Ubiquitous / Corbis.

Chapter 30: pg. 661 © Bettmann / CORBIS; pg. 662 © Mike Kemp / In Pictures / Corbis; pg. 666 © Bettmann / CORBIS; pg. 668 © David Lees / CORBIS; pg. 673 © Gideon Mendel / Corbis.

Chapter 31: pg. 681 © Frederic Pitchal / Sygma / Corbis; pg. 686 © Bettmann / CORBIS; pg. 690 © Bob Krist / CORBIS.

Chapter 32: pg. 698 © Wally McNamee / CORBIS; pg. 699 © Reuters / CORBIS; pg. 705 © Jacques Langevin / Sygma / Corbis; pg. 709 © Peter Turnley / CORBIS; pg. 715 Hulton Archive / Getty Images; pg. 718 © Robert Maass / CORBIS.

Chapter 33: pg. 724 © Karlheinz Schindler / dpa / Corbis; pg. 725 © Andrew Holbrooke / Corbis; pg. 728 © Robert Wallis / Corbis; pg. 730 © David Turnley / CORBIS; pg. 734 © Reuters / CORBIS; pg. 743 © Gary Trotter / Eye Ubiquitous / Corbis.

Chapter 34: pg. 757 © Gary Knight / VII / Corbis; pg. 761 © Alberto Pizzoli / Sygma / Corbis; pg. 768 © Brooks Kraft / CORBIS; pg. 774 © Thierry Tronnel / Corbis; pg. 777 © Jean-Michel Turpin / Corbis.

---

*All images, unless otherwise noted, are within the public domain.

INDEX